清华ＭＢＡ核心课程英文版教材

战略管理 概念与案例

Sixteenth Edition

Strategic Management
Concepts and Cases: A Competitive Advantage Approach

[美] 弗雷德·R. 戴维 （Fred R. David）
福里斯特·R. 戴维 （Forest R. David）   著

第16版

清华大学出版社
北京

北京市版权局著作权合同登记号　图字：01-2017-8968

图书在版编目（CIP）数据

战略管理：概念与案例：第 16 版 = Strategic Management：Concepts and Cases, A Competitive Advantage Approach：英文 /（美）弗雷德·R.戴维(Fred R. David)，（美）福里斯特·R.戴维(Forest R.David) 著. —北京：清华大学出版社，2018（2024.2重印）

（清华 MBA 核心课程英文版教材）

ISBN 978-7-302-50087-2

Ⅰ.①战… Ⅱ.①弗… ②福… Ⅲ.①企业战略—战略管理—研究生—教材—英文 Ⅳ.①F272

中国版本图书馆 CIP 数据核字(2018)第 097803 号

责任编辑：梁云慈
封面设计：常雪影
责任印制：杨　艳

出版发行：清华大学出版社
　　　　网　　址：https://www.tup.com.cn, https://www.wqxuetang.com
　　　　地　　址：北京清华大学学研大厦 A 座　　　　　邮　　编：100084
　　　　社 总 机：010-83470000　　　　　　　　　　　邮　　购：010-62786544
　　　　投稿与读者服务：010-62776969, c-service@tup.tsinghua.edu.cn
　　　　质量反馈：010-62772015, zhiliang@tup.tsinghua.edu.cn
印 装 者：三河市龙大印装有限公司
经　　销：全国新华书店
开　　本：203mm×260mm　　　　　　　　　　　　　印　　张：41.25
版　　次：2018 年 6 月第 1 版　　　　　　　　　　　印　　次：2024 年 2 月第 5 次印刷
定　　价：105.00 元

产品编号：077117-02

出 版 说 明

　　为了适应经济全球化的发展趋势，满足国内广大读者了解、学习和借鉴国外先进的管理经验和掌握经济理论前沿动态的需求，清华大学出版社与国外著名出版公司合作影印出版一系列英文版经济管理方面的图书。我们所选择的图书，基本上是已再版多次、在国外深受欢迎并被广泛采用的优秀教材，绝大部分是该领域中较具权威性的经典之作。在本书的出版过程中，我们得到了清华大学李东红老师的支持、帮助和鼓励，在此表示谢意！

　　由于原作者所处国家的政治、经济和文化背景等与我国不同，对书中所持观点，敬请广大读者在阅读过程中注意加以分析和鉴别。

　　我们期望这套影印书的出版对我国经济科学的发展能有所帮助，对我国经济管理专业的教学能有所促进。

　　欢迎广大读者给我们提出宝贵的意见和建议；同时也欢迎有关的专业人士向我们推荐您所接触到的国外优秀图书。

清华大学出版社

2018.1

总序

世纪之交，中国与世界的发展呈现最显著的两大趋势——以网络为代表的信息技术的突飞猛进，以及经济全球化的激烈挑战。无论是无远弗届的互联网，还是日益密切的政治、经济、文化等方面的国际合作，都标示着 21 世纪的中国是一个更加开放的中国，也面临着一个更加开放的世界。

教育，特别是管理教育总是扮演着学习与合作的先行者的角色。改革开放以来，尤其是 20 世纪 90 年代之后，为了探寻中国国情与国际上一切优秀的管理教育思想、方法和手段的完美结合，为了更好地培养高层次的"面向国际市场竞争、具备国际经营头脑"的管理者，我国的教育机构与美国、欧洲、澳洲以及亚洲一些国家和地区的大量的著名管理学院和顶尖跨国企业建立了长期密切的合作关系。以清华大学经济管理学院为例，2000 年，学院顾问委员会成立，并于 10 月举行了第一次会议，2001 年 4 月又举行了第二次会议。这个顾问委员会包括了世界上最大的一些跨国公司和中国几家顶尖企业的最高领导人，其阵容之大、层次之高，超过了世界上任何一所商学院。在这样高层次、多样化、重实效的管理教育国际合作中，教师和学生与国外的交流机会大幅度增加，越来越深刻地融入到全球性的教育、文化和思想观念的时代变革中，我们的管理教育工作者和经济管理学习者，更加真切地体验到这个世界正发生着深刻的变化，也更主动地探寻和把握着世界经济发展和跨国企业运作的脉搏。

我国管理教育的发展，闭关锁国、闭门造车是绝对不行的，必须同国际接轨，按照国际一流的水准来要求自己。正如朱镕基同志在清华大学经济管理学院成立十周年时所发的贺信中指出的那样："建设有中国特色的社会主义，需要一大批掌握市场经济的一般规律，熟悉其运行规则，而又了解中国企业实情的经济管理人才。清华大学经济管理学院就要敢于借鉴、引进世界上一切优秀的经济管理学院的教学内容、方法和手段，结合中国的国情，办成世界第一流的经管学院。"作为达到世界一流的一个重要基础，朱镕基同志多次建议清华的 MBA 教育要加强英语教学。我体会，这不仅因为英语是当今世界交往中重要的语言工具，是连接中国与世界的重要桥梁和媒介，而且更是中国经济管理人才参与国际竞争，加强国际合作，实现中国企业的国际战略的基石。推动和实行英文教学并不是目的，真正的目的在于培养学生——这些未来的企业家——能够具备同国际竞争对手、合作伙伴沟通和对抗的能力。按照这一要求，清华大学经济管理学院正在不断推动英语教学的步伐，使得英语不仅是一门需要学习的核心课程，而且渗透到各门专业课程的学习当中。

课堂讲授之外，课前课后的大量英文原版著作、案例的阅读对于提高学生的英文水平也是非常关键的。这不仅是积累相当的专业词汇的重要手段，而且是对学习者思维方式的有效训练。

　　我们知道，就阅读而言，学习和借鉴国外先进的管理经验和掌握经济理论动态，或是阅读翻译作品，或是阅读原著。前者属于间接阅读，后者属于直接阅读。直接阅读取决于读者的外文阅读能力，有较高外语水平的读者当然喜欢直接阅读原著，这样不仅可以避免因译者的疏忽或水平所限而造成的纰漏，同时也可以尽享原作者思想的真实表达。而对于那些有一定外语基础，但又不能完全独立阅读国外原著的读者来说，外文的阅读能力是需要加强培养和训练的，尤其是专业外语的阅读能力更是如此。如果一个人永远不接触专业外版图书，他在获得国外学术信息方面就永远会比别人差半年甚至一年的时间，他就会在无形中减弱自己的竞争能力。因此，我们认为，有一定外语基础的读者，都应该尝试一下阅读外文原版，只要努力并坚持，就一定能过了这道关，到那时就能体验到直接阅读的妙处了。

　　在掌握大量术语的同时，我们更看重读者在阅读英文原版著作时对于西方管理者或研究者的思维方式的学习和体会。我认为，原汁原味的世界级大师富有特色的表达方式背后，反映了思维习惯，反映了思想精髓，反映了文化特征，也反映了战略偏好。知己知彼，对于跨文化的管理思想、方法的学习，一定要熟悉这些思想、方法所孕育、成长的文化土壤，这样，有朝一日才能真正"具备国际战略头脑"。

　　以往，普通读者购买和阅读英文原版还有一个书价的障碍。一本外版书少则几十美元，多则上百美元，一般读者只能望书兴叹。随着全球经济合作步伐的加快，目前在出版行业有了一种新的合作出版的方式，即外文影印版，其价格几乎与国内同类图书持平。这样一来，读者可以不必再为书价发愁。清华大学出版社这些年在这方面一直以独特的优势领先于同行。早在1997年，清华大学出版社敢为人先，在国内最早推出一批优秀商学英文版教材，规模宏大，在企业界和管理教育界引起不小的轰动，更使国内莘莘学子受益良多。

　　为了配合清华大学经济管理学院推动英文授课的急需，也为了向全国更多的 MBA 试点院校和更多的经济管理学院的教师和学生提供学习上的支持，清华大学出版社再次隆重推出与世界著名出版集团合作的英文原版影印商学教科书，也使广大工商界人士、经济管理类学生享用到最新最好质优价廉的国际教材。

　　祝愿我国的管理教育事业在社会各界的大力支持和关心下不断发展、日进日新；祝愿我国的经济建设在不断涌现的大批高层次的面向国际市场竞争、具备国际经营头脑的管理者的勉力经营下早日中兴。

赵纯均 教授

清华大学经济管理学院

目　录

案例

Contents

Chapter 8 Strategy Generation and Selection 247

Chapter 9 Strategy Implementation 285

Chapter 10 Strategy Execution   321

Chapter 11 Strategy Monitoring   359

Appendix Guidelines for Case Analysis   385

Cases

Service Firms

Manufacturing Firms

Preface

Why Adopt This Text?

This textbook is trusted across five continents to provide managers the latest skills and concepts needed to effectively formulate and efficiently implement a strategic plan—a game plan, if you will—that can lead to sustainable competitive advantage for any type of business. The Association to Advance Collegiate Schools of Business (AACSB) International increasingly advocates a more skills-oriented, practical approach in business books, which this text provides, rather than a theory-based approach. *Strategic Management Concepts and Cases: A Competitive Advantage Approach* meets all AACSB International guidelines for the strategic-management course at both the graduate and undergraduate levels, and previous editions have been used at more than 500 colleges and universities globally. We believe you will find this sixteenth edition to be the best textbook available for communicating both the excitement and value of strategic management. Concise and exceptionally well organized, this text is now available in English, Chinese, Spanish, Thai, German, Japanese, Farsi, Indonesian, Indian, Vietnamese, and Arabic. A version in Russian is being negotiated. In addition to universities, hundreds of companies, organizations, and governmental bodies use this text as a management guide.

An MBA student using this text recently wrote the following:

> Dear Dr. David: I am in the midst of my MBA at Adams State University here in Colorado. I'm 7 of 12 classes in with a 4.0 average. As a result, I've been through about 14 textbooks (not to mention the 60 or so I went through for my BBA at the University of California (UC)-Berkeley. This is the first time I've written to the author of a textbook. Why? Because the David book is by far the best textbook I have ever used. It's clear. It's accurate. It's not full of opinion masquerading as fact! You, sir, are to be commended. Usually when I spend an insane amount of money on a text, I'm broke. But your text is worth every cent, and I'll keep it forever. Well done sir! Respectively, Eric Seiden, MBA Student in Littleton, Colorado (August 10, 2015)

Eric N. Sims, a professor who has used this text for his classes at Sonoma State University in California, says:

> I have read many strategy books. I am going to use the David book. What I like—to steal a line from Alabama coach Nick Saban—is your book teaches "a process." I believe at the end of your book, you can actually help a company do strategic planning. In contrast, other books teach a number of near and far concepts related to strategy.

A recent reviewer of this textbook shares his opinion:

> One thing I admire most about the David text is that it follows the fundamental sequence of strategy formulation, implementation, and evaluation. There is a basic flow from vision/mission to internal/external environmental scanning, to strategy development, selection, implementation, and evaluation. This has been, and continues to be, a hallmark of the David text. Many other strategy texts are more disjointed in their presentation, and thus confusing to the student, especially at the undergraduate level.

New to This Edition

1. This 16th edition is 40 percent new and improved from the prior edition.
2. A brand new **COHESION CASE** on Nestlé S.A. (2016) is provided. Nestlé is one of the largest and most successful food producing companies in the world, known for its innovations and effective management. Students apply strategy concepts to Nestlé at the end of each chapter through new, innovative Assurance of Learning Exercises.

3. Brand-new one-page **MINI-CASES** appear at the end of each chapter, complete with questions designed to apply chapter concepts. Provided for the first time ever in this text, the mini-cases focus on the following companies:

    Chapter 1: Ryanair Holdings PLC
    Chapter 2: Airbus Group SE
    Chapter 3: Etihad Airways
    Chapter 4: Tiger Brands
    Chapter 5: Citizen Holdings Company
    Chapter 6: Bank of China
    Chapter 7: Woolworths Limited
    Chapter 8: Hyundai Motor Company
    Chapter 9: Tata Motors Limited
    Chapter 10: Horizon Pharma
    Chapter 11: Broadcom Limited

4. Original, half-page **ACADEMIC RESEARCH CAPSULES** are presented in each chapter to showcase how new strategic-management research is impacting business practice. Two capsules per chapter are provided—for the first time ever in this text.

5. At the end of each chapter are new sections titled **IMPLICATIONS FOR STRATEGISTS** and **IMPLICATIONS FOR STUDENTS** that highlight how companies can best gain and sustain competitive advantages.

6. Brand new and updated **EXEMPLARY COMPANY CAPSULES** appear at the beginning of each chapter and showcase a company that is employing strategic management exceptionally well. The capsules focus on the following companies:

    Chapter 1: Singapore Airlines Limited
    Chapter 2: Honda Motor Company
    Chapter 3: Bank Audi
    Chapter 4: Petronas
    Chapter 5: Samsung Electronics Limited
    Chapter 6: Vodafone
    Chapter 7: Michelin
    Chapter 8: Unilever
    Chapter 9: Royal Dutch Shell
    Chapter 10: Accenture
    Chapter 11: BHP Billiton Limited

7. Chapter 2, Outside–USA Strategic Planning, is shortened by 30 percent but provides new coverage of cultural and conceptual strategic-management differences across countries. Doing business globally has become a necessity in most industries.

8. Chapter 3, Ethics, Social Responsibility, and Sustainability, provides extensive new coverage of ethics, workplace romance, flirting, hiring away rival firms' employees, wildlife welfare, and sustainability. "Good ethics is good business."

9. Chapter 5, Vision and Mission Analysis, is 60 percent new, due to current research and practice that reveals the need for "these statements to be more customer-oriented." Unique to strategic-management texts, the sustainability discussion is strengthened in this edition to promote and encourage firms to conduct operations with respect for the environment—an important concern for consumers, companies, society, and AACSB International.

10. Twenty-four unique **ASSURANCE OF LEARNING EXERCISES** appear at the end of chapters to apply chapter concepts. The exercises prepare students for strategic-management case analysis. An additional excellent exercise for each chapter is provided in the *Chapter Instructor's Resource Manual.*

11. More than 200 new **EXAMPLES** bring the chapters to life.

12. At the end of chapters are 33 new **REVIEW QUESTIONS** related to chapter content.

13. All the Current Readings at the end of the chapters are new, and up-to-date research and theories of seminal thinkers are included. However, practical aspects of strategic management are center stage and the trademark of this text.

14. Every sentence and paragraph has been scrutinized, modified, clarified, streamlined, updated, and improved to enhance the content and caliber of presentation.

15. An enhanced, continually updated **AUTHOR WEBSITE** (www.strategyclub.com) provides new author videos, case and chapter updates, sample case analyses, and the popular, FREE EXCEL STUDENT TEMPLATE. The template enables students to more easily develop strategic-planning matrices, tables, and analyses needed for case analysis.

New Case Features

1. All 29 cases focus on exciting, well-known companies, effective for students to apply strategy concepts.
2. All 29 cases are undisguised, featuring real organizations in real industries using real names (nothing is fictitious in any case).
3. All 29 cases feature an organization and industry undergoing strategic change.
4. All 29 cases provide ample, excellent quantitative information, so students can prepare a defensible strategic plan.
5. All 29 cases are written in a lively, concise writing style that captures the reader's interest.
6. All 29 cases are "comprehensive," focusing on multiple business functions, rather than a single problem or issue.
7. All 29 cases provide an organizational chart and a vision and mission statement—important strategy concepts.
8. All 29 cases are supported by an excellent teacher's note, provided to professors in a new *Case Instructor's Resource Manual.*
9. All 29 cases facilitate coverage of all strategy concepts, but as revealed in the new Concepts by Cases Matrix, some cases especially exemplify some concepts, enabling professors to effectively use an assortment of cases with various chapters in the text.
10. All 29 cases have been class-tested to ensure that they are interesting, challenging, and effective for illustrating strategy concepts.
11. All 29 cases appear in no other textbooks, thus offering a truly fresh, new, up-to-date learning platform.
12. The 29 cases represent an excellent mix of firms performing really well and some performing very poorly, including 12 service-based organizations, and 17 manufacturing-based firms.
13. All 29 case companies have excellent websites in English that provide detailed financial information, history, sustainability statements, ethics statements, and press releases, so students can easily access current information to apply strategy concepts.

Time-Tested Features

1. This text meets all AACSB International guidelines that support a practitioner orientation rather than a theory/research approach. It offers a skills-oriented process for developing a vision and mission statement; performing an external audit; conducting an internal assessment; and formulating, implementing, and evaluating strategies.
2. The author's writing style is concise, conversational, interesting, logical, lively, and supported by numerous current examples.
3. A simple, integrative strategic-management model appears in all chapters and on the inside back cover. The model is widely used by strategic-planning consultants and companies worldwide.
4. An exciting, new Cohesion Case on Nestlé S.A. (2016) follows Chapter 1 and is revisited at the end of each chapter, allowing students to apply strategic-management concepts and techniques to a real company as the text develops, thus preparing students for case analysis as the course evolves.
5. End-of-chapter Assurance of Learning Exercises apply chapter concepts and techniques in a challenging, meaningful, and enjoyable manner. Twenty-four exercises apply text material to the Cohesion Case; while others apply textual material to a college or university and some exercises send students into the business world to explore important strategy topics.

6. There is excellent pedagogy, including Learning Objectives opening each chapter as well as Key Terms, Current Readings, Discussion Questions, and Assurance of Learning Exercises ending each chapter.
7. The various strategy-formulation issues are outstanding, covering topics such as business ethics, global versus domestic operations, vision and mission, matrix analysis, partnering, joint venturing, competitive analysis, value chain analysis, governance, and matrices for assimilating and evaluating information.
8. Strategy-implementation issues are covered thoroughly and include items such as corporate culture, organizational structure, outsourcing, marketing concepts, financial analysis, business ethics, whistleblowing, bribery, pay and performance linkages, and workplace romance.
9. A systematic, analytical "process" is presented that includes nine matrices: IFEM, EFEM, CPM, SWOT, BCG, IE, GRAND, SPACE, and QSPM.
10. Both the chapter material and case material is published in color.
11. Chapters-only and e-book versions of the text are available.
12. Custom-case publishing is available whereby an instructor can combine chapters from this text with cases from a variety of sources or select any number of the 29 cases provided.
13. For the chapter material, an outstanding ancillary package includes a comprehensive *Chapter Instructor's Resource Manual, Case Instructor's Resource Manual,* Test Bank, TestGen, and Chapter PowerPoints.

Why Is This Text Different/Better Than Other Strategic-Management Texts?

Strategic Management Concepts and Cases: A Competitive Advantage Approach is by far the most practical, skills-oriented strategic management textbook on the market. This text is designed to enable students to learn "how to do strategic planning," rather than simply memorize seminal theories in strategy. Students using this text follow an integrative model that appears in every chapter as the "process" unfolds. Students learn how to construct strategic planning matrices, such as the Strengths, Weaknesses, Opportunities, and Threats (SWOT) and the Boston Consulting Group (BCG) matrices. Readers also learn how to perform strategic-planning analyses, such as earnings-per-share/earnings-before-interest-and-taxes (EPS/EBIT) and corporate valuation. The focus throughout this text is on "learning by doing." This overarching, differentiating aspect has been improved with every edition and has led to this text becoming perhaps the leading strategic-management text globally, now available in 10 languages. The practical, skills-oriented approach is manifested through eight specific features:

1. A Cohesion Case that appears after Chapter 1 with 24 end-of-chapter assurance of learning exercises, many that apply concepts to the Cohesion Case, thus allowing students to gain practice doing strategic planning by performing analysis. No other strategic-management textbook provides a Cohesion Case or an array of end-of-chapter exercises.
2. A strategy formulation analytical framework in Chapter 8 integrates nine widely used planning matrices (IFEM, EFEM, CPM, SWOT, BCG, IE, SPACE, GRAND, and QSPM) into three stages (Input, Matching, and Decision), which guide the strategic-planning process in all companies. Firms gather strategic information (Input), array key external with internal factors (Matching), and then make strategic decisions (Decision).
3. A far wider coverage of strategy topics than any other strategic-management textbook, for two primary reasons: (a) As firms formulate and implement strategies, a wide variety of functional business topics arise and (b) as the capstone, integrative course in nearly all Schools of Business, strategic management entails students applying functional business skills to case companies.

4. This text provides 29 comprehensive, exciting, exceptionally up-to-date cases designed to apply chapter concepts as students develop a strategic plan for the case companies. For example, every case includes (a) the company's vision/mission statements (if the firm has one); (b) the company's by-segment revenue breakdown (since allocating resources divisions is perhaps the key strategy decision made by firms); (c) the company's organizational chart (since structure is a key strategy topic); and (d) the company's financial statements so students can show the impact of a proposed strategic plan on a firm's financial statements. Thus, the cases take a total-firm, multifunctional approach, which by definition is the nature of strategic management. In addition, this text offers end-of-chapter mini-cases to further apply chapter concepts.

5. More coverage of business ethics, social responsibility, and sustainability is provided in this text than in any other strategic-management textbook, including topics such as bribery, workplace romance, devising codes of ethics, taking a position (or not) on social issues, and wildlife welfare—topics that other textbooks do not mention, even though companies continually face strategic decisions in these areas.

6. This text offers more coverage of global/international issues than any other strategic-management textbook, including topics such as how business culture and practice vary across countries, as well as how taxes, tariffs, political stability, and economic conditions vary across countries—all framed from a strategic planning perspective.

7. The conversational, concise writing style is supported by hundreds of current examples, all aimed at arousing and maintaining the reader's interest as the "process" unfolds from start to finish. The unique writing style is in stark contrast to some strategic-management books that seem to randomly present theory and research for the sake of discussion, rather than material being presented in a logical flow that emulates the actual practice of strategic planning among companies and organizations.

8. This text is supported by outstanding ancillaries, including author-developed manuals, and an author website at **www.strategyclub.com** that offers practical author-developed videos, templates, sample case analyses, special resources, and even a Facebook page for the text. Pearson Education also offers outstanding support materials for instructors and students. For more information, visit **www.pearsonglobaleditions.com/David**.

Instructor Resources

At the Instructor Resource Center, **www.pearsonglobaleditions.com/David**, instructors can easily register to gain access to a variety of instructor resources available with this text in downloadable format. If assistance is needed, our dedicated technical support team is ready to help with the media supplements that accompany this text. Visit **https://support.pearson.com/getsupport/s/** for answers to frequently asked questions and toll-free user support phone numbers.

The following supplements are available with this text:

- *Case Instructor's Resource Manual*
- *Chapter Instructor's Resource Manual*
- **Test Bank**
- **TestGen® Computerized Test Bank**
- **PowerPoint Presentation**

The Case Rationale

Case analysis remains the primary learning vehicle used in most strategic-management classes, for five important reasons:

1. Analyzing cases gives students the opportunity to work in teams to evaluate the internal operations and external issues facing various organizations and to craft strategies that can lead these firms to success. Working in teams gives students practical experience in solving problems as part of a group. In the business world, important decisions are generally made within groups; strategic-management students learn to deal with overly aggressive group members as well as timid, noncontributing group members. This experience is valuable because strategic-management students are near graduation and soon enter the working world full time.

2. Analyzing cases enables students to improve their oral and written communication skills as well as their analytical and interpersonal skills by proposing and defending particular courses of action for the case companies.

3. Analyzing cases allows students to view a company, its competitors, and its industry concurrently, thus simulating the complex business world. Through case analysis, students learn how to apply concepts, evaluate situations, formulate strategies, and resolve implementation problems.

4. Analyzing cases allows students to apply concepts learned in many business courses. Students gain experience dealing with a wide range of organizational problems that impact all the business functions.

5. Analyzing cases gives students practice in applying concepts, evaluating situations, formulating a "game plan," and resolving implementation problems in a variety of business and industry settings.

The New Concepts by Cases Matrix

All 29 cases facilitate coverage of all strategy concepts, but as revealed by grey cells, some cases especially exemplify some key strategy concepts. The Concepts by Cases matrix enables professors to effectively utilize different cases to assure student learning of various chapter concepts. Note from the grey boxes that two, three, or four cases are used to test each strategic-management concept. This new, innovative ancillary promises to elevate the case learning method to new heights in teaching strategic management.

Case Number	Service Firms	Key Strategic-Management Concepts	Strategy Model/Process	Vision/Mission Statements	Competitive Profile Matrix	Porter's Five Forces	EFE Matrix	Resource Based View	Financial Ratios & Breakeven	Value Chain Analysis	IFE Matrix	Strategy Types	Porter's Five Generic Strategies
Case 1	Krispy Kreme Doughnuts, Inc.									■			
Case 2	Domino's Pizza, Inc.					■						■	
Case 3	Dunkin' Brands Group, Inc.				■	■							
Case 4	United Parcel Service, Inc.												
Case 5	FedEx Corporation												
Case 6	Citigroup Inc.												
Case 7	JPMorgan Chase & Co.												
Case 8	Polaris Industries, Inc.												
Case 9	The Emirates Group											■	
Case 10	Walt Disney Company							■			■		
Case 11	Facebook, Inc.												
Case 12	World Wildlife Fund									■			
	Manufacturing Firms												
Case 13	Ford Motor Company							■					
Case 14	Bayerische Motoren Werke (BMW)	■											
Case 15	Exxon Mobil Corporation									■			
Case 16	Embraer S.A.										■		
Case 17	Apple Inc.				■							■	
Case 18	International Business Machines Corporation												
Case 19	Microsoft Corporation												
Case 20	Lenovo Group Limited								■				
Case 21	Nikon Corporation												
Case 22	Netgear, Inc.								■				
Case 23	Crocs, Inc.			■	■								
Case 24	L'Oréal SA			■	■								
Case 25	Avon Products, Inc.												
Case 26	Revlon, Inc.	■											
Case 27	Under Armour, Inc.												■
Case 28	Pearson Plc.							■				■	
Case 29	Snyder's-Lance, Inc.	■									■		■

	First Mover Advantages	Outsourcing	SWOT Matrix	SPACE Matrix	BCG & IE Matrices	Grand Strategy & QSPM	Governance	Organizational Structure	Organizational Culture	Human Resources Management	Market Segmentation & Production	EPS-EBIT Analysis	Projected Financial Statements	Company Valuation	Balanced Scorecard	Business Ethics	Environmental Sustainability	Foreign Business Culture

Acknowledgments

Many persons have contributed time, energy, ideas, and suggestions for improving this text over many editions. The strength of this text is largely attributed to the collective wisdom, work, and experiences of strategic-management professors, researchers, students, and practitioners. Names of particular individuals whose published research is referenced in this edition are listed alphabetically in the Name Index. To all individuals involved in making this text so popular and successful, we are indebted and thankful.

Many special persons and reviewers contributed valuable material and suggestions for this edition. We would like to thank our colleagues and friends at Auburn University, Mississippi State University, East Carolina University, the University of South Carolina, Campbell University, the University of North Carolina at Pembroke, and Francis Marion University. We have taught strategic management at all these universities. Scores of students and professors at these schools helped shape the development of this text.

We thank the following guest writers who contributed a case(s) to this sixteenth edition:

Meredith E. David, Baylor University

Mark L. Frigo, DePaul University

Debora J. Gilliard, Metropolitan State University of Denver

David Lynn Hoffman, Metropolitan State University of Denver

Edward Moore, Liberty University

Alvaro Polanco, Baylor University

Lori Radulovich, Baldwin Wallace University

Raj Selladurai, Indiana University Northwest

Diana Tsaw, California Lutheran University

John D. Varlaro, Johnson & Wales University

Jason Willoughby, Elizabethtown Community College

We thank you, the reader, for investing the time and effort to read and study this text. It will help you formulate, implement, and evaluate strategies for any organization with which you become associated. We hope you come to share our enthusiasm for the rich subject area of strategic management and for the systematic learning approach taken in this text. We welcome and invite your suggestions, ideas, thoughts, comments, and questions regarding any part of this text or the ancillary materials. Please contact Dr. Fred R. David at the following e-mail: **freddavid9@gmail.com**, or write him at the School of Business, Francis Marion University, Florence, SC 29501. We sincerely appreciate and need your input to continually improve this text in future editions. Your willingness to draw our attention to specific errors or deficiencies in coverage or exposition will especially be appreciated.

Thank you for using this text.

Fred R. David and Forest R. David

Global Acknowledgments

Pearson would also like to thank and acknowledge the following people for reviewing the global edition content and sharing their feedback to help improve the material

Nazih K. El-Jor, Lebanese American University

Georg Hauer, Stuttgart Technology University of Applied Sciences

Goh See Kwong, Taylor's University

Anneleen Michiels, University of Leuven

Sununta Siengthai, Asian Institute of Technology

1

Strategic Management Essentials

LEARNING OBJECTIVES

After studying this chapter, you should be able to do the following:

1-1. Describe the strategic-management process.

1-2. Discuss the three stages of strategy formulation, implementation, and evaluation activities.

1-3. Explain the need for integrating analysis and intuition in strategic management.

1-4. Define and give examples of key terms in strategic management.

1-5. Illustrate the comprehensive strategic-management model.

1-6. Describe the benefits of engaging in strategic management.

1-7. Explain why some firms do no strategic planning.

1-8. Describe the pitfalls in actually doing strategic planning.

1-9. Discuss the connection between business and military strategy.

ASSURANCE OF LEARNING EXERCISES

The following exercises are found at the end of this chapter:

W hen CEOs from the big three U.S. automakers—Ford, General Motors (GM), and Chrysler—showed up several years ago without a clear strategic plan to ask congressional leaders for bailout monies, they were sent home with instructions to develop a clear strategic plan for the future. Austan Goolsbee, one of President Barack Obama's top economic advisers, said, "Asking for a bailout without a convincing business plan was crazy." Goolsbee also said, "If the three auto CEOs need a bridge, it's got to be a bridge to somewhere, not a bridge to nowhere."[1] This text gives the instructions on how to develop a clear strategic plan—a bridge to somewhere rather than nowhere.

The chapter provides an overview of strategic management. It introduces a practical, integrative model of the strategic-management process, and it defines basic activities and terms in strategic management.

At the beginning of each chapter, a different company is showcased doing an exemplary job applying strategic-planning concepts, tools, and techniques. The first company featured for excellent strategic management practices is Singapore Airlines, Ltd., ranked amongst the top 15 carriers worldwide and one of the best managed companies in the world. In 2010, Goh Choon Phong was made the CEO of the flag carrier of Singapore. At the end of each chapter, a new, one-page, mini-case on a company is provided with respective questions that examine various concepts, tools, and techniques presented.

What Is Strategic Management?

Once there were two company presidents who competed in the same industry. These two presidents decided to go on a camping trip to discuss a possible merger. They hiked deep into the woods. Suddenly, they came upon a grizzly bear that rose up on its hind legs and snarled. Instantly, the first president took off his knapsack and got out a pair of jogging shoes. The second president said, "Hey, you can't outrun that bear." The first president responded, "Maybe I can't

Singapore Airlines Limited (SIA)

A 5-star airline, Singapore Airlines (SIA) operates the world's longest non-stop commercial flight from Singapore to Los Angeles and Newark and other trans-Pacific flights, and provides passenger services across more than 30 countries.

Strategically well managed, its diversified businesses include aircraft handling and engineering. SIA owns SilkAir, an airline company overseeing regional flights catering to small capacity requirements in secondary cities, and Tigerair, a low fare airline that serves 37 destinations across 12 countries. In Asia, SilkAir helps passengers travel in over 30 cities. The company is the official sponsor of Singapore's national football team and has continued to market the iconic Singapore Girl, a prominent element that depicts the flight attendants of the airline and is pegged as the central image for the brand.

SIA was acknowledged as the best Asian airline in the Business Traveler Awards 2014. According to a survey by *Fortune* in 2015, it was ranked as the best international airline for business travel and best customer service. The airline has often ranked as one of the most admired company in the world outside the United States. Apart from being acknowledged for their service and efficient operations, SIA has also been commended for their business performance.

SIA's 2014–2015 *Annual Report* reveals that the company carried 18,737 passengers that fiscal year, up from 18,628 the previous year, and had revenue of $15,566 million, up from $15,244 the prior year. In their 2014–2015 *Annual Report*, the company reported net profits of $368 million, up from $359 million the prior year.

In July 2015, SIA reported that its net profit in the first quarter was twice the amount made in the previous year due to lower oil prices, hence, lower fuel expenses for the airline. The airline saw a net profit of SGD $91.2 million ($67 million), up 162 percent from the same period in the previous year. In July 2015, all talks about acquiring a stake in South Korea's Jeju Air had ended. Instead SIA chose to respond to budget airlines, which were a bigger threat for SIA with their increasing market share in Southeast Asia, by focusing on expanding in Australia, Thailand, and India. An investment in Jeju Air would have given it more access to North Asia, including China.

Source: Based on company documents.

outrun that bear, but I surely can outrun you!" This story captures the notion of strategic management, which is to gain and sustain competitive advantage.

What Is a Cohesion Case?

A distinguishing, popular feature of this text is the Cohesion Case, named so because a written case on a company appears at the end of this chapter, and then all other chapters feature end-of-chapter Assurance of Learning Exercises to apply strategic-planning concepts, tools, and techniques to the Cohesion Case company. Nestlé S.A. is featured as the new Cohesion Case in this edition, because Nestlé is a well-known, well-managed global firm undergoing strategic change. By working through the Nestlé-related exercises at the end of each chapter, students become well prepared to develop an effective strategic plan for any company assigned to them (or their team) to perform a strategic-management case analysis. Case analysis is a core part of almost every strategic-management course globally.

Defining Strategic Management

Strategic management is the art and science of formulating, implementing, and evaluating cross-functional decisions that enable an organization to achieve its objectives. As this definition implies, strategic management focuses on integrating management, marketing, finance and accounting, production and operations, research and development (R&D), and information systems to achieve organizational success. The term *strategic management* in this text is used synonymously with the term **strategic planning**. The latter term is more often used in the business world, whereas the former is often used in academia. Sometimes the term *strategic management* is used to refer to strategy formulation, implementation, and evaluation, with *strategic planning* referring only to strategy formulation. The purpose of strategic management is to exploit and create new and different opportunities for tomorrow; **long-range planning**, in contrast, tries to optimize for tomorrow the trends of today.

The term *strategic planning* originated in the 1950s and was popular between the mid-1960s and the mid-1970s. During these years, strategic planning was widely believed to be the answer for all problems. At the time, much of corporate America was "obsessed" with strategic planning. Following that boom, however, strategic planning was cast aside during the 1980s as various planning models did not yield higher returns. The 1990s, however, brought the revival of strategic planning, and the process is widely practiced today in the business world. Many companies today have a *chief strategy officer (CSO)*. McDonald's hired a new CSO in October 2015.

A strategic plan is, in essence, a company's game plan. Just as a football team needs a good game plan to have a chance for success, a company must have a good strategic plan to compete successfully. Profit margins among firms in most industries are so slim that there is little room for error in the overall strategic plan. A strategic plan results from tough managerial choices among numerous good alternatives, and it signals commitment to specific markets, policies, procedures, and operations in lieu of other, "less desirable" courses of action.

The term *strategic management* is used at many colleges and universities as the title for the capstone course in business administration. This course integrates material from all business courses, and, in addition, introduces new strategic-management concepts and techniques being widely used by firms in strategic planning.

Stages of Strategic Management

The **strategic-management process** consists of three stages: strategy formulation, strategy implementation, and strategy evaluation. **Strategy formulation** includes developing a vision and a mission, identifying an organization's external opportunities and threats, determining internal strengths and weaknesses, establishing long-term objectives, generating alternative strategies, and choosing particular strategies to pursue. Strategy-formulation issues include deciding what new businesses to enter, what businesses to abandon, whether to expand operations or diversify, whether to enter international markets, whether to merge or form a joint venture, and how to avoid a hostile takeover.

Because no organization has unlimited resources, strategists must decide which alternative strategies will benefit the firm most. Strategy-formulation decisions commit an organization to specific products, markets, resources, and technologies over an extended period of time. Strategies determine long-term competitive advantages. For better or worse, strategic decisions have major multifunctional consequences and enduring effects on an organization. Top managers have the best perspective to understand fully the ramifications of strategy-formulation decisions; they have the authority to commit the resources necessary for implementation.

Strategy implementation requires a firm to establish annual objectives, devise policies, motivate employees, and allocate resources so that formulated strategies can be executed. Strategy implementation includes developing a strategy-supportive culture, creating an effective organizational structure, redirecting marketing efforts, preparing budgets, developing and using information systems, and linking employee compensation to organizational performance.

Strategy implementation often is called the "action stage" of strategic management. Implementing strategy means mobilizing employees and managers to put formulated strategies into action. Often considered to be the most difficult stage in strategic management, strategy implementation requires personal discipline, commitment, and sacrifice. Successful strategy implementation hinges on managers' ability to motivate employees, which is more an art than a science. Strategies formulated but not implemented serve no useful purpose.

Interpersonal skills are especially critical for successful strategy implementation. Strategy-implementation activities affect all employees and managers in an organization. Every division and department must decide on answers to questions such as "What must we do to implement our part of the organization's strategy?" and "How best can we get the job done?" The challenge of implementation is to stimulate managers and employees throughout an organization to work with pride and enthusiasm toward achieving stated objectives.

Strategy evaluation is the final stage in strategic management. Managers desperately need to know when particular strategies are not working well; strategy evaluation is the primary means for obtaining this information. All strategies are subject to future modification because external and internal factors constantly change. Three fundamental strategy-evaluation activities are (1) reviewing external and internal factors that are the bases for current strategies, (2) measuring performance, and (3) taking corrective actions. Strategy evaluation is needed because success today is no guarantee of success tomorrow! Success always creates new and different problems; complacent organizations experience demise.

Formulation, implementation, and evaluation of strategy activities occur at three hierarchical levels in a large organization: corporate, divisional or strategic business unit, and functional. By fostering communication and interaction among managers and employees across hierarchical levels, strategic management helps a firm function as a competitive team. Most small businesses and some large businesses do not have divisions or strategic business units; they have only the corporate and functional levels. Nevertheless, managers and employees at these two levels should be actively involved in strategic-management activities.

Peter Drucker says the prime task of strategic management is thinking through the overall mission of a business—

> that is, of asking the question, "What is our business?" This leads to the setting of objectives, the development of strategies, and the making of today's decisions for tomorrow's results. This clearly must be done by a part of the organization that can see the entire business; that can balance objectives and the needs of today against the needs of tomorrow; and that can allocate resources of men and money to key results.[2]

Integrating Intuition and Analysis

Edward Deming once said, "In God we trust. All others bring data." The strategic-management process can be described as an objective, logical, systematic approach for making major decisions in an organization. It attempts to organize qualitative and quantitative information in a way that allows effective decisions to be made under conditions of uncertainty. Yet strategic management is not a pure science that lends itself to a nice, neat, one-two-three approach.

Based on past experiences, judgment, and feelings, most people recognize that **intuition** is essential to making good strategic decisions. Intuition is particularly useful for making decisions in situations of great uncertainty or little precedent. It is also helpful when highly interrelated variables exist or when it is necessary to choose from several plausible alternatives. Some managers and owners of businesses profess to have extraordinary abilities for using intuition alone in devising brilliant strategies. For example, Will Durant, who organized GM, was described by Alfred Sloan as "a man who would proceed on a course of action guided solely, as far as I could tell, by some intuitive flash of brilliance. He never felt obliged to make an engineering hunt for the facts. Yet at times, he was astoundingly correct in his judgment."[3] Albert Einstein acknowledged the importance of intuition when he said, "I believe in intuition and inspiration. At times I feel certain that I am right while not knowing the reason. Imagination is more important than knowledge, because knowledge is limited, whereas imagination embraces the entire world."[4]

Although some organizations today may survive and prosper because they have intuitive geniuses managing them, many are not so fortunate. Most organizations can benefit from strategic management, which is based on integrating intuition and analysis in decision making. Choosing an intuitive or analytic approach to decision making is not an either-or proposition. Managers at all levels in an organization inject their intuition and judgment into strategic-management analyses. Analytical thinking and intuitive thinking complement each other.

Operating from the I've-already-made-up-my-mind-don't-bother-me-with-the-facts mode is not management by intuition; it is management by ignorance.[5] Drucker says, "I believe in intuition only if you discipline it. 'Hunch' artists, who make a diagnosis but don't check it out with the facts, are the ones in medicine who kill people, and in management kill businesses."[6] As Henderson notes:

> The accelerating rate of change today is producing a business world in which customary managerial habits in organizations are increasingly inadequate. Experience alone was an adequate guide when changes could be made in small increments. But intuitive and experience-based management philosophies are grossly inadequate when decisions are strategic and have major, irreversible consequences.[7]

In a sense, the strategic-management process is an attempt to duplicate what goes on in the mind of a brilliant, intuitive person who knows the business and assimilates and integrates that knowledge using analysis to formulate effective strategies.

Adapting to Change

The strategic-management process is based on the belief that organizations should continually monitor internal and external events and trends so that timely changes can be made as needed. The rate and magnitude of changes that affect organizations are increasing dramatically, as evidenced by how the drop in oil prices caught so many firms by surprise. Firms, like organisms, must be "adept at adapting" or they will not survive. To survive, all organizations must astutely identify and adapt to change. The strategic-management process is aimed at allowing organizations to adapt effectively to change over the long run. Waterman noted:

> In today's business environment, more than in any preceding era, the only constant is change. Successful organizations effectively manage change, continuously adapting their bureaucracies, strategies, systems, products, and cultures to survive the shocks and prosper from the forces that decimate the competition.[8]

On a political map, the boundaries between countries may be clear, but on a competitive map showing the real flow of financial and industrial activity, the boundaries have largely disappeared. The speedy flow of information has eaten away at national boundaries so that people worldwide readily see for themselves how other people live and work. We have become a borderless world with global citizens, global competitors, global customers, global suppliers, and global distributors! Many firms headquartered in the United States are challenged by outside-U.S.–based companies in many industries. For example, Toyota, Honda, Yamaha, Suzuki, Volkswagen, Samsung, and Kia have huge market shares in the United States.

The need to adapt to change leads organizations to key strategic-management questions, such as "What kind of business should we become?" "Are we in the right field(s)?" "Should we reshape our business?" "What new competitors are entering our industry?" "What strategies should we pursue?" "How are our customers changing?" "Are new technologies being developed that could put us out of business?"

The Internet promotes endless comparison shopping, enabling consumers worldwide to band together to demand discounts. The Internet has transferred power from businesses to individuals. Buyers used to face big obstacles when attempting to get the best price and service, such as limited time and data to compare, but now consumers can quickly scan hundreds of vendor offerings. Both the number of people shopping online and the average amount they spend is increasing dramatically. Digital communication has become the name of the game in marketing. Consumers today are flocking to blogs, sending tweets, watching and posting videos on YouTube, and spending hours on Tumbler, Facebook, Reddit, Instagram, and LinkedIn, instead of watching television, listening to the radio, or reading newspapers and magazines. Facebook recently unveiled features that further marry these social sites to the wider Internet. Facebook users can now log onto various business shopping sites from their social site, so their friends can see what items they have purchased from what companies. Facebook wants their members to use their identities to manage *all* their online identities. Most traditional retailers boost in-store sales using their websites to promote in-store promotions.

Key Terms in Strategic Management

Before we further discuss strategic management, we should define nine key terms: *competitive advantage, strategists, vision and mission statements, external opportunities and threats, internal strengths and weaknesses, long-term objectives, strategies, annual objectives,* and *policies.*

Competitive Advantage

Strategic management is all about gaining and maintaining **competitive advantage**. This term can be defined as any activity a firm does especially well compared to activities done by rival firms, or any resource a firm possesses that rival firms desire.

Having fewer fixed assets than rival firms can provide major competitive advantages. For example, Apple has virtually no manufacturing facilities of its own, and rival Sony has 57 electronics factories. Apple relies almost entirely on contract manufacturers for production of all its products, whereas Sony owns its own plants. Having fewer fixed assets has enabled Apple to remain financially lean.

According to CEO Paco Underhill of Envirosell, "Where it used to be a polite war, it's now a 21st-century bar fight, where everybody is competing with everyone else for the customers' money." Shoppers are "trading down: Nordstrom is taking customers from Neiman Marcus and Saks Fifth Avenue, T.J. Maxx and Marshalls are taking customers from most other stores in the mall, and Family Dollar is taking revenues from Walmart.[9] Getting and keeping competitive advantage is essential for long-term success in an organization. In mass retailing, big-box companies, such as Walmart, Best Buy, and Sears, are losing competitive advantage to smaller stores, reflecting the dramatic shift in mass retailing to becoming smaller. As customers shift more to online purchases, less brick and mortar is definitely better for sustaining competitive advantage in retailing. Walmart Express stores of less than 40,000 square feet each, rather than its 185,000-square-foot Supercenters, and Office Depot's new 5,000-square-foot stores are examples of smaller is better.

Normally, a firm can sustain a competitive advantage for only a certain period because of rival firms imitating and undermining that advantage. Thus, it is not adequate simply to obtain competitive advantage. A firm must strive to achieve **sustained competitive advantage** by (1) continually adapting to changes in external trends and events and internal capabilities, competencies, and resources; and (2) effectively formulating, implementing, and evaluating strategies that capitalize on those factors.

Strategists

Strategists are the individuals most responsible for the success or failure of an organization. They have various job titles, such as *chief executive officer, president, owner, chair of the board, executive director, chancellor, dean,* and *entrepreneur.* Jay Conger, professor of organizational behavior at the London Business School and author of *Building Leaders*, says, "All strategists have to be chief learning officers. We are in an extended period of change. If our leaders aren't highly adaptive and great models during this period, then our companies won't adapt either, because ultimately leadership is about being a role model."

Strategists help an organization gather, analyze, and organize information. They track industry and competitive trends, develop forecasting models and scenario analyses, evaluate corporate and divisional performance, spot emerging market opportunities, identify business threats, and develop creative action plans. Strategic planners usually serve in a support or staff role. Usually found in higher levels of management, they typically have considerable authority for decision making in the firm. The CEO is the most visible and critical strategic manager. Any manager who has responsibility for a unit or division, responsibility for profit and loss outcomes, or direct authority over a major piece of the business is a strategic manager (strategist).

In the last few years, the position of CSO has become common in many organizations, including Sun Microsystems, Network Associates, Clarus, Lante, Marimba, Sapient, Commerce One, BBDO, Cadbury Schweppes, General Motors, Ellie Mae, Cendant, Charles Schwab, Tyco, Campbell Soup, Morgan Stanley, and Reed-Elsevier. This corporate officer title represents recognition of the growing importance of strategic planning in business. Franz Koch, the CSO of German sportswear company Puma AG, was recently promoted to CEO of Puma. When asked about his plans for the company, Koch said on a conference call, "I plan to just focus on the long-term strategic plan." Academic Research Capsule 1-1 reveals when CSOs are most often hired.

Strategists differ as much as organizations do, and these differences must be considered in the formulation, implementation, and evaluation of strategies. Strategists differ in their attitudes, values, ethics, willingness to take risks, concern for social responsibility, concern for profitability, concern for short-run versus long-run aims, and management style—some will not even consider various types of strategies because of their personal philosophies. The founder of Hershey, Milton Hershey, built the company so that he could afford to manage an orphanage. From corporate profits, Hershey today cares for about 900 boys and 1,000 girls in its boarding school for pre-K through grade 12.

Athletic coaches are also strategists. Football, basketball, baseball, soccer, and in fact most athletic contests are often won or lost based a team's game plan. For example, a basketball coach may plan to fast break and play up-tempo, rather than play more half court, if the players are smaller and faster, or if the team has more depth than the opposing team. A few great college basketball coaches today are Mike Krzyzewski at Duke, John Calipari at Kentucky, Jim Boeheim at Syracuse, and Tom Izzo at Michigan State. Great college basketball coaches years ago included John Wooden, Jim Valvano, Dean Smith, and Bobby Knight. Another great coach of yesteryear was Nolan Richardson, who developed excellent game plans and, in 1994, as the first black head coach at a major university in the South, led the Arkansas Razorbacks men's basketball team to

ACADEMIC RESEARCH CAPSULE 1-1

When Are Chief Strategy Officers (CSOs) Hired/Appointed?

An increasing number of firms are employing a chief strategy officer (CSO). In an article published in 2014, Menz and Sheef examined 200 S&P 500 firms over a 5-year period to examine what factors contribute to firms hiring a CSO and what factors contribute to a CSO affecting a firm's financial performance. Of the sampled firms, on average, during the study, 42 percent employed a CSO. Although many factors may lead to a firm's decision to appoint a CSO, the authors focused on five key areas that prior research suggests as most important and most likely to lead to a CSO appointment:

1) As the business portfolio increases (e.g., the firm becomes more diversified)

2) As acquisition activity expands
3) As alliance activity increases
4) As a firm's size grows
5) As top management team interdependence increases

Results of the Menz and Sheef study reveal that an increase in management interdependence and growth in acquisition activity were most commonly associated with hiring a new CSO.

Source: Based on Markus Menz and Christine Sheef, "Chief Strategy Officers: Contingency Analysis of Their Presence in Top Management Teams," *Strategic Management Journal* 35, no. 3 (March 2014): 461–471.

TABLE 1-1 Ten Famous, Strategic-Planning–Relevant Quotes from NFL Coaches

1. "Perfection is not attainable. But if we chase perfection, we can catch excellence." —*Vince Lombardi, Head Coach Green Bay Packers (1959–67)*
2. "Leadership is a matter of having people look at you and gain confidence…. If you're in control, they're in control." —*Tom Landry, Head Coach Dallas Cowboys (1960–88)*
3. "On a team, it's not the strength of the individual players, but it is the strength of the unit and how they all function together." —*Bill Belichick, Head Coach New England Patriots (2000– Present), New York Jets (1999), Cleveland Browns (1991–95)*
4. "If you want to win, do the ordinary things better than anyone else does them day in and day out." —*Chuck Noll, Head Coach Pittsburgh Steelers (1969–91)*
5. "Leaders are made, they are not born. They are made by hard effort, which is the price which all of us must pay to achieve any goal that is worthwhile." —*Vince Lombardi, Head Coach Green Bay Packers (1959–67)*
6. "Try not to do too many things at once. Know what you want, the number one thing today and tomorrow. Persevere and get it done." —*George Allen, Head Coach Los Angeles Rams (1957, 1966–70), Chicago Bears (1958–65), Washington Redskins (1971–77)*
7. "You fail all the time, but you aren't a failure until you start blaming someone else." —*Bum Phillips, Head Coach Houston Oilers (1975–80), New Orleans Saints (1981–85)*
8. "Success demands singleness of purpose." —*Vince Lombardi, Head Coach Green Bay Packers (1959–67)*
9. "Stay focused. Your start does not determine how you're going to finish." —*Herm Edwards, Head Coach New York Jets (2001–05), Kansas City Chiefs (2006–08)*
10. "Nobody who ever gave his best regretted it." —*George S. Halas, Head Coach Chicago Bears (1933–42, 1946–55, 1958–67)*

Source: A variety of sources.

win the NCAA college basketball national championship versus Duke.[10] Switching to football, some inspirational, strategic-planning–related quotes from legendary National Football League (NFL) coaches are provided in Table 1-1.

Vision and Mission Statements

Many organizations today develop a **vision statement** that answers the question "What do we want to become?" Developing a vision statement is often considered the first step in strategic planning, preceding even development of a mission statement. Many vision statements are a single sentence. For example, the vision statement of Stokes Eye Clinic in Florence, South Carolina, is "Our vision is to take care of your vision."

Mission statements are "enduring statements of purpose that distinguish one business from other similar firms. A mission statement identifies the scope of a firm's operations in product and market terms."[11] It addresses the basic question that faces all strategists: "What is our business?" A clear mission statement describes the values and priorities of an organization. Developing a mission statement compels strategists to think about the nature and scope of present operations and to assess the potential attractiveness of future markets and activities. A mission statement not only broadly charts the future direction of an organization but it also serves as a constant reminder to its employees of why the organization exists and what the founders envisioned when they put their fame and fortune (and names) at risk to breathe life into their dreams.

External Opportunities and Threats

External opportunities and **external threats** refer to economic, social, cultural, demographic, environmental, political, legal, governmental, technological, and competitive trends and events that could significantly benefit or harm an organization in the future. Opportunities and threats are largely beyond the control of a single organization—thus the word *external*. Some general categories of opportunities and threats are listed in Table 1-2, but be mindful that dollars, numbers, percentages, ratios, and quantification are essential, so strategists can assess the magnitude

TABLE 1-2 Some General Categories of Opportunities and Threats

- Availability of capital can no longer be taken for granted.
- Consumers expect green operations and products.
- Marketing is moving rapidly to the Internet.
- Commodity food prices are increasing.
- An oversupply of oil is driving oil and gas prices down.
- Computer hacker problems are increasing.
- Intense price competition is plaguing most firms.
- Unemployment and underemployment rates remain high globally.
- Interest rates are low but rising.
- Product life cycles are becoming shorter.
- State and local governments are financially weak.
- Drug cartel–related violence is increasing in Mexico.
- Winters are colder and summers are hotter than usual.
- Birth rates are declining in most countries.
- Global markets offer the highest growth in revenues.
- New laws are passed.
- Competitors introduce new products.
- National catastrophes occur.
- The value of the Euro is rebounding.
- The separation between the rich and poor is growing.
- Social media networking is greatly expanding.
- The Russian ruble has dropped 60 percent in value.

of opportunities and threats and take appropriate actions. For example, in Table 1-2, rather than saying "Marketing is moving rapidly to the Internet," strategists who take the time to do research would find, for example, that "spending on online advertisements globally rose about 25 percent in 2014, according to eMarketer, and represented about 39 percent of total advertising spending in the United States.[12] Strategies must be formulated and implemented based on specific factual information to the extent possible—because so much is at stake in having a good game plan.

External trends and events are creating a different type of consumer and consequently a need for different types of products, services, and strategies. Many companies in many industries face the severe threat of online sales eroding brick-and-mortar sales. A competitor's strength could be a threat, or a rival firm's weakness could be an opportunity.

A basic tenet of strategic management is that firms need to formulate strategies to take advantage of external opportunities and avoid or reduce the impact of external threats. For this reason, identifying, monitoring, and evaluating external opportunities and threats are essential for success. This process of conducting research and gathering and assimilating external information is sometimes called **environmental scanning** or *industry analysis*. Lobbying is one activity that some organizations use to influence external opportunities and threats.

Internal Strengths and Weaknesses

Internal strengths and **internal weaknesses** are an organization's controllable activities that are performed especially well or poorly. They arise in the management, marketing, finance/accounting, production/operations, research and development, and management information systems (MIS) activities of a business. Identifying and evaluating organizational strengths and weaknesses in the functional areas of a business is an essential strategic-management activity. Organizations strive to pursue strategies that capitalize on internal strengths and eliminate internal weaknesses.

Strengths and weaknesses are determined relative to competitors. *Relative deficiency or superiority is important information.* Also, strengths and weaknesses can be determined by elements of *being* rather than *performance*. For example, a strength may involve ownership of natural resources or a historic reputation for quality. Strengths and weaknesses may be determined relative to a firm's own objectives. For instance, high levels of inventory turnover may not be a strength for a firm that seeks never to stock-out.

In performing a strategic-management case analysis, it is important to be as divisional as possible when determining and stating internal strengths and weaknesses. In other words, for a company such as Walmart saying, "Sam Club's revenues grew 11 percent in the recent quarter," is much better than Walmart couching all of its internal factors in terms of the firm as a *whole*. "Being divisional" will enable strategies to be more effectively formulated because in strategic planning, firms must allocate resources among divisions (segments) of the firm (that is, by product, region, customer, or whatever the various units of the firm are), such as Walmart's Sam's Club versus Walmart's Supercenters, or Walmart's Mexico segment versus Walmart's Europe segment.

Both internal and external factors should be stated as specifically as possible, using numbers, percentages, dollars, and ratios, as well as comparisons over time to rival firms. *Specificity is important because strategies will be formulated and resources allocated based on this information.* The more specific the underlying external and internal factors, the more effectively strategies can be formulated and resources allocated. Determining the numbers takes more time, but survival of the firm often is at stake, so doing some research and incorporating numbers associated with key factors is essential.

Internal factors can be determined in a number of ways, including computing ratios, measuring performance, and comparing to past periods and industry averages. Various types of surveys also can be developed and administered to examine internal factors, such as employee morale, production efficiency, advertising effectiveness, and customer loyalty.

Long-Term Objectives

Objectives can be defined as specific results that an organization seeks to achieve in pursuing its basic mission. Long-term means more than one year. Objectives are essential for organizational success because they provide direction; aid in evaluation; create synergy; reveal priorities; focus coordination; and provide a basis for effective planning, organizing, motivating, and controlling activities. Objectives should be challenging, measurable, consistent, reasonable, and clear. In a multidimensional firm, objectives are needed both for the overall company and each division.

Strategies

Strategies are the means by which **long-term objectives** will be achieved. Business strategies may include geographic expansion, diversification, acquisition, product development, market penetration, retrenchment, divestiture, liquidation, and joint ventures. Strategies currently being pursued by some companies are described in Table 1-3.

Strategies are potential actions that require top-management decisions and large amounts of the firm's resources. They affect an organization's long-term prosperity, typically for at least five years, and thus are future-oriented. Strategies also have multifunctional and multidivisional consequences and require consideration of both the external and internal factors facing the firm.

Annual Objectives

Annual objectives are short-term milestones that organizations must achieve to reach long-term objectives. Like long-term objectives, annual objectives should be measurable, quantitative, challenging, realistic, consistent, and prioritized. They must also be established at the corporate, divisional, and functional levels in a large organization. Annual objectives should be stated in terms of management, marketing, finance/accounting, production/operations, R&D, and MIS accomplishments. A set of annual objectives is needed for each long-term objective. These objectives are especially important in strategy implementation, whereas long-term objectives are particularly important in strategy formulation. Annual objectives provide the basis for allocating resources.

TABLE 1-3 Sample Strategies in Action in 2015

General Electric Company (GE)
General Electric Company recently sold its appliance business to Sweden-based Electrolux AB for $3.3 billion, leaving GE focused almost entirely on finance and big-ticket industrial equipment, such as power turbines, locomotives, and aircraft engines. GE's CEO Jeff Immelt, when asked "What is GE?," recently responded with the word *energy,* rather than *insurance, plastics, media, consumer finance,* or *appliances*. Founded by Thomas Edison in 1889 and originally named Edison General Electric Company, GE is returning to its roots as an energy company. The company has spent about $14 billion lately buying oil-and-gas service companies, while divesting dishwashers, radios, stoves, microwaves, and toasters.

Chuy's (CHUY)
Chuy's is a chain of 59 small Mexican restaurants scattered across the United States. It is not "fast casual," like Chipotle Mexican Grill; rather, it is a sit-down, table-service restaurant that is uniquely festive, including, for example, Elvis shrines and complimentary Happy Hour nacho bars served out of makeshift car trunks. The décor also includes walls that feature customer-submitted snapshots of their pet dogs. Chuy's uniqueness and strategies are working great, as revenue soared 20 percent to $64.1 million in its latest quarter. The company opened 11 more locations in the last 12 months. At the individual restaurant level, Chuy's reported a 3 percent improvement in comps, comprised of a 1.3 percent increase in customers and a 1.7 percent bump in the average check. Chuy's comparable restaurant sales have increased for 17 consecutive quarters. Unlike Chipotle, which recently increased prices, Chuy's has absorbed numerous commodity increases, keeping most of its menu items below $10.

Source: Company documents and a variety of sources.

Policies

Policies are the means by which annual objectives will be achieved. Policies include guidelines, rules, and procedures established to support efforts to achieve stated objectives. Policies are guides to decision making and address repetitive or recurring situations. Usually, policies are stated in terms of management, marketing, finance/accounting, production/operations, R&D, and MIS activities. They may be established at the corporate level and apply to an entire organization, at the divisional level and apply to a single division, or they may be established at the functional level and apply to particular operational activities or departments.

Like annual objectives, policies are especially important in strategy implementation because they outline an organization's expectations of its employees and managers. Policies allow consistency and coordination within and between organizational departments. Policy change is sometimes difficult. For example, years ago, it was unquestioningly accepted that people could smoke in their offices, in restaurants, in hotels, and on airplanes. But as people and companies became educated about the harms of smoking—not only to smokers but also to nonsmokers —policy in businesses began to change. Even with the vast changes in smoking in public areas, smoking rates are still high. In the United States, Kentucky takes the lead in having more smokers than in any other state: 30.2 percent of residents, followed by West Virginia and Mississippi; Utah has the lowest rate (12.2%), followed by California and Minnesota.[13] In the United States overall, 20.5 percent of men smoke, compared to 15.8 percent of women. For a brief time, people thought the answer might be "tobacco-less" cigarettes, as electronic cigarettes hit the market. Unfortunately, however, the product still injects nicotine into the smoker's body.

Substantial research suggests that a healthier workforce can more effectively and efficiently implement strategies. Smoking has become a heavy burden for Europe's state-run social welfare systems, with smoking-related diseases costing more than $100 billion a year. Smoking also is a huge burden on companies worldwide, so firms are continually implementing policies to curtail smoking. Starbucks has banned smoking within 25 feet of its 7,000 stores not located inside another retail establishment.

The Strategic-Management Model

The strategic-management process can best be studied and applied using a model. Every model represents some kind of process. The framework illustrated in Figure 1-1 is a widely accepted, comprehensive model of the strategic-management process.[14] This model does not guarantee success, but it does represent a clear and practical approach for formulating, implementing, and evaluating strategies. Relationships among major components of the strategic-management process are shown in the model, which appears in all subsequent chapters with appropriate areas shaped to show the particular focus of each chapter. This text is organized around this model because the model reveals how organizations actually do strategic planning. Three important questions to answer in developing a strategic plan are as follows:

Where are we now?

Where do we want to go?

How are we going to get there?

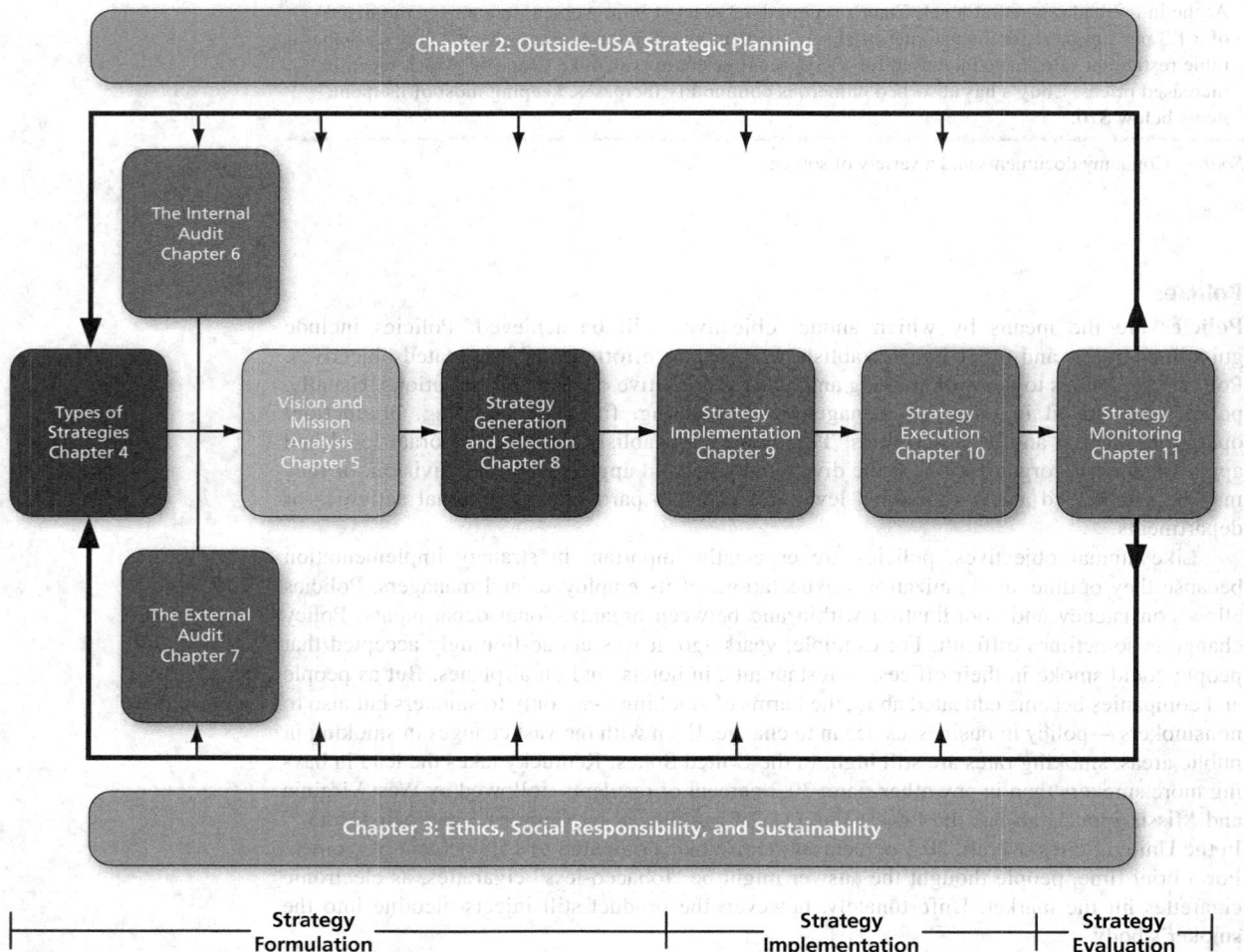

FIGURE 1-1

A Comprehensive Strategic-Management Model

Source: Fred R. David, adapted from "How Companies Define Their Mission," *Long Range Planning* 22, no. 3 (June 1988): 40, © Fred R. David.

Identifying an organization's existing vision, mission, objectives, and strategies is the logical starting point for strategic management because a firm's present situation and condition may preclude certain strategies and may even dictate a particular course of action. Every organization has a vision, mission, objectives, and strategy, even if these elements are not consciously designed, written, or communicated. The answer to where an organization is going can be determined largely by where the organization has been!

The strategic-management process is dynamic and continuous. A change in any one of the major components in the model can necessitate a change in any or all of the other components. For instance, African countries coming online could represent a major opportunity and require a change in long-term objectives and strategies; a failure to accomplish annual objectives might require a change in policy; or a major competitor's change in strategy might require a change in the firm's mission. Therefore, strategy formulation, implementation, and evaluation activities should be performed on a continual basis, not just at the end of the year or semiannually. The strategic-management process never really ends.

Note in the **strategic-management model** that business ethics, social responsibility, and environmental sustainability issues impact all activities in the model, as discussed in Chapter 3. Also, note in the model that global and international issues impact virtually all strategic decisions, as described in detail in Chapter 2.

The strategic-management process is not as cleanly divided and neatly performed in practice as the strategic-management model suggests. Strategists do not go through the process in lockstep fashion. Generally, there is give-and-take among hierarchical levels of an organization. Many organizations conduct formal meetings semiannually to discuss and update the firm's vision, mission, opportunities, threats, strengths, weaknesses, strategies, objectives, policies, and performance. These meetings are commonly held off-premises and are called **retreats**. The rationale for periodically conducting strategic-management meetings away from the work site is to encourage more creativity and candor from participants. Good communication and feedback are needed throughout the strategic-management process. The Academic Research Capsule 1-2 reveals what activity is most important in the strategic-management process.

Application of the strategic-management process is typically more formal in larger and well-established organizations. Formality refers to the extent that participants, responsibilities, authority, duties, and approach are specified. Smaller businesses tend to be less formal. Firms that compete in complex, rapidly changing environments, such as technology companies, tend to be more formal in strategic planning. Firms that have many divisions, products, markets, and technologies also tend to be more formal in applying strategic-management concepts. Greater formality in applying the strategic-management process is usually positively associated with organizational success.[15]

Benefits of Engaging in Strategic Management

Strategic management allows an organization to be more proactive than reactive in shaping its own future; it allows an organization to initiate and influence (rather than just respond to) activities—and thus to exert control over its own destiny. Small business owners, chief executive

ACADEMIC RESEARCH CAPSULE 1-2

What Activity Is Most Important in the Strategic-Management Process?

Recent research has examined the strategic-management process and concluded that perhaps the most important "activity" is the feedback loop, because strategy must be thought of as a "verb rather than a noun." Rose and Cray contend that strategy is a "living, evolving conceptual entity," and as such must be engulfed in flexibility. "Flexibility" should also be reflected in the structures put in place to monitor and modify strategic plans. Flexibility safeguards should increasingly be known and practiced throughout the firm, especially at lower levels of the organization. The stages of strategic management (formulation, implementation, and evaluation) are so fluid as

to be virtually indistinguishable when one starts and the other ends. Thus, in the comprehensive model illustrated, the encompassing feedback loop is vitally important to enable firms to readily adapt to changing conditions. A significant change in any activity (box) in the model could necessitate change(s) in other activities.

Source: Based on Wade Rose and David Cray "The Role of Context in the Transformation of Planned Strategy into Implemented Strategy," *International Journal of Business Management and Economic Research* 4, no. 3 (2013): 721–737.

officers, presidents, and managers of many for-profit and nonprofit organizations have recognized and realized the benefits of strategic management.

Historically, the principal benefit of strategic management has been to help organizations formulate better strategies through the use of a more systematic, logical, and rational approach for decision making. In addition, the process, rather than the decision or document, is also a major benefit of engaging in strategic management. Through involvement in the process (i.e., dialogue and participation), managers and employees become committed to supporting the organization. *Communication is a key to successful strategic management.* Communication *may be the most important word in management.* Figure 1-2 illustrates this intrinsic benefit of a firm engaging in strategic planning. Note that all firms need all employees "on a mission" to help the firm succeed.

Dale McConkey said, "Plans are less important than planning." The manner in which strategic management is carried out is therefore exceptionally important. A major aim of the process is to achieve understanding and commitment from all managers and employees. Understanding may be the most important benefit of strategic management, followed by commitment. When managers and employees understand what the organization is doing and why, they often feel a part of the firm and become committed to assisting it. This is especially true when employees also understand links between their own compensation and organizational performance. Managers and employees become surprisingly creative and innovative when they understand and support the firm's mission, objectives, and strategies. A great benefit of strategic management, then, is the opportunity that the process provides to empower individuals. **Empowerment** is the act of strengthening employees' sense of effectiveness by encouraging them to participate in decision making and to exercise initiative and imagination, and rewarding them for doing so. William Fulmer said, "You want your people to run the business as it if were their own."

Strategic planning is a learning, helping, educating, and supporting process, not merely a paper-shuffling activity among top executives. Strategic-management dialogue is more important than a nicely bound strategic-management document. The worst thing strategists can do is develop strategic plans themselves and then present them to operating managers to execute. Through involvement in the process, line managers become "owners" of the strategy. Ownership of strategies by the people who have to execute them is a key to success!

Although making good strategic decisions is the major responsibility of an organization's owner or chief executive officer, both managers and employees must also be involved in strategy formulation, implementation, and evaluation activities. Participation is a key to gaining commitment for needed changes. An increasing number of corporations and institutions are using strategic management to make effective decisions. But strategic management is not a guarantee for success; it can be dysfunctional if conducted haphazardly.

Financial Benefits

Organizations that use strategic-management concepts are generally more profitable and successful than those that do not. Businesses using strategic-management concepts show significant improvement in sales, profitability, and productivity compared to firms without systematic

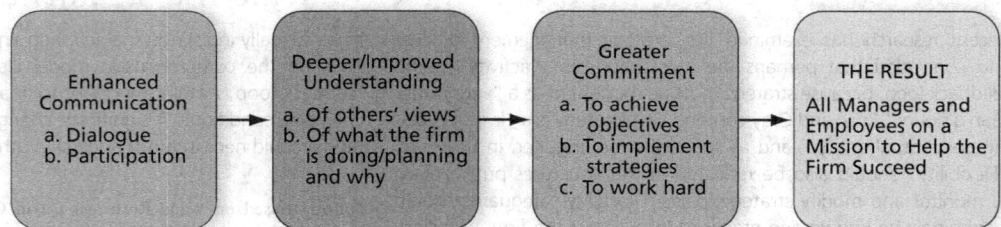

| Enhanced Communication a. Dialogue b. Participation | → | Deeper/Improved Understanding a. Of others' views b. Of what the firm is doing/planning and why | → | Greater Commitment a. To achieve objectives b. To implement strategies c. To work hard | → | THE RESULT All Managers and Employees on a Mission to Help the Firm Succeed |

FIGURE 1-2
Benefits to a Firm That Does Strategic Planning

planning activities. High-performing firms tend to do systematic planning to prepare for future fluctuations in their external and internal environments. Firms with management systems that utilize strategic-planning concepts, tools, and techniques generally exhibit superior long-term financial performance relative to their industry.

High-performing firms seem to make more informed decisions with good anticipation of both short- and long-term consequences. In contrast, firms that perform poorly often engage in activities that are shortsighted and do not reflect good forecasting of future conditions. Strategists of low-performing organizations are often preoccupied with solving internal problems and meeting paperwork deadlines. They typically underestimate their competitors' strengths and overestimate their own firm's strengths. They often attribute weak performance to uncontrollable factors such as a poor economy, technological change, or foreign competition.

More than 100,000 businesses in the United States fail annually. Business failures include bankruptcies, foreclosures, liquidations, and court-mandated receiverships. Although many factors besides a lack of effective strategic management can lead to business failure, the planning concepts and tools described in this text can yield substantial financial benefits for any organization.

Nonfinancial Benefits

Besides helping firms avoid financial demise, strategic management offers other tangible benefits, such as enhanced awareness of external threats, improved understanding of competitors' strategies, increased employee productivity, reduced resistance to change, and a clearer understanding of performance–reward relationships. Strategic management enhances the problem-prevention capabilities of organizations because it promotes interaction among managers at all divisional and functional levels. Firms that have nurtured their managers and employees, shared organizational objectives with them, empowered them to help improve the product or service, and recognized their contributions can turn to them for help in a pinch because of this interaction.

In addition to empowering managers and employees, strategic management often brings order and discipline to an otherwise floundering firm. It can be the beginning of an efficient and effective managerial system. Strategic management may renew confidence in the current business strategy or point to the need for corrective actions. The strategic-management process provides a basis for identifying and rationalizing the need for change to all managers and employees of a firm; it helps them view change as an opportunity rather than as a threat. Some nonfinancial benefits of a firm utilizing strategic management, according to Greenley, are increased discipline, improved coordination, enhanced communication, reduced resistance to change, increased forward thinking, improved decision making, increased synergy, and more effective allocation of time and resources.[16]

Why Some Firms Do No Strategic Planning

Some firms do no strategic planning, and some firms do strategic planning but receive no support from managers and employees. Ten reasons (excuses) often given for poor or no strategic planning in a firm are as follows:

1. No formal training in strategic management
2. No understanding of or appreciation for the benefits of planning
3. No monetary rewards for doing planning
4. No punishment for not planning
5. Too busy "firefighting" (resolving internal crises) to plan ahead
6. View planning as a waste of time, since no product/service is made
7. Laziness; effective planning takes time and effort; time is money
8. Content with current success; failure to realize that success today is no guarantee for success tomorrow; even Apple Inc. is an example
9. Overconfident
10. Prior bad experience with strategic planning done sometime/somewhere

Pitfalls in Strategic Planning

Strategic planning is an involved, intricate, and complex process that takes an organization into uncharted territory. It does not provide a ready-to-use prescription for success; instead, it takes the organization through a journey and offers a framework for addressing questions and solving problems. Being aware of potential pitfalls and being prepared to address them is essential to success.

Here are some pitfalls to watch for and avoid in strategic planning:

- Using strategic planning to gain control over decisions and resources
- Doing strategic planning only to satisfy accreditation or regulatory requirements
- Too hastily moving from mission development to strategy formulation
- Failing to communicate the plan to employees, who continue working in the dark
- Top managers making many intuitive decisions that conflict with the formal plan
- Top managers not actively supporting the strategic-planning process
- Failing to use plans as a standard for measuring performance
- Delegating planning to a "planner" rather than involving all managers
- Failing to involve key employees in all phases of planning
- Failing to create a collaborative climate supportive of change
- Viewing planning as unnecessary or unimportant
- Becoming so engrossed in current problems that insufficient or no planning is done
- Being so formal in planning that flexibility and creativity are stifled[17]

Comparing Business and Military Strategy

A strong military heritage underlies the study of strategic management. Terms such as *objectives, mission, strengths*, and *weaknesses* were first formulated to address problems on the battlefield. According to *Webster's New World Dictionary*, strategy is "the science of planning and directing large-scale military operations, of maneuvering forces into the most advantageous position prior to actual engagement with the enemy."[18] The word *strategy* comes from the Greek *strategos*, which refers to a military general and combines *stratos* (the army) and *ago* (to lead). The history of strategic planning began in the military. A key aim of both business and military strategy is "to gain competitive advantage." In many respects, business strategy is like military strategy, and military strategists have learned much over the centuries that can benefit business strategists today.

Both business and military organizations try to use their own strengths to exploit competitors' weaknesses. If an organization's overall strategy is wrong (ineffective), then all the efficiency in the world may not be enough to allow success. Business or military success is generally not the happy result of accidental strategies. Rather, success is the product of both continuous attention to changing external and internal conditions and the formulation and implementation of insightful adaptations to those conditions. The element of surprise provides great competitive advantages in both military and business strategy; information systems that provide data on opponents' or competitors' strategies and resources are also vitally important.

A fundamental difference between military and business strategy is that business strategy is formulated, implemented, and evaluated with an assumption of *competition*, whereas military strategy is based on an assumption of *conflict*. Nonetheless, military conflict and business competition are so similar that many strategic-management techniques apply equally to both. Business strategists have access to valuable insights that military thinkers have refined over time. Superior strategy formulation and implementation can overcome an opponent's superiority in numbers and resources.

Born in Pella in 356 BCE, Alexander the Great was king of Macedon, a state in northern ancient Greece. Tutored by Aristotle until the age of 16, Alexander had created one of the largest empires of the ancient world by the age of 30, stretching from the Ionian Sea to the Himalayas. Alexander was undefeated in battle and is considered one of history's most successful commanders. He became the measure against which military leaders even today compare themselves, and military academies throughout the world still teach his strategies and tactics. Alexander the Great once said, "Greater is an army of sheep led by a lion, than an army of lions led by a sheep." This quote reveals the overwhelming importance of an excellent strategic plan for any organization to succeed. The legendary Alabama football coach Bear Bryant asserted, "I will defeat the opposing coach's team with my players, but if given a week's notice, I could defeat the opposing coach's team with his players and he take my players."

Both business and military organizations must adapt to change and constantly improve to be successful. Too often, firms do not change their strategies when their environment and competitive conditions dictate the need to change. Gluck offered a classic military example of this:

> When Napoleon won, it was because his opponents were committed to the strategy, tactics, and organization of earlier wars. When he lost—against Wellington, the Russians, and the Spaniards—it was because he, in turn, used tried-and-true strategies against enemies who thought afresh, who were developing the strategies not of the last war but of the next.[19]

Sun Tzu's *The Art of War* has been applied to many fields well outside of the military. Much of the text is about how to fight wars without actually having to do battle: It gives tips on how to outsmart one's opponent so that physical battle is not necessary. As such, the book has found application as a training guide for many competitive endeavors that do not involve actual combat, such as in devising courtroom trial strategy or acquiring a rival company. There are business books applying its lessons to office politics and corporate strategy. Many Japanese companies make the book required reading for their top executives. The book is a popular read among Western business managers who have turned to it for inspiration and advice on how to succeed in competitive business situations.

The Art of War has also been applied in the world of sports in preparing for athletic contests. NFL coach Bill Belichick is known to have read the book and used its lessons to gain insights in preparing for games. Australian cricket coaches, as well as Brazilian association football coaches Luis Felipe Scolari and Carolos Alberto Parreira, embraced the text. Scolari made the Brazilian World Cup squad of 2002 study the ancient work during their successful campaign.

Similarities can be construed from Sun Tzu's writings to the practice of formulating and implementing strategies among businesses today. Table 1-4 provides narrative excerpts from *The Art of War*. As you read through the table, consider which of the principles of war apply to business strategy as companies today compete aggressively to survive and grow.

TABLE 1-4 Excerpts from Sun Tzu's *The Art of War* Writings

- War is a matter of vital importance to the state: a matter of life or death, the road either to survival or ruin. Hence, it is imperative that it be studied thoroughly.
- Warfare is based on deception. When near the enemy, make it seem that you are far away; when far away, make it seem that you are near. Hold out baits to lure the enemy. Strike the enemy when he is in disorder. Avoid the enemy when he is stronger. If your opponent is of choleric temper, try to irritate him. If he is arrogant, try to encourage his egotism. If enemy troops are well prepared after reorganization, try to wear them down. If they are united, try to sow dissension among them. Attack the enemy where he is unprepared, and appear where you are not expected. These are the keys to victory for a strategist. It is not possible to formulate them in detail beforehand.
- A speedy victory is the main object in war. If this is long in coming, weapons are blunted and morale depressed. When the army engages in protracted campaigns, the resources of the state will fall short. Thus, while we have heard of stupid haste in war, we have not yet seen a clever operation that was prolonged.
- Generally, in war the best policy is to take a state intact; to ruin it is inferior to this. To capture the enemy's entire army is better than to destroy it; to take intact a regiment, a company, or a squad is better than to destroy it. For to win one hundred victories in one hundred battles is not the epitome of skill. To subdue the enemy without fighting is the supreme excellence. Those skilled in war subdue the enemy's army without battle.

- The art of using troops is this: When ten to the enemy's one, surround him. When five times his strength, attack him. If double his strength, divide him. If equally matched, you may engage him with some good plan. If weaker, be capable of withdrawing. And if in all respects unequal, be capable of eluding him.
- Know your enemy and know yourself, and in a hundred battles you will never be defeated. When you are ignorant of the enemy but know yourself, your chances of winning or losing are equal. If ignorant both of your enemy and of yourself, you are sure to be defeated in every battle.
- He who occupies the field of battle first and awaits his enemy is at ease, and he who comes later to the scene and rushes into the fight is weary. And therefore, those skilled in war bring the enemy to the field of battle and are not brought there by him. Thus, when the enemy is at ease, be able to tire him; when well fed, be able to starve him; when at rest, be able to make him move.
- Analyze the enemy's plans so that you will know his shortcomings as well as his strong points. Agitate him to ascertain the pattern of his movement. Lure him out to reveal his dispositions and to ascertain his position. Launch a probing attack to learn where his strength is abundant and where deficient. It is according to the situation that plans are laid for victory, but the multitude does not comprehend this.
- An army may be likened to water, for just as flowing water avoids the heights and hastens to the lowlands, so an army should avoid strength and strike weakness. And as water shapes its flow in accordance with the ground, so an army manages its victory in accordance with the situation of the enemy. And as water has no constant form, there are in warfare no constant conditions. Thus, one able to win the victory by modifying his tactics in accordance with the enemy situation may be said to be divine.
- If you decide to go into battle, do not announce your intentions or plans. Project "business as usual."
- Unskilled leaders work out their conflicts in courtrooms and battlefields. Brilliant strategists rarely go to battle or to court; they generally achieve their objectives through tactical positioning well in advance of any confrontation.
- When you do decide to challenge another company (or army), much calculating, estimating, analyzing, and positioning bring triumph. Little computation brings defeat.
- Skillful leaders do not let a strategy inhibit creative counter-movement. Nor should commands from those at a distance interfere with spontaneous maneuvering in the immediate situation.
- When a decisive advantage is gained over a rival, skillful leaders do not press on. They hold their position and give their rivals the opportunity to surrender or merge. They do not allow their forces to be damaged by those who have nothing to lose.
- Brilliant strategists forge ahead with illusion, obscuring the area(s) of major confrontation, so that opponents divide their forces in an attempt to defend many areas. Create the appearance of confusion, fear, or vulnerability so the opponent is helplessly drawn toward this illusion of advantage.

Note: Substitute the words *strategy* or *strategic planning* for *war* or *warfare*.

Source: Sun Tzu's The Art of War Writings, 1910, Lionel Giles.

IMPLICATIONS FOR STRATEGISTS

Figure 1-3 reveals that to gain and sustain competitive advantages, a firm must create and nurture a clear vision and mission, and then systematically formulate, implement, and evaluate strategies. Consistent business success rarely happens by chance; it most often results from careful planning followed by diligent, intelligent, hard work. If the process were easy, every business would be successful. Consistent success requires that strategists gather and assimilate relevant data, make tough trade-off decisions among various options that would benefit the firm, energize and reward employees, and continually adapt to change. To survive and prosper, a business must gain and sustain at least several major competitive advantages over rival firms.

The strategic-management process represents a systematic means for creating, maintaining, and strengthening a firm's competitive advantages. This text provides step-by-step guidance throughout the process to help strategists gain and sustain a firm's competitive advantages. As the eleven chapters unfold, more than 100 key elements of the process, ranging from developing portfolio matrices to managing workplace romance, are examined to help strategists lead the firm in delivering prosperity to shareholders, customers, and employees. The eleven chapters provide a clear, planned, journey through the strategic-management process, with numerous highlights accented along the way, so strategists can perform essential analyses and anticipate and resolve potential problems in leading their firm to success.

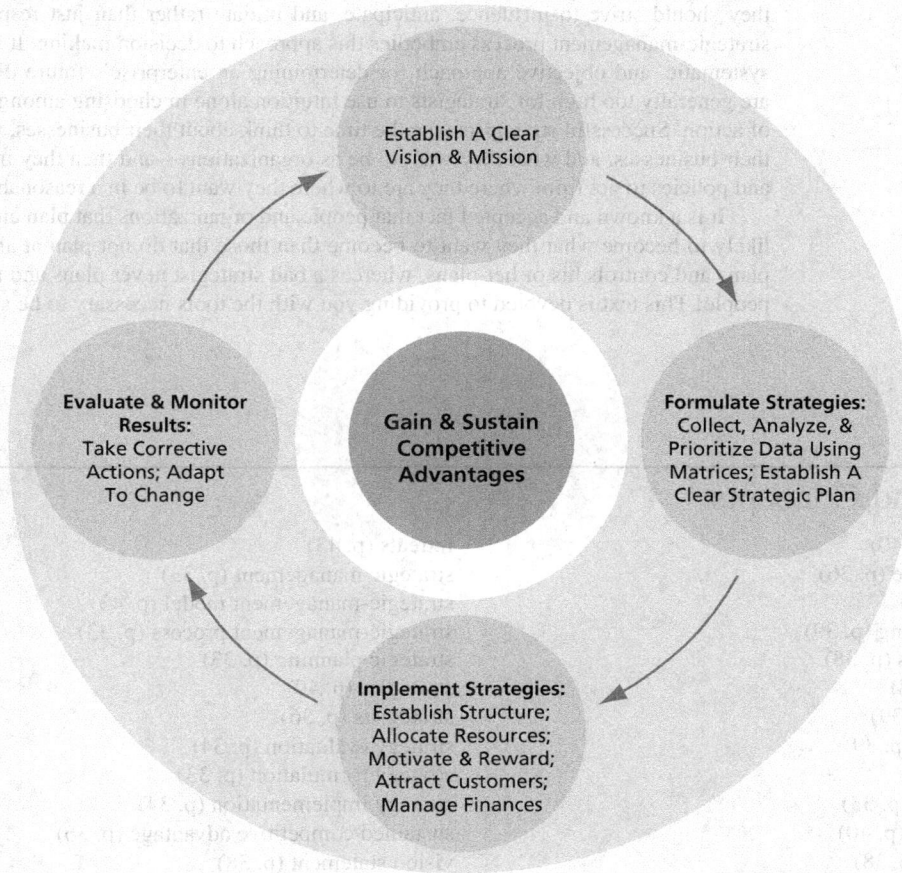

Establish A Clear
Vision & Mission

Formulate Strategies:
Collect, Analyze, &
Prioritize Data Using
Matrices; Establish A
Clear Strategic Plan

Gain & Sustain
Competitive
Advantages

Implement Strategies:
Establish Structure;
Allocate Resources;
Motivate & Reward;
Attract Customers;
Manage Finances

Evaluate & Monitor
Results:
Take Corrective
Actions; Adapt
To Change

FIGURE 1-3

How to Gain and Sustain Competitive Advantages

IMPLICATIONS FOR STUDENTS

In performing strategic-management case analysis, emphasize throughout your project, beginning with the first page or slide, where your firm has competitive advantages and disadvantages. More importantly, emphasize throughout how you recommend the firm sustain and grow its competitive advantages and how you recommend the firm overcome its competitive disadvantages. Pave the way early and often in your presentation for what you ultimately recommend your firm should do over the next three years. The notion of competitive advantage should be integral to the discussion of every page or PowerPoint slide. Therefore, avoid being merely *descriptive* in your written or oral analysis; rather, be *prescriptive*, insightful, and forward-looking throughout your project.

Chapter Summary

All firms have a strategy, even if it is informal, unstructured, and sporadic. All organizations are heading somewhere, but unfortunately some organizations do not know where they are going. The old saying "If you do not know where you are going, then any road will lead you there!" accents the need for organizations to use strategic-management concepts and techniques. The strategic-management process is becoming more widely used by small firms, large companies, nonprofit institutions, governmental organizations, and multinational conglomerates alike. The process of empowering managers and employees has almost limitless benefits.

Organizations should take a proactive rather than a reactive approach in their industry, and they should strive to influence, anticipate, and initiate rather than just respond to events. The strategic-management process embodies this approach to decision making. It represents a logical, systematic, and objective approach for determining an enterprise's future direction. The stakes are generally too high for strategists to use intuition alone in choosing among alternative courses of action. Successful strategists take the time to think about their businesses, where they are with their businesses, and what they want to be as organizations—and then they implement programs and policies to get from where they are to where they want to be in a reasonable period of time.

It is a known and accepted fact that people and organizations that plan ahead are much more likely to become what they want to become than those that do not plan at all. A good strategist plans and controls his or her plans, whereas a bad strategist never plans and then tries to control people! This text is devoted to providing you with the tools necessary to be a good strategist.

Key Terms and Concepts

annual objectives (p. 40)
competitive advantage (p. 36)
empowerment (p. 44)
environmental scanning (p. 39)
external opportunities (p. 38)
external threats (p. 38)
internal strengths (p. 39)
internal weaknesses (p. 39)
intuition (p. 34)
long-range planning (p. 33)
long-term objectives (p. 40)
mission statements (p. 38)
policies (p. 41)

retreats (p. 43)
strategic management (p. 33)
strategic-management model (p. 43)
strategic-management process (p. 33)
strategic planning (p. 33)
strategies (p. 40)
strategists (p. 36)
strategy evaluation (p. 34)
strategy formulation (p. 33)
strategy implementation (p. 34)
sustained competitive advantage (p. 36)
vision statement (p. 38)

Issues for Review and Discussion

1-1. Discount airlines are competing more aggressively with Singapore Airline. How could Singapore Airline best compete with these rivals?

1-2. Does Singapore Airlines have its strategic plan posted on its website? Should the company do so? Why or why not?

1-3. Compare and contrast the activities involved in strategy formulation and those in strategy implementation.

1-4. Given the political and economic collapse of various Middle Eastern countries, identify a list of companies for which gaining and sustaining competitive advantage has permanently changed.

1-5. There is a dramatic shift in mass retailing to become smaller. Give four reasons for this phenomenon, with corporate examples of each.

1-6. Avoid being merely descriptive in your written or oral case analysis; rather, be prescriptive, insightful, and forward-looking throughout your project. Explain the statement and discuss its significance.

1-7. As cited in the chapter, Dale McConkey says, "plans are less important than planning." In terms of strategic management and its benefits, what does McConkey mean?

1-8. In terms of developing a strategic plan, explain what Edward Deming means by "In God we trust. All others bring data."

1-9. In an organization, at which three hierarchal levels would strategy formulation, implementation, and evaluation activities occur?

1-10. Explain Einstein's rationale for saying "Imagination is more important than knowledge." Would you agree with Einstein? Why or why not?

1-11. Explain Drucker's statement "I believe in intuition only if you discipline it." Do you agree with it? Give reasons for your answer.

1-12. Strategic management is all about gaining and maintaining competitive advantage. Explain whether you agree or disagree with the help of examples.

1-13. Based on the chapter's definition of strategists, identify the top three strategists you have personally spoken to, and interacted with.

1-14. Would the collapse of the euro be a major threat, or opportunity, for your college or university? Why or why not? In your opinion, what is the probability of such a collapse?

1-15. Strategic management is not a panacea for success and can be dysfunctional if conducted haphazardly. In this context, give five examples of potential "haphazard" aspects of the planning process.

1-16. Explain how and why firms use social networks these days to gain a competitive advantage.

1-17. Compare and contrast vision statements with mission statements.

1-18. Identify the top 10 external factors that you feel are affecting your university. Rank them with one being most important.

1-19. In order of importance, list six benefits of a firm engaging in strategic management.

1-20. Rank six reasons, in order of their importance, why firms don't have strategic plans.

1-21. Identify six guidelines required while conducting strategic management activities.

1-22. Discuss how relevant you think Sun Tzu's *Art of War* writings are, for firms today, in developing and carrying out a strategic plan.

1-23. Determine the ways and means by which strategic planning is conducted at your college or university. Report your findings to your class.

1-24. Go to the author website (www.strategyclub.com) and describe the strategic-planning products offered.

1-25. Compare and contrast the extent to which strategic-planning concepts are used by companies in your country versus companies in the United States.

1-26. Would strategy formulation or strategy implementation concepts differ more across countries? Why?

1-27. Compare strategic planning with long-range planning.

1-28. Which three activities comprise strategy evaluation? Why is strategy evaluation important, even for successful firms?

1-29. Explain how a firm can achieve sustained competitive advantage.

1-30. Identify and give an overview of three social networking sites that firms use to gain competitive advantage.

1-31. List four strategists whom you know personally. Rank them on their effectiveness as a leader in their organization.

1-32. List six characteristics of objectives and give an example of each.

1-33. Conduct an Internet research to determine what percentage of your country's population smoke. What implications does this have for firms in your country?

1-34. List four financial and four nonfinancial benefits of a firm engaging in strategic planning.

1-35. Discuss the comparisons between business strategy and military strategy.

1-36. Briefly explain whether strategic planning should be more of a people-oriented process than a paper process.

1-37. Do you agree with the fact that strategic planning should not be controlled by technicians? Briefly explain the reasons for your answer.

1-38. According to Sun Tzu, warfare is based on deception. Should strategic planning be based on deception? Explain.

1-39. Explain Sun Tzu's statement "Generally, in war the best policy is to take a state intact; to ruin it is inferior to this." Is this true in corporate strategic planning? Explain.

1-40. What is Singapore Airlines' competitive advantage? How can this advantage be sustained?

1-41. Are there any compelling reasons why the external audit, and internal audit, should not be conducted simultaneously?

1-42. Which stage of strategic management do you feel is the most important? Give reasons for your answer.

1-43. Should strategic planning be more open or closed (i.e., hidden or transparent)? Why?

1-44. Discuss the extent to which strategic-planning concepts would be applicable to individuals managing their own lives.

1-45. Strengths and weaknesses should be determined relative to competitors, or by elements of being, or relative to a firm's own objectives. Explain.

1-46. What are the three stages in strategic management? Which stage is more analytical? Which relies most on empowerment to be successful? Which relies most on statistics? Justify your answers.

1-47. What two factors most often are associated with companies hiring a Chief Strategy Officer?

1-48. What is the most important activity in the strategic-management process?

1-49. Create a diagram illustrating how to gain and sustain competitive advantages.

MINI-CASE ON RYANAIR LIMITED (RYAAY)

IS RYANAIR'S WEBSITE ITS STRATEGIC MARKETING TOOL?

Source: © 123rf.com

Headquartered in Dublin, Ireland, Ryanair was set up by the Ryan family and began operating in 1985 with a share capital of £1 only, and a staff of 25 individuals.

According to the International Air Transport Association (IATA) report in 2013, the low-cost airline, with its main bases at Dublin and London Stansted Airports, was considered the largest European airline in terms of domestic, international, and scheduled passenger figures and passenger-kilometers. The airline has 1,600 flights scheduled daily across 185 destinations, with 300 Boeing 737-800 jets in operation.

The airline is growing rapidly, serving 35 countries in Africa (Morocco), and the Middle East (Cyprus and Israel), and Europe. In 2014, the airline saw an increase in traffic by 11 percent. The operations outgrew its previous office space at the Dublin Airport, and in April, 2014, Ryanair's new €20m Dublin Head Office in Airside Business Park, which was around 100,000 square feet, was officially opened. In the same year, Ryanair launched its "Always Getting Better" program to address things that customers did not appreciate. It also agreed to purchase up to 200 Boeing 737 Max 8s (100 confirmed and 100 options) for over $22 billion. In December 2015, the airline opened an operating base at Milan Malpensa Airport.

The key trends for Ryanair over recent years are shown below (year ending March, 2015):

	2010	2011	2012	2013	2014	2015
Total operating revenue (€m)	2,988.1	3,629.5	4,390.2	4,884.0	5,036.7	5,654.0
Operating income (€m)	402.1	488.2	683.2	718.2	658.6	1,042.9
Profit before taxation (€m)	341.0	420.9	633.0	650.9	591.4	982.4
Profit after taxation (€m)	305.3	374.6	560.4	569.3	522.8	866.7

Source: Based on data from Ryanair FY 2015 Results, March 2015, © RyanAir, www.investor.ryanair.com.

In December 2014, Ryanair announced that it would inaugurate its 72nd base in 2015 in the Azores. In 2016, Ryanair will work towards developing a low-cost airline named VivaCan. The airline service has projected to have provided service to 160 million passengers in 2024.

Questions

1. Visit Ryanair's website. Compare its website with one of its competitor, like Spirit Air, and give recommendations on how Ryanair can utilize its website as a strategic marketing tool to enhance its competitiveness. How can it improve the website to function more effectively and enhance the company's efficiency in serving its potential customers?
2. Can you identify any strengths and weaknesses of Ryanair based on information provided in the case and the data given in the table above?

Current Readings

Alber, Laura. "The CEO of Williams-Sonoma on Blending Instinct with Analysis." *Harvard Business Review* 92.9 (2014): 41–44. *Business Source Premier*. Web. 5 Sept. 2014.

Courtney, Hugh, Dan Lovallo, and Carmina Clarke. "Deciding How to Decide (Cover Story)." *Harvard Business Review* 91.11 (2013): 62–70. *Business Source Premier*. Web. 5 Sept. 2014.

Hon, Alice H. Y., Matt Bloom, and J. Michael Crant. "Overcoming Resistance to Change and Enhancing Creative Performance." *Journal of Management* 40.3 (2014): 919–941. *Business Abstracts with Full Text (H. W. Wilson)*. Web, 5 Sept. 2014.

Martin, Roger L. "The Big Lie of Strategic Planning." *Harvard Business Review* 92.1/2 (2014): 78–84. *Business Source Premier*. Web. 5 Sept. 2014.

Priem, Richard L., John E. Butler, and Sali Li. "Toward Reimagining Strategy Research: Retrospection and Prospection on the 2011 AMR Decade Award Article." *Academy of Management Review* 38.4 (2013): 471–489. *Business Source Premier*. Web. 5 Sept. 2014.

Rosenzweig, Phil. "What Makes Strategic Decisions Different (Cover Story)." *Harvard Business Review* 91.11 (2013): 88–93. *Business Source Premier*. Web. 5 Sept. 2014.

Weaver, Gary R., Scott J. Reynolds, and Michael E. Brown. "Moral Intuition: Connecting Current Knowledge to Future Organizational Research and Practice." *Journal of Management* 40.1 (2014): 100–129. *Business Abstracts with Full Text (H. W. Wilson)*. Web. 5 Sept. 2014.

Endnotes

1. Kathy Kiely, "Officials Say Auto CEOs Must Be Specific on Plans," *USA Today*, November 24, 2008, 3B.

2. Peter Drucker, *Management: Tasks, Responsibilities, and Practices* (New York: Harper & Row, 1974), 611.

3. Alfred Sloan, Jr., *Adventures of the White Collar Man* (New York: Doubleday, 1941), 104.

4. Quoted in Eugene Raudsepp, "Can You Trust Your Hunches?" *Management Review* 49, no. 4 (April 1960): 7.

5. Stephen Harper, "Intuition: What Separates Executives from Managers," *Business Horizons* 31, no. 5 (September–October 1988): 16.

6. Ron Nelson, "How to Be a Manager," *Success* (July–August 1985): 69.

7. Bruce Henderson, *Henderson on Corporate Strategy* (Boston: Abt Books, 1979), 6.

8. Robert Waterman, Jr., *The Renewal Factor: How the Best Get and Keep the Competitive Edge* (New York: Bantam, 1987). See also *BusinessWeek*, September 14, 1987, 100; and *Academy of Management Executive* 3, no. 2 (May 1989): 115.

9. Jayne O'Donnell, "Shoppers Flock to Discount Stores," *USA Today*, February 25, 2009, B1.

10. Richie Brand, "Nolan Richardson Scored a Championship Career," *Investor's Business Daily* (November 14, 2014): A3.

11. John Pearce, II, and Fred David, "The Bottom Line on Corporate Mission Statements," *Academy of Management Executive* 1, no. 2 (May 1987): 109.

12. Jack Marshall, "Online Ads Lure Cash, But Losses Still Mount," *Wall Street Journal* (August 18, 2014), B1.

13. Mike Esterl, Karishma Mehrotra, and Valerie Bauerlein, "America's Smokers: Still 40 Million Strong," *Wall Street Journal* (July 16, 2014), B1.

14. Fred R. David, "How Companies Define Their Mission," *Long Range Planning* 22, no. 1 (February 1989): 91.

15. G. L. Schwenk and K. Schrader, "Effects of Formal Strategic Planning in Financial Performance in Small Firms: A Meta-Analysis," *Entrepreneurship and Practice* 3, no. 17 (1993): 53–64. See also C. C. Miller and L. B. Cardinal, "Strategic Planning and Firm Performance: A Synthesis of More Than Two Decades of Research," *Academy of Management Journal* 6, no. 27 (1994): 1649–1665; Michael Peel and John Bridge, "How Planning and Capital Budgeting Improve SME Performance," *Long Range Planning* 31, no. 6 (October 1998): 848–856; Julia Smith, "Strategies for Start-Ups," *Long Range Planning* 31, no. 6 (October 1998): 857–872.

16. Gordon Greenley, "Does Strategic Planning Improve Company Performance?" *Long Range Planning* 19, no. 2 (April 1986): 106.

17. Adapted from www.des.calstate.edu/limitations.html and www.entarga.com/stratplan/purposes.html

18. Victoria Neufeldt, ed. *Webster's New World Dictionary*, 4th ed. (Hoboken, NJ: Pearson, 1998). Pearson purchased this dictionary from Simon & Schuster in 1998, but sold it to IDG Books in 1999.

19. Frederick Gluck, "Taking the Mystique Out of Planning," *Across the Board* (July–August 1985), 59.

THE COHESION CASE

Nestlé S.A. - 2016

BY FOREST R. DAVID AND MEREDITH E. DAVID

www.nestle.com (NSRGY)

Source: © Danny
Kosmayer.123rf

Headquartered in Vevey, Switzerland, Nestlé is one of the largest food producing companies in the world providing quality, healthy, and tasty treats and meals for all ages. Nestlé's diversified portfolio includes notable product categories like baby foods, pet foods, dairy products, coffee, frozen goods, bottled water, and weight management products. Across this range of products, the top Nestlé brands include Milo, Häagen-Dazs, Carnation milk, Coffee Mate, Nescafe, Perrier, DiGiorno, Stouffers, Lean Cuisine, Nesquik, Purina pet foods, Butterfinger, Baby Ruth, and Nestlé Toll House among others. Nestlé also has many brands under a specific product category. For example, it has over 70 bottled water brands in its portfolio, and over 100 chocolate & confectionary brands. Nestlé reported that in 2014 of the group's sales was 91.6 billion Swiss Francs (CHF) or approximately $98.8 billion USD based on 2014 average exchange rates. This indicated that the sales in 2014 were down a minimal 500 million CHF from 2013, approximately 0.6 percent. In the 2014 sales breakdown for the firm that competes globally, the United States accounts for 28 percent; Latin America and Caribbean, 15 percent; Europe, 28 percent; and Asia, Oceania, and Africa, 29 percent.

During the first half of 2015, Nestlé faced a food contamination scare in India and was forced to recall its range of instant noodles Maggi, from the shelves in the Indian market costing the company 66 million Swiss francs ($67 million); Nestlé also had to pay a $100 million USD fine. Overall, Nestlé's sales declined slightly to 42.84 billion Swiss francs ($43.70 billion) from 42.98 billion francs a year earlier. The group's net profit fell 2.5 percent to 4.52 billion francs. So while Nestlé, like many other food companies, saw a particular slump in frozen food sales, at constant rates, their sales had improved. The slump, especially in the United States of America, was due to a shift in consumer perception toward food products that they feel are fresh or natural. Even though frozen vegetables and freshly farmed products are often as wholesome as each other, people still view frozen meals and snacks as having more preservatives, sugar, and sodium.

Despite this chill over the frozen food market, Nestlé's research and development team has recently focused its effort on revamping frozen-food brands Lean Cuisine and Stouffer's, with an eye on product-packaging and health attributes. Though the company is still struggling with the strong franc and its product recall in India that resulted in its first ever quarterly loss in India, in 2015 the revenue in the Americas increased 5.2 percent from the 3.7 percent growth in the first quarter. This growth was driven mainly by increased pricing. Nestlé's CEO, Paul Bulcke, recently diversified the company into skin health, spending almost $5 billion in 2014 to acquire L'Oréal S.A.'s stake in a joint venture, and rights to sell certain medical products from Valeant Pharmaceuticals International Inc.

In the third quarter of 2015, Nestlé inaugurated its third Nespresso plant, at Romont Switzerland. This move is a strategic, long-term plan for Nestlé with a focus on producing its new large-cup Vertuo Line, a coffee machine that will compete with Keurig Green Mountain's K-cup. Nestlé's North American Nespresso sales grew with its 2014 launch of the Vertuo Line, and it now has 36 new boutiques in the United States. The coffee capsule market in the United States is worth $5 billion and, thus, is a key growth market for Nespresso—flourishing in Europe, but nascent in the United States. The company spent around 300 million Swiss francs ($308.29 million) to construct the Romont plant. While the plant has a capacity to employ 300-400 workers, it has 125 employees.

Copyright by Fred David Books LLC. www.strategyclub.com (Written by Forest R. David)

History

The first thing most people instantly associate Nestlé with is chocolate products, but Nestlé's roots are embedded in milk products, in particular baby formula. Nestlé's roots can be traced back to 1866 when the Anglo-Swiss Condensed Milk Company first opened a milk factory in Cham, Switzerland. Nestlé was actually founded one year later in 1867 when a German pharmacist, Henri Nestlé, saved a neighbor's child in Vevey, Switzerland, from starvation with a mixture comprising cow's milk, wheat flour, and sugar. Fittingly enough, Nestlé's first logo was that of a mother bird feeding her new hatchlings.

Nestlé benefitted from World War I, which had created a shortage of food and governments were seeking contracts to help feed its militaries. By the end of the War, the firm had grown from a few factories to over 40 across various countries. Notable product launches after World War I included Nescafe in 1938 and Nestea a few years later. At the conclusion of World War II, Nestlé saw rapid growth, adding many new product lines and even diversifying by purchasing a stake in Paris based cosmetics maker L'Oréal. In the early 1990s, Nestlé benefited tremendously from the fall of communism in the former Soviet Union and Eastern Europe. Nestlé diversified into the pet food business in 2001 with the acquisition of Ralston Purina. Nestlé went on to purchase the American baby food giant Gerber in 2007 and Wyeth Nutrition from Pfizer Nutrition a few years later, strengthening its baby nutrition business. In 2014, Nestlé expanded its Nestlé Skin Health S.A. business to capitalize on the growing trends of global skin care. Part of Nestlé's motivation for these acquisitions was to shift their business more towards nutrition and health from simply candy, food, canned goods, and other less nutritious products.

Internal Issues

Organizational Structure

Nestlé operates from a strategic business unit (SBU) type organizational structure as illustrated on the company website's About Us section; Exhibit 1 provides a list of Nestlé's top executives along with their title. It should be noted that there is one woman (Patrice Bula) among 16 top executives; providing opportunities in upper management for women is an area Nestlé should work on improving in the future.

Vision and Mission

Nestlé does not use the terms vision or mission, but on the company website's About Us section, the firm clearly states that it is "committed to enhancing people's lives by offering tastier and healthier food and beverage choices at all stages of life and at all times of the day." Nestlé prides itself on being ethical and nonnegotiable on quality and safety.

EXHIBIT 1 Nestlé's Top Executive Team

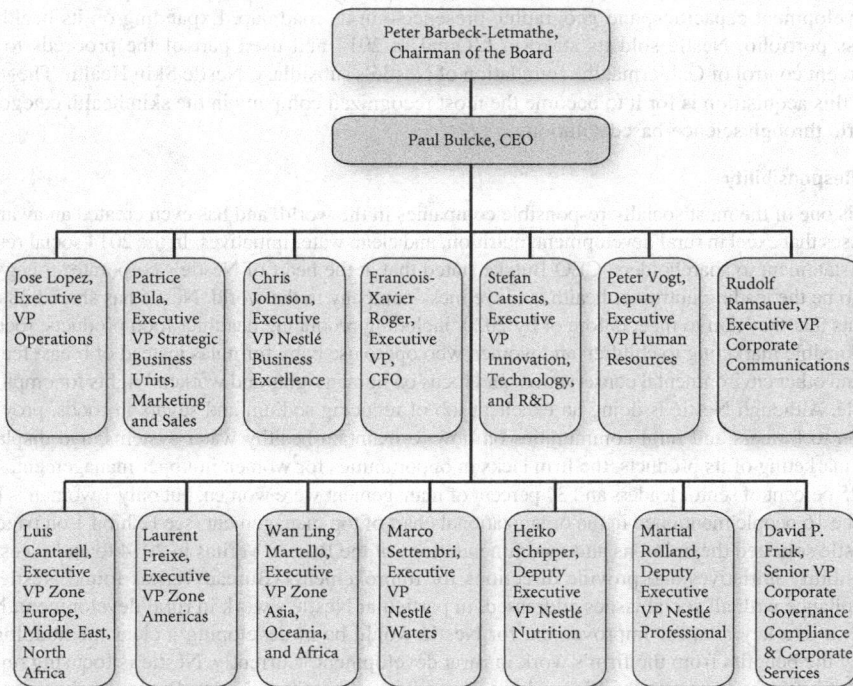

Strategy

Being a global organization, Nestlé's strategy has always displayed a competitive focus. Their corporate roadmap is threefold.

Nestlé has certain operational pillars that include innovation, consumer engagement, and operational efficiency.

Nestlé also has certain growth drivers. One such growth driver for the group is in its image transformation from a packaged food company to one that focuses on nutrition, health, and wellness. While it has no plans to stop selling chocolate, coffee, ice cream, and other food products that it is world famous for, Nestlé is actively engaged in offering healthier food options to its customers. The firm has the largest research and development budget of any food company and it aims use this to produce healthier and tastier food options, from infant formula to products designed for senior citizens. Nestlé has recently reduced the amount of salt, sugar, and saturated fats in many of its products as a means of improving the nutrition quotient, and enhancing other flavors so as to not reduce the taste of these products. One key area that Nestlé will focus on improving in December 2015 is its Policy on Marketing Communication to Children. The company will be looking at phasing out their marketing communication in schools and increasing their focus on health and wellness education through various mediums including the television. Nestlé currently has a series running in both Mexico and the Philippines to better target children.

The global ice cream market's growth expectation was to go from $67 billion in 2014 to $71 billion in 2015, with Unilever and Nestlé having one third of that market share. However, consumers who are more aware of and concerned about healthy diets prefer smaller treats and niche brands with healthier ingredients to large blocks of ice cream. As part of their focus on premiumization, Nestlé is putting up some bulk ice cream businesses for sale, while entering new markets, acquiring start-ups, and introducing new products. Independent brands like the United Kingdom's Jude's, America's Ciao Bella, China Mengniu Dairy, and R&R Ice Cream in Europe are gaining market share. Nestlé sells the banana-like Peelin' Pops, as well as Häagen-Dazs and Movenpick, but some of its consumer ice cream operations have already been sold. More of its ice cream business, which provides the company about $4 billion of its $95 billion in annual revenue, is likely to be divested. In 2015, Nestlé sold its South African ice cream business to R&R Ice Cream. Nestlé's wants its operations to focus on nutrition and health. According to an analyst at the Swiss private bank Vontobel, Nestlé may not want to increase its share in the unhealthy ice cream business.

Nestlé also looks at its competitive advantages—having unmatched product portfolio, research and development capacities, and geographic presence—in its roadmap. Expanding on its health and wellness portfolio, Nestlé sold its stake in L'Oréal in 2014 and used part of the proceeds to gain 100 percent control of Galderma, the foundation of Nestlé's subsidiary, Nestlé Skin Health. The vision behind this acquisition is for it to become the most recognized company in the skin health category in the world through science-based solutions.

Social Responsibility

Nestlé is one of the most socially responsible companies in the world, and has even created an award for businesses that excel in rural development, nutrition, and clean water initiatives. In the 2014 social responsibility statement to shareholders, CEO Bulcke stated that at the heart of Nestlé's corporate strategy is a desire to be the leading nutrition, health, and wellness-company in the world. Nestlé has shared 38 commitments that they aim to meet before or by 2020, including producing healthier food products, focusing on responsible marketing to children and women who opt to use baby formulas instead of breast feeding, water and other environmental conservation, and focus on human rights and workers' rights for employees at Nestlé. Although Nestlé is doing an excellent job of reducing sodium and sugars in foods, providing direction to farmers and rural communities on how to maintain healthy water systems, and displaying ethical marketing of its products, the firm lacks in opportunities for women in upper management. As of 2014, 25 percent of senior leaders and 34 percent of management were women, but only 1 woman is listed out of the 16 people mentioned in the organizational chart of top management (see Exhibit 1 on page 55).

Nestlé solicited the opinions and recommendations of the Bureau Veritas in 2014 to audit its social responsibility initiatives and provide directions for improvements. Bureau Veritas found Nestlé was in compliance with all social issues addressed, in particular Nestlé's work in rural development. Moving forward, a key area for improvement for Nestlé would be in developing a clear methodology to quantify the benefits from the firm's work in rural development. Currently, Nestlé is focusing on case studies of just a few areas where it is working on rural development activities. Bureau Veritas also suggested Nestlé provide increased disclosure to stakeholders on its R&D programs that are transforming Nestlé from a food and beverage business to a health, nutrition and wellness business.

Nestlé has received numerous accolades for its commitment to being socially responsible. In 2013, Nestlé ranked 3rd among global food providers in the Access to Nutrition Index, which measures firms on a variety of factors such as governance, ethical marketing, accessibility, product labeling, and other parameters. In October 2014, Nestlé received a score of 96 out of 100 from the Climate Disclosure Index and received a maximum score of 20 from the Carbon Disclosure Project Water. Also in 2014, the Dow Jones Sustainability Index assigned a score of 88 to Nestlé, placing the firm second in its industry.

Despite numerous accolades, in August 2015 Nestlé was sued in California for allegedly knowingly allowing a Thai supplier that employed slave labor to provide fish for its Fancy Feast cat food products. According to the class action lawsuit filed by the Hagens Berman law firm, Nestlé imports around 28 million pounds of seafood-based pet products to the United States through Thai Union Frozen Products PCL. The ingredients in those products have been said to be the result of slave labor. The lawsuit alleges that male individuals are often taken from certain areas in Thailand, Myanmar, and Cambodia, and sold to companies like Thai Union. These individuals work for around 20 hours a day with little pay, and if their work doesn't meet standard requirements they are severely punished. Although protection of human rights is one of Nestlé's corporate principles, Steve Berman, managing partner of the Hagens Berman law firm, had said that keeping these from the public has allowed Nestlé to mislead millions of consumers, who support and encourage slave labor in the production of its pet food without even knowing it.

Research & Development

Nestlé has the largest R&D network and budget of any food company in the world, with total R&D expenses of 1.6 billion CHF in 2014 that amounted to 1.8 percent of total sales. Hershey and Mondelez (producers of Cadbury, Nabisco, and other products) by comparison had no R&D expenses listed on their respective income statement in 2014. Nestlé has 34 R&D facilities with over 5,000 employees around the world working to provide healthier food options for consumers. Switzerland is the base for almost two-thirds of Nestlé's research and development. While these expenses are still relatively small in relation to total revenues, Nestlé is aiming to transform itself from merely a food company to a health and wellness company. With its strategy to produce healthier food and baby formulas, and to enter into the skin care market, research and development is likely to become of increased strategic importance for Nestlé moving forward. In fact, Nestlé plans to open R&D centers in the United States for frozen foods, and in Shanghai for skin care products focused on an aging population.

Finance

Nestlé's revenues dropped marginally in 2014 as revealed in Exhibit 2, but its net income increased 43 percent. Total assets, as shown in Exhibit 3, increased 10 percent in 2014 mostly due to a 10 percent increase in the company's goodwill and intangibles.

Segments

Nestlé is well diversified within the food industry with a range, for example, from pet food and skin care products. Exhibit 4 below reveals Nestlé's 2014 and 2013 revenues over its 7 segments. Note that sales dropped in 5 product categories in 2014, only increasing in the Nutrition and Health Science segment and the Water segment. The year 2014 as a whole was slow for many in the food industry, so Nestlé's sales are not out of line with industry norms. Nestlé's increase in Nutrition and Health Science sales is in line with the firm's overall strategy of becoming increasingly a health and wellness firm, rather than solely a packaged-food company.

EXHIBIT 2 Nestlé's Income Statements (in millions CHF)

Report Date	December 31, 2014	December 31, 2013
Revenues	91,612	92,158
Cost of goods sold	(47,553)	(48,111)
Other operating expenses net	(33,154)	(30,979)
EBIT	10,905	13,068
Interest expense	(637)	(631)
EBT	10,268	12,437
Tax	(3,367)	(3,256)
Income from associates	8,003	1,264
Net income	**14,904**	**10,445**

Source: Based on Nestlé's 2014 *Consolidated Financial Statements Report,* pages 58–59.

EXHIBIT 3 Nestlé's Balance Sheets (in millions CHF)

Report Date	December 31, 2014	December 31, 2013
Assets		
Cash and equivalents	7,448	6,415
Accounts receivable	13,459	12,206
Inventory	9,172	8,382
Other current assets	3,882	3,063
Total current assets	33,961	30,066
Property, plant & equipment	28,421	26,895
Goodwill	34,557	31,039
Intangible assets	19,800	12,673
Other assets	16,711	19,769
Total assets	**133,450**	**120,442**
Liabilities		
Accounts payable	17,437	16,072
Short term debt	8,810	11,380
Other current liabilities	6,648	5,465
Total current liabilities	32,895	32,917
Long term debt	12,396	10,363
Deferred income taxes	3,191	2,643
Employee benefits	8,081	6,279
Other liabilities	5,003	4,101
Total liabilities	**61,566**	**56,303**
Treasury stock	(3,918)	(2,196)
Translation reserve	(17,255)	(20,811)
Retained earnings	90,981	85,260
Other	2,076	1,885
Total equity	**71,884**	**64,139**
Total liabilities & equity	**133,450**	**120,442**

Source: Based on Nestlé's 2014 *Consolidated Financial Statements Report*, pages 60–61.

EXHIBIT 4 Nestlé's Sales (in millions of CHF)

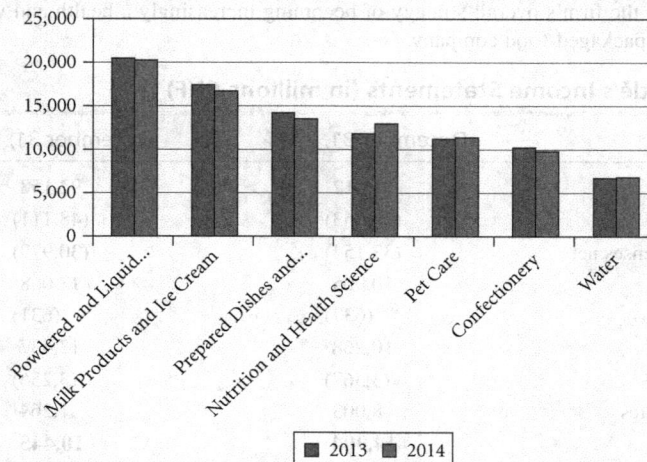

Source: Based on Nestlé's 2014 *Annual Report*, p. 43.

EXHIBIT 5 Nestlé's 2014 Operating Profit Breakdown

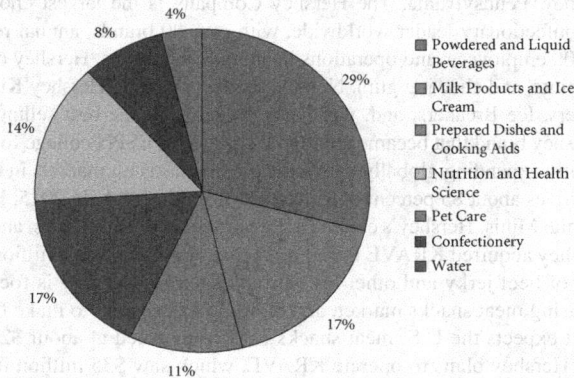

Legend:
- Powdered and Liquid Beverages
- Milk Products and Ice Cream
- Prepared Dishes and Cooking Aids
- Nutrition and Health Science
- Pet Care
- Confectionery
- Water

Source: Based on Nestlé's 2014 *Annual Report*, p. 43.

Exhibit 5 represents Nestlé's operating profits for each division during 2014. Note that Nestlé Water profits only comprise 4 percent of the company total. Nevertheless, Nestlé's sales and profits are quite diversified, with no one product category generating more than 30 percent of total 2014 operating profits.

Much like Nestlé's product categories, Nestlé's geographical diversification is quite good, with roughly a quarter of 2014 revenues divided between Europe, North America, Asia, and the rest of the world as shown by Exhibit 6. It is quite remarkable that Nestlé is not overly dependent on any one region. If needed, Nestlé should divert its resources to more profitable regions. For example, in 2014 Nestlé's sales in Brazil, Philippines, and Russia increased 10.6, 9.4, and 13.4 percent respectively, based on local currency (not taking into account exchanges rates with the Swiss Franc). These three nations are fairly sizable in volume as well, with Brazil producing the 4th largest revenues of any country served by Nestlé, and Philippines and Russia ranking 8th and 12th globally in Nestlé's total sales. No other country in the top 12 experienced growth in local currency over 3 percent, with several reporting lower sales in 2014 than 2013. Nestlé did suffer from the depreciation of the Russian ruble, Mexican peso, and Australian dollar in 2014. The first half of 2015, however, continued to indicate a slowdown in emerging markets, especially China, while established markets remained stable.

Competitors

Nestlé competes primarily in the food and beverage business with 70 percent of operating profits derived from these products and the remaining profits derived relatively evenly between skin care and pet food products. Within the food and beverage business, Nestlé finds itself competing with global chocolate giants, Hershey, Mars and others, along with firms such as French-based Danone, European focused Nomad Foods, U.S.-based Kraft, and many more. In the skin care business, Nestlé competes with a slew of consumer products firms such as giant Unilever. On pet foods, Nestlé competes with familiar competitors such as the world leader in pet food, which may be surprising to some, Mars. Del Monte, along with Procter & Gamble (P&G) are also in the pet food business.

EXHIBIT 6 Nestlé's 2014 Sales Breakdown by Geographic Region

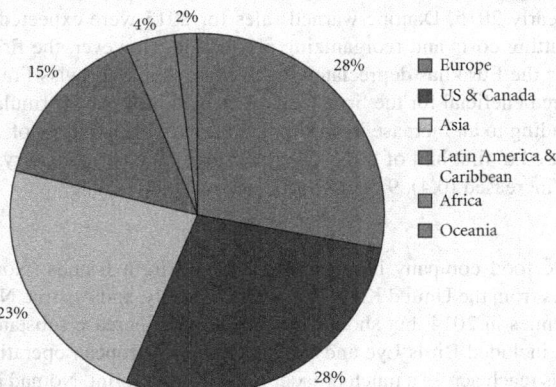

Legend:
- Europe
- US & Canada
- Asia
- Latin America & Caribbean
- Africa
- Oceania

Source: Based on Nestlé's 2014 *Annual Report*, p. 47.

Hershey

Headquartered in Hershey, Pennsylvania, The Hershey Company is the largest chocolate producer in North America and a confectionary leader worldwide, with over 80 brands, annual revenues of over $7 billion, with about 20,000 employees, and operations in about 80 countries. Hershey offers chocolates as well as other candies, mints, and chewing gum. Notable products include Hershey Kisses, Mr. Goodbar, Twizzlers, Jolly Ranchers, Ice Breakers, and, what may arguably be the best selling candy bar on the planet —Reese's, a Hershey brand that became an official sponsor of ESPN college football game day, in 2015. Hershey is currently expanding globally with strategic emphasis on markets in China and Mexico, but the company still derives about 85 percent of its revenue from the USA. In 2015, Hershey introduced products like KitKat White Minis, Hershey's caramels, Reese's Spreads Snacksters, and Graham Dippers.

In early 2015, Hershey acquired KRAVE Pure Foods, Inc. for about $300 million. KRAVE, founded in 2009, is a maker of beef jerky and other high-protein snacks. Hershey is focusing on getting a share of the ever-increasing meat snacks market, and building its capacity to make foods that consumers want to snack on. It expects the U.S. meat snacks category, valued at about $2.5 billion, to grow at a double-digit pace. Hershey plans to operate KRAVE, which saw $35 million in sales in 2014, as a single business unit in the North America division; KRAVE's founder, Mr. Sebastiani, continues to head the business as the company's president.

Mars, Inc.

Mars is the second largest candy manufacturer in the United States and the third largest privately-held company in the United States according to *Forbes*. Headquartered in McLean, Virginia, and having annual sales of over $30 billion, Mars, like Nestlé, is well diversified with six business units consisting of chocolate, drinks, food, symbio-science, pet care, and Wrigley chewing gum. Mars blockbuster chocolate brands include: Snickers, Milky Way, M&Ms, Dove, Bounty, 3 Musketeers, Starburst, Skittles, among others. Mars' annual revenue in 2014 was about $35 billion, more than 50 percent higher than in 2007, largely due to the firm's 2008 acquisition of Wrigley. Since patenting recipes is difficult and producing chocolate is secretive, Mars does not allow visitors to its kitchens in its factories and facilities. Mars' first blockbuster product back in 1923 was the Milky Way candy bar.

Market researcher Euromonitor International recently reported that Mars' market share in the USA rose to 28 percent from 24 percent. To further battle Hershey, Mars in 2014 opened a new 500,000 square foot chocolate factory in Topeka, Kansas at a cost of $270 million. Almost every day, the factory cranks out around 39 million peanut M&M's and 8 million miniature Snickers candy bars.

Like Nestlé, Mars advocates globally sustainability of the cocoa resource but has received criticism in recent years over purchasing cocoa from West African farms that use child labor. Mars is also one of the world's biggest producers of dog food and pet-care products. Mars' Wrigley division produces chewing gums, confectionery products, and a variety of other products ranging from Uncle Ben's rice to Flavia coffee. Pedigree, Greenies, and Whiskas are some of the pet-food brands under Mars. Interestingly, chocolate is Mars' second-largest business globally, behind pet care.

Danone

Danone is a global company based in Paris, France with 21 billion euros in revenue in 2014. The firm has four key operating segments—dairy products, water, baby nutrition, and medical nutrition, representing 52, 21, 20, and 7 percent of revenues respectively. Danone is also fairly diverse geographically with sales of approximately 40, 24 and 36 percent in Europe, North America, and Other respectively. With the close overlap on products and markets served, Danone is a significant competitor to Nestlé on many key areas. In early 2015, Danone warned sales for 2015 were expected to decline and the company planned on cutting costs and reorganizing production. However, the first half of 2015 was profitable for Danone as the Euro has depreciated much more than the Swiss Franc, making conversions back to Euros more beneficial for the firm. Chinese demand for baby formula was also strong in the first half of 2015 leading to an increase in worldwide Early Nutrition sales of 11 percent from the first half of 2015 compared to first half of 2014. Over the same time period, Dairy, Waters, and Medical Nutrition decreased/increased (0.4), 9.5 and 8.1 respectively at Danone.

Nomad Foods

Nomad Foods is a large food company based in the British Virgin Islands. Nomad derives nearly 90 percent of its revenues from the United Kingdom, Germany, Italy, and Austria. Nomad reported over 1.5 billion euros in revenues in 2014, but should see this number increase substantially with its 2015 purchase of Iglo, which included Birds Eye and Findus Group's European operations for $2.8 billion USD expanding the firms reach across a much broader European footprint. Nomad is focused primarily on the frozen food market, and is now targeting possible U.S. acquisitions.

External Issues

Flavor Enhancers

There is a growing awareness of sugars harmful effects on people in particular high-fructose corn syrup and salt. Hershey is a high-profile example of the move away from high-fructose corn syrup that has may fuel weight gain and diabetes, using sugar in some of its products as a replacement for high-fructose corn syrup. However, the American Medical Association stated that restricting the use of syrup is not supported with enough evidence. The Corn Refiners Association, through research by firms like Mintel and Nielsen, analyzed perceptions of sweeteners and observed that 67 percent of consumers felt specific sweetener types were less important than moderation. In the food and beverage industry, soda constitutes a large portion of the high-fructose corn syrup market. Hunt's ketchup is one product to have reverted to using corn syrup after having tried more sugar because there was no change in the sales. The U.S. Food and Drug Administration (FDA) had denied requests made by some companies to have their sweetening agent renamed "corn sugar" on nutrition labels. In addition to this, in July 2015 the FDA proposed forcing food producing companies to add the percent daily value of added sugar on all nutrition labels like the percent daily allowance of salt, fat, and other ingredients, which are listed on the product labels. Any added sugar, just as in the case of corn syrup, can have dramatic effects on the body. Added sugars are linked to diabetes, tooth decay, heart problems, weight gain, and many other health problems.

In response to sugar being harmful, there is a growing global demand for artificial sweeteners as a means to reduce calories, stabilize blood sugar levels, and just an overall healthier choice rather than raw sugar. However, to date, research in this area is not conclusive as some studies reveal artificial sweeteners are similar to raw sugar once ingested. Europe has banned several artificial sweetener products such as Stevia and aspartame from lack on conclusive research, but other nations such as Japan and the United States have been using the same sweeteners for decades. Never the less, there is a growing public awareness toward both raw and artificial sugars.

Another common flavor enhancer found in food is salt. Table salt has been linked to water retention, high blood pressure, stomach cancer, osteoporosis, and killing of beneficial bacterial in the body. Many medical researches recommend limiting salt consumption to 6 grams a day, however the World Health Organization suggests the average person consumes between 9 and 12 grams of salt daily. Many food companies are attempting to reduce the amount of sodium in their products as global awareness increases on the harmful effects of a high salt diet. Nestlé, for example is experimenting with reducing both salt and sugar from its foods and replacing them with natural flavorings.

Cocoa Prices

Over 100 years ago, chocolate was generally considered a luxury for the rich and out of the grasp of lower income customers. However, today consumers in emerging markets worldwide are able to afford increasingly higher quality chocolates that require better and higher percentages of cocoa. Unlike other crops such as corn or soybeans, cocoa is more difficult to produce and cocoa prices are expected to rise substantially moving forward, according to the International Cocoa Organization (ICO).

Typically cocoa trees take upwards of 10 years to mature and many trees now are old, not yielding the same number or quality of beans. Farmers are also switching to more profitable crops, even as the price per ton of cocoa approaches $3,000 per ton. Analysts estimate the cocoa price would need to be $3,500 per ton to maintain current production rates from farmers. In fact the ICO expects the demand to production ratio to be the highest ever by 2018, since it started keeping records in 1960. In 2013 alone, worldwide consumption of cocoa beans was up 32 percent from 2012 and Chinese demand is projected to rise 5 percent annually through 2018. To help combat the new demand, Mars and Nestlé have spent millions to educate farmers in West Africa on proper techniques and in developing new types of cocoa trees. The Ebola virus outbreak in West Africa threatened hundreds of cocoa farms.

North American based Blommer Chocolate Company is a top cocoa processor and one of the main suppliers to rival Hershey and other chocolate producing companies. Blommer is expanding its processing capacity to meet strong chocolate demand in the United States. Nevertheless, chocolate companies are facing tough choices that include raising prices, reducing portion sizes, or even using less cocoa in its products. As early as 2006, Hershey started using substitutes for cocoa butter in the production of Krackel and Mr. Goodbar which resulted in the firm having to change the label "milk chocolate" to "made with chocolate" or "chocolate candy" to comply with the FDA protocols for labeling of chocolate food items. Hershey however is now switching both Krackel and Mr. Goodbar back to solid milk chocolate, meaning the bars will contain at least 10 percent cocoa per FDA regulations to be called milk chocolate.

Potential Taxes and Health-Minded Public

There is a growing awareness worldwide to unhealthy eating, especially when it comes to sugars, processed foods, and animal fats. Many different governments (local, regional and national) have (or plan to) increased taxes or flat out banned unhealthy items. Taxes are viewed by governments much like tobacco taxes as a way not only to curb citizens' consumption but also as an additional means of revenues. For example, Connecticut recently proposed a 2 percent additional tax on all soda, suggesting it would provide $144 million in annual revenues and reduce soda consumption in the state. New York City has banned most sugary drinks 16oz and larger from being served. The Navajos Nation, the largest American Indian Reservation in the United States with 300,000 members, is proposing a tax of up to 7 percent on fatty snacks and soda, up from the current level of 5 percent, while healthy food items are excluded from taxation. Former NBA star Yao Ming is campaigning in his home country of China to promote healthier eating and exercise habits. Mexico recently passed legislation to significantly tax both sugary drinks and high calorie items such as candy. Peru, Uruguay, and Costa Rica banned all junk food from public schools, including candy bars, back in 2012. Many other nations in Latin America require red or yellow circles around sugar content on items depending on their sugar content. All of these actions and trends are a threat to Nestlé.

Increasing obesity is a major problem among the world's population. Processed sugar negatively impacts the body by increasing your chances of tooth decay, obesity, and diabetes, and additionally can significantly increase ones chances of getting heart disease and even cancer. Scientific tests reveal that sugar is basically a food for cancer cells and people that drink 2 soft drinks a week are 87 percent more likely to develop pancreatic cancer. For comparison, a Nestlé Butterfinger and Baby Ruth contain 29 and 33 grams of sugar respectively, and a can of cola contains around 39g of sugar. Sugar is also believed to be damaging to your skin, looks and overall mood. Moving forward, Nestlé could consider increased marketing of dark chocolate, which contain good antioxidants, but is much higher in saturated fat than milk chocolate and contains high levels of sugar. Sugar free candy has also been linked to cancer and weight gain, partly because artificial sweeteners are not healthy.

By 2017, almost 150 artificial ingredients, like artificial sweeteners, preservatives and artificial flavor enhancers, will be discarded from Panera Bread Company's kitchens. Food companies are increasingly eliminating unnatural and unhealthy ingredients. For example, natural colorings made from turmeric and paprika will replace Kraft Heinz Company's artificial colorings in its macaroni and cheese product, and PepsiCo's Diet Pepsi will see a switch from artificial sweetener aspartame to sucralose. After an environmental advocacy group said it found nanoparticles, through laboratory tests, in the Dunkin Donut's white powdered sugar, the company will do away with titanium dioxide (a whitening agent used in sunscreen) from its recipes. Nanoparticles, like titanium dioxide, may cause damage to cells and tissues.

Hair Care, Skin Care, Cosmetics

The hair care, skin care and cosmetic industry in the USA accounts for over $55 billion in annual sales and enjoyed a growth rate of nearly 6 percent from 2010 through 2014. Much like many food products, consumers still purchased beauty products at relatively high rates even during the recession. Growth is projected to continue through 2020 at rate of nearly 4 percent. Hair care and skin care products are the two largest revenue producing contributions to the industry as a whole with revenues each of approximately $13 billion totaling just short of 50 percent of total revenues combined. Higher marketing and R&D expenses, along with a growing concern for reduced packaging, animal safety, and product safety all negatively hurt profits. Consumers also are quick to switch from brand to brand, and are showing less brand loyalty presenting both threats and opportunities for producers. There is also a growing influx of imported products from around the world on all price points. Generally perceived higher quality products are imported from Europe, where perceived lower quality and lower priced products are imported from Mexico and China. Skin care products continue to grow as a percent of total industry market share as more and more people are using these products, including men. In 2014, skin care products barely trailed hair care products in industry wide sales, but are expected to be the largest revenue producing product category moving forward. Firms promote anti-aging treatments and wrinkle reducing creams. Even creams promoted to remove back circles from under the eyes are available. Sunscreen is also in this category. Estée Lauder's CEO recently suggested that men's skin care products may outpace company-wide growth at his firm moving forward.

Activist Shareholders

Food and beverage companies have been popular targets for activist shareholders because of their bloated lackluster growth. In August 2015, Bill Ackman disclosed a stake in Mondelēz International, spurring speculation that he would seek cost cuts and potentially a sale. Similarly ConAgra Foods and

Boulder Brands have recently faced calls for shakeups. So far however, activist investors have mainly targeted U.S. food companies, but Nestlé's underperformance is attracting prying eyes. Nestlé is grappling with falling demand for its biscuits and peanut-milk beverages in China and the recall in India of its popular Maggi instant noodles. Its frozen-food business is not performing well.

Given the activist shareholder environment, Nestlé may want to consider divesting its frozen-food division, along with the company's 23.2 percent stake in cosmetics maker L'Oréal S.A. Nestlé could add 21 billion euros ($23 billion) of cash flow through 2018 by gradually reducing its stake in L'Oréal, said Jeff Stent, an analyst at Exane BNP Paribas. Nestlé could use that money to boost its share buyback or to make acquisitions. Additionally, an activist shareholder could require Nestlé to sell is its skin-health business. Nestlé acquired full control of the Galderma wrinkle treatment and acne medication business from joint-venture partner L'Oréal in 2014, but skincare does not fit well with food and beverages.

To significantly impact Nestlé, an activist investor would need at least a 1 percent stake, said Urs Beck, a fund manager at EFG Asset Management. That would cost more than $2 billion. Jenny Craig and PowerBar are two examples of businesses that Nestlé acquired, held onto for too long and got depressed prices for in later divestitures. The political environment in Switzerland also gives activist investors another reason to "go for" Nestlé. Switzerland has instituted a "fat-cat" referendum that gives shareholders more say over salaries and the ability to eject an entire board. Even Nestlé's Chairman Peter Brabeck-Letmathe has said new Swiss laws threaten the company's long-term strategy. A new proposal that would allow investors to sue management and directors, even amid opposition by most shareholders, is also flawed, he has said. "Activist shareholders and plaintiffs' lawyers would be granted free reign," Brabeck-Lemathe says.

Future

Nestlé has many internal and external issues to consider as the company struggles to help feed the world and reward shareholders, employees, and customers. The company is determined to become a renowned nutrition and corporate wellness company, but many of its products still are unhealthy for consumption.

Nestlé needs a clear strategic plan going forward. Develop a three-year strategic plan for Nestlé S.A. that will enable the company to meet its many obligations to the many shareholders who expect to see the company grow both revenues and profits annually.

ASSURANCE OF LEARNING EXERCISES

EXERCISE 1A
Assess Singapore Airlines' Most Recent Quarterly Performance Data

Purpose

This exercise will enable you to analyze business strategies and practice examining the progress a firm is making in executing its strategic plan. Singapore Airlines utilizes excellent strategic management as showcased at the beginning of Chapter 1.

Instructions

Step 1	Go to Singapore Airlines' website. Find the *About Us* section, which is usually on the bottom left hand corner of the home page, and then click on *Investor Relations*.
Step 2	Review Singapore Airlines' most recent quarterly report or half-year report.
Step 3	Examine the change in performance variables and statistics for that most recent quarter or half-year report.
Step 4	Based on your observations, what are strategic changes you think were made during that time period? What additional changes in your view are still needed? Do the statistics and numbers reveal any key problem areas? How well do you think the company is faring using the strategic management processes they currently have in place?

EXERCISE 1B
Gather Strategy Information on Nestlé S.A.

Purpose

The purpose of this exercise is to get you familiar with strategy terms introduced and defined in this chapter. Let's apply these terms to the Cohesion Case on Nestlé S.A. (traded as NSRGY).

Instructions

Step 1   Go to the Nestlé Global corporate website. Scroll to the bottom of the site and find Investors; click on Publications and download the most recent *Annual Review* report. The *Annual Review* contains excellent information for developing a list of internal strengths and weaknesses for Nestlé.

Step 2   From your college library website, download a copy of Standard & Poor's *Industry Surveys* for the food industry. This document will contain excellent information for developing a list of external opportunities and threats facing Nestlé. You could also refer to Citi group's credit cards page, IBIS World, ValueLine, and Mergent Online, if these sources are available in your college library.

Step 3   Using the Internet, find out and print information about Nestlé's two major competitors: Danone (DANOY) and Mondelēz International (MDLZ).

Step 4   Using the Nestlé Cohesion Case and with the help of the information gathered above, identify what you consider to be Nestlé's three major strengths, three major weaknesses, three major opportunities, and three major threats. Each factor listed for this exercise must include a percentage (%), number (#), dollar ($), or ratio (employees per share) to reveal some quantified fact or trend. These factors provide the underlying basis for a strategic plan because a firm strives to take advantage of strengths, improve weaknesses, avoid threats, and capitalize on opportunities. Estimate the numbers as needed.

Step 5   Through class discussion, compare your lists of external and internal factors to those developed by other students and add to your lists of factors. Keep this information for use in later exercises at the end of other chapters.

Step 6   Be mindful that whatever case company is assigned to you or your team this semester, you can start to update the information on your company by following the steps listed for any publicly held firm.

EXERCISE 1C
Get Familiar with the Free Excel Student Template

Purpose

Every week companies, like Nestlé, update their websites with notes and articles on important strategic decisions and information. This exercise is designed to help strategic-management students become familiar with the free Excel student template for the case analysis offered by the authors.

Instructions

Step 1   Go to the www.strategyclub.com website. Download the free Excel student template.

Step 2   Write a one-page summary summarizing the template and explaining why and how the template will benefit you the most in this course.

Step 3   Submit your report to your professor.

EXERCISE 1D
Evaluate an Oral Student Presentation

Purpose

Quite often in a strategic-management course, a team of students is required to give a 15 to 20 minute case analysis oral presentation. This exercise gives you insight on some do's and don'ts regarding oral presentations.

Instructions

Step 1   Go to www.strategyclub.com website and watch the live student case analysis presentation given there on Barnes & Noble.

Step 2   Critique the presentation. What are four aspects that you liked most and four aspects that you liked least?

EXERCISE 1E
Strategic Planning at Nestlé S.A.

Purpose

The purpose of this exercise is to give you practical knowledge and experience in investigating the strategic plan of large, publicly held firms such as Nestlé S.A. An important aspect of formulating a strategic plan is to assess the strategic plans of rival firms. For this exercise, you are in the top management team of M&M Mars, a large chocolate company that competes with Nestlé in the confectionery business worldwide.

Instructions

Step 1   Go to Nestlé's website and review the company's recent *Annual Report*. List as clearly as you can the five major strategies that Nestlé is pursuing worldwide.

Step 2   Go to Mars, Inc.'s website and determine as best you can what the privately-held firm is doing worldwide to compete with Nestlé.

Step 3   Write a one-page paper that summarizes your assessment of Nestlé's strategic plan as compared to Mars's strategic plan. Include whether you feel being privately held, as Mars is, enables a firm to conceal its strategic plan from rival firms. Do you feel it is advantageous to keep strategies secret from shareholders, employees, creditors, suppliers, and other stakeholders? What would be the advantages of being publicly held?

Step 4   Prepare to give your class an overview of your findings.

EXERCISE 1F
Interview Local Strategists

Purpose

This exercise is designed to give you practical experience in learning how strategists in your city or town formulate and implement strategies. This information can be used to compare and contrast concepts presented in this textbook with practices of local strategists. Recall that strategists include owners of businesses, directors of nonprofit organizations, top managers of large firms, CEOs, presidents, and many others.

Instructions

Step 1   Contact several business owners or top managers. Find three organizations that do strategic planning. Make an appointment to visit with three strategists of the businesses.

Step 2   Interview them, asking the following questions.
- How do you decide which strategies to implement in this organization?
- How often do you change strategies or take a fresh look at existing strategies?
- How many persons assist you in formulating strategies?
- Does your organization have written mission, vision, and objective statements?
- Is the strategic-planning process in your company more secret or open in regards to process and procedure? Which approach do you feel is best? Why?

Step 3   Prepare answers and report back to your professor.

Source: © BelliniFrancescoM81/Fotolia

Outside-USA Strategic Planning

LEARNING OBJECTIVES

After studying this chapter, you should be able to do the following:

2-1. Discuss the nature of doing business globally, including language and labor union issues.

2-2. Explain the advantages and disadvantages of doing business globally.

2-3. Discuss the global challenge facing firms and why this is a strategic issue.

2-4. Discuss tax rates and tax inversions as strategic issues.

2-5. Compare and contrast American business culture versus foreign business cultures; explain why this is a strategic issue.

2-6. Discuss the business culture found in Mexico, Japan, China, and India; explain why this is a strategic issue.

2-7. Discuss the business climate in Africa, China, Indonesia, India, Japan, Mexico, and Vietnam; explain why this is a strategic issue.

ASSURANCE OF LEARNING EXERCISES

The following exercises are found at the end of this chapter:

EXERCISE 2A Nestlé S.A. Wants to Enter Africa. Help Them.

EXERCISE 2B Assess Differences in Culture across Countries

EXERCISE 2C Honda Motor Company Wants to Do Business in Vietnam. Help Them.

EXERCISE 2D Does My University Recruit in Foreign Countries?

Global considerations impact virtually all strategic decisions, as illustrated in Figure 2-1 with white shading. The boundaries of countries no longer can define the limits of our imaginations. To see and appreciate the world from the perspective of others has become a matter of survival for businesses. The underpinnings of strategic management hinge on managers gaining an understanding of competitors, markets, prices, suppliers, distributors, governments, creditors, shareholders, and customers worldwide. The price and quality of a firm's products and services must be competitive on a worldwide basis, not just on a local basis. Shareholders expect substantial revenue growth, so doing business globally is one of the best ways to achieve this end. As indicated in the exemplary company shown next, Honda Motor Company effectively and successfully does business globally.

The Nature of Doing Business Globally

Exports of goods and services from the United States account for only 13.5 percent of U.S. gross domestic product, so the nation is still largely a domestic, continental economy. What happens inside the United States largely determines the strength of the economic recovery. In contrast, as a percent of gross domestic product (GDP), exports comprise 45.6 percent of the German economy, 22.6 percent of the Chinese economy, and 187 percent of the Singapore economy (http://data.worldbank.org/indicator/NE.EXP.GNFS.ZS). Singapore's number is so high because it imports oil and other products and then re-exports them globally. A point here is that the United States has substantial room for improvement in doing business globally based on the 11 percent exports to the GDP number.

EXEMPLARY **COMPANY** SHOWCASED

Honda Motor Company (HMC)

Honda, headquartered in Minato, Tokyo, Japan, is the world's largest manufacturer of motorcycles and of internal combustion engines. It annually produces and sells thousands of scooters, water pumps, lawn and garden equipment tools, tillers, outboard motors, robotics, jet engines, and solar cells. Honda, which has about 180,000 employees, is annually ranked as one of the most respected companies in the world by *Fortune*.

Honda recently invested another $215 million in its Ohio operations, pushing the company's total to $2.7 billion in North American operations in only the past three years. The majority of the money was spent on an expansion of manufacturing capabilities at the company's Anna Engine Plant, Ohio, while the remainder was spent on a new building in Marysville, Ohio. Honda already has the strongest foothold of any Japanese automaker, and produces more cars with U.S.-sourced parts than any automaker other than General Motors. Nine of Honda's 16 mass-market cars are made with over half American made parts, according to the survey—that's more than Ford.

Honda recently built a new car factory in Ityrapina, Brazil, which is approximately 120 miles northwest of Sao Paulo, doubling its capacity in that country to 240,000 cars a year. The existing Honda factory in Brazil is in Sumare, a city of around 100,000, located halfway between Ityrapina and Sao Paulo. The cost of the new factory, including the purchase of the 1,433 acres, is about $435 million. The factory employs approximately 2,000 people, and produces the Honda Fit.

Source: Based on company documents.

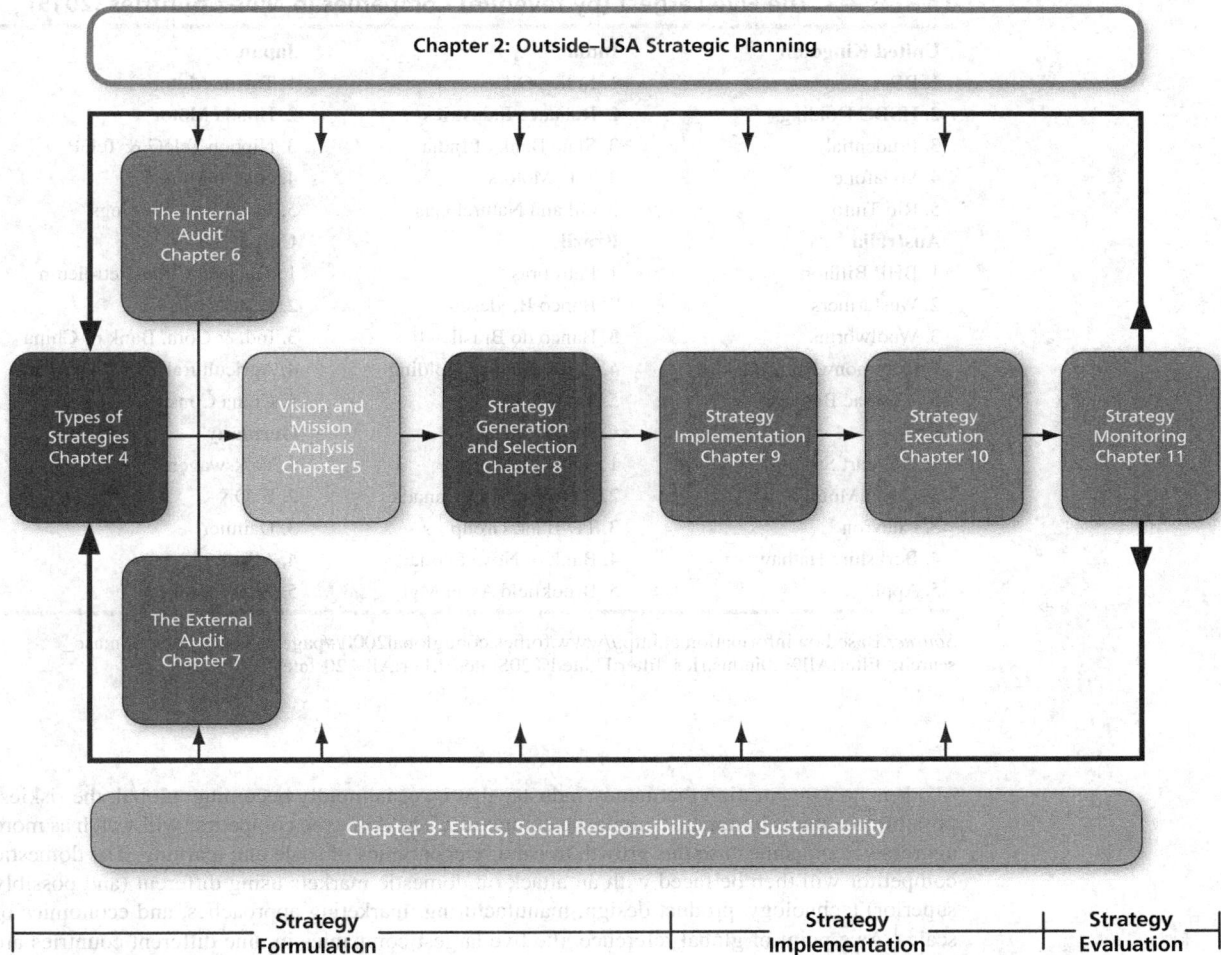

FIGURE 2-1

A Comprehensive Strategic-Management Model

Source: Fred R. David, adapted from "How Companies Define Their Mission," *Long Range Planning* 22, no. 3 (June 1988): 40, © Fred R. David.

A world market has emerged from what previously was a multitude of distinct national markets, and the climate for international business today is more favorable than in years past. Mass communication and high technology have created similar patterns of consumption in diverse cultures worldwide. This means that many companies may find it difficult to survive by relying solely on domestic markets.

Globalization is a process of doing business worldwide, so strategic decisions are made based on global profitability of the firm rather than just domestic considerations. A global strategy seeks to meet the needs of customers worldwide, with the highest value at the lowest cost. This may mean locating production in countries with the lowest labor costs or abundant natural resources, locating research and complex engineering centers where skilled scientists and engineers can be found, and locating marketing activities close to the markets to be served.

A **global strategy** includes designing, producing, and marketing products with global needs in mind, instead of considering individual countries alone. A global strategy integrates actions against competitors into a worldwide plan. Today, there are global buyers and sellers and the instant transmission of money and information across continents.

TABLE 2-1 The Five Largest (by revenue) Companies in Nine Countries (2015)

United Kingdom	India	Japan
1. BP	1. Indian Oil	1. Toyota Motor
2. HSBC Holdings	2. Reliance Industries	2. Honda Motor
3. Prudential	3. State Bank of India	3. Nippon TeleG & TeleP
4. Vodafone	4. Tata Motors	4. Nissan Motor
5. Rio Tinto	5. Oil and Natural Gas	5. Japan Post Holdings
Australia	**Brazil**	**China**
1. BHP Billiton	1. Petrobras	1. Sinopec–China Petroleum
2. Wesfarmers	2. Banco Bradesco	2. PetroChina
3. Woolworths	3. Banco do Brasil	3. Ind. & Com. Bank of China
4. Commonwealth Bank	4. Itau Unibanco Holding	4. Agricultural Bank of China
5. Westpac Banking	5. Vale	5. China Construction Bank
USA	**Canada**	**Germany**
1. Walmart Stores	1. Suncor Energy	1. Volkswagen
2. ExxonMobil	2. Royal Bank of Canada	2. E. ON
3. Chevron	3. TD Bank Group	3. Daimier
4. Berkshire Hathaway	4. Bank of Nova Scotia	4. Allianz
5. Apple	5. Brookfield Asset Mgt.	5. BMW Group

Source: Based on information at http://www.forbes.com/global2000/#page:4_sort:0_direction:asc_
search:_filter:All%20industries_filter:United%20States_filter:All%20states

It is no exaggeration that in any industry that is, or is rapidly becoming, global, the riskiest possible posture is to remain a domestic competitor. The domestic competitor will watch as more aggressive companies use this growth to capture economies of scale and learning. The domestic competitor will then be faced with an attack on domestic markets using different (and possibly superior) technology, product design, manufacturing, marketing approaches, and economies of scale.[1] As a point of global reference, the five largest companies in nine different countries are listed in Table 2-1.

Multinational Firms

Organizations that conduct business operations across national borders are called **international firms** or **multinational corporations**. The strategic-management process is conceptually the same for multinational firms as for purely domestic firms; however, the process is more complex for international firms as a result of more variables and relationships. The social, cultural, demographic, environmental, political, governmental, legal, technological, and competitive opportunities and threats that face a multinational corporation are almost limitless, and the number and complexity of these factors increase dramatically with the number of products produced and the number of geographic areas served. Millions of small businesses do business everyday outside their home country by interacting with customers though websites, smartphones, and social media. All of Africa, and places such as Cuba and Iran, are becoming more desirable for business every day.

More time and effort are required to identify and evaluate external trends and events in multinational corporations than in domestic corporations. Geographic distance, cultural and national differences, and variations in business practices often make communication between domestic headquarters and overseas operations difficult. Strategy implementation can be more difficult because different cultures have different norms, values, and work ethics. Multinational corporations (MNCs) face unique and diverse risks, such as expropriation of assets, currency losses through exchange rate fluctuations, unfavorable foreign court interpretations of contracts and agreements, social/political disturbances, import/export restrictions, tariffs, and trade barriers. Strategists in MNCs are often confronted with the need to be globally competitive and nationally responsive at the same time. With the rise in world commerce, government and regulatory bodies are more closely monitoring foreign business practices. The U.S. Foreign Corrupt Practices Act, for example, monitors business practices in many areas.

Before entering international markets, firms should scan relevant journals and patent reports, seek the advice of academic and research organizations, participate in international trade fairs, form partnerships, and conduct extensive research to broaden their contacts and diminish the risk of doing business in new markets. Firms can also offset some risks of doing business internationally by obtaining insurance from the U.S. government's Overseas Private Investment Corporation (OPIC). The decision to expand operations into foreign markets—that is, to globalize—is one of the most important strategic decisions made by companies. Thus, variables that influence how, when, where, and why to internationalize have attracted much attention in scholarly journals. Recent research reveals that countries are attractive not only because of their own institutions but also as a function of their serving as a platform for entry into other regions.[2] Therefore, multinational firms make globalization decisions with special consideration in mind for how a particular region/country will facilitate the firm's further globalization into other regions/countries.

Different Languages Globally

A strategic issue facing many firms is whether to publish their website material in different languages, given that most of the world's population does not speak English. Pioneering work to document the number of different languages spoken has been done by the Summer Institute of Linguistics (SIL) International. That organization today publishes 2,508 translations of the Christian Bible, and has compiled a catalogue of the world's languages, called the *Ethnologue,* which lists 6,909 distinct languages being spoken. Of that total, only 230 are spoken in Europe and 2,197 in Asia. But in Papua, New Guinea, 830 different languages are spoken by 3.9 million people, and in France, the *Ethnologue* cites 10 languages being spoken, including Picard, Gascon, Provençal, Allemannisch, Alsace, Breton, and French. Academic Research Capsule 2-1 reveals that most languages will permanently disappear by the end of this century.

Labor Unions across Europe

Prevalence of unions is a relevant factor in many strategic decisions, such as where to locate stores or factories. There is great variation across Europe in regards to levels of union membership, ranging from 74 percent of employees in Finland and 71 percent in Sweden to 9 percent in Lithuania and 8 percent in France. However, percentage of union membership is not the only indicator of strength. In France, for example, unions have repeatedly shown that despite low levels of membership, they are able to mobilize workers in mass strikes and demonstrations to great effect.

ACADEMIC RESEARCH CAPSULE 2-1

How Many Languages Are There Globally?

When businesses consider offering their products or services globally, or manufacturing and securing resources outside their own country, language barriers arise. Interacting with people who speak a different language is one of many variables that complicate doing business globally—yet millions of businesses need to do more business globally. Thankfully, translations to and from most mainstream languages such as English, Spanish, French, German, and Chinese are easily done with online programs, and there are millions of multilingual people.

The implication for businesses doing business globally is that the total number of languages spoken globally is decreasing quite dramatically. For example, in North America, many Native American languages are disappearing yearly, a common phenomenon all over the world. Whenever any language ceases to be learned by young children, that language generally does not survive the death of current native speakers. In North America, about 75 languages are spoken by only a handful of older people, and those languages are expected to become extinct. About 25 percent of the world's languages have fewer than a thousand remaining speakers. By the year 2099, analysts estimate that roughly one half of the 6,909 languages listed by *Ethnologue* will disappear. By 2115, researchers say there will be only 600 left on the planet.

Source: Based on information from the website http://www.linguisticsociety .org/content/how-many-languages-are-there-world; and John McWhorter, "What the World Will Speak in 2115," *Wall Street Journal,* January 4, 2015, C1–C2.

The average level of union membership across the whole of the European Union (EU), weighted by the numbers employed in the different member states, is 23 percent, compared to about 11 percent in the United States. The European average is held down by relatively low levels of membership in some of the larger EU states: Germany with 18 percent, France with 8 percent, Spain with 19 percent, and Poland with 12 percent. The three smallest states—Cyprus, Luxembourg, and Malta—have levels well above the average.

The four Nordic countries of Denmark, Sweden, Finland, and Norway have 67, 70, 74, and 52 percent, respectively, of all employees as members of unions. In part this is because, as in Belgium, which also has above-average levels of union density, unemployment and other social benefits are normally paid out through the union. High union density in the Nordic countries also reflects an approach that sees union membership as a natural part of employment. Central and Eastern Europe nations generally have below-average levels of union membership. In Poland, for example, 12 percent of employees are estimated to be union members. Level of union membership is clearly trending downward all over Europe. The two exceptions appear to be Ireland and Italy, where union membership is slowly growing.

Advantages and Disadvantages of Doing Business Globally

Firms have numerous reasons for formulating and implementing strategies that initiate, continue, or expand involvement in business operations across national borders. Perhaps the greatest advantage is that firms can gain new customers for their products and services, thus increasing revenues. Growth in revenues and profits is a common organizational objective and often an expectation of shareholders because it is a measure of organizational success. Potential advantages to initiating, continuing, or expanding international operations are as follows:

1. Firms can gain new customers for their products.
2. Foreign operations can absorb excess capacity, reduce unit costs, and spread economic risks over a wider number of markets.
3. Foreign operations can allow firms to establish low-cost production facilities in locations close to raw materials or cheap labor.
4. Competitors in foreign markets may not exist, or competition may be less intense than in domestic markets.
5. Foreign operations may result in reduced tariffs, lower taxes, and favorable political treatment.
6. Joint ventures can enable firms to learn the technology, culture, and business practices of other people and to make contacts with potential customers, suppliers, creditors, and distributors in foreign countries.
7. Economies of scale can be achieved from operation in global rather than solely domestic markets. Larger-scale production and better efficiencies allow higher sales volumes and lower-price offerings.
8. A firm's power and prestige in domestic markets may be significantly enhanced if the firm competes globally. Enhanced prestige can translate into improved negotiating power among creditors, suppliers, distributors, and other important groups.

The availability, depth, and reliability of economic and marketing information in different countries vary extensively, as do industrial structures, business practices, and the number and nature of regional organizations. There are also numerous potential disadvantages of initiating, continuing, or expanding business across national borders, such as the following:

1. Foreign operations could be seized by nationalistic factions.
2. Firms confront different and often little-understood social, cultural, demographic, environmental, political, governmental, legal, technological, economic, and competitive forces when doing business internationally. These forces can make communication difficult in the firm.

3. Weaknesses of competitors in foreign lands are often overestimated, and strengths are often underestimated. Keeping informed about the number and nature of competitors is more difficult when doing business internationally.

4. Language, culture, and value systems differ among countries, which can create barriers to communication and problems managing people.

5. Gaining an understanding of regional organizations such as the European Economic Community, the Latin American Free Trade Area, the International Bank for Reconstruction and Development, and the International Finance Corporation is difficult but is often required in doing business internationally.

6. Dealing with two or more monetary systems can complicate international business operations.

The Global Challenge

Few companies can afford to ignore the presence of international competition. Firms that seem insulated and comfortable today may be vulnerable tomorrow; for example, foreign banks do not yet compete or operate in most of the United States, but this too is changing. Thomson Reuters annually compiles a list of the world's most innovative companies, using metrics that include patent activity, R&D investment, success rate, globalization, and influence. For the first time ever, Japan (39%) overtook the United States (36%) in 2014 as having the most innovative companies in the world. Top U.S. firms making the list included Apple, Lockheed Martin, Google, Microsoft, Intel, and IBM, whereas some top Asian companies on the top-100 list included Samsung, Fujitsu, Hitachi, Canon, and for the first time, a Chinese company, Huawei.

The U.S. economy is becoming much less American. A world economy and monetary system are emerging. Corporations in every corner of the globe are taking advantage of the opportunity to obtain customers globally. Markets are shifting rapidly and, in many cases, converging in tastes, trends, and prices. Innovative transport systems are accelerating the transfer of technology. Shifts in the nature and location of production systems, especially to China and India, are reducing the response time to changing market conditions. China has more than 1.3 billion residents and a dramatically growing middle class anxious to buy goods and services.

More and more countries around the world are welcoming foreign investment and capital. As a result, labor markets have steadily become more international. East Asian countries are market leaders in labor-intensive industries, Brazil offers abundant natural resources and rapidly developing markets, and Germany offers skilled labor and technology. The drive to improve the efficiency of global business operations is leading to greater functional specialization. This is not limited to a search for the familiar low-cost labor in Latin America or Asia. Other considerations include the cost of energy, availability of resources, inflation rates, tax rates, and the nature of trade regulations.

Many countries are quite protectionist, and this position can impact companies' strategic plans. **Protectionism** refers to countries imposing tariffs, taxes, and regulations on firms outside the country to favor their own companies and people. Most economists argue that protectionism harms the world economy because it inhibits trade among countries and invites retaliation.

Advancements in telecommunications are drawing countries, cultures, and organizations worldwide closer together. Foreign revenue as a percentage of total company revenues already exceeds 50 percent in hundreds of U.S. firms, including ExxonMobil, Gillette, Dow Chemical, Citicorp, Colgate-Palmolive, and Texaco. A primary reason why most domestic firms do business globally is that growth in demand for goods and services outside the United States is considerably higher than inside. For example, the domestic food industry is growing just 3 percent per year, so Kraft Foods, the second-largest food company in the world behind Nestlé, is focusing on foreign acquisitions. Shareholders and investors expect sustained growth in revenues from firms; satisfactory growth for many firms can only be achieved by capitalizing on demand outside the United States. Joint ventures and partnerships between domestic and foreign firms are becoming the rule rather than the exception!

Fully 95 percent of the world's population lives outside the United States, and this group is growing 70 percent faster than the U.S. population. The lineup of competitors in virtually all industries is global. General Motors and Ford compete with Toyota and Hyundai. General Electric and Westinghouse battle Siemens and Mitsubishi. Caterpillar and John Deere compete with Komatsu. Goodyear battles Michelin, Bridgestone/Firestone, and Pirelli. Boeing competes with Airbus. Only a few U.S. industries—such as furniture, printing, retailing, consumer packaged goods, and retail banking—are not yet greatly challenged by foreign competitors. But many products and components in these industries too are now manufactured in foreign countries. International operations can be as simple as exporting a product to a single foreign country or as complex as operating manufacturing, distribution, and marketing facilities in many countries.

New research examined in Academic Research Capsule 2-2 sheds some light on how firms decide where to expand.

It is clear that different industries become global for different reasons. The need to amortize massive research and development (R&D) investments over many markets is a major reason why the aircraft manufacturing industry became global. Monitoring globalization in one's industry is an important strategic-management activity. Knowing how to use that information for one's competitive advantage is even more important. For example, firms may look around the world for the best technology and select one that has the most promise for the largest number of markets. When firms design a product, they design it to be marketable in as many countries as possible. When firms manufacture a product, they select the lowest-cost source, which may be Japan for semiconductors, Sri Lanka for textiles, Malaysia for simple electronics, and Europe for precision machinery.

Tax Rates and Tax Inversions

Tax Rates

Tax rates in countries are important in strategic decisions regarding where to build manufacturing facilities or retail stores or even where to acquire other firms. High corporate tax rates deter investment in new factories and also provide strong incentives for corporations to avoid and evade taxes. Corporate tax rates vary considerably across countries and companies. As indicated in Table 2-2, the top national statutory corporate tax rates in 2015 among sample countries ranged from 0 percent in Bermuda to 55 percent in the United Arab Emirates (UAE). Note that some countries have a flat tax, which often, on adoption, triggers a surge in foreign direct investment. Signet Jewelers Ltd., owner of Kay's Jewelers, Zale Corporation, and Jared the Galleria of Jewelry, is headquartered in Bermuda for a reason: zero corporate taxes.

The United States requires companies to pay the difference between lower foreign taxes and the U.S. corporate-tax rate of 35 percent when they bring their international earnings home. In contrast, the territorial system that many other countries use allows companies to pay little to no taxes on foreign profits above what they have already paid abroad. The United States is the only nation that imposes taxes on foreign earnings. Thus, to avoid paying U.S. taxes on income made in other countries, many U.S. companies are cash-rich outside the United States, but cash-poor inside

ACADEMIC RESEARCH CAPSULE 2-2

How Do Firms Decide Where to Expand?

Considerable prior research has examined the relative attractiveness of various countries to expand operations, quite often from a "need to exploit resources in host countries" perspective. A recent article focused on the nature of institutions, such as schools, laws, and health care, rather than resources, such as oil, gas, minerals, and labor, in the decision to expand operations to other countries. Arregle and colleagues report that it does indeed matter which region(s) are chosen for expansion. More specifically, Arregle and colleagues have found that companies seek to expand primarily to regions that have institutions similar to their own institutions, or at least similar to the institutions in other regions where the firm already has operations. The "institutions factor" may be more important than the "resources factor" in internationalization decisions.

Source: Based on Jean-Luc Arregle, Tuyah Miller, Michael Hitt, and Paul Beamish, "Do Regions Matter?" An Integrated Institutional and Semi-Globalization Perspective on the Internationalization of MNEs," *Strategic Management Journal* 34 (2013): 910–934.

TABLE 2-2 Corporate Tax Rates across Countries in 2015 (from high to low)

Country/Region	Corporate Tax Rate (%)
United Arab Emirates (UAE)	55.00
Chad	40.00
USA	35.00
Brazil	34.00
France	33.33
Germany	33.00
India	30.00
Mexico	30.00
Italy	27.50
Japan	25.50
Israel	25.00
Austria	25.00
China Mainland	25.00
Portugal	25.00
Finland	24.50
U.K.	23.00
Ukraine	21.00
Estonia	21.00
Russia	20.00
Greece	20.00
Croatia	20.00
Libya	20.00
Netherlands	20.00
Turkey	20.00
Poland	19.00
Czech Republic	19.00
Hungary	19.00
Singapore	17.00
Canada	15.00
China Hong Kong	16.50
Romania	16.00
Latvia	15.00
Lithuania	15.00
Ireland	12.50
Serbia	10.00
Bulgaria	10.00
Cyprus	10.00
Bermuda	0.00

Source: Based on information at http://www.worldwide-tax.com/#partthree, retrieved January 1, 2015.

the United States, and they bring cash back to the United States only as needed. For example, Microsoft has $15+ billion in cash reserves on its balance sheet, but only about 15 percent of that money is housed in the United States. General Electric and Apple have a similar policy to avoid paying U.S. corporate taxes. Emerson Electric has $2 billion in cash with almost all of it in Europe and Asia, so the firm borrows money in the United States rather than bringing its cash back and paying a 35 percent corporate U.S. tax on corporate profits minus whatever tax it has already paid overseas. Johnson & Johnson keeps virtually all of its $24+ billion in cash outside the United States, as does Illinois Tool Works Inc. Whirlpool has 85 percent of its cash offshore. Bruce Nolop, former CFO of Pitney Bowes, explains it this way: "You end up with the really peculiar result where you are borrowing money in the United States, while you show cash on the balance sheet that is trapped overseas. It is a totally inefficient capital structure." The U.S. tax system, unfortunately for Americans, is structured so that companies can cut their tax bill by shifting income offshore to lower-tax countries.

Since the 1980s, most countries have been steadily lowering their tax rates, but the United States has not cut its top statutory corporate tax rate since 1993. Canada recently achieved its goal of having the most business-friendly tax system of the Group of Seven (G-7) nations, which include Canada, France, Germany, Italy, Japan, the United Kingdom and the United States. In January 2014, Canada's federal corporate tax rate automatically fell to 15 percent from 16.5 percent as the last installment of a series of corporate rate cuts launched in 2006 by the administration of Prime Minister Stephen Harper, who had campaigned on the promise to lower Canada's overall federal corporate tax rate by one third. More recently, the United Kingdom lowered its federal tax rate to 23 percent.

Other factors besides the corporate tax rate obviously affect companies' decisions of where to locate plants and facilities and whether to acquire other firms. For example, the large, affluent market and efficient infrastructure in both Germany and Britain attract companies, but the high labor costs and strict labor laws there keep other companies away. The rapidly growing GDP in Brazil and India attracts companies, but violence and political unrest in Middle East countries deter investment. Perhaps the United States should lower its rate to reward companies that invest in jobs domestically. Lowering the U.S. corporate tax rate should also reduce unemployment and spur growth domestically.

Tax Inversions

An increasing number of U.S. companies are reincorporating in foreign countries to reduce their tax burden, and doing this typically by acquiring a foreign firm. For example, Illinois-based AbbVie recently acquired Dublin-based Shire PLC for $54 billion and Pennsylvania-based Mylan acquired Abbott Laboratories' overseas generic drugs segment for $5.3 billion. Whenever a U.S. firm acquires a foreign firm and adopts that firm's lower tax rate or establishes a holding company in a foreign country and adopts that firm's lower tax rate, the transaction is called an **inversion**. Inversions are becoming common out of fear that politicians will soon eliminate that cross-border tax strategy. The U.S. Treasury Department installed some new rules in September 2014 to curtail inversions, but those rules had little effect. Under consideration currently are U.S.-based Pfizer and Medtronic bidding for Actavis (based in Ireland) and Covidien (based in Ireland), respectively, and Chiquita (based in Charlotte, NC) recently acquiring Fyffes (based in Ireland). Ireland in particular is taking steps to close the best-known corporate tax loophole.

Tax inversions have led to a higher dollar value of mergers and acquisitions in the United States in 2014–2015 than in the past 10 years. Inversions are common because the old alternative strategy of simply reincorporating in, say Bermuda or the Cayman Islands, has been virtually eliminated by politicians. Mylan, like many firms, used its foreign acquisition to reincorporate in the Netherlands, and then transfer pretax income from their domestic operations to their foreign parent through intercompany debt. Similarly, Salix Pharmaceuticals in North Carolina recently acquired an Italian drug company and reincorporated in Ireland in the process. Congress's Joint Committee on Taxation says eliminating inversions would yield $19.46 billion more in tax revenue for the United States over 10 years, but this will likely not get done for several years.

American Versus Foreign Business Culture

To be successful in world markets, U.S. managers must obtain a better knowledge of historical, cultural, and religious forces that motivate and drive people in other countries. For multinational firms, knowledge of business culture variation across countries can be essential for gaining and sustaining competitive advantage. An excellent website to visit on this topic is www.worldbusinessculture.com, where you may select any country in the world and check out how business culture varies in that country versus other lands. In Japan, for example, business relations operate within the context of **Wa**, which stresses group harmony and social cohesion. In China, business behavior revolves around **guanxi**, or personal relations. In South Korea, activities involve concern for **inhwa**, or harmony based on respect of hierarchical relationships, including obedience to authority.[3]

In Europe, it is generally true that the farther north on the continent, the more participatory the management style. Most European workers are unionized and enjoy more frequent vacations and holidays than U.S. workers. A 90-minute lunch break plus 20-minute morning and afternoon breaks are common in European firms. Many Europeans resent pay-for-performance, commission salaries, and objective measurement and reward systems. This is true especially of workers in southern Europe. Many Europeans also find the notion of team spirit difficult to grasp because the unionized environment has dichotomized worker–management relations throughout Europe.

A weakness of some U.S. firms in competing with Pacific Rim firms is a lack of understanding of Asian cultures, including how Asians think and behave. Spoken Chinese, for example, has more in common with spoken English than with spoken Japanese or Korean. Managers in the United States consistently put more weight on being friendly and liked, whereas Asian and European managers often exercise authority without this concern. Americans tend to use first names instantly in business dealings with foreigners, but foreigners find this presumptuous. In Japan, for example, first names are used only among family members and intimate friends; even longtime business associates and coworkers shy away from the use of first names. Table 2-3 lists other cultural differences or pitfalls that would benefit U.S. managers.

Managers from the United States place greater emphasis on short-term results than do foreign managers. In marketing, for example, Japanese managers strive to achieve "everlasting customers," whereas many Americans strive to make a one-time sale. Marketing managers in Japan see making a sale as the beginning, not the end, of the selling process. This is an important distinction. Japanese managers often criticize U.S. managers for worrying more about shareholders, whom they do not know, than employees, whom they do know. Americans refer to "hourly employees," whereas many Japanese companies still refer to "lifetime employees."

Rose Knotts summarized some important cultural differences between U.S. and foreign managers.[4] Awareness and consideration of these differences can enable a manager to be more effective, regardless of his or her own nationality.

1. Americans place an exceptionally high priority on time, viewing time as an asset. Many foreigners place more worth on relationships. This difference results in foreign managers often viewing U.S. managers as "more interested in business than people."
2. Personal touching and distance norms differ around the world. Americans generally stand about three feet from each other when carrying on business conversations, but Arabs and

TABLE 2-3 Cultural Pitfalls That May Help You Be a Better Manager

- Waving is a serious insult in Greece and Nigeria, particularly if the hand is near someone's face.
- Making a "good-bye" wave in Europe can mean "No," but it means "Come here" in Peru.
- In China, last names are written first.
- A man named Carlos Lopez-Garcia should be addressed as Mr. Lopez in Latin America but as Mr. Garcia in Brazil.
- Breakfast meetings are considered uncivilized in most foreign countries.
- Latin Americans are, on average, 20 minutes late to business appointments.
- Direct eye contact is impolite in Japan.
- Do not cross your legs in any Arab or many Asian countries—it is rude to show the sole of your shoe.
- In Brazil, touching your thumb and first finger—an American "Okay" sign—is the equivalent of raising your middle finger.
- Nodding or tossing your head back in southern Italy, Malta, Greece, and Tunisia means "No." In India, this body motion means "Yes."
- Snapping your fingers is vulgar in France and Belgium.
- Folding your arms across your chest is a sign of annoyance in Finland.
- In China, leave some food on your plate to show that your host was so generous that you could not finish.
- Do not eat with your left hand when dining with clients from Malaysia or India.
- One form of communication works the same worldwide. It is the smile—so take that along wherever you go.

Africans stand about one foot apart. Touching another person with the left hand in business dealings is taboo in some countries.

3. Family roles and relationships vary in different countries. For example, males are valued more than females in some cultures, and peer pressure, work situations, and business interactions reinforce this phenomenon.

4. Business and daily life in some societies are governed by religious factors. Prayer times, holidays, daily events, and dietary restrictions, for example, need to be respected by managers not familiar with these practices in some countries.

5. Time spent with the family and the quality of relationships are more important in some cultures than the personal achievement and accomplishments espoused by the traditional U.S. manager.

6. Many cultures around the world value modesty, team spirit, collectivity, and patience much more than competitiveness and individualism, which are so important in the United States.

7. Punctuality is a valued personal trait when conducting business in the United States, but it is not revered in many of the world's societies.

8. Eating habits also differ dramatically across cultures. For example, belching is acceptable in some countries as evidence of satisfaction with the food that has been prepared. Chinese culture considers it good manners to sample a portion of each food served.

9. To prevent social blunders when meeting with managers from other lands, one must learn and respect the rules of etiquette of others. Sitting on a toilet seat is viewed as unsanitary in most countries, but not in the United States. Leaving food or drink after dining is considered impolite in some countries, but not in China. Bowing instead of shaking hands is customary in many countries. Some cultures view Americans as unsanitary for locating toilet and bathing facilities in the same area, whereas Americans view people of some cultures as unsanitary for not taking a bath or shower every day.

10. Americans often do business with individuals they do not know, unlike businesspersons in many other cultures. In Mexico and Japan, for example, an amicable relationship is often mandatory before conducting business.

In many countries, effective managers are those who are best at negotiating with government bureaucrats, rather than those who inspire workers. Many U.S. managers are uncomfortable with nepotism, which is practiced in some countries. The United States defends women from sexual harassment, defends minorities from discrimination, and allows gay marriage, but not all countries embrace the same values. American managers in China have to be careful about how they arrange office furniture because Chinese workers believe in **feng shui**, the practice of harnessing natural forces. Also, U.S. managers in Japan have to be careful about **nemaswashio**, whereby Japanese workers expect supervisors to alert them privately of changes rather than informing them in a meeting. Japanese managers have little appreciation for versatility, expecting all managers to be the same. In Japan, "If a nail sticks out, you hit it into the wall," says Brad Lashbrook, an international consultant for Wilson Learning.

Probably the biggest obstacle to the effectiveness of U.S. managers—or managers from any country working in another—is the fact that it is almost impossible to change the attitude of a foreign workforce. "The system drives you; you cannot fight the system or culture," says Bill Parker, president of Phillips Petroleum in Norway. For example, in the Middle East, gifts should not be made of pigskin, and should not be any type of alcohol, because Muslins do not eat pork or drink alcohol. In India, cows are revered, so no leather gifts.

Communication Differences across Countries

Communication may be the most important word in strategic management. Americans increasingly interact with managers in other countries, so it is important to understand communication differences across countries. Americans sometimes come across as intrusive, manipulative, and garrulous; this impression may reduce their effectiveness in communication. Asian managers view extended periods of silence as important for organizing and evaluating one's thoughts, whereas U.S. managers have a low tolerance for silence. Sitting through a conference without talking is unproductive in the United States, but it is viewed as positive in Japan if one's silence helps preserve unity. Managers from the United States are much more action-oriented than their counterparts around the world; they rush to appointments, conferences, and meetings—and then feel the day has been productive. But for many foreign managers, resting, listening, meditating, and thinking is considered productive.

Most Japanese managers are reserved, quiet, distant, introspective, and other oriented, whereas most U.S. managers are talkative, insensitive, impulsive, direct, and individual-oriented. Americans often perceive Japanese managers as wasting time and carrying on pointless conversations, whereas U.S. managers often use blunt criticism, ask prying questions, and make quick decisions. These kinds of communication differences have disrupted many potentially productive Japanese–American business endeavors. Viewing the Japanese communication style as a prototype for all Asian cultures is a stereotype that must be avoided.

Like many Asian and African cultures, the Japanese are nonconfrontational. They have a difficult time saying "no," so you must be vigilant at observing their nonverbal communication. Rarely refuse a request, no matter how difficult or nonprofitable it may appear at the time. In communicating with Japanese, phrase questions so that they can answer *yes*—for example, "Do you disagree with this?" Group decision making and consensus are vitally important. The Japanese often remain silent in meetings for long periods of time and may even close their eyes when they want to listen intently.

Business Culture across Countries[5]

Managers, marketers, salespersons, and virtually all businesspersons can be more effective in doing business with persons and companies in other countries if they have an understanding and appreciation of business culture variation across countries. Thus, let's focus here on a few countries to compare and contrast their business cultures with the U.S. business culture.

Mexico's Business Culture

Mexico is an authoritarian society in terms of schools, churches, businesses, and families. Employers seek workers who are agreeable, respectful, and obedient, rather than innovative, creative, and independent. Mexican workers tend to be activity-oriented rather than problem solvers. When visitors walk into a Mexican business, they are impressed by the cordial, friendly atmosphere. This is almost always true because Mexicans desire harmony rather than conflict; desire for harmony is part of the social fabric in worker–manager relations. There is a much lower tolerance for adversarial relations or friction at work in Mexico as compared to that in the United States.

Mexican employers are paternalistic, providing workers with more than a paycheck, but in return they expect allegiance. Weekly food baskets, free meals, free bus service, and free day care are often part of compensation. The ideal working condition for a Mexican worker is the family model, with people all working together, doing their share, according to their designated roles. Mexican workers do not expect or desire a work environment in which self-expression and initiative are encouraged. American business embodies individualism, achievement, competition, curiosity, pragmatism, informality, spontaneity, and doing more than expected on the job, whereas Mexican businesses stress collectivism, continuity, cooperation, belongingness, formality, and doing exactly what is told.

In Mexico, business associates rarely entertain each other at their homes, which are places reserved exclusively for close friends and family. Business meetings and entertaining are nearly always done at a restaurant. Preserving one's honor, saving face, and looking important are also exceptionally important in Mexico. This is why Mexicans do not accept criticism and change easily; many find it humiliating to acknowledge having made a mistake. A meeting among employees and managers in a business located in Mexico is a forum for giving orders and directions rather than for discussing problems or participating in decision making. Mexican workers want to be closely supervised, cared for, and corrected in a civil manner. Opinions expressed by employees are often regarded as back talk in Mexico. Mexican supervisors are viewed as weak if they explain the rationale for their orders to workers.

In general, Mexicans do not feel compelled to follow rules that are not associated with a particular person in authority they work for or know well. Thus, signs to wear earplugs or safety glasses, or attendance or seniority policies, and even one-way street signs are often ignored. Whereas Americans follow the rules, Mexicans often do not. Life is simply slower in Mexico than in the United States. The first priority is often assigned to the last request, rather than to the first. Telephone systems break down. Banks may suddenly not have pesos. Phone repair can take a month. Electricity for an entire plant or town can be down for hours or even days. Business and government offices may open and close at odd hours. Buses and taxis may be hours off schedule. Meeting times for appointments are not rigid. Tardiness is common everywhere. Effectively doing business in Mexico requires knowledge of the Mexican way of life, culture, beliefs, and customs.

When greeting others, Mexican women normally pat each other on the right forearm or shoulder rather than shake hands. Men normally shake hands or, if close friends, use the traditional hug and back slapping upon greeting. If visiting a person's home in Mexico, bring a gift such as flowers or sweets, but avoid both marigolds and red flowers because they symbolize negativity. White flowers are an excellent choice. Arrive up to 30 minutes late, but definitely not early. If you receive a gift, open it immediately and react enthusiastically. At dinner, do not sit until you are invited to, and wait to be told where to sit. This is true in most foreign countries as well as in the United States. Do not begin eating until the hostess starts. Only men give toasts in Mexico. It is also polite to leave some food on your plate after a meal. For business appointments, as opposed to home visits, it is best to arrive on time, although your Mexican counterparts may be up to 30 minutes late. Do not get irritated at their lack of punctuality.

Mexicans often judge or stereotype a person by who introduces them, and changing that first impression is difficult in business. Expect to answer questions about personal background, family, and life interests—because Mexicans consider trustworthiness and character to be of upmost importance. Mexicans are status conscious, so business titles and rank are important. Face-to-face meetings are preferred over telephone calls, letters, or e-mail. Negotiations in Mexico include a fair amount of haggling, so do not give a best offer first.

Japan's Business Culture

Due to its dwindling workforce and aging population, Japan is increasingly promoting women into managerial positions. Recent statistics show that only 10 percent of managers in Japan are currently women, compared with 31 percent in Singapore, 38 percent in Germany, and 43 percent in the United States.[6] Therefore, Prime Minister Shinzo Abe of Japan has proclaimed a goal to fill 30 percent of leadership positions in Japan with women by 2020. Abe recently filled five open positions in his own cabinet with women. A key reason that Japanese women have historically not advanced to managerial positions is the business culture of notorious long work hours. Although Japan's powerful business lobby, Keidanren, currently has no women on its 24-member board of directions, the body has mandated its member companies to publicize their gender equity strategies and progress—and Keidanren itself plans to appoint women into board positions. Suppression, exploitation, and even persecution of women are severe problems in many countries, especially in the Middle East and to a lesser extent in the Far East. However, Japan is taking a leadership role by aggressively reversing its historical underutilization of women in business.

The Japanese people place great importance on group loyalty and consensus—a concept called *Wa*. Nearly all corporate activities in Japan encourage Wa among managers and employees. Wa requires that all members of a group agree and cooperate; this results in constant discussion and compromise. Japanese managers evaluate the potential attractiveness of alternative business decisions in terms of the long-term effect on the group's Wa. This is why silence, used for pondering alternatives, can be a plus in a formal Japanese meeting. Discussions potentially disruptive to Wa are generally conducted in informal settings, such as at a bar, so as to minimize harm to the group's Wa. Entertaining is an important business activity in Japan because it strengthens Wa. Formal meetings are often conducted in informal settings. When confronted with disturbing questions or opinions, Japanese managers tend to remain silent, whereas Americans tend to respond directly, defending themselves through explanation and argument.

Americans have more freedom to control their own fates than do the Japanese. The United States offers more upward mobility to its people, as indicated below:

America is not like Japan and can never be. America's strength is the opposite: It opens its doors and brings the world's disorder in. It tolerates social change that would tear most other societies apart. This openness encourages Americans to adapt as individuals rather than as a group. Americans go west to California to get a new start; they move east to Manhattan to try to make the big time; they move to Vermont or to a farm to get close to the soil. They break away from their parents' religions or values or class; they rediscover their ethnicity. They go to night school; they change their names.[7]

In Japan, a person's age and status are of paramount importance, whether in the family unit, the extended family, or a social or business situation. Schoolchildren learn early that the oldest person in the group is to be honored. Older folks are served first and their drinks are poured for them. Greetings in Japan are formal and ritualized, so wait to be introduced, because it may be viewed as impolite to introduce yourself, even in a large gathering. Foreigners may shake hands, but the traditional form of greeting in Japan is to bow. The deeper you bow, the more respect you show, but at least bow the head slightly in greetings.

Chocolates or small cakes are excellent gifts in Japan, but do not give lilies, camellias, lotus blossoms, or white flowers, because they all are associated with funerals. Do not give potted plants because they encourage sickness, although a bonsai tree is always acceptable. Give items in odd numbers, but avoid the number 9. Gifts are not opened when received. If going to a Japanese home, remove your shoes before entering and put on the slippers left at the doorway. Leave shoes pointing away from the doorway you are about to walk through. If going to the toilet in a Japanese home, put on the toilet slippers and remove them when you exit.

Learn how to use chopsticks before visiting Japan and do not pierce food with chopsticks. Never point the chopsticks. Japanese oftentimes slurp their noodles and soup, but mixing other food with rice is inappropriate. Instead of mixing, eat a bit of rice and then a bit of food. To signify that you do not want more rice or drink, leave some in the bowl or glass. Conversation over dinner is generally subdued because the Japanese prefer to savor their food.

Unlike Americans, Japanese prefer to do business on the basis of personal relationships rather than impersonally speaking over the phone or by written correspondence. Therefore, build and maintain relationships by sending greeting, thank-you, birthday, and seasonal cards. You need to be a good "correspondent" to effectively do business with the Japanese. Punctuality is important, so arrive on time for meetings and be mindful that it may take several meetings to establish a good relationship. The Japanese are looking for a long-term relationship. Always give a small gift as a token of your appreciation, and present it to the most senior person at the end of any meeting.

Business cards are exchanged in Japan constantly and with excitement. Invest in quality business cards and keep them in pristine condition. Do not write on them. Have one side of your card translated in Japanese and give it to the person with the Japanese side facing the recipient. Business cards are generally given and received with two hands and a slight bow. Examine any business card you receive carefully.

India's Business Culture

According to statistics from the United Nations, India's rate of female participation in the labor force is 34.2 percent, which is quite low, especially because women make up 42 percent of college graduates in India. But even Indian women with a college degree are expected to let their careers take a back seat to caring for their husband, children, and elderly parents. "The measures of daughterly guilt are much higher in Indian women than in other countries," says Sylvia Ann Hewlett, president of the Center for Work-Life Policy, a Manhattan think tank, who headed a recent study on the challenges Indian women face in the workplace.[8] Hewlett adds, "Since taking care of elderly parents usually becomes a reality later in a woman's career, it takes them out of the workplace just when they should be entering top management roles." That is why gender disparities at Indian companies unfortunately grow more pronounced at higher levels of management.

Like in many Asian cultures, people in India do not like to say *no*, verbally or nonverbally. Rather than disappoint you, they often will say something is not available, will offer you the response that they think you want to hear, or will be vague with you. This behavior should not be considered dishonest. Shaking hands is common in India, especially in the large cities among the more educated who are accustomed to dealing with westerners. Men may shake hands with other men and women may shake hands with other women; however, there are seldom handshakes between men and women because of religious beliefs.

Indians believe that giving gifts eases the transition into the next life. Gifts of cash are common, but do not give frangipani or white flowers, because they represent mourning. Yellow, green, and red are lucky colors, so remember that when you wrap gifts. Because Hindus consider cows to be sacred, do not give gifts made of leather. Before entering an Indian's house, take off your shoes, just as you would in China or Japan. Politely turn down the host's first offer of tea, coffee, or snacks. You will be asked again and again. Saying no to the first invitation is part of the protocol. Be mindful that neither Hindus nor Sikhs eat beef, and many are vegetarians. Muslims do not eat pork or drink alcohol. Lamb, chicken, and fish are the most commonly served main courses. Table manners are somewhat formal, but much Indian food is eaten with the fingers. Like most places in the world, wait to be told where and when to sit at dinner. Women in India typically serve the men and eat later. You may be asked to wash your hands before and after sitting down to a meal. Always use your right hand to eat, whether using utensils or your fingers. Leave a small amount of food on your plate to indicate that you are satisfied. Finishing all your food means that you are still hungry, which is true in Egypt, China, Mexico, and many countries.

Indians prefer to do business with those with whom they have established a relationship built on mutual trust and respect. Punctuality is important. Indians generally do not trust the legal system, and someone's word is often sufficient to reach an agreement. Do not disagree publicly with anyone in India. Titles such as professor, doctor, or engineer are important in India, as is a person's age, university degree, caste, and profession. Use the right hand to give and receive business cards. Business cards need not be translated into Hindi but always present your business card so the recipient may read the card as it is handed to him or her. This is a nice, expected gesture in most countries around the world.

Business Climate across Countries

The World Bank and the International Finance Corporation annually rank 189 countries in terms of their respective ease of doing business (http://www.doingbusiness.org/rankings). The index ranks nations from 1 (best) to 189 (worst). For each nation, the ranking is calculated as the simple average of the percentile rankings on how easy is it to (1) start a business, (2) deal with construction permits, (3) register property, (4) get credit, (5) protect investors, (6) pay taxes, (7) trade across borders, (8) enforce contracts, (9) resolve insolvency, and (10) get electricity.

Table 2-4 reveals the 2014 "Ease of Doing Business" rankings for the top 10 nations in six regions of the world. Note, for example, that Norway is rated the sixth best country on the planet for doing business, the United States is ranked seventh, and Colombia is the best country in South America. This information can be helpful for strategists (and students) deciding where to locate new operations, and where to focus new efforts.

TABLE 2-4 The Top 10 Countries/Regions That Are Easiest To Do Business With Across Continents

Overall Best	East Asia Pacific	East Europe Central Asia	Latin America Caribbean	Mid-East & North Africa	Sub-Saharan Africa	South Asia
1. Singapore	Singapore	Georgia	Colombia	UAE	Mauritius	Sri Lanka
2. New Zealand	China Hong Kong	Latvia	Peru	S. Arabia	S. Africa	Nepal
3. China Hong Kong	Malaysia	Lithuania	Mexico	Qatar	Rwanda	Maldives
4. Denmark	China Taiwan	Macedonia	Puerto Rico	Bahrain	Botswana	Bhutan
5. South Korea	Thailand	Montenegro	Jamaica	Tunisia	Seychelles	Pakistan
6. Norway	Samoa	Bulgaria	Guatemala	Oman	Nambia	India
7. USA	Tonga	Armenia	Trinidad/Tobago	Morocco	Swaziland	Bangladesh
8. UK	Mongolia	Romania	Uruguay	Kuwait	Zambia	Afghanistan
9. Finland	Vanuatu	Hungary	Costa Rico	Malta	Cabo Verde	NA
10. Australia	Vietnam	Turkey	Dom. Republic	Lebanon	Mozambique	NA

Source: Based on information at http://www.doingbusiness.org/rankings, retrieved on January 1, 2005.

Africa's Business Climate

Recently, 25 African countries held democratic elections, whereas two decades ago only 3 African countries were considered democracies. Currencies in Africa are stabilizing and many countries are fund-raising to build modern highways, ports, and power grids. Many African and non-African companies are launching operations in Africa due to the rapidly growing middle class and an average GDP growth of 5 percent for the continent through 2017. Also, the World Bank says food demand across Africa will double between 2012 and 2020.

Morocco has the highest Internet penetration among all countries in Africa, with 51 percent, followed by Egypt (36%), Kenya (tied with Nigeria at 28%), Senegal (18%), South Africa (17%), Angola (15%), Algeria (14%), Ghana (14%), and Tanzania (12%).[9] All other African countries have less than 6 percent Internet penetration among their residents. The article was based on research published by the consulting firm McKinsey, which estimates that only 16 percent of Africans have access to the Internet. McKinsey predicts that by 2025, 50 percent of Africans will be online.

Nigeria (GDP = $510B) recently surpassed South Africa (GDP = $320B) as having the continent's largest gross domestic product.[10] In 2014, Nissan Motor assembled thousands of cars in Nigeria, General Electric began building $10 billion worth of new turbines for power plants, and Procter & Gamble (P&G) opened a second diaper factory. Nigeria's population will be seven times larger than South Africa by 2050, even though the country still has problems with infrastructure, unemployment, crime, and poverty.

A recent article in the *Wall Street Journal* (7-13-15, p. B1) reported that Ethiopia is the newest country where garment companies are shifting manufacturing work; Kenya also is receiving numerous new "clothing" factories. VF Corporation that makes such brands as Lee, Wrangler, and Timberland, as well as Calvin Klein and PVH Corporation that makes Tommy Hilfiger, are all mentioned in the article as increasingly shifting their production operations to Africa. Such companies are shifting work to Africa from China, Bangladesh, Vietnam, Cambodia, India, Sri Lanka, and Turkey, primarily due to exceptionally low wages. For example, the article reports that Chinese garment workers earn between $155 to $297 a month, compared to workers in Bangladesh and Ethiopia that earn about $67 and $21 a month respectively. Many African countries also grow cotton and that is a plus for textile companies, but the lowest wages on the planet, coupled with improving infrastructure and stability, is the real draw.

Table 2-5 provides a summary of the economic situation in 12 African countries. Note that Angola is rated lowest in terms of doing business, whereas South Africa is rated highest. Recent regime changes in Egypt, Tunisia, Libya, and Algeria may spur further investment in Africa as democracy and capitalism strengthens. Many multinational companies are now gaining first mover advantages by engaging Africa at all levels. Today, 40 percent of Africans live in the cities—a proportion close to China and India. *The general stereotype of Africa is rapidly changing from subsistence farmers avoiding lions to millions of smartphone-carrying consumers in cities purchasing products.*

Africa has the world's largest deposits of platinum, chrome, and diamonds—and many Chinese companies in particular are investing there. Africa's largest food retailer, Shoprite Holdings, has more than 1,000 stores in 17 countries. Shoprite is a potential acquisition target being considered by European retailers Carrefour and Tesco. Diageo PLC sells Guinness beer,

TABLE 2-5 Sampling of African Countries: Ease-of-Doing-Business Rankings

	Population in Millions	Ease of Doing Business among All Countries	Capital City
South Africa	49	43 out of 183	Pretoria
Tunisia	11	60 out of 183	Tunis
Ghana	24	70 out of 183	Accra
Morocco	32	71 out of 183	Rabat
Kenya	39	136 out of 183	Nairobi
Egypt	79	112 out of 183	Cairo
Ethiopia	86	132 out of 183	Addis Ababa
Uganda	33	150 out of 183	Kampala
Nigeria	150	170 out of 183	Abuja
Sudan	41	160 out of 183	Khartoum
Mozambique	22	127 out of 183	Maputo
Angola	13	181 out of 183	Luanda

Source: Based on information at http://www.doingbusiness.org/rankings, retrieved on January 1, 2015.

Smirnoff vodka, Baileys liqueur, and Johnnie Walker whiskey in more than 40 countries across Africa. Nestlé S.A. now has more than 25 factories in Africa.

All of Africa is coming online, representing huge opportunities for countless companies. McKinsey & Co. estimates that within 5 years another 220 million Africans that today can meet only basic needs will join the middle class as consumers.[11] There are more than 950 million people who live in Africa.

Brazil's Business Climate

Brazil's biggest trading partner is China, but as China's economy has slowed, Brazil's economy has deteriorated. In August 2015, consumer confidence in Brazil is at a record low, unemployment has increased to 8.3 percent, inflation is nearing 10 percent, and corruption scandals have left President Dilma Rouseseff with approval ratings below 10 percent. Demand for Brazil's commodities, especially soybeans and iron ore, has declined sharply, so Brazilian businesses are laying off workers and cutting spending. Lower commodity prices cost Brazil $12 billion in foreign sales through the first half of 2015 alone. Brazil's currency, the real, declined 30 percent versus the US dollar in the last twelve months; Brazil's stock market is down 22 percent in the last twelve months; Brazil's economy is shrinking at about 1.7 percent annually. Economists now predict prolonged stagnation for Brazil. Marcos Troyjo, a former Brazilian diplomat who now is at Columbia University, says: "We went from Brazil mania to Brazil nausea; we are now looking at a lost decade." Instead of negative growth, Brazil reported 7+ percent annual GDP growth in 2010–2012 making it a BRIC (Brazil, Russia, India, China) high performer. But that was then. Also hurting Brazil now has been the fall in oil prices since that country is (or was) a big exporter of oil.

Indonesia's Business Climate

A Pacific archipelago comprised of thousands of islands, Indonesia's stock market was the top performer in 2014 among all Asian countries, and was also the top performer in five out of the last seven years in Asia. Indonesia's currency is the rupiah and its economy is one of the fastest growing in Asia, behind China and the Philippines. Indonesia's GDP is expected to grow 5.7 percent in 2015. As Southeast Asia's largest economy, Indonesia elected a new legislature and president in 2014. Despite its large population and densely populated regions, Indonesia has the world's second-highest level of biodiversity, with vast areas of wilderness and abundant natural resources.

India's Business Climate

The GDP of India in 2015 is expected to reach 8.3 percent, making it the world's fastest-growing large economy, and the first time that India's growth rate has exceeded that of China since the 1990s. China's GDP for 2015 is expected to slow to 6.8 percent.

By a landslide, India elected a new prime minister in May 2014, Narendra Modi. Modi has introduced excellent policies to jump-start India's economy, boosting profits at companies ranging from banks to cement makers. In support of Modi and India's future, money managers worldwide poured more than $17 billion into Indian stocks in 2014—the most of any developing country tracked by the Institute of International Finance. India's S&P Index grew nearly 40 percent in 2014. The country is the world's tenth-largest economy, but its economy pre-Modi was stagnant due to cumbersome bureaucracy and poor infrastructure. India grew faster (5.6%) in 2014 than any BRIC (Brazil, Russia, India, and China) country. India's economy is expected to grow 6.4 percent in 2015. Modi's political party has the ruling majority in the India legislature for the first time in 30 years. India is benefiting greatly from low prices for oil and gas, India's biggest import.

India's state Parliament of Rajasthan recently overhauled its local labor laws by making it easier for companies with as many as 300 employees to fire workers and avoid other contentious provisions of strict labor-protection laws. Modi is using various Indian states where his Bharatiya Janata Party has control to test his greater economic openness policies. He believes, for example, that manufacturers will now relocate to Rajasthan, and the neighboring state of Haryana has suggested it may follow Rajasthan. Modi is trying to revitalize India's manufacturing sector by taking the following steps immediately: reducing the powers of labor inspectors, replacing onerous paperwork with digital submissions, removing restrictions on women working at night, improving factory conditions for workers, easing regulations on hiring apprentices, and facilitating overtime.

Foreign firms may now own 100 percent of some Indian retail ventures, up from a previous 51 percent a few years ago. One company taking advantage of this change in the law is IKEA, which recently opened 25 new stores in India. India has also greatly reduced the expensive government subsidies on diesel fuel. Indian banks are lowering interest rates to spur growth. The country is implementing a 5-year road map to improve its finances, aiming to narrow its budget deficit of 5.3 percent of GDP to 3 percent by 2017. Complicating matters in India are high interest rates and budget deficits. The Indian Parliament recently approved higher overseas ownership in their insurance and pension investments sectors of the economy.

The Indian government is slowly improving the country's education system, but an enormous amount of work remains. Only 74 percent of Indian men and 48 percent of Indian women are literate, compared to 96 percent of men and 88 percent of women in China. India's "knowledge economy" employs only about 2.23 million people out of 750 million available.

At present, only 15 percent of India's citizens enter higher education, and the government hopes to increase this to 21 percent by 2017. The Indian Institutes of Technology—a group of universities focused on engineering and technology—are world renowned, but offer only a miniscule 7,000 places to students each year. There is elaborate red tape required to establish and operate any business in India. Also, the country's tax code is archaic and many new sectors are not even open to foreign direct investment. However, India will surpass China as the most populated country in 2030. Its highest density growth and population is in the northwest and east-central areas of the country. India has a literacy rate now of 74 percent, up from 65 percent a decade ago.

Japan's Business Climate

Japan's new Prime Minister Shinzo Abe was reelected on a mandate to revive the economy. Hopes for Abe's "Three Arrows" of hyper-easy monetary policy, government spending, and reforms such as deregulation were tarnished after Japan's economy slipped into a recession in Q3 2014, following a national sales tax increase from 5 to 8 percent aimed primarily at reducing Japan's huge public debt, the worst among advanced nations. But the sales tax increase hurt ordinary Japanese citizens. However, the falling yen has hurt small businesses and consumers by raising the cost of imported goods. Abe is pushing hard now for Japanese companies to raise wages of their employees, because company stock prices and profits are up and ordinary citizens are suffering. Abe says if wages do not rise as quickly as prices, households will cut back on spending, endangering a desired economic recovery in Japan.

Prime Minister Abe wants to restart nuclear reactors that were taken offline after the 2011 Fukushima disaster. As of 2015, all 48 of Japan's reactors are offline. Abe likely will stay in power in Japan through 2018, becoming one of Japan's rare long-term leaders. His historically pro-business Liberal Democratic Party (LBD), together with its junior coalition partner, the Komeito party, now controls more than two thirds of the lower house. Abe also wants to revitalize Japan's military to help confront growing aggression from China and North Korea, and to be able to respond to incidents such as the recent ISIS beheading of two Japanese journalists.

Mexico's Business Climate

South Korea's Kia Motors is building a $1 billion assembly near Monterrey, Mexico, joining Mazda Motors, Honda Motors, Audi AG, BMW AG, Renault S.A., Nissan Motors, and Daimler AG, all of which are shifting automobile assembly operations to Mexico. The country of Mexico is now (2015) the fourth-largest auto exporter in the world, behind Japan, Germany, and South Korea. Mexico's auto industry now employs one of every six Mexican factor workers and comprises one third of all exports from Mexico.

No country was hurt more in the last decade by the rise of China than Mexico, but Chinese policy today is to boost wages and therefore boost consumer spending. The Boston Consulting Group estimates that "China's average manufacturing wage exceeded Mexico's in 2012 for the first time, when accounting for differences in productivity; Mexican workers typically produce more per hour than Chinese workers."[12] The average wage plus benefits across Mexico is $3.50 an hour. This fact, coupled with China's rising wages and slowing growth and Mexico's close proximity to the United States, represents a great opportunity for Mexico to recoup much of the manufacturing prowess it lost in the last decade to China.

Foreign direct investment (FDI) in Mexico has surged to exceed $30 billion annually, led by automobile manufacturers such as Volkswagen AG building new factories, and auto-parts suppliers such as Delphi Automotive PLC following. Home Depot will soon have 150 stores in Mexico. The FDI surge is expected to last at least through 2018, spurred by low wages, government policies that allow foreign companies to import raw materials without paying duties or tariffs, a 30 percent corporate tax rate, and rising wages in China. Note in Table 2-6 that Mexico rose to 39th place (from 53rd place) in the last two years among all nations in terms of ease of doing business.

Mexico is especially attractive for manufacturing products that are bulky or costly to transport, such as automobiles. However, a key variable hurting Mexico is drug-related violence. Mexico's homicide rate exceeds 15 people per 100,000, compared with a per capita rate of about 5.0 in the United States and 1.1 in China. If Mexico can improve its security situation as it intends, then hundreds of additional firms may consider returning to Mexico from China (and India).

Vietnam's Business Climate

Internet penetration has grown to 44 percent among Vietnam's 90 million people, up from 12 percent a decade ago.[13] Unlike another communist country, North Korea, Vietnam is booming for business. The market for e-commerce in Vietnam generates $4 billion in revenue annually and is growing dramatically. Telecommunications companies in Vietnam, such as Viettel Mobile and Vietnam Mobile Telecom Services, provide the lowest data prices in the world at just over $3 per gigabyte. The Vietnamese are among the most prevalent watchers of videos on smartphones in the world. The number of active mobile social-media accounts in Vietnam rose 41 percent from January 2014 to January 2015—a higher growth rate than China, India, or Brazil. Facebook has over 30 million active users in Vietnam, up from 8.5 million in 2012. Even the smallest businesses in the United States (and elsewhere) can easily reach and sell to consumers in Vietnam, who yearn for new products and services. (Interestingly, the most recent foreign translation of this textbook, *Strategic Management,* has been translated into Vietnamese.)

TABLE 2-6 Sampling of North and South American Countries: Ease-of-Doing-Business Rankings

	Population in Millions	Ease of Doing Business among All Countries	Capital City
USA	308	7 out of 183	Washington, DC
Canada	34	16 out of 183	Ottawa
Chile	17	41 out of 183	Santiago
Peru	30	35 out of 183	Lima
Mexico	112	39 out of 183	Mexico City
Argentina	41	124 out of 183	Buenos Aires
Brazil	199	120 out of 183	Brasilia
Ecuador	15	115 out of 183	Quito
Bolivia	10	157 out of 183	La Paz
Venezuela	27	182 out of 183	Caracas

Source: Based on information at http://www.doingbusiness.org/rankings, retrieved on January 1, 2015.

IMPLICATIONS FOR STRATEGISTS

Figure 2-2 reveals that doing business globally is increasingly a pre-requisite for success even for the smallest of firms. An estimated 95 percent of consumers globally live outside the United States; firms can grow and gain economies of scale by serving these consumers. Staying domestic oftentimes gives rival firms major competitive advantages. There are about 190 countries on seven continents.

Whatever product/service your company has to offer, it would likely be well received in many nations, and it may be strategically best for your firm to outsource operations, procure resources, and use a labor force away from home, to gain and sustain competitive advantages at home.

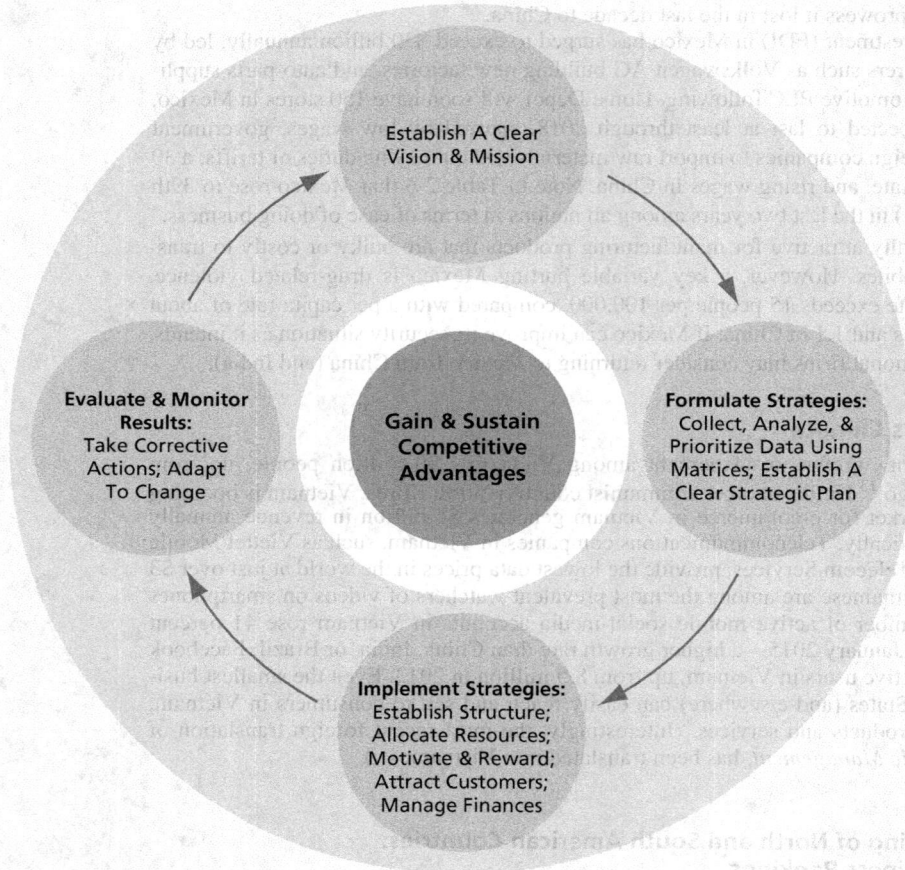

Establish A Clear
Vision & Mission

Formulate Strategies:
Collect, Analyze, &
Prioritize Data Using
Matrices; Establish A
Clear Strategic Plan

Gain & Sustain
Competitive
Advantages

Evaluate & Monitor
Results:
Take Corrective
Actions; Adapt
To Change

Implement Strategies:
Establish Structure;
Allocate Resources;
Motivate & Reward;
Attract Customers;
Manage Finances

FIGURE 2-2
How to Gain and Sustain Competitive Advantages

IMPLICATIONS FOR STUDENTS

Even the smallest businesses today regularly serve customers globally and gain competitive advantages and economies of scale by doing so. Many iconic U.S. businesses, such as Tupperware, obtain more than 80 percent of their revenue from outside the United States. Therefore, in performing a strategic-management case analysis, you must evaluate the scope, magnitude, and nature of what your company is doing globally compared to rival firms. Then, determine what your company should be doing to garner global

business. Continuously throughout your presentation or written report, compare your firm to rivals in terms of global business and make recommendations based on careful analysis. Be "prescriptive and insightful" rather than "descriptive and mundane" with every slide presented to pave the way for your specific recommendations with costs regarding global reach of your firm. Continually compare and contrast what you are recommending versus what the company is actually doing or planning to do.

Chapter Summary

The population of the world has surpassed 7 billion. Just as they did for centuries before Columbus reached America, businesses search for new opportunities beyond their national boundaries for centuries to come. There has never been a more internationalized and economically competitive society than today's model. Some U.S. industries, such as textiles, steel, and consumer electronics, are in disarray as a result of the international challenge.

Success in business increasingly depends on offering products and services that are competitive on a world basis, not just on a local basis. If the price and quality of a firm's products and services are not competitive with those available elsewhere in the world, the firm may soon face extinction. Global markets have become a reality in all but the most remote areas of the world. Certainly throughout the United States, even in small towns, firms feel the pressure of world competitors.

This chapter has provided some basic global information that can be essential to consider in developing a strategic plan for any organization. The advantages of engaging in international business may well offset the drawbacks for most firms. It is important in strategic planning to be effective, and the nature of global operations may be the key component in a plan's overall effectiveness.

Key Terms and Concepts

feng shui (p. 78)
global strategy (p. 69)
globalization (p. 69)
guanxi (p. 76)
international firms (p. 70)
inhwa (p. 76)

inversion (p. 76)
multinational corporations (p. 70)
nemaswashio (p. 78)
protectionism (p. 73)
Wa (p. 76)

Issues for Review and Discussion

⭐ **2-1.** Honda Motor Company has been very successful in recent years. What percentage of Honda's revenues comes from the United States versus Europe? How does this percentage compare with rival firms?

⭐ **2-2.** Why are consumption patterns becoming similar worldwide? What are the strategic implications of this trend?

⭐ **2-3.** What are the major differences between the United States operations and multinational operations that affect strategic management?

⭐ **2-4.** Why is globalization of industries a common factor today?

⭐ **2-5.** Compare and contrast the United States with foreign cultures in terms of doing business.

⭐ **2-6.** List six reasons why strategic management is more complex in a multinational firm.

⭐ **2-7.** Do you feel that protectionism is good or bad for the world economy? Why?

⭐ **2-8.** How many different languages are the in the world?

⭐ **2-9.** Why are some industries more "global" than others? Discuss.

⭐ **2-10.** *Wa, guanxi* and *inhwa* are important management terms in Japan, China, and Korea respectively. What would be analogous terms to describe American management practices?

⭐ **2-11.** Why do many Europeans also find the notion of "team spirit" in a work environment difficult to grasp?

2-12. In China *feng shui* is important in business, while in Japan *nemaswashio* is deemed important. What are the analogous American terms and practices?

2-13. Describe the business culture in Mexico.

2-14. Describe the business culture in Japan.

2-15. Compare tax rates in the United States versus other countries. What impact could these differences have on "keeping jobs at home?"

2-16. Discuss the requirements for doing business in India.

2-17. Select any four countries in which Honda Motor Company operates. Evaluate their operations in those countries.

2-18. Based on the points of comparisons discussed in this chapter compare and contrast business practices and cultures in Europe with the U.S. business culture.

2-19. In 2016, China devalued its currency substantially. What impact does that have within and outside China?

2-20. What five countries in Asia have the highest GDP? What are its implications for Nestlé?

2-21. Africa is rapidly joining the world economic community. Give 10 examples to justify this.

2-22. Which six African countries do you feel are most suitable for foreign investment?

2-23. Compare business practice and culture in your own country versus the United States.

2-24. What is required to be done in a strategic-management case analysis?

2-25. Select three countries in South America. Prepare a one-page summary for each to reveal their attractiveness for foreign direct investment. For each of the three countries, prepare a one-page summary analyzing their suitability for foreign direct investment.

2-26. Compare sexual harassment policies and practices in your country with those in the United States.

2-27. Discuss the business culture in Australia.

2-28. In terms of presenting flowers as business gifts, compare and contrast the practices and customs across three countries.

2-29. Discuss how business etiquette at dinner varies across countries.

2-30. Make a good argument for keeping the statutory corporate tax rate in the United States the highest in the world. Make a counterargument.

2-31. Is the number languages increasing or decreasing globally? What are the strategic implications?

2-32. Which country recently achieved its goal of having the most business-friendly tax system of the Group of Seven (G-7) nations—Canada, France, Germany, Italy, Japan, the United Kingdom, and the United States?

ASSURANCE OF LEARNING EXERCISES

EXERCISE 2A
Nestlé S.A. Wants to Enter Africa. Help Them.

Purpose

More and more companies every day begin doing business in Africa and websites provide a lot of information to help compare and contrast business cultures across countries. Research is necessary to determine the best strategy for being the first mover in many African countries (that is, being the first competitor doing business in various countries).

Instructions

Step 1	Search the Internet and print a map of Africa.
Step 2	Look for demographic data on any 10 African countries and print the details.
Step 3	Gather competitive information regarding the presence of Nestlé companies doing business in Africa.
Step 4	List, in prioritized order, eight countries that you would recommend for Nestlé to enter. Remember that Country 1 would be the one you consider best and Country 2 is the next best.
Step 5	List, in a prioritized order, three cities in each of the eight African countries where you believe Nestlé should build distribution centres. Justify your choices.

EXERCISE 2B

Assess Differences in Culture across Countries

Purpose

Persons in your country are more effective in dealing with business people from other countries if they have some awareness and understanding of differences in culture across countries. This exercise will help increase your knowledge and understanding of various countries' business culture, making you a more effective manager and communicator with people and organizations globally. This is a fun exercise that provides information for your class regarding some of these key differences.

Instructions

Step 1	Identify four individuals who either grew up in a foreign country or have lived in a foreign country for more than a year. Interview those four persons. Try to have four different countries represented.
Step 2	During each interview, develop a list of eight key differences between your country's business style and customs and that particular country's style and custom in terms of various aspects of speech, meetings, meals, relationships, friendships, and communication, which could impact business dealings.
Step 3	Develop a 15-minute PowerPoint presentation for your class and discuss, summarizing your findings. In your speech to the class, identify the persons you interviewed and the length of time those persons lived in their respective countries. Frame your presentation as if you are giving advice to top managers regarding expansion into those countries.
Step 4	Submit a hard copy of your presentation to your professor.

EXERCISE 2C

Honda Motor Company Wants to Do Business in Vietnam. Help Them.

Purpose

More and more companies every day decide to begin doing business in Vietnam. Research is necessary to determine the best strategy for being competitive in Vietnam. Review the opening chapter boxed insert and Honda Motor Company's website, as well as the information about Vietnam in the chapter.

Instructions

Step 1	Print a map of Vietnam.
Step 2	Print the demographic data on 10 cities in Vietnam.
Step 3	Gather competitive information regarding the presence of automobile companies doing business in Vietnam.
Step 4	Develop a prioritized list of five cities in which you would recommend Honda build and expand their business operations.

EXERCISE 2D
Does My University Recruit in Foreign Countries?

Purpose

A competitive climate is emerging among colleges and universities around the world. Colleges and universities in Europe and Japan are increasingly recruiting U.S. students to offset declining enrolments. Foreign students already make up more than one-third of the student body at many American universities. The purpose of this exercise is to identify particular colleges and universities in foreign countries that represent a competitive threat to your college.

Instructions

Step 1   Select a foreign country. Conduct research to determine the number and nature of colleges and universities in that country. What are the major educational institutions in that country? What programs are those institutions recognized for offering? What percentage of undergraduate and graduate students attending those institutions are citizens of your country? Do these institutions actively recruit students from your country? Are any of the Schools of Business at the various universities AACSB International accredited?

Step 2   Prepare a report for the class that summarizes your research findings. Present your report to the class.

MINI-CASE ON AIRBUS GROUP SE (AIR.PA)

HOW WELL IS AIRBUS PERFORMING GLOBALLY?

Source: © Bocman1973.Shutterstock

Headquartered in Toulouse, France, Airbus Group SE is a European multinational aerospace and defense company that consists of the three business divisions: Airbus, Airbus Defense and Space, and Airbus Helicopters. Airbus competes heavily with Boeing for making commercial airliners and military aircraft. For the first half of Airbus Group SE's' fiscal 2015 year, revenues were $31.8 billion, up 6 percent from the prior year. The company's operating income of $2.1 billion was also up 6 percent, and earnings per share were up 34 percent at $2.13 for the first half of 2015.

Airbus added 348 new planes to its order book in the first half of 2015, nearly double the prior year period, rising 94.5 percent to $59.3 billion. The company's backlog of work to be done is now valued at $1.02 trillion. Simply put, Airbus has all engines running at full steam. The company recently finalized its biggest order, $26.5 billion deal with India's budget airline, IndiGo, which ordered 250 A320neo family aircraft for $27 billion. The aircraft is a more fuel efficient Airbus, delivering on low-cost fares and enabling the company to grow further.

Airbus is also scheduled to deliver seven A330s in 2017 and a further eight to China Eastern Airlines Corporation in 2018. It will also help China Eastern Airlines to meet rising passenger demand for mid and long routes. According to the International Air Transport Association, China will be the world's largest air passenger market by 2034.

Question

1. At the Airbus website (www.airbus.com), determine the percentage breakdown of Airbus revenues across continents. What is the company's strategy with regards to global expansion? Is that strategy working well for the company?

Current Readings

Alessandri, Todd M., and Anju Seth. "The Effects of Managerial Ownership on International and Business Diversification: Balancing Incentives and Risks." *Strategic Management Journal*, 35, issue 13 (December 2014): 2064–2075.

Berman, Jonathan, Brad Smith, and Eniola Ladapo. "Seven Reasons Why Africa's Time Is Now: Interaction." *Harvard Business Review* 91, no. 12 (2013): 22.

Bremmer, Ian. "The New Rules of Globalization." *Harvard Business Review* 92, no. 1/2 (2014): 103–107.

Chand, Masud, and Rosalie L. Tung. "The Aging of the World's Population and Its Effects on Global Business." *Academy of Management of Perspectives* 28 (November 2014): 409–429.

Mazrouei, Hanan A., and Richard J. Pech. "The Expatriate as Company Leader in the UAE: Cultural Adaptation." *Journal of Business Strategy*, no. 1 (2015): 33–40.

Schneckenberg, Dirk. "Open Innovation and Knowledge Networking in a Multinational Corporation." *Journal of Business Strategy* 36, no. 1 (2015): 14–24.

Tate, Wendy L., et al. "Global Competitive Conditions Driving the Manufacturing Location Decision." *Business Horizons* 57, no. 3 (2014): 381–390.

Endnotes

1. Frederick Gluck, "Global Competition in the 1990s," *Journal of Business Strategy* (Spring 1983): 22–24.
2. Arregle, Jean-Luc, Toyah Miller, Michael Hitt, and Paul Beamish, "Do Regions Matter? An Integrated Institutional and Semiglobalization Perspective on the Internationalization of MNEs," *Strategic Management Journal*, 34 (2013): 910–934.
3. Jon Alston, "Wa, Guanxi, and Inhwa: Managerial Principles in Japan, China and Korea," *Business Horizons* 32, no. 2 (March–April 1989): 26.
4. Rose Knotts, "Cross-Cultural Management: Transformations and Adaptations," *Business Horizons* (January–February 1989): 29–33.
5. Some of the narrative in this section is based on information at http://kwintessential.co.uk/resources/country-profiles.html and http://www.kwintessential.co.uk/resources/global-etiquette/
6. Toko Sekiguchi, "Japan Seeks New Salarywomen," *Wall Street Journal*, September 12, 2014, A9.
7. Stratford Sherman, "How to Beat the Japanese?" *Fortune* (April 10, 1989): 45.
8. Mehul Srivastava, "Keeping Women on the Job in India," *Bloomberg Businessweek,* March 7–13, 2011, 11–12.
9. Sarah Childress, "Telecom Giants Battle for Kenya," *Wall Street Journal*, January 14, 2011, B1.
10. Drew Hinshaw, "Nigeria Economy Takes Lead in Continent," *Wall Street Journal,* April 7, 2014, A13.
11. Emmanuel Tumanjong, "Prying Open Africa's Web Reach," *Wall Street Journal,* January 10, 2014, B6.
12. David Luhnow and Bob Davis, "For Mexico, an Edge on China," *Wall Street Journal,* September 17, 2012, A12.
13. James Hookway, "Vietnam's Mobile Revolution," *Wall Street Journal,* June 15, 2015, B4.

Source: © nobeatsofierce.Shutterstock

③

Ethics, Social Responsibility, and Sustainability

LEARNING OBJECTIVES

After studying this chapter, you should be able to do the following:

3-1. Explain why good ethics is good business in strategic management.

3-2. Explain why whistle-blowing, bribery, and workplace romance are strategic issues.

3-3. Discuss why social responsibility and policy are key issues in strategic planning.

3-4. Discuss the nature of environmental sustainability and why it is a key issue in strategic planning.

3-5. Explain why animal welfare is a strategic issue for firms.

ASSURANCE OF LEARNING EXERCISES

The following exercises are found at the end of this chapter:

EXERCISE 3A   Sustainability and Nestlé

EXERCISE 3B   How Does My Municipality Compare to Others on Being Pollution-Safe?

EXERCISE 3C   Compare Nestlé versus Mars, Inc. on Social Responsibility

EXERCISE 3D   How Do You Rate Nestlé's Sustainability Efforts?

EXERCISE 3E   The Ethics of Spying on Competitors

Although the three sections of this chapter [(1) business ethics, (2) social responsibility, and (3) environmental sustainability] are distinct, the topics are quite related. For example, many people consider it unethical for a firm to be socially irresponsible or to treat animals inhumanely. **Business ethics** can be defined as principles of conduct within organizations that guide decision making and behavior. Good business ethics is a prerequisite for good strategic management; good ethics is just good business! **Social responsibility** refers to actions an organization takes beyond what is legally required to protect or enhance the well-being of living things. **Sustainability** refers to the extent that an organization's operations and actions protect, mend, and preserve rather than harm or destroy the natural environment. Polluting the environment, for example, is unethical, irresponsible, and in many cases illegal, as is treating pigs, cows, chickens, and turkeys inhumanely. Business ethics, social responsibility, and environmental sustainability issues therefore are interrelated and impact all areas of the strategic-management process, as illustrated in Figure 3-1 with white shading.

An example of a high-performing, highly ethical, privately held company is Bank Audi S.A.L., the largest Lebanese bank integrating CSR and sustainability into core business activities. Another high-performing, highly ethical, publicly held company is Chipotle Mexican Grill, which recently stopped selling a pork product at one third of its U.S. restaurants because one of its suppliers failed an animal welfare audit. That particular supplier could not ensure that pigs have outdoor access or "deeply bedded barns" instead of being raised in tight cages. In response, Chipotle stopped offering carnitas, or pork meat, in its burritos or bowls. An increasing number of firms like Chipotle are raising their standards for animal welfare in terms of its beef, pork, and poultry suppliers raising animals with respect and also avoid using various antibiotics and growth hormones. A Chipotle spokesman remarked, "This is fundamentally an animal welfare decision and is rooted in our unwillingness to compromise our standards where animal welfare is concerned; we hope the vendor will solve its problems and return as a regular supplier for Chipotle."

Why "Good Ethics is Good Business"

The Institute of Business Ethics (IBE) recently did a study titled "Does Business Ethics Pay?" and concluded that companies displaying a "clear commitment to ethical conduct" consistently outperform companies that do not display ethical conduct. Philippa Foster Black of the IBE

Bank Audi S.A.L

As of 2015, Bank Audi S.A.L., headquartered in Beirut, Lebanon, is the largest Lebanese bank, employing 6,720 individuals, including 3,087 employees in Lebanon. Its total assets amounted to 63,783 billion Lebanese pounds (around $42 billion); customer deposits were 54,430 billion Lebanese pounds ($36 billion); and it had a net profit of 305 billion Lebanese pounds ($200 million) in the first half of 2015. Over the last decade, Bank Audi's strategy included regional expansion. Apart from Lebanon, it operates across Egypt, Qatar, Saudi Arabia, Syria, Jordan, and Sudan; it also operates in France, Switzerland and Monaco. It is exploring opportunities in Sub-Saharan Africa, which may prove to be advantageous for the company as Africa becomes more interesting for the Turkish market. With its Latin American clients leading to a turnover of $2.1 billion in 2014, Bank Audi plans to begin operations in Latin America and make the most of its Latin American employees in Lebanon and Switzerland.

In 2014, Bank Audi began integrating CSR and sustainability into core business activities. It continued implementing its Environmental and Social Management System that guided its approach in evaluating the environmental and social risks associated with its corporate and commercial activities. In an attempt to reduce its carbon footprint and increase environmental awareness within the company, and among the youth, Bank Audi initiated an employee-volunteering program called "Be a Hero for a Day," with employees representing a culture of ethics and responsibility.

Source: Based on information from Bank Audi Group's website, http://www.bankaudi.com.lb; and http://www.bankaudi.com.lb/GroupWebsite/openAudiFile.aspx?id=2783.

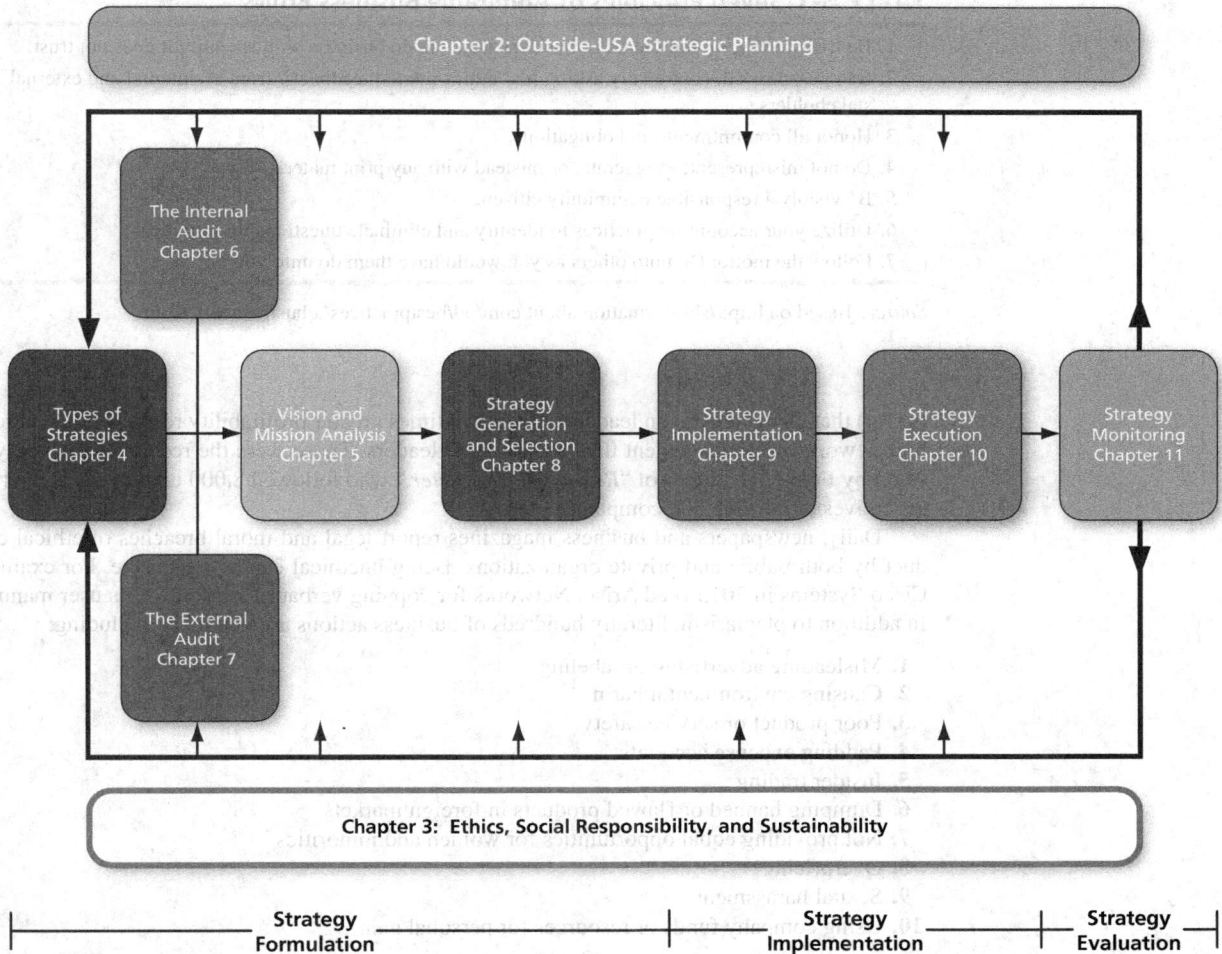

FIGURE 3-1
A Comprehensive Strategic-Management Model

Source: Fred R. David, adapted from "How Companies Define Their Mission," *Long Range Planning* 22, no. 3 (June 1988): 40,
© Fred R. David.v

stated, "Not only is ethical behavior in business life the right thing to do in principle, it pays off in financial returns." Alan Simpson remarked, "If you have integrity, nothing else matters. If you don't have integrity, nothing else matters." Good ethics is good business. Bad ethics can derail even the best strategic plans. This chapter provides an overview of the importance of business ethics in strategic management. Table 3-1 provides some results of the IBE study.

Does It Pay to Be Ethical?

A rising tide of consciousness about the importance of business ethics is sweeping the United States and the rest of the world. Strategists such as CEOs and business owners are the individuals primarily responsible for ensuring that high ethical principles are espoused and practiced in an organization. All strategy formulation, implementation, and evaluation decisions have ethical ramifications.

As indicated in Academic Research Capsule 3-1, it does pay to be ethical; high-performing companies generally exhibit high business ethics. *Investor's Business Daily* reported on 7-20-15

TABLE 3-1 Seven Principles of Admirable Business Ethics

1. Be trustworthy; no individual or business wants to do business with an entity it does not trust.
2. Be open-minded, continually asking for "ethics-related feedback" from all internal and external stakeholders.
3. Honor all commitments and obligations.
4. Do not misrepresent, exaggerate, or mislead with any print materials.
5. Be visibly a responsible community citizen.
6. Utilize your accounting practices to identify and eliminate questionable activities.
7. Follow the motto: Do unto others as you would have them do unto you.

Source: Based on http://sbinformation.about.com/od/bestpractices/a/businessethics.htm

(p. A4) that character-driven leaders deliver five times greater profitability results and 26 percent higher workforce engagement than self-focused leaders. Those were the results of a seven-year study by Fred Kiel, author of "*Return on Character*," who followed 8,000 employees and 84 top executives of Fortune 500 companies.

Daily, newspapers and business magazines report legal and moral breaches of ethical conduct by both public and private organizations. Being unethical can be expensive. For example, Cisco Systems in 2015 sued Arista Networks for copying verbatim sections of its user manuals. In addition to plagiarism, literally hundreds of business actions are unethical, including:

1. Misleading advertising or labeling
2. Causing environmental harm
3. Poor product or service safety
4. Padding expense accounts
5. Insider trading
6. Dumping banned or flawed products in foreign markets
7. Not providing equal opportunities for women and minorities
8. Overpricing
9. Sexual harassment
10. Using company funds or resources for personal gain

Increasingly, executives' and managers' personal and professional decisions are placing them in the crosshairs of angry shareholders, disgruntled employees, and even their own boards

ACADEMIC RESEARCH CAPSULE 3-1

What Can We Learn from High-Performance Companies?

Research at DePaul University in Chicago by Frigo and Litman found a pattern of strategic activities of high-performance companies. Their research involved screening the financial performance of more than 15,000 public companies using 30 years of financial data and identifying about 100 high-performance companies. Here are three lessons from high-performance companies studied:

1) ***Commitment to Return on Investment and Ethical Business Conduct***: High-performance companies demonstrate a strong commitment to creating shareholder value by focusing on sustainable return on investment (ROI). These companies achieve superior ROI and growth while adhering to ethical business conduct, such as Johnson & Johnson, which is famous for its credo as a foundation for ethical business conduct at the company.

2) ***Focus on Unmet Customer Needs in Growing Market Segments***: To avoid commoditization, high-performance companies concentrate on fulfilling unmet customer needs and target growing market segments. Harley-Davidson targets customer needs (lifestyle, freedom, community) with their unique Harley experience while pursuing a growing customer group (the Baby Boom generation).

3) ***Innovate Offerings***: High-performance companies constantly reexamine their products and services (their offerings), modifying existing ones and developing new ones that will better fulfill customers' unmet needs. For example, Apple demonstrate this characteristic through its innovation strategy.

Source: Based on Mark L. Frigo and Joel Litman, *DRIVEN: Business Strategy, Human Actions and the Creation of Wealth, Strategy and Execution* (Chicago: Strategy & Execution LLC, 2008).

of directors—making the imperious CEO far more vulnerable to personal, public, and corporate missteps than ever before. "Certainly, anybody who is doing something that can be construed as unethical, immoral or greedy is being taken to task," says Paul Dorf of Compensation Resources, a consultant to boards of directors.[1]

Social media and business-centric websites such as glassdoor.com and vault.com as well as disclosure mandates required under Sarbanes-Oxley are just several among hundreds of outlets that today quickly spread fact and rumor about the inside dealings of corporations and organizations, revealing ethical breaches and internal business practices that may never have surfaced years ago. Wendy Patrick, who teaches business ethics at San Diego State University, states, "God forbid anyone who isn't squeaky-clean these days or misrepresents their credentials. Anything embarrassing and you begin to question everything. If you aren't making good decisions in your personal life, it can bleed over to your career (professional life)."

How to Establish an Ethics Culture

A new wave of ethics issues has recently surfaced related to product safety, employee health, sexual harassment, AIDS in the workplace, smoking, acid rain, affirmative action, waste disposal, foreign business practices, cover-ups, takeover tactics, conflicts of interest, employee privacy, inappropriate gifts, and security of company records. A key ingredient for establishing an ethics culture is to develop a clear **code of business ethics**. Internet fraud, hacking into company computers, spreading viruses, and identity theft are other unethical activities that plague every sector of online commerce.

As indicated in Academic Research Capsule 3-2, anyone is prone to be unethical in a business, so Donald Palmer provides six procedures to establish an ethics culture.

Merely having a code of ethics, however, is not sufficient to ensure ethical business behavior. A code of ethics can be viewed as a public relations gimmick, a set of platitudes, or window dressing. To ensure that the code is read, understood, believed, and remembered, periodic ethics workshops are needed to sensitize people to workplace circumstances in which ethics issues may arise.[2] If employees see examples of punishment for violating the code as well as rewards for upholding the code, this reinforces the importance of a firm's code of ethics. The website www.ethicsweb.ca/codes provides guidelines on how to write an effective code of ethics.

Reverend Billy Graham once said, "When wealth is lost, nothing is lost; when health is lost, something is lost; when character is lost, all is lost." An ethics "culture" needs to permeate organizations! To help create an ethics culture, Citicorp developed a business ethics board game that is played by thousands of employees worldwide. Called "The Word Ethic," this game asks players business ethics questions, such as "How do you deal with a customer who offers you football tickets in exchange for a new, backdated IRA?" Diana Robertson at the Wharton School

ACADEMIC RESEARCH CAPSULE 3-2

Who Is Prone to Be Unethical in a Business?

Prior research suggests that being unethical is abnormal, rare, and most often perpetrated by people who are abhorrent. However, Donald Palmer recently reported that misconduct is a normal phenomenon and that wrongdoing is as prevalent as "rightdoing," and that misconduct is most often done by people who are primarily good, ethical, and socially responsible. Palmer reports that individuals engage in unethical activities due to a plethora of structure, processes, and mechanisms inherent in the functioning of organizations—and, importantly, all of us are candidates to be unethical under the right circumstances in any organization. Implications of this new research abound for managers. In light of his findings, Palmer concludes that organizations should implement the following six procedures as soon as possible:

1) Punish wrongdoing swiftly and severely when it is detected.
2) Be careful to hire employees who possess high ethical standards.
3) Develop socialization programs to reinforce desired cultural values.
4) Alter chains of command so subordinates report to more than one superior.
5) Develop a culture whereby subordinates may challenge their superior's orders when they seem questionable.
6) Develop a better understanding of internal policies, procedures, systems, and mechanisms that could lead to misconduct.

Source: Based on Donald Palmer, "The New Perspective on Organizational Wrongdoing," *California Management Review*, 56, no. 1 (2013): 5–23.

of Business believes the game is effective because it is interactive. Many organizations have developed a code-of-conduct manual outlining ethical expectations and giving examples of situations that commonly arise in their businesses.

One reason strategists' salaries are high is that they must take the moral risks of the firm. Strategists are responsible for developing, communicating, and enforcing the code of business ethics for their organizations. Although primary responsibility for ensuring ethical behavior rests with a firm's strategists, an integral part of the responsibility of all managers is to provide ethics leadership by constant example and demonstration. Managers hold positions that enable them to influence and educate many people. This makes managers responsible for developing and implementing ethical decision making. Gellerman and Drucker, respectively, offer some good advice for managers:

> All managers risk giving too much because of what their companies demand from them. But the same superiors who keep pressing you to do more, or to do it better, or faster, or less expensively, will turn on you should you cross that fuzzy line between right and wrong. They will blame you for exceeding instructions or for ignoring their warnings. The smartest managers already know that the best answer to the question "How far is too far?" is don't try to find out.[3]

> A man (or woman) might know too little, perform poorly, lack judgment and ability, and yet not do too much damage as a manager. But if that person lacks character and integrity—no matter how knowledgeable, how brilliant, how successful—he destroys. He destroys people, the most valuable resource of the enterprise. He destroys spirit. And he destroys performance. This is particularly true of the people at the head of an enterprise because the spirit of an organization is created from the top. If an organization is great in spirit, it is because the spirit of its top people is great. If it decays, it does so because the top rots. As the proverb has it, "Trees die from the top." No one should ever become a strategist unless he or she is willing to have his or her character serve as the model for subordinates.[4]

No society anywhere in the world can compete long or successfully with people stealing from one another or not trusting one another, with every bit of information requiring notarized confirmation, with every disagreement ending up in litigation, or with government having to regulate businesses to keep them honest. Being unethical is a recipe for headaches, inefficiency, and waste. History has proven that the greater the trust and confidence of people in the ethics of an institution or society, the greater its economic strength. Business relationships are built mostly on mutual trust and reputation. Short-term decisions based on greed and questionable ethics will preclude the necessary self-respect to gain the trust of others. More and more firms believe that ethics training and an ethics culture create strategic advantage. According to Max Killan, "If business is not based on ethical grounds, it is of no benefit to society, and will, like all other unethical combinations, pass into oblivion."

Whistle-Blowing, Bribery, and Workplace Romance

As social media and technology have become commonplace globally, three business ethics topics—whistle-blowing, bribery, and workplace romance—have become important strategic issues facing companies. Missteps in any of these three areas can severely harm an organization.

Whistle-Blowing

Whistle-blowing refers to employees reporting any unethical violations they discover or see in the firm. Employees should practice whistle-blowing, and organizations should have policies that encourage whistle-blowing. Three individuals recently received $170 million for helping investigators obtain a record $16.65 billion penalty against Bank of America for inflating the value of mortgage properties and selling defective loans to investors. The whistle-blower payouts are among the highest ever in financial institution cases. Thousands of firms warn managers and employees that failing to report an ethical violation by others could bring discharge. The Securities and Exchange Commission (SEC) recently strengthened its whistle-blowing policies, virtually mandating that anyone seeing unethical activity report such behavior.

Whistle-blowers in the corporate world receive up to 25 percent of the proceeds of legal proceedings against firms for wrongdoing. Such payouts are becoming more and more common. J.P. Morgan Chase employee Keith Edwards recently received a $63.9 million payout for his whistle-blowing tips that led J.P. Morgan to pay $614 million to the U.S. government for illegally approving thousands of FHA loans and hundreds of VA loans that did not meet underwriting requirements. The SEC recently paid $30 million to a non-U.S. citizen whistle-blower who reported an ongoing fraud matter. Sean McKessy, the SEC's whistle-blower top executive, commented about the case, "Whistleblowers from all over the world should feel similarly incentivized to come forward with credible information about potential violations of the U.S. securities laws."

An accountant who recently tipped off the IRS that his employer was skimping on taxes received $4.5 million in the first IRS whistle-blower award. The accountant's tip netted the IRS $20 million in taxes and interest from the errant financial-services firm. The award represented a 22 percent cut of the taxes recovered. The IRS program, designed to encourage tips in large-scale cases, mandates awards of 15 to 30 percent of the amount recouped. "It's a win-win for both the government and taxpayers. These are dollars that are being returned to the U.S. Treasury that otherwise wouldn't be," said lawyer Eric Young.

Ethics training programs should include messages from the CEO or owner of the business, emphasizing ethical business practices, the development and discussion of codes of ethics, and procedures for discussing and reporting unethical behavior. Firms can align ethical and strategic decision making by incorporating ethical considerations into strategic planning, by integrating ethical decision making into the performance appraisal process, by encouraging whistle-blowing, and by monitoring departmental and corporate performance regarding ethical issues.

Avoid Bribery

Managers, employees, and firms must avoid bribery. **Bribery** is defined by *Black's Law Dictionary* as the offering, giving, receiving, or soliciting of any item of value to influence the actions of an official or other person in discharge of a public or legal duty. A **bribe** is a gift bestowed to influence a recipient's conduct. The gift may be any money, goods, actions, property, preferment, privilege, emolument, object of value, advantage, or merely a promise or undertaking to induce or influence the action, vote, or influence of a person in an official or public capacity. Bribery is a crime in most countries of the world, including the United States.[5] For example, Avon Products has been plagued by bribery charges over the last 8 years. French engineering firm Alstom S.A. recently pleaded guilty to criminal charges that the company paid tens of millions of dollars in a "widespread" bribery scheme to win energy contracts globally. Alstom paid a fine of $772 million for falsifying financial records and paying bribes to win contracts around the world.

The U.S. Foreign Corrupt Practices Act (FCPA) governs bribery in the United States and has stepped up enforcement. This act, and a new provision in the Dodd-Frank financial-regulation law, allows company employees or others who bring cases of financial fraud, such as bribery, to the government's attention to receive up to 30 percent of any sum recovered. Bribery suits against a company also expose the firm to shareholder lawsuits. Hewlett-Packard (HP) recently paid $108 million to resolve bribery investigations in Russia, Poland, and Mexico. The HP bribery activities included the use of slush funds and shell companies to funnel monies to politicians, as well as free trips to Las Vegas with free cash to gamble.

A recent *Wall Street Journal* article titled "Bribery Law Dos and Don'ts" provides a synopsis of the recent 130-page document released by the U.S. Justice Department and the SEC to respond to complaints from companies that ambiguity in the FCPA has forced them to abandon business in high-risk countries and spend millions of dollars investigating themselves.[6] Numerous examples of bribery are given, such as "providing a $12,000 birthday trip for a government official from Mexico that includes visits to wineries and museums" and "$10,000 spent on a government official for drinks, dinners, and entertainment." The U.S. Justice Department and the SEC each file about 100 bribery cases annually.

The United Kingdom Bribery Law forbids any company doing any business in the United Kingdom from bribing foreign or domestic officials to gain competitive advantage. The British law is more stringent even than the similar U.S. FCPA. The British Bribery Law carries a maximum 10-year prison sentence for those convicted of bribery. The law stipulates that "failure to prevent bribery" is an offense and stipulates that facilitation payments, or payments to gain access, are not a valid defense to prevent bribery. The United Kingdom law applies even to bribes between private businesspersons, and if the individual who makes the payment does not realize the transaction was a bribe, he or she is still liable. The new bribery law is being enforced by Britain's Serious Fraud Office (SFO) and boosts the maximum penalty for bribery from 7 years to 10 years in prison, and sets no limits on fines. More and more nations are taking a tougher stance against corruption, and companies worldwide are installing elaborate programs to avoid running afoul of the FCPA or the SFO.

In some foreign countries, paying bribes and kickbacks has historically been acceptable. But now, antibribery and extortion initiatives are advocated by many organizations, including the World Bank, the International Monetary Fund, the European Union (EU), the Council of Europe, the Organization of American States, the Pacific Basin Economic Council, the Global Coalition for Africa, and the United Nations. Tipping is even now considered bribery in some countries. Taking business associates to lavish dinners and giving them expensive holiday gifts and even outright cash may have been expected in some countries, such as South Korea and China, but there is now stepped-up enforcement of bribery laws virtually everywhere. The world's third-largest commercial aircraft manufacturer, Embraer S.A., headquartered in Brazil, is currently being investigated for allegedly paying a $3.5 million bribe to a Dominican Republic Air Force colonel, who then pressured Dominican legislators to approve a $92 million contract for Embraer to provide attack planes to that country.

Several pharmaceutical companies, including Merck, AstraZeneca PLC, Bristol-Myers Squibb, and GlaxoSmithKline PLC, are currently being investigated for allegedly paying bribes in certain foreign countries to boost sales and speed approvals. Four types of violations are being reviewed: bribing government-employed doctors to purchase drugs, paying company sales agents commissions that are passed along to government doctors, paying hospital committees to approve drug purchases, and paying regulators to win drug approvals. Johnson & Johnson recently paid $70 million to settle allegations that it paid bribes to doctors in Greece, Poland, and Romania to use their surgical implants and to prescribe its drugs. Pfizer paid $60 million to resolve similar probes to win business overseas.

Workplace Romance

Workplace romance is an intimate relationship between two consenting employees, as opposed to **sexual harassment**, which the Equal Employment Opportunity Commission (EEOC) defines broadly as unwelcome sexual advances, requests for sexual favors, and other verbal or physical conduct of a sexual nature. Sexual harassment (and discrimination) is illegal, unethical, and detrimental to any organization and can result in expensive lawsuits, lower morale, and reduced productivity.

Workplace romance between two consenting employees simply happens, so the question is generally not whether to allow the practice, or even how to prevent it, but rather how best to manage the phenomena. An organization probably should not strictly forbid workplace romance because such a policy could be construed as an invasion of privacy, overbearing, or unnecessary. Some romances actually improve work performance, adding a dynamism and energy that translates into enhanced morale, communication, creativity, and productivity.[7]

However, it is important to note that workplace romance can be detrimental to workplace morale and productivity, for a number of reasons that include:

1. Favoritism complaints can arise.
2. Confidentiality of records can be breached.
3. Reduced quality and quantity of work can become a problem.
4. Personal arguments can lead to work arguments.
5. Whispering secrets can lead to tensions and hostilities among coworkers.
6. Sexual harassment (or discrimination) charges may ensue, either by the involved female or a third party.
7. Conflicts of interest can arise, especially when well-being of the partner trumps well-being of the company.

In some states, such as California, managers can be held personally liable for damages that arise from workplace romance. Organizations should establish guidelines or policies that address workplace romance, for at least six reasons:

1. Guidelines can enable the firm to better defend against and avoid sexual harassment or discrimination charges.

2. Guidelines can specify reasons (such as the seven listed previously) why workplace romance may not be a good idea.

3. Guidelines can specify resultant penalties for romancing partners if problems arise.

4. Guidelines can promote a professional and fair work atmosphere.

5. Guidelines can help assure compliance with federal, state, and local laws and recent court cases.

6. Lack of any guidelines sends a lackadaisical message throughout the firm.

Workplace romance guidelines should apply to all employees at all levels of the firm and should specify certain situations in which affairs are especially discouraged, such as supervisor and subordinate. Company guidelines or policies in general should discourage workplace romance because "the downside risks generally exceed the upside benefits" for the firm. Best Buy CEO Brian Dunn recently resigned when directors learned of his inappropriate relationship with a young subordinate, which was a violation of that company's code of ethics. Based in Fremont, California, IGate Corp. fired its CEO, Phaneesh Murthy, recently for allegedly failing to report a workplace romance relationship that turned into a sexual harassment issue with a subordinate.

Flirting is a step down from workplace romance, but a full-page *Wall Street Journal* article titled "The New Rules of Flirting" reveal the dos and don'ts of flirting.[8] Flirting is defined by researchers as "romantic behavior that is ambiguous and goal oriented," or said differently, "ambiguous behavior with potential sexual or romantic overtones that is goal-oriented." A few flirting rules given in the article are:

1. Do not flirt with someone you know is looking for a relationship if you are not interested in a new relationship.

2. Do flirt within a relationship that you want to strengthen.

3. Do not flirt to make your partner jealous because this is manipulative behavior.

4. Flirting between power differences, such as boss and employee or professor and student, usually leads to trouble, as many defendants in sexual harassment complaints know.

5. Do not make physical contact with the person you are flirting with, unless it is within a desired relationship.

Among colleges and universities, the federal Office of Civil Rights (OCR) has stepped up its investigation of sexual harassment cases brought forward by female students against professors. Numerous institutions are currently being investigated. At no charge to the student, the OCR will investigate a female student's claim if evidence is compelling.

A *Wall Street Journal* article recapped U.S. standards regarding boss and subordinate love affairs at work.[9] Only 5 percent of all firms sampled had no restrictions on such relationships; 80 percent of firms have policies that prohibit relationships between a supervisor and a subordinate. Only 4 percent of firms strictly prohibited such relationships, but 39 percent of firms had policies that required individuals to inform their supervisors whenever a romantic relationship begins with a coworker. Only 24 percent of firms required the two persons to be in different departments.

In Europe, romantic relationships at work are largely viewed as private matters and most firms have no policies on the practice. However, European firms are increasingly adopting explicit, U.S.-style sexual harassment laws. The U.S. military strictly bans officers from dating or having sexual relationships with enlistees. At the World Bank, sexual relations between a supervisor and an employee are considered "a de facto conflict of interest which must be resolved to avoid favoritism." World Bank president Paul Wolfowitz recently was forced to resign as a result of a relationship he had with a bank staff person.

A recent *Bloomberg Businessweek* article reports that employees are filing sexual harassment complaints as a way to further their own job security. Many of these filings are increasingly third-party individuals not even directly involved in the relationship but alleging their own job was impacted. Largely the result of the rise of third-party discrimination claims, the EEOC recovers about $500 million on behalf of office romance victims.[10]

Social Responsibility and Policy

Some strategists agree with Ralph Nader, who proclaims that organizations have tremendous social obligations. Nader points out, for example, that ExxonMobil has more assets than most countries, and because of this, such firms have an obligation to help society cure its many ills.

ACADEMIC RESEARCH CAPSULE 3-3

Does It Pay to Be Socially Responsible?

Economists generally say *no*, and philanthropists say *yes* to this question. Recent research by Barnett and Salomon examined the relationship between corporate social performance (CSP) and corporate financial performance (CFP). They hypothesized, and then confirmed, that the CSP–CFP relationship is U-shaped. Specifically, Barnett and Salomon reported that firms with low CSP have higher CFP than firms with moderate CSP, but firms with high CSP have the highest CFP. They also found that firms with the highest CSP

generally have the highest CFP. In addition, the researchers reported that the accrual of social responsibility deeds causes the benefits of CSP to increase at a higher rate than the costs, producing an eventual upturn in the CSP–CFP relationship.

Source: Based on Michael Barnett and Robert Salomon, "Does It Pay to Be Really Good? Addressing the Shape of the Relationship Between Social and Financial Performance," *Strategic Management Journal*, 33 (2012): 1304–1320.

Other people, however, agree with the economist Milton Friedman, who asserts that organizations have no obligation to do any more for society than is legally required. Friedman may contend that it is irresponsible for a firm to give monies to charity.

Do you agree more with Nader or Friedman? Surely we can all agree that the first social responsibility of any business must be to make enough profit to cover the costs of the future, because if this is not achieved, no other social responsibility can be met. Indeed, no social need can be met if the firm fails. Strategists should examine social problems in terms of potential costs and benefits to the firm and focus on social issues that could benefit the firm most. For example, if a firm avoids cutting jobs to protect employees' livelihood, and that decision forces the firm to liquidate, then all the employees lose their jobs. As indicated in Academic Research Capsule 3-3, most economists suggest that firms should not engage much, if any, in philanthropy, because simply making a profit is difficult, and shareholders expect a high return on their investment.

Design and Articulate a Social Policy

The term **social policy** embraces managerial philosophy and thinking at the highest level of the firm, which is why the topic is covered in this text. Social policy concerns what responsibilities the firm has to employees, consumers, environmentalists, minorities, communities, shareholders, and other groups. After decades of debate, many firms still struggle to determine appropriate social policies. The impact of society on business and vice versa is becoming more pronounced each year. Corporate social policy should be designed and articulated during strategy formulation, set and administered during strategy implementation, and reaffirmed or changed during strategy evaluation.[11]

Firms should strive to engage in social activities that have economic benefits. Merck & Co. once developed the drug ivermectin for treating river blindness, a disease caused by a fly-borne parasitic worm endemic in poor tropical areas of Africa, the Middle East, and Latin America. In an unprecedented gesture that reflected its corporate commitment to social responsibility, Merck then made ivermectin available at no cost to medical personnel throughout the world. Merck's action highlights the dilemma of orphan drugs, which offer pharmaceutical companies no economic incentive for profitable development and distribution. Merck did, however, garner substantial goodwill among its stakeholders for its actions.

Social Policies on Retirement

Some countries around the world are facing severe workforce shortages associated with their aging populations. The percentage of persons age 65 or older exceeds 20 percent in Japan, Italy, and Germany—and will reach 20 percent in 2018 in France. In 2036, the percentage of persons age 65 or older will reach 20 percent in the United States and China. Unlike the United States, Japan is reluctant to rely on large-scale immigration to bolster its workforce. Instead, Japan provides incentives for its elderly to work until ages 65 to 75. Western European countries are doing the opposite, providing incentives for its elderly to retire at ages 55 to 60. The International Labor Organization says 71 percent of Japanese men ages 60 to 64 work, compared to 57 percent of American men and just 17 percent of French men in the same age group.

TABLE 3-2 The Ten Best Socially Responsible Companies in the World

1. Microsoft
2. Google
3. Walt Disney Company
4. BMW
5. Apple
6. Daimler (Mercedes-Benz)
7. Volkswagen
8. Sony
9. Colgate-Palmolive
10. LEGO Group

Source: Based on information at http://www.forbes.com/pictures/efkk45mmlm/no-1-microsoft/

Sachiko Ichioka, a typical 67-year-old man in Japan, says, "I want to work as long as I'm healthy. The extra money means I can go on trips, and I'm not a burden on my children." Better diet and health care have raised Japan's life expectancy now to 82, the highest in the world. Japanese women are having, on average, only 1.28 children compared to 2.04 in the United States. Keeping the elderly at work, coupled with reversing the old-fashioned trend of keeping women at home, are Japan's two key remedies for sustaining its workforce in factories and businesses. This prescription for dealing with problems associated with an aging society should be considered by many countries around the world. The Japanese government is phasing in a shift from age 60 to age 65 as the date when a person may begin receiving a pension, and premiums paid by Japanese employees are rising while payouts are falling. Unlike the United States, Japan has no law against discrimination based on age.

Worker productivity increases in Japan are not able to offset declines in number of workers, thus resulting in a decline in overall economic production. Like many countries, Japan does not view immigration as a good way to solve this problem. Japan's shrinking workforce has become such a concern that the government just recently allowed an unspecified number of Indonesian and Filipino nurses and caregivers to work in Japan for two years. The number of working-age Japanese—those between ages 15 and 64—is projected to shrink to 70 million by 2030. Using foreign workers is known as *gaikokujin roudousha* in Japanese. Many Filipinos have recently been hired now to work in agriculture and factories throughout Japan.

Forbes best companies globally in regard to being socially responsible are listed in Table 3-2. Bill Gates, former CEO of the number-one ranked firm Microsoft, established the well-known Bill and Melinda Gates Foundation, which sets a high standard for any person or company.

Environmental Sustainability

The ecological challenge facing all organizations requires managers to formulate strategies that preserve and conserve natural resources and control pollution. Special natural environment issues include ozone depletion, global warming, depletion of rain forests, destruction of animal habitats, protecting endangered species, developing biodegradable products and packages, waste management, clean air, clean water, erosion, destruction of natural resources, and pollution control. Firms increasingly are developing green product lines that are biodegradable or are made from recycled products. Green products sell well. Managing the health of the planet requires an understanding of how international trade, competitiveness, and global resources are connected. Managing environmental affairs, for example, can no longer be simply a technical function performed by specialists in a firm; more emphasis must be placed on developing an environmental perspective among all employees and managers of the firm.

Businesses must not exploit and decimate the natural environment. Mark Starik at George Washington University believes, "Halting and reversing worldwide ecological destruction and deterioration is a strategic issue that needs immediate and substantive attention by all businesses and managers." According to the International Standards Organization, the word **environment** is defined as "surroundings in which an organization operates, including air, water, land, natural resources, flora, fauna, humans, and their interrelation." This chapter illustrates how many firms are gaining competitive advantage by being good stewards of the natural environment.

Employees, consumers, governments, and societies are especially resentful of firms that harm rather than protect the natural environment. Conversely, people today are especially appreciative of firms that conduct operations in a way that mends, conserves, and preserves the natural environment. Consumer interest in businesses preserving nature's ecological balance and fostering a clean, healthy environment is high.

What Firms Are the Best Stewards?

Lennar Corporation, the nation's second-largest homebuilder, now offers solar panels as standard equipment on thousands of its new homes, especially in the southwestern United States. Homeowners can either lease the solar panels from Lennar or purchase the panels outright. Even with oil and gas prices at decade lows, solar panels have become quite cost effective, and "exhumes good ethics rather than bad fumes." Walmart is installing solar panels on its stores in California and Hawaii, providing as much as 30 percent of the power in some stores. It may go national with solar power if this test works well. Also moving to solar energy is department-store chain Kohl's Corp., which is converting 64 of its 80 California stores to use solar power. There are big subsidies for solar installations in some states.

In October of every year, three world-renowned corporate sustainability rankings are published: (1) the Dow Jones Sustainability Index (DJSI), (2) the Carbon Disclosure Project, and (3) *Newsweek's* "Green" rankings. The DJSI annually reveals the best corporations in the world in various industries in terms of sustainability. Note in Table 3-3 that Sodexo, for example, leads all

TABLE 3-3 The Best "Environmental Sustainability" Company in Various Industries (2014–2015)

Company	Industry
BMW AG	Automobiles & Components
AG Westpac Banking	Banks
Siemens AG	Capital Goods
SGS SA	Commercial & Professional Services
LG Electronics Inc	Consumer Durables & Apparel
Sodexo	Consumer Services
ING Group NV	Diversified Financials
Thai Oil PCL	Energy
Woolworths Ltd	Food & Staples Retailing
Unilever NV	Food, Beverage & Tobacco
Abbott Laboratories	Health Care Equipment & Services
Kao Corp	Household & Personal Products
Swiss Re AG	Insurance
Akzo Nobel NV	Materials
Telenet Group Holding NV	Media
Roche Holding AG	Pharmaceuticals & Biotechnology
GPT Group	Real Estate
Lotte Shopping Co Ltd	Retailing
Taiwan Semiconductor Manufacturing	Semiconductors
Wipro Ltd	Software & Services
Alcatel Lucent	Technology Hardware & Equipment
Telecom Italia SpA	Telecommunication Services
Air France-KLM	Transportation
EDP Energias de Portugal SA	Utilities

Source: Based on information at http://www.sustainability-indices.com/review/annual-review-2014.jsp

"consumer services" companies in "environmental sustainability;" consumer services includes providing food services in the cafeteria at many colleges and universities.

The strategies of both companies and countries are increasingly scrutinized and evaluated from a natural environment perspective. Companies (e.g., Walmart) now monitor not only the price their vendors offer for products but also how those products are made in terms of environmental practices, as well as safety and infrastructure soundness—particularly of Southeast Asia factories. A growing number of business schools offer separate courses and even a concentration in environmental management.

In terms of megawatts of wind power generated by various states in the nation, Texas's 8,000 megawatts dwarfs all other states. Minnesota also is making substantial progress in wind power generation. New Jersey recently outfitted 200,000 utility poles with solar panels. A *Wall Street Journal* (6-29-15, p. B1) article says Hawaii leads all states in the most electricity per capita (21%) generated from solar or wind. A new Hawaii mandates that 100 percent of the state's electricity be supplied by wind turbines and solar panels by 2045. States that get the most electricity per capita from residential solar panels are Hawaii 168 watts per capita, followed by California at 47, Arizona at 44, and New Jersey at 25.

Sustainability Reports

A **sustainability report** reveals how a firm's operations impact the natural environment. This document discloses to shareholders information about the firm's labor practices, product sourcing, energy efficiency, environmental impact, and business ethics practices.

No business wants a reputation as being a polluter. A bad sustainability record will hurt the firm in the market, jeopardize its standing in the community, and invite scrutiny by regulators, investors, and environmentalists. Governments increasingly require businesses to behave responsibly and require, for example, that businesses publicly report the pollutants and wastes their facilities produce. It is simply good business for any business to provide a sustainability report annually to the public.

With 60,000 suppliers and more than $350 billion in annual sales, Walmart works with its suppliers to make sure they provide such reports. Many firms use the Walmart sustainability report as a benchmark guideline, and model to follow in preparing their own report. Walmart encourages and expects its 1.35 million U.S. employees to adopt what it calls Personal Sustainability Projects, which include such measures as organizing weight-loss or smoking-cessation support groups, biking to work, or starting recycling programs. Employee wellness can be a part of sustainability. Home Depot, the world's second-largest retailer behind Walmart, recently more than doubled its offering of environmentally friendly products such as all-natural insect repellent. Home Depot has made it much easier for consumers to find its organic products by using special labels similar to Timberland's (the outdoor company) Green Index tags.

The Global Reporting Initiative recently issued a set of detailed reporting guidelines specifying what information should go into sustainability reports. The proxy advisory firm Institutional Shareholder Services reports that an increasing number of shareholder groups are pushing firms to provide sustainability information annually. Two companies that released sustainability reports for the first time were Hyatt Hotels & Resorts and Las Vegas Sands Corporation. Rival firm Hilton Worldwide does not have a stand-alone sustainability report, but Marriott and Wyndham Worldwide do release annual sustainability reports and report excellent reductions in energy, water, waste, and carbon dioxide emissions.

Managers and employees of firms must be careful not to become scapegoats blamed for company environmental wrongdoings. Harming the natural environment can be unethical, illegal, and costly. When organizations today face criminal charges for polluting the environment, they increasingly turn on their managers and employees to win leniency. Employee firings and demotions are becoming common in pollution-related legal suits. Managers were fired at Darling International, Inc., and Niagara Mohawk Power Corporation for being indirectly responsible for their firms polluting water. Managers and employees today must be careful not to ignore, conceal, or disregard a pollution problem, or they may find themselves personally liable.

A few years ago, firms could get away with placing "green" terminology on their products and labels, using such terms as *organic, green, safe, earth-friendly, nontoxic,* or *natural* because there were no legal or generally accepted definitions. Today, however, these terms carry much more specific connotations and expectations. Uniform standards defining environmentally responsible company actions are rapidly being incorporated into the legal landscape. It has become more and more difficult for firms to make "green" claims when their actions are not substantive, comprehensive, or even true. Lack of standards once made consumers cynical about corporate environmental claims, but those claims today are increasingly being challenged in courts. According to Joel Makower, "One of the main reasons to truly become a green firm is for your employees. They're the first group that needs assurance than any claims you make hold water."[12]

Around the world, political and corporate leaders now realize that the "business green" topic is not going away and in fact is gaining ground rapidly. Strategically, companies more than ever must demonstrate to their customers and stakeholders that their green efforts are substantive and set the firm apart from competitors. A firm's social performance (facts and figures) must back up their rhetoric and be consistent with sustainability standards.

The Office of Environmental Affairs

Many companies are moving environmental affairs from the staff side of the organization to the line side, thus making the corporate environmental group report directly to the chief operating officer. Firms that manage environmental affairs will enhance relations with consumers, regulators, vendors, and other industry players, substantially improving their prospects of success. Environmental strategies could include developing or acquiring green businesses, divesting or altering environment-damaging businesses, striving to become a low-cost producer through waste minimization and energy conservation, and pursuing a differentiation strategy through green-product features. In addition, firms could include an environmental representative on their board of directors, conduct regular environmental audits, implement bonuses for favorable environmental results, become involved in environmental issues and programs, incorporate environmental values in mission statements, establish environmentally oriented objectives, acquire environmental skills, and provide environmental training programs for company employees and managers.

Preserving the environment should be a permanent part of doing business, for the following reasons:

1. Consumer demand for environmentally safe products and packages is high.
2. Public opinion demanding that firms conduct business in ways that preserve the natural environment is strong.
3. Environmental advocacy groups now have more than 20 million Americans as members.
4. Federal and state environmental regulations are changing rapidly and becoming more complex.
5. More lenders are examining the environmental liabilities of businesses seeking loans.
6. Many consumers, suppliers, distributors, and investors shun doing business with environmentally weak firms.
7. Liability suits and fines against firms having environmental problems are on the rise.

More firms are becoming environmentally proactive—doing more than the bare minimum to develop and implement strategies that preserve the environment. The old undesirable alternative of being environmentally reactive—changing practices only when forced to do so by law or consumer pressure—more often today leads to high clean-up costs, liability suits, reduced market share, reduced customer loyalty, and higher medical costs. In contrast, a proactive policy views environmental pressures as opportunities and includes such actions as developing green products and packages, conserving energy, reducing waste, recycling, and creating a corporate culture that is environmentally sensitive.

ISO 14000/14001 Certification

Based in Geneva, Switzerland, the International Organization for Standardization (ISO) is a network of the national standards institutes of 147 countries, with one member per country. The ISO is the world's largest developer of sustainability standards. Widely accepted all over the world, ISO standards are voluntary because it has no legal authority to enforce their implementation; the organization itself does not regulate or legislate. Governmental agencies in various countries, such as the Environmental Protection Agency (EPA) in the United States, have adopted ISO standards as part of their regulatory framework, and the standards are the basis of much legislation. Adoptions are sovereign decisions by the regulatory authorities, governments, or companies concerned. Businesses and municipalities should consider becoming ISO certified to help attract business.

ISO 14000 refers to a series of voluntary standards in the environmental field. The ISO 14000 family of standards concerns the extent to which a firm minimizes harmful effects on the environment caused by its activities and continually monitors and improves its own environmental performance. These standards have been adopted by thousands of firms and municipalities worldwide to certify to their constituencies that they are conducting business in an environmentally friendly manner; these standards offer a universal technical benchmark for environmental compliance that more and more firms are requiring not only of themselves but also of their suppliers and distributors. Included in the ISO 14000 series are the ISO 14001 standards in fields such as environmental auditing, environmental performance evaluation, environmental labeling, and life-cycle assessment.

ISO 14001 is a set of standards adopted by thousands of firms worldwide to certify to their constituencies that they are conducting business in an environmentally friendly manner. The ISO 14001 standard offers a universal technical standard for environmental compliance that more and more firms are requiring not only of themselves but also of their suppliers and distributors.

According to the ISO 14001 standard, a community or organization is required to put in place and implement a series of practices and procedures that, when taken together, result in an **environmental management system (EMS)**. The ISO 14001 is not a technical standard and as such does not in any way replace technical requirements embodied in statutes or regulations. It also does not set prescribed standards of performance for organizations. Not being certified with ISO 14001 can be a strategic disadvantage for towns, counties, and companies because people today expect organizations to minimize or, even better, to eliminate environmental harm they cause.[13] There are six major requirements of an EMS under ISO 14001:

1. Show commitments to prevention of pollution, continual improvement in overall environmental performance, and compliance with all applicable statutory and regulatory requirements.
2. Identify all aspects of the organization's activities, products, and services that could have a significant impact on the environment, including those that are not regulated.
3. Set performance objectives and targets for the management system that link back to three policies: (a) prevention of pollution, (b) continual improvement, and (c) compliance.
4. Meet environmental objectives that include training employees, establishing work instructions and practices, and establishing the actual metrics by which the objectives and targets will be measured.
5. Conduct an audit operation of the EMS.
6. Take corrective actions when deviations from the EMS occur.

Wildlife Welfare

Consumers globally are becoming increasingly intolerant of any business or nation that directly or indirectly destroys wildlife, especially endangered wildlife, such as tigers, elephants, whales, songbirds, and coral reefs. Affected businesses range from retailers that sell ivory chess pieces to restaurants that sell whale meat. The United States recently crushed over 6 tons of elephant ivory as part of a global effort to combat elephant poaching; one elephant is killed every 16 minutes.[14] The Chinese government recently destroyed more than 6.1 tons of elephant ivory to help stop illegal ivory smuggling that is fueling poaching and decimating elephant populations in Africa. There are today less than 100,000 elephants in Africa, down from more than 300,000 in 2002, primarily because the demand for ivory remains robust in Asia, particularly China.

African giraffes are in danger of becoming extinct due to hunting and poaching in Africa that has decimated the giraffe population. There are only about 80,000 giraffes left in the wild, down from 140,000 giraffes 15 years ago. Fewer than 300 West African giraffes remain in Niger, and only 700 Rothschild's giraffes remain in Uganda and Kenya. Poaching is especially detrimental in eastern and central Africa, partly because some people (in Tanzania) erroneously believe the giraffe's meat and/or bone marrow is an HIV cure.

Many New Zealanders, supported by Australians, are outraged about Japan's large-scale whaling operations in the Antarctic. Japan recently issued permits allowing its whalers to kill up to 935 Antarctica minkes, 50 fin whales, and 50 humpbacks as part of "research into sustainable hunting." Whale meat is regarded as a delicacy in Japan and can fetch up to US$38 for 100 grams. Japan ironically is a member of the International Whaling Commission that has banned commercial whaling in a 31 million square-mile area around Antarctica known as the Southern Ocean Whale Sanctuary. Unfortunately, South Korea recently resumed whaling, despite a 1986 moratorium on commercial whaling. Many countries are upset with whaling, including Australia, where the Prime Minister Julia Gillard asserted, "We are completely opposed to whaling; there's no excuse for scientific whaling." Only a few countries—such as Norway, Japan, and Russia—favor and engage in commercial whaling. Norway was soundly criticized globally in mid-2015 for launching whale-hunting expeditions, to follow up on their killing 729 whales the prior year, the most annual whale killings by Norway in two decades. Countries, municipalities, and companies increasingly run the risk of being boycotted and exposed for direct or indirect wildlife endangering practices.

About 50 million sharks are killed every year solely to cut off (and sell) their fins.[15] Although "shark-finning" was outlawed in U.S. waters in 2000, the law does not ban fin imports or serving the fins in food, so about 57 metric tons of fins are imported in the United States annually. Only eight U.S. states have laws banning the sale of shark fins in food: Hawaii, Oregon, Washington, Illinois, California, Maryland, New York, and Delaware. The problem is much worse in some countries, especially China. More than 25 percent of the world's shark species now face extinction, according to the International Union for Conservation of Nature.

Table 3-4 reveals the impact that bad environmental policies have on songbirds and coral reefs, two of nature's many ecosystems.

TABLE 3-4   Songbirds and Coral Reefs Need Help

Songbirds

Please be a good steward of the natural environment to save our songbirds. Bluebirds are one of 76 songbird species in the United States that have dramatically declined in numbers in the last two decades. Not all birds are considered songbirds, and why birds sing is not clear. Some scientists say they sing when calling for mates or warning of danger, but many scientists now contend that birds sing for sheer pleasure. Songbirds include chickadees, orioles, swallows, mockingbirds, warblers, sparrows, vireos, and the wood thrush. "These birds are telling us there's a problem, something's out of balance in our environment," says Jeff Wells, bird conservation director for the National Audubon Society. Songbirds may be telling us that their air or water is too dirty or that we are destroying too much of their habitat. People collect Picasso paintings and save historic buildings. "Songbirds are part of our natural heritage. Why should we be willing to watch songbirds destroyed any more than allowing a great work of art to be destroyed?" asks Wells. Whatever message songbirds are singing to us today about their natural environment, the message is becoming less and less heard nationwide. Listen when you go outside today. Each of us as individuals, companies, states, and countries should do what we reasonably can to help improve the natural environment for songbirds.[16] A recent study concludes that 67 of the 800 bird species in the United States are endangered, and another 184 species are designated of "conservation concern." The birds of Hawaii are in the greatest peril.

Coral Reefs

Please be a good steward of the natural environment to save our coral reefs. The ocean covers more than 71 percent of the earth. The destructive effect of commercial fishing on ocean habitats coupled with increasing pollution runoff into the ocean and global warming of the ocean have decimated fisheries, marine life, and coral reefs around the world. The unfortunate consequence of fishing over the last century has been overfishing, with the principal reasons being politics and greed. Trawl fishing with nets destroys coral reefs and has been compared to catching squirrels by cutting down forests because bottom nets scour and destroy vast areas of the ocean. The great proportion of marine life caught in a trawl is "by-catch" juvenile fish and other life that are killed and discarded. Warming of the ocean as a result of carbon dioxide emissions also kills thousands of acres of coral reefs annually. The total area of fully protected marine habitats in the United States is only about 50 square miles, compared to some 93 million acres of national wildlife refuges and national parks on the nation's land. A healthy ocean is vital to the economic and social future of the nation—and, indeed, all countries of the world. Everything we do on land ends up in the ocean, so we all must become better stewards of this last frontier on earth to sustain human survival and the quality of life.[17]

Food Suppliers and Animal Welfare

Humane treatment of animals matters! Walmart, other retailers, and restaurants are demanding that food suppliers treat animals better, and consumers are flocking to organic foods. Thus, numerous food companies, such as Tyson Foods, the largest U.S. meatpacker, are phasing out use of human antibiotics and are "housing" animals more humanely. Walmart says its suppliers must begin to "raise animals with sufficient space for them to express normal behaviors and freedom from discomfort." Walmart wants the use of battery cages for chickens, gestation crates for hogs, and veal crates for cows to be eliminated, although such small confined areas are currently used to raise many chickens, pigs, and cows in the United States. Wayne Pacelle, CEO of the Humane Society of the United States, wants Walmart to set a timeline for compliance. Parents want their children to eat food raised without use of growth hormones and antibiotics. Sales of organic milk, eggs, and other food products are booming, even at the higher prices. Walmart is by far the largest grocer in the United States, with grocery accounting for 56 percent of the company's $288 billion in sales in 2014.[18]

IMPLICATIONS FOR STRATEGISTS

Figure 3-2 reveals that the whole strategic-management process is designed to gain and sustain competitive advantages, but all can be lost with ethical violations, ranging from bribery to sexual harassment to selling whale meat. Trees die from the top; strategists are at the top of the firm. Consequently, strategists must set an exemplary example personally and professionally to establish and continually reinforce an organizational culture for "doing the right thing." Social responsibility and environmental sustainability policies, practices, and procedures must reinforce that good ethics is good business," and that good ethics is the foundation for everything we do and say."

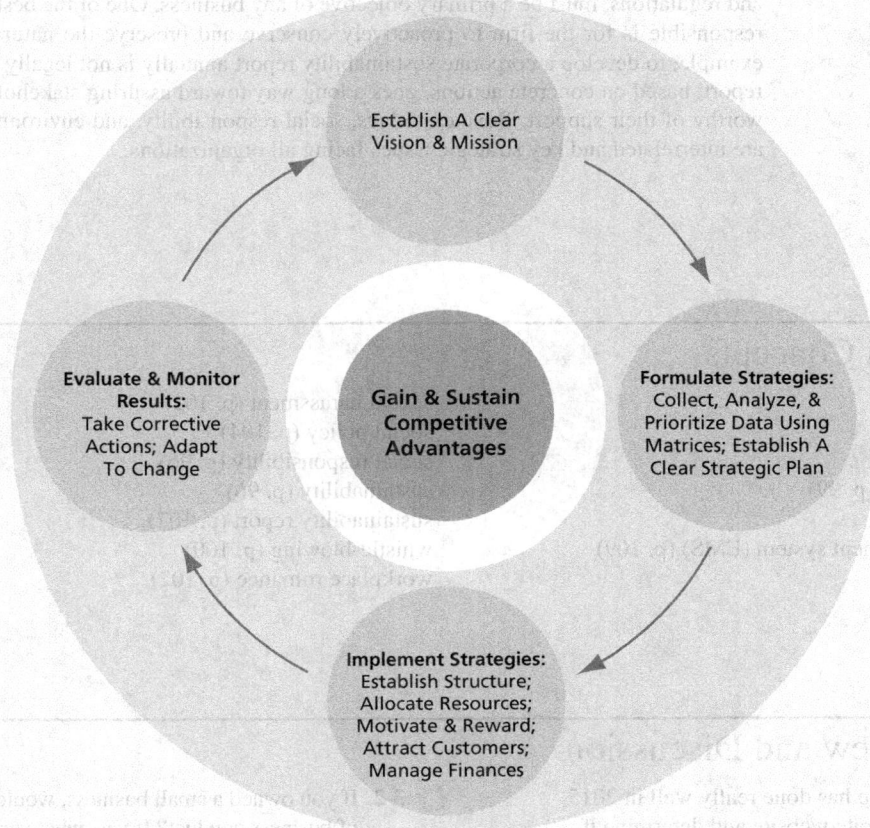

FIGURE 3-2
How to Gain and Sustain Competitive Advantages

IMPLICATIONS FOR STUDENTS

No company or individual wants to do business with someone who is unethical or is insensitive to natural environment concerns. It is no longer admirable simply to be environmentally proactive; today, it is expected, and in many respects is the law. Firms are being compared to rival firms every day on sustainability and ethics behavior, actually every minute on Facebook, Twitter, LinkedIn, and YouTube. Issues presented in this chapter therefore comprise a competitive advantage or disadvantage for all organizations. Thus, you should include in your case analysis recommendations for your firm to exceed stakeholder expectations on ethics, sustainability, and social responsibility. Make comparisons to rival firms to show how your firm can gain or sustain competitive advantage on these issues. Reveal suggestions for the firm to be a good corporate citizen and promote that for competitive advantage. Be mindful that the first responsibility of any business is to stay in business, so use cost/benefit analysis as needed to present your recommendations effectively.

Chapter Summary

In a final analysis, ethical standards come out of history and heritage. Our predecessors have left us with an ethical foundation on which to build. Even the legendary football coach Vince Lombardi knew that some things were worth more than winning, and he required his players to have three kinds of loyalty: to God, to their families, and to the Green Bay Packers, "in that order." Employees, customers, and shareholders have become less and less tolerant of business ethics violations in firms, and more and more appreciative of model ethical firms. Information-sharing across the Internet increasingly reveals such model firms versus irresponsible firms.

Consumers across the country and around the world appreciate firms that do more than is legally required to be socially responsible. But staying in business, while adhering to all laws and regulations, must be a primary objective of any business. One of the best ways to be socially responsible is for the firm to proactively conserve and preserve the natural environment. For example, to develop a corporate sustainability report annually is not legally required, but such a report, based on concrete actions, goes a long way toward assuring stakeholders that the firm is worthy of their support. Business ethics, social responsibility, and environmental sustainability are interrelated and key strategic issues facing all organizations.

Key Terms and Concepts

bribe (p. 101)
bribery (p. 101)
business ethics (p. 96)
code of business ethics (p. 99)
environment (p. 105)
environmental management system (EMS) (p. 109)
ISO 14000 (p. 109)
ISO 14001 (p. 109)

sexual harassment (p. 102)
social policy (p. 104)
social responsibility (p. 96)
sustainability (p. 96)
sustainability report (p. 107)
whistle-blowing (p. 100)
workplace romance (p. 102)

Issues for Review and Discussion

⭐ **3-1.** Bank Audi Group has done really well in 2015. Visit their corporate website and determine if business ethics and sustainability issues may be key reasons for their success.

⭐ **3-2.** If you owned a small business, would you develop a code of business conduct? If yes, what variables would you include? If no, how would you ensure that ethical business standards were being followed by your employees?

⭐ 3-3. What is the relationship between personal ethics and business ethics? Are they, or should they be the same?

⭐ 3-4. How can firms best ensure that their code of business ethics is read, understood, believed, remembered, and acted upon?

⭐ 3-5. Why is it important not to view the concept of "whistle blowing" as "tattle-telling" or "ratting" on another employee?

3-6. List six desired results of "ethics training programs," in terms of recommended business ethics policies or procedures in the firm.

3-7. Discuss bribes. Would actions like politicians adding earmarks in legislation or pharmaceutical salespersons giving away drugs to physicians constitute bribery? Identify three business activities that would constitute bribery and three actions that would not.

3-8. How could a strategist's attitude toward social responsibility affect a firm's strategy? On a 1-to-10 scale, ranging from Nader's view to Friedman's view, what is your attitude toward social responsibility?

3-9. How do social policies on retirement differ in various countries around the world?

⭐ 3-10. Who is prone to be unethical in a business according to Donald Palmer's research?

⭐ 3-11. Given Donald Palmer's research, what should organizations do to help assure an ethical work environment?

3-12. According to Barnett and Salomon, does it pay to be socially responsible? Discuss with specifics from the chapter.

ASSURANCE OF LEARNING EXERCISES

EXERCISE 3A
Sustainability and Nestlé

Purpose

Headquartered in Vevey, Switzerland, Nestlé is the largest food company in the world measured by revenues. Nestlé has hundreds of products that include cereals, coffee, dairy products, pet foods, snacks, baby food, and bottled water. Thirty of Nestlé's brands have annual sales of over 1 billion Swiss francs (about $1.1 billion), including Nespresso, Nescafé, Kit Kat, Smarties, Nesquick, Stouffers, Vittel, and Maggi. Nestlé has around 450 factories, operates in 86 countries, and employs around 328,000 people. Sustainability reports are increasingly becoming expected or even required by business organizations. This exercise can give you practice in evaluating a company's sustainability efforts. At the company's website, read about the three key sustainability areas that the firm engages in: Nutrition, CSV-Water, and Rural Development.

Instructions

Step 1   Conduct research to evaluate and determine the six best aspects of Nestlé's sustainability efforts.

Step 2   Evaluate and analyze the sustainability efforts of competitors Danone (stock symbol DANOY) and Mondelēz International, Inc. (stock symbol = MDLZ).

Step 3   Prepare a report for the class giving your assessment of Nestlé's sustainability work versus rival firms Danone and Mondelēz International, Inc.

EXERCISE 3B
How Does My Municipality Compare to Others on Being Pollution-Safe?

Purpose

Sometimes it is difficult to know how safe a particular municipality or county is regarding industrial and agricultural pollutants. A website that provides consumers and businesses excellent information in this regard is http://scorecard.goodguide.com. This type information is often used in assessing where to locate new business operations.

Instructions

Step 1   Go to http://scorecard.goodguide.com/. Put in your zip code. Print off the information available for your city/county regarding pollutants.

Step 2   Prepare a comparative analysis of your municipality versus state and national norms on pollution issues. Does your locale receive an A, B, C, D, or F?

EXERCISE 3C
Compare Nestlé versus Mars, Inc. on Social Responsibility

Purpose

This exercise aims to familiarize you with corporate social responsibility programs.

Instructions

Step 1   Go to Nestlé's Code of Business Conduct which is provided at the corporate website by clicking on About Us and then click on Business Principles.

Step 2   Go to Mars' corporate website at, visit the "about mars" page, and read about the Five Principles of Mars.

Step 3   Compare Nestlé's business ethics and social responsibility efforts with those of Mars, Inc. Summarize your findings in a three-page report for your professor.

EXERCISE 3D
How Do You Rate Nestlé's Sustainability Efforts?

Purpose

This exercise aims to familiarize you with corporate sustainability programs.

Instructions

Step 1   Go to www.nestle.com and click on Environmental Sustainability down the left column. Review the sustainability information in this section of the website.

Step 2   On a separate sheet of paper, list five aspects that you like most and five aspects that you like least about Nestlé's environmental sustainability efforts.

Step 3   Provide a two-page executive summary of your assessment of Nestlé's sustainability efforts.

EXERCISE 3E
The Ethics of Spying on Competitors

Purpose

This exercise gives you an opportunity to discuss in class ethical and legal issues related to methods being used by many companies to spy on competing firms. Gathering and using information about competitors is an area of strategic management that Japanese firms do more proficiently than American firms.

Instructions

On a separate sheet of paper, write down numbers 1 to 18. For the 18 spying activities that follow, indicate whether or not you believe the activity is ethical or unethical and legal or illegal. Place either an *E* for ethical or *U* for unethical, and either an *L* for legal or an *l* for illegal for each activity. Compare your answers to those of your classmates and discuss any differences.

1. Buying competitors' garbage
2. Dissecting competitors' products
3. Taking competitors' plant tours anonymously
4. Counting tractor-trailer trucks leaving competitors' loading bays
5. Studying aerial photographs of competitors' facilities
6. Analyzing competitors' labor contracts
7. Analyzing competitors' help-wanted ads
8. Quizzing customers and buyers about the sales of competitors' products
9. Infiltrating customers' and competitors' business operations
10. Quizzing suppliers about competitors' level of manufacturing
11. Using customers to buy out phony bids
12. Encouraging key customers to reveal competitive information
13. Quizzing competitors' former employees
14. Interviewing consultants who may have worked with competitors
15. Hiring key managers away from competitors
16. Conducting phony job interviews to get competitors' employees to reveal information
17. Sending engineers to trade meetings to quiz competitors' technical employees
18. Quizzing potential employees who worked for or with competitors

HOW ETHICAL AND SUSTAINABLE IS ETIHAD AIRWAYS?

Source: © Lucky Business. Shutterstock

Headquartered in Khalifa City, Abu Dhabi, Etihad Airways is the second-largest airline of the United Arab Emirates (UAE). Operating more than 1,000 flights every week to destinations in the Middle East, Africa, Europe, Asia, Australia, and the Americas, Etihad has a fleet of 119 aircrafts since August, 2015. Apart from transporting passengers, Etihad also operates Etihad Holidays and Etihad Cargo and recently established its own airline alliance, *Etihad Airways Partners,* which includes Alitalia, Jet Airways, Airberin, Niki, Air Serbia, Air Seychelles, and Etihad Regional. Booking for these airlines is consolidated under one network.

In August 2015, Etihad Airways received two awards for "Best Sustainability Communication Program" and "Sustainability Manager of the Year" at the Abu Dhabi Sustainability Group's (ADSG) award ceremony. ADSG is focused on promoting sustainability management in Abu Dhabi through learning and knowledge-sharing opportunities provided to the government, private companies, and not-for-profit organizations. Having strategically worked towards sustainability, Etihad Airways received an award for its "BIOjet: Flight Path to Sustainability" program and its Head of Sustainability, Linden Coppell, won the award for Sustainability Manager of the Year.

Questions

1. At the Etihad website, click on About Us section, go through its Corporate Responsibility section, and evaluate Etihad's record on sustainability and business ethics.
2. Visit Etihad's corporate profile on the website, scroll down to the Executive Team and click on it. You will be able to view the pictures of Etihad's nine top executives. There are no women. Explain whether you think this represents an ethical issue or not.

Source: Based on company documents.

Current Readings

Barnett, Michael L. "Why Stakeholders Ignore Firm Misconduct: A Cognitive View." *Journal of Management* 40, no. 3 (2014): 676–702.

Hanson, William R., and Jeffrey R. Moore, "Business Student Moral Influencers: Unseen Opportunities for Development?" *Academy of Management Journal Learning and Education* 13 (December 2014): 525–546.

Hess, Megan F., and Earnest Broughton. "Fostering an Ethical Organization from the Bottom Up and the Outside In." *Business Horizons* (July 2014): 541–561.

Jones, David A., Chelsea R. Willness, and Sarah Madey. "Why Are Job Seekers Attracted by Corporate Social Performance? Experimental and Field Tests of Three Signal-Based Mechanisms." *Academy of Management Journal* 57, no. 2 (2014): 383–404.

Lubin, David A., and Daniel C. Esty. "Bridging the Sustainability Gap." *MIT Sloan Management Review* 55, no. 4 (2014): 18–21.

Paine, Lynn S. "Sustainability in the Boardroom." *Harvard Business Review* 92, no. 7/8 (2014): 86–94.

Perrott, Bruce E. "Building the Sustainable Organization: An Integrated Approach." *Journal of Business Strategy* 36, no. 1 (2015): 41–51.

Rangan, Kasturi, Lisa Chase, and Sohel Karim. "The Truth about CSR." *Harvard Business Review* (January–February 2015).

Reilly, Anne H., and Katherine A. Hynan. "Corporate Communication, Sustainability, and Social Media: It's Not Easy (Really) Being Green," *Business Horizons* 57, no. 6 (January–February 2015): 747–758.

Scott, Brent A., Adela S. Garza, Donald E. Conlon, and You Jin Kim. "Why Do Managers Act Fairly in the First Place? A Daily Investigation of "Hot" and "Cold" Motives and Discretion," *Academy of Management Journal,* December 1, 2014, vol. 47, no. 6, pp. 1571–1591.

Sonenshein, Scott, Katherine A., Decelles, and Jane E. Dutton. "It's Not Easy Being Green: The Role of Self-Evaluations in Explaining Support of Environmental Issues." *Academy of Management Journal* 57, no. 1 (2014): 7–37.

Unruh, Gregory. "The Sweet Spot of Sustainability Strategy." *MIT Sloan Management Review* 55, no. 1 (2013): 16–19.

Washburn, Nathan T., and Donald Lange. "Does Your Company Seem Socially Irresponsible?" *MIT Sloan Management Review* 55, no. 1 (2013): 10–11.

Endnotes

1. http://www.usatoday.com/money/companies/management/story/2012-05-14/ceo-firings/54964476/1

2. Joann Greco, "Privacy—Whose Right Is It Anyhow?" *Journal of Business Strategy* (January–February 2001): 32.

3. Ashby Jones and JoAnn Lublin, "New Law Prompts Blowing Whistle," *Wall Street Journal*, November 1, 2010, B1.

4. Saul Gellerman, "Why 'Good' Managers Make Bad Ethical Choices," *Harvard Business Review* 64, no. 4 (July–August 1986): 88.

5. www.wikipedia.org

6. Joe Palazzolo and Christopher Matthews, "Bribery Law Do's and Don'ts," *Wall Street Journal* (November 15, 2012): B1.

7. http://www.businessknowhow.com/manage/romance.htm

8. Elizabeth Bernstein "The New Rules of Flirting," *Wall Street Journal*, November 13, 2012, D1.

9. Phred Dvorak, Bob Davis, and Louise Radnofsky, "Firms Confront Boss-Subordinate Love Affairs," *Wall Street Journal*, October 27, 2008, B5.

10. Spencer Morgan, "The End of the Office Affair," *Bloomberg Businessweek*, September 20–26, 2010, 74.

11. Archie Carroll and Frank Hoy, "Integrating Corporate Social Policy into Strategic Management," *Journal of Business Strategy* 4, no. 3 (Winter 1984): 57.

12. Kerry Hannon, "Businesses' Green Opportunities Are Wide, But Complex," *USA Today*, January 2, 2009, 5B.

13. Adapted from the www.iso14000.com website and the www.epa.gov website.

14. Ana Campoy, "Crushing Illegal Ivory Trade," *Wall Street Journal,* November 15, 2013, p. A3. See also, Dinny McMahon, "Chinese Officials Destroy Tons of Illegal Ivory," *Wall Street Journal,* January 7, 2014, p. A10.

15. Zusha Elinson, "Shark-Fin Bans Hard to Police," *Wall Street Journal*, February 25, 2014, A3.

16. Tom Brook, "Declining Numbers Mute Many Birds' Songs," *USA Today*, September 11, 2001, 4A.

17. John Ogden, "Maintaining Diversity in the Oceans," *Environment*, April 2001, 29–36.

18. Based on Sarah Nassauer, "Wal-Mart: Food Suppliers Must Treat Animals Better," *Wall Street Journal,* May 23–24, 2015, p. B3.

Source: © Bruder Jakob/Fotolia

Types of Strategies

LEARNING OBJECTIVES

After studying this chapter, you should be able to do the following:

4-1. Identify and discuss eight characteristics of objectives and ten benefits of having clear objectives.

4-2. Define and give an example of eleven types of strategies.

4-3. Identify and discuss the three types of "Integration Strategies."

4-4. Give specific guidelines when market penetration, market development, and product development are especially effective strategies.

4-5. Explain when diversification is an effective business strategy.

4-6. List guidelines for when retrenchment, divestiture, and liquidation are especially effective strategies.

4-7. Identify and discuss Porter's five generic strategies.

4-8. Compare (a) cooperation among competitors, (b) joint venture and partnering, and (c) merger/acquisition as key means for achieving strategies.

4-9. Discuss tactics to facilitate strategies, such as (a) being a first mover, (b) outsourcing, and (c) reshoring.

4-10. Explain how strategic planning differs in for-profit, not-for-profit, and small firms.

ASSURANCE OF LEARNING EXERCISES

The following exercises are found at the end of this chapter:

Hundreds of companies today have embraced strategic planning in their quest for higher revenues and profits. Kent Nelson, former chair of UPS, explains why his company created a new strategic-planning department: "Because we're making bigger bets on investments in technology, we can't afford to spend a whole lot of money in one direction and then find out five years later it was the wrong direction."[1]

This chapter brings strategic management to life with many contemporary examples. Sixteen types of strategies are defined and exemplified, including Michael Porter's generic strategies: cost leadership, differentiation, and focus. Guidelines are presented for determining when each strategy is most appropriate to pursue. An overview of strategic management in nonprofit organizations, governmental agencies, and small firms is provided. As showcased next, Petronas is an example company that for many years has exemplified excellent strategic management, especially through its Upstream and Downstream business focus.

Long-Term Objectives

Long-term objectives represent the results expected from pursuing certain strategies. Strategies represent the actions to be taken to accomplish long-term objectives. The time frame for objectives and strategies should be consistent, usually from 2 to 5 years. Without long-term objectives, an organization would drift aimlessly toward some unknown end. It is hard to imagine an organization or an individual being successful without clear objectives. You probably have worked hard the last few years striving to achieve an objective to graduate with a business degree. Success only rarely occurs by accident; rather, it is the result of hard work directed toward achieving certain objectives.

Long-term objectives are needed at the corporate, divisional, and functional levels of an organization. They are an important measure of managerial performance. Many practitioners and academicians attribute a significant part of U.S. industry's competitive decline to the short-term, rather than long-term, strategy orientation of managers in the United States. Arthur D. Little argues that bonuses or merit pay for managers today must be based to a greater extent on long-term objectives and strategies. An example framework for relating objectives to performance

---

PETRONAS (PGAS.KL)

Established in 1974, Petroliam Nasional Berhad (PETRONAS), headquartered in Kuala Lumpur, Malaysia, is an integrated oil and gas multinational company. Responsible for the national oil and gas resources, PETRONAS explores, develops, and produces these resources and delivers energy to meet the country's growing demands. The only Malaysian company to feature in the Fortune Global 500 list, it operates in over 35 countries and is engaged in a wide spectrum of petroleum activities. Its Upstream business explores, produces, and monetizes oil and gas resources, and its Downstream business focuses on marketing and distribution strategies to enhance the value of resources. Its successful management of legal and maintenance activities in 2014 enabled PETRONAS to shift its focus to raising utilization rate by 5 percent in 2015. In 2014, while profit decreased by 27 percent, the group saw a 4 percent growth in revenue, which was driven by higher production, higher liquefied natural gas (LNG) sales volume, and favorable U.S. Dollar exchange rate movement. Revenue derived from PETRONAS provides roughly 45 percent of the Malaysian government's annual budget.

Taking advantage of being an integrated chain and its strategic location in South East Asia, a region with fast growing chemical consumers, it is focusing on three long-term objectives— operational excellence, marketing and sales excellence, and innovation excellence. As part of its strategies, PETRONAS is pursuing backward integration by purchasing its ships to transport its oil and gas, especially its LNG. This will provide low cost, direct access to LNG shipping capacity. PETRONAS, operating the world's first floating LNG facility, is also in the process of constructing one of the largest LNG facilities in British Columbia.

Source: Based on company documents.

TABLE 4-1 Varying Performance Measures by Organizational Level

Organizational Level	Basis for Annual Bonus or Merit Pay
Corporate	75% based on long-term objectives
	25% based on annual objectives
Division	50% based on long-term objectives
	50% based on annual objectives
Function	25% based on long-term objectives
	75% based on annual objectives

evaluation is provided in Table 4-1. A particular organization could tailor these guidelines to meet its own needs, but incentives should be attached to both long-term and annual objectives.

Characteristics and Benefits of Objectives

Objectives should be quantitative, measurable, realistic, understandable, challenging, hierarchical, obtainable, and congruent among organizational units. Each objective should also be associated with a timeline. Objectives are commonly stated in terms such as *growth in assets, growth in sales, profitability, market share, degree and nature of diversification, degree and nature of vertical integration, earnings per share*, and *social responsibility*. Clearly established objectives offer many benefits. They provide direction, allow synergy, assist in evaluation, establish priorities, reduce uncertainty, minimize conflicts, stimulate exertion, and aid in both the allocation of resources and the design of jobs. Objectives provide a basis for consistent decision making by managers whose values and attitudes differ. Objectives serve as standards by which individuals, groups, departments, divisions, and entire organizations can be evaluated.

Table 4-2 reveals the desired characteristics of objectives, and Table 4-3 summarizes the benefits of having clear objectives.

Financial versus Strategic Objectives

Two types of objectives are especially common in organizations: financial and strategic objectives. **Financial objectives** include those associated with growth in revenues, growth in earnings, higher dividends, larger profit margins, greater return on investment, higher earnings per share, a rising stock price, improved cash flow, and so on; whereas **strategic objectives** include things such as a larger market share, quicker on-time delivery than rivals, shorter design-to-market times than rivals, lower costs than rivals, higher product quality than rivals, wider geographic coverage than rivals, achieving technological leadership, consistently getting new or improved products to market ahead of rivals, and so on.

Although financial objectives are especially important in firms, oftentimes there is a trade-off between financial and strategic objectives such that crucial decisions have to be made. For example, a firm can do certain things to maximize short-term financial objectives that would harm long-term strategic objectives. To improve financial position in the short run through higher

TABLE 4-2 Eight Desired Characteristics of Objectives

1. Quantitative
2. Measurable
3. Realistic
4. Understandable
5. Challenging
6. Hierarchical
7. Obtainable
8. Congruent across departments

TABLE 4-3 Ten Benefits of Having Clear Objectives

1. Provide direction by revealing expectations
2. Allow synergy
3. Assist in evaluation by serving as standards
4. Establish priorities
5. Reduce uncertainty
6. Minimize conflicts
7. Stimulate exertion
8. Aid in allocation of resources
9. Aid in design of jobs
10. Provide basis for consistent decision making

prices may, for example, jeopardize long-term market share. The dangers associated with trading off long-term strategic objectives with near-term bottom-line performance are especially severe if competitors relentlessly pursue increased market share at the expense of short-term profitability. Amazon, for example, went many years operating without profits but gaining market share. And there are other trade-offs between financial and strategic objectives, related to riskiness of actions, concern for business ethics, the need to preserve the natural environment, and social responsibility issues. Both financial and strategic objectives should include both annual and long-term performance targets. Ultimately, the best way to sustain competitive advantage over the long run is to relentlessly pursue strategic objectives that strengthen a firm's business position over rivals. Financial objectives can best be met by focusing first and foremost on achieving strategic objectives that improve a firm's competitiveness and market strength.

Avoid Not Managing by Objectives

Mr. Derek Bok, former President of Harvard University, once said, "If you think education is expensive, try ignorance." The idea behind this saying also applies to establishing objectives, because strategists should avoid the following ways of "not managing by objectives."

- *Managing by Extrapolation* —Adheres to the principle "If it ain't broke, don't fix it." The idea is to keep on doing the same things in the same ways because things are going well.
- *Managing by Crisis* —Based on the belief that the true measure of a really good strategist is the ability to solve problems. Because there are plenty of crises and problems to go around for every person and organization, strategists ought to bring their time and creative energy to bear on solving the most pressing problems of the day. Managing by crisis is actually a form of reacting, letting events dictate the *what* and *when* of management decisions.
- *Managing by Subjectives* —Built on the idea that there is no general plan for which way to go and what to do; just do the best you can to accomplish what you think should be done. In short, "Do your own thing, the best way you know how" (sometimes referred to as *the mystery approach to decision making* because subordinates are left to figure out what is happening and why).
- *Managing by Hope* —Based on the fact that the future is laden with great uncertainty and that if we try and do not succeed, then we hope our second (or third) attempt will succeed. Decisions are predicated on the hope that they will work and that good times are just around the corner, especially if luck and good fortune are on our side![2]

Types of Strategies

The model illustrated in Figure 4-1 provides a conceptual basis for applying strategic management. Defined and exemplified in Table 4-4, alternative strategies that an enterprise could pursue can be categorized into 11 actions: forward integration, backward integration, horizontal integration, market penetration, market development, product development, related diversification,

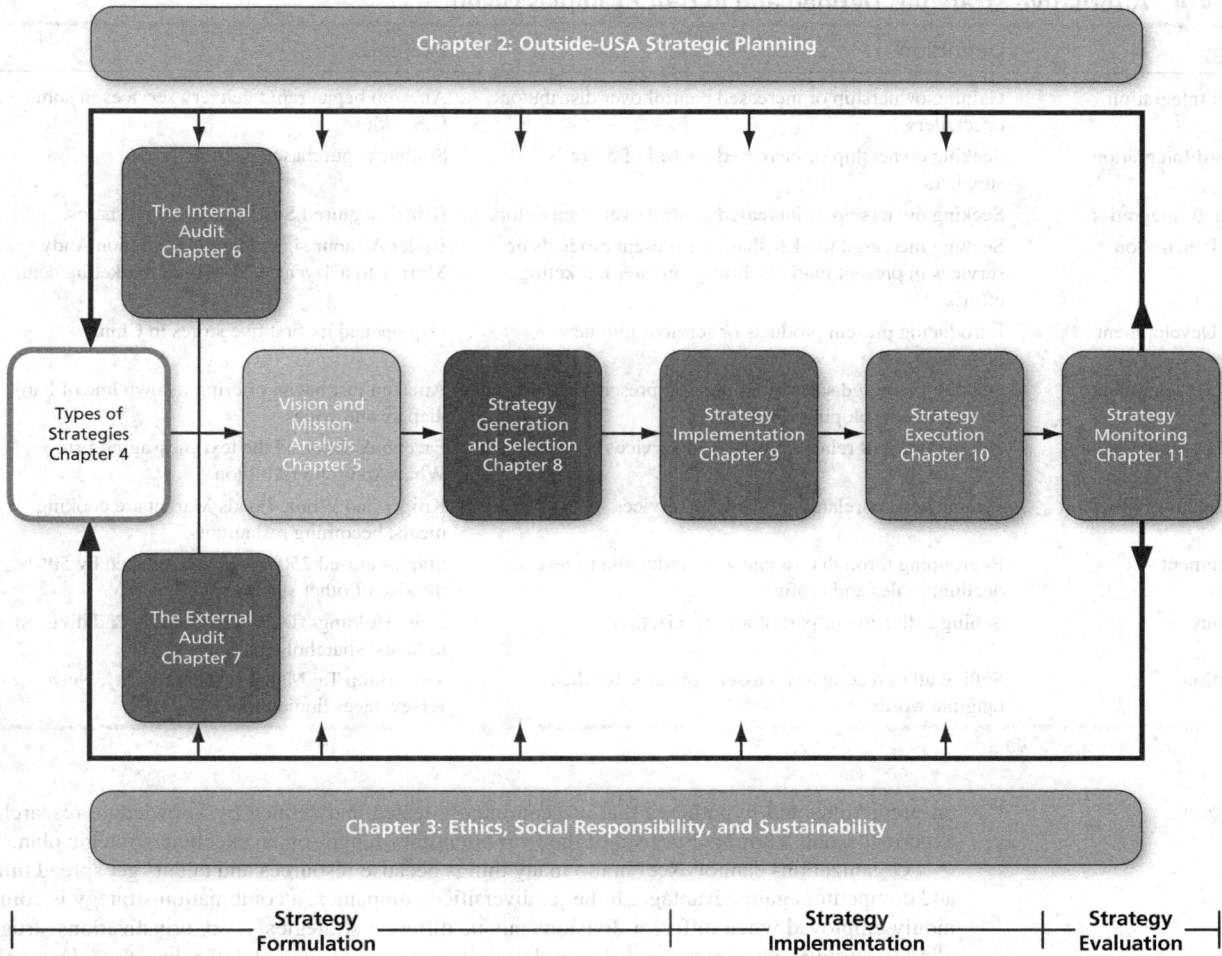

FIGURE 4-1

A Comprehensive Strategic-Management Model

Source: Fred R. David, adapted from "How Companies Define Their Mission," *Long Range Planning* 22, no. 3 (June 1988): 40, © Fred R. David.

unrelated diversification, retrenchment, divestiture, and liquidation. Each alternative strategy has countless variations. For example, market penetration can include adding salespersons, increasing advertising expenditures, couponing, and using similar actions to increase market share in a given geographic area.

Most organizations simultaneously pursue a combination of two or more strategies, but a **combination strategy** can be exceptionally risky if carried too far. No organization can afford to pursue all the strategies that might benefit the firm. Difficult decisions must be made. Priorities must be established. Organizations, like individuals, have limited resources. Both organizations and individuals must choose among alternative strategies and avoid excessive indebtedness.

Hansen and Smith explain that strategic planning involves "choices that risk resources and trade-offs that sacrifice opportunity." In other words, if you have a strategy to go north, then you must buy snowshoes and warm jackets (spend resources) and forgo the opportunity of "faster population growth in southern states." You cannot have a strategy to go north and then take a step east, south, or west "just to be on the safe side." Firms spend resources and focus on a finite number of opportunities in pursuing strategies to achieve an uncertain outcome in the future. Strategic planning is much more than a roll of the dice; it is an educated wager based

TABLE 4-4 Alternative Strategies Defined and Recent Examples Given

Strategy	Definition	Example
Forward Integration	Gaining ownership or increased control over distributors or retailers	Amazon began rapid delivery services in some U.S. cities.
Backward Integration	Seeking ownership or increased control of a firm's suppliers	Starbucks purchased a coffee farm.
Horizontal Integration	Seeking ownership or increased control over competitors	BB&T acquired Susquehanna Bancshares.
Market Penetration	Seeking increased market share for present products or services in present markets through greater marketing efforts	Under Armour signed tennis champion Andy Murray to a 4-year, $23 million marketing deal.
Market Development	Introducing present products or services into new geographic area	Gap opened its first five stores in China.
Product Development	Seeking increased sales by improving present products or services or developing new ones	Amazon just began offering its own line of baby diapers and wipes.
Related Diversification	Adding new but related products or services	Facebook acquired the text-messaging firm WhatsApp for $19 billion.
Unrelated Diversification	Adding new, unrelated products or services	Kroger and Whole Foods Market are cooking meals, becoming restaurants.
Retrenchment	Regrouping through cost and asset reduction to reverse declining sales and profit	Staples closed 250 stores and reduced by 50% the size of other stores.
Divestiture	Selling a division or part of an organization	Sears Holdings divested its Land's End division to Sears' shareholders.
Liquidation	Selling all of a company's assets, in parts, for their tangible worth	The Trump Taj Mahal in Atlantic City, New Jersey, faces liquidation.

on predictions and hypotheses that are continually tested and refined by knowledge, research, experience, and learning. Survival of the firm oftentimes hinges on an excellent strategic plan.[3]

Organizations cannot excel in too many things because resources and talents get spread thin and competitors gain advantage. In large, diversified companies, a combination strategy is commonly employed when different divisions pursue different strategies. Also, organizations struggling to survive may simultaneously employ a combination of several defensive strategies, such as divestiture, liquidation, and retrenchment.

Levels of Strategies

Strategy making is not just a task for top executives. Middle- and lower-level managers also must be involved in the strategic-planning process to the extent possible. In large firms, there are actually four levels of strategies: corporate, divisional, functional, and operational—as illustrated in Figure 4-2. However, in small firms, there are three levels of strategies: company, functional, and operational.

The persons primarily responsible for having effective strategies at the various levels include the CEO or business owner at the corporate level; the president or executive vice president at the divisional level; the chief finance officer (CFO), chief information officer (CIO), human resource manager (HRM), chief marketing officer (CMO), and so on at the functional level; and the plant manager, regional sales manager, and so on at the operational level. It is important that all managers at all levels participate and understand the firm's strategic plan to help ensure coordination, facilitation, and commitment, while avoiding inconsistency, inefficiency, and miscommunication.

Integration Strategies

Forward integration and backward integration are sometimes collectively referred to as **vertical integration**. Vertical integration strategies allow a firm to gain control over distributors and suppliers, whereas **horizontal integration** refers to gaining ownership and/or control over competitors. Vertical and horizontal actions by firms are broadly referred to as **integration strategies**.

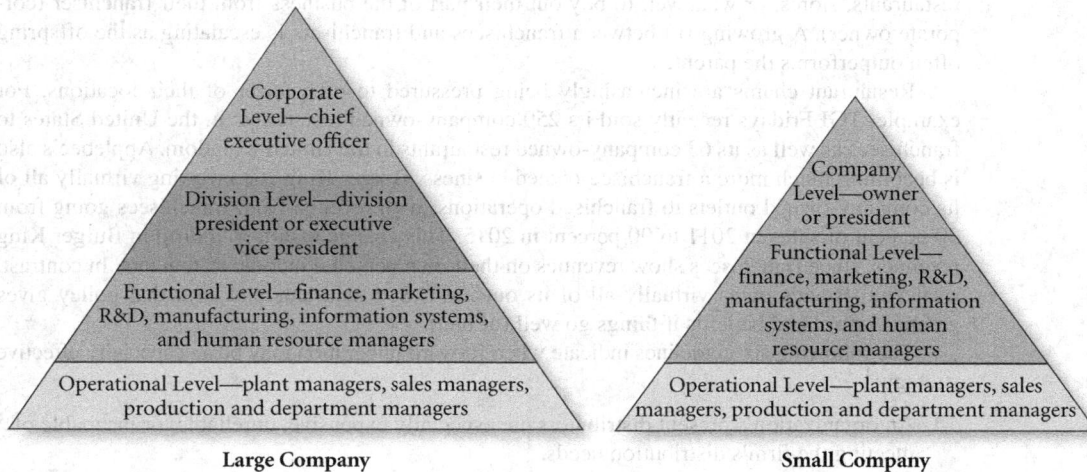

FIGURE 4-2
Levels of Strategies with Persons Most Responsible

Forward Integration

Forward integration involves gaining ownership or increased control over distributors or retailers. Increasing numbers of manufacturers (suppliers) are pursuing a forward integration strategy by establishing websites to sell their products directly to consumers.

In a forward integration move, Coca-Cola recently signed a 10-year partnership with Green Mountain Coffee Roasters, maker of the Keurig single-serve coffeemaker, to offer for the first time a Coca-Cola drink through a K-Cup. Coca-Cola thus plans to sell Coke through the at-home beverage system Keurig K-Cup. With the partnership, Coca-Cola also acquired 10 percent of the Green Mountain company for about $1.25 billion. Green Mountain now has a similar partnership with Campbell Soup to brew a cup of chicken broth in a K-Cup.

Based in Cincinnati and having more than 2,600 grocery stores, Kroger recently acquired Viatcost.com to expand its push into online groceries, partly so as not to concede the same-day food delivery market to Amazon.com. FedEx and UPS are both using forward integration, paying the United States Post Office (USPS) to ship their packages. Today, USPS delivers about 2.5 million packages daily for FedEx, or about one third of FedEx's express-mail U.S.-bound mailings.

Amazon is forward integrating into the "installation business." When you buy, for example, a ceiling fan or car stereo from Amazon, the company now wants to install it for you for a fee—at least in three cities (Los Angeles, New York, and Seattle). Amazon's new program is called Amazon Local Services and is another step by the company to erode brick-and-mortar's 90 percent market share of retail sales in the United States. In addition, Amazon is developing a new mobile application that recruits and pays ordinary people to be carriers of packages as they travel, doing away with the need for FedEx, UPS, and even the United States Postal Service. This new Amazon forward integration strategy is known as "On My Way" and is still being tested to resolve potential issues such as what happens if the package is damaged, or even stolen, by the transporter.

Taco Bell also wants to ring your doorbell and deliver you the goods. Fast food delivery is already a strategy at some rival firms, such as Jimmy John's sandwich shop; Burger King has been offering delivery in select markets for a couple of years now; Starbucks is testing delivery.

An effective means of implementing forward integration is **franchising**. Approximately 2,000 companies in about 50 different industries in the United States use franchising to distribute their products or services. Businesses can expand rapidly by franchising because costs and opportunities are spread among many individuals. Total sales by franchises in the United States are annually about $1 trillion. There are about 800,000 franchise businesses in the United States. However, a growing trend is for franchisees, who, for example, may operate 10 franchised restaurants, stores, or whatever, to buy out their part of the business from their franchiser (corporate owner). A growing rift between franchisees and franchisers is escalating as the offspring often outperforms the parent.

Restaurant chains are increasingly being pressured to own fewer of their locations. For example, TGI Fridays recently sold its 250 company-owned restaurants in the United States to franchisees as well as its 63 company-owned restaurants in the United Kingdom. Applebee's also is becoming much more a franchisee-owned business. Burger King is converting virtually all of its company-owned outlets to franchised operations, with revenue from franchisees going from 30 percent of sales in 2011 to 90 percent in 2015. This change results in a drop in Burger King revenues, since franchisees show revenues on their own personal income statements. In contrast, rival Yum Brands owns virtually all of its outside-U.S. restaurants and says that policy gives greater control and benefits if things go well (or bad).

The following six guidelines indicate when forward integration may be an especially effective strategy:[4]

1. An organization's present distributors are especially expensive, unreliable, or incapable of meeting the firm's distribution needs.
2. The availability of quality distributors is so limited as to offer a competitive advantage to those firms that promote forward integration.
3. An organization competes in an industry that is growing and is expected to continue to grow markedly; this is a factor because forward integration reduces an organization's ability to diversify if its basic industry falters.
4. An organization has both the capital and human resources needed to manage the new business of distributing its own products.
5. The advantages of stable production are particularly high; this is a consideration because an organization can increase the predictability of the demand for its output through forward integration.
6. Present distributors or retailers have high profit margins; this situation suggests that a company could profitably distribute its own products and price them more competitively by integrating forward.

Backward Integration

Backward integration is a strategy of seeking ownership or increased control of a firm's suppliers. This strategy can be especially appropriate when a firm's current suppliers are unreliable, too costly, or cannot meet the firm's needs. Starbucks recently purchased its first coffee farm—a 600-acre property in Costa Rica. This backward integration strategy was utilized primarily to develop new coffee varieties and to test methods to combat a fungal disease known as coffee rust that plagues the industry. Manufacturers as well as retailers purchase needed materials from suppliers.

The huge wine and beer producer, Constellation Brands, recently purchased several glass-bottle factories after experiencing problems with several suppliers of their bottles. Constellation acquired a controlling interest in a Mexican Anheuser-Busch glass-bottle factory, giving Constellation ownership now of more than 50 percent of the glass bottles it uses.

Some industries, such as automotive and aluminum producers, are reducing their historical pursuit of backward integration. Instead of owning their suppliers, companies negotiate with several outside suppliers. Ford and Chrysler buy more than half of their component parts from outside suppliers such as TRW, Eaton, General Electric (GE), and Johnson Controls. **De-integration** makes sense in industries that have global sources of supply. Companies today shop around, play one seller against another, and go with the best deal. Global competition is also spurring firms to reduce their number of suppliers and to demand higher levels of service and quality from those they keep. Although traditionally relying on many suppliers to ensure uninterrupted supplies and low prices, many U.S. firms now are following the lead of Japanese firms, which have far fewer suppliers and closer, long-term relationships with those few. "Keeping track of so many suppliers is onerous," said Mark Shimelonis, formerly of Xerox.

Seven guidelines when backward integration may be an especially effective strategy are:[5]

1. An organization's present suppliers are especially expensive, unreliable, or incapable of meeting the firm's needs for parts, components, assemblies, or raw materials.

2. The number of suppliers is small and the number of competitors is large.
3. An organization competes in an industry that is growing rapidly; this is a factor because integrative-type strategies (forward, backward, and horizontal) reduce an organization's ability to diversify in a declining industry.
4. An organization has both capital and human resources to manage the new business of supplying its own raw materials.
5. The advantages of stable prices are particularly important; this is a factor because an organization can stabilize the cost of its raw materials and the associated price of its product(s) through backward integration.
6. Present suppliers have high profit margins, which suggest that the business of supplying products or services in a given industry is a worthwhile venture.
7. An organization needs to quickly acquire a needed resource.

Horizontal Integration

Seeking ownership of or control over a firm's competitors, horizontal integration is arguably the most common growth strategy. Thousands of mergers, acquisitions, and takeovers among competitors are consummated annually. Nearly all these transactions aim for increased economies of scale and enhanced transfer of resources and competencies. Kenneth Davidson makes the following observation about horizontal integration:

> The trend towards horizontal integration seems to reflect strategists' misgivings about their ability to operate many unrelated businesses. Mergers between direct competitors are more likely to create efficiencies than mergers between unrelated businesses, both because there is a greater potential for eliminating duplicate facilities and because the management of the acquiring firm is more likely to understand the business of the target.[6]

In the cigarette industry, Reynolds American recently acquired Lorillard for $25 billion. The merger combined Reynolds' Pall Mall and Camel brands (with 8.1 percent market share each in the United States) with Lorillard's Newport brand (with 12.2 market share) to combat industry leader Altria's Marlboro brand that commands 40.2 percent market share in the United States. As part of the transaction, to combat antitrust concerns, Reynolds CEO Susan Cameron said her company will divest Lorillard's Blu e-cigarette to Imperial Tobacco (another rival firm), while keeping and growing Reynolds' Vuse e-cigarette. Reynolds also divested its Kool, Winston, Salem, and Maverick brands to Imperial.

Both Dollar General and Dollar Tree recently competed for months to acquire Family Dollar. The winner, Dollar Tree, is reducing prices and converting Family Dollar stores into bright, clean, friendly places. Dollar Tree still sells more items for a dollar or less, whereas Family Dollar sells more branded merchandise. About 5,000 Dollar Tree stores and 8,300 Family Dollar stores now compete with industry leader Dollar General's 11,500 stores.

Charter Communications (CHTR) recently acquired (1) Time Warner Cable (TWC) for $55.33 billion and (2) Bright House Networks for $10.4 billion, creating a giant U.S. TV and Internet firm. The new Charter has nearly 24 million customers, below the leader Comcast's (CMCSK) 27.2 million customers. Comcast owns NBCUniversal. Charter also lags AT&T (T), whose recent merger with DirecTV (DTV) gave AT&T 26.4 million TV customers and 16.1 million fixed Internet customers, as well as tens of millions of wireless customers. Several major factors are spurring horizontal integration in the TV and Internet business, including that cable providers are rapidly losing TV subscribers, and pressure from online video services such as Netflix (NFLX), Hulu, and Amazon is increasing dramatically.

The following five guidelines indicate when horizontal integration may be an especially effective strategy:[7]

1. An organization can gain monopolistic characteristics in a particular area or region without being challenged by the federal government for "tending substantially" to reduce competition.
2. An organization competes in a growing industry.
3. Increased economies of scale provide major competitive advantages.
4. An organization has both the capital and human talent needed to successfully manage an expanded organization.

5. Competitors are faltering as a result of a lack of managerial expertise or a need for particular resources that an organization possesses; note that horizontal integration would not be appropriate if competitors are doing poorly because in that case overall industry sales are declining.

Intensive Strategies

Market penetration, market development, and product development are sometimes referred to as **intensive strategies** because they require intensive efforts if a firm's competitive position with existing products is to improve.

Market Penetration

A **market penetration** strategy seeks to increase market share for present products or services in present markets through greater marketing efforts. This strategy is widely used alone and in combination with other strategies. Market penetration includes increasing the number of salespersons, increasing advertising expenditures, offering extensive sales promotion items, or increasing publicity efforts. For example, Anheuser annually purchases several $4.5+ million, 30-second advertising slots during the Super Bowl.

Tiffany & Co. recently began using same-sex couples in advertising, preceded by J. Crew casting one of its designers and his boyfriend in a catalogue. Gap uses a handsome couple in a billboard, and Jeremiah Brent and Nate Berkus appear in a Banana Republic advertising campaign.

The following five guidelines indicate when market penetration may be an especially effective strategy:[8]

1. Current markets are not saturated with a particular product or service.
2. The usage rate of present customers could be increased significantly.
3. The market shares of major competitors have been declining while total industry sales have been increasing.
4. The correlation between dollar sales and dollar marketing expenditures historically has been high.
5. Increased economies of scale provide major competitive advantages.

Market Development

Market development involves introducing present products or services into new geographic areas. For example, Whirlpool recently acquired Indesit, an Italian company that sells appliances, in order to double Whirlpool's size in Europe, where the company has struggled to compete against Electrolux AB of Sweden, LG Electronics Inc. of South Korea, and Haier Group of China. Indesit had 13 percent of the major appliance market share in eastern Europe and Whirlpool had 5 percent, so now 18 percent of the major appliances sold in eastern Europe are Whirlpool. In western Europe, the Indesit acquisition gave Whirlpool a 17 percent market share behind the leader, BSH Bosch & Siemens Hausgerate GmbH's 20 percent.

The largest online video-streaming company, Netflix, recently launched it services into France, Germany, Belgium, and Switzerland, as well as eastern and southern Europe, and expects to be a global service provider by 2018. Netflix's major rival in Europe is Vivendi SA's pay-TV unit Canal Plus that offers Netflix-like services through its Canal Play services.

These six guidelines indicate when market development may be an especially effective strategy:[9]

1. New channels of distribution are available that are reliable, inexpensive, and of good quality.
2. An organization is successful at what it does.
3. New untapped or unsaturated markets exist.
4. An organization has the needed capital and human resources to manage expanded operations.
5. An organization has excess production capacity.
6. An organization's basic industry is rapidly becoming global in scope.

Product Development

Product development is a strategy that seeks increased sales by improving or modifying present products or services. Product development usually entails large research and development expenditures. Walt Disney Company recently developed a Disney Baby line of products and services that it expects to become a powerful baby brand for customers ages 0 to 2. Bob Chapek, president of Disney Consumer Products, stated, "This gives Disney the opportunity to reach out to moms when magical moments begin; there is no more special occasion than the birth of a baby."

The action camera company, GoPro, recently unveiled new high- and low-end cameras. GoPro is the leading producer of wearable and durable high-definition video cameras used by outdoor enthusiasts such as scuba divers and surfers. Based in San Mateo, California, GoPro's rival firms include Sony, Canon, Garmin, and Polaroid, but GoPro is doing great by selling products in more than 100 countries and through more than 25,000 retail outlets.

The new Apple Watch is actually a wrist-top computer, and now competes with various Android-powered devices from Motorola and Samsung Electronics. "Wearable computers" are good for the people to monitor their healthiness among countless other things. The firm Sensoria is making smart garments, including smart socks, which yes, are washable. Opportunities for product development strategies are endless, given rapid technological changes occurring daily.

These following five guidelines indicate when product development may be an especially effective strategy to pursue:[10]

1. An organization has successful products that are in the maturity stage of the product life cycle; the idea here is to attract satisfied customers to try new (improved) products as a result of their positive experience with the organization's present products or services.
2. An organization competes in an industry that is characterized by rapid technological developments.
3. Major competitors offer better-quality products at comparable prices.
4. An organization competes in a high-growth industry.
5. An organization has especially strong research and development capabilities.

Diversification Strategies

The two general types of **diversification strategies** are **related diversification** and **unrelated diversification**. Businesses are said to be *related* when their value chains possess competitively valuable cross-business strategic fits; businesses are said to be *unrelated* when their value chains are so dissimilar that no competitively valuable cross-business relationships exist.[11] Most companies favor related diversification strategies to capitalize on synergies as follows:

- Transferring competitively valuable expertise, technological know-how, or other capabilities from one business to another
- Combining the related activities of separate businesses into a single operation to achieve lower costs
- Exploiting common use of a well-known brand name
- Cross-business collaboration to create competitively valuable resource strengths and capabilities[12]

Diversification strategies are becoming less popular because organizations are finding it more difficult to manage diverse business activities. In the 1960s and 1970s, the trend was to diversify to avoid being dependent on any single industry, but the 1980s saw a general reversal of that thinking. Diversification is still on the retreat. Michael Porter, of the Harvard Business School, commented, "Management found it couldn't manage the beast." Businesses are still selling, closing, or spinning off less profitable or "different" divisions to focus on their core businesses. For example, ITT recently divided itself into three separate, specialized companies. At one time, ITT owned everything from Sheraton hotels and Hartford Insurance to the maker of Wonder Bread and Hostess Twinkies. About the ITT breakup, analyst Barry Knap said, "Companies generally are not very efficient diversifiers; investors usually can do a better job of that by purchasing stock in a variety of companies." Rapidly appearing new technologies, new products, and fast-shifting buyer preferences make diversification difficult.

Diversification must do more than simply spread business risks across different industries; after all, shareholders could accomplish this by simply purchasing equity in different firms across different industries or by investing in mutual funds. Diversification makes sense only to the extent that the strategy adds more to shareholder value than what shareholders could accomplish acting individually. Any industry chosen for diversification must be attractive enough to yield consistently high returns on investment and offer potential across the operating divisions for synergies greater than those entities could achieve alone. Many strategists contend that firms should "stick to the knitting" and not stray too far from the firms' basic areas of competence.

A few companies today, however, pride themselves on being conglomerates, from small firms such as Pentair Inc. and Blount International to huge companies such as Textron, Berkshire Hathaway, Allied Signal, Emerson Electric, GE, Viacom, Amazon, Google, Disney, and Samsung. Conglomerates prove that focus and diversity are not always mutually exclusive. In an unattractive industry, for example, diversification makes sense, such as for Philip Morris, because cigarette consumption is declining, product liability suits are a risk, and some investors reject tobacco stocks on principle.

Related Diversification

Alcoa recently diversified further into the jet-engine parts industry by acquiring Firth Rixson Ltd. for nearly $3 billion. The move away from total reliance on aluminum puts Alcoa in position to become a major player in the aerospace jet-engine market. Jet engines utilize a lot of aluminum but still this strategy is best classified as related diversification rather than forward integration due to the new high-tech competencies required.

With its new Apply Pay product being linked with iBeacon so stores can detect and locate iPhone users via a Bluetooth wireless signal as they enter the premises, Apple recently entered the online payments business, competing directly with PayPal. Using their iPhone and/or Apple Watch, consumers can now make retail purchases by tapping their device at participating checkout registers. Apple is basically diversifying into the banking business with these new products, but the threat to PayPal in particular is spurring eBay and Google to cooperate in this arena.

The guidelines for when related diversification may be an effective strategy are as follows.[13]

1. An organization competes in a no-growth or a slow-growth industry.
2. Adding new, but related, products would significantly enhance the sales of current products.
3. New, but related, products could be offered at highly competitive prices.
4. New, but related, products have seasonal sales levels that counterbalance an organization's existing peaks and valleys.
5. An organization's products are currently in the declining stage of the product's life cycle.
6. An organization has a strong management team.

Unrelated Diversification

Privately held Mars Inc., best known for its M&M chocolates and its Mars and Snickers candy bars, recently became the world's largest pet-food company, purchasing 80 percent of Procter & Gamble's pet-food brands for $2.9 billion, to go with its own Whiskas, Pedigree, and Royal Canin pet brands. Mars has over 25 percent market share in the global pet-food industry, slightly ahead of Nestlé S.A., which owns Purina and Friskies.

Google now offers an electric-powered driverless car that has no steering wheel, brake, or gas pedal; rather, the car is equipped with buttons for go and stop, and travels at a top speed of 25 mph. Further diversifying, Google recently acquired Skybox Imaging to collect and provide data from the sky using satellites that collect daily photos and video of the Earth. With the acquisition, Google is also trying to cover the globe with fast Internet access from the sky, using balloons, drones, and satellites.

Honda Motor Company diversified in 2015 by developing, producing, and marketing its first business jet, named the HondaJet HA-420 that has a range of 1,180 miles and a top speed of 420 knots, and can carry seven passengers. This new product competes directly with the Cessna Citation M2 and Embraer Phenom 100E business jets. These business jets sell for about $4.5 million each.

An unrelated diversification strategy favors capitalizing on a portfolio of businesses that are capable of delivering excellent financial performance in their respective industries, rather than striving to capitalize on value chain strategic fits among the businesses. Firms that employ unrelated diversification continually search across different industries for companies that can be acquired for a deal and yet have potential to provide a high return on investment. Pursuing unrelated diversification entails being on the hunt to acquire companies whose assets are undervalued, companies that are financially distressed, or companies that have high-growth prospects but are short on investment capital.

Given below are 10 guidelines when unrelated diversification may be an especially effective strategy.[14]

1. Revenues derived from an organization's current products or services would increase significantly by adding the new, unrelated products.
2. An organization competes in a highly competitive or a no-growth industry, as indicated by low industry profit margins and returns.
3. An organization's present channels of distribution can be used to market the new products to current customers.
4. New products have countercyclical sales patterns compared to an organization's present products.
5. An organization's basic industry is experiencing declining annual sales and profits.
6. An organization has the capital and managerial talent needed to compete successfully in a new industry.
7. An organization has the opportunity to purchase an unrelated business that is an attractive investment opportunity.
8. Financial synergy exists between the acquired and acquiring firm. (Note that a key difference between related and unrelated diversification is that the former should be based on some commonality in markets, products, or technology, whereas the latter is based more on profit considerations.)
9. Existing markets for an organization's present products are saturated.
10. Antitrust action could be charged against an organization that historically has concentrated on a single industry.

Defensive Strategies

In addition to integrative, intensive, and diversification strategies, organizations also could pursue defensive strategies such as retrenchment, divestiture, or liquidation.

Retrenchment

Retrenchment occurs when an organization regroups through cost and asset reduction to reverse declining sales and profits. Sometimes called a *turnaround* or *reorganizational strategy*, retrenchment is designed to fortify an organization's basic distinctive competence. During retrenchment, strategists work with limited resources and face pressure from shareholders, employees, and the media. Retrenchment can involve selling off land and buildings to raise needed cash, pruning product lines, closing marginal businesses, closing obsolete factories, automating processes, reducing the number of employees, and instituting expense control systems.

Levi Strauss & Co. recently cut 20 percent of its nonretail and nonmanufacturing workforce as part of a retrenchment strategy aimed at streamlining the firm's operations and generating cost savings of nearly $200 million per year. The 160-year-old company headquartered in San Francisco is having trouble competing in the intensely competitive retail clothing industry, marked by fleeting fashions and "sale only" shoppers.

Cisco Systems recently removed 6,000 employees from its payrolls, comprising 8 percent of the company's total workforce. The routing and switching system company is experiencing declining revenue and profits. The Turner Broadcasting division of Time Warner recently deleted 1,475 jobs, or 10 percent of its workforce. The Turner division generates about half of Time Warner's operating profit and has more than 5,000 full-time employees in its home city of Atlanta. Staples closed 170 stores in North America in 2014, and closed another 55 stores in 2015.

In some cases, declaring **bankruptcy** can be an effective retrenchment strategy. Bankruptcy can allow a firm to avoid major debt obligations and to void union contracts. There are five major types of bankruptcy: Chapter 10, Chapter 11, Chapter 2, Chapter 12, and Chapter 13. The first type, *Chapter 10 bankruptcy*, is a liquidation procedure used only when a corporation sees no hope of being able to operate successfully or to obtain the necessary creditor agreement. All the organization's assets are sold in parts for their tangible worth. Several hundred thousand companies declare Chapter 10 bankruptcy annually.

Chapter 11 bankruptcy applies to municipalities. Detroit, Michigan, is the largest U.S. city to declare bankruptcy, but others include Stockton, California, and Birmingham, Alabama.

Chapter 2 bankruptcy allows organizations to reorganize and come back after filing a petition for protection. Quiznos recently filed Chapter 2 bankruptcy as its 2,100 stores simply cannot compete with rival Subway's 41,000 stores. Quiznos collects a 7 percent royalty fee and another 4 percent advertising from is disgruntled franchisees, compared to the industry average 6 percent royalty fee and 2 percent marketing fee. The average Quiznos store has about $300,000 in annual revenue, down from $425,000 a few years ago.

Also, Sbarro recently filed Chapter 2 bankruptcy for a second time in less than three years. The pizza chain blamed its recent financial troubles on "an unprecedented decline in mall traffic." Based in Melville, New York, Sbarro is a privately held firm with about 800 stores in more than 40 countries.

An artificial-sapphire producer for Apple, GT Advanced Technologies, recently filed for bankruptcy, soon after Apple decided to go with glass screens rather than sapphire. GT's stock price dropped 93 percent the same day the bankruptcy news released. By using sapphire, Apple was hoping for a more scratch- and shatter-resistant cover for its smartphones, but decided instead to use hardened glass.

Chapter 12 bankruptcy was created by the Family Farmer Bankruptcy Act of 1986. This law provides special relief to family farmers with debt equal to or less than $1.5 million.

Chapter 13 bankruptcy is a reorganization plan similar to Chapter 2, but it is available only to small businesses owned by individuals with unsecured debts of less than $100,000 and secured debts of less than $350,000. The Chapter 13 debtor is allowed to operate the business while a plan is being developed to provide for the successful operation of the business in the future.

Five guidelines for when retrenchment may be an especially effective strategy to pursue are as follows:[15]

1. An organization has a clearly distinctive competence but has failed consistently to meet its objectives and goals over time.
2. An organization is one of the weaker competitors in a given industry.
3. An organization is plagued by inefficiency, low profitability, poor employee morale, and pressure from stockholders to improve performance.
4. An organization has failed to capitalize on external opportunities, minimize external threats, take advantage of internal strengths, and overcome internal weaknesses over time; that is, when the organization's strategic managers have failed (and possibly will be replaced by more competent individuals).
5. An organization has grown so large so quickly that major internal reorganization is needed.

Divestiture

Selling a division or part of an organization is called **divestiture**. It is often used to raise capital for further strategic acquisitions or investments. Divestiture can be part of an overall retrenchment strategy to rid an organization of businesses that are unprofitable, that require too much capital, or that do not fit well with the firm's other activities. Divestiture has also become a popular strategy for firms to focus on their core businesses and become less diversified.

The largest consumer-products company in the world, Procter & Gamble (P&G), is in the process of divesting (selling) more than half of its brands (nearly 100) in order to focus on its core brands (about 80). With brands such as Pampers, Tide, Era, Cheer, Metamucil, Clairol, Wella, Oral-B, Duracell, Fixodent, Ivory, and Clearblue (pregnancy tests), P&G has 23 brands that have more than $1 billion annual sales each. Ivory might be divested, as Americans have increasingly opted for body washes and liquid hand soap over plain bar soaps.

Airbus Group NV is in the process of divesting its defense assets in order to focus solely on its commercial-airplane business. Airbus is selling its secure-communications business, Fairchild Controls, as well as Rostock System-Technik, AvDef, ESG, and its Atlas Elektronik naval-technology joint venture with ThyseenKrupp AG. Airbus is also divesting its 46 percent nonvoting interest in Dassault Aviation SA that makes France's Rafale combat jets and Falcon business jets.

A version of divestiture occurs when a corporation splits into two or more parts. For example, Hewlett-Packard (HP) recently separated its personal computer and printer businesses from its corporate hardware and services operations. Most often, divested segments become separate, publically traded companies. Many large conglomerate firms are employing this strategy. Sometimes this strategy is a prelude to the firm selling the separated part(s) to a rival firm, such as HP's corporate hardware and services business perhaps merging with EMC Corporation. PepsiCo is under pressure to split its soft drinks division away from its snacks operations. Even General Electric is facing pressure from investors to spin off some of its diverse operations ranging from power plants to locomotives to MRI machines. Dupont is splitting off a segment that generates 20 percent of its revenue. Gannet Company, owner of *USA Today* and *Wall Street Journal*, recently split their print-publishing business from their television-film business.

In 2014 alone, corporations globally split off about $2 trillion worth of subsidiaries. Part of the reason for splitting diversified firms is that the homogenous parts are generally much more attractive for potential buyers. Most times, the acquiring firms desire to promote homogeneity to complement their own operations, rather than heterogeneity, and are willing to pay for homogeneity. For example, Fiat Chrysler Automobiles NV recently "spun off" its Ferrari segment into a separate IPO, possibly raising as much as $10 billion for Fiat. In the United States, Ferrari sports cars are priced between $190,000 and $400,000, with limited edition models exceeding $3 million each.

Germany's huge power utility, E.ON SE, recently split into two companies, one focusing on the utility's green energy initiatives, while the other company is comprised of the firm's conventional power-generation operations. Germany is in the midst of an aggressive policy to phase out all of its nuclear energy power plants by 2025.

Here are some guidelines for when divestiture may be an especially effective strategy to pursue:[16]

1. An organization has pursued a retrenchment strategy and failed to accomplish needed improvements.
2. To be competitive, a division needs more resources than the company can provide.
3. A division is responsible for an organization's overall poor performance.
4. A division is a misfit with the rest of an organization; this can result from radically different markets, customers, managers, employees, values, or needs.
5. A large amount of cash is needed quickly and cannot be obtained reasonably from other sources.
6. Government antitrust action threatens an organization.

Liquidation

Selling all of a company's assets, in parts, for their tangible worth is called **liquidation**; it is associated with Chapter 10 bankruptcy. Liquidation is a recognition of defeat and consequently can be an emotionally difficult strategy. However, it may be better to cease operating than to continue losing large sums of money. For example, based in New York City, Crumbs Bake Shop, the nation's largest cupcake company, filed for Chapter 10 bankruptcy liquidation of its 65 stores in 12 states and Washington, DC. Crumbs Bake Shop was famous for selling giant cupcakes in flavors such as Red Velvet, Cookie Dough, and Girl Scouts Thin Mints. The company notified all its 165 full-time employees and 655 part-time hourly employees that the business was closing. Crumbs' last day on the Nasdaq was June 30, 2014, at a stock price of 11 cents.

The midwestern retailer, Alco Stores, in early 2015 liquidated (closed) all its stores after earlier operating under Chapter 2 bankruptcy. Founded in 1901 as a general-merchandising store in Abilene, Kansas, Alco had major offices both in Abilene and in Coppell, Texas. More than 3,000 employees lost their job as Alco liquidated its assets.

Based in Bonita Springs, Florida, one of the largest distributors of magazines in the United States, Source Interlink Distribution, recently liquidated, laying off its 6,000 employees and forgoing its $750 million a year in revenue. Source Interlink had played a major role in arranging for printed magazines to be distributed to retailers, large and small.

These three guidelines indicate when liquidation may be an especially effective strategy to pursue:[17]

1. An organization has pursued both a retrenchment strategy and a divestiture strategy, and neither has been successful.
2. An organization's only alternative is bankruptcy. Liquidation represents an orderly and planned means of obtaining the greatest possible amount of cash for an organization's assets. A company can legally declare bankruptcy first and then liquidate various divisions to raise needed capital.
3. The stockholders of a firm can minimize their losses by selling the organization's assets.

Michael Porter's Five Generic Strategies

Probably the three most widely read books on competitive analysis in the 1980s were Michael Porter's *Competitive Strategy* (1980), *Competitive Advantage* (1985), and *Competitive Advantage of Nations* (1989). According to Porter, strategies allow organizations to gain competitive advantage from three different bases: cost leadership, differentiation, and focus. Porter calls these bases **generic strategies**.

Cost leadership emphasizes producing standardized products at a low per-unit cost for consumers who are price sensitive. Two alternative types of cost leadership strategies can be defined. Type 1 is a *low-cost* strategy that offers products or services to a wide range of customers at the lowest price available on the market. Type 2 is a *best-value* strategy that offers products or services to a wide range of customers at the best price-value available on the market. The best-value strategy aims to offer customers a range of products or services at the lowest price available compared to a rival's products with similar attributes. Both Type 1 and Type 2 strategies target a large market.

Porter's Type 3 generic strategy is **differentiation**, a strategy aimed at producing products and services considered unique to the industry and directed at consumers who are relatively price insensitive.

Focus means producing products and services that fulfill the needs of small groups of consumers. Two alternative types of focus strategies are Type 4 and Type 5. Type 4 is a low-cost focus strategy that offers products or services to a small range (niche group) of customers at the lowest price available on the market. Examples of firms that use the Type 4 strategy include Jiffy Lube International and Pizza Hut, as well as local used car dealers and hot dog restaurants. Type 5 is a best-value focus strategy that offers products or services to a small range of customers at the best price-value available on the market. Sometimes called "focused differentiation," the best-value focus strategy aims to offer a niche group of customers the products or services that meet their tastes and requirements better than rivals' products do. Both Type 4 and Type 5 focus strategies target a small market. However, the difference is that Type 4 strategies offer products or services to a niche group at the lowest price, whereas Type 5 offers products and services to a niche group at higher prices but loaded with features so the offerings are perceived as the best value. Bed-and-breakfast inns and local retail boutiques are examples of Type 5 firms.

Porter's five strategies imply different organizational arrangements, control procedures, and incentive systems. Larger firms with greater access to resources typically compete on a cost leadership or differentiation basis, whereas smaller firms often compete on a focus basis. Porter's five generic strategies are illustrated in Figure 4-3. Note that a differentiation strategy (Type 3) can be pursued with either a small target market or a large target market. However, it is not effective to pursue a cost leadership strategy in a small market because profits margins are generally too small. Likewise, it is not effective to pursue a focus strategy in a large market because economies of scale would generally favor a low-cost or best-value cost leadership strategy to gain or sustain competitive advantage.

Porter stresses the need for strategists to perform cost-benefit analyses to evaluate "sharing opportunities" among a firm's existing and potential business units. Sharing activities and

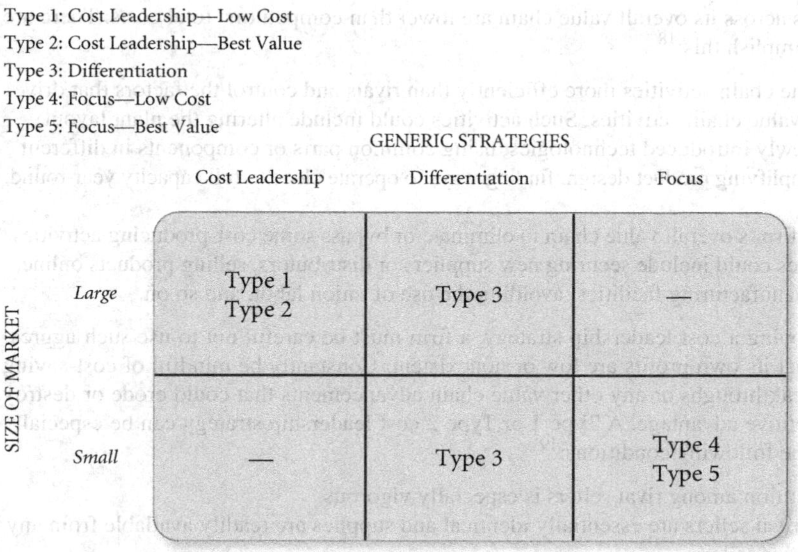

Type 1: Cost Leadership—Low Cost
Type 2: Cost Leadership—Best Value
Type 3: Differentiation
Type 4: Focus—Low Cost
Type 5: Focus—Best Value

GENERIC STRATEGIES

	Cost Leadership	Differentiation	Focus
Large	Type 1 Type 2	Type 3	—
Small	—	Type 3	Type 4 Type 5

SIZE OF MARKET

FIGURE 4-3

Porter's Five Generic Strategies

Source: Based on Michael E. Porter, *Competitive Strategy: Techniques for Analyzing Industries and Competitors* (New York: Free Press, 1980), 35–40.

resources enhances competitive advantage by lowering costs or increasing differentiation. In addition to prompting sharing, Porter stresses the need for firms to effectively "transfer" skills and expertise among autonomous business units to gain competitive advantage. Depending on factors such as type of industry, size of firm, and nature of competition, various strategies could yield advantages in cost leadership, differentiation, and focus.

Cost Leadership Strategies (Type 1 and Type 2)

A primary reason for pursuing forward, backward, and horizontal integration strategies is to gain low-cost or best-value cost leadership benefits. But cost leadership generally must be pursued in conjunction with differentiation. A number of cost elements affect the relative attractiveness of generic strategies, including economies or diseconomies of scale achieved, learning and experience curve effects, the percentage of capacity utilization achieved, and linkages with suppliers and distributors. Other cost elements to consider in choosing among alternative strategies include the potential for sharing costs and knowledge within the organization, research and development (R&D) costs associated with new product development or modification of existing products, labor costs, tax rates, energy costs, and shipping costs.

Striving to be the low-cost producer in an industry can be especially effective when the market is composed of many price-sensitive buyers, when there are few ways to achieve product differentiation, when buyers do not care much about differences from brand to brand, or when there are a large number of buyers with significant bargaining power. The basic idea is to underprice competitors and thereby gain market share and sales, entirely driving some competitors out of the market. Companies employing a low-cost (Type 1) or best-value (Type 2) cost leadership strategy must achieve their competitive advantage in ways that are difficult for competitors to copy or match. If rivals find it relatively easy or inexpensive to imitate the leader's cost leadership methods, the leaders' advantage will not last long enough to yield a valuable edge in the marketplace. Recall that for a resource to be valuable, it must be either rare, hard to imitate, or not easily substitutable. To employ a cost leadership strategy successfully, a firm must ensure that its total costs across its overall value chain are lower than competitors' total costs. There are two ways to accomplish this:[18]

1. Perform value chain activities more efficiently than rivals and control the factors that drive the costs of value chain activities. Such activities could include altering the plant layout, mastering newly introduced technologies, using common parts or components in different products, simplifying product design, finding ways to operate close to full capacity year-round, and so on.
2. Revamp the firm's overall value chain to eliminate or bypass some cost-producing activities. Such activities could include securing new suppliers or distributors, selling products online, relocating manufacturing facilities, avoiding the use of union labor, and so on.

When employing a cost leadership strategy, a firm must be careful not to use such aggressive price cuts that its own profits are low or nonexistent. Constantly be mindful of cost-saving technological breakthroughs or any other value chain advancements that could erode or destroy the firm's competitive advantage. A Type 1 or Type 2 cost leadership strategy can be especially effective under the following conditions:[19]

1. Price competition among rival sellers is especially vigorous.
2. Products of rival sellers are essentially identical and supplies are readily available from any of several eager sellers.
3. There are few ways to achieve product differentiation that have value to buyers.
4. Most buyers use the product in the same ways.
5. Buyers incur low costs in switching their purchases from one seller to another.
6. Buyers are large and have significant power to bargain down prices.
7. Industry newcomers use introductory low prices to attract buyers and build a customer base.

A successful cost leadership strategy usually permeates the entire firm, as evidenced by high efficiency, low overhead, limited perks, intolerance of waste, intensive screening of budget requests, wide spans of control, rewards linked to cost containment, and broad employee participation in cost control efforts. Some risks of pursuing cost leadership are that competitors may imitate the strategy, thus driving overall industry profits down; technological breakthroughs in the industry may make the strategy ineffective; or buyer interest may swing to other differentiating features besides price. The dollar stores are well known for their low-cost leadership strategies.

Differentiation Strategies (Type 3)

Different strategies offer different degrees of differentiation. Differentiation does not guarantee competitive advantage, especially if standard products sufficiently meet customer needs or if rapid imitation by competitors is possible. Durable products protected by barriers to quick copying by competitors are best. Successful differentiation can mean greater product flexibility, greater compatibility, lower costs, improved service, less maintenance, greater convenience, or more features. Product development is an example of a strategy that offers the advantages of differentiation.

A differentiation strategy should be pursued only after a careful study of buyers' needs and preferences to determine the feasibility of incorporating one or more differentiating features into a unique product that showcases the desired attributes. A successful differentiation strategy allows a firm to charge a higher price for its product and to gain customer loyalty because consumers may become strongly attached to the differentiation factors. Special features that differentiate one's product can include superior service, spare parts availability, engineering design, product performance, useful life, gas mileage, or ease of use.

A risk of pursuing a differentiation strategy is that the unique product may not be valued highly enough by customers to justify the higher price. When this happens, a cost-leadership strategy easily will defeat a differentiation strategy. Another risk of pursuing a differentiation strategy is that competitors may quickly develop ways to copy the differentiating features. Firms thus must find durable sources of uniqueness that cannot be imitated quickly or cheaply by rival firms.

Common organizational requirements for a successful differentiation strategy include strong coordination among the R&D and marketing functions and substantial amenities to attract scientists and creative people. Firms can pursue a differentiation (Type 3) strategy based on many different competitive aspects. Differentiation opportunities exist or can potentially be developed anywhere along the firm's value chain, including supply chain activities, product R&D activities, production and technological activities, manufacturing activities, human resource management activities, distribution activities, or marketing activities.

The most effective differentiation bases are those that are hard or expensive for rivals to duplicate. Competitors are continually trying to imitate, duplicate, and outperform rivals along any differentiation variable that has yielded competitive advantage. For example, when U.S. Airways cut its prices, Delta quickly followed suit. When Caterpillar instituted its quick-delivery-of-spare-parts policy, John Deere soon followed suit. To the extent that differentiating attributes are tough for rivals to copy, a differentiation strategy will be especially effective, but the sources of uniqueness must be time consuming, cost prohibitive, and simply too burdensome for rivals to match. A firm, therefore, must be careful when employing a differentiation (Type 3) strategy. Buyers will not pay the higher differentiation price unless their perceived value exceeds the price they are currently paying.[20] Based on such matters as attractive packaging, extensive advertising, quality of sales presentations, quality of website, list of customers, professionalism, size of the firm, or profitability of the company, perceived value may be more important to customers than actual value.

A Type 3 differentiation strategy can be especially effective under the following four conditions:[21]

1. There are many ways to differentiate the product or service and many buyers perceive these differences as having value.
2. The buyer's needs and uses are diverse.
3. Few rival firms are following a similar differentiation approach.
4. Technological change is fast paced and competition revolves around rapidly evolving product features.

Focus Strategies (Type 4 and Type 5)

A successful focus strategy depends on an industry segment that is of sufficient size, has good growth potential, and is not crucial to the success of other major competitors. Strategies such as market penetration and market development offer substantial focusing advantages. Midsize and large firms can effectively pursue focus-based strategies only in conjunction with differentiation or cost leadership–based strategies. All firms essentially follow a differentiated strategy. Because only one firm can differentiate itself with the lowest cost, the remaining firms in the industry must find other ways to differentiate their products.

Focus strategies are most effective when consumers have distinctive preferences or requirements and when rival firms are not attempting to specialize in the same target segment. For example, Clorox Company, which obtains 80 percent of its revenue from the United States, is focusing on brands viewed as environmentally friendly. Marriott continues to focus on its hotel business by announcing plans to double its hotels in Asia to 275 by 2017, especially growing its China-based hotels to about 125 from 60 and covering nearly 75 percent of Chinese provinces. Reasoning for Marriott's strategy is that Chinese tourists are traveling at home and abroad in dramatically increased numbers, up 21 percent on average year after year.

Risks of pursuing a focus strategy include the possibility that numerous competitors will recognize the successful focus strategy and copy it or that consumer preferences will drift toward the product attributes desired by the market as a whole. An organization using a focus strategy may concentrate on a particular group of customers, geographic markets, or particular product-line segments to serve a well-defined but narrow market better than competitors who serve a broader market.

A low-cost (Type 4) or best-value (Type 5) focus strategy can be especially attractive under these conditions:[22]

1. The target market niche is large, profitable, and growing.
2. Industry leaders do not consider the niche to be crucial to their own success.

3. Industry leaders consider it too costly or difficult to meet the specialized needs of the target market niche while taking care of their mainstream customers.

4. The industry has many different niches and segments, thereby allowing a focuser to pick a competitively attractive niche suited to its own resources.

5. Few, if any, other rivals are attempting to specialize in the same target segment.

Means for Achieving Strategies

Cooperation among Competitors

Fierce competitors for decades, Apple and IBM recently formed an alliance to cooperate in developing apps and selling iPhones and iPads. For Apple, the alliance allows the company to expand the reach of its products into the business world, whereas for IBM the alliance allows the firm to move more of its business software onto mobile devices. In a joint interview with IBM CEO Virginia Rometty, Apple's CEO Tim Cook observed, "In 1984, we were competitors, but today, I don't think you can find two more complementary companies." Apple and IBM are today developing more than 100 apps together.

Also fierce competitors for decades, Apple and Google recently agreed to share rights to digital content with any consumer who buys a Disney movie using the Disney Movies Anywhere app. Previously, both Apple and Google had restricted movies, TV shows, and other content to its own family of iOS or Android-powered devices, respectively. Now, both Apple and Google pay Walt Disney Company a wholesale rate for each copy of a Disney film that they sell, regardless of the type device people use.

Strategies that stress cooperation among competitors are being used more. For collaboration between competitors to succeed, both firms must contribute something distinctive, such as technology, distribution, basic research, or manufacturing capacity. But a major risk is that unintended transfers of important skills or technology may occur at organizational levels below where the deal was signed.[23] Information not covered in the formal agreement often gets traded in the day-to-day interactions and dealings of engineers, marketers, and product developers. Firms often give away too much information to rival firms when operating under cooperative agreements! Tighter formal agreements are needed.

Perhaps the best example of rival firms in an industry forming alliances to compete against each other is the airline industry. Today, there are three major alliances: Star, SkyTeam, and Oneworld. Joint ventures and cooperative arrangements among competitors demand a certain amount of trust if companies are to combat paranoia about whether one firm will injure the other. Increasing numbers of domestic firms are joining forces with competitive foreign firms to reap mutual benefits. Kathryn Harrigan at Columbia University contends, "Within a decade, most companies will be members of teams that compete against each other."

Often, U.S. companies enter alliances primarily to avoid investments, being more interested in reducing the costs and risks of entering new businesses or markets than in acquiring new skills. In contrast, *learning from the partner* is a major reason why Asian and European firms enter into cooperative agreements. American firms, too, should place learning high on the list of reasons to be cooperative with competitors. Companies in the United States often form alliances with Asian firms to gain an understanding of their manufacturing excellence, but Asian competence in this area is not easily transferable. Manufacturing excellence is a complex system that includes employee training and involvement, integration with suppliers, statistical process controls, value engineering, and design. In contrast, U.S. know-how in technology and related areas can be imitated more easily. Therefore, U.S. firms need to be careful not to give away more intelligence than they receive in cooperative agreements with rival Asian firms.

Academic Research Capsule 4-1 examines whether international alliances are more effective with competitors or noncompetitors.

Joint Venture and Partnering

Joint venture is a popular strategy that occurs when two or more companies form a temporary partnership or consortium for the purpose of capitalizing on some opportunity. Often, the two or more sponsoring firms form a separate organization and have shared equity ownership in the new entity.

ACADEMIC RESEARCH CAPSULE 4-1

Are International Alliances More Effective with Competitors or Noncompetitors?

Recent research reveals that small- and medium-size firms expanding into other countries should form alliances with noncompetitors rather than with rival firms. Alliances with competitors are more costly, directly and indirectly, and provide redundant knowledge and resources, leading researchers to conclude that small- and medium-size firms should strive to form alliances with noncompetitors rather than competitors whenever possible. Researchers report that the benefits of allying with competitors are offset by higher monitoring and control costs. Also, competing firms oftentimes share less knowledge than they could or should. Even though small- and medium-size firms typically have resource constraints as they expand globally and need alliances to grow, research shows that alliances with noncompetitors are positively associated with international performance, whereas alliances with competitors are negatively related. These findings are based on a recent study involving 162 British and U.S. private small- and medium-sized businesses.

Source: Based on K. Brouthers & P. Dimitratos, "International Alliances with Competitors and Non-Competitors: The Disparate Impact on SME International Performance," *Strategic Entrepreneurship Journal*, 8, no. 2 (June 2014): 167–182.

Other types of cooperative arrangements include research and development partnerships, cross-distribution agreements, cross-licensing agreements, cross-manufacturing agreements, and joint-bidding consortia. Although joint ventures and partnerships are increasingly preferred over mergers as a means for achieving strategies, they are not always successful, for four primary reasons:

1. Managers who must collaborate daily in operating the venture are not involved in forming or shaping the venture.
2. The venture may benefit the partnering companies but may not benefit customers, who then complain about poorer service or criticize the companies in other ways.
3. The venture may not be supported equally by both partners. If supported unequally, problems arise.
4. The venture may begin to compete more with one of the partners than the other.[24]

Joint ventures are being used increasingly because they allow companies to improve communications and networking, to globalize operations, and to minimize risk. They are formed when a given opportunity is too complex, uneconomical, or risky for a single firm to pursue alone, or when an endeavor requires a broader range of competencies and know-how than any one firm can marshal. Kathryn Rudie Harrigan, summarizes the trend toward increased joint venturing:

> In today's global business environment of scarce resources, rapid rates of technological change, and rising capital requirements, the important question is no longer "Shall we form a joint venture?" Now the question is "Which joint ventures and cooperative arrangements are most appropriate for our needs and expectations?" followed by "How do we manage these ventures most effectively?"[25]

In a global market tied together by the Internet, joint ventures, partnerships, and alliances are proving to be a more effective way to enhance corporate growth than mergers and acquisitions.[26] Strategic partnering takes many forms, including outsourcing, information sharing, joint marketing, and joint research and development. There are today more than 10,000 joint ventures formed annually—more than all mergers and acquisitions. Walmart's successful joint venture with Mexico's Cifra is indicative of how a domestic firm can benefit immensely by partnering with a foreign company to gain substantial presence in that new country. Technology also is a major reason behind the need to form strategic alliances, with the Internet linking widely dispersed partners. For example, IBM recently signed partnerships with both Twitter and Facebook, enabling IBM to mine information from Twitter's 302 million monthly active users and Facebook's 1.4 billion users. With data from those partnerships, IBM is using its cloud analytics and data analytics services to help companies create social data-enabled apps. The leading data analytics, or business analytics, company is Tableau Software, followed by Qlik Technologies.

Although evidence is mounting that firms should use partnering as a means for achieving strategies, most U.S. firms in many industries—such as financial services, forest products, metals, and retailing—still operate in a merge or acquire mode to obtain growth. Partnering is not yet taught at most business schools and is often viewed within companies as a financial issue rather than a strategic issue. However, partnering has become a core competency, a strategic issue of such high importance.

Six guidelines for when a joint venture may be an especially effective means for pursuing strategies are:[27]

1. A privately owned organization is forming a joint venture with a publicly owned organization. There are some advantages to being privately held, such as closed ownership. There are also some advantages of being publicly held, such as access to stock issuances as a source of capital. Sometimes the unique advantages of being privately and publicly held can be synergistically combined in a joint venture.
2. A domestic organization is forming a joint venture with a foreign company. A joint venture can provide a domestic company with the opportunity for obtaining local management in a foreign country, thereby reducing risks such as expropriation and harassment by host country officials.
3. The distinct competencies of two or more firms complement each other especially well.
4. Some project is potentially profitable but requires overwhelming resources and risks.
5. Two or more smaller firms have trouble competing with a large firm.
6. There is a need to quickly introduce a new technology.

Merger/Acquisition

Merger and acquisition are two commonly used ways to pursue strategies. A **merger** occurs when two organizations of about equal size unite to form one enterprise. An **acquisition** occurs when a large organization purchases (acquires) a smaller firm or vice versa. If a merger or acquisition is not desired by both parties, it is called a **hostile takeover**, as opposed to a **friendly merger**. Most mergers are friendly, but the number of hostile takeovers is on the rise. Not all mergers are effective and successful. For example, soon after Halliburton acquired Baker Hughes, Halliburton's stock price declined 11 percent. So, a merger between two firms can yield great benefits, but the price and reasoning must be right. Some key reasons why many mergers and acquisitions fail are provided in Table 4-5.

There were far more global mergers and acquisitions in 2014 than in any year since 2007, exceeding $3.5 billion. Three contributory reasons for this trend are (1) the desire of diversified firms to "spin off" segments into separate companies that are then acquired by other firms, (2) the desire of firms to acquire similar companies in countries with low corporate tax rates and to shift company profits from the United States through those countries, and (3) the desire of shareholders for firms to continually grow revenues. Often, growth is most effective through acquisition, as opposed to internal (organic) growth.

In the United States, mergers and acquisitions totaled $1.52 trillion in 2014, comprising 45 percent of global deals, up from $998 billion, or 43 percent, the prior year. The data firm Dealogic reported in mid-2015 that global mergers and acquisitions in 2015 likely will hit an all-time record of $4.58 trillion.

TABLE 4-5   Nine Reasons Why Many Mergers and Acquisitions Fail

1. Integration difficulties
2. Inadequate evaluation of target
3. Large or extraordinary debt
4. Inability to achieve synergy
5. Too much diversification
6. Managers overly focused on acquisitions
7. Too large an acquisition
8. Difficult to integrate different organizational cultures
9. Reduced employee morale due to layoffs and relocations

However, the U.S. Treasury Department's new rules cracking down on tax inversions, where a company acquires a foreign company in order to avoid paying federal taxes, will likely somewhat curtail the number of mergers and acquisitions going forward. More than 10,000 mergers transpire annually in the United States, with same-industry combinations predominating. A general market consolidation is occurring in many industries, especially energy, banking, insurance, defense, and health care, but also in pharmaceuticals, food, airlines, accounting, publishing, computers, retailing, financial services, and biotechnology. Table 4-6 presents the potential benefits of merging with or acquiring another firm.

A **leveraged buyout (LBO)** occurs when a corporation's shareholders are bought (hence *buyout*) by the company's management and other private investors using borrowed funds (hence *leverage*). Besides trying to avoid a hostile takeover, other reasons for initiating an LBO include whenever a particular division(s) does not fit into an overall corporate strategy, or whenever selling a division could raise needed cash. An LBO converts a public firm into a private company.

Private-Equity Acquisitions

Private equity (PE) firms are acquiring and taking private a wide variety of companies almost daily in the business world. For example, one of the world's largest private-equity firms, Apollo Global Management LLC, recently acquired 577 Chuck E. Cheese stores, the party pizza and arcade game venues, in 47 states and 10 foreign countries or territories. Apollo paid about $950 million for the parent company, CEC Entertainment, or a 12 percent premium over the company's stock price. Chuck E. Cheese's profit and revenue has been on the decline of late and the number of birthday parties hosted falling. Another large PE firm, Carlyle Group LP, recently acquired Johnson & Johnson's blood-testing business for $4.15 billion.

Private equity firms are an integral part of the business world, especially in the United States but also in Europe, Asia, and, more recently, Latin America. Private equity firms such as Kohlberg Kravis Roberts (KKR) have jumped aggressively back into the business of acquiring and selling firms, and releasing new initial public offerings (IPO). A large PE firm, Cerberus Capital Management, recently bought the second-largest U.S. grocery store chain, Safeway Inc., based in Pleasanton, California, for $9.4 billion. Cerberus already owns Albertsons, the fifth-largest U.S. grocery store chain. Cerberus plans to unite the two companies' distribution and purchasing operations to save money and compete better with major rivals, Wal-Mart Stores and Kroger.

Headquartered in Phoenix, Arizona, PetSmart was acquired in December 2014 by London-based PE firm BC Partners for $8.8 billion, the largest U.S. private equity deal of the year. PetSmart reportedly had received a joint bid offer from KKR and Clayton Dubilier & Rice, and a bid from Apollo, all PE firms. PetSmart operates 1,387 retail pet stores in the United States, Canada, and Puerto Rico. BC Partners paid $83 per share for PetSmart, a 6.86 percent premium over PetSmart's closing stock price.

TABLE 4-6 Eleven Potential Benefits of Merging with or Acquiring Another Firm

1. To provide improved capacity utilization
2. To make better use of the existing sales force
3. To reduce managerial staff
4. To gain economies of scale
5. To smooth out seasonal trends in sales
6. To gain access to new suppliers, distributors, customers, products, and creditors
7. To gain new technology
8. To gain market share
9. To enter global markets
10. To gain pricing power
11. To reduce tax obligations

The intent of virtually all PE acquisitions is to buy firms at a low price and sell them later at a high price, arguably just good business. Private equity firms also are buying companies from other PE firms, such as Clayton, Dubilier & Rice's recent purchase of David's Bridal from Leonard Green & Partners LP for $1.05 billion. Such PE-to-PE acquisitions are called **secondary buyouts**. In addition, PE firms especially, but other firms too, sometimes borrow money simply to fund dividend payouts to themselves, a controversial practice known as **dividend recapitalizations**. Critics say dividend recapitalization saddles a company with debt, thus burdening its operations.

Tactics to Facilitate Strategies

Strategists use numerous tactics to accomplish strategies, including being a "first mover," outsourcing, and reshoring. There are advantages and disadvantages of such tactics, as discussed next.

First Mover Advantages

First mover advantages refer to the benefits a firm may achieve by entering a new market or developing a new product or service prior to rival firms. As indicated in Table 4-7, some advantages of being a first mover include securing access to rare resources, gaining new knowledge of key factors and issues, and carving out market share and a position that is easy to defend and costly for rival firms to overtake. First mover advantages are analogous to taking the high ground first, which puts one in an excellent strategic position to launch aggressive campaigns and to defend territory. Being the first mover can be an excellent strategy when such actions (1) build a firm's image and reputation with buyers; (2) produce cost advantages over rivals in terms of new technologies, new components, new distribution channels, and so on; (3) create strongly loyal customers, and (4) make imitation or duplication by a rival difficult or unlikely.

To sustain the competitive advantage gained by being the first mover, a firm needs to be a fast learner. There are, however, risks associated with being the first mover, such as unexpected and unanticipated problems and costs that occur from being the first firm doing business in the new market. Therefore, being a slow mover (also called *fast follower* or *late mover*) can be effective when a firm can easily copy or imitate the lead firm's products or services. If technology is advancing rapidly, slow movers can often leapfrog a first mover's products with improved second-generation products. Samsung is an example in the smartphone business. Apple has always been a good example of a first mover firm.

First mover advantages tend to be greatest when competitors are roughly the same size and possess similar resources. If competitors are not similar in size, then larger competitors can wait while others make initial investments and mistakes, and then respond with greater effectiveness and resources. Lenovo has done this of late, as has Volkswagen.

Outsourcing and Reshoring

The second largest U.S. airline by traffic, United Continental Holdings, recently outsourced its check-in, baggage-handling, and customer service jobs to vendors who perform the duties at a lower cost. **Outsourcing** involves companies hiring other companies to take over various parts of

TABLE 4-7   Five Benefits of a Firm Being the First Mover

1. Secure access and commitments to rare resources.
2. Gain new knowledge of critical success factors and issues.
3. Gain market share and position in the best locations.
4. Establish and secure long-term relationships with customers, suppliers, distributors, and investors.
5. Gain customer loyalty and commitments.

their functional operations, such as human resources, information systems, payroll, accounting, customer service, and even marketing.

For more than a decade, U.S. and European companies have been outsourcing their manu-facturing, tech support, and back-office work, but most insisted on keeping research and devel-opment activities in-house. However, an ever-growing number of firms today are outsourcing their product design to Asian developers. China and India are becoming increasingly important suppliers of intellectual property. The details of what work to outsource, to whom, where, and for how much can challenge even the biggest, most sophisticated companies. And some outsourcing deals do not work out, such as the J. P. Morgan Chase deal with IBM and Dow Chemical's deal with Electronic Data Systems. Both outsourcing deals were abandoned after several years. India has become a booming place for outsourcing.

Table 4-8 reveals some of the potential benefits that firms strive to achieve through outsourc-ing. Notice that benefit #1 is that outsourcing is oftentimes used to access lower wages in foreign countries.

Reshoring is the new term that refers to U.S. companies planning to move some of their manufacturing back to the United States. Many U.S. companies plan to *reshore* in 2016–2017 for the following reasons: a desire to get products to market faster and respond rapidly to customer orders, savings from reduced transportation and warehousing, improved quality and protection of intellectual property, pressure to increase U.S. jobs.[28] "Made in the USA" is making a come-back. Walmart, for example, is spending an added $250 billion in the next 10 years on USA-made goods. Consequently, numerous Walmart suppliers, such as Element Electronics based in Eden Prairie, Minnesota, are bringing manufacturing and assembly operations back to the United States. Element now assembles flat screen televisions in Winnsboro, South Carolina. Whirlpool and General Electric have also reshored some of their production operations back to the United States. However, the management consulting firm A. T. Kearney reports that reshor-ing has stalled, and that U.S. firms are increasingly producing goods in lower-cost countries.[29] The strength of the dollar also has led U.S. firms to look outside the United States more and more to produce goods. The high value of the dollar makes U.S. goods more expensive overseas and

TABLE 4-8 Thirteen Potential Benefits of Outsourcing

1. *Cost savings:* Access lower wages in foreign countries.
2. *Focus on core business:* Focus resources on developing the core business rather than being distracted by other functions.
3. *Cost restructuring:* Outsourcing changes the balance of fixed costs to variable costs by moving the firm more to variable costs. Outsourcing also makes variable costs more predictable.
4. *Improve quality:* Improve quality by contracting out various business functions to specialists.
5. *Knowledge:* Gain access to intellectual property and wider experience and knowledge.
6. *Contract:* Gain access to services within a legally binding contract with financial penalties and legal redress. This is not the case with services performed internally.
7. *Operational expertise:* Gain access to operational best practice that would be too difficult or time consuming to develop in-house.
8. *Access to talent:* Gain access to a larger talent pool and a sustainable source of skills, especially science and engineering.
9. *Catalyst for change:* Use an outsourcing agreement as a catalyst for major change that cannot be achieved alone.
10. *Enhance capacity for innovation:* Use external knowledge to supplement limited in-house capac-ity for product innovation.
11. *Reduce time to market:* Accelerate development or production of a product through additional capability brought by the supplier.
12. *Risk management:* Manage risk by partnering with an outside firm.
13. *Tax benefit:* Capitalize on tax incentives to locate manufacturing plants to avoid high taxes in various countries.

makes imports to the United States cheaper. However, seven benefits of reshoring back into the United States are as follows:

1. Stable wages
2. Reduced gas and electricity costs
3. Excellent security to protect designs from overseas copycats
4. Enable closer tabs on quality control and supply chains
5. Excellent economy with consumers purchasing more
6. Less shipment costs with consumers nearby
7. Excellent human rights, education, legal, and political systems that promote freedom and opportunity for citizens

Strategic Management in Nonprofit, Governmental, and Small Firms

Nonprofit organizations are basically just like for-profit companies except for two major differences: (1) nonprofits do not pay taxes and (2) nonprofits do not have shareholders to provide capital. In virtually all other ways, these two types of organizations are like one another. Nonprofits have employees, customers, creditors, suppliers, and distributors as well as financial budgets, income statements, balance sheets, cash flow statements, and so on. Nonprofit organizations embrace strategic planning just as much as for-profit firms, and perhaps even more, because equity capital is not an alternative source of financing. Nonprofits also have competitors that want to put them out of business.

The strategic-management process is being used effectively by countless nonprofit and governmental organizations, such as the Girl Scouts, Boy Scouts, the Red Cross, chambers of commerce, educational institutions, medical institutions, public utilities, libraries, government agencies, zoos, cities, and churches. The nonprofit sector, surprisingly, is by far the largest employer in the United States. Many nonprofit and governmental organizations outperform private firms and corporations on innovativeness, motivation, productivity, and strategic management.

Compared to for-profit firms, nonprofit and governmental organizations may be totally dependent on outside financing. Especially for these organizations, strategic management provides an excellent vehicle for developing and justifying requests for needed financial support. Nonprofits and governmental organizations owe it to their constituencies to garner and use monies wisely; that requires excellent strategy formulation, implementation, and evaluation.

Educational Institutions

The world of higher education is rapidly moving to online courses and degrees. The American Council on Education, an association for higher education presidents, is considering allowing free, online courses to be eligible for credit toward a degree and eligible for transfer credit. Educational institutions are more frequently using strategic-management techniques and concepts. Richard Cyert, former president of Carnegie Mellon University, said, "I believe we do a far better job of strategic management than any company I know." Population shifts nationally from the Northeast and Midwest to the Southeast and West are but one factor causing trauma for educational institutions that have not planned for changing enrollments. Ivy League schools in the Northeast are recruiting more heavily in the Southeast and West. This trend represents a significant change in the competitive climate for attracting the best high school graduates each year. Online degrees are a threat to traditional colleges and universities. "You can put the kids to bed and go to law school," says Andrew Rosen, chief operating officer of Kaplan Education Centers, a subsidiary of the Washington Post Company. Reduced state and federal funding for higher education has resulted in more aggressive fund raising by colleges and universities. President Obama's call for free community college education for all could also erode attendance in four-year colleges' 100- and 200-level courses. All institutions of higher learning need an excellent strategic plan to survive and prosper.

Medical Organizations

Declining occupancy rates, deregulation, and accelerating growth of health maintenance organizations, preferred provider organizations, urgent care centers, outpatient surgery centers, diagnostic centers, specialized clinics, and group practices are other major threats facing hospitals today. Many private and state-supported medical institutions are in financial trouble as a result of traditionally taking a reactive rather than a proactive approach in dealing with their industry. Originally intended to be warehouses for people dying of tuberculosis, smallpox, cancer, pneumonia, and infectious disease, hospitals are creating new strategies today as advances in the diagnosis and treatment of chronic diseases are undercutting that previous mission. Hospitals are beginning to bring services to the patient as much as bringing the patient to the hospital; health care is more and more being concentrated in the home and in the residential community rather than on the hospital campus. Current strategies being pursued by many hospitals include creating home health services, establishing nursing homes, and forming rehabilitation centers. Backward integration strategies that some hospitals are pursuing include acquiring ambulance services, waste disposal services, and diagnostic services. Millions of people annually research medical ailments online, causing a dramatic shift in the balance of power between doctor, patient, and hospitals.

Governmental Agencies and Departments

Federal, state, county, and municipal agencies and departments, such as police departments, chambers of commerce, forestry associations, and health departments, are responsible for formulating, implementing, and evaluating strategies that use taxpayers' dollars in the most cost-effective way to provide services and programs. Strategic-management concepts are generally required and thus widely used to enable governmental organizations to be more effective and efficient.

Strategists in governmental organizations operate with less strategic autonomy than their counterparts in private firms. Public enterprises generally cannot diversify into unrelated businesses or merge with other firms. Governmental strategists usually enjoy little freedom in altering the organizations' missions or redirecting objectives. Legislators and politicians often have direct or indirect control over major decisions and resources. Strategic issues get discussed and debated in the media and legislatures. Issues become politicized, resulting in fewer strategic choice alternatives. There is now more predictability in the management of public sector enterprises.

Government agencies and departments are finding that their employees get excited about the opportunity to participate in the strategic-management process and thereby have an effect on the organization's mission, objectives, strategies, and policies. In addition, government agencies are using a strategic-management approach to develop and substantiate formal requests for additional funding.

Small Firms

"Becoming your own boss" is a dream for millions of people and a reality for millions more. Almost everyone wants to own a business—from teens and college students, who are signing up for entrepreneurial courses in record numbers, to those older than age 65, who are forming more companies every year. However, the January 3, 2015, issue of the *Wall Street Journal* (page A1) reported that the percentage of people under age 30 who own private businesses has reached a 24-year low in the United States, to about 3.6 percent, down from 10.6 percent in 1989. The stereotype that 20-somethings are entrepreneurial risk-takers is simply false, as millions of young adults struggle in underpaid jobs to maintain their own household, rather than living with their parents. Reasons for the decline vary, but reduced bank lending for small business startups, more indebtedness among young people, and increasing numbers of competitors due to the Internet, all contribute to a more risk-averse, under-30 age group for becoming entrepreneur strategists.

The strategic-management process is just as vital for small companies as it is for large firms. From their inception, all organizations have a strategy, even if the strategy just evolves from day-to-day operations. Even if conducted informally or by a single owner or entrepreneur, the strategic-management process can significantly enhance small firms' growth and prosperity. However, a lack of strategic-management knowledge is a serious obstacle for many small business owners, as is a lack of sufficient capital to exploit external opportunities and a day-to-day cognitive frame of reference. Research indicates that strategic management in small firms is more informal than in large firms, but small firms that engage in strategic management generally outperform those that do not.

Academic Research Capsule 4-2 reveals the key attributes of great entrepreneurs, many of whom never went to college and never were an expert at their trade.

ACADEMIC RESEARCH CAPSULE 4-2

What Attributes Do Great Entrepreneurs Possess?

Many people dream of becoming a professional football player, musician, doctor, or entrepreneur, but many of us do not think we have the perceived special skills required to become greatly successful. Most aspiring entrepreneurs mistakenly believe those special skills are mandatory versus other skill sets we devalue. Baron and Henry carefully examined what attributes most great entrepreneurs possess, and found that many great strategists began as great entrepreneurs, including Michael Dell, Steve Jobs, Milton Hershey, Walt Disney, Henry Ford, and Bill Gates. Baron and Henry report that neither "years of experience" nor "God given natural ability" are top attributes that explain the success of most entrepreneurs. There does indeed need to be some level of natural "special" competence, but importantly, most of us are competent enough to become surprisingly successful at any endeavor we choose.

Baron and Henry found that most aspiring entrepreneurs can gain or already have the necessary experience in a particular area, and additional experience yields only incremental improvements; they contend that experience, in fact, can become an inhibiting factor. This finding is surprising because experience is highly valued in most professions, especially by those making hiring decisions. Many students, for example, when applying for jobs, are told, "You don't have enough work experience." So, if innate talent (special skills) and experience are not overriding keys to entrepreneurial success, what is? Baron and Henry provide the answer, reporting that the dominating, overriding factor accounting for the success of most great entrepreneurs is that they possess a high level of **deliberate practice**. Deliberate practice is best described as "an intense focusing on all aspects related to a subject matter or business idea." Deliberate practice goes well beyond hard work or routine practice, so much so that even the most successful entrepreneurs cannot engage in deliberate practice for more than a few hours each day. This characteristic includes examining yourself as a person, your competition, and a wide array of factors related to the entrepreneurial endeavor at hand. Several antecedents of deliberate practice include strong motivation, self-efficacy, self-discipline, delayed gratification, and self-control. Other factors are determination, strong work ethic, goal-oriented, dedication, time management, and "being on a mission."

Deliberate practice entails working "hard and smart" simultaneously; it is all about developing and utilizing a strategic mental approach to the endeavor at hand, rather than having a special innate talent or gaining 20 years of experience. Mr. Disney, Ford, Dell, Gates, Hershey, and Jobs utilized deliberate practice right out of the gate, rather than waiting to obtain innate talent or work experience. These great entrepreneurs (strategists) generally had neither innate talent nor years of work experience. Baron and Henry assert that anyone can become great through deliberate practice. Thus, do not get discouraged by having minimal innate talent or work experience. Rather, use the deliberate practice process to become successful in your chosen endeavor.

Source: Based on R. A. Baron & R. Henry, "How Entrepreneurs Acquire the Capacity to Excel: Insights from Research on Expert Performance," *Strategic Entrepreneurship Journal*, 4 (2019): 49–65. (*Note:* This is the most downloaded article in this journal in the last five years.)

IMPLICATIONS FOR STRATEGISTS

Figure 4-4 reveals that to gain and sustain competitive advantages, firms must collect, analyze, and prioritize large amounts of information in order to make excellent decisions. A "strategic plan" is very much akin to an athletic team's "game plan" in the sense that both a strategic plan and a game plan are developed after carefully studying rival firms (teams); success of the firm (or team) depends greatly on that plan being a better plan than the rival's plan. Any strategist, much like any coach, puts his or her firm in great jeopardy of failure if the opposing strategist (coach) has a better strategic plan.

Substantial deliberate practice, as discussed in Academic Research Capsule 4-2, is required to create, identify, nurture, and exploit competitive advantages that can lead to success. Parity (and commoditization) is becoming commonplace in both business and athletics; as parity increases, the intrinsic value of the overarching strategic plan, or game plan, increases exponentially.

For example, in college football, great parity exists among teams such as Auburn, Alabama, Ohio State, Florida State, Kansas State, Oregon, Arizona State, Michigan State, and Michigan, so the game plan can make the difference between winning and losing.

Most of the strategies described in this chapter would separately yield substantial benefits for firms, but no firm has sufficient resources to pursue more than a few basic strategies. Thus, strategists must select from a number of excellent alternatives, eliminate other excellent options, and consider risks, tradeoffs, costs, and other key factors. Any strategist, or coach, that gets "outstrategized" by his or her opposing strategist (or coach) puts his or her firm (or team) at a major disadvantage. Being outcoached can doom even a superior team (or firm). Therefore, in Chapter 8 we examine six additional analytical tools being widely used by strategists to help develop a winning strategic plan.

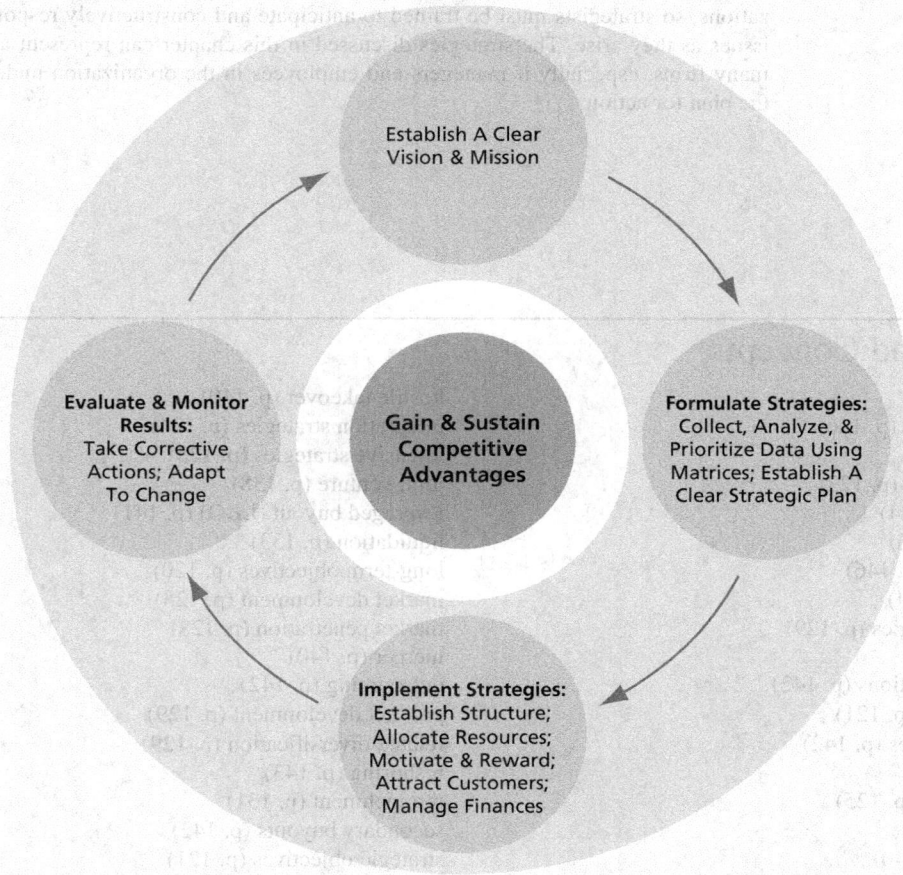

FIGURE 4-4

How to Gain and Sustain Competitive Advantages

IMPLICATIONS FOR STUDENTS

Numerous alternative strategies could benefit any firm, but your strategic-management case analysis should result in specific recommendations that you decide will best provide the firm with competitive advantages. Because company recommendations with costs comprise the most important pages or slides in your case project, introduce bits of that information early in the presentation as relevant supporting material is presented to justify your expenditures. Your recommendations page(s) itself should therefore be a summary of suggestions mentioned throughout your paper or presentation, rather than being a surprise shock to your reader or audience. You may even want to include with your recommendations insight as to why certain other feasible strategies were not chosen for implementation. That information, too, should be anchored in the notion of competitive advantage and disadvantage with respect to perceived costs and benefits. If someone asks, "What is the difference between recommendations and strategies?", respond with "Recommendations are alternative strategies actually selected for implementation."

Chapter Summary

The main appeal of any managerial approach is the expectation that it will enhance organizational performance. This is especially true of strategic management. Through involvement in strategic-management activities, managers and employees achieve a better understanding of an organization's priorities and operations. Strategic management allows organizations to be efficient, but more important, it allows them to be effective. Although strategic management does not guarantee organizational success, the process allows proactive rather than reactive decision making. Strategic management may represent a radical change in philosophy for some organizations, so strategists must be trained to anticipate and constructively respond to questions and issues as they arise. The strategies discussed in this chapter can represent a new beginning for many firms, especially if managers and employees in the organization understand and support the plan for action.

Key Terms and Concepts

acquisition (p. 140)
backward integration (p. 126)
bankruptcy (p. 132)
combination strategy (p. 123)
cost leadership (p. 134)
de-integration (p. 126)
deliberate practice (p. 146)
differentiation (p. 134)
diversification strategies (p. 129)
divestiture (p. 132)
dividend recapitalizations (p. 142)
financial objectives (p. 121)
first mover advantages (p. 142)
focus (p. 134)
forward integration (p. 125)
franchising (p. 125)
friendly merger (p. 140)
generic strategies (p. 134)
horizontal integration (p. 124)

hostile takeover (p. 140)
integration strategies (p. 124)
intensive strategies (p. 128)
joint venture (p. 138)
leveraged buyout (LBO) (p. 141)
liquidation (p. 133)
long-term objectives (p. 120)
market development (p. 128)
market penetration (p. 128)
merger (p. 140)
outsourcing (p. 142)
product development (p. 129)
related diversification (p. 129)
reshoring (p. 143)
retrenchment (p. 131)
secondary buyouts (p. 142)
strategic objectives (p. 121)
unrelated diversification (p. 129)
vertical integration (p. 124)

Issues for Review and Discussion

⭐ **4-1.** For Petronas, featured at the beginning of the chapter, give a hypothetical strategy for each of the following categories: market penetration, related diversification, divestiture, and retrenchment.

⭐ **4-2.** For Petronas, featured at the beginning of the chapter, give a hypothetical strategy for each of the following categories: market development, unrelated diversification, backward integration, and product development.

4-3. Identify five situations when forward integration is a particularly good strategy. Forward integration involves gaining ownership or increased control over distributors or retailers. Increasing numbers of manufacturers (suppliers) are pursuing a forward integration strategy

by establishing websites to sell their products directly to consumers.

⭐ **4-4.** What three strategies defined in the chapter do you feel are most widely used by small businesses?

4-5. Should non-profit organizations post their strategic plan on their website? What about corporations? Why?

4-6. Give some guidelines of when divestiture is a particularly effective strategy. Selling a division or part of an organization is called divestiture. It is often used to raise capital for further strategic acquisitions or investments.

4-7. Which two strategies do you consider the best for Nestle to pursue? Why?

4-8. Give some examples of Type 4 and Type 5 focus strategies according to Porter's generic strategy approach.

4-9. List three industries where cooperation among competitors is most likely and explain why.

4-10. Do a Google search on joint ventures. What important new concepts did you learn that were not presented in the chapter?

4-11. Identify three joint ventures that have worked especially well in the past.

4-12. List four important reasons why many mergers and acquisitions fail.

⭐ **4-13.** Explain how strategic management differs in governmental organizations as compared to educational institutions.

⭐ **4-14.** Explain how and why Petronas has been so successful in recent years.

4-15. List six characteristics of objectives and an example of each.

4-16. In order of importance, rank six major benefits of a firm having objectives.

4-17. Give a hypothetical example of forward integration, backward integration, and horizontal integration for Volkswagen.

4-18. Give a hypothetical example of market penetration, market development, and product development for Toyota Motors.

4-19. Give a hypothetical example of related diversification and an example of unrelated diversification for Google.

⭐ **4-20.** Give a hypothetical example of retrenchment and divestiture for Wal-Mart. Students' answers may vary.

4-21. When would market development generally be the preferred strategy over backward or forward integration?

4-22. Why is it not advisable to pursue too many strategies at once?

4-23. What conditions, externally and internally, would be desired/necessary for a firm to diversify?

⭐ **4-24.** List and describe the five types of bankruptcy. If your college or university had to declare bankruptcy, which type would be appropriate?

4-25. Explain why you believe some analysts consider Michael Porter's generic strategies to be too few and too vague.

4-26. Explain the difference between joint ventures and partnerships as a means for achieving various strategies

4-27. List the pros and cons of a hostile versus friendly takeover of another firm.

4-28. In order of importance, list six reasons why many mergers and acquisitions fail.

⭐ **4-29.** In order of importance, list six potential benefits of two firms merging.

4-30. What are the major advantages and disadvantages of diversification?

4-31. List three ways a country could prevent its companies from outsourcing jobs to other countries.

4-32. How does strategic management differ in for-profit and nonprofit organizations?

4-33. Identify three local businesses in your city. What three strategies do these three firms pursue? List the strategies in order of prevalence.

⭐ **4-34.** With different types of strategies, how can firms best cope with the turbulent, high-velocity markets or uncertainty in the business environment?

4-35. Based on the information given for Petronas, what three strategies are being pursued by the firm?

4-36. Prepare a strategic-management case analysis presentation referring to the chapter's "Implications for Students" section.

4-37. Identify three companies that use outsourcing effectively. Explain how and why those firms utilize this management approach.

4-38. What are the pros and cons of a firm merging with a rival firm?

4-39. Discuss the nature of as well as the pros and cons of a "friendly merger" versus "hostile takeover" in acquiring another firm. Give an example of each.

⭐ **4-40.** The big USA appliance maker, Whirlpool, recently acquired Indesit, an Italian company that sells appliances, in order to double Whirlpool's size in Europe, where the company has struggled to compete against Electrolux AB of Sweden, LG Electronics Inc. of South Korea, and Haier Group of China. Indesit had 13 percent of the major appliance market share in Eastern Europe and Whirlpool had 5 percent, so now Whirlpool has 18 percent. What type strategy is this for Whirlpool?

4-41. The world's largest furniture retailer, IKEA based in Stockholm, Sweden, recently entered the insurance business, including child, pregnancy, and home insurance products being available at many IKEA stores. IKEA has over 59 million members of its Club, customers who regularly shop at its stores, and now these folks can purchase insurance. What type strategy is this for IKEA?

4-42. Are international alliances more effective with competitors or non-competitors?

ASSURANCE OF LEARNING EXERCISES

EXERCISE 4A
Market Development for Petronas

Purpose
Petronas is featured in the opening chapter case as a firm that engages in excellent strategic planning, despite being hurt recently by falling oil prices. The purpose of this exercise is to give you practice extending a company's global strategy into new geographic regions.

Instructions

Step 1   Visit the website and review the company's latest *Annual Report*. Especially assess where and in what respect does Petronas do business in Asia, Australia, and the Middle East. Identify six countries that Petronas currently does not do business with.

Step 2   Based on your analysis in Step 1, evaluate the six countries identified in terms of their business culture, environment, and attractiveness for Petronas to begin doing business there.

Step 3   Rank order the six countries identified and evaluated in terms of a proposed plan for Petronas to begin doing business in these places. Prepare a two-page executive summary to support your suggested plan.

EXERCISE 4B
Alternative Strategies for Petronas

Purpose
This exercise will give you practice labeling hypothetical strategies that a firm could pursue.

Instructions
For each of the strategies listed below, identify a hypothetical strategy that you believe may be good for Petronas to pursue. Refer to Chapter 6 for a description of the strategies.

1. Forward Integration
2. Backward Integration
3. Horizontal Integration
4. Market Penetration
5. Market Development
6. Product Development
7. Related Diversification
8. Unrelated Diversification
9. Retrenchment
10. Divestiture
11. Liquidation

EXERCISE 4C
Private-Equity Acquisitions

Purpose
As stock prices increase and companies become more cash-rich, private-equity firms such as Kohlberg Kravis Roberts (KKR) have jumped aggressively back into the business of acquiring and selling firms. Private-equity firms have unleashed a wave of new initial public offerings (IPOs). Apollo Global Management is a large private-equity firms that owns many companies. The purpose of this exercise is to give you practice identifying and evaluating the nature and role of private-equity acquisitions in Europe.

Instructions

Step 1   Identify the top five IPOs in Europe in the last 12 months.

Step 2   Identify the top five private-equity firms in Europe.

Step 3   Prepare a two-page executive summary of the nature and role of private-equity acquisitions in Europe in the last 12 months. Include your expectations over the next 12 months for this activity to increase or decrease across Europe. Give supporting rationales.

EXERCISE 4D
The Strategies of Nestlé S.A.: 2015–2017

Purpose

In performing strategic management case analysis, you can find information about the company's actual and planned strategies. Comparing what is planned versus what you recommend is an important part of case analysis. Do not recommend what the firm actually plans, unless in-depth analysis of the situation reveals those strategies to be the best among all feasible alternatives. This exercise gives you experience conducting library and Internet research to determine what Nestlé plans to do in 2015–2017.

Instructions

Step 1 Go the Nestlé's corporate website as well as the www.finance.yahoo.com website. Locate information about Nestlé's recent strategic actions.

Step 2 Prepare a three-page report titled "Strategies Being Pursued by Nestlé in 2015–2017."

EXERCISE 4E
Lessons in Doing Business Globally

Purpose

The purpose of this exercise is to discover some important lessons learned by local businesses that do business internationally.

Instructions

Contact several local business leaders by telephone. Find at least three firms that engage in international or export operations. Visit the owner or manager of each business in person. Ask the businessperson to give you several important lessons that his or her firm has learned in globally doing business. Record the lessons on paper and report your findings to the class.

EXERCISE 4F
What Are Petronas' Strategies in 2015–2017?

Purpose

In performing strategic management case analysis, you should find information about the company's actual and planned strategies. Comparing what is planned versus what you recommend is an important part of case analysis. Do not recommend what the firm actually plans, unless in-depth analysis of the situation reveals those strategies to be the best among all feasible alternatives. This exercise gives you experience conducting library and Internet research to determine what Petronas plans to do in 2015–2017.

Instructions

Step 1 Go to the Petronas corporate website. Study the information provided there.

Step 2 Prepare a three-page report titled "Strategies Being Pursued by Petronas in 2015–2017."

EXERCISE 4G
What Strategies Are Most Risky?

Purpose

This exercise encourages you to think about the relative riskiness of various strategies.

Instructions

Step 1 List the strategies defined in Chapter 6 in order of low risk to high risk.

Step 2 Write a synopsis that explains your rankings.

EXERCISE 4H
Explore Bankruptcy

Purpose

Bankruptcy is becoming more and more common among business firms. This exercise is designed to enhance your knowledge of bankruptcy.

Instructions

Identify five firms in your country that are operating under bankruptcy. Compare and contrast the nature of the bankruptcy among these firms.

EXERCISE 4I
Examine Strategy Articles

Purpose

Strategy articles can be found weekly in journals, magazines, and newspapers. By reading and studying strategy articles, you can gain a better understanding of the strategic management process. Several of the best journals in which to find corporate strategy articles are: *Advanced Management Journal, Business Horizons, Long Range Planning, Journal of Business Strategy,* and *Strategic Management Journal.* These journals are devoted to reporting the results of empirical research in management. They apply strategic management concepts to specific organizations and industries. They introduce new strategic management techniques and provide short case studies on selected firms. Other good journals in which to find strategic management articles are *Harvard Business Review, Sloan Management Review, California Management Review, Academy of Management Review, Academy of Management Journal, Academy of Management Executive, Journal of Management,* and *Journal of Small Business Management.* In addition to journals, many magazines regularly publish articles that focus on business strategies. Several of the best magazines in which to find applied strategy articles are: *Dun's Business Month, Fortune, Forbes, Business Week, Inc.,* and *Industry Week.* Newspapers such as *USA Today, Wall Street Journal, New York Times,* and *Barron's* cover strategy events when they occur—for example, a joint venture announcement, a bankruptcy declaration, a new advertising campaign start, acquisition of a company, divestiture of a division, a chief executive officer's hiring or firing, or a hostile takeover attempt. In combination, journal, magazine, and newspaper articles can make the strategic-management course more exciting. These sources provide information about the strategies of for-profit and non-profit organizations.

Instructions

Step 1   Go to your college library and find a recent journal article that focuses on a strategic management topic. Select your article from one of the journals listed previously, not from a magazine. Copy the article and bring it to class.

Step 2   Give a 3-minute oral report summarizing the most important information in your article. Include comments giving your personal reaction to the article. Pass your article around in class.

EXERCISE 4J
Classify Some Strategies

Purpose

This exercise can improve your understanding of various strategies by giving you experience classifying strategies. This skill will help you use the strategy-formulation tools presented later. Consider the following 12 (actual or possible) strategies by various firms:

1. Dunkin' Donuts is increasing the number of its U.S. stores to over 15,000.
2. Brown-Forman Corp. selling its Hartmann luggage and leather-goods business.
3. Motorola, which makes TVs, acquired Terayon Communication, a supplier of TV equipment.
4. Macy's department stores adding bistros and Starbucks coffee shops at many of its stores.
5. Dell allowing Wal-Mart to begin selling its computers. This was its first move away from direct mail order selling of computers.
6. Motorola cutting 7,500 additional jobs.

7. Hilton Hotels building 55 new properties in Russia, the United Kingdom, and Central America.
8. Video-sharing website YouTube launching its services in nine new countries.
9. Cadbury Schweppes PLC slashing 7,500 jobs, shedding product variations, and closing factories globally.
10. General Electric selling its plastics division for $11.6 million to Saudi Basic Industries Corp. of Saudi Arabia.
11. Cadbury Schweppes PLC, the maker of Trident gum, buying Turkish gum maker Intergum.
12. Limited Brands selling its Express and Limited divisions to focus on its Victoria's Secret and Bath & Body Works divisions.

Instructions

Step 1   On a separate sheet of paper, write down numbers 1 to 12. These numbers correspond to the strategies described.

Step 2   What type of strategy best describes the 12 actions cited? Indicate your answers.

Step 3   Exchange papers with a classmate, and grade each other's paper as your instructor gives the right answers.

MINI-CASE ON TIGER BRANDS LIMITED

IS TIGER BRANDS STRATEGICALLY READY TO COMPETE AND COOPERATE?

Headquartered in Bryanston, South Africa, Tiger Brands Limited has been one of the largest manufacturers and marketers of food, home and personal care brands, and baby products in Southern Africa for several decades. Founded in 1921, the consumer goods company has used expansion, acquisitions, and joint ventures to achieve a distribution network that now spans across more than 22 African countries. Apart from its operations in South Africa, Tiger Brands also has interests in international food businesses in Chile, Zimbabwe, Nigeria, Kenya, and Cameroon. For the period October 2014 to March 2015, Tiger Brands reported a 9 percent increase in operating profit from domestic businesses; the total group turnover increased by 7 percent to 15.9 billion South African Rand, while operating profit before the IFRS 2 charges declined by 3 percent to 1.7 billion South African Rand.

Source: © MaraZe. Shutterstock

In 2010, the Competition Commission found Tiger Brands, and its competitors Pioneer Foods and Premier Foods, guilty of anti-competitive behavior and conspiring to increase the price of bread. However, Pioneer settled on a penalty of nearly 1 billion South African Rand and Premier was granted immunity for co-operating with the commission, while Tiger Brands, despite co-operating had to pay a fine of nearly 90 million South African Rand.

Tiger Brands' statements of vision and mission, posted on their corporate website, include its aim to be the world's most admired brand for consumer packaged-goods in emerging markets. Tiger Brands is also working towards being a high performing, fast–moving company that operates across the globe in several emerging territories.

Questions

1. How well does Tiger Brand's vision and mission statements help narrow down feasible alternative strategies available for the firm?
2. Does Tiger Brand pursue a cost leadership, differentiation, or focus strategy? Evaluate its strategic approach in comparison to its competitors.

Source: Based on company documents.

Current Readings

Cabral, Sandro, Bertrand Quelin, and Walmir Maia. "Outsourcing Failure and Reintegration: The Influence of Contractual and External Factors." *Long Range Planning* 47, no. 6 (December 2014): 365–378.

Dobni, C. Brooke, Mark Klassen, and W. Thomas Nelson. "Innovation Strategy in the US: Top Executives Offer Their Views." *Journal of Business Strategy* 36, no. 1 (2015): 3–13.

Fogarty, David, and Peter C. Bell. "Should You Outsource Analytics?" *MIT Sloan Management Review* 55, no. 2 (2014): 41–45.

MacCormack, Alan, Fiona Murray, and Erika Wagner. "Spurring Innovation through Competitions." (Cover Story). *MIT Sloan Management Review* 55, no. 1 (2013): 25–32.

Martinez-Jerez, F. Asis. "Rewriting the Playbook for Corporate Partnerships." *MIT Sloan Management Review* 55, no. 2 (2014): 63–70.

Mckinley, William, Scott Latham, and Michael Braun. "Organizational Decline and Innovation: Turnarounds and Downward Spirals." *Academy of Management Review* 39, no. 1 (2014): 88–110.

Nadkarni, Sucheta, and Jianhong Chen. "Bridging Yesterday, Today, and Tomorrow: CEO Temporal Focus, Environmental Dynamism, and Rate of New Product Introduction." *Academy of Management Journal* 57 (December 2014): 1,810–1,833.

Roloff, Julia, Michael S. Ablander, and Dilek Z. Nayir. "The Supplier Perspective: Forging Strong Partnerships with Buyers." *Journal of Business Strategy* 36, no. 1 (2015): 25–32.

Rubera, Gaia, and Gerard J. Tetlis. "Spinoffs versus Buyouts: Profitability of Alternate Routes for Commercializing Innovations." *Strategic Management Journal*, 35, no. 13 (December 2014): 2,043–2,052.

Smith, Wendy K. "Dynamic Decision Making: A Model of Senior Leaders Managing Strategic Paradoxes." *Academy of Management Journal* 57 (December 2014): 1,592–1,623.

Trahms, Cheryl A., Hermann Achidi Ndofor, and David G. Sirmon. "Organizational Decline and Turnaround: A Review and Agenda for Future Research." *Journal of Management* 39, no. 5 (2013): 1,277–1,307.

Endnotes

1. John Byrne, "Strategic Planning—It's Back," *BusinessWeek* (August 26, 1996): 46.
2. Steven C. Brandt, *Strategic Planning in Emerging Companies* (Reading, MA: Addison-Wesley, 1981). Reprinted with permission of the publisher.
3. F. Hansen and M. Smith, "Crisis in Corporate America: The Role of Strategy," *Business Horizons* (January–February 2003): 9.
4. Based on F. R. David, "How Do We Choose among Alternative Growth Strategies?" *Managerial Planning* 33, no. 4 (January–February 1985): 14–17, 22.
5. Ibid.
6. Kenneth Davidson, "Do Megamergers Make Sense?" *Journal of Business Strategy* 7, no. 3 (Winter 1987): 45.
7. David, "How Do We Choose."
8. Ibid.
9. Ibid.
10. Ibid.
11. Arthur Thompson Jr., A. J. Strickland III, and John Gamble, *Crafting and Executing Strategy: Text and Readings* (New York: McGraw-Hill/Irwin, 2005), 241.
12. Michael E. Porter, *Competitive Strategy: Techniques for Analyzing Industries and Competitors* (New York: Free Press, 1980), 53–57, 318–319.
13. David, "How Do We Choose."
14. Ibid.
15. Ibid.
16. Ibid.
17. Ibid.
18. Michael Porter, *Competitive Advantage* (New York: Free Press, 1985), 97. See also Arthur Thompson Jr., A. J. Strickland III, and John Gamble, *Crafting and Executing Strategy: Text and Readings* (New York: McGraw-Hill/Irwin, 2005), 117.
19. Arthur Thompson Jr., A. J. Strickland III, and John Gamble, *Crafting and Executing Strategy: Text and Readings* (New York: McGraw-Hill/Irwin, 2005), 125–126.
20. Porter, *Competitive Advantage,* 160–162.
21. Thompson, Strickland, and Gamble, *Crafting and Executing Strategy,* 129–130.
22. Ibid., 134.

23. Gary Hamel, Yves Doz, and C. K. Prahalad, "Collaborate with Your Competitors—and Win," *Harvard Business Review* 67, no. 1 (January–February 1989): 133.

24. Matthew Schifrin, "Partner or Perish," *Forbes* (May 21, 2001): 32.

25. Kathryn Rudie Harrigan, "Joint Ventures: Linking for a Leap Forward," *Planning Review* 14, no. 4 (July–August 1986): 10.

26. Schifrin, "Partner or Perish," p. 26.

27. David, "How Do We Choose."

28. James Hagerty, "Some Firms Opt to Bring Manufacturing Back to USA," *Wall Street Journal,* July 18, 2012, B8.

29. James Hagerty, "Offshoring Outpaces 'Reshoring,'" *Wall Street Journal*, December 15, 2014, B3.

Source: © Paylessimages/Fotolia

Vision and Mission Analysis

LEARNING OBJECTIVES

After studying this chapter, you should be able to do the following:

5-1. Describe the nature and role of vision statements in strategic management.

5-2. Describe the nature and role of mission statements in strategic management.

5-3. Discuss the process of developing a vision and mission statement.

5-4. Discuss how clear vision and mission statements can benefit other strategic-management activities.

5-5. Describe the characteristics of a good mission statement.

5-6. Identify the components of mission statements.

5-7. Evaluate mission statements of different organizations and write effective vision and mission statements.

ASSURANCE OF LEARNING EXERCISES

The following exercises are found at the end of this chapter:

EXERCISE 5A	Examine Potential Changes Needed in a Firm's Vision/Mission
EXERCISE 5B	Studying an Alternative View of Mission Statement Content
EXERCISE 5C	Evaluate Mission Statements
EXERCISE 5D	Evaluate the Vision and Mission Statements of Unilever, Nestlé's Competitor
EXERCISE 5E	Selecting the Best Vision and Mission Statements in a Given Industry
EXERCISE 5F	Write an Excellent Vision and Mission Statement for Novartis AG

This chapter focuses on the concepts and tools needed to evaluate and write business vision and mission statements. It also provides a practical framework for developing and creating effective vision and mission statements. Actual mission statements from large and small organizations and for-profit and nonprofit enterprises are presented and critiqued. The exemplary company examined in the beginning of this chapter, Samsung Electronics, is exemplary in terms of both its vision and mission concepts as well as its strategic management.

We can perhaps best understand vision and mission by focusing on a business when it is first started. In the beginning, a new business is simply a collection of ideas. Starting a new business rests on a set of beliefs that the new organization can offer some product or service to some customers in some geographic area using some type of technology at a profitable price. A new business owner typically believes his or her philosophy of the new enterprise will result in a favorable public image, and the business concept can be effectively communicated to and adopted by important constituencies. When the set of beliefs about a business at its inception is put into writing, the resulting document mirrors the same basic ideas that underlie vision and mission statements. As a business grows, owners or managers find it necessary to revise the founding set of beliefs, but those original ideas usually are reflected in the revised statements of vision and mission.

Vision and mission statements often can be found in the front of annual reports. They often are displayed throughout a firm's premises and are distributed with company information sent to constituencies. The statements are part of numerous internal reports, such as loan requests, supplier agreements, labor relations contracts, business plans, and customer service agreements.

Vision Statements: What Do We Want to Become?

It is especially important for managers and executives in any organization to agree on the basic vision that the firm strives to achieve in the long term. A **vision statement** should answer the basic question, "What do we want to become?" A clear vision provides the foundation for developing a comprehensive mission statement. Many organizations have both a vision and mission

Samsung Electronics Co. Limited (SSNLF)

Headquartered in Suwon, South Korea, Samsung is the world's largest information company. With over 270,000 employees, Samsung has assembly plants and sales networks across 88 countries. A leader amongst smartphone manufacturer, Samsung also leads in the production of electronic components like lithium-ion batteries, semiconductors chips, and tablet computers.

Samsung's values and philosophy are provided on the About Us section of the company's website. Samsung's vision statement, posted on their website, states that the company aims to develop innovative technologies and efficient processes to enter new territories, improve people's lives, and carry on as a leader in the digital platform. The company's mission statement is called a statement of philosophy Right beneath the firm's vision and mission on the website, the company's core values are listed and described under five categories: People, Excellence, Change, Integrity, and Co-Prosperity. The website also provides the company's Vision 2020 which reinforces the firm's mission statement. The firm is exemplary in terms of both its vision and mission concepts as well as its strategic management.

Source: Based on company documents.

statement, but the vision statement should be established first and foremost. The vision statement should be short, preferably one sentence, and as many managers as possible should have input into developing the statement. Where there is no vision, the people perish (Proverbs 29:18).

For many, if not most, corporations, profit rather than mission or vision is the primary motivator. But profit alone is not enough to motivate people. Profit is perceived negatively by many stakeholders of a firm. For example, employees may see profit as something that they earn and management then uses and even gives away to shareholders. Although this perception is undesired and disturbing to management, it clearly indicates that both profit and vision are needed to motivate a workforce effectively.

When employees and managers together shape or fashion the vision and mission statements for a firm, the resultant documents can reflect the personal visions that managers and employees have in their hearts and minds about their own futures. Shared vision creates a commonality of interests that can lift workers out of the monotony of daily work and put them into a new world of opportunity and challenge.

Although typically a single sentence, vision statements need to be written from a customer perspective. For example, eBay's vision is "To provide a global trading platform where practically anyone can trade practically anything." Vision statements need to do more than identify the product/service a firm offers. The old Ford Motor Company vision, for example, was product-oriented: "To make the automobile accessible to every American," but today Ford has a more effective customer-oriented vision statement: "To provide personal mobility for people around the world." Examples of vision statements are provided in Table 5-1.

Vision Statement Analysis

At a minimum, a vision statement should reveal the type of business the firm engages. For example, to have a vision that says, "to become the best retailing firm in the USA" is much too broad, because that firm could be selling anything from boats to bunnies. Notice here how Starbucks' vision statement is improved.

STARBUCKS VISION STATEMENT (PARAPHRASED)

Starbucks strives to be the premier roaster and retailer of specialty coffee globally.

STARBUCKS "IMPROVED" VISION STATEMENT

Starbucks' vision is to be the most well-known, specialty coffee, tea, and pastry restaurant in the world, offering sincere customer service, a welcoming atmosphere, and unequaled quality.

AUTHOR COMMENTS

- The first vision statement does not state what the company wants to become. Nor does it acknowledge the firm's movement into specialty tea offerings. It is not as customer-oriented as needed.
- The improved vision statement reveals the company's aspirations for the future and acknowledges that upscale tea and pastries complement their premium coffee offerings.

TABLE 5-1 Vision Statement Examples

- General Motors' vision is to be the world leader in transportation products and related services. *(Author comment: Good statement)*
- PepsiCo's responsibility is to continually improve all aspects of the world in which we operate— environment, social, economic—creating a better tomorrow than today. *(Author comment: Statement is too vague; it should reveal how the firm's food and beverage business benefits people)*
- Royal Caribbean's vision is to empower and enable our employees to deliver the best vacation experience for our guests, thereby generating superior returns for our shareholders and enhancing the well-being of our communities. *(Author comment: Statement is good but could end after the word* guests*)*

Sources: Courtesy General Motors; © 2013 PepsiCo Inc. Used with permission; Courtesy Royal Caribbean.

Mission Statements: What Is Our Business?

Current thought on mission statements is based largely on guidelines set forth in the mid-1970s by Peter Drucker, who is often called "the father of modern management" for his pioneering studies at General Motors and for his 22 books and hundreds of articles. Drucker believes that asking the question "What is our business?" is synonymous with asking "What is our mission?" An enduring statement of purpose that distinguishes one organization from other similar enterprises, the **mission statement** is a declaration of an organization's "reason for being." It answers the pivotal question "What is our business?" A clear mission statement is essential for effectively establishing objectives and formulating strategies.

Sometimes called a **creed statement**, a statement of purpose, a statement of philosophy, a statement of beliefs, a statement of business principles, or a statement "defining our business," a mission statement reveals what an organization wants to be and whom it wants to serve. All organizations have a reason for being, even if strategists have not consciously transformed this reason into writing. As illustrated with white shading in Figure 5-1, carefully prepared statements of vision and mission are widely recognized by both practitioners and academicians as the

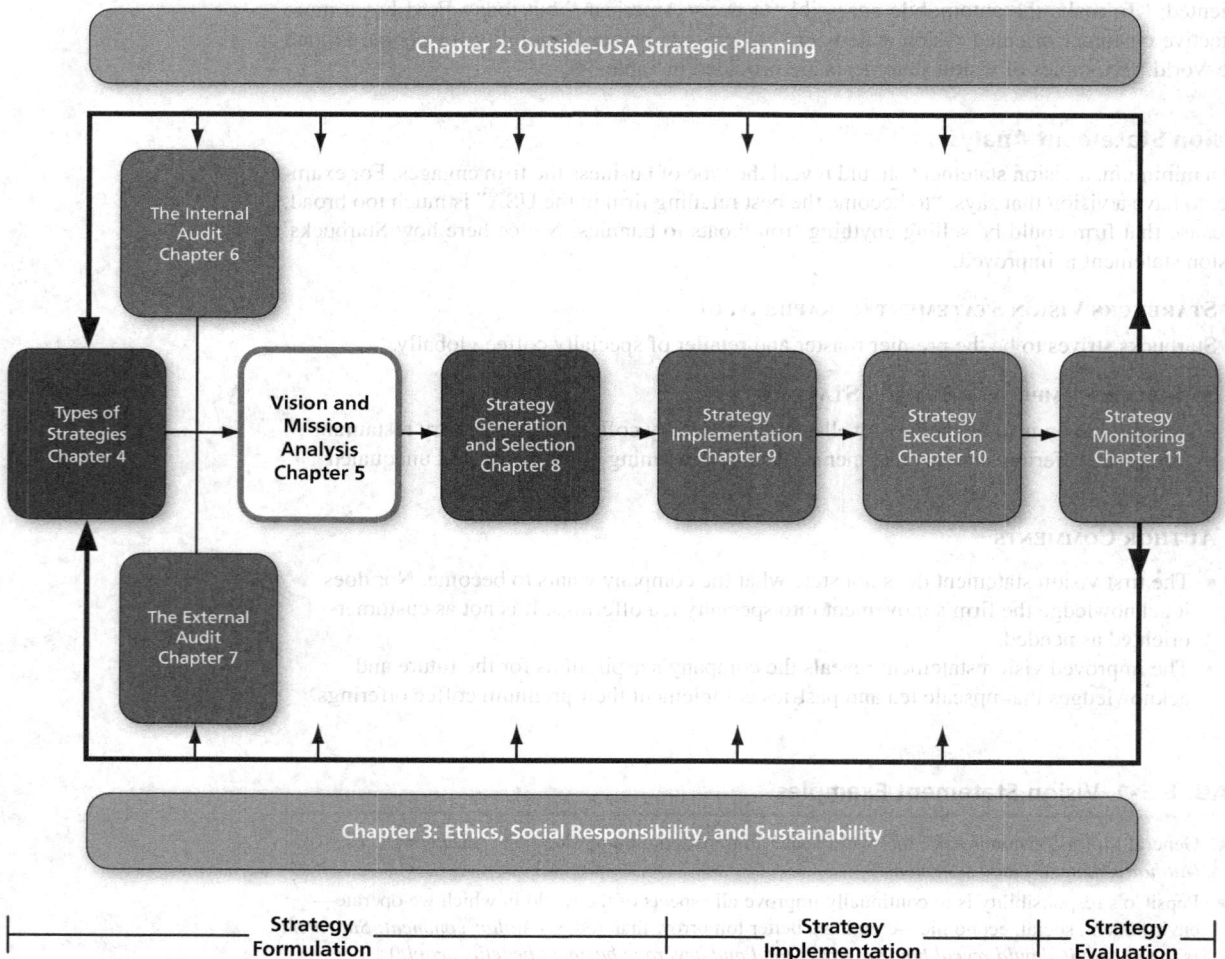

FIGURE 5-1

A Comprehensive Strategic-Management Model

Source: Fred R. David, adapted from "How Companies Define Their Mission," *Long Range Planning* 22, no. 3 (June 1988): 40, © Fred R. David.

first step in strategic management. Drucker has the following to say about mission statements (paraphrased):

> A mission statement is the foundation for priorities, strategies, plans, and work assignments. It is the starting point for the design of jobs and organizational structures. Nothing may seem simpler or more obvious than to know what a company's business is. A lumber mill makes lumber, an airline carries passengers and freight, and a bank lends money. But "What is our business?" is almost always a difficult question and the right answer is usually anything but obvious. The answer to this question is the first responsibility of strategists.[1]

Some strategists spend almost every moment of every day on administrative and tactical concerns; those who rush quickly to establish objectives and implement strategies often overlook the development of a vision and mission statement. This problem is widespread even among large organizations. Many corporations in the United States have not yet developed a formal vision or mission statement. An increasing number of organizations, however, are developing these statements.

Some companies develop mission statements simply because owners or top management believe it is fashionable, rather than out of any real commitment. However, as described in this chapter, firms that develop and systematically revisit their vision and mission statements, treat them as living documents, and consider them to be an integral part of the firm's culture realize great benefits. For example, managers at Johnson & Johnson (J&J) meet regularly with employees to review, reword, and reaffirm the firm's vision and mission. The entire J&J workforce recognizes the value that top management places on this exercise, and these employees respond accordingly.

The Process of Developing Vision and Mission Statements

As indicated in the strategic-management model, clear vision and mission statements are needed before alternative strategies can be formulated and implemented. As many managers as possible should be involved in the process of developing these statements because, through involvement, people become committed to an organization.

A widely used approach to developing a vision and mission statement is first to select several articles (such as those listed as Current Readings at the end of this chapter) about these statements and ask all managers to read these as background information. Then, ask managers to individually prepare a vision and mission statement for the organization. A facilitator or committee of top managers should then merge these statements into a single document and distribute the draft statements to all managers. A request for modifications, additions, and deletions is needed next, along with a meeting to revise the document. To the extent that all managers have input into and support the final documents, organizations can more easily obtain managers' support for other strategy formulation, implementation, and evaluation activities. Thus, the process of developing vision and mission statements represents a great opportunity for strategists to obtain needed support from all managers in the firm.

During the process of developing vision and mission statements, some organizations use discussion groups of managers to develop and modify existing statements. Other organizations hire an outside consultant or facilitator to manage the process and help draft the language. At times an outside person with expertise in developing such statements, who has unbiased views, can manage the process more effectively than an internal group or committee of managers. Decisions on how best to communicate the vision and mission to all managers, employees, and external constituencies of an organization are needed when the documents are in final form. Some organizations even create a videotape to explain the statements and how they were developed.

An article by Campbell and Yeung emphasizes that the process of developing a mission statement should create an "emotional bond" and "sense of mission" between the organization and its employees.[2] Commitment to a company's strategy and intellectual agreement on the strategies to be pursued do not necessarily translate into an emotional bond; hence, strategies that have been formulated may not be implemented. These researchers stress that an emotional bond comes when an individual personally identifies with the underlying values and behavior of a firm, thus turning intellectual agreement and commitment to strategy into a sense of mission. Campbell and Yeung also differentiate between the terms *vision* and *mission*, saying that vision is "a possible and desirable future state of an organization" that includes specific goals, whereas mission is more associated with behavior and the present.

The Importance (Benefits) of Vision and Mission Statements

The importance (benefits) of vision and mission statements to effective strategic management is well documented in the literature, although research results are mixed. As indicated in Academic Research Capsule 5-1, there is a positive relationship between mission statements and measures of financial performance.

In actual practice, wide variations exist in the nature, composition, and use of both vision and mission statements. King and Cleland recommend that organizations carefully develop a written mission statement in order to reap the following benefits:

1. To make sure all employees/managers understand the firm's purpose or reason for being.
2. To provide a basis for prioritization of key internal and external factors utilized to formulate feasible strategies.
3. To provide a basis for the allocation of resources.
4. To provide a basis for organizing work, departments, activities, and segments around a common purpose.[3]

Reuben Mark, former CEO of Colgate, maintains that a clear mission increasingly must make sense internationally. Mark's thoughts on vision are as follows:

> When it comes to rallying everyone to the corporate banner, it's essential to push one vision globally rather than trying to drive home different messages in different cultures. The trick is to keep the vision simple but elevated: "We make the world's fastest computers" or "Telephone service for everyone." You're never going to get anyone to charge the machine guns only for financial objectives. It's got to be something that makes people feel better, feel a part of something.[4]

ACADEMIC RESEARCH CAPSULE 5-1

The Mission Statement/Firm Performance Linkage

A meta-analysis of 20 years of empirical research on mission statements concluded that "there is a small positive relationship between mission statements and measures of financial organizational performance" (Desmidt et al., 2011, p. 468). However, research in marketing explains that customer satisfaction has a strong positive relationship with organizational performance (Devasagayam et al., 2013). Indeed, researchers have noted that "managers increasingly tend to see customer satisfaction as a valuable intangible asset" (Luo et al., 2012, p. 745). Thus, mission statements designed from a customer perspective could positively impact organizational performance by enhancing customer satisfaction. If written from a customer perspective, mission statements could spur employees, salespersons, and managers to provide exemplary customer service, which arguably would enhance customer loyalty and translate into customers being "on a mission"

to seek out, use, and promote the firm's products and services. Written from a customer perspective, mission statements may indeed "accomplish their mission."

Sources: Based on S. Desmidt, A. Prinzie, & A. Decramer, A. "Looking for the Value of Mission Statements: A Meta-Analysis of 20 Years of Research," *Management Decision,* 49, no. 3 (2011): 468–483; R. Devasagayam, N. R. Stark, & L. S. Valestin, "Examining the Linearity of Customer Satisfaction: Return on Satisfaction as an Alternative," *Business Perspectives and Research* 1, no. 2 (2013): 1–8; X. Luo, J. Wieseke, & C. Homburg, "Incentivizing CEOs to Build Customer- and Employee-Firm Relations for Higher Customer Satisfaction and Firm Value," *Journal of the Academy of Marketing Science* 40, no. 6 (2012): 45–758; M. E. David, Forest R. David, & Fred R. David, "Mission Statement Theory and Practice: A Content Analysis and New Direction," *International Journal of Business, Marketing, and Decision Sciences* 7, no. 1 (Summer 2014): 95–109.

A Resolution of Divergent Views

Another benefit of developing a comprehensive mission statement is that divergent views among managers can be revealed and resolved through the process. The question "What is our business?" can create controversy. Raising the question often reveals differences among strategists in the organization. Individuals who have worked together for a long time and who think they know each other suddenly may realize that they are in fundamental disagreement. For example, in a college or university, divergent views regarding the relative importance of teaching, research, and service often are expressed during the mission statement development process. Negotiation, compromise, and eventual agreement on important issues are needed before people can focus on more specific strategy-formulation activities.

Considerable disagreement among an organization's strategists over vision and mission statements can cause trouble if not resolved. For example, unresolved disagreement over the business mission was one of the reasons for W. T. Grant's bankruptcy and eventual liquidation. Top executives of the firm, including Ed Staley and Lou Lustenberger, were firmly entrenched in opposing positions that W. T. Grant should be like Kmart or JC Penney, respectively. W. T. Grant decided to become a bit like both Kmart and JC Penney; this compromise was a huge strategic mistake. In other words, top executives of W. T. Grant never resolved their vision/mission issue, which ultimately led to the firm's disappearance.[5]

Too often, strategists develop vision and mission statements only when the organization is in trouble. Of course, the documents are needed then. Developing and communicating a clear mission during troubled times indeed may have spectacular results and may even reverse decline. However, to wait until an organization is in trouble to develop a vision and mission statement is a gamble that characterizes irresponsible management. According to Drucker, the most important time to ask seriously, "What do we want to become?" and "What is our business?" is when a company has been successful:

> Success always obsoletes the very behavior that achieved it, always creates new realities, and always creates new and different problems. Only the fairy tale story ends, "They lived happily ever after." It is never popular to argue with success or to rock the boat. It will not be long before success will turn into failure. Sooner or later, even the most successful answer to the question "What is our business?" becomes obsolete.[6]

In multidivisional organizations, strategists should ensure that divisional units perform strategic-management tasks, including the development of a statement of vision and mission. Each division should involve its own managers and employees in developing a vision and mission statement that is consistent with and supportive of the corporate mission. Ten benefits of having a clear mission and vision are provided in Table 5-2.

An organization that fails to develop a vision statement, as well as a comprehensive and inspiring mission statement, loses the opportunity to present itself favorably to existing and

TABLE 5-2 Ten Benefits of Having a Clear Mission and Vision

1. Achieve clarity of purpose among all managers and employees.
2. Provide a basis for all other strategic planning activities, including internal and external assessment, establishing objectives, developing strategies, choosing among alternative strategies, devising policies, establishing organizational structure, allocating resources, and evaluating performance.
3. Provide direction.
4. Provide a focal point for all stakeholders of the firm.
5. Resolve divergent views among managers.
6. Promote a sense of shared expectations among all managers and employees.
7. Project a sense of worth and intent to all stakeholders.
8. Project an organized, motivated organization worthy of support.
9. Achieve higher organizational performance.
10. Achieve synergy among all managers and employees.

potential stakeholders. All organizations need customers, employees, and managers, and most firms need creditors, suppliers, and distributors. Vision and mission statements are effective vehicles for communicating with important internal and external stakeholders. The principal benefit of these statements as tools of strategic management is derived from their specification of the ultimate aims of a firm. Vision and mission statements reveal the firm's shared expectations internally among all employees and managers. For external constituencies, the statements reveal the firm's long-term commitment to responsible, ethical action in providing a needed product and/or service for customers.

Characteristics of a Mission Statement

A mission statement is a declaration of attitude and outlook. It usually is broad in scope for at least two major reasons. First, a good mission statement allows for the generation and consideration of a range of feasible alternative objectives and strategies without unduly stifling management creativity. Excess specificity would limit the potential of creative growth for the organization. However, an overly general statement that does not exclude any strategy alternatives could be dysfunctional. Apple Computer's mission statement, for example, should not open the possibility for diversification into pesticides—or Ford Motor Company's into food processing.

Second, a mission statement needs to be broad to reconcile differences effectively among, and appeal to, an organization's diverse **stakeholders**, the individuals and groups of individuals who have a special stake or claim on the company. Thus, a mission statement should be **reconciliatory**. Stakeholders include employees, managers, stockholders, boards of directors, customers, suppliers, distributors, creditors, governments (local, state, federal, and foreign), unions, competitors, environmental groups, and the general public. Stakeholders affect and are affected by an organization's strategies, yet the claims and concerns of diverse constituencies vary and often conflict. For example, the general public is especially interested in social responsibility, whereas stockholders are more interested in profitability. Claims on any business literally may number in the thousands, and they often include clean air, jobs, taxes, investment opportunities, career opportunities, equal employment opportunities, employee benefits, salaries, wages, clean water, and community services. All stakeholders' claims on an organization cannot be pursued with equal emphasis. A good mission statement indicates the relative attention that an organization will devote to meeting the claims of various stakeholders.

The fine balance between specificity and generality is difficult to achieve, but it is well worth the effort. George Steiner offers the following insight on the need for a mission statement to be broad in scope:

> Most business statements of mission are expressed at high levels of abstraction. Vagueness nevertheless has its virtues. Mission statements are not designed to express concrete ends, but rather to provide motivation, general direction, an image, a tone, and a philosophy to guide the enterprise. An excess of detail could prove counterproductive since concrete specification could be the base for rallying opposition. Precision might stifle creativity in the formulation of an acceptable mission or purpose. Once an aim is cast in concrete, it creates a rigidity in an organization and resists change. Vagueness leaves room for other managers to fill in the details.[7]

As indicated in Table 5-3, in addition to being broad in scope, an effective mission statement should not be too lengthy; recommended length is less than 150 words. An effective mission statement should arouse positive feelings and emotions about an organization; it should be inspiring in the sense that it motivates readers to action. A mission statement should be enduring. All of these are desired characteristics of a statement. An effective mission statement generates the impression that a firm is successful, has direction, and is worthy of time, support, and investment—from all socioeconomic groups of people.

A business mission reflects judgments about future growth directions and strategies that are based on forward-looking external and internal analyses. The statement should provide useful criteria for selecting among alternative strategies. A clear mission statement provides a basis

CHAPTER 5 • VISION AND MISSION ANALYSIS **165**

TABLE 5-3 Characteristics of a Mission Statement

1. Broad in scope; does not include monetary amounts, numbers, percentages, ratios, or objectives
2. Fewer than 150 words in length
3. Inspiring
4. Identifies the utility of a firm's products
5. Reveals that the firm is socially responsible
6. Reveals that the firm is environmentally responsible
7. Includes nine components: customers, products or services, markets, technology, concern for survival/growth/profits, philosophy, self-concept, concern for public image, concern for employees
8. Reconciliatory
9. Enduring

for generating and screening strategic options. The statement of mission should be sufficiently broad to allow judgments about the most promising growth directions and those considered less promising.

A Customer Orientation

An effective mission statement describes an organization's purpose, customers, products or services, markets, philosophy, and basic technology. According to Vern McGinnis, a mission statement should (1) define what the organization is and what the organization aspires to be, (2) be limited enough to exclude some ventures and broad enough to allow for creative growth, (3) distinguish a given organization from all others, (4) serve as a framework for evaluating both current and prospective activities, and (5) be stated in terms sufficiently clear to be widely understood throughout the organization.[8] The mission statement should reflect the anticipations of customers. Rather than developing a product and then trying to find a market, the operating philosophy of organizations should be to identify customers' needs and then provide a product or service to fulfill those needs.

Good mission statements identify the utility of a firm's products to its customers. This is why AT&T's mission statement focuses on communication rather than on telephones; it is why ExxonMobil's mission statement focuses on energy rather than on oil and gas; it is why Union Pacific's mission statement focuses on transportation rather than on railroads; it is why Universal Studios' mission statement focuses on entertainment rather than on movies. A major reason for developing a mission statement is to attract customers who give meaning to an organization. The following utility statements are relevant in developing a mission statement:

Do not offer me things.

Do not offer me clothes. Offer me attractive looks.

Do not offer me shoes. Offer me comfort for my feet and the pleasure of walking.

Do not offer me a house. Offer me security, comfort, and a place that is clean and happy.

Do not offer me books. Offer me hours of pleasure and the benefit of knowledge.

Do not offer me CDs. Offer me leisure and the sound of music.

Do not offer me tools. Offer me the benefits and the pleasure that come from making beautiful things.

Do not offer me furniture. Offer me comfort and the quietness of a cozy place.

Do not offer me things. Offer me ideas, emotions, ambience, feelings, and benefits.

Please, do not offer me *things*.

Components of a Mission Statement

Mission statements can and do vary in length, content, format, and specificity. Most practitioners and academicians of strategic management feel that an effective statement should include the nine **mission statement components** given here. Because a mission statement is often the most visible and public part of the strategic-management process, it is important that it includes not only the characteristics as summarized in Table 5-3 but also the following nine components:

1. *Customers*—Who are the firm's customers?
2. *Products or services*—What are the firm's major products or services?
3. *Markets*—Geographically, where does the firm compete?
4. *Technology*—Is the firm technologically current?
5. *Survival, growth, and profitability*—Is the firm committed to growth and financial soundness?
6. *Philosophy*—What are the basic beliefs, values, aspirations, and ethical priorities of the firm?
7. *Self-concept (distinctive competence)*—What is the firm's major competitive advantage?
8. *Public image*—Is the firm responsive to social, community, and environmental concerns?
9. *Employees*—Are employees a valuable asset of the firm?[9]

To exemplify how mission statements could be written from a customer perspective, a component-by-component example for a charter boat fishing company is provided in Table 5-4. Note the charter company's customers are "outdoor enthusiasts." "Customers" is a key component to include in a mission statement, but simply including the word *customer* or *consumer* does not qualify that component to be considered "written from a customer perspective." The statement needs to identify more precisely the target groups of customers. All nine components in Table 5-4 are written from a customer perspective. For example, regarding the "product/ service" component, the charter fishing company provides "memories for a lifetime"—thus revealing the "utility" of the service offered. Regarding the "distinctive competence" component, whereby the firm reveals the major competitive advantage its products/services provide, the statement says: "for customer enjoyment and safety, we provide the most experienced staff in the industry."

Evaluating and Writing Mission Statements

There is no one best mission statement for a particular organization, so when it comes to evaluating mission statements, good judgment is required. Ideally, the statement will provide more than simply inclusion of a single word such as *products* or *employees* regarding a respective

TABLE 5-4 Mission Statement Components Written from a Customer Perspective

1. *Customers*—Our customers are outdoor enthusiasts seeking fishing excitement and adventure.
2. *Products or services*—We provide fast, clean boats, all the bait and tackle needed, and friendly first mates to create memories for a lifetime.
3. *Markets*—Our fleet of fast, clean vessels operate all along the Florida Gulf Coast.
4. *Technology*—Our vessels are equipped with the very latest safety and fish finding equipment to ensure that customers comfortably are "catching rather than just fishing."
5. *Survival, growth, and profitability*—Our prices are as low as possible to provide customers great value in conjunction with high employee morale and a reasonable return for our owners.
6. *Philosophy*—We assure customers the upmost courtesy and care as our motto on every vessel is to follow the Golden Rule.
7. *Self-concept*—For customer enjoyment and safety, we provide the most experienced staff in the industry.
8. *Public image*—Our vessels use emission-friendly engines; we strive to bring repeat tourists to all communities where we operate.
9. *Employees*—Our on-the-water and off-the-water employees are "on a mission" to help customers have a great time.

Source: Based on Meredith E. David, Forest R. David, & Fred R. David, "Mission Statement Theory and Practice: A Content Analysis and New Direction," *International Journal of Business, Marketing, and Decision Sciences* 7, no. 1 (Summer 2014): 95–109.

component. Why? Because the statement should motivate stakeholders to action, as well as be customer-oriented, informative, inspiring, and enduring.

Two Mission Statements Critiqued

Perhaps the best way to develop a skill for writing and evaluating mission statements is to study actual company missions. Thus, Table 5-5 provides a component-by-component critique of two actual mission statements from PepsiCo, and Royal Caribbean. The Royal Caribbean statement includes only six of the nine components, comprises 86 words total, and lacks a customer perspective. The Royal Caribbean statement merely includes the word *customer(s)*, which is inadequate to be considered written from a customer perspective.

Five Mission Statements Revised

As additional guidance for practitioners (and students), five actual mission statements are revised/rewritten from a customer perspective and presented in Table 5-6. The improved statements include all nine components written from a customer perspective, and, additionally, are inspiring, concise, and comprised of fewer than 90 words each. Regarding the "customer" component, the new Best Buy statement refers to "individuals and businesses"; the new Lowe's statement refers to "homebuilders and homeowners"; and the improved Crocs statement refers to "men, women, and children." In contrast, the Crocs, Best Buy, Rite Aid, and Lowe's actual statements merely include (or not) the word *customer* or *consumer*. The statements are revised to potentially enhance customer satisfaction, especially if communicated to customers by marketers, and backed by company commitment to and implementation of the mission message. The proposed statement for the footwear company Crocs, Inc., for example, talks about "dependable and lasting comfort all day," whereas the UPS proposed statement talks about "the most timely, dependable, and accurate delivery times in the world."

Two Mission Statements Proposed

The process by which mission statements are developed and the exact language/wording included in the statement can significantly impact their effectiveness as a tool for strategic management and marketing strategy. Firms strive to have customers exhibit an emotional bond with the firm's

TABLE 5-5 Two Mission Statements Critiqued

The numbers in parentheses correspond to the nine mission statement components.

PepsiCo

We aspire to make PepsiCo the world's (3) premier consumer products company, focused on convenient foods and beverages (2). We seek to produce healthy financial rewards for investors (5) as we provide opportunities for growth and enrichment to our employees (9), our business partners and the communities (8) in which we operate. And in everything we do, we strive to act with honesty, openness, fairness and integrity (6). *(Author comment: Statement lacks three components: Customers (1), Technology (4), and Distinctive Competence (7); 62 words)*

Royal Caribbean

We are loyal to Royal Caribbean and Celebrity and strive for continuous improvement in everything we do. We always provide service with a friendly greeting and a smile (7). We anticipate the needs of our customers and make all efforts to exceed our customers' expectations. We take ownership of any problem that is brought to our attention. We engage in conduct that enhances our corporate reputation and employee morale (9). We are committed to act in the highest ethical manner and respect the rights and dignity of others. (6). *(Author comment: Statement lacks six components: Customers (1), Products/Services (2), Markets (3), Technology (4), Survival/Growth/Profits (5), and Public Image (8); 86 words)*

Source: Based on Meredith E. David, Forest R. David, & Fred R. David, "Mission Statement Theory and Practice: A Content Analysis and New Direction," *International Journal of Business, Marketing, and Decision Sciences* 7, no. 1 (Summer 2014): 95–109. Also based on information found at the various corporate websites. © 2013 PepsiCo Inc. Used with Permission. Courtesy Royal Caribbean.

TABLE 5-6 Five Mission Statements Revised

The numbers in parentheses correspond to the nine mission statement components.

Rite Aid

We are on a mission to offer the best possible drugstore experience for people of all ages (1) around the United States (3). We have a state-of-the-art information system (4) that provides our pharmacists (9) with warnings of any possible drug interactions to help better ensure customer safety (8). We are determined to improve our customers' overall health through our wellness programs (5). We offer an extensive line of other beauty, food, drink, cosmetic, and vitamin products through our alliance with GNC (2). We believe in treating our customers like family (6) and strive to maintain our reputation as the most personable drugstore (7). *(88 words total)*

Best Buy

We are committed to providing individuals and businesses (1) the latest high-tech products (2) at the lowest prices of any retail store (7). Serving North America, China, and other markets (3), all Best Buy employees (9) are exceptionally knowledgeable about the products we offer. We believe good ethics is good business (6) and use business analytics (4) to better understand customer trends. We strive to make a profit for our shareholders (5) and be a good community citizen everywhere we operate (8). *(72 words)*

Lowe's

We are committed to exceeding the expectations of our homebuilder, homeowner, and other customers (1). We offer superior home improvement products (2) and expert advice (7) at nearly 2,000 Lowe's stores in the United States, Canada, and Mexico (3). We have a best-in-class electronic in-store tracking system (4) to help customers. We continue to create jobs (8) in all communities where we operate. Up to 80 percent of our employees work on a full-time basis (9) and have high ethical standards (6). We put the customer first as we strive to grow profitably for our shareholders (8). *(88 words)*

United Parcel Service (UPS)

We strive to be the most timely and dependable parcel and freight forwarding delivery service (2) in the world (3). By implementing the latest tracking technology (4), we are able to profitably grow (5) by offering individuals and businesses (1) dependable and accurate delivery times (7). We promote from within to improve morale among all employees (9). Our philosophy (6) is to responsibly balance the needs of our customers, employees, shareholders, and communities (8) in an exemplary manner. *(68 words)*

Crocs, Inc.

Crocs is committed to providing profound comfort, fun and innovation in all the shoe models (2) we produce. Through our Croslite technology (4) (7), we are able to provide men, women, and children (1) dependable and lasting comfort all day. We strive to expand our brand throughout the world (3) and are able to save on costs (5), while protecting the environment (8) with our package-less shoes. We adhere to the belief that good ethics is good business (6) in all that we do as we strive to take care of our employees and shareholders. *(85 words)*

Source: Based on Meredith E. David, Forest R. David, & Fred R. David, "Mission Statement Theory and Practice: A Content Analysis and New Direction," *International Journal of Business, Marketing, and Decision Sciences* 7, no. 1 (Summer 2014): 95–109.

products/services and be "on a mission" to use and promote those offerings. Mission statements should be developed and used to foster customer satisfaction and create a bond between a firm and its customers. Involving marketers and sales representatives in the mission statement development process, coupled with including the nine components written from a customer perspective, could enable firms to create an emotional bond with customers, and enhance the likelihood that salespersons would be "on a mission" to provide excellent customer service. Avon and L'Oréal's customers, for example, often portray an emotional bond or attachment to the firm's products.

Proposed, exemplary mission statements for Avon and L'Oréal are provided in Table 5-7. These rival firms have uniquely different competitive advantages in that Avon utilizes door-to-door sales representatives to gain competitive advantage, whereas L'Oréal markets products in thousands of retail outlets. The proposed Avon and L'Oréal statements have the characteristics described earlier,

TABLE 5-7 Two Exemplary, Proposed Mission Statements

The numbers in parentheses correspond to the nine mission statement components.

Avon

Our mission is to provide women (1) quality fragrances, cosmetics, and jewelry (2) at reasonable prices backed by outstanding customer service provided by our thousands of door-to-door sales representatives (7, 9) operating globally (3). We use the latest technology (4) to profitably develop and market products desired by women all over the world (5). Avon representatives put integrity first (6) in setting a good example in every community (8) they operate—as they sell beauty. *(58 words)*

L'Oréal

Our mission is to design, produce, and distribute the world's best fragrances, perfumes, and personal care products (2) to women, men, and children (1) by utilizing the latest technological improvements (4). We empower our highly creative team of researchers to develop safe, eco-friendly (7) products that will enable our firm to profitably grow (5) through thousands of retail outlets. We strive to be one of the most socially responsible (8) firms on the planet (3) and appreciate our employees (9) making that happen, while following the "golden rule" in all that we do (6). *(85 words)*

Source: Based on Meredith E. David, Forest R. David, & Fred R. David, "Mission Statement Theory and Practice: A Content Analysis and New Direction," *International Journal of Business, Marketing, and Decision Sciences* 7, no. 1 (Summer 2014): 95–109.

and include the nine components written from a customer perspective. The proposed Avon statement includes the nine components in 58 words, and provides a basis for an emotional bond to be established between the firm and its customers. For example, the Avon statement reveals that if you purchase Avon products, you will be rewarded with "outstanding customer service provided by a personal sales representative who adheres to the highest ethical standards, while providing fragrances, cosmetics, and jewelry that exhibit the highest technological advancements." There is quite a lot in that brief statement that an Avon customer can become loyal to, especially when the Avon marketing representative reinforces the statement with her actions.

Also written from a customer perspective, the proposed L'Oréal mission statement provides a basis for an emotional bond to be formed between the firm and its customers. Potential customers are reassured in the statement that the L'Oréal's fragrances, perfumes, and personal care products are "organic" and developed by excellent teams of researchers. In addition, the statement reveals that L'Oréal does great philanthropy work and follows the "golden rule" in all endeavors. Customers may become more dedicated to L'Oréal when they see the company's marketing communications reinforce the basic content given in the proposed mission statement. Loyal customers are a competitive advantage for any firm.

IMPLICATIONS FOR STRATEGISTS

Figure 5-2 reveals that establishing and nurturing an effective vision and mission is a vital first step in gaining and maintaining competitive advantages. Businesses succeed by attracting and keeping customers, and they do this by providing better value for customers than do their rival firms. Marketers continually assess customers' changing needs and wants and make appropriate adjustments in the design and delivery of products and services to sustain competitive advantage. Developing and communicating a clear business vision and mission is essential because without an effective vision and mission statements, a firm's short-term actions may be counterproductive to long-term interests. A clear vision and mission provides direction for all subsequent activities that endeavor to see customers, employees, and shareholders concurrently "on a mission" to see the firm succeed.

Vision and mission statements are not just words that look nice when framed or engraved; they provide a basis for strategy and action; they reveal the reason a business opens its doors every day, the reason salespersons sell, the reason customers buy, and the reason employees work. The statements ideally are the passion behind the company, the foundation for employee morale, and the basis for customer loyalty. Written from a customer perspective and included in both oral and written communication with customers, the statements could be used to attract and keep customers. Vision and mission statements do matter. Marketers pursue projects and managers make daily decisions mindful of the firm's basic vision, mission, and resources. Managers work hard every day trying to motivate employees. Executives are on a mission to present the firm favorably to many stakeholders. A clear vision and mission enables strategists to lead the way as a firm strives to gain, sustain, and grow its customer base and competitive advantages.

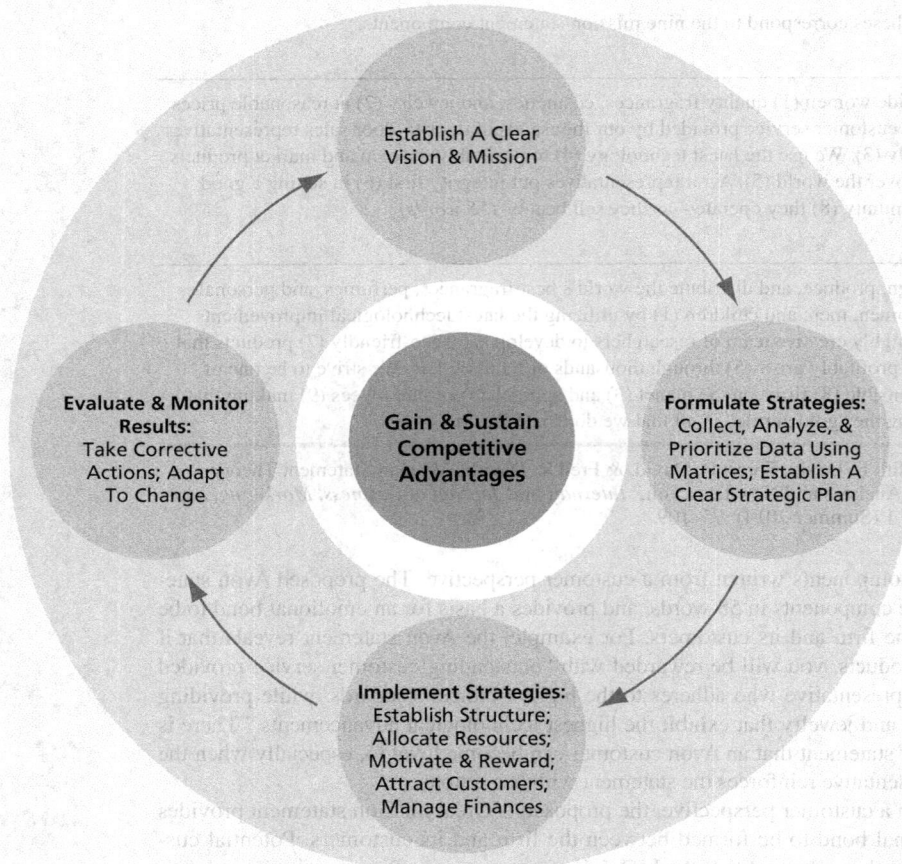

FIGURE 5-2
How to Gain and Sustain Competitive Advantages

IMPLICATIONS FOR STUDENTS

Because gaining and sustaining competitive advantage is the essence of strategic management, when presenting your vision and mission statements as part of a case analysis, be sure to address the "self-concept (distinctive competence)" component. Compare your recommended vision and mission statement with the firm's existing statements, and with rival firms' statements to clearly reveal how your recommendations or strategic plan enables the firm to gain and sustain competitive advantage. Your proposed mission statement

should certainly include the nine components and nine characteristics, but in your vision or mission discussion, focus on competitive advantage. In other words, be prescriptive, forward-looking, and insightful—couching your vision/mission overview in terms of how you believe the firm can best gain and sustain competitive advantage. Do not be content with merely showing a nine-component comparison of your proposed statement with rival firms' statements, although that would be nice to include in your analysis.

Chapter Summary

Every organization has a unique purpose and reason for being. This uniqueness should be reflected in vision and mission statements. The nature of a business vision and mission can represent either a competitive advantage or disadvantage for the firm. An organization achieves a heightened sense of purpose when strategists, managers, and employees develop and communicate a clear business vision and mission. Drucker says that developing a clear business vision and mission is the "first responsibility of strategists."

A good mission statement reveals an organization's customers; products or services; markets; technology; concern for survival, growth, and profitability; philosophy; self-concept; concern for public image; and concern for employees. These nine basic components serve as a practical framework for evaluating and writing mission statements. As the first step in strategic management, the vision and mission statements provide direction for all planning activities. As indicated next in the mini-case, Citizen Holdings' vision and mission statement is clear and working well for the company.

Well-designed vision and mission statements are essential for formulating, implementing, and evaluating strategy. Developing and communicating a clear business vision and mission are the most commonly overlooked tasks in strategic management. Without clear statements of vision and mission, a firm's short-term actions can be counterproductive to long-term interests. Vision and mission statements always should be subject to revision, but, if carefully prepared, they will require infrequent major changes. Organizations usually reexamine their vision and mission statements annually. Effective vision and mission statements stand the test of time.

Vision and mission statements are essential tools for strategists—a fact illustrated in a short story told by Porsche's former CEO Peter Schultz (paraphrased):

> Three guys were at work building a large church. All were doing the same job, but when each was asked what his job was, the answers varied: "Pouring cement," the first replied; "Earning a paycheck," responded the second; "Helping to build a cathedral," said the third. Few of us can build cathedrals. But to the extent we can see the cathedral in whatever cause we are following, the job seems more worthwhile. Good strategists and a clear mission help us find those cathedrals in what otherwise could be dismal issues and empty causes.[10]

Key Terms and Concepts

employees (p. 166)
public image (p. 166)
survival, growth, and profitability (p. 166)
creed statement (p. 160)
customers (p. 166)
markets (p. 166)
mission statement (p. 160)
mission statement components (p. 166)

philosophy (p. 166)
products or services (p. 166)
reconciliatory (p. 164)
self-concept (distinctive competence) (p. 166)
stakeholders (p. 164)
technology (p. 166)
vision statement (p. 158)

Issues for Review and Discussion

5-1. Develop (or find) a mission statement for Samsung Electronics. Analyze the company's mission statement in light of the guidelines in Chapter 4.

5-2. Summarize Samsung's successful global strategy for the last decade. Can that strategy be as successful in 2016? Explain.

5-3. See if you can find a vision statement for Samsung. If not, write a proposed vision statement for the company.

5-4. Should the mission statement components vary in importance depending on type of business? If yes, how would their relative importance vary for Samsung versus Singapore Airlines?

5-5. List three things you are on a mission to accomplish in the next three years. How relevant is the concept of vision/mission to an individual in their personal and professional life? Explain.

5-6. Conduct a Google search for the key words "mission statement." What are the two best websites in your opinion that provide example mission statements?

5-7. Write a vision statement for your university. Write a vision statement for your School (or College) of Business within the university.

5-8. If you just purchased a 10-employee company, how would you establish a clear vision and mission?

5-9. Search the web for six mission statement examples. Evaluate the six statements and bring your analysis to class.

5-10. How and why could the process of developing a vision and mission statement vary across countries?

5-11. In order of importance, list six benefits of having a clearly defined vision and mission statement.

5-12. Only the fairytale ends with a "they lived happily ever after." What is the relevance of this statement to the concepts vision and mission statement?

5-13. Define "reconciliatory" and give an example of how this "characteristic" can be met in a mission statement.

⭐ **5-14.** List the nine mission statement components. Give an example of each component for your college or university.

5-15. In order of importance, rank seven characteristics of a mission statement.

5-16. Write a vision and mission statement for a local restaurant in your area.

5-17. Write an excellent sentence for Samsung, which includes four mission statement components.

5-18. Within a given industry, compare the mission statements of three companies in your country versus three competing companies from the United States. How do they differ?

5-19. Does Singapore Airlines have its vision and mission statement posted on its website? Should the company? Why or why not?

5-20. How often do you think a firm's vision and mission statements should be changed? Why?

5-21. Explain how a mission statement can be "reconciliatory." Give an example.

5-22. Do local fast food restaurants need a mission statement posted in their place of business? Why or why not?

⭐ **5-23.** Understand the "Implications for Students" and explain how a team of students should couch their mission statement discussion of slides in a presentation.

⭐ **5-24.** List the four most important characteristics of a mission statement for a small retail store. Explain.

5-25. Give an example of how the "product" component of a mission statement could have a customer orientation for a charter fishing company.

5-26. Give an example of how the "technology" component of a mission statement could have a customer orientation for a charter fishing company.

5-27. Give an example of how the "philosophy" component of a mission statement could have a customer orientation for a charter fishing company.

ASSURANCE OF LEARNING EXERCISES

EXERCISE 5A
Examine Potential Changes Needed in a Firm's Vision/Mission

Purpose
Samsung Electronics is featured in the opening chapter insert as a firm that engages in excellent strategic planning. This exercise gives you practice examining the change or needed change in a company's vision and mission statements, given a change in the company's product offerings. Visit the Samsung corporate website. Samsung's vision statement is posted on their website, as: "Samsung is dedicated to developing innovative technologies and efficient processes that create new markets, enrich people's lives and continue to make Samsung a digital leader." The company's mission statement is called a statement of philosophy and also is given on the corporate website. Samsung does an excellent job in strategic management.

Instructions
Step 1   Evaluate Samsung's vision and mission statements in light of the characteristics and components in Chapter 5.
Step 2   Write improved vision and mission statements for Samsung Electronics given shortcomings of the statements based on Chapter 4 concepts and Samsung's new products being rolled out globally.

EXERCISE 5B
Studying an Alternative View of Mission Statement Content

Purpose
This exercise presents a somewhat different view of mission statements as compared to concepts presented in Chapter 5. For example, according to Bart, 1997, a mission statement consists of three essential components:

1. Key market—Who is your target client/customer?
2. Contribution—What product or service do you provide to that client?
3. Distinction—What makes your product or service unique, so that the client would choose you? For example, if you locate McDonald's mission statement on the Internet, Bart's essential components are covered in the following ways:
   - Key Market: the fast food customer worldwide
   - Contribution: tasty and reasonably-priced food prepared in a high-quality manner
   - Distinction: delivered consistently (world-wide) in a low-key décor and friendly atmosphere.

Instructions

Compare and contrast the guidelines presented by Bart with the guidelines presented in Chapter 5.

Source: Based on information at Christopher K. Bart. "Sex, Lies, and Mission Statements," *Business Horizons*, p. 9–18, November, 1997.

EXERCISE 5C
Evaluate Mission Statements

Purpose

A business mission statement is an integral part of strategic management. It provides direction for formulating, implementing, and evaluating strategic activities. This exercise will give you practice evaluating mission statements, a skill that is a prerequisite to writing a good mission statement. The mission statement for Nestlé is given below:

Instructions

Step 1   On a separate sheet of paper, write the nine mission statement components down the left side.

Step 2   Write "yes" or "no" beside each number to indicate whether you feel the Nestlé mission statement has included the respective component. For any component that you record a "no," write a good sentence to encompass that component.

Step 3   Submit your paper to your instructor for a grade.

EXERCISE 5D
Evaluate the Vision and Mission Statements of Unilever, Nestlé's Competitor

Purpose

There is always room for improvement in regard to an existing vision and mission statement. A major competitor to Nestlé is Unilever. Those two firms for example produce one third of all the ice cream sold on the planet. Go to the Unilever's website, visit the "our vision" page, and review their corporate vision statement and purpose (mission) statement.

Instructions

Step 1   On a separate sheet of paper, write the nine mission statement components down the left side.

Step 2   Write "yes" or "no" beside each number to indicate whether you feel the Unilever mission statement has included the respective component. For any component that you record a "no," write a good sentence to encompass that component.

Step 3   Turn your paper in to your instructor for a grade.

Step 4   Write a new and improved vision statement for Unilever.

EXERCISE 5E
Selecting the Best Vision and Mission Statements in a Given Industry

Purpose

This exercise is designed to get you familiar with existing vision and mission statements in an industry of your choice.

Instructions

Identify companies in an industry that you are interested in working in one day. Find five company vision statements and five company mission statements. Rank your five vision statements and your five mission statements in order of attractiveness, with 1 being the best and 5 being the worst. Give a rationale for your rankings.

EXERCISE 5F

Write an Excellent Vision and Mission Statement for Novartis AG

Purpose

This exercise is designed to give you practice developing from scratch or improving an existing vision and mission statement.

Instructions

Step 1   Go to the Novartis AG website and look for the company's vision statement and mission statement. Look at https://www.novartis.com/about-us. Recall from Chapter 4 that companies use different names or titles for these documents.

Step 2   Prepare an improved vision and mission statement for Novartis AG whether or not you were able to find these statements on the company's website or in the firm's *Annual Report*.

MINI-CASE ON CITIZEN HOLDINGS COMPANY LIMITED (CIZN)

DOES CITIZEN HOLDINGS' HAVE A CLEAR VISION OR MISSION?

Source: © georgy Kopytin.123rf

Citizen Holdings, headquartered in Nishitokyo, Japan, manufactures Cincom precision lathe machine tools as well as Citizen and Bulova watches. The company has five segments—watches and clocks, machine tools, devices and components, electronic products, and other products.

The financial results for the first quarter of the fiscal year ending March 31, 2016, saw the watches and clocks segment increase profits, with net sales of ¥43.0 billion (up 13.3 percent year-on-year) and operating income of ¥4.5 billion (up 101.3 percent year-on-year). The machine tools segment achieved higher sales but lower profits, with net sales of ¥12.2 billion (up 5.4 percent year-on-year) and operating income of ¥1.2 billion (down 12.5 percent year-on-year). The devices and components segment saw net sales of ¥19.8 billion (up 18.9 percent year-on-year) and operating income of ¥1.7 billion (up 3.1 percent year-on-year). However, the electronic products segment fell in both sales and profit, with net sales of ¥5.7 billion (down 11.3 percent year-on-year) and operating income of ¥0.0 billion (down 99.9 percent year-on-year), and the other product segment, as a whole, recorded lower sales but higher profits, with net sales of ¥2.7 billion and operating loss of ¥0.1 billion.

For the three months ended June 30, 2015, Citizen's sales amounted to ¥83,690 million, a 10.2 percent increase from the previous year. The company's operating income for the three months ending June 30, 2015 was ¥6,350 million, which was a 39 percent increase from the previous year. For now Citizen Holdings Company is ticking along very nicely.

Questions

1. Visit the corporate index on Citizen's global website. This provides Citizen's corporate profile. Check whether a vision/mission statement is given. If yes, evaluate that statement in light of the content provided in the chapter. If no vision or mission is found, write an excellent vision and mission statement for the bank.
2. On the About Us section of the company's website, go to the message section. It appears that the CEO of Citizen Holdings, Toshio Tokura, has a vision for the company. It is "Aiming to be a 'Solid Global Company'." Is that slogan useful as a vision statement? Explain.

Source: Based on company documents.

Current Readings

Bartkus, Barbara, Myron Glassman, and R. Bruce McAfee. "Mission Statements: Are They Smoke and Mirrors?" *Business Horizons* 43, no. 6 (November–December 2000): 23.

Binns, Andy, et al. "The Art of Strategic Renewal." *MIT Sloan Management Review* 55, no. 2 (2014): 21–23.

Birkinshaw, Julian, Nicolai J. Foss, and Siegwart Lindenberg. "Combining Purpose with Profits." *MIT Sloan Management Review* 55, no. 3 (2014): 49–56.

Braun, S., J. S. Wesche, D., Frey, S. Weisweller, & C. Paus. "Effectiveness of Mission Statements in Organizations—A Review." *Journal of Management & Organization*, 18 (2012): 430–444.

Canton, Andrew M., Chad Murphy, and Jonathan R. Clark. "A (Blurry) Vision of the Future: How Leader Rhetoric about Ultimate Goals Influences Performance." *Academy of Management Journal,* 57 (December 2014): 1,544–1,570.

Church Mission Statements, http://www.missionstatements.com/church_mission_statements.html

Collins, David J., and Michael G. Rukstad. "Can You Say What Your Strategy Is?" *Harvard Business Review* (April 2008): 82. Company Mission Statements, http://www.mission-statements.com/company_mission_statements.html

Conger, Jay A., and Douglas A. Ready. "Enabling Bold Visions." *MIT Sloan Management Review* 49, no. 2 (Winter 2008): 70.

Craig, Nick, and Scott Snook. "From Purpose to Impact." *Harvard Business Review* 92, no. 5 (2014): 104–111.

David, Meredith E., Forest R. David, and Fred R. David. "Mission Statement Theory and Practice: A Content Analysis and New Direction." *International Journal of Business, Marketing, and Decision Sciences* 7, no. 1 (Summer 2014): 95–109.

Day, George S., and Paul Schoemaker. "Peripheral Vision: Sensing and Acting on Weak Signals." *Long Range Planning* 37, no. 2 (April 2004): 117.

Desmidt, S., A. Prinzie, and A. Decramer. "Looking for the Value of Mission Statements: A Meta-Analysis of 20 Years of Research." *Management Decision*, 49 (2011): 468–483.

Devasagayam, R., N. R. Stark, and L. S. Valestin. "Examining the Linearity of Customer Satisfaction: Return on Satisfaction as an Alternative." *Business Perspectives and Research*, 1 (2013): 1–8.

Hollensbe, Elaine, Charles Wookey, Loughlin Hickey, and Gerard George, "Organizations with Purpose." *Academy of Management Journal* 57, no. 5 (October 2014): 1227–1234.

Ibarra, Herminia, and Otilia Obodaru. "Women and the Vision Thing." *Harvard Business Review* (January 2009): 62–71.

Lissak, Michael, and Johan Roos. "Be Coherent, Not Visionary." *Long Range Planning* 34, no. 1 (February 2001): 53.

Luo, X, J. Wieseke, and C. Homburg. "Incentivizing CEOs to Build Customer- and Employee-Firm Relations for Higher Customer Satisfaction and Firm Value." *Journal of the Academy of Marketing Science,* 40 (2012): 745–758.

MacMillan, Martin I. "Managing Your Mission—Critical Knowledge." *Harvard Business Review* (January–February 2015).

Newsom, Mi Kyong, David A. Collier, and Eric O. Olsen. "Using 'Biztainment' to Gain Competitive Advantage." *Business Horizons* (March–April 2009): 167–166.

Nonprofit Organization Mission Statements, http://www.missionstatements.com/nonprofit_mission_statements.html

Palmer, T. B., and J. C. Short. "Mission Statements in U.S. Colleges of Business: An Empirical Examination of Their Content with Linkages to Configurations and Performance." *Academy of Management Learning & Education* 7 (2008): 454–470.

Peyrefitte, Joe, and Forest R. David. "A Content Analysis of the Mission Statements of United States Firms in Four Industries." *International Journal of Management*, 23 (2006): 296–301.

Powers, E. L. "Organizational Mission Statement Guidelines Revisited." *International Journal of Management & Information Systems* 16 (2012): 281–290.

Rarick, C., and J. Vitton. "Mission Statements That Make Cents." *Journal of Business Strategy,* 16 (1995): 11–12.

Restaurant Mission Statements, http://www.missionstatements.com/restaurant_mission_statements.html

School Mission Statements, http://www.missionstatements.com/school_mission_statements.html

Sidhu, J. "Mission Statements: Is It Time to Shelve Them?" *European Management Journal* 21 (2003): 439–446.

Smith, M., R. B. Heady, P. P. Carson, and K. D. Carson. "Do Missions Accomplish Their Missions? An Exploratory Analysis of Mission Statement Content and Organizational Longevity." *The Journal of Applied Management and Entrepreneurship* 6 (2001): 75–96.

Endnotes

1. Peter Drucker, *Management: Tasks, Responsibilities, and Practices* (New York: Harper & Row, 1974), 61.
2. Andrew Campbell and Sally Yeung, "Creating a Sense of Mission," *Long Range Planning* 24, no. 4 (August 1991): 17.
3. W. R. King and D. I. Cleland, *Strategic Planning and Policy* (New York: Van Nostrand Reinhold, 1979), 124.
4. Brian Dumaine, "What the Leaders of Tomorrow See," *Fortune* (July 3, 1989), 50.
5. "How W. T. Grant Lost $175 Million Last Year," *Business Week* (February 25, 1975), 75.
6. Drucker, *Management*, 88.
7. John Pearce II, "The Company Mission as a Strategic Tool," *Sloan Management Review* 23, no. 3 (Spring 1982): 74.
8. George Steiner, *Strategic Planning: What Every Manager Must Know* (New York: The Free Press, 1979), 160.
9. David, Meredith E., David, Forest R., and David, Fred R. "Mission Statement Theory and Practice: A Content Analysis and New Direction," International Journal of Business, Marketing, and Decision Sciences, Vol. 7, No. 1, Summer 2014, 95-109.
10. http://ezinearticles.com/?Elements-of-a-Mission-Statement&id=3846671

Source: © Dabarti CGI.Shutterstock

The Internal Audit

LEARNING OBJECTIVES

After studying this chapter, you should be able to do the following:

6-1. Describe the nature and role of an internal assessment in formulating strategies.

6-2. Discuss why organizational culture is so important in formulating strategies.

6-3. Identify the basic functions (activities) that make up management and their relevance in formulating strategies.

6-4. Identify the basic functions of marketing and their relevance in formulating strategies.

6-5. Discuss the nature and role of finance/accounting in formulating strategies.

6-6. Discuss the nature and role of production/operations in formulating strategies.

6-7. Discuss the nature and role of research and development (R&D) in formulating strategies.

6-8. Discuss the nature and role of management information systems (MIS) in formulating strategies.

6-9. Explain value chain analysis and its relevance in formulating strategies.

6-10. Develop and use an Internal Factor Evaluation (IFE) Matrix.

ASSURANCE OF LEARNING EXERCISES

The following exercises are found at the end of this chapter:

This chapter focuses on identifying and evaluating a firm's strengths and weaknesses in the functional areas of business, including management, marketing, finance, accounting, production/operations, research and development (R&D), and management information systems (MIS). Relationships among these areas of business are examined. Also, strategic implications of important functional area concepts are explained. In addition, this chapter describes the process of performing an internal audit. The resource-based view (RBV) of strategic management is introduced, as is value chain analysis (VCA) and benchmarking.

Showcased here for exemplary strategic management, Vodafone does an excellent job using its strengths to capitalize on external opportunities. Expanding rapidly globally, Vodafone is the world's second largest mobile telecommunications, behind China Mobile, and is attracting potential customers globally.

The Nature of an Internal Audit

All organizations have strengths and weaknesses in the functional areas of business. No enterprise is equally strong or weak in all areas. Maytag, for example, is known for excellent production and product design, whereas Procter & Gamble is known for superb marketing. Internal strengths and weaknesses, coupled with external opportunities and threats and clear vision and mission statements, provide the basis for establishing objectives and strategies. Objectives and strategies are established with the intention of capitalizing on internal strengths and overcoming weaknesses. The internal-audit part of the strategic-management process is illustrated in Figure 6-1 with white shading.

EXEMPLARY COMPANY SHOWCASED

Vodafone Group Plc (VOD)

Vodafone is based in London, the United Kingdom, and is considered to be the second largest mobile telecommunications. It holds and operates networks in 30 countries with partner networks in almost 60 countries. Vodafone recently announced results for the six months ended September 30, 2015. The Group highlighted organic service revenue growth of 1.0 percent and indicated that its revenue fell by 2.3 percent to £20.3 billion. The 2015 results was the company's fifth consecutive quarter of improving revenue trends, with a second quarter organic service revenue growth of 1.2 percent. The company's website states that EBITDA was up by 1.9 percent to £5.8 billion. Increasing operating and acquisition costs related to Project Spring were offset by service revenue growth, with the phasing out of Project Spring being reflected in the company's free cash outflow of £0.5 billion. While the interim dividend per share increased by 2.2 percent, Vodafone had a net debt £28.9 billion, or £25.4 billion net of $5.2 billion Verizon loan notes.

Vodafone's revenue for the six months that ended September 30, 2015, for Europe was €12,104, up 1.8 percent from the prior period, and for Africa, Middle East, and Asia Pacific (AMAP) was €5,889, down 1.7 percent from the previous year. The company's operating profit for that six-month period was € 933, up 1.7 percent from the prior period. Vodafone now has 29.9 million 4G customers and provides 4G coverage to 80 percent of Europe. Vodafone also saw other positive statistics, including an H1 mobile data traffic growth of 75 percent, an increase in the average usage per customer in Europe, 12.5 million broadband customers, and marketing high speed broadband to 66 million homes in Europe. In the commercial front Vodafone had 2.7 million mobile contract net adds and 0.5 million net new broadband customers in H1. In the second quarter, the enterprise revenue was above 29.2 percent, machine-to-machine, and the Group's global enterprise above 7.3 percent. While sustaining its commercial momentum in emerging markets, Vodafone's preparations for IPO in India are in progress.

Source: Based on company documents.

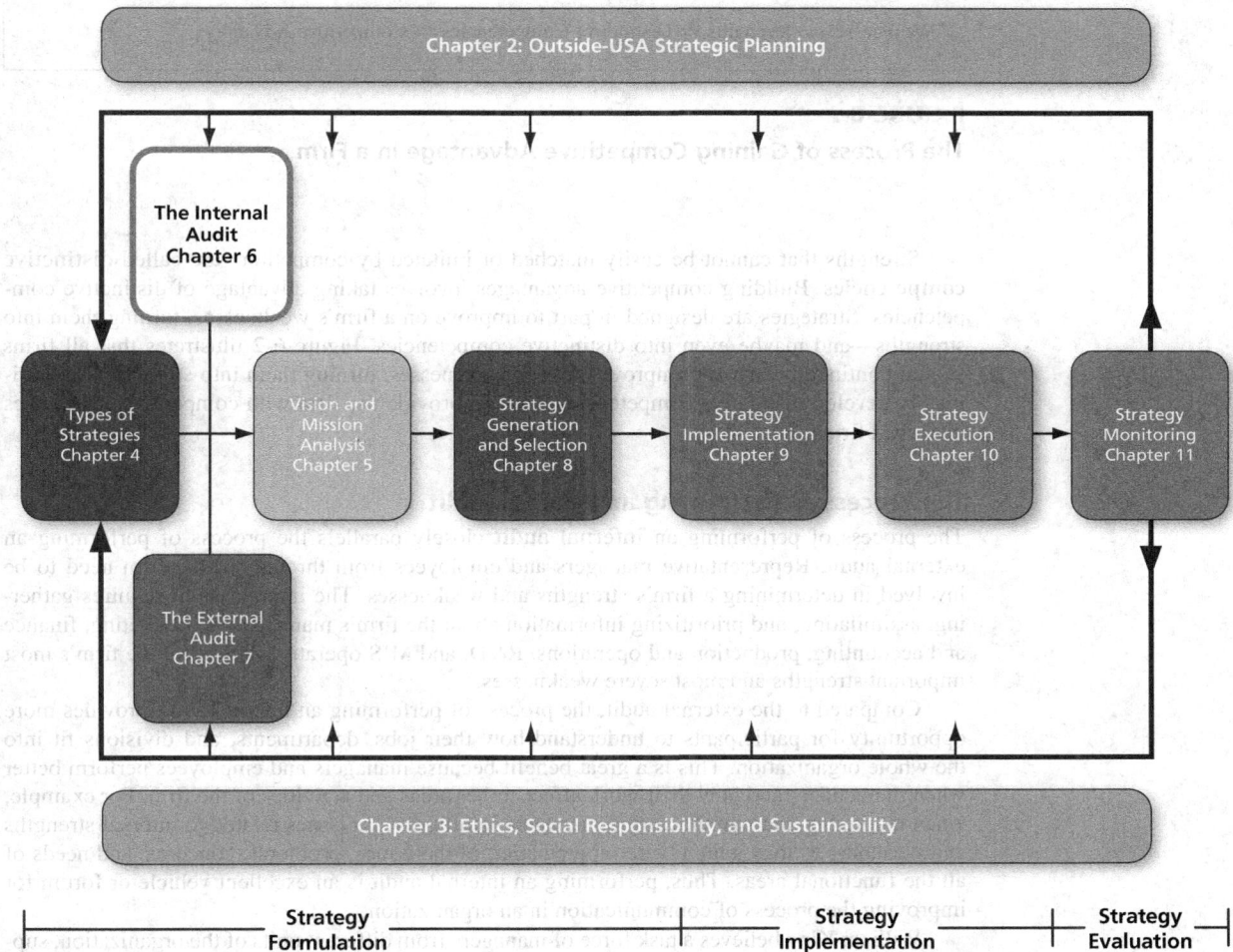

FIGURE 6-1

A Comprehensive Strategic-Management Model

Source: Fred R. David, adapted from "How Companies Define Their Mission," *Long Range Planning* 22, no. 3 (June 1988): 40, © Fred R. David.

Key Internal Forces

It is impossible in a strategic-management text to review in depth all the material presented in courses such as marketing, finance, accounting, management, management information systems, and production and operations; there are many subareas within these functions, such as customer service, warranties, advertising, packaging, and pricing under marketing. However, strategic planning must include a detailed assessment of how the firm is doing in all internal areas. A complete internal assessment is vital to help a firm formulate, implement, and evaluate strategies to enable it to gain and sustain competitive advantages.

For different types of organizations, such as hospitals, universities, and government agencies, the functional business areas differ. In a hospital, for example, functional areas may include cardiology, hematology, nursing, maintenance, physician support, and receivables. Functional areas of a university can include athletic programs, placement services, housing, fund-raising, academic research, counseling, and intramural programs. Regardless of the type or size of firm, effective strategic planning hinges on identification and prioritization of internal strengths and weaknesses.

Weaknesses ⇒ Strenghts ⇒ Distinctive Competencies ⇒ Competitive Advantage

FIGURE 6-2
The Process of Gaining Competitive Advantage in a Firm

Strengths that cannot be easily matched or imitated by competitors are called **distinctive competencies**. Building competitive advantages involves taking advantage of distinctive competencies. Strategies are designed in part to improve on a firm's weaknesses, turning them into strengths—and maybe even into distinctive competencies. Figure 6-2 illustrates that all firms should continually strive to improve on their weaknesses, turning them into strengths, and ultimately develop distinctive competencies that can provide the firm with competitive advantages over rival firms.

The Process of Performing an Internal Audit

The process of performing an **internal audit** closely parallels the process of performing an external audit. Representative managers and employees from throughout the firm need to be involved in determining a firm's strengths and weaknesses. The internal audit requires gathering, assimilating, and prioritizing information about the firm's management, marketing, finance and accounting, production and operations, R&D, and MIS operations to reveal the firm's most important strengths and most severe weaknesses.

Compared to the external audit, the process of performing an internal audit provides more opportunity for participants to understand how their jobs, departments, and divisions fit into the whole organization. This is a great benefit because managers and employees perform better when they understand how their work affects other areas and activities of the firm. For example, when marketing and manufacturing managers jointly discuss issues related to internal strengths and weaknesses, they gain a better appreciation of the issues, problems, concerns, and needs of all the functional areas. Thus, performing an internal audit is an excellent vehicle or forum for improving the process of communication in an organization.

William King believes a task force of managers from different units of the organization, supported by staff, should be charged with determining the 20 most important strengths and weaknesses that should influence the future of the firm. According to King,

> The development of conclusions on the 20 most important organizational strengths and weaknesses can be, as any experienced manager knows, a difficult task, when it involves managers representing various organizational interests and points of view. Developing a 20-page list of strengths and weaknesses could be accomplished relatively easily, but a list of the 20 most important ones involves significant analysis and negotiation. This is true because of the judgments that are required and the impact which such a list will inevitably have as it is used in the formulation, implementation, and evaluation of strategies.[1]

Strategic planning is most successful when managers and employees from all functional areas work together to provide ideas and information. Financial managers, for example, may need to restrict the number of feasible options available to operations managers, or R&D managers may develop products for which marketing managers need to set higher objectives. A key to organizational success is effective coordination and understanding among managers from all functional business areas. Through involvement in performing an internal strategic-management audit, managers from different departments and divisions of the firm come to understand the nature and effect of decisions in other functional business areas in their firm. Knowledge of these relationships is critical for effectively establishing objectives and strategies. Financial ratio analysis, for example, exemplifies the complexity of relationships among the functional areas of business. A declining return on investment or profit margin ratio could, for example, be the result of ineffective marketing, poor management policies, R&D errors, or a weak MIS.

The Resource-Based View

Some researchers emphasize the importance of the internal-audit part of the strategic-management process by comparing it to the external audit. Robert Grant, for example, concluded that the internal audit is more important, saying:

> In a world where customer preferences are volatile, the identity of customers is changing, and the technologies for serving customer requirements are continually evolving, an externally focused orientation does not provide a secure foundation for formulating long-term strategy. When the external environment is in a state of flux, the firm's own resources and capabilities may be a much more stable basis on which to define its identity. Hence, a definition of a business in terms of what it is capable of doing may offer a more durable basis for strategy.[2]

The **resource-based view (RBV)** approach to competitive advantage contends that internal resources are more important for a firm than external factors in achieving and sustaining competitive advantage. In contrast to the Industrial Organization (I/O) theory presented in the previous chapter, proponents of the RBV view/theory contend that organizational performance will primarily be determined by internal resources that can be grouped into three all-encompassing categories: physical resources, human resources, and organizational resources.[3] *Physical resources* include all plant and equipment, location, technology, raw materials, and machines; *human resources* include all employees, training, experience, intelligence, knowledge, skills, and abilities; and *organizational resources* include firm structure, planning processes, information systems, patents, trademarks, copyrights, databases, and so on. A firm's resources can be tangible, such as labor, capital, land, plant, and equipment, or resources can be intangible, such as culture, knowledge, brand equity, reputation, and intellectual property. Since tangible resources can more easily be bought and sold, intangible resources are often more important for gaining and sustaining competitive advantage.

Resource-based view theory asserts that resources are actually what helps a firm exploit opportunities and neutralize threats. As indicated in the Academic Research Capsule 6-1, RBV theory may be helpful in identifying diversification targets.

The basic premise of the RBV is that the mix, type, amount, and nature of a firm's internal resources should be considered first and foremost in devising strategies that can lead to sustainable competitive advantage. Managing strategically according to the RBV involves developing and exploiting a firm's unique resources and capabilities, and continually maintaining and strengthening those resources. The theory asserts that it is advantageous for a firm to pursue a strategy that is not currently being implemented by any competing firm. When other firms are unable to duplicate a particular strategy, then the focal firm has a sustainable competitive advantage, according to RBV theorists.

A resource can be considered valuable to the extent that it is (1) rare, (2) hard to imitate, or (3) not easily substitutable. Often called **empirical indicators**, these three characteristics of resources enable a firm to implement strategies that improve its efficiency and effectiveness and lead to a sustainable competitive advantage. The more a resource(s) is rare (not held by many

ACADEMIC RESEARCH CAPSULE 6-1

Does RBV Theory Determine Diversification Targets?

Recent research by Neffke and Henning basically says the answer to this question is *yes*. Their empirical evidence reveals that it is the nature of a firm's human capital, more than any other variable in the firm's value chain, that impacts that firm's choice of diversification targets. Specifically, firms select acquisition targets that offer opportunities to leverage existing human resources. Neffke and Henning report that firms are far more likely to diversify into industries that have ties to the firms' core RBV activities in terms of their existing workforce, rather than into industries without such ties. In fact, the researchers report that "firms are over 100 times more likely to diversify into industries to which the firms' internal human assets are strongly complementary, rather than into industries for which such skill-relatedness linkages are weak."

Source: Based on F. Neffke & M. Henning, "Skill Relatedness and Firm Diversification," *Strategic Management Journal* 34 (2013): 297–316.

firms in the industry), hard to imitate (hard to copy or achieve), and/or not easily substitutable (invulnerable to threat of substitution from different products), the stronger a firm's competitive advantage will be and the longer it will last.

Integrating Strategy and Culture

Every business entity has a unique organizational culture that impacts strategic-planning activities. **Organizational culture** is "a pattern of behavior that has been developed by an organization as it learns to cope with its problem of external adaptation and internal integration, and that has worked well enough to be considered valid and to be taught to new members as the correct way to perceive, think, and feel."[4] This definition emphasizes the importance of matching external with internal factors in making strategic decisions. Organizational culture captures the subtle, elusive, and largely unconscious forces that shape a workplace. Remarkably resistant to change, culture can represent a major strength or weakness for any firm. It can be an underlying reason for strengths or weaknesses in any of the major business functions.

Defined in Table 6-1, **cultural products** include values, beliefs, rites, rituals, ceremonies, myths, stories, legends, sagas, language, metaphors, symbols, folktales, and heroes and heroines. These products or dimensions are levers that strategists can use to influence and direct strategy formulation, implementation, and evaluation activities. An organization's culture compares to an individual's personality in the sense that no two organizations have the same culture and no two individuals have the same personality. Both culture and personality are enduring and can be warm, aggressive, friendly, open, innovative, conservative, liberal, harsh, or likable.

At Google and Facebook, for example, the cultures are informal. Google employees are encouraged to wander the halls on employee-sponsored scooters and brainstorm on public whiteboards provided everywhere. In contrast, the culture at Procter & Gamble (P&G) is so rigid that employees jokingly call themselves "Proctoids." Despite this difference, the two companies are swapping employees and participating in each other's staff training sessions. Why? One reason is that P&G spends more money on advertising than any other company and Google desires more of P&G's roughly $8 billion in annual advertising expenses.

TABLE 6-1 Examples of Cultural Products Defined

Rites	Planned sets of activities that consolidate various forms of cultural expressions into one event
Ceremonies	Several rites connected together
Rituals	Standardized sets of behaviors used to manage anxieties
Myths	Narratives of imagined events, usually not supported by facts
Sagas	Historical narratives describing the unique accomplishments of a group and its leaders
Legends	Handed-down narratives of some wonderful event, usually not supported by facts
Stories	Narratives usually based on true events
Folktales	Fictional stories
Symbols	Any object, act, event, quality, or relation used to convey meaning
Language	The manner in which members of a group communicate
Metaphors	Shorthand of words used to capture a vision or to reinforce old or new values
Values	Life-directing attitudes that serve as behavioral guidelines
Beliefs	Understanding of particular phenomena
Heroes/Heroines	Individuals greatly respected

Source: Based on H. M. Trice and J. M. Beyer, "Studying Organizational Cultures through Rites and Ceremonials," *Academy of Management Review* 9, no. 4 (October 1984): 655.

Dimensions of organizational culture permeate all the functional areas of business. It is something of an art to uncover the basic values and beliefs that are deeply buried in an organization's rich collection of stories, language, heroes, and rituals, but cultural products can represent both important strengths and weaknesses. Culture is an aspect of an organization that can no longer be taken for granted in performing an internal strategic-management audit, because culture and strategy must work together.

The strategic-management process takes place largely within a particular organization's culture. Lorsch found that executives in successful companies are emotionally committed to the firm's culture, but he concluded that culture can inhibit strategic management in two basic ways. First, managers frequently miss the significance of changing external conditions because they are blinded by strongly held beliefs. Second, when a particular culture has been effective in the past, the natural response is to stick with it in the future, even during times of major strategic change.[5] An organization's culture must support the collective commitment of its people to a common purpose. It must foster competence and enthusiasm among managers and employees.

Organizational culture significantly affects business decisions and must therefore be evaluated during an internal strategic-management audit. If strategies can capitalize on cultural strengths, such as a strong work ethic or highly ethical beliefs, then management often can swiftly and easily implement changes. However, if the firm's culture is not supportive, strategic changes may be ineffective or even counterproductive. A firm's culture can become antagonistic to new strategies, with the result being confusion and disorientation.

Table 6-2 provides some example (possible) aspects of an organization's culture. Note that you might want to ask employees and managers to rate the degree that the dimension characterizes the firm. When one firm acquires another firm, integrating the two cultures effectively can be vital for success. For example, in Table 6-2, one firm may score mostly 1s (low) and the other firm may score mostly 5s (high), which would present a challenging strategic problem.

An organization's culture should infuse individuals with enthusiasm for implementing strategies. Allarie and Firsirotu emphasized the need to understand culture:

> Culture provides an explanation for the insuperable difficulties a firm encounters when it attempts to shift its strategic direction. Not only has the "right" culture become the essence and foundation of corporate excellence, it is also claimed that success or failure of reforms hinges on management's sagacity and ability to change the firm's driving culture in time and in time with required changes in strategies.[6]

Internal strengths and weaknesses associated with a firm's culture sometimes are overlooked because of the interfunctional nature of this phenomenon. This is a key reason why strategists

TABLE 6-2   Fifteen Example (Possible) Aspects of an Organization's Culture

Dimension	Low	Degree		High
1. Strong work ethic; arrive early and leave late	1	2	3 4	5
2. High ethical beliefs; clear code of business ethics followed	1	2	3 4	5
3. Formal dress; shirt and tie expected	1	2	3 4	5
4. Informal dress; many casual dress days	1	2	3 4	5
5. Socialize together outside of work	1	2	3 4	5
6. Do not question supervisor's decision	1	2	3 4	5
7. Encourage whistle-blowing	1	2	3 4	5
8. Be health conscious; have a wellness program	1	2	3 4	5
9. Allow substantial "working from home"	1	2	3 4	5
10. Encourage creativity, innovation, and open-mindedness	1	2	3 4	5
11. Support women and minorities; no glass ceiling	1	2	3 4	5
12. Be highly socially responsible; be philanthropic	1	2	3 4	5
13. Have numerous meetings	1	2	3 4	5
14. Have a participative management style	1	2	3 4	5
15. Preserve the natural environment; have a sustainability program	1	2	3 4	5

need to view and understand their firm as a sociocultural system. Success is oftentimes determined by linkages between a firm's culture and strategies. The challenge of strategic management today is to bring about the changes in organizational culture and individual mind-sets that are needed to support the formulation, implementation, and evaluation of strategies.

Management

The **functions of management** consist of five basic activities: planning, organizing, motivating, staffing, and controlling. An overview of these activities is provided in Table 6-3. These activities must be examined in strategic planning because an organization should continually capitalize on its strengths and improve on its weaknesses in these five areas.

Planning

The only thing certain about the future of any organization is change, and **planning** is the essential bridge between the present and the future that increases the likelihood of achieving desired results. Planning is the process by which a person (1) determines whether to attempt a task, (2) works out the most effective way of reaching desired objectives, and (3) prepares to overcome unexpected difficulties with adequate resources. Planning is the start of the process by which an individual or business may turn empty dreams into achievements. Planning enables one to avoid the trap of working extremely hard but achieving little.

TABLE 6-3 The Basic Functions of Management

Function	Description	Stage of Strategic-Management Process When Most Important
Planning	Planning consists of all those managerial activities related to preparing for the future, such as forecasting, establishing objectives, devising strategies, and developing policies.	Strategy Formulation
Organizing	Organizing includes all those managerial activities that result in a structure of task and authority relationships, such as organizational design, job specialization, job descriptions, span of control, coordination, job design, and job analysis.	Strategy Implementation
Motivating	Motivating involves efforts directed toward shaping human behavior. Specific topics include leadership, communication, work groups, behavior modification, delegation of authority, job enrichment, job satisfaction, needs fulfillment, organizational change, employee morale, and managerial morale.	Strategy Implementation
Staffing	Staffing refers to human resource (HR) activities, such as wage and salary administration, employee benefits, interviewing, hiring, firing, training, management development, employee safety, equal employment opportunity, and union relations.	Strategy Implementation
Controlling	Controlling refers to all those managerial activities directed toward ensuring that actual results are consistent with planned results. Key areas of concern include quality control, financial control, sales control, inventory control, expense control, analysis of variances, rewards, and sanctions.	Strategy Evaluation

Planning is an up-front investment in success. It helps a firm achieve maximum effect from a given effort. It also enables a firm to take into account relevant factors and focus on the critical ones. Planning helps ensure that the firm can be prepared for all reasonable eventualities and for all changes that will be needed. The act of planning allows a firm to gather the resources needed and carry out tasks in the most efficient way possible. It also enables a firm to conserve its own resources, avoid wasting ecological resources, make a fair profit, and be seen as an effective, useful firm. Furthermore, planning enables a firm to identify precisely what is to be achieved and to detail precisely the who, what, when, where, why, and how needed to achieve desired objectives. It empowers a firm to assess whether the effort, costs, and implications associated with achieving desired objectives are warranted.[7] Planning is the cornerstone of effective strategy formulation, and even though it is considered the foundation of management, it is commonly the task that managers neglect most. Planning is essential for successful strategy implementation and strategy evaluation, largely because organizing, motivating, staffing, and controlling activities depend on good planning.

Planning can have a positive impact on organizational and individual performance. It allows an organization to identify and take advantage of external opportunities as well as minimize the impact of external threats. Planning is more than extrapolating from the past and present into the future (long-range planning). It also includes developing a mission, forecasting future events and trends, establishing objectives, and choosing strategies to pursue.

An organization can develop synergy through planning. **Synergy** exists when everyone pulls together as a team that knows what it wants to achieve; synergy is the 2 + 2 = 5 effect. By establishing and communicating clear objectives, employees and managers can work together toward desired results. Synergy can result in powerful competitive advantages. The strategic-management process itself is aimed at creating synergy in an organization.

In addition, planning allows a firm to adapt to changing markets and thus shape its destiny. It enables an organization to be proactive, to anticipate, and to influence, rather than being primarily reactive strategies. Successful organizations strive to control their own futures rather than merely react to external forces and events as they occur. Historically, organisms and organizations that have not adapted to changing conditions have become extinct.

Organizing

The purpose of **organizing** is to achieve coordinated effort by defining task and authority relationships. Organizing means determining who does what and who reports to whom. There are countless examples in history of well-organized enterprises successfully competing against—and in some cases defeating—much stronger but less-organized firms. A well-organized firm generally has motivated managers and employees who are committed to seeing the organization succeed. Resources are allocated more effectively and used more efficiently in a well-organized firm than in a disorganized firm.

The organizing function of management can be viewed as consisting of three sequential activities: breaking down tasks into jobs (work specialization), combining jobs to form departments (departmentalization), and delegating authority. *Breaking down tasks* into jobs requires the development of job descriptions and job specifications. These tools clarify for both managers and employees what particular jobs entail. In *The Wealth of Nations*, published in 1776, Adam Smith cited the advantages of work specialization in the manufacture of pins:

> One man draws the wire, another straightens it, a third cuts it, a fourth points it, a fifth grinds it at the top for receiving the head. Ten men working in this manner can produce 48,000 pins in a single day, but if they had all wrought separately and independently, each might at best produce twenty pins in a day.[8]

Combining jobs to form departments results in an organizational structure, span of control, and a chain of command. Changes in strategy often require changes in structure because positions may be created, deleted, or merged. Organizational structure dictates how resources are allocated and how objectives are established in a firm. Allocating resources and establishing objectives geographically, for example, is much different from doing so by product or customer. The most common types of structure are functional, divisional, strategic business unit, and matrix. These designs are discussed in Chapter 10.

Delegating authority is an important organizing activity, as evidenced in the old saying, "You can tell how good a manager is by observing how his or her department functions when he or she isn't there." Employees today are more educated and more capable of participating in organizational decision making than ever before. In most cases, they expect to be delegated authority and responsibility and to be held accountable for results. Delegation of authority is embedded in the strategic-management process.

Motivating

Motivating is the process of influencing people to accomplish specific objectives.[9] Motivation explains why some people work hard and others do not. Objectives, strategies, and policies have little chance of succeeding if employees and managers are not motivated to implement strategies once they are formulated. The motivating function of management includes at least four major components: leadership, group dynamics, communication, and organizational change.

When managers and employees of a firm strive to achieve high levels of productivity, this indicates that the firm's strategists are good leaders. Good leaders establish rapport with subordinates, empathize with their needs and concerns, set a good example, and are trustworthy and fair. Leadership includes developing a vision of the firm's future and inspiring people to work hard to achieve that vision. Kirkpatrick and Locke reported that certain traits also characterize effective leaders: knowledge of the business, cognitive ability, self-confidence, honesty, integrity, and drive.[10] Stressing the importance of leadership, Sun Tzu stated, "Weak leadership can wreck the soundest strategy."

Research suggests that democratic behavior on the part of leaders results in more positive attitudes toward change and higher productivity than does autocratic behavior. According to Drucker:

Leadership is not a magnetic personality. That can just as well be demagoguery. It is not "making friends and influencing people." That is flattery. Leadership is the lifting of a person's vision to higher sights, the raising of a person's performance to a higher standard, the building of a person's personality beyond its normal limitations.[11]

Because social media has come to dominate the conversation at all levels of personal and professional life, Frank Guglielmo in *The Social Leader* reports that the best leaders today do not function like generals. Rather, Guglielmo observes, "Leaders today need to be more concerned with their span of influence than their span of control; agendas are negotiated, not dictated; information is shaped, not controlled; and accountability is shared, not monitored."[12] Selladurai and Carraher in *Servant Leadership: Research and Practice* (2014) promote the idea that true leadership requires a dissolution of autocratic thinking in favor of leading by guiding and encouraging.

An organization's system of communication determines whether strategies can be implemented successfully. Good two-way communication is vital for gaining support for departmental and divisional objectives and policies. Top-down communication can encourage bottom-up communication. The strategic-management process becomes a lot easier when subordinates are encouraged to discuss their concerns, reveal their problems, provide recommendations, and give suggestions. A primary reason for instituting strategic management is to build and support effective communication networks throughout the firm.

The manager of tomorrow must be able to get his [or her] people to commit themselves to the business, whether they are machine operators or junior vice-presidents. The key issue will be empowerment, a term whose strength suggests the need to get beyond merely sharing a little information and a bit of decision making.[13]

Staffing

The management function of **staffing**, or **human resource (HR) management**, includes activities such as recruiting, interviewing, testing, selecting, orienting, training, developing, caring for, evaluating, rewarding, disciplining, promoting, transferring, demoting, and dismissing employees, as well as managing union relations. Staffing activities play a major role in strategy-implementation efforts, and for this reason, HR managers are becoming more actively involved in the strategic-management process. It is important to identify strengths and weaknesses in the staffing area.

The complexity and importance of HR activities have increased to such a degree that all but the smallest organizations generally have a full-time human resource manager. Numerous court cases that directly affect staffing activities are decided each day. Organizations and individuals can be penalized severely for not following federal, state, and local laws and guidelines related to staffing. Line managers simply cannot stay abreast of all the legal developments and requirements regarding staffing. The HR department coordinates staffing decisions in the firm so that an organization as a whole meets legal requirements. This department also provides needed consistency in administering company rules, wages, policies, and employee benefits as well as collective bargaining with unions.

Human resource management is particularly challenging for international companies. For example, the inability of spouses and children to adapt to new surroundings can be a staffing problem in overseas transfers. The problems include premature returns, job performance slumps, resignations, discharges, low morale, marital discord, and general discontent. Firms such as Ford Motors and ExxonMobil screen and interview spouses and children before assigning families to overseas positions. Similarly, 3M Corporation introduces children to peers in the target country and offers spouses educational benefits.

Some companies, such as LRN Corporation and Ruppert Landscape, have recently dissolved their HR departments in order to flatten organizational structures, shift accountability for employees closer to managers, and to take advantage of outsourcing payroll, benefits, and other HR activities for greater efficiency and quality.[14]

Controlling

The **controlling** function of management includes all of those activities undertaken to ensure that actual operations conform to planned operations. All managers in an organization have controlling responsibilities, such as conducting performance evaluations and taking necessary action to minimize inefficiencies. The controlling function of management is particularly important for effective strategy evaluation. Controlling consists of four basic steps:

1. Establishing performance standards
2. Measuring individual and organizational performance
3. Comparing actual performance to planned performance standards
4. Taking corrective actions

Measuring individual performance is often conducted ineffectively or not at all in organizations. Some reasons for this shortcoming are that evaluations can create confrontations that most managers prefer to avoid, can take more time than most managers are willing to give, and can require skills that many managers lack. No single approach to measuring individual performance is without limitations. For this reason, an organization should examine various methods, such as the graphic rating scale, the behaviorally anchored rating scale, and the critical incident method, and then develop or select a performance-appraisal approach that best suits the firm's needs. Increasingly, firms are striving to link organizational performance with managers' and employees' pay.

Management Audit Checklist of Questions

The following checklist of questions can help determine specific strengths and weaknesses in the functional area of business. An answer of *no* to any question could indicate a potential weakness, although the strategic significance and implications of negative answers, of course, will vary by organization, industry, and severity of the weakness. Positive or *yes* answers to the checklist questions suggest potential areas of strength.

1. Does the firm use strategic-management concepts?
2. Are company objectives and goals measurable and well communicated?
3. Do managers at all hierarchical levels plan effectively?
4. Do managers delegate authority well?
5. Is the organization's structure appropriate?

6. Are job descriptions and job specifications clear?
7. Is employee morale high?
8. Are employee turnover and absenteeism low?
9. Are organizational reward and control mechanisms effective?

Marketing

Marketing can be described as the process of defining, anticipating, creating, and fulfilling customers' needs and wants for products and services. There are seven basic **functions of marketing**: (1) customer analysis, (2) selling products and services, (3) product and service planning, (4) pricing, (5) distribution, (6) marketing research, and (7) cost/benefit analysis.[15] Understanding these functions helps strategists identify and evaluate marketing strengths and weaknesses—a vital strategy-formulation activity.

Customer Analysis

Customer analysis—the examination and evaluation of consumer needs, desires, and wants—involves administering customer surveys, analyzing consumer information, evaluating market positioning strategies, developing customer profiles, and determining optimal market segmentation strategies. Customer profiles can reveal the demographic characteristics of an organization's customers. Buyers, sellers, distributors, salespeople, managers, wholesalers, retailers, suppliers, and creditors can all participate in gathering information to successfully identify customers' needs and wants. Successful organizations continually monitor present and potential customers' buying patterns. Business analytics has become an integral part of customer analysis and strategic planning.

Selling Products and Services

Successful strategy implementation generally rests on the ability of an organization to sell some product or service. **Selling** includes many marketing activities, such as advertising, sales promotion, publicity, personal selling, sales force management, customer relations, and dealer relations. The effectiveness of various selling tools for consumer and industrial products varies. Personal selling is most important for industrial goods companies, whereas advertising is most important for consumer goods companies. Determining organizational strengths and weaknesses in the selling function of marketing is an important part of performing an internal strategic-management audit.

Advertising can be expensive, a primary reason marketing is a major business function to be studied carefully. Without marketing, even the best products and services have little chance of being successful. Companies paid in excess of $4 million per 30-second spots during the 2015 Super Bowl. Anheuser-Busch just tallied its 28th year as the exclusive beer advertiser at the Super Bowl, buying a whopping 3.5 minutes of advertising time for Budweiser and Bud Light. George Parker argues that there may be no relationship at all between ads and sales:

> If someone were to do a truly analytical study of the Super Bowls of the last 20 years, I guarantee there would be no correlation between the ads and increases or declines in sales. The only way you can directly measure the effect of advertising is in direct marketing, which is a targeted promotion that provides an immediate point of sale, like an email campaign that encourages recipients to make a direct purchase or inquiry.[16]

Recent research reveals that the most effective marketing methods for firms with fewer than 500 employees is the company website (50%), Facebook and/or other social media sites such as Twitter (27%), and yellow pages and other (23%).[17] Nearly 2 million firms of all sizes now pay to advertise on Facebook, up from about 1 million 18 months ago. Spending on online advertisements globally is increasing about 25 percent annually, according to edMarketer, and represents about 39 percent of total advertising spending in the United States.[18]

Advertising on television is on a downward spiral, according to Time Warner, Discovery Communications, and Comcast. "Upfront" ads for the 2014–2015 TV season declined about 6 percent. Heavy marketers, such as Allstate and Mondelez International, now openly speak about shifting TV ad dollars to digital platforms. Allstate shifted 20 percent of its TV ad dollars to digital from 2013 to 2015 and that is typical. Ad giant Omnicom Group is advising its clients to shift 10 to 25 percent of their TV ad dollars to digital.

Chief marketing officers (CMOs), such as Eduardo Conrado at Motorola, now spend more than 50 percent of their budget on technology to manage activities such as online marketing and social media.[19] Marketing is becoming technical, with software to track and target customers and manage customer relationships, predict consumer behavior, run online storefronts, analyze social media, manage websites, and craft targeted advertisements. In response to this trend, IBM is shifting its attention from CIOs to chief marketing officers (CMOs) as their primary clients.

The world's largest social network, Facebook, may epitomize where the advertising industry is going. Facebook allows a company to "leverage the loyalty" of its best customers. If you have recently gotten engaged and updated your Facebook status, you may start seeing ads from local jewelers who have used Facebook's automated ad system to target you. Facebook enables any firm today to effectively target its exact audience with perfect advertising.[20] In performing a strategic-planning analysis, in addition to comparing rival firms' websites, it is important to compare rival firms' handling of social media issues.

One of the last off-limit advertising outlets has historically been books, but with the proliferation of e-books, marketers are experimenting more and more with advertising to consumers as they read e-books. New ads are being targeted based on the book's content and the demographic profile of the reader. Digital e-book companies such as Wowio and Amazon are trying to insert ads between chapters and along borders of digital pages. Random House says its e-books will soon include ads, but only with author approval.

Product and Service Planning

Product and service planning includes activities such as test marketing; product and brand positioning; devising warranties; packaging; determining product options, features, style, and quality; deleting old products; and providing for customer service. Product and service planning is particularly important when a company is pursuing product development or diversification.

One of the most effective product and service planning techniques is **test marketing**. Test markets allow an organization to test alternative marketing plans and to forecast future sales of new products. In conducting a test market project, an organization must decide how many cities to include, which cities to include, how long to run the test, what information to collect during the test, and what action to take after the test has been completed. Test marketing is used more frequently by consumer goods companies than industrial goods companies. The technique can enable an organization to avoid substantial losses by revealing weak products and ineffective marketing approaches before large-scale production begins.

Pricing

Procter & Gamble is currently embroiled in a shampoo price war with Unilever PLC in the U.S. hair care industry. Unilever's TRESemme, Alberto VO5, Clear, and Dove brands have been taking market share from P&G's Pantene and Old Spice brands, but both firms are now simultaneously cutting prices and spending heavily on advertising to "cripple" the other.

Five major stakeholders affect **pricing** decisions: consumers, governments, suppliers, distributors, and competitors. Sometimes an organization will pursue a forward integration strategy primarily to gain better control over prices charged to consumers. Governments can impose constraints on price fixing, price discrimination, minimum prices, unit pricing, price advertising, and price controls. For example, the Robinson-Patman Act prohibits manufacturers and wholesalers from discriminating in price among channel member purchasers (suppliers and distributors) if competition is injured.

Competing organizations must be careful not to coordinate discounts, credit terms, or condition of sale; not to discuss prices, markups, and costs at trade association meetings; and not to arrange to issue new price lists on the same date, rotate low bids on contracts, or uniformly restrict production to maintain high prices. Strategists should view price from both a short-run and a long-run perspective because competitors can copy price changes with relative ease. Often a dominant firm will aggressively match all price cuts by competitors.

Intense price competition, coupled with Internet price-comparative shopping, has reduced profit margins to bare minimum levels for most companies. Target recently joined Best Buy in offering to match online prices of rival retailers. Both companies are seeking to combat "showrooming" by shoppers who check out products in their stores but buy them on rival's websites. Both Target and Best Buy are matching prices from Amazon.com, Walmart.com, and Toysrus.com.

In contrast to popular opinion, online sales are more expensive for companies than brick-and-mortar sales, after factoring in the cost of shipping, handling, and the higher rates of returns.[21] For example, Kohl's Corporation reports that its profitability online is less than half of its store business, and even WalMart reports that it will lose money online at least through 2016. Primark, the European discount retailer, avoids online retailing "because it deems it to be unprofitable." However, online sales exceeded $294 billion, or 9 percent of all retail sales, in the United States in 2014, but analysts expect those numbers to increase to $414 billion and 11 percent by 2018.

During the 2014 Christmas shopping season, Amazon changed prices on as many as 80 million products during a single day, creating havoc for companies such as Walmart, Best Buy, and Toys "R" Us that had already announced they will not be undersold and would match any competitors' prices in a printed flyer or website. Because of pricing flexibility and variation, retail shopping has become much more challenging for savvy customers, and much more work for brick-and-mortar store managers empowered to meet all competitor prices.

Distribution

Distribution includes warehousing, distribution channels, distribution coverage, retail site locations, sales territories, inventory levels and location, transportation carriers, wholesaling, and retailing. Most producers today do not sell their goods directly to consumers. Various marketing entities act as intermediaries; they bear a variety of names such as wholesalers, retailers, brokers, facilitators, agents, vendors—or simply distributors. Some of the most complex and challenging decisions facing a firm concern product distribution. Intermediaries flourish in our economy because many producers lack the financial resources and expertise to carry out direct marketing. Manufacturers who could afford to sell directly to the public often can gain greater returns by expanding and improving their manufacturing operations.

Successful organizations identify and evaluate alternative ways to reach their ultimate market. Possible approaches vary from direct selling to using just one or many wholesalers and retailers. Strengths and weaknesses of each channel alternative should be determined according to economic, control, and adaptive criteria. Organizations should consider the costs and benefits of various wholesaling and retailing options. They must consider the need to motivate and control channel members and the need to adapt to changes in the future. Once a marketing channel is chosen, an organization usually must adhere to it for an extended period of time.

Marketing Research

Marketing research is the systematic gathering, recording, and analyzing of data about problems relating to the marketing of goods and services. Marketing researchers employ numerous scales, instruments, procedures, concepts, and techniques to gather information; their research can uncover critical strengths and weaknesses. Marketing-research activities support all of the major business functions of an organization. Organizations that possess excellent marketing research skills have a competitive advantage. According to the president of PepsiCo,

> Looking at the competition is the company's best form of market research. The majority of our strategic successes are ideas that we borrow from the marketplace, usually from a small regional or local competitor. In each case, we spot a promising new idea, improve on it, and then out-execute our competitor.[22]

Cost/Benefit Analysis

The seventh function of marketing is **cost/benefit analysis**, which involves assessing the costs, benefits, and risks associated with marketing decisions. Three steps are required to perform a cost/benefit analysis: (1) compute the total costs associated with a decision, (2) estimate the total benefits from the decision, and (3) compare the total costs with the total benefits. When expected benefits exceed total costs, an opportunity becomes more attractive. Sometimes the variables included in a cost/benefit analysis cannot be quantified or even measured, but usually reasonable estimates can be made to allow the analysis to be performed. One key factor to be considered is risk. Cost/benefit analysis should also be performed when a company is evaluating alternative ways to be socially responsible.

The practice of cost/benefit analysis differs among countries and industries. Some of the main differences include the types of impacts that are included as costs and benefits within appraisals, the extent to which impacts are expressed in monetary terms, and differences in the discount rate. Government agencies across the world rely on a basic set of key cost/benefit indicators, including the following:

1. Net present value (NPV)
2. Present value of benefits (PVB)
3. Present value of costs (PVC)
4. Benefit cost ratio (BCR) = PVB/PVC
5. Net benefit = PVB − PVC
6. NPV/k (where k is the level of funds available)[23]

Marketing Audit Checklist of Questions

The following questions about marketing must be examined in strategic planning:

1. Are markets segmented effectively?
2. Is the organization positioned well among competitors?
3. Has the firm's market share been increasing?
4. Are present channels of distribution reliable and cost effective?
5. Does the firm have an effective sales organization?
6. Does the firm conduct market research?
7. Are product quality and customer service good?
8. Are the firm's products and services priced appropriately?
9. Does the firm have an effective promotion, advertising, and publicity strategy?
10. Are marketing, planning, and budgeting effective?
11. Do the firm's marketing managers have adequate experience and training?
12. Is the firm's Internet presence excellent as compared to rivals?

Finance and Accounting

Financial condition is often considered the single-best measure of a firm's competitive position and overall attractiveness to investors. Determining an organization's financial strengths and weaknesses is essential to effectively formulating strategies. A firm's liquidity, leverage, working capital, profitability, asset utilization, cash flow, and equity can eliminate some strategies as being feasible alternatives. Financial factors often alter existing strategies and change implementation plans.

Finance/Accounting Functions

According to James Van Horne, the **functions of finance/accounting** comprise three decisions: the investment decision, the financing decision, and the dividend decision.[24] **Financial ratio analysis** is the most widely used method for determining an organization's strengths and weaknesses in the investment, financing, and dividend areas. Because the functional areas of business are so closely related, financial ratios can signal strengths or weaknesses in management, marketing, production, R&D, and MIS activities. Financial ratios are equally applicable in for-profit and nonprofit organizations. Even though nonprofit organizations obviously would not have return-on-investment or earnings-per-share ratios, they would routinely monitor many other special ratios. For example, a church would monitor the ratio of dollar contributions to the number of members, whereas a zoo would monitor dollar food sales to number of visitors. A university would monitor number of students divided by number of professors. Therefore, be creative when performing ratio analysis for nonprofit organizations, for they strive to be financially sound just as for-profit firms do. Nonprofit organizations need strategic planning just as much as for-profit firms.

The **investment decision**, also called **capital budgeting**, is the allocation and reallocation of capital and resources to projects, products, assets, and divisions of an organization. After strategies are formulated, capital budgeting decisions are required to successfully implement strategies. The **financing decision** determines the best capital structure for the firm and includes examining various methods by which the firm can raise capital (for example, by issuing stock, increasing debt, selling assets, or using a combination of these approaches). The financing decision must consider both short-term and long-term needs for working capital. Two key financial ratios that indicate whether a firm's financing decisions have been effective are the debt-to-equity ratio and the debt-to-total-assets ratio.

Dividend decisions concern issues such as the percentage of earnings paid to stockholders, the stability of dividends paid over time, and the repurchase or issuance of stock. Dividend decisions determine the amount of funds that are retained in a firm compared to the amount paid out to stockholders. Three financial ratios that are helpful in evaluating a firm's dividend decisions are the earnings-per-share ratio, the dividends-per-share ratio, and the price-earnings ratio.

The benefits of paying dividends to investors must be balanced against the benefits of internally retaining funds, and there is no set formula on how to balance this trade-off. In 2014–2016, companies are aggressively boosting their dividends paid to shareholders. Companies are also buying back their own stock (called *Treasury stock*) at record levels. For the reasons listed here, dividends are sometimes paid out even when the firm has incurred a negative annual net income, and/or even if the funds could be better reinvested in the business, and/or even if the firm has to obtain outside sources of capital to pay for the dividends:

1. Paying cash dividends is customary for some firms. Failure to do so could be thought of as a stigma. A dividend change is a signal about the future.
2. Dividends represent a sales point for investment bankers. Some institutional investors can buy only dividend-paying stocks.
3. Shareholders often demand dividends, even in companies with great opportunities for reinvesting all available funds.
4. A myth exists that paying dividends will result in a higher stock price.

Financial Ratios

Financial ratios are computed from an organization's income statement and balance sheet. Computing financial ratios is like taking a photograph—the results reflect a situation at just one point in time. Comparing ratios over time and to industry averages is more likely to result in meaningful statistics that can be used to identify and evaluate strengths and weaknesses. Trend analysis, illustrated in Figure 6-3, is a useful technique that incorporates both the time and industry average dimensions of financial ratios. Note that the dotted lines reveal projected ratios.

Financial ratio analysis should be conducted on three separate fronts:

1. *How has each ratio changed over time?* This information provides a means of evaluating historical trends. Examine whether each ratio has been historically increasing, decreasing, or nearly constant. For example, a 10 percent profit margin could be bad if the trend has been down 20 percent each of the last three years. But a 10 percent profit margin could be excellent if the trend has been up, up, up. Analysts often calculate the percentage change in a ratio from one year to the next to assess historical financial performance on that dimension. Large percent changes can be especially relevant.
2. *How does each ratio compare to industry norms?* A firm's inventory turnover ratio may appear impressive at first glance but may pale when compared to industry standards or norms. Industries can differ dramatically on certain ratios. For example, grocery companies have a high inventory turnover, whereas automobile dealerships have a lower turnover. Therefore, comparison of a firm's ratios within its particular industry can be essential in determining strengths and weaknesses.

Current ratio

Profit margin
(percent)

FIGURE 6-3

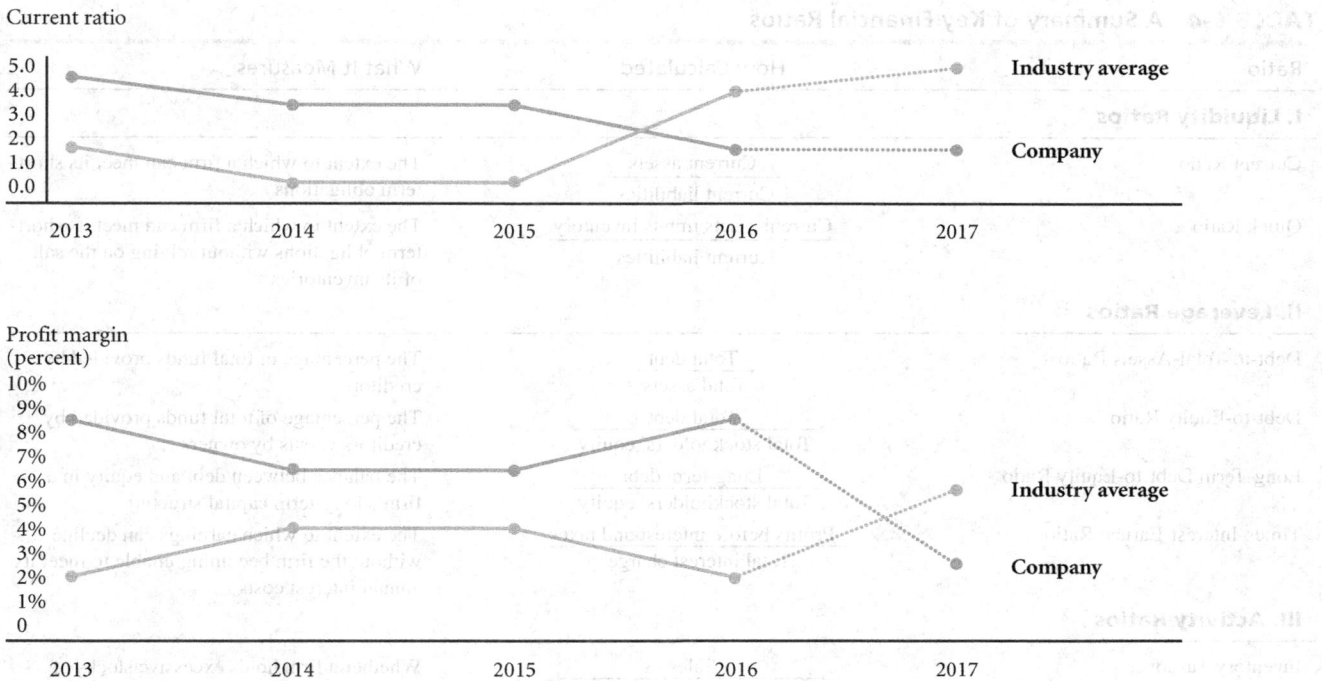

The Process of Gaining Competitive Advantage in a Firm

3. **How does each ratio compare with key competitors?** Oftentimes competition is more intense between several competitors in a given industry or location than across all rival firms in the industry. When this is true, financial ratio analysis should include comparison to those key competitors. For example, if a firm's profitability ratio is trending up over time and compares favorably to the industry average, but it is trending down relative to its leading competitor, there may be reason for concern.

Financial ratio analysis is not without some limitations. For example, financial ratios are based on accounting data, and firms differ in their treatment of such items as depreciation, inventory valuation, R&D expenditures, pension plan costs, mergers, and taxes. Also, seasonal factors can influence comparative ratios. Therefore, conformity to industry composite ratios does not establish with certainty that a firm is performing normally or that it is well managed. Likewise, departures from industry averages do not always indicate that a firm is doing especially well or badly. For example, a high inventory turnover ratio could indicate efficient inventory management and a strong working capital position, but it also could indicate a serious inventory shortage and a weak working capital position.

Another limitation of financial ratios in terms of including them as key internal factors in the upcoming IFE Matrix is that financial ratios are not very "actionable" in terms of revealing potential strategies needed (i.e., because they generally are based on performance of the overall firm). For example, to include as a key internal factor that the firm's "current ratio increased from 1.8 to 2.1" is not as "actionable" as "the firm's fragrance division revenues increased 18 percent in Africa in 2015." Recall from the prior chapter the importance of selecting *"actionable responses"* as key factors, both externally and internally, upon which to formulate strategies. Selecting "actionable" key factors is vital to successful strategic planning.

Table 6-4 provides a summary of key financial ratios showing how each ratio is calculated and what each ratio measures. However, all the ratios are not significant for all industries and companies. For example, accounts receivable turnover and average collection period are not meaningful to a company that takes only cash receipts. As indicated in Table 6-4, key financial ratios can be classified into the following five types: liquidity, leverage, activity, profitability, and growth.

TABLE 6-4   A Summary of Key Financial Ratios

Ratio	How Calculated	What It Measures
I. Liquidity Ratios		
Current Ratio	$$\frac{\text{Current assets}}{\text{Current liabilities}}$$	The extent to which a firm can meet its short-term obligations
Quick Ratio	$$\frac{\text{Current assets minus inventory}}{\text{Current liabilities}}$$	The extent to which a firm can meet its short-term obligations without relying on the sale of its inventories
II. Leverage Ratios		
Debt-to-Total-Assets Ratio	$$\frac{\text{Total debt}}{\text{Total assets}}$$	The percentage of total funds provided by creditors
Debt-to-Equity Ratio	$$\frac{\text{Total debt}}{\text{Total stockholders' equity}}$$	The percentage of total funds provided by creditors versus by owners
Long-Term Debt-to-Equity Ratio	$$\frac{\text{Long-term debt}}{\text{Total stockholders' equity}}$$	The balance between debt and equity in a firm's long-term capital structure
Times-Interest-Earned Ratio	$$\frac{\text{Profits before interest and taxes}}{\text{Total interest charges}}$$	The extent to which earnings can decline without the firm becoming unable to meet its annual interest costs
III. Activity Ratios		
Inventory Turnover	$$\frac{\text{Sales}}{\text{Inventory of finished goods}}$$	Whether a firm holds excessive stocks of inventories and whether a firm is slowly selling its inventories compared to the industry average
Fixed Assets Turnover	$$\frac{\text{Sales}}{\text{Fixed assets}}$$	Sales productivity and plant and equipment utilization
Total Assets Turnover	$$\frac{\text{Sales}}{\text{Total assets}}$$	Whether a firm is generating a sufficient volume of business for the size of its asset investment
Accounts Receivable Turnover	$$\frac{\text{Annual credit sales}}{\text{Accounts receivable}}$$	The average length of time it takes a firm to collect credit sales (in percentage terms)
Average Collection Period	$$\frac{\text{Accounts receivable}}{\text{Total credit sales/365 days}}$$	The average length of time it takes a firm to collect on credit sales (in days)
IV. Profitability Ratios		
Gross Profit Margin	$$\frac{\text{Sales minus cost of goods sold}}{\text{Sales}}$$	The total margin available to cover operating expenses and yield a profit
Operating Profit Margin	$$\frac{\text{Earnings before interest and taxes EBIT}}{\text{Sales}}$$	Profitability without concern for taxes and interest
Net Profit Margin	$$\frac{\text{Net income}}{\text{Sales}}$$	After-tax profits per dollar of sales
Return on Total Assets (ROA)	$$\frac{\text{Net income}}{\text{Total assets}}$$	After-tax profits per dollar of assets; this ratio is also called return on investment (ROI)
Return on Stockholders' Equity (ROE)	$$\frac{\text{Net Income}}{\text{Total stockholders' equity}}$$	After-tax profits per dollar of stockholders' investment in the firm
Earnings Per Share (EPS)	$$\frac{\text{Net income}}{\text{Number of shares of common stock outstanding}}$$	Earnings available to the owners of common stock
Price-Earnings Ratio	$$\frac{\text{Market price per share}}{\text{Earnings per share}}$$	Attractiveness of firm on equity markets
V. Growth Ratios		
Sales	Annual percentage growth in total sales	Firm's growth rate in sales
Net Income	Annual percentage growth in profits	Firm's growth rate in profits
Earnings Per Share	Annual percentage growth in EPS	Firm's growth rate in EPS
Dividends Per Share	Annual percentage growth in dividends per share	Firm's growth rate in dividends per share

Breakeven Analysis

Because consumers remain price sensitive, many firms have lowered prices to compete. As a firm lowers prices, its **breakeven (BE) point** in terms of units sold increases, as illustrated in Figure 6-4. The breakeven point can be defined as the quantity of units that a firm must sell for its total revenues (TR) to equal its total costs (TC). Note that the before and after chart in Figure 6-4 reveals that the TR line rotates to the right with a decrease in price, thus increasing the quantity (Q) that must be sold just to break even. Increasing the breakeven point is thus a huge drawback of lowering prices. Of course when rivals are lowering prices, a firm may have to lower prices anyway to compete. However, the breakeven concept should be kept in mind because it is so important, especially in recessionary times.

The before and after charts in Figure 6-5 show that increasing **fixed costs (FC)** raises a firm's breakeven quantity. The figure also reveals that adding fixed costs such as more stores, or more plants, or even more advertising as part of a strategic plan also raises the TC line, which makes the intersection of the TC and TR lines at a point farther down the Quantity axis. Increasing a firm's FC therefore significantly raises the quantity of goods that must be sold to break even. This is not just theory for the sake of theory. Firms with less fixed costs, such as Apple and Amazon.com, have lower breakeven points, which give them a decided competitive advantage in harsh economic times. Figure 6-5 reveals that adding fixed costs—such as plant, equipment, stores, advertising, and land—may be detrimental whenever there is doubt that significantly more units can be sold to offset those expenditures.

Firms must be cognizant of the fact that lowering prices and adding fixed costs could be a catastrophic double whammy because the firm's breakeven quantity needed to be sold is increased dramatically. Figure 6-6 illustrates this double whammy. Note how far the breakeven point shifts with both a price decrease and an increase in fixed costs. If a firm does not break even, then it will of course incur losses, and losses are not good, especially sustained losses.

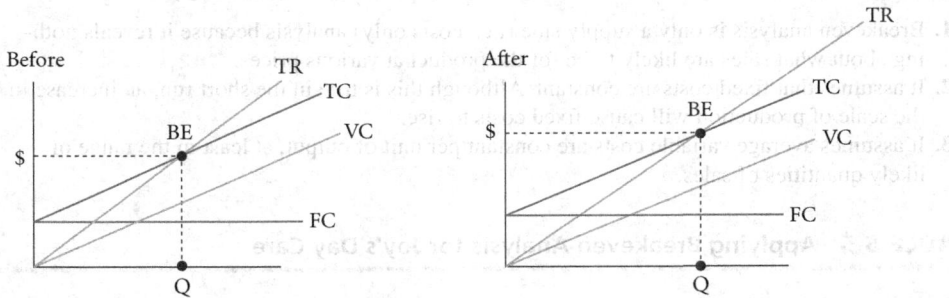

FIGURE 6-4
A Before and After Breakeven Chart When Prices Are Lowered

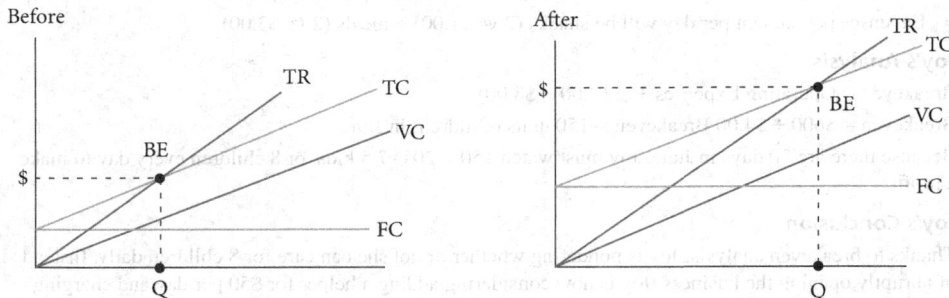

FIGURE 6-5
A Before and After Breakeven Chart When Fixed Costs are Increased

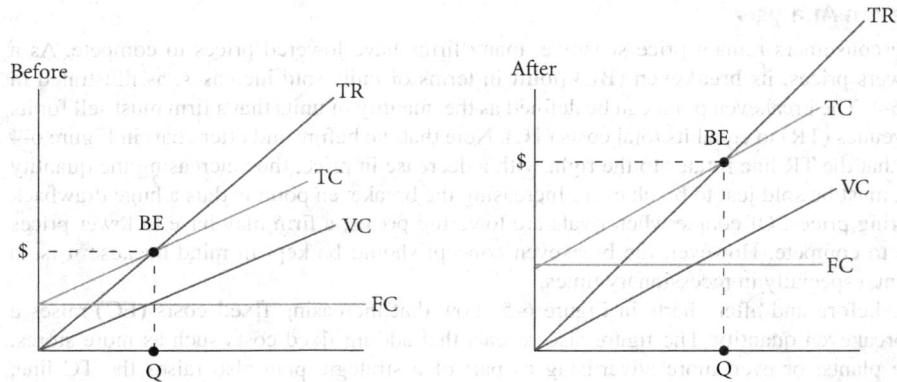

FIGURE 6-6

A Before and After Breakeven Chart When Prices Are Lowered and Fixed Costs Are Increased

Finally, note in Figures 6-4, 6-5, and 6-6 that **variable costs (VC)**, such as labor and materials, when increased, have the effect of raising the breakeven point, too. Raising VC is reflected by the VC line shifting left or becoming steeper. When the TR line remains constant, the effect of increasing VC is to increase TC, which increases the point at which TR = TC = BE.

The formula for calculating the breakeven point is BE Quantity = TFC divided by (price − VC). In other words, the quantity or units of product that need to be sold for a firm to break even given in Table 6-5. Suffice it to say here that various strategies can have dramatically beneficial or harmful effects on the firm's financial condition because of the concept of breakeven analysis.

There are some limitations of breakeven analysis, including the following points:

1. Breakeven analysis is only a supply side (i.e., costs only) analysis because it reveals nothing about what sales are likely to be for the product at various prices.
2. It assumes that fixed costs are constant. Although this is true in the short run, an increase in the scale of production will cause fixed costs to rise.
3. It assumes average variable costs are constant per unit of output, at least in the range of likely quantities of sales.

TABLE 6-5 Applying Breakeven Analysis for Joy's Day Care

Seeing a need for childcare in her town, Joy is considering opening her own day-care service. Joy's Day Care needs to be affordable, so Joy would like to care for each child for $12 a day. But Joy also wants to make money. She needs to know how many children she will have to watch per day to make money. Joy gathered the following information about her potential new business.

- The month of June has 20 workdays, Monday through Friday for 4 weeks.
- Insurance and rent on her business will be $200 and $400, respectively, per month.
- Expenses per student per day will be snacks (2 @ $1.00) + meals (2 @ $3.00).

Joy's Analysis

Breakeven = Operating Expenses ÷ ($12.00 − $8.00)

Breakeven = $600 ÷ $4.00 Breakeven = 150 units (children) in June.

Because there are 20 days in June, Joy must watch 150 ÷ 20 = 7.5 kids, or 8 children every day to make a profit.

Joy's Conclusion

Thanks to breakeven analysis, Joy is pondering whether or not she can care for 8 children daily. Instead of abruptly opening the business, Joy is now considering adding a helper for $50 per day and charging $20 per student per day. How many students now would Joy have to care for to make a profit under this scenario? (Answer 6.6 = 7) What do you think would be an ideal scenario for Joy in planning for her new business?

4. It assumes that the quantity of goods produced is equal to the quantity of goods sold (i.e., there is no change in beginning or ending inventory).
5. In multiproduct companies, it assumes that the relative proportions of each product sold and produced are constant (i.e., the sales mix is constant).[25]

Finance/Accounting Audit Checklist

Some finance/accounting questions that should be examined in any strategic analysis of the firm are given here:

1. Where is the firm financially strong and weak as indicated by financial ratio analyses?
2. Can the firm raise needed short-term capital?
3. Can the firm raise needed long-term capital through debt or equity?
4. Does the firm have sufficient working capital?
5. Are capital budgeting procedures effective?
6. Are dividend payout policies reasonable?
7. Does the firm have good relations with its investors and stockholders?
8. Are the firm's financial managers experienced and well trained?
9. Is the firm's debt situation excellent?

Production/Operations

The **production/operations function** of a business consists of all those activities that transform inputs into goods and services. production/operations management deals with inputs, transformations, and outputs that vary across industries and markets. A manufacturing operation transforms or converts inputs such as raw materials, labor, capital, machines, and facilities into finished goods and services. The extent to which a manufacturing plant's output reaches its potential output is called **capacity utilization**, a key strategic variable. The higher the capacity utilization, the better; otherwise, equipment may sit idle.

As indicated in Table 6-6, Roger Schroeder suggests that production/operations management comprises five functions or decision areas: process, capacity, inventory, workforce, and quality.

Production/operations activities often represent the largest part of an organization's human and capital assets. In most industries, the major costs of producing a product or service are incurred within operations, so production/operations can have great value as a competitive weapon in a company's overall strategy. Strengths and weaknesses in the five functions of production can mean the success or failure of an enterprise.

TABLE 6-6 The Basic Functions (Decisions) within Production/Operations

Decision Areas	Example Decisions
1. Process	These decisions include choice of technology, facility layout, process flow analysis, facility location, line balancing, process control, and transportation analysis. Distances from raw materials to production sites to customers are a major consideration.
2. Capacity	These decisions include forecasting, facilities planning, aggregate planning, scheduling, capacity planning, and queuing analysis. Capacity utilization is a major consideration.
3. Inventory	These decisions involve managing the level of raw materials, work-in-process, and finished goods, especially considering what to order, when to order, how much to order, and materials handling.
4. Workforce	These decisions involve managing the skilled, unskilled, clerical, and managerial employees by caring for job design, work measurement, job enrichment, work standards, and motivation techniques.
5. Quality	These decisions are aimed at ensuring that high-quality goods and services are produced by caring for quality control, sampling, testing, quality assurance, and cost control.

Source: Based on R. Schroeder, *Operations Management* (New York: McGraw-Hill, 1981), p. 12.

Increasingly in production settings, a new breed of robots called **collaborative machines**, are working alongside people. The robots, priced as low as $20,000 and becoming widely used even in small businesses, do not take lunch breaks or sick days or require health insurance, and they can work nonstop all night tirelessly if needed. Unlike larger robots that cost much more, collaborative machines are more flexible, oftentimes doing one task one day and a different task the next day. At Panek Precision Inc., an Northbrook, Illinois-based machine shop, Mr. Panek states, "Having robots has allowed us to move our existing workers into more useful tasks, such as monitoring more-advanced machines that require human tending." Workers are generally quite receptive to collaborative machines, even giving them names, such as "Fred" at Stuller Inc., a jewelry factory in Lafayette, Louisiana, and "Baxter" at K'NEX Brands, a toy maker in Hatfield, Pennsylvania.[26]

Many production/operations managers are finding that cross-training of employees can help their firms respond faster to changing markets. Cross-training can increase efficiency, quality, productivity, and job satisfaction. For example, at General Motors' Detroit gear and axle plant, costs related to product defects were reduced 400 percent in 2 years as a result of cross-training workers. As shown in Table 6-7, James Dilworth has outlined implications of several types of strategic decisions a company might make.

Production/Operations Audit Checklist

Questions such as the following should be examined:

1. Are supplies of raw materials, parts, and subassemblies reliable and reasonable?
2. Are facilities, equipment, machinery, and offices in good condition?
3. Are inventory-control policies and procedures effective?
4. Are quality-control policies and procedures effective?
5. Are facilities, resources, and markets strategically located?
6. Does the firm have technological competencies?

TABLE 6-7 Implications of Various Strategies on Production/Operations

Various Strategies	Implications
1. Become a low-cost provider	Creates high barriers to entry
	Creates larger market
	Requires longer production runs and fewer product changes
2. Become a high-quality provider	Requires more quality-assurance efforts
	Requires more expensive equipment
	Requires highly skilled workers and higher wages
3. Provide great customer service	Requires more service people, service parts, and equipment
	Requires rapid response to customer needs or changes in customer tastes
	Requires a higher inventory investment
4. Be the first to introduce new products	Has higher research and development costs
	Has high retraining and tooling costs
5. Become highly automated	Requires high capital investment
	Reduces flexibility
	May affect labor relations
	Makes maintenance more crucial
6. Minimize layoffs	Serves the security needs of employees and may develop employee loyalty
	Helps attract and retain highly skilled employees

Source: Based on J. Dilworth, *Production/Operations Management: Manufacturing and Nonmanufacturing,* 2nd ed. Copyright © 1983 by Random House, Inc.

Research and Development

The fifth major area of internal operations that should be examined for specific strengths and weaknesses as input into formulating strategies is **research and development (R&D)**. Many firms today conduct no R&D, and yet many other companies depend on successful R&D activities for survival. Firms pursuing a product-development strategy especially need to have a strong R&D orientation. High-tech firms, such as Microsoft, spend a much larger proportion of their revenues on R&D. A key decision for many firms is whether to be a "first mover" or a "late follower" (i.e., spend heavily on R&D to be the first to develop radically new products, or spend less on R&D by imitating/duplicating/improving on products after rival firms develop them).

Organizations invest in R&D because they believe that such an investment will lead to a superior product or service and will give them competitive advantages. Research and development expenditures are directed at developing new products before competitors do, at improving product quality, or at improving manufacturing processes to reduce costs. However, a recent study reported that the stock price appreciation of technology companies in the lowest third of R&D spending have consistently outperformed companies in the highest third over 1-, 3-, 5-, and 10-year periods since 1977, with a 5-year average outperformance of 8 percent.[27] In the study, some big R&D underspenders whose stock price significantly outperformed were Micron Technology, Seagate Technology, Western Digital, and Apple. The study reported in *Investor's Business Daily* accents the need to formulate and implement an effective R&D spending strategy consistent with overall corporate strategy and objectives.

Effective management of the R&D function requires a strategic and operational partnership between R&D and the other vital business functions. A spirit of partnership and mutual trust between general and R&D managers is evident in the best-managed firms today. Managers in these firms jointly explore; assess; and decide the what, when, where, why, and how much of R&D. Priorities, costs, benefits, risks, and rewards associated with R&D activities are discussed openly and shared. The overall mission of R&D has thus become broad based, including supporting existing businesses, helping launch new businesses, developing new products, improving product quality, improving manufacturing efficiency, and deepening or broadening the company's technological capabilities.[28]

Internal and External Research and Development

Four approaches to determining research and development budget allocations commonly are used: (1) financing as many project proposals as possible, (2) using a percentage-of-sales method, (3) budgeting about the same amount that competitors spend for R&D, or (4) deciding how many successful new products are needed and working backward to estimate the required R&D investment. The strengths (capabilities) and weaknesses (limitations) of R&D play a major role in strategy formulation and strategy implementation.

Most firms have no choice but to continually develop new and improved products because of changing consumer needs and tastes, new technologies, shortened product life cycles, and increased domestic and foreign competition. A shortage of ideas for new products, increased global competition, increased market segmentation, strong special-interest groups, and increased government regulations are several factors making the successful development of new products more and more difficult, costly, and risky. In the pharmaceutical industry, for example, only one of every few thousand drugs created in the laboratory ends up on pharmacists' shelves.

Research and Development Audit

Questions such as the following should be asked in performing a research and development audit:

1. Does the firm have R&D facilities? Are they adequate?
2. If outside R&D firms are used, are they cost effective?
3. Are the organization's R&D personnel well qualified?
4. Are R&D resources allocated effectively?
5. Are management information and computer systems adequate?
6. Is communication between R&D and other organizational units effective?
7. Are present products technologically competitive?

Management Information Systems

Billions of bits of information are now "in the cloud." Information ties all business functions together and provides the basis for all managerial decisions. It is the cornerstone of all organizations. Information represents a major source of competitive management advantage or disadvantage. Assessing a firm's internal strengths and weaknesses in information systems is a critical dimension of performing an internal audit.

A purpose of a management information system is to improve the performance of an enterprise by improving the quality of managerial decisions. An effective information system thus collects, codes, stores, synthesizes, and presents information in such a manner that it answers important operating and strategic questions. The heart of an information system is a database containing the kinds of records and data important to managers.

A **management information system (MIS)** receives raw material from both the external and internal evaluation of an organization. It gathers data about marketing, finance, production, and personnel matters internally, and social, cultural, demographic, environmental, economic, political, governmental, legal, technological, and competitive factors externally. Data are integrated in ways needed to support managerial decision making.

Starbucks is an example firm with an outstanding management information system that begins with more than 7 million weekly transactions taking place at Starbucks registers, and 16 percent of those are made from a mobile device. Surprisingly, Starbucks transactions comprise about 90 percent of all mobile pay transactions in the United States. And Starbucks is reportedly developing a stand-alone e-payment system that its customers may use anywhere, anytime, to buy anything. Such a system would compete with Apple Pay, Google's Wallet, eBay's PayPal, and CurrentC used by WalMart and CVS Health.

Managing Voluminous Consumer Data

Recent research by the Pew Research Center reveals that more than 50 percent of all consumers are concerned about the volume of their personal data on the Internet.[29] Basically, every time you get online and do anything at any website with any company or anybody, that information is dissected to determine your patterns of behavior; resultant information is disseminated to marketers. Every time you swipe a card, click, log in, text, tweet, email, or call, your behavior is being tracked. Consider a few facts:

1. The number of times the online activity of an average Internet user is tracked every day is estimated to be 2,000-plus.
2. Facebook and Twitter can track the activity of visitors at 1,205 and 868 of the most popular websites, respectively, on the Internet.
3. The estimated annual value to Facebook of a "very active" versus "relatively inactive" female user is $27.61 and $12.37, respectively, due to their dissemination of the information to marketers.
4. People are so worried about their privacy that 86 percent of them have taken steps to conceal their digital footprints.
5. More than 25 percent of Americans have downloaded advertisement-blocking tools so companies cannot so easily access data about the users.[30]

ACADEMIC RESEARCH CAPSULE 6-2

New Trends in Managing Big Data

Business analytics can identify and analyze patterns, but perhaps more importantly, they can reveal the likelihood of an event, and that information can be worth millions and even billions of dollars to companies, organizations, and governments. In analyzing big data, two trends in analysis have emerged. First, the typical statistical approach of relying on p values to establish the significance of a finding is becoming less trusted because, with extremely high sample sizes, "almost everything" becomes significant. In contrast, the focus of analysis is shifting more to the size and variance explained (i.e., examining for example R-squared). Stepwise regression and cluster analysis are becoming more widely used to supplement traditional p-value analyses. Second, in analyzing big data, there is a shift from focusing largely on aggregates or averages to focusing also on outliers, because outliers oftentimes reveal (predict) critical

innovations, trends, disruptions, and revolutions on the horizon. In essence, knowing more about "who is not your customer and why" may be as (or more) important than knowing about your customer. Perceptual mapping and multidimensional scaling are being more widely used to explore outlier patterns. By 2018, global data analytics software is expected to reach $21.7 billion, a 64 percent increase from 2012. Leading firms providing the software include IBM, SAP, Oracle, Microsoft, Qlik Technologies, Tibco Software, and Tableau Software.

Source: Based on G. George, M. Haas, & A. Pentland, "Big Data and Management," *Academy of Management Journal* 52, no. 2 (April 2014): 321–326. See also P. Barlas, "Data Analytics Gets in the Sports Game," *Investor's Business Daily,* July 11, 2014, A1.

Academic Research Capsule 6-2 reveals key trends in analyzing big data.

Management Information Systems Audit

Questions such as the following should be asked when conducting this audit:

1. Do all managers in the firm use the information system to make decisions?
2. Is there a chief information officer or director of information systems position in the firm?
3. Are data in the information system updated regularly?
4. Do managers from all functional areas of the firm contribute input to the information system?
5. Are there effective passwords for entry into the firm's information system?
6. Are strategists of the firm familiar with the information systems of rival firms?
7. Is the information system user-friendly?
8. Do all users of the information system understand the competitive advantages that information can provide firms?
9. Are computer training workshops provided for users of the information system?
10. Is the firm's information system continually being improved in content and user-friendliness?

Value Chain Analysis

According to Porter, the business of a firm can best be described as a *value chain,* in which total revenues minus total costs of all activities undertaken to develop and market a product or service yields value.[31] All firms in a given industry have a similar value chain, which includes activities such as obtaining raw materials, designing products, building manufacturing facilities, developing cooperative agreements, and providing customer service. A firm will be profitable so long as total revenues exceed the total costs incurred in creating and delivering the product or service. Firms should strive to understand not only their own value chain operations but also those of their competitors, suppliers, and distributors.

Value chain analysis (VCA) refers to the process whereby a firm determines the costs associated with organizational activities from purchasing raw materials to manufacturing product(s) to marketing those products. Value chain analysis aims to identify where low-cost advantages or disadvantages exist anywhere along the value chain from raw material to customer service activities. The VCA process can enable a firm to better identify its own strengths and weaknesses, especially as compared to competitors' value chain analyses and their own data examined over time.

Substantial judgment may be required in performing a VCA because different items along the value chain may impact other items positively or negatively, at times creating complex interrelationships. For example, exceptional customer service may be especially expensive yet may reduce the costs of returns and increase revenues. Cost and price differences among rival firms can have their origins in activities performed by suppliers, distributors, creditors, or even shareholders. The initial step in implementing VCA is to divide a firm's operations into specific activities or business processes. Then the analyst attempts to attach a cost to each discrete activity; the costs could be in terms of both time and money. Finally, the analyst converts the cost data into information by looking for competitive cost strengths and weaknesses that may yield competitive advantage or disadvantage. Conducting a value chain analysis is supportive of the research-based view's examination of a firm's assets and capabilities as sources of distinctive competence.

When a major competitor or new market entrant offers products or services at low prices, this may be because that firm has substantially lower value chain costs or perhaps the rival firm is just waging a desperate attempt to gain sales or market share. Thus, VCA can be critically important for a firm in monitoring whether its prices and costs are competitive. An example value chain is illustrated in Figure 6-7. There can be more than a hundred particular value-creating activities associated with the business of producing and marketing a product or service, and each one of the activities can represent a competitive advantage or disadvantage for the firm. The combined costs of all the various activities in a company's value chain define the firm's cost of doing business. Firms should determine where cost advantages and disadvantages in their value chain occur *relative* to the value chain of rival firms.

Value chains differ immensely across industries and firms. Whereas a paper products company, such as Stone Container, would include on its value chain timber farming, logging, pulp mills, and papermaking, a company such as Hewlett-Packard would include programming, peripherals, software, hardware, and laptops. A motel would include food, housekeeping, check-in and check-out operations, website, reservations system, and so on. However, all firms should use value chain analysis to develop and nurture a core competence and convert this competence into a distinctive competence. A **core competence** is a VCA that a firm performs especially well. When a core competence evolves into a major competitive advantage, then it is called a *distinctive competence.* Figure 6-8 illustrates this process.

More and more companies are using VCA to gain and sustain competitive advantage by being especially efficient and effective along various parts of the value chain. For example, Walmart has built powerful value advantages by focusing on exceptionally tight inventory control and volume purchasing of products. In contrast, computer companies compete aggressively along the distribution end of the value chain. Price competitiveness is a key component of competitiveness for both mass retailers and computer firms.

Benchmarking

Benchmarking is an analytical tool used to determine whether a firm's value chain analysis is competitive compared to those of rivals and thus conducive to winning in the marketplace. Benchmarking entails measuring costs of value chain activities across an industry to determine "best practices" among competing firms for the purpose of duplicating or improving on those best practices. Benchmarking enables a firm to take action to improve its competitiveness by identifying (and improving on) value chain activities where rival firms have comparative advantages in cost, service, reputation, or operation.

A comprehensive survey on benchmarking was recently commissioned by the Global Benchmarking Network, a network of benchmarking centers representing 22 countries. More than 450 organizations responded from over 40 countries. Here are two important results:

1. Mission and vision statements along with customer (client) surveys are the most used (77 percent of organizations) of 20 improvement tools, followed by SWOT (strengths, weaknesses, opportunities, threats) analysis (72 %), and informal benchmarking (68 %). Performance benchmarking was used by 49 percent and best practice benchmarking was used by 39 percent of respondents.
2. The tools that are likely to increase the most in popularity over the next 3 years are performance benchmarking, informal benchmarking, SWOT, and best practice benchmarking. More than 60 percent of organizations not currently using these tools indicated they are likely to use them in the next 3 years.[32]

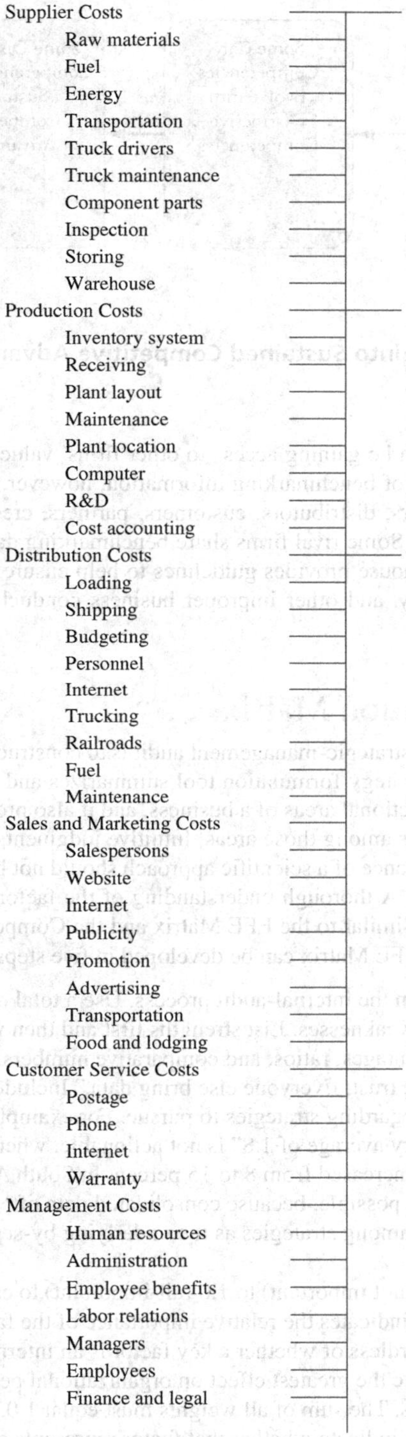

Supplier Costs

    Raw materials

    Fuel

    Energy

    Transportation

    Truck drivers

    Truck maintenance

    Component parts

    Inspection

    Storing

    Warehouse

Production Costs

    Inventory system

    Receiving

    Plant layout

    Maintenance

    Plant location

    Computer

    R&D

    Cost accounting

Distribution Costs

    Loading

    Shipping

    Budgeting

    Personnel

    Internet

    Trucking

    Railroads

    Fuel

    Maintenance

Sales and Marketing Costs

    Salespersons

    Website

    Internet

    Publicity

    Promotion

    Advertising

    Transportation

    Food and lodging

Customer Service Costs

    Postage

    Phone

    Internet

    Warranty

Management Costs

    Human resources

    Administration

    Employee benefits

    Labor relations

    Managers

    Employees

    Finance and legal

FIGURE 6-7

An Example Value Chain for a Typical Manufacturing Firm

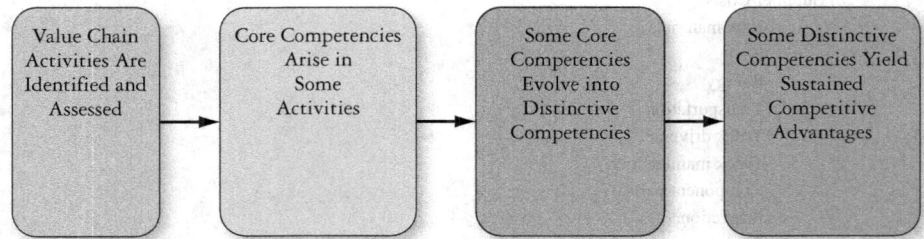

FIGURE 6-8

Transforming Value Chain Activities into Sustained Competitive Advantage

The hardest part of benchmarking can be gaining access to other firms' value chain analyses with associated costs. Typical sources of benchmarking information, however, include published reports, trade publications, suppliers, distributors, customers, partners, creditors, shareholders, lobbyists, and willing rival firms. Some rival firms share benchmarking data. However, the International Benchmarking Clearinghouse provides guidelines to help ensure that restraint of trade, price fixing, bid rigging, bribery, and other improper business conduct do not arise between participating firms.

The Internal Factor Evaluation Matrix

A summary step in conducting an internal strategic-management audit is to construct an **Internal Factor Evaluation (IFE) Matrix**. This strategy-formulation tool summarizes and evaluates the major strengths and weaknesses in the functional areas of a business, and it also provides a basis for identifying and evaluating relationships among those areas. Intuitive judgments are required in developing an IFE Matrix, so the appearance of a scientific approach should not be interpreted to mean this is an all-powerful technique. A thorough understanding of the factors included is more important than the actual numbers. Similar to the EFE Matrix and the Competitive Profile Matrix (CPM) described in Chapter 7, an IFE Matrix can be developed in five steps:

1. List key internal factors as identified in the internal-audit process. Use a total of 20 internal factors, including both strengths and weaknesses. List strengths first and then weaknesses. Be as specific as possible, using percentages, ratios, and comparative numbers. Recall that Edward Deming said, "In God we trust. Everyone else bring data." Include *actionable* factors that can provide insight regarding strategies to pursue. For example, the factor "Our Quick Ratio is 2.1 versus industry average of 1.8" is not actionable, whereas the factor "Our chocolate division's ROI increased from 8 to 15 percent in South America" is actionable. Also, be as *divisional* as possible, because consolidated data oftentimes is not as revealing or useful in deciding among strategies as the underlying by-segment or division data.

2. Assign a weight that ranges from 0.0 (not important) to 1.0 (all-important) to each factor. The weight assigned to a given factor indicates the relative importance of the factor to being successful in the firm's industry. Regardless of whether a key factor is an internal strength or weakness, factors considered to have the greatest effect on organizational performance should be assigned the highest weights. The sum of all weights must equal 1.0.

3. Assign a 1 to 4 rating to each factor to indicate whether that factor represents a major weakness (rating = 1), a minor weakness (rating = 2), a minor strength (rating = 3), or a major strength (rating = 4). Note that strengths must receive a 3 or 4 rating and weaknesses must receive a 1 or 2 rating. Ratings are thus company-based, whereas the weights in step 2 are industry-based.

4. Multiply each factor's weight by its rating to determine a weighted score for each variable.

5. Sum the weighted scores for each variable to determine the total weighted score for the organization.

Regardless of how many factors are included in an IFE Matrix, the total weighted score can range from a low of 1.0 to a high of 4.0, with the average score being 2.5. Total weighted scores well below 2.5 characterize organizations that are weak internally, whereas scores significantly above 2.5 indicate a strong internal position. Like the EFE Matrix, an IFE Matrix should include 20 key factors. The number of factors has no effect on the range of total weighted scores because the weights always sum to 1.0.

When a key internal factor is both a strength and a weakness, the factor may be included twice in the IFE Matrix, and a weight and rating assigned to each statement. For example, the Playboy logo both helps and hurts Playboy Enterprises; the logo attracts customers to *Playboy* magazine, but it keeps the Playboy cable channel out of many markets. Be as quantitative as possible when stating factors. Use monetary amounts, percentages, numbers, and ratios to the extent possible.

An example IFE Matrix is provided in Table 6-8 for a retail computer store. The table reveals that the two most important factors to be successful in the retail computer store business are "Revenues from repair/service in the store" and "Employee morale." Note that the store is doing best on "Average customer purchase" amount and "In-store technical support." The store is having major problems with its carpet, bathroom, paint, and checkout procedures. Note also that the matrix contains substantial quantitative data rather than vague statements; this is excellent. Overall, this store receives a 2.5 total weighted score, which on a 1 to 4 scale is exactly average/halfway, indicating there is definitely room for improvement in store operations, strategies, policies, and procedures.

The IFE Matrix provides important information for strategy formulation. For example, this retail computer store might want to hire another checkout person and repair its carpet, paint, and bathroom problems. Also, the store may want to increase advertising for its repair/services, because that is a really important (weight 0.15) factor to being successful in this business.

An actual IFE Matrix for Forjas Taurus S.A. is provided in Table 6-9. Headquartered in Porto Alegre, Brazil, Taurus manufactures and sells military and civilian pistols, submachine guns, rifles, ammunition, bulletproof vests, motorbike helmets, and more. Note that the total weighted score of 2.53 is barely above the average of 2.50. Note, too, that the most important

TABLE 6-8 Sample Internal Factor Evaluation Matrix for a Retail Computer Store

Key Internal Factors	Weight	Rating	Weighted Score
Strengths			
1. Inventory turnover increased from 5.8 to 6.7.	0.05	3	0.15
2. Average customer purchase increased from $97 to $128.	0.07	4	0.28
3. Employee morale is excellent.	0.10	3	0.30
4. In-store promotions resulted in 20% increase in sales.	0.05	3	0.15
5. Newspaper advertising expenditures increased 10%.	0.02	3	0.06
6. Revenues from repair/service in the store up 16%.	0.15	3	0.45
7. In-store technical support personnel have MIS college degrees.	0.05	4	0.20
8. Store's debt-to-total assets ratio declined to 34%.	0.03	3	0.09
9. Revenues per employee up 19%.	0.02	3	0.06
Weaknesses			
1. Revenues from software segment of store down 12%.	0.10	2	0.20
2. Location of store negatively impacted by new Highway 34.	0.15	2	0.30
3. Carpet and paint in store somewhat in disrepair.	0.02	1	0.02
4. Bathroom in store needs refurbishing.	0.02	1	0.02
5. Revenues from businesses down 8%.	0.04	1	0.04
6. Store has no website.	0.05	2	0.10
7. Supplier on-time delivery increased to 2.4 days.	0.03	1	0.03
8. Often customers have to wait to check out	0.05	1	0.05
Total	**1.00**		**2.50**

TABLE 6-9 An Actual IFE Matrix for Forjas Taurus S.A.

Strengths	Weight	Rating	Weighted Score
1. Taurus offers low prices for pistols and small arms in the USA.	0.09	4	0.36
2. Taurus had a 15.7% increase in net revenue.	0.07	4	0.28
3. Taurus has 51% market share in Brazil's motorcycle helmet industry.	0.06	3	0.18
4. Taurus has reduced the percentage of sales devoted to income tax from 3.11% to 2.82%.	0.06	3	0.18
5. Taurus produces a diverse range of products in different markets.	0.05	3	0.15
6. Taurus is a qualified supplier of products to Brazil's armed forces.	0.05	4	0.20
7. Taurus and ammo-maker Companha Brasileira de Cartuchos dominate Brazil's small arms industry.	0.04	4	0.16
8. Taurus provides weapons for Brazil's military, state, and civil police.	0.03	4	0.12
9. Taurus has good brand recognition within the USA.	0.03	4	0.12
10. Taurus's employee morale is good.	0.02	4	0.08
Weaknesses			
1. Adjusted EBIT is down 23%.	0.08	1	0.08
2. Total revenue in the domestic market is down 10.5%.	0.08	2	0.16
3. Gross margin fell from 38.1% to 29.9%.	0.07	1	0.07
4. Taurus's stock price has plummeted to less than 1.0.	0.07	1	0.07
5. Revenue from products in the metallurgy and plastics segment, excluding helmets, is down 7%.	0.04	2	0.08
6. Taurus has very little presence in Europe and Asia.	0.04	2	0.08
7. Taurus has a reputation for poor customer service.	0.04	2	0.08
8. There was a recent 23.6% increase in operating expenses.	0.03	1	0.03
9. Taurus reported a net income loss of over $32 million.	0.03	1	0.03
10. Taurus has poor quality control—a Taurus pistol discharged in Sao Paulo without pulling the trigger.	0.02	1	0.02
TOTALS	**1.00**		**2.53**

factor in the industry (Weight = 0.09) is price, and Taurus does excellent (Rating = 4) in selling low-priced firearms.

In multidivisional firms, each autonomous division or strategic business unit should construct an IFE Matrix. Divisional matrices then can be integrated to develop an overall corporate IFE Matrix. Be as divisional as possible when developing a corporate IFE Matrix. Also, in developing an IFE Matrix, do not allow more than 30 percent of the key factors to be financial ratios, because financial ratios are generally the result of many factors, so it is difficult to know what particular strategies should be considered based on financial ratios. For example, a firm would have no insight on whether to sell in Brazil or South Africa to take advantage of a high corporate ROI ratio.

IMPLICATIONS FOR STRATEGISTS

Figure 6-9 illustrates that to gain and sustain competitive advantages, a firm must formulate strategies that capitalize on internal strengths across all its products, services, and regions, and continually improve on its internal weaknesses. This must be done in a cost-effective manner, even though large outlays of human and financial capital may be required for various strategies deemed best to pursue. Thus, long-term commitments often accompany a given strategic plan. Breakeven analysis, value chain analysis, and the IFE Matrix are especially useful strategic planning tools in formulating strategies, especially in performing the internal assessment. Coupled with the vision/mission and external audit, the internal audit must be performed methodically and carefully because survival of the firm could hinge on an excellent strategic plan being created. Strategists should follow the guidelines presented in this chapter and throughout this book to help assure that their firm is heading in the right direction for the right reasons, and rewarding the right people, for doing the right things, in the right places.

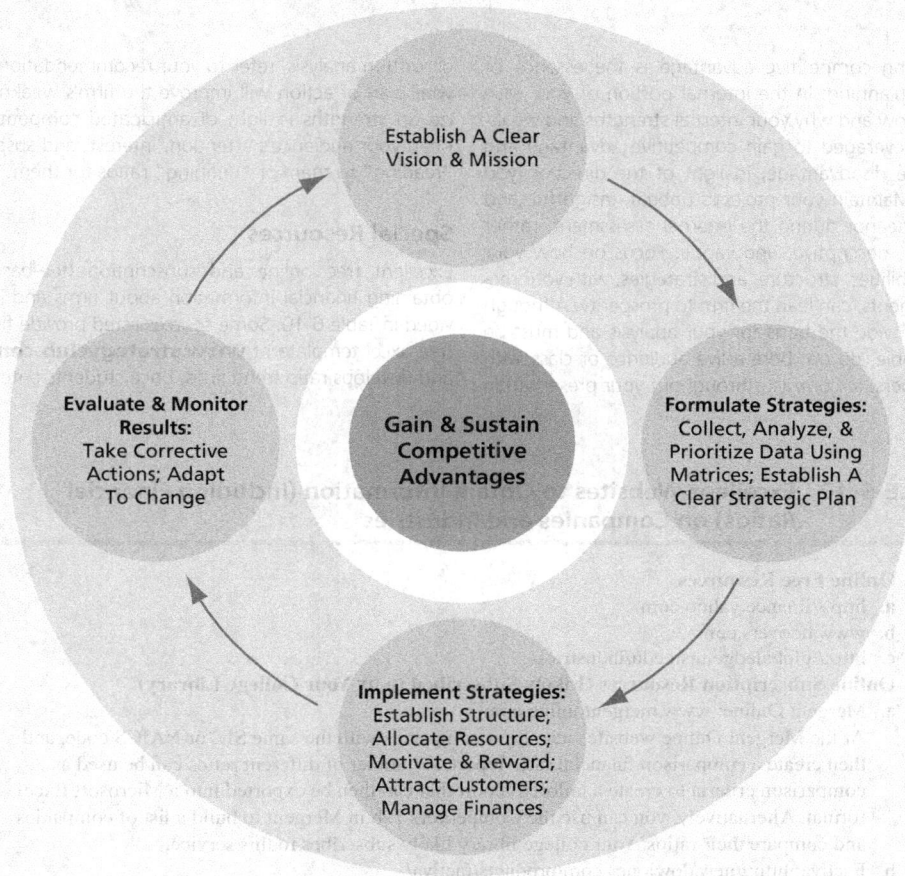

FIGURE 6-9

How to Gain and Sustain Competitive Advantages

Upstream versus Downstream Activities

The primary means for gaining and sustaining competitive advantages for most companies are shifting downstream. Recent research by Dawar reveals that in most industries today, **upstream activities**—such as supply chain management, production, and logistics—are being commoditized or outsourced by firms, whereas **downstream activities** related to consumer behavior are becoming the primary means for gaining and sustaining competitive advantage.[33] Dawar reports that the sources of competitive advantage are shifting away from production processes inside the firm to customers and markets outside the firm. Businesses are increasingly gaining competitive advantage by proactively shaping customers' point-of-purchase behavior, rather than firms using focus groups, surveys, and social media to determine what customers want. An early glimpse of this shift came a few years ago when Apple's Steve Jobs was asked how much market research led to the iPad. Jobs responded, "None. It's not the consumers' job to

know what they want." Activities that attract customers by making it easier, compelling, and convenient for them to purchase the firm's products and services in many ways are leading to sustained competitive advantage much more so than altering internal mechanisms. Figure 6-10 illustrates this shifting source of competitive advantage in most industries.

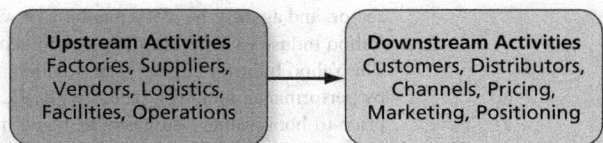

Upstream Activities
Factories, Suppliers, Vendors, Logistics, Facilities, Operations

Downstream Activities
Customers, Distributors, Channels, Pricing, Marketing, Positioning

FIGURE 6-10

The Shifting Source of Competitive Advantage

IMPLICATIONS FOR STUDENTS

Gaining and sustaining competitive advantage is the essence or purpose of strategic planning. In the internal portion of your case analysis, emphasize how and why your internal strengths and weaknesses can both be leveraged to gain competitive advantage and overcome competitive disadvantage, in light of the direction you are taking the firm. Maintain your project's upbeat, insightful, and forward-thinking demeanor during the internal assessment, rather than being mundane, descriptive, and vague. Focus on how your firm's resources, capabilities, structure, and strategies, with your recommended improvements, can lead the firm to prosperity. Although the numbers must provide the basis for your analysis and must be accurate and reasonable, do not bore a live audience or class with overreliance on numbers. In contrast, throughout your presentation or written analysis, refer to your recommendations, explaining how your plan of action will improve the firm's weaknesses and capitalize on strengths in light of anticipated competitor countermoves. Keep your audience's attention, interest, and suspense, rather than "reading" to them or "defining" ratios for them.

Special Resources

Excellent free online and subscription (fee-based) resources for obtaining financial information about firms and industries are provided in Table 6-10. Some sources listed provide financial ratios. The free excel template at **www.strategyclub.com** calculates ratios and develops ratio trend lines, once students enter in relevant data.

TABLE 6-10   Excellent Websites to Obtain Information (Including Financial Ratios) on Companies and Industries

---

1. **Online Free Resources**
   a. http://finance.yahoo.com
   b. www.hoovers.com
   c. http://globaledge.msu.edu/industries/
2. **Online Subscription Resources (Likely Subscribed to by Your College Library)**
   a. Mergent Online: www.mergentonline.com
      At the Mergent Online website, search for companies with the same SIC or NAICS code, and then create a comparison financial ratio report. A number of different ratios can be used as comparison criteria to create a tailored report that can then be exported into a Microsoft Excel format. Alternatively, you can use the Competitors Tab in Mergent to build a list of companies and compare their ratios. Your college library likely subscribes to this service.
   b. Factiva: http://new.dowjones.com/products/factiva/
      At the Factiva website, first use the Companies & Markets tab to search for a company. Next, click "Reports" and choose the "Ratio Comparison Report" to get a company's ratios compared to industry averages. Your college library likely subscribes to this service.
   c. S&P NetAdvantage: http://www.standardandpoors.com/products-services/industry_surveys/en/us
      At the S&P NetAdvantage website, company and industry ratios are provided in two different sections of the database: (1) the Compustat Excel Analytics section of a particular company's information page and (2) in the data from the S&P Industry Surveys. Your college library likely subscribes to this service.
   d. Onesource: www.avention.com/OneSource
      Onesource is a good source for financial ratio information. Search for a particular company and then click on the link for "Ratio Comparisons" on the left side of the company information page. The data in Onesource will compare your company against the industry, against the sector, and against the stock market as a whole.
   e. Yahoo Industry Center: http://biz.yahoo.com/ic/
      The Yahoo Industry Center is an excellent free resource that allows you to browse industries by performance rankings, including ROE, P/E ratio, market cap, price change, profit margin, price-to-book value, long-term debt, and more.
3. **Hardcopy Reference Books for Financial Ratios in Most Libraries**
   a. Robert Morris Associate's *Annual Statement Studies:* An excellent source of financial ratio information.
   b. Dun & Bradstreet's *Industry Norms & Key Business Ratios:* An excellent source of financial ratio information.

Source: Based on a variety of sources.

Chapter Summary

Management, marketing, finance/accounting, production/operations, R&D, and MIS represent the core operations of most businesses and the source of competitive advantages. A strategic-management audit of a firm's internal operations is vital to organizational health. Many companies still prefer to be judged solely on their bottom-line performance. However, it is essential that strategists identify and evaluate internal strengths and weaknesses to effectively formulate and choose among alternative strategies. The Internal Factor Evaluation Matrix, coupled with the Competitive Profile Matrix, the External Factor Evaluation Matrix, and clear statements of vision and mission provide the basic information needed to successfully formulate competitive strategies. The process of performing an internal audit represents an opportunity for managers and employees throughout the organization to participate in determining the future of the firm. Involvement in the process can energize and mobilize managers and employees.

Understanding both external and internal factors and relationships among them (see SWOT analysis in Chapter 8) is the key to effective strategy formulation. Because both external and internal factors continually change, strategists seek to identify and take advantage of positive changes and buffer against negative changes in a continuing effort to gain and sustain a firm's competitive advantage. This is the essence and challenge of strategic management, and oftentimes survival of the firm hinges on this work.

Key Terms and Concepts

activity ratios (p. 194)
benchmarking (p. 202)
breakeven (BE) point (p. 195)
capacity utilization (p. 197)
capital budgeting (p. 192)
collaborative machines (p. 198)
controlling (p. 187)
core competence (p. 202)
cost/benefit analysis (p. 190)
cultural products (p. 182)
customer analysis (p. 188)
distinctive competencies (p. 180)
distribution (p. 190)
dividend decisions (p. 192)
downstream activities (p. 207)
empirical indicators (p. 181)
financial ratio analysis (p. 191)
financing decision (p. 192)
fixed costs (FC) (p. 195)
functions of finance/accounting (p. 191)
functions of management (p. 184)
functions of marketing (p. 188)
growth ratios (p. 194)
human resource (HR) management (p. 186)

internal audit (p. 180)
Internal Factor Evaluation (IFE) Matrix (p. 204)
investment decision (p. 192)
leverage ratios (p. 194)
liquidity ratios (p. 194)
management information system (MIS) (p. 200)
marketing research (p. 190)
motivating (p. 186)
organizational culture (p. 182)
organizing (p. 185)
planning (p. 184)
pricing (p. 189)
product and service planning (p. 189)
production/operations function (p. 197)
profitability ratios (p. 194)
research and development (R&D) (p. 199)
resource-based view (RBV) (p. 181)
selling (p. 188)
staffing (p. 186)
synergy (p. 185)
test marketing (p. 189)
upstream activities (p. 207)
value chain analysis (VCA) (p. 201)
variable costs (VC) (p. 196)

Issues for Review and Discussion

⭐ **6-1.** Volkswagen (VW) Group has been very successful in the last decade. Research VW and see if they have strategic planning. Create a report of your findings for your class.

6-2. Visit Volkswagen's (VW) corporate website. See the list of top executives for VW and create an organizational chart for the company.

6-3. Given the 15 example (possible) aspects of an organization's culture as presented in the chapter, rate a company you are very familiar with in terms of the extent to which each culture item exists. Explain.

6-4. Rank the seven functions of marketing in order of importance for a small hardware business.

⭐ **6-5.** Develop a quantitative problem to show your understanding of cost/benefit analysis. Students' answers will vary depending on the quantitative problem they feature.

6-6. Develop a quantitative problem to show that you understand breakeven analysis. Students' answers will vary depending on the quantitative problem they feature.

6-7. For Volkswagen's (VW), determine their most recent dividend payout amount per share. How has that amount changed over the last 12 months?

⭐ **6-8.** List some advantages and disadvantages of a company paying dividends versus reinvesting that money in the company, and striving for stock price increase as the primary way to reward investors.

⭐ **6-9.** Illustrate a breakeven chart for Volkswagen (VW). Explain how it may work for the organization.

6-10. Volkswagen (VW) has historically spent more on R&D than almost any other automobile company in the world. What are the major advantages and disadvantages of this strategy?

⭐ **6-11.** Perform a value chain analysis for an organization of your choice.

6-12. Discuss the relationship between benchmarking and value chain analysis.

6-13. Explain why the ratings in an IFE Matrix should be 4 or 3 for strengths, and 1 or 2 for weaknesses as compared to the EFE Matrix, where the ratings should be 1, 2, 3, or 4 among both the opportunities and threats.

6-14. Compare the financial ratio analysis for Volkswagen (VW) on the four different websites identified in the chapter. Which site do you like best? Why?

6-15. Conduct a Google search for value chain analysis. In a two-page report, discuss the concepts presented in the chapter.

⭐ **6-16.** What competitive advantages would Amazon have over Wal-Mart stores in doing business outside the United States?

6-17. How could the "process of performing an internal audit" differ across countries, given varying global management styles?

6-18. Why is sole reliance on financial ratios an ineffective means of deriving internal strengths and weaknesses?

6-19. Give an example of two resources for a fast-food chain that you believe meet the three "empirical indicators" criteria.

6-20. Prepare a culture assessment table, as presented in the chapter, for a local business that you are familiar with. Rate the business on the 15 culture criteria presented in the chapter. What are the implications of your ratings on the strategic planning process within that firm?

6-21. Why is human resource management particularly challenging for international firms?

6-22. List some specific characteristics of advertisements, in the wake of a lingering recession in Europe.

6-23. How do changes in the value of the dollar affect pricing of products of global firms?

6-24. Historically, what has been the attitude of technology firms toward paying dividends? Give some examples.

6-25. Describe Singapore as a place to locate or start a business.

6-26. Visit the www.strategyclub website, and describe the strategic planning products offered.

6-27. Develop a value chain analysis for a large global firm and its primary rival firm.

⭐ **6-28.** Identify four major strengths and weaknesses each, of your college or university. Rank each factor in terms of importance.

6-29. Search the Internet for financial information on Volkswagen (VW). Identify three financial ratios where the firm is weak and three financial ratios the firm is strong.

⭐ **6-30.** What five cultural products do you feel are most important? Justify your selections.

6-31. Rate the company where you work, or would like to work, on the fifteen aspects of culture listed in the chapter.

6-32. Develop a breakeven chart for a company, which simultaneously lays off employees and closes facilities.

6-33. Financial ratio analysis should be conducted on three separate fronts. What are these fronts and which is most important?

6-34. Explain breakeven analysis using three graphs that show changes in breakeven given: 1) a change in price, 2) a change in advertising expenditures, and 3) a change in labor costs.

6-35. Why is breakeven analysis such an important strategic planning concept?

6-36. What are the basic functions of production/operations in a large manufacturing company? Why are these factors important in an internal strategic management audit?

6-37. Explain benchmarking

6-38. Go to the www.strategyclub.com website and review the benefits of using the free excel template.

6-39. For the Nestlé Cohesion Case, what do you consider as the company's four major strengths and four major weaknesses?

6-40. Prepare a financial ratio analysis for Nestlé. Include comparative ratios for a rival and for the industry.

⭐ **6-41.** Explain how Nestlé could utilize breakeven analysis.

6-42. Explain how top executives of Nestle could utilize Porter's Five Forces Model to aid the firm in strategic planning.

6-43. Could Nestlé and Mars, Inc. being rival companies hinder the two firms from cooperating with each other on R&D or facilitate the gathering and assimilation of competitive intelligence of one or the other firm?

6-44. Since Nestlé is so divisional, how could the company best develop a corporate IFE Matrix for various Divisional IFE Matrices?

6-45. When is it more important to capitalize on strengths than improve on weaknesses in strategic planning?

6-46. Why is inclusion of about 20 factors recommended in the IFE Matrix, rather than about 10 factors or about 40 factors?

6-47. Do you think the RBV view or the I/O theorists view is more accurate in performing a strategic analysis? What would be the important implications for a business?

6-48. Does the RBV Theory help in determining diversification targets?

6-49. How does the cost of sales compare between online versus brick-and-mortar sales approaches?

6-50. Does spending more on research and development usually positively impact stock price appreciation?

ASSURANCE OF LEARNING EXERCISES

EXERCISE 6A

Develop a Corporate IFE Matrix for Volkswagen Group

Purpose

Volkswagen (VW) Group is featured in the opening chapter case as a firm that engages in excellent strategic planning despite its recent legal/ethical pollution fiasco. VW has four major geographic business segments. Each of these divisions of VW would prepare their own IFE matrices, which would be assimilated to develop an overall corporate IFE matrix. This exercise gives you practice developing divisional IFE matrices and assimilating those into an overall corporate IFE matrix.

Instructions

Step 1	Review VW's most recent *Annual Report* in regards to the company's four geographic business segments, which are North America, South America, Asia-Pacific, and Europe.
Step 2	Review the latest S&P *Industry Survey* for companies that produce and market automobiles.
Step 3	Develop a divisional IFE matrix for each of VW's business segments.
Step 4	Assimilate your divisional IFE matrices into an overall corporate IFE matrix for VW.

EXERCISE 6B

Should Volkswagen Deploy More (or Less) Resources Outside of Europe?

Purpose

As indicated in the opening chapter boxed insert, Volkswagen (VW) receives more revenue from outside its home base of Europe than from inside Europe. This exercise gives you practice analyzing domestic versus global revenue base so that more effective strategies can be formulated and implemented.

Instructions

Step 1	Go to the VW's website and review the company's most recent *Annual Report*. Be careful to note the financial, management, and marketing information available for each geographic

region. Let all regions outside Europe, for purposes of this exercise, be referred to as Global, and Europe be referred to as domestic for VW.

Step 2   Go to www.finance.yahoo.com and review the last 45 days of Headlines for VW. Take note of public information related to VW as well as to General Motors (GM), Ford, Honda, and Toyota.

Step 3   Prepare a three-page executive summary to reveal whether you feel VW should be placing more or less emphasis on operations outside of Europe. Provide supporting tables, #'s, ratios, and narrative.

EXERCISE 6C
Apply Breakeven Analysis

Purpose

Breakeven analysis is one of the simplest yet underused analytical tools in management. It helps provide a dynamic view of the relationships among sales, costs, and profits. A better understanding of breakeven analysis can enable an organization to formulate and implement strategies more effectively. This exercise will show you how to calculate breakeven points mathematically.

The formula for calculating breakeven point is BE Quantity = TFC/P – VC. In other words, the quantity (Q) or units of product that need to be sold for a firm to break even is total fixed costs (TFC) divided by (Price per Unit – Variable Costs per Unit).

Instructions

Step 1   Assume an airplane company has fixed costs of $100 million and variable costs per unit of $2 million. The planes sell for $3 million each. What is the company's breakeven point in terms of the number of planes that need to be sold just to break even?

Step 2   If the airplane company wants to make a profit of $99 million annually, how many planes will it have to sell?

Step 3   If the company can sell 200 airplanes in a year, how much annual profit will the firm make?

EXERCISE 6D
Perform a Financial Ratio Analysis for Nestlé

Purpose

Financial ratio analysis is one of the best techniques for identifying and evaluating internal strengths and weaknesses. Potential investors and current shareholders look closely at firms' financial ratios, making detailed comparisons to industry averages and to previous periods of time. Financial ratio analysis provides vital information for developing an IFE Matrix.

Instructions

Step 1   On a separate sheet of paper, write down numbers 1 to 20. Referring to Nestlé's income statement and balance sheet, calculate 20 financial ratios for 2015.

Step 2   In a second column, indicate whether you consider each ratio to be a strength, weakness, or neutral factor for Nestlé.

EXERCISE 6E
Construct an IFE Matrix for Nestlé

Purpose

This exercise will give you experience developing an IFE matrix. Identifying and prioritizing factors to include in an IFE matrix fosters communication among functional and divisional managers. Preparing an IFE matrix allows human resources,' marketing's, production/operations,' finance/ accounting's, R&D's, and management information systems' managers to articulate their concerns and thoughts regarding the business condition of the firm. This results in an improved collective understanding of the business.

Instructions

Step 1   Join with two other individuals to form a three-person team. Develop an IFE matrix for Nestlé.

Step 2   Compare your team's IFE matrix with other teams' IFE matrices. Discuss any major differences.

Step 3   What strategies do you think would allow Nestlé to capitalize on its major strengths? What strategies would allow Nestlé to improve upon its major weaknesses?

EXERCISE 6F
Analyze Your College or University's Internal Strategic Situation

Purpose
This exercise is excellent for doing together as a class and will help in evaluating your university's major strengths and weaknesses. An organization's strategies are largely based on striving to take advantage of strengths and improving on weaknesses.

Instructions

Step 1 As a class, determine your college or university's major internal strengths and weaknesses. List 10 strengths and 10 weaknesses.

Step 2 Get everyone in class to rank their factors with 1 being most important and 10 being least important.

Step 3 Gather up everyone's papers, count the numbers, and in that manner create a prioritized list of the key internal strengths and weaknesses facing your college.

MINI-CASE ON BANK OF CHINA LIMITED (BACHF)

WHAT IS THE NATURE OF BANK OF CHINA'S GROWTH?

Headquartered in Beijing, China, the Bank of China (BOC) is the oldest bank in the country. As China's most international and diversified bank, BOC has offices in 37 countries/regions, including China Taiwan, Portugal, Canada, Singapore, China Hong Kong, and London. During BOC's first fiscal quarter of 2015, which ended June 30, BOC reported an estimated profit of RMB47.77 billion and a profit attributable to equity holders of RMB45.84 billion, an increase of 1.21 percent and 1.05 percent respectively compared to the prior year period. It is indicated in the investor section of the bank's website that its financial performance at the end of 2014 was excellent. Due to slowing growth in China, the Shanghai stock market crashed in July–August, 2015, wiping out $5 trillion in value that had been accumulated earlier in the year. However, bank stocks, such as the stock of BOC, led a slight recovery in late August. The central bank of China cut interest rates and reduced the amount of required reserves for banks, aiding a slight recovery.

Source: © Dang Liu.Shutterstock

Questions

1. Visit the About Us section of the bank's website. Go through the information under Organization section and review BOC's branch offices globally. How has the number of branches changed in the last six months, given that virtually all banks in the United States are closing branches rather than opening them, primarily due to the slow shift of banking to an online business model from a brick-and-mortar one?

2. Visit the investor section on the BOC website and review its financial condition. Compute three key ratios. Rate the bank's financial condition on an A, B, C, D, or F grading system.

3. Describe BOC's most recent financial performance?

4. Visit BOC's investor relations section on its website and check the investor services. Click on 2015 interim results, available under the results presentation, and make a note the top six executives pictured at this website. Determine whether the top twenty executives of Bank of China include any females or minorities. Is this a problem for the company or it is typical of the bank hierarchy among firms in China?

Source: Based on company documents; "Serving Society, Delivering Excellence," Bank of China, 2015 Interim Results, August 28, 2015.

Current Readings

Acito, Frank, and Vijay Khatri. "Business Analytics: Why Now and What Next?" *Business Horizons* 57, no. 5 (2014): 565–570.

Chen, Chien-Ming, Magali A. Delmas, and Marvin B. Lieberman. "Production Frontier Methodologies and Efficiency as a Performance Measure in Strategic Management Research." *Strategic Management Journal* 36, no. 1 (January 2015): 19–36.

Davenport, Thomas H. "What Businesses Can Learn from Sports Analytics." *MIT Sloan Management Review* 55, no. 4 (2014): 10–13.

George, Gerard, Martine R. Haas, and Alex Pentland. "Big Data and Management." *Academy of Management Journal* (April 2014): 321–338.

Hayashi, Alden M. "Thriving in a Big Data World." *MIT Sloan Management Review* 55, no. 2 (2014): 35–39.

Howard, Dana, W. Glynn Mangold, and Tim Johnston. "Managing Your Social Campaign Strategy Using Facebook, Twitter, Instagram, YouTube & Pinterest: An Interview with Dana Howard, Social Media Marketing Manager." *Business Horizons* 57, no. 5 (2014): 657–665.

Kiron, David, Pamela Kirk Prentice, and Renee Boucher Ferguson. "Raising the Bar with Analytics." *MIT Sloan Management Review* 55, no. 2 (2014): 29–33.

Kuratko, Donald F., Jeffrey S. Hornsby, and Jeffrey G. Covin. "Diagnosing a Firm's Internal Environment for Corporate Entrepreneurship." *Business Horizons* 57, no.1 (2014): 37–47.

Ross, Jeanne W., Cynthia M. Beath, and Anne Quaadgras. "You May Not Need Big Data After All." *Harvard Business Review* 91, no.11 (2013).

Sampler, Jeffrey L., and Michael J. Earl. "What's Your Information Footprint?" *MIT Sloan Management Review* 55, no. 2 (2014): 96–97.

Thomas, Roberta J., et al. "Developing Tomorrow's Global Leaders." *MIT Sloan Management Review* 55, no. 1 (2013): 12–13.

Wuyts, Stefan, and Shantanu Dutta. "Benefiting from Alliance Portfolio Diversity: The Role of Past Internal Knowledge Creation Strategy." *Journal of Management* 40 (2014).

Endnotes

1. Reprinted by permission of the publisher from "Integrating Strength–Weakness Analysis into Strategic Planning," by William King, *Journal of Business Research* 2, no. 4: 481. Copyright 1983 by Elsevier Science Publishing Co., Inc.

2. Robert Grant, "The Resource-Based Theory of Competitive Advantage: Implications for Strategy Formulation," *California Management Review* (Spring 1991): 116.

3. J. B. Barney, "Firm Resources and Sustained Competitive Advantage," *Journal of Management* 17 (1991): 99–120; J. B. Barney, "The Resource-Based Theory of the Firm," *Organizational Science* 7 (1996): 469; J. B. Barney, "Is the Resource-Based 'View' a Useful Perspective for Strategic Management Research? Yes." *Academy of Management Review* 26, no. 1 (2001): 41–56.

4. Edgar Schein, *Organizational Culture and Leadership* (San Francisco: Jossey-Bass, 1985), 9.

5. John Lorsch, "Managing Culture: The Invisible Barrier to Strategic Change," *California Management Review* 28, no. 2 (1986): 95–109.

6. Y. Allarie and M. Firsirotu, "How to Implement Radical Strategies in Large Organizations," *Sloan Management Review* (Spring 1985): 19.

7. www.mindtools.com/plfailpl.html
8. Adam Smith, *The Wealth of Nations* (New York: Modern Library, 1937), 3–4.
9. Richard Daft, *Management*, 3rd ed. (Orlando, FL: Dryden Press, 1993), 512.
10. Shelley Kirkpatrick and Edwin Locke, "Leadership: Do Traits Matter?" *Academy of Management Executive* 5, no. 2 (May 1991): 48.
11. Peter Drucker, *Management Tasks, Responsibilities, and Practice* (New York: Harper & Row, 1973), 463.
12. Michael Mink, "Stay Atop Social Media," *Investor's Business Daily*, October 7, 2014, A4.
13. Brain Dumaine, "What the Leaders of Tomorrow See," *Fortune, July 3, 1999*, 51.
14. Lauren Weber and Rachael Feintzeig, "Is It a Dream or a Drag? Companies without HR," *Wall Street Journal,* April 9, 2014, B1.
15. J. Evans, and B. Bergman, *Marketing* (New York: Macmillan, 1982), 17.
16. http://www.ibtimes.com/super-bowl-ads-2014-what-does-4-million-really-buy-you-1551884
17. Sarah Needleman and Jack Marshall, "Small Businesses Grapple with Facebook," *Wall Street Journal,* August 7, 2014, B5.
18. Jack Marshall, "Online Ads Lure Cash, But Losses Still Mount," *Wall Street Journal,* August 18, 2014, B1.
19. Spencer Ante, "As Economy Cools, IBM Furthers Focus on Marketers," *Wall Street Journal,* July 18, 2012, B3.
20. Brad Stone, "See Your Friends," *Bloomberg Businessweek* (September 27–October 3, 2010): 65–69.
21. Suzanne Kapner, "Higher Web Sales Drag on Retailers," *Wall Street Journal,* December 2, 2014, B1.
22. Quoted in Robert Waterman, Jr., "The Renewal Factor," *BusinessWeek* (September 14, 1987): 108.
23. http://en.wikipedia.org/wiki/Cost-benefit_analysis
24. J. Van Horne, *Financial Management and Policy* (Upper Saddle River, NJ: Prentice-Hall, 1974): 10.
25. http://en.wikipedia.org/wolo/Break-even_(economics)
26. Timothy Aeppel, "Robots Work Their Way into Small Factories," *Wall Street Journal,* September 18, 2004, B1.
27. Patrick Seitz, "Largest Tech R&D Spenders Not Top Stock Performers," *Investor's Business Daily,* July 8, 2014, A5.
28. Philip Rousebi, Kamal Saad, and Tamara Erickson, "The Evolution of Third Generation R&D," *Planning Review* 19, no. 2 (March–April 1991): 18–26.
29. Based on Elizabeth Dwoskin, "Big Data: Give Me Back My Privacy," *Wall Street Journal,* March 24, 2014, R1–R4.
30. Ibid.
31. Michael Porter, *Competition Strategy: Techniques for Analyzing Industries and Competitors* (New York: Free Press, 1980), 34–44.
32. http://en.wikipedia.org/siki/Benchmarking
33. Niraj Dawar, "When Marketing Is Strategy," *Harvard Business Review* (December 2013): 101–108.

Source: © industrieblick/Fotolia

The External Audit

LEARNING OBJECTIVES

After studying this chapter, you should be able to do the following:

7-1. Describe the nature and purpose of an external assessment in formulating strategies.

7-2. Identify and discuss 10 external forces that must be examined in formulating strategies: economic, social, cultural, demographic, environmental, political, governmental, legal, technological, and competitive.

7-3. Explain Porter's Five Forces Model and its relevance in formulating strategies.

7-4. Describe key sources of information used for locating vital external information.

7-5. Discuss forecasting tools and techniques.

7-6. Explain how to develop and use an External Factor Evaluation (EFE) Matrix.

7-7. Explain how to develop and use a Competitive Profile Matrix.

ASSURANCE OF LEARNING EXERCISES

The following exercises are found at the end of this chapter:

EXERCISE 7A Michelin and Africa: An External Assessment

EXERCISE 7B Preparing a CPM for Michelin Based on Countries Rather Than Companies

EXERCISE 7C Develop Divisional Michelin EFE Matrices

EXERCISE 7D Developing an EFE Matrix for Nestlé S.A.

EXERCISE 7E The External Audit

EXERCISE 7F Develop a Competitive Profile Matrix for Michelin

EXERCISE 7G Develop a Competitive Profile Matrix for Nestlé

EXERCISE 7H Analyzing Your College or University's External Strategic Situation

This chapter examines the tools and concepts needed to conduct an *external strategic-management* audit (sometimes called **environmental scanning** or **industry analysis**). An **external audit** focuses on identifying and evaluating trends and events beyond the control of a single firm, such as increased foreign competition, population shifts to coastal areas of the United States, an aging society, and taxing Internet sales. An external audit reveals key opportunities and threats confronting an organization, so managers can formulate strategies to take advantage of the opportunities and avoid or reduce the impact of threats. This chapter presents a practical framework for gathering, assimilating, and analyzing external information. The Industrial Organization (I/O) view of strategic management is discussed.

The company showcased here for practicing exemplary strategic management is Michelin Manufacturing Company. Michelin is a huge tire manufacturer rivaling Bridgestone, a world leader in aircraft and earthmover tires. Apart from establishing and following a strict code of ethics within the organization, Michelin is fundamentally opposed to child and forced labor, in full compliance with the principles of the International Labor Organization (ILO). This chapter addresses whether companies should take a stand on political and societal issues. Do you think companies should?

Michelin (MGDDF)

Headquartered in Clemont-Ferrand in the Auvergne region of France, Michelin is a huge tire manufacturer rivaling Bridgestone, and is a leader in aircraft and earthmover tires. Michelin owns BFGoodrich, Kleber, Riken, Komoran, and the Uniroyal tire brands, as well as the Warrior brand in China. Over 175 million tires are produced by Michelin annually for various vehicles, while new and replacement tires are supplied to the passenger car and truck markets. Additionally, Michelin is also known in the culinary world for its Red Guide reference books and restaurant star awards, and about 10 million travel guides and maps are published by it every year.

Michelin introduced two new Enduro bicycle tires, reentering the bike racing business. To provide mountain bike riders with high-performance tires, Michelin has partnered with two famous bikers: Fabien Barel, three-time world downhill champion, and Pierre Edouard Ferry, free ride champion. The new Michelin bike tires were developed by the Michelin Group engineers, aided by the two bikers, after working on it for two and a half years. Michelin's new Pilot Sport Cup 2 is the only tire certified for two new high-powered sports cars-the Ferrari 458 Speciale and the Porsche 918 Spyder. Michelin's Pilot Sport 3 tires equip the new Peugeot 308, making the car more energy efficient while delivering outstanding safety, handling, and longevity. For the Peugeot 208 HYbrid FE, Michelin developed a range of tall and narrow tires with a longer rim diameter and better performance.

Michelin produces tires throughout Europe but also has manufacturing facilities in the USA, Canada, Brazil, Thailand, Japan, Italy, and several other countries. Michelin has more than 65,000 people and has 40 production sites in Europe, which accounts for 40 percent of the company's operations. In Europe, Michelin is consolidating its position on high added-value production by reorganizing its activities in the United Kingdom and Italy. In these two countries, Michelin, under its reorganization, will be spending 265 million euros to modernize manufacturing plants and facilities along with the logistics network. With more than 4,000 employees, 80 percent of whom work on production sites, the Italian branch oversees over 10 percent of the European processes. By 2020, Michelin will have invested around 180 million euros in its Italian manufacturing lines, strengthening the sites at Cuneo and Alessandria, to extensively develop the country's automobile tire volumes.

Source: Based on company documents.

The Purpose and Nature of an External Audit

The purpose of an external audit is to develop a finite list of opportunities that could benefit a firm as well as threats that should be avoided. As the term *finite* suggests, the external audit is not aimed at developing an exhaustive list of every possible factor that could influence the business; rather, it is aimed at identifying key variables that offer **actionable responses**. Firms should be able to respond either offensively or defensively to the factors by formulating strategies that take advantage of external opportunities or that minimize the impact of potential threats. Figure 7-1 illustrates with white shading how the external audit fits into the strategic-management process.

Key External Forces

External forces can be divided into five broad categories: (1) economic forces; (2) social, cultural, demographic, and natural environment forces; (3) political, governmental, and legal forces; (4) technological forces; and (5) competitive forces. Relationships among these forces and an

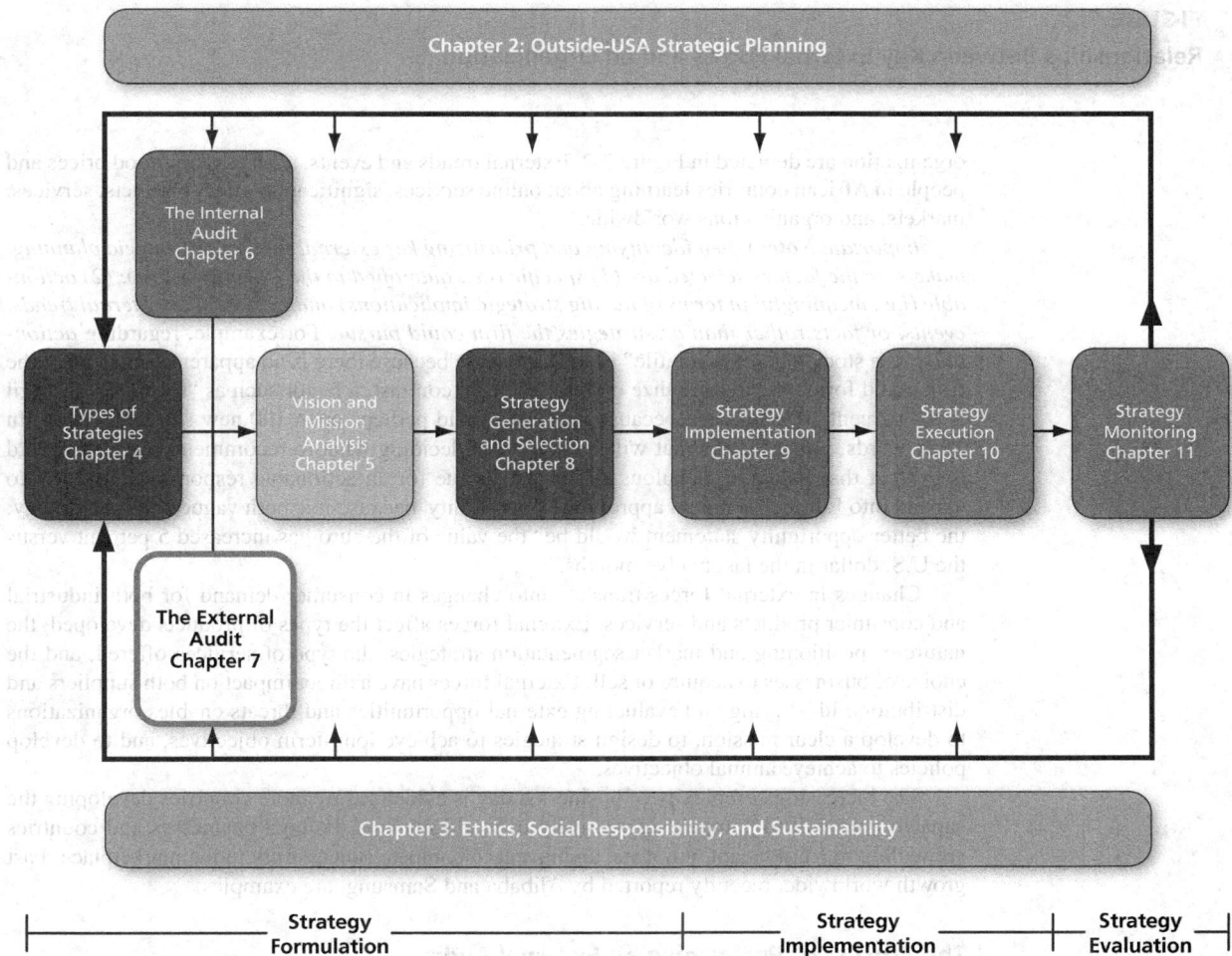

FIGURE 7-1

A Comprehensive Strategic-Management Model

Source: Fred R. David, adapted from "How Companies Define Their Mission," *Long Range Planning* 22, no. 3 (June 1988): 40, © Fred R. David.

Economic forces	Competitors	
Social, cultural, demographic, and natural environment forces	Suppliers	AN ORGANIZATION'S
	Distributors	OPPORTUNITIES AND
Political, legal, and governmental forces	Creditors	THREATS
	Customers	
Technological forces	Employees	
	Communities	
Competitive forces	Managers	

FIGURE 7-2

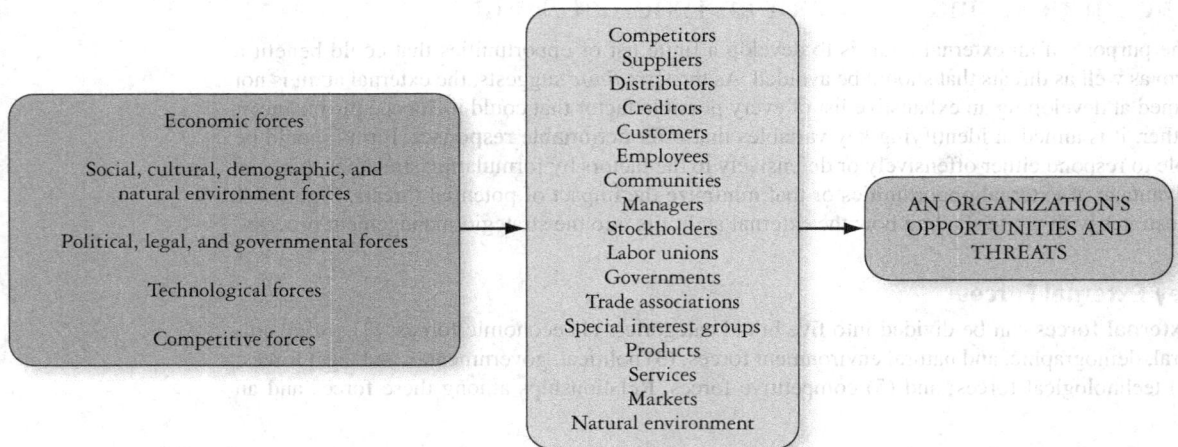

Relationships Between Key External Forces and an Organization

organization are depicted in Figure 7-2. External trends and events, such as rising food prices and people in African countries learning about online services, significantly affect products, services, markets, and organizations worldwide.

Important Note: When identifying and prioritizing key external factors in strategic planning, make sure the factors selected are (1) specific (i.e., quantified to the extent possible); (2) actionable (i.e., meaningful in terms of having strategic implications) and (3) stated as external trends, events, or facts rather than as strategies the firm could pursue. For example, regarding *actionable*, "the stock market is volatile" is not actionable because there is no apparent strategy that the firm could formulate to capitalize on that factor. In contrast, a factor such as "the GDP of Brazil is 6.8 percent" is actionable because the firm should perhaps open 100 new stores in Brazil. In other words, select factors that will be helpful in deciding what to recommend the firm should do, rather than selecting nebulous factors too vague for an actionable response. Similarly, "to expand into Europe" is not an appropriate opportunity, because it is both vague and is a strategy; the better opportunity statement would be "the value of the euro has increased 5 percent versus the U.S. dollar in the last twelve months."

Changes in external forces translate into changes in consumer demand for both industrial and consumer products and services. External forces affect the types of products developed, the nature of positioning and market segmentation strategies, the type of services offered, and the choice of businesses to acquire or sell. External forces have a direct impact on both suppliers and distributors. Identifying and evaluating external opportunities and threats enables organizations to develop a clear mission, to design strategies to achieve long-term objectives, and to develop policies to achieve annual objectives.

The increasing complexity of business today is evidenced by more countries developing the capacity and will to compete aggressively in world markets. Foreign businesses and countries are willing to learn, adapt, innovate, and invent to compete successfully in the marketplace. Fast growth worldwide, recently reported by Alibaba and Samsung, are examples.

The Process of Performing an External Audit

The process of performing an external audit must involve as many managers and employees as possible. As emphasized in previous chapters, involvement in the strategic-management process can lead to understanding and commitment from organizational members. Individuals appreciate having the opportunity to contribute ideas and to gain a better understanding of their firm's industry, competitors, and markets. Key external factors can vary over time and by industry.

CHAPTER 7 • THE EXTERNAL AUDIT

To perform an external audit, a company first must gather competitive intelligence and information about economic, social, cultural, demographic, environmental, political, governmental, legal, and technological trends. Individuals can be asked to monitor various sources of information, such as key magazines, trade journals, and newspapers—and use online sources such as those listed later in this chapter in Table 7-8. These persons can submit periodic scanning reports to the person(s) who coordinate the external audit. This approach provides a continuous stream of timely strategic information and involves many individuals in the external-audit process. Suppliers, distributors, salespersons, customers, and competitors represent other sources of vital information.

After information is gathered, it should be assimilated and evaluated. A meeting or series of meetings of managers is needed to collectively identify the most important opportunities and threats facing the firm. A prioritized list of these factors must be obtained by requesting that all managers individually rank the factors identified, from 1 (for the most important opportunity/threat) to 20 (for the least important opportunity/threat). Instead of ranking factors, managers could simply place a checkmark by their most important "top 10 factors." Then, by summing the rankings, or the number of checkmarks, a prioritized list of factors is revealed. Prioritization is absolutely essential in strategic planning because no organization can do everything that would benefit the firm; tough choices among good choices have to be made.

The Industrial Organization (I/O) View

The **Industrial Organization** view of strategic planning advocates that external (industry) factors are more important than internal ones for gaining and sustaining competitive advantage. Proponents of the I/O view, such as Michael Porter, contend that organizational performance will be primarily determined by industry forces, such as falling gas prices that no single firm can control. Porter's Five-Forces Model, presented later in this chapter, is an example of the I/O perspective, which focuses on analyzing external forces and industry variables as a basis for getting and keeping competitive advantage.

Competitive advantage is determined largely by competitive positioning within an industry, according to I/O advocates. Managing strategically from the I/O perspective entails firms striving to compete in attractive industries, avoiding weak or faltering industries, and gaining a full understanding of key external factor relationships within that attractive industry. I/O theorists contend that external factors—such as economies of scale, barriers to market entry, product differentiation, the economy, and level of competitiveness—are more important than internal resources, capabilities, structure, and operations.

The I/O view has enhanced the understanding of strategic management. However, the authors contend that it is not a question of whether external or internal factors are more important in gaining and maintaining competitive advantage. In contrast, effective integration and understanding of *both* external and internal factors is the key to securing and keeping a competitive advantage. In fact, as discussed in Chapter 8, matching key external opportunities and threats with key internal strengths and weaknesses provides the basis for successful strategy formulation.

Ten External Forces That Affect Organizations

Economic Forces

Economic factors have a direct impact on the potential attractiveness of various strategies. For example, high underemployment (minimum wage-type employment) in the United States bodes well for discount firms such as Dollar Tree, T.J. Maxx, Walmart, and Subway, but hurts thousands of traditional-priced retailers in many industries. Although the Dow Jones Industrial Average is high, corporate profits are high, dividend increases are up sharply, gas prices are low, and emerging markets are growing, millions of people work for minimum wages or are unemployed. As a result of droughts, commodity prices are up sharply, especially food, which is contributing to rising inflation fears. Many firms are switching to part-time rather than full-time employees to avoid having to pay health benefits.

To take advantage of Canada's robust economy and eager-to-spend people, many firms are adding facilities in Canada, including T.J. Maxx opening Marshalls stores and Tanger Outlet

TABLE 7-1 Key Economic Variables to Be Monitored

Shift to a service economy in the USA	Demand shifts for different goods and services
Availability of credit	Income differences by region and consumer groups
Level of disposable income	Price fluctuations
Propensity of people to spend	Foreign countries' economic conditions
Interest rates	Monetary and fiscal policies
Inflation rates	Stock market trends
Gross domestic product trends	Tax rate variation by country and state
Consumption patterns	European Economic Community (EEC) policies
Unemployment trends	Organization of Petroleum Exporting Countries
Value of the dollar in world markets	(OPEC) policies
Import/export factors	

Factory Centers stores opening. Canada is one of the most economically prosperous countries in the world. Although interrelated, every country has its own economic situation, and those situations impact where companies choose to spend money and do business.

Interest rates, stock prices, and discretionary income are slowly rising. As stock prices increase, the desirability of equity as a source of capital increases. When the market rises, consumer and business wealth expands. A few important economic variables that often represent opportunities and threats for organizations are provided in Table 7-1. Be mindful that in strategic planning and case analysis, relevant economic variables such as those listed must be quantified and actionable to be useful.

An example of an economic variable is "value of the dollar" that recently hit a 7-year high compared to the yen, a 9-year high compared to the euro, a 5-year high compared to the Australian dollar, and an 11-year high to some other currencies. The high dollar makes it cheap for Americans to travel abroad, but expensive for foreigners to travel to the United States, thus hurting the U.S. tourism business. Trends in the dollar's value have significant and unequal effects on companies in different industries and in different locations. Agricultural and petroleum industries are hurt by the dollar's rise against the currencies of Mexico, Brazil, Venezuela, and Australia. Generally, a strong or high dollar makes U.S. goods more expensive in overseas markets. This worsens the U.S. trade deficit.

Domestic firms with big overseas sales, such as McDonald's, also are hurt by a strong dollar. Its revenue from abroad is lowered because, for example, 100 euros earned in Europe, when translated back to U.S. dollars for reporting purposes, is worth maybe $75. To combat this "loss," some companies try to raise prices in their European or Mexican stores, but that carries a risk of alienating shoppers, angering retailers, and giving local competitors a price edge. Some advantages of a strong dollar, however, are that (1) companies with substantial outside U.S. operations see their overseas expenses, such as salaries paid in euros, become cheaper; (2) it gives U.S. companies greater firepower for international acquisitions; and (3) companies importing goods have greater buying power because their dollars now go further overseas. Table 7-2 lists 10 advantages of a strong U.S. dollar for U.S. firms.

TABLE 7-2 Ten Advantages of a Strong Dollar for Domestic Firms

1. Leads to lower exports
2. Leads to higher imports
3. Makes U.S. goods expensive for foreign consumers
4. Helps keep inflation low
5. Allows U.S. firms to purchase raw materials cheaply from other countries
6. Allows USA to service its debt better
7. Spurs foreign investment
8. Encourages Americans to travel abroad
9. Leads to lower oil prices because oil globally is priced in U.S. dollars
10. Encourages Americans to spend money because they can buy more for their money

Social, Cultural, Demographic, and Natural Environment Forces

Social, cultural, demographic, and environmental changes impact strategic decisions on virtually all products, services, markets, and customers. Small, large, for-profit, and nonprofit organizations in all industries are being staggered and challenged by the opportunities and threats arising from changes in social, cultural, demographic, and environmental variables. In every way, the United States is much different today than it was yesterday, and tomorrow promises even greater changes.

The United States is becoming older and less white. The oldest among the 76 million baby boomers plan to retire soon, and this has lawmakers and younger taxpayers concerned about who will pay their Social Security, Medicare, and Medicaid. Individuals age 65 and older in the United States as a percentage of the population will rise to 18.5 percent by 2025. The oldest American as of January 1, 2015, is 116-year-old Gertrude Weaver of Little Rock, Arkansas. Weaver is the second-oldest person in the world, behind Misao Okawa of Japan, according to the Gerontology Research Group.

The trend toward an older United States is good news for restaurants, hotels, airlines, cruise lines, tours, resorts, theme parks, luxury products and services, recreational vehicles, home builders, furniture producers, computer manufacturers, travel services, pharmaceutical firms, automakers, and funeral homes. Older Americans are especially interested in health care, financial services, travel, crime prevention, and leisure. The world's longest-living people are the Japanese. By 2050, the Census Bureau projects that the number of Americans age 100 and older will increase to over 834,000 from just under 100,000 centenarians in the country in 2000. Americans age 65 and over will increase from 12.6 percent of the U.S. population in 2000 to 20.0 percent by the year 2050. The aging U.S. population affects the strategic orientation of nearly all organizations.

Retail shoppers in the United States are increasingly buying online, resulting in a persistent 5 to 7 percent decline in store traffic among almost all retail stores, prompting chains to slow or cease store openings.[1] Research reveals that growth in store counts at the 100 largest retailers by revenue slowed to 2 percent in 2014 from more than 12 percent in 2011. Consumer tastes and trends are changing as people wander through stores less, opting more and more to use their mobile phones and computers to research prices and cherry-pick promotions. Sales derived from online purchases are rapidly increasing.

The historical trend of people moving from the Northeast and Midwest to the Sunbelt and West has slowed, but there remains a steady migration to coastal areas. Hard-number data related to this trend can represent key opportunities for many firms and thus can be essential for successful strategy formulation, including where to locate new plants and distribution centers and where to focus marketing efforts.

Fortune recently ranked the largest 100 U.S. cities according to the best managed and worst managed.[2] A variety of factors were included, such as the area's economy, job market, crime level, and welfare of the population. The best-managed city is Irvine, California, followed by Fremont, California; Plano, Texas; Lincoln, Nebraska; Virginia Beach, Virginia; Scottsdale, Arizona; Seattle, Washington; Austin, Texas; Chesapeake, Virginia; and Raleigh, North Carolina.

By 2075, the United States will have no racial or ethnic majority. This forecast is aggravating tensions over issues such as immigration and affirmative action. Hawaii, California, and New Mexico already have no majority race or ethnic group. The population of the world recently surpassed 7 billion; the United States has slightly more than 310 million people. That leaves literally billions of people outside the United States who may be interested in the products and services produced through domestic firms. Remaining solely domestic is an increasingly risky strategy, especially as the world population continues to grow to an estimated 8 billion in 2028 and 9 billion in 2054.

Social, cultural, demographic, and environmental trends are shaping the way Americans live, work, produce, and consume. New trends are creating a different type of consumer and, consequently, a need for different products, new services, and updated strategies. One trend is that there are now more U.S. households with people living alone or with unrelated people than there are households consisting of married couples with children. Another is that U.S. households are making more and more purchases online.

Some important social, cultural, demographic, and environmental variables that represent opportunities or threats for virtually all organizations is given in Table 7-3. Be mindful that in

TABLE 7-3 Key Social, Cultural, Demographic, and Natural Environment Variables

Population changes by race, age, and geographic area	Attitudes toward retirement
Regional changes in tastes and preferences	Energy conservation
Number of marriages	Attitudes toward product quality
Number of divorces	Attitudes toward customer service
Number of births	Pollution control
Number of deaths	Attitudes toward foreign peoples
Immigration and emigration rates	Energy conservation
Social Security programs	Social programs
Life expectancy rates	Number of churches
Per capita income	Number of church members
Social media pervasiveness	Social responsibility issues

strategic planning and case analysis, relevant social, cultural, demographic, and natural environment factors for a particular business must be *quantified* and *actionable* to be useful.

Political, Governmental, and Legal Forces

Political issues and stances do matter for business and do impact strategic decisions, especially in today's world of instant tweeting and emailing. Various industries, such as aerospace and their supplier firms, typically support and lobby for Republicans, whereas other industries, such as automotive and their supplier firms, generally support Democrats. National, state, and local elections impact businesses, with ongoing healthy debate concerning the pros and cons of each party's agenda for business.

For industries and firms that depend heavily on government contracts or subsidies, political forecasts can be the most important part of an external audit. Changes in patent laws, antitrust legislation, tax rates, and lobbying activities can affect firms significantly. The increasing global interdependence among economies, markets, governments, and organizations makes it imperative that firms consider the possible impact of political variables on the formulation and implementation of competitive strategies.

Various countries worldwide are resorting to protectionism to safeguard their own industries. European Union (EU) nations, for example, have tightened their own trade rules and resumed subsidies for their own industries, while barring imports from certain other countries. The EU recently restricted imports of U.S. chicken and beef. India is increasing tariffs on foreign steel. Russia perhaps has instituted the most protectionist measures by raising tariffs on most imports and subsidizing its own exports. Despite these measures taken by other countries, the United States has largely refrained from "Buy American" policies and protectionist measures, although there are increased tariffs on French cheese and Italian water. Many economists say trade constraints will make it harder for global economic growth.

Local, state, and federal laws, as well as regulatory agencies and special-interest groups, can have a major impact on the strategies of small, large, for-profit, and nonprofit organizations. Many companies have altered or abandoned strategies in the past because of political or governmental actions. In the academic world, as state budgets have dropped in recent years, so too has state support for colleges and universities. Resulting from the decline in funds received from the state, many institutions of higher learning are doing more fund-raising on their own—naming buildings and classrooms, for example, for donors.

Some companies take public stands on political issues. For example, Starbucks' recent support of same-sex marriage in its home state of Washington was praised by a number of prominent rights activists. Today, all states allow same-sex marriage. But the Seattle-based coffee chain's outspoken opponents, such as the National Organization for Marriage (NOM), has vowed to make Starbucks (along with other companies that support same-sex marriage) pay a "price" for this stance. "Middle Eastern countries are hostile to lesbian, gay, bisexual, and transgender (LGBT) rights. So, for example, in Qatar, in the Middle East, we've begun working to make sure that there's some price to be paid for this," Brian Brown of the NOM said. "These are not countries that look kindly on same-sex marriage. And this is where Starbucks wants to expand, as well as India."

Recently, CVS Caremark stopped selling tobacco products at its 7,600 stores, becoming the first U.S. drugstore chain to remove cigarettes from the store—and at the same time changed its corporate name to CVS Health. Nontobacco consumers and the medical community in general applauded the CVS announcement. With the announcement, CVS said its tobacco ban will result in the firm losing about $4 billion in annual sales. Euromonitor International reports that cigarette sales in the United States declined 31.3 percent from 2003 to 2013. However, smoking is still cited as the leading cause of preventable death in the country, killing more than 480,000 Americans per year. Within weeks after the CVS announcement, 24 states, Washington DC, and three U.S. territories sent coordinated letters to the CEOs of Walmart, Rite-Aid, Safeway, Kroger, and Walgreens, asking them to stop selling tobacco products.

In mid-2015, the United States normalized relations with Cuba, ending 54 years of hostility. This event represents an opportunity for numerous companies to do business with Cuba. On 7-20-15, Cuba raised its flag over its new embassy in Washington, D.C. For example, Carnival Corporation has won approval to begin cruising to Cuba and back, marking the first time in over 50 years that a cruise line can travel to and from Cuba.

A political debate still rages in the United States regarding sales taxes on the Internet. Walmart, Target, and other large retailers are pressuring state governments to collect sales taxes from Amazon.com. Big brick-and-mortar retailers are backing a coalition called the Alliance for Main Street Fairness, which is leading political efforts to change sales-tax laws in more than a dozen states. According to Walmart's executive Raul Vazquez, "The rules today don't allow brick-and-mortar retailers to compete evenly with online retailers, and that needs to be addressed."

Federal, state, local, and foreign governments are major regulators, deregulators, subsidizers, employers, and customers of organizations. Political, governmental, and legal factors, therefore, can represent major opportunities or threats for both small and large organizations. Politicians decide on tax rates. State and local income taxes and property taxes impact where companies locate facilities and where people desire to live. The five states, in rank order, with the lowest overall state taxes, and the five states with the highest state taxes, are shown here.[3]

Lowest State Taxes	Highest State Taxes
1. Wyoming	1. New York
2. Alaska	2. California
3. Nevada	3. Nebraska
4. Florida	4. Connecticut
5. South Dakota	5. Illinois

Regarding *only* state income taxes (rather than property, local, and sales taxes, too), seven states have zero (0.00) state income taxes: Texas, Nevada, Alaska, Florida, South Dakota, Washington, and Wyoming. States with the highest income tax are California (13.3%), Hawaii (11%), Oregon (9.90%), Minnesota (9.85%), Iowa (8.98%), and New Jersey (8.97%).

The extent that a state is unionized can be a significant political factor in strategic-planning decisions as related to manufacturing plant location and other operational matters. The size of U.S. labor unions has fallen sharply in the last decade as a result in large part of erosion of the U.S. manufacturing base. Organized public-sector labor issues are being debated in many state legislatures. Wisconsin, for example, recently passed a law eliminating most collective-bargaining rights for the state's public-employee unions. That law sets a precedent that many other states may follow to curb union rights as a way to help state budgets become solvent. Ohio is close to passing a similar bill that will curb union rights for 400,000 public workers. Among states, New York continues to have the highest union membership rate (24.1%) and North Carolina has the lowest rate (2.9%).

Some political, governmental, and legal variables that can represent key opportunities or threats to organizations are provided in Table 7-4, but in stating these for a particular company, the factors should be both *quantitative* and *actionable*.

TABLE 7-4 Some Political, Governmental, and Legal Variables

Environmental regulations	USA vs. other country relationships
Number of patents	Political conditions in foreign countries
Changes in patent laws	Global price of oil changes
Equal employment laws	Local, state, and federal laws
Level of defense expenditures	Import–export regulations
Unionization trends	Tariffs
Antitrust legislation	Local, state, and national elections

Technological Forces

A variety of new technologies such as the Internet of Things, 3D printing, the cloud, mobile devices, biotech, analytics, autotech, robotics, and artificial intelligence are fueling innovation in many industries, and impacting strategic-planning decisions. Businesses are using mobile technologies and applications to better determine customer trends and employing advanced analytics data to make enhanced strategy decisions. The vast increase in the amount of data coming from mobile devices is driving the development of advanced analytics applications. In fact, by 2018, machine-to-machine devices ranging from wearable Web access devices and utility meters and sensors in cars will account for 35 percent of global Internet network-connected devices, up from 18.6 percent today.[4] A primary reason that Cisco Systems has recently entered the data analytics business is that sales of hardware, software, and services connected to the Internet of Things is expected to increase to $7.1 billion by 2020 from about $2.0 billion in 2015.

Rapid technological advances in mobile and electronic banking have led banks to close branch offices at dramatically increasing rates in the United States. The total number of branch locations has dropped below 90,000, the lowest total number in the United States in a decade. Too offset closing branch offices, U.S. banks are ramping up mobile and online services, such as allowing customers to make deposits simply by snapping photos of checks with smartphones and emailing them. Many banks now allow customers to transfer money to other customers via smartphones. At Bank of America, for example, nearly 15 percent of all checks deposited by customers come from snapping pictures on smartphones or tablet computers. Not a single state in the United States reported an increase in the number of branch bank locations in recent years.[5] Florida leads all states in branch bank closures, followed by Pennsylvania. Technology is rapidly changing the competitive landscape in banking, and many other industries characterized by brick-and-mortar stores.

Monitoring online reviews about your business, large or small, has become a burdensome but an essential task, especially given emergence of social-media channels, such as Twitter, that empowers opinionated customers. Research is clear that benign neglect of a company's online reputation could quickly hurt sales, especially given the new normal behavior of customers consulting their smartphones for even the smallest of purchases.[6]

A number of organizations are establishing two positions in their firms: **chief information officer (CIO)** and **chief technology officer (CTO)**, reflecting the growing importance of **information technology (IT)** in strategic management. A CIO and CTO work together to ensure that information needed to formulate, implement, and evaluate strategies is available where and when it is needed. These individuals are responsible for developing, maintaining, and updating a company's information database. The CIO is more a manager, managing the firm's relationship with stakeholders; the CTO is more a technician, focusing on technical issues such as data acquisition, data processing, decision-support systems, and software and hardware acquisition.

Global cybersecurity spending by critical infrastructure industries exceeds $50 billion annually, and is rising more than 10 percent annually.[7] Security is a major concern for all businesses, yet complete security is something most businesses cannot financially afford to install. Hackers recently stole 40 million of Target Corporation's customers' credit- and debit-card numbers, along with passcodes and passwords. Building firewalls and triplicate systems can be expensive. Similarly, J.P. Morgan reported that 76 million of their customers' contact information was recently stolen in a cybersecurity breach. Sony, too, was recently a victim of a massive cyber-attack.

Results of technological advancements are varied, as shown in the following list:

1. They represent major opportunities and threats that must be considered in formulating strategies.
2. They can dramatically affect organizations' products, services, markets, suppliers, distributors, competitors, customers, manufacturing processes, marketing practices, and competitive position.
3. They can create new markets, result in a proliferation of new and improved products, change the relative competitive cost positions in an industry, and render existing products and services obsolete.
4. They can reduce or eliminate cost barriers between businesses, create shorter production runs, create shortages in technical skills, and result in changing values and expectations of employees, managers, and customers.
5. They can create new competitive advantages that are more powerful than existing advantages.

No company or industry today is insulated against emerging technological developments. In high-tech industries, identification and evaluation of key technological opportunities and threats can be the most important part of the external strategic-management audit.

Competitive Forces

An important part of an external audit is identifying rival firms and determining their strengths, weaknesses, capabilities, opportunities, threats, objectives, and strategies. George Salk stated, "If you're not faster than your competitor, you're in a tenuous position, and if you're only half as fast, you're terminal."

Collecting and evaluating information on competitors is essential for successful strategy formulation. Identifying major competitors is not always easy because many firms have divisions that compete in different industries. Many multidivisional firms do not provide sales and profit information on a divisional basis for competitive reasons. Also, privately held firms do not publish any financial or marketing information. Addressing questions about competitors, such as those presented in Table 7-5, is important in performing an external audit.

Competition in virtually all industries is intense—and sometimes cutthroat. For example, Walgreens and CVS pharmacies are located generally across the street from each other and battle

TABLE 7-5   Key Questions About Competitors

1. What are the strengths of our major competitors?
2. What are the weaknesses of our major competitors?
3. What are the objectives and strategies of our major competitors?
4. How will our major competitors most likely respond to current economic, social, cultural, demographic, environmental, political, governmental, legal, technological, and competitive trends affecting our industry?
5. How vulnerable are the major competitors to our alternative company strategies?
6. How vulnerable are our alternative strategies to successful counterattack by our major competitors?
7. How are our products or services positioned relative to major competitors?
8. To what extent are new firms entering and old firms leaving this industry?
9. What key factors have resulted in our present competitive position in this industry?
10. How have the sales and profit rankings of our major competitors in the industry changed over recent years? Why have these rankings changed that way?
11. What is the nature of supplier and distributor relationships in this industry?
12. To what extent could substitute products or services be a threat to our competitors?

each other every day on price and customer service. Most automobile dealerships also are located close to each other. Dollar General, Dollar Tree, and Family Dollar compete intensely on price to attract customers away from each other and away from Walmart and Target.

Seven characteristics describe the most competitive companies:

1. Strive to continually increase market share.
2. Use the vision/mission as a guide for all decisions.
3. Realize that the adage "If it's not broke, don't fix it" has been replaced by "Whether it's broke or not, fix it;" in other words, continually strive to improve everything about the firm.
4. Continually adapt, innovate, improve—especially when the firm is successful.
5. Strive to grow through acquisition whenever possible.
6. Hire and retain the best employees and managers possible.
7. Strive to stay cost-competitive on a global basis.[8]

Competitive intelligence (CI), as formally defined by the Society of Competitive Intelligence Professionals (SCIP), is a systematic and ethical process for gathering and analyzing information about the competition's activities and general business trends to further a business's own goals (SCIP website). Good competitive intelligence in business, as in the military, is one of the keys to success. The more information and knowledge a firm can obtain about its competitors, the more likely the firm can formulate and implement effective strategies. Major competitors' weaknesses can represent external opportunities; major competitors' strengths may represent key threats.

Various legal and ethical ways to obtain competitive intelligence include the following:

- Hire top executives from rival firms.
- Reverse engineer rival firms' products.
- Use surveys and interviews of customers, suppliers, and distributors.
- Conduct drive-by and on-site visits to rival firm operations.
- Search online databases.
- Contact government agencies for public information about rival firms.
- Systematically monitor relevant trade publications, magazines, and newspapers.

Information gathering from employees, managers, suppliers, distributors, customers, creditors, and consultants also can make the difference between having superior or just average intelligence and overall competitiveness. The Fuld website explains that competitive intelligence is *not* the following:

Is not spying

Is not a crystal ball

Is not a simple Google search

Is not one-size-fits-all

Is not useful if no one is listening

Is not a job for one, smart person

Is not a fad

Is not driven by software or technology

Is not based on internal assumptions about the market

Is not a spreadsheet.[9]

The three basic objectives of a CI program are (1) to provide a general understanding of an industry and its competitors, (2) to identify areas in which competitors are vulnerable and to assess the impact strategic actions would have on competitors, and (3) to identify potential moves that a competitor might make that would endanger a firm's position in the market.[10] Competitive information is equally applicable for strategy formulation, implementation, and evaluation decisions. An effective CI program allows all areas of a firm to access consistent and verifiable information in making decisions. All members of an organization—from the CEO to custodians—are valuable intelligence agents and should feel themselves to be a part of the CI process. Special characteristics of a successful CI program include flexibility, usefulness, timeliness, and cross-functional cooperation.

Competitive intelligence is not corporate espionage; after all, 95 percent of the information a company needs to make strategic decisions is available and accessible to the public. Sources of competitive information include trade journals, want ads, newspaper articles, and government filings, as well as customers, suppliers, distributors, competitors themselves, and the Internet. Unethical tactics such as bribery, wiretapping, and computer hacking should never be used to obtain information. All the information a company needs can be collected without resorting to unethical tactics.

Porter's Five-Forces Model

Former chair and CEO of PepsiCo Wayne Calloway said, "Nothing focuses the mind better than the constant sight of a competitor that wants to wipe you off the map." As illustrated in Figure 7-3, **Porter's Five-Forces Model** of competitive analysis is a widely used approach for developing strategies in many industries. The intensity of competition among firms varies widely across industries. Table 7-6 reveals the average gross profit margin and earnings per share (EPS) for firms in different industries. Note the substantial variation among industries. For example, note that industry operating margins range from 4 to 34 percent, whereas industry

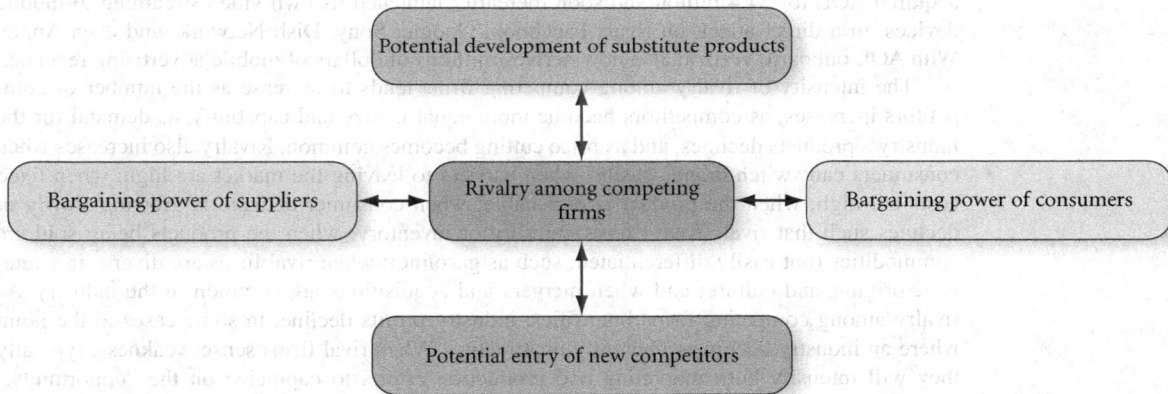

FIGURE 7-3
The Five-Forces Model of Competition

TABLE 7-6   Competitiveness Across a Few Industries (2015 data)

	Operating Margin (%)	EPS ($)
Pharmaceutical	13.0	0.61
Telecommunications	14.0	1.25
Fragrances/Cosmetics	12.0	2.23
Banking	34.0	1.58
Bookstores	6.0	0.16
Food Manufacturers	4.0	0.63
Oil and Gas	10.0	2.03
Airlines	10.0	0.09
Machinery/Construction	7.0	0.96
Paper Products	5.0	0.27

Source: Based on company data.

EPS values range from −16 to 2.23. Note that food manufacturers have the lowest average profit margin (2.3), which implies fierce competition in that industry. Intensity of competition is highest in lower-return industries. The collective impact of competitive forces is so brutal in some industries that the market is clearly "unattractive" from a profit-making standpoint. Rivalry among existing firms is severe, new rivals can enter the industry with relative ease, and both suppliers and customers can exercise considerable bargaining leverage. According to Porter, a Harvard Business School professor, the nature of competitiveness in a given industry can be viewed as a composite of five forces:

1. Rivalry among competing firms
2. Potential entry of new competitors
3. Potential development of substitute products
4. Bargaining power of suppliers
5. Bargaining power of consumers

Rivalry Among Competing Firms

Rivalry among competing firms is usually the most powerful of the five competitive forces. The strategies pursued by one firm can be successful only to the extent that they provide competitive advantage over the strategies pursued by rival firms. Changes in strategy by one firm may be met with retaliatory countermoves, such as lowering prices, enhancing quality, adding features, providing services, extending warranties, and increasing advertising. For example, Verizon recently acquired AOL for $4.4 billion and soon thereafter launched its own video streaming to mobile devices, in a direct attack on rivals Facebook, Google, Sony, Dish Network, and even Apple. With AOL onboard, Verizon also now derives millions of dollars of mobile advertising revenue.

The intensity of rivalry among competing firms tends to increase as the number of competitors increases, as competitors become more equal in size and capability, as demand for the industry's products declines, and as price cutting becomes common. Rivalry also increases when consumers can switch brands easily; when barriers to leaving the market are high; when fixed costs are high; when the product is perishable; when consumer demand is growing slowly or declines such that rivals have excess capacity or inventory; when the products being sold are commodities (not easily differentiated, such as gasoline); when rival firms are diverse in strategies, origins, and culture; and when mergers and acquisitions are common in the industry. As rivalry among competing firms intensifies, industry profits decline, in some cases to the point where an industry becomes inherently unattractive. When rival firms sense weakness, typically they will intensify both marketing and production efforts to capitalize on the "opportunity." Table 7-7 summarizes conditions that cause high rivalry among competing firms.

TABLE 7-7   Conditions That Cause High Rivalry Among Competing Firms

1. When the number of competing firms is high
2. When competing firms are of similar size
3. When competing firms have similar capabilities
4. When the demand for the industry's products is falling
5. When the product or service prices in the industry is falling
6. When consumers can switch brands easily
7. When barriers to leaving the market are high
8. When barriers to entering the market are low
9. When fixed costs are high among competing firms
10. When the product is perishable
11. When rivals have excess capacity
12. When consumer demand is falling
13. When rivals have excess inventory
14. When rivals sell similar products/services
15. When mergers are common in the industry

Potential Entry of New Competitors

Whenever new firms can easily enter a particular industry, the intensity of competitiveness among firms increases. Barriers to entry, however, can include the need to gain economies of scale quickly, the need to gain technology and specialized know-how, the lack of experience, strong customer loyalty, strong brand preferences, large capital requirements, lack of adequate distribution channels, government regulatory policies, tariffs, lack of access to raw materials, possession of patents, undesirable locations, counterattack by entrenched firms, and potential saturation of the market.

Despite numerous barriers to entry, new firms sometimes enter industries with higher-quality products, lower prices, and substantial marketing resources. The strategist's job, therefore, is to identify potential new firms entering the market, to monitor the new rival firms' strategies, to counterattack as needed, and to capitalize on existing strengths and opportunities. When the threat of new firms entering the market is strong, incumbent firms generally fortify their positions and take actions to deter new entrants, such as lowering prices, extending warranties, adding features, or offering financing specials.

The Walt Disney Company is nearing completion of its Shanghai Disneyland, a $4.4 billion complex set to open in China in 2016, complete with hotels, restaurants, retail shops, and other amenities. However, a rival firm, DreamWorks Animation SKG, is nearing completion of a $3.1 billion entertainment district named Dream Center in Shanghai right beside Disneyland and says its facility will also open in 2016. Although expensive to build, theme parks are becoming more popular globally. Time Warner's Warner Brothers is building Harry Potter attractions around the world, including a converted movie studio outside London.

Potential Development of Substitute Products

In many industries, firms are in close competition with producers of substitute products in other industries. Examples are plastic container producers competing with glass, paperboard, and aluminum can producers, and acetaminophen manufacturers competing with other manufacturers of pain and headache remedies. The presence of substitute products puts a ceiling on the price that can be charged before consumers will switch to the substitute product. Price ceilings equate to profit ceilings and more intense competition among rivals. Producers of eyeglasses and contact lenses, for example, face increasing competitive pressures from laser eye surgery. Producers of sugar face similar pressures from artificial sweeteners. Newspapers and magazines face substitute-product competitive pressures from the Internet and 24-hour cable television. The magnitude of competitive pressure derived from the development of substitute products is generally evidenced by rivals' plans for expanding production capacity, as well as by their sales and profit growth numbers.

Competitive pressures arising from substitute products increase as the relative price of substitute products declines and as consumers' costs of switching decrease. The competitive strength of substitute products is best measured by the inroads into the market share those products obtain, as well as those firms' plans for increased capacity and market penetration.

Bargaining Power of Suppliers

The bargaining power of suppliers affects the intensity of competition in an industry, especially when there are few suppliers, when there are few good substitute raw materials, or when the cost of switching raw materials is especially high. It is often in the best interest of both suppliers and producers to assist each other with reasonable prices, improved quality, development of new services, just-in-time deliveries, and reduced inventory costs, thus enhancing long-term profitability for all concerned.

Firms may pursue a backward integration strategy to gain control or ownership of suppliers. This strategy is especially effective when suppliers are unreliable, too costly, or not capable of meeting a firm's needs on a consistent basis. Firms generally can negotiate more favorable terms with suppliers when backward integration is a commonly used strategy among rival firms in an industry.

However, in many industries it is more economical to use outside suppliers of component parts than to self-manufacture the items. This is true, for example, in the outdoor power equipment industry, where producers (such as Murray) of lawn mowers, rotary tillers, leaf blowers, and edgers generally obtain their small engines from outside manufacturers (such as Briggs & Stratton) that specialize in such engines and have huge economies of scale.

In more and more industries, sellers are forging strategic partnerships with select suppliers in an effort to (1) reduce inventory and logistics costs (e.g., through just-in-time deliveries), (2) accelerate the availability of next-generation components, (3) enhance the quality of the parts and components being supplied and reduce defect rates, and (4) squeeze out important cost savings for both themselves and their suppliers.[11]

Bargaining Power of Consumers

When customers are concentrated or large in number or buy in volume, their bargaining power represents a major force affecting the intensity of competition in an industry. Rival firms may offer extended warranties or special services to gain customer loyalty whenever the bargaining power of consumers is substantial. Bargaining power of consumers also is higher when the products being purchased are standard or undifferentiated. When this is the case, consumers often can negotiate selling price, warranty coverage, and accessory packages to a greater extent.

The bargaining power of consumers can be the most important force affecting competitive advantage. Consumers gain increasing bargaining power under the following circumstances:

1. If they can inexpensively switch to competing brands or substitutes
2. If they are particularly important to the seller
3. If sellers are struggling in the face of falling consumer demand
4. If they are informed about sellers' products, prices, and costs
5. If they have discretion in whether and when they purchase the product[12]

Sources of External Information

A wealth of strategic information is available to organizations from both published and unpublished sources. *Unpublished sources* include customer surveys, market research, speeches at professional and shareholders' meetings, television programs, interviews, and conversations with stakeholders. *Published sources* of strategic information include periodicals, journals, reports, government documents, abstracts, books, directories, newspapers, and manuals. A company website is usually an excellent place to start to find information about a firm, particularly on the Investor Relations web pages.

There are many excellent websites for gathering strategic information, but three that the authors use routinely are:

1. http://finance.yahoo.com
2. www.hoovers.com
3. http://globaledge.msu.edu/industries/

An excellent source of industry information is provided by Michigan State University at http://globaledge.msu.edu/industries/. Industry profiles provided at that site are an excellent source for information, news, events, and statistical data for any industry. In addition to a wealth of indices, risk assessments, and interactive trade information, a wide array of global resources are provided.

Most college libraries subscribe to many excellent online business databases that can then be used free by students to gather information to perform a strategic management case analysis. Simply ask your reference librarian. Especially good sources of information are described in Table 7-8.

Forecasting Tools and Techniques

Forecasts are educated assumptions about future trends and events. Forecasting is a complex activity because of factors such as technological innovation, cultural changes, new products, improved services, stronger competitors, shifts in government priorities, changing social values,

TABLE 7-8 Great Online Sources of Company and Industry Information

- **IBISWorld**—Provides online USA Industry Reports (NAICS), U.S. Industry iExpert Summaries, and U.S. Business Environment Profiles. A global version of IBIS is also available.
- **Lexis-Nexis Academic**—Provides online access to newspaper articles (including *New York Times* and *Washington Post*) and business information (including SEC filings).
- **Lexis-Nexis Company Dossier**—Provides online access to extensive, current data on 13 million companies. It collects and compiles information into excellent documents.
- **Mergent Online**—Provides online access to Mergent's (formerly Moody's/FISOnline) Manuals, which include trend, descriptive, and statistical information on hundreds of public companies and industries. Company income statements and balance sheets are provided.
- **Regional Business News**—Provides comprehensive full-text coverage for regional business publications; incorporates coverage of more than 80 regional business publications covering all metropolitan and rural areas within the United States.
- **Standard & Poor's NetAdvantage**—Provides online access to Standard & Poor's *Industry Surveys*, stock reports, corporation records, *The Outlook*, mutual fund reports, and more.
- **Value Line Investment Survey**—Provides excellent online information and advice on approximately 1,700 stocks, more than 90 industries, the stock market, and the economy. Company income statements and balance sheets are provided.

Source: Based on information at www.fmarion.edu/library.

unstable economic conditions, and unforeseen events. Managers often must rely on published forecasts to effectively identify key external opportunities and threats.

A sense of the future permeates all action and underlies every decision a person makes. People eat expecting to be satisfied and nourished in the future. People sleep assuming that in the future they will feel rested. They invest energy, money, and time because they believe their efforts will be rewarded in the future. They build highways assuming that automobiles and trucks will need them in the future. Parents educate children on the basis of forecasts that they will need certain skills, attitudes, and knowledge when they grow up. The truth is we all make implicit forecasts throughout our daily lives. The question, therefore, is not whether we should forecast but rather how we can best forecast to enable us to move beyond our ordinarily unarticulated assumptions about the future. Can we obtain information and then make educated assumptions (forecasts) to better guide our current decisions to achieve a more desirable future state of affairs? Assumptions must be made based on facts, figures, trends, and research. Strive for the firm's assumptions to be more accurate than rival firm's assumptions.

Sometimes organizations must develop their own projections. Most organizations forecast (project) their own revenues and profits annually. Organizations sometimes forecast market share or customer loyalty in local areas. Because forecasting is so important in strategic management and because the ability to forecast (in contrast to the ability to use a forecast) is essential, selected forecasting tools are examined further here.

No forecast is perfect—some are even wildly inaccurate. This fact accents the need for strategists to devote sufficient time and effort to study the underlying bases for published forecasts and to develop internal forecasts of their own. Key external opportunities and threats can be effectively identified only through good forecasts. Accurate forecasts can provide major competitive advantages for organizations. Accurate forecasts are vital to the strategic-management process and to the success of organizations.

Making Assumptions

Planning would be impossible without assumptions. McConkey defines assumptions as the "best present estimates of the impact of major external factors, over which the manager has little if any control, but which may exert a significant impact on performance or the ability to achieve desired results."[13] Strategists are faced with countless variables and imponderables that can be neither controlled nor predicted with 100 percent accuracy. Wild guesses should never be made in formulating strategies, but reasonable assumptions based on available information must *always* be made.

By identifying future occurrences that could have a major effect on the firm and by making reasonable assumptions about those factors, strategists can carry the strategic-management process forward. Assumptions are needed only for future trends and events that are most likely to have a significant effect on the company's business. Based on the best information at the time, assumptions serve as checkpoints on the validity of strategies. If future occurrences deviate significantly from assumptions, strategists know that corrective actions may be needed. Without reasonable assumptions, the strategy-formulation process could not proceed effectively. Firms that have the best information generally make the most accurate assumptions, which can lead to major competitive advantages.

Business Analytics

Business analytics is an MIS technique that involves using software to mine huge volumes of data to help executives make decisions. Sometimes called *predictive analytics, machine learning,* or *data mining,* this software enables a researcher to assess and use the aggregate experience of an organization, which is a priceless strategic asset for a firm. The history of a firm's interaction with its customers, suppliers, distributors, employees, rival firms, and more can all be tapped with **data mining** to generate predictive models. Business analytics is similar to the actuarial methods used by insurance companies to rate customers by the chance of positive or negative outcomes. Every business is basically a risk management endeavor! Therefore, like insurance companies, all businesses can benefit from measuring, tracking, and computing the risk associated with hundreds of strategic and tactical decisions made every day. Business analytics enables a company to benefit from measuring and managing risk.

As more and more products become commoditized (so similar as to be indistinguishable), competitive advantage more and more hinges on improvements to business processes. Business analytics can provide a firm with proprietary business intelligence regarding, for example, which segment(s) of customers choose your firm versus those who defer, delay, or defect to a competitor and why. Business analytics can reveal where competitors are weak so that marketing and sales activities can be directly targeted to take advantage of resultant opportunities (knowledge). In addition to understanding consumer behavior better, which yields more effective and efficient marketing, business analytics also is being used to slash expenses by, for example, withholding retention offers from customers who are going to stay with the firm anyway, or managing fraudulent transactions involving invoices, credit-card purchases, tax returns, insurance claims, mobile phone calls, online ad clicks, and more.

A key distinguishing feature of business analytics is that it enables a firm to learn from experience and to make current and future decisions based on prior information. Deriving robust predictive models from data mining to support hundreds of commonly occurring business decisions is the essence of learning from experience. The mathematical models associated with business analytics can dramatically enhance decision making at all organizational levels and all stages of strategic management. In a sense, art becomes science with business analytics resulting from the mathematical generalization of thousands, millions, or even billions of prior data points to discover patterns of behavior for optimizing the deployment of resources.

Netflix has used business analytics lately to mount a comeback in the industry and to grow dramatically its customer base. Netflix uses data analysis increasingly to refine its movie recommendations to particular customers as well as to identify which movies and television shows to license or develop. A recent article by Willhite defines *business analytics* as "the art and science of collecting and combing through vast amounts of information for insights that aren't apparent on a smaller scale."[14] Data mining, and using an analytical approach to all phases of strategic management, is rapidly burgeoning into a necessary prerequisite for success in hundreds of firms globally. This book advocates a systematic, analytical approach to strategic planning because otherwise emotion, politics, "experience," and subjectivity too often prevent identification and consideration of key facts, figures, and trends in choosing among numerous feasible alternative strategies, and implementing and monitoring the execution of those strategies.

The big data analytics firm, Splunk, reports ever-increasing revenues and profits as it capitalizes on a growing market for helping companies find better ways to manage increasing amounts of data coming in from mobile phones, PCs, global positioning systems, and other electronic devices. Splunk CEO Godfrey Sullivan says companies have "a massive thirst to better understand their customers, as well as the data coming through the enterprise from a variety of sources."

IBM's annual business analytics revenues of about $40 billion are growing about 15 percent every quarter, compared to the industry growing about 15 percent annually. IBM's acquisition of SPSS for $1.2 billion, among other recent acquisitions, launched the firm heavily into the business analytics consulting business. Other business analytics firms are Oracle, Tableau Software, Rocket Fuel, and Cisco Systems.

The External Factor Evaluation Matrix

An **External Factor Evaluation (EFE) Matrix** allows strategists to summarize and evaluate economic, social, cultural, demographic, environmental, political, governmental, legal, technological, and competitive information, illustrated earlier in Figure 7-2. The EFE Matrix can be developed in five steps:

1. List 20 key external factors as identified in the external-audit process, including both opportunities and threats that affect the firm and its industry. List the opportunities first and then the threats. Be as specific as possible, using percentages, ratios, and comparative numbers whenever possible. Recall that Edward Deming said, "In God we trust. Everyone else bring data." In addition, utilize "actionable" factors as defined earlier in this chapter.
2. Assign to each factor a weight that ranges from 0.0 (not important) to 1.0 (very important). The weight indicates the relative importance of that factor to being successful in the firm's industry. Opportunities often receive higher weights than threats, but threats can receive high weights if they are especially severe or threatening. Appropriate weights can be determined by comparing successful with unsuccessful competitors or by discussing the factor and reaching a group consensus. The sum of all weights assigned to the factors must equal 1.0.
3. Assign a rating between 1 and 4 to each key external factor to indicate how effectively the firm's current strategies respond to the factor, where 4 = the response is superior, 3 = the response is above average, 2 = the response is average, and 1 = the response is poor. Ratings are based on effectiveness of the firm's strategies. Ratings are thus company-based, whereas the weights in Step 2 are industry-based. It is important to note that both threats and opportunities can receive a 1, 2, 3, or 4.
4. Multiply each factor's weight by its rating to determine a weighted score.
5. Sum the weighted scores for each variable to determine the total weighted score for the organization.

Regardless of the number of key opportunities and threats included in an EFE Matrix, the highest possible total weighted score for an organization is 4.0 and the lowest possible total weighted score is 1.0. The average total weighted score is 2.5. A total weighted score of 4.0 indicates that an organization is responding in an outstanding way to existing opportunities and threats in its industry. In other words, the firm's strategies effectively take advantage of existing opportunities and minimize the potential adverse effects of external threats. A total score of 1.0 indicates that the firm's strategies are not capitalizing on opportunities or avoiding external threats.

An example of an EFE Matrix is provided in Table 7-9 for a local 10-theater cinema complex. Observe in the table that the most important factor to being successful in this business is "Trend toward healthy eating eroding concession sales," as indicated by the 0.12 weight. Also note that the local cinema is doing excellent in regard to handling two factors, "TDB University is expanding 6 percent annually" and "Trend toward healthy eating eroding concession sales." Perhaps the cinema is placing flyers on campus and also adding yogurt and healthy drinks to its concession menu. Note that you may have a 1, 2, 3, or 4 anywhere down the Rating column. Observe also that the factors are stated in quantitative terms to the extent possible, rather than being stated in vague terms. Quantify the factors as much as possible in constructing an EFE Matrix. Note also that all the factors are "actionable" instead of being something like "The economy is bad." Finally, note that the total weighted score of 2.58 is above the average (midpoint) of 2.5, so this cinema business is doing pretty well, taking advantage of the external opportunities

TABLE 7-9 EFE Matrix for a Local 10-Theater Cinema Complex

Key External Factors	Weight	Rating	Weighted Score
Opportunities			
1. Two new neighborhoods developing within 3 miles	0.09	1	0.09
2. TDB University is expanding 6% annually	0.08	4	0.32
3. Major competitor across town recently closed	0.08	3	0.24
4. Demand for going to cinemas growing 10%	0.07	2	0.14
5. Disposable income among citizens up 5% in prior year	0.06	3	0.18
6. Rowan County is growing 8% annually in population	0.05	3	0.15
7. Unemployment rate in county declined to 3.1%	0.03	2	0.06
Threats			
8. Trend toward healthy eating eroding concession sales	0.12	4	0.48
9. Demand for online movies and DVDs growing 10%	0.06	2	0.12
10. Commercial property adjacent to cinemas for sale	0.06	3	0.18
11. TDB University installing an on-campus movie theater	0.04	3	0.12
12. County and city property taxes increasing 25%	0.08	2	0.16
13. Local religious groups object to R-rated movies	0.04	3	0.12
14. Movies rented at local Red Box's up 12%	0.08	2	0.16
15. Movies rented last quarter from Time Warner up 15%	0.06	1	0.06
TOTAL	**1.00**		**2.58**

and avoiding the threats facing the firm. There is definitely room for improvement, though, because the highest total weighted score would be 4.0. As indicated by ratings of 1, this business needs to capitalize more on the "Two new neighborhoods developing [nearby]" opportunity and the "movies rented from … Time Warner" threat. Notice also that there are many percentage-based factors among the group. Be quantitative to the extent possible! Note, too, that the ratings range from 1 to 4 on both the opportunities and threats.

An actual EFE Matrix for the largest U.S. homebuilder, D. R. Horton, is given in Table 7-10. Note that the most important external threat facing the company, as indicated by a weight of 0.10, deals with labor and supplier costs. The key factors are listed in order beginning with the most important (highest weight). Notice how specific the factors are stated—specificity is essential. Also note that following DRH's EFE Matrix, an "author commentary" is given in Table 7-11, providing the rationale for each factor included.

Author commentary on each factor in the D. R. Horton EFE Matrix is given in Table 7-11 to provide insight on the thinking that needs to support not only inclusion of respective factors but also various weights and ratings assigned. Recall that mathematically, 0.04 is 33 percent more important than 0.03, and a rating of 3 is 50 percent higher than a rating of 2. Small judgments are helpful in moving forward toward larger decisions related to deployment of resources and money across regions and products.

The Competitive Profile Matrix

The **Competitive Profile Matrix (CPM)** identifies a firm's major competitors and its particular strengths and weaknesses in relation to a sample firm's strategic position. The weights and total weighted scores in both a CPM and an EFE have the same meaning. However, *critical success factors* in a CPM include both internal and external issues; therefore, the ratings refer to strengths and weaknesses, where 4 = major strength, 3 = minor strength, 2 = minor weakness, and 1 = major weakness. The critical success factors in a CPM are not grouped

TABLE 7-10 An Actual EFE Matrix for the Homebuilder D. R. Horton

Opportunities	Weight	Rating	Weighted Score
1. The 10 fastest-growing states by population are SC, WA, AZ, FL, SD, NV, TX, CO, UT, and ND.	0.12	3	0.36
2. Most new technological advances in residential building have come in the form of green building.	0.08	2	0.16
3. New home sales are up over 40% (compared to 20% in resales) with the South being up 38% and the West being up 49%.	0.08	3	0.24
4. Lennar's starting prices are about 10% more nationwide.	0.06	3	0.18
5. More than 80% of people over the age of 65 own a home.	0.05	2	0.10
6. Corporate social responsibility pays; 53% of consumers said they would pay up to 10% more for a product from a CSR firm.	0.04	1	0.04
7. It is more affordable to buy than it is to rent in 98 out of 100 U.S. metros.	0.02	2	0.04
8. Interest rates have fallen 0.25% in the last year.	0.02	2	0.04
9. The availability of credit has increased 16%.	0.02	3	0.06
10. The level of disposable income has increased 5%.	0.01	3	0.03

Threats	Weight	Rating	Weighted Score
1. Framing lumber has increased 45%. YTD wages per hour are up 3.1%, cement costs are up 3.8%, and lumber costs are up 6.1%.	0.10	2	0.20
2. Lennar is growing faster than any other top-5 builder; Lennar has built 69% more homes, compared to DRH's 44%.	0.08	3	0.24
3. Lennar operates using an "everything's included" approach (supplying luxury items as standard features).	0.06	2	0.12
4. Lennar is building in just as many, if not more, communities in the South and Southwest (some of the fastest-growing areas).	0.05	2	0.10
5. USA has the lowest number of mortgage applications in 2 years.	0.05	3	0.15
6. 76% of the public are dissatisfied with the direction of the country, with 48% being very dissatisfied.	0.05	3	0.15
7. FHA mortgage insurance premiums increased 5 to 10 basis points and the time until termination significantly increased.	0.04	3	0.12
8. Lennar has a superior website (includes community involvement, how to take care of your home, why buy now).	0.03	2	0.06
9. Homeowner percentage fell from 69% to 65% between 2005 and 2015.	0.02	3	0.06
10. Personal savings rate is 5.7%, up from 4.9% 6 months ago.	0.02	3	0.06
TOTALS	**1.00**		**2.51**

into opportunities and threats as they are in an EFE. In a CPM, the ratings and total weighted scores for rival firms can be compared to the sample firm. This comparative analysis provides important internal strategic information. Avoid assigning the same rating to firms included in your CPM analysis.

A sample CPM is provided in Table 7-12. In this example, the two most important factors to being successful in the industry are "advertising" and "global expansion," as indicated by weights of 0.20. If there were no weight column in this analysis, note that each factor then would be equally important. Thus, having a weight column makes for a more robust analysis because it enables the analyst to assign higher and lower numbers to capture perceived or actual levels of importance. Note in Table 7-12 that Company 1 is strongest on "product quality," as indicated by a rating of 4, whereas Company 2 is strongest on "advertising." Overall, Company 1 is strongest, as indicated by the total weighted score of 3.15 and Company 3 is weakest.

TABLE 7-11 Author Commentary on Each Factor in the D. R. Horton EFE Matrix

Opportunities

1. These states will need more new homes than average because the populations are the fastest growing.
2. Building using more green technologies could result in creating a preference and increased revenue/profit, because customers are increasingly make green requests.
3. Since new homes, especially in the South and the West, are on the rise, there is an opportunity to build more homes, increasing revenue/profit/market share.
4. Building and selling lower-priced homes is a competitive advantage for DRH because consumers are price conscious.
5. Many senior citizens look to downsize, so they could be specifically targeted to increase sales.
6. By increasing its corporate social responsibility position, DRH could build a preference for its homes.
7. If it is more affordable to buy than rent, people will want to build (or buy), and DRH is the largest homebuilder in the USA.
8. With low interest rates, a mortgage is more affordable; therefore, consumers are inclined to build (or buy)—a plus for DRH.
9. If it is easier than before to obtain a mortgage, more consumers will do so. This creates an opportunity for DRH.
10. If consumers have more money to spend, some will want to spend it on a home. This creates an opportunity for DRH.

Threats

1. Increased costs of labor and supplies make new homes less affordable, so fewer people will want one.
2. Lennar is gaining economies of scale on DRH, enabling Lennar to price lower.
3. Lennar creates the perception that they have a higher quality, because they do not "nickel and dime" customers; this hurts DRH.
4. Lennar aims to take market share from DRH by building in more and more communities.
5. If consumers are seeking fewer mortgages, then fewer homes are being sought.
6. As consumers become worried about the country, they become more conservative and are less likely to buy a home.
7. As the FHA becomes less amenable to approving mortgages, this trend hurts DRH.
8. Because everybody does research online, Lennar's superior website could hurt DRH.
9. If the percentage of people that own a home is decreasing, then fewer new homes would be needed.
10. If consumers are saving more, they are spending less, perhaps less even on housing.

TABLE 7-12 An Example Competitive Profile Matrix

Critical Success Factors	Weight	Company 1 Rating	Company 1 Score	Company 2 Rating	Company 2 Score	Company 3 Rating	Company 3 Score
Advertising	0.20	1	0.20	4	0.80	3	0.60
Product Quality	0.10	4	0.40	3	0.30	2	0.20
Price Competitiveness	0.10	3	0.30	2	0.20	1	0.10
Management	0.10	4	0.40	3	0.20	1	0.10
Financial Position	0.15	4	0.60	2	0.30	3	0.45
Customer Loyalty	0.10	4	0.40	3	0.30	2	0.20
Global Expansion	0.20	4	0.80	1	0.20	2	0.40
Market Share	0.05	1	0.05	4	0.20	3	0.15
Total	**1.00**		**3.15**		**2.50**		**2.20**

Note: The ratings values are as follows: 1 = major weakness, 2 = minor weakness, 3 = minor strength, 4 = major strength. As indicated by the total weighted score of 2.20, Company 3 is weakest overall. Only eight critical success factors are included for simplicity; in actuality, however, this is too few.

TABLE 7-13   An Actual CPM for D. R. Horton

Critical Success Factors	Weight	D. R. Horton		Lennar		PulteGroup	
		Rating	Score	Rating	Score	Rating	Score
1. Price	0.16	4	0.64	3	0.48	2	0.32
2. Market Share	0.14	4	0.56	3	0.42	2	0.28
3. Geographical Coverage	0.12	4	0.48	2	0.24	3	0.36
4. Quality	0.10	2	0.20	4	0.40	3	0.30
5. Customer Service	0.09	2	0.18	3	0.27	4	0.36
6. Profitability	0.08	3	0.24	4	0.32	2	0.16
7. Financial Position	0.07	3	0.21	2	0.14	4	0.28
8. Energy Efficiencies	0.06	2	0.12	3	0.18	4	0.24
9. Growth	0.06	3	0.18	4	0.24	2	0.12
10. Website	0.05	3	0.15	4	0.20	2	0.10
11. Warranty Issues	0.04	3	0.12	2	0.08	4	0.16
12. Social Responsibility	0.03	2	0.06	3	0.09	4	0.12
Totals	**1.00**		**3.14**		**3.06**		**2.80**

Other than the critical success factors listed in the sample CPM, factors often included in this analysis include breadth of product line, effectiveness of sales distribution, proprietary or patent advantages, location of facilities, production capacity and efficiency, experience, union relations, technological advantages, and e-commerce expertise.

Just because one firm receives a 3.20 overall rating and another receives a 2.80 in a CPM, it does not necessarily follow that the first firm is precisely 14.3 percent better than the second, but it does suggest that the first firm is better in some areas. Regarding weights in a CPM or EFE Matrix, be mindful that 0.08 is mathematically 33 percent higher than 0.06, so even small differences can reveal important perceptions regarding the relative importance of various factors. The aim with numbers is to assimilate and evaluate information in a meaningful way that aids in decision making.

An actual CPM is provided in Table 7-13, again for the largest homebuilder in the United States, D. R. Horton. Note that the two rival firms, Lennar and PulteGroup, receive higher ratings on "Quality" than D. R. Horton. Also note the factors are listed beginning with the most important (highest weight). D. R. Horton, Lennar, and PulteGroup are headquartered in Fort Worth, Texas; Miami, Florida; and Atlanta, Georgia; respectively.

IMPLICATIONS FOR STRATEGISTS

Figure 7-4 reveals that to gain and sustain competitive advantages, strategists must collect, analyze, and prioritize information regarding the firm's competitors, as well as identify and consider relevant social, demographic, economic, and technology trends and events impacting the firm and its industry. This engineering hunt for the facts is essential because expensive, and sometimes irreversible, strategies are ultimately formulated and implemented based on that information. This chapter reveals that quantified, organized, prioritized, actionable external information is a key ingredient for making decisions that culminate in a winning strategic plan. Increasingly, business analytics is being used to identify key external trends that may otherwise go unnoticed from casual observation. The External Factor Evaluation Matrix and Competitive Profile Matrix presented in this chapter are excellent strategic-planning tools for assimilating and prioritizing information to enhance decision making.

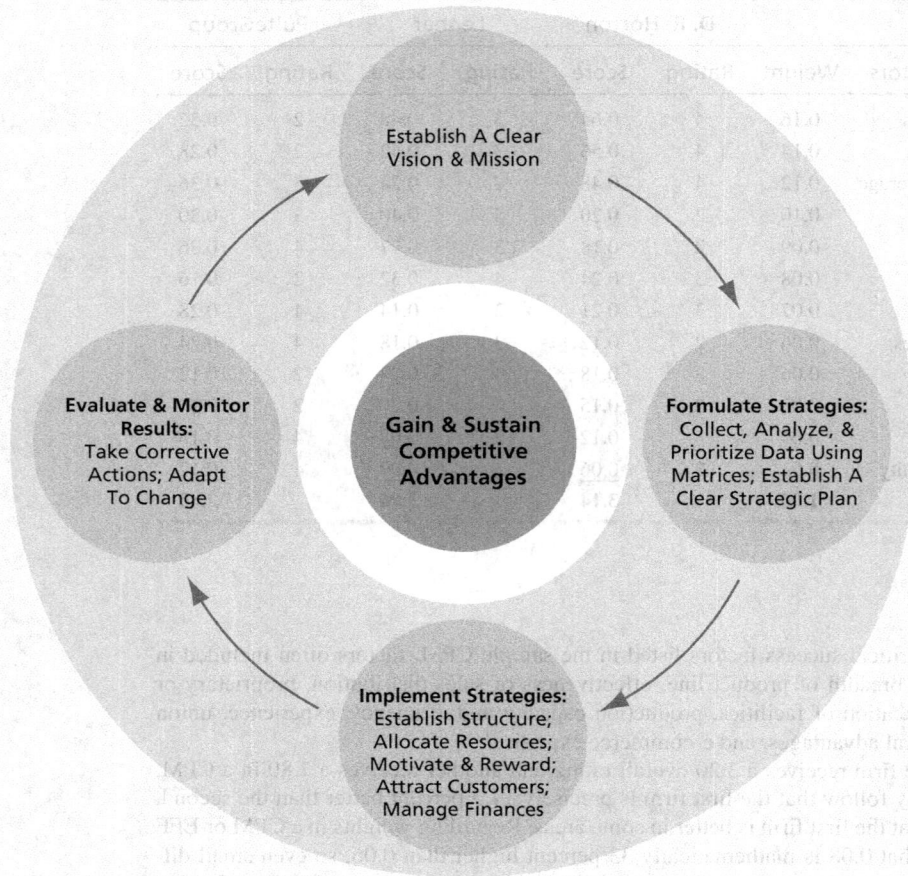

FIGURE 7-4

How to Gain and Sustain Competitive Advantages

IMPLICATIONS FOR STUDENTS

In developing and presenting your external assessment for your firm, be mindful that gaining and sustaining competitive advantage is the overriding purpose of developing the EFE Matrix and CPM. During this section of your written or oral project, emphasize how and why particular factors can yield competitive advantage for the firm. In other words, instead of robotically going through the weights and ratings (which, by the way, are critically important), highlight various factors in light of where you are leading the firm. Make it abundantly clear in your discussion how your firm, with your suggestions, can subdue rival firms or at least profitably compete with them. Showcase during this section of your project the key underlying reasons how and why your firm can prosper among rivals. Remember to be *prescriptive*, rather than *descriptive*, in the manner that you present your entire project. If presenting your project orally, be self-confident and passionate rather than timid and uninterested. Definitely "bring the data" throughout your project, because "vagueness" is the most common downfall of students in case analyses.

Chapter Summary

Increasing turbulence in markets and industries around the world means the external audit has become an explicit and vital part of the strategic-management process. This chapter provided a framework for collecting and evaluating economic, social, cultural, demographic, environmental, political, governmental, legal, technological, and competitive information. Firms that do not mobilize and empower their managers and employees to identify, monitor, forecast, and evaluate key external forces may fail to anticipate emerging opportunities and threats and, consequently, may pursue ineffective strategies, miss opportunities, and invite organizational demise. Firms not taking advantage of e-commerce and social media networks are technologically falling behind.

A major responsibility of strategists is to ensure development of an effective external-audit system. This includes using information technology to devise a competitive intelligence system that works. The external-audit approach described in this chapter can be used effectively by any size or type of organization. Typically, the external-audit process is more informal in small firms, but the need to understand key trends and events is no less important for these firms. The EFE Matrix and Porter's Five-Forces Model can help strategists evaluate the market and industry, but these tools must be accompanied by good intuitive judgment. Multinational firms especially need a systematic and effective external-audit system because external forces among foreign countries vary so greatly.

Key Terms and Concepts

actionable responses (p. 219)
business analytics (p. 234)
chief information officer (CIO) (p. 226)
chief technology officer (CTO) (p. 226)
competitive intelligence (CI) (p. 228)
Competitive Profile Matrix (CPM) (p. 236)
data mining (p. 234)
environmental scanning (p. 218)

external audit (p. 218)
External Factor Evaluation (EFE) Matrix (p. 235)
external forces (p. 219)
Industrial Organization (I/O) (p. 221)
industry analysis (p. 218)
information technology (IT) (p. 226)
Porter's Five-Forces Model (p. 229)

Issues for Review and Discussion

7-1. Michelin has been very successful in the last decade. In your opinion, what strategy changes would Michelin need in 2016?

7-2. Of the many competitors it has, which firm do you think worries Michelin most about? Why? Prepare a Competitive Profile Matrix (CPM) that includes Michelin and the rival firm you identified.

7-3. A political debate in the United States concerns sales taxes on the Internet. Most states do not collect a sales tax on online products. How does the situation in any country of Europe compare with the United States, in terms of sales tax on items purchased online? What is the strategic implication for companies?

7-4. The size of American labor unions have fallen sharply in the last decade, mostly due to the erosion of the U.S. manufacturing base. How does the situation in any country of Europe compare to the United States in this regard? What is the strategic implication for companies?

7-5. List four reasons why some countries in Europe are struggling economically in comparison to Asian countries. What is the strategic implication for companies?

7-6. Does the Arab Spring, in the Middle East, represent more of an opportunity or threat to companies? Explain.

7-7. Identify two companies that you think would have a 1.5 total weighted score on their EFE Matrix. Why? Identify two companies that would have a 3.5 total weighted score on their EFE Matrix. Why?

7-8. Read and summarize Chapter 10's "Implications for Students," which emphasizes on gaining and sustaining competitive advantage as the overriding purpose of developing the EFE Matrix and the CPM.

7-9. List the 10 key external forces that give rise to opportunities and threats. Give a specific example of each force, for your college or university.

7-10. Give four reasons why you agree or do not agree with I/O theorists.

7-11. Regarding economic variables, list in order of importance six specific factors that you feel greatly impact your college or university.

7-12. Explain why U.S.-based firms, such as McDonald's, greatly benefit from a weak dollar.

7-13. Regarding social, cultural, demographic, and natural environment variables, list in order of importance six specific factors that you feel most greatly impact your college or university.

7-14. Regarding political, governmental, and legal variables, list in order of importance six specific factors that you feel most greatly impact your college or university.

7-15. Choose any four industries and explain how wireless technology is impacting four industries.

7-16. Discuss the pros and cons of gathering and assimilating competitive intelligence.

7-17. Using Porter's Five-Forces Model, explain competitiveness for a local fast food restaurant.

⭐ **7-18.** Identify an industry in which "bargaining power of suppliers" is the most important factor among Porter's variables.

7-19. Develop an EFE Matrix for your college or university.

7-20. Distinguish between ratings and weights in an EFE Matrix.

7-21. List 10 external trends or facts pertaining specifically to your country that would impact companies in your city.

7-22. Develop a CPM for a company that you or your parents have been employed.

⭐ **7-23.** Discuss the ethics of gathering competitive intelligence.

7-24. Discuss the ethics of cooperating with rival firms.

7-25. Contact your college library. Ask if they have the S&P Industry Surveys in hardcopy (or online) in the library. If they do, print out the relevant report for a company that you are familiar with.

7-26. Your boss develops an EFE Matrix that includes 54 factors. How would you suggest reducing the number of factors to 20?

7-27. List the 10 external areas that give rise to opportunities and threats. Give an example of each for IBM.

7-28. Compare the ratings in an EFE Matrix with those in a CPM in terms of meaning and definition.

7-29. Discuss the I/O view or approach to strategic planning.

7-30. List in order of importance what you feel are the six major advantages of a weak dollar for a U.S.-based firm.

⭐ **7-31.** List in order of importance what you feel are the six major advantages of a weak euro for a Europe-based firm headquartered in a country that has the euro as its currency.

⭐ **7-32.** Cooperating with competitors is becoming more common. What are the advantages and disadvantages of this for a company?

7-33. Regarding sources of external information, visit the www.finance.yahoo.com website and enter IBM; click on Headlines, and identify three major new initiatives the company has undertaken.

7-34. Differentiate between making assumptions and making wild guesses about future opportunities, and threats facing business firms.

7-35. Explain how the external assessment would, or should be different for non-profit organizations versus corporations.

7-36. Apply Porter's Five-Forces Model to IBM. What strategic implications arise in that analysis?

7-37. Compare and contrast competitive intelligence programs across several organizations that you are familiar with.

7-38. The value of the dollar was recently extremely high, a seven year high to the yen, a two-year high to the euro, and a five-year high to the Australian dollar. What impact does that have on Americans traveling abroad and foreigners traveling to the USA? Does the same analogous effect happen with your country's currency?

7-39. Should a company take a political stand against smoking, potentially losing millions of customers that smoke?

7-40. Global cybersecurity spending by critical infrastructure industries exceeds $50 billion annually, and is rising above 10 percent annually. Security is major concern for all businesses, yet complete security is something most businesses cannot financially afford to install. Discuss.

ASSURANCE OF LEARNING EXERCISES

EXERCISE 7A
Michelin and Africa: An External Assessment

Purpose
Michelin is featured in the opening chapter case as a firm that engages in excellent strategic planning. This exercise gives you practice conducting an external strategic management audit to determine if Africa is the new, best place for Michelin to produce and market products and services. For example, considerable underground mining occurs in much of Africa. The new MICHELIN XTXL tire is available in 25-inch for underground mining vehicles. The new tires offer enhanced safety and productivity and are available in sizes 26.5R25 and 29.5R25. Tests indicate that the new tires offer increases of 10 percent in longevity, 20 percent in puncture resistance, and 30 percent in load capacity.

Instructions
Step 1   Research the business climate in 10 African countries.

Step 2   Prepare an EFE Matrix for Michelin based solely on the opportunities and threats that Michelin will face in doing business in the 10 African countries you have chosen.

Step 3   Based on your research, list the 10 African countries you selected in rank order of attractiveness for Michelin to focus efforts upon. Give a one-sentence rationale for each country's ranking.

EXERCISE 7B
Preparing a CPM for Michelin Based on Countries Rather Than Companies

Purpose
Countries are similar to companies in that they compete with each other for investment dollars and economic development.

Instructions
Step 1   Revisit the research you collected and analyzed in the above exercise.

Step 2   Prepare a CPM that reveals your assessment of three African countries in terms of their relative strengths and weaknesses based on what you deem to be the most critical success factors.

EXERCISE 7C
Develop Divisional Michelin EFE Matrices

Purpose
Michelin has five major geographic divisions: Europe, North America, Asia, South America, and Africa/India/Middle-East. The company faces fierce but different competitors in each segment. The external opportunities and threats that Michelin faces are different in each geographic segment, so each segment prepares its own list of key external success factors. This external analysis is critically important in strategic planning because a firm needs to exploit opportunities and avoid or, at least, mitigate threats. The purpose of this exercise is to develop divisional EFE matrices that Michelin could use in developing an overall corporate EFE Matrix.

Instructions
Step 1   Go to the http://www.michelinman.com/US/en/homepage.html website. Review the company's most recent *Annual Report*.

Step 2   Determine and review Michelin's major geographic segments.

Step 3   Conduct research to determine what you believe are the four major threats and the four major opportunities critical to strategic planning within Michelin's geographic segments. Review the relevant *Standard and Poor's* Industry Survey documents for each segment.

Step 4   Develop divisional EFE Matrices for Michelin. Work within a team of students if your instructor so requests but you will need an EFE Matrix for each segment.

Step 5   Prioritize the 20 threats and the 20 opportunities developed in the prior step so that corporate Michelin top executives can better develop a corporate EFE Matrix.

Step 6   Let's say Michelin has their operations segmented by domestic versus global. Based on your research, prepare an EFE Matrix for Michelin's domestic operations and another EFE Matrix for Michelin's global Operations. Let Europe be domestic and all other regions be global.

EXERCISE 7D
Developing an EFE Matrix for Nestlé S.A.

Purpose
This exercise will provide practice developing an EFE Matrix. An EFE Matrix summarizes the results of an external audit. This is an important tool widely used by strategists.

Instructions
Step 1   Join with two other students in class and prepare an EFE Matrix for Nestlé. Refer back to the Cohesion Case and to Exercise 1B, if necessary, to identify external opportunities and threats. Use the information in the *Standard and Poor's* Industry Surveys that you copied as part of Assurance of Learning Exercise 1B. Be sure not to include strategies as opportunities, but do include as many monetary amounts, percentages, numbers, and ratios as possible.

Step 2   All three-person teams participating in this exercise should record their EFE total weighted scores on the board. Put your initials after your score to identify it as your teams.

Step 3   Compare the total weighted scores. Which team's score came closest to the instructor's answer? Discuss reasons for variation in the scores reported on the board.

EXERCISE 7E
The External Audit

Purpose
This exercise will help you become familiar with important sources of external information available in your college or university library. A key part of preparing an external audit is searching the Internet and examining published sources of information for relevant economic, social, cultural, demographic, environmental, political, governmental, legal, technological, and competitive trends and events. External opportunities and threats must be identified and evaluated before strategies can be formulated effectively.

Instructions

Step 1	Select a company or business from a country other than your own. Conduct an external audit for this company. Find opportunities and threats in recent issues of newspapers and magazines. Search for information using the Internet. Use the following websites: http://marketwatch.multexinvestor.com; www.hoovers.com; http://moneycentral.msn.com; http://finance.yahoo.com; www.clearstation.com; and https://us.etrade.com/e/t/invest/markets
Step 2	On a separate sheet of paper, list 10 opportunities and 10 threats that face this company. Be specific in stating each factor.
Step 3	Include a bibliography to reveal where you found the information.
Step 4	Write a three-page summary of your findings, and submit it to your instructor.

EXERCISE 7F
Develop a Competitive Profile Matrix for Michelin

Purpose
Monitoring competitors' performance and strategies is a key aspect of an external audit. This exercise is designed to give you practice evaluating the competitive position of organizations in a given industry and assimilating that information in a CPM.

Instructions

Step 1	Join with two other students in class and prepare an EFE Matrix for Nestlé. Refer back to the Cohesion Case and to Exercise 1B, if necessary, to identify external opportunities and threats. Use the information in the *Standard and Poor's* Industry Surveys that you copied as part of Assurance of Learning Exercise 1B. Be sure not to include strategies as opportunities, but do include as many monetary amounts, percentages, numbers, and ratios as possible.
Step 2	On a separate sheet of paper, prepare a CPM that includes Michelin and its two leading competitors: Bridgestone Corporation and Goodyear Tire and Rubber Company.
Step 3	Turn in your CPM for a class work grade.

EXERCISE 7G
Develop a Competitive Profile Matrix for Nestlé

Purpose
Monitoring competitors' performance and strategies is a key aspect of an external audit. This exercise is designed to give you practice evaluating the competitive position of organizations in a given industry and assimilating that information in the form of a CPM.

Instructions

Step 1	Gather information from Assurance of Learning Exercise 1B. Also, turn back to the Cohesion Case and review the section on competitors.
Step 2	On a separate sheet of paper, prepare a CPM that includes Mars and Mondelēz International
Step 3	Turn in your CPM for a class work grade.

EXERCISE 7H
Analyzing Your College or University's External Strategic Situation

Purpose
This exercise is excellent for doing together as a class.

Instructions

As a class, determine your college or university's major external opportunities and threats. List 10 opportunities and 10 threats. Then, get everyone in class to rank their factors with 1 being most important and 10 being least important. Then, gather up everyone's paper, count the numbers, and in that manner create a prioritized list of the key external opportunities and threats facing your college.

MINI-CASE ON WOOLWORTHS LIMITED (WOW)

IS WOOLWORTHS LOSING ITS EDGE TO ALDI?

Headquartered in Bella Vista, Australia, Woolworths Limited is the largest retail company in Australia and New Zealand, and the largest food retailer in both countries. The largest division is Woolworths Supermarkets (colloquially known as "Woolies"), a huge grocery store chain in Australia.

Woolworths Supermarkets, and rival Coles, form a near duopoly of Australian supermarkets, together accounting for about 80 percent of the Australian market. However, the expansion of discount supermarket chain Aldi, headquartered in Essen, Germany is gaining market share in Australia. Woolworths currently operates 872 stores across Australia. Woolworth's net profit for fiscal 2014 was $2.45 billion, and fiscal 2015 is to come in slightly lower than that number. However, Aldi has over 10,000 stores globally, including over 350 in Australia. Woolworth's CEO, Grant O'Brien, announced his retirement in mid-2015, so a global search is underway to find a replacement.

Source: © Elena Efimova. Shutterstock

Questions

1. Visit Woolworth's company website (http://www.woolworths.com.au) and evaluate their commitment to the natural environment.
2. Visit Aldi's website, www.aldi.com, and develop a competitive analysis for Woolworths as per what Aldi is doing and the extent to which Aldi is a threat in Australia. What can and should Woolworths do to combat the threat?

Source: Based on company documents.

Current Readings

Howard-Grenville, Jennifer, et al. "Climate Change and Management." *Academy of Management Journal* (June 2014): 615–641.

Kiron, David, et al. "How Serious Is Climate Change to Business?" *MIT Sloan Management Review* 55, no.1 (2013): 75–76.

Roberts, Carter. "Strategy Migration in a Changing Climate." *Harvard Business Review* 92, no. 5 (2014): 42.

Endnotes

1. Shelly Banjo and Paul Ziobro, "Shoppers Flee Physical Stores," *Wall Street Journal,* August 6, 2014, B1.
2. http://247wallst.com/special-report/2014/01/02/the-best-and-worst-run-cities-in-america-2/
3. http://wallethub.com/edu/best-worst-states-to-be-a-taxpayer/2416/#complete-rankings
4. Pete Barlas, "Cisco Systems Dart into Data Analytics," *Wall Street Journal,* December 11, 2014, A5.
5. Saabira Chaudhuri, "Banks Leave More Branches," *Wall Street Journal,* January 28, 2014, C1.
6. Roger Yu, "Online Rep Crucial for Small Companies," *USA Today,* October 30, 2012, 5B.
7. Danny Yadron, "Companies Wrestle with the Cost of Security," *Wall Street Journal,* February 26, 2014, B3.
8. Bill Saporito, "Companies That Compete Best," *Fortune* (May 22, 1989): 36.
9. http://www.fuld.com/what-is-competitive-intelligence
10. John Prescott and Daniel Smith, "The Largest Survey of 'Leading-Edge' Competitor Intelligence Managers," *Planning Review* 17, no. 3 (May–June 1989): 6–13.
11. Arthur Thompson, Jr., A. J. Strickland III, and John Gamble, *Crafting and Executing Strategy: Text and Readings* (New York: McGraw-Hill/Irwin, 2005): 63.
12. Michael E. Porter, *Competitive Strategy: Techniques for Analyzing Industries and Competitors* (New York: Free Press, 1980): 24–27.
13. Dale McConkey, "Planning in a Changing Environment," *Business Horizons* 31, no. 5 (September–October 1988): 67.
14. James Willhite, "Getting Started in 'Big Data,'" *Wall Street Journal*, February 4, 2014, B7.

Source: © motorlka/Fotolia

Strategy Generation and Selection

LEARNING OBJECTIVES

After studying this chapter, you should be able to do the following:

8-1. Describe the strategy analysis and choice process.

8-2. Diagram and explain the three-stage strategy-formulation analytical framework.

8-3. Diagram and explain the Strengths-Weaknesses-Opportunities-Threats (SWOT) Matrix.

8-4. Diagram and explain the Strategic Position and Action Evaluation (SPACE) Matrix.

8-5. Diagram and explain the Boston Consulting Group (BCG) Matrix.

8-6. Diagram and explain the Internal-External (IE) Matrix.

8-7. Diagram and explain the Grand Strategy Matrix.

8-8. Diagram and explain the Quantitative Strategic Planning Matrix (QSPM).

8-9. Discuss the role of organizational culture in strategic analysis and choice.

8-10. Identify and discuss important political considerations in strategy analysis and choice.

8-11. Discuss the role of a board of directors (governance) in strategic planning.

ASSURANCE OF LEARNING EXERCISES

The following exercises are found at the end of this chapter:

EXERCISE 8A	Should Unilever Penetrate Southeast Asia Further?
EXERCISE 8B	Perform a SWOT Analysis for Unilever's Global Operations
EXERCISE 8C	Prepare a BCG Matrix for Unilever
EXERCISE 8D	Develop a SWOT Matrix for Nestlé S.A.
EXERCISE 8E	Develop a SPACE Matrix for Nestlé S.A.
EXERCISE 8F	Develop a BCG Matrix for Nestlé S.A.
EXERCISE 8G	Develop a QSPM for Nestlé S.A.
EXERCISE 8H	Develop a SPACE Matrix for Unilever
EXERCISE 8I	Develop a BCG Matrix for Your College or University
EXERCISE 8J	Develop a QSPM for a Company That You Are Familiar With
EXERCISE 8K	Formulate Individual Strategies

S trategy analysis and choice largely involve making subjective decisions based on objective information. This chapter introduces important concepts that can help strategists generate feasible alternatives, evaluate those alternatives, and choose a specific course of action. Behavioral aspects of strategy formulation are featured, including politics, culture, ethics, and social responsibility considerations. Modern tools for formulating strategies are described, and the appropriate role of a board of directors is discussed. As showcased next, Unilever Plc launched the Unilever Sustainable Living Plan, a part of the company's larger goal to double the size of its business while reducing our environmental footprint, and increasing its positive social impact.

The Strategy Analysis and Choice Process

As indicated by Figure 8-1 with white shading, this chapter focuses on generating and evaluating alternative strategies, as well as selecting strategies to pursue. Strategy analysis and choice seek to determine alternative courses of action that could best enable the firm to achieve its mission and objectives. The firm's present strategies, objectives, vision, and mission, coupled with the external and internal audit information, provide a basis for generating and evaluating feasible alternative strategies. This systematic approach is the best way to avoid an organizational crisis. Rudin's Law states, "When a crisis forces choosing among alternatives, most people choose the worst possible one."

Unless a desperate situation confronts the firm, alternative strategies will likely represent incremental steps that move the firm from its present position to a desired future position. Alternative strategies do not come out of the wild blue yonder; they are derived from the firm's vision, mission, objectives, external audit, and internal audit; they are consistent with, or build on, past strategies that have worked well.

The Process of Generating and Selecting Strategies

Strategists never consider all feasible alternatives that could benefit the firm because there are an infinite number of possible actions and an infinite number of ways to implement those actions. Therefore, a manageable set of the most attractive alternative strategies must be developed, examined, prioritized, and selected. The advantages, disadvantages, trade-offs, costs, and benefits of these strategies should be determined. This section discusses the process that many

EXEMPLARY COMPANY SHOWCASED

Unilever Plc (UL)

The Anglo–Dutch Unilever is the world's third-largest consumer goods company behind Procter & Gamble and Nestlé, offering a product portfolio that ranges from food and beverages to personal care products. While operating as a single business entity and under the same directors, Unilever is a dual listed company comprising Unilever N.V. based in Rotterdam, Netherlands, and Unilever Plc, London. Of its 450 brands, some of Unilever's best selling products include Aviance, Ben & Jerry's, Dove, Knorr, Lipton, Heartbrand ice creams, Hellmann's, Sunsilk, and PG Tips. In an effort to help the marine environment, the use of microplastics in all personal care products was phased out by Unilever. Their strategies focus on sustainable and ethical activities.

After selling selling its Slim-Fast brand to Kainos Capital, Unilever recently acquired Talenti Gelato & Sorbetto, a Minneapolis-based packaged gelato company in the United States. Unilever acquired Procter & Gamble's Zest brand outside of North America and the Caribbean, and it also acquired Camay and its global operations, which resulted in $225 million turnover for Unilever in the most recent fiscal year.

For the fourth year in a row, Unilever received an 'A' for Performance by global NGO CDP (formally the Carbon Disclosure Project) and was included in 'The A List: The CDP Climate Performance Leadership Index 2015' (CPLI). The company also achieved the maximum disclosure score of 100, up from 99 in 2014 and 85 in 2013. Only 11 companies received an 'A' in the Consumer Staples sector, and only 113 (5%) participating companies have ever been awarded an 'A' Performance Band rating. Also, Unilever was recently included among CDP's elite UK FTSE 350 Climate Performance Leadership companies. Unilever's Chief Sustainability Officer, Jeff Seabright, was featured in a short film marking the release of the CDP Climate 2015 results.

Source: Based on company documents.

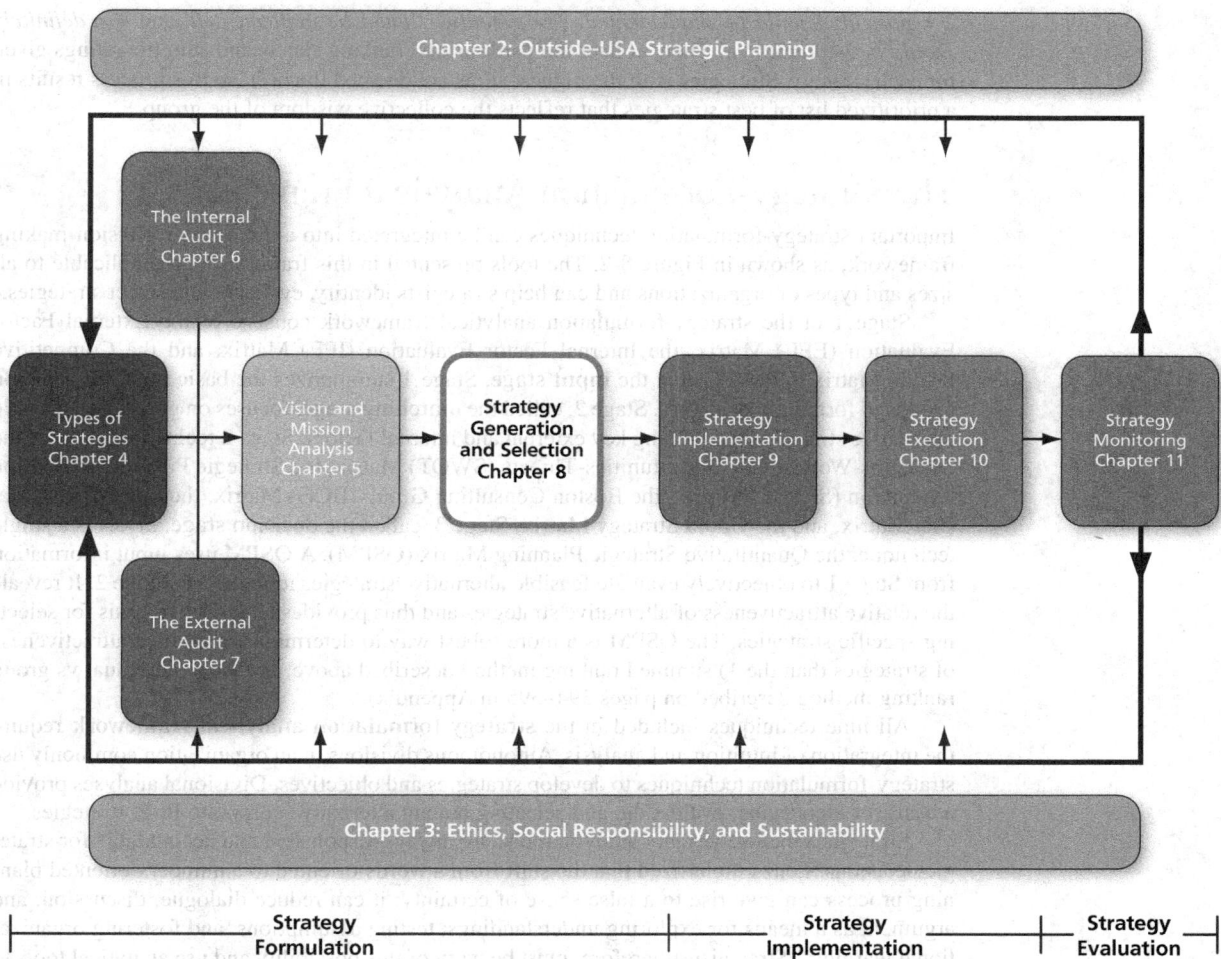

FIGURE 8-1

A Comprehensive Strategic-Management Model

Source: Fred R. David, adapted from "How Companies Define Their Mission," *Long Range Planning* 22, no. 3 (June 1988): 40, © Fred R. David.

firms use to determine an appropriate set of alternative strategies. Recommendations (strategies selected to pursue) come from alternative strategies formulated.

Identifying and evaluating alternative strategies should involve many of the managers and employees who previously assembled the organizational vision and mission statements, performed the external audit, and conducted the internal audit. Representatives from each department and division of the firm should be included in this process, as was the case in previous strategy-formulation activities. Involvement provides the best opportunity for managers and employees to gain an understanding of what the firm is doing and why and to become committed to helping the firm accomplish its objectives.

All participants in the strategy analysis and choice activity should have the firm's external and internal audit information available. This information, coupled with the firm's vision and mission statements, will help participants crystallize in their own minds particular strategies that they believe could benefit the firm most. Creativity should be encouraged in this thought process.

Alternative strategies proposed by participants should be considered and discussed in a meeting or series of meetings. Proposed strategies should be listed in writing. When all feasible strategies identified by participants are given and understood, the strategies should be individually ranked in order of attractiveness by each participant, with 1 = *should not be implemented*,

2 = *possibly should be implemented*, 3 = *probably should be implemented*, and 4 = *definitely should be implemented*. Then, collect the participants' ranking sheets and sum the ratings given for each strategy. Strategies with the highest sums are deemed the best, so this process results in a prioritized list of best strategies that reflects the collective wisdom of the group.

The Strategy-Formulation Analytical Framework

Important strategy-formulation techniques can be integrated into a three-stage decision-making framework, as shown in Figure 8-2. The tools presented in this framework are applicable to all sizes and types of organizations and can help strategists identify, evaluate, and select strategies.

Stage 1 of the strategy-formulation analytical framework consists of the External Factor Evaluation (EFE) Matrix, the Internal Factor Evaluation (IFE) Matrix, and the Competitive Profile Matrix (CPM). Called the **input stage**, Stage 1 summarizes the basic input information needed to formulate strategies. Stage 2, called the **matching stage**, focuses on generating feasible alternative strategies by aligning key external and internal factors. Stage 2 techniques include the Strengths-Weaknesses-Opportunities-Threats (SWOT) Matrix, the Strategic Position and Action Evaluation (SPACE) Matrix, the Boston Consulting Group (BCG) Matrix, the Internal-External (IE) Matrix, and the Grand Strategy Matrix. Stage 3, called the **decision stage**, involves a single technique, the Quantitative Strategic Planning Matrix (QSPM). A QSPM uses input information from Stage 1 to objectively evaluate feasible alternative strategies identified in Stage 2. It reveals the relative attractiveness of alternative strategies and thus provides an objective basis for selecting specific strategies. The QSPM is a more robust way to determine the relative attractiveness of strategies than the 1) summed ranking method described above, or the 2) individual vs group ranking method described on pages 394–395 in Appendix).

All nine techniques included in the **strategy-formulation analytical framework** require the integration of intuition and analysis. Autonomous divisions in an organization commonly use strategy-formulation techniques to develop strategies and objectives. Divisional analyses provide a basis for identifying, evaluating, and selecting among alternative corporate-level strategies.

Strategists themselves, not analytic tools, are always responsible and accountable for strategic decisions. Lenz emphasized that the shift from a words-oriented to a numbers-oriented planning process can give rise to a false sense of certainty; it can reduce dialogue, discussion, and argument as a means for exploring understandings, testing assumptions, and fostering organizational learning.[1] Strategists, therefore, must be wary of this possibility and use analytical tools to facilitate, rather than to diminish, communication. Without objective information and analysis, personal biases, politics, prejudices, emotions, personalities, and halo error (the tendency to put too much weight on a single factor) oftentimes play a dominant role in the strategy-formulation process, undermining effectiveness. Thus, an analytical approach is essential for achieving maximum effectiveness in strategic planning.

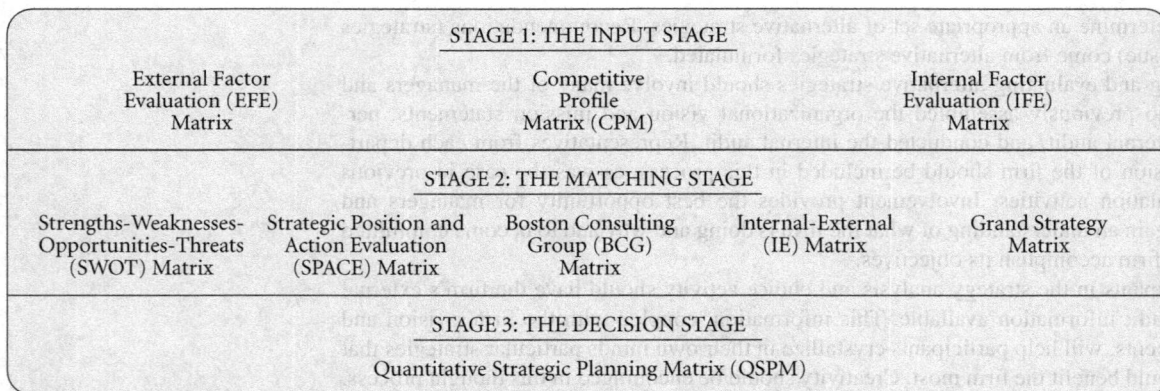

STAGE 1: THE INPUT STAGE		
External Factor Evaluation (EFE) Matrix	Competitive Profile Matrix (CPM)	Internal Factor Evaluation (IFE) Matrix

STAGE 2: THE MATCHING STAGE				
Strengths-Weaknesses-Opportunities-Threats (SWOT) Matrix	Strategic Position and Action Evaluation (SPACE) Matrix	Boston Consulting Group (BCG) Matrix	Internal-External (IE) Matrix	Grand Strategy Matrix

STAGE 3: THE DECISION STAGE
Quantitative Strategic Planning Matrix (QSPM)

FIGURE 8-2
The Strategy-Formulation Analytical Framework

The Input Stage

Procedures for developing an EFE Matrix, an IFE Matrix, and a CPM were presented in Chapters 6 and 7. Information derived from the EFE Matrix, IFE Matrix, and CPM provides basic input information for the matching and decision stage matrices described in this chapter.

The input tools require strategists to quantify subjectivity during early stages of the strategy-formulation process. Making small decisions in the input matrices regarding the relative importance of external and internal factors allows strategists to more effectively generate, prioritize, evaluate, and select among alternative strategies. Good intuitive judgment is always needed in determining appropriate weights and ratings, but keep in mind that a rating of 3, for example, is mathematically 50 percent more important than with a rating of 2, so small differences matter.

The Matching Stage

Strategy is sometimes defined as the match an organization makes between its internal resources and skills and the opportunities and risks created by its external factors.[2] The matching stage of the strategy-formulation framework consists of five techniques that can be used in any sequence: the SWOT Matrix, the SPACE Matrix, the BCG Matrix, the IE Matrix, and the Grand Strategy Matrix. These tools rely on information derived from the input stage to match external opportunities and threats with internal strengths and weaknesses. **Matching** external and internal key factors is the essential for effectively generating feasible alternative strategies. For example, a firm with excess working capital (an internal strength) could take advantage of the cell phone industry's 20 percent annual growth rate (an external opportunity) by acquiring Cellfone, Inc. This example portrays simple one-to-one matching. In most situations, external and internal relationships are more complex, and the matching requires multiple alignments for each strategy generated. Successful matching of key external and internal factors depends on those underlying key factors being *specific, actionable, and divisional* to the extent possible. The basic concept of matching is illustrated in Table 8-1.

The Decision Stage

As indicated above, participants could individually rate strategies on a 1-to-4 scale as to desirability, and then sum the ratings from all participants, so that a prioritized list of the best strategies could be achieved. However, the QSPM, described later in this chapter, offers a more robust procedure to determine the relative attractiveness of alternative strategies.

The SWOT Matrix

The **Strengths-Weaknesses-Opportunities-Threats (SWOT) Matrix** is an important matching tool that helps managers develop four types of strategies: SO (strengths-opportunities) strategies, WO (weaknesses-opportunities) strategies, ST (strengths-threats) strategies, and WT (weaknesses-threats) strategies.[3] Matching key external and internal factors is the most difficult part of developing a SWOT Matrix, as it requires good judgment—and there is no one best set of matches. Note in Table 8-1 that the first, second, third, and fourth strategies are SO, WO, ST, and WT strategies, respectively.

SO strategies use a firm's internal strengths to take advantage of external opportunities. All managers would like their organization to be in a position in which internal strengths can be used to take advantage of external trends and events. Organizations generally will pursue WO, ST,

TABLE 8-1 Matching Key External and Internal Factors to Formulate Alternative Strategies

Key Internal Factor	Key External Factor	Resultant Strategy
Excess working capital (an internal strength)	+ Annual growth of 20 percent in the cell phone industry (an external opportunity)	= Acquire Cellfone, Inc.
Insufficient capacity (an internal weakness)	+ Exit of two major foreign competitors from the industry (an external opportunity)	= Pursue horizontal integration by buying competitors' facilities
Strong research and development expertise (an internal strength)	+ Decreasing numbers of younger adults (an external threat)	= Develop new products for older adults
Poor employee morale (an internal weakness)	+ Rising health-care costs (an external threat)	= Develop a new wellness program

or WT strategies to get into a situation in which they can apply SO strategies. When a firm has major weaknesses, it will strive to overcome them and make them strengths. When an organization faces major threats, it will seek to avoid them to concentrate on opportunities.

WO strategies aim at improving internal weaknesses by taking advantage of external opportunities. Sometimes key external opportunities exist, but a firm has internal weaknesses that prevent it from exploiting those opportunities. For example, there may be a high demand for electronic devices to control the amount and timing of fuel injection in automobile engines (opportunity), but a certain auto parts manufacturer may lack the technology required for producing these devices (weakness). One possible WO strategy would be to acquire this technology by forming a joint venture with a firm having competency in this area. An alternative WO strategy would be to hire and train people with the required technical capabilities.

ST strategies use a firm's strengths to avoid or reduce the impact of external threats. This does not mean that a strong organization should always meet threats in the external environment head-on. An example ST strategy occurred when Texas Instruments used an excellent legal department (a strength) to collect nearly $700 million in damages and royalties from nine Japanese and Korean firms that infringed on patents for semiconductor memory chips (threat). Rival firms that copy ideas, innovations, and patented products are a threat in many industries.

WT strategies are defensive tactics directed at reducing internal weakness and avoiding external threats. An organization faced with numerous external threats and internal weaknesses may indeed be in a precarious position. In fact, such a firm may have to fight for its survival, merge, retrench, declare bankruptcy, or choose liquidation.

A schematic representation of the SWOT Matrix is provided in Figure 8-3. Note that a SWOT Matrix is composed of nine cells. As shown, there are four key factor cells, four strategy cells, and one cell that is always left blank (the upper-left cell). The four strategy cells, labeled *SO*, *WO*, *ST*, and *WT*, are developed after completing four key factor cells, labeled *S*, *W*, *O*, and *T*. The process of constructing a SWOT Matrix can be summarized in eight steps, as follows:

1. List the firm's key external opportunities.
2. List the firm's key external threats.
3. List the firm's key internal strengths.
4. List the firm's key internal weaknesses.
5. Match internal strengths with external opportunities, and record the resultant SO strategies in the appropriate cell.
6. Match internal weaknesses with external opportunities, and record the resultant WO strategies.
7. Match internal strengths with external threats, and record the resultant ST strategies.
8. Match internal weaknesses with external threats, and record the resultant WT strategies.

Some important aspects of a SWOT Matrix are evidenced in Figure 8-3. For example, note that both the internal and external factors and the SO, ST, WO, and WT strategies are stated in quantitative terms. This is important! For example, regarding the second SO number 2 and ST number 1 strategies, if the analyst just said, "Add new repair and service persons," the reader might think that 20 new repair and service persons are needed. Actually only 2 are needed. So, with strategies, as with the underlying key external and internal factors, *be specific, actionable, and divisional* to the extent possible.

It is also important to include the "S1, O2" type notation after each strategy in a SWOT Matrix. This notation reveals the rationale for each alternative strategy. Strategies do not appear out of the blue. Note in Figure 8-3 how this notation reveals the internal and external factors that were matched to formulate desirable strategies. For example, note that this retail computer store business may need to "purchase land to build new store" because a new Highway 34 will make its location less desirable. The notation (W2, O2) and (S8, T3) in Figure 8-3 exemplifies this matching process.

The purpose of SWOT analysis and each Stage 2 matching tool is to generate feasible alternative strategies, not to select or determine which strategies are best. Not all of the strategies developed in the SWOT Matrix will be selected for implementation. No firm has sufficient capital or resources to implement every strategy formulated.

The strategy-formulation guidelines provided in Chapter 4 can enhance the process of matching key external and internal factors. For example, when an organization has both the capital and human resources needed to distribute its own products (internal strength) and distributors are unreliable, costly, or incapable of meeting the firm's needs (external threat), forward integration can be an attractive ST strategy. When a firm has excess production capacity (internal weakness)

	Strengths	Weaknesses
	1. Inventory turnover up 5.8 to 6.7	1. Software revenues in store down 12 percent
	2. Average customer purchase up $97 to $128	2. Location of store hurt by new Hwy 34
	3. Employee morale is excellent	3. Carpet and paint in store in disrepair
	4. In-store promotions = 20 percent increase in sales	4. Bathroom in store needs refurbishing
	5. Newspaper advertising expenditures down 10 percent	5. Total store revenues down 8 percent
	6. Revenues from repair and service in store up 16 percent	6. Store has no website
	7. In-store technical support persons have MIS degrees	7. Supplier on-time-delivery up to 2.4 days
	8. Store's debt-to-total-assets ratio down 34 percent	8. Customer checkout process too slow
		9. Revenues per employee up 19 percent
Opportunities	**WO Strategies**	**WO Strategies**
1. Population of city growing 10 percent	1. Add four new in-store promotions monthly (S4, O3)	1. Purchase land to build new store (W2, O2)
2. Rival computer store opening one mile away	2. Add two new repair and service persons (S6, O5)	2. Install new carpet, paint, and bath (W3, W4, O1)
3. Vehicle traffic passing store up 12 percent	3. Send flyer to all seniors over age 55 (S5, O5)	3. Up website services by 50 percent (W6, O7, O8)
4. Vendors average six new products a year		4. Launch mailout to all realtors in city (W5, O7)
5. Senior citizen use of computers up 8 percent		
6. Small business growth in area up 10 percent		
7. Desire for websites up 18 percent by realtors		
8. Desire for websites up 12 percent by small firms		
Threats	**ST Strategies**	**WT Strategies**
1. Best Buy opening new store in one year nearby	1. Hire two more repair persons and market these new services (S6, S7, T1)	1. Hire two new cashiers (W8, T1, T4)
2. Local university offers computer repair	2. Purchase land to build new store (S8, T3)	2. Install new carpet, paint, and bath (W3, W4, T1)
3. New bypass Hwy 34 in 1 year will divert traffic	3. Raise out-of-store service calls from $60 to $80 (S6, T5)	
4. New mall being built nearby		
5. Gas prices up 14 percent		
6. Vendors raising prices 8 percent		

FIGURE 8-3

A SWOT Matrix for a Retail Computer Store

and its basic industry is experiencing declining annual sales and profits (external threat), related diversification can be an effective WT strategy.

Although the SWOT Matrix is widely used in strategic planning, the analysis does have some limitations.[4] First, SWOT does not show how to achieve a competitive advantage, so it must not be an end in itself. The matrix should be the starting point for a discussion on how proposed strategies could be implemented as well as cost/benefit considerations that ultimately could lead to competitive advantage. Second, SWOT is a static assessment (or snapshot) in time. A SWOT Matrix can be like studying a single frame of a motion picture where you see the lead characters and the setting but have no clue as to the plot. As circumstances, capabilities, threats, and strategies change, the dynamics of a competitive environment may not be revealed in a single matrix. Third, SWOT analysis may lead the firm to overemphasize a single internal or external factor in formulating strategies. There are interrelationships among the key internal and external factors that SWOT does not reveal that may be important in devising strategies. Fourth, there are no weights, ratings, or numbers in a SWOT analysis. Finally, the relative attractiveness of alternative strategies is not provided.

The Strategic Position and Action Evaluation (SPACE) Matrix

The **Strategic Position and Action Evaluation (SPACE) Matrix**, another important Stage 2 matching tool, is illustrated in Figure 8-4. Its four-quadrant framework indicates whether aggressive, conservative, defensive, or competitive strategies are most appropriate for a given organization. The axes of the SPACE Matrix represent two internal dimensions (**financial position [FP]** and **competitive position [CP]**) and two external dimensions (**stability position [SP]** and **industry position [IP]**). These four factors are perhaps the most important determinants of an organization's overall strategic position.[5]

It is helpful here to elaborate on the difference between the SP and IP axes. The term *SP* refers to the volatility of profits and revenues for firms in a given industry. Thus, SP volatility (stability) is based on the expected impact of changes in core external factors such as technology, economy, demographic, seasonality, and so on. The higher the frequency and magnitude of changes in a given industry, the more unstable the SP becomes. An industry can be stable or unstable on SP, yet high or low on IP. The smartphone industry, for instance, would be unstable (–6 or –7) on SP yet high growth on IP, whereas the canned food industry would be stable (–1 or –2) on SP yet low growth on IP.

Depending on the type of organization, numerous variables could make up each of the dimensions represented on the axes of the SPACE Matrix. Factors that were included in the firm's EFE

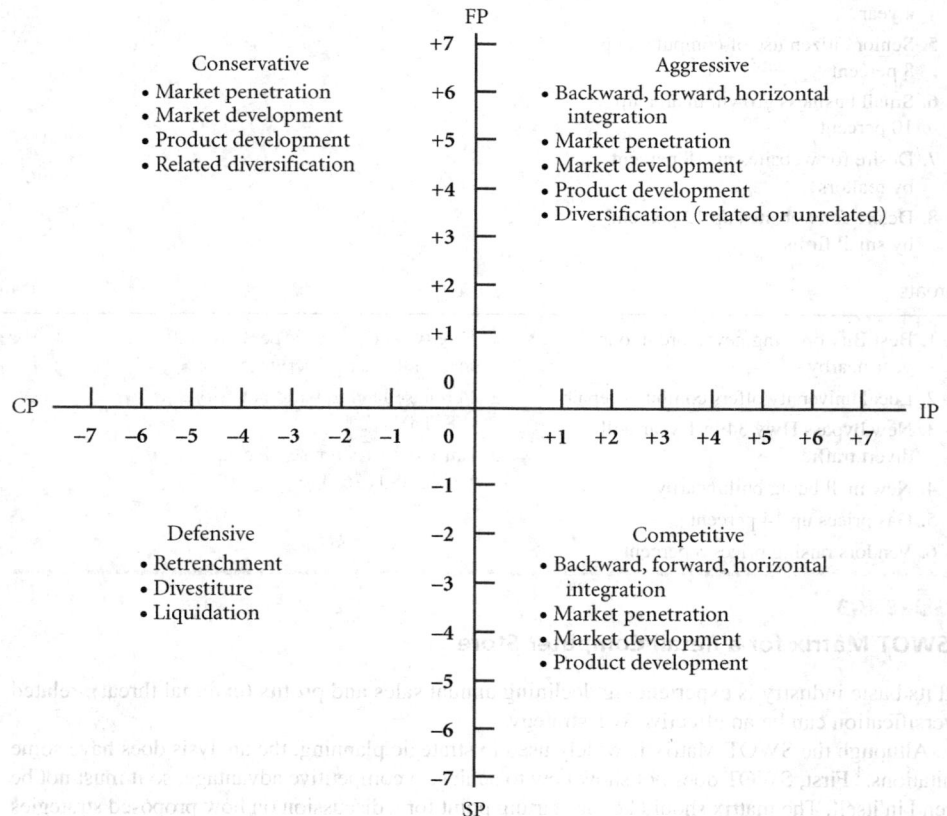

FIGURE 8-4
The SPACE Matrix

Source: Based on H. Rowe, R. Mason, and K. Dickel, *Strategic Management and Business Policy: A Methodological Approach* (Reading, MA: Addison-Wesley Publishing Co. Inc., © 1982), 155.

and IFE Matrices should be considered in developing a SPACE Matrix. Other variables commonly included are given in Table 8-2. For example, return on investment, leverage, liquidity, working capital, and cash flow are commonly considered to be determining factors of an organization's financial position (FP). Like the SWOT Matrix, the SPACE Matrix should be both tailored to the particular organization being studied and based on factual information to the extent possible.

The process of developing a SPACE Matrix can be summarized in six steps, as follows:

1. Select a set of variables to define financial position (FP), competitive position (CP), stability position (SP), and industry position (IP).
2. Assign a numerical value ranging from +1 (worst) to +7 (best) to each of the variables that make up the FP and IP dimensions. Assign a numerical value ranging from –1 (best) to –7 (worst) to each of the variables that make up the SP and CP dimensions. On the FP and CP axes, make comparisons to competitors. On the IP and SP axes, make comparisons to other industries. On the SP axis, know that a –7 denotes highly unstable industry conditions, whereas –1 denotes highly stable.
3. Compute an average score for FP, CP, IP, and SP by summing the values given to the variables of each dimension and then by dividing by the number of variables included in the respective dimension.
4. Plot the average scores for FP, IP, SP, and CP on the appropriate axis in the SPACE Matrix.
5. Add the two scores on the x-axis and plot the resultant point on X. Add the two scores on the y-axis and plot the resultant point on Y. Plot the intersection of the new (x, y) coordinate.
6. Draw a **directional vector** from the origin of the SPACE Matrix (0,0) through the new (x, y) coordinate. That vector, being located in a particular quadrant, reveals particular strategies the organization should consider.

Some example strategy profiles that can emerge from SPACE analysis are shown in Figure 8-5. The directional vector associated with each profile suggests the type of strategies to pursue: aggressive, conservative, defensive, or competitive. Specifically, when a firm's directional vector is located in the **Aggressive Quadrant** (upper right) of the SPACE Matrix, an organization is in an excellent position to use its internal strengths to (1) take advantage of external opportunities, (2) overcome internal weaknesses, and (3) avoid external threats. Therefore, market penetration, market

TABLE 8-2 Example Factors That Make Up the SPACE Matrix Axes

Internal Strategic Position	External Strategic Position
Financial Position (FP)	*Stability Position (SP)*
Return on investment	Technological changes
Leverage	Rate of inflation
Liquidity	Demand variability
Working capital	Price range of competing products
Cash flow	Barriers to entry into market
Inventory turnover	Competitive pressure
Earnings per share	Ease of exit from market
Price earnings ratio	Risk involved in business
Competitive Position (CP)	*Industry Position (IP)*
Market share	Growth potential
Product quality	Profit potential
Product life cycle	Financial stability
Customer loyalty	Extent leveraged
Capacity utilization	Resource utilization
Technological know-how	Ease of entry into market
Control over suppliers and distributors	Productivity, capacity utilization

Source: Based on H. Rowe, R. Mason, & K. Dickel, *Strategic Management and Business Policy: A Methodological Approach* (Reading, MA: Addison-Wesley Publishing Co. Inc., © 1982), 155–156.

development, product development, backward integration, forward integration, horizontal integration, or diversification, can be feasible, depending on the specific circumstances that face the firm.

When a particular company is known, the analyst must be much more specific in terms of recommended strategies. For example, instead of saying market penetration is a recommended

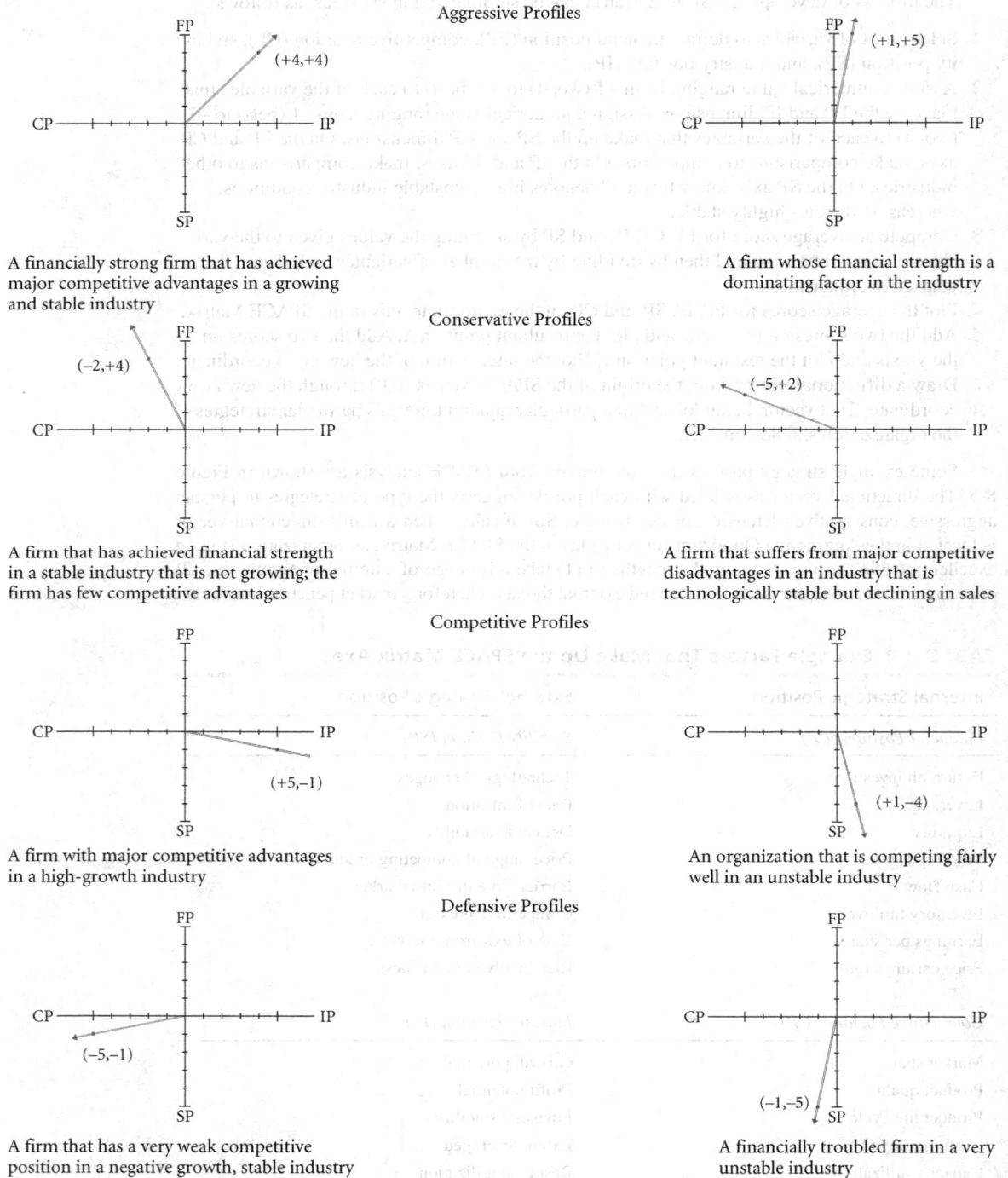

Aggressive Profiles

A financially strong firm that has achieved major competitive advantages in a growing and stable industry

A firm whose financial strength is a dominating factor in the industry

Conservative Profiles

A firm that has achieved financial strength in a stable industry that is not growing; the firm has few competitive advantages

A firm that suffers from major competitive disadvantages in an industry that is technologically stable but declining in sales

Competitive Profiles

A firm with major competitive advantages in a high-growth industry

An organization that is competing fairly well in an unstable industry

Defensive Profiles

A firm that has a very weak competitive position in a negative growth, stable industry

A financially troubled firm in a very unstable industry

FIGURE 8-5

Example Strategy Profiles

Source: Based on H. Rowe, R. Mason, and K. Dickel, *Strategic Management and Business Policy: A Methodological Approach* (Reading, MA: Addison-Wesley Publishing Co. Inc., © 1982), 155.

strategy when your vector is located in the Conservative Quadrant, say that adding 34 new stores in India is a recommended strategy. This is an important point for students doing case analyses because whenever a particular company is known, then terms such as *market development* are too vague to use. That term could refer to adding a manufacturing plant in Thailand or Mexico or South Africa. Thus, be *specific* to the extent possible regarding implications of all the matrices presented herein this chapter. Vagueness can be disastrous in strategic management. Avoid terms such as *expand, increase, decrease,* and *grow*—be more specific than that! *Reveal how your proposed strategies could enable your company to rotate/shift its SPACE vector more toward the Aggressive Quadrant.*

The directional vector may appear in the **Conservative Quadrant** (upper left) of the SPACE Matrix, which implies staying close to the firm's basic competencies and not taking excessive risks. Conservative strategies most often include market penetration, market development, product development, and related diversification. The directional vector may be located in the **Defensive Quadrant** (lower left) of the SPACE Matrix, which suggests the firm should focus on improving internal weaknesses and avoiding external threats. Defensive strategies include retrenchment, divestiture, liquidation, and related diversification. Finally, the directional vector may be located in the **Competitive Quadrant** (lower right) of the SPACE Matrix, indicating competitive strategies. Competitive strategies include backward, forward, and horizontal integration; market penetration; market development; and product development.

Note that a SPACE Matrix has some limitations:

1. It is a snapshot in time.
2. There are more than four dimensions that firms could/should be rated on.
3. The directional vector could fall directly on an axis, or could even go nowhere if the coordinate is (0,0).
4. Implications of the exact angle of the vector within a quadrant are unclear.
5. The relative attractiveness of alternative strategies generated is unclear.
6. Key underlying internal and external factors are not explicitly considered.

A SPACE Matrix for Domino's Pizza, Inc. is provided in Figure 8-6. Note the SPACE vector for Domino's is located in the Competitive Quadrant (lower right), based primarily on

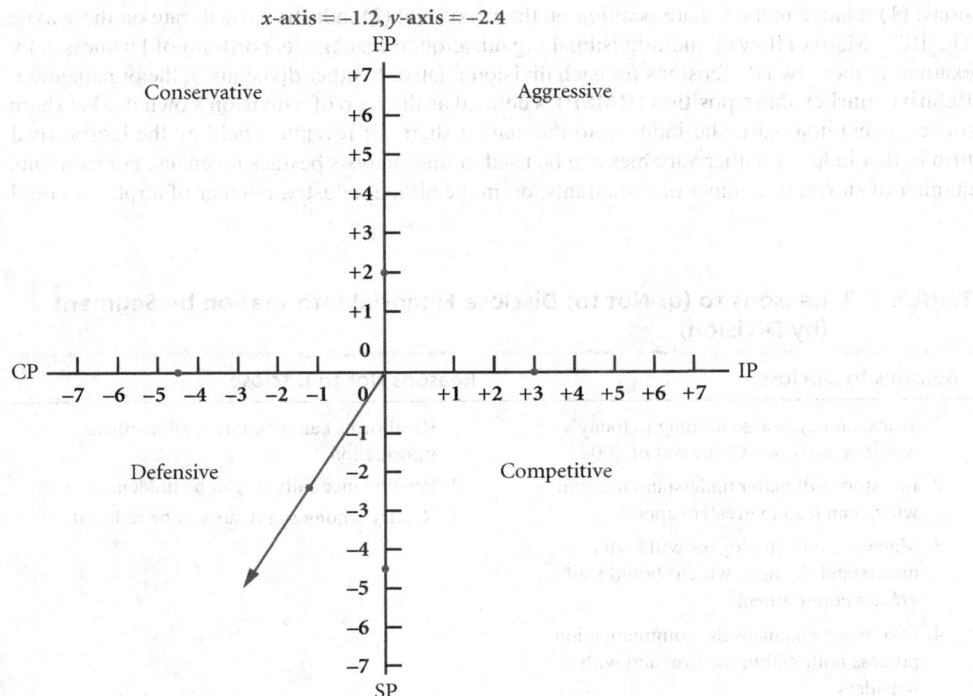

FIGURE 8-6
A SPACE Matrix for Domino's Pizza

three factors: (1) the company's $1.5 billion in long-term debt, (2) intense competition within the fast-food industry, and (3) offering products that are generally not a healthy food choice. Domino's should consider adding a line of salads to their menu to shift the SPACE vector into the Aggressive Quadrant (upper right); adding salads would likely benefit Domino's financially, thus moving the SPACE point on the vertical (y-axis) up.

In performing strategic-management case analysis, prepare the SPACE Matrix (and all matrices) based on the point in time of your analysis rather than a desired future point in time. However, in your discussion of implications, be sure to comment on what you recommend the firm should do to improve its situation. Focus more on implications of matrices than on "number crunching" in your actual oral delivery of a case analysis.

The Boston Consulting Group (BCG) Matrix

Based in Boston and having 6,200 consultants worldwide, the Boston Consulting Group (BCG) has 87 offices in 45 countries, and annually ranks in the top five of *Fortune*'s list of the "100 Best Companies to Work For." The Boston Consulting Group is a private management consulting firm that specializes in strategic planning.

Autonomous divisions (also called *segments* or *profit centers*) of an organization make up what is called a **business portfolio**. When a firm's divisions compete in different industries, a separate strategy often must be developed for each business. The **Boston Consulting Group (BCG) Matrix** and the Internal-External (IE) Matrix are designed specifically to enhance a multidivisional firm's efforts to formulate strategies. Allocating resources across divisions is arguably the most important strategic decision facing multidivisional firms. Multidivisional firms range in size from small, three-restaurant, mom-and-pop firms, to huge conglomerates such as Walt Disney Company, to universities that have various schools or colleges—and they all need to use portfolio analysis.

In a *Form 10K* or *Annual Report*, some companies do not disclose financial information by segment, in which case a BCG portfolio analysis may not be possible by persons external to the firm. However, reasons to disclose by segment financial information in a *Form 10K* more than offset the reasons not to disclose, as indicated in Table 8-3.

The BCG Matrix graphically portrays differences among divisions based on two dimensions: (1) relative market share position on the x-axis and (2) industry growth rate on the y-axis. The BCG Matrix allows a multidivisional organization to manage its portfolio of businesses by examining these two dimensions for each division relative to other divisions in the organization. **Relative market share position (RMSP)** is defined as the ratio of a division's own market share (or revenues) in a particular industry to the market share (or revenues) held by the largest rival firm in that industry. Other variables can be used in this analysis besides revenues. For example, number of stores, or number of restaurants, or, in the airline industry, number of airplanes could

TABLE 8-3 Reasons to (or Not to) Disclose Financial Information by Segment (by Division)

Reasons to Disclose	Reasons Not to Disclose
1. Transparency is a good thing in today's world of Sarbanes-Oxley Act of 2002.	1. Rival firms can obtain free competitive information.
2. Investors will better understand the firm, which can lead to greater support.	2. Performance failures can be hidden.
3. Managers and employees will better understand the firm, which should lead to greater commitment.	3. Rivalry among segments can be reduced.
4. Disclosure enhances the communication process both within the firm and with outsiders.	

TABLE 8-4 Current Market Share Data for Cigarette and Beer Brands

What Percentage of People Smoke What Cigarette Brands in the USA?		What Beer Brands Annually Sell the Most Million Barrels in the USA?	
Marlboro	40.2 %	Bud Light	381
Newport	12.2	Coors Light	182
Pall Mall	8.1	Budweiser	160
Camel	8.1	Miller Lite	137
Winston	2.4	Corona Extra	74
Pyramid	2.3	Samuel Adams	23
Doral	2.0	Sierra Nevada	10
USA Gold	1.9	New Belgium	8
Kool	1.8		
Other	21.0		
Total	100.0		

Source: Based on M. Esterl & P. Evans, "Reynolds, Lorillard Strike a Match," *Wall Street Journal,* July 6, 2014, B4. See also M. Esterl & T. Mickle, "Beer Conglomerates Cultivate Their Crafty Side," *Wall Street Journal,* December 29, 2014, B1.

be used for comparative purposes to determine relative market share position. In the cigarette industry, for example, Newport's relative market share position is 12.2/40.2 = 0.303, and Miller Lite's relative market share position is 137/381 = 0.359 (see Table 8-4).

Relative market share position is given on the *x*-axis of the BCG Matrix. The midpoint on the *x*-axis usually is set at 0.50, corresponding to a division that has half the market share of the leading firm in the industry. The *y*-axis represents the **industry growth rate (IGR)** in sales, measured in percentage terms—that is, the average annual increase in revenue for all firms in an industry. The growth rate percentages on the *y*-axis could range from −20 to +20 percent, with 0.0 being the midpoint. The average annual increase in revenues for several leading firms in the industry would be a good estimate of the value. Also, various sources such as the *S&P Industry Surveys* and www.finance.yahoo.com (click on Competitors) would provide this value. These numerical ranges on the *x*- and *y*-axes are often used, but other numerical values could be established as deemed appropriate for particular organizations, such as −10 to +10 percent on the *y*-axis.

Based on each division's respective (*x, y*) coordinate, each segment can be properly positioned (centered) in a BCG Matrix. Divisions located in Quadrant I (upper right) of the BCG Matrix are called "Question Marks," those located in Quadrant II (upper left) are called "Stars," those located in Quadrant III (lower left) are called "Cash Cows," and those divisions located in Quadrant IV (lower right) are called "Dogs." The following list describes the four BCG quadrants.

- *Question Marks*—Divisions in Quadrant I (upper right) have a low relative market share position, yet they compete in a high-growth industry. Generally these firms' cash needs are high and their cash generation is low. These businesses are called **question marks** because the organization must decide whether to strengthen them by pursuing an intensive strategy (market penetration, market development, or product development) or to sell them.
- *Stars*—Divisions in Quadrant II (upper left) represent the organizations' best long-run opportunities for growth and profitability, and are therefore called **stars**. Divisions with a high relative market share and a high industry growth rate should receive substantial investment to maintain or strengthen their dominant positions. Forward, backward, and horizontal integration; market penetration; market development; and product development are appropriate strategies for these divisions to consider, as indicated in Figure 8-7.
- *Cash Cows*—Divisions in Quadrant III (lower left) have a high relative market share position but compete in a low-growth industry. Called **cash cows** because they generate cash in excess of their needs, they are often milked. Many of today's cash cows were

RELATIVE MARKET SHARE POSITION

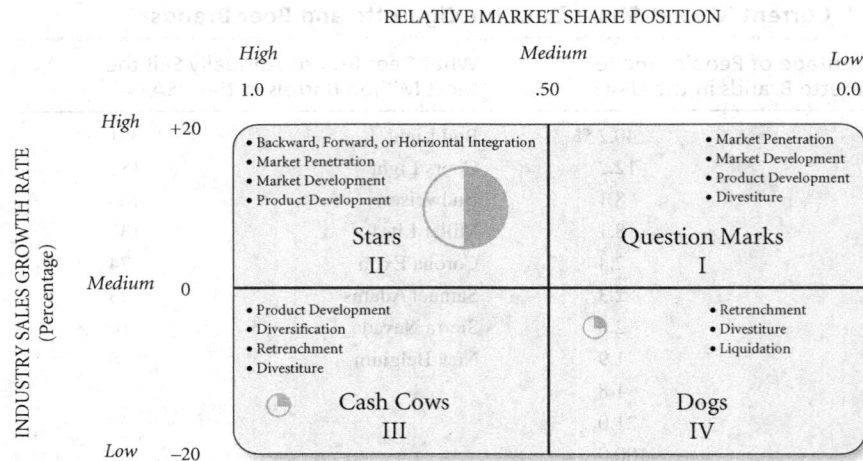

FIGURE 8-7
The BCG Matrix

Source: Based on the BCG Portfolio Matrix from the Product Portfolio Matrix, © 1970, The Boston Consulting Group.

yesterday's stars. Cash cow divisions should be managed to maintain their strong position for as long as possible. Product development or diversification may be attractive strategies for strong cash cows. However, as a cash cow division becomes weak, retrenchment or divestiture can become more appropriate.

- *Dogs*—Divisions in Quadrant IV (lower right) have a low relative market share position and compete in a slow- or no-market-growth industry; they are **dogs** in the firm's portfolio. Because of their weak internal and external position, these businesses are often liquidated, divested, or trimmed down through retrenchment. When a division first becomes a dog, retrenchment can be the best strategy to pursue because many dogs have bounced back, after strenuous asset and cost reduction, to become viable, profitable divisions.

The basic BCG Matrix appears in Figure 8-7. Each circle represents a separate division. The size of the circle corresponds to the proportion of corporate revenue generated by that business unit, and the pie slice indicates the proportion of corporate profits generated by that division.

The major benefit of the BCG Matrix is that it draws attention to the cash flow, investment characteristics, and needs of an organization's various divisions. The divisions of many firms evolve over time: dogs become question marks, question marks become stars, stars become cash cows, and cash cows become dogs in an ongoing counterclockwise motion. Less frequently, stars become question marks, question marks become dogs, dogs become cash cows, and cash cows become stars (in a clockwise motion). In some organizations, no cyclical motion is apparent. Over time, organizations should strive to achieve a portfolio of divisions that are stars.

An example of a BCG Matrix is provided in Figure 8-8, which illustrates an organization composed of five divisions with annual sales ranging from $5,000 to $60,000. Division 1 has the greatest sales volume, so the circle representing that division is the largest one in the matrix. The circle corresponding to Division 5 is the smallest because its sales volume ($5,000) is least among all the divisions. The pie slices within the circles reveal the percent of corporate profits contributed by each division. As shown, Division 1 contributes the highest profit percentage, 39 percent, as indicated by 39 percent of the area within circle 1 being shaded. Notice in the diagram that Division 1 is considered a star, Division 2 is a question mark, Division 3 is also a question mark, Division 4 is a cash cow, and Division 5 is a dog.

The BCG Matrix, like all analytical techniques, has some limitations. For example, viewing every business as a star, cash cow, dog, or question mark is an oversimplification; many businesses

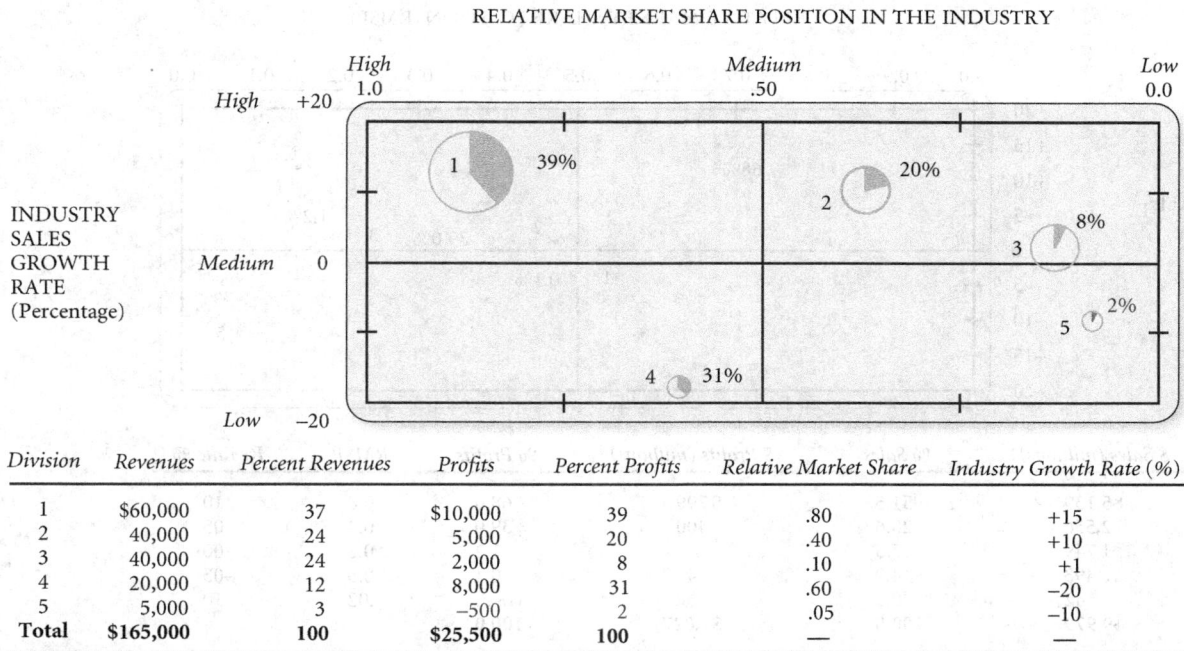

Division	Revenues	Percent Revenues	Profits	Percent Profits	Relative Market Share	Industry Growth Rate (%)
1	$60,000	37	$10,000	39	.80	+15
2	40,000	24	5,000	20	.40	+10
3	40,000	24	2,000	8	.10	+1
4	20,000	12	8,000	31	.60	−20
5	5,000	3	−500	2	.05	−10
Total	$165,000	100	$25,500	100	—	—

FIGURE 8-8

An Example BCG Matrix

fall right in the middle of the BCG Matrix and thus are not easily classified. Furthermore, the BCG Matrix does not reflect if various divisions or their industries are growing over time; that is, the matrix has no temporal qualities, but rather it is a snapshot of an organization at a given point in time. Finally, other variables besides relative market share position and industry growth rate in sales, such as size of the market and competitive advantages, are important in making strategic decisions about various divisions.

Another example BCG Matrix is provided in Figure 8-9. As you can see, Division 5 had an operating loss of $188 million.

The Internal-External (IE) Matrix

The **Internal-External (IE) Matrix** positions an organization's various divisions (segments) in a nine-cell display, illustrated in Figure 8-10. The IE Matrix is similar to the BCG Matrix in that both tools involve plotting a firm's divisions in a schematic diagram; this is why they are both called *portfolio matrices*. Also, in both the BCG and IE Matrices, the size of each circle represents the percentage of sales contribution of each division, and pie slices reveal the percentage of profit contribution of each division. But there are four important differences between the BCG Matrix and the IE Matrix, as follows:

1. The *x* and *y* axes are different.
2. The IE Matrix requires more information about the divisions than does the BCG Matrix.
3. The strategic implications of each matrix are different. For these reasons,
4. The IE Matrix has nine quadrants versus four in a BCG Matrix.

For the previous four reasons, strategists in multidivisional firms often develop both the BCG Matrix and the IE Matrix in formulating alternative strategies. A common practice is to develop a BCG Matrix and an IE Matrix for the present, and then develop projected matrices to reflect expectations of the future. This before-and-after analysis can be very effective in an oral presentation, enabling students (or strategists) to pave the way for (justify or give some rationale for) their recommendations across divisions of the firm.

RELATIVE MARKET SHARE POSITION (RMSP)

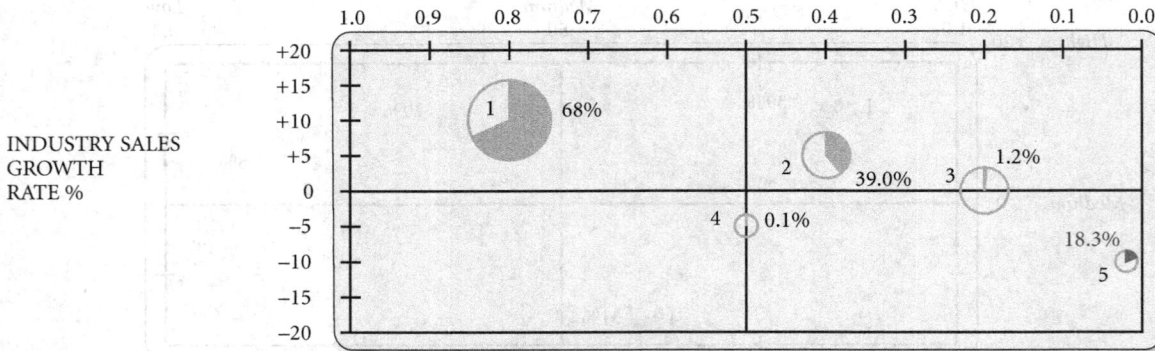

Division	$ Sales (millions)	% Sales	$ Profits (millions)	% Profits	RMSP	IG Rate %
1	$5,139	51.5	$799	68.0	0.8	10
2	2,556	25.6	400	39.0	0.4	05
3	1,749	17.5	12	1.2	0.2	00
4	493	4.9	4	0.1	0.5	−05
5	42	0.5	−188	(18.3)	.02	−10
Total	$9,979	100.0	$1,027	100.0		

FIGURE 8-9

An Example BCG Matrix

THE IFE TOTAL WEIGHTED SCORES

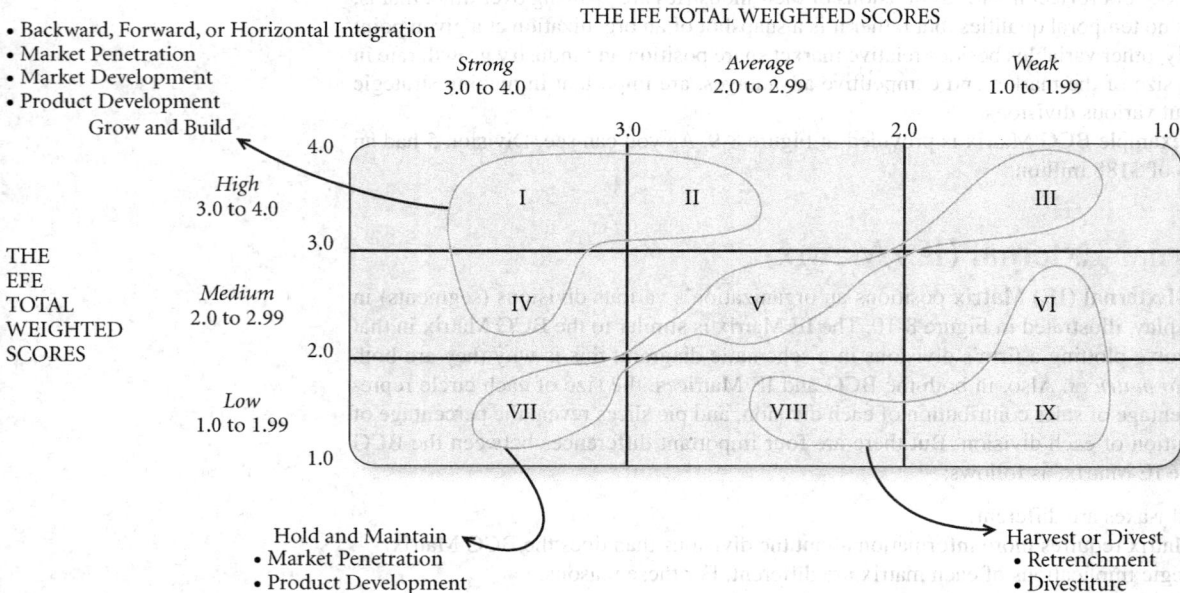

FIGURE 8-10

The Internal-External (IE) Matrix

Source: The IE Matrix was developed from the General Electric (GE) Business Screen Matrix. For a description of the GE Matrix, see Michael Allen, "Diagramming GE's Planning for What's WATT," in R. Allio and M. Pennington, eds., *Corporate Planning: Techniques and Applications* l par; New York: AMACOM, 1979.

The IE Matrix is based on two key dimensions: (1) the IFE total weighted scores on the x-axis and (2) the EFE total weighted scores on the y-axis. Recall that each division of an organization should construct an IFE Matrix and an EFE Matrix for its part of the organization, but oftentimes in performing case analysis, strategic-management students are asked to simply estimate divisional IFE and EFE scores, rather than prepare those underlying matrices for every division. Anyway, the total weighted scores derived from the divisions allow construction of the corporate-level IE Matrix. On the x-axis of the IE Matrix, an IFE total weighted score of 1.0 to 1.99 represents a weak internal position; a score of 2.0 to 2.99 is considered average; and a score of 3.0 to 4.0 is strong. Similarly, on the y-axis, an EFE total weighted score of 1.0 to 1.99 is considered low; a score of 2.0 to 2.99 is medium; and a score of 3.0 to 4.0 is high. Circles, representing divisions, are positioned in an IE Matrix based on their (x, y) coordinate.

Despite having nine cells (or quadrants), the IE Matrix has three major regions that have different strategy implications, as follows:

- *Region 1*—The prescription for divisions that fall into cells I, II, or IV can be described as *grow and build*. Intensive (market penetration, market development, and product development) or integrative (backward integration, forward integration, and horizontal integration) strategies can be most appropriate for these divisions. This is the best region for divisions, given their high IFE and EFE scores. Successful organizations are able to achieve a portfolio of businesses positioned in Region 1.
- *Region 2*—The prescription for divisions that fall into cells III, V, or VII can be described as *hold and maintain* strategies; market penetration and product development are two commonly employed strategies for these types of divisions.
- *Region 3*—The prescription for divisions that fall into cells VI, VIII, or IX can be described as *harvest or divest*.

An example of a four-division IE Matrix is given in Figure 8-11. As indicated by the positioning of the four circles, *grow and build* strategies are appropriate for Divisions 1, 2, and 3. But Division 4 is a candidate for *harvest or divest*. Division 2 contributes the greatest percentage of company sales and thus is represented by the largest circle. Division 1 contributes the greatest proportion of total profits; it has the largest-percentage pie slice.

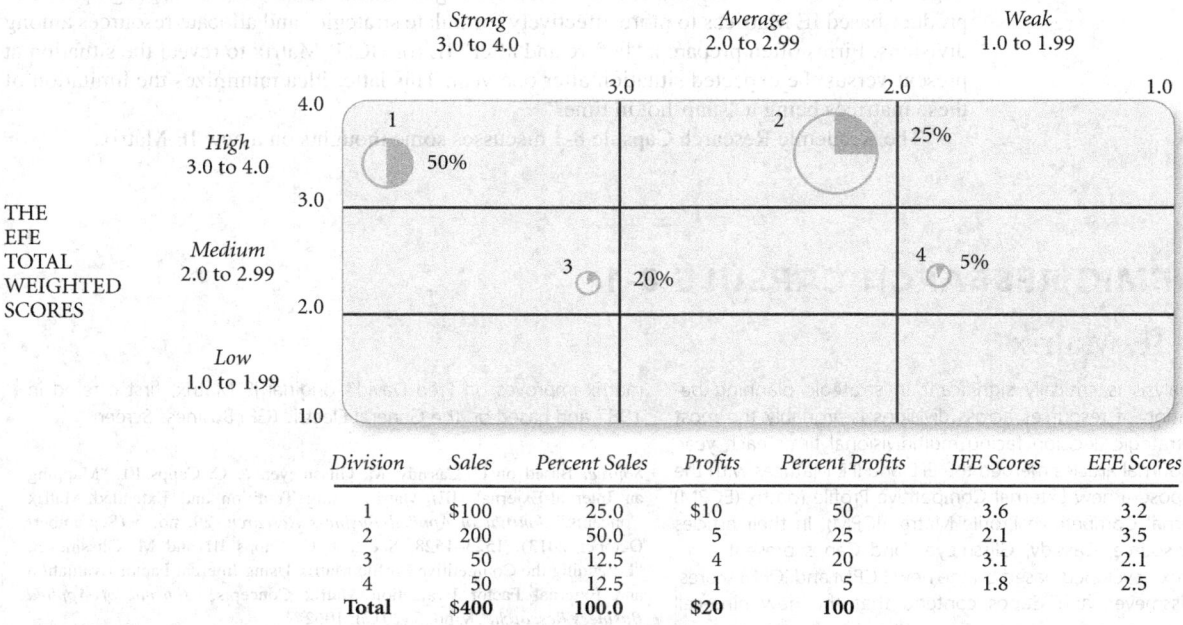

THE IFE TOTAL WEIGHTED SCORES

Division	Sales	Percent Sales	Profits	Percent Profits	IFE Scores	EFE Scores
1	$100	25.0	$10	50	3.6	3.2
2	200	50.0	5	25	2.1	3.5
3	50	12.5	4	20	3.1	2.1
4	50	12.5	1	5	1.8	2.5
Total	**$400**	**100.0**	**$20**	**100**		

FIGURE 8-11

An Example IE Matrix

THE IFE TOTAL WEIGHTED SCORES

	Strong 3.0 to 4.0	Average 2.0 to 2.99	Weak 1.0 to 1.99

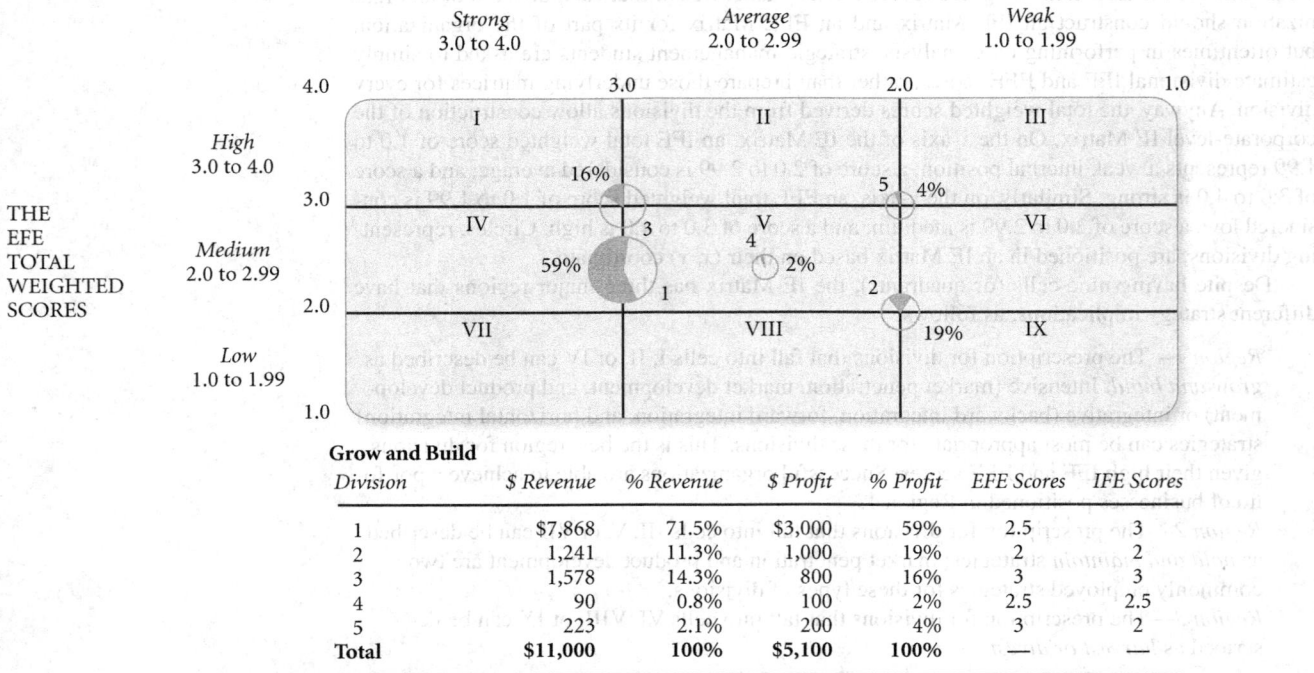

FIGURE 8-12
The IE Matrix

Grow and Build

Division	$ Revenue	% Revenue	$ Profit	% Profit	EFE Scores	IFE Scores
1	$7,868	71.5%	$3,000	59%	2.5	3
2	1,241	11.3%	1,000	19%	2	2
3	1,578	14.3%	800	16%	3	3
4	90	0.8%	100	2%	2.5	2.5
5	223	2.1%	200	4%	3	2
Total	**$11,000**	**100%**	**$5,100**	**100%**	—	—

An example five-division IE Matrix is given in Figure 8-12. Note that Division 1 has the largest revenues (as indicated by the largest circle) and the largest profits (as indicated by the largest pie slice) in the matrix. It is common for organizations to develop both geographic and product-based IE Matrices to more effectively formulate strategies and allocate resources among divisions. Firms often prepare a "before and after" IE (or BCG) Matrix to reveal the situation at present versus the expected situation after one year. This latter idea minimizes the limitation of these matrices being a "snapshot in time."

The Academic Research Capsule 8-1 discusses some thoughts on a new IE Matrix.

ACADEMIC RESEARCH CAPSULE 8-1

A New IE Matrix

Portfolio analysis is critically significant in strategic planning because allocation of resources across divisions is arguably the most important strategic decision facing multidivisional firms each year. Two recent journal articles merged the EFE and IFE Matrices with the CPM to propose a new External Competitive Profile Matrix (ECPM) and an Internal Competitive Profile Matrix (ICPM). In their articles cited in the source, Cassidy, Glissmeyer, and Capps present a revised IE Matrix developed based on the new ECPM and ICPM scores. Cassidy, Glissmeyer, and Capps contend that the new nine-cell matrix improves on Fred David's original IE Matrix, first offered in 1987 and based on the General Electric (GE) Business Screen.

Source: Based on C. Cassidy, M. Glissmeyer, & C. Capps III, "Mapping an Internal-External (IE) Matrix Using Tradition and Extended Matrix Concepts," *Journal of Applied Business Research*, 29, no. 5 (September/October 2013): 1523–1528. See also C. Capps III and M. Glissmeyer, "Extending the Competitive Profile Matrix Using Internal Factor Evaluation and External Factor Evaluation Matrix Concepts," *Journal of Applied Business Research*, 28, no. 5 (2012): 1062

The Grand Strategy Matrix

In addition to the SWOT Matrix, SPACE Matrix, BCG Matrix, and IE Matrix, the **Grand Strategy Matrix** has become a popular tool for formulating alternative strategies. All organizations can be positioned in one of the Grand Strategy Matrix's four strategy quadrants. A firm's divisions likewise could be positioned. As illustrated in Figure 8-13, the Grand Strategy Matrix is based on two evaluative dimensions: (1) competitive position on the x-axis and (2) market (industry) growth on the y-axis. Any industry whose annual growth in sales exceeds 5 percent could be considered to have rapid growth. Appropriate strategies for an organization to consider are listed in sequential order of attractiveness in each quadrant of the Grand Strategy Matrix.

Firms located in Quadrant I of the Grand Strategy Matrix are in an excellent strategic position. For these companies, continued concentration on current markets (market penetration and market development) and products (product development) is an appropriate strategy. It is unwise for a Quadrant I firm to shift notably from its established competitive advantages. When a Quadrant I organization has excessive resources, then backward, forward, or horizontal integration may be effective strategies. When a Quadrant I firm is too heavily committed to a single product, then related diversification may reduce the risks associated with a narrow product line. Quadrant I firms can afford to take advantage of external opportunities in several areas. They can take risks aggressively when necessary.

Firms positioned in Quadrant II need to evaluate their present approach to the marketplace seriously. Although their industry is growing, they are unable to compete effectively; they need to determine why the firm's current approach is ineffective and how the company can best change to improve its competitiveness. Because Quadrant II organizations are in a rapid market growth industry, an intensive strategy (as opposed to integrative or diversification) is usually the first option that should be considered. However, if the firm is lacking a distinctive competence

RAPID MARKET GROWTH

Quadrant II
1. Market development
2. Market penetration
3. Product development
4. Horizontal integration
5. Divestiture
6. Liquidation

Quadrant I
1. Market development
2. Market penetration
3. Product development
4. Forward integration
5. Backward integration
6. Horizontal integration
7. Related diversification

WEAK COMPETITIVE POSITION — STRONG COMPETITIVE POSITION

Quadrant III
1. Retrenchment
2. Related diversification
3. Unrelated diversification
4. Divestiture
5. Liquidation

Quadrant IV
1. Related diversification
2. Unrelated diversification
3. Joint ventures

SLOW MARKET GROWTH

FIGURE 8-13
The Grand Strategy Matrix

Source: Based on Roland Christensen, Norman Berg, and Malcolm Salter, *Policy Formulation and Administration* (Homewood, IL: Richard D. Irwin, 1976), 16–18.

or competitive advantage, then horizontal integration is often a desirable alternative. As a last resort, divestiture or liquidation should be considered. Divestiture can provide funds needed to acquire other businesses or buy back shares of stock.

Quadrant III organizations compete in slow-growth industries and have weak competitive positions. These firms must make some drastic changes quickly to avoid further decline and possible liquidation. Extensive cost and asset reduction (retrenchment) should be pursued first. An alternative strategy is to shift resources away from the current business into different areas (diversify). If all else fails, the final options for Quadrant III businesses are divestiture or liquidation.

Finally, Quadrant IV businesses have a strong competitive position but are in a slow-growth industry. These firms have the strength to launch diversified programs into more promising growth areas: Quadrant IV businesses have characteristically high cash-flow levels and limited internal growth needs and often can pursue related or unrelated diversification successfully. Quadrant IV firms also may pursue joint ventures.

Even with the Grand Strategy Matrix, be certain that you always, whenever possible, state your alternative strategies in *specific, actionable, and divisional* terms to the extent possible. When you know the particular firm, such as in strategic-management case analysis, avoid using terms such as *divestiture,* for example. Rather, specify the exact division to be sold. Also, be sure to use the free Excel student template at www.strategyclub.com that facilitates construction of all strategic planning matrices.

The Decision Stage: The Quantitative Strategic Planning Matrix (QSPM)

Other than ranking strategies to achieve the prioritized list, there is only one analytical technique in the literature designed to determine the relative attractiveness of feasible alternative actions. The **Quantitative Strategic Planning Matrix (QSPM)**, which comprises Stage 3 of the strategy-formulation analytical framework, objectively indicates which alternative strategies are best.[6] The QSPM uses input from Stage 1 analyses and matching results from Stage 2 analyses to decide objectively among alternative strategies. That is, the EFE Matrix, IFE Matrix, and CPM that comprise Stage 1, coupled with the SWOT Matrix, SPACE Matrix, BCG Matrix, IE Matrix, and Grand Strategy Matrix that comprise Stage 2, provide the needed information for setting up the QSPM (Stage 3). The QSPM is a tool that allows strategists to evaluate alternative strategies objectively, based on previously identified external and internal key success factors. Like other strategy-formulation analytical tools, the QSPM requires assignment of ratings (called attractiveness scores), but making "small" rating decisions enables strategists to make effective "big" decisions, such as which country to spend a billion dollars in to sell a product.

The basic format of the QSPM is illustrated in Table 8-5. Note that the left column of a QSPM consists of key external and internal factors (from Stage 1), and the top row consists of feasible alternative strategies (from Stage 2). Specifically, the left column of a QSPM consists of information obtained directly from the EFE Matrix and IFE Matrix. In a column adjacent to the key success factors, the respective weights received by each factor in the EFE Matrix and the IFE Matrix are recorded.

The top row of a QSPM consists of alternative strategies derived from the SWOT Matrix, SPACE Matrix, BCG Matrix, IE Matrix, and Grand Strategy Matrix. These matching tools usually generate similar feasible alternatives. However, not every strategy suggested by the matching techniques has to be evaluated in a QSPM. Strategists should compare several viable alternative strategies in a QSPM. Make sure your strategies are stated in specific terms, such as "Open 275 new stores in Indonesia" rather than "Expand globally" or "Open new stores in Africa." Ultimately, a dollar value must be established for each recommended strategy; it would be impossible to establish a dollar value for "expand globally."

Conceptually, the QSPM determines the relative attractiveness of various strategies based on the extent that key external and internal factors are capitalized on or improved. The relative attractiveness of each strategy within a set of alternatives is computed by determining the cumulative impact of each external and internal factor. Any number of sets of alternative strategies can

TABLE 8-5 The Quantitative Strategic Planning Matrix (QSPM)

Key Factors	Weight	Strategy 1	Strategy 2	Strategy 3
			Strategic Alternatives	
Key External Factors				
Economy				
Political/Legal/Governmental				
Social/Cultural/Demographic/ Environmental				
Technological				
Competitive				
Key Internal Factors				
Management				
Marketing				
Finance/Accounting				
Production/Operations				
Research and Development				
Management Information Systems				

be included in the QSPM, and any number of strategies can make up a given set, but only strategies within a given set are evaluated relative to each other. For example, one set of strategies may include diversification, whereas another set may include issuing stock and selling a division to raise needed capital. These two sets of strategies are totally different, and the QSPM evaluates strategies only within sets. Note in Table 8-5 that three strategies are included, and they make up just one set.

A Quantitative Strategic Planning Matrix for a retail computer store is provided in Table 8-6. This example illustrates all the components of the QSPM: strategic alternatives, key factors, weights, attractiveness scores (AS), total attractiveness scores (TAS), and the sum total attractiveness score. The three new terms just introduced—(1) attractiveness scores, (2) total attractiveness scores, and (3) the sum total attractiveness score—are defined and explained as the six steps required to develop a QSPM are discussed:

Step 1: *Make a list of the firm's key external opportunities and threats and internal strengths and weaknesses in the left column of the QSPM.* This information should be taken directly from the EFE Matrix and IFE Matrix. (The Excel template at www.strategyclub.com can facilitate this process.)

Step 2: *Assign weights to each key external and internal factor.* These weights are identical to those in the EFE Matrix and IFE Matrix. The weights are presented in a straight column just to the right of the external and internal factors.

Step 3: *Examine the Stage 2 (matching) matrices, and identify alternative strategies that the organization should consider implementing.* Record these strategies in the top row of the QSPM. Group the strategies into mutually exclusive sets if possible.

Step 4: *Determine the Attractiveness Scores (AS),* defined as numerical values that indicate the relative attractiveness of each strategy considering a single external or internal factor. **Attractiveness Scores (AS)** are determined by examining each key external or internal factor, one at a time, and asking the question, "Does this factor affect the choice of strategies being made?" If the answer to this question is *yes,* then the strategies should be compared relative to that key factor. Specifically, AS should be assigned to each strategy to indicate the relative attractiveness of one strategy over others, considering the particular factor. The range for AS is 1 = *not attractive,* 2 = *somewhat attractive,* 3 = *reasonably attractive,* and 4 = *highly attractive.* By "attractive," we mean the extent

TABLE 8-6 A QSPM for a Retail Computer Store

		STRATEGIC ALTERNATIVES			
		1 Buy New Land and Build New Larger Store		2 Fully Renovate Existing Store	
Key Factors	Weight	AS	TAS	AS	TAS
Opportunities					
1. Population of city growing 10%	0.10	4	0.40	2	0.20
2. Rival computer store opening one mile away	0.10	2	0.20	4	0.40
3. Vehicle traffic passing store up 12%	0.08	1	0.08	4	0.32
4. Vendors average six new products/year	0.05	—		—	
5. Senior citizen use of computers up 8%	0.05	—		—	
6. Small business growth in area up 10%	0.05	—		—	
7. Desire for websites up 18% by realtors	0.04	—		—	
8. Desire for websites up 12% by small firms	0.03	—		—	
Threats					
1. Best Buy opening new store nearby in one year	0.15	4	0.60	3	0.45
2. Local university offers computer repair	0.08	—		—	
3. New bypass for Hwy 34 in one year will divert traffic	0.12	4	0.48	1	0.12
4. New mall being built nearby	0.08	2	0.16	4	0.32
5. Gas prices up 14%	0.04	—		—	
6. Vendors raising prices 8%	0.03	—		—	
Total	**1.00**				
Strengths					
1. Inventory turnover increased from 5.8 to 6.7	0.05	—		—	
2. Average customer purchase increased from $97 to $128	0.07	2	0.14	4	0.28
3. Employee morale is excellent	0.10	—		—	
4. In-store promotions resulted in 20% increase in sales	0.05	—		—	
5. Newspaper advertising expenditures increased 10%	0.02	—		—	
6. Revenues from repair/service segment of store up 16%	0.15	4	0.60	3	0.45
7. In-store technical support personnel have MIS college degrees	0.05	—		—	
8. Store's debt-to-total-assets ratio declined to 34%	0.03	4	0.12	2	0.06
9. Revenues per employee up 19%	0.02	—		—	
Weaknesses					
1. Revenues from software segment of store down 12%	0.10	—		—	
2. Location of store negatively impacted by new Highway 34	0.15	4	0.60	1	0.15
3. Carpet and paint in store somewhat in disrepair	0.02	1	0.02	4	0.08
4. Bathroom in store needs refurbishing	0.02	1	0.02	4	0.08
5. Revenues from businesses down 8%	0.04	3	0.12	4	0.16
6. Store has no website	0.05	—		—	
7. Supplier on-time delivery increased to 2.4 days	0.03	—		—	
8. Often customers have to wait to check out	0.05	2	0.10	4	0.20
Total	**1.00**		**3.64**		**3.27**

that one strategy, compared to others, enables the firm to either capitalize on the strength, improve on the weakness, exploit the opportunity, or avoid the threat. Work row by row in developing a QSPM. If the answer to the previous question is *no*, indicating that the respective key factor has no effect on the specific choice being made, then do not assign AS to the strategies in that set. Use a dash to indicate that the key factor does not affect the choice being made. *Note:* If you assign an AS score to one strategy, then assign an AS score(s) to the other—in other words, if one strategy receives a dash—then all others must receive a dash in a given row. Also, in the Excel template provided at www.strategyclub.com, zeros are used instead of dashes.

Step 5: *Compute the Total Attractiveness Scores.* Total Attractiveness Scores (TAS) are defined as the product of multiplying the weights (Step 2) by the AS (Step 4) in each row. The TAS indicate the relative attractiveness of each alternative strategy, considering only the impact of the adjacent external or internal critical success factor. The higher the TAS, the more attractive the strategic alternative (considering only the adjacent critical success factor).

Step 6: *Compute the Sum Total Attractiveness Score.* Add TAS in each strategy column of the QSPM. The **Sum Total Attractiveness Scores (STAS)** reveal which strategy is most attractive in each set of alternatives. Higher scores indicate more attractive strategies, considering all the relevant external and internal factors that could affect the strategic decisions. The magnitude of the difference between the STAS in a given set of strategic alternatives indicates the relative desirability of one strategy over another.

In Table 8-6, two alternative strategies—(1) buy new land and build new larger store and (2) fully renovate existing store—are being considered by a computer retail store. Note by the Sum Total Attractiveness Scores of 3.64 versus 3.27 that the analysis indicates the business should buy new land and build a new larger store. Note the use of dashes to indicate which factors do not affect the strategy choice being considered. If a particular factor affects one strategy, but not the other, it affects the choice being made, so AS should be recorded for both strategies. Never rate one strategy and not the other. Note also in Table 8-6 that there are no consecutive 1s, 2s, 3s, or 4s across any row in a QSPM; never assign the same AS score across a row. Always prepare a QSPM working row by row. Also, if you have more than one strategy in the QSPM, then let the AS scores range from 1 to "the number of strategies being evaluated." This will enable you to have a different AS score for each strategy. These are all important guidelines to follow in developing a QSPM. In actual practice, the store did purchase the new land and build a new store; the business also did some minor refurbishing until the new store was operational.

There should be a rationale for each AS score assigned. Note in the first row of Table 8-6 that the "Population of city growing 10 percent" opportunity could be capitalized on best by Strategy 1, "Buy New Land and Build New, Larger Store," so an AS score of 4 was assigned to Strategy 1. Attractiveness Scores, therefore, are not mere guesses; they should be rational, defensible, and reasonable. Mathematically, the AS score of 4 in row 1 suggests Strategy 1 is 100 percent more attractive than Strategy 2, whose AS score was 2 (since $4 - 2 = 2$ and 2 divided by $2 = 100$ percent).

Positive Features and Limitations of the QSPM

A positive feature of the QSPM is that sets of strategies can be examined sequentially or simultaneously. For example, corporate-level strategies could be evaluated first, followed by division-level strategies, and then function-level strategies. There is no limit to the number of strategies that can be evaluated or the number of sets of strategies that can be examined at once using the QSPM.

Another positive feature of the QSPM is that it requires strategists to integrate pertinent external and internal factors into the decision process. Developing a Quantitative Strategic Planning Matrix makes it less likely that key factors will be overlooked or weighted inappropriately. It draws attention to important relationships that affect strategy decisions. Although developing a QSPM requires Attractiveness Scores (AS) decisions, those small decisions enhance the probability that the final strategic decisions will be best for the organization. A QSPM can be used by small and large, for-profit and nonprofit organizations.[7]

The Quantitative Strategic Planning Matrix has two limitations. First, it always requires informed judgments regarding AS scores, but quantification is helpful throughout the strategic-planning process to minimize halo error and various biases. Attractiveness Scores are not mere guesses. Be reminded that a 4 is 33 percent more important than a 3; making good small decisions is important for making good big decisions, such as deciding among various strategies to implement. Second, a limitation of the QSPM is that it can be only as good as the prerequisite information and matching analyses on which it is based.

Cultural Aspects of Strategy Analysis and Choice

As defined in Chapter 6, organizational culture includes the set of shared values, beliefs, attitudes, customs, norms, rites, rituals, personalities, heroes, and heroines that describe a firm. Culture is the unique way an organization does business. It is the human dimension that creates solidarity and meaning, and it inspires commitment and productivity in an organization when strategy changes are made. All human beings have a basic need to make sense of the world, to feel in control, and to make meaning. When events threaten meaning, individuals react defensively. Managers and employees may even sabotage new strategies in an effort to recapture the status quo. For these reasons, it is beneficial to view strategy analysis and choice from a cultural perspective, because success often rests on the degree of support that strategies receive from a firm's culture. If a firm's strategies are supported by an organization's culture, then managers often can implement changes swiftly and easily. However, if a supportive culture does not exist and is not cultivated, then strategy changes may be ineffective or even counterproductive. A firm's culture can become antagonistic to new strategies, and the result of that antagonism may be confusion and disarray.

Strategies that require fewer cultural changes may be more attractive because extensive changes can take considerable time and effort. Whenever two firms merge, it becomes especially important to evaluate and consider culture-strategy linkages. Organizational culture can be the primary reason for difficulties a firm encounters when it attempts to shift its strategic direction, as the following statement explains:

> Not only has the "right" corporate culture become the essence and foundation of corporate excellence, but success or failure of needed corporate reforms hinges on management's sagacity and ability to change the firm's driving culture in time and in tune with required changes in strategies.[8]

The Politics of Strategy Analysis and Choice

All organizations are political. Unless managed, political maneuvering consumes valuable time, subverts organizational objectives, diverts human energy, and results in the loss of some valuable employees. Sometimes political biases and personal preferences get unduly embedded in strategy choice decisions. Internal politics affect the choice of strategies in all organizations. The hierarchy of command in an organization, combined with the career aspirations of different people and the need to allocate scarce resources, guarantees the formation of coalitions of individuals who strive to take care of themselves first and the organization second, third, or fourth. Coalitions of individuals often form around key strategy issues that face an enterprise. A major responsibility of strategists is to guide the development of coalitions, to nurture an overall team concept, and to gain the support of key individuals and groups of individuals.

In the absence of objective analyses, strategy decisions too often are based on the politics of the moment. With development of improved strategy-formation analytical tools, political factors become less important in making strategic decisions. In the absence of objectivity, political factors sometimes dictate strategies, and this is unfortunate. Managing political relationships is an integral part of building enthusiasm and esprit de corps in an organization.

A classic study of strategic management in nine large corporations examined the political tactics of successful strategists.[9] Successful strategists were found to let weakly supported ideas and proposals die through inaction and to establish additional hurdles or tests for strongly supported ideas considered unacceptable but not openly opposed. Successful strategists kept a low political profile on unacceptable proposals and strived to let most negative decisions come from subordinates or a group consensus, thereby reserving their personal vetoes for big issues and crucial moments. Successful strategists did a lot of chatting and informal questioning to stay abreast of how things were progressing and to know when to intervene. They led strategy but did not dictate it. They gave few orders, announced few decisions, depended heavily on informal questioning, and sought to probe and clarify until a consensus emerged.

Successful strategists generously and visibly rewarded key thrusts that succeeded. They assigned responsibility for major new thrusts to **champions**, the individuals most strongly identified with the idea or product and whose futures were linked to its success. They stayed alert to the symbolic impact of their own actions and statements so as not to send false signals that could stimulate movements in unwanted directions.

Successful strategists ensured that all major power bases within an organization were represented in, or had access to, top management. They interjected new faces and new views into considerations of major changes. This is important because new employees and managers generally have more enthusiasm and drive than employees who have been with the firm a long time. New employees do not see the world the same old way; nor do they act as screens against changes. Successful strategists minimized their own political exposure on highly controversial issues and in circumstances in which major opposition from key power centers was likely. In combination, these findings provide a basis for managing political relationships in an organization.

Because strategies must be effective in the marketplace and capable of gaining internal commitment, the following tactics used by politicians for centuries can aid strategists:

1. Achieving desired results is more important that imposing a particular method; therefore, consider various methods and choose, whenever possible, the one(s) that will afford the greatest commitment from employees/managers.
2. Achieving satisfactory results with a popular strategy is generally better than trying to achieve optimal results with an unpopular strategy.
3. Often, an effective way to gain commitment and achieve desired results is to shift from specific to general issues and concerns.
4. Often, an effective way to gain commitment and achieve desired results is to shift from short-term to long-term issues and concerns.
5. Middle-level managers must be genuinely involved in and supportive of strategic decisions, because successful implementation will hinge on their support.[10]

Boards of Directors: Governance Issues

A **board of directors** is a group of individuals elected by the ownership of a corporation to have oversight and guidance over management and to look out for shareholders' interests. The act of oversight and direction is referred to as **governance**. The National Association of Corporate Directors defines *governance* as "the characteristic of ensuring that long-term strategic objectives and plans are established and that the proper management structure is in place to achieve those objectives, while at the same time making sure that the structure functions to maintain the corporation's integrity, reputation, and responsibility to its various constituencies." Boards are held accountable for the entire performance of an organization. Boards of directors are increasingly sued by shareholders for mismanaging their interests. New accounting rules in the United States and Europe now enhance corporate-governance codes and require much more extensive financial disclosure among publicly held firms. The roles and duties of a board of directors can be divided into four broad categories, as indicated in Table 8-7.

Shareholders are increasingly wary of boards of directors. Most directors globally have ended their image as rubber-stamping friends of CEOs. Boards are more autonomous than

TABLE 8-7 Board of Director Duties and Responsibilities

1. CONTROL AND OVERSIGHT OVER MANAGEMENT
   a. Select the Chief Executive Officer (CEO).
   b. Sanction the CEO's team.
   c. Provide the CEO with a forum.
   d. Ensure managerial competency.
   e. Evaluate management's performance.
   f. Set management's salary levels, including fringe benefits.
   g. Guarantee managerial integrity through continuous auditing.
   h. Chart the corporate course.
   i. Devise and revise policies to be implemented by management.

2. ADHERENCE TO LEGAL PRESCRIPTIONS
   a. Keep abreast of new laws.
   b. Ensure the entire organization fulfils legal prescriptions.
   c. Pass bylaws and related resolutions.
   d. Select new directors.
   e. Approve capital budgets.
   f. Authorize borrowing, new stock issues, bonds, and so on.

3. CONSIDERATION OF STAKEHOLDERS' INTERESTS
   a. Monitor product quality.
   b. Facilitate upward progression in employee quality of work life.
   c. Review labor policies and practices.
   d. Improve the customer climate.
   e. Keep community relations at the highest level.
   f. Use influence to better governmental, professional association, and educational contacts.
   g. Maintain good public image.

4. ADVANCEMENT OF STOCKHOLDERS' RIGHTS
   a. Preserve stockholders' equity.
   b. Stimulate corporate growth so that the firm will survive and flourish.
   c. Guard against equity dilution.
   d. Ensure equitable stockholder representation.
   e. Inform stockholders through letters, reports, and meetings.
   f. Declare proper dividends.
   g. Guarantee corporate survival.

ever and continually mindful of and responsive to legal and institutional-investor scrutiny. Boards are more cognizant of auditing and compliance issues and more reluctant to approve excessive compensation and perks. Boards stay much more abreast today of public scandals that attract shareholder and media attention. Increasingly, boards of directors monitor and review executive performance carefully without favoritism to executives, representing shareholders rather than the CEO. Boards are more proactive today, whereas in years past they were often merely reactive. These are all reasons why the chair of the board of directors should not also serve as the firm's CEO. In North America, the number of new incoming CEOs that also serve as Chair of the Board has declined to about 10 percent today from about 50 percent in 2001. Academic Research Capsule 8-2 reveals "how many" board of director members are ideal.

Until recently, individuals serving on boards of directors did most of their work sitting around polished mahogany tables. However, Hewlett-Packard's directors, among many others, now log on to their own special board website twice a week and conduct business based on

ACADEMIC RESEARCH CAPSULE 8-2

How Many Board of Directors Members Are Ideal?

Recent research reveals that companies with fewer board members outperform larger boards, largely because having fewer directors facilitates deeper debates, more nimble decision making, and greater accountability. For example, there are only 8 members on Apple's board, and Apple is doing great. Recent research reveals that among companies with a market capitalization of at least $10 billion, smaller boards produced substantially higher shareholder returns between 2011 and 2014. Research also shows that 9-person boards perform much better, for example, than 14- to 15-member boards. As a result of this recent research, many companies are reducing their number of board members. Another benefit of fewer board members is that CEOs are more often reprimanded (or dismissed) if needed. Dr. David Yermack, a finance professor at New York University's business school, reports that smaller boards are generally more decisive, more cohesive, more hands-on, and have more informal meetings and fewer committees. Netflix is another example of a company with a small board,

only 7 members, who debate extensively before approving important management moves. Netflix is doing great. In contrast, Eli Lilly & Co. has 14 board members who find it "too big to encourage the kinds of discussions you want, because drilling down on different issues simply takes too long; members feel constrained even asking a second or third question." Bank of America has 15 directors—too many to be efficient. In addition, the chair of the board should rarely, if ever, be the same person as the CEO, as discussed. In summary, companies should seek to reduce their board of directors to fewer than 10 persons, whenever possible—and strategy students should examine this issue in their assigned case companies.

Source: Based on Joann Lublin, "Are Smaller Boards Better for Investors?" *Wall Street Journal*, August 27, 2014. Also based on Den Favaro, Per-Ola Karlsson, and Gary Neilson, "The $112 Billion CEO Succession Problem," *Strategy + Business*, PwC Strategy (May 4, 2015).

extensive confidential briefing information posted there by the firm's top management team. Then the board members meet face-to-face fully informed every two months to discuss the biggest issues facing the firm. New board involvement policies are aimed at curtailing lawsuits against board members.

Today, boards of directors are composed mostly of outsiders who are becoming more involved in organizations' strategic management. The trend in the United States is toward much greater board member accountability with smaller boards, now averaging 12 members rather than 18 as they did a few years ago. *BusinessWeek* recently evaluated the boards of most large U.S. companies and provided the following "principles of good governance":

1. Never have more than two of the firm's executives (current or past) on the board.
2. Never allow a firm's executives to serve on the board's audit, compensation, or nominating committee.
3. Require all board members to own a large amount of the firm's equity.
4. Require all board members to attend at least 75 percent of all meetings.
5. Require the board to meet annually to evaluate its own performance, without the CEO, COO, or top management in attendance.
6. Never allow the CEO to be chairperson of the board.
7. Never allow interlocking directorships (where a director or CEO sits on another director's board).[11]

Jeff Sonnerfeld, associate dean of the Yale School of Management, comments, "Boards of directors are now rolling up their sleeves and becoming much more closely involved with management decision making." Company CEOs and boards are required to personally certify financial statements; company loans to company executives and directors are illegal; and there is faster reporting of insider stock transactions. Just as directors place more emphasis on staying informed about an organization's health and operations, they are also taking a more active role in ensuring that publicly issued documents are accurate representations of a firm's status. Failure to accept responsibility for auditing or evaluating a firm's strategy is considered a serious breach of a director's duties. Legal suits are becoming more common against directors for fraud, omissions, inaccurate disclosures, lack of due diligence, and culpable ignorance about a firm's operations.

IMPLICATIONS FOR STRATEGISTS

This chapter has revealed six new matrices widely used by strategists to gain and sustain a firm's competitive advantages, the core purpose of strategic planning, as illustrated in Figure 8-14. Five of the six are matching tools, SWOT, SPACE, BCG, IE, and GRAND, coupled with the single decision-making tool, QSPM. Whereas some consulting firms and some textbooks advocate using only one or two matrices in strategic planning, our experience is that all six tools introduced in this chapter are uniquely valuable. Coupled with the External Factor Evaluation Matrix, the Competitive Profile Matrix, and the Internal Factor Evaluation Matrix from earlier

chapters, the nine tools together give strategists the best means for leading a firm down the narrow path to success. Rarely is the path to success wide or easy, due to parity, commoditization, imitation, duplication, substitute products, global competitors, and the willingness and ability of consumers to switch allegiances and loyalties. Employees expect strategists to formulate a superior "game plan," so their hard work implementing the strategic plan will yield job security, good compensation, and ultimately happiness for employees.

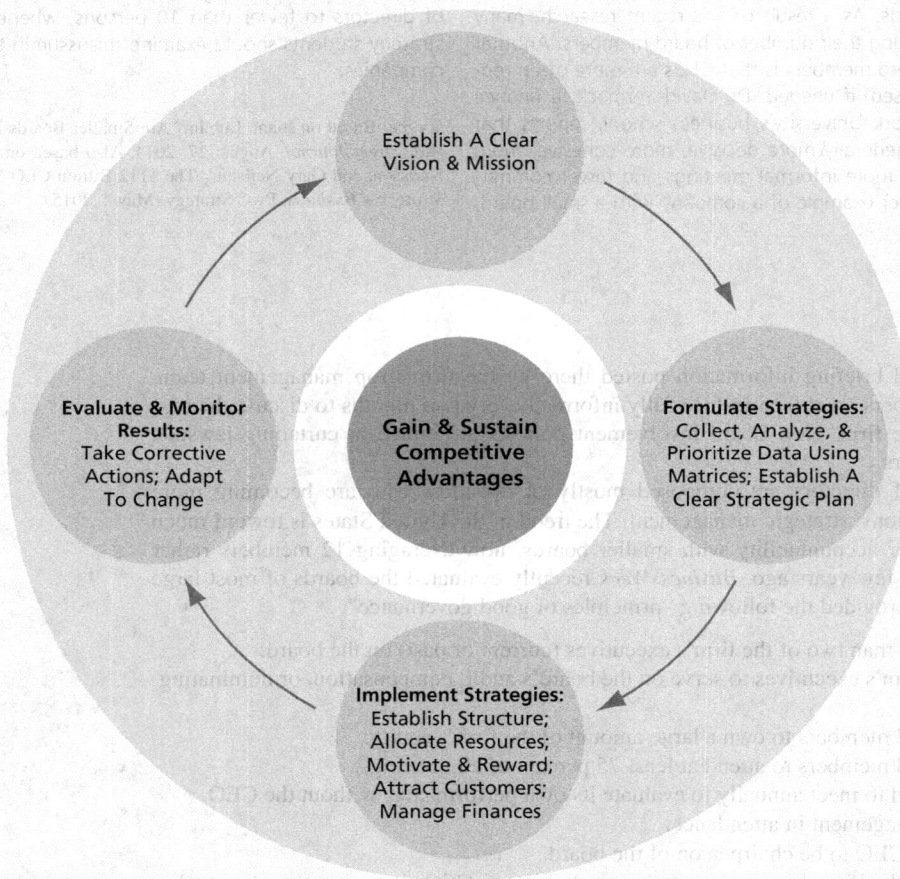

FIGURE 8-14

How to Gain and Sustain Competitive Advantages

IMPLICATIONS FOR STUDENTS

In preparing the strategy-formulation matrices presented in this chapter, it is important to avoid "wild guesses," but at the same time to become comfortable with "excellent estimates," as needed, based on research, to move forward with appropriate matrices. Sometimes students are so accustomed (due to their accounting and finance classes especially) to being counted wrong if their answer is

off at the third decimal place, that it takes a while in a strategic management class to realize that businesses make "excellent estimates based on research" all the time, because no one is sure what tomorrow will bring. So, if you can make reasonable estimates, move forward with particular matrices. For example, with the BCG Matrix, if segment information is not provided, enter only a single circle in the matrix for the overall firm, rather than two or more circles for the divisions. But be mindful that multiple circles could be included based on the number of stores, or the number of customers, rather than traditional dollar revenue numbers, so do not rush to the conclusion that portfolio information is not available.

To generate and decide on alternative strategies that will best gain and sustain competitive advantages, your SWOT, SPACE, BCG, IE, Grand, and QSPM need to be developed accurately. However, in covering those matrices in an oral presentation, focus more on the implications of those analyses than the nuts-and-bolts calculations. In other words, as you go through those matrices in a presentation, your goal is not to prove to the class that you did the calculations correctly. They expect accuracy and clarity and certainly you should have that covered. It is the implications of each matrix that your audience will be most interested in, so use these matrices to pave the way for your recommendations with costs, which generally come just a page or two deeper into the project. A good rule of thumb is to spend at least an equal amount of time on the implications as the actual calculations of each matrix when presented. This approach will improve the delivery aspect of your presentation or paper by maintaining the high interest level of your audience. Focusing on implications rather than calculations will also encourage questions from the audience when you finish. Silence from an audience is a bad sign because silence could mean your audience was asleep, disinterested, or did not feel you did a good job. Also, utilize the free Excel student template at www.strategyclub.com as needed.

The Sarbanes-Oxley Act resulted in scores of boardroom overhauls among publicly traded companies. Board audit committees must now have at least one financial expert as a member, and meet 10 or more times per year, rather than 3 of 4 times as they did prior to the act. The act put an end to the "country club" atmosphere of most boards and shifted power from CEOs to directors. Although aimed at public companies, the act has also had a similar impact on privately owned companies. A board of directors should conduct an annual strategy audit in much the same fashion that it reviews the annual financial audit.

Recent research reveals that about 31 percent of boards of directors have served a decade or longer, and there is a movement nationwide to replace highly tenured board members with fresh, new talent.[12] Many companies have a mandatory retirement age of 75 for board members, but analysts expect that age limit to drop due to new technological prowess and the tendency to investigate new ideas.

Women make up only 19.2 percent of board members at companies in the S&P 500, but in 2014, 29 percent of new board members appointed were women, and the number of companies with no women on the board dropped to 18 from 25 the prior year.[13] Analysts say it is no longer acceptable for a company to have zero board members who are women. For example, Twitter's board was all men at the time of its initial public offering (IPO) and this fact drew widespread criticism, and makes a firm more vulnerable to discrimination lawsuits.

Chapter Summary

The essence of strategy formulation is an assessment of whether an organization is doing the right things and how it can be more effective in what it does. Every organization should be wary of becoming a prisoner of its own strategy, for even the best strategies become obsolete sooner or later. Regular reappraisal of strategy helps management avoid complacency. Objectives and strategies should be consciously developed and coordinated and should not merely evolve out of day-to-day operating decisions.

An organization with no sense of direction and no coherent strategy precipitates its own demise. When an organization does not know where it wants to go, it usually ends up some place it does not want to be. Every organization needs to consciously establish and communicate clear objectives and strategies. Any organization, whether military, product-oriented, service-oriented, governmental, or even athletic, must develop and execute good strategies to win. A good offense without a good defense, or vice versa, usually leads to defeat. Developing strategies that use strengths to capitalize on opportunities could be considered an offense, whereas strategies designed to improve on weaknesses while avoiding threats could be termed defensive. Every organization has some external opportunities and threats and internal strengths and weaknesses that can be aligned to formulate feasible alternative strategies.

Modern strategy-formulation tools and concepts described in this chapter are integrated into a practical three-stage framework. Tools such as the SWOT Matrix, SPACE Matrix, BCG Matrix, IE Matrix, and QSPM can significantly enhance the quality of strategic decisions, but they should never be used to dictate the choice of strategies. Behavioral, cultural, and political aspects of strategy generation and selection are always important to consider and manage. Because of increased legal pressure from outside groups, boards of directors are assuming a more active role in strategy analysis and choice. This is a positive trend for organizations.

Key Terms and Concepts

Aggressive Quadrant (p. 255)
Attractiveness Scores (AS) (p. 267)
board of directors (p. 271)
Boston Consulting Group (BCG) Matrix (p. 258)
business portfolio (p. 258)
cash cows (p. 259)
champions (p. 271)
competitive position (CP) (p. 254)
Competitive Quadrant (p. 257)
Conservative Quadrant (p. 257)
decision stage (p. 250)
Defensive Quadrant (p. 257)
directional vector (p. 255)
dogs (p. 260)
financial position (FP) (p. 254)
governance (p. 271)
Grand Strategy Matrix (p. 265)
halo error (p. 250)
industry growth rate (p. 259)
industry position (IP) (p. 254)

input stage (p. 250)
Internal-External (IE) Matrix (p. 261)
matching (p. 251)
matching stage (p. 250)
Quantitative Strategic Planning Matrix (QSPM) (p. 266)
question marks (p. 259)
relative market share position (RMSP) (p. 258)
SO strategies (p. 251)
stability position (SP) (p. 254)
stars (p. 259)
Strategic Position and Action Evaluation (SPACE) Matrix (p. 254)
strategy-formulation analytical framework (p. 250)
Strengths-Weaknesses-Opportunities-Threats (SWOT) Matrix (p. 251)
ST strategies (p. 252)
Sum Total Attractiveness Scores (STAS) (p. 269)
Total Attractiveness Scores (TAS) (p. 269)
WO strategies (p. 252)
WT strategies (p. 252)

Issues for Review and Discussion

⭐ 8-1. Unilever has done really well for decades. How does Unilever do so well? How can they continue to prosper?

⭐ 8-2. Give an internal and external strength of Unilever. Show how those two factors are related to reveal a feasible alternative strategy.

8-3. What do you believe are the three major external opportunities that Unilever faces?

8-4. Develop a SPACE Matrix for Unilever. Explain the implications of your Matrix.

8-5. Develop a BCG Matrix for Unilever. Explain the implications of your Matrix.

8-6. Develop a QSPM for Unilever that includes two strategies, six internal factors, and six external factors. What strategy appears to be best for Unilever to pursue?

8-7. Do a Google search using the key terms "boards of directors." What new information did you learn that was not given in the chapter?

8-8. In preparing a SPACE Matrix, which axis would the European political and economic unrest fall under?

8-9. In preparing a BCG Matrix, what would be the best range for the IGR axis as applied to the beverage industry?

⭐ **8-10.** List four reasons why the IE Matrix is widely considered to be superior to the BCG Matrix.

8-11. Is there a limit to the number of strategies that could be examined in a QSPM? Why?

⭐ **8-12.** Go to Adidas' website and examine what you can find about the company's board of directors. Evaluate Adidas' board based on guidelines presented in the chapter.

8-13. Explain why the CEO of a firm should not also be chairperson of the board of directors.

8-14. In preparing a QSPM, what should be done if the TAS for each strategy are identical?

8-15. Understand the "Implications for Students" section and discuss what is to be in mind while preparing strategy-formulation matrices.

8-16. Develop a Grand Strategy Matrix for Unilever and include one rival firm.

8-17. Explain what should be done if the SPACE vector co-ordinate point is (0,0).

⭐ **8-18.** Why is it important to work row by row instead of column by column in preparing a QSPM?

8-19. When constructing a SPACE Matrix, would it be appropriate to use a 1 to 10 scale for all axes?

8-20. If Unilever has the leading market share in Russia, where along the top axis of a BCG Matrix would their Russia Operations be plotted?

⭐ **8-21.** Develop a SWOT Matrix for yourself.

⭐ **8-22.** Why is "matching" internal with external factors such an important strategic management activity?

8-23. Illustrate the strategy formulation framework that includes three stages and nine analytical tools. Which stage and tool do you feel is most important? Why?

8-24. Develop an example SWOT Matrix for your college or university with two items in each quadrant. Make sure your strategies clearly exemplify "matching" and show this with (S1, T2) type notation.

8-25. Develop an example SPACE Matrix for a global company that you are familiar with. Include two factors for each of the four axes (SP, IP, SP, and CP).

8-26. What would be an appropriate SP rating for Unilever?

8-27. Discuss the pros and cons of divulging divisional information to stakeholders.

8-28. Develop an example BCG Matrix for a company that has three divisions with revenues of 4, 8, and 12 and profits of 5, 3, and 2, respectively.

8-29. Develop a SPACE Matrix for a firm that is a weak competitor competing in a slow growing and unstable industry. Label axes and quadrants clearly.

8-30. Discuss the limitations of a BCG analysis and the limitations of a SPACE analysis.

8-31. Prepare an IE Matrix for a company with two divisions that have 30 and 60 in revenues to go with 10 and 15 in profits.

8-32. Develop a Grand Strategy Matrix with two example companies in each quadrant, i.e., companies that you know something about and that you would place in those quadrants.

8-33. Develop a QSPM for yourself—given two strategies: 1) go to graduate school or 2) begin working full-time.

8-34. Would a QSPM analysis be useful without the weight column? Why or why not?

8-35. Discuss the characteristics of successful strategists in terms of political factions within the firm.

8-36. In order of attractiveness to you, rank the political Tactics presented in Chapter 9.

8-37. For a business in your city, list in order of importance the top eight board-of-director duties and responsibilities listed in the chapter.

8-38. Discuss the pros and cons of Sweden's new board-of director rule regarding women.

8-39. Develop a SPACE Matrix for your college or university.

8-40. Develop a BCG Matrix for your college or university.

8-41. Explain the limitations of the BCG, SPACE, and SWOT.

8-42. Develop a QSPM for a local company that you are familiar with.

8-43. Write a short essay that reveals your recommendations to firms, regarding disclosure of financial information.

8-44. Explain why a before and after BCG and IE analysis can be useful in presenting a strategic plan for consideration.

8-45. Find an example of a company, on the Internet, which has both a Cash Cow and a Question Mark division.

8-46. Regarding a Grand Strategy Matrix, identify two companies that would be located in your judgment in each quadrant—identify eight firms total.

8-47. For a non-profit company, list in order of importance the top 10 board-of-director duties and responsibilities.

8-48. Regarding the principles of good governance in the chapter, list in order of importance the top seven guidelines.

⭐ **8-49.** List some limitations of the SPACE Matrix.

⭐ **8-50.** Since 40.2 percent of all cigarettes sold are Marlboro, followed by 12.2 percent for Newport, what is Newport's relative market share position in a BCG Matrix sense?

⭐ **8-51.** How many board of directors members are ideal?

ASSURANCE OF LEARNING EXERCISES

EXERCISE 8A
Should Unilever Penetrate Southeast Asia Further?

Purpose

Unilever is featured in the opening chapter case as a firm that engages in excellent strategic planning. Unilever is the world's third-largest consumer goods company (behind Procter & Gamble and Nestlé). Some of Unilever's best selling brands are Aviance, Ben & Jerry's, Dove, Flora/Becel, Hellmann's, Knorr, Lipton, Lux/Radox, Omo/Surf, Sunsilk, Toni & Guy, VO5, Wall's, and PG Tips.

The purpose of this exercise is to give you experience investigating a particular region of the world to determine whether a firm should expand more into that region of the world. Unilever has recently begun construction of a new factory in Yangon, Myanmar, and by 2015 expects to provide direct and indirect employment for over 2,000 people in Myanmar. The company currently employs close to 200 Myanmar employees at its factory in Thailand, of which a number are being moved back to Myanmar to help kick-start its operations in the country.

Instructions

Step 1	Go to the Unilever website and download the company's most recent *Annual Report*. Examine the narrative and tables related to their operations in Southeast Asia.
Step 2	Research the competitive climate and business culture of Myanmar and two other countries in Southeast Asia as well as the operations of rival Nestlé.
Step 3	Develop six recommendations for Unilever based on your assessment of their present and potential operations in Southeast Asia.

EXERCISE 8B
Perform a SWOT Analysis for Unilever's Global Operations

Purpose

Unilever's global and domestic business segments could be required to submit a SWOT analysis annually to corporate top executives who merge divisional analyses into an overall corporate analysis. This exercise will give you practice performing a SWOT analysis.

Instructions

Step 1	Review Unilever's global operations as described in the company's most recent *Annual Report*. Unilever recently acquired 82 percent of the Russia-based beauty company Kalina.
Step 2	Review industry and competitive information pertaining to Unilever's global operations, especially as compared to rival Procter & Gamble.
Step 3	Join with two other students in class. Together, develop a global SWOT Matrix for Unilever's global business segment. Follow all the SWOT guidelines provided in the chapter, including (S4, T3)-type notation at the end of each strategy. Include three strategies in each of the four (SO, ST, WT, WO) quadrants. Avoid generic strategy terms such as Forward Integration.
Step 4	Turn in your team-developed SWOT Matrix to your professor for a class work grade.

EXERCISE 8C
Prepare a BCG Matrix for Unilever

Purpose

This exercise will give you practice preparing both a by-product and a by-region-based BCG Matrix. Unilever has four major product segments of the company: Personal Care, Food, Refreshment, and

Home Care. The company also has three major geographic segments: Europe, The Americas, and Asia/AMET/RUB.

Instructions

Step 1   Review Unilever's global operations as described in the company's most recent *Annual Report* and *Form 10K*.

Step 2   Prepare a up-to-date BCG matrices for Unilever's 1) four product categories and 2) three geographic divisions.

Step 3   Write a two-page executive summary to reveal the strategic implications of your analyses.

EXERCISE 8D
Develop a SWOT Matrix for Nestlé S.A.

Purpose

The most widely used strategy formulation technique among firms worldwide is the SWOT Matrix. This exercise requires development of a SWOT Matrix for Nestlé. Matching key external and internal factors in a SWOT Matrix requires good intuitive and conceptual skills. You will improve with practice in developing a SWOT Matrix.

Instructions

Recall from Exercise 7B that you already may have determined Nestlé's external opportunities/threats and internal strengths/weaknesses. This information could be used to complete this exercise. Follow the steps outlined as follows:

Step 1   On a separate sheet of paper, construct a large nine-cell diagram that will represent your SWOT Matrix. Appropriately label the cells.

Step 2   Record Nestlé's opportunities/threats and strengths/weaknesses in your diagram.

Step 3   Match key external and internal factors to generate feasible alternative strategies for Nestlé. Record SO, WO, ST, and WT strategies in appropriate cells of the SWOT Matrix. Use the proper notation to indicate the rationale for the strategies. Try to include four strategies in each of the four strategy cells.

Step 4   Compare your SWOT Matrix to other students' SWOT Matrices. Discuss any major differences.

EXERCISE 8E
Develop a SPACE Matrix for Nestlé S.A.

Purpose

Should Nestlé pursue aggressive, conservative, competitive, or defensive strategies? Develop a SPACE Matrix for Nestlé to answer this question. Elaborate on the strategic implications of your directional vector. Be specific in terms of strategies that could benefit Nestlé.

Instructions

Step 1   Join with two other persons in your class and develop a joint SPACE Matrix for Nestlé.

Step 2   Diagram your SPACE Matrix on the board. Compare your matrix with other teams' matrices.

Step 3   Discuss the implications of your SPACE Matrix.

EXERCISE 8F
Develop a BCG Matrix for Nestlé S.A.

Purpose

Portfolio matrices are widely used by multidivisional organizations to help identify and select strategies to pursue. A BCG analysis identifies particular divisions that should receive fewer resources than others. It may identify some divisions to be divested. This exercise can give you practice developing a BCG Matrix.

Instructions

Step 1   Place the following five column headings at the top of a separate sheet of paper: Divisions, Revenues, Profits, Relative Market Share Position, and Industry Growth Rate. Down the far left of your page, list Nestlé's by-product segments. Turn back to the Cohesion Case and find information to fill in all the cells in your data table.

Step 2   Complete 1) a BCG and 2) an IE Matrix for Nestlé.

Step 3   Compare your BCG Matrix to other students' matrices. Discuss any major differences.

EXERCISE 8G
Develop a QSPM for Nestlé S.A.

Purpose

This exercise can give you practice developing a Quantitative Strategic Planning Matrix (QSPM) to determine the relative attractiveness of various strategic alternatives.

Instructions

Step 1   Join with two other students in class to develop a joint QSPM for Nestlé.

Step 2   Go to the board and record your strategies and their Sum Total Attractiveness Scores. Compare your team's strategies and sum total attractiveness scores to those of other teams. Be sure not to assign the same AS score in a given row. Recall that dashes should be inserted all the way across a given row when used.

Step 3   Discuss any major differences.

EXERCISE 8H
Develop a SPACE Matrix for Unilever

Purpose

Should Unilever pursue aggressive, conservative, competitive, or defensive strategies? Develop a SPACE Matrix for Unilever to answer this question. Elaborate on the strategic implications of your directional vector. Be specific in terms of strategies that could benefit Unilever.

Instructions

Step 1   Join with two other persons in class and develop a joint SPACE Matrix for Unilever.

Step 2   Diagram your SPACE Matrix on the board. Compare your matrix with other teams' matrices.

Step 3   Discuss the implications of your SPACE Matrix.

EXERCISE 8I
Develop a BCG Matrix for Your College or University

Purpose

Developing a BCG Matrix for many nonprofit organizations, including colleges and universities, is a useful exercise. Of course, there are no profits for each division or department—and in some cases no revenues. However, be creative in performing a BCG Matrix. For example, the pie slice in the circles can represent the number of majors receiving jobs on graduation, the number of faculty teaching in that area, or some other variable that you believe is important to consider. The size of the circles can represent the number of students majoring in particular departments or areas.

Instructions

Step 1   Develop a BCG Matrix for your university. Include all academic schools, departments, or colleges.

Step 2   Diagram your BCG Matrix on the blackboard.

Step 3   Discuss differences among the BCG Matrices on the board.

EXERCISE 8J
Develop a QSPM for a Company That You Are Familiar with

Purpose

This exercise can give you practice developing a Quantitative Strategic Planning Matrix (QSPM) to determine the relative attractiveness of various strategic alternatives.

Instructions

Step 1   Join with two other students in class to develop a joint QSPM for a company that all of you are familiar with.

Step 2   Record your strategies and their Sum Total Attractiveness Scores. Compare your team's strategies and sum total attractiveness scores to those of other teams. Be sure not to assign the same AS score in a given row. Recall that dashes should be inserted all the way across a given row when used.

Step 3   Discuss any major differences.

EXERCISE 8K

Formulate Individual Strategies

Purpose

Individuals and organizations are alike in many ways. Each has competitors, and each should plan for the future. Every individual and organization faces some external opportunities and threats and has some internal strengths and weaknesses. Both individuals and organizations establish objectives and allocate resources. These and other similarities make it possible for individuals to use many strategic management concepts and tools. This exercise is designed to demonstrate how the SWOT Matrix can be used by an individual to plan his or her future. As one nears completion of a college degree and begins interviewing for jobs, planning can be particularly important.

Instructions

Construct a SWOT Matrix. Include what you consider to be your major external opportunities, your major external threats, your major strengths, and your major weaknesses. An internal weakness may be a low grade point average. An external opportunity may be that your university offers a graduate program that interests you. Match key external and internal factors by recording in the appropriate cell of the matrix alternative strategies or actions that would allow you to capitalize on your strengths, overcome your weaknesses, take advantage of your external opportunities, and minimize the impact of external threats. Be sure to use the appropriate matching notation in the strategy cells of the matrix. Because every individual (and organization) is unique, there is no one right answer to this exercise.

MINI-CASE ON HYUNDAI MOTOR COMPANY (HYMTF)

HOW WOULD A BCG FOR HYUNDAI LOOK LIKE?

Source: © ronfromyork.
Shutterstock

Hyundai Motor Company is a large multinational automotive manufacturer based in Seoul, South Korea, that also owns a 32.8 percent of Kia Motors. Currently the fourth largest vehicle manufacturer in the world, Hyundai operates the world's largest integrated automobile manufacturing facility in Ulsan, South Korea. With around 75,000 employees globally, Hyundai sells automobiles across 193 countries with the help of around 6,000 dealerships and showrooms.

In August 2015, the five largest auto brands in China are Volkswagen, General Motors, Nissan Motor, Hyundai Motor, and Toyota Motor. Among these five companies, only Toyota is on track to meet its full-year 2015 target, while Hyundai is performing the worst. Specifically, in the first-half of 2015, Toyota's China sales rose 10 percent, on track to meet their 20 percent full-year's growth target. In contrast, Hyundai's China sales fell 8 percent although the company has a 3 percent full-year growth target. Hyundai recently posted its lowest monthly China sales figure in four years, selling

54,160 cars in July, 2015, down 32 percent from a year ago. Hyundai Motor stock price dropped 4.1 percent in Seoul in one day due to weak China data and strong Korean won. Currency movements of the won versus the Japanese yen and the Chinese yuan heavily impact automobile sales.

Questions

1. On a BCG Matrix for Hyundai, what would be the RMSP value for company's operations in South Korea?
2. On a BCG Matrix for Hyundai, what would be an appropriate IGR value for the company's operations in China?
3. HYMTF stock sold for $39 on 21 August, 2015. If the stock price rises 39 percent as expected, what would the price become?

Source: Based on company documents from automobile companies.

Current Readings

Barton, Dominic, and Mark Wiseman. "Where Boards Fall Short." *Harvard Business Review* (January–February 2015).

Beckman, Christine M., et al. "Relational Pluralism in De Novo Organizations: Boards of Directors as Bridges or Barriers to Diverse Alliance Portfolios?" *Academy of Management Journal* 57, no. 2 (2014): 460–483.

Donaldson, Lex, Steven D. Charlier, and Jane X. J. Qiu. "Corrigendum to Organizational Portfolio Analysis: Focusing on Risk Inside the Corporation." *Long Range Planning* 45, no. 4 (2012): 235–257.

Hacklin, F., B. Battistini, and G. Von Krogh. "Strategic Choices in Converging Industries." *MIT Sloan Management Review* 55, no. 1 (2013): 65–73.

Joseph, John, William Ocasio, and Mary-Hunter McDonnell. "The Structural Elaboration of Board Independence: Executive Power, Institutional Logics, and the Adoption of CEO-Only Board Structures in U.S. Corporate Governance." *Academy of Management Journal* 57 (December 2014): 1834–1858.

Misangyi, Vilmos F., and Abhijith G. Acharya. "Substitutes or Complements? A Configurational Examination of Corporate Governance Mechanisms." *Academy of Management Journal* 57 (December 2014): 1681–1705.

Reuer, J. J., E. Klijn, and C. S. Lioukas. "Board Involvement in International Joint Ventures." *Strategic Management Journal*, 35, no. 11 (November 2014): 1626–1644.

Tihanyi, Laszio, Scott Graffin, and Gerard George. "Rethinking Governance in Management Research." *Academy of Management Journal* 57 (December 2014): 1535–1543.

Zhu, David H., and James D Westphal. "How Directors' Prior Experience with Other Demographically Similar CEOs Affects Their Appointments onto Corporate Boards and the Consequences for CEO Compensation." *Academy of Management Journal* 57, no. 3 (2014): 791–813.

Endnotes

1. R. T. Lenz, "Managing the Evolution of the Strategic Planning Process," *Business Horizons* 30, no. 1 (January–February 1987): 37.
2. Robert Grant, "The Resource-Based Theory of Competitive Advantage: Implications for Strategy Formulation," *California Management Review* (Spring 1991): 114.
3. Heinz Weihrich, "The TOWS Matrix: A Tool for Situational Analysis," *Long Range Planning* 15, no. 2 (April 1982): 61. *Note:* Although Dr. Weihrich first modified SWOT analysis to form the TOWS matrix, the acronym SWOT is much more widely used than TOWS in practice. See also Marilyn Helms and Judy Nixon, "Exploring SWOT Analysis—Where Are We Now?"

Journal of Strategy and Management 3, no. 3 (2010): 215–251.
4. Greg Dess, G. T. Lumpkin, and Alan Eisner, *Strategic Management: Text and Cases* (New York: McGraw-Hill/Irwin, 2006), 72.
5. Adapted from H. Rowe, R. Mason, and K. Dickel, *Strategic Management and Business Policy: A Methodological Approach* (Reading, MA: Addison-Wesley, 1982), 155–156.
6. Fred David, "The Strategic Planning Matrix—A Quantitative Approach," *Long Range Planning* 19, no. 5 (October 1986): 102; Andre Gib and Robert Margulies, "Making Competitive Intelligence Relevant to the User," *Planning Review* 19, no. 3 (May–June 1991): 21.

7. Meredith E. David, Forest R. David, and Fred R. David, "The QSPM: A New Marketing Tool," Presented at the International Academy of Business and Public Administration Disciplines (IABPAD) Meeting in Dallas, Texas, April 2015.

8. Y. Allarie and M. Firsirotu, "How to Implement Radical Strategies in Large Organizations," *Sloan Management Review* 26, no. 3 (Spring 1985): 19. Another excellent article is P. Shrivastava, "Integrating Strategy Formulation with Organizational Culture," *Journal of Business Stratgegy* 5, no. 3 (Winter 1985): 103–111.

9. James Brian Quinn, *Strategies for Changes: Logical Incrementalism* (Homewood, IL: Irwin, 1980), 128–145.

These political tactics are listed in A. Thompson and A. Strickland, *Strategic Management: Concepts and Cases* (Plano, TX: Business Publications, 1984), 261.

10. William Guth and Ian Macmillan, "Strategy Implementation versus Middle Management Self-Interest," *Strategic Management Journal* 7, no. 4 (July–August 1986): 321.

11. Louis Lavelle, "The Best and Worst Boards," *BusinessWeek,* October 7, 2002, 104–110.

12. Joann Lublin, "Boards' Longtimers Face Pressure to Move On," *Wall Street Journal*, December 24, 2014, B6.

13. Rachel Feintzeig, "Changes Ahead for Women on Boards," *Wall Street Journal*, January 13, 2015, B1.

Strategy Implementation

LEARNING OBJECTIVES

After studying this chapter, you should be able to do the following:

9-1. Identify and describe strategic marketing issues vital for strategy implementation.

9-2. Explain why social media marketing is an important strategy-implementation tool.

9-3. Explain why market segmentation is an important strategy-implementation tool.

9-4. Explain how to use product positioning (perceptual mapping) as a strategy-implementation tool.

9-5. Identify and describe strategic finance/accounting issues vital for strategy implementation.

9-6. Perform EPS/EBIT analysis to evaluate the attractiveness of debt versus stock as a source of capital to implement strategies.

9-7. Develop projected financial statements to reveal the impact of strategy recommendations.

9-8. Determine the cash value of any business using four corporate evaluation methods.

9-9. Discuss IPOs, keeping cash offshore, and issuing corporate bonds as strategic decisions that face many firms.

9-10. Discuss the nature and role of research and development (R&D) in strategy implementation.

9-11. Explain how management information systems (MISs) impact strategy-implementation efforts.

ASSURANCE OF LEARNING EXERCISES

The following exercises are found at the end of this chapter:

S trategies can be implemented successfully only when an organization markets its goods and services effectively and raises needed working capital. This chapter examines marketing, finance/accounting, research and development (R&D), and management information systems (MIS) issues that are central to effective strategy implementation. Special topics include market segmentation, market positioning, evaluating the worth of a business, determining to what extent debt or stock should be used as a source of capital, developing projected financial statements, contracting R&D outside the firm, and creating an information support system. Manager and employee involvement and participation are essential for success in marketing, finance and accounting, R&D, and MIS activities.

A football quarterback can call the best play possible in the huddle, but that does not mean the play will go for a touchdown. The team may even lose yardage unless the play is executed (implemented) well. Royal Dutch Shell (Shell) is implementing strategies especially well, as described below.

Strategy implementation generally impacts the lives of everyone in an organization. In some situations, individuals may not have participated in the strategy-formulation process at all and may not appreciate or understand the thought that went into strategy formulation, nor accept the work required for strategy implementation. There may even be foot dragging or resistance on their part. Managers and employees who do not understand the business and are not committed to the business may attempt to sabotage strategy-implementation efforts in hopes that the organization will return to its old ways. The strategy-implementation stage of the strategic-management process is highlighted in Figure 9-1 as illustrated with white shading.

Strategic Marketing Issues

Countless marketing variables affect the success or failure of strategy implementation efforts. Some strategic marketing issues or decisions are as follows:

1. How to make advertisements more interactive to be more effective
2. How to take advantage of Facebook and Twitter conservations about the company and industry

Royal Dutch Shell Plc (RDS.A)

On September 2015, Royal Dutch Shell (Shell) announced the termination of its oil drilling activities in the Arctic offshore of Alaska. Incorporated in the United Kingdom but headquartered in the Netherlands, Shell ranks second globally among the largest oil and gas companies. It has worldwide reserves of the equivalent of 14.2 billion barrels of oil.

Oman, Nigeria, and the United Kingdom account for most of Shell's crude oil production, but the company is also spending a lot on converting oil sands in Alberta to synthetic oil through its Athabasca Oil Sands Project. With operations across 90 countries and in 44,000 gas stations, Shell is regarded as the world's largest retail fuel network. Vertically integrated, Shell explores, produces, refines, transports, and sells oil related products and chemicals. Upstream, Downstream, and Corporate are the three primary segments that the company has. Exploring for and retrieving crude oil and natural gas constitutes Shell's Upstream segment along with the liquefaction and transportation of gas, producing wind energy, and using oil sands to extract bitumen. The production, supply, and distribution and marketing activities for Shell's oil products and chemicals are taken care of by its Downstream segment. The Corporate segment includes all support functions, such as operations, legal, accounting, and maintenance.

For the second quarter of 2015, Shell's revenues were USD 70,969.53 million and the firm reported earnings of USD 3,907.14 million, and an EPS of USD 1.22. All of these numbers represented a significant drop from the prior year period, as oil and gas prices globally dropped significantly due to rising levels of supply coupled with lower demand.

Source: Based on company documents.

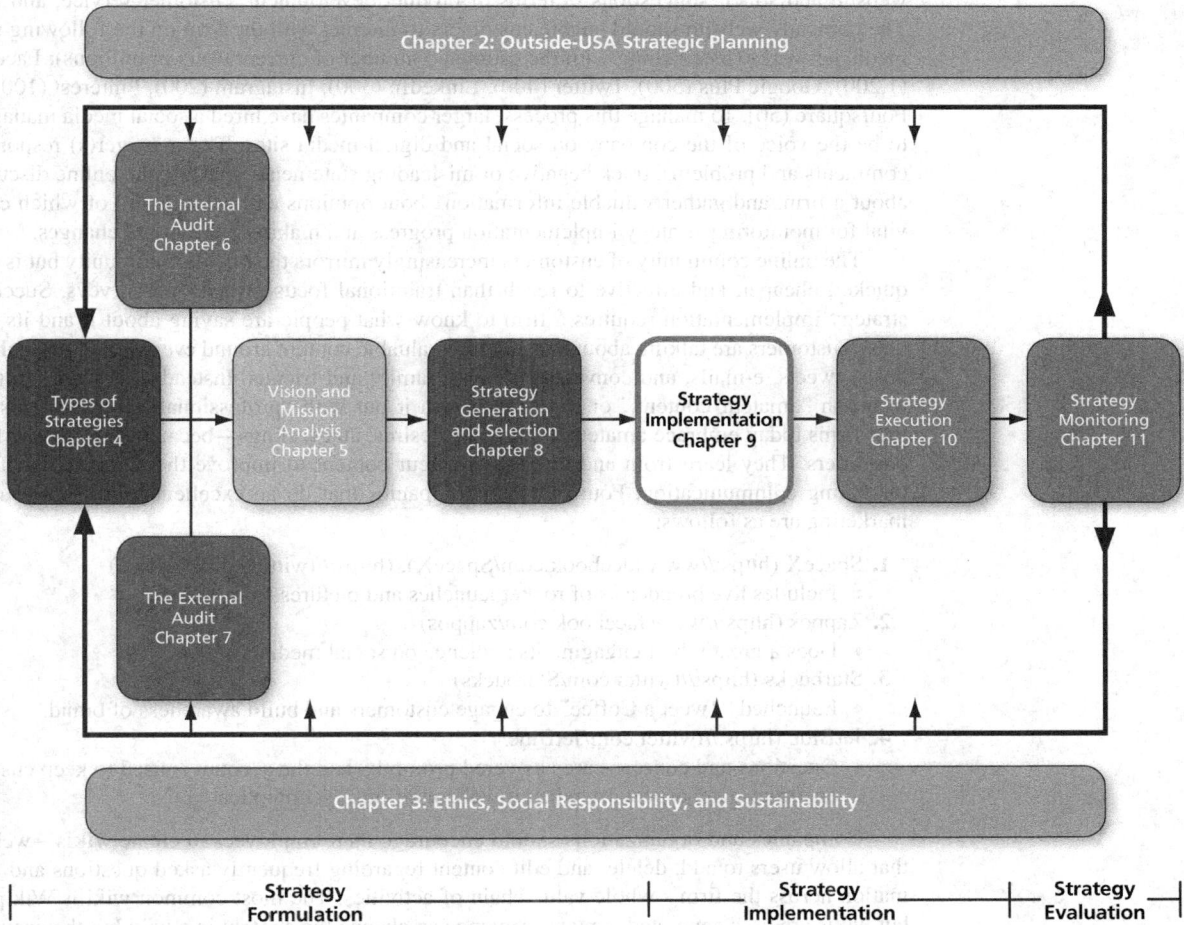

FIGURE 9-1
A Comprehensive Strategic-Management Model

Source: Fred R. David, adapted from "How Companies Define Their Mission," *Long Range Planning* 22, no. 3 (June 1988): 40, © Fred R. David.

3. To use exclusive dealerships or multiple channels of distribution
4. To use heavy, light, or no TV advertising versus online advertising
5. To limit (or not) the share of business done with a single customer
6. To be a price leader or a price follower
7. To offer a complete or limited warranty
8. To reward salespeople based on straight salary, commission, or a combination salary and commission

Three marketing activities especially important in strategy implementation are listed below and then discussed:

1. Engage customers in social media.
2. Segment markets effectively.
3. Develop and use product-positioning/perceptual maps.

Social Media Marketing

Social media marketing has become an important strategic issue. Marketing has evolved to be more about building a two-way relationship with consumers than just informing consumers about a product or service. Marketers increasingly must get customers involved in the company website and solicit suggestions in terms of product development, customer service, and ideas. The company website should enable customers to interact with the firm on the following social media networks (listed along with the estimated number of current users in millions): Facebook (1,200), Google Plus (500), Twitter (400), LinkedIn (300), Instagram (200), Pinterest (100), and Foursquare (50). To manage this process, larger companies have hired a social media manager(s) to be the voice of the company on social and digital media sites. The manager(s) responds to comments and problems, track negative or misleading statements, manage the online discussion about a firm, and gather valuable information about opinions and desires—all of which can be vital for monitoring strategy implementation progress and making appropriate changes.

The online community of customers increasingly mirrors the offline community but is much quicker, cheaper, and effective to reach than traditional focus groups and surveys. Successful strategy implementation requires a firm to know what people are saying about it and its products. Customers are talking about and creating valuable content around every brand through blog posts, tweets, e-mails, and conversations with family and friends. Instead of ignoring or trying to quash "amateur content," or trying to drown it out with "professional advertisements," the best firms today embrace amateurs' opinions, desires, and feelings—because they are the firms' customers. They learn from and leverage amateur content to improve the authenticity of their marketing communication. Four example companies that do an excellent job of social media marketing are as follows:

1. SpaceX (https://www.facebook.com/SpaceX); (https://twitter.com/SpaceX)
   • Includes live broadcasts of rocket launches and pictures from space.
2. Zappos (https://www.facebook.com/zappos)
   • Does a great job of engaging its audience on social media.
3. Starbucks (https://twitter.com/Starbucks)
   • Launched "Tweet a Coffee" to engage customers and build awareness of brand.
4. JetBlue (https://twitter.com/JetBlue/)
   • Questions and concerns are answered promptly, and the account is used to keep customers up-to-date, especially when travel conditions get complicated.

Companies and organizations should encourage their employees to create **wikis**—websites that allow users to add, delete, and edit content regarding frequently asked questions and information across the firm's whole value chain of activities. The most common wiki is Wikipedia, but wikis are user-generated content. Anyone can change the content in a wiki but the group and other editors can change the content submitted.

Firms benefit immensely by providing incentives to customers to share their thoughts, opinions, and experiences on the company website. Encourage customers to network among themselves on topics of their choosing on the company website. The company website must not be just about the company—it must be all about the customer too. Perhaps offer points, discounts, or coupons on the website for customers who provide ideas, suggestions, or feedback. Drive traffic to the company website, and then keep customers at the website for as long as possible with daily new material, updates, excitement, and offers. Encourage and promote customer participation and interaction. Customers trust other customers' opinions more than a company's marketing pitch, and the more they talk freely, the more the firm can learn how to improve its product, service, and marketing. Marketers should monitor blogs daily to determine, evaluate, and influence opinions being formed by customers. Customers must not feel like they are a captive audience for advertising at a firm's website. Table 9-1 provides new principles of marketing according to Parise, Guinan, and Weinberg.[1]

Wells Fargo and Bank of America **tweet** (Twitter.com) customers to describe features of bank products. Some banks are placing marketing videos on YouTube. UMB Financial of Kansas City, Missouri, tweets about everything from the bank's financial stability to the industry's prospects. Steve Furman, Discover's director of e-commerce, says the appeal of social networking is that it provides "pure, instant" communication with customers.[2]

Although the exponential increase in social networking has created huge opportunities for marketers, it also has produced some severe threats. Perhaps the greatest threat is that any kind of negative publicity travels fast online. Seemingly minor ethical and questionable actions can catapult these days into huge public relations problems for companies as a result of the monumental online social and business communications.

TABLE 9-1 The New Principles of Marketing

1. Do not just talk at consumers—work with them throughout the marketing process.
2. Give consumers a reason to participate.
3. Listen to—and join—the conversation outside your company's website.
4. Resist the temptation to sell, sell, sell. Instead attract, attract, attract.
5. Do not control online conversations; let it flow freely.
6. Find a "marketing technologist," a person who has three excellent skill sets (marketing, technology, and social interaction).
7. Embrace instant messaging and chatting.

Source: Based on Salvatore Parise, Patricia Guinan, and Bruce Weinberg, "The Secrets of Marketing in a Web 2.0 World," *Wall Street Journal,* December 15, 2008, R1.

Increasingly, people living in underdeveloped and poor nations around the world have smartphones, but oftentimes no computers. This is opening up even larger markets to online marketing. People in remote parts of Indonesia, Egypt, and Africa represent the fastest-growing customer base for many companies, including Opera Software ASA, a Norwegian maker of Internet browsers for mobile devices.

People ages 18 to 27 spend more time weekly on the Internet than watching television, listening to the radio, and watching DVDs combined. Most companies have come to the realization that social networking and video sites are better means of reaching customers than spending so many marketing dollars on traditional yellow pages, television, magazine, radio, or newspaper ads.

New companies such as Autonet Mobile based in San Francisco are selling new technology equipment for cars so that everyone in the vehicle can be online except, of course, the driver. This technology is accelerating the movement from hard media to web-based media. With this technology, when the vehicle drives into a new location, information on shows, museums, hotels, and other attractions in the location can be instantly downloaded.

Digital advertising spending on social media and mobile devices increased nearly 17 percent to $50 billion in the United States in 2014, comprising 28 percent of total ad spending in the nation; however, about 36 percent of all traffic on the Internet is fake, being the result of bogus computers programmed to visit websites to take advantage of marketers who typically pay for ads whenever they are loaded when a user visits a webpage, regardless if the user is an actual person.[3] Criminals can erect websites and deliver phony traffic and collect payments from advertisers through middlemen, oftentimes in third-world countries. This fraud problem is becoming so severe that Bob Liodice, CEO of the Association of National Advertisers, observes, "The total digital-media ad budget is being questioned and totally challenged; marketers want to spend more money in digital, but until there is more transparency on how their money is being spent, many hold back."[4]

The ad-fraud detection firm White Ops reports that more than $6 billion of online ads in the United States annually are paid to "fraudsters." Digital advertising is here to stay, no doubt, but there is a need to be increasingly careful of automated (fake) systems/websites/individuals securing your ad monies.

Market Segmentation

Market segmentation and product positioning rank as marketing's most important contributions to strategic management. **Market segmentation** can be defined as the subdividing of a market into distinct subsets of customers according to needs and buying habits. For example, eBay recently initiated a new market segmentation strategy to target consumers under 18 years old. "We're definitely looking at ways to legitimately bring younger people in," said Devin Wenig at eBay. "We won't allow a 15-year-old unfettered access to the site. We would want a parent, an adult, as a ride-along. But the age 18 and up group [is] an increasingly savvy and desirable consumer segment for us."

Market segmentation is important in strategy implementation for at least three major reasons. First, strategies such as market development, product development, market penetration,

TABLE 9-2 The Marketing Mix Component Variables

Product	Place	Promotion	Price
Quality	Distribution channels	Advertising	Level
Features and options	Distribution coverage	Personal selling	Discounts and
Style	Outlet location	Sales promotion	allowances
Brand name	Sales territories	Publicity	Payment terms
Packaging	Inventory levels and locations		
Product line	Transportation carriers		
Warranty			
Service level			
Other services			

Source: Based on E. Jerome McCarthy, *Basic Marketing: A Managerial Approach,* 9th ed. (Homewood, IL: Richard D. Irwin, Inc., 1987), 37–44. Used with permission.

and diversification require increased sales through new markets and products. To implement these strategies successfully, new or improved market-segmentation approaches are required. Second, market segmentation allows a firm to operate with limited resources because mass production, mass distribution, and mass advertising are not required. Market segmentation enables a small firm to compete successfully with a large firm by maximizing per-unit profits and per-segment sales. And third, market segmentation decisions directly affect **marketing mix variables**: product, place, promotion, and price, as indicated in Table 9-2. Geographic and demographic bases for segmenting markets are the most commonly employed, as illustrated in Table 9-3.

Evaluating potential market segments requires strategists to determine the characteristics and needs of consumers, to analyze consumer similarities and differences, and to develop consumer group profiles. Segmenting consumer markets is generally much simpler and easier than segmenting industrial markets, because industrial products, such as electronic circuits and forklifts, have multiple applications and appeal to diverse customer groups.

Segmentation is a key to matching supply and demand, which is one of the thorniest problems in customer service. Segmentation often reveals that large, random fluctuations in demand actually consist of several small, predictable, and manageable patterns. Matching supply and demand allows factories to produce desirable levels without extra shifts, overtime, and subcontracting. Matching supply and demand also minimizes the number and severity of stock-outs. The demand for hotel rooms, for example, can be dependent on foreign tourists, businesspersons, and vacationers. Focusing separately on these three market segments, however, can allow hotel firms to more effectively predict overall supply and demand.

Banks now are segmenting markets to increase effectiveness. "You're dead in the water if you aren't segmenting the market," observes Anne Moore, president of a bank consulting firm in Atlanta. The Internet makes market segmentation easier today because consumers naturally form "communities" on the Web.

To aid in segmenting markets and targeting specific groups of customers, companies commonly tag each of their active customers with three "retention" values:

- Tag 1: Is this customer at high risk of canceling the company's service? One of the most common indicators of high-risk customers is a drop off in usage of the company's service. For example, in the credit card industry this could be signaled through a customer's decline in spending on his or her card.
- Tag 2: Is this customer worth retaining? This determination boils down to whether the postretention profit generated from the customer is predicted to be greater than the cost incurred to retain the customer. Customers need to be managed as investments.
- Tag 3: What retention tactics should be used to retain this customer? For customers who are deemed "save-worthy," it is essential for the company to know which save tactics are most likely to be successful. Tactics commonly used range from providing "special" customer discounts to sending customers communications that reinforce the value proposition of the given service.[5]

TABLE 9-3 Alternative Bases for Market Segmentation

Variable	Typical Breakdowns
Geographic	
Region	Pacific, Mountain, West North Central, West South Central, East North Central, East South Central, South Atlantic, Middle Atlantic, New England
County Size	A, B, C, D
City Size	Under 5,000; 5,000–20,000; 20,001–50,000; 50,001–100,000; 100,001–250,000; 250,001–500,000; 500,001–1,000,000; 1,000,001–4,000,000; 4,000,001 or over
Density	Urban, suburban, rural
Climate	Northern, southern
Demographic	
Age	Under 6, 6–11, 12–19, 20–34, 35–49, 50–64, 65+
Gender	Male, female
Family Size	1–2, 3–4, 5+
Family Life Cycle	Young, single; young, married, no children; young, married, youngest child under 6; young, married, youngest child 6 or over; older, married, with children; older, married, no children under 18; older, single; other
Income	Under $10,000; $10,001–$15,000; $15,001–$20,000; $20,001–$30,000; $30,001–$50,000; $50,001–$70,000; $70,001–$100,000; over $100,000
Occupation	Professional and technical; managers, officials, and proprietors; clerical and sales; craftspeople; foremen; operatives; farmers; retirees; students; housewives; unemployed
Education	Grade school or less; some high school; high school graduate; some college; college graduate
Religion	Catholic, Protestant, Jewish, Islamic, other
Race	White, Asian, Hispanic, African American
Nationality	American, British, French, German, Scandinavian, Italian, Latin American, Middle Eastern, Japanese
Psychographic	
Social Class	Lower lowers, upper lowers, lower middles, upper middles, lower uppers, upper uppers
Personality	Compulsive, gregarious, authoritarian, ambitious
Behavioral	
Use Occasion	Regular occasion, special occasion
Benefits Sought	Quality, service, economy
User Status	Nonuser, ex-user, potential user, first-time user, regular user
Usage Rate	Light user, medium user, heavy user
Loyalty Status	None, medium, strong, absolute
Readiness Stage	Unaware, aware, informed, interested, desirous, intending to buy
Attitude toward Product	Enthusiastic, positive, indifferent, negative, hostile

Source: Adapted from Philip Kotler, *Marketing Management: Analysis, Planning and Control*, © 1984: 256. Adapted by permission of Prentice-Hall, Inc., Upper Saddle River, New Jersey.

The idea with retention-based segmentation is to examine and compare the attributes of active customers with the attributes of prior customers in order to better target potential customers with similar attributes. Using the theory that "birds of a feather flock together," the approach is based on the assumption that active customers will have similar retention outcomes as those of their comparable predecessor. This whole process is possible through business analytics or **data mining**.

People all over the world are congregating into virtual communities on the web by becoming members, customers, and visitors of websites that focus on an endless range of topics. People essentially segment themselves by nature of the websites that comprise their "favorite places," and many of these websites sell information regarding their "visitors." Businesses and groups of individuals all over the world pool their purchasing power in websites to get volume discounts. Through its Connect feature, Facebook uses a type of mobile advertising that targets consumers based on the apps they use from their phones. Connect lets users log into millions of websites and apps with their Facebook identity, so the company then targets ads based on that data. Facebook can also track what people do on their apps. Google uses similar means to gather (and sell) market segmentation data.

Product Positioning and Perceptual Mapping

After markets have been segmented so that the firm can target particular customer groups, the next step is to find out what customers want and expect. This takes analysis and research. A severe mistake is to assume the firm knows what customers want and expect. Countless research studies reveal large differences between how customers define service and rank the importance of different service activities versus how companies view services. Many firms have become successful by filling the gap between what customers versus companies see as good service. What the customer believes is good service is paramount, not what the producer believes service should be.

Product positioning (sometimes called **perceptual mapping**) entails developing schematic representations that reflect how products or services compare to those of the competitors on dimensions most important to success in the industry. Product positioning is widely used for deciding how to meet the needs and wants of particular consumer groups. The technique can be summarized in five steps:

1. Select key criteria that effectively differentiate products or services in the industry.
2. Diagram a two-dimensional product-positioning map with specified criteria on each axis.
3. Plot major competitors' products or services in the resultant four-quadrant matrix.
4. Identify areas in the positioning map where the company's products or services could be most competitive in the given target market. Look for vacant areas (niches).
5. Develop a marketing plan to position the company's products or services appropriately.

Because just two criteria can be examined on a single product-positioning (perceptual) map, multiple maps are often developed to assess various approaches to strategy implementation. **Multidimensional scaling** could be used to examine three or more criteria simultaneously, but this technique is beyond the scope of this text. Some rules for using product positioning as a strategy-implementation tool are the following:

1. Look for the hole or **vacant niche**, which is a segment of the market currently not being served.
2. Do not serve two segments with the same strategy. Usually, a strategy successful with one segment cannot be directly transferred to another segment.
3. Do not position yourself in the middle of the map. The middle usually indicates a strategy that is not clearly perceived to have any distinguishing characteristics. This rule can vary with the number of competitors. For example, when there are only two competitors, as in U.S. presidential elections, the middle becomes the preferred strategic position.[6]

An effective product-positioning strategy meets two criteria: (1) it uniquely distinguishes a company from the competition and (2) it leads customers to expect slightly less service than a company can deliver. Network Equipment Technology is an example of a company that keeps customer expectations slightly below perceived performance. This is a constant challenge for marketers. Firms need to inform customers about what to expect and then exceed the promise. Underpromise and overdeliver! That is a key for excellent strategy implementation.

The product positioning map, or perceptual map, in Figure 9-2 shows consumer perceptions of various automobiles on the two dimensions of sporty and conservative and classy and affordable. This sample of consumers felt Porsche was the sportiest and classiest of the cars in the study (top right corner) and Plymouth was the most practical and conservative (bottom left corner). Car manufacturers focus their marketing efforts on various target groups, or design features in their vehicles, based on research and survey information illustrated in perceptual maps. Perceptual maps can aid marketers in being more effective in spending money to promote products. Products, brands, or companies positioned close to one another are perceived as similar

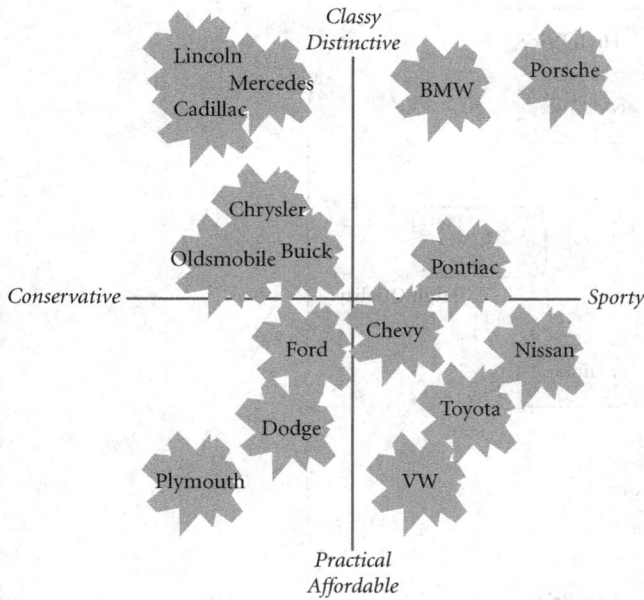

FIGURE 9-2
A Perceptual Map for the Automobile Industry

Source: Based on info at http://en.wikipedia.org/wiki/Perceptual_mapping.

on the relevant dimensions. For example, in Figure 9-2, consumers see Lincoln, Mercedes, and Cadillac as similar. They are close competitors and form a competitive grouping. A company considering the introduction of a new or improved model may look for a vacant niche on a perceptual map. Some perceptual maps use different size circles to indicate the sales volume or market share of the various competing products.

Perceptual maps may also display consumers' ideal points. These points reflect ideal combinations of the two dimensions as seen by a consumer. Dots are often used to represent one respondent's ideal combination of the two dimensions. Areas where there is a cluster of ideal points indicates a **market segment**. Areas without ideal points are sometimes referred to as **demand voids**. A company considering introducing a new product will look for areas with a high density of ideal points. They will also look for areas without competitive rivals (a vacant niche), perhaps best done by placing both the (1) ideal points and (2) competing products on the same map.

Companies commonly develop several perceptual maps to better understand competitive advantages and disadvantages versus rival companies. For example, the largest homebuilder in the United States, D. R. Horton (DRH), competes with Pulte, Lennar, KB Home, and other homebuilders. Figures 9-3, 9-4, and 9-5 reveal recently developed D. R. Horton perceptual maps. Note the author commentary provided for each illustration.

Author Commentary

AUTHOR COMMENTARY ON FIGURE 9-3 Price versus Quality is used in a perceptual map because these two factors are often viewed as the most important considerations when purchasing a home. The average sale price per DRH home is lower than any other major homebuilders in the United States, which is why they are the lowest on the perceptual map. Oftentimes, however, being the low-cost provider can mean actual, or perceived, low quality. The map reveals that DRH is above only KB Home in quality. Quality was determined through interpreting online ratings of the companies, as well as reviewing all of the competitor's websites for proof that quality was being provided. Note that Lennar is the closet to DRH on the Price versus Quality perceptual map.

AUTHOR COMMENTARY ON FIGURE 9-4 When buying or building a new home, consumers not only want to make sure it can be built where they want it but also with the layout or options they desire. By comparing coverage maps of the largest homebuilders in the United States, it was concluded that DRH has the highest geographical coverage of all the competitors. Additionally,

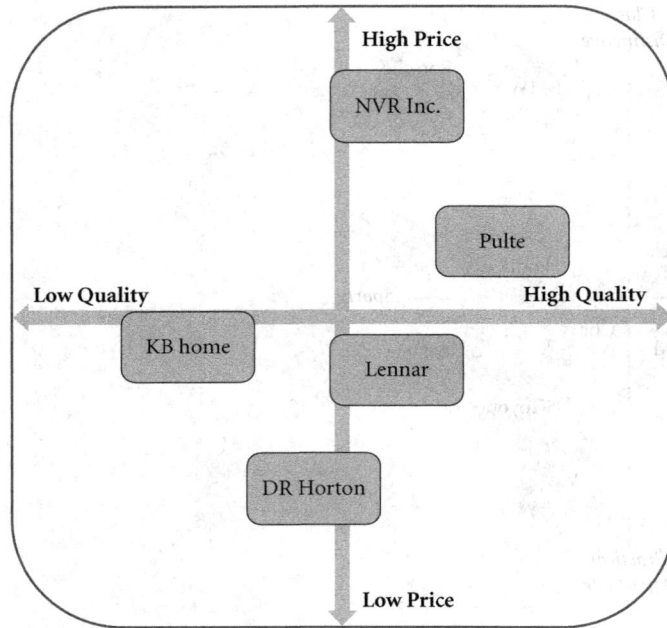

FIGURE 9-3
A DRH Perceptual Map—Price versus Quality

through a review of the homebuilder's websites, it was determined that DRH has the largest
quantity of options and layouts for new homes. Neither of these facts should come as a surprise,
as DRH does hold the title of "Largest Home Builder in the USA." Rival firms are placed
accordingly on the perceptual map. Note that Lennar is the closest to DRH on the Number of
Options and Layouts versus Geographical Coverage perceptual map.

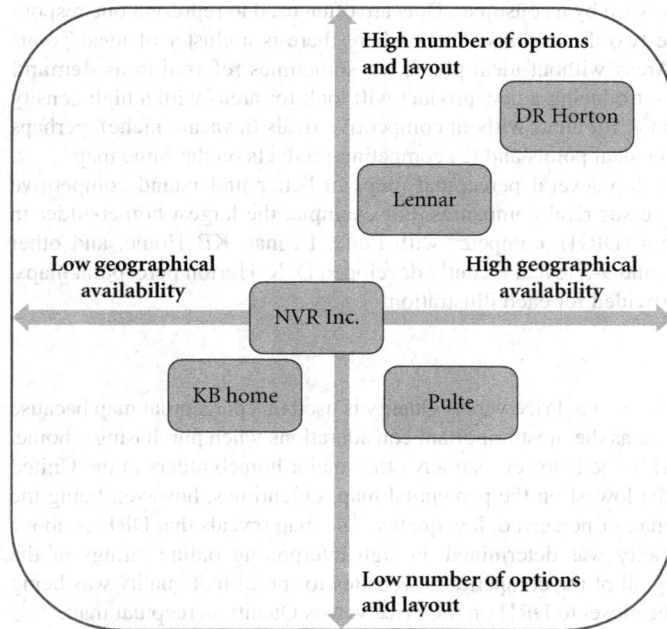

FIGURE 9-4
A DRH Perceptual Map—Number of Options/Layouts
versus Geographical Availability

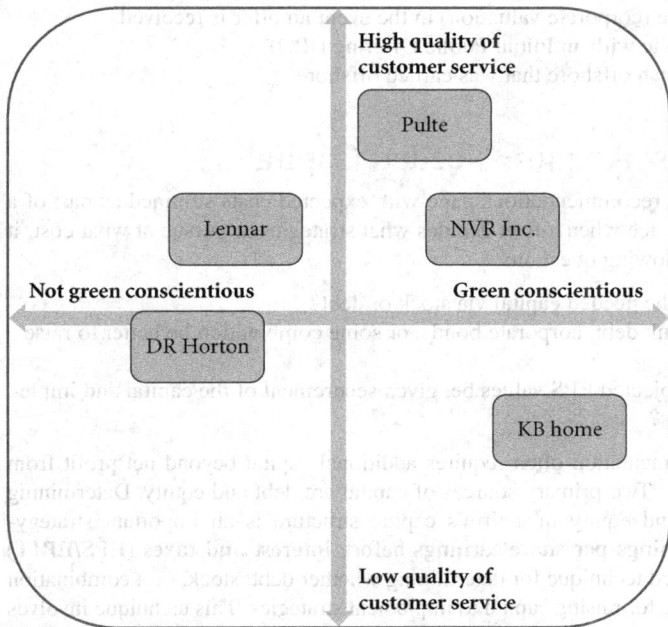

FIGURE 9-5
A DRH Perceptual Map—Quality of Customer Service
versus Extent the Firm is Green Conscientious

AUTHOR COMMENTARY ON FIGURE 9-5 Consumers increasingly are concerned with what and from whom they are purchasing. Thus, customer service and green conscientiousness are often key factors considered by consumers. After examining online ratings of the largest homebuilders and reviewing competitor's websites, it was determined that DRH has, at best, average customer service. There were numerous complaints at several websites, and not very many resolutions, or ways to find resolutions. Furthermore, through a review of the competitors' websites, it appears that DRH is the least green conscientious builder among the major players. It had very little, if any, mention of green considerations, whereas some firms had very involved and detailed sections on their web pages about green building. Note that Lennar is the closest to DRH on the Quality of Customer Service versus Extent the Firm is Green Conscientious perceptual map.

Strategic Finance/Accounting Issues

Several finance/accounting concepts central to strategy implementation are acquiring needed capital, developing projected financial statements, preparing financial budgets, and evaluating the worth of a business. Some examples of decisions that may require finance and accounting policies are:

1. To raise capital with short-term debt, long-term debt, preferred stock, or common stock
2. To lease or buy fixed assets
3. To determine an appropriate dividend payout ratio
4. To use last-in, first-out (LIFO), first-in, first-out (FIFO), or a market-value accounting approach
5. To extend the time of accounts receivable
6. To establish a certain percentage discount on accounts within a specified period of time
7. To determine the amount of cash that should be kept on hand

Five especially important finance/accounting activities central to strategy implementation are listed below and then discussed:

1. Acquire needed capital to implement strategies; perform EPS/EBIT analysis
2. Develop projected financial statements to show expected impact of strategies implemented

3. Determine the firm's value (corporate valuation) in the event an offer is received
4. Decide whether to go public with an Initial Public Offering (IPO)
5. Decide whether to keep cash offshore that was earned offshore

EPS/EBIT Analysis: Acquire Needed Capital

When students complete their recommendations page with expected costs summed as part of a case analysis, or in actual practice when a firm decides what strategies to pursue at what cost, it is necessary to address the following questions:

1. Can the company obtain the needed capital via stock or debt?
2. Would common stock, bank debt, corporate bonds, or some combination be better to raise needed capital?
3. What would the firm's projected EPS values be, given securement of the capital and implementation of the strategies?

Successful strategy implementation often requires additional capital beyond net profit from operations or the sale of assets. Two primary sources of capital are debt and equity. Determining an appropriate mix of debt and equity in a firm's capital structure is an important strategy-implementation decision. **Earnings per share/earnings before interest and taxes (EPS/EBIT) analysis** is the most widely used technique for determining whether debt, stock, or a combination of the two is the best alternative for raising capital to implement strategies. This technique involves an examination of the impact that debt versus stock financing has on earnings per share (EPS) under various expectations for EBIT, given specific recommendations (strategies to be implemented).

Theoretically, an enterprise should have enough debt in its capital structure to boost its return on investment by applying debt to products and projects earning more than the cost of the debt. In low-earning periods, too much debt in the capital structure of an organization can endanger stockholders' returns and jeopardize company survival. Fixed debt obligations generally must be met, regardless of circumstances. This does not mean that stock issuances are always better than debt for raising capital. When the cost of capital (interest rates) is low, debt may be better than stock to obtain capital, but the analysis still must be performed because high stock prices usually accompany low interest rates, making stock issuances attractive for obtaining capital. Some special concerns with stock issuances are dilution of ownership, effect on stock price, and the need to share future earnings with all new shareholders.

Another popular way for a company to raise capital is to issue corporate bonds, which is analogous to going to the bank and borrowing money, except that with bonds, the company obtains the funds from investors rather than banks. Especially when a company's balance sheet is strong and its credit rating excellent, issuing bonds can be an effective, and certainly an alternative way to raise needed capital. In 2014, companies around the world issued more than $1 trillion in corporate bonds, more than 4 percent higher than the prior year. Thus, even with high stock prices, the low interest rate environment enticed companies to increasingly use debt to (1) finance growth, (2) pay dividends, and (3) buy back their own stock (called **treasury stock**). In fact, in 2014, companies sold corporate bonds at the fastest pace ever, led by Apple, Numericable Group (a French firm), Oracle, Petrobras, Cisco, and Bank of America. Twitter recently raised $1.5 billion by offering **convertible bonds** in two chunks of $650 million. The word *convertible* means the bonds can be converted into shares of stock in some cases. Companies lately have been flocking to the convertible bond market to raise cash, as many investors look for less volatility in their investments. Medtronic, the Minneapolis medical-device-maker, recently eclipsed even Apple's $12 billion bond sale and Alibaba's $8 billion bond sale. Medtronic raised $17 billion selling bonds, enabling the company to finance its $43 billion purchase of Ireland's Covidien PLC. Companies are selling bonds at a hectic rate in order to finance strategies at low interest rates, since rates are expected to climb in 2016–2017.

Before explaining EPS/EBIT analysis, it is important to know that EPS is *earnings per share,* which is net income divided by number of shares outstanding. Another term for *shares outstanding* is *shares issued*. In addition, know that the denominator of EPS is reduced when a firm buys its own stock (treasury stock), thus increasing the overall EPS value. Also know that EBIT is earnings before interest and taxes, or as it is sometimes called, operating income. EBT is earnings before tax. EAT is earnings after tax.

The purpose of EPS/EBIT analysis is to determine whether all debt, all stock, or some combination of debt and stock yields the highest EPS values for the firm. Earnings per share is perhaps the best measure of success of a company, so it is widely used in making the capital acquisition decision. It reflects the common "maximizing shareholders' wealth" overarching corporate objective. By chance if profit maximization is the company's goal, then in performing an EPS/EBIT analysis, you may focus more on the EAT row than the EPS row. Large companies may have millions of shares outstanding, so even small differences in EPS across different financing options can equate to large sums of money saved by using that highest EPS value alternative. Any number of combination debt/stock (D/S) scenarios, such as 70/30 D/S or 30/70 D/S, may be examined in an EPS/EBIT analysis. The free Excel template at www.strategyclub.com can enable easy calculation of various scenarios of financing options.

Perhaps the best way to explain EPS/EBIT analysis is by working through an example for the XYZ Company, as provided in Table 9-4. Note that 100 percent stock is the best financing alternative as indicated by the EPS values of 0.0279 and 0.056. An EPS/EBIT chart can be constructed to determine the breakeven point, where one financing alternative becomes more attractive than another. Figure 9-4 reveals that issuing common stock is the best financing alternative for the XYZ Company. As noted in Figure 9-6, the top row (EBIT) on the x-axis is graphed with the bottom row (EPS) on the y-axis, and the highest plotted line reveals the best method. Sometimes the plotted lines will interact, so a graph is especially helpful in making the capital acquisition decision, rather than solely relying on a table of numbers.

All analytical tools have limitations and EPS/EBIT analysis is no exception. But unless you have a compelling reason to overturn the highest last row EPS values dictating the best financing option, then indeed those highest values along the bottom row should dictate the financing decision, because EPS is arguably the best measure of organizational performance, and thus is the best variable to examine in deciding which financing option is best. Seven potential limitations of EPS/EBIT analysis are here:

1. *Flexibility is a limitation.* As an organization's capital structure changes, so does its flexibility for considering future capital needs. Using all debt or all stock to raise capital in the

TABLE 9-4 EPS/EBIT Analysis for the XYZ Company

Input Data	The Number	How Determined
$ Amount of Capital Needed	$100 million	Estimated $ cost of recommendations
EBIT Range	$20 to $40 million	Estimate based on prior year EBIT and recommendations for the coming year(s)
Interest Rate	5 percent	Estimate based on cost of capital
Tax Rate	30 percent	Use prior year %: taxes divided by income before taxes, as given on income statement
Stock Price	$50	Use most recent stock price
# Shares Outstanding	500 million	For the debt columns, enter the existing # shares outstanding. For stock columns, use the existing # shares outstanding + the # new shares that must be issued to raise the needed capital (i.e., based on stock price). So divide the stock price into the $ amount of capital needed.

	100% Debt		100% Stock		50/50 Debt/Stock Combo	
$ EBIT	20,000,000	40,000,000	20,000,000	40,000,000	20,000,000	40,000,000
$ Interest	5,000,000	5,000,000	0	0	2,500,000	2,500,000
$ EBT	15,000,000	35,000,000	20,000,000	40,000,000	17,500,000	37,500,000
$ Taxes	4,500,000	10,500,000	6,000,000	12,000,000	5,250,000	11,250,000
$ EAT	10,500,000	24,500,000	14,000,000	28,000,000	12,250,000	26,250,000
# Shares	500,000,000	500,000,000	502,000,000	502,000,000	501,000,000	501,000,000
$ EPS	0.0210	0.049	0.0279	0.056	0.0245	0.0523

Conclusion: The best financing alternative is 100% stock because the EPS values are largest; the worst financing alternative is 100% debt because the EPS values are lowest.

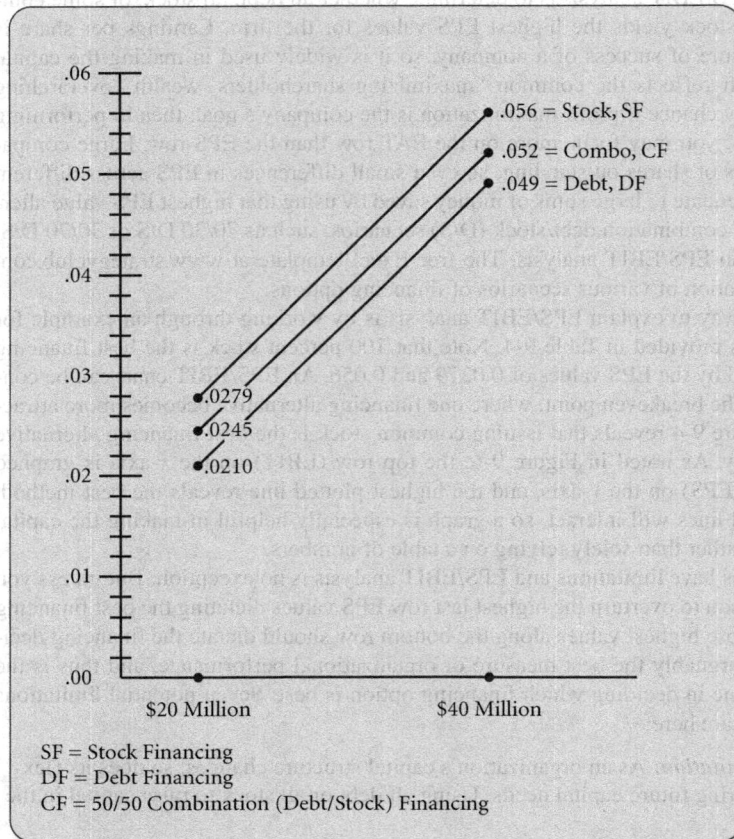

FIGURE 9-6
An EPS/EBIT Chart for the XYZ Company

present may impose fixed obligations, restrictive covenants, or other constraints that could severely reduce a firm's ability to raise additional capital in the future.

2. *Control is a limitation.* When additional stock is issued to finance strategy implementation, ownership and control of the enterprise are diluted. This can be a serious concern in today's business environment of hostile takeovers, mergers, and acquisitions. Dilution of ownership could be a problem, and if so, debt could be better than stock regardless of determined EPS values in the analysis.

3. *Timing is a limitation..* If interest rates are expected to rise, then debt could be better than stock, regardless of the determined EPS values in the analysis. In times of high stock prices, stock may prove to be the best alternative from both a cost and a demand standpoint.

4. *Extent leveraged is a limitation.* If the firm is already too highly leveraged versus industry average ratios, then stock may be best regardless of determined EPS values in the analysis.

5. *Continuity is a limitation.* The analysis assumes stock price, tax rate, and interest rates are constant during all economic conditions.

6. *EBIT ranges are a limitation.* The estimated EBIT low and high values are estimated based on the prior year, plus the impact of strategies to be implemented.

7. *Dividends are a limitation.* If EPS values are highest for the "all-stock scenario," and if the firm pays dividends, then more funds will leave the firm due to dividends if the all stock scenario is selected.

Table 9-5 provides an EPS/EBIT analysis for Boeing Company. Notice in the analysis that the combination stock/debt options vary from 30/70 to 70/30. Any number of combinations

TABLE 9-5 EPS/EBIT Analysis for Boeing Company (M = in millions)

Amount Needed: $10,000 M
Interest Rate: 5%
Tax Rate: 7%
Stock Price: $53.00
# of Shares Outstanding: 826 M

	Common Stock Financing			Debt Financing		
	Recession	Normal	Boom	Recession	Normal	Boom
EBIT	1,000.00	2,500.00	5,000.00	1,000.00	2,500.00	5,000.00
Interest	0.00	0.00	0.00	500.00	500.00	500.00
EBT	1,000.00	2,500.00	5,000.00	500.00	2,000.00	4,500.00
Taxes	70.00	175.00	350.00	35.00	140.00	315.00
EAT	930.00	2,325.00	4,650.00	465.00	1,860.00	4,185.00
# Shares	1,014.68	1,014.68	1,014.68	826.00	826.00	826.00
EPS	**0.92**	**2.29**	4.58	**0.56**	**2.25**	**5.07**

	70% Stock—30% Debt			70% Debt—30% Stock		
	Recession	Normal	Boom	Recession	Normal	Boom
EBIT	1,000.00	2,500.00	5,000.00	1,000.00	2,500.00	5,000.00
Interest	150.00	150.00	150.00	350.00	350.00	350.00
EBT	850.00	2,350.00	4,850.00	650.00	2,150.00	4,650.00
Taxes	59.50	164.50	339.50	45.50	150.50	325.50
EAT	790.50	2,185.50	4,510.50	604.50	1,999.50	4,324.50
# Shares	958.08	958.08	958.08	882.60	882.60	882.60
EPS	**0.83**	**2.28**	**4.71**	**0.68**	**2.27**	**4.90**

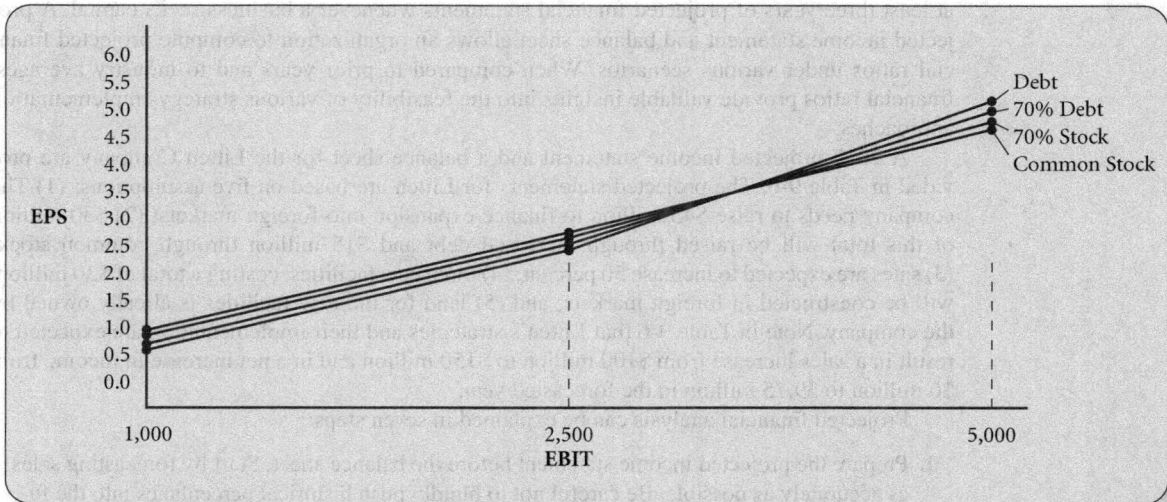

Conclusion: Boeing should use common stock to raise capital in a recession (see 0.92) or a normal (see 2.29) economic conditions but should use debt financing under boom conditions (see 5.07).

could be explored. However, sometimes in preparing the EPS/EBIT graphs, the lines will intersect, thus revealing breakeven points at which one financing alternative becomes more or less attractive than another. The slope of these lines will be determined by a combination of factors, including stock price, interest rate, number of shares, and amount of capital needed. Also, it should be emphasized here that the best financing alternatives are indicated by the highest EPS values. In Table 9-5, the 7 percent tax rates was computed from Boeing's income statement by dividing taxes paid by income before taxes. Always calculate the tax rate in this manner.

In Table 9-5, note that Boeing should use stock to raise capital in a recession (see 0.92) or in normal (see 2.29) economic conditions but should use debt financing under boom conditions (see 5.07). Let us calculate here the "# Shares" figure of 1,014.68 given under Boeing's stock alternative. Divide $10,000 M funds needed by the stock price of $53 = 188.68 M new shares to be issued + the 826 M shares outstanding already = 1014.68 M shares under the stock scenario. Along the final row, EPS is the number of shares outstanding divided by EAT in all columns.

Note in Table 9-5 that a dividends row is absent from the Boeing analysis. The more shares outstanding, the more dividends to be paid (if the firm indeed pays dividends). To consider dividends in an EPS/EBIT analysis, simply insert another row for "Dividends" right below the "EAT" row and then insert an "Earnings After Taxes and Dividends" row. Considering dividends would make the analysis more robust.

In the Boeing graph, notice that there is a breakeven point between the normal and boom range of EBIT where the debt option overtakes the 70/30 D/S option as the best financing alternative. A breakeven point (where two lines cross each other) is the EBIT level where various financing alternatives represented by lines crossing are equally attractive in terms of EPS. The Boeing graph indicates that EPS values are highest for the 100 percent debt option at high EBIT levels. The graph also reveals that the EPS values for 100 percent debt increase faster than the other financing options as EBIT levels increase beyond the breakeven point. At low levels of EBIT, however, the Boeing graph indicates that 100 percent stock is the best financing alternative because the EPS values are highest.

Projected Financial Statements

Projected financial statement analysis is a technique that allows an organization to examine the expected results of strategies being implemented. This analysis can be used to forecast the impact of various implementation decisions (e.g., to increase promotion expenditures by 50 percent to support a market-development strategy or to increase research and development expenditures by 70 percent to support product development). Most financial institutions require at least three years of projected financial statements whenever a business seeks capital. A projected income statement and balance sheet allows an organization to compute projected financial ratios under various scenarios. When compared to prior years and to industry averages, financial ratios provide valuable insights into the feasibility of various strategy-implementation approaches.

A 2017 projected income statement and a balance sheet for the Litten Company are provided in Table 9-6. The projected statements for Litten are based on five assumptions: (1) The company needs to raise $45 million to finance expansion into foreign markets; (2) $30 million of this total will be raised through increased debt and $15 million through common stock; (3) sales are expected to increase 50 percent; (4) three new facilities, costing a total of $30 million, will be constructed in foreign markets; and (5) land for the new facilities is already owned by the company. Note in Table 9-6 that Litten's strategies and their implementation are expected to result in a sales increase from $100 million to $150 million and in a net increase in income from $6 million to $9.75 million in the forecasted year.

Projected financial analysis can be explained in seven steps:

1. Prepare the projected income statement before the balance sheet. Start by forecasting sales as accurately as possible. Be careful not to blindly push historical percentages into the future with regard to revenue (sales) increases. Be mindful of what the firm did to achieve those past sales increases, which may not be appropriate for the future unless the firm takes similar or analogous actions (such as opening a similar number of stores, for example). If dealing with a manufacturing firm, also be mindful that if the firm is operating at 100 percent capacity running three 8-hour shifts per day, then probably new manufacturing facilities (land, plant, and equipment) will be needed to increase sales further.

2. Use the percentage-of-sales method to project cost of goods sold (CGS) and the expense items in the income statement. For example, if CGS is 70 percent of sales in the prior year

TABLE 9-6 A Projected Income Statement and Balance Sheet for the Litten Company (in millions)

	Prior Year 2016	Projected Year 2017	Remarks
PROJECTED INCOME STATEMENT			
Sales	$100	$150.00	50% increase
Cost of Goods Sold	70	105.00	70% of sales
Gross Margin	30	45.00	
Selling Expense	10	15.00	10% of sales
Administrative Expense	5	7.50	5% of sales
Earnings Before Interest and Taxes	15	22.50	
Interest	3	3.00	
Earnings Before Taxes	12	19.50	
Taxes	6	9.75	50% rate
Net Income	**6**	**9.75**	
Dividends	2	5.00	
Retained Earnings	4	4.75	
PROJECTED BALANCE SHEET			
Assets			
Cash	5	7.75	Plug figure
Accounts Receivable	2	4.00	100% increase
Inventory	20	45.00	
Total Current Assets	27	56.75	
Land	15	35.00	Purchased land
Plant and Equipment	50	80.00	Add three new plants at $10 million each
Less Depreciation	10	20.00	
Net Plant and Equipment	40	60.00	
Total Fixed Assets	55	75.00	
Total Assets	**82**	**151.75**	
Liabilities			
Accounts Payable	10	10.00	
Notes Payable	10	10.00	
Total Current Liabilities	20	20.00	
Long-Term Debt	40	70.00	Borrowed $30 million
Additional Paid-in-Capital	20	35.00	Issued 100,000 shares at $150 each
Retained Earnings	2	6.75	$2 + $4.75
Total Liabilities and Net Worth	**82**	**151.75**	

(as it is in Table 9-6), then use that same percentage to calculate CGS in the future year—unless there is a reason to use a different percentage. Items such as interest, dividends, and taxes must be treated independently and cannot be forecasted using the percentage-of-sales method.

3. Calculate the projected net income.
4. Subtract from the net income any dividends to be paid for that year. This remaining net income is retained earnings (RE). Bring this retained earnings amount for that year (NI − DIV = RE) over to the balance sheet by adding it to the prior year's RE shown on the balance sheet. In other words, every year, a firm adds its RE for that particular year (from the income statement) to its historical RE total on the balance sheet. Therefore, the RE amount on the balance sheet is a cumulative number rather than money available for

strategy implementation. Note that retained earnings is the first projected balance sheet item to be entered. As a result of this accounting procedure in developing projected financial statements, the RE amount on the balance sheet is usually a large number. However, it also can be a low or even negative number if the firm has been incurring losses. The only way for RE to decrease from one year to the next on the balance sheet is (1) if the firm incurred an earnings loss that year or (2) the firm had positive net income for the year but paid out dividends more than the net income. Be mindful that RE is the key link between a projected income statement and balance sheet, so be careful to make this calculation correctly.

5. Project the balance sheet items, beginning with retained earnings and then forecasting shareholders' equity, long-term liabilities, current liabilities, total liabilities, total assets, fixed assets, and current assets (in that order), working from the bottom to the top of the balance sheet.

6. Use the cash account as the plug figure—that is, use the cash account to make the assets total the liabilities and net worth. Then make appropriate adjustments. For example, if the cash needed to balance the statements is too small (or too large), make appropriate changes to borrow more (or less) money than planned. If the projected cash account number is too high, a firm could reduce the cash number and concurrently reduce a liability or equity account the same amount to keep the statement in balance. Rarely is the cash account number perfect on the first pass-through, so adjustments are needed and made.

7. List commentary (remarks) on the projected statements. Any time a significant change is made in an item from a prior year to the projected year, an explanation (comment) should be provided. Comments/remarks are essential because otherwise changes can be difficult to understand.

The U.S. Securities and Exchange Commission (SEC) conducts fraud investigations if projected numbers are misleading or if they omit information that is important to investors. Projected statements must conform with generally accepted accounting principles (GAAP) and must not be designed to hide poor expected results. The Sarbanes-Oxley Act requires CEOs and CFOs of corporations to personally sign their firms' financial statements attesting to their accuracy. These executives could thus be held personally liable for misleading or inaccurate statements. Some firms still "inflate" their financial projections and call them "pro formas," so investors, shareholders, and other stakeholders must still be wary of different companies' financial projections.[7]

On financial statements, different companies use different terms for various items, such as *revenues* or *sales* used for the same item. *Net income, earnings,* or *profits* can refer to the same item on an income statement, depending on the company.

Projected Financial Statement Analysis for D. R. Horton

Because so many strategic management students have limited experience developing projected financial statements, let us apply the steps outlined on the previous pages to the largest American homebuilder company by revenues, D. R. Horton (DRH). The projected statements, developed on January 14, 2014, considered that D.R. Horton would go forward with the following four recommendations in 2014–2016, and incur the following expected costs:

1. Acquire four building products firms: (a) Universal Forest Products, (b) Scotch and Gulf Lumber, (c) United Plywood and Lumber, and (d) Dixie Plywood. **Total Cost = $850 million**

2. Expand home-building services to North and South Dakota to gain 5% of the market by the end of 2016. (Start with an office in Bismarck, ND, the second-largest city in ND. It is close enough to the ND/SD border to serve both states, and it is located where Bismarck and Minneapolis can both help serve Fargo/Moorhead. If all goes well, place a second location in Rapid City, SD, the second-largest city in SD. It is located where Rapid City and Minneapolis can both help serve Sioux Falls, and is located close enough to Casper, WY, and Scottsbluff, NE, for possible future service expansions.) **Total Cost = $232 million**

3. Increase the number of communities that DRH services by 50% in California and Nevada by 2016 (20 more communities in California and 10 more communities in Nevada). **Total Cost = $290 million**

4. Develop and launch a nationwide marketing campaign. Topics should include D. R. Horton's low prices in the industry (while still stressing they provide value),

TABLE 9-7 DRH's Actual and Projected Income Statements (in millions)

	Actual Year 2013	Projected 2014	Projected 2015	Projected 2016
Sales	$6,259.00	$10,607.94	$12,520.69	$14,776.03
Costs of Goods Sold	$4,854.00	$8,570.14	$10,115.44	$11,937.52
Gross Margin	$1,405.00	$2,037.81	$2,405.25	$2,838.50
Selling & Administrative	$766.00	$1,298.24	$1,532.33	$1,808.35
Other Operating	−$15.00	−$25.42	−$30.01	−$35.41
EBIT	$654.00	$764.99	$902.93	$1,065.57
Interest	$5.00	$8.47	$10.00	$11.80
Other Income	$9.00	$15.25	$18.00	$21.25
EBT	$658.00	$771.77	$910.93	$1,075.01
Taxes	$195.00	$228.72	$269.96	$318.58
Net Income	**$463.00**	**$543.05**	**$640.97**	**$756.43**
Dividends	$60.20	$70.45	$72.57	$74.74
Retained Earnings	$402.80	$472.60	$568.41	$681.69

home owning is still more cost effective than renting, green solutions offered by DRH, corporate social responsibility efforts by DRH, and targeting the 55 to 75 age group for buying homes. **Total Cost = $35 million**

Based on these recommendations, DHR's actual and projected income statements are given in Table 9-7. Note the large increase in sales in 2014 were due to DRH potentially acquiring four smaller homebuilder companies. Note also at the bottom of Table 9-7 the dividends to be paid and resultant annual retained earnings to be carried forward to the DRH projected balance sheets. Commentary regarding DRH's actual and projected income statements is provided in Table 9-8.

Table 9-9 reveals DRH's actual and projected balance sheets given the four recommendations listed earlier and the annual retained earnings carried forward to the balance sheet. Table 9-10 provides commentary regarding the projected balance sheet changes.

Note in Table 9-9 that DRH increased its retained earnings on the projected balance sheets correctly, expecting to pay out the dividend amounts indicated in Table 9-8. Note in Table 9-9

TABLE 9-8 Comments Regarding DRH's Actual and Projected Income Statements

In millions	Comments
Sales	New home building up 18% in last year. 15% increase year to year seems fair (works out to about 15% in the housing market and 10% in building supplies). Plus, the goal of 1% increase in market share (0.33%/yr). Plus, $3,000 in year 1 from acquisitions.
Costs of Goods Sold	80.8% of sales after acquisitions
Gross Margin	
Selling and Admin. Expense	12.25% of sales
Other Operating Expenses	0.25% of sales
EBIT	
Interest	0.08% of sales
Other Income	0.14% of sales
EBT	
Taxes	29.65% of EBT
Net Income	
Dividends	3% increase year to year. Plus, $8.2M in year 1 from acquisitions.
Retained Earnings	NI − Dividends

TABLE 9-9 DRH's Actual and Projected Balance Sheets (in millions)

	Actual Year 2013	Projected Year 2014	Projected Year 2015	Projected Year 2016
Assets				
Cash	$937.00	$1,091.30	$891.72	$652.53
Inventory	$6,197.00	$7,955.96	$9,390.52	$11,082.02
Deferred Income Taxes	$587.00	$994.87	$1,174.25	$1,385.77
Other Current Assets	$77.00	$99.00	$99.00	$99.00
Total Current Assets	$7,798.00	$10,141.12	$11,555.49	$13,294.06
Land, Plant, and Equipment	$237.00	$924.76	$943.40	$962.98
Less Depreciation	$130.00	$500.00	$530.00	$560.00
Goodwill	$39.00	$199.00	$199.00	$199.00
Other Long-Term Assets	$913.00	$981.40	$1,053.23	$1,128.64
Total Fixed Assets	$1,059.00	$1,605.16	$1,665.63	$1,730.62
Total Assets	**$8,857.00**	**$11,746.28**	**$13,221.12**	**$14,949.94**
Liabilities				
Accounts Payable	$400.00	$583.44	$688.64	$812.68
Taxes Payable	$60.00	$60.00	$60.00	$60.00
Accrued Liabilities	$211.00	$318.24	$375.62	$443.28
Other Current Liabilities	$615.00	$615.00	$615.00	$615.00
Total Current Liabilities	$1,286.00	$1,576.68	$1,739.26	$1,930.96
Long-Term Debt	$3,509.00	$4,959.00	$5,702.85	$6,558.28
Minority Interest	$3.00	$3.00	$3.00	$3.00
Total Noncurrent Liabilities	$3,512.00	$4,962.00	$5,705.85	$6,561.28
Total Liabilities	$4,798.00	$6,538.68	$7,445.11	$8,492.24
Additional Paid-in Capital	$2,042.00	$2,218.00	$2,218.00	$2,218.00
Common Stock	$3.00	$3.00	$3.00	$3.00
Retained Earnings	$2,146.00	$3,118.60	$3,687.01	$4,368.70
Treasury Stock	–$134.00	–$134.00	–$134.00	–$134.00
Other Accumulated Income	$2.00	$2.00	$2.00	$2.00
Total Stockholders' Equity	$4,059.00	$5,207.60	$5,776.01	$6,532.44
Total Liabilities and Net Worth	**$8,857.00**	**$11,746.28**	**$13,221.12**	**$14,949.94**

that the projections show DRH not buying back any of its own stock (treasury stock), as indicated by the $134 number staying unchanged. Many companies lately have been aggressively buying their own stock, reflecting optimism about their future. However, some analysts argue that stock buybacks eat cash that a firm could better use to grow the firm. Stock buybacks do however reduce a firm's number of shares outstanding, which increases a firm's EPS, so firms reap this "intangible benefit" with stock buybacks. Sometimes firms will thus increase their treasury stock near the end of the quarter, or near the end of the year, to "artificially" inflate their EPS, which oftentimes makes the stock price go up. For example, FedEx bought $2.8 billion worth of its own stock in its 2014 fiscal fourth quarter, contributing 15 cents to the company's EPS of $2.10, thus beating Wall Street's expectation of $1.95. In fact, 25 percent of the S&P 500 companies in the third quarter of 2014 alone increased their EPS by 4 percent or more simply by buying back their own stock.

Corporate Valuation

Evaluating the worth of a business is central to strategy implementation because numerous strategies are often implemented by acquiring other firms. In addition, some strategies, such as retrenchment and divestiture, may result in the sale of a division of an organization or of the firm itself. Thus, thousands of transactions occur each year in which businesses are bought or sold in

TABLE 9-10 Comments Regarding DRH's Actual and Projected Balance Sheets

	Comments
Assets	
Cash	Plug Variable
Inventory	75% of sales after acquisitions
Deferred Income Taxes	9.4% of sales
Other Current Assets	$22 increase in year one due to acquisition
Total Current Assets	
Land, Plant, and Equipment	Currently 63 locations, Average = 3.75 million. Upgrading 5 facilities at 50% and adding 2 new facilities in the next 3 years. Plus 5% average increase with market share per year. Plus $670 in year 1 from acquisitions
Less Depreciation	$340 increase in year 1 from acquisitions plus 30 million per year
Goodwill	$160 increase due to acquisitions
Other Long-Term Assets	Increase at the same percentage as Land, Plant, and Equipment, less acquisitions
Total Fixed Assets	
Total Assets	
Liabilities	
Accounts Payable	5.5% of sales after acquisitions
Taxes Payable	
Accrued Liabilities	3.0% of sales after acquisitions
Other Current Liabilities	
Total Current Liabilities	
Long-Term Debt	Borrowed $1450 for acquisitions and expansions in year 1. Plus 15% thereafter.
Minority Interest	
Total Noncurrent Liabilities	
Total Liabilities	
Additional Paid-in Capital	$176 increase in year one due to acquisitions
Common Stock	
Retained Earnings	Prior RE + the new annual RE
Treasury Stock	
Other Income	
Total Stockholders' Equity	
Total Liabilities and SE	

the United States. In all these cases, it is necessary to establish the financial worth or cash value of a business to successfully implement strategies.

Corporate valuation is not an exact science; value is sometimes in the eye of the beholder. Companies desire to sell high and buy low, and negotiation normally takes place in both situations. The valuation of a firm's worth is based on financial facts, but common sense and good judgment enter into the process because it is difficult to assign a monetary value to some factors—such as a loyal customer base, a history of growth, legal suits pending, dedicated employees, a favorable lease, a bad credit rating, or good patents—that may not be reflected in a firm's financial statements. Also, different valuation methods will yield different totals for a firm's worth, and no prescribed approach is best for a certain situation. Evaluating the worth of a business truly requires both qualitative and quantitative skills.

Before we examine four methods widely used for corporate valuation, let's examine the concepts of goodwill, premium, and discount a bit further because these issues directly relate to corporate valuation. FASB Rule 142 requires companies to admit once a year if the premiums they paid for acquisitions, called **goodwill**, were a waste of money. Goodwill is not a good thing

ACADEMIC RESEARCH CAPSULE 9-1

When Should We Overpay to Acquire a Firm?

Scholars have long been interested in the decision-making process regarding when firms pay premiums versus discounts for acquired firms. Paying high acquisition premiums inflate a firm's goodwill, and has often been criticized in research. Acquisition premiums the last few years have averaged 25 to 40 percent, but sometimes exceed 100 percent. Prior research suggests that high premiums generally have negative impacts on acquisition performance. Scholars have explored the how and why of excessive premium decisions to determine if overconfidence or hubris on the part of chief executive officers (CEOs) is the culprit. Specifically, Zhu recently reported that board members' influence on premium versus discount decisions

may not always be beneficial. In particular, Zhu reports a tendency for directors to support low premiums when their average prior premium was low, but directors tend to support paying high premiums when their average prior premium was relatively high. Due to this "group bias," Zhu questions the extent (or whether) members of a firm's board of directors should be involved with acquisition purchase decisions.

Source: Based on Zhu, David, "Group Polarization on Corporate Boards: Theory and Evidence on Board Decisions about Acquisition Premiums," *Strategic Management Journal*, 34 (2013): 800–822.

to have on a balance sheet. J. Crew Group Inc., for example, recently wrote down the value of the goodwill on its balance sheet by 57 percent, or $536 million. Hewlett-Packard, Boston Scientific, Frontier Communications, and Republic Services carry more goodwill on their balance sheet than their market (or book) value. This is a signal that their goodwill should be "written down," which means "reduced and recorded as an expense on the income statement." Jack Ciesielski, publisher of Analyst's Accounting Observer, says, "Writing down goodwill is an admission that the company screwed up when it budgeted what an acquired firm is worth." Sometimes it is OK to pay more for a company than its book value if the firm has technology or patents you need or economies of scale you desire or even to reduce competitive pricing pressure, but, like buying a house, paying a "premium" for a company is almost always not a good thing. Acquiring at a "discount" is far better for shareholders. Because goodwill write-down accounting rules involve projections and judgments, companies have leeway for when to write down goodwill, and by how much. If the purchase price is less than the stock price times the number of shares outstanding (rather than more), that difference is called a **discount**. For example, Clayton Doubilier & Rice LLC recently acquired Emergency Medical Services (EMS) Corp. for $2.9 billion, a 9.4 percent discount below EMS's stock price of $64.00. Academic Research Capsule 9-1 addresses the premium versus discount issue.

Corporate Valuation Methods

Four methods are often used to determine the monetary value of a company; these four methods are described below.

METHOD 1 The Net Worth Method = Total Shareholders' Equity (SE) – (Goodwill + Intangibles) Other terms for Total Shareholders' Equity are Total Owners' Equity or Net Worth, but this line item near the bottom of a balance sheet represents the sum of common stock, additional paid-in capital, and retained earnings. After calculating total SE, subtract goodwill and intangibles if these items appear as assets on the firm's balance sheet. Whereas intangibles include copyrights, patents, and trademarks, goodwill arises only if a firm acquires another firm and pays more than the book value for that firm

METHOD 2 The Net Income Method = Net Income × Five
The second approach for measuring the monetary value of a company grows out of the belief that the worth of any business should be based largely on the future benefits its owners may derive through net profits. A conservative rule of thumb is to establish a business's worth as five times the firm's current annual profit. A 5-year average profit level could also be used. When using this approach, remember that firms normally suppress earnings in their financial statements to minimize taxes. Note in Table 9-11 that Method 2 results in the lowest corporate valuation of all methods for all three firms. If you were acquiring a business, this might be a good first offer, but likely Method 2 does not produce a value you would want to begin with if you are selling your business.

TABLE 9-11 Company Worth Analysis for Amazon.com, Ross Stores, and Panera Bread Company (in millions, except stock price and EPS)

Input Data	Amazon.com	Ross Stores	Panera Bread
$ Shareholders' Equity (SE)	9,746	2,007	699
$ Net Income (NI)	274	837	196
$ Stock Price (SP)	307	90	160
$ EPS	7.59	4.24	6.80
# of Shares Outstanding	463	205	27
$ Goodwill	2,656	0	123
$ Intangibles	0	0	79
$ Total Assets	40,159	3,896	1,180
Company Worth Analyses			
1. SE – Goodwill – Intangibles	7,090	2,007	497
2. Net Income × 5	1,370	4,185	980
3. (Stock Price/EPS) × NI	142,572	17,766	4,611
4. # of Shares Out × Stock Price	142,141	18,450	4,320
5. Four Method Average	$73,293	$10,604	$2,602
$ Goodwill/$ Total Assets	6.6%	0	10.4%

If a firm's net income is negative, theoretically Method 2 yields a negative number, implying that the firm would pay you to acquire them. Of course, when you acquire another firm, you obtain all of the firm's debt and liabilities, so theoretically this would be possible.

METHOD 3 Price-Earnings Ratio Method = (Stock Price ÷ EPS) × NI
To use this method, divide the market price of the firm's common stock by the annual earnings per share (EPS) and multiply this number by the firm's average net income for the past five years. Notice in Table 9-12 this method yields an answer close to Method 4. Algebraically, this method is identical to Method 4, if earnings and # of shares figures are taken at the same point in time.

METHOD 4 Outstanding Shares Method = # of Shares Outstanding × Stock Price
To use this method, simply multiply the number of shares outstanding (or issued) by the market price per share. If the purchase price is more than this amount, the additional dollars are called a **premium**. The outstanding shares method may also be called the **market value** or **market capitalization** or **book value** of the firm. The premium is a per-share dollar amount that a person or firm is willing to pay beyond the book value of the firm to control (acquire) the other company.

Table 9-11 provides the cash value analyses for three companies—Amazon.com, Ross Stores, and Panera Bread Company at year-end 2014. Note in Table 9-11 that Panera Bread Company's $ Goodwill to $ Total Assets is high at 10.4 percent, indicating that a tenth of the company's assets are "Goodwill," which is not good.

Notice in Table 9-11 there is significant variation among the four methods used to determine cash value. For example, the worth of Amazon ranged from $1.3 billion to $142 billion. Obviously, if you were selling your company, you would seek the larger values, whereas if purchasing a company you would seek the lower values. In practice, substantial negotiation takes place in reaching a final compromise (or averaged) amount.

In addition to preparing to buy or sell a business, corporate valuation analysis is oftentimes performed when dealing with the following issues: bank loans, tax calculations, retirement packages, death of a principal, divorce, partnership agreements, and IRS audits. Practically, it is just good business to have a reasonable understanding of what a firm is worth. This knowledge protects the interests of all parties involved.

TABLE 9-12 The Top 20 College Football Programs in Terms of Monetary Value (all numbers are in millions of $)

Team	Revenue	Net Income	Team Value
1. Texas Longhorns	109	82	139
2. Notre Dame Fighting Irish	78	46	117
3. Alabama Crimson Tide	89	47	110
4. LSU Tigers	74	48	105
5. Michigan Wolverines	81	58	104
6. Florida Gators	75	49	94
7. Oklahoma Sooners	70	45	92
8. Georgia Bulldogs	66	40	91
9. Ohio State Buckeyes	61	38	83
10. Nebraska Cornhuskers	56	35	80
11. Auburn Tigers	75	39	77
12. Arkansas Razorbacks	61	32	74
13. USC Trojans	58	35	73
14. Texas A&M Aggies	54	36	72
15. Penn State Nittany Lions	59	30	71
16. Wisconsin Badgers	51	19	70
17. Washington Huskies	56	33	66
18. South Carolina Gamecocks	49	24	65
19. Oregon Ducks	54	33	64
20. Tennessee Volunteers	55	28	63

Source: Based on information from the U.S. Department of Education as of February 1, 2014, and http://www.forbes.com/forbes/welcome/.

Table 9-12 provides a list of U.S. college football teams ranked in terms of their monetary value. Note that the Texas Longhorns are Number 1, followed by the Notre Dame Fighting Irish. Also observe that there are eight Southeastern Conference (SEC) teams among the top 20. In calculating the team value amounts, analysts made various cash flow adjustments, so the amounts are generally less than the "net income times five" formula described in Method 2. Net income times two (or three) is much closer to actual figures reported for the monetary value of college football programs.

IPOs, Cash Management, and Corporate Bonds

Go Public With An IPO?

Hundreds of companies annually hold **initial public offerings (IPOs)** to move from being private to being public. In 2014, the number of firms going public was at its fastest pace in years, as investors bid aggressively for new shares of new companies, paying on average 14.5 times annual sales for firms. The average U.S. IPO stock price in 2014 increased 19 percent, rewarding investors.[8] However, nearly three quarters of the firms going public in 2014 were unprofitable, and most had annual sales of less than $50 million. In addition to Alibaba, some of the most successful IPOs in 2014 were GoPro, maker of the popular action photography camera, whose stock hit the market mid-year priced at $24 and rose to $71 for a 195 percent total return. Also in 2014, the IPO from Immune Design, a large pharmaceutical firm, saw its initial stock price of $12 rise to $34, up 184 percent. There were 275 IPOs on the U.S. stock markets in 2014, up from 222 the prior year. However, not all initial public offering stock prices increased. Even Facebook's stock dropped dramatically after its IPO, although it eventually recovered nicely.

"Going public" means selling off a percentage of a company to others to raise capital; consequently, it dilutes the owners' control of the firm. Going public is not recommended for companies with less than $10 million in sales because the initial costs can be too high for the firm to generate sufficient cash flow to make going public worthwhile. One dollar in four is the average total cost paid to lawyers, accountants, and underwriters when an initial stock issuance is under $1 million; $1 in $20 will go to cover these costs for issuances over $20 million. In addition to initial costs involved with a stock offering, there are costs and obligations associated with reporting and management in a publicly held firm. For firms with more than $10 million in sales, going public can provide major advantages. It can allow the firm to raise capital to develop new products, build plants, expand, grow, and market products and services more effectively.

Keep Cash Offshore is Earned Offshore?

Many U.S. firms have most of the cash on their balance sheet in overseas accounts, since a large percentage of their revenues are derived in foreign countries. Many such firms prefer to leave their cash outside the United States because to use those funds to pay dividends or purchase treasury stock, for example, would trigger a big U.S. corporate income tax payment. During calendar year 2014, U.S.-based companies added $206 billion to their stockpiles of offshore profits, recorded as "Cash" on their balance sheet. Keeping earnings (cash) in banks in low-tax countries has resulted in U.S. multinational companies having now accumulated $1.95 trillion in cash held outside the United States, up 11.8 percent from a year earlier, according to securities filings from 307 corporations reviewed by Bloomberg News. Three U.S.-based companies in particular—Microsoft, Apple, and IBM—added $37.5 billion, or 18.2 percent of the total increase in 2014. So, when you see "Cash" on a firm's balance sheet, that cash may not be readily available, given the firm may prefer not to pay U.S. taxes on those "foreign" earnings. The federal government is currently considering legislation to tax those foreign cash accounts, such as pay a one-time tax of 10 percent and bring all that cash back to U.S. banks, but nothing has been decided so far.

Issue Corporate Bonds for What Purpose?

Corporations normally issue bonds to raise capital for acquisitions, to refinance debt, and to fund various strategies expected to yield long-term profits. However, increasingly, companies are issuing bonds to buy back their own stock and to pay cash dividends to shareholders. This practice has become a concern. For example, in the first half of 2015, at least ten junk-rated or B-rated companies, including Sirius XM Holdings, Nathan's Famous (Hotdogs), and McGraw-Hill Education, issued more than $5.4 billion in bonds at least in part to finance paying out cash dividends and buying back company stock. For all of 2014, 30 companies issued more than $14.8 billion of bonds for the same purpose. Companies in the S&P 500 in 2014 paid out a record $93.4 billion in dividends and repurchased $148 billion worth of stock—partly (or largely) by issuing corporate bonds. Stock buybacks in 2015 are on pace to exceed $600 billion, a huge increase. The CFO of Legg Mason says "debt analysts hate companies' practice of using debt to fund buybacks."[9] A strategic decision facing corporations therefore, is whether to issue bonds to raise capital to pacify shareholders with cash dividends and purchase company stock, or to issue bonds to finance strategies carefully formulated to yield greater revenues and profits.

Strategic Research and Development (R&D) Issues

Research and development (R&D) personnel can play an integral part in strategy implementation. These individuals are generally charged with developing new products and improving old products effectively. R&D persons perform tasks that include transferring complex technology, adjusting processes to local raw materials, adapting processes to local markets, and altering products to particular tastes and specifications. Strategies such as product development, market penetration, and related diversification require that new products be successfully developed and that old products be significantly improved.

Technological improvements that affect consumer and industrial products and services shorten product life cycles. Companies in virtually every industry rely on the development of new products and services to fuel profitability and growth. Surveys suggest that the most successful

TABLE 9-13 R&D Involvement in Selected Strategy-Implementation Situations

Type of Organization	Strategy Being Implemented	R&D Activity
Pharmaceutical company	Product development	Test the effects of a new drug on different subgroups.
Boat manufacturer	Related diversification	Test the performance of various keel designs under various conditions.
Plastic container manufacturer	Market penetration	Develop a biodegradable container.
Electronics company	Market development	Develop a telecommunications system in a foreign country.

organizations use an R&D strategy that ties external opportunities to internal strengths and is linked with objectives. Well-formulated R&D policies match market opportunities with internal capabilities. Strategic R&D issues include the following:

1. To emphasize product or process improvements.
2. To stress basic or applied research.
3. To be a leader or follower in R&D.
4. To develop robotics or use manual-type processes.
5. To spend a high, average, or low amount of money on R&D.
6. To perform R&D within the firm or contract R&D to outside firms.
7. To use university researchers or private-sector researchers.

Research and development policy among rival firms often varies dramatically. Various pharmaceutical firms, for example, have a philosophical disagreement over the merits of heavy investment to discover new drugs, versus waiting for others to spend the money and then follow up with similar products. Table 9-13 gives some examples of R&D activities that could be required for successful implementation of various strategies. Many U.S. utility, energy, and automotive companies have charged their R&D departments with determining how the firm can effectively reduce its gas emissions.

Many firms wrestle with the decision to acquire R&D expertise from external firms or to develop R&D expertise internally. The following guidelines can be used to help make this decision:

1. If the rate of technical progress is slow, the rate of market growth is moderate, and there are significant barriers to possible new entrants, then in-house R&D is the preferred solution. The reason is that R&D, if successful, will result in a temporary product or process monopoly that the company can exploit.
2. If technology is changing rapidly and the market is growing slowly, then a major effort in R&D may be risky because it may lead to the development of an ultimately obsolete technology or one for which there is no market.
3. If technology is changing slowly but the market is growing quickly, there generally is not enough time for in-house development. The prescribed approach is to obtain R&D expertise on an exclusive or nonexclusive basis from an outside firm.
4. If both technical progress and market growth are fast, R&D expertise should be obtained through acquisition of a well-established firm in the industry.[10]

There are at least three major R&D approaches for implementing strategies, as discussed here:

1. The first approach is to be the first firm to market new technological products. This is a glamorous and exciting strategy but also a dangerous one. Firms such as 3M, Apple, and General Electric have been successful with this method, but many other pioneering firms have fallen, with rival firms seizing the initiative.
2. The second approach is to be an innovative imitator of successful products, thus minimizing the risks and costs of a "startup." This approach entails allowing a pioneer firm to develop the first version of the new product and to demonstrate that a market exists. Then, laggard firms develop a similar product. This strategy requires excellent R&D and marketing personnel.

3. The third approach is to be a low-cost producer by mass-producing products similar to but less expensive than products recently introduced. As a new product is accepted by customers, price becomes increasingly important in the buying decision. Also, mass marketing replaces personal selling as the dominant selling strategy. This approach requires substantial investment in plant and equipment, but fewer expenditures in R&D than the other two approaches. Dell and Lenovo have utilized this third approach to gain competitive advantage.

R&D spending in China increased to about $285 billion in 2014, up 22 percent from 2012. In contrast, R&D spending in the United States grew about 4 percent to $465 billion during the same period. Analysts expect R&D spending in China to surpass U.S. R&D spending by 2022.[11] For example, Shenzhen-based Huawei Technologies, the second-largest telecom-equipment firm in the world behind Ericsson, spends almost $6 billion annually on R&D. Huawei's R&D center in Shanghai employs more than 10,000 engineers, many of whom have computer science advanced degrees. Lenovo, another Chinese firm spending billions on R&D, just opened its huge new hub for R&D in the central Chinese city of Wuhan. China's Fuzhou Rockchip Electronics and Allwinner Technology are rapidly trying to catch up in the mobile processor chips industry with the U.S. Qualcomm and Nvidia Corp. Generally speaking, Chinese firms are "on a mission" to eventually lead the world in technological advancements.

Perhaps the most current trend in R&D has been lifting the veil of secrecy whereby firms, even major competitors, join forces to develop new products. Collaboration is on the rise as a result of new competitive pressures, rising research costs, increasing regulatory issues, and accelerated product development schedules. Companies are also turning to consortia at universities for their R&D needs; more than 600 research consortia are now in operation in the United States.

Strategic Management Information Systems (MIS) Issues

Firms that gather, assimilate, and evaluate external and internal information most effectively are gaining competitive advantages over other firms. Having an effective **management information system (MIS)** may be the most important factor in differentiating successful from unsuccessful firms. The process of strategic management is facilitated immensely in firms that have an effective information system. Information collection, retrieval, and storage can be used to create competitive advantages in ways such as cross-selling to customers, monitoring suppliers, keeping managers and employees informed, coordinating activities among divisions, and managing funds. Like inventory and human resources, information is now recognized as a valuable organizational asset that can be controlled and managed. Firms strive to implement strategies using the best information.

A good information system can allow a firm to reduce costs. For example, online orders from salespersons to production facilities can shorten materials ordering time and reduce inventory costs. Direct communications between suppliers, manufacturers, marketers, and customers can link together elements of the value chain as though they were one organization. Improved quality and service often result from an improved information system.

Firms are increasingly concerned about computer hackers and are taking specific measures to secure and safeguard corporate communications, files, orders, and business. Thousands of companies today are plagued by computer hackers, who may include disgruntled employees, competitors, sociopaths, thieves, spies, and hired agents. Computer vulnerability is a huge, strategic, expensive headache. The first big hacking of 2015 happened at the health insurer Anthem Inc., exposing 80 million customers' personal information. Two recent hackings occurred at Home Depot, exposing 56 million customers' information, and a month later, at J.P. Morgan Chase, exposing 76 million customers' information. Millions of companies are vulnerable to hackers.

In many firms, information technology is allowing employees to work at home or anywhere, anytime. The mobile concept of work allows employees to work the traditional 9-to-5 workday across any of the 24 time zones around the globe. Desktop videoconferencing allows employees to "beam in" whenever needed. Any manager or employee who travels a lot away from the office is a good candidate for working at home. Salespersons and consultants are good examples, but any person whose job largely involves talking to others or handling information could operate at home with the proper MIS.[12]

Mobile Tracking of Employees

Mobile devices and inexpensive monitoring software now enable companies to know where employees are, eavesdrop on their phone calls, and do other things such as know whether or not a driver is wearing his/her seatbelt. More than 40 percent of businesses that send employees out on service calls today track the location and movement of those employees by their company-owned/provided hand-held devices or vehicles.[13] Some employees complain that various monitoring practices are an invasion of privacy, but businesses contend that such measures improve workplace safety and productivity, while also reducing theft and protecting against discrimination.

No federal laws currently prevent businesses from using GPS devices to monitor employees, nor does federal law require businesses to disclose to employees whether they are using such techniques. In fact, in the United States, only two states currently require businesses to tell employees if their electronic communications—including e-mails, instant messages, texts,

IMPLICATIONS FOR STRATEGISTS

Figure 9-7 reveals that to gain and sustain competitive advantages, firms must attract customers and manage their finances better than the best rival firms. Thus, being good is most usually not good enough; being superior is often required. Perceptual mapping and market segmentation, as described in this chapter, are vitally important tools for strategists to make sure that monies devoted to advertising, promotion, publicity, and selling are wisely used. Marketing expenditures can be unnecessarily exorbitant if not based on clear product positioning analyses, target marketing, and customer analysis.

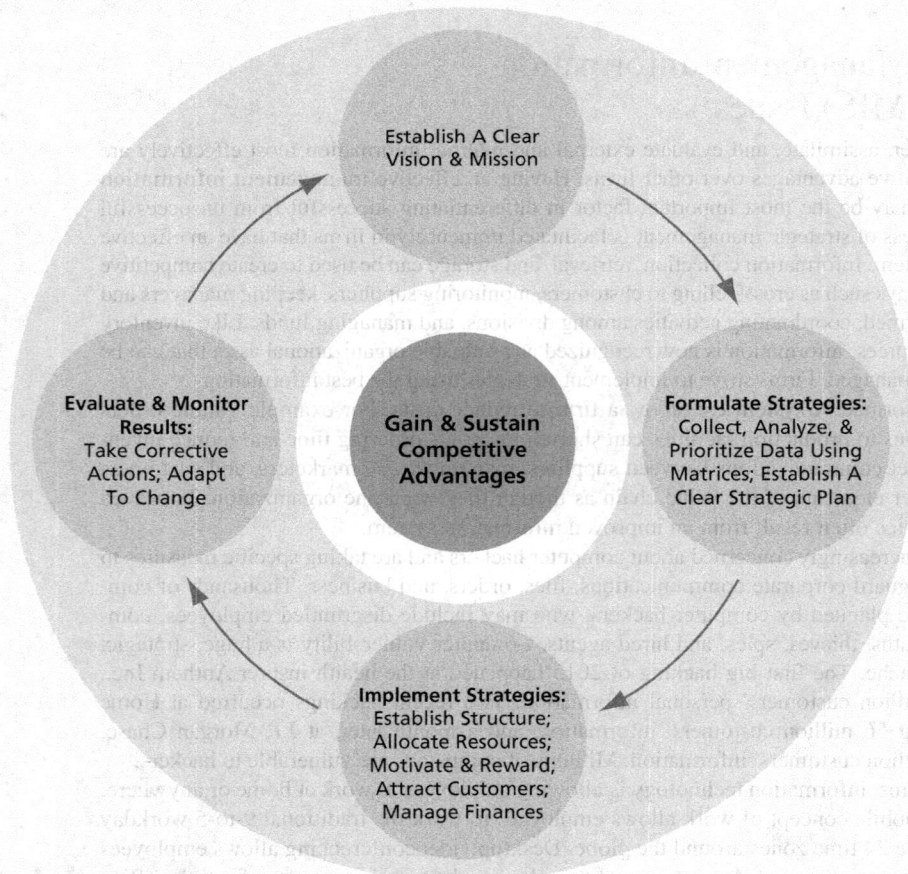

FIGURE 9-7
How to Gain and Sustain Competitive Advantages

According to Figure 9-7, strategists must manage the firm's financial resources exceptionally well, better than strategists at rival firms, especially using corporate valuation analysis, EPS/EBIT analysis, and projected financial statement analysis. It is difficult to make a dollar of profit; every dollar saved is like a dollar earned. Dollars matter and successful strategy implementation is dependent on superior "dollar management." Its take dollars to gain and sustain competitive advantage, and strategists are entrusted with dollar management.

IMPLICATIONS FOR STUDENTS

Regardless of your business major, be sure to capitalize on that special knowledge in delivering your strategic-management case analysis. Whenever the opportunity arises in your oral or written project, reveal how your firm can gain and sustain competitive advantage using your marketing, finance and accounting, or MIS recommendations. Continuously compare your firm to your firm's rivals and draw insights and conclusions so that your recommendations come across as well conceived. Never shy away from the EPS/EBIT or projected financial statement analyses, because your audience must be convinced that what you recommend is financially feasible and worth the dollars to be spent. Spend sufficient time on the nuts-and-bolts of those analyses, so fellow students (and your professor) will be assured that you did them correctly and reasonably. Too often, when students rush at the end, it means their financial statements are overly optimistic or incorrectly developed—so avoid that issue. The marketing, finance and accounting, R&D, and MIS aspects of your recommended strategies must ultimately work together to gain and sustain competitive advantage for the firm—so point that out frequently. By the way, the free student Excel template at www.strategyclub.com can help immensely in performing EPS/EBIT analysis.

photos, and websites visited—are being monitored; the two states are Delaware and Connecticut. MIS tracking technology today has permeated many industries and is utilized by thousands of businesses ranging from landscaping firms to restaurants. And, in many of the businesses, employees do not realize that their actions, location, and habits are being monitored whenever they are on the job.

Mobile Apps for Customers

Companies are increasingly developing mobile apps for customers and using resultant data to devise improved strategies for attracting customers. For example, hotels are rapidly developing apps to help speed up check-in for travelers, including letting customers go straight to their rooms by using their smartphone to unlock doors. In November 2014, Starwood Hotels and Resorts became the first hotel to let guests unlock doors with their phones. Starwood Hotels requires the phone to actually touch a pad on the outside of the door to open it—to make sure if there is a knock on the door late at night and a guest goes to the peephole to see who is there, the guest's phone in his or her pocket will not accidently unlock the door. Some hotel chains, such as Marriott, are holding off on using smartphones as keys until potential security issues can be resolved.

Hilton Worldwide is the second hotel chain, behind Starwood, to announce plans for mobile room keys, which it plans to roll out at the end of 2015 at some U.S. properties. In all 4,000 Hilton properties worldwide, guests can also use maps on the Hilton app to select a specific room. However, guests who like personal interaction at check-in, such as to ask about pool hours or whatever, can still opt for a more leisurely check-in. Hotels eventually would like all travelers to be comfortable using mobile apps on their iPad, smartphone, or smartwatch to request a wakeup call, purchase suite upgrades, book spa treatments, request room service, and open their room door.

Chapter Summary

Successful strategy implementation depends on cooperation among all functional and divisional managers in an organization. Marketing departments are commonly charged with implementing strategies that require significant increases in sales revenues in new areas and with new or improved products. Finance and accounting managers must devise effective strategy-implementation approaches at low cost and minimum risk to that firm. Research and development managers have to transfer complex technologies or develop new technologies to successfully implement strategies. Information systems managers are being called on more and more to provide leadership and training for all individuals in the firm. The nature and role of marketing, finance/accounting, R&D, and MIS activities, coupled with the management, production/operations, and human resource activities described in Chapter 10, largely determine organizational success.

Key Terms and Concepts

book value (p. 307)
convertible bonds (p. 296)
data mining (p. 291)
demand void (p. 293)
discount (p. 306)
EPS/EBIT analysis (p. 296)
goodwill (p. 305)
initial public offerings (IPOs) (p. 308)
management information system (MIS) (p. 311)
market capitalization (p. 307)
market segment (p. 293)
market segmentation (p. 289)
market value (p. 307)

marketing mix variables (p. 290)
multidimensional scaling (p. 292)
outstanding shares method (p. 307)
perceptual mapping (p. 292)
premium (p. 307)
price-earnings ratio method (p. 307)
product positioning (p. 292)
projected financial statement analysis (p. 300)
treasury stock (p. 296)
tweet (p. 288)
vacant niche (p. 292)
wikis (p. 288)

Issues for Review and Discussion

⭐ **9-1.** Royal Dutch Shell Plc has been successful for decades. Analyze their year-end 2015 financials. List six points that best summarize Shell's performance in 2015.

9-2. Explain how to develop an advertising strategy.

⭐ **9-3.** Illustrate a product-positioning map for Royal Dutch Shell. Include three rival firms in your matrix.

9-4. Illustrate a product-positioning map for your college or university.

⭐ **9-5.** List and explain the advantages and disadvantages of using debt versus equity, as a means of raising capital.

9-6. List in order of importance the limitations of the EPS/EBIT analysis.

9-7. Consider the Cohesion Case on Nestlé. Calculate that company's tax rate, which is a common calculation needed in performing EPS/EBIT analysis.

9-8. Review the website of a company that you are familiar with. Discuss the extent to which that organization has instituted the new principles of marketing according to Parise, Guinan, and Weinberg.

9-9. For companies in general, identify and discuss three opportunities and three threats associated with social networking activities on the Internet.

⭐ **9-10.** "Television viewers are passive viewers of ads whereas Internet users take an active role in choosing what to look at—so customers on the Internet are tougher for

marketers to reach." Do you agree or disagree with the statement? Explain your answer.

9-11. How important or relevant do you believe purpose-based marketing is for organizations today?

⭐ **9-12.** Why is it essential for organizations to segment markets and target particular groups of consumers?

9-13. Explain how and why the Internet makes market segmentation easier?

9-14. A product-positioning rule given in the chapter is that "when there are only two competitors, the middle becomes the preferred strategic position." Illustrate this for the cruise ship industry where two firms, Carnival and Royal Caribbean, dominate. Illustrate this for the commercial airliner building industry where Boeing and Airbus dominate.

9-15. How would dividends affect an EPS/EBIT analysis? Would it be correct to refer to "earnings after taxes, interest, and dividends" as retained earnings for a given year?

9-16. In performing an EPS/EBIT analysis, where does the first row of (EBIT) numbers come from?

9-17. In performing an EPS/EBIT analysis, where does the tax rate percentage come from?

9-18. What amount of dividends did Royal Dutch Shell pay in 2015? How much of 2015's earnings did Shell reinvest back into the company?

9-19. Show algebraically that the price earnings ratio formula is identical to the number of shares outstanding multiplied by the stock price formula. Why are the values obtained from these two methods sometimes different?

9-20. In accounting terms, distinguish between intangibles and goodwill on a balance sheet. Why do these two items generally stay the same on projected financial statements?

9-21. What are the three major R&D approaches to implementing strategies? Which approach would you prefer as owner of a small software company? Why?

⭐ 9-22. Explain in your own words the process of developing projected financial statement analysis.

9-23. In developing projected financial statements, why should the preparer not use historical percentages too heavily?

9-24. Explain five methods for determining the cash value of a company.

9-25. Given the seven R&D policies mentioned in the chapter, which four do you feel would be best for Audi to utilize? Why?

⭐ 9-26. Illustrate an EPS/EBIT chart that reflects negative EPS values.

9-27. Define a vacant niche using an example.

9-28. Define and give an example of wikis and tweets.

⭐ 9-29. List the marketing mix variables. Give an example of each.

9-30. Show algebraically that the price earnings ratio method of calculating the cash value of a company is identical to the number of shares outstanding multiplied by the stock price method.

⭐ 9-31. Define and give an example of, goodwill and intangibles.

9-32. Differentiate between capital surplus and additional paid in capital on a balance sheet. Capital Surplus is a comparison of two years, for example, to reflect the capital situation, such as stocks, performing in the two years.

9-33. What transaction links a projected income statement with a projected balance sheet?

9-34. Explain the benefits of a before-and-after product-positioning map.

9-35. Explain how Hewlett-Packard (HP) should conduct market segmentation.

9-36. Determine the cash value of HP using the methods described in this chapter.

9-37. What are convertible bonds?

9-38. With regard to financial ratios, what is an indirect benefit of increasing Treasury Stock during the last fiscal quarter of a year?

9-39. If a firm's long-term debt rises from $110 million to $215 million, what percent increase is that?

ASSURANCE OF LEARNING EXERCISES

EXERCISE 9A
Prepare an EPS/EBIT Analysis for Royal Dutch Shell Plc

Purpose

Shell is featured in the opening chapter case as a firm that engages in excellent strategic planning. By some measures, Shell is the second largest oil and gas company in the world and one of the largest firm globally. Incorporated in the United Kingdom but headquartered in the Netherlands, Shell has worldwide reserves of 14.2 billion barrels of oil equivalent. An important part of effective strategic management is wisely using debt versus equity for raising capital. This exercise gives you practice in preparing an EPS/EBIT analysis for a company to determine whether debt versus equity or some combination of the two is best for the firm to expand and grow.

Instructions

Step 1 Shell needs to raise $1billion to acquire a rival firm in Southeast Asia.
Step 2 Prepare an EPS/EBIT analysis to determine whether Shell should use stock or debt to raise the needed capital.
Step 3 Prepare a two-page executive summary to provide justification for your financing decision.

EXERCISE 9B
Develop a Product-Positioning Map for Nestlé S.A.

Purpose

Organizations continually monitor how their products and services are positioned relative to competitors. This information is especially useful for marketing managers, but is also used by other managers and strategists.

Instructions

Step 1 On a separate sheet of paper, develop a product-positioning map for Nestlé. Include three rival firms in your diagram, perhaps Unilever, Danone, and Mondelēz International.
Step 2 Compare your product-positioning maps with those diagrammed by other students. Discuss any major differences.

EXERCISE 9C
Perform an EPS/EBIT Analysis for Nestlé S.A.

Purpose

An EPS/EBIT analysis is one of the most widely used techniques for determining the extent that debt and/or stock should be used to finance strategies to be implemented. This exercise can give you practice performing EPS/EBIT analysis.

Instructions

In order to expand into Africa, Nestlé needs to raise $1 billion. Determine whether Nestlé should use all debt, all stock, or a 50–50 combination of debt and stock to finance this market-development strategy. Assume a 20 percent tax rate, 3 percent interest rate, Nestle stock price of $30 per share, and an annual dividend of $0.50 per share of common stock. The EBIT range for 2015 is between $1.0 billion and $2 billion. A total of 500 million shares of common stock are outstanding. Develop an EPS/EBIT chart to reflect your analysis.

EXERCISE 9D
Prepare Projected Financial Statements for Nestlé S.A.

Purpose

This exercise is designed to give you experience preparing projected financial statements. Pro forma analysis is a central strategy-implementation technique because it allows managers to anticipate and evaluate the expected results of various strategy-implementation approaches.

Instructions

Step 1 Work with a classmate. Develop a 2016 projected income statement and balance sheet for Nestlé. Assume that Nestlé plans to raise $900 million in 2016 to begin serving Africa, and plans to obtain 50 percent financing from a bank and 50 percent financing from a stock issuance. Make other assumptions as needed, and state them clearly in written form. Use Nestlé's website as needed.

Step 2 Compute Nestlé's current ratio, debt-to-equity ratio, and return on investment for 2014 and 2015. How do your 2016 projected ratios compare to the 2014 and 2015 ratios? Why is it important to make this comparison?

Step 3 Bring your projected statements to class and discuss any problems or questions you encountered.

Step 4 Compare your projected statements to the statements of other students. What major differences exist between your analysis and the work of other students?

EXERCISE 9E
Determine the Cash Value of Nestlé S.A.

Purpose

It is simply good business practice to periodically determine the financial worth or cash value of your company. This exercise gives you practice determining the total worth of a company using several methods. Use data as given in the Cohesion Case or the data from the Nestlé website.

Instructions

Step 1 Calculate the financial worth of Nestlé based on four methods: 1) the net worth or stockholders' equity, 2) the future value of Nestlé's earnings, 3) the price-earnings ratio, and 4) the outstanding shares method. In dollars, how much is Nestlé worth?

Step 2 Compare your analyses and conclusions with those of other students.

EXERCISE 9F
Develop a Product-Positioning Map for Your College

Purpose

Organizations continually monitor how their products and services are positioned relative to competitors. This information is especially useful for marketing managers, but is also used by other managers and strategists.

Instructions

Step 1 On a separate sheet of paper, develop a product-positioning map for your college or university.

Step 2 On the board, draw a diagram of your product-positioning map. Compare your product-positioning map with those diagrammed by other students. Discuss any major differences.

EXERCISE 9G
Do Banks Require Projected Financial Statements?

Purpose

The purpose of this exercise is to explore the practical importance and use of projected financial statements in the banking business.

Instructions

Visit with two local bankers and seek answers to the questions that follow. Record the answers you receive, and report your findings to the class.

- Does your bank require projected financial statements as part of a business loan application?
- How does your bank use projected financial statements when they are part of a business loan application?
- What special advice do you give potential business borrowers in preparing projected financial statements?

MINI-CASE ON TATA MOTORS LIMITED (TTM)

Source: © dragunov.Shutterstock

Headquartered in Mumbai, India, Tata Motors is one of the largest multinational manufacturing companies. It manufactures commercial and passenger vehicles—cars, trucks, vans, coaches, buses, construction equipment, and military vehicles. Tata Motors has several auto manufacturing and assembly plants, and research and development centers located across India, including in Jameshedpur, Lucknow, and Pune. With a solid base in the country, Tata Motors has also built its operations in Argentina, South Africa, Thailand, and the United Kingdom. In 2014, the company was ranked the world's 287th biggest corporation in Fortune's Global 500 list. Marketing its products through dealership, sales, services, and spare parts network, the company produces well-known models like the Nano, Safari, Aria, Zest, Bolt, and Venture brand names, as well as Xenon XT brand name.

For a fourth straight quarter, the decline in China sales of Jaguar Land Rover (JLR), a subsidiary of Tata Motors, dragged down the company's profits. Jaguar's net income fell 49 percent to 27.7 billion rupees ($434 million) in the quarter ended in June, 2015. Its retail sales plunged 33 percent in China that quarter, which lead to a 1 percent decline in worldwide deliveries. The luxury unit has cut its sales targets and prices in China as all automakers brace for a slowdown in the world's biggest auto market. Tata Motors' earnings for the second quarter of 2015 were also hurt by a prolonged slump in sales of its light commercial vehicles in India. Tata's revenue fell 5.7 percent to 610.2 billion rupees. Sales at the luxury unit declined 6.5 percent to 5 billion pounds. Shares of Tata Motors stock has slumped 29 percent over the past six months making it the second-worst performer on the S&P BSE Sensex, which has lost 1.7 percent in the period. Sales of the Tata's Evoque sport utility vehicle were also lower in China.

The company's vision statement, posted on the corporate website, states that by 2025, the company's commitment to delivering improved quality of life will be available to 25 percent of the global population, making Tata one of the 25 most admired global brands and one of the most valuable companies in the world. Its mission is to use its leadership experience, long-term value creation, and the trust it has built to improve the quality of life of its consumers around the world.

Questions

1. How has the value of the Indian rupee changed compared to China's yuan and the US dollar in the last six months? How does this impact Tata?
2. In the About Us section of the company's website, go to the corporate governance section and click on the values and purpose link. Evaluate Tata's vision and mission statement mentioned in this section. Discuss the potential implications of Tata's vision and mission on the firm's competitive advantages.

Source: Based on company documents.

Current Readings

Bell, R. Greg, Igor Filatotchev, and Ruth V. Aguilera. "Corporate Governance and Investors' Perceptions of Foreign IPO Value: An Institutional Perspective." *Academy of Management Journal* 57, no. 1 (2014): 301–320.

Changhyun, Kim, and Richard A. Bettis. "Cash Is Surprisingly Valuable as a Strategic Asset." *Strategic Management Journal*, 35, issue 13 (December 2014): 2053–2063.

Dawar, Niraj. "When Marketing Is Strategy." *Harvard Business Review* 91, no. 12 (2013): 100–108.

Glen, Roy, Christy Suciu, and Christopher Baughn. "The Need for Design Thinking in Business Schools." *Academy of Management Journal Learning and Education* 13 (December 2014): 653–667.

Kodama, Matt, and Bill Ladd. "Mapping the Cyberwar Battlefield." *Harvard Business Review* 91, no. 9 (2013): 32–33.

Wang, R. D., and J. M. Shaver, "Competition-Driven Repositioning," *Strategic Management Journal* 35, no. 11 (November 2014): 1,585–1,604.

Yang, Yi, Vadake K. Narayanan, and Donna M. De Carolis. "The Relationship between Portfolio Diversification and Firm Value: The Evidence from Corporate Venture Capital Activity." *Strategic Management Journal* 35, no. 13 (December 2014): 1993–2011.

Endnotes

1. Salvatore Parise, Patricia Guinan, and Bruce Weinberg, "The Secrets of Marketing in a Web 2.0 World," *Wall Street Journal*, December 15, 2008, R1.

2. Kathy Chu and Kim Thai, "Banks Jump on Twitter Wagon," *USA Today*, May 12, 2009, B1.

3. Suzanne Vranica, "Man vs. Bot: The Online-Ad Wars," *Wall Street Journal*, March 24, 2014, B1 & B5.

4. Ibid.

5. Gupta, Sunil, and Donald R. Lehmann, *Managing Customers as Investments: The Strategic Value of Customers in the Long Run* ("Customer Retention" section) (Upper Saddle River, NJ: Pearson Education/ Wharton School Publishing, 2005).

6. Ralph Biggadike, "The Contributions of Marketing to Strategic Management," *Academy of Management Review* 6, no. 4 (October 1981): 627.

7. Michael Rapoport, "Pro Forma Is a Hard Habit to Break," *Wall Street Journal*, September 18, 2003, B3A.

8. Telis Demos, "Companies Rush to Join IPO Surge," *Wall Street Journal*, March 7, 2014, p. A1.

9. Based on Maxwell Murphy and Mike Cherney, "Bond-Funded Buybacks Draw Skeptics," *Wall Street Journal*, June 16, 2015, p. B6.

10. Pier Abetti, "Technology: A Key Strategic Resource," *Management Review* 78, no. 2 (February 1989): 38.

11. Juro Osawa and Paul Mozur, "The Rise of China's Innovation Engine," *Wall Street Journal*, January 17, 2004, B1.

12. Adapted from Edward Baig, "Welcome to the Officeless Office," *Businessweek*, June 26, 1995.

13. Spencer Ante and Lauren Weber, "Memo to Workers: The Boss Is Watching," *Wall Street Journal*, October 28, 2013, B1, B6.

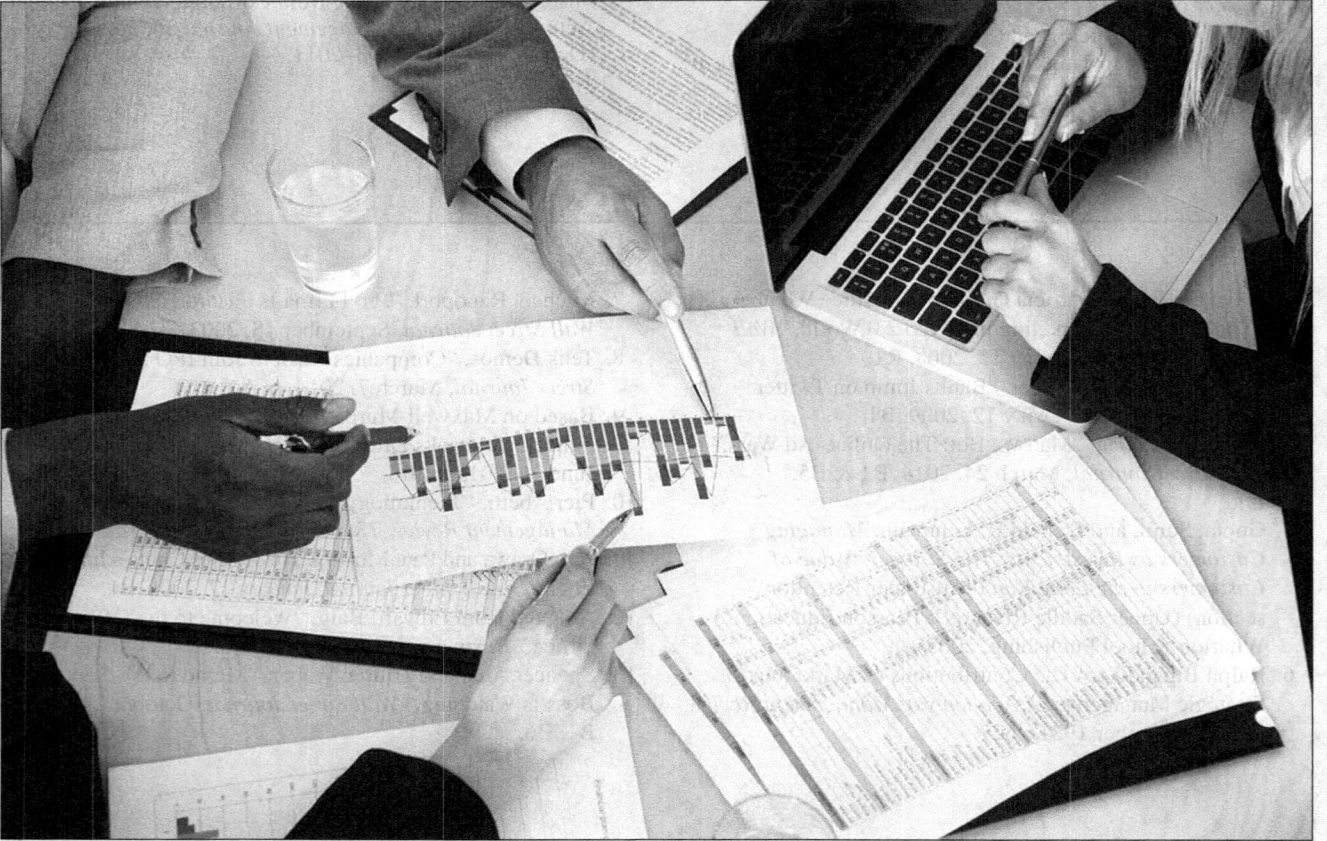

10

Strategy Execution

LEARNING OBJECTIVES

After studying this chapter, you should be able to do the following:

10-1. Describe the transition from formulating to implementing strategies

10-2. Discuss five reasons why annual objectives are essential for effective strategy implementation.

10-3. Identify and discuss six reasons why policies are essential for effective strategy implementation.

10-4. Explain the role of resource allocation and managing conflict in strategy implementation.

10-5. Discuss the need to match a firm's structure with its strategy.

10-6. Identify, diagram, and discuss seven different types of organizational structure.

10-7. Identify and discuss fifteen dos and don'ts in constructing organizational charts.

10-8. Discuss four strategic production/operations issues vital for successful strategy implementation.

10-9. Discuss seven strategic human resource issues vital for successful strategy implementation.

ASSURANCE OF LEARNING EXERCISES

The following exercises are found at the end of this chapter:

EXERCISE 10A Develop an Organizational Chart for Accenture Plc

EXERCISE 10B Assess Accenture's Philanthropy Efforts

EXERCISE 10C Revise Nestlé's Organizational Chart

EXERCISE 10D Explore Objectives

EXERCISE 10E Understanding Your University's Culture

The strategic-management process does not end with deciding what strategy or strategies to pursue. There must be a translation of strategic thought into action. This translation is much easier if managers and employees of the firm understand the business, feel a part of the company, and through involvement in strategy-formulation activities have become committed to helping the organization succeed. Without understanding and commitment, strategy-implementation efforts face major problems. Vince Lombardi commented, "The best game plan in the world never blocked or tackled anybody."

Implementing strategy affects an organization from top to bottom, including all the functional and divisional areas of a business. This chapter focuses on management, operations, and human resource issues most critical for successful strategy implementation, whereas Chapter 9 focuses on marketing, finance/accounting, R&D, and management information systems (MIS) strategic issues. As showcased next, Accenture, the world's largest consulting firm by revenue, is a model company for motivating employees, by providing employee benefits and being specially aware of the needs and priorities of female employees.

Even the most technically perfect strategic plan will serve little purpose if it is not implemented. Many organizations tend to spend an inordinate amount of time, money, and effort on developing the strategic plan, treating the means and circumstances under which it will be implemented as afterthoughts! Change comes through implementation and evaluation, not through the plan. A technically imperfect plan that is implemented well will achieve more than the perfect plan that never gets off the paper on which it is typed.[1]

Transitioning from Formulating to Implementing Strategies

The strategy-implementation stage of strategic management is revealed in Figure 10-1, as illustrated with white shading. Successful strategy formulation does not guarantee successful strategy implementation. It is always more difficult to do something (strategy implementation) than to say you are going to do it (strategy formulation)! Although inextricably linked, strategy implementation is fundamentally different from strategy formulation.

EXEMPLARY COMPANY SHOWCASED

Accenture Plc (ACN)

Accenture, based in Dublin, Ireland, employs around 275,000 individuals and provides service to clients in over 120 countries. Regarded as one of the largest consulting firms, in terms of revenue, Accenture's largest employee base is in India, with almost 100,000 employees compared to the 50,000 in the United States. Accenture's 39 industry subgroups fall under its five operating groups—financial services; resources; communications, media, and technology; products; and health and public service.

Accenture is a model company for providing employee benefits and for taking care of women. In the United States and Cananda, Accenture introduced a range of of parental benefits for its employees, including offering to pay for breast milk to be shipped home to infants while their mothers travelled for work. This benefit put Accenture in league with IBM, and fellow consulting firm Ernst and Young. In the United States, Accenture will not only pay for the packaging of the milk and will bear shipping costs but will also make hospital-grade breast pumps available to its female employees. Among its other initiatives, employees are given an opportunity to work locally, and every year they are provided with back-up dependent care for children for 80 hours. The company also provides online parenting education for its employees in the United States. The paid parental leave for birth mothers was increased from eight weeks to 16 weeks while other primary caregivers were allowed eight weeks leave.

In August 2015, U.K.-based Total Logistics, an independent logistics and supply chain consultancy, was acquired by Accenture. Total Logistics supports clients in the retail and consumer goods industries, automotive and industrial equipment industries, and those in the life sciences industry. In 2014, Accenture's supply chain management and procurement applications increased by 10.8 percent to $9.9 billion, beating most software markets.

Source: Based on company documents.

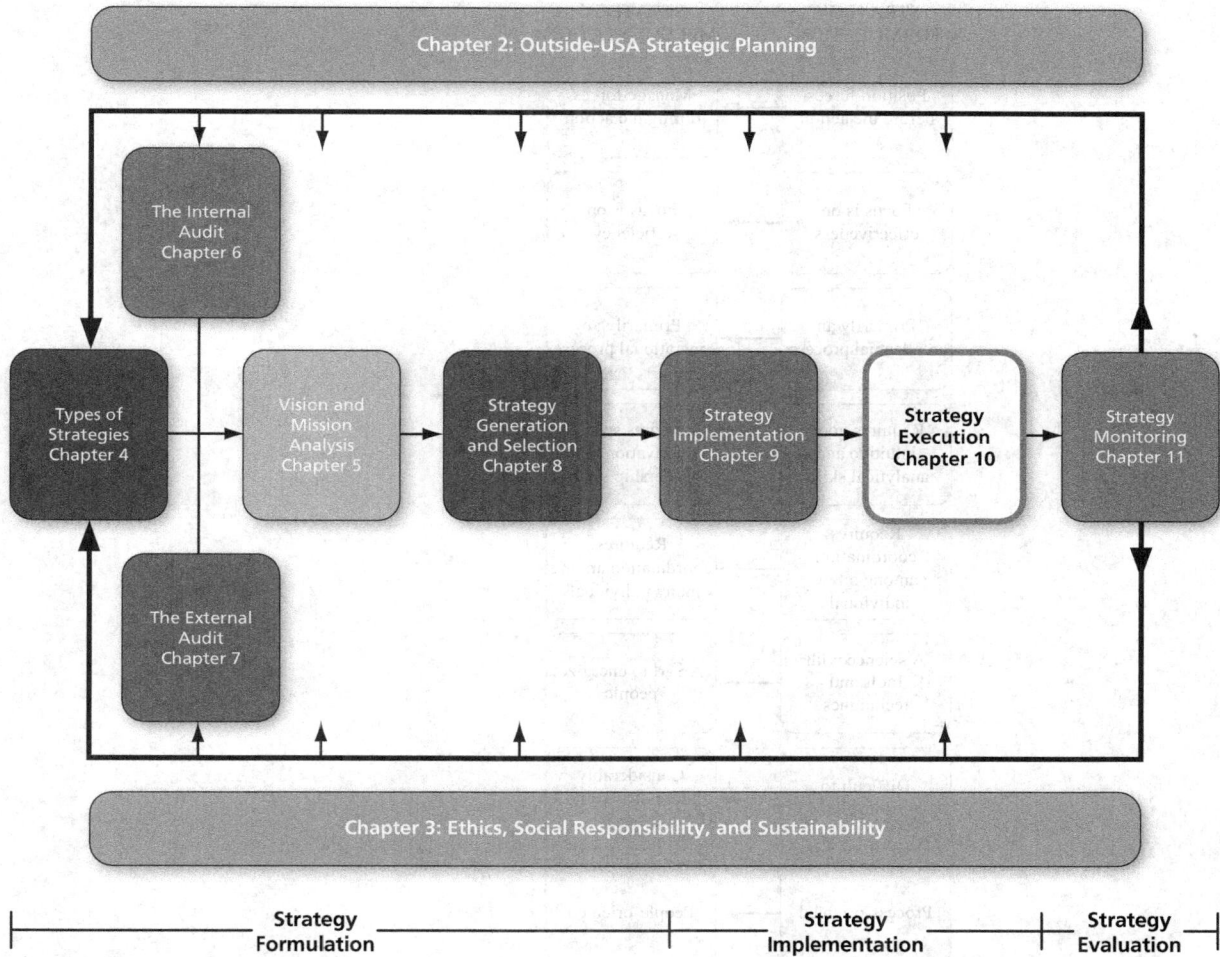

FIGURE 10-1

Comprehensive Strategic-Management Model

Source: Fred R. David, adapted from "How Companies Define Their Mission," *Long Range Planning* 22, no. 3 (June 1988): 40, © Fred R. David.

In all but the smallest organizations, the transition from strategy formulation to strategy implementation requires a shift in responsibility from strategists to divisional and functional managers. Implementation problems can arise because of this shift in responsibility, especially if strategy-formulation decisions come as a surprise to middle- and lower-level managers. Managers and employees are motivated more by perceived self-interests than by organizational interests, unless the two coincide. This is a primary reason why divisional and functional managers should be involved as much as possible in both strategy-formulation and strategy-implementation activities. Strategy formulation and implementation can be contrasted in the ways illustrated in Figure 10-2.

Strategy-formulation concepts and tools do not differ greatly for small, large, for-profit, or nonprofit organizations. However, strategy implementation varies substantially among different types and sizes of organizations. Implementing strategies requires such actions as altering sales territories, adding new departments, closing facilities, hiring new employees, changing an organization's pricing strategy, developing financial budgets, developing new employee benefits, establishing cost-control procedures, changing advertising strategies, building new facilities, training new employees, transferring managers among divisions, and building a better management information system. These types of activities obviously differ greatly among manufacturing, service, and governmental organizations.

STRATEGY FORMULATION	STRATEGY IMPLEMENTATION
Position forces before the action	Manage forces during the action
Focus is on effectiveness	Focus is on efficiency
Primarily an intellectual process	Primarily an operational process
Requires good intuitive and analytical skills	Requires special motivation and leadership skills
Requires coordination among a few individuals	Requires coordination among many individuals
A science with tools and techniques	An art to energize people
Difficult to do well	Considerably more difficult to do well
Process-oriented	People-oriented
Primary responsibility of top managers	Primary responsibility of mid and lower-level managers

FIGURE 10-2

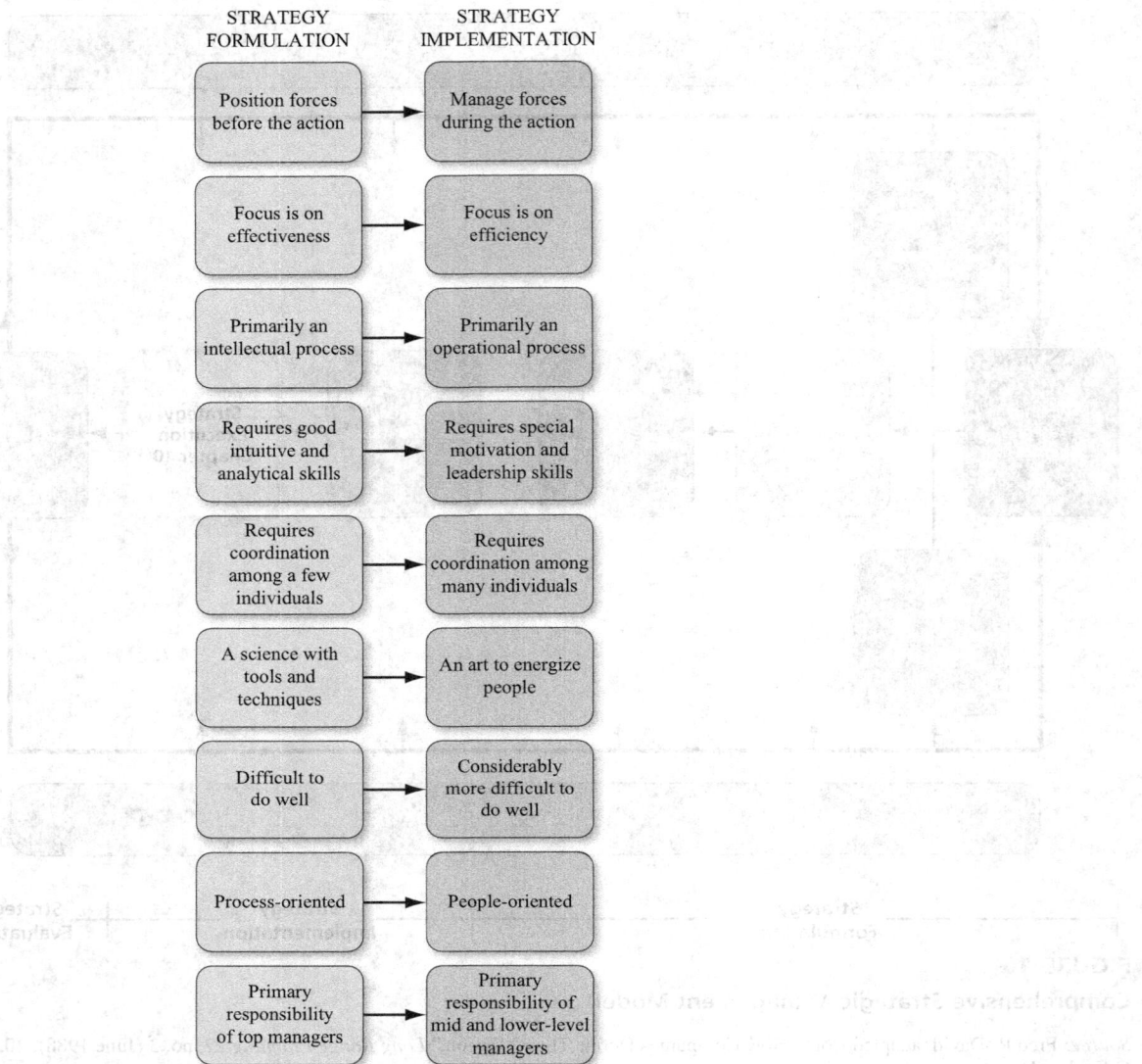

Contrasting Strategy Formulation with Strategy Implementation

The Need for Clear Annual Objectives

Annual objectives are desired milestones an organization needs to achieve to ensure successful strategy implementation. Annual objectives are essential for strategy implementation for five primary reasons:

1. They represent the basis for allocating resources.
2. They are a primary mechanism for evaluating managers.
3. They enable effective monitoring of progress toward achieving long-term objectives.
4. They establish organizational, divisional, and departmental priorities.
5. They are essential for keeping a strategic plan on track.

Considerable time and effort should be devoted to ensuring that annual objectives are well conceived, consistent with long-term objectives, and supportive of strategies to be implemented. Active participation in establishing annual objectives is needed for the preceding reasons listed.

Approving, revising, or rejecting annual objectives is much more than a rubber-stamp activity. The purpose of annual objectives can be summarized as follows:

Annual objectives serve as guidelines for action, directing and channeling efforts and activities of organization members. They provide a source of legitimacy in an enterprise by justifying activities to stakeholders. They serve as standards of performance. They serve as an important source of employee motivation and identification. They give incentives for managers and employees to perform. They provide a basis for organizational design.[2]

Clearly stated and communicated objectives are critical to success in all types and sizes of firms. Annual objectives are often stated in terms of profitability, growth, and market share by business segment, geographic area, customer groups, and product. Figure 10-3 illustrates how

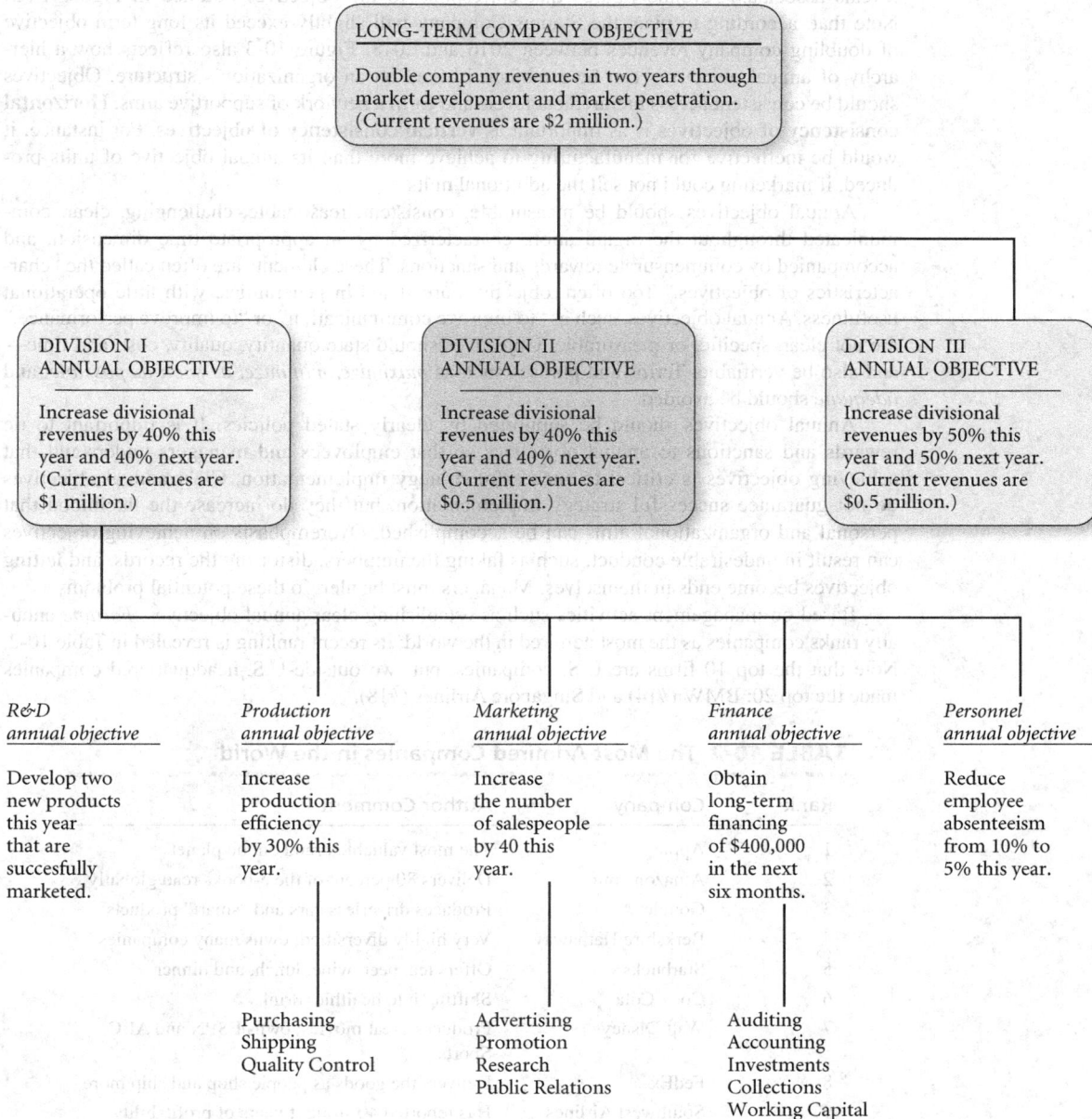

LONG-TERM COMPANY OBJECTIVE

Double company revenues in two years through market development and market penetration. (Current revenues are $2 million.)

DIVISION I ANNUAL OBJECTIVE

Increase divisional revenues by 40% this year and 40% next year. (Current revenues are $1 million.)

DIVISION II ANNUAL OBJECTIVE

Increase divisional revenues by 40% this year and 40% next year. (Current revenues are $0.5 million.)

DIVISION III ANNUAL OBJECTIVE

Increase divisional revenues by 50% this year and 50% next year. (Current revenues are $0.5 million.)

R&D annual objective

Develop two new products this year that are succesfully marketed.

Production annual objective

Increase production efficiency by 30% this year.

Marketing annual objective

Increase the number of salespeople by 40 this year.

Finance annual objective

Obtain long-term financing of $400,000 in the next six months.

Personnel annual objective

Reduce employee absenteeism from 10% to 5% this year.

Purchasing
Shipping
Quality Control

Advertising
Promotion
Research
Public Relations

Auditing
Accounting
Investments
Collections
Working Capital

FIGURE 10-3

The Stamus Company's Hierarchy of Aims

TABLE 10-1 The Stamus Company's Revenue Expectations (in $ millions)

	2016	2017	2018
Division I Revenues	1.0	1.400	1.960
Division II Revenues	0.5	0.700	0.980
Division III Revenues	0.5	0.750	1.125
Total Company Revenues	**2.0**	**2.850**	**4.065**

the Stamus Company could establish annual objectives based on long-term objectives. Table 10-1 reveals associated revenue figures that correspond to the objectives outlined in Figure 10-3. Note that, according to plan, the Stamus Company will slightly exceed its long-term objective of doubling company revenues between 2016 and 2018. Figure 10-3 also reflects how a hierarchy of annual objectives can be established based on an organization's structure. Objectives should be consistent across hierarchical levels and form a network of supportive aims. **Horizontal consistency of objectives** is as important as **vertical consistency of objectives**. For instance, it would be ineffective for manufacturing to achieve more than its annual objective of units produced, if marketing could not sell the additional units.

Annual objectives should be measurable, consistent, reasonable, challenging, clear, communicated throughout the organization, characterized by an appropriate time dimension, and accompanied by commensurate rewards and sanctions. These elements are often called the "characteristics of objectives." Too often, objectives are stated in generalities, with little operational usefulness. Annual objectives, such as "to improve communication" or "to improve performance," are not clear, specific, or measurable. Objectives should state quantity, quality, cost, and time—and also be verifiable. Terms and phrases such as *maximize, minimize, as soon as possible,* and *adequate* should be avoided.

Annual objectives should be supported by clearly stated policies. It is important to tie rewards and sanctions to annual objectives so that employees and managers understand that achieving objectives is critical to successful strategy implementation. Clear annual objectives do not guarantee successful strategy implementation, but they do increase the likelihood that personal and organizational aims can be accomplished. Overemphasis on achieving objectives can result in undesirable conduct, such as faking the numbers, distorting the records, and letting objectives become ends in themselves. Managers must be alert to these potential problems.

Based on management activities such as establishing clear annual objectives, *Fortune* annually ranks companies as the most admired in the world; its recent ranking is revealed in Table 10-2. Note that the top 10 firms are U.S. companies, but two outside-U.S.-headquartered companies made the top 20: BMW (#14) and Singapore Airlines (#18).

TABLE 10-2 The Most Admired Companies in the World

Rank	Company	Author Comment
1	Apple	The most valuable brand on the planet
2	Amazon.com	Delivers 80 percent of the e-books read globally
3	Google	Produces driverless cars and "smart" products
4	Berkshire Hathaway	Very highly diversified; owns many companies
5	Starbucks	Offers tea, beer, wine, lunch, and dinner
6	Coca-Cola	Shifting into healthier drinks
7	Walt Disney	Produces great movies; owns ESPN and ABC Sports
8	FedEx	Delivers the goods as people shop and ship more
9	Southwest Airlines	Has reported 40 straight years of profitability
10	General Electric	Highly diversified; competes in many industries

Source: Based on information at http://fortune.com/worlds-most-admired-companies/apple-1/

The Need for Clear Policies

Policies refer to specific guidelines, methods, procedures, rules, forms, and administrative practices established to support and encourage work toward stated goals. Changes in a firm's strategic direction do not occur automatically. On a day-to-day basis, policies are needed to make a strategy work. Policies facilitate solving recurring problems and guide the implementation of strategy. Policies are essential instruments for strategy implementation, for at least six reasons:

1. Policies set boundaries, constraints, and limits on the kinds of administrative actions that can be taken to reward and sanction behavior.
2. Policies let both employees and managers know what is expected of them, thereby increasing the likelihood that strategies will be implemented successfully.
3. Policies provide a basis for management control and allow coordination across organizational units.
4. Policies reduce the amount of time managers spend making decisions. Policies also clarify what work is to be done and by whom.
5. Policies promote delegation of decision making to appropriate managerial levels where various problems usually arise.
6. Policies clarify what can and cannot be done in pursuit of an organization's objectives.

As an example, some companies have a policy that bans employees from accessing their personal social media sites during work hours. Some companies are more stringent than others regarding social media policy. An excerpt from Gap, Inc.'s social media policy asserts, "Unless you are an authorized Social Media Manager for Gap, do not let social media affect your job performance." Many organizations have a policy manual that serves to guide and direct behavior. Policies can apply to all divisions and departments (such as, "We are an equal opportunity employer"). Some policies apply to a single department ("Employees in this department must take at least one training and development course each year"). Whatever their scope and form, policies serve as a mechanism for implementing strategies and obtaining objectives. Policies should be stated in writing whenever possible. They represent the means for carrying out strategic decisions. Sometimes policies can be controversial, as described in the mini-case at the end of this chapter for Horizon Pharma.

Examples of policies that support a company strategy, a divisional objective, and a departmental objective are given in Table 10-3. Some example issues that may require a management policy are provided in Table 10-4.

Allocate Resources and Manage Conflict

Allocate Resources

All organizations have at least four types of resources (or assets) that can be used to achieve desired objectives: (1) financial resources, (2) physical resources, (3) human resources, and (4) technological resources. **Resource allocation** can be defined as distributing an organization's "assets" across products, regions, and segments according to priorities established by annual objectives. Allocating resources is a vital strategy-implementation activity. Strategic management itself is sometimes referred to as a "resource allocation process."

In organizations that do no strategic planning, resource allocation is often based on political or personal factors and bias, rather than being based on clear analysis and thought. Strategists should be wary of a number of factors that commonly prohibit effective resource allocation, including an overprotection of resources, too great an emphasis on short-run financial criteria, organizational politics, vague strategy targets, a reluctance to take risks, and a lack of sufficient knowledge. Below the corporate level, there often exists an absence of systematic thinking about resources allocated and strategies of the firm. Effective resource allocation does not guarantee successful strategy implementation because programs, personnel, controls, and commitment must breathe life into the resources provided. Yavitz and Newman explain why:

> Managers normally have many more tasks than they can do. Managers must allocate time and resources among these tasks. Pressure builds up. Expenses are too high. The CEO wants a good financial report for the third quarter. Strategy formulation and implementation

TABLE 10-3 A Hierarchy of Policies

Company Strategy
Acquire a chain of retail stores to meet our sales growth and profitability objectives.

Supporting Policies
1. "All stores will be open from 8 AM to 8 PM Monday through Saturday." (This policy could increase retail sales if stores currently are open only 40 hours a week.)
2. "All stores must submit a Monthly Control Data Report." (This policy could reduce expense-to-sales ratios.)
3. "All stores must support company advertising by contributing 5 percent of their total monthly revenues for this purpose." (This policy could allow the company to establish a national reputation.)
4. "All stores must adhere to the uniform pricing guidelines set forth in the Company Handbook." (This policy could help assure customers that the company offers a consistent product in terms of price and quality in all its stores.)

Divisional Objective
Increase the division's revenues from $10 million in 2016 to $15 million in 2018.

Supporting Policies
1. "Beginning in January 2017, each one of this division's salespersons must file a weekly activity report that includes the number of calls made, the number of miles traveled, the number of units sold, the dollar volume sold, and the number of new accounts opened." (This policy could ensure that salespersons do not place too great an emphasis in certain areas.)
2. "Beginning in January 2017, this division will return to its employees 5 percent of its gross revenues in the form of a Christmas bonus." (This policy could increase employee productivity.)
3. "Beginning in January 2017, inventory levels carried in warehouses will be decreased by 30 percent in accordance with a just-in-time (JIT) manufacturing approach." (This policy could reduce production expenses and thus free funds for increased marketing efforts.)

Production Department Objective
Increase production from 20,000 units in 2016 to 30,000 units in 2018.

Supporting Policies
1. "Beginning in January 2017, employees will have the option of working up to 20 hours of overtime per week." (This policy could minimize the need to hire additional employees.)
2. "Beginning in January 2017, perfect attendance awards in the amount of $100 will be given to all employees who do not miss a workday in a given year." (This policy could decrease absenteeism and increase productivity.)
3. "Beginning in January 2017, new equipment must be leased rather than purchased." (This policy could reduce tax liabilities and thus allow more funds to be invested in modernizing production processes).

TABLE 10-4 Some Issues That May Require a Management Policy

- To offer extensive or limited management development workshops and seminars
- To centralize or decentralize employee-training activities
- To recruit through employment agencies, college campuses, or newspapers
- To promote from within or to hire from the outside
- To promote on the basis of merit or on the basis of seniority
- To tie executive compensation to long-term or annual objectives
- To offer numerous or few employee benefits
- To negotiate directly or indirectly with labor unions
- To delegate authority for large expenditures or to centrally retain this authority
- To allow much, some, or no overtime work
- To establish a high- or low-safety stock of inventory
- To use one or more suppliers
- To buy, lease, or rent new production equipment
- To greatly or somewhat stress quality control
- To establish many or only a few production standards
- To operate one, two, or three shifts
- To discourage using insider information for personal gain
- To discourage sexual harassment
- To discourage smoking at work
- To discourage insider trading
- To discourage moonlighting

activities often get deferred. Today's problems soak up available energies and resources. Scrambled accounts and budgets fail to reveal the shift in allocation away from strategic needs to currently squeaking wheels.[3]

Manage Conflict

Honest differences of opinion, turf protection, and competition for limited resources can inevitably lead to conflict. **Conflict** can be defined as a disagreement between two or more parties on one or more issues. Establishing annual objectives can lead to conflict because individuals have different expectations, perceptions, schedules, pressures, obligations, and personalities. Misunderstandings between line managers (such as production supervisors) and staff managers (such as human resource specialists) can occur. For example, a collection manager's objective of reducing bad debts by 50 percent in a given year may conflict with a divisional objective to increase sales by 20 percent. Conflict must be managed for strategy implementation to be successful. Managing conflict is a strategic issue in most, if not all, organizations.

Establishing objectives can lead to conflict because managers and strategists must make trade-offs, such as whether to emphasize short-term profits or long-term growth, profit margin or market share, market penetration or market development, growth or stability, high risk or low risk, and social responsiveness or profit maximization. Trade-offs are necessary because no firm has sufficient resources to pursue all strategies that would benefit the firm. Table 10-5 reveals some important management trade-off decisions required in strategy implementation. Strategic planning necessitates making effective trade-off decisions.

Conflict is not always bad. An absence of conflict can signal indifference and apathy. Conflict can serve to energize opposing groups into action and may help managers identify problems. General George Patton once said, "If everyone is thinking alike, then somebody isn't thinking."

Various approaches for managing and resolving conflict can be classified into three categories: avoidance, defusion, and confrontation. **Avoidance** includes such actions as ignoring the problem in hopes that the conflict will resolve itself or physically separating the conflicting individuals (or groups). **Defusion** can include playing down differences between conflicting parties while accentuating similarities and common interests, compromising so that there is neither a clear winner nor loser, resorting to majority rule, appealing to a higher authority, or redesigning present positions. **Confrontation** is exemplified by exchanging members of conflicting parties so that each can gain an appreciation of the other's point of view or holding a meeting at which conflicting parties present their views and work through their differences.

Match Structure with Strategy

Changes in strategy often require changes in the way an organization is structured, for two major reasons. First, structure largely dictates how objectives and policies will be established. For example, objectives and policies established under a geographic organizational structure are

TABLE 10-5 Some Management Trade-Off Decisions Required in Strategy Implementation

To emphasize short-term profits or long-term growth

To emphasize profit margin or market share

To emphasize market development or market penetration

To lay off or furlough

To seek growth or stability

To take high risk or low risk

To be more socially responsible or more profitable

To outsource jobs or pay more to keep jobs at home

To acquire externally or to build internally

To restructure or reengineer

To use leverage or equity to raise funds

To use part-time or full-time employees

TABLE 10-6 Symptoms of an Ineffective Organizational Structure

1. Too many levels of management
2. Too many meetings attended by too many people
3. Too much attention being directed toward solving interdepartmental conflicts
4. Too large a span of control
5. Too many unachieved objectives
6. Declining corporate or business performance
7. Losing ground to rival firms
8. Revenue or earnings divided by number of employees or number of managers is low compared to rival firms

couched in geographic terms. Objectives and policies are stated largely in terms of products in an organization whose structure is based on product groups. The structural format for developing objectives and policies can significantly impact all other strategy-implementation activities.

The second major reason why changes in strategy often require changes in structure is that structure dictates how resources will be allocated. If an organization's structure is based on customer groups, then resources will be allocated in that manner. Similarly, if an organization's structure is set up along functional business lines, then resources are allocated by functional areas. Unless new or revised strategies place emphasis in the same areas as old strategies, structural reorientation commonly becomes a part of strategy implementation.

Alfred Chandler promoted the notion that "changes in strategy lead to changes in organizational structure." Structure should be designed to facilitate the strategic pursuit of a firm and, therefore, follow strategy. Without a strategy or reasons for being (mission), companies find it difficult to design an effective structure. There is no one optimal organizational design or structure for a given strategy or type of organization. What is appropriate for one organization may not be appropriate for a similar firm, although successful firms in a given industry do tend to organize themselves in a similar way. For example, consumer goods companies tend to emulate the divisional structure-by-product form of organization. Small firms tend to be functionally structured (centralized). Medium-sized firms tend to be divisionally structured (decentralized). Large firms tend to use a **strategic business unit (SBU) structure** or matrix structure.

When a firm changes its strategy, the existing organizational structure may become ineffective. As indicated in Table 10-6, symptoms of an ineffective organizational structure include too many levels of management, too many meetings attended by too many people, too much attention being directed toward solving interdepartmental conflicts, too large a span of control, and too many unachieved objectives. Changes in structure can facilitate strategy-implementation efforts, but changes in structure should not be expected to make a bad strategy good, to make bad managers good, or to make bad products sell.

Structure undeniably can and does influence strategy. Strategies formulated must be workable, so if a certain new strategy requires massive structural changes, it may not be an attractive choice. In this way, structure can shape the choice of strategies. But a more important concern is determining what types of structural changes are needed to implement new strategies and how these changes can best be accomplished.

Types of Organizational Structure

Structure matters! There are seven basic types of organizational structure: (1) functional, (2) divisional by geographic area, (3) divisional by product, (4) divisional by customer, (5) divisional by process, (6) strategic business unit (SBU), and (7) matrix. Companies, like people and armies, strive to be better organized/structured than rivals, because better organization can yield tremendous competitive advantages. There are countless examples throughout history of incidents, battles, and companies where superior organization overcame massive odds against the entity.

The Functional Structure

The most widely used structure is the functional or centralized type because this structure is the simplest and least expensive of the seven alternatives. A **functional structure** groups tasks and

TABLE 10-7 Advantages and Disadvantages of a Functional Organizational Structure

Advantages	Disadvantages
1. Simple and inexpensive	1. Accountability forced to the top
2. Capitalizes on specialization of business activities such as marketing and finance	2. Delegation of authority and responsibility not encouraged
3. Minimizes need for elaborate control system	3. Minimizes career development
4. Allows for rapid decision making	4. Low employee and manager morale
	5. Inadequate planning for products and markets
	6. Leads to short-term, narrow thinking
	7. Leads to communication problems

activities by business function, such as production and operations, marketing, finance and accounting, research and development, and management information systems. A university may structure its activities by major functions that include academic affairs, student services, alumni relations, athletics, maintenance, and accounting. Besides being simple and inexpensive, a functional structure also promotes specialization of labor, encourages efficient use of managerial and technical talent, minimizes the need for an elaborate control system, and allows rapid decision making. Some disadvantages of a functional structure are that it forces accountability to the top, minimizes career development opportunities, and is sometimes characterized by low employee morale, line or staff conflicts, poor delegation of authority, and inadequate planning for products and markets. Table 10-7 summarizes the advantages and disadvantages of a functional organizational structure.

A functional structure often leads to short-term and narrow thinking that may undermine what is best for the firm as a whole. For example, the research and development department may strive to overdesign products and components to achieve technical elegance, whereas manufacturing may argue for low-frills products that can be mass produced more easily. Thus, communication is often not as good in a functional structure. Schein gives an example of a communication problem in a functional structure:

> The word "marketing" will mean product development to the engineer, studying customers through market research to the product manager, merchandising to the salesperson, and constant change in design to the manufacturing manager. Then when these managers try to work together, they often attribute disagreements to personalities and fail to notice the deeper, shared assumptions that vary and dictate how each function thinks.[4]

Most large companies have abandoned the functional structure in favor of decentralization and improved accountability. However, a large company that still operates from a functional type of organizational design is Nucor. Headquartered in Charlotte, North Carolina, Nucor's executive management team consists of eight white, male persons (lack of diversity is not good; see http://www.nucor.com/governance/executives/). A large producer of steel products, Nucor has no apparent division heads, and John Ferriola is both CEO and Chairman of the Board (holding those two titles is not good).

The Divisional Structure

The **divisional (decentralized) structure** is the second-most common type. Divisions are sometimes referred to as *segments, profit centers,* or *business units.* As a small organization grows, it has more difficulty managing different products and services in different markets. Some form of divisional structure generally becomes necessary to motivate employees, control operations, and compete successfully in diverse locations. The divisional structure can be organized in one of four ways: (1) by geographic area, (2) by product *or* service, (3) by customer, or (4) by process. With a divisional structure, functional activities are performed both centrally and in each separate division.

Sun Microsystems recently reduced the number of its business units from seven to four. Kodak recently reduced its number of business units from seven by-customer divisions to five by-product divisions. As consumption patterns become increasingly similar worldwide, a by-product structure is becoming more effective than a by-customer or a by-geographic type of divisional structure. In the restructuring, Kodak eliminated its global operations division and distributed those responsibilities across the new by-product divisions.

A divisional structure has some clear advantages. First and perhaps foremost, accountability is clear. That is, divisional managers can be held responsible for sales and profit levels. Because a divisional structure is based on extensive delegation of authority, managers and employees can easily see the results of their good or bad performances. As a result, employee morale is generally higher in a divisional structure than it is in a centralized structure. Other advantages of the divisional design are that it creates career development opportunities for managers, allows local control of situations, leads to a competitive climate within an organization, and allows new businesses and products to be added easily.

The divisional design is not without some limitations, however. Perhaps the most important limitation is that a divisional structure is costly, for a number of reasons. First, each division requires functional specialists who must be paid. Second, there exists some duplication of staff services, facilities, and personnel; for instance, functional specialists are also needed centrally (at headquarters) to coordinate divisional activities. Third, managers must be well qualified because the divisional design forces delegation of authority; better-qualified individuals require higher salaries. A divisional structure can also be costly because it requires an elaborate, headquarters-driven control system. Fourth, competition between divisions may become so intense that it is dysfunctional and leads to limited sharing of ideas and resources for the common good of the firm. Table 10-8 summarizes the advantages and disadvantages of divisional organizational structure.

A *divisional structure by geographic area* is appropriate for organizations whose strategies need to be tailored to fit the particular needs and characteristics of customers in different geographic areas. This type of structure can be most appropriate for organizations that have similar branch facilities located in widely dispersed areas. A divisional structure by geographic area allows local participation in decision making and improved coordination within a region. Due to steady declines in revenues among its U.S. restaurants, McDonald's recently created a new organizational structure for its operations in the United States, replacing three regions with four geographic zones to better respond to local tastes. McDonald's U.S. President Mike Andres said, "What has worked for McDonald's USA for the past decade is not sufficient to propel the business forward in the future." The footwear maker, Crocs, Inc., also uses the divisional-by-region type of structure, as illustrated in Figure 10-4.

The *divisional structure by product (or services)* is most effective for implementing strategies when specific products or services need special emphasis. Also, this type of structure is widely used when an organization offers only a few products or services or when an organization's products or services differ substantially. The divisional structure allows strict control over and attention to product lines, but it may also require a more skilled management force and reduced top management control.

TABLE 10-8 Advantages and Disadvantages of a Divisional Organizational Structure

Advantages	Disadvantages
1. Clear accountability	1. Can be costly
2. Allows local control of local situations	2. Duplication of functional activities
3. Creates career development chances	3. Requires a skilled management force
4. Promotes delegation of authority	4. Requires an elaborate control system
5. Leads to competitive climate internally	5. Competition among divisions can become so intense as to be dysfunctional
6. Allows easy adding of new products or regions	6. Can lead to limited sharing of ideas and resources
7. Allows strict control and attention to products, customers, or regions	7. Some regions, products, or customers may receive special treatment

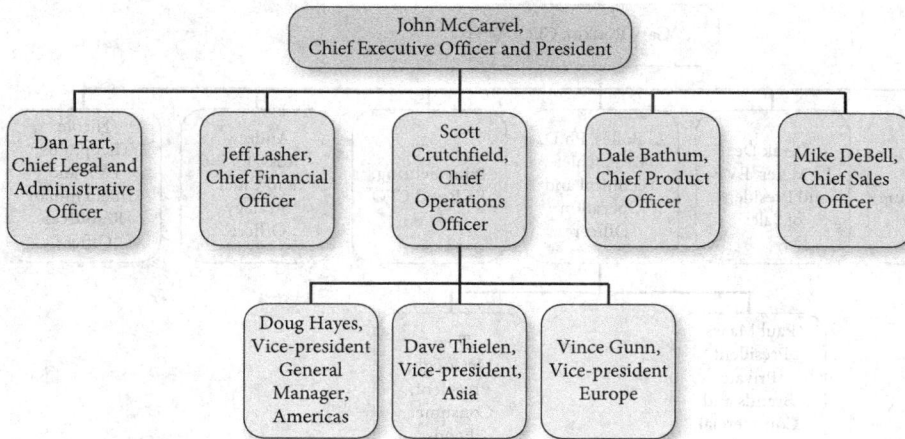

FIGURE 10-4
Divisional Organizational Structure of Crocs, Inc.

When a few major customers are of paramount importance and many different services are provided to these customers, then a *divisional structure by customer* can be the most effective way to implement strategies. This structure allows an organization to cater effectively to the requirements of clearly defined customer groups. For example, book-publishing companies often organize their activities around customer groups, such as colleges, secondary schools, and private commercial schools. Some airline companies have two major customer divisions: (1) passengers and (2) freight or cargo services. Utility companies often use (1) commercial, (2) residential, and (3) industrial as their divisions by customer.

Headquartered in New York City, Time Warner Cable (TWC) recently changed its organizational structure from a divisional-by-geographic region to a divisional-by-customer design. Time Warner is now organized by reference to its customer groups served (residential, business, or media clients) and the functions necessary to serve those customers. The company now has three business units—(1) Residential Services, (2) Business Services, and (3) Media Services—reporting to the chief operating officer (COO) Rob Marcus.

A *divisional structure by process* is similar to a functional structure, because activities are organized according to the way work is actually performed. However, a key difference between these two designs is that functional departments are not accountable for profits or revenues, whereas divisional process departments are evaluated on these criteria. An example of a divisional structure by process is a manufacturing business organized into six divisions: electrical work, glass cutting, welding, grinding, painting, and foundry work. In this case, all operations related to these specific processes would be grouped under the separate divisions. Each process (division) would be responsible for generating revenues and profits. The divisional structure by process can be particularly effective in achieving objectives when distinct production processes represent the thrust of competitiveness in an industry.

The Strategic Business Unit (SBU) Structure

As the number, size, and diversity of divisions in an organization increase, controlling and evaluating divisional operations become increasingly difficult for strategists. Increases in sales often are not accompanied by similar increases in profitability. The span of control becomes too large at top levels of the firm. For example, in a large conglomerate organization composed of 90 divisions, such as ConAgra, the chief executive officer could have difficulty even remembering the first names of divisional presidents. In multidivisional organizations, an SBU structure can greatly facilitate strategy-implementation efforts. ConAgra has put its many divisions into two primary SBUs: (1) consumer foods and (2) private brands and commercial foods. ConAgra's SBU structure is illustrated in Figure 10-5. Commercial foods are "food for restaurants," whereas consumer foods are "food in grocery stores."

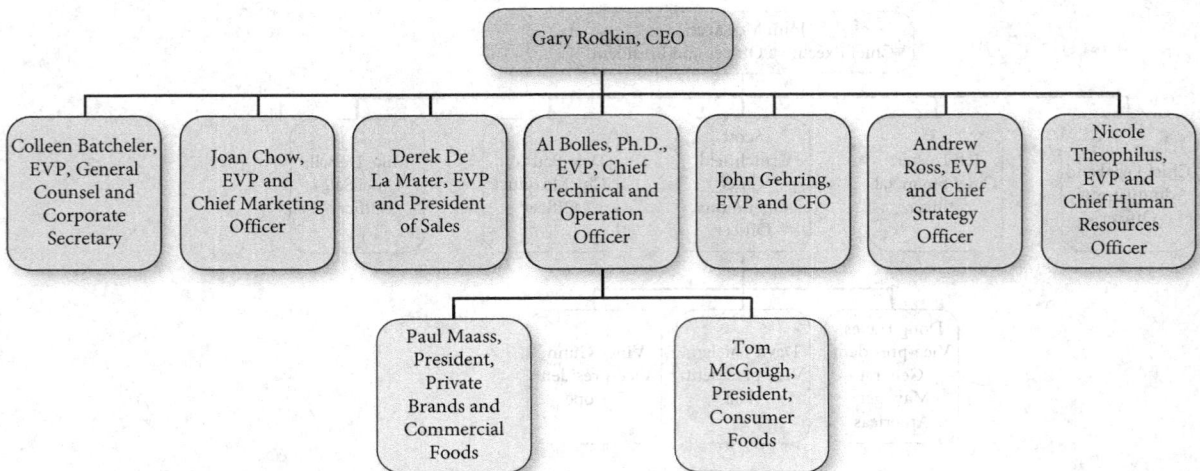

FIGURE 10-5

ConArgra's SBU Organizational Structure

Source: Based on information at the company's *Form 10k*.

The strategic business unit structure groups similar divisions into SBUs and delegates authority and responsibility for each unit to a senior executive who reports directly to the chief executive officer. This change in structure can facilitate strategy implementation by improving coordination between similar divisions and channeling accountability to distinct business units. In a 100-division conglomerate, the divisions could perhaps be regrouped into 10 SBUs according to certain common characteristics, such as competing in the same industry, being located in the same area, or having the same customers.

Two disadvantages of an SBU structure are that it requires an additional layer of management, which increases salary expenses. Also, the role of the group vice president is often ambiguous. However, these limitations often do not outweigh the advantages of improved coordination and accountability. Another advantage of the SBU structure is that it makes the tasks of planning and control by the corporate office more manageable. Halliburton operates from an SBU structure with the divisions based on process, as described at www.halliburton.com (click on About Us, then click Company Profile). In June 2015, Microsoft changed its organizational structure to become three by-product strategic business units: (1) Windows and Devices Group (WDG), (2) Cloud and Enterprise (C+E), and (3) Applications and Services Group (ASG).

The Matrix Structure

A **matrix structure** is the most complex of all designs because it depends on both vertical and horizontal flows of authority and communication (hence the term *matrix*). In contrast, functional and divisional structures depend primarily on vertical flows of authority and communication. A matrix structure can result in higher overhead because it creates more management positions. Other disadvantages of a matrix structure that contribute to overall complexity include dual lines of budget authority (a violation of the unity-of-command principle), dual sources of reward and punishment, shared authority, dual reporting channels, and a need for an extensive and effective communication system.

Despite its complexity, the matrix structure is widely used in many industries, including construction, health care, research, and defense. As indicated in Table 10-9, some advantages of a matrix structure are that project objectives are clear, there are many channels of communication, workers can see the visible results of their work, shutting down a project can be accomplished relatively easily, and it facilitates the use of specialized personnel, equipment, and facilities. Functional resources are shared in a matrix structure, rather than duplicated as in a divisional structure. Individuals with a high degree of expertise can divide their time as needed among projects, and they in turn develop their own skills and competencies more than in other structures.

TABLE 10-9 Advantages and Disadvantages of a Matrix Structure

Advantages	Disadvantages
1. Clear project objectives	1. Requires excellent vertical and horizontal flows of communication
2. Results of their work clearly seen by employees	2. Costly because creates more manager positions
3. Easy to shut down a project	3. Violates unity of command principle
4. Facilitates uses of special equipment, personnel, and facilities	4. Creates dual lines of budget authority
5. Shared functional resources instead of duplicated resources, as in a divisional structure	5. Creates dual sources of reward and punishment
	6. Creates shared authority and reporting
	7. Requires mutual trust and understanding

A typical matrix structure is illustrated in Figure 10-6. Note that the letters (A through Z4) refer to managers. For example, if you were manager A, you would be responsible for financial aspects of Project 1, and you would have two bosses: the Project 1 Manager on site and the CFO off site.

For a matrix structure to be effective, organizations need participative planning, training, clear mutual understanding of roles and responsibilities, excellent internal communication, and mutual trust and confidence. The matrix structure is being used more frequently by U.S. businesses because firms are pursuing strategies that add new products, customer groups, and technology to their range of activities. Out of these changes are coming product managers, functional managers, and geographic-area managers, all of whom have important strategic responsibilities. When several variables, such as product, customer, technology, geography, functional area, and line of business, have roughly equal strategic priorities, a matrix organization can be an effective structural form.

Dos and Don'ts in Developing Organizational Charts

Students analyzing strategic-management cases (and actual corporate executives) oftentimes revise and improve a firm's organizational structure. This section provides some basic guidelines for this endeavor. There are some basic dos and don'ts in regard to devising or constructing organizational charts, especially for midsize to large firms. First of all, reserve the title *CEO* for the top executive of the firm. Don't use the title *president* for the top person; use it for the division top managers if there are divisions within the firm. Also, do not use the title *president* for functional business executives. They should have the title *chief*, or *vice president*, or *manager*, or *officer*, such as "Chief Information Officer," or "VP of Human Resources." Furthermore, do not recommend a dual title (such as *CEO and president*) for just one executive.

Do not let a single individual be both chairman of the board and CEO of a company, although Seifi Ghasemi was recently named as the new CEO, President, and Chairman of the large industrial-gas provider Air Products & Chemicals Inc. Also, Home Depot recently appointed their CEO Craig Menear to also be the company's chairman of the board. Menear is the first person to hold both CEO and chairman titles of Home Depot since the company's co-founder, Bernie Marcus. Actually, *chairperson* is much better than *chairman* for a top board person's title. A significant movement among corporate America is to split the chairperson of the board and the CEO positions in publicly held companies.[5] The movement includes asking the New York Stock Exchange and Nasdaq to adopt listing rules that would require separate positions. About 50 percent of companies in the S&P 500 stock index have separate positions, up from 22 percent in 2002, but this still leaves plenty of room for improvement. Among European and Asian companies, the split in these two positions is much more common. For example, 79 percent of British companies split the positions, and all virtually German and Dutch companies split the position.

Directly below the CEO, it is best to have a COO (chief operating officer) with any division presidents reporting directly to the COO. On the same level as the COO and also reporting to the CEO, draw in your functional business executives, such as a CFO (chief financial officer), VP of human resources, a CSO (chief strategy officer), a CIO (chief information officer), a CMO (chief marketing officer), a VP of R&D, a VP of legal affairs, an investment relations officer, maintenance officer, and so on. Note in Figure 10-6 that these positions are labeled and placed

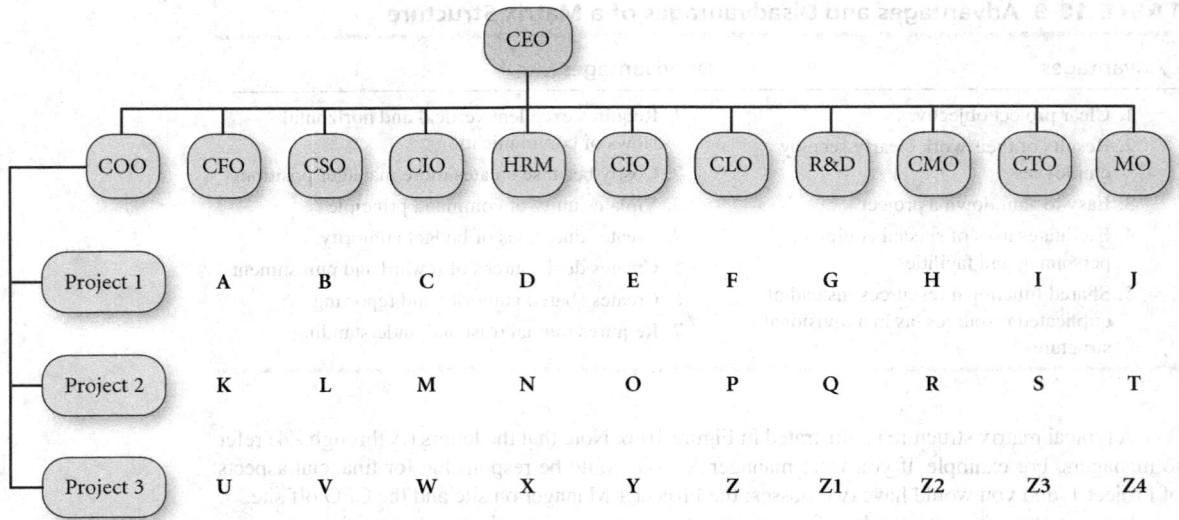

Chief Executive Officer (CEO)
Chief Finance Officer (CFO)
Chief Strategy Officer (CSO)
Chief Information Officer (CIO)
Human Resources Manager (HRM)
Chief Operating Officer (COO)
Chief Legal Officer (CLO)
Research & Development Officer (R&D)
Chief Marketing Officer (CMO)
Chief Technology Officer (CTO)
Competitive Intelligence Officer (CIO)
Maintenance Officer (MO)

FIGURE 10-6

Typical Top Managers of a Large Firm

appropriately in a matrix structure, which, as shown, generally include project managers rather than division presidents reporting to a COO. However, note in Academic Research Capsule 10-1 the COO position is losing favor in North America.

In developing an organizational chart, avoid having a particular person reporting to more than one person in the chain of command. This would violate the unity-of-command principle of management that "every employee should have just one boss." Also, do not have the CFO, CIO, CSO, human resource officer, or other functional positions report to the COO. All these positions report directly to the CEO.

A recent article (*WSJ*, 8-25-15, p. B5) reveals that since 2009 there has been a 40 percent rise in the number of chief accounting officers (CAO) among American companies. CAO's now do much more than just manage the company's books and prepare financial statements. Companies increasingly need a CAO that can stand up and debate strategic issues related to how best to balance the balance sheet, and know when and how to recognize revenue, and know how to report results using both USA and foreign standards (GAAP vs IFRS). CAO's are more and more signing the company's financial filings, making them personally liable for any mistakes or improprieties – along with the CFO and CEO. As more and more firms acquire foreign firms and even relocate their headquarters offshore (inversion), a CAO is needed who knows both USA and foreign insurance and accounting practices. Garu Kabureck, former CAO at Xerox Corp. says: "I think what happened over the last 15 years in the USA is that the accounting function started to separate from the controller function." In a firm, a controller is typically more focused on budgeting and planning, whereas the CAO is responsible for the in's and out's of global bookkeeping. The CAO also interacts closely with the board's audit committee, as well with outside firms auditing the company.

A relatively new, but increasingly popular, top management position, is the Chief Design Officer (CDO). Johnson & Johnson (J&J), for example, just hired a chief design officer, Ernesto

ACADEMIC RESEARCH CAPSULE 10-1

Why Is the COO Position Being Deleted in Many Organizations?

The COO position is increasingly being deleted in U.S. companies. Twitter recently divided the duties of its COO among all managers. McDonald's, Tiffany & Co., and Yahoo recently deleted their COO position. In fact, the percentage of large companies in the United States with COOs has declined almost every year for a decade, to about 36 percent today. Health-care and industrial companies are least likely to have a COO today. A senior executive search firm, Crist Kolder Associates, reports that the percentage of Fortune 500 and S&P 500 companies with a COO has declined steadily from 48 percent in 2000 to 36 percent in 2014. An accounting firm, PricewaterhouseCoopers, suggests there are four reasons why companies are phasing out the COO position: (1) flatten their structure, (2) eliminate a layer of management, (3) reduce costs, and (4) expand the CEO's authority and responsibility. Digital communications and even social media today enable a CEO oftentimes to perform COO duties. However, three situations that especially warrant having a COO include (1) whenever the CEO lacks operational experience, (2) whenever the firm desires to be transparent about their CEO succession plans, and (3) whenever the CEO needs to lead a restructuring or transformation of the firm. Although historically a stepping-stone position to the CEO position, many companies now delegate the traditional duties of a COO to the CEO or to other positions, such as the CFO or to the chief brand officer. Deleting the COO position does increase the span of control of the CEO, spreading him or her thinly, which is not a good idea for many companies.

Interestingly, as the COO position has declined, the chief financial officer (CFO) position has increased in responsibility and prevalence. An example is the CFO position at Twitter Inc., where Anthony Noto is being groomed perhaps to become that company's CEO. Noto was recently also given head responsibility for marketing at Twitter. In the last year, it was Noto who initiated and coordinated the major business deals and acquisitions at Twitter.

Source: Based on Feintzeig, Rachel, "COOs Join Endangered Species List," *Wall Street Journal*, June 13, 2014, B1. Also based on Crist Kolder Associates, "Trends in CEO Recruiting and Succession," *Volatility Report 2014;* http://strategy-business.com/article/00328 published by PricewaterhouseCoopers; and Yoree Koh, "Ascent of Twitter CFO Creates a Power Center," *Wall Street Journal*, June 15, 2015, B1 and B4.

Quinteros, to be a liaison between the chief marketing officer (CMO) and R&D. The CDO position has equal status with the CMO position at J&J, PepsiCo, and Phillips Electronics NV—because "a product that is wonderfully designed sells itself, and has a huge benefit on the marketing side," said J&J's Sandi Peterson, who created the CDO position at J&J.

If a firm is large with numerous divisions, an SBU type of structure would be more appropriate to reduce the span of control reporting to the COO. One never knows for sure if a proposed or actual structure is indeed most effective for a particular firm. Declining financial performance signals a need for altering the structure. Some important guidelines to follow in devising organizational charts for companies are provided in Table 10-10.

TABLE 10-10 Fifteen Guidelines for Developing an Organizational Chart

1. Instead of *chairman* of the board, make it *chairperson* of the board.
2. Make sure the board of directors reveals diversity in race, ethnicity, gender, and age.
3. Make sure the chair of the board is not also the CEO or president of the company.
4. Make sure the CEO of the firm does not also carry the title *president*.
5. Reserve the title *president* for the division heads of the firm.
6. Make sure the firm has a COO.
7. Make sure only presidents of divisions report to the COO.
8. Make sure functional executives such as CFO, CIO, CMO, CSO, R&D, CLO, CTO, and HRM report to the CEO, not the COO.
9. Make sure every executive has one boss, so lines in the chart should be drawn accordingly, assuring unity of command.
10. Make sure span of control is reasonable, probably no more than 10 persons reporting to any other person.
11. Make sure diversity in race, ethnicity, gender, and age is well represented among corporate executives.
12. Avoid a functional type structure for all but the smallest firms.
13. Decentralize, using some form of divisional structure, whenever possible.
14. Use an SBU type structure for large, multidivisional firms.
15. Make sure executive titles match product names as best possible in division-by-product and SBU-designated firms.

Strategic Production/Operations Issues

Production/operations capabilities, limitations, and policies can significantly enhance or inhibit the attainment of objectives. Production processes typically constitute more than 70 percent of a firm's total assets. Thus, a major part of the strategy-implementation process takes place at the production site. Strategic production-related decisions on plant size, plant location, product design, choice of equipment, kind of tooling, size of inventory, inventory control, quality control, cost control, use of standards, job specialization, employee training, equipment and resource utilization, shipping and packaging, and technological innovation can determine the success or failure of strategy-implementation efforts.

Four production/operations issues—(1) restructuring/reengineering, (2) managing resistance to change, (3) deciding where/how to produce goods, and (4) managing an ESOP—are especially important for successful strategy implementation and are therefore discussed next.

Restructuring and Reengineering

Restructuring and reengineering are becoming commonplace on the corporate landscape across the United States and Europe. **Restructuring** involves reducing the size of the firm in terms of number of employees, number of divisions or units, and number of hierarchical levels in the firm's organizational structure. This reduction in size is intended to improve both efficiency and effectiveness. Restructuring is concerned primarily with shareholder well-being rather than employee well-being.

The primary benefit sought from restructuring is cost reduction. For some highly bureaucratic firms, restructuring can actually rescue the firm from global competition and demise. But the downside of restructuring can be reduced employee commitment, creativity, and innovation that accompanies the uncertainty and trauma associated with pending and actual employee layoffs. Avon Products recently restructured, reducing its six commercial business units down to two—(1) Developed Markets and (2) Developing Markets—essentially going to a divisional by geographic region type structure.

The recent falling euro and weak economy in Europe forced many European companies to downsize, laying off managers and employees. This practice was historically rare in Europe because labor unions and laws required lengthy negotiations or huge severance checks before workers could be terminated. In contrast to the United States, labor union executives of large European firms sit on most boards of directors. Job security in European companies is slowly moving toward a U.S. business model, in which firms lay off almost at will. From banks in Milan to factories in Mannheim, European employers are starting to show people the door in an effort to streamline operations, increase efficiency, and compete against already slim and trim U.S. firms. European firms still prefer to downsize by attrition and retirement, rather than by blanket layoffs because of culture, laws, and unions.

In contrast to restructuring, reengineering is concerned more with employee and customer well-being than shareholder well-being. **Reengineering** involves reconfiguring or redesigning work, jobs, and processes for the purpose of improving cost, quality, service, and speed. Reengineering does not usually affect the organizational structure or chart, nor does it imply job loss or employee layoffs. Whereas restructuring is concerned with eliminating or establishing, shrinking or enlarging, and moving organizational departments and divisions, the focus of reengineering is changing the way work is actually carried out. Reengineering is characterized by many tactical (short-term, business-function-specific) decisions, whereas restructuring is characterized by strategic (long-term, affecting all business functions) decisions.

Developed by Motorola in 1986 and made famous by CEO Jack Welch at General Electric and more recently by Robert Nardelli, former CEO of Home Depot, **Six Sigma** is a quality-boosting process improvement technique that entails training several key persons in the firm in the techniques to monitor, measure, and improve processes and eliminate defects. Six Sigma has been widely applied across industries from retailing to financial services. For example, CEO Dave Cote at Honeywell and CEO Jeff Immelt at General Electric spurred acceptance of Six Sigma, which aims to improve work processes and eliminate waste by training "select" employees who are given judo titles such as Master Black Belts, Black Belts, and Green Belts. Target Corp. claims more than $100 million in savings over the past six years resulting from its Six Sigma program.

Six Sigma was criticized in a *Wall Street Journal* article that cited many example firms whose stock price fell for a number of years after adoption of Six Sigma. The technique's reliance on the special group of trained employees is problematic and its use within retail firms such as Home Depot has not been as successful as in manufacturing firms.[6]

Manage Resistance to Change

No organization or individual can escape change. But the thought of change raises anxieties because people fear economic loss, inconvenience, uncertainty, and a break in normal social patterns. Almost any change in structure, technology, people, or strategies has the potential to disrupt comfortable interaction patterns. For this reason, people resist change. The strategic-management process can impose major changes on individuals and processes. Reorienting an organization to get people to think and act strategically is not an easy task. Strategy implementation can pose a threat to many managers and employees. New power and status relationships are anticipated and realized. New formal and informal groups' values, beliefs, and priorities may be largely unknown. Managers and employees may become engaged in resistance behavior as their roles, prerogatives, and power in the firm change. Disruption of social and political structures that accompany strategy execution must be anticipated and considered during strategy formulation and managed during strategy implementation.

Resistance to change may be the single-greatest threat to successful strategy implementation. Resistance regularly occurs in organizations in the form of sabotaging production machines, absenteeism, filing unfounded grievances, and an unwillingness to cooperate. People often resist strategy implementation because they do not understand what is happening or why changes are taking place. In that case, employees may simply need accurate information. Successful strategy implementation hinges on managers' ability to develop an organizational climate conducive to change. Change must be viewed by managers and employees as an opportunity for the firm to compete more effectively, rather than being seen as a threat to everyone's livelihood.

Resistance to change can emerge at any stage or level of the strategy-implementation process. Although there are various approaches for implementing changes, three commonly used strategies are a force change strategy, an educative change strategy, and a rational or self-interest change strategy. A **force change strategy** involves giving orders and enforcing those orders; this strategy has the advantage of being fast, but it is plagued by low commitment and high resistance. The **educative change strategy** is one that presents information to convince people of the need for change; the disadvantage of an educative change strategy is that implementation becomes slow and difficult. However, this type of strategy evokes greater commitment and less resistance than does the force change strategy. Finally, a **rational change strategy** or **self-interest change strategy** is one that attempts to convince individuals that the change is to their personal advantage. When this appeal is successful, strategy implementation can be relatively easy. However, implementation changes are seldom to everyone's advantage.

Strategists can take a number of positive actions to minimize managers' and employees' resistance to change. For example, individuals who will be affected by a change should be involved in the decision to make the change and in decisions about how to implement the change. Strategists should anticipate changes and develop and offer training and development workshops so that managers and employees can adapt to those changes. They also need to effectively communicate the need for changes. Strategy implementation is basically a process of managing change.

The most successful organizations today continuously adapt to changes in the competitive environment. It is not sufficient today to simply react to change. Managers need to anticipate change and be the creator of change. Viewing change as a continuous process is in stark contrast to an old management doctrine regarding change, which was to unfreeze behavior, change the behavior, and then refreeze the new behavior. The new "continuous organizational change" philosophy should mirror the popular "continuous quality improvement philosophy."

Decide Where and How to Produce Goods

In China, about 700,000 assembly workers at manufacturing contractors such as Foxconn put together Apple products. It would be virtually impossible to bring those jobs to the United States for at least three reasons. First of all, Foxconn—China's largest private employer and

TABLE 10-11 Production Management and Strategy Implementation

Type of Organization	Strategy Being Implemented	Production System Adjustments
Hospital	Adding a cancer center (Product Development)	Purchase specialized equipment and add specialized people.
Bank	Adding 10 new branches (Market Development)	Perform site location analysis.
Beer brewery	Purchasing a barley farm operation (Backward Integration)	Revise the inventory control system.
Steel manufacturer	Acquiring a fast-food chain (Unrelated Diversification)	Improve the quality control system.
Computer company	Purchasing a retail distribution chain (Forward Integration)	Alter the shipping, packaging, and transportation systems.

the manufacturer of an estimated 40 percent of the world's consumer electronic devices—pays its assembly workers far less than U.S. labor laws would allow. A typical salary is about $18 a day. Second, unlike U.S. plants, Foxconn and other Chinese manufacturing operations house employees in dormitories and can send hundreds of thousands of workers to the assembly lines at a moment's notice. On the lines, workers are subjected to what most Americans would consider unbearable long hours and tough working conditions. That system gives tech companies the efficiency needed to race products out the door, so speed is a bigger factor than pay. Finally, most of the component suppliers for Apple and other technology giants are also in China or other Asian countries. That geographic clustering gives companies the flexibility to change a product design at the last minute and still ship on time.

Examples of adjustments in production systems that could be required to implement various strategies are provided in Table 10-11 for both for-profit and nonprofit organizations. For instance, note that when a bank formulates and selects a strategy to add 10 new branches, a production-related implementation concern is site location. The largest bicycle company in the United States, Huffy, recently ended its own production of bikes and now contracts out those services to Asian and Mexican manufacturers. Huffy focuses instead on the design, marketing, and distribution of bikes, but it no longer produces bikes itself. The Dayton, Ohio, company closed its plants in Ohio, Missouri, and Mississippi.

Just-in-time (JIT) production approaches have withstood the test of time. Just-in-time significantly reduces the costs of implementing strategies. Parts and materials are delivered to a production site just as they are needed, rather than being stockpiled as a hedge against later deliveries. Harley-Davidson reports that at one plant alone, JIT freed $22 million previously tied up in inventory and greatly reduced reorder lead time.

Factors that should be studied before locating production facilities include the availability of major resources, the prevailing wage rates in the area, transportation costs related to shipping and receiving, the location of major markets, political risks in the area or country, and the availability of trainable employees. Some of these factors explain why many manufacturing operations in China are moving back to Mexico, or to Vietnam, or even back to the United States. Table 10-12 lists ways that companies today are reducing labor, production, and operations costs to stay financially sound.

Employee Stock Ownership Plans (ESOPs)

Besides reducing worker alienation and stimulating productivity, **employee stock ownership plans (ESOPs)** allow firms other benefits, such as substantial tax savings. An ESOP is a tax-qualified, defined-contribution, employee-benefit plan whereby employees purchase stock of the company through borrowed money or cash contributions. These plans empower employees to work as owners; this is a primary reason why the number of ESOPs have grown dramatically to more than 10,000 firms covering more than 14 million employees. Today, ESOPs control more than $600 billion in corporate stock in the United States. "The ownership culture really makes a difference, when management is a facilitator, not a dictator," observes Corey Rosen, executive

TABLE 10-12 Labor Cost-Saving Tactics

Salary freeze
Hiring freeze
Salary reductions
Reduction of employee benefits
Increase in employee contribution to health-care premiums
Reduction of employee 401(k)/403(b) match
Reduction of employee workweek
Mandatory furlough (temporary layoff)
Voluntary furlough
Temporary instead of full-time employees
Contract employees instead of full-time employees
Volunteer buyouts (Walt Disney is doing this)
Production halt for three days a week (Toyota Motor is doing this)
Layoffs
Early retirement
Reducing or eliminating bonuses

Source: Based on Mattioli, Dana, "Employers Make Cuts Despite Belief Upturn Is Near," *Wall Street Journal,* April 23, 2009, B4.

TABLE 10-13 The Ten Largest ESOP Companies in the United States

Company	Headquarters Location	# Employees (in thousands)
Publix Super Markets	Lakeland, Florida	160
Daymon Worldwide	Stamford, Connecticut	35
CH2M Hill	Englewood, Colorado	26
Lifetouch	Eden Prairie, Minnesota	25
Price Chopper	Schenectady, New York	23
Penmac	Springfield, Missouri	18
Amsted Industries	Chicago, Illinois	16
Houchens Industries	Bowling Green, Kentucky	15
WinCo Foods	Boise, Idaho	15
Parsons	Pasadena, California	15

director of the National Center for Employee Ownership. The 10 largest employee-owned companies are listed in Table 10-13.

Strategic Human Resource Issues

Any organization is only as good as its people! Thus, human resource issues can make or break successful strategy implementation. Thus, seven human resource issues are discussed further in this section, as follows: (1) linking performance and pay to strategy, (2) balancing work life with home life, (3) developing a diverse work force, (4) using caution in hiring a rival's employees, (5) creating a strategy-supportive culture, (6) using caution in monitoring employees' social media, and (7) developing a corporate wellness program.

Linking Performance and Pay to Strategy

An organization's compensation system needs to be aligned with strategic outcomes. Decisions on salary increases, promotions, merit pay, and bonuses need to support the long-term and annual objectives of the firm. A dual bonus system based on both annual and long-term objectives can be helpful in linking performance and pay to strategies. The percentage of a manager's annual bonus attributable to short-term versus long-term results should vary by hierarchical level in the organization. It is important that bonuses not be based solely on short-term results, because such a system ignores long-term company strategies and objectives.

To better link performance and pay to strategies, many companies have recently instituted policies to allow their shareholders to vote on executive compensation policies. Back in 2007, Aflac was the first U.S. firm to voluntarily give shareholders an advisory vote on executive compensation. Apple did the same in 2008, as did H&R Block. Several companies that instituted say-on-pay policies more recently were Ingersoll-Rand, Verizon, Motorola, Occidental Petroleum, and Hewlett-Packard. Firms are also establishing profit sharing, gain sharing, and bonus systems. More than 30 percent of U.S. companies have profit-sharing plans, but critics emphasize that too many factors affect profits for this to be a good criterion. Taxes, pricing, or an acquisition would wipe out profits, for example. Also, firms try to minimize profits in a sense to reduce taxes.

For employee (rather than executive) bonuses and incentives, only 16 percent of U.S. companies are now using stock price, down from 29 percent in 2009.[7] Instead, companies are using profit in order to more closely link employees' incentives to spending and budget decisions. PepsiCo, for example, recently began using profit and cash flow instead of stock price to focus managers on profit and cash-flow targets. PepsiCo's CFO, Hugh Johnston, remarked, "The change allows our employees to make decisions about spending and profit trade-offs themselves, rather than simply being handed a budget to follow; it's something they can wrap their arms around and say, 'Now I understand how I can impact PepsiCo's stock price.'" For upper-level executives, stock price is still the major variable used for compensation incentives, but for mid- and lower-level managers and employees, stock price is dependent on too many extraneous variables for it to be an effective compensation variable.

Gain sharing requires employees or departments to establish performance targets; if actual results exceed objectives, all members get bonuses. More than 26 percent of U.S. companies use some form of gain sharing; about 75 percent of gain-sharing plans have been adopted since 1980. Carrier, a subsidiary of United Technologies, has had excellent success with gain sharing in its six plants in Syracuse, New York; Firestone's tire plant in Wilson, North Carolina, has experienced similar success with gain sharing.

Criteria such as sales, profit, production efficiency, quality, and safety could also serve as bases for an effective **bonus system**. If an organization meets certain understood, agreed-on profit objectives, every member of the enterprise should share in the harvest. A bonus system can be an effective tool for motivating individuals to support strategy-implementation efforts. BankAmerica, for example, recently overhauled its incentive system to link pay to sales of the bank's most profitable products and services. Branch managers receive a base salary plus a bonus based both on the number of new customers and on sales of bank products. Every employee in each branch is also eligible for a bonus if the branch exceeds its goals. Thomas Peterson, a top BankAmerica executive, says, "We want to make people responsible for meeting their goals, so we pay incentives on sales, not on controlling costs or on being sure the parking lot is swept."

A combination of reward strategy incentives, such as salary raises, stock options, fringe benefits, promotions, praise, recognition, criticism, fear, increased job autonomy, and awards, can be used to encourage managers and employees to push hard for successful strategic implementation. The range of options for getting people, departments, and divisions to actively support strategy-implementation activities in a particular organization is almost limitless. Merck, for example, recently gave each of its 37,000 employees a 10-year option to buy 100 shares of Merck stock at a set price of $127.

In an effort to cut costs and increase productivity, more and more Japanese companies are switching from seniority-based pay to performance-based approaches. Toyota has switched to a full merit system for 20,000 of its 70,000 white-collar workers. Fujitsu, Sony, Matsushita Electric Industrial, and Kao also have switched to merit pay systems. This switching is hurting morale at some Japanese companies, which have trained workers for decades to cooperate rather than to compete and to work in groups rather than individually.

Richard Brown, CEO of Electronic Data Systems (EDS), once said,

You have to start with an appraisal system that gives genuine feedback and differentiates performance. Some call it ranking people. That seems a little harsh. But you can't have a manager checking a box that says you're either stupendous, magnificent, very good, good, or average. Concise, constructive feedback is the fuel workers use to get better. A company that doesn't differentiate performance risks losing its best people.[8]

Balance Work Life and Home Life

More women than men earn both undergraduate and graduate degrees in the United States, but a wage disparity still persists between genders at all education levels.[9] Women, on average, make 25 percent less than men. The average age today for U.S. women to get married is 30 years old for those with a college degree, and 26 years old for those with only a high school degree. About 29 percent of both men and women in the United States today have a college degree, whereas in 1970, only 8 percent of women and 14 percent of men had college degrees. In March 2015, the U.S. Census Bureau and American Association of University Women revealed that among full-time, year-round workers, women are paid, on average, 78 percent as much as men. The pay gap discrepancy between genders has not moved much in a decade. Catherine Rampell at the *Washington Post* reports that among 342 professions, women earn more than men in only *nine*. (For more information, see the two charts given at http://jobs.aol.com/articles/2015/03/24/charts-illustrate-gender-wage-gap/)

Work and family strategies now represent a competitive advantage for those firms that offer such benefits as elder care assistance, flexible scheduling, job sharing, adoption benefits, on-site summer camp, employee help lines, pet care, and even lawn service referrals. New corporate titles such as Work and Life Coordinator and Director of Diversity are becoming common. Globally, it is widely acknowledged that the best countries for working women are Iceland, Norway, Sweden, Finland, and Denmark, all of which rate above the United States. According to the World Economic Forum's 2014 report on the global gender gap overall, the United States, in fact, ranked number 20 overall.

Working Mother magazine annually published its listing of "The 100 Best Companies for Working Mothers" (www.workingmother.com). Three especially important variables used in the ranking were availability of flextime, advancement opportunities, and equitable distribution of benefits. Other important criteria are compressed weeks, telecommuting, job sharing, childcare facilities, maternity leave for both parents, mentoring, career development, and promotion for women. *Working Mother's* top 10 best companies for working women in 2014 are provided in Table 10-14. *Working Mother* also conducts extensive research to determine the best U.S. firms for women of color.

A corporate objective to become more lean and mean must today include consideration for the fact that a good home life contributes immensely to a good work life. The work and family issue is no longer just a women's issue. Some specific measures that firms are taking to address this issue are providing spouse relocation assistance as an employee benefit; supplying company resources for family recreational and educational use; establishing employee country clubs, such

TABLE 10-14 Top Ten Companies for Working Women

Company	# Employees	% Women	Headquarters
1. Abbott	18,400	47	Abbott Park, Illinois
2. Deloitte	45,900	42	New York, New York
3. Discovery Communications	3,600	53	Silver Spring, Maryland
4. Ernst & Young LLP	31,500	46	New York, New York
5. General Mills	16,500	40	Minneapolis, Minnesota
6. IBM	430,000	30	Armonk, New York
7. Prudential Financial	19,800	51	Newark, New Jersey
8. PwC	36,500	45	New York, New York
9. WellStar Health System	13,200	82	Marietta, Georgia
10. Zoetis	4,200	40	Florham Park, New Jersey

Source: Based on information at the Working Mother website, January 1, 2015.

TABLE 10-15 The 26 Fortune 500 Women CEOs in 2015 (up from 21 in 2013)

CEO	Company	Fortune 500 Rank
Mary Barra	GM	(#7)
Meg Whitman	HP	(#17)
Virginia Rometty	IBM	(#23)
Patricia Woertz	Archer Daniels Midland	(#27)
Indra Nooyi	PepsiCo, Inc.	(#43)
Marillyn Hewson	Lockheed Martin	(#59)
Safra Catz (co-CEO)	Oracle	(#82)
Ellen Kullman	DuPont	(#86)
Irene Rosenfeld	Mondelez International	(#89)
Phebe Novakovic	General Dynamics	(#99)
Carol Meyrowitz	TJX Companies	(#108)
Lynn Good	Duke Energy	(#123)
Ursula Burns	Xerox Corporation	(#137)
Deanna Mulligan	Guardian	(#245)
Kimberly Bowers	CST Brands	(#266)
Debra Reed	Sempra Energy	(#267)
Barbara Rentler	Ross Stores	(#277)
Sheri McCoy	Avon Products	(#282)
Denise M. Morrison	Campbell Soup	(#315)
Susan Cameron	Reynolds American	(#329)
Heather Bresch	Mylan	(#377)
Ilene Gordon	Ingredion	(#412)
Jacqueline Hinman	CH2M Hill	(#437)
Kathleen Mazzarella	Graybar Electric	(#449)
Lisa Su	Advanced Micro Devices	(#474)
Gracia Martore	Gannett	(#481)

Source: Fortune, http://fortune.com/2013/05/09/women-ceos-in-the-fortune-500/.

as those at IBM and Bethlehem Steel; and creating family and work interaction opportunities. A study by Joseph Pleck of Wheaton College found that in companies that do not offer paternity leave for fathers as a benefit, most men take short, informal paternity leaves anyway by combining vacation time and sick days.

Some organizations have developed family days, when family members are invited into the workplace, taken on plant or office tours, dined by management, and given a chance to see exactly what other family members do each day. Family days are inexpensive and increase the employee's pride in working for the organization. Flexible working hours during the week are another human resource response to the need for individuals to balance work life and home life.

There is great room for improvement in removing the glass ceiling domestically, especially considering that women make up 47 percent of the U.S. labor force. **Glass ceiling** refers to the invisible barrier in many firms that bars women and minorities from top-level management positions. The United States is a leader globally in promoting women and minorities into mid- and top-level managerial positions in business. However, only 5.2 percent (26/500) of Fortune 500 firms have a woman CEO. Academic Research Capsule 10-2 reveals that women CEOs more often than men lead firms to be more philanthropic (giving). Table 10-15 gives the 26 Fortune 500 Women CEOs in 2015. These women are excellent role models for women globally.

Develop a Diverse Workforce

Chief Executive Officer Rosalind Brewer, the first African American woman to lead a Walmart business unit, is turning Walmart's SAM's Club into a $100 billion business. A recent study by McKinsey & Co. revealed that Asian companies' average return on equity improves from 15

ACADEMIC RESEARCH CAPSULE 10-2

How Do Women vs. Men CEOs Perform?

It is widely acknowledged in the literature that increased presence of women executives and directors leads firms to make greater philanthropic contributions. Marquis and Lee concluded that women executives and directors seek to strengthen external relationships of the firm through corporate philanthropy. Recent research also indicates that firms need to be much more proactive in public relations efforts announcing a new female CEO, due to a "guilt by association" effect. Specifically, female CEOs, unlike their male counterparts, are subject to criticism simply by being among a small group for such top executive women. Thus, a firm should actively take steps to bring legitimacy to a female CEO by highlighting her qualifications and accomplishments, while minimizing gender-related stereotypes. Investors react more negatively to the appointment of female CEOs than to male counterparts, partly because of media reports, rather than any legitimate performance differences. Recent research also reveals that women (and people of color) are more likely than white men to be promoted CEO of weakly performing firms.

Source: Based on Marquis, Christopher, & Matthew Lee, "Who Is Governing Whom? Executives, Governance, and the Structure of Generosity in Large U.S. Firms." *Strategic Management Journal*, 34 (2013): 483–497. See also Dixon-Fowler, Heather, Alan Ellstrand, and Jonathan Johnson, "Strength in Numbers or Guilt by Association? Intragroup Effects of Female Chief Executive Announcements," *Strategic Management Journal*, 34 (April 2013): 1488–1501; and Cook, Alison, and Christy Glass, "Above the Glass Ceiling: When Are Women and Racial/Ethnic Minorities Promoted to CEO?" *Strategic Management Journal*, 7 (July 2014): 1080–1089.

to 22 percent when more and more women hold high-level positions.[10] Wang Jin at McKinsey remarks, "Women tend to be stronger in terms of collaboration and people development, while men tend to be stronger in individual decision making. By having more women at the senior level, companies are helping to improve organizational health as well as financial performance."[11]

An organization can perhaps be most effective when its workforce mirrors the diversity of its customers. For global companies, this goal can be optimistic, but it is a worthwhile goal. The customer base in every country includes gay persons. Thus, retailers are increasingly using gay couples in advertisements. Tiffany recently promoted the company's first same-sex couples in advertising, preceded by J. Crew. Gap, and Banana Republic using gay couples in advertising campaigns.

Six benefits of having a diverse workforce are as follows:

1. Women and minorities have different insights, opinions, and perspectives that should be considered.
2. A diverse workforce portrays a firm committed to nondiscrimination.
3. A workforce that mirrors a customer base can help attract customers, build customer loyalty, and design/offer products/services that meet customer needs/wants.
4. A diverse workforce helps protect the firm against discrimination lawsuits.
5. Women and minorities represent a huge additional pool of qualified applicants.
6. A diverse workforce strengthens a firm's social responsibility and ethical position.

The percentage of women on corporate boards in Australia increased from 8.3 in 2010 to more than 16 percent in 2016.[12] Malaysia and South Korea are also making excellent progress integrating women into upper levels of management and subsidizing companies that build childcare facilities and help women juggle work and family life. In contrast, women in India still are expected to care for their family and extended family; many women in India often have an abortion if they know their fetus is a girl. Overall, in Asia, women comprise only 6 percent of corporate board seats, compared to 17 percent in Europe and 15 percent in the United States. However, there are currently 24 countries globally with female presidents, chancellors, or prime ministers – the 22 pictured in Table 10-16, plus Switzerland (Simonetta Sommaruga) and Croatia (Kolinda Grabar-Kitarovic).

Use Caution in Hiring a Rival's Employees

A recent article titled "Dos and Don'ts of Poaching Workers" in *Investor's Business Daily* gives guidelines to consider before hiring a rival firm's employees.[13] The practice of hiring employees from rival firms has a long tradition, but increasingly in our lawsuit-happy environment, firms must consider whether that person(s) had access to the "secret sauce formula, customer list, programming algorithm, or any proprietary or confidential information" of the rival firm. If the

TABLE 10-16 Female Presidents, Chancellors, and Prime Ministers of Countries (as of 2015)

#	Country	Pic	Leader	In office since:	Notes
1	Germany		Chancellor **Angela Merkel**	Nov. 22, 2005 -	elected
2	Liberia		President **Ellen Johnson-Sirleaf**	Jan. 16, 2006 -	elected
3	Argentina		President **Cristina Fernandez de Kirchner**	Dec. 10, 2007 -	elected
4	Bangledesh		Prime Minister **Sheikh Hasina Wajed**	Jan. 6, 2009 -	elected
5	Lithuania		President **Dalia Grybauskaite**	Jul. 12, 2009 -	elected
6	Costa Rica		President **Laura Chinchilla**	May 8, 2010 -	elected
7	Trinidad and Tobago		Prime Minister **Kamla Persad-Bissessar**	May 26, 2010 -	elected
8	Brazil		President **Dilma Rousseff**	Jan. 1, 2011 -	elected
9	Kosovo		President **Atifete Jahjaga**	Apr. 7, 2011 -	elected
10	Denmark		Prime Minister **Helle Thorning-Schmidt**	Oct. 3, 2011 -	elected
11	Jamaica		Prime Minister **Portia Simpson Miller**	Jan. 5, 2012 -	elected
12	Malawi		President **Joyce Banda**	Apr. 7, 2012 -	succeeded

#	Country	Pic	Leader	In office since:	Notes
13	South Korea		President **Park Geun-hye**	Feb. 25, 2013 -	elected
14	Slovenia		Prime Minister **Alenka Bratusek**	Mar. 20, 2013 -	elected
15	Cyprus (North)		Prime Minister **Sibel Siber**	Jun. 13, 2013 -	appointed
16	Senegal		Prime Minister **Aminata Touré**	Sep. 3, 2013 -	appointed
17	Norway		Prime Minister **Erna Solberg**	Oct. 16, 2013 -	elected
18	Latvia		Prime Minister **Laimdota Straujuma**	Jan. 22, 2014 -	elected
19	Central African Republic		President **Catherine Samba-Panza**	Jan. 23, 2014 -	appointed
20	Chile		President **Michelle Bachelet**	Mar. 11, 2014 -	elected
21	Malta		President **Marie-Louise Coleiro Preca**	Apr. 7, 2014 -	elected
22	Poland	Not Available	Prime Minister **Ewa Kopacz**	Apr. 7, 2014 -	elected

Source: Based on information at http://www.jjmccullough.com/charts_rest_female-leaders.php. Used with permission.

person has that information and joins your firm, lawsuits could follow that hiring, especially if the person was under contract at the rival firm or had signed a "noncompete agreement." The article says that to help safeguard the firm from this potential problem, a "well-written employee handbook" addressing the issue is necessary. The article talks about Hewlett-Packard (HP) recently hiring an IBM general manager, and IBM suing HP over the hiring, and in that case lost, but this type of legal action is becoming more commonplace.

According to Wayne Perrett, human resource manager for ComAp in Roscoe, Illinois, "A company does not want to become known as one that "steals" employees from competitors; that is bad for ethics and bad for business." Thus, it is not illegal to interview and hire employees from rival firms, and it has been done for centuries, but increasingly this is becoming a strategic issue to be managed, to avoid litigation.

TABLE 10-17 Ways and Means for Altering an Organization's Culture

1. Recruitment
2. Training
3. Transfer
4. Promotion
5. Restructuring
6. Reengineering
7. Role modeling
8. Positive reinforcement
9. Mentoring
10. Revising vision and/or mission
11. Redesigning physical spaces/facades
12. Altering reward system
13. Altering organizational policies, procedures, and practices

Create a Strategy-Supportive Culture

All organizations have a unique **culture**. For example, at Facebook, Inc., employees are given unusual freedom to choose and change assignments. Even low-level employees are encouraged to question and criticize managers. Facebook employees are rated on a normal distribution curve (Bell curve), which creates a hectic, intense work environment, where past accomplishments mean little, compared to what you have done lately for the firm. Managers are not revered at Facebook as bosses; rather, they are regarded as helpers.

Strategists should strive to preserve, emphasize, and build on aspects of an existing culture that support proposed new strategies. Aspects of an existing culture that are antagonistic to a proposed strategy should be identified and changed. Changing a firm's culture to fit a new strategy is usually more effective than changing a strategy to fit an existing culture. As indicated in Table 10-17, numerous techniques are available to alter an organization's culture, including recruitment, training, transfer, promotion, restructure of an organization's design, role modeling, positive reinforcement, and mentoring.

Schein indicated that the following elements are most useful in linking culture to strategy:

1. Formal statements of organizational philosophy, charters, creeds, materials used for recruitment and selection, and socialization
2. Designing of physical spaces, facades, and buildings
3. Deliberate role modeling, teaching, and coaching by leaders
4. Explicit reward and status system and promotion criteria
5. Stories, legends, myths, and parables about key people and events
6. What leaders pay attention to, measure, and control
7. Leader reactions to critical incidents and organizational crises
8. How the organization is designed and structured
9. Organizational systems and procedures
10. Criteria used for recruitment, selection, promotion, leveling off, retirement, and "excommunication" of people[14]

When Volkswagen AG recently acquired Porsche, there was concern that the autocratic style of 75-year-old Volkswagen Chairman Ferdinand Piech would be at odds with Porsche's informal culture. Porsche had for a long time placed a premium on individual effort among its engineers and designers, often encouraging competition among groups to come up with new design ideas and innovations. Time will tell if Volkswagen and Porsche can meld their cultures into a competitive advantage.

In the personal and religious side of life, the impact of loss and change is easy to see.[15] Memories of loss and change often haunt individuals and organizations for years. Ibsen wrote, "Rob the average man of his life illusion and you rob him of his happiness at the same stroke."[16] When attachments to a culture are severed in an organization's attempt to change direction, employees and managers often experience deep feelings of grief. This phenomenon commonly occurs when external conditions dictate the need for a new strategy. Managers and employees often struggle to find meaning in a situation that changed many years before. Some people find comfort in memories; others find solace in the present. Weak linkages between strategic management and organizational culture can jeopardize performance and success. Deal and Kennedy emphasized that making strategic changes in an organization always threatens a culture:

> People form strong attachments to heroes, legends, the rituals of daily life, the hoopla of extravaganza and ceremonies, and all the symbols of the workplace. Change strips relationships and leaves employees confused, insecure, and often angry. Unless something can be done to provide support for transitions from old to new, the force of a culture can neutralize and emasculate strategy changes.[17]

Use Caution in Monitoring Employees' Social Media

Many companies monitor employees' and prospective employees' social media activities, and have the legal right to do so, but there are many pros and cons of this activity. Proponents of companies monitoring employees' social media activities emphasize that (1) a company's reputation in the marketplace can easily be damaged by disgruntled employees venting on social media sites and (2) social media records can be subpoenaed, like email, and used as evidence against the company. Proponents say companies have a responsibility to know the nature of employees' communication through social media as related to clients, patients, suppliers, distributors, coworkers, managers, technology, patents, procedures, policies, and much more. To ignore social media communication by employees, proponents say, is irresponsible and too risky for the firm. Using social media to research and screen job candidates, various companies report finding provocative/inappropriate photos and information related to potential employees' bias, stereotypes, prejudices, drinking, and using drugs that led to rejection of the candidate. Companies should never use social media to discriminate based on age, race, ethnic background, religion, sexuality, or handicapped issues.

However, arguments against the practice of companies monitoring employees' social media activities say it is an invasion of privacy and too often becomes "a fishing expedition" sifting through tons of personal information irrelevant to a company or its business. Positions on political issues, gun rights, or immigration are all examples topics where company researchers may "not like" individuals with different belief systems than their own. In a recent study, 77 percent of employers said they conduct Internet searches of prospective employees, and 35 percent have rejected job applicants because of information they found.[18] Rejecting potential employees because of private behavior unrelated to work is unfair. In addition, whenever a company discovers through social media that an employee or potential employee is Muslim, disabled, gay, or over 40 years old, for example, and then denies a promotion or hires someone else, that "social media discovery information" could be the basis of a discrimination suit against the firm. For some jobs, such as law enforcement, due diligence may require firms to monitor social media activities to help assure their entire workforce is not involved in drugs, child pornography, gangs, and so on.

On balance, companies generally should monitor employee and potential employee's social media activities whenever they have a reason to believe the person is engaged in illegal or unethical conduct—but to systematically investigate every employee and job candidate's social media activities is arguably counterproductive. The bottom line is that companies have the *legal right* to monitor employees' conduct, but have the *legal duty* to do so only if there is sufficient reason for concern.

Develop a Corporate Wellness Program

Corporate wellness has become a major strategic issue in companies. If you owned a company and paid the health insurance of employees, would you desire to have a healthy workforce? Your likely answer is *yes*, because health insurance premiums are more costly for an unhealthy workforce.

Corporate wellness programs have proliferated in recent years due in part to the Affordable Care Act, which increased the maximum incentives and penalties employers may use to encourage employee well-being.[19] Most companies therefore now have both "carrots," such as giving employee discounts on insurance premiums or even extra cash, and "sticks," such as imposing surcharges on premiums for those who do not make progress towards getting healthy. For example, the state of Maryland installed penalties up to $450 per person for 2017 on any employee who fails to undergo certain screenings or treatment plans. Similarly at CVS Health, employees pay an extra $600 if they do not comply with certain health policies. Some employers, however, face lawsuits for violating the Americans with Disabilities Act that forbids employers from requiring medical exams and making disability-related inquiries. At Caesars, employees may reduce their insurance premiums by $40 per paycheck if they participate in the firm's wellness program, and additionally can obtain a $250 annual bonus if they improve their healthiness over the year. Companies are increasingly instituting wellness programs to curtail growing health-care costs.

JetBlue has a corporate wellness program called LifeVest, where the firm gives $500 to employees who improve their body mass index. However, a recent report from the Bipartisan Policy Center's CEO Council on Health and Innovation concluded that "results from studies examining the return on investment of wellness programs are mixed." Despite mixed results, 74 percent of firms with wellness programs are increasing incentives "paid and charged" to employees to be and stay healthy, up from 57 percent a few years ago.

About 2.1 billion people globally, or 29 percent of the world's population, are obese, with most of those people living in developed countries.[20] From 1980 to 2013, the prevalence of obesity rose by 27.5 percent for adults and 47.1 percent for children. The percentage of a nation's population that is obese, from the most obese countries, are the United States, China, India, Russia, Brazil, Mexico, Egypt, Germany, Pakistan, and Indonesia.[21] Corporate wellness programs are largely aimed at reducing workforce obesity.

Recent articles detail how companies such as Johnson & Johnson (J&J), Lowe's Home-Improvement, the supermarket chain H-E-B, and Healthwise report impressive returns on investment of comprehensive, well-run employee wellness programs, sometimes as high as six to one.[22] A recent study by Fidelity Investments and the National Business Group on Health reports that nearly 90 percent of employers today offer some kind of wellness incentives or prizes to employees who "get healthier," up from 59 percent in 2009. For example, JetBlue Airways offers employees money—$25 for teeth cleanings, $400 for completing an Ironman triathlon, and so forth. Furniture company KI has all its employees divided into four groups based on "healthiness" with the most healthy people paying $1,000 less on health insurance premiums than the least healthy employees.

Chevron and Biltmore provide exemplary wellness programs that think beyond diet and exercise and focus also on stress management by assisting employees with such issues as divorce, serious illness, death and grief recovery, child rearing, and care of aging parents. Biltmore's two-day health fairs twice a year focus on physical, financial, and spiritual wellness. At Lowe's headquarters, an impressive spiral staircase in the lobby makes climbing the stairs more appealing than riding the elevator. Such practices as "providing abundant bicycle racks," "conducting walking meetings," and "offering five-minute stress breaks" are becoming common at companies to promote a corporate wellness culture.

Whole Foods Market, headquartered in Austin, Texas, is another outstanding corporate wellness company with its employees receiving a 30 percent discount card on all products sold in their stores "if they maintain and document a healthy lifestyle." In addition, Wegman's Food Markets, headquartered in Rochester, New York, has an excellent corporate wellness program. Scotts Miracle-Gro Company (based in Marysville, Ohio), IBM, and Microsoft are implementing wellness programs, requiring employees to get healthier or pay higher insurance premiums. Employees who do get healthier win bonuses, free trips, and pay lower premiums; nonconforming employees pay higher premiums and receive no "healthy" benefits. Wellness of employees has become a strategic issue for many firms. Most firms require a health examination as a part of an employment application, and healthiness is more and more becoming a hiring factor. Michael Porter, coauthor of *Redefining Health Care*, says, "We have this notion that you can gorge on hot dogs, be in a pie-eating contest, and drink every day, and society will take care of you. We can't afford to let individuals drive up company costs because they're not willing to address their own health problems."

TABLE 10-18 Seven Keys to Staying Healthy, Living to 100, and Being a "Well" Employee

1. Eat nutritiously—Eat a variety of fruits and vegetables daily because they have ingredients that the body uses to repair and strengthen itself.

2. Stay hydrated—Drink plenty of water to aid the body in eliminating toxins and to enable body organs to function efficiently; the body is mostly water.

3. Get plenty of rest—The body repairs itself during rest, so get at least seven hours of sleep nightly, preferably eight hours.

4. Get plenty of exercise—Exercise vigorously at least 30 minutes daily so the body can release toxins and strengthen vital organs.

5. Reduce stress—The body's immune system is weakened when one is under stress, making the body vulnerable to many ailments, so keep stress to a minimum.

6. Do not smoke—Smoking kills, no doubt about it anymore.

7. Take vitamin supplements—Consult your physician, but because it is difficult for diet alone to supply all the nutrients and vitamins needed, supplements can be helpful in achieving good health and longevity.

Source: Based on Etter, Lauren, "Trans Fats: Will They Get Shelved?" *Wall Street Journal*, December 8, 2006, A6. See also Fuhrman, Joel, MD, *Eat to Live* (Boston: Little, Brown, 2003).

Seven key lifestyle habits listed in Table 10-18 may significantly improve health and longevity.

The Equal Employment Opportunity Commission (EEOC) is presently investigating Honeywell International because the firm recently asked employees to participate in a voluntary health screening of their cholesterol, body mass index, and other health measures as part of the firm's corporate wellness program. The EEOC has a problem with the Honeywell provision that employees choosing not to sit for the medical screenings could face up to $4,000 in surcharges and lost incentives in 2015. This is only the third EECO investigation of any company's corporate wellness program, the other two being Flamgea Inc, owned by Nordic Group, and Orion Energy Systems, when employees were fired for not participating or their insurance cancelled for not participating in the firm's corporate wellness program. The EEOC got involved in the Honeywell matter when two employees filed discrimination charges under the Americans with Disabilities Act, after being requested to participate in the firm's health screenings. The Affordable Care Act specifically encourages firms to reward as well as penalize employees who do or do not meet specific health goals, such as lowering blood sugar, weight, or cholesterol. Honeywell's program applies to spouses of employees when those persons are covered too by the firm's health insurance plans. Health insurance is expensive and companies desire a healthy workforce.

About 38 percent of companies now cover weight-loss bariatric surgery for employees, according to the Society for Human Resource Management (SHRM). Many companies now promote weight-reduction programs under the banner of wellness programs. Some companies are promoting and even paying for newly approved weight-loss drugs, such as Belviq, Qsymia, and Contrave. The Equal Employment Opportunity Commission (EEOC) is set to release guidance to employers regarding dos and don'ts related to corporate wellness programs.

IMPLICATIONS FOR STRATEGISTS

Figure 10-7 reveals that to gain and sustain competitive advantages, firms must be exceptionally well organized, and must allocate resources appropriately across products, services, and regions. Employees must know clearly what rewards and benefits they will receive if the firm does well; this knowledge will help motivate the workforce to work hard. As indicated in this chapter, other management policies and procedures also are needed to facilitate superior strategic implementation, including respect for women and minorities, linking compensation to firm performance, encouraging corporate wellness, and nurturing an organizational culture that treats all people with respect. If strategists do an exceptional job with the management, production/operations, and human resource issues related to strategy implementation, as described in this chapter, the firm is well on its way to success. But there are also critically important marketing and financial strategy implementation issues, as examined in the next chapter.

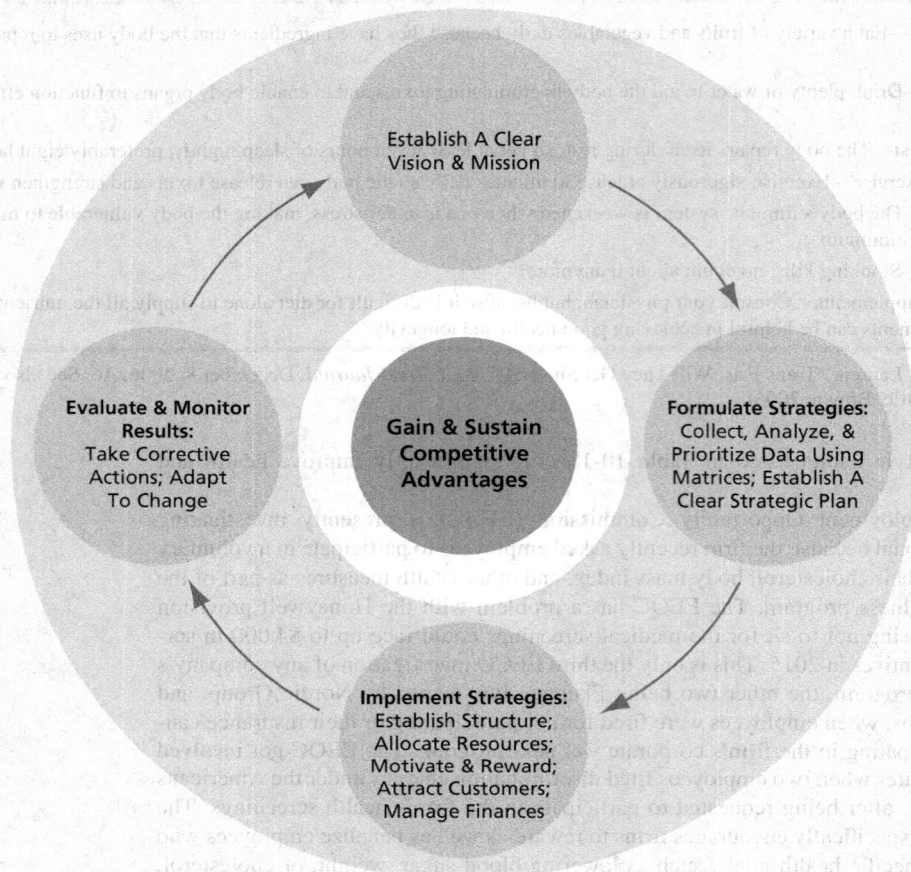

FIGURE 10-7
How to Gain and Sustain Competitive Advantages

IMPLICATIONS FOR STUDENTS

An integral part of managing a firm is continually and systematically seeking to gain and sustain competitive advantage through effective planning, organizing, motivating, staffing, and controlling. Rival firms engage in these same activities, so emphasize in your strategic-management case analysis how your firm can best implement your recommendations. Remember to be prescriptive rather than descriptive on every page or slide in your project, meaning to be insightful, forward-looking, and analytical, rather than just describing operations. It is easy to *describe* a company but it is difficult to *analyze* a company. Strategic-management case analysis is about *analyzing* a company and its industry, uncovering ways and means for the firm to best gain and sustain competitive advantage. So, communicate throughout your project how your firm, and especially your recommendations, will lead to improved growth and profitability versus rival firms. Avoid vagueness and generalities throughout your project, as your audience or reader seeks great ideas backed up by great analyses. Be analytical and prescriptive rather than vague and descriptive in highlighting every slide you show an audience.

A key consideration in devising an organizational structure concerns the divisions. Note whether the divisions (if any) of a firm presently are established based on geography, customer, product, or process. If the firm's organizational chart is not available, you often can devise a chart based on the titles of executives. An important case analysis activity is for you to decide how the divisions of a firm should be organized for maximum effectiveness. Even if the company presently has no divisions, determine whether it would operate better with divisions. In other words, which type of divisional breakdown do you (or your group or team) feel would be best for the firm in allocating resources, establishing objectives, and devising compensation incentives? This important strategic decision faces many midsize and large firms (and teams of students analyzing a strategic-management case).

Be mindful that all firms have functional staff below their top executive and often readily provide this information, so be wary of concluding prematurely that a particular firm uses a functional structure. If you see the word *president* in the titles of executives, coupled with financial-reporting segments, such as by product or geographic region, then the firm is currently divisionally structured.

Chapter Summary

Successful strategy formulation does not at all guarantee successful strategy implementation. Although inextricably interdependent, strategy formulation and strategy implementation are characteristically different. In a single word, strategy implementation means *change*. It is widely agreed that *the real work begins after strategies are formulated.* Successful strategy implementation requires the support of, as well as discipline and hard work, from motivated managers and employees. It is sometimes frightening to think that a single individual can irreparably sabotage strategy-implementation efforts.

Formulating the right strategies is not enough because managers and employees must be motivated to implement those strategies. Management issues considered central to strategy implementation include matching organizational structure with strategy, linking performance and pay to strategies, creating an organizational climate conducive to change, managing political relationships, creating a strategy-supportive culture, adapting production and operations processes, and managing human resources. Establishing annual objectives, devising policies, and allocating resources are central strategy-implementation activities common to all organizations. Depending on the size and type of the organization, other management issues could be equally important to successful strategy implementation.

Key Terms and Concepts

annual objectives (p. 324)
avoidance (p. 329)
bonus system (p. 342)
conflict (p. 329)
confrontation (p. 329)
culture (p. 348)
defusion (p. 329)
divisional (decentralized) structure by geographic area, product, customer, or process (p. 331)
educative change strategy (p. 339)
employee stock ownership plans (ESOPs) (p. 340)
force change strategy (p. 339)
functional structure (p. 330)
gain sharing (p. 342)

glass ceiling (p. 344)
horizontal consistency of objectives (p. 326)
just-in-time (JIT) (p. 340)
matrix structure (p. 334)
policies (p. 327)
rational change strategy (p. 339)
reengineering (p. 338)
resistance to change (p. 339)
resource allocation (p. 327)
restructuring (p. 338)
self-interest change strategy (p. 339)
Six Sigma (p. 338)
strategic business unit (SBU) structure (p. 330)
vertical consistency of objectives (p. 326)

Issues for Review and Discussion

10-1. Accenture is a strong firm globally. What are the three major threats you see that Accenture may face in a country of your choice?

10-2. List in order of importance the six management issues you feel are most central to strategy implementation. Give your rationale.

10-3. List the five major benefits of a firm having clearly defined annual objectives.

10-4. Which approach to conflict resolution would you use to resolve a disagreement between top-level managers, regarding a firm's strategic plan?

10-5. Illustrate a functional organizational chart.

10-6. Create a diagram for a divisional organizational chart.

10-7. Discuss recent trends and facts regarding corporate wellness programs in the United States.

10-8. Illustrate a matrix organizational chart.

10-9. List ten "dos and don'ts" regarding development of organizational charts.

10-10. Compare and contrast restructuring and reengineering.

10-11. Describe five ways a firm could link performance and pay to strategies.

10-12. List in order of importance, eight ways and means for altering an organization's culture. Explain why.

10-13. Why are so many firms today installing corporate wellness programs?

10-14. Discuss how business attitudes towards "balancing work life and home life" vary across three countries that you are familiar with.

10-15. Discuss the glass ceiling in your country versus the United States.

⭐ 10-16. Discuss ESOPs in your country compared to the United States.

10-17. In order of importance, in your opinion, list six advantages of a matrix organizational structure.

10-18. Determine whether your college or university has a corporate wellness program.

10-19. Do you think horizontal consistency of objectives is as important as vertical consistency? Explain using an example.

10-20. Define policies. Give four examples of policies for a bank.

10-21. Discuss your preference on each of the trade-off decisions required for strategy implementation. Explain why.

⭐ 10-22. List three categories or approaches for conflict resolution. Which approach would you use for a salesperson who may have had a disagreement with a client, regarding the value of a property to be listed for sale?

⭐ 10-23. In order of importance, list six symptoms of an ineffective organizational structure.

10-24. Explain why the functional organizational structure is the most widely used around the world.

10-25. List the advantages and disadvantages of a functional versus divisional structure.

10-26. How should a firm decide between a divisional-by-product versus divisional-by-region type organizational chart?

10-27. A divisional structure-by-process organizational chart is quite uncommon. Give two examples of the type of companies where this would be appropriate.

10-28. Illustrate a matrix-type structure for a hospital.

⭐ 10-29. Compare and contrast restructuring with reengineering.

10-30. Explain why it is so important to link performance and pay to strategies.

10-31. Describe five tests that are often used to determine whether a performance-pay plan will benefit an organization.

10-32. Describe three commonly used strategies to minimize employee resistance to change. Which approach would you most often use? Why?

10-33. Give a hypothetical example of each labor cost-saving tactic listed in the chapter. Students' answers may vary.

10-34. Use the Internet to find five companies in your country, which operate based on an ESOP. Present your list to the class.

10-35. Provide the advantages and disadvantages of a firm operating based on an ESOP.

10-36. Visit www.workingmother.com and find five examples of firms that are outstanding for working mothers, and that have business locations in your city.

10-37. Only 26 of the *Fortune* 500 CEOs are women. Conduct an Internet research to identify five companies in your country that have women CEOs. Why do you think there are such few women CEOs?

10-38. List four benefits of having a diverse workforce.

10-39. Explain why corporate wellness programs are becoming increasingly popular.

⭐ 10-40. Define and give an example of Six Sigma.

10-41. Define a glass ceiling. Provide an example.

10-42. How many divisions would a firm have to have for you to recommend an SBU type structure? Why?

10-43. Explain when a matrix-type structure may be the most effective for an organization.

10-44. How would you link compensation of your employees to performance of your business?

10-45. Compare and contrast women versus men in terms of serving as CEO of a company.

10-46. Name six countries that have or have had a female President.

⭐ 10-47. Is it a good management practice to hire away employees from rival companies? Discuss.

ASSURANCE OF LEARNING EXERCISES

EXERCISE 10A

Develop an Organizational Chart for Accenture Plc

Purpose

Accenture is featured in the opening chapter case as a firm that engages in excellent strategic planning. This exercise gives you practice developing an organizational chart.

Instructions

Step 1   Visit the https://www.accenture.com/in-en/ website. Review the company's most recent *Annual Report*. Note the list of top managers of the firm.

Step 2   Develop an organizational chart for Accenture based on the titles of their top executives.

Step 3   Develop a recommended organizational chart for Accenture based on the guidelines presented in Chapter 3.

EXERCISE 10B

Assess Accenture's Philanthropy Efforts

Purpose

Accenture recently awarded Quest Alliance India an additional grant of US$623,000 to help Quest provide approximately 3,000 disadvantaged young people with career and workplace skills. The grant brings Accenture's direct support to Quest Alliance India to more than US$950,000 since 2009. This exercise gives you practice comparing a company's philanthropy efforts versus its major rivals.

Step 1   Visit Accenture's website and click on the Citizenship and Values hotlink. Review Accenture's sustainability efforts.

Step 2   Identify Accenture's major competitors.

Step 3   Compare and contrast Accenture's sustainability efforts versus its two major competitors.

EXERCISE 10C

Revise Nestlé's Organizational Chart

Purpose

Developing and altering organizational charts is an important skill for strategists to possess. This exercise can improve your skill in altering an organization's hierarchical structure in response to new strategies being formed.

Instructions

Step 1   Develop an organizational chart for Nestlé. On a separate sheet of paper, answer the following questions:

- What type of organizational chart have you illustrated for Nestlé?
- What improvements would you recommend for the Nestlé organizational chart? Give your reasoning for each suggestion.

Step 2   Now consider the following:

- What aspects of your Nestlé chart do you especially like?
- What type of organizational chart do you believe would best suit Nestlé? Why?

EXERCISE 10D

Explore Objectives

Purpose

The purpose of this exercise is to bridge the gap between key topics in Chapter 3 versus what companies are doing in your area with regard to having clearly defined objectives.

Instructions

Do sufficient research to discover five businesses in your local area that have clearly defined objectives. Discuss the nature and role of objectives in these firms.

EXERCISE 10E

Understanding Your University's Culture

Purpose

It is something of an art to uncover the basic values and beliefs that are buried deeply in an organization's rich collection of stories, language, heroes, heroines, and rituals, yet culture can be the most important factor in implementing strategies.

Instructions

Step 1	On a separate sheet of paper, list the following terms: *hero/heroine, belief, metaphor, language, value, symbol, story, legend, saga, folktale, myth, ceremony, rite,* and *ritual.*
Step 2	For your college or university, give examples of each term. If necessary, speak with faculty, staff, alumni, administration, or fellow students of the institution to identify examples of each term.
Step 3	Report your findings to the class. Tell the class how you feel regarding cultural products being consciously used to help implement strategies.

MINI-CASE ON HORIZON PHARMA (HZNP)

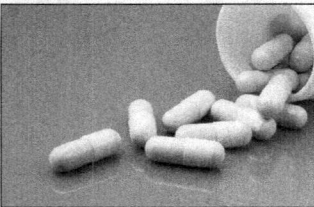

DOES HORIZON PHARMA HAVE A FORMAL STRUCTURE?

Source: © Triff. Shutterstock

Headquartered in Dublin, Ireland, Horizon Pharma develops and markets medicines, especially ones for treating arthritis, pain, and inflammatory diseases. Horizon has been on a buying spree. In September 2014, for a $660 million deal, the company acquired Vidara Therapeutics International; in October 2014, under a deal worth $45 million, the company acquired the U.S. sales and marketing rights to the osteoarthritis drug Pennsaid from Nuvo Research; and in May 2015, Hyperion Therapeutics was acquired by Horizon Pharma for $1.1 billion, increasing their orphan disease drug portfolio and increased their product range to seven with RAVICTI and BUPHENYL coming onboard. For a price of almost $3 billion, Horizon Pharma had hoped to acquire DepoMed (DEPO), which would have meant a premium of 42 percent of DEPO's closing price as of July 2015. However, Horizon had to withdraw their offer after a court ruling on the company's improper use of confidential information.

Horizon is focused on identifying, developing, acquiring, and commercializing a range of medical products that are accessible and will address different medical needs. In 2015, the third quarter saw net sales of $226.5 million, increasing by more than 200 percent in comparison to the previous year, and 31 percent up from the second quarter in 2015. The net income in 2015, for the third quarter, was $3.3 million, a 57 percent increase from the same quarter in the previous year.

The profitable growth was mainly due to strong sales growth in the business units— primary care ($56.9 million), orphan ($28.7 million), and specialty ($11.7 million). As part of its strategy for 2015, Horizon's orphan and primary care business units were given new medicines in the third quarter. Horizon received the European Commission's approval for RAVICTI oral liquid treatment in 2015, and is expecting to launch this product in 2017. In 2015, the drug RAYOS, under Horizon's specialty division, saw sales of $11.7 million, an increase of 106 percent in comparison to the third quarter of the previous year, while the sales of LODOTRA increased 36 percent. Horizon Pharma's strategy of growing through acquisition seems to be the right medicine for the company so far.

Questions

1. Visit Horizon's website and go through the senior management section. The company lists its top 21 corporate executives and their respective titles. Based on this information, what type of organizational structure is Horizon using?
2. Based on the information at the website given above, what are three good and three bad aspects of Horizon's organizational structure?

Source: Based on company documents.

Current Readings

Brinker, Scott, and Laura McLellan. "The Rise of the Chief Marketing Technologist." *Harvard Business Review* 92, no. 7/8 (2014): 82–85.

Ganster, Daniel C., and Christopher C. Rosen. "Work Stress and Employee Health: A Multidisciplinary Review." *Journal of Management* 39, no. 5 (2013): 1085–1122.

Gedmin, Jeffrey. "Our Mania for Measuring (and Remeasuring) Well-Being." *Harvard Business Review* 91, no. 9 (2013): 38.

Hewlett, Sylvia Ann, Melinda Marshall, and Laura Sherbin. "How Diversity Can Drive Innovation." *Harvard Business Review* 91, no.12 (2013): 30.

Hirsch, Peter. B. "Being Awkward: Creating Conscious Culture Change." *Journal of Business Strategy* 36, no. 1 (2015): 52–55.

Hoobler, Jenny M., Grace Lemmon, and Sandy J. Wayne. "Women's Managerial Aspirations: An Organizational Development Perspective." *Journal of Management* 40, no. 3 (2014): 703–730.

Ibarra, Herminia, Robin Ely, and Deborah Kolb. "Women Rising: The Unseen Barriers." (Cover Story). *Harvard Business Review* 91, no. 9 (2013): 60–67.

Krause, Ryan, Matthew Semadeni, and Albert A. Cannella. "CEO Duality: A Review and Research Agenda." *Journal of Management* 40, no. 1 (2014): 256–286.

Puranam, Phanish, Oliver Alexy, and Markus Reitzig. "What's 'New' about New Forms of Organizing?" *Academy of Management Review* 39, no. 2 (2014): 162–180.

Riccò, Rossella and Marco. "Diversity Challenge: An Integrated Process to Bridge the 'Implementation Gap.'" *Business Horizons* 57, no. 2 (2014): 235–245.

Wagner, Stephan, M. Kristoph, K. R. Ullrich, and Sandra Transchel. "The Game Plan dor Aligning the Organization." *Business Horizons* 57, no. 2 (2014): 189–201.

Endnotes

1. Dale McConkey, "Planning in a Changing Environment," *Business Horizons* (September–October 1988): 66.
2. A. G. Bedeian and W. F. Glueck, *Management,* 3rd ed. (Chicago: Dryden, 1983), 212.
3. Boris Yavitz and William Newman, *Strategy in Action: The Execution, Politics, and Payoff of Business Planning* (New York: The Free Press, 1982), 195.
4. E. H. Schein, "Three Cultures of Management: The Key to Organizational Learning," *Sloan Management Review* 38, 1 (1996): 9–20.
5. Joann Lublin, "Chairman-CEO Split Gains Allies," *Wall Street Journal*, March 30, 2009, B4.
6. Karen Richardson, "The 'Six Sigma' Factor for Home Depot," *Wall Street Journal*, January 4, 2007, C3.
7. Emily Chasan, "Stock Loses Some Sway on Pay," *Wall Street Journal,* October 30, 2012. B4.
8. Richard Brown, "Outsider CEO: Inspiring Change with Force and Grace," *USA Today,* July 19, 1999, 3B.
9. Conor Dougherty, "Strides by Women, Still a Wage Gap," *Wall Street Journal*, March 1, 2011, A3. See also David Jackson and Mimi Hall, "Women Gain in Education and Longevity," *USA Today*, March 2, 2011, 5A.
10. Kathy Chu, "Asian Women Fight Barriers," *Wall Street Journal,* July 2, 2012, B4.
11. Ibid.
12. Ibid.
13. Sheila Riley, "The Dos and Don'ts of Poaching Workers," *Investor's Business Daily*, March 31, 2014, A10.
14. E. H. Schein, "The Role of the Founder in Creating Organizational Culture," *Organizational Dynamics* (Summer 1983): 13–28.
15. T. Deal and A. Kennedy, "Culture: A New Look Through Old Lenses," *Journal of Applied Behavioral Science* 19, no. 4 (1983): 498–504.
16. H. Ibsen, "The Wild Duck," in O. G. Brochett and L. Brochett (Eds.), *Plays for the Theater* (New York: Holt, Rinehart and Winsstron, 1967); R. Pascale, "The Paradox of 'Corporate Culture': Reconciling Ourselves to Socialization," *California Management Review* 28, no. 2 (1985): 26, 37–40.
17. T. Deal and A. Kennedy, *Corporate Cultures: The Rites and Rituals of Corporate Life* (Reading, MA: Addison-Wesley, 1982), 256.
18. Nancy Flynn and Lewis Maltby, "Should Companies Monitor Their Employees' Social Media?" *Wall Street Journal*, May 12, 2014, R1.
19. Lauren Weber, "A Health Check for Wellness Programs," *Wall Street Journal,* October 8, 2014, B1, B8.
20. Betsy McKay, "About 30% of Word Is Overweight," *Wall Street Journal,* May 30, 2014.
21. Ibid.
22. Leonard Berry, Ann Mirabito, and William Baun, "What's the Hard Return on Employee Wellness Programs?" *Harvard Business Review,* December 210, 104–112. See also Jen Wieczner, "Your Company Wants to Make You Healthy," *Wall Street Journal,* December 17, 2014, B1.

Strategy Monitoring

LEARNING OBJECTIVES

After studying this chapter, you should be able to do the following:

11-1. Discuss the strategy-evaluation process, criteria, and methods used.

11-2. Discuss three activities that comprise strategy evaluation.

11-3. Describe and develop a Balanced Scorecard.

11-4. Identify and describe published sources of strategy-evaluation information.

11-5. Identify and describe six characteristics of an effective strategy-evaluation system.

11-6. Discuss the nature and role of contingency planning in strategy evaluation.

11-7. Explain the role of auditing in strategy evaluation.

11-8. Identify and discuss three twenty-first-century challenges in strategic management.

11-9. Identify and describe 17 guidelines for effective strategic management.

ASSURANCE OF LEARNING EXERCISES

The following exercises are found at the end of this chapter:

EXERCISE 11A   Evaluate BHP Billiton's Strategies

EXERCISE 11B   Prepare a Strategy-Evaluation Report for Nestlé S.A.

EXERCISE 11C   Prepare a Balanced Scorecard for Nestlé S.A.

EXERCISE 11D   Evaluate Your University's Strategies

The best formulated and best implemented strategies become obsolete as a firm's external and internal environments change. It is essential, therefore, that strategists systematically review, evaluate, and control the execution of strategies. This chapter presents a framework that can guide managers' efforts to evaluate strategic-management activities, to make sure they are working, and to make timely changes. Guidelines are presented for formulating, implementing, and evaluating strategies. Perth-based petroleum company, BHP Billiton is the exemplary company showcased because the firm continually evaluates its strategies and takes prompt corrective actions as needed.

The Strategy-Evaluation Process, Criteria, and Methods

The strategic-management process results in decisions that can have significant, long-lasting consequences. Erroneous strategic decisions can inflict severe penalties and can be exceedingly difficult, if not impossible, to reverse. Therefore, most strategists agree that strategy evaluation is vital to an organization's well-being; timely evaluations can alert management to problems or potential problems before a situation becomes critical. The strategy-evaluation process includes three basic activities:

1. Examine the underlying bases of a firm's strategy.
2. Compare expected results with actual results.
3. Take corrective actions to ensure that performance conforms to plans.

Figure 11-1 illustrates the strategy-evaluation stage of the strategic-management process (see white shading). Adequate and timely feedback is the cornerstone of effective strategy evaluation. Strategy evaluation can be no better than the information on which it is based. Too much pressure from top managers may result in lower managers contriving numbers they think will be satisfactory. Strategy evaluation can be a complex and sensitive undertaking. Too much emphasis on evaluating strategies may be expensive and counterproductive. No one likes to be evaluated too closely! The more managers attempt to evaluate the behavior of others, the less control they have. Yet too little or no evaluation can create even worse problems. Strategy evaluation is essential to

BHP Billiton (BHP)

Perth-based Anglo-Australian BHP Billiton is a multinational mining and petroleum company, arguably the largest mining company in the world and is ranked among the ten largest companies in terms of market capitalization. Apart from its crude oil and natural gas holdings, BHP is also regarded as one of the leading producers of natural resources, producing and developing resources like iron ore, coal, copper, and aluminum.

In the third quarter of 2015, BHP's total petroleum production decreased by four percent to 64.5 million barrels of oil equivalents (MMboe). For the 2016 financial year, BHP has planned for a petroleum capital expenditure of $2.9 billion, which includes onshore capital expenditure of $1.4 billion, falling from the previous year's $3 billion by six percent. Account for $1.5 billion, BHP's conventional capital expenditure focuses on high-return drilling opportunities in the Gulf of Mexico and Australia, while also weighing projects at Bass Strait and North West Shelf. The third quarter's crude oil, condensate and natural gas liquids production was 30.7 MMboe, falling by one percent, while its onshore liquids volumes rose by 17 percent to 13.5 MMboe. BHP's third quarter natural gas production fell by 7 percent.

As part of their strategy going forward, Chesapeake Energy received $4.75 billion from BHP for all of its shale assets, its 487,000 acres of mineral rights leases, and 420 miles (680 km) of the north central Arkansas pipeline located in the United States. Almost 415 million cubic feet of natural gas is produced every day from the mineral leases acquired. Over the next decade, the company plans to spend $800 million to $1 billion each year to developing the fields and further increase production.

Source: Based on company documents.

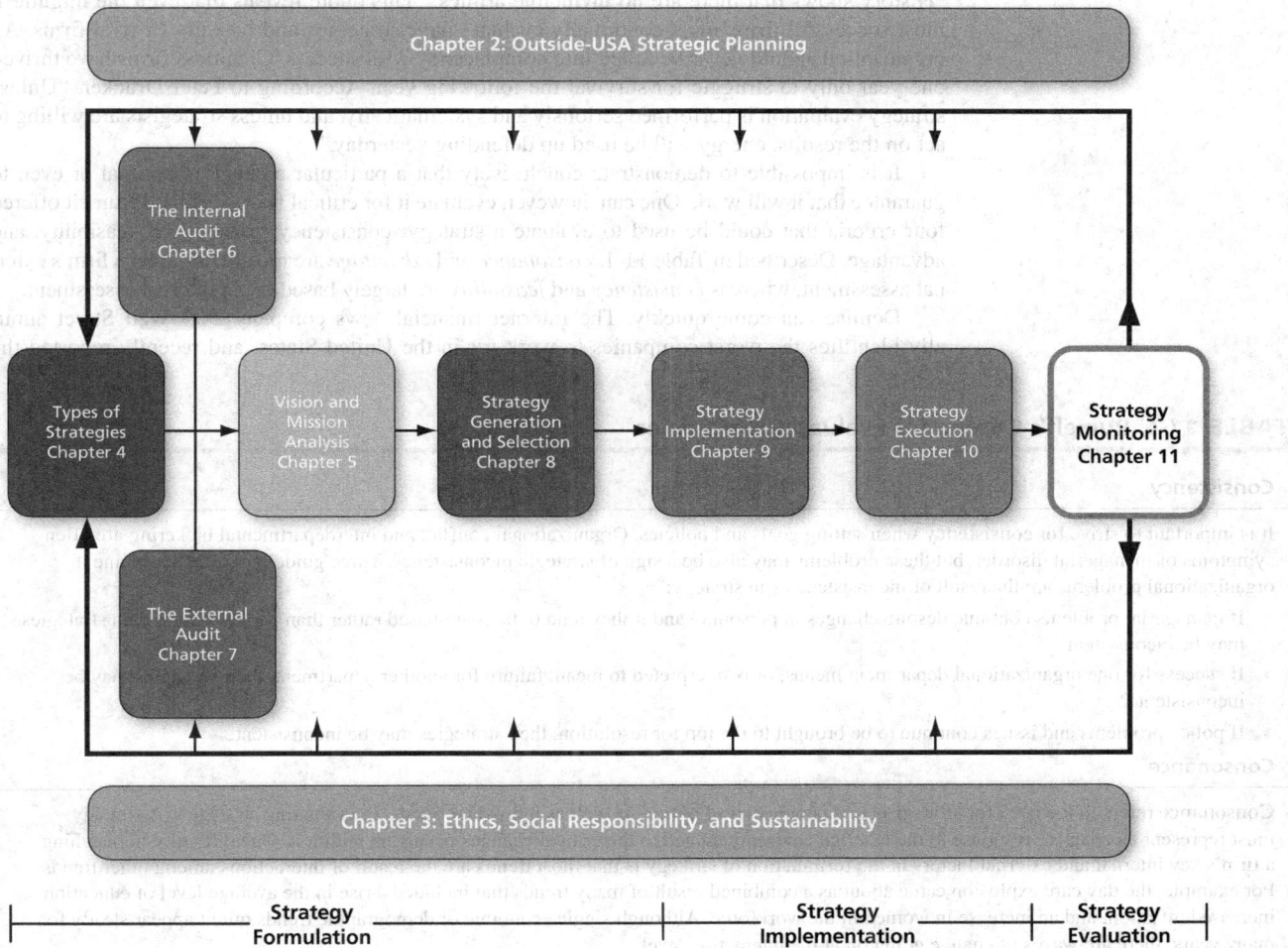

FIGURE 11-1

A Comprehensive Strategic-Management Model

Source: Fred R. David, adapted from "How Companies Define Their Mission," *Long Range Planning* 22, no. 3 (June 1988): 40, © Fred R. David.

ensure that stated objectives are being achieved. Strategists need to create an organizational culture where strategy evaluation is viewed as an opportunity to make the firm better, so the firm can compete better, so everyone in the firm can do better, sharing in the firm's increased profitability.

In many organizations, strategy evaluation is simply an appraisal of how well an organization has performed. Have the firm's assets increased? Has there been an increase in profitability? Have sales increased? Have productivity levels increased? Have profit margin, return on investment, and earnings-per-share ratios increased? Some firms argue that their strategy must have been correct if the answers to these types of questions are affirmative. Well, the strategy or strategies may have been correct, but this type of reasoning can be misleading because strategy evaluation must have both a long-run and short-run focus. Strategies often do not affect short-term operating results until it is too late to make needed changes.

Strategy evaluation is important because organizations face dynamic environments in which key external and internal factors often change quickly and dramatically. Success today is no guarantee of success tomorrow! Joseph Stalin was a ruthless leader (from 1928 on) and premier (from 1941 on) of the Soviet Union until his death in 1953. A famous quote from Stalin was:

"History shows that there are no invincible armies." This quote reveals that even the mightiest, most successful firms must continually evaluate their strategies and be wary of rival firms. An organization should never be lulled into complacency with success. Countless firms have thrived one year only to struggle for survival the following year. According to Peter Drucker, "Unless strategy evaluation is performed seriously and systematically, and unless strategists are willing to act on the results, energy will be used up defending yesterday."

It is impossible to demonstrate conclusively that a particular strategy is optimal or even to guarantee that it will work. One can, however, evaluate it for critical flaws. Richard Rumelt offered four criteria that could be used to evaluate a strategy: consistency, consonance, feasibility, and advantage. Described in Table 11-1, *consonance* and *advantage* are mostly based on a firm's external assessment, whereas *consistency* and *feasibility* are largely based on an internal assessment.

Demise can come quickly. The Internet financial news company 24/7 Wall Street annually identifies the worst companies to work for in the United States, and recently reported the

TABLE 11-1 Rumelt's Criteria for Evaluating Strategies

Consistency

It is important to strive for **consistency** when setting goals and policies. Organizational conflict and interdepartmental bickering are often symptoms of managerial disorder, but these problems may also be a sign of strategic inconsistency. Three guidelines help determine if organizational problems are the result of inconsistencies in strategy:

- If managerial problems continue despite changes in personnel and if they tend to be issue-based rather than people-based, then strategies may be inconsistent.
- If success for one organizational department means, or is interpreted to mean, failure for another department, then strategies may be inconsistent.
- If policy problems and issues continue to be brought to the top for resolution, then strategies may be inconsistent.

Consonance

Consonance refers to the need for strategists to examine *sets of trends*, as well as individual trends, in evaluating strategies. A strategy must represent an adaptive response to the external environment and to the critical changes occurring within it. One difficulty in matching a firm's key internal and external factors in the formulation of strategy is that most trends are the result of interactions among other trends. For example, the day care explosion came about as a combined result of many trends that included a rise in the average level of education, increased inflation, and an increase in women in the workforce. Although single economic or demographic trends might appear steady for many years, there are waves of change going on at the interaction level.

Feasibility

A strategy must neither overtax available resources nor create unsolvable subproblems. The final broad test of strategy is its **feasibility**; that is, can the strategy be attempted within the physical, human, and financial resources of the enterprise? The financial resources of a business are the easiest to quantify and are normally the first limitation against which strategy is evaluated. It is sometimes forgotten, however, that innovative approaches to financing are often possible. Devices, such as captive subsidiaries, sale-leaseback arrangements, and tying plant mortgages to long-term contracts, have all been used effectively to help win key positions in suddenly expanding industries. A less quantifiable, but actually more rigid, limitation on strategic choice is that imposed by individual and organizational capabilities. In evaluating a strategy, it is important to examine whether an organization has demonstrated in the past that it possesses the abilities, competencies, skills, and talents needed to carry out a given strategy.

Advantage

A strategy must provide for the creation or maintenance of a competitive **advantage** in a selected area of activity. Competitive advantages normally are the result of superiority in one of three areas: (1) resources, (2) skills, or (3) position. The idea that the positioning of one's resources can enhance their combined effectiveness is familiar to military theorists, chess players, and diplomats. Position can also play a crucial role in an organization's strategy. Once gained, a good position is defensible—meaning that it is so costly to capture that rivals are deterred from full-scale attacks. Positional advantage tends to be self-sustaining so long as the key internal and environmental factors that underlie it remain stable. This is why entrenched firms can be almost impossible to unseat, even if their raw skill levels are only average. Although not all positional advantages are associated with size, it is true that larger organizations tend to operate in markets and use procedures that turn their size into advantage, whereas smaller firms seek product or market positions that exploit other types of advantage. The principal characteristic of good position is that it permits the firm to obtain advantage from policies that would not similarly benefit rivals without the same position. Therefore, in evaluating strategy, organizations should examine the nature of positional advantages associated with a given strategy.

Source: Adapted from Richard Rumelt, "The Evaluation of Business Strategy," in W. F. Glueck (ed.), *Business Policy and Strategic Management* (New York: McGraw-Hill, 1980), 359–367. Used with permission.

worst company to be Books-A-Million, followed by Express Scripts, Frontier Communications, Jos. A. Bank Clothiers, Brookdale Senior Living, Dillards, ADT, hhgregg, Family Dollar Stores, Children's Place, and, the 11th worst, Radio Shack.[1]

Strategy evaluation is becoming increasingly difficult with the passage of time, for many reasons. Domestic and world economies were more stable in years past, product life cycles were longer, product development cycles were longer, technological advancement was slower, change occurred less frequently, there were fewer competitors, foreign companies were generally weak, and there were more regulated industries. Other reasons why strategy evaluation is more difficult today include the following trends:

1. A dramatic increase in the environment's complexity
2. The increasing difficulty of predicting the future with accuracy
3. The increasing number of variables
4. The rapid rate of obsolescence of even the best plans
5. The increase in the number of both domestic and world events affecting organizations
6. The decreasing time span for which planning can be done with any degree of certainty[2]

A fundamental problem facing managers today is how to effectively manage a workforce in light of modern organizational demands for greater flexibility, innovation, creativity, and initiative from employees.[3] Managers need empowered employees acting responsibly and never putting the well-being of the business at risk. The potential costs to companies in terms of damaged reputations, fines, missed opportunities, and diversion of management's attention are enormous, and bad news oftentimes spreads like wildfire over social media. Too much pressure to achieve specific goals can lead to dysfunctional behavior. For example, Nordstrom, the upscale fashion retailer known for outstanding customer service, was subjected to lawsuits and fines when employees underreported hours worked to increase their sales per hour—the company's primary performance criterion.

The Process of Evaluating Strategies

Strategy evaluation is necessary for all sizes and kinds of organizations. Strategy evaluation should initiate managerial questioning of expectations and assumptions, should trigger a review of objectives and values, and should stimulate creativity in generating alternatives and formulating criteria of evaluation.[4] Regardless of the size of the organization, a certain amount of "management by wandering around" at all levels is essential to effective strategy evaluation. Strategy-evaluation activities should be performed on a continuing basis, rather than at the end of specified periods of time or just after problems occur. Waiting until the end of the year, for example, could result in a firm closing the barn door after the horses have already escaped.

Evaluating strategies on a continuous rather than on a periodic basis allows benchmarks of progress to be established and more effectively monitored. Some strategies take years to implement; consequently, associated results may not become apparent for years. Successful strategies combine patience with a willingness to promptly take corrective actions when necessary. There always comes a time when corrective actions are needed in an organization! Centuries ago, a writer (perhaps Solomon) made the following observations about change:

There is a time for everything,
A time to be born and a time to die,
A time to plant and a time to uproot,
A time to kill and a time to heal,
A time to tear down and a time to build,
A time to weep and a time to laugh,
A time to mourn and a time to dance,
A time to scatter stones and a time to gather them,
A time to embrace and a time to refrain,
A time to search and a time to give up,
A time to keep and a time to throw away,
A time to tear and a time to mend,
A time to be silent and a time to speak,
A time to love and a time to hate,
A time for war and a time for peace.[5]

Managers and employees of the firm should be continually aware of progress being made toward achieving the firm's objectives. As key success factors change, organizational members should be involved in determining appropriate corrective actions. If assumptions and expectations deviate significantly from forecasts, then the firm should renew strategy-formulation activities, perhaps sooner than planned. In strategy evaluation, like strategy formulation and strategy implementation, people make the difference. Through involvement in the process of evaluating strategies, managers and employees become committed to keeping the firm moving steadily toward achieving objectives.

The Three Strategy-Evaluation Activities

Table 11-2 summarizes the three strategy-evaluation activities in terms of key questions that should be addressed, alternative answers to those questions, and appropriate actions for an organization to take. Notice that corrective actions are almost always needed except when (1) external and internal factors have not significantly changed and (2) the firm is progressing satisfactorily toward achieving stated objectives. Relationships among strategy-evaluation activities are illustrated in Figure 11-2.

Reviewing Bases of Strategy

As shown in Figure 11-2, **reviewing the underlying bases of an organization's strategy** could be approached by developing a revised EFE Matrix and IFE Matrix. A **revised IFE Matrix** should focus on changes in the organization's management, marketing, finance and accounting, production and operations, research and development (R&D), and management information systems (MIS) strengths and weaknesses. A **revised EFE Matrix** should indicate how effective a firm's strategies have been in response to key opportunities and threats. This analysis could also address such questions as the following:

1. How have competitors reacted to our strategies?
2. How have competitors' strategies changed?
3. Have major competitors' strengths and weaknesses changed?
4. Why are competitors making certain strategic changes?
5. Why are some competitors' strategies more successful than others?
6. How satisfied are our competitors with their present market positions and profitability?
7. How far can our major competitors be pushed before retaliating?
8. How could we more effectively cooperate with our competitors?

Numerous external and internal factors can prevent firms from achieving long-term and annual objectives. Externally, actions by competitors, changes in demand, changes in technology, economic

TABLE 11-2 A Strategy-Evaluation Assessment Matrix

Have Major Changes Occurred in the Firm's Internal Strategic Position?	Have Major Changes Occurred in the Firm's External Strategic Position?	Has the Firm Progressed Satisfactorily Toward Achieving Its Stated Objectives?	Result
No	No	No	Take corrective actions
Yes	Yes	Yes	Take corrective actions
Yes	Yes	No	Take corrective actions
Yes	No	Yes	Take corrective actions
Yes	No	No	Take corrective actions
No	Yes	Yes	Take corrective actions
No	Yes	No	Take corrective actions
No	No	Yes	Continue present strategic course

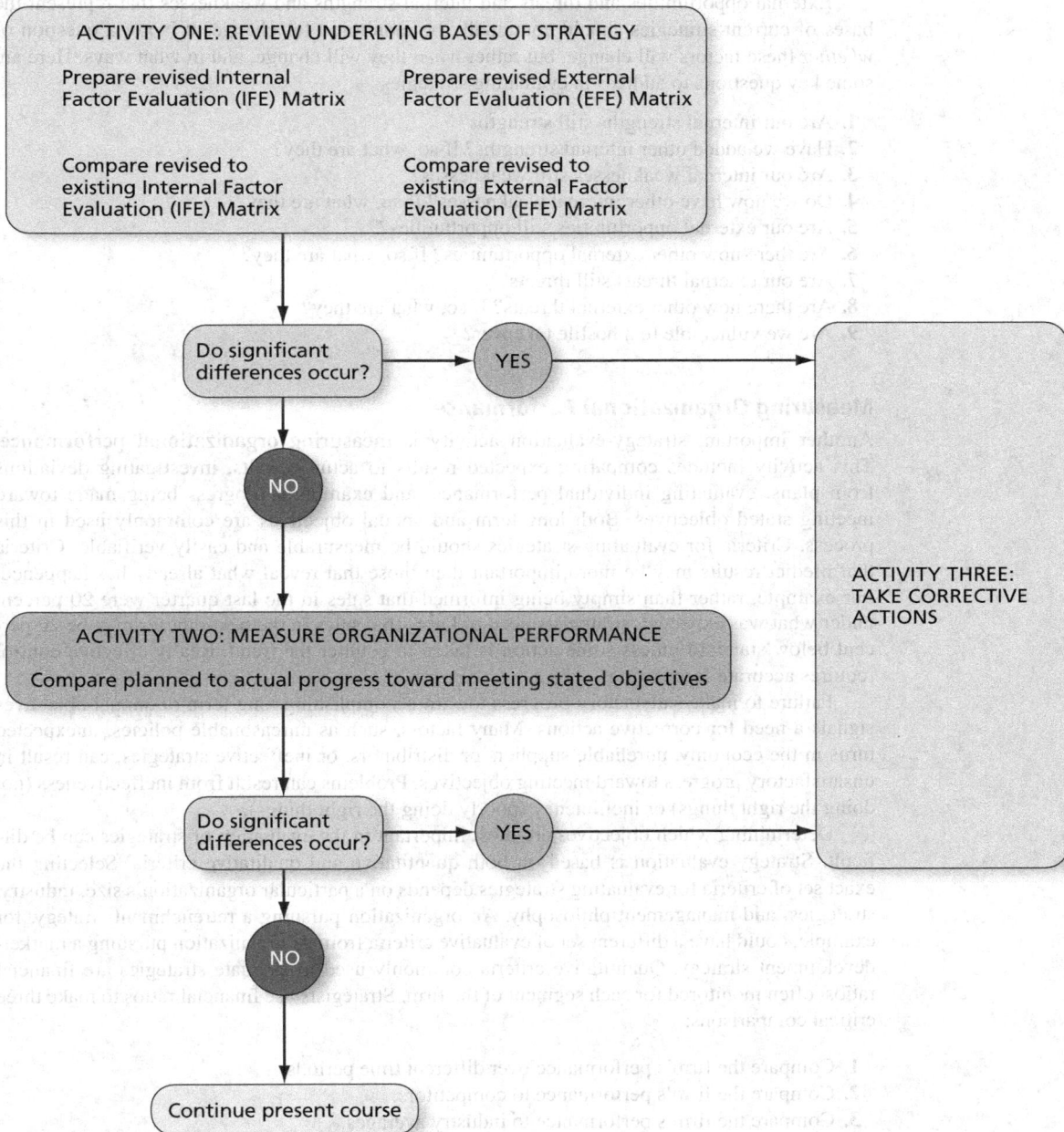

ACTIVITY ONE: REVIEW UNDERLYING BASES OF STRATEGY

Prepare revised Internal
Factor Evaluation (IFE) Matrix

Prepare revised External
Factor Evaluation (EFE) Matrix

Compare revised to
existing Internal Factor
Evaluation (IFE) Matrix

Compare revised to
existing External Factor
Evaluation (EFE) Matrix

Do significant
differences occur?   →   YES   →   ACTIVITY THREE:
TAKE CORRECTIVE
ACTIONS

NO

ACTIVITY TWO: MEASURE ORGANIZATIONAL PERFORMANCE

Compare planned to actual progress toward meeting stated objectives

Do significant
differences occur?   →   YES

NO

Continue present course

FIGURE 11-2
A Strategy-Evaluation Framework

changes, demographic shifts, and governmental actions may prevent objectives from being accomplished. Internally, ineffective strategies may have been chosen or implementation activities may have been poor. Objectives may have been too optimistic. Thus, failure to achieve objectives may not be the result of unsatisfactory work by managers and employees. All organizational members need to know this to encourage their support for strategy-evaluation activities. Organizations desperately need to know as soon as possible when their strategies are not effective. Sometimes managers and employees on the front lines discover this well before strategists.

External opportunities and threats and internal strengths and weaknesses that represent the bases of current strategies should continually be monitored for change. It is not a question of *whether* these factors will change, but rather *when* they will change, and in what ways. Here are some key questions to address in evaluating strategies:

1. Are our internal strengths still strengths?
2. Have we added other internal strengths? If so, what are they?
3. Are our internal weaknesses still weaknesses?
4. Do we now have other internal weaknesses? If so, what are they?
5. Are our external opportunities still opportunities?
6. Are there now other external opportunities? If so, what are they?
7. Are our external threats still threats?
8. Are there now other external threats? If so, what are they?
9. Are we vulnerable to a hostile takeover?

Measuring Organizational Performance

Another important strategy-evaluation activity is **measuring organizational performance**. This activity includes comparing expected results to actual results, investigating deviations from plans, evaluating individual performance, and examining progress being made toward meeting stated objectives. Both long-term and annual objectives are commonly used in this process. Criteria for evaluating strategies should be measurable and easily verifiable. Criteria that predict results may be more important than those that reveal what already has happened. For example, rather than simply being informed that sales in the last quarter were 20 percent under what was expected, strategists need to know that sales in the next quarter may be 20 percent below standard unless some action is taken to counter the trend. Really effective control requires accurate forecasting.

Failure to make satisfactory progress toward accomplishing long-term or annual objectives signals a need for corrective actions. Many factors, such as unreasonable policies, unexpected turns in the economy, unreliable suppliers or distributors, or ineffective strategies, can result in unsatisfactory progress toward meeting objectives. Problems can result from ineffectiveness (not doing the right things) or inefficiency (poorly doing the right things).

Determining which objectives are most important in the evaluation of strategies can be difficult. Strategy evaluation is based on both quantitative and qualitative criteria. Selecting the exact set of criteria for evaluating strategies depends on a particular organization's size, industry, strategies, and management philosophy. An organization pursuing a retrenchment strategy, for example, could have a different set of evaluative criteria from an organization pursuing a market-development strategy. Quantitative criteria commonly used to evaluate strategies are financial ratios, often monitored for each segment of the firm. Strategists use financial ratios to make three critical comparisons:

1. Compare the firm's performance over different time periods.
2. Compare the firm's performance to competitors.
3. Compare the firm's performance to industry averages.

Many variables can and should be included in measuring organizational performance. As indicated in Table 11-3, typically a favorable or unfavorable variance is recorded monthly, quarterly, and annually, and resultant actions needed are then determined.

Some potential problems are associated with using only quantitative criteria for evaluating strategies. First, most quantitative criteria are geared to annual objectives rather than long-term objectives. Also, different accounting methods can provide different results on many quantitative criteria. Third, intuitive judgments are almost always involved in deriving quantitative criteria. Thus, qualitative criteria are also important in evaluating strategies. Human factors such as high absenteeism and turnover rates, poor production quality and quantity rates, or low employee satisfaction can be underlying causes of declining performance. Marketing, finance and accounting, R&D, or MIS factors can also cause financial problems. The need for a "balanced" quantitative/qualitative approach in evaluating strategies gives rise in a moment to discussion of the balanced scorecard.

TABLE 11-3 A Sample Framework for Measuring Organizational Performance

Factor	Actual Result	Expected Result	Variance	Action Needed
Corporate Revenues				
Corporate Profits				
Corporate ROI				
Region 1 Revenues				
Region 1 Profits				
Region 1 ROI				
Region 2 Revenues				
Region 2 Profits				
Region 2 ROI				
Product 1 Revenues				
Product 1 Profits				
Product 1 ROI				
Product 2 Revenues				
Product 2 Profits				
Product 2 ROI				

Some additional key questions that reveal the need for qualitative judgments in strategy evaluation are as follows:

1. How good is the firm's balance of investments between high-risk and low-risk projects?
2. How good is the firm's balance of investments between long-term and short-term projects?
3. How good is the firm's balance of investments between slow-growing markets and fast-growing markets?
4. How good is the firm's balance of investments among different divisions?
5. To what extent are the firm's alternative strategies socially responsible?
6. What are the relationships among the firm's key internal and external strategic factors?
7. How are major competitors likely to respond to particular strategies?

Taking Corrective Actions

The final strategy-evaluation activity, **taking corrective actions**, requires making changes to competitively reposition a firm for the future. As indicated in Table 11-4, examples of changes that may be needed are altering an organization's structure, replacing one or more key individuals, selling a division, or revising a business mission. Other changes could include establishing or revising objectives, devising new policies, issuing stock to raise capital, adding additional salespersons, differently allocating resources, or developing new performance incentives. Taking corrective actions does not necessarily mean that existing strategies will be abandoned or even that new strategies must be formulated.

The probabilities and possibilities for incorrect or inappropriate actions increase geometrically with an arithmetic increase in personnel. Any person directing an overall undertaking must check on the actions of the participants as well as the results they have achieved. If either the actions or results do not comply with preconceived or planned achievements, then corrective actions are needed.[6]

McDonald's is currently taking extensive corrective actions after recently reporting steep declines in its revenues and profits. A company spokesman said, "We will diligently work to enhance our marketing, simplify our menu, and implement a more locally driven organizational structure to increase relevance with consumers." In taking corrective actions, McDonald's recently fired a CEO, hired another CEO, shuffled its management ranks, created a new organizational structure, and revamped its menu.

TABLE 11-4 Corrective Actions Possibly Needed to Correct Unfavorable Variances

1. Alter the firm's structure.
2. Replace one or more key individuals.
3. Divest a division.
4. Alter the firm's vision or mission.
5. Revise objectives.
6. Alter strategies.
7. Devise new policies.
8. Install new performance incentives.
9. Raise capital with stock or debt.
10. Add or terminate salespersons, employees, or managers.
11. Allocate resources differently.
12. Outsource (or rein in) business functions.

No organization can survive as an island; no organization can escape change. Taking corrective actions is necessary to keep an organization on track toward achieving stated objectives. In his thought-provoking books *Future Shock* and *The Third Wave*, Alvin Toffler argued that business environments are becoming so dynamic and complex that they threaten people and organizations with **future shock,** which occurs when the nature, types, and speed of changes overpower an individual's or organization's ability and capacity to adapt. Strategy evaluation enhances an organization's ability to adapt successfully to changing circumstances.

Taking corrective actions raises employees' and managers' anxieties. Research suggests that participation in strategy-evaluation activities is one of the best ways to overcome individuals' resistance to change. According to Erez and Kanfer, individuals accept change best when they have a cognitive understanding of the changes, a sense of control over the situation, and an awareness that necessary actions are going to be taken to implement the changes.[7]

Strategy evaluation can lead to strategy-formulation and/or strategy-implementation changes, or no changes at all. Strategists cannot escape having to revise strategies and implementation approaches sooner or later. Hussey and Langham offered the following insight on taking corrective actions:

> Resistance to change is often emotionally based and not easily overcome by rational argument. Resistance may be based on such feelings as loss of status, implied criticism of present competence, fear of failure in the new situation, annoyance at not being consulted, lack of understanding of the need for change, or insecurity in changing from well-known and fixed methods. It is necessary, therefore, to overcome such resistance by creating situations of participation and full explanation when changes are envisaged.[8]

Corrective actions should place an organization in a better position to capitalize on internal strengths; to take advantage of key external opportunities; to avoid, reduce, or mitigate external threats; and to improve internal weaknesses. Corrective actions should have a proper time horizon and an appropriate amount of risk. They should be internally consistent and socially responsible. Perhaps most important, corrective actions strengthen an organization's competitive position in its basic industry. Continuous strategy evaluation keeps strategists close to the pulse of an organization and provides information needed for an effective strategic-management system. Carter Bayles described the benefits of strategy evaluation as follows:

> Evaluation activities may renew confidence in the current business strategy or point to the need for actions to correct some weaknesses, such as erosion of product superiority or technological edge. In many cases, the benefits of strategy evaluation are much more far-reaching, for the outcome of the process may be a fundamentally new strategy that will lead, even in a business that is already turning a respectable profit, to substantially increased earnings. It is this possibility that justifies strategy evaluation, for the payoff can be very large.[9]

The Balanced Scorecard

Do a Google search using the keywords *balanced scorecard images* and you will see more than 100 currently used balanced scorecards. Note the wide variation in format evidenced through the images. Developed in the early 1990s by Harvard Business School professors Robert Kaplan and David Norton, and refined continually through today, the **Balanced Scorecard** is a strategy evaluation and control technique. Balanced Scorecard derives its name from the perceived need of firms to "balance" financial measures that are oftentimes used exclusively in strategy evaluation and control with nonfinancial measures such as product quality and customer service. An effective Balanced Scorecard contains a carefully chosen combination of strategic and financial objectives tailored to the company's business.

As a tool to manage and evaluate strategy, the Balanced Scorecard is currently in use at Sears, United Parcel Service, 3M Corporation, Heinz, and hundreds of other firms. For example, 3M Corporation has a financial objective to achieve annual growth in earnings per share of 10 percent or better, as well as a strategic objective to have at least 30 percent of sales come from products introduced in the past four years. The overall aim of the Balanced Scorecard is to "balance" shareholder objectives with customer and operational objectives. Obviously, these sets of objectives interrelate and many even conflict. For example, customers want low price and high service, which may conflict with shareholders' desire for a high return on their investment. The Balanced Scorecard concept is consistent with the notions of continuous improvement in management (CIM) and total quality management (TQM).

The Balanced Scorecard basic premise is that firms should establish objectives and evaluate strategies on criteria other than financial measures. Financial measures and ratios are vitally important in strategic planning, but of equal importance are factors such as customer service, employee morale, product quality, pollution abatement, business ethics, social responsibility, community involvement, and other such items. In conjunction with financial measures, these "softer" factors comprise an integral part of both the objective-setting process and the strategy-evaluation process. A Balanced Scorecard for a firm is simply a listing of all key objectives to work toward, along with an associated time dimension of when each objective is to be accomplished, as well as a primary responsibility or contact person, department, or division for each objective.

The Balanced Scorecard is an important strategy-evaluation tool that allows firms to evaluate strategies from four perspectives: financial performance, customer knowledge, internal business processes, and learning and growth. Its analysis requires that firms seek answers to the following questions and use that information, in conjunction with financial measures, to adequately and more effectively evaluate strategies being implemented:

1. Is the firm continually improving and creating value along measures such as innovation, technological leadership, product quality, operational process efficiencies, and so on?
2. Is the firm sustaining and even improving on its core competencies and competitive advantages?
3. How satisfied are the firm's customers?

A sample Balanced Scorecard is provided in Table 11-5. Notice that the firm examines six key issues in evaluating its strategies: (1) Customers, (2) Managers/Employees, (3) Operations/Processes, (4) Community/Social Responsibility, (5) Business Ethics/Natural Environment, and (6) Financial. The basic form of a Balanced Scorecard may differ for different organizations. The Balanced Scorecard approach to strategy evaluation aims to balance long-term with short-term concerns, to balance financial with nonfinancial concerns, and to balance internal with external concerns. The Balanced Scorecard would be constructed differently—that is, adapted to particular firms in various industries with the underlying theme or thrust being the same, which is to evaluate the firm's strategies based on both key quantitative and qualitative measures.

The Balanced Scorecard Institute has a Certification Program that includes two levels of certification: Balanced Scorecard Master Professional (BSMP) and Balanced Scorecard Professional (BSP), both of which are offered in association with George Washington University and are achievable through public workshop participation. The website for this program is http://www.balancedscorecard.org/

The Graphic Communications Group Limited (GCGL), Ghana's leading print media organization, recently adopted the Balanced Scorecard to monitor quantitative and qualitative targets set by itself and its staff. A recent article reports that the Balanced Scorecard is used by 65 percent of

TABLE 11-5 An Example Balanced Scorecard

Area of Objectives	Measure or Target	Time Expectation	Primary Responsibility
Customers			
1.			
2.			
3.			
4.			
Managers/Employees			
1.			
2.			
3.			
4.			
Operations/Processes			
1.			
2.			
3.			
4.			
Community/Social Responsibility			
1.			
2.			
3.			
4.			
Business Ethics/Natural Environment			
1.			
2.			
3.			
4.			
Financial			
1.			
2.			
3.			
4.			

Fortune 500 companies.[10] Other companies using the Balanced Scorecard in Ghana are the Social Security and National Insurance Thrust (SSNIT), the Volta River Authority (VRA), Electricity Company of Ghana (ECG), and the Ghana Revenue Authority (GRA). The Managing Director of GCGL, Mr. Kenneth Ashigbey, sees the Balanced Scorecard as a roadmap that will help his company connect its strategy to its vision. The vision of the GCGL "to become the dominant multimedia group in West Africa, telling the African story." Along with adopting the Balanced Scorecard system, GCGL's mission was rewritten "to empower our audience and customers everywhere with authentic information and excellent products through visionary leadership and strong brands." Ashigbey says with the introduction of the Balanced Scorecard, the ultimate objective of GCGL is "to be a leading and top-of-the-mind multimedia company in English-speaking West Africa by 2017." He also says about the BSC: "We will maintain our leadership position in print media and become one of the top three multimedia organizations in terms of circulation, audience reach, advert spend and sales revenue." Ashigbey refers to the Balanced Scorecard as "a tool for employees to understand how their respective day-to-day work contributes to the company's success." As part of the Balanced Scorecard, GCGL set for itself eight core values, which include leadership in all that it does, exhibition of high level of professionalism and integrity, commitment to excellence, customer focus, and working as a team. The firm also set four strategic themes: business growth, operational excellence, service excellence, and innovation.

CHAPTER 11 • STRATEGY MONITORING

Published Sources of Strategy-Evaluation Information

Sydney Finkelstein, professor of management at the Tuck School of Business at Dartmouth, annually releases his list of the worst CEOs each year.[11] For the year 2014, Finkelstein reported that among the worst CEOs were Dick Costolo, CEO of Twitter; Eddie Lampert, CEO of Sears Holdings; Phillip Clarke, CEO of Tesco, a British supermarket chain; Dov Charney, CEO of American Apparel; and Ricardo Espírito Santo Silva Salgado, CEO of Banco Espírito, the second largest bank in Portugal.

A number of publications are helpful in evaluating a firm's strategies. For example, *Fortune* annually identifies and evaluates the Fortune 1000 (the largest manufacturers) and the Fortune 50 (the largest retailers, transportation companies, utilities, banks, insurance companies, and diversified financial corporations in the United States). *Fortune* ranks the best and worst performers on various factors, such as return on investment, sales volume, and profitability. Annually, the publication publishes its strategy-evaluation research in an article titled "World's Most Admired Companies." Nine key attributes serve as evaluative criteria: people management, innovativeness, products quality, financial soundness, social responsibility, use of assets, long-term investment, global competitiveness, and quality of management. *Fortune's* 2014 evaluation in Table 11-6 reveals the most admired companies.

Businessweek, Industry Week, and *Dun's Business Month* periodically publish detailed evaluations of U.S. businesses and industries. Although published sources of strategy-evaluation information focus primarily on large, publicly held businesses, the comparative ratios and related information are widely used to evaluate small businesses and privately owned firms as well.

Characteristics of an Effective Strategy Evaluation System

The strategy-evaluation process must exhibit several characteristics to be effective. First, strategy-evaluation activities must be economical; too much information can be just as bad as too little information, and too many controls can do more harm than good. Strategy-evaluation activities also should be meaningful; they should specifically relate to a firm's objectives. They should

TABLE 11-6 Fortune's 20 Most Admired Companies in 2014

1. Apple
2. Amazon.com
3. Google
4. Berkshire Hathaway
5. Starbucks
6. Coca-Cola
7. Walt Disney
8. FedEx
9. Southwest Airlines
10. General Electric
11. American Express
12. Costco Wholesale
13. Nike
14. BMW
15. Procter & Gamble
16. IBM
17. Nordstrom
18. Singapore Airlines
19. Johnson & Johnson
20. Whole Foods Market

Source: Based on information at http://www.haygroup.com/ww/best_companies/index.aspx?id=155

provide managers with useful information about tasks over which they have control and influence. Strategy-evaluation activities should provide timely information; on occasion and in some areas, managers may need information on a daily or even continuous basis. For example, when a firm has diversified by acquiring another firm, evaluative information may be needed frequently. In contrast, in an R&D department, daily or even weekly evaluative information could be dysfunctional. Approximate information that is timely is generally more desirable as a basis for strategy evaluation than accurate information that does not depict the present. Frequent measurement and rapid reporting may frustrate control rather than give better control. The time dimension of control must coincide with the time span of the event being measured.

Strategy-evaluation processes should be designed to provide a true picture of what is happening. For example, in a severe economic downturn, productivity and profitability ratios may drop alarmingly, although employees and managers are actually working harder. Strategy evaluations should fairly portray this type of situation. Information derived from the strategy-evaluation process should facilitate action and should be directed to those individuals in the organization who need to take action based on it. Managers commonly ignore evaluative reports that are provided only for informational purposes; not all managers need to receive all reports. Controls need to be action-oriented rather than information-oriented. The strategy-evaluation process should not dominate decisions; it should foster mutual understanding, trust, and common sense. No department should fail to cooperate with another in evaluating strategies. Strategy evaluations should be simple, not too cumbersome, and not too restrictive. Complex strategy-evaluation systems often confuse people and accomplish little. The test of an effective evaluation system is its usefulness, not its complexity.

Large organizations require a more elaborate and detailed strategy-evaluation system because it is more difficult to coordinate efforts among different divisions and functional areas. Managers in small companies often communicate daily with each other and their employees and do not need extensive evaluative reporting systems. Familiarity with local environments usually makes gathering and evaluating information much easier for small organizations than for large businesses. But the key to an effective strategy-evaluation system may be the ability to convince participants that failure to accomplish certain objectives within a prescribed time is not necessarily a reflection of their performance.

There is no one ideal strategy-evaluation system. The unique aspects of an organization, including its size, management style, purpose, problems, and strengths, can determine a strategy-evaluation and control system's final design. Robert Waterman offered the following observation about successful organizations' strategy-evaluation and control systems:

> Successful companies treat facts as friends and controls as liberating. Morgan Guaranty and Wells Fargo not only survive but thrive in the troubled waters of bank deregulation, because their strategy evaluation and control systems are sound, their risk is contained, and they know themselves and the competitive situation so well. Successful companies have a voracious hunger for facts. They see information where others see only data. Successful companies maintain tight, accurate financial controls. Their people don't regard controls as an imposition of autocracy but as the benign checks and balances that allow them to be creative and free.[12]

Contingency Planning

A basic premise of good strategic management is that firms strive to be proactive, planning ways to deal with unfavorable and favorable events before they occur. Too many organizations prepare contingency plans just for unfavorable events; this is a mistake, because both minimizing threats and capitalizing on opportunities can improve a firm's competitive position.

Regardless of how carefully strategies are formulated, implemented, and evaluated, unforeseen events, such as strikes, boycotts, natural disasters, arrival of foreign competitors, and government actions, can make a strategy obsolete. To minimize the impact of potential threats, organizations should develop contingency plans as part of their strategy-evaluation process. **Contingency plans** can be defined as alternative plans that can be put into effect if certain key events do not occur as expected. Only high-priority areas require the insurance of contingency plans. Strategists cannot and should not try to cover all bases by planning for all possible contingencies. But in any case, contingency plans should be as simple as possible.

Some contingency plans commonly established by firms include the following:

1. If a major competitor withdraws from particular markets as intelligence reports indicate, what actions should our firm take?
2. If our sales objectives are not reached, what actions should our firm take to avoid profit losses?
3. If demand for our new product exceeds plans, what actions should our firm take to meet the higher demand?
4. If certain disasters occur—such as loss of computer capabilities; a hostile takeover attempt; loss of patent protection; or destruction of manufacturing facilities because of earthquakes, tornadoes, or hurricanes—what actions should our firm take?
5. If a new technological advancement makes our new product obsolete sooner than expected, what actions should our firm take?

Too many organizations discard alternative strategies not selected for implementation although the work devoted to analyzing these options would render valuable information. Alternative strategies not selected for implementation can serve as contingency plans in case the strategy or strategies selected do not work. When strategy-evaluation activities reveal the need for a major change quickly, an appropriate contingency plan can be executed in a timely way. Contingency plans can promote a strategist's ability to respond quickly to key changes in the internal and external bases of an organization's current strategy. For example, if underlying assumptions about the economy turn out to be wrong and contingency plans are ready, then managers can make appropriate changes promptly. Sometimes, external or internal conditions present unexpected opportunities. When such opportunities occur, contingency plans could allow an organization to quickly capitalize on them. Linneman and Chandran report that contingency planning gives users, such as DuPont, Dow Chemical, Consolidated Foods, and Emerson Electric, three major benefits, as follows:

1. It enables quick responses to change.
2. It prevents panic in crisis situations.
3. It makes managers more adaptable by encouraging them to appreciate just how variable the future can be.

In addition, Linneman and Chandran suggest that effective contingency planning involves a five-step process, as follows:

1. Identify both good and bad events that could jeopardize strategies.
2. Determine when the good and bad events are likely to occur.
3. Determine the expected pros and cons of each contingency event.
4. Develop contingency plans for key contingency events.
5. Determine early warning trigger points for key contingency events.[13]

Auditing

A frequently used tool in strategy evaluation is the audit. **Auditing** is defined by the American Accounting Association (AAA) as "a systematic process of objectively obtaining and evaluating evidence regarding assertions about economic actions and events to ascertain the degree of correspondence between these assertions and established criteria, and communicating the results to interested users."[14]

Auditors examine the financial statements of firms to determine whether they have been prepared according to **generally accepted accounting principles (GAAP)** and whether they fairly represent the activities of the firm. Independent auditors use a set of standards called **generally accepted auditing standards (GAAS).** Public accounting firms often have a consulting arm that provides strategy-evaluation services.

The new era of **international financial reporting standards (IFRS)** is approaching in the United States, and businesses need to go ahead and get ready to use IFRS. Many U.S. companies now report their finances using both the old GAAP and the new IFRS. "If companies don't prepare, if they don't start three years in advance," warns business professor Donna Street at the University of Dayton, "they're going to be in big trouble." The GAAP standards are comprised of 25,000 pages, whereas the IFRS comprises only 5,000 pages, so in that sense IFRS is less cumbersome.

This accounting switch from GAAP to IFRS in the United States will cost businesses millions of dollars in fees and upgraded software systems and training. Certified public accountants in the United States need to study global accounting principles, and business schools should go ahead and begin teaching students the new accounting standards. Most large accounting firms and multinational firms favor the switch to IFRS, saying it will simplify accounting, make it easier for investors to compare firms across countries, and make it easier to raise capital globally. But many smaller firms oppose the upcoming change, believing it will be too costly; some firms are uneasy about the idea of giving an international body the authority to write accounting rules for the United States. Some firms also would pay higher taxes because last in, first out (LIFO) inventory methods are not allowed under IFRS. The International Accounting Standards Board (IASB) has publicly expressed "regret" over the slowness in the United States of adopting IFRS.

The U.S. Chamber of Commerce supports a change, saying it will lead to much more cross-border commerce and will help the United States compete in the world economy. Already the European Union and 113 nations have adopted or soon plan to use international rules, including Australia, China, India, Mexico, and Canada. So, the United States is likely to adopt IFRS rules, but this switch could unleash a legal and regulatory nightmare. A few U.S. multinational firms already use IFRS for their foreign subsidiaries, such as United Technologies (UT), which derives more than 60 percent of its revenues from abroad and is already training its entire staff to use IFRS.

Movement to IFRS from GAAP encompasses a company's entire operations, including auditing, oversight, cash management, taxes, technology, software, investing, acquiring, merging, importing, exporting, pension planning, and partnering. Switching from GAAP to IFRS is also likely to be plagued by gaping differences in business customs, financial regulations, tax laws, politics, and other factors. One critic of the upcoming switch is Charles Niemeier of the Public Company Accounting Oversight Board, who says the switch "has the potential to be a Tower of Babel," costing firms millions when they do not even have thousands to spend.

Others say the switch will help U.S. companies raise capital abroad and do business with firms abroad. Perhaps the biggest upside of the switch is that IFRS rules are more streamlined and less complex than GAAP. Lenovo is a big advocate of IFRS, as it desires to be a world company rather than a U.S. or Chinese company, so the faster the switch to IFRS, the better for them. The bottom line is that IFRS is coming to the United States, likely sooner rather than later.

Twenty-First-Century Challenges in Strategic Management

Three particular challenges or decisions that face all strategists today are (1) deciding whether the process should be more an art or a science, (2) deciding whether strategies should be visible or hidden from stakeholders, and (3) deciding whether the process should be more top-down or bottom-up in their firm.[15]

The Art or Science Issue

This book is consistent with most of the strategy literature in advocating that strategic management be viewed more as a science than an art. This perspective contends that firms need to systematically assess their external and internal environments, conduct research, carefully evaluate the pros and cons of various alternatives, perform analyses, and then decide on a particular course of action. In contrast, Mintzberg's notion of "crafting" strategies embodies the artistic model, which suggests that strategic decision making be based primarily on holistic thinking, intuition, creativity, and imagination.[16] Mintzberg and his followers reject strategies that result from objective analysis, preferring instead subjective imagination. "Strategy scientists" reject strategies that emerge from emotion, hunch, creativity, and politics. Proponents of the artistic view often consider strategic planning exercises to be time poorly spent. The Mintzberg philosophy insists on informality, whereas strategy scientists (and this text) insist on more formality.

Mintzberg refers to strategic planning as an "emergent" process, whereas strategy scientists use the term *deliberate* process.[17]

The answer to the art-versus-science question is one that strategists must decide for themselves, and certainly the two approaches are not mutually exclusive. The CEO of Williams-Sonoma, Laura Alber, recently stated, "I've found that the very best solutions arise from a willingness to blend art with science, ideas with data, and instinct with analysis." In deciding which approach is more effective, however, consider that the business world today has become increasingly complex and more intensely competitive. There is less room for error in strategic planning. Recall that Chapter 1 discussed the importance of intuition, experience, and subjectivity in strategic planning, and even the weights and ratings discussed in Chapters 6, 7, and 8 certainly require good judgment. But the idea of deciding on strategies for any firm without thorough research and analysis, at least in the mind of these authors, is unwise. Certainly, in smaller firms there can be more informality in the process compared to larger firms, but even for smaller firms, a wealth of competitive information is available on the Internet and elsewhere and should be collected, assimilated, and evaluated before deciding on a course of action on which survival of the firm may hinge. The livelihood of countless employees and shareholders may hinge on the effectiveness of strategies selected. Too much is at stake to be less than thorough in formulating strategies. It is not wise for a strategist to rely too heavily on gut feeling and opinion instead of research data, competitive intelligence, and analysis in formulating strategies.

The Visible or Hidden Issue

An interesting aspect of any competitive analysis discussion is whether strategies themselves should be secret or open within firms. The Chinese warrior Sun Tzu and military leaders today strive to keep strategies secret, because war is based on deception. But for business organizations, secrecy may not be best. Keeping strategies secret from employees and stakeholders at large could severely inhibit employee and stakeholder communication, understanding, and commitment, as well as forgo valuable input that these persons could have regarding formulation or implementation of that strategy. Thus, strategists in a particular firm must decide for themselves whether the risk of rival firms easily knowing and exploiting a firm's strategies is worth the benefit of improved employee and stakeholder motivation and input. Most executives agree that some strategic information should remain confidential to top managers, and that steps should be taken to ensure that such information is not disseminated beyond the inner circle. For a firm that you may own or manage, would you advocate openness or secrecy in regard to strategies being formulated and implemented?

There are certainly good reasons to keep the strategy process and strategies themselves visible and open rather than hidden and secret. There are also good reasons to keep strategies hidden from all but top-level executives. Strategists must decide for themselves what is best for their firms. This text comes down largely on the side of being visible and open, but certainly this may not be best for all strategists and all firms. As pointed out in Chapter 1, Sun Tzu argued that all war is based on deception and that the best maneuvers are those not easily predicted by rivals. Business and war are analogous in many respects.

Four reasons to be completely open with the strategy process and resultant decisions are these:

1. Managers, employees, and other stakeholders can readily contribute to the process. They often have excellent ideas. Secrecy would forgo many excellent ideas.
2. Investors, creditors, and other stakeholders have greater basis for supporting a firm when they know what the firm is doing and where the firm is going.
3. Visibility promotes democracy, whereas secrecy promotes autocracy. Domestic firms and most foreign firms prefer democracy over autocracy as a management style.
4. Participation and openness enhance understanding, commitment, and communication within the firm.

However, four reasons why some firms prefer to conduct strategic planning in secret and keep strategies hidden from all but the highest-level executives are as follows:

1. Free dissemination of a firm's strategies may easily translate into competitive intelligence for rival firms who could exploit the firm given that information.
2. Secrecy limits criticism, second guessing, and hindsight.
3. Participants in a visible strategy process become more attractive to rival firms who may lure them away.
4. Secrecy limits rival firms from imitating or duplicating the firm's strategies and undermining the firm.

The obvious benefits of the visible versus hidden extremes suggest that a working balance must be sought between the apparent contradictions. Parnell says that in a perfect world all key individuals both inside and outside the firm should be involved in strategic planning, but in practice, particularly sensitive and confidential information should always remain strictly confidential to top managers.[18] This balancing act is difficult but essential for survival of the firm.

The Top-Down or Bottom-Up Approach

Proponents of the top-down approach contend that top executives are the only persons in the firm with the collective experience, acumen, and fiduciary responsibility to make key strategy decisions. In contrast, bottom-up advocates argue that lower- and middle-level managers and employees who will be implementing the strategies need to be actively involved in the process of formulating the strategies to ensure their support and commitment. Recent strategy research and this text emphasize the bottom-up approach, but earlier work by Schendel and Hofer stressed the need for firms to rely on perceptions of their top managers in strategic planning.[19] Strategists must reach a working balance of the two approaches in a manner deemed best for their firms at a particular time, while being cognizant of the fact that current research supports the bottom-up approach, at least among U.S. firms. Increased education and diversity of the workforce at all levels are reasons why middle- and lower-level managers—and even nonmanagers—should be invited to participate in the firm's strategic planning process, at least to the extent that they are willing and able to contribute.

Guidelines for Effective Strategic Management

Failing to follow certain guidelines in conducting strategic management can foster criticisms of the process and create problems for the organization. Issues such as "Is strategic management in our firm a people process or a paper process?" should be addressed. Some organizations spend an inordinate amount of time developing a strategic plan, but then fail to follow through with effective implementation. Change and results in a firm come through implementation, not through formulation, although effective formulation is critically important for successful implementation. Continual evaluation of strategies is also essential because the world changes so rapidly that existing strategies can need modifying often.

Strategic management must not become a self-perpetuating bureaucratic mechanism. Rather, it must be a self-reflective learning process that familiarizes managers and employees in the organization with key strategic issues and feasible alternatives for resolving those issues. Strategic management must not become ritualistic, stilted, orchestrated, or too formal, predictable, and rigid. Words supported by numbers, rather than numbers supported by words, should represent the medium for explaining strategic issues and organizational responses. A key role of strategists is to facilitate continuous organizational learning and change.

R. T. Lenz offers six guidelines for effective strategic management:

1. Keep the process simple and easily understandable.
2. Eliminate vague planning jargon.
3. Keep the process nonroutine; vary assignments, team membership, meeting formats, settings, and even the planning calendar.
4. Welcome bad news and encourage devil's advocate thinking.

5. Do not allow technicians to monopolize the planning process.

6. To the extent possible, involve managers from all areas of the firm.[20]

An important guideline for effective strategic management is open-mindedness. A willingness and eagerness to consider new information, new viewpoints, new ideas, and new possibilities is essential; all organizational members must share a spirit of inquiry and learning. Strategists such as chief executive officers, presidents, owners of small businesses, and heads of government agencies must commit themselves to listen to and understand managers' positions well enough to be able to restate those positions to the managers' satisfaction. In addition, managers and employees throughout the firm should be able to describe the strategists' positions to the satisfaction of the strategists. This degree of discipline will promote understanding and learning.

No organization has unlimited resources. No firm can take on an unlimited amount of debt or issue an unlimited amount of stock to raise capital. Therefore, no organization can pursue all the strategies that potentially could benefit the firm. Strategic decisions, then, always have to be made to eliminate some courses of action and to allocate organizational resources among others. Most organizations can afford to pursue only a few corporate-level strategies at any given time. It is a critical mistake for managers to pursue too many strategies at the same time, thereby spreading the firm's resources so thin that all strategies are jeopardized.

Strategic decisions require trade-offs such as long-range versus short-range considerations or maximizing profits versus increasing shareholders' wealth. There are ethics issues, too. Strategy trade-offs require subjective judgments and preferences. In many cases, a lack of objectivity in formulating strategy results in a loss of competitive posture and profitability. Most organizations today recognize that strategic-management concepts and techniques can enhance the effectiveness of decisions. Subjective factors such as attitudes toward risk, concern for social responsibility, and organizational culture will always affect strategy-formulation decisions, but organizations need to be as objective as possible in considering qualitative factors. Table 11-7 summarizes important guidelines for the strategic-planning process to be effective.

TABLE 11-7 Seventeen Guidelines for the Strategic-Planning Process to Be Effective

1. It should be a people process more than a paper process.

2. It should be a learning process for all managers and employees.

3. It should be words supported by numbers rather than numbers supported by words.

4. It should be simple and nonroutine.

5. It should vary assignments, team memberships, meeting formats, and even the planning calendar.

6. It should challenge the assumptions underlying the current corporate strategy.

7. It should welcome bad news.

8. It should welcome open-mindedness and a spirit of inquiry and learning.

9. It should not be a bureaucratic mechanism.

10. It should not become ritualistic, stilted, or orchestrated.

11. It should not be too formal, predictable, or rigid.

12. It should not contain jargon or arcane planning language.

13. It should not be a formal system for control.

14. It should not disregard qualitative information.

15. It should not be controlled by "technicians."

16. Do not pursue too many strategies at once.

17. Continually strengthen the "good ethics is good business" policy.

IMPLICATIONS FOR STRATEGISTS

Figure 11-3 reveals on the far left that strategists must systematically, continuously, and carefully evaluate and monitor results by product, region, territory, segment, store, department, and even by individual, so that timely corrective actions can be taken to keep the firm on track. Quarterly, weekly, and even daily, companies have to adapt to changes that occur externally and internally, because even the best strategic plan needs periodic adjusting as rival firms adjust and launch new initiatives and products in new areas. As described in this chapter, the balanced scorecard is widely used by strategists to help manage the strategy evaluation process.

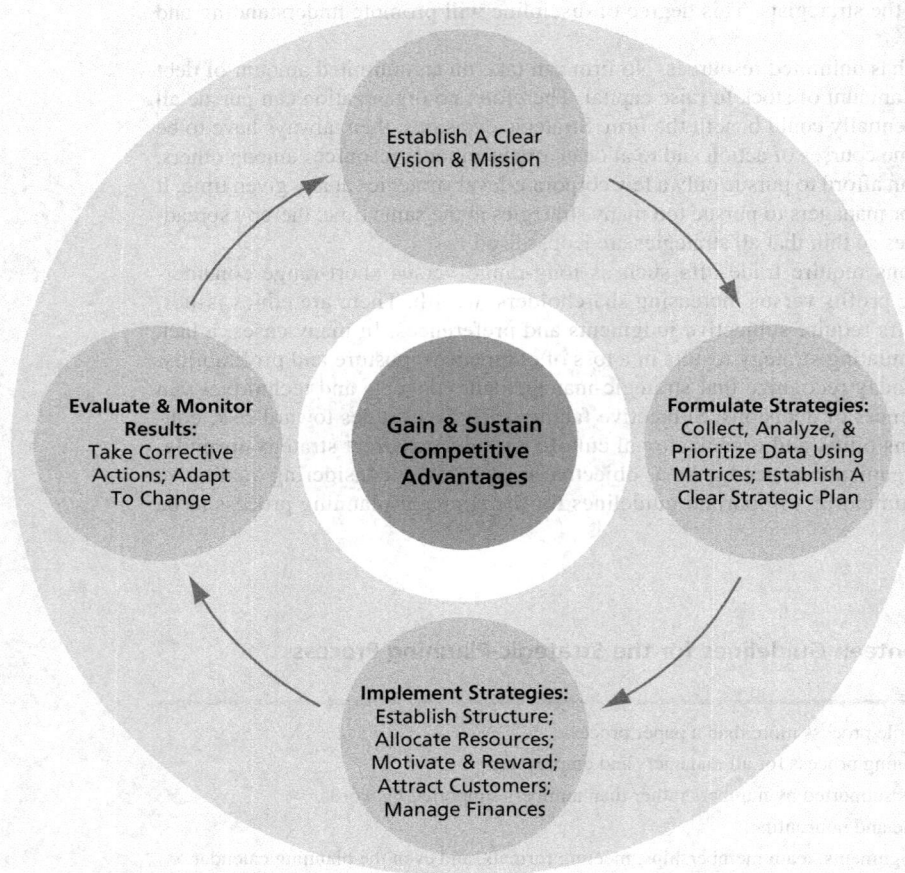

Establish A Clear Vision & Mission

Formulate Strategies: Collect, Analyze, & Prioritize Data Using Matrices; Establish A Clear Strategic Plan

Gain & Sustain Competitive Advantages

Implement Strategies: Establish Structure; Allocate Resources; Motivate & Reward; Attract Customers; Manage Finances

Evaluate & Monitor Results: Take Corrective Actions; Adapt To Change

FIGURE 11-3
How to Gain and Sustain Competitive Advantages

IMPLICATIONS FOR STUDENTS

In performing your case analysis, develop and present a Balanced Scorecard that you recommend to help your firm monitor and evaluate progress toward stated objectives. Effective, timely evaluation of strategies can enable a firm to adapt quickly to changing conditions, and a Balanced Scorecard can assist in this endeavor. Couch your discussion of the Balanced Scorecard in terms of competitive advantage versus rival firms.

Chapter Summary

Effective strategy evaluation allows an organization to capitalize on internal strengths as they develop, to exploit external opportunities as they emerge, to recognize and defend against threats, and to mitigate internal weaknesses before they become detrimental.

Strategists in successful organizations take the time to formulate, implement, and then evaluate strategies deliberately and systematically. Good strategists move their organization forward with purpose and direction, continually evaluating and improving the firm's external and internal strategic positions. Strategy evaluation allows an organization to shape its own future rather than allowing it to be constantly shaped by remote forces that have little or no vested interest in the well-being of the enterprise.

Although not a guarantee for success, strategic management allows organizations to make effective long-term decisions, to execute those decisions efficiently, and to take corrective actions as needed to ensure success. Computer networks and the Internet help to coordinate strategic-management activities and to ensure that decisions are based on good information. A key to effective strategy evaluation and to successful strategic management is an integration of intuition and analysis:

A potentially fatal problem is the tendency for analytical and intuitive issues to polarize. This polarization leads to strategy evaluation that is dominated by either analysis or intuition, or to strategy evaluation that is discontinuous, with a lack of coordination among analytical and intuitive issues.[21] Strategists in successful organizations realize that strategic management is first and foremost a people process. It is an excellent vehicle for fostering organizational communication. People are what make the difference in organizations.

The real key to effective strategic management is to accept the premise that the planning process is more important than the written plan, that the manager is continuously planning and does not stop planning when the written plan is finished. The written plan is only a snapshot as of the moment it is approved. If the manager is not planning on a continuous basis—planning, measuring, and revising—the written plan can become obsolete the day it is finished. This obsolescence becomes more of a certainty as the increasingly rapid rate of change makes the business environment more uncertain.[22]

Key Terms and Concepts

advantage (p. 362)
auditing (p. 373)
Balanced Scorecard (p. 369)
consistency (p. 362)
consonance (p. 362)
contingency plans (p. 372)
feasibility (p. 362)
future shock (p. 368)
generally accepted accounting principles (GAAP) (p. 373)

generally accepted auditing standards (GAAS) (p. 373)
international financial reporting standards (IFRS) (p. 373)
measuring organizational performance (p. 366)
reviewing the underlying bases of an organization's strategy (p. 364)
revised EFE Matrix (p. 364)
revised IFE Matrix (p. 364)
taking corrective actions (p. 367)

Issues for Review and Discussion

11-1. BHP Billiton has been very successful in the last decade. What is the major reason for its success?

11-2. Visit BHP Billiton's website and evaluate the firm's strategies, which are currently being implemented.

11-3. Discuss the nature and implications of the upcoming accounting switch from GAAP to IFRS in the United States.

⭐ **11-4.** Ask an accounting professor at your college or university the following question and report back to the class—"To what extent would my learning the IFRS standards on my own give me a competitive advantage in the job market?"

⭐ **11-5.** Give an example of "consonance," other than the one provided by Rumelt in this chapter.

11-6. "Evaluating strategies on a continuous rather than a periodic basis is desired." Discuss the pros and cons of this statement.

11-7. How often should an organization's vision or mission be changed, in light of strategy evaluation activities?

11-8. Compare Mintzberg's notion of "crafting" strategies with the notion of "gathering and assimilating information" to formulate strategies, mentioned in this book.

11-9. Do you believe strategic management is more of an art or science? Explain.

11-10. Do you feel strategic management should be more a top-down or bottom-up process in a firm? Briefly explain your answer.

11-11. Do you think strategic management should be more visible or hidden, as a process in a firm? Explain.

11-12. Develop a balanced scorecard for BHP Billiton.

11-13. Develop a Balanced Scorecard for your college or university.

11-14. Discuss contingency planning.

11-15. Identify some important financial ratios, which are useful in evaluating a firm's strategies.

⭐ **11-16.** How often should a firm formally evaluate its strategies?

11-17. Under what conditions are corrective actions not required in the strategy-evaluation process?

11-18. Define and discuss auditing as it relates to strategy evaluation.

11-19. List 10 characteristics of an effective evaluation system.

⭐ **11-20.** Go to *Fortune* magazine's website and identify several firms nearest you that are listed among the most admired companies in the world according to *Fortune*.

⭐ **11-21.** Ask the dean of your school to describe how their department evaluates strategies. Present your findings to the class.

11-22. Identify four firms that provide their strategic plans on their websites, and four that do not. Should firms do this? Explain your answer.

⭐ **11-23.** About what percent of Fortune 500 companies use a Balanced Scorecard?

⭐ **11-24.** Among Fortune's most admired company list for 2015, what two companies made the list that are headquartered outside the USA?

⭐ **11-25.** To what extent do you prefer the art versus science approach to developing strategies for a company?

ASSURANCE OF LEARNING EXERCISES

EXERCISE 11A
Evaluate BHP Billiton's Strategies

Purpose

BHP Billiton is featured in the opening chapter case as a firm that engages in excellent strategic planning. BHP is an Anglo-Australian multinational mining and petroleum company headquartered in Perth, Australia. BHP also has major offices in London. BHP is arguably the world's largest mining company and among the top ten largest companies in the world measured by market capitalization. BHP is among the world's top producers of iron ore, coal, aluminum, copper, manganese, nickel, silver, uranium, and potash. BHP also has crude oil and natural gas holdings. BHP may soon divest its diamond assets. This exercise can give you practice evaluating a company's strategies.

Instructions

Step 1	Go to BHP Billiton's website and navigate to the Investors & Media section. Review recent news releases for BHP Billiton.
Step 2	Determine what new strategies BHP is pursuing.
Step 3	Evaluate BHP's newest strategies based on concepts presented in Chapter 2.
Step 4	Prepare a strategy evaluation report for BHP.

EXERCISE 11B
Prepare a Strategy-Evaluation Report for Nestlé S.A.

Purpose

This exercise can give you experience locating strategy-evaluation information. Use of the Internet coupled with published sources of information can significantly enhance the strategy-evaluation process. Performance information on competitors, for example, can help put into perspective a firm's own performance.

Instructions

Step 1	Search the Internet for information on Nestlé. Prepare a strategy-evaluation report for your instructor. Include in your report a summary of Nestlé's strategies and performance in 2015 and a summary of your conclusions regarding the effectiveness of Nestlé's strategies.
Step 2	Based on your analysis, do you feel that Nestlé is pursuing effective strategies? What recommendations would you offer to Nestlé's chief executive officer?

EXERCISE 11C
Prepare a Balanced Scorecard for Nestlé S.A.

Purpose

This exercise can give you experience developing a Balanced Scorecard for a corporation.

Instructions

Step 1	Compile all information that you have collected on Nestlé.
Step 2	Join with three other students in class. Jointly develop a 20-item Balanced Scorecard for the company.
Step 3	Appoint a spokesperson for your team to give a three-minute overview to the class regarding the substance of your Balanced Scorecard.

EXERCISE 11D
Evaluate Your University's Strategies

Purpose

An important part of evaluating strategies is determining the nature and extent of changes in an organization's external opportunities and threats as well as internal strengths and weaknesses. Changes in these underlying key factors can indicate a need to change or modify the firm's strategies.

Instructions

As a class, discuss positive and negative changes in your university's external and internal factors during your college career. Begin by listing on the board new or emerging opportunities and threats. Then identify strengths and weaknesses that have changed significantly during your college career. In light of the external and internal changes that were identified, discuss whether your university's strategies need modifying. Are there any new strategies that you would recommend? Make a list to recommend to your department chair, dean, president, or chancellor.

MINI-CASE ON BROADCOM LIMITED (AVGO)

HOW COULD A BALANCED SCORECARD BENEFIT BROADCOM?

Source: © asharkyu. Shutterstock

Jointly headquartered in San Jose, California, and Singapore, Broadcom Technologies (earlier known as Avago Technologies) designs, develops, and supplies analogue, digital, and optoelectronics components and systems. In May 2015, Avago had announced its plans to acquire Broadcom Technologies for $37 billion (a combination of $17 billion cash and $20 billion in shares). This acquisition significantly increased Broadcom's patent position in sectors like communication technologies, making it the ninth largest patent-holder in semiconductor vendor's category. Broadcom's varied product portfolio has four target markets, including wireless communications, enterprise storage, wired infrastructure, and industrial.

In August 2015, Broadcom announced the release of products—40G bidirectional (BiDi) multimode fiber (MMF) QSFP + transceiver module, and the AFBR-79EBPZ—that were designed for high-speed data center interconnect and networking applications. Broadcom provided a cost-effective solution to upgrade Ethernet in the data center with its 40 GbE links on existing LC duplex multimode fiber.

In October 2015, Broadcom Technologies released an industry-first new multi-reader HDD read channel in silicon, supporting product development of next-generation HDD controllers with high-performance data rates and enabling Array Reader Magnetic Recording (ARMR) to provide densities greater than 1.3 Tb/in^2. Capacity gains enabled by the HDD read channels are almost 10 times more than the previous generation channel technologies. In addition to this, the new technology is more cost-effective than the previous single-reader HDD system on chips (SoCs); the new technology doesn't have any performance limitations, making it ideal for deploying in all HDD enterprise and consumer markets.

Questions

1. On Broadcom's website, under the leadership section, the company reveals its top executives. A balanced scorecard sometimes examines the number of men versus women in the hierarchy. What is the breakdown for Broadcom? Is this good management? Are there minorities represented?

2. From the corporate website, assess the extent that Broadcom does an effective job evaluating strategies.

Source: Based on company documents.

Current Readings

DaSilva, Carlos M., and Peter Trkman. "Business Model: What It Is and What It Is Not." *Long Range Planning* 47, issue 6 (December 2014): 379–389.

Drummond, Helga. "Escalation of Commitment: When to Stay the Course?" *Academy of Management Perspectives* 28 (November 2014): 430–446.

Kownatzki, Maximilian, et al. "Corporate Control and the Speed of Strategic Business Unit Decision Making." *Academy of Management Journal* 56, no. 5 (2013): 1295–1324.

Endnotes

1. Based on information at http://finance.yahoo.com/news/america-worst-companies-152240176.html

2. Dale McConkey, "Planning in a Changing Environment," *Business Horizons* (September–October 1988): 64.

3. Robert Simons, "Control in an Age of Empowerment," *Harvard Business Review* (March–April 1995), 80.

4. Dale Zand, "Reviewing the Policy Process," *California Management Review* 21, no. 1 (Fall 1978): 37.

5. Ecclesiastes. 3:1–8.

6. Claude George Jr., *The History of Management Thought* (Upper Saddle River, NJ: Prentice Hall, 1968), 165–166.

7. M. Erez and F. Kanfer, "The Role of Goal Acceptance in Goal Setting and Task Performance," *Academy of Management Review* 8, no. 3 (July 1983): 457.

8. D. Hussey and M. Langham, *Corporate Planning: The Human Factor* (Oxford, England: Pergamon, 1979), 138.

9. Carter Bayles, "Strategic Control: The President's Paradox," *Business Horizons* 20, no. 4 (August 1977): 18.

10. Based on information at http://graphic.com.gh/archive/Business-News/graphic-adopts-balanced-scorecard.html

11. Based on information at http://finance.yahoo.com/news/the-worst-ceos-of-2014-191156277.html

12. Robert Waterman, Jr., "How the Best Get Better," *BusinessWeek*, September 14, 1987, 105.

13. Robert Linneman and Rajan Chandran, "Contingency Planning: A Key to Swift Managerial Action in the Uncertain Tomorrow," *Managerial Planning* 29, no. 4 (January–February 1981): 23–27.

14. American Accounting Association, *Report of Committee on Basic Auditing Concepts*, 1971, 15–74.

15. John Parnell, "Five Critical Challenges in Strategy Making," *SAM Advanced Management Journal* 68, no. 2 (Spring 2003): 15–22.

16. Henry Mintzberg, "Crafting Strategy," *Harvard Business Review* (July–August 1987): 66–75.

17. Henry Mintzberg and J. Waters, "Of Strategies, Deliberate and Emergent," *Strategic Management Journal* 6, no. 2 (1985): 257–272.

18. Parnell, "Five Critical Challenges," 15–22.

19. D. E. Schendel and C. W. Hofer (Eds.), *Strategic Management* (Boston: Little, Brown, 1979).

20. R. T. Lenz, "Managing the Evolution of the Strategic Planning Process," *Business Horizons* 30, no. 1 (January–February 1987): 39.

21. Michael McGinnis, "The Key to Strategic Planning: Integrating Analysis and Intuition," *Sloan Management Review* 26, no. 1 (Fall 1984): 49.

22. McConkey, "Planning in a Changing Environment," 72.

STRATEGIC-MANAGEMENT CASE ANALYSIS

Guidelines for Case Analysis

LEARNING OBJECTIVES

After studying the appendix, you should be able to do the following:

1. Describe the case method for learning strategic-management concepts.

2. Identify the steps in preparing a comprehensive written case analysis.

3. Describe how to give an effective oral case analysis presentation.

4. Discuss special tips for doing a case analysis.

The purpose of this section is to help you analyze strategic-management cases. Numerous guidelines and suggestions are presented as well as steps to follow. Be sure to use the author website (www.strategyclub.com), which provides sample case analyses, sample presentations, author videos, case and chapter updates, and especially the free Excel student template.

What Is a Strategic-Management Case?

A *strategic-management case* describes an organization's external and internal conditions and raises issues concerning the firm's vision, mission, strategies, objectives, and policies. Most of the information in a strategic-management case is established fact, but some information may be opinions, judgments, and beliefs. Strategic-management cases are more comprehensive than those you may have studied in other courses. They generally include a description of important internal (management, marketing, finance/accounting, production/operations, research and development (R&D), management information systems) and external issues. A case puts you at the scene of the action by describing a firm's situation at some point in time. Strategic-management cases are written to give you practice applying strategic-management concepts. The case method for studying strategic management is often called *learning by doing*.

Guidelines for Preparing Case Analyses

The Need for Practicality

There is no such thing as a complete case, and no case ever gives you all the information you need for conducting analyses and making recommendations. Likewise, in the business world, strategists never have all the information they need to make decisions: Information may be unavailable or too costly to obtain, or it may take too much time to obtain. So, in analyzing cases, do what strategists do every day—make reasonable assumptions about unknowns, perform appropriate analyses, and make decisions. *Be practical.* For example, in performing a projected financial analysis, make reasonable assumptions and proceed to show what impact your recommendations are expected to have on the organization's financial position. Avoid saying, "I don't have enough information." Always supplement the information provided in a case with Internet and library research.

The Need for Justification

There is no single best solution or one right answer to a case, so it is important to give ample justification for your recommendations. In the business world, strategists oftentimes do not know if their decisions are right until resources have been allocated and consumed. Then it is often too late to reverse a decision. Therefore, in your project, amply justify your recommendations, from the beginning to the end of your written or oral presentation.

The Need for Realism

Avoid recommending a course of action beyond an organization's means. *Be realistic.* No organization can possibly pursue all the strategies that could potentially benefit the firm. Estimate how much capital will be required to implement your recommendation. Determine whether debt, stock, or a combination of debt and stock could be used to obtain the capital. Make sure your suggestions are feasible. Do not prepare a case analysis that omits all arguments and information not supportive of your recommendations. Rather, present the major advantages and disadvantages of several feasible alternatives. Try not to exaggerate, stereotype, prejudge, or overdramatize. Strive to demonstrate that your interpretation of the evidence is reasonable and objective.

The Need for Specificity

Do not make broad generalizations such as, "The company should pursue a market penetration strategy." Be specific by telling *what, why, when, how, where,* and *who*. Failure to use specifics is the single major shortcoming of most oral and written case analyses. For example, in an internal audit, say, "The firm's current ratio fell from 2.2 in 2015 to 1.3 in 2016, and this is considered to be a major weakness," instead of "The firm's financial condition is bad." But recall from what you have read that selected external and internal factors need to be "*actionable*" to the extent possible, and financial ratios in general are not actionable. Rather than concluding from a Strategic Position and Action Evaluation (SPACE) Matrix that a firm should be defensive be more specific, saying, "The firm should consider closing three plants, laying off 280 employees, and divesting itself of its chemical division, for a net savings of $20.2 million in 2017." Use ratios, percentages, numbers, and dollar estimates. Businesspeople dislike generalities and vagueness.

The Need for Originality

Do not necessarily recommend the course of action that the firm plans to take or actually undertook, even if those actions resulted in improved revenues and earnings. The aim of case analysis is for you to consider all the facts and information relevant to the organization at the time, to generate feasible alternative strategies, to choose among those alternatives, and to defend your recommendations. Support your position with charts, graphs, ratios, analyses, and the like. *Be original.* Compare and contrast what you recommend versus what the company plans to do or is doing.

The Need to Contribute

Strategy formulation, implementation, and evaluation decisions are commonly made by a group of individuals rather than by a single person. (See the individual versus group decision-making exercise at the end of this Appendix.) Your professor will likely divide the class into three- or four-person teams and ask you to prepare written or oral case analyses. Members of a team, in class or in the business world, differ on their aversion to risk, their concern for short-run versus long-run benefits, their attitudes toward social responsibility, and their views concerning globalization. There are no perfect people, so there are no perfect strategies. Be open-minded to others' views. *Be a good listener and a good contributor.*

Your professor may ask the whole class to prepare a case for class discussion. Preparing a case for class discussion means that you need to read the case before class, make notes regarding the organization's external opportunities and threats as well as internal strengths and weaknesses, perform appropriate analyses, and come to class prepared to offer and defend some specific recommendations. Be excited about strategic management. Be a class leader.

The Case Method Versus Lecture Approach

The *case method* of teaching involves a classroom situation in which students do most of the talking; your professor facilitates discussion by asking questions and encouraging student interaction regarding ideas, analyses, and recommendations. Be prepared for a discussion along the lines of "What would you do, why would you do it, when would you do it, and how would you do it?" Prepare answers to the following types of questions:

- What are the firm's most important external opportunities and threats?
- What are the organization's major strengths and weaknesses?
- How would you describe the organization's financial condition?
- What are the firm's existing strategies and objectives?
- Who are the firm's competitors, and what are their strategies?
- What objectives and strategies do you recommend for this organization? Explain your reasoning. How does what you recommend compare to what the company plans?
- How could the organization best implement what you recommend? What implementation problems do you envision? How could the firm avoid or solve those problems?

The Cross-Examination

Take a stand on the issues and support your position with objective analyses and outside research. Strive to apply strategic-management concepts and tools in preparing your case for class discussion. Seek defensible arguments and positions. Support opinions and judgments with facts, reasons, and evidence. Crunch the numbers before class! Be willing to describe your recommendations to the class without fear of disapproval. Respect the ideas of others, but be willing to go against the majority opinion when you can justify a better position.

Case analysis gives you the opportunity to learn more about yourself, your colleagues, strategic management, and the decision-making process in organizations. The rewards of this experience will depend on the effort you put forth. Discussing cases in class is exciting and challenging. Expect views counter to those you present. Different students will place emphasis on different aspects of an organization's situation and submit different recommendations for scrutiny and rebuttal. Cross-examination discussions commonly arise, just as they occur in a real business organization. Avoid being a silent observer.

Preparing a Written Case Analysis

In addition to asking you to prepare a case for class discussion, your professor could ask you to prepare a written case analysis. Written reports are generally more structured and more detailed than an oral presentation. Always avoid using jargon, vague or redundant words, acronyms, abbreviations, sexist language, and ethnic or racial slurs. And watch your spelling! Use short sentences and paragraphs and simple words and phrases. Use quite a few subheadings. Arrange issues and ideas from the most important to the least important. Use the active voice rather than the passive voice for all verbs; for example, say "Our team recommends that the company diversify" rather than "It is recommended by our team to diversify." Use many examples to add specificity and clarity. Tables, figures, pie charts, bar charts, timelines, and other kinds of exhibits help communicate important points and ideas. Sometimes a picture *is* worth a thousand words.

The Executive Summary

Your professor could ask you to focus the written case analysis on a particular aspect of the strategic-management process, such as (1) to identify and evaluate the organization's existing vision, mission, objectives, and strategies; or (2) to propose and defend specific recommendations for the company; or (3) to develop an industry analysis by describing the competitors, products, selling techniques, and market conditions in a given industry. These types of written reports are sometimes called *executive summaries*. An executive summary usually ranges from three to five pages of text in length, plus exhibits.

The Comprehensive Written Analysis

If asked to develop a *comprehensive written analysis*, picture yourself as a consultant who has been asked by a company to conduct a study of its external and internal environment and to make specific recommendations for its future. Prepare exhibits to support your recommendations. Highlight exhibits with discussion in the paper. Comprehensive written analyses are usually about 20 pages in length, plus 20 exhibits. Throughout your written analysis, emphasize how your proposed strategies will enable the firm to gain and sustain competitive advantage. Visit www.strategyclub.com for examples.

Steps in Preparing a Comprehensive Written Analysis

In preparing a *written* case analysis, you should follow the steps outlined here, which correlate to the stages in the strategic-management process and the chapters in this text. (Note—More detailed steps, including a minute-by-minute breakdown, are given later in this Appendix.)

Step 1　Identify the firm's existing vision, mission, objectives, and strategies.
Step 2　Develop vision and mission statements for the organization.
Step 3　Identify the organization's external opportunities and threats.
Step 4　Construct a Competitive Profile Matrix (CPM).
Step 5　Construct an External Factor Evaluation (EFE) Matrix.
Step 6　Identify the organization's internal strengths and weaknesses.
Step 7　Construct an Internal Factor Evaluation (IFE) Matrix.

Step 8   Prepare a Strengths-Weaknesses-Opportunities-Threats (SWOT) Matrix, Strategic Position and Action Evaluation (SPACE) Matrix, Boston Consulting Group (BCG) Matrix, Internal-External (IE) Matrix, Grand Strategy Matrix, and Quantitative Strategic Planning Matrix (QSPM) as appropriate. Give advantages and disadvantages of alternative strategies.

Step 9   Recommend specific strategies and long-term objectives. Show how much your recommendations will cost. Clearly itemize these costs for each projected year. Compare your recommendations to actual strategies planned by the company.

Step 10   Specify how your recommendations can be implemented and what results you can expect. Prepare forecasted ratios and projected financial statements. Present a timetable or agenda for action.

Step 11   Recommend specific annual objectives and policies.

Step 12   Recommend procedures for strategy review and evaluation.

Making an Oral Presentation

Your professor may ask you to prepare a case analysis, individually or as a group, and present your analysis to the class. Oral presentations are usually graded on two parts: content and delivery. *Content* refers to the quality, quantity, correctness, and appropriateness of analyses presented, including such dimensions as logical flow through the presentation, coverage of major issues, use of specifics, avoidance of generalities, absence of mistakes, and feasibility of recommendations. *Delivery* includes such dimensions as audience attentiveness, clarity of visual aids, appropriate dress, persuasiveness of arguments, tone of voice, eye contact, and posture. Great ideas are of no value unless others can be convinced of their merit through clear communication. The guidelines presented here can help you make an effective oral presentation. Present a united front when presenting as a team. Always say "we did such and such" and "we recommend such and such," rather than, "I did the financial ratios" or "I recommend such and such." A light or humorous introduction can be effective at the beginning of a presentation.

Controlling Your Voice

An effective rate of speaking ranges from 100 to 125 words per minute. Practice your presentation aloud to determine if you are talking too fast. Individuals commonly speak too fast when they are nervous. Breathe deeply before and during the presentation to help yourself slow down. Have a cup of water available; pausing to take a drink will wet your throat, give you time to collect your thoughts, control your nervousness, slow you down, and signal to the audience a change in topic.

Avoid a monotone voice by placing emphasis on different words or sentences. Speak loudly and clearly, but do not shout. Silence can be used effectively to break a monotone voice. Stop at the end of each sentence, rather than running sentences together with *and* or *uh*.

Managing Body Language

Be sure not to fold your arms, lean on the podium, put your hands in your pockets, or put your hands behind you. Maintain a straight posture, with one foot slightly in front of the other. Do not turn your back to the audience; doing so is not only rude but it also prevents your voice from projecting well. Avoid using too many hand gestures, too. On occasion, leave the podium or table and walk toward your audience, but do not walk around too much. Never block the audience's view of your visual aids.

Maintain good eye contact throughout the presentation. This is the best way to persuade your audience. There is nothing more reassuring to a speaker than to see members of the audience nod in agreement or smile. Try to look everyone in the eye at least once during your presentation, but focus more on individuals who look interested than on those who seem bored. To stay in touch with your audience, use humor and smiles as appropriate throughout your presentation. No presentation should ever be dull!

Speaking from Notes

Be sure not to read to your audience; doing so puts people to sleep. Perhaps worse than reading is merely reciting what you have memorized. Do not try to memorize anything. Rather, practice unobtrusively using notes. Make sure your notes are written clearly so you will not flounder when trying to read your own writing. Include only main ideas on your note cards. Keep note cards on a podium or table if possible so that you will not drop them or get them out of order; walking with note cards tends to be distracting.

Constructing Visual Aids

Make sure your visual aids are legible to individuals in the back of the room. Using color to highlight special items is a good idea. Avoid putting complete sentences on visual aids; rather, use short phrases and then orally elaborate on issues as you make your presentation. Generally, there should be no more than four to six lines of text on each visual aid. Use clear headings and subheadings. Do not use many handouts or your audience may concentrate on them instead of you during the presentation.

Answering Questions

It is best to field questions at the end of your presentation, rather than during the presentation itself. Encourage questions, and take your time to respond to each one. Answering questions can be persuasive because it involves you with the audience. If a team is giving the presentation, the audience should direct questions to a specific person. During the question-and-answer period, be polite, confident, and courteous. Avoid verbose responses. Do not get defensive with your answers, even if a hostile or confrontational question is asked. Staying calm during potentially disruptive situations, such as a cross-examination, reflects self-confidence, maturity, poise, and command of the particular company and its industry. Stand up throughout the question-and-answer period.

Tips for Success in Case Analysis

Strategic-management students who have used this text over 15 editions offer you the following tips for success in doing case analysis.

1. Use the www.strategyclub.com website resources. The free Excel student template is especially useful as are the sample PowerPoint case analyses.
2. In preparing your external assessment, use the online databases subscribed to by your college library.
3. Go to http://finance.yahoo.com and enter your company's stock symbol. Also, enter your firm's major rival's stock symbol. Become knowledgeable about key trends and issues in your industry.
4. View your case analysis and presentation as a product that must have some competitive factor to favorably differentiate it from the case analyses of other students.
5. Develop a mind-set of *why*, continually questioning your own and others' assumptions and assertions.
6. Seek the help of professors in other specialty areas when necessary, and mention them by name in your presentation.
7. A goal of case analysis is to improve your ability to think clearly in ambiguous and confusing situations; do not get frustrated that there is no single best answer.
8. Work hard to develop the ability to formulate reasonable, consistent, and creative plans; put yourself in the strategist's position.
9. Develop confidence in using quantitative tools for analysis.
10. Strive for excellence in writing and in the technical preparation of your case. Prepare informative and neat charts, tables, diagrams, and graphs.
11. Pay attention to detail.
12. Think through alternative implications fully and realistically. The consequences of decisions are not always apparent. They often impact many different aspects of a firm's operations.
13. Provide answers to such fundamental questions as *what, when, where, why, who,* and *how.*

14. Do not merely recite ratios or present figures. Rather, develop ideas and conclusions concerning the possible trends. Use figures to support what your team is recommending.
15. Your analysis should be as detailed and specific as possible.
16. Emphasize the Recommendations and Strategy Implementation sections. A common mistake is to spend too much time on the external or internal analysis parts of your paper or presentation. The recommendations and implementation sections are the most important part.
17. Throughout your case analysis, emphasize how your proposed strategic plan will enable the firm to gain and sustain competitive advantage.
18. When working as a team, do most of the work individually. Use team meetings mostly to assimilate work. This approach is most efficient.
19. During the presentation, keep good posture, eye contact, and voice tone, and project confidence. Do not get defensive under any conditions or with any questions.
20. Prepare your case analysis in advance of the due date to allow time for reflection and practice. Do not procrastinate.
21. Other students will have strengths in functional areas that will complement your weaknesses, so develop a cooperative spirit that moderates competitiveness in group work.
22. When preparing a case analysis as a group, divide into separate teams to work on the external analysis and internal analysis.
23. Maintain a good sense of humor.
24. Capitalize on the strengths of each member of the group; volunteer your services in your areas of strength.
25. Set goals for yourself and your team; budget your time to attain them.
26. Foster attitudes that encourage group participation and interaction. Do not be hasty to judge group members.
27. Be prepared to work. There will be times when you will have to do more than your share. Accept it, and do what you have to do to move the team forward.
28. Think of your case analysis as if it were really doing this for a company.
29. To uncover flaws in your analysis let one person in the group actively play the devil's advocate.
30. Do not schedule excessively long group meetings; two-hour sessions are about right.
31. Push your ideas hard enough to get them listened to, but then let up; listen to others and try to follow their lines of thinking; follow the flow of group discussion, recognizing when you need to get back on track.
32. Develop a case-presentation style that is direct, assertive, and convincing; be concise, precise, fluent, and correct.
33. Have fun when at all possible. Preparing a case is frustrating at times, but enjoy it while you can; it may be several years before you are playing CEO again.
34. Get things written down (drafts) as soon as possible.
35. Neatness is a real plus; your case analysis should look professional.
36. Let someone else read and critique your presentation several days before you present it.
37. Make special efforts to get to know your group members. This leads to more openness in the group and allows for more interchange of ideas.
38. Be constructively critical of your group members' work. Do not dominate group discussions. Be a good listener and contributor.
39. Include this project on your resume as class work is accomplished.
40. Apply for a full-time job at the case company for which you prepared this strategic plan.
41. For every slide you show in an oral presentation, point out how the information supports your recommendations for the firm.
42. Make certain that your key external and internal factors are quantitative, divisional, and actionable to the extent possible.

Sample Case Analysis Outline

There are musicians who play wonderfully without notes and there are chefs who cook wonderfully without recipes, but most of us prefer a more orderly cookbook approach, at least in the first attempt at doing something new. Therefore, the eight minute-by-minute steps shown in Table 1

TABLE 1 Recommended Outline for Delivering a 27-Minute Oral Case Presentation

I. INTRODUCTION (1 MINUTE)
a. Introduce yourselves by name and major. Establish the time setting of your case and analysis. Prepare your strategic plan for the three years forthcoming.
b. Introduce your company and its products or services; capture interest.
c. Show the outline of your presentation and tell who is doing what parts.

II. VISION AND MISSION (2 MINUTES)
a. Show existing vision and mission statements if available from the firm's website, annual report, or elsewhere.
b. Show your "improved" vision and mission and tell how and why it is different.
c. Compare your vision and mission to a leading competitor's statements.

III. INTERNAL ASSESSMENT (5 MINUTES)
a. Give your financial ratio analysis. Highlight especially good and bad ratios. Do not give definitions of the ratios and do not highlight all the ratios.
b. Show the firm's organizational chart found or "created based on executive titles." Identify the type of chart as well as good and bad aspects. Unless all white males comprise the chart, peoples' names are generally not important because positions reveal structure.
c. Present your improved organizational chart. Tell how and why it is different.
d. Show a market positioning map with firm and competitors. Discuss the map in light of strategies you envision for firm versus competitors' strategies.
e. Identify the marketing strategy of the firm in terms of good and bad points versus competitors and in light of strategies you envision for the firm.
f. Show a map locating the firm's operations. Discuss in terms of strategies you envision. Perhaps show a value chain analysis chart.
g. Discuss (and perhaps show) the firm's website and Facebook page in terms of good and bad points compared to rival firms.
h. Show your "value of the firm" analysis.
i. List the firm's 20 most important strengths and weaknesses. Go over highly rated factors without "reading" any verbatim. Make sure you key internal factors are quantitative, divisional, and actionable to the extent possible.
j. Show and highlight your Internal Factor Evaluation (IFE) Matrix.

IV. EXTERNAL ASSESSMENT (5 MINUTES)
a. Identify and discuss major competitors. Use pie charts, maps, tables, or figures to show the intensity of competition in the industry. Pave the way for your recommendations.
b. Show your Competitive Profile Matrix. Include 15 factors and two competitors.
c. Summarize key industry trends citing Standard & Poor's *Industry Survey* and IBIS World information. Highlight key external (economic, social, cultural, demographic, geographic, technological, political, legal, governmental, and natural environment) trends as they impact the firm.
d. List the firm's 20 most important opportunities and threats. Make sure your opportunities are not stated as strategies. Go over highly weighted factors without "reading" any verbatim. Make sure your key external factors are quantitative, divisional, and actionable to the extent possible.
e. Show and highlight your External Factor Evaluation (EFE) Matrix.

V. STRATEGY FORMULATION (7 MINUTES)
a. Show and highlight your SWOT Matrix, focusing on the strategies you ultimately will recommend.
b. Show and explain your SPACE Matrix. Focus more on the implications than the numbers. Strategies must be specific; avoid vague terms such as *market penetration*.
c. Show your Boston Consulting Group (BCG) Matrix. Focus more on the implications than the numbers. Do multiple BCG Matrices if possible, including domestic versus global, or another geographic breakdown. Develop a product BCG if at all possible. Comment on each matrix as per strategies you recommend. Develop this matrix even if you do not know the profits per division and even if you have to estimate the axes information. However, make no wild guesses on axes or revenue/profit information.
d. Show and highlight your Internal-External (IE) Matrix.
e. Show and highlight your Grand Strategy Matrix.
f. Show your Quantitative Strategic Planning Matrix (QSPM). Be sure to explain your strategies. Do not go back over the internal and external factors.
g. Present your recommendations page. This is the most important page in your presentation. Be specific in terms of both strategies and estimated costs of those strategies. *Total your estimated costs.* You should have 10 or more strategies. Divide your strategies into two groups: (1) Existing Strategies to Be Continued and (2) New Strategies to Be Started.

VI. STRATEGY IMPLEMENTATION (4 MINUTES)
a. Show and highlight your earnings per share/earnings before interest and taxes (EPS/EBIT) analysis to reveal whether stock, debt, or a combination is best to finance your recommendations. Graph the analysis.
b. Show your projected income statement and balance sheet. Relate changes in the items to your recommendations rather than blindly going with historical percentage changes. Be sure to show the retained earnings calculation and the results of your EPS/EBIT decision.
c. Show your projected financial ratios and highlight several key ratios to show the benefits of your strategic plan.

VII. STRATEGY EVALUATION (1 MINUTE)
a. Prepare a Balanced Scorecard to show your expected financial and nonfinancial objectives recommended for the firm.

VIII. CONCLUSION (2 MINUTES)
a. Compare and contrast your strategic plan versus the company's own plans for the future.
b. Thank audience members for their attention. Genuinely seek and gladly answer questions.

---

may serve as a basic outline for you in presenting a strategic plan for your firm's future. This outline is not the only approach used in business and industry for communicating a strategic plan, but this approach is time-tested, it does work, and it does cover all of the basics. You may amend the content, tools, and concepts given to suit your own company, audience, assignment, and circumstances, but it helps to know and understand the rules before you start breaking them.

Recommended Time Allocation for Presenting a Case Analysis
Your professor may allow between 15 and 40 minutes for your case presentation; the outline in Table 1 is provided for a 27-minute presentation. Be sure in an oral presentation to manage time, knowing that your recommendations and associated costs are the most important part. If you are only allowed 15 minutes of presentation time, prepare (1) a condensed slide show and (2) a full slide show of your case analysis, using the condensed for presentation purposes and the full to submit to your professor. Good luck.

ASSURANCE OF LEARNING EXERCISE
Strategic Planning for Gruma SAB

Purpose
Strategic-management classes are usually composed of a team of students who perform case analysis as described in the text. The purpose of this exercise is to examine whether individual decision making is better than group decision making. Academic research suggests that groups make better decisions than individuals about 80 percent of the time. No company has sufficient resources to implement all strategies that would benefit the firm. Thus, tough choices have to be made. Ranking strategies as to their relative attractiveness (1 = most attractive, 2 = next most attractive, etc.) is a commonly used procedure to help determine which actions to fund. Oftentimes, a group of managers will jointly rank strategies and compare their ranking to other groups. This ranking process may be used to determine the relative attractiveness of feasible alternative strategies.

Completing this exercise will reveal whether you as an individual make better strategic decisions than your group or team. This is a fun exercise that also gives you experience selecting among feasible alternative strategies for a company.

The Situation
Headquartered in Monterrey, Gruma is the largest tortilla producer in the world. Gruma uses corn and wheat flour and other ingredients to produce grits, cereals, tortilla chips, taco shells, sauces, snacks, pasta, potato chips, and more. Top Gruma food brand names are Mission, Guerrero, Calidad,

Maseca, and Tortimasa. The company also produces Tortec and Batitech machines that produce tortilla and tortilla chips that are sold to restaurants, supermarkets, and other food service providers. One special feature of Gruma's machines and products is the use of a dry production method rather than using wet dough. Gruma's method yields lower costs and superior product uniformity. Over the last 10 years, Gruma has acquired several competing firms, including Albuquerque Tortilla Company, Casa de Oro Foods, and Archer Daniels Midlands stake in Azteca Milling. Gruma operates 101 production facilities serving over 113 countries and employs 18,000. On July 22, 2015, the company announced excellent results for its second quarter of 2015 (2Q15). During the course of 2Q15, Gruma made capital investments worth 33 million U.S. dollars, most of which was spent on technology improvements, expanding the installed capacity of the firm's tortilla and corn flour production plants in Mexicali, building a new plant to produce tostadasin in Tijuana, Mexico, and building a tortilla plant in Russia. Despite doing really well, Gruma wants to do better. It is trying to decide what strategies would be best for the company going forward. Following are 12 strategies that are being considered.

The Strategies

1. **Backward integration.** Purchase a 10,000-acre corn and wheat farm to gain better control over supplies needed for production operations.
2. **Forward integration (a).** Acquire Chipotle Mexican Grill (CMG). Chipotle is a chain of about 1,700 restaurants in the United States, United Kingdom, Canada, and Europe, specializing in burritos, tacos, and salads. *Chipotle* is Spanish for "smoked or fried jalapeno chili pepper."
3. **Forward integration (b).** Acquire Chuy's (CHUY). Chuy's is a chain of 59 small Mexican restaurants in the United States. Chuy's is not "fast casual" like Chipotle, but rather is a sit-down table-service restaurant that is uniquely festive. Chuy's revenue soared 20 percent to $64.1 million in its latest quarter. Chuy's opened 11 more locations in the last year.
4. **Horizontal integration.** Acquire Grupo Bimbo, S.A.B. de C.V. Founded in 1945 in Mexico City, Grupo Bimbo employs over 129,000 and does business worldwide with167 plants, but the company's principal operations are in Mexico and the United States. Top brands in Mexico include Bimbo, Marinela, Barcel, and Ricolino.
5. **Market development (a).** Build a manufacturing plant in China to begin servicing that country.
6. **Market development (b).** Build a manufacturing plant in South Africa to begin servicing all of Africa.
7. **Market penetration (a).** Launch an advertising, promotion, and publicity campaign in Mexico to increase market share in Mexico.
8. **Market penetration (b).** Launch an advertising, promotion, and publicity campaign in the United States to increase market share in the country.
9. **Product development (a).** Develop, produce, and launch a full line of organic tortillas, chips, and taco shells.
10. **Product development (b).** Develop, produce, and launch new products, including spaghetti, linguine, and bread.
11. **Related diversification.** Acquire the Prego trademark brand name pasta sauce from Campbell Soup Company. Prego pasta sauce is available in 19 different flavors, including marinara, traditional, mini meatball, zesty mushroom, and roasted garlic parmesan. Several Prego flavors are made with all organic ingredients.
12. **Unrelated diversification.** Acquire a construction company in Mexico, such as one of the following companies: Cemex, Grupo Villacero, Tubacero, Lamosa, or ICA.

The Task

Your task is to rank the 12 preceding strategies in terms of their relative attractiveness for Gruma, where 1 = the most attractive strategy to pursue, 2 = the next most attractive strategy, and so on to 12 = the least attractive strategy to pursue. Rank the strategies first as an individual, and then as part a group. Then, listen to the EXPERT ranking and rationale. In this manner, this exercise enables you to determine what individual(s) and what group(s) in class make the best strategic decisions (i.e., that come closest to the expert ranking).

TABLE 2 Strategic Planning for Gruma: Individual versus Group Decision Making

Strategy	Column Number				
	(1) My Rank	(2) Group Rank	(3) EXPERT Rank	(4) Absolute Value 1–3	(5) Absolute Value 2–3
1. Backward integration					
2. Forward integration (a)					
3. Forward integration (b)					
4. Horizontal integration					
5. Market development (a)					
6. Market development (b)					
7. Market penetration (a)					
8. Market penetration (b)					
9. Product development (a)					
10. Product development (b)					
11. Related diversification					
12. Unrelated diversification					
Sum of Columns 1, 2, 4, & 5					

Note: The expert ranking and rationale are given in the *Chapter Instructor's Manual.*

The Steps

1. Fill in Column 1 in Table 2 to reveal your individual ranking of the relative attractiveness of the proposed strategies. For example, if you feel backward integration is the seventh-best option, then enter 7 into Column 1 beside backward integration.
2. Fill in Column 2 in the table to reveal your group's ranking of the relative attractiveness of the proposed strategies. For example, if your group believes backward integration is the third-best option, then enter 3 into Column 2 beside backward integration.
3. Fill in Column 3 in the table to reveal the expert's ranking of the relative attractiveness of the proposed strategies.
4. Fill in Column 4 in the table to reveal the absolute difference between Column 1 and Column 3 to reveal how well you performed as an individual in this exercise. (Note: Absolute difference disregards negative numbers.)
5. Fill in Column 5 in the Table to reveal the absolute difference between Column 2 and Column 3 to reveal how well your group performed in this exercise.
6. Sum Column 4. Sum Column 5.
7. Compare the Column 4 sum with the Column 5 sum. If your Column 4 sum is less than your Column 5 sum, then you performed better as an individual than as a group. If you did better than your group, your performance was especially good.
8. The Individual Winner(s): The individual(s) with the lowest Column 4 sum is the WINNER.
9. The Group Winners(s): The group(s) with the lowest Column 5 score is the WINNER.

Strategic Management Cases

Krispy Kreme Doughnuts, Inc., 2015

www.krispykreme.com, KKD

Headquartered in Winston-Salem, North Carolina, Krispy Kreme Doughnuts (KKD) serves doughnuts and coffee as well as other snack items. The company has locations in 23 different countries. Many Krispy Kreme shops are factory shops where customers can watch doughnuts being made and purchase fresh hot doughnuts as well. The factory stores are responsible for servicing local grocery stores and convenience stores. The KK Supply Chain provides raw materials for both franchise and company-owned stores in the doughnut-making process. Krispy Kreme storeowners must purchase all materials from KK Supply Chain. Krispy Kreme reported total revenues in fiscal year end February 2015 of $490 million (up from $460 million the prior year) with about 90 percent of revenues derived from the United States.

For the fiscal first quarter (Q1) of 2015, Krispy Kreme's revenue rose 9 percent year-over-year to $132.5 million, driven almost entirely by a 17.3 percent increase in Krispy Kreme's store count. For that quarter, the company's domestic same-store sales rose 5.2 percent, but its international franchise same-store sales declined 1.7 percent. Overall for Q1 of 2015, the company's adjusted net income was $16.6 million, or $0.24 per share. The company's EPS number was up at least by the KKD buying back 391,300 shares of its stock for $7.4 million.

Copyright by Fred David Books LLC. www.strategyclub.com (Written by Forest R. David)

History

Krispy Kreme traces its roots back to 1933 when Vernon Rudolph bought a doughnut shop in Paducah, Kentucky. After selling doughnuts in Kentucky, Tennessee, and West Virginia, the store known today as Krispy Kreme was moved to Winston-Salem. Krispy Kreme doughnuts were sold to grocery stores at first, but became so popular with customers that they requested the option to buy the doughnuts fresh and hot from the store, thus launching the doughnut factory retail store and selling directly to the public.

Krispy Kreme grew quickly over the next four decades before being sold to Beatrice Foods Company in 1976. Shortly after the purchase by Beatrice, in 1982, several Krispy Kreme franchisees purchased the company back from Beatrice Foods and quickly established the current Doughnut Theater style of factory stores where by customers can watch doughnuts being made. It was not until 1996 that KKD finally expanded outside the Southeast by opening a store in New York City, followed in 2001 by opening its first store outside the United States, in Canada. The company went public with its IPO launch in April 2000.

In the United Kingdom, KKD just concocted a single, gigantic box that holds 2,400 doughnuts. The box (11.4 feet by 3 feet) was filled with doughnuts and required eight KKD employees to deliver it to 360 Resourcing Solutions. The box was part of a promotion for the new "Krispy Kreme Occasions" division that customizes doughnut offerings for corporate events or special occasions such as weddings and other celebrations. The division sells doughnut "towers" for special events or even personalized doughnuts with customized, chocolate nameplates or corporate logos. The company has no plans to create another box, but it is happy to sell 100 of the so-called double-dozen boxes for about $2,600.

Krispy Kreme opened its first store in India in 2013 in Bangalore, Karnataka, and now there are seven in that city. Also in 2013, KKD began opening stores in Colombia, with a total of 25 planned, as the first South American country for the company. In late 2013, KKD opened its first store in Taipei, Taiwan. In 2014, KKD opened its first shop in Chennai in southern India.

Internal Issues

Vision/Mission

Krispy Kreme Doughnuts does not appear to have a published vision statement. The company's mission statement, however, is given as follows:

Consumers are our lifeblood, the center of the doughnut

There is no substitute for quality in our service to consumers

Impeccable presentation is critical wherever Krispy Kreme is sold

We must produce a collaborative team effort that is unexcelled

We must cast the best possible image in all that we do

We must never settle for "second best;" we deliver on our commitments

We must coach our team to ever-better results. (*Source:* Company documents)

Distribution

Krispy Kreme doughnuts are sold in KKD stores, grocery stores, convenience stores, gas stations, Walmart, and Target stores in the United States. Internationally, the doughnuts are sold in Loblaws supermarkets, Petro-Canada gas stations, and as freestanding stores in Canada, along with BP Service Stations and BP Travel Centers and 7-Eleven stores in Australia. In the United Kingdom, Tesco supermarkets, Tesco Extra, and most Tesco service stations carry KKD products, and service stations Moto, Welcome Break, and Road Chef also carry self-service KKD cabinets. Today, KKD has locations in the United Kingdom, Australia, Turkey, the Dominican Republic, Kuwait, Mexico, Puerto Rico, China Taiwan, South Korea, Malaysia, Thailand, Indonesia, the Philippines, Japan, China Mainland, the United Arab Emirates, Qatar, Saudi Arabia, Bahrain, China Hong Kong, and Ethiopia.

Organizational Structure

As illustrated in Exhibit 1, KKD basically has two segments: USA and International. Note the company does not have a Chief Operating Officer (COO), Chief Administrative Officer (CAO), or Chief Strategy Officer (CSO). However, KKD reports revenues by geographic region, but is not structured geographically. In fact, the company appears to be structurally functionally, rather than divisionally.

EXHIBIT 1 KKD's Organizational Structure

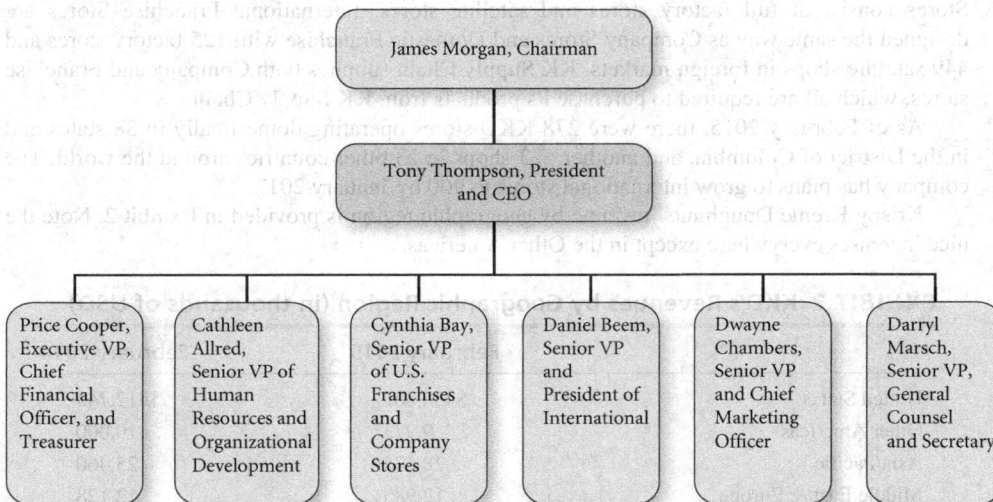

Source: A depiction based on author's best judgment.

Strategy

Krispy Kreme Doughnuts has long prided itself on hot fresh doughnuts and a one of a kind taste. As you can easily watch at a KKD factory store Doughnut Theater, the original glazed doughnut is fried before it heads toward a glazing waterfall to be covered in a sugary signature glaze. There is only one supplier of KKD's signature glaze. In addition to entertaining guests, KKD feels the Doughnut Theater also reveals the firm's commitment to quality and freshness. To help attract customers into the store, the original hot doughnuts sign is lit during peak production hours, generally early in the mornings and late at night, when customers are most likely to visit the stores. In essence, KKD's strategy is hot fresh doughnuts, but the firm also sells its products in gas stations, grocery stores, and other retail outlets. About 50 percent of all KKD revenue is derived from wholesale outlets, so the firm plans to work on ways to improve the freshness and quality of its doughnuts sold in various retail locations.

The company is transitioning toward smaller factory shops that will focus on retail rather than wholesale customers. This strategy appears more in line with the firm's new marketing approach. Many new stores in the southeastern United States will be company owned, whereas new smaller factory stores outside the southeast are more likely to be operated under franchisee agreements.

Krispy Kreme Doughnuts has long helped the communities with fund-raisers, even offering special packaging at times. Fund-raisers are under the firm's "local relationship marketing" strategy. The company does a good job attracting customers from local businesses and families. About 55 percent of all domestic transactions are for doughnut orders of 1 dozen or more. However, this is also partly explained by the volume discount provided for such orders. International orders of a dozen or more doughnuts at a time are a significant portion of sales as well, indicating that doughnut consumption habits are more homogeneous globally than some may believe. The company likes to mention homogeneity as a part of its "sharing concept," which is a key aspect of the firm's global marketing strategy.

In early 2014, KKD and Keurig Green Mountain Coffee agreed to create both decaf and regular Krispy Kreme coffee for Keurig coffee makers. Customers can purchase the products at both Keurig and KKD websites as well as at KKD factory stores, grocery, retail, and other channels throughout the United States. Krispy Kreme also has a new line of iced coffee. About 89 percent of all KKD's retail sales are derived from doughnuts, with the industry average closer to 50 percent of sales being derived from doughnuts. KKD is late to capitalize on selling coffee and other drinks, but the company is making efforts.

Segments

Krispy Kreme Doughnuts is broken down into (1) Company Stores, (2) Domestic Franchise, (3) International Franchise, and (4) KK Supply Chain. Company Stores and Domestic Franchise stores are similar, only differing in ownership. Both Company Stores and Domestic Franchise Stores consist of full factory stores and satellite stores. International Franchise Stores are designed the same way as Company Stores and Domestic Franchise with 125 factory stores and 449 satellite shops in foreign markets. KK Supply Chain supplies both Company and Franchise stores, which all are required to purchase its products from KK Supply Chain.

As of February 2015, there were 278 KKD stores operating domestically in 38 states and in the District of Columbia, and another 523 shops in 23 other countries around the world. The company has plans to grow international stores to 900 by January 2017.

Krispy Kreme Doughnuts' revenue by geographic region is provided in Exhibit 2. Note the nice increases everywhere except in the Other Americas.

EXHIBIT 2 KKD's Revenues by Geographic Region (in thousands of USD)

	February 2015	February 2014
United States	$438,801	$412,743
Other Americas	9,973	10,000
Asia/Pacific	28,575	25,460
Middle East & Europe	12,985	12,128
Total Revenues	**490,334**	**460,331**

Source: Based on KKD *Annual Report*, 2015, page 23.

EXHIBIT 3 KKD's Revenues by Company-Owned versus Franchise (in thousands of USD)

	Revenues		Operating Income	
	February 2015	February 2014	February 2015	February 2014
Company Stores	$325,306	$306,825	$9,287	$11,334
Domestic Franchise	13,450	11,839	8,103	8,083
International Franchise	28,598	25,607	20,026	17,977
KKD Supply Chain After Adjustments	122,980	116,060	41,823	36,953
Totals	**490,334**	**460,331**	**79,239**	**74,347**

Source: Based on KKD *Annual Report*, 2015 page 41.

Revenues and operating income by company-owned versus franchised stores are provided in Exhibit 3. Notice nice increases across the board, with international franchise lagging slightly.

Krispy Kreme Doughnuts' revenues by retail versus wholesale are provided in Exhibit 4. Note that retail sales are the highest, accounting for 49 percent of 2014 revenues. However, collectively, wholesale sales accounted for 51 percent of total revenues led by grocers and mass merchants such as Walmart at 31 percent of total sales.

Finance

The fiscal year for Krispy Kreme Doughnuts ends in February. The company had an outstanding 2013 (ending February 1, 2014) on most financial areas. The firm's stock price was up over 100 percent, revenues increased 6 percent, and the company reported a 65 percent increase in net income. Much of the increases can be attributed to opening 80 new locations around the world, but KKD also reported 6.7 percent increase in comparable store sales. The company's CEO indicated in the spring of 2014 that overseas markets remain strong for the firm, with many new store openings having long lines for up to 3 months after opening. The CFO, Douglas Muir, retired in 2015, turning the reins over to Price Cooper. Also, KKD is increasing its $80 million stock buyback to $105 million in 2015.

The company's most recent income statement and balance sheet are provided in Exhibits 5 and 6, respectively.

External Issues

The doughnut market in the United States is a $13 billion industry, with about 25 percent of sales coming from bulk doughnuts in the 1 dozen-size box and up. Another 40 percent of sales come from drinks with half of this being derived from coffee. Major rival Dunkin' Brands accounts for much of these sales with their popular coffee offerings. Yeast doughnuts account for about 10 percent of industrywide sales. Doughnut holes and other varieties account for about 10 percent. There are thousands of "mom-and-pop" doughnut and coffee shops globally.

EXHIBIT 4 KKD's Revenues by Retail versus Wholesale

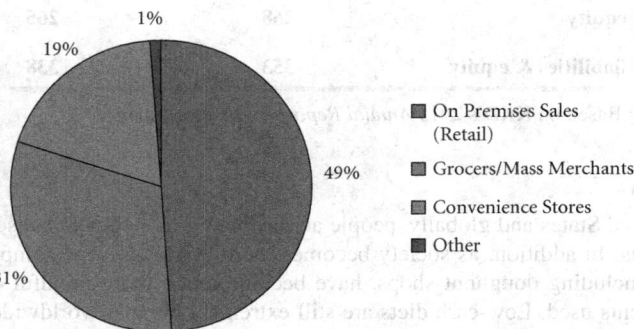

Source: Based on KKD *Annual Report*, 2014, page 44.

EXHIBIT 5 Income Statement (in millions of USD)

Report Date	February 2, 2015	February 2, 2014
Revenues	$490	$460
Operating expenses	441	413
EBIT	49	47
Interest and other benefit	0.8	1.5
EBT	48	45
Tax	18	10
Net income	**30**	**34**

Source: Based on KKD's 2015 *Annual Report*.

EXHIBIT 6 Balance Sheet (in millions of USD)

Report Date	February 2, 2015	February 2, 2014
Assets		
Cash and equivalents	$51	$56
Accounts receivable	28	25
Inventories	18	17
Deferred tax	23	23
Other current assets	8	6
Total current assets	128	127
Property, plant, & equipment	116	93
Goodwill and intangibles	30	24
Deferred tax	68	83
Other assets	11	11
Total assets	**353**	**338**
Liabilities		
Short-term debt	—	—
Accounts payable	49	17
Taxes	1	2
Other current liabilities	0	27
Total current liabilities	50	46
Long-term debt	9	2
Other liabilities	26	25
Total liabilities	**85**	**73**
Common stock	311	338
Retained earnings	(43)	(73)
Total equity	**268**	**265**
Total liabilities & equity	**353**	**338**

Source: Based on KKD's 2015 *Annual Report*, and Yahoo Finance.

Eating Healthy

Both in the United States and globally, people are becoming more health conscious in their diet and food choices. In addition, as society becomes more litigious, firms competing in the fast-food industry, including doughnut shops, have become much more mindful of product labeling and ingredients used. Low-carb diets are still extremely popular worldwide and many have even made low-carb eating a lifestyle. Some cities and other governments around the world, for example, are imposing laws that restrict portion sizes of soft drinks and other sugary-laden snack sizes. Competitors of KKD, including Dunkin' Brands and Starbucks, have already diversified their menu options to include healthier choices. However, still, when most people want a dough-nut, they want it to taste good and view it as a treat, so the outlook for doughnut shops remains positive, especially outside of North America, where the market is not saturated.

Coffee Prices

Like many commodities, the price of coffee is subject to wild price fluctuations. Brazil accounts for about 40 percent of worldwide coffee production. Droughts in Brazil, fungal infections, and defores-tation of the rain forest have caused prices to swing greatly. The fungal infection in 2014 accounted for $1 billion in lost revenues; coffee production could drop as much as 40 percent in the coming years. Also, a global acceptance to "fair trade" providing farmers a fair wage and educational pro-grams for their farming efforts has also contributed to higher prices. In addition, a growing middle class in developing countries has provided upward pressure on coffee prices. In total, coffee prices doubled from 2013 to 2014. The good news for consumers is that coffee prices paid will not be felt much more than a nickel or dime per cup at a restaurant, according to most analysts.

Competitors

Top doughnut competitors are Dunkin' Brands, Tim Hortons, as well as Starbucks for coffee and other snacks. The global market looks promising for American donut firms and Canadian-based Tim Hortons. Dunkin' Brands accounts for about 54 percent of the total doughnut shop market share. Krispy Kreme and Tim Hortons each account for about 5 percent of the U.S. doughnut market share. Regarding coffee shops, Starbucks accounts for 35 percent, Dunkin' Brands for 25 percent, and Tim Hortons and KKD 2 percent each of the U.S. coffee shop market share in total revenues. Exhibit 7 shows the summary financial information for KKD and its rival firms.

Dunkin' Brands Group (DNKN)

Headquartered in Canton, Massachusetts, Dunkin' Brands is a global distributor of coffee, baked goods, and their famous ice cream served under the Baskin Robbins name brand. There are 11,000 Dunkin' Donuts restaurants in 40 states and 32 foreign countries, as well as 7,300 Baskin-Robbins restaurants in 43 states and 46 foreign countries. Many Dunkin' Donuts restaurants also contain a Baskin-Robbins within them, and all but 36 Dunkin' Donuts and Baskin-Robbins stores are franchisee owned. About two thirds of all Dunkin' restaurants in the United States have a drive-through that caters to customers, especially morning customers on their way to work. The majority of Dunkin' Donuts and Baskin-Robbins stores outside the United States are located in Asia and the Middle East, with South Korea and Japan having the most stores.

After an infusion of cash from going public with its IPO in 2011, Dunkin' started to aggres-sively expand within the United States and internationally, opening 700 Dunkin' Donuts and Baskin-Robbins worldwide in 2014 alone. Dunkin' is opening 65 stores in Brazil between 2014 and 2016. The company is also introducing a European flavor to over 100 restaurants that now offer soft seating areas with low tables in earthy colors and contemporary lights. Implemented in 2014 was a company rewards program that enables Dunkin' to understand its customers better and learn ways to meet their demand and desires more efficiently.

EXHIBIT 7 Summary Financial Information for KKD versus Rival Firms

	Krispy Kreme	Dunkin' Brands	Starbucks
# Employees	2,800	1,584	191,000
$ Net Income	30 M	176 M	2,068 M
$ Revenue	490 M	749 M	16,477 M
$ Revenue/Employee	175,000	473,000	86,000
$ EPS Ratio	0.46	1.70	1.69
Market Cap.	1.24 B	5.32 B	81.83 B

Source: Based on company documents.

With 99 percent of all Dunkin' Donuts stores under the franchisee system, most of Dunkin's revenues are derived from a 5.4 percent royalty payment franchisees pay on gross sales to the company. Baskin-Robbins franchisees pay around 5.0 percent. These numbers are U.S.-based only, as international based Dunkin' and Baskin-Robbins pay 2.1 percent and 0.7 percent royalty rates, with Baskin-Robbins stores also paying for certain ice cream products. U.S.-based stores also pay advertising fees of 5 percent of gross sales.

Financially, 2014 was a banner year for Dunkin' Brands with revenues increasing 5 percent to $748 million, buoyed by 790 new restaurants that were opened worldwide in 2013 with 439 of these outside the United States. With new additions and improving business and prospects in foreign markets, Dunkin', like KKD, also experienced a large increase in net income of around 17 percent in 2014. Also noteworthy of late is Dunkin's increases in royalty income, franchise fees, and higher margins on Baskin Robbins ice cream products.

Tim Hortons

Tim Hortons is the largest doughnut and coffee retailer in Canada. Founded in Hamilton, Ontario, in 1964, the firm sells premium coffee, espresso, teas, and many other hot and cold beverages including fruit smoothies. Food items sold include soups, sandwiches, wraps, and many other choices. The company's mainstay, however, is donuts for which the firm was founded. There are over 850 Tim Hortons locations throughout the United States. The company also offers its products in self-service kiosk machines. In 2014, the company generated over $634 million in the United States alone. Tim Hortons was recently acquired by Burger King Worldwide.

Starbucks

Starbucks is the world's largest specialty coffee retailer with over 18,000 stores in 60 different countries. In addition to offering a variety of hot and cold coffee drinks, Starbucks also offers pastries, muffins, cookies, and other dessert-type items. As of 2014, Starbucks expanded its line of products to include beer, wine, chocolate fondue, and even chicken skewers at around 40 of its locations. The company also owns Seattle's Best Coffee and Torrefazione Italia coffee brands. Customers frequently purchase Starbucks coffee and ready-made coffee drinks at grocery stores, gas stations, and department stores.

An important way Starbucks has historically differentiated itself from rivals KKD and Dunkin' Brands was by its perception as a more premium coffee offered in a variety of flavors. With Dunkin' Brands responding similarly with its product line, Starbucks is now using sales of beer, wine, and upgraded snacks and food as a means of attracting customers in the late afternoon and early evening—a time when sales are historically slower. Starbucks also maintains its position as more of a sit-down-and-relax establishment, unlike most KKD and Dunkin' Donuts stores. Starbucks has enjoyed over a 100 percent stock price increase from January 2013 to the summer 2015 and a new income increase of 50 percent from fiscal year end 2012 to fiscal year end 2014.

Future

Krispy Kreme Doughnuts is slowly shifting its focus from wholesale to more of a retail presence. Currently around 50 percent of revenues are derived from each source. However, KKD has always prided itself on hot fresh doughnuts that customers purchase directly from factory stores. As a result, the firm is building smaller-sized factory stores to better serve the retail customer directly. The company is also expanding its footprint internationally. In December 2014, KKD opened its 100th store in South Korea, a 3,200-square-foot doughnut theater facility with the full viewing area and the famous "Hot Doughnuts Now" sign. Also, in early 2015, KKD agreed with Doughnuts Café to establish 15 Krispy Kreme facilities in the greater Saint Petersburg, Russia, area by 2020.

As KKD has expanded and become a global brand, rival firms and other food-producing companies are eyeing the possibility of acquiring the company. In early 2015, Jollibee Foods Corp., based in the Philippines, was considered by many analysts to be a serious contender to purchase KKD, as Jollibee management looks to add an American-based food company to its portfolio. Between growing both domestically and internationally, moving into a more retail-focused strategy, hedging off potential takeovers, and a growing awareness of a healthy eating public, KKD needs a clear strategic plan. Devise a three-year plan for CEO Morgan moving forward.

Domino's Pizza, Inc., 2013

www.dominos.com, DPZ

Based in Ann Arbor, Michigan, Domino's is the largest pizza delivery company in the USA having a 22.5 percent share of the pizza delivery market. Domino's digital ordering channels include online ordering at www.dominos.com, mobile ordering at http://mobile.dominos.com, and ordering on iPhone, Kindle Fire, and Android apps. More than $2 billion of Domino's pizza is ordered online annually. There are more than 10,300 Domino's stores in over 70 countries. Domino's had sales of over $7.4 billion in 2012, with $3.6 billion of that coming from the USA.

Copyright by Fred David Books LLC. (Written by Forest R. David)

History

Growing up in foster homes most of their childhood, Tom Monaghan and his brother James borrowed $900 in 1960 to purchase a mom-and-pop pizza store in Ypsilanti, Michigan, named Domi-Nick's. After trading his brother James a Volkswagen Beetle for his half of the business in 1961, Tom changed the store name in 1965 from Domi-Nick's to Domino's Pizza Inc. The company experienced steady growth during the 1960s, and by 1978, there were 200 Domino's stores in the USA. During the 1980s, the company expanded rapidly both in the USA and internationally. By the end of the decade, Domino's had more than 5,000 stores in the USA, Canada, United Kingdom, Japan, Australia, and Colombia. By 1998, there were more than 6,000 Dominos, with 1,500 located outside the USA. Tom Monaghan retired in 1998 and sold 93 percent of the company (worth $1 billion) to Bain Capital Inc. In the six years following the sale, Domino's enjoyed great success under Bain Capital and in 2004 Domino's became a publically traded company on the New York Stock Exchange under the ticker symbol DPZ. The initial stock price was $16 per share and placed a value on the company at more than $2 billion (double the price Bain paid).

Domino's changed its 49-year-old recipe at year end 2009 and started a heavily advertised marketing campaign called "new inspired pizza." Domino's stock price appreciated from around $8 a share at the start of 2010 to $60 in mid-2003. Fueled by the new recipe and new products, Domino's celebrated its 50th anniversary in 2010 and was awarded best pizza chain in 2010 and 2011 by *Pizza Today magazine*, marking the first time ever that the same pizza chain had received the award in consecutive years. Domino's CEO Patrick Doyle was named the best CEO of 2011 by CNBC. Domino's was recently ranked number 1 in *Forbes magazine's* "Top 20 Franchises for the Money" list.

About 96 percent of Domino's stores are owned by franchisees. There are very few company-owned Domino's stores.

Corporate Philosophy and Mission Statement

Domino's does not have a stated vision statement, but the company mission statement is as follows: "Exceptional franchisees and team members on a mission to be the best pizza delivery company in the world." Domino's "guiding principles" are based on the concept of one united brand, system and team:

- putting people first;
- striving to make every customer a loyal customer;
- delivering with smart hustle and positive energy; and
- winning by improving results every day. (2012 *Annual Report*)

Organizational Structure

As indicated in Exhibit 1, Domino's has 11 top executives, mostly executive vice-presidents (EVPs). It appears that Domino's operates from a functional organizational structure with Doyle being "where the buck stops," although for a firm of this size, a divisional or strategic business

EXHIBIT 1 Domino's Organizational Chart

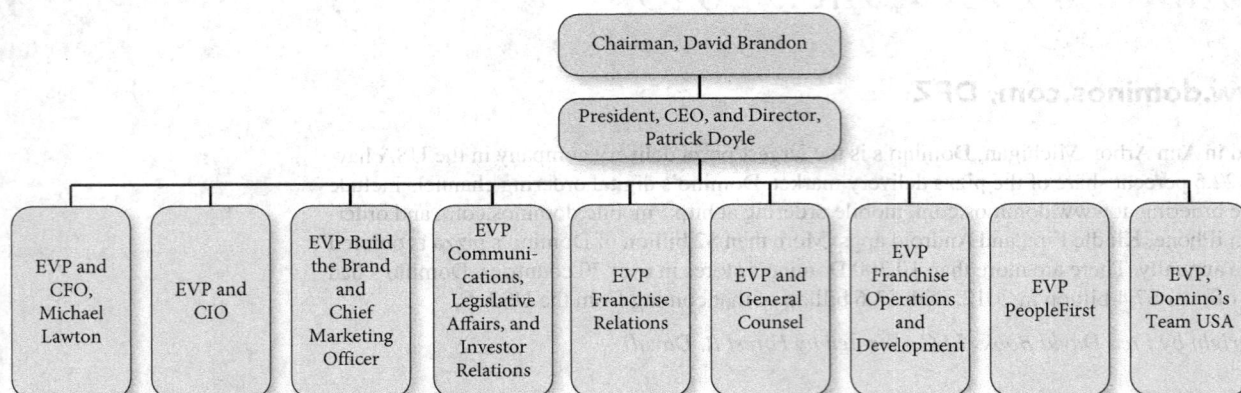

```
                            Chairman, David Brandon
                                     |
                          President, CEO, and Director,
                                 Patrick Doyle
```

| EVP and CFO, Michael Lawton | EVP and CIO | EVP Build the Brand and Chief Marketing Officer | EVP Communications, Legislative Affairs, and Investor Relations | EVP Franchise Relations | EVP and General Counsel | EVP Franchise Operations and Development | EVP PeopleFirst | EVP, Domino's Team USA |

unit type structure by region (or by franchised versus company owned) may be more effective in promoting delegation of authority, responsibility, and accountability.

Business Segments

Domino's provides financial information for four key business segments: (1) domestic company-owned stores, (2) domestic franchise stores, (3) domestic supply chain, and (4) international. Note in Exhibit 2 that the largest revenue-generating segment is the domestic supply chain with more than 50 percent of all revenue. Note also the large revenue numbers for the relatively few company owned stores, because each Domino's domestic franchisee owns his or her own store(s) and reports their revenues on their own personal financial statements rather than Domino's. From franchisees, Domino's reports only the royalties and advertising fees it receives from franchisees as revenue. The financial data for the international supply chain centers are included in the international division, not under the domestic supply chain division. Also note in Exhibit 2 the slight revenue decline in 2012 for domestic company-owned stores.

Exhibit 3 reveals that for 2012, Domino's international stores had the highest growth in revenue, followed by U.S. company-owned stores. However the sales growth among all three segments slowed in 2012.

Exhibit 4 reveals that Domino's growth in number of stores is highest outside the USA, with the actual number of company-owned stores in the USA falling to 388. About 10,000 employees work for Domino's, but counting all workers for all franchisees, this number is closer to 205,000.

EXHIBIT 2 Finances by Segment (in millions)

Business Segment	Revenue, 2012	Revenue, 2011	Revenue, 2010	Revenue Increase (%)
Domestic company-owned stores	$324	$336	$345	(3.6)
Domestic franchise	195	187	173	4.3
Domestic supply chain	942	928	876	1.5
International	217	201	176	8.0
TOTAL	$1,678	$1,652	$1,571	1.6

Source: Company documents.
Note: Domino's 2012 year ended 1-31-13.

EXHIBIT 3 Same Store Sales Growth (Percent)

	U.S. company-owned stores	U.S. franchise-owned stores	International stores
2008	−2.2	−5.2	6.2
2009	−0.9	0.6	4.3
2010	9.7	10.0	6.9
2011	4.1	3.4	6.8
2012	1.3	3.2	5.2

Source: Company documents.

EXHIBIT 4 Growth: Total Number of Domino's Stores

	U.S. company-owned stores	U.S. franchise-owned stores	International stores
2008	489	4,558	3,736
2009	466	4,461	4,072
2010	454	4,475	4,422
2011	394	4,513	4,835
2012	388	4,540	5,327

Source: Company documents.

Domestic Supply Chain

Domino's domestic supply chain supplies franchisees with dough, vegetables, ovens, uniforms, and much more, enabling better control, pizza consistency, and timely delivery of products. This backward integration strategy enables Domino's to offer pizza at lower prices and allows store managers to focus on store operations rather than mixing dough on site, prepping vegetables, and bargaining with independent suppliers for ingredients. Domino's has 16 regional dough-manufacturing and supply chain centers and leases a fleet of more than 400 trucks to aid in delivering products to stores twice a week. However, Dominos' franchisees are not required to purchase supplies from Domino's, but interestingly more than 99 percent do purchase all its supplies from the company's domestic supply chain segment. To ensure this division remains viable, Domino's provides profit-sharing incentives to franchisees to buy its products from Domino's. In addition to the 16 domestic supply chain centers, Domino's also operates 6 supply chain centers outside the USA.

Domestic Stores

The company's domestic stores division includes a network of 4,540 stores operated by 1,026 franchisees and 388 company-owned stores in the USA. Domino's desires to have all of its stores owned and operated by franchisees, but if certain stores are underperforming, Domino's often will purchase these stores in hopes of turning them around and then refranchising them at a later date. Domino's uses company-owned stores as test sites for new products, promotions, new potential store layout improvements, and as test sites for prospective new franchisees.

Although the typical franchisee of Domino's operates 4 stores, the nine largest franchisees operate more than 50 stores, including the largest domestic franchisee that operates 135 stores. Currently, Domino's has 1,077 different domestic franchisees with the average franchisee being in Domino's system for an impressive 14 years. Much of this longevity can be attributed to Domino's requiring prospective franchisees to manage a store for 1 year before entering into a long-term contract with Domino's. Domino's feels this system is unique to the pizza industry and provides a competitive advantage over rival pizza firms.

International Division

Domino's has 5,327 franchise stores outside the USA. The company's international revenues as a percent of total revenues increased to 13.0 percent in 2012, up from 11.2 percent in 2010. Exhibit 5 provides is a breakdown of Domino's stores in the top 10 markets, which account for

EXHIBIT 5 Top 10 Countries/Regions Where Domino's Are Located

Country/Region	Number of Stores, 2011	Number of Stores, 2012	% Change
United Kingdom	670	720	7.5
Mexico	577	581	0.7
Australia	450	464	3.1
India	439	522	25.7
South Korea	358	372	3.9
Canada	354	368	3.9
Turkey	220	284	29.0
Japan	205	245	19.5
France	195	215	10.3
China Taiwan	141	140	–

Source: Company documents.

more than 75 percent of all Domino's international stores. Note that the United Kingdom has the most Domino's of all countries, followed by Mexico. Among the company's six "international" supply chain centers, four of these are in Canada, one is in Alaska, and one is in Hawaii. (It is unclear why Domino's categorizes Alaska and Hawaii as international). As with Domestic franchisee stores, most of the company's revenue in the international division comes from royalty payments and advertising, as well as the sales of food and supplies to certain markets (predominantly Canada, Alaska, and Hawaii). Note in Exhibit 5 the rapid growth in Domino's stores in India, Turkey, and Japan. The largest Domino's franchisee outside the USA operates 911 stores.

Internal Issues

Domino's has a vertically integrated supply chain where they have backward control to some extent over many of its supplies such as dough, veggies, equipment, and uniforms and forward control over around 400 retail stores that are company owned. Domino's offers little to nothing in terms of healthy food options on the menu, such as salads or fruit. Although this approach enables Domino's to focus exclusively on pizza, this practice also increases the firm's vulnerability to the increasingly health-minded customer and possible government mandates for fast-food restaurants to stop using certain ingredients and preservatives, and potentially forcing all restaurants to label all nutrition information on the menu at the point of sale. Such a law would not be favorable to Domino's.

Domino's attributes much of its success to an incentive-based system for franchisees in which it actively shares in profits through increasing demand for new stores and through purchasing supplies from the Domino's supply chain. Domino's individual franchisee stores and company-owned stores also enjoy a simple and effective store layout enabling pizza delivery and carryout orders to be processed and executed efficiently as compared to many competitors. Unlike Domino's, many rival pizza firms use a dine-in business model, which is much more costly than Domino's strategy. Competitive advantages such as these make Domino's an attractive franchisee option in the quick-service restaurant (QSR) market because overhead and investment is generally cheaper than competing firms.

Sustainability
Sustainability refers to the extent that an organization's operations and actions protect, mend, and preserve rather than harm or destroy the natural environment. Many firms today develop an annual sustainability report, similar to an annual report, to reveal to stakeholders its actions and commitment to sustainability. However, Domino's does not produce an annual sustainability report nor does the company have a sustainability statement on its website.

Advertising and Sales Force

Dominos domestic stores contributed 5.5 percent of all retail sales to support national and local advertising campaigns. Domino's expects this rate to remain unchanged for the foreseeable future. Much of those monies are devoted to mass-mail flyers promoting specials at the local Domino's.

Domino's Pulse Point-of-Sale System

To maximize efficiencies and provide timely financial and marketing data, Domino's requires all stores to install and use its PULSE system that now exists in all company-owned stores and 98 percent of franchisee-owned stores. The system enables touch-screen ordering that improves order accuracy and efficiency and provides the driver with directions and the best route to take for multiple deliveries, saving time and money. In addition, the PULSE system better enables Domino's to ensure it receives full royalties from all transactions in what is often a cash business, assuming the franchisees are honest and always use the PULSE system when receiving orders.

Finance

Domino's recent income statements and balance sheets are provided in Exhibits 6 and 7, respectively. Note that Domino's revenues increased 2.6 percent in 2012 and the firm's long-term debt rose slightly to $1.53 billion. Note the company has zero goodwill on its balance sheet.

EXHIBIT 6 Domino's Pizza, Statements of Income (In thousands, except per share amounts)

	2010	2011	2012
REVENUES:			
Domestic company-owned stores	$ 345,636	$ 336,349	$ 323,652
Domestic franchise	173,345	187,007	195,000
Domestic supply chain	875,517	927,904	942,219
International	176,396	200,933	217,568
Total revenues	1,570,894	1,652,193	1,678,439
COST OF SALES:			
Domestic company-owned stores	278,297	267,066	247,391
Domestic supply chain	778,510	831,665	843,329
International	75,498	82,946	86,381
Total cost of sales	1,132,305	1,181,677	1,177,101
OPERATING MARGIN	438,589	470,516	501,338
GENERAL AND ADMINISTRATIVE	210,887	211,371	219,007
INCOME FROM OPERATIONS	227,702	259,145	282,331
INTEREST INCOME	244	296	304
INTEREST EXPENSE	(96,810)	(91,635)	(101,448)
OTHER	7,809	–	–
INCOME BEFORE PROVISION FOR INCOME TAXES	138,945	167,806	181,187
PROVISION FOR INCOME TAXES	51,028	62,445	68,795
NET INCOME	$ 87,917	$ 105,361	$ 112,392
EARNINGS PER SHARE:			
Common Stock—basic	$ 1.50	$ 1.79	$ 1.99
Common Stock—diluted	$ 1.45	$ 1.71	$ 1.91

Source: 2012 Form 10K, p. 50.

EXHIBIT 7 Domino's Pizza, Balance Sheets (In thousands except share and per share amounts)

	2011	2012
ASSETS		
CURRENT ASSETS:		
Cash and cash equivalents	$ 50,292	$ 54,813
Restricted cash and cash equivalents	92,612	60,015
Accounts receivable, net of reserves of $5,446 in 2011 and $5,906 in 2012	87,200	94,103
Inventories	30,702	31,061
Notes receivable, net of reserves of $324 in 2011 and $630 in 2012	945	1,858
Prepaid expenses and other	12,232	11,210
Advertising fund assets, restricted	36,281	37,917
Deferred income taxes	16,579	15,290
Total current assets	326,843	306,267
PROPERTY, PLANT AND EQUIPMENT:		
Land and buildings	23,714	24,460
Leasehold and other improvements	79,518	80,279
Equipment	171,726	168,452
Construction in Process	6,052	9,967
	281,010	283,158
Accumulated depreciation and amortization	(188,610)	(191,713)
Property, plant and equipment, net	92,400	91,445
OTHER ASSETS:		
Investments in marketable securities, restricted	1,538	2,097
Notes receivable, less current portion, net of reserves of $1,735 in 2011 and $814 in 2012	5,070	3,028
Deferred financing costs, net of accumulated amortization of $25,590 in 2011 and $5,201 in 2012	16,051	34,787
Goodwill	16,649	16,598
Capitalized software, net of accumulated amortization of $51,274 in 2011 and $48,381 in 2012	8,176	11,387
Other assets, net of accumulated amortization of $4,070 in 2011 and $4,404 in 2012	8,958	8,635
Deferred income taxes	4,858	3,953
Total other assets	61,300	80,485
Total assets	$ 480,543	$ 478,197

LIABILITIES AND STOCKHOLDERS' DEFICIT		
CURRENT LIABILITIES:	2011	2012
Current portion of long-term debt	$ 904	$ 24,349
Accounts payable	69,714	77,414
Accrued compensation	21,691	21,843
Accrued interest	15,775	15,035
Insurance reserves	13,023	12,964
Legal reserves	10,069	5,025
Advertising fund liabilities	36,281	37,917
Other accrued liabilities	29,718	34,951
Total current liabilities	$ 197,175	$ 229,498

EXHIBIT 7 Continued

	2011	2012
LONG-TERM LIABILITIES:		
Long-term debt, less current portion	$ 1,450,369	$ 1,536,443
Insurance Reserves	21,334	24,195
Deferred income taxes	5,021	7,001
Other accrued liabilities	16,383	16,583
Total long-term liabilities	1,493,107	1,584,222
Total liabilities	1,690,282	1,813,720
COMMITMENTS AND CONTINGENCIES		
STOCKHOLDERS' DEFICIT:		
Common stock, par value $0.01 per share;	577	563
170,000,000 shares authorized; 57,741,208 in 2011		
and 56,313,249 in 2012 issued and outstanding		
Preferred stock, par value $0.01 per share; 5,000,000	–	–
shares authorized, none issued		
Additional paid-in capital	–	1,664
Retained deficit	(1,207,915)	(1,335,364)
Accumulated other comprehensive loss	(2,401)	(2,386)
Total stockholders' deficit	(1,209,739)	(1,335,523)
Total liabilities and stockholders' deficit	$ 480,543	$ 478,197

Source: 2012 *Form 10K*, pp 48-49.

Competitors

Competition in both the USA and international pizza-delivery and carry-out business is extremely intense, with Pizza Hut (owned by Yum Brands) being the largest competitor in the industry. Pizza Hut's revenues are more than 60 percent greater than Domino's. Papa John's and Little Caesars are also fierce rivals in the industry. In fact, Little Caesars was listed as the fastest-growing pizza chain in 2010, with revenues up 13.6 percent over 2009, followed by Pizza Hut's 8 percent increase and Domino's 7.2 percent increase. In addition to the three main rivals, Domino's faces intense competition from many local mom-and-pop pizza stores, frozen pizzas from the grocery store, as well as hundreds of non-pizza fast-food options. Pizza Hut, Domino's, and Papa John's account for 51 percent of all consumer spending on pizza delivery stores in the USA, with the other 49 percent coming from regional or mom-and-pop establishments.

Internationally, Pizza Hut and Domino's are the main players in the industry, but various countries have numerous national companies and thousands of mom-and-pop pizza and Italian restaurants vie for business as well. As with the domestic market, some customers consider local pizza stores to offer better quality products than large chains and are willing to pay marginally higher prices for this perceived quality.

Another competitor is Pizza Inn Holdings, Inc., based in The Colony, Texas. Pizza Inn owns 10 stores and franchises out 300 more stores.

Pizza Hut

A division of Yum Brands, Pizza Hut is based in Plano, Texas, and operates more than 7,200 restaurants in the USA and more than 5,600 restaurants internationally in more than 90 countries. In contrast to Domino's, almost all Pizza Huts are dine-in restaurants. Pizza Huts serve pan pizza, as well as its thin n' crispy, stuffed crust, hand tossed, and sicilian. Other menu items include pasta, salads, and sandwiches. Pizza Huts offer dine-in service at its famous red-roofed restaurants, as well as carryout and delivery service. About 15 percent of all Pizza Huts are company-operated, whereas the remaining stores are franchised. The world's largest fast food company, YUM Brands also owns and operates Kentucky Fried Chicken (KFC), Long John Silvers, and Taco Bell. Pizza Hut is Domino's major pizza rival outside of the USA.

Papa John's International, Inc.

Headquartered in Louisville, Kentucky, and founded in 1985, Papa John's operates 3,883 pizza restaurants with 3,255 of these being franchisee-owned and 628 being company-owned stores. Papa John's has restaurants in all 50 U.S. states and 32 foreign markets. The company currently has 16,500 full-time employees and markets its pizza under the slogan "better ingredients, better pizza." Between 2001 and 2012, Papa John's was ranked number one (by the American Customer Satisfaction Index) among national pizza chains for 10 of the 11 years during this period. The company reported revenue of more than $1.2 billion for year-end 2011, and consistent with the industry, it shows no revenue allocated to research and development. Papa John's carries $75 million in goodwill on its balance sheet; founder and CEO John Schnatter owns more than 20 percent of the chain. Papa John's offers several different pizza styles and topping choices, as well as a few specialty pies such as The Works and The Meats. Papa John's stores typically offer delivery and carryout service only.

Exhibit 8 provides a comparison between Domino's and Papa John's. Note that Domino's appears to generate more revenue with less employees, but that is not true because employees at franchised stores are not Domino's employees. Pizza Inn's 57 employees work at company-owned restaurants, not franchised stores.

Pizza Inn Holdings, Inc.

Pizza Inn is a relatively small chain of franchised quick-service pizza restaurants, with more than 300 locations in the USA and the Middle East. Pizza Inns offer pizzas, pastas, and sandwiches, along with salads and desserts. Most locations offer buffet-style and table service, whereas other units are strictly delivery and carryout units. The chain also has limited-menu express carryout units in convenience stores and airport terminals, and on college campuses. Pizza Inn's domestic locations are concentrated in more than 15 southern states, with about half located in Texas and North Carolina.

Little Caesars

Headquartered in Detroit, Michigan, and privately held, Little Caesars is famous for its advertising slogan, "Pizza! Pizza!" which was introduced in 1979. The phrase refers to two pizzas being offered for the comparable price of a single pizza from competitors. In November 2010, Little Caesars introduced Pizza! Pizza! Pantastic, denying that the return of "Pizza! Pizza!" had any relationship to the recent success of Domino's. Little Caesars operates under its parent Little Caesars Enterprises and is estimated to be the fourth largest pizza chain in the USA. Little Caesars operates in 30 foreign countries.

External Issues

Domino's competes in the Quick Service Restaurant (QSR) pizza category, which consists of two categories: 1) delivery and 2) carry-out. Delivery revenues for the industry in 2012 were $9.6 billion, up only slightly the last few years. The delivery portion accounts for 30 percent of

EXHIBIT 8 A Comparison Between Domino's and Papa John's

	Domino's	Papa John's	Pizza Inn Holdings
Revenue	1.65B	1.24B	43.5M
Market Capitalization	1.76B	1.16B	20.1M
Gross Margin	0.29	0.31	0.12
Net Income	98.99M	55.97M	888K
EPS	1.63	2.24	0.10
Price/Earnings Ratio	18.67	21.69	24.51
Number of Employees	10K	16.5K	57

EPS, earnings per share.
Source: Company documents.

the total QSP pizza revenues. However, the carry-out portion of the industry grew revenues from $14.1 billion in 2011 to $14.6 billion in 2012. Domino's is the market leader in delivery and second largest in carry-out. Outside of the USA, pizza delivery is underdeveloped, with Domino's and one rival being the only firms.

Nutrition Concerns

An area of concern for all fast-food establishments, including pizza stores, is the growing health-minded customer, as well as the growing pressure from government agencies to label all products with nutrition information. There have been battles between the restaurant industry and government agencies for many years, but much like the tobacco industry (in respect to labeling its products). It appears the war is close to being lost for the restaurant industry. Domino's itemizes nutrition information on its website, but forces the customer to add the calories for crust, sauce, cheese, and topping, and then divide by the number of slices to derive the total calorie count per slice. After doing the calculations, one large slice of hand-tossed pepperoni pizza for example has 300 calories and 12 grams of fat, and there are 8 slices in a pizza. To complicate matters for restaurants such as Domino's, it is difficult to provide accurate nutrition labels when there can be an almost endless combination of ingredients on a pizza. For example, someone may order a large sausage pizza with onions and olives whereas someone else might order extra cheese and tomatoes. Having to print out nutrition labels for all these combinations would be quite costly as opposed to a restaurant like McDonald's where it can print the nutrition label on the Big Mac because there is uniformity in ingredients and the label is understood to be for the base item. However, Domino's PULSE system could possibly be adjusted to resolve this potential issue.

Chipotle Mexican Grill claims to only use meat and dairy products from free-ranging cattle, as opposed to cattle injected with growth hormones. Domino's Pizza markets its pizzas as having gluten-free crust. This is an attempt to win over health-conscious customers, comply with government regulations, and make current customers feel a little less guilty about eating pizza. The tug of war between customers, governments, lawyers, and the restaurant industry on health issues is likely to continue for some time.

In response to these challenges, many restaurants have opted for healthy menu options. Wendy's, for example, has promoted several meal combinations that contain less than 10 grams of fat. All of these items were originally on its menu, just not marketed in that manner. Wendy's has added side salads and fruit to help cut down on calories, fat, and sodium. Subway is also famous for marketing its products as healthy alternatives to other fast-food options. Domino's, and many pizza competitors, offer few to no menu options for the health-conscious consumer.

Barriers to Entry

Barriers to entry are relatively low for the restaurant industry, but rivalry (competitiveness) among firms is exceptionally high. One large contributing factor for the low barriers to entry is many small entrepreneurs can open mom-and-pop establishments and bypass the franchise fees, royalties, selection process, and so on of owning a franchised restaurant and lease an existing building relatively cheap. However, even avoiding high fixed costs, variable costs are often high and small-scale entrepreneurs are not able to compete with larger franchise stores, who can better negotiate pricing on food, packaging, and other supplies. In the QSR industry, the bargaining power of consumers is quite powerful, availability of restaurant options in most places is abundant, and consequently there is intense price competitiveness among rival firms. Even if you are sure you want pizza for lunch or dinner, you likely have many options.

Economic Factors

The current landscape in the QSR business is a bimodal population distribution with a large population of bargain-minded customers seeking deals on cheaper end fast food options, and another population of more affluent consumers targeting middle to higher-end restaurants. Domino's is well positioned strategically to target the first group of consumers because there are many more of them; Domino's often has excellent sales and discounts to target this group.

Among the subset of customers who are value shoppers, many of these are also shoppers of quality and are willing to wait in line a little longer or pay a little more for better quality food products. Domino's has recently capitalized on this well with the introduction of its artisan pizzas and new recipes (or higher quality products) for its crust, sauce, and cheeses. In addition, Domino's offers many pick up specials. Although an inconvenience over delivery, many customers in today's climate are willing to tolerate a degree of inconvenience that they historically were not if they can get a better deal.

Similar to Domino's, many restaurant owners in the fast-food industry have experienced stronger growth in international markets than domestic markets. This trend is expected to continue, especially in China and other developing nations because many U.S. fast-food options are still novel, even in Europe. According to the S&P Industry Surveys, QSRs are expected to see a sales increase of 3 percent in 2012 and orders to increase 1.5 percent as a result in large part of consumers trading down to cheaper restaurant alternatives. There also is a steadily growing international appetite for U.S. fast food and an improving global economy. These positive trends are expected to continue into 2013 and should bode well for Domino's with its strong international presence.

Ethics and Corporate Citizenship

Domino's has two extensive "Code of Ethics" documents on its website: one statement for its employees and one statement for its executives. The documents outline matters such as: conflicts of interest, how to report unethical conduct, fair dealing with all employees, compliance with laws, proper way to use company assets, and much more.

In addition to Domino's Code of Ethics statements, the company is noted for its corporate citizenship record in particular with St. Jude Children's Research Hospital. Since 2006, Domino's has donated more than $12 million to St. Jude and has hosted pizza parties for patients and its families on St. Jude properties.

In 1986, Domino's launched its Pizza Partners Foundation with a mission of "team members helping team members." The foundation is 100-percent funded by team member and franchise contributions and has disbursed nearly $12 million to aid team members facing crisis situations such as fire, illness, or other personal tragedies.

The Future

As CEO Doyle and his management team contemplate the future direction of Domino's, it has much to consider. Should the firm continue its aggressive market development strategies and accept the risk associated with expanding into markets it has little expertise operating within? What new geographic locations or regions should Domino's focus? Should Domino's simply follow Pizza Hut's international rollout of stores? How would this expansion affect the corporate structure of Domino's? Would restructuring by geographic division and thus establishing offices in Asia, the Middle East, and South America better enable them to manage these more risky environments? Can Domino's afford this financially? Should Domino's consider offering salads or a line of healthy menu options? Should Domino's purchase trucks to deliver its products rather than incurring such heavy leasing expenses?

Domino's needs a clear three-year strategic plan. Prepare this document for the company.

Dunkin' Brands Group, Inc., 2015

www.dunkinbrands.com, DNKN

Headquartered in Canton, Massachusetts, Dunkin' Brands (Dunkin') sells hot and cold coffee and baked goods, as well as hard-serve ice cream, using a near-100 percent franchised business model. With 11,300 Dunkin' Donuts restaurants in 40 states and 32 foreign countries, and 7,500 Baskin-Robbins restaurants in 43 states and 46 foreign countries, Dunkin' is one of the world's largest franchisors of quick-service restaurants (QSR). All but 36 Dunkin' Donuts and Baskin-Robbins are franchisee-owned. In the last few years, more and more customers are coming into Dunkin' restaurants and spending more and more money when they are there. About 70 percent of all Dunkin' stores have a drive thru, which caters to consumers in a hurry. Dunkin' is a speed leader among QSR, even given increased ticket volume and menu complexity.

Dunkin' recently launched a loyalty and rewards program that enables the company to collect data from customers to determine their habits. For example, if you normally visit Dunkin' Donuts in the morning, the firm may soon send you offers to purchase some donuts in the afternoon or evening. Companies increasingly are using business analytics to make strategic decisions. Major rival firms in the coffee retailing business include Starbucks, Krispy Kreme Doughnuts, and Tim Hortons. Dunkin' especially caters to the on-the-go consumer looking for a quick coffee and breakfast. One potential weakness for Dunkin' is that the firm does not offer many healthy food options for health-conscious customers.

Coffee prices rose 50 percent in 2014 due to drought conditions in South America, especially since Brazil endured its worst drought in decades. The 2014 coffee harvest in Brazil was the lowest in three years. To take up the slack, Colombia, the world's number-two Arabica grower, was increasing production, but Colombia only produces about one quarter as much coffee as Brazil.

Dunkin' Brands is performing quite well. In mid-2015, Dunkin' announced agreements with seven franchise groups to open 51 new restaurants in Virginia and West Virginia over the next several years. Of the seven groups, only one is a new franchisee while the rest are existing franchisees/franchise groups. For Q1 of 2015, the company's revenues increased 8.1 percent year-over-year to $185.9 million, driven partly by revenue from the Dunkin' K-Cup pack licensing agreement with Keurig Green Mountain, Inc.

Copyright by Fred David Books LLC. www.strategyclub.com (Written by Meredith E. David)

History

Independently in the 1940s, Bill Rosenberg founded the first Dunkin' Donut restaurant, and Burt Baskin and Irv Robbins each founded a chain of ice cream shops that eventually combined to form Baskin-Robbins. Baskin-Robbins and Dunkin' Donuts were acquired by Allied Domecq in 1973 and 1989, respectively, and renamed Dunkin' Brands, Inc. in 2004. Allied was acquired in 2005 by Pernod Ricard, who soon sold the firm to Bain Capital Partners, LLC, The Carlyle Group, and Thomas H. Lee Partners, L.P. In 2011, Dunkin' Brands became listed on the NASDAQ Global Select Market under the symbol "DNKN."

Dunkin' Donuts

Bill Rosenberg opened his first donut restaurant, Kettle Donuts, in 1948, in Quincy, Massachusetts. The name changed to Dunkin' Donuts in 1950. Rosenberg sold franchisees to others as early as 1955. The 100th restaurant opened in 1963, the 1,000th in 1979, and the 3,000th in 1992. In 1996, bagels were introduced to the Dunkin' Donuts menu and breakfast sandwiches the following year.

In 2013, Dunkin' Donuts received the No. 1 ranking for customer loyalty in the coffee category by Brand Keys for eight years running, and was rated by CREST in December 2013 as number-one in iced regular/decaf/flavored coffee, number-one in hot regular/decaf/flavored coffee, number-one in donut category, and number-one in bagel and muffin category.

The following year, Dunkin' Donuts reentered the United Kingdom, 20 years after it exited the country, with its first store opening in Harrow, London. In Canada, Dunkin' Donuts has lost a substantial percent of its market share in recent years, and now has only five restaurants, all in Quebec. Dunkin's Canadian decline is largely due to rival donut firm Tim Hortons.

Baskin-Robbins
In 1945, brothers-in-law Burt Baskin and Irv Robbins owned different ice cream parlors, Burton's Ice Cream and Snowbird Ice Cream, both in Glendale, California. The separate companies merged in 1953 and the number of ice cream flavors increased to 31. That year, Baskin-Robbins hired Carson-Roberts Advertising who recommended adoption of the number 31 as well as the pink (cherry) and brown (chocolate) polka dots and typeface. In the 1970s, the company went international, opening stores in Japan, Saudi Arabia, Korea, and Australia. Baskin-Robbins was the first company to introduce ice cream cakes to the public, and the first to offer both hand scooped and Soft Serve ice cream. In some places, such as Malaysia, Baskin-Robbins gives 31 percent off their hand-packed ice cream on the 31st of a month.

Today, Baskin-Robbins is the world's largest chain of ice cream specialty shops serving premium ice cream, specialty-frozen desserts, and beverages to more than 300 million customers annually. In 2014, the company was named the top U.S. ice cream and frozen dessert franchise by *Entrepreneur* magazine.

Vision/Mission
Dunkin's vision statement is given on the corporate website as follows: "Serving Responsibly— To be recognized as a company that responsibly serves our guests, franchisees, employees, communities, business partners, and the interests of our planet."

Dunkin's mission statement is also given on the corporate website, but it is titled "Our Priorities." The statement has four parts: Our People, Our Guests, Our Neighborhoods, and Our Planet. For example, regarding Our People, the statement reads: "From our employees and franchisees to the farmers who grow our coffee, we believe in treating everyone with respect and fairness so they are empowered to reach their goals."

Organizational Structure

In 2014, Dunkin' extended Chairman and CEO Nigel Travis's employment contract through December 2018. Mr. Travis, age 64, joined Dunkin' Brands as CEO in December 2008; his contract was to expire in 2016. Besides Mr. Travis, other top executives at Dunkin' are listed in Exhibit 1. Notice there is no Chief Operating Officer and Mr. Travis is both the Chairman and CEO. Also notice there are no women or minorities among the top nine executives.

Regarding Dunkin's number of employees, since the company is nearly 100 percent franchised, workers are employed and paid by the franchisee, rather than by Dunkin'. Dunkin' has no unionized employees.

EXHIBIT 1 Dunkin' Brands' Organizational Chart

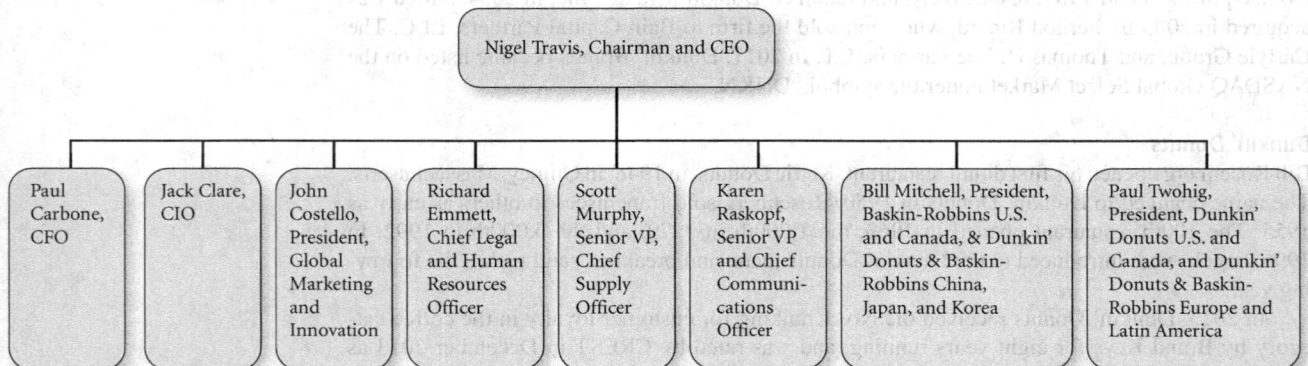

Source: Based on information at Dunkin' Brands' corporate website.

Internal Issues

Strategy

Dunkin' is opening 65 Dunkin' Donuts stores in Brazil's capital of Brasilia and surrounding states by 2016, through a licensing agreement with OLH Group. The new stores will be primarily in the capital city of Brasilia and the state of Goias. Dunkin' also has plans to open an additional 80 stores in Brazil outside of the capital area by 2018. Dunkin's largest South American presence to date is in Colombia with 171 restaurants. In 2014, Dunkin' opened about 700 Dunkin' Donuts and Baskin-Robbins stores worldwide. Store cannibalization is becoming a problem in some areas as the firm increasingly opens new stores in close proximity to existing stores. Dunkin' restaurants are most heavily concentrated in the New England region of the United States. Dunkin' franchisees are currently overhauling restaurant décor into a "sip and sit" atmosphere, with over 100 restaurants now offering soft seating areas, as well as high and low tables and stools. The new décor features earthy colors, contemporary lights, coffee-housed themed artwork, free Wi-Fi, power outlets, flat panel televisions, and digital menus.

To keep revenues flowing around the clock, Dunkin' Donuts (and rival Starbucks) now offer more dinner-friendly foods. "Though breakfast remains our core, today people are seeking all-day dining, and they want to eat what they want, when they want it and where they want it," says John Costello, Dunkin' Donuts president of global marketing and innovation. Thus, Dunkin' Donuts in late 2014 introduced a dinner staple (steak) and made a steak sandwich as well as a wrap with eggs permanent additions to its menu. Only 40 percent of Dunkin' Donuts' sales come after 11 AM, leaving a lot of room for growth in that arena, especially at the more than 2,300 Dunkin' Donuts in the United States that are open 24 hours. Most Dunkin' Donuts, Costello said, are open until 10 PM.

Sustainability

Dunkin' Brands has a current Corporate Sustainability Report (CSR) posted on their website. The CSR details how Dunkin' is progressing toward improving on its environmental goals and objectives. For example, the Dunkin' Donuts & Baskin-Robbins Community Foundation (DDBRCF) recently partnered with Feeding America to support such initiatives as the BackPack Program to provide hungry children with nutritious and easy-to-prepare food to take home on weekends, and to support the School Pantry Program, which helps alleviate child hunger in America.

Franchise Fees

In the United States, Dunkin' Donuts franchisees pay a royalty of about 5.4 percent of gross sales to the company, and Baskin-Robbins franchisees pay about 5.0 percent. However, outside the United States, Dunkin' Donut franchisees, on average, pay a royalty rate of only 2.1 percent. For the Baskin-Robbins brand outside the United States, Dunkin' does not generally receive royalty payments from franchisees; instead, it earns revenue from such franchisees by selling ice cream products to them, so the royalty rate in this segment is about 0.7 percent. Dunkin' franchisees in the United States also pay advertising fees of about 5 percent of gross sales.

Segments

Dunkin' Brands operates in four segments: (1) Dunkin' Donuts U.S., (2) Dunkin' Donuts International, (3) Baskin-Robbins International, and (4) Baskin-Robbins U.S. The two Dunkin' Donuts U.S. and International segments generated 2014 revenues of about $568 million, or about 76 percent of the firm's total segment revenues, of which $549 million was in the U.S. segment and $20 million was in the international segment. As calendar 2015 began, there were 11,275 Dunkin' Donuts stores—8,047 in the United States and 3,228 in 32 countries outside the United States.

The two Baskin-Robbins segments generated 2014 annual revenues of about $122 million in the international segment and about $43 million in the U.S. segment. As calendar 2015 began, there were 7,546 Baskin-Robbins stores—5,068 were international in 46 countries outside the United States, and 2,478 were in the United States.

In Q4 of 2015, Dunkin' Brands' franchisees and licensees opened another 260 restaurants worldwide, including 141 Dunkin' Donuts U.S. locations, 75 Baskin-Robbins International

EXHIBIT 2 Dunkin' Brands' Number of Restaurants at Year-End

	2014	2013	2012
Dunkin' Donuts U.S.	8,047	7,677	7,306
Dunkin' Donuts International	3,228	3,181	3,043
Baskin-Robbins U.S.	2,478	2,467	2,463
Baskin-Robbins International	5,068	4,833	4,556
Total	**18,821**	**18,158**	**17,368**

outlets, 46 Dunkin' Donuts International units. Also, two Baskin-Robbins U.S. locations were closed. Additionally, Dunkin' Donuts U.S. franchisees remodeled 172 restaurants during the quarter. Exhibit 2 provides a breakdown of Dunkin' Brands' restaurants.

Since Dunkin' Brands is nearly 100 percent franchised, revenues derived from selling both ice cream and donuts to consumers is reported on the franchisees' financial statements, rather than on Dunkin's financial statements. Thus, the company generates revenue from five primary sources: royalty income and fees, rental income from restaurant properties leased, sales of ice cream products to franchisee, retail store revenue at company-owned stores, and licensing of the Dunkin' Donuts brand for products sold in nonfranchised outlets (such as retail packaged coffee).

Outside the United States, Dunkin' stores are predominantly located in Asia and the Middle East, which accounted for about 70 and 16 percent, respectively, of international franchisee-reported sales in 2014.

Dunkin' Donuts

The Dunkin' Donuts brand has evolved into a predominantly coffee-based concept, with approximately 57 percent of Dunkin' Donuts' U.S. franchisee-reported sales for fiscal year 2013 generated from coffee and other beverages. Dunkin' Donuts has centralized manufacturing locations (CMLs) that are franchisee-owned and operated for producing donuts and bakery goods. The CMLs deliver freshly baked products to Dunkin' Donuts restaurants on a daily basis with consistent quality. At year-end 2013, there were 114 Dunkin' CMLs of varying size and capacity in the United States. However, some Dunkin' Donuts restaurants produce donuts and bakery goods on-site rather than relying on CMLs. Some of those stand-alone Dunkin' Donuts restaurants supply other local Dunkin' Donuts restaurants that do not have access to CMLs.

Dunkin's coffee supplier, National DCP LLC, hedges coffee prices with farmers, protecting Dunkin' from rapid swings in coffee price. Coffee prices have been rising of late, due to inclement weather, especially a drought in South America. Consequently, the price of Robusta coffee beans is high, whereas Arabica coffee bean prices are lower. Dunkin' is positioned well somewhat because on the Dunkin' website, it says, "We use 100% Arabica coffee beans."

Exhibit 3 provides a breakdown of Dunkin' Donuts' restaurants outside the United States, and income globally.

Baskin-Robbins

Dunkin' Brands outsources all its manufacturing and distribution of ice cream products for the domestic Baskin-Robbins brand franchisees to Dean Foods. Dunkin's Baskin-Robbins U.S. segment has reported comparable store sales growth in each of the last three fiscal years. The company's "31 flavors" offer consumers a different flavor for each day of the month. Baskin-Robbins USA franchise system has sales of about $520 million, or 5.5 percent of Dunkin's global franchisee-reported sales.

About 65 percent of Baskin-Robbins restaurants are located outside of the United States and operate primarily through joint ventures and country or territorial license arrangements with "master franchisees." The Baskin-Robbins international franchise system, predominantly located across Asia and the Middle East, generated franchisee-reported sales of $2.0 billion in 2013, or 22.1 percent of Dunkin' Brands' global franchisee-reported sales.

The number of Baskin-Robbins outside of the United States are revealed in Exhibit 4, as well as the segment's income globally.

EXHIBIT 3 The Number of Dunkin' Donuts Outside the United States and Income Globally (in thousands of USD)

	2014 # Stores	2013 # Stores
South Korea	902	827
Middle East	338	386
Other	1,941	2,015
Total	**3,181**	**3,228**
Dunkin' Donuts U.S.		
Income		
Royalty income	$362,342	$337,170
Franchise fees	36,192	29,445
Rental income	91,918	92,049
Sales at company-owned stores	24,976	22,765
Other revenues	5,751	3,970
Total revenues	**521,179**	**485,399**
Segment profit	**379,751**	**355,274**
Dunkin' Donuts International		
Income		
Royalty income	$14,249	$13,474
Franchise fees	3,531	1,715
Rental income	133	179
Other revenues	403	117
Total revenues	**18,316**	**15,485**
Segment profit	**7,479**	**9,670**

EXHIBIT 4 The Number of Baskin-Robbins Outside the United States and Income Globally (in thousands of USD)

	2014 # Stores	2013 # Stores
South Korea	1,065	1,106
Japan	1,157	1,170
Middle East	706	754
Other	1,805	2,030
Total	**4,833**	**5,068**
Baskin-Robbins U.S.		
Income		
Royalty income	$25,728	$25,768
Franchise fees	1,160	775
Rental income	3,420	3,949
Sales of ice cream products	3,808	3,942
Sales at company-owned stores	—	157
Other revenues	8,036	7,483
Total revenues	**42,152**	**42,074**
Segment profit	**27,081**	**26,274**
Baskin-Robbins International		
Income		
Royalty income	$9,109	$9,301
Franchise fees	1,665	1,292
Rental income	535	561
Sales of ice cream products	108,435	90,717
Other revenues	589	104
Total revenues	**120,333**	**101,975**
Segment profit	**54,321**	**42,004**

Finance

Dunkin' Brands' revenues in 2014 were $748.7 million, up 4.9 percent year over year. Adjusted earnings per share were $1.74, up 13.7 percent over the prior year. For that quarter, Dunkin' Brands declared a quarterly dividend of 26.5 cents per share of common stock, an increase of 15 percent from the prior quarter. The increased dividend was paid on March 18, 2015 of record as of March 9.

Dunkin' Brands' income statement and balance sheet are provided in Exhibits 5 and 6, respectively.

EXHIBIT 5 Dunkin' Brands' Income Statement (in thousands of USD)

Report Date	December 27, 2014	December 28, 2013
Revenues	$748,709	$713,840
Operating expenses	432,535	436,631
Operating income	22,684	27,527
EBIT	338,858	304,736
Interest	83,125	86,648
EBT	255,733	218,088
Tax	80,170	71,784
Other items	794	599
Net income	**176,357**	**146,903**

Source: Based on p. 52 in Dunkin's 2014 *Form 10K.*

EXHIBIT 6 Dunkin' Brands' Balance Sheet (in thousands of USD)

Report Date	December 27, 2014	December 27, 2013
Cash	$208,080	$256,933
Accounts receivable	105,060	79,765
Inventories	—	—
Other current assets	129,478	125,062
Total current assets	442,618	461,760
Property, plant & equipment	182,061	182,858
Equity investments	164,493	170,644
Goodwill & intangibles	2,317,167	2,343,803
Other assets	71,044	75,625
Total assets	**3,177,383**	**3,234,690**
Short-term debt	3,852	5,000
Accounts payable	13,814	12,445
Other current liabilities	337,853	326,853
Total current liabilities	355,519	344,298
Long-term debt	1,807,081	1,818,609
Deferred income taxes	540,339	561,714
Other liabilities	99,494	97,781
Total liabilities	**2,802,433**	**2,822,402**
Noncontrolling interest	6,991	4,930
Common stock	104	107
Retained earnings	(711,531)	(779,741)
Treasury stock	—	(10,773)
Paid in capital and other	1,079,386	1,197,765
Total equity	**367,959**	**407,358**
Total liabilities, noncontrolling interest, & equity	**3,177,383**	**3,234,690**

Source: Based on p. 51 in Dunkin's 2014 *Form 10K.*

Competitors

There are thousands of "mom-and-pop" doughnut shops globally. However, Krispy Kreme Doughnuts (KKD), Starbucks, Dunkin' Brands Group, and Tim Hortons (now owned by Restaurant Brands) are dominant rivals, and have been increasing coffee and doughnuts sales annually. For example, total sales in 2014 for KKD, Starbucks, and Dunkin' Brands Group, increased 6.5, 10.1, and 4.9 percent, respectively. All four companies have aggressive expansion plans. Krispy Kreme Doughnuts is in an aggressive growth mode and plans to expand in a way similar to that of Dunkin' Brands, which plans to double its Dunkin' Donuts store count to around 15,000 in the United States alone. Krispy Kreme plans to increase its 800 stores worldwide to 1,300 by 2017.

Exhibit 7 provides some comparative information about Dunkin' Brands, Krispy Kreme Doughnuts, and Starbucks. Revenue per employee is not really applicable due to franchising, whereas the persons are employees of the franchisee and not Dunkin'.

Starbucks Corporation (SBUX)

Starbucks is the world's largest specialty coffee retailer with more than 18,000 coffee shops in 60 countries. It offers coffee drinks and pastries, roasted beans, coffee accessories, and teas. The company owns about 9,400 of its own shops (mostly in the United States), while licensees and franchisees operate roughly 8,650 units worldwide (primarily in shopping centers and airports). In 2014, Starbucks began offering beer and wine, as well as fancy snacks, chicken skewers, chocolate fondue, and other items. By year-end 2014, only 40 Starbucks offered these new items. The company also owns the Seattle's Best Coffee and Torrefazione Italia coffee brands. Starbucks markets its coffee through grocery stores and licenses its brand for other food and beverage products. The company is determined to get the afternoon and evening customer, whereas historically it has mainly been a breakfast place. That is why the beer, wine, and more food is being rolled out at more and more Starbucks outlets.

The company sees afternoon and dinner also as a way to differentiate itself from Dunkin' Donuts and Krispy Kreme Doughnuts that historically have been more about quick service than sit down and stay, which is the venue Starbucks plans to enter aggressively globally. Starbucks now offers 10 standard small dinner plates as part of its evening menu, such as truffle macaroni and cheese. There are also five choices of red wine, three white wines, a sparkling rose, and prosecco.

Krispy Kreme Doughnuts (KKD)

Krispy Kreme Doughnuts is chain of doughnut outlets with about 695 locations throughout the United States and in about 20 other countries. The shops are popular for their glazed doughnuts that are served fresh and hot out of the fryer, as well as cake and filled doughnuts, crullers, and fritters. Hot coffee and other beverages also are sold. KKD outlets are almost all owned and operated by franchisees; the company owns and operates 90 locations. Aside from doughnuts and coffee, no other food items of substance are offered. The company markets its doughnuts through grocery stores and supermarkets.

Green Mountain Coffee Roasters Inc. (GMCR) and KKD have agreed to widen the home-made single-serve coffee options for Keurig users, whereby KKD's upcoming coffees—Smooth and Decaf—will be available in K-Cup packs for Keurig brewers. Krispy Kreme's K-Cup packs

EXHIBIT 7 Dunkin' Donuts versus Rival Firms

	Dunkin'	Krispy Kreme	Starbucks
# Employees	1,150	2,500	191,000
$ Net Income	$176 M	$34 M	$2,068 M
$ Revenue	$748 M	$460 M	$16,447 M
$ Revenue/Employee	NA	$184,000	$86,110
$ EPS Ratio	$1.65	$0.55	$3.30
Market Cap.	$5.0 B	$1.4 B	$66.7 B

will be available at the online shopping sites of Keurig and KKD, along with the participating KKD shops, grocery, and many other retail outlets. The convenience of Keurig brewers will enhance the popularity of KKD coffee among Keurig fans.

The fiscal fourth-quarter results for KKD on March 12, 2014, saw revenue rise 3.3 percent to $112.7 million. Company-owned same-store sales rose 1.6 percent, and franchise same-store sales soared 6.7 percent. Adjusted net income grew 37 percent to $8.3 million. It was the fifth full year and 21st quarter in a row of same-store KKD sales gains.

Tim Hortons, Inc.

Tim Hortons is Canada's leading quick-service restaurant brand, having more than 4,250 coffee and donut shops across the country, and in several U.S. states. Tim Hortons was acquired by Burger King Worldwide in late 2014 in an $11 billion deal, and BKW immediately created Restaurant Brands International (RBI). RBI is now the second largest global quick-service restaurant in the world. Today, BKW is headquartered in Oakville, outside of Toronto, Canada.

The Tim Horton menu features a variety of coffees and cappuccino, along with donuts, Dutchies, bagels, and other baked goods. In addition, Tim Hortons serves a lunch menu of soup, sandwiches, and chili. The chain includes freestanding as well as kiosk and mall-based outlets; all but about 20 of the locations are operated by franchisees. The company owns the Cold Stone Creamery ice cream shop chain. Tim Hortons' revenues in a recent quarter increased 10.7 percent, and adjusted earnings-per-share grew 6 percent.

External Issues

Barriers to Entry

Barriers to entry are relatively low for the restaurant industry, but rivalry (competitiveness) among firms is exceptionally high. One large contributing factor for the low barriers to entry is many small entrepreneurs can open mom-and-pop establishments and bypass the franchise fees, royalties, selection process, and so on, of owning a franchised restaurant and lease an existing building at a relatively low price. There are thousands of mom-and-pop donut shops across the United States and likely tens of thousands of small ice cream places. However, even avoiding high fixed costs, variable costs are often high, and small-scale entrepreneurs are not able to compete with larger franchise stores that can better negotiate pricing on food, packaging, and other supplies. In the QSR industry, the bargaining power of consumers is quite powerful, availability of restaurant options in most places is abundant, and consequently there is intense price competitiveness among rival firms. Even if you are sure you want a donut or ice cream, you likely have many options.

Future

Dunkin' Brands reported slower sales growth slow in Q4 of 2014 as it faced intensifying competition for on-the-go customers in the mornings. Sales for Dunkin' Donuts USA edged up 1.4 percent in the period, down from the growth of 3.5 percent a year ago. Analysts say the slowdown comes as more competitors have pushed into the breakfast category, a relative bright spot in the fast-food industry. For example, Yum Brands' Taco Bell segment recently reported that its quarterly sales rose 7 percent in its U.S. locations, boosted by its national breakfast launch. Dunkin' CEO Nigel Travis says, "If you think about it, everyone's getting into the breakfast space."

Rival Burger King provides breakfast and coffee to millions of customers through thousands of restaurants located near Dunkin' Donuts restaurants. Now, in addition, Burger King owns Tim Hortons, and looks to put those restaurants near Dunkin' Donuts restaurants, especially in the northeastern United States. CEO Nigel Travis at Dunkin' Brands needs a three-year strategic plan. Do you have any suggestions to help Mr. Travis?

United Parcel Service, Inc., 2013

www.ups.com, UPS

Headquartered in Atlanta, Georgia, United Parcel Service (UPS) is the largest logistics company in the world based on revenue and package volume. Operating in the air delivery and freight services industry, UPS delivers packages up to 150 pounds across the USA and to 220 countries worldwide. Serving customers since 1907, UPS operates a fleet of more than 100,000 cars, vans, trucks, tractors, and motorcycles and more than 530 aircraft and uses 35,000 transport cargo containers. In addition, UPS has 39,100 drop boxes, 2,100 customer centers, 4,700 independently owned UPS stores, and perhaps most importantly, 83,900 drivers.

UPS's Q2 of 2013 revenue increased 1.2 percent as the company's daily international package volume improved 5 percent and domestic volume grew 1.9 percent from the prior year. For Q2, UPS delivered 15.7 million packages per day, an increase of 2.3 percent over the prior-year period. The company's domestic Q2 revenue improved to $8.24 billion, up 2.3 percent; domestic revenue per piece was up 0.3 percent. The company's daily package volume improved 1.9 percent, compared to the same period last year, driven by residential shipments from e-commerce customers. Declining letter volume led to a 1.5 percent drop in Next Day Air. For Q2 of 2013, UPS's international daily package volume grew 5.0 percent and revenue increased 1.6 percent to $3.06 billion. Daily Export shipments increased 5.0 percent, led by Europe and Asia. Customers globally continue to trade down to slower moving solutions, resulting in a 3.4 percent decline in UPS's export revenue per piece.

UPS global air network is headquartered in Louisville, Kentucky, where the company can process 416,000 packages per hour! UPS has numerous other airport hubs across the USA and in Germany, Canada, China Hong Kong, Singapore, China Taiwan, and China Mainland. A member of both the Dow Jones 30 Composite and Dow Transportation indexes, UPS employs 399,000 full-time employees (323,000 in the USA and 76,000 outside of the USA). A total of 349,000 of these employees were members of a union. UPS operates under three principle segments: (1) U.S. Domestic Package, (2) International Package, and the newer and much smaller (3) Supply Chain and Freight segment. UPS's major competitors are FedEx and the United States Postal Service.

Although UPS's primary business is the timely delivery of packages and documents, the company has extended its capabilities in recent years to encompass the broader spectrum of services known as supply chain solutions, such as freight forwarding, customs brokerage, fulfillment, returns, financial transaction, and even repairs. UPS is also a leading provider of less-than-truckload transportation services.

Copyright by Fred David Books LLC. (Written by Forest R. David)

History

UPS was founded in 1907 by teenagers Claude Ryan and Jim Casey as the American Messenger Company in Seattle, Washington. The teenagers saw an opportunity with the limited telephone and automobile options to run errands, carry notes, and make home deliveries for drugstores. The early strategy of UPS was to compete on cost by offering the best prices while maintaining dependable and courtesy service.

By 1913, the telephone was more common, reducing the need for messenger services, so the American Messenger Company changed its name to Merchant's Parcel Delivery and merged with Evert McCabe's to focus almost exclusively on package delivery of drugstore and grocery store packages to people's homes. The acquisition of Evert McCabe's added motorcycles and a single Ford Motel T to the business, so by 1916 "UPS" had an expanding fleet of delivery vehicles. Soon the company expanded its business to also deliver department store packages to homes in the Seattle area.

Geographic expansion continued throughout the 1920s, including air service, and the company expanded into cities along the entire Pacific coast. The company changed its name to United Parcel Service and moved its headquarters to New York. UPS continued to grow over the years, and in 1975 the company began serving Toronto, Canada, marking the first time UPS served customers outside the USA. The following year, UPS began operations in Germany, and then in 1989, with the purchase of a British document company, UPS was serving customers virtually worldwide.

The 1990s saw UPS adapt well to the growing presence of electronic data and package tracking. The company moved its headquarters to Atlanta, Georgia, in 1994. Operating as a private company for the first 90 years, UPS offered 10 percent of its stock to the public in 1999, giving the company the ability to raise capital through equity and make acquisitions more easily.

UPS's 1999 acquisitions of Challenge Air resulted in UPS becoming the largest air cargo carrier in Latin America. Other acquisitions in the United Kingdom and Poland expanded UPS's global reach throughout Europe. UPS has to date acquired more than 40 companies ranging from shipping and trucking to finance and international trade services.

UPS's supply chain solutions capabilities are available to clients in over 220 countries and territories. UPS's 2012 revenues increased 1.9 percent to $54.1 billion, but net income decreased 78.8 percent to $807 million. The company's 2012 return on assets (ROA) dropped to 2.2 percent, from 11.1 percent the prior year. In 2013, UPS is trying to close on its acquisition of the European firm, TNT Express, for $6.8 billion, which will expand its presence in the European and Asian markets.

Internal Issues

Vision and Mission
The UPS vision is provided on the company website, as follows:

Our goal is to synchronize the world of commerce by developing business solutions that create value and competitive advantages for our customers.

The company provides the following mission statement on its website:

Mission: What We Seek to Achieve

- Grow our global business by serving the logistics needs of customers, offering excellence and value in all that we do.

- Maintain a financially strong company—with broad employee ownership—that provides a long-term competitive return to our shareowners.

- Inspire our people and business partners to do their best, offering opportunities for personal development and success.

- Lead by example as a responsible, caring, and sustainable company making a difference in the communities we serve.

UPS describes the nature of its business in the following way:

As the world's largest package delivery company and a leading global provider of specialized transportation and logistics services, UPS continues to develop the frontiers of logistics, supply chain management, and e-Commerce … combining the flows of goods, information, and funds.

Sustainability
UPS provides an elaborate Sustainability Report on its website, after giving the following sustainability statement:

UPS is committed to operating our business in a socially, environmentally and economically responsible manner. We publish annual programs on goal attainment.

UPS was recently recognized as one of only 10 U.S. corporations to receive an A+ for superior transparency from companies registered with the Global Reporting Initiative (GRI). "One of the guiding principles to UPS's sustainability strategy is our commitment to transparency," UPS Chairman and CEO Scott Davis wrote in the organization's 2011 Sustainability Report. "We are disclosing more information than ever.... We have reported our five-year progress, successes and challenges. Now, we are focused ahead." Chief Sustainability Officer Scott Wicker reported that UPS now uses a "materiality matrix" to track how the company's interests match or differ from those of other stakeholders. A recent GRI report recognized UPS for (a) driving 85 million fewer miles, saving 8.4 million gallons of fuel and 83,000 metric tons of carbon dioxide emissions using advanced route-planning technology, (b) expanding telematics technology to eliminate more than 98 million minutes of engine idling time, saving 653,000 gallons of fuel, and (c) earning the highest Carbon Disclosure Project score among all U.S. companies, and tying with three others for the top score in the world.

Speaking at *Fortune's* Brainstorm Green 2012, UPS Chief Operations Officer (COO) David Abney said: "Sustainability is a way of life. It's always high on our radar screen." The UPS Foundation, the charitable arm of the firm, recently started a long-term effort to support employee volunteer activities to plant more than 1 million trees around the world, beginning with tree-planting initiatives in China, Canada, Haiti, the Netherlands, Norway, Russia, Uganda, and the United States by the end of 2013. UPS was rated #1 in *Fortune* Magazine's 2012 "World's Most Admired" for the Delivery Industry.

Culture and Ethics

The company code of ethics is provided at on the UPS website under Governance Documents (http://www.investors.ups.com/phoenix.zhtml?c=62900&p=irol-govhighlights).

Additionally, UPS has what it refers to on its website as a "distinctive culture." The statement reads as follows:

We believe that the dedication of our employees results in large part from our distinctive "employee-owner" concept. Our employee stock ownership tradition dates from 1927, when our founders, who believed that employee stock ownership was a vital foundation for successful business, first offered stock to employees. To facilitate employee stock ownership, we maintain several stock-based compensation programs.

The company's brown-clothed drivers and employees and brown trucks symbolize the firm's commitment to a distinctive culture, anchored by employee ownership of a large part of the firm. UPS is highly unionized.

After donating $150,000 to the Irving-based Boy Scouts of America, UPS announced recently that the company will no longer fund them, until gay scouts and leaders are allowed to be members. The *Atlanta Business Chronicle* reported that the Gay & Lesbian Alliance Against Defamation (GLADD) said it was told by UPS that under revised guidelines of The UPS Foundation, it will not support organizations that are unable to attest to having a policy that aligns with the foundation's nondiscrimination policy.

Organizational Structure

Among UPS's top eight corporate executives, there are two women and one African American. Exhibit 1 reveals UPS's current organizational chart. Note the company uses a divisional-by-geographic region structure.

Strategy

During calendar 2012, UPS opened 12 new dedicated health care facilities on four continents, bringing the company total to 37. UPS strives daily to provide customers competitive prices and excellent services worldwide. UPS benefits from several key trends in the marketplace, including (a) expansion of global trade, (b) growth in emerging markets,

EXHIBIT 1 UPS's Organizational Structure

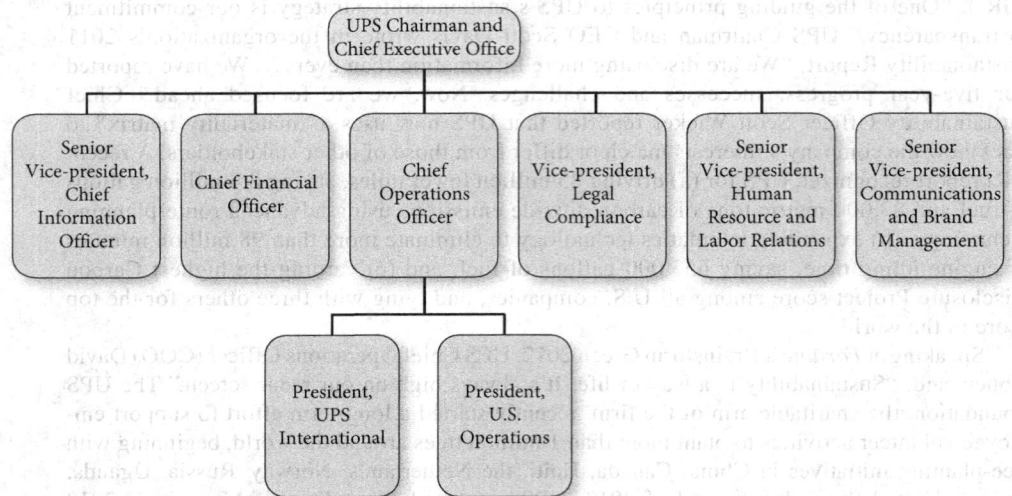

Source: Based on information on the company's website.

(c) outsourcing, (d) retail commercial growth, and (e) increasing trade across borders. These are reasons why UPS recently acquired Italy-based Pieffe Group, a pharmaceutical logistics company that helps enhance the trust that European-based pharmaceutical and biotech companies have for UPS to handle the delivery of its products and services. UPS's principle strategy is to identify successful businesses outside the USA and form alliances with them in the hope of eventually acquiring them. China remains the key emerging market with air hubs in Shanghai and Shenzhen. Recent UPS Chinese investments include adding intra-Asia and around-the-world flight frequencies, striving to serve customers more efficiently in Asia, Europe, and around the world. UPS already services more than 40 Asian nations through more than 20 alliances. In Vietnam alone, since a 2010 alliance, UPS's volume in that country has doubled.

UPS plans to increase its market share in Europe, where half of all its international revenue derives from; strong growth is expected to continue in Germany, the United Kingdom, France, Italy, Spain, and the Netherlands. Despite lingering economic troubles in Europe, UPS is expanding its European Air hub in Cologne, Germany, by 70 percent to a total capacity of 190,000 packages per hour. For reference, this is still well short of the hub in Louisville, Kentucky, that processes more than 400,000 packages per hour. The expansion of the Cologne hub was completed in 2013. In addition, the 2012 acquisition of Belgium-based Kiala S.A. enables e-commerce retailers to offer its customers timely delivery to retail locations or people's homes.

UPS's 2009 acquisition of Turkey-based Unsped Paket Servisi has led to double-digit growth to and from that country. South and Central America economies are growing along with Mexico, and UPS is currently well positioned in those countries as well.

Effective December 31, 2012, UPS instituted a 4.5 percent rate increase for UPS Air and U.S.-originating International Services shipments. UPS breaks the rate increase into two parts: a 6.5 percent base rate on UPS Air and International Services minus a two percentage point reduction in fuel surcharges on such shipments. UPS Ground base rates also increased on that date, by 5.9 percent, mitigated by a single percentage point reduction in the fuel surcharge, resulting in an average 4.9 percent price hike. UPS Next Day Air Freight, Second Day Air Freight, and Three-Day Freight rates for shipments among U.S., Canadian, and Puerto Rican locations also rose by 4.9 percent.

UPS recently closed on its $6.58 billion deal to acquire TNT Express N.V., an international courier delivery-services company with headquarters in Hoofddorp, Netherlands. Competing primarily with FedEx and DHL, TNT Express has fully owned operations in 65 countries and delivers documents, parcels, and pieces of freight to more than 200 countries. The company recorded sales of more than €7.2 billion in 2011. As part of the deal, UPS is seeking to avoid concessions that would hinder the company's plan to double its operations in Europe through the acquisition of TNT whose air operations were at issue because companies outside the European Union cannot hold stakes of more than 49 percent in airlines. The TNT Express deal will mark the largest acquisition ever for UPS.

To expand its global healthcare distribution facility network in the Asia Pacific region, UPS recently opened new facilities in Hangzhou and Shanghai, China, and Sydney, Australia. These openings bring the total number of UPS dedicated healthcare facilities around the globe to 36, encompassing more than a half-million square meters of space. The UPS strategy is to invest in its global healthcare network to become the largest medical products transporter in the world. Increased globalization and growing healthcare consumption in emerging markets are the impetus for this strategy. The new distribution centers serve multinational and regional healthcare manufacturers across the Asia Pacific region.

Segments

UPS's top 20 customers account for less than 10 percent of the company's revenue. UPS has major air hubs in Hartford, CN; Ontario, CA; Philidalphia, PA; Rockford, IL and outside of the United States in Hamilton, Ontario; Cologne, Germany; Shanghai China; Shenzhen, China; Raipei, Taiwan, China; Incheon, South Korea; Hong Kong, China; and Singapore. UPS reports revenues and operating profits in three different segments: (1) U.S. Domestic Package, (2) International Package, and (3) Supply Chain and Freight. Exhibit 2 reveals that UPS's Supply Chain and Freight division accounts for about 17 percent of all revenue and 10 percent of all operating profits. Also note that more than half of UPS's profits come from its U.S. operations, so there is a lot of room for growth globally, which is another reason for the TNT Express acquisition. But South America, Australia, and to a lesser degree, Asia, are not UPS strongholds to say the least.

EXHIBIT 2 Selected Income Statement Data

	Years Ended December 31,				
	2012	2011	2010	2009	2008
Revenue:					
U.S. Domestic Package	$ 32,856	$ 31,717	$ 29,742	$ 28,158	$ 31,278
International Package	12,124	12,249	11,133	9,699	11,293
Supply Chain & Freight	9,147	9,139	8,670	7,440	8,915
Total revenue	**54,127**	**53,105**	**49,545**	**45,297**	**51,486**
Operating expenses:					
Compensation and benefits	33,102	27,575	26,557	25,933	29,826
Other	19,682	19,450	17,347	15,856	20,041
Total operating expenses	52,784	47,025	43,904	41,789	49,867
Operating profit (loss):					
U.S. Domestic Package	459	3,764	3,238	1,919	823
International Package	869	1,709	1,831	1,279	1,246
Supply Chain and Freight	15	607	572	310	(450)
Total operating profit	1,343	6,080	5,641	3,508	1,619

Source: 2012 *Form 10K*, p. 21.

EXHIBIT 3 U.S. Domestic Package Operations

	Year Ended December 31,			% Change
	2012	2011	2010	2012/2011
Average Daily Package Volume (in thousands):				
Next Day Air	1,277	1,206	1,205	5.9%
Deferred	1,031	975	941	5.7%
Ground	11,588	11,230	11,140	3.2%
Total Avg. Daily Package Volume	13,896	13,411	13,286	3.6%
Average Revenue Per Piece:				
Next Day Air	$ 19.93	$ 20.33	$ 19.14	(2.0)%
Deferred	13.06	13.32	12.50	(2.0)%
Ground	7.89	7.78	7.43	1.4%
Total Avg. Revenue Per Piece	$ 9.38	$ 9.31	$ 8.85	0.8%
Operating Days in Period	252	254	253	
Revenue (in millions):				
Next Day Air	$ 6,412	$ 6,229	$ 5,835	2.9%
Deferred	3,392	3,299	2,975	2.8%
Ground	23,052	22,189	20,932	3.9%
Total Revenue	$ 32,856	$ 31,717	$ 29,742	3.6%

Source: UPS 2012 *Form 10K*, p. 24.

U.S. Domestic Package Segment

UPS's U.S. Domestic Package division reported revenues of $32.8 billion in 2012, up from $31.7 billion in 2011, a 3.6 percent increase. Operating profits decreased around 87.8 percent during this same time period. This division of UPS focuses on timely delivery of small packages across the USA offers customers same-, next-, two-, and three-day alternatives or standard shipping depending on how fast the delivery is needed. UPS delivers more than 11 million packages daily in the USA with most being delivered between one to three business days. Within this segment, UPS has an alliance with the United States Postal Service (USPS) called SurePost, a service for customers who are sending or receiving nonurgent lightweight shipments in which UPS handles the long haul ground transportation and USPS makes the final home delivery. Note in Exhibit 3, UPS's "Next Day Air" and their "Deferred" business reported declines in business in 2012 versus 2011. Note in Exhibit 2 the 88 percent drop in UPS's 2012 operating profit in their domestic segment.

International Package Segment

UPS's International Package Reporting Segment includes all package operations outside the USA. This segment offers a wide selection of price and delivery options, such as Express Plus, Express, and Express Saver for urgent shipments. More traditional shipments that do not require express service can use UPS Worldwide. In addition, customers in the USA, Mexico, Canada, and Europe can use UPS Transborder Standard delivery services for its shipments.

Among the international regions served, Europe is the largest UPS customer and accounts for around half of the company's international revenue. UPS expects Europe to continue being a large revenue source in the future because of the fragmented nature of the market in Europe and the fact that exports make up a large part of Europe's gross domestic product (GDP). Additionally, UPS's TNT Express acquisition will nearly double UPS's business in Europe.

Asia is somewhat of a new frontier for UPS, but that continent offers the fastest growth opportunities. Note in Exhibit 4 that UPS's international segment reported quite a few negative numbers in 2012 versus 2011.

EXHIBIT 4 International Package Operations

	Year Ended December 31,			% Change
	2012	2011	2010	2012/2011
Average Daily Package Volume (in thousands):				
Domestic	1,427	1,444	1,403	(1.2)%
Export	972	942	885	3.2%
Total Avg. Daily Package Volume	2,399	2,386	2,288	0.5%
Average Revenue Per Piece:				
Domestic	$ 7.04	$ 7.17	$ 6.66	(1.8)%
Export	36.88	37.85	36.77	(2.6)%
Total Avg. Revenue Per Piece	$ 19.13	$ 19.28	$ 18.31	(0.8)%
Operating Days in Period	252	254	253	
Revenue (in Millions):				
Domestic	$ 2,531	$ 2,628	$ 2,365	(3.7)%
Export	9,033	9,056	8,234	(0.3)%
Cargo	560	565	534	(0.9)%
Total Revenue	$12,124	$12,249	$11,133	(1.0)%
Operating Expenses (in millions):				
Operating Expenses	$11,255	$10,540	$ 9,302	6.8%
Defined Benefit Plan Mark-to-Market Charge	(941)	(171)	(42)	
Adjusted Operating Expenses	$10,314	$10,369	$ 9,260	(0.5)%
Operating Profit (in millions) and Operating Margin:				
Operating Profit	$ 869	$ 1,709	$ 1,831	(49.2)%

Source: UPS's 2012 *Form 10K*, p. 28.

Supply Chain and Freight

UPS's Supply Chain and Freight segment includes logistics services, UPS freight business, and financial offerings through UPS Capital. As of December 2012, UPS managed supply chains in more than 195 countries and territories with more than 35 million square feet of distribution space. Because of the complex nature of supply chains, UPS offers the following services: freight forwarding, customs brokerage, logistics and distribution, UPS freight, and UPS capital.

UPS is the second-largest freight forwarding company in the USA and is among the top six internationally. A freight forwarder or forwarding agent is a person or company that organizes shipments for individuals or companies to get large orders from the manufacturer to market or final point of distribution. A forwarder is not typically a carrier but is an expert in supply chain management. In other words, a freight forwarder is a "travel agent" for the cargo industry, or a third-party logistics provider. Thus, instead of transporting cargo, UPS oftentimes just facilitates the movement of cargo ranging from raw agricultural products to manufactured goods. Cargo can travel on a variety of carrier types, including ships, airplanes, trucks, railroads, or all of these modes, and oftentimes not on UPS-owned assets.

UPS Freight is the long-haul segment of UPS providing long distance transportation of packages in all 50 states, several U.S. territories, and Mexico. UPS Capital aids customers in export and import financing, as well as protecting goods and payment solutions.

Finance

For calendar 2012, UPS's overall volume grew 2.8 percent. The company's business-to-business volume showed no growth, partly due to the increasing migration of traditional retail to on-line retail. UPS's income statements are provided in Exhibit 5. Balance sheets are provided in Exhibit 6.

EXHIBIT 5 UPS's Income Statements (in millions, except per share amounts)

	Years Ended December 31,		
	2012	2011	2010
Revenue	$ 54,127	$ 53,105	$ 49,545
Operating Expenses:			
Compensation and benefits	33,102	27,575	26,557
Repairs and maintenance	1,228	1,286	1,131
Depreciation and amortization	1,858	1,782	1,792
Purchased transportation	7,354	7,232	6,640
Fuel	4,090	4,046	2,972
Other occupancy	902	943	939
Other expenses	4,250	4,161	3,873
Total Operating Expenses	52,784	47,025	43,904
Operating Profit	1,343	6,080	5,641
Other Income and (Expense):			
Investment income	24	44	3
Interest expense	(393)	(348)	(354)
Total Other Income and (Expense)	(369)	(304)	(351)
Income Before Income Taxes	974	5,776	5,290
Income Tax Expense	167	1,972	1,952
Net Income	$ 807	$ 3,804	$ 3,338
Basic Earnings Per Share	$ 0.84	$ 3.88	$ 3.36
Diluted Earnings Per Share	$ 0.83	$ 3.84	$ 3.33

Source: UPS's 2012 *Form 10K*, p. 58.

EXHIBIT 6 UPS's Balance Sheets (in millions)

	December 31,	
	2012	2011
ASSETS		
Current Assets:		
Cash and cash equivalents	$ 7,327	$ 3,034
Marketable securities	597	1,241
Accounts receivable, net	6,111	6,246
Deferred income tax assets	583	611
Other current assets	973	1,152
Total Current Assets	15,591	12,284
Property, Plant and Equipment, Net	17,894	17,621
Goodwill	2,173	2,101
Intangible Assets, Net	603	585
Investments and Restricted Cash	307	303
Derivative Assets	535	483
Deferred Income Tax Assets	684	118
Other Non-Current Assets	1,076	1,206
Total Assets	$ 38,863	$ 34,701

EXHIBIT 6 Continued

	December 31,	
	2012	2011
LIABILITIES AND SHAREOWNERS' EQUITY		
Current Liabilities:		
Current maturities of long-term debt and commercial paper	$ 1,781	$ 33
Accounts payable	2,278	2,300
Accrued wages and withholdings	1,927	1,843
Self-insurance reserves	763	781
Other current liabilities	1,641	1,557
Total Current Liabilities	8,390	6,514
Long-Term Debt	11,089	11,095
Pension and Postretirement Benefit Obligations	11,068	5,505
Deferred Income Tax Liabilities	48	1,900
Self-Insurance Reserves	1,980	1,806
Other Non-Current Liabilities	1,555	773
Shareowners' Equity:		
Class A common stock (225 and 240 shares issued in 2012 and 2011)	3	3
Class B common stock (729 and 725 shares issued in 2012 and 2011)	7	7
Additional paid-in capital		
Retained earnings	7,997	10,128
Accumulated other comprehensive loss	(3,354)	(3,103)
Deferred compensation obligations	78	88
Less: Treasury stock (1 and 2 shares in 2012 and 2011)	(78)	(88)
Total Equity for Controlling Interests	4,653	7,035
Noncontrolling Interests	80	73
Total Shareowners' Equity	4,733	7,108
Total Liabilities and Shareowners' Equity	$ 38,863	$ 34,701

Source: UPS's 2012 *Form 10K*, p. 57.

External Issues

Changing Consumer Behavior

More and more people are no longer willing to pay more for an overnight delivery service. They would rather wait another day for the goods to be delivered, instead of paying a premium for quicker delivery. This change in customer preferences and attitude appears to be permanent, regardless of the economy.

Companies Exporting More

UPS anticipates that most high-tech companies expect to export more cell phones, tablets, and other electronics over the next several years to growing middle-class populations in developing nations. The Barack Obama administration has a goal to double exports by 2015. Scott Davis, UPS chief executive officer, is on the President's Export Council and has touted free trade agreements as critical for boosting U.S. exports and the economy. A free trade agreement between the USA and Panama will soon go into effect, following on the heels of such agreements with Colombia and South Korea. Some analysts expect that high-tech product sales and shipments are expected to grow by 22 percent in India, the Middle East, and Africa over the next three to five years. Those same analysts expect such sales increases to range from 18 percent in Brazil and 19 percent in the rest of South America to 15 percent in Eastern Europe, 13 percent in Korea, and 8 percent in China and in other Asian nations.

Many executives are planning to modify its distribution networks to handle more volume at East Coast ports once a wider Panama Canal is opened to bigger ships around 2015. Quite a few companies plan to shift from air to ocean freight when that happens, so many East Coast ports are heavily investing in dredging and other projects to be able to accept bigger ships. Both FedEx and UPS have already seen a shift in demand for shipping products cheaper, such as by sea, rather than premium-priced express air services, because of the weakening global economy.

Internet and Catalog Purchasing

About 40 percent of total UPS shipments are from businesses-to-consumers, compared with about one-third from a few years ago. It expects these shipments, typically from large catalog or Internet retailers, to grow to half of all packages during the holiday season. Consumers are expected to do more and more online shopping. UPS and its smaller rival FedEx can benefit twice when consumers shop online: UPS ships the gift to the receiver, and it also ships the unwanted presents that are later returned. Online sales are expected to grow at four times the pace of traditional retail sales in 2012. This trend is helping UPS's earnings despite weakness in trade between businesses. Business-to-business shipments are typically between a manufacturer and a retailer, and are closely tied to industrial production.

Competitors

As indicated in Exhibit 7, UPS competes with USPS and FedEx. Another large competitor is DHL International. Exhibit 6 reveals that UPS generates more revenue per employee than either the USPS or FedEx. Note how low the USPS is on revenue per employee.

USPS

USPS incurred a record loss of $15.9 billion for its fiscal year 2012, which it blamed primarily on a mandate to set aside billions of dollars for a retirement heath fund. The USPS loss included $11.1 billion in defaulted payments it owes to "prefund" health benefits for future retirees. Postal officials have complained for years about these prepayments, which are required by Congress, to pay for future retirees. The USPS points out that other federal agencies do not have similar mandates for prefunding.

The $15.9 billion loss was more than triple the $5.1 billion in loss the USPS posted in the prior year. Fredric Rolando, president of the National Association of Letter Carriers, recently blamed the congressionally mandated prefunding for the bulk of USPS's financial woes. The USPS is highly unionized.

USPS has been struggling with declines in mail revenue for a variety of reasons, including everyone's transition to e-mail. To combat massive losses, USPS plans to cut 150,000 workers through 2015, reduce existing staffers' work hours and hike the price on first-class stamps by 3 cents to 49 cents. USPS officials are considering a scale back of delivery service to five days, ceasing its low-volume, low-revenue, Saturday service. The notion of five-day service however is intensely unpopular in Congress and unlikely to prevail.

EXHIBIT 7 Comparing UPS to Rivals

	USPS	UPS	FedEx
Number of Employees	551K	222K	230K
Net Income ($)	—	3.26B	2.02B
Revenue ($)	65.7B	53.66B	42.95B
Revenue ($)/Employee	119K	241K	187K
EPS Ratio ($)	—	3.38	6.40
Market Capitalization	—	66.8B	27.1B

EPS, earnings per share.

Unlike other federal agencies, the USPS does not technically receive taxpayer support, though it has borrowed $15 billion from the U.S. Treasury.

FedEx

Headquartered in Memphis, Tennessee, FedEx is the world's number-1 express transportation provider, delivering about 3.5 million packages daily to more than 220 countries and territories from about 2,000 FedEx Office shops. FedEx owns and operates a fleet of about 690 aircraft and more than 50,000 motor vehicles and trailers. To complement its express delivery business, FedEx Ground provides small-package ground delivery in North America, and less-than-truckload (LTL) carrier FedEx Freight hauls larger shipments. FedEx Office Stores offer a variety of document-related and other business services and serve as retail hubs for other FedEx units.

FedEx is spending $100 million to build a new 134,000-square-meter international express and cargo hub, to be up and running at the airport in Pudong, China, by 2017. FedEx said it will be capable of handling 36,000 parcels and documents per hour. The new facility's annual sorting capacity may reach more than 90 million items, meeting the demand in the next 20 years.

Shanghai is forecast to become the world's top air cargo hub by 2015, with a throughput of more than 5 million tons. Major domestic airlines have based 80 percent of its freight capacities at the Pudong airport, which now ranks number 3 by cargo turnover, after Hong Kong and Memphis.

FedEx is expanding its services across the USA, Canada, and Mexico. The company is expanding its Priority next-day services in its FedEx Freight segment by opening a new service center in Rochester, New York, that will cater to 13 U.S. and Canadian markets dealing in cross-border shipments to and from Toronto and Montreal. In Mexico, FedEx recently added two new service centers—one each in Culiacán and Silao—to strengthen its freight network in northwestern and north central part of Mexico. FedEx is building a new hub in Guangzhou, China, for catering to 100 new Chinese cities within the next five years.

As for acquisitions, FedEx completed the take over of Polish courier company, Opek Sp. z o.o., and French B2B Express transportation company, TATEX, both in mid-2012. Then FedEx acquired Rapidão Cometa, a Brazilian transportation and logistics company. These acquisitions should provide FedEx greater operational efficiencies, provide a competitive edge, generate significant long-term synergies, support international business growth, and drive higher profitability.

DHL

Headquartered in Germany and privately held, DHL is a gigantic package delivery company that constitutes the express delivery and logistics business segments of its parent, Deutsche Post. DHL is a leader in the worldwide market for express delivery services, operating through four divisions: Express, Global Forwarding and Freight Forwarding, Mail, and Supply Chain. (Mail service in Germany is handled by the Deutsche Post brand; DHL handles all of the Global Mail business). DHL's Express courier service network spans more than 220 countries and territories using a fleet of 32,000 vehicles and about 250 aircraft. DHL's supply chain division maintains some 23 million square meters (almost 250 million square feet) of warehouse space.

The Future

UPS is on the hunt for businesses similar to TNT Express in Europe that it recently acquired. Similar businesses in Asia, Australia, South America, and Africa would enable UPS to extend its services globally. More than half of UPS's revenues still comes from the USA, yet 95 percent of the world's population lives outside the USA. More and more people are buying and selling online, which is a key positive trend for UPS in the future. A key threat however is that rival FedEx is aggressive and savvy and also on the hunt to make acquisitions. FedEx does not like being number 2 in the global packaging business. Help UPS develop a clear strategic plan going forward.

FedEx Corporation, 2015

FDX, www.fedex.com

Headquartered in Memphis, Tennessee, and founded in 1971, FedEx is one of the largest express freight delivery companies in the world, having about 57,000 drop-off locations, 700 aircraft, and 62,000 vehicles. FedEx does business in over 220 countries and employs over 220,000 workers. The company is comprised of subsidiaries: FedEx Ground, FedEx Express, FedEx Freight, and FedEx Services. Revenues for fiscal year-end of May 2014 were $45 billion, or about $10 billion less than top competitor United Parcel Service (UPS). In fact, rival UPS is spending $2 billion to expand internationally in Asia, Europe, and the Americas, and is modernizing its U.S. operations to automatically sort packages. UPS expects its revenues to rise 7 percent annually through 2018, so FedEx needs an excellent strategic plan going forward.

In April 2015, FedEx offered to acquire Dutch delivery firm TNT Express N.V. (TNTEY) for approximately $8.75 per share, or $4.8 billion (€4.4 billion). However on July 13, 2015, the European Commission (EC) raised concerns about competition being restrained in the event of the deal materializing. As the antitrust watchdog of the European Union, the EC is investigating whether the impending deal, involving two key global players in the field of small package delivery, abides by the EU Merger Regulation. The EC is concerned that the combined entity, if approved, would dominate the market for small packages, thereby stifling competition in the space and causing prices to soar.

Copyright by Fred David Books LLC. www.strategyclub.com (Written by Forest R. David)

History

FedEx traces its history to 1971, when Frederick Smith (the current CEO) bought a controlling interest in Arkansas Aviation Sales. The frustration of being unable to effectively deliver packages in 2 days created the idea of determining a more effective way to handle freight. Smith named his new company Federal Express in hopes of obtaining a contract with the Federal Reserve Bank and to draw public interest though the term *Federal*. The contract proposal with the Federal Reserve was denied, but the company officially began operating in 1973 with 14 small aircraft from Memphis, Tennessee, by delivering 186 packages to 25 different U.S. cities. Federal Express did not officially change its name to FedEx until 1994.

FedEx first turned a profit in 1975 and was instrumental in lobbying for the deregulation of air cargo that was passed in 1977. Deregulation allowed FedEx to use larger aircraft, and today, FedEx is the world's largest all cargo fleet. The firm reached $1 billion in sales in 1983, marking the first ever for a U.S. company to reach this level of revenues without mergers or acquisitions within 10 years of operations. After a series of international acquisitions, FedEx starting offering services to Europe, Asia, and China through a 1995 acquisition.

In 2014, about 90 percent of FedEx's $1.2 billion investments were to boost capacity or infrastructure. As Christmas approached, the company hired about 50,000 seasonal workers, up from 40,000 the prior year. The investment is designed to address the rapid growth of consumer goods ordered online. Peak volume, referring to the busiest day of the year, had climbed dramatically in recent years for FedEx, to 26-plus million packages on one day near Christmas. That busiest day recently jumped 40 percent at rival UPS, to 31 million packages. Last-minute, holiday online free shipping deals have proliferated in recent years.

Internal Issues

Organizational Structure
FedEx uses a divisional-by-product organizational structure, but the firm does not appear to have executives with popular titles such as COO, CTO, CSO, HRM, or R&D. Exhibit 1 provides a probable schematic of the company structure.

EXHIBIT 1 FedEx's Organizational Structure

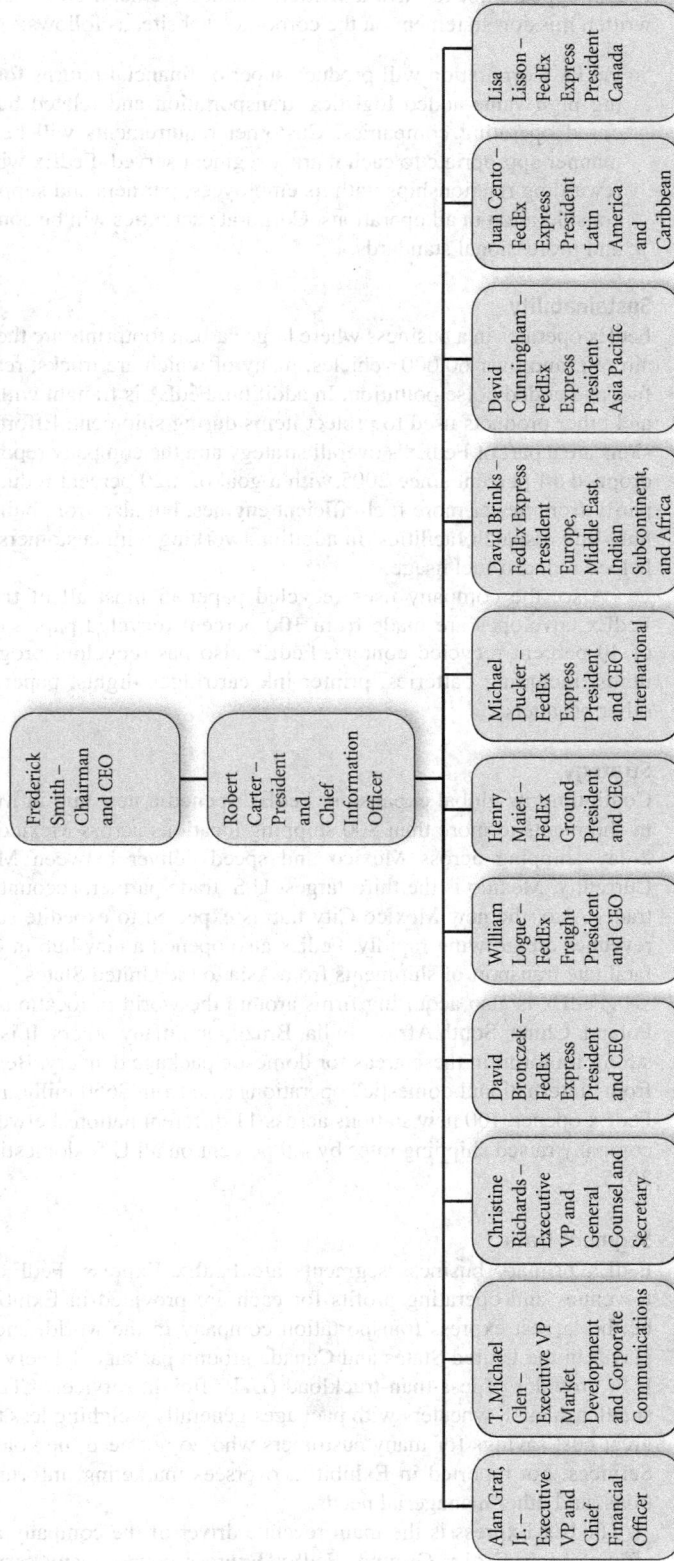

Frederick Smith – Chairman and CEO

Robert Carter – President and Chief Information Officer

- Alan Graf, Jr. – Executive VP and Chief Financial Officer
- T. Michael Glen – Executive VP Market Development and Corporate Communications
- Christine Richards – Executive VP and General Counsel and Secretary
- David Bronczek – FedEx Express President and CEO
- William Logue – FedEx Freight President and CEO
- Henry Maier – FedEx Ground President and CEO
- Michael Ducker – FedEx Express President and CEO International
- David Brinks – FedEx Express President Europe, Middle East, Indian Subcontinent, and Africa
- David Cunningham – FedEx Express President Asia Pacific
- Juan Cento – FedEx Express President Latin America and Caribbean
- Lisa Lisson – FedEx Express President Canada

Source: Based on FedEx's 2014 *Annual Report.*

Vision/Mission

FedEx appears not to have a written vision statement. However, the company does provide a written mission statement on the corporate website, as follows:

> FedEx Corporation will produce superior financial returns for its shareowners by providing high value-added logistics, transportation and related business services through focused operating companies. Customer requirements will be met in the highest quality manner appropriate to each market segment served. FedEx will strive to develop mutually rewarding relationships with its employees, partners and suppliers. Safety will be the first consideration in all operations. Corporate activities will be conducted to the highest ethical and professional standards.

Sustainability

FedEx operates in a business where large carbon footprints are the norm. Operating a fleet of 700 aircraft, and over 60,000 vehicles, many of which are trucks, results in a large consumption of fuel and added noise pollution. In addition, FedEx is fraught with excess packaging boxes, tape, and other products used to protect items during shipment. Efforts made to reduce carbon emissions are a part of FedEx's overall strategy and the company reports its fleet miles per gallon has dropped 14 percent since 2005 with a goal of a 20 percent reduction by 2020. The declines are partly from newer more fuel-efficient engines, but also from building more strategically located hubs and dispatch facilities. In addition, working with customers on their own supply chain has helped reduced fuel usage.

Also, the company uses recycled paper in most all of their shipping packaging. Most FedEx envelopes are made from 100 percent recycled paper, and boxes contain a minimum of 40 percent recycled content. FedEx also has recycling programs in place for a variety of items, including batteries, printer ink cartridges, lights, paper, oil, tires, plastics, and many other products.

Strategy

Continuing its global expansion, FedEx opened a new hub in Mexico City in 2014 to help aid in shipments to more than 800 shipping locations across Mexico. The hub should better enable 2-day shipping across Mexico and speed deliver between Mexico and the United States. Currently, Mexico is the third-largest U.S. trade partner, accounting for 13.5 percent of all U.S. trade. Also, the new Mexico City hub is expected to expedite service to Latin America, where revenues are growing rapidly. FedEx also opened a new hub in Osaka, Japan, in 2014 to better facilitate transport of shipments from Asia to the United States.

FedEx is also acquiring firms around the world in locations such as the United Kingdom, Poland, China, South Africa, India, Brazil, and many others. It is FedEx's strategy to establish a strong footprint in these areas for domestic package delivery. Between 2011 and 2014, revenues from "international domestic" operations rose from $650 million to $1.4 billion. Across Europe, FedEx opened 100 new stations across 11 different nations between 2011 and May of 2014. The company raised shipping rates by 4.9 percent on all U.S. domestic and imported mail in January 2015.

Segment Data

FedEx primary business segments are FedEx Express, FedEx Ground, and FedEx Freight. Revenues and operating profits for each are provided in Exhibit 2. FedEx Express claims to be the largest express transportation company in the world, and FedEx Ground is a principle player in the United States and Canada ground package delivery system. FedEx Freight is a top U.S. provider of less-than-truckload (LTL) freight services. LTL includes shipments on trucks smaller than 18 wheelers with packages generally weighing less than 150 pounds. This provides great cost savings for many customers who do not need the volume of a full-size truck. FedEx Services, not reported in Exhibit 2, oversees marketing, information technology, communications, and other managerial needs.

FedEx Express is the main revenue driver of the company although it does not operate as efficiently as FedEx Ground. FedEx Express covers many services focused on timely delivery but also on cost savings if expenses are more important than time. The business segment

EXHIBIT 2 FedEx's Revenues and Operating Income by Segment (in millions of USD)

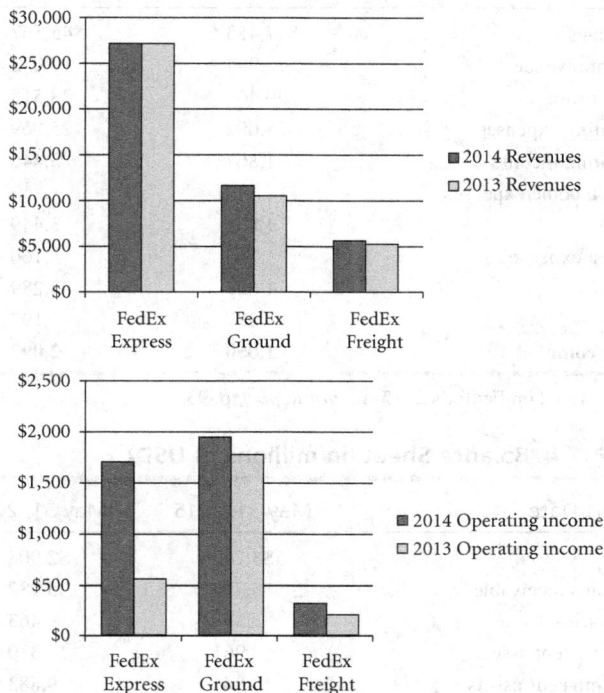

Source: Based on company documents.

provides worldwide delivery in anywhere from 1 to 5 business days based on client needs. Total U.S. and international revenues from FedEx Express were $11.6 billion and $8.7 billion, respectively, in 2014. In addition to $8.7 billion in international revenues, FedEx Express also reported $1.4 billion in revenues from "international domestic." FedEx Express is continuing its acquisition of foreign companies to establish domestic services for those areas. Freight accounted for $4.1 billion of FedEx Express's 2014 revenues. FedEx Express plans on an increase in expenses in 2015 and 2016 as the segment modernizes its airline and trucking fleet.

FedEx Ground offers services to nearly 100 percent of all U.S. residences and most Canadian residences as well. The segment specializes in package delivery. FedEx SmartPost business uses the United States Postal Service (USPS) to deliver smaller packages that are less time sensitive. However, SmartPost only generated $983 million of the $11,617 million the segment reported in 2014. Daily average package volume for FedEx Ground and FedEx SmartPost are $4,588 and $2,186 million, respectively. FedEx Ground receives on average $9.10 per package, whereas SmartPost generates $1.78 of revenue per package.

FedEx Freight, like FedEx Express and FedEx Ground, reported improved financial numbers in each of the last three years, as revealed in Exhibit 2.

Finance

FedEx reported 2015 revenues of $47.4 billion with net income of over $1 billion (down from over $2 billion in 2014), as revealed in Exhibit 3. The firm paid 35 percent taxes in fiscal year 2015, and has over $3 billion in goodwill on the balance sheet, as indicated in Exhibit 4. FedEx has been in an aggressive share buyback program, buying back 2.7 million shares in fiscal 2013 for an average price of $90.96 and 36.8 million shares in fiscal 2014 (ended in May) for an average price of $131.83. The company's stock price was trading for over $173 a share in February of 2015. FedEx has cash of $2.9 billion and expects enough liquidly moving forward without needing additional debt.

EXHIBIT 3 Income Statement (in millions of USD)

Report Date	May 31, 2015	May 31, 2014
Revenues	$47,453	$45,567
Cost of revenue	16,984	17,052
Gross profit	30,469	28,515
Operating expenses	28,602	25,069
Operating income	1,867	3,446
Other income/expenses	(5)	3
EBIT	1,862	3,449
Interest expense	235	160
EBT	1,627	3,289
Tax	577	1,192
Net income	**1,050**	**2,097**

Source: Based on FedEx's 2015 *Annual Report,* p. 93.

EXHIBIT 4 Balance Sheet (in millions of USD)

Report Date	May 31, 2015	May 31, 2014
Cash	$3,763	$2,908
Accounts receivable	5,719	5,982
Inventories	498	463
Other current assets	961	330
Total current assets	**10,941**	**9,683**
Property, plant & equipment	20,875	19,550
Goodwill	3,810	—
Intangible assets	—	—
Other assets	1,443	1,047
Total assets	**37,069**	**33,070**
Current debt	19	1
Accounts payable	5,948	5,311
Total current liabilities	**5,957**	**5,312**
Long-term debt	7,249	4,736
Deferred liabilities	2,639	3,078
Other liabilities	6,231	4,667
Total liabilities	**22,076**	**17,793**
Common stock	32	32
Retained earnings	16,900	20,429
Treasury stock	(4,897)	(4,133)
Paid in capital and other	2,958	(1,051)
Total equity	**14,993**	**15,277**
Total liabilities & equity	**37,069**	**33,070**

Source: Based on FedEx's 2015 *Annual Report,* p. 91.

Competitors

A summary of key statistics for large package delivery firms is provided in Exhibit 5. Note that FedEx has nearly double the earnings per share (EPS) as UPS, despite having half the net income.

FedEx competes primarily with UPS and the U.S. Postal Service in the United States, and with UPS and Deutsche Post internationally. The U.S. Mail Delivery Services segment accounts

EXHIBIT 5 FedEx versus Rival Firms

	FedEx	UPS	U.S. Postal Service
# Employees	231,500	213,200	488,000
$ Net Income	$2.1 B	$4.4 B	($5.5 B)
$ Revenue	$45.5 B	$55.4 B	$67.8 B
$ Revenue/Employee	$196,544	$259,849	$128,9344
$ EPS Ratio	$7.89	$4.02	—
Market Cap.	$49 B	$91 B	—

Source: Based on FedEx's 2014 company documents.

EXHIBIT 6 Percent Market Share of Key Global Players

	FedEx	UPS	Others
USA Mailbox Rentals	6%	13%	*81%
USA Mail Delivery	26%	38%	*46%
Cargo Airplanes (Non USA)	19%	10%	**71%
Mail Delivery (Non USA)	20%	24%	***56%

*United States Postal Service not included in this data.

**Air France-KLM SA, Deutsche Lufthansa AG, Emirates account for approximately 16% total with approximately equal market shares.

***Deutsche Post (parent to DHL International) accounts for around 19%.

Source: From various company reports (such as IBIS, headings changed).

for over $90 billion in annual revenues, with a 3 percent projected annual growth rate over the next 5 years. Approximately 55 percent of the $90 billion is derived from ground delivery services, whereas 29 and 8 percent, respectively, are derived from domestic and international air delivery services. Delivery services outside the United States currently are a $200 billion industry with 3 to 4 percent annual growth expected through 2020, taking the overall projected industry revenues to over $250 billion by 2020.

Traditionally, FedEx, UPS, US Postal Service, Deutsche Post, TNT International, and large national postal services in other nations were the main drivers of package delivery, along with many smaller local companies. However, with e-commerce growing, new delivery competitors such as Google, eBay, and Amazon are offing delivery services. As of now, many of these delivery services are same day and only in large cities such as Manhattan, Los Angeles, and San Francisco. It is unclear whether Amazon and Alibaba can also become package delivery giants; however, they have eroded into margins of the big transport firms such as UPS and FedEx. With Amazon's size and package volume, the firm can negotiate attractive shipping prices for its customers. Exhibit 6 reveals market share data for rival firms in the package delivery industry.

United Parcel Service (UPS)

Headquartered in Atlanta, Georgia, UPS was founded in 1907 and competes in the package delivery business as well as providing logistics and financial services in both the United States and internationally. UPS is broken down into three operating segments: U.S. Domestic Package, International Package, and Supply Chain & Freight. UPS's Package segments deliver packages to over 220 countries and the Supply Chain & Freight Segment aids businesses in financing, risk mitigation, supply chain design, consulting services, and much more in 195 countries.

United Parcel Service has reported total revenues of $58.2 billion in 2015, up from $55.4 billion the prior year. The company's 2014 net income, however, declined to $3.0 billion from $4.3 billion the prior year. About 75 percent of company revenues are derived from U.S. operations. By segments, U.S. Packaging, International Packaging, and Supply Chain & Freight account for about 62, 22, and 16 percent of total revenues, respectively. Total revenues associated from air package delivery are about $6 billion, or 11 percent, of total revenues, leaving UPS ground the single-largest driver of corporate revenues.

UPS operates over 103,000 vehicles and owns 33,000 package containers. Kentucky-based UPS Airlines, a division of UPS, operates the world's second-largest cargo aircraft fleet with 240 aircraft. UPS Airlines processes 416,000 packages per hour and has hubs in China, Germany, Canada, and many states. In 2012, UPS was denied permission to acquire competitor TNT Express on monopolistic concerns. UPS is actively expanding internally, and completed a 70 percent expansion of its hub in Cologne, Germany, in November 2012. In addition, UPS has acquired multiple firms in Latin America, Europe, and Asia-Pacific over the last several years.

In 2014, UPS announced it is expanding its service that allows customers to pick up packages at convenience stores, dry cleaners, UPS shops, and many other businesses. UPS has found many customers browse online, then shop in stores, because they are unable to sign for packages delivered to their home during working hours. For $5 per package or $40 annual membership, customers can have packages dropped off at a specified pick-up location. The strategy has worked well in Europe, which currently has over 12,000 pick-up locations with plans to expand to over 20,000 in Europe alone by year-end 2015. Receiving a fee to drop off at central locations is a bonanza for UPS. The firm has determined that saving 1 second per driver per day will result in $14.5 million in savings annually.

CEO David Abney in Fall 2014 outlined UPS's commitment to becoming more a global player, especially with respect to China and Vietnam. Abney also indicated Africa will become more of a global player in the future and possibly Mexico will become a larger player as manufacturing plants want to relocate closer to the United States, as fuel prices and labor wages in Asia increase.

United States Postal Service (USPS)

Beginning with the Pony Express and stagecoaches, the United States Postal Service (USPS) is the oldest postal service in the country, existing for over 235 years. Currently, USPS employs 488,000 workers, making it the third-largest employer in the United States, behind Walmart and the federal government. USPS daily reaches over 150 million residences, businesses, and post office boxes, delivering about 155 billion pieces of mail to 971,000 delivery points. USPS delivers around 40 percent of the world's total mail volume with its fleet of over 218,000 vehicles.

The United States Postal Service is divided into five business segments: (1) First Class Mail, (2) Standard Mail, (3) Packages, (4) International, and (5) Periodicals. Revenues for the segments in 2013 were $28, $17, $12.5, $3, and $1.6 billion, respectively. Total revenues for 2014 were $67.8 billion, about the same as in 2013. Operating expenses were $73 billion in 2014, resulting in a $5.5 billion loss. The USPS lost $4.9 billion in 2013 and $15.9 billion in 2012.

The USPS continues to consolidate mail-processing centers and reduce delivery days on Standard Mail offerings. The firm also is aggressively training employees better to reduce waste, making many rural post offices part-time post offices, and offering discounts up to 58 percent to customers who mail 50,000 parcels a year. These cost saving plans are expected to save the USPS around $500 million annually. However, UPS and FedEx have questions regarding how the USPS can offer discounts to customers, when both UPS and FedEx are being forced to raise prices. With respect to USPS' lower prices, UPS's management recently stated in that it should "raise a red flag," especially since the organization is currently operating at a loss. UPS management went further, accusing USPS of charging higher rates on first-class letters, where customers have little choice or bargaining power on who to do business with. In addition, both UPS and FedEx have accused USPS of offering subsidies to customers to ship with them and even charging less for package deliver than revenues derived. USPS's proprietary pricing information does not allow FedEx or UPS to get a clear picture of the situation, but both FedEx and UPS are threating antitrust lawsuits against USPS. As a result of USPS' moves, its package business has grown over 20 percent annually from 2009 to 2014. By law, the USPS must pay its own way, and does not receive tax payer support.

The USPS workforce is heavily unionized, being represented by four labor unions: (1) American Postal Workers Union (APWU); (2) National Association of Letter Carriers (NALC); (3) National Rural Letter Carriers Association (NRLCA); and (4) National Postal Mail Handlers Union (NPMHU). All jobs at USPS not in one of the three main categories of employment are covered with the clerks by the APWU. Some union policies are quite restrictive on the postal service. For example, it is standard policy after a letter carrier has served 360 days, he or she may be represented by the NALC for reduced working hours, or for "just cause" any issue determined to be unfavorable by the union member. As mail volume continues to decrease, due to the increased use of email, bank draft billing, and the transition from junk mail advertising to Internet, USPS is constantly downsizing operations, replacing many positions with machines and consolidating mail routes. The forced pre-funding requirements for retirement benefits costs the USPS about $5.5 billion annually.

Deutsche Post (DPW.DE)

Considered the world's largest courier company, Deutsche Post employs 488,000 workers and reported 2014 revenues of €29.4 billion, or approximately $35 billion USD (up 8.1 percent from the prior year), and profits of €1.38 billion, or approximately $1.65 billion USD (down 9.1 percent from prior year). Headquartered in Bonn, Germany, Deutsche Post serves customers in over 220 countries. The company currently trades under the ticker symbol DPW on the Xetra in Germany. The company most directly competes with FedEx and UPS through DHL Express, a shipping company it acquired in 2005.

External Issues

Air Freight Demand

Demand for air cargo rose over 2 percent from May 2013 to May 2014. High jet fuel prices historically was to blame for many customers switching to trucking and slower means of transportation, favoring lower cost over more timely arrival of products. However, with oil prices falling dramatically in 2014–2015, demand for air freight is rising. Domestic freight accounts for about 20 percent of total air cargo ton-mile revenues, with FedEx Express and UPS accounting for 80 percent of this total. International freight demand was up less than 1 percent between both the United States and Europe as well as the United States and Asia in early 2014, improving from 3 to 4 percent declines in 2013. Even with an improving economy and lower oil prices, freight demand outlook for international packages by air travel is murky due to competition from large ocean shipping companies, new ports, and quicker shipping times.

International Markets

International markets continue to be important for future growth in the airfreight industry. In 2014, international markets accounted for over 50 percent of the airfreight ton-miles and have been increasing steadily since then. Domestic volumes are growing around 4 percent a year, whereas volumes in Asia are growing nearly 20 percent a year. Both FedEx and UPS have capitalized on these trends, especially in China, but also in Germany, to help facilitate a growing European market as well. International rates tend to offer a higher margin as well, since many customers internationally disproportionally use next day service, which carries a significant price premium.

Less than Truck Load (LTL)

FedEx Ground and UPS both compete in the LTL segment that accounts for about 6 percent of the total trucking industry. Annual revenues in the LTL are over $50 billion with both FedEx Ground and UPS accounting for the majority shares. The LTL typical haul consists of 1,000 to 1,500 pounds and is normally used by business-to-business or retail-to-consumer segments, such as Amazon sending shipments to customers. The LTL system also requires a large hub structure, which both UPS and FedEx Ground have. In LTL, labor costs are high, with many drivers being represented by the International Brotherhood of Teamsters Union.

Natural Gas Powered Trucks

The trucking industry had high hopes for natural gas powered trucks, especially in the United States, where natural gas is plentiful but sales have lagged expectations. In 2013, sales were around 8,700 trucks and around 10,000 in 2014. However, analysts were expecting 16,000 natural gas powered trucks to be sold in 2014. Premiums on the trucks upwards of 33 percent have caused pause with potential customers, combined with cheaper diesel fuel prices during the same time. Also, only in select parts of the South and West are there reliable natural-gas fueling stations. Natural gas powered trucks do save around $1.70 per equivalent gallon on fuel after taking into account diesel trucks are 20 percent more fuel efficient. In the end, it takes around

4 years at current fuel prices to recover the price premium paid for a natural gas powered truck. However, UPS has a fleet of around 300 gas-powered trucks and 700 tractors. In addition, UPS has helped finance several natural-gas filling stations.

Future

From Summer 2014 into early 2015, oil prices fell nearly 60 percent in the United States, in what many would consider a boom for trucking companies such as FedEx. But as CEO of Old Dominion Trucking pointed out, much of the oil price is passed on to consumers, and rising or falling prices do not directly impact trucking business. FedEx, in fact, missed its second quarter 2014 earnings estimates, reporting $2.14 EPS versus Wall Street estimates of $2.22 EPS. The difference was blamed mostly on reduced fuel surcharges stemming from the drop in oil prices, which FedEx was unable to pass along to consumers as the price of oil dropped. Nevertheless, FedEx is still doing great; second-quarter 2014 profits were up 23 percent from the same quarter in 2013, and revenue was up 5 percent over the same period. UPS's stock price dropped nearly 15 percent in one week in January 2015 after reporting flat earnings and a 6 percent sales gain. In response to UPS's news and growing concerns, FedEx's CEO was quoted as saying "We are not UPS."

FedEx acquired GENCO Distribution System, Inc. in January 2015. The GENCO acquisition is expected to further FedEx's commitment to its customers by improving logistics offerings. GENCO is a large third-party logistic provider in the United States and Canada. FedEx plans to allow GENCO to operate as a subsidiary and keep its management team. The new subsidiary will, however, report through FedEx's Ground business segment.

FedEx is flying high. In mid-2015, the company signed a deal to buy 50 additional Boeing Co (BA.N) 767-300 freighters in the biggest order ever for the plane, allowing Boeing to extend its production line well into the next decade. The deal includes options for another 50 767Fs and is worth $9.97 billion at list prices. The new aircraft are being delivered to FedEx Express over the fiscal years 2018 to 2023. This deal brings FedEx's orders for 767Fs to 106 and extends the company's drive to modernize its fleet.

FedEx needs a clear strategic plan moving forward. Help CEO Smith prepare this document.

Citigroup Inc., 2015

www.citigroup.com, C

Headquartered in New York City, Citigroup is a diversified financial services holding company formally divided into Citicorp and Citi Holdings. Citi Holdings contains the noncore businesses and comprises only about 6 percent of the overall company. The Citicorp segment provides global banking, advisory services, derivative services, brokerage, mortgages, auto loans, and much more. Citigroup is the largest banking enterprise in the world based on geographic coverage with operations in 160 nations and over 16,000 offices worldwide with 251,000 full-time employees. Citigroup is world's largest credit card issuer with over 900 million retail accounts with various well-known brands.

Senator Elizabeth Warren in December 2014 took to the Senate floor and gave a barn-burning speech attacking Citigroup for being unethical. Warren's rhetoric called out by name Citigroup for economic problems in the United States, and blamed Citi for costing millions of Americans their jobs and homes. Warren stated that Citi was bailed out with half a trillion dollars of taxpayer money, and then used their fortunes to buy Congress, and make it more likely they will be bailed out again. There are numerous business ethics issues associated with Citigroup, but Senator Warren pointed out that five top economic advisors to Presidents Bush and Obama were/are Citi alumni.

During Q2 of 2015, Citigroup continued to wind down its Citi Holdings division by reducing that segment's assets another $32 billion, or 22 percent, from the prior-year period. In Q2, Citi sold about $32 billion of the remaining assets in Citi Holdings, including OneMain Financial, the largest business remaining in Citi Holdings. Citi Holdings maintained profitability in Q2 of 2015, contributing to Citigroup's reported net income of $4.8 billion, compared to $181 million in the prior-year period. Citicorp revenues, net of interest expense, increased 2 percent from the prior-year period to $17.8 billion.

Copyright by Fred David Books LLC. www.strategyclub.com (Written by Forest R. David)

History

Citigroup traces its roots to 1812 when the Citi Bank of New York was formed with $2 million in assets. The bank was founded by Samuel Osgood, who served as the nation's first postmaster-general as well as a soldier, and legislator, and is associated with the founding fathers of the United States. Osgood was keen on foreign trade with nations. His bank financed much of the War of 1812 against England and also the railroad advancement in the middle 1800s. Citi was instrumental in financing the transatlantic cable that brought New York and London instant communication in 1866. By 1895, the bank was the largest in the United States. Citi was the first American bank to surpass $1 billion in assets and eventually became the largest bank in the world in 1929. In 1976, the bank was officially named Citibank and in 1998 it merged with Travelers Group to create a $140 billion firm with assets of $700 billion, changing its name to Citigroup. However, Travelers Group was divested in 2002. Still under government oversight following the subprime mortgage crisis in 2008, Citi failed Federal Reserve stress tests in 2012 and 2014. Citi reported net income of $13.7 billion in 2013 and had a market capitalization of $162 billion in late 2014.

In 2015, Citigroup sold its Japanese retail operations to Sumitomo Mitsui Banking Corp. for $400 million, ending this Citigroup problematic, money-losing segment. With this divestiture, Citigroup lost 740,000 customers in Japan.

Internal Issues

Organizational Structure

Citigroup operates from a hybrid, complex organizational structure, but it most resembles a strategic business unit (SBU) design, with the two groups being Institutional Clients and Global Consumer Banking. Citigroup's probable chain of command is illustrated in Exhibit 1.

EXHIBIT 1 Citigroup's Organizational Structure

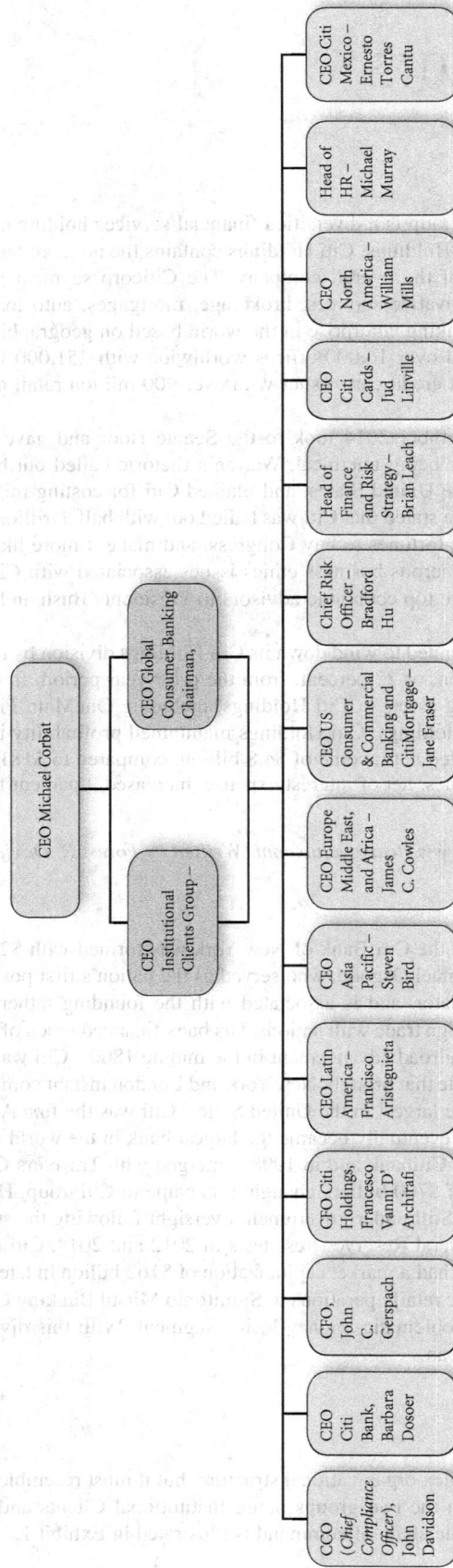

CEO Michael Corbat

CEO Institutional Clients Group –

CEO Global Consumer Banking Chairman,

CCO (Chief Compliance Officer), John Davidson

CEO Citi Bank, Barbara Desoer

CFO, John C. Gerspach

CFO Citi Holdings, Francesco Vanni D' Archirafi

CEO Latin America – Francisco Aristeguieta

CEO Asia Pacific – Steven Bird

CEO Europe Middle East, and Africa – James C. Cowles

CEO US Consumer & Commercial Banking and CitiMortgage – Jane Fraser

Chief Risk Officer – Bradford Hu

Head of Finance and Risk Strategy – Brian Leach

CEO Citi Cards – Jud Linville

CEO North America – William Mills

Head of HR – Michael Murray

CEO Citi Mexico – Ernesto Torres Cantu

Source: Based on information from Citigroup's recent *Annual Report.*

444

Vision/Mission

Citigroup does not have a vision statement. However, at the corporate website, Citigroup provides a mission statement, as follows: "Citi works tirelessly to serve individuals, communities, institutions and nations. With 200 years of experience meeting the world's toughest challenges and seizing its greatest opportunities, we strive to create the best outcomes for our clients and customers with financial solutions that are simple, creative, and responsible. An institution connecting over 1,000 cities, 160 countries, and millions of people, we are your global bank; we are Citi."

Strategy

Citigroup has recently resolved a significant portion of its mortgage litigation, and cut Citi Holdings annual loss in half. Citi Holdings now accounts for only 6 percent of the balance sheet. CEO Corbat has shifted his strategy from selling assets in Citi Holdings to cutting costs, in an attempt to break even in the near future. Recently, all 101 countries Citi does business in were sorted into four categories, or buckets, to better help prioritize resources.

In late 2014, Citigroup was close to fully spinning off OneMain Financial, which would remove Citi's exposure to its U.S. subprime-lending unit. Although the unit suffered major losses during the financial crisis, it has been profitable since 2012. OneMain targets customers that may not qualify for traditional bank loans, so divesting this business would help Citi avoid any unnecessary scrutiny from the government or stakeholders. This is the second time since 2009 that Citi has tried to sell OneMain, but the price was not right at the time. Subprime lending, contrary to public opinion, has become a more attractive business of late. If Citi is successful in the divesture, it will take several years to fully divest 100 percent of its holdings in OneMain.

Ethical Issues

Citigroup incurred charges of $3.5 billion in Q4 of 2014 to cover legal and restructuring costs. The bank allocated $2.7 billion of that amount to cover legal costs associated with investigations into currency trading, the manipulation of a key interest rate, as well as anti-money laundering and related probes. The remaining $800 million was spent reducing the bank's headcount and reducing the number of its physical branch offices. Investigators at Citi recently found $235 million in falsified invoices reported through a financing program in Mexico. Citi's problems in Mexico go hand in hand with the Federal Reserve in 2014 citing Citi for failing a stress test. In late 2014, it was speculated that Mr. Medina-Mora, the head of the consumer-banking unit in Mexico, plans to step down amid further scandal at Banamex (Citi's Mexico Unit). Citigroup was stricken with another $400 million in fraud by the oil services firm Oceanografia (also tied to Banamex) in 2014. Citi fired 12 Banamex employees over the Oceanografia incident. Banamex remains one of Citigroup's best assets and is the second largest bank in Mexico. Banamex has earned Citi over $1 billion in net income over the last several years, even during the financial crisis.

Segments

Citigroup reports in two segments: Citicorp and Citi Holdings. The Citicorp business includes Global Consumer Banking, Securities and Banking, and Transaction Services. Citi Holdings accounts for only 6 percent of the total balance sheet for Citigroup and the firm is currently cutting costs further in this segment. Note in Exhibit 2 that Citi Holdings had a loss of $3.3 billion in 2014. Citicorp specializes in providing global bank operations for consumers and businesses and is also closely tied to many emerging markets, with a heavy focus on Latin America.

Citigroup's Global Consumer Banking (GCB) segment is the largest in terms of revenues of any other segment and includes Citigroup's four geographical Regional Consumer Banking (RCB) businesses. The segment reported $37,753 million in sales during fiscal 2014. These banks provide services to retail customers, commercial banking, credit cards, and other financial services. As of January 2014, Citi had 3,729 branches in 36 different countries. As of January 2015, Citi operated 3,280 branches in 35 countries. The main strategy of the GCB is to become the top bank of choice among the affluent worldwide, with a focus on metropolitan areas. Retail banking accounted for $17 billion and cards accounted for $21 billion in 2013 across all geographic markets in GCB.

Citigroup's Institutional Clients group consists of Securities and Banking (S&B) and Transaction Services. The segment focuses on offering products for corporations, governments,

EXHIBIT 2 Segment Data for Citigroup (in millions of USD)

	2014		2013	
	Revenues	Income	Revenues	Income
Global Consumer Banking				
North America	$ 19,645	$ 4,421	$19,778	$ 3,910
EMEA	1,358	(7)	1,449	35
Latin America	9,204	1,204	9,318	1,337
Asia	7,546	1,320	7,624	1,481
Total	37,753	6,938	38,169	6,763
Institutional Clients Group				
North America	12,345	3,896	11,473	3,143
EMEA	9,513	1,984	10,020	2,432
Latin America	4,237	1,337	4,692	1,628
Asia	7,172	2,304	7,382	2,211
Total	33,267	9,521	33,567	9,414
Corporate/Other	47	(5,593)	121	(630)
Citi Holdings	5,815	(3,366)	4,566	(1,917)
Citi Totals*	$76,882	$ 7,313	$76,419	$13,673

*Reflects discontinued operations removed.
Based on Citigroup Financial Supplement, http://www.citigroup.com/citi/investor/qer.htm

institutions, and high net worth individuals and reported $33,267 million in revenues for fiscal year 2014. S&B offers customers cash, fixed income, foreign currency, equity, and commodity products. The segment also offers corporate lending, prime brokerage, derivative services, and many other services. Fixed income markets earned $13 billion, followed by total investment banking and equity markets earning $4 and $3 billion, respectively, in 2013 across all geographic markets in S&B. The Transaction Services business serves corporations, financial institutions, and the public sector worldwide. Most all business in the segment is related to foreign transactions, with most income coming from fees and the spread in interest revenue on trade loans. In total, the Transaction Services business serves institutions in the United States and 140 countries, with $3 trillion in global transactions daily. The business serves 85 percent of the Fortune 500 companies, through 10 regional processing centers.

Finance
Citigroup's recent income statement and balance sheet are provided in Exhibits 3 and 4, respectively. Note the decline in net income in 2014. The statements are condensed somewhat from the company's actual statements in its *Annual Report*.

Competitors
A comparative analysis of Citigroup with rivals J. P. Morgan and Bank of America is provided in Exhibit 5. Note that Citigroup trails both J. P. Morgan and Bank of America on every statistic presented, except total number of employees, with all three banks roughly equal on employment numbers.

J. P. Morgan Chase (JPM)
Founded in 1799 and headquartered in New York City, JPM is the largest bank in the United States, with 2013 revenues of $96 billion and assets over $2.4 trillion. The firm employs over 242,000 people. The firm divides its operations in two distinct areas: (1) Consumer and Community Banking and (2) Corporate and Investment Bank. Services offered under the consumer and community banking include credit cards, auto loans, student loans, home mortgage, business mortgages, and banking for both individuals and businesses. J. P. Morgan's Corporate

EXHIBIT 3 Citigroup's Income Statement (in millions of USD)

	December 31, 2014	December 31, 2013
Revenues	$76,882	$76,419
Operating expenses	55,051	48,408
Operating income	21,831	28,011
Other expenses	7,467	8,514
EBIT	14,364	19,497
Interest expense	–	–
EBT	14,364	19,497
Tax	6,864	5,867
EAT	7,500	13,630
Other items	(187)	43
Net income	**7,313**	**$13,673**

Source: Based on Citigroup's 2014 Annual Report p. 134.

EXHIBIT 4 Citigroup's Balance Sheet (in millions of USD)

Report Date	December 31, 2014	December 31, 2013
Cash	$402,767	$455,927
Accounts receivable	28,419	25,674
Total current assets	431,186	481,601
Property, plant & equipment	–	–
Goodwill	23,592	25,009
Intangibles	4,566	5,056
Trading account	296,786	285,928
Total investments	333,443	308,980
Net loans	628,641	645,824
Other assets	124,316	127,984
Total assets	**1,842,530**	**1,880,382**
Current debt	231,773	262,456
Accounts payable	52,180	53,707
Other current liabilities	899,332	968,273
Total current liabilities	1,183,285	1,284,436
Long-term debt	362,116	329,878
Other liabilities	85,084	59,935
Total liabilities	**1,630,485**	**1,674,249**
Common stock	31	31
Preferred stock	10,468	6,738
Retained earnings	118,201	111,168
Treasury stock	(2,929)	(1,658)
Paid in capital and other	86,274	89,854
Total equity	**212,045**	**206,133**
Total liabilities & equity	**1,842,530**	**1,880,382**

Source: Based on Citigroup's 2014 Annual Report p. 136.

EXHIBIT 5 Citigroup versus Rival Firms (Net Income, Revenue, and Market Cap., (in millions of USD))

	Citigroup	J. P. Morgan	Bank of America
# Employees	241,000	241,000	223,000
$ Net Income	7,313	17,923	11,431
$ Revenue	76,882	96,381	101,697
$ Revenue/Employee	319,012	399,921	456,040
$ EPS Ratio	2.20	5.29	0.36
Market Cap.	142,000	202,000	159,000

Source: Based on company documents and a variety of sources.

and Investment Bank deals with investment banking, securities, equity markets, fixed income, and other corporate related financing related activities.

Exhibit 6 reveals JPM's 2013 financial breakdown by segment. The largest revenue and income driver is the Consumer & Community Banking. Top services provided here are ATMs, online banking, business banking, mortgage banking, credit cards, student loans, among others. The worst performing segment was Corporate/Private Equity, which serves to monitor the four other segments. The bank was scheduled to divest $3.5 billion of its physical commodities business to Swiss trading firm Mercuria in 2014, but the deal was cut to an all-cash $800 million deal, including JPM's Henry Bath & Sons Ltd., which is a chain of metals warehouses. JPM is actively looking to divest the full $3.5 billion of its physical commodity assets and is currently in search of potential suitors. Despite the sale, JPM plans to remain trading commodities, including storing precious metals.

J. P. Morgan continues to pay out $4 billion in consumer aid required with its settlement with the Justice Department in 2013 largely over the subprime mortgage issues. The bank announced in 2014 it should receive credit for $869 million from actions that include lower mortgage debts for low-income homeowners and lending to similar potential buyers. The $869 million in credit steams from providing $7.6 billion in mortgage relief.

In 2014, JPM suffered a security breach that released contact information for 76 million households and 7 million small businesses. Fortunately, no sensitive account data was breached. CEO Dimon has pledged to double the bank's security measures in the next 5 years from $250 million to $500 million. Although a potential risk for other big banks, there is no evidence any other large banks were affected by breaches.

Bank of America

Headquartered in Charlotte, North Carolina, Bank of America is a huge bank in the both the United States and the global banking industry. Its top brand name is Merrill Lynch. Bank of America does business in all 50 states and in 40 countries, with 230,000 full-time employees. The bank had year-end 2013 revenues of over $100 billion and total assets over $2 trillion. The bank's real estate segment has lately been the poorest performing, with a net loss in 2013 of over

EXHIBIT 6 JPM's Segment Data (in millions of USD)

Segment	2013 Revenues	2013 Income
Consumer and Community Banking	$46,026	$10,749
Corporate and Investment Bank	34,225	8,546
Commercial Banking	6,973	2,575
Asset Management	11,320	2,031
Corporate/Private Equity	1,254	(5,978)
Total	**99,798**	**17,923**

Source: Based on J. P. Morgan's 2013 *Annual Report*, page 85.

$5 billion. The bank's Global Banking segment is its investment bank and the Global Markets segment focuses on fixed income and equity markets. The Global Markets segment also includes a high concentration in energy and commodities markets.

Bank of America continues to be plagued by litigation stemming from the subprime era. The bank has faced nearly twice the litigation than either J. P. Morgan or Citigroup. The bank estimates that litigation demands have cannibalized 30 percent of profit in 2013 and 2014. Further troubling for Bank of America is the SEC debating on whether the bank should face further business restrictions after meeting its agreed upon litigation requirements. In particular, the SEC is considering how quickly Bank of America should be able to issue stocks and bonds without a SEC review. As of 2014, the bank had spent $75 billion to settle lawsuits, pay fines, and other litigation processes, much related to the 2008 purchase of Countrywide Financial and in the process acquiring many bad loans.

Online Banks
Online banks are growing rapidly in number and taking market share from large banks. The website http://www.mybanktracker.com/best-online-banks rates 30-plus online banks in the United States in terms of having low fees, low interest rates, excellent technology, and great customer service. Exhibit 7 reveals in rank order the top 5 Internet banks in the United States. The only bank to remain in the top 5 since 2011 is Ally Bank, which held the #1 spot in 2011. With low interest rates, some online banks such as Ally Bank are offering interest payments on money market funds around 1,000 percent more than many brick-and-mortar banks. As of November 2014, Ally was offering 0.80 percent on money market funds with many tradition banks offering interest rates of 0.01 percent.

External Issues

U.S. Investment Banking and Securities
The investment banking and securities business is a $148 billion operation in the United States, dominated by Bank of America, J. P. Morgan Chase, Citigroup, Morgan Stanley, and Goldman Sachs, with U.S. market shares of 12, 11, 8, 8, and 8 percent, respectively. Approximately 53 percent of the industry revenues are derived from other firms. The industry is currently improving from the subprime loan era where, from 2009 to 2014, revenues declined industry wide at an annualized rate of over 4 percent. However, the outlook moving forward from 2014 to 2019 is for a growth rate over 4 percent. Replacing the subprime loan market as key growth initiatives are underwriting of equity services and mergers and acquisitions (M&A) advising fees. Large banks have enjoyed many new IPOs and a high level of M&A activity in the last 2 years. Underwriting equities and M&A advising fees account for around 15 and 17 percent of total U.S. bank revenues. Underwriting debt and trading and related services account for about 30 and 24 percent of total U.S. industrywide revenues.

Firms also use investment banks to aid in raising capital by issuing bonds (debt). Trading services account for 24 percent of the investment banking and securities business and include principal trading and market making, proprietary trading, and prime brokerage. Principle trading and market making is what most people think of when they think of trading. Here, the bank takes the client's money and buys a stock or some other security and the client then waits for the security to appreciate (hopefully) in value before selling. Banks charge a fee for this service, much like any online stockbroker would. The investment banks also are able to capitalize on the differences in the "ask and bid," known as the *spread prices*. Proprietary trading is also considered part of the trading services portfolio of many banks; however, its use is declining. Simply, proprietary

EXHIBIT 7 The Top Five Online Banks in the United States

1. Sally Mae Bank
2. Ally Bank
3. Bank of Internet
4. Capital One 360
5. Discover Bank

trading is when the bank places its trades on a particular security before the trades of its clients, ensuring a better price for itself. However, the Volcker Rule in the Dodd-Frank Wall Street Reform and Consumer Protection Act of 2010 places limitations on proprietary trading and the future of proprietary trading impact on overall revenues for investment banks should be greatly reduced. Banks also engage in lending to hedge funds in order to buy securities on margin.

With the increase in mergers and acquisitions in recent years, along with divestitures and other restructurings, investment banks have made significant profits on financial advisory services. Mergers and acquisitions alone account for over 17 percent of U.S. banking and securities revenues, and other advisory fees account for about 5 percent of total revenues. Corporate financial services on various loans generate 9 percent of industry revenue. Low rates worldwide have limited higher returns in this business.

Unlike commercial banks, many U.S. investment banks also control a significant portion of the global investment banking business. Bank of America, Citigroup, and J. P. Morgan all account for approximately 12 percent each of total revenues. Two large non-U.S.-based banks, Barclays and Deutsche Bank AG, each account for around 6 percent of total revenues.

U.S. Commercial Banking

The U.S. commercial banking industry provides loans to commercial and consumers from funds deposited in the bank. The industry makes money from fees and from the spread on money deposited compared to a higher interest rate of the same money loaned back out. Interest rates are affected by Federal Funds Rate, Prime Rate, and the respective consumers' credit scores. In the United States, there is a $426 billion industry that is just now starting to grow gain, after annualized growth rates less than 2 percent from 2009 to 2014. Approximately 40 percent of all loans are considered to be based on real estate, and another 27 percent for depository services (bank accounts and other similar services). Individual loans and loans to commercial operations account for about 15 percent each of the market. Most loans to individuals are in the form of auto, marine, or recreational vehicles. Personal loans for housing are not included under this industry.

In the global commercial banking industry, large U.S. players have very little market share, and no single player has more than a 4 percent market share. Key players include the Industrial and Commercial Bank of China, Bank of America, J. P. Morgan, and Wells Fargo. The balance of competitors account for over 85 percent of total revenues generated.

U.S. Credit Card Industry

The U.S. credit card business is a $90 billion industry with profits in excess of $30 billion and growth rates expected to be around 2.5 percent annualized through 2020. The industry is slowly recovering from an annual negative growth rate of 3.5 percent from 2009 to 2014. The six major players in the market control nearly 85 percent of revenues, with American Express being the single market leader with a 20 percent market share. Capital One, Bank of America, and J. P. Morgan all enjoy market shares between 15 and 18 percent; Citigroup and Discovery have market shares of 9 and 7 percent, respectively. The industry makes money from three key areas: interest income, interchange fees, and cardholder fees. All three revenue streams account for approximately one third each of total revenues. Interest charged on U.S. credit cards now ranges from 12 to 19 percent and is largely dependent on the customer's credit score. Interchange fees are the fees firms like MasterCard and Visa charge merchants for accepting a customer's card. The higher the fees, the higher the profits for banks, and MasterCard and Visa often raise fees to attract banks into selecting their particular card. The United States has some of the highest credit card fees in the world, and with increased competition from other credit card players, there is expected to be downward pressure on card fees in the future.

A growing trend in the United States is the use of mobile payments through providers such as Apple and Google, which use processing firms Visa and MasterCard. It remains to be seen if new players such as Apple and Google can create their own brands and bypass the banks in gaining access directly to the major credit card companies. However, consumers in Europe have been using mobile phone payments for around a decade now with growing popularity and use. The new technology does bring growing awareness to security issues and the perceived dangers of a digital currency as data is increasingly stored on Internet accessible systems. Recent security breaches, such as Home Depot and J. P. Morgan, are examples of potential problems that could escalate in the future. New competitors—for example, Bitcoin and PayPal—also may increasingly take market share away from the larger banks, along with possibly Apple and Google, if they can enter into direct agreements with MasterCard and Visa, and totally bypass the banks all together.

U.S. Loans

The loan business in the United States is a $90 billion industry with profits of $14 billion. The industry is largely dependent on the health of the housing market. With low interest rates, many homeowners have refinanced lately. The extended outlook for the industry is to generate $95 billion by 2019. The industry is heavily fragmented with Bank of America, Citigroup, J. P. Morgan, and Wells Fargo, all accounting for just over 26 percent of the total industrywide revenues, fairly evenly distributed among the four. The balance of 75 percent is comprised of thousands of other banks, mostly regional in nature. There are currently over 5,500 different commercial banks in the United States.

Latin America Growth Slows

Latin America is expected to have its slowest growth in 2014 at 1.2 percent having grown only 2.5 and 3 percent, respectively, in 2012 and 2013. The World Bank projects 2015 growth of 2.2 percent. Much of the drawdown can be explained by a rising U.S. dollar and lower commodity prices, which many Latin American nations rely on heavily. Slowdown is also contributed to China, a large buyer of many Latin American commodities, along with the United States tapering and then ending its Quantitative Easing programs. Venezuela, largely dependent on oil, is experiencing inflation of over 60 percent, and Argentina has double-digit inflation itself. Both nations are expected to experience gross domestic product contractions of 2.9 and 1.5 percent, respectively. Highlights in the region include Mexico, which grew 2.5 percent in 2014. Mexico is also a large business partner for Citigroup and should remain strong moving forward. The largest-growing country in Latin America, with respect to gross domestic product, is Colombia, with nearly 5 percent growth in 2014.

Future

Banks, including Citigroup, are largely dependent on the spread between short- and long-term interest rates, referred to as the yield curve. When short-term rates are low, and long-term rates are high, bank profits tend to be higher, as they are able to pay relatively low interest rates on CDs and savings, while charging higher rates on automobile, housing, business and other loans. This spread is where the banks make money. In 2015, interest rates have been rising slowly in the United States.

Automobile sales were up in both 2014 and 2015 as customers are buying new and larger vehicles as the price of oil has dropped. This is a potential windfall for banks but only to the extent that rates start to increase. With the European Central Bank, Japan, Australia, and other top economies are engaging in their own quantitative easing programs, rates will not likely move higher in these regions throughout 2015. While the U.S. Federal Reserve plans to start raising rates in late 2015, they may be unable to do so because the increasing dollar value has already put a burden on U.S. corporations, hurting profits in overseas markets. One aspect that is positive for Citigroup moving forward is that the firm receives over 50 percent of revenues from its Global Consumer segment from the United States, with rates likely to rise in the nation quicker than in overseas markets.

JPMorgan Chase & Co., 2013

www.jpmorganchase.com, JPM

Headquartered in New York City, JPMorgan & Chase (JPM) is a financial holding company that competes worldwide, serving customers for more than 200 years, making it one of the oldest financial intuitions in the USA. Considered to be the largest bank in the USA, JPM has total assets of more than $2.3 trillion and employs more than 240,000 people in more than 60 countries around the globe. JPM's stock is one of the 30 components of the Dow Jones Industrial Average. The hedge fund unit of JPM is one of the largest in the USA.

JPM in mid-2013 announced plans to stop trading in physical commodities, but in August 2013, JPM purchased the over-the-counter business in commodity derivatives of Switzerland's UBS AG. The deal excluded precious metals and index-based trades, but included hedge positions on financial exchanges. Zurich-based UBS is closing the majority of its commodities "flow" trading business involving raw materials and financial derivatives as part of its slimming down and laying off 10,000 employees.

JPM operates under two principle brands, (1) JPMorgan and (2) Chase. The JPMorgan brand focuses on large multinational corporations, governments, wealthy individuals, and institutional investors. The Chase brand is further divided into two distinct segments: (1) consumer business and (2) commercial banking business. The Chase consumer business includes such businesses as traditional bank branches, ATMs, credit cards, home finance, retirement and investing, and merchant services among others. The Chase commercial banking business includes such areas as business credit, corporate client banking, commercial term lending, and community development. The two JPM brands overlap so much in terms of regions and products that the company does not report revenues or income by the two brands.

Copyright by Fred David Books LLC. (Written by Forest R. David)

History

Dating back to 1799, JPM is one of the oldest financial institutions in the world. The heritage of the House of Morgan traces its roots to the partnership of Drexel, Morgan & Co., which in 1895 was renamed J.P. Morgan & Co. Arguably the most influential financial institution of its era, J.P. Morgan & Co. financed the formation of the United States Steel Corporation, which took over the business of Andrew Carnegie and others and was the world's first billion-dollar corporation. In 1895, J.P. Morgan & Co. supplied the United States government with $62 million in gold to float a bond issue and restore the treasury surplus of $100 million. In 1892, the company began to finance the New York, New Haven, and Hartford Railroad and led it through a series of acquisitions that made it the dominant railroad transporter in New England. Although his name was big, Morgan owned only 19 percent of Morgan assets. The rest was owned by the Rothschild family following a series of bailouts and rescues attributed by some to Morgan's stubborn will and seemingly "nonexistent" investment savvy.

In 2004, JPM merged with Chicago-based Bank One Corp., bringing on board current chairman and Chief Executive Officer (CEO) Jamie Dimon as president and Chief Operating Officer and designating him as CEO William Harrison, Jr.'s successor. Dimon's pay was pegged at 90 percent of Harrison's. Dimon quickly made his influence felt by embarking on a cost-cutting strategy, and replaced former JPMorgan Chase executives in key positions with Bank One executives—many of whom were with Dimon at Citigroup. Dimon became CEO and chairman of JPM in 2006.

JPM has acquired more than 1,200 financial institutions over its life. Several key acquisitions during the last 20 years include in 1991 Chemical Banking Corp., the second largest bank in the USA and in 1995, First Chicago Corp., the largest bank in the Midwest. The acquisition responsible for the current name of the company was in 2000 when J.P. Morgan & Co. merged with The Chase Manhattan Corp. In 2010, JPM acquired Cazenove, an advisory and underwriting joint venture established in 2004 in the United Kingdom. Since 2010, JPM has refrained from making acquisitions that had historically been its trademark.

Internal Issues

Vision and Mission

JPM does not list a formal mission statement, but the company vision statement is:

> At JPMorgan Chase, we want to be the best financial services company in the world. Because of our great heritage and excellent platform, we believe this is within our reach.

Organizational Structure

Some analysts contend that JPM has organizational design problems because there are numerous CEOs, no presidents, dual-title individuals, lack of a clear JP Morgan-versus-Chase dichotomy, and overall, too many top-level executives. As best as can be determined, the existing organizational chart for JPM is given in Exhibit 1. Note that Jamie Dimon is both chairman of the board and CEO, a practice being shunned by more and more by corporations.

In 2013, the company replaced its Chief Financial Officer, Doug Braunstein, with Marianne Lake, who is now one of the most powerful women on Wall Street. Lake joins asset-management chief Mary Erdoes as the only two women on the bank's elite 14-member operating committee.

Ethics Issues

JPM has an extensive Code of Conduct and Code of Ethics posted on its website. Part of the company's code of conduct says in part: "The Code is based on our fundamental understanding that no one at JPMorgan Chase should ever sacrifice integrity—or give the impression that they have—even if they think it would help the firm's business." The company's code of ethics is more lengthy, and says in part: "The purpose of this Code of Ethics is to promote honest and ethical conduct and compliance with the law, particularly as related to the maintenance of the firm's financial books and records and the preparation of its financial statements."

Despite having extensive ethical-based statements, JPM has had its fair share of ethical issues over the years. In January 2011, JPM admitted that it wrongly overcharged several thousand military families for their mortgages, including active-duty personnel in Afghanistan. The bank also admitted it improperly foreclosed on more than a dozen military families; both actions were in clear violation of the Service Members Civil Relief Act, which automatically lowers mortgage rates to 6 percent and bars foreclosure proceedings of active-duty personnel. The overcharges may have never come to light were it not for legal action taken by Marine Capt. Jonathan Rowles, a fighter pilot. Both Captain Rowles and his spouse Julia accused Chase of violating the law and harassing the couple for nonpayment.

In April 2012, hedge fund insiders became aware that the market in credit default swaps was possibly being affected by the activities of Bruno Iksil, a trader for JPM, referred to as "the London whale" in reference to the huge positions he was taking. Heavy opposing bets to his positions are known to have been made by traders, including another branch of JPM that purchased the derivatives offered by JPM in such high volume. Early reports were denied and minimized by the firm in an attempt to minimize exposure. Major losses of $2 billion were reported by the firm in May 2012 in relationship to these trades and updated to $4.4 billion on July 13, 2012. The disclosure, which resulted in headlines in the media, did not disclose the exact nature of the trading involved, which remains in progress and as of June 28, 2012, was continuing to produce losses that could total as much as $9 billion under worst case scenarios. The item traded, possibly related to CDX IG 9, an index based on the default risk of major U.S. corporations, has been described as a "derivative of a derivative." On the company's emergency conference call, JPM CEO Jamie Dimon said the strategy was "flawed, complex, poorly reviewed, poorly executed, and poorly monitored." The episode is being investigated by the Federal Reserve, the Securities and Exchange Commission (SEC), and the FBI.

Strategy

JPM strategies revolve around the areas of (a) international expansion of its wholesale business and global corporate bank, (b) small business growth, (c) commodities, (d) growth in branch network, and (e) growth in private client business.

EXHIBIT 1 JPM's Organizational Chart

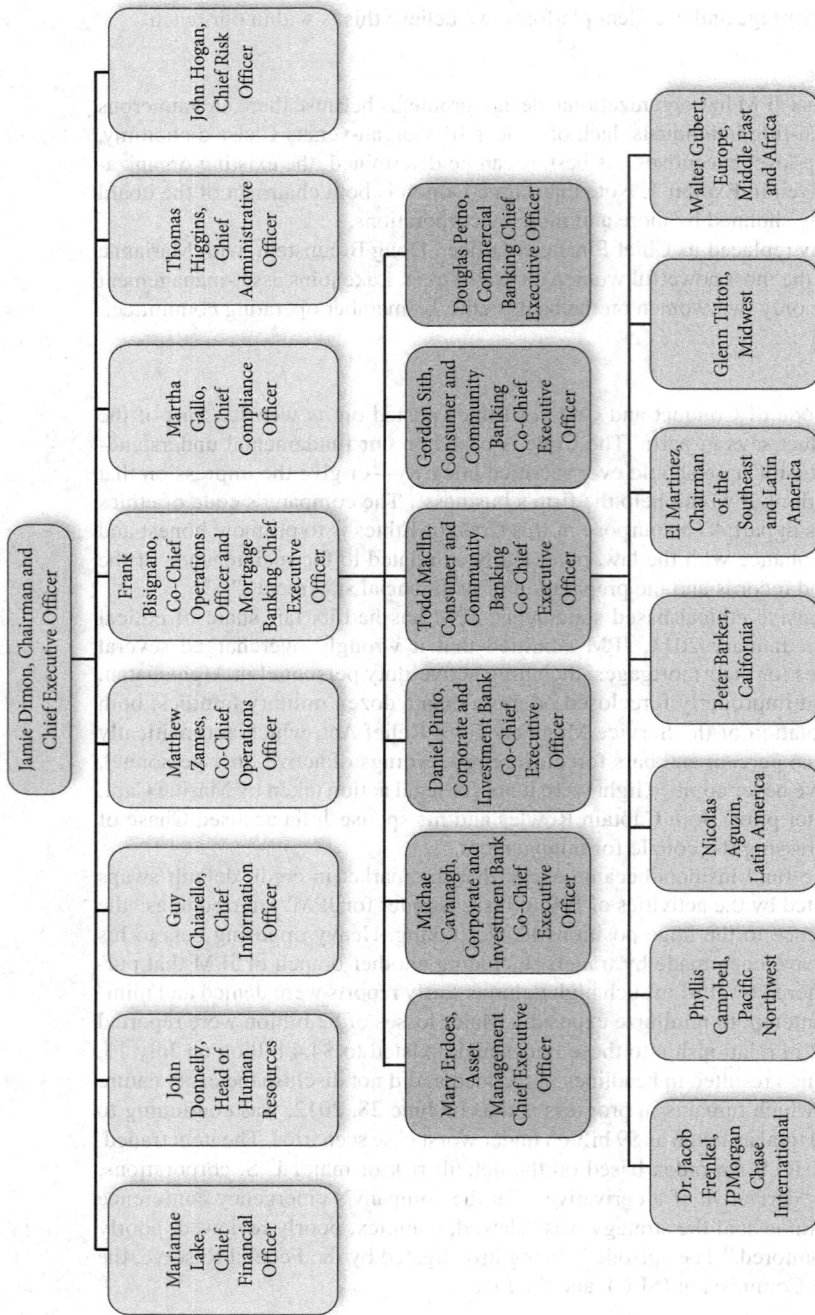

Jamie Dimon, Chairman and Chief Executive Officer

- Marianne Lake, Chief Financial Officer
- John Donnelly, Head of Human Resources
- Guy Chiarello, Chief Information Officer
- Matthew Zames, Co-Chief Operations Officer
- Frank Bisignano, Co-Chief Operations Officer and Mortgage Banking Chief Executive Officer
- Martha Gallo, Chief Compliance Officer
- Thomas Higgins, Chief Administrative Officer
- John Hogan, Chief Risk Officer

- Mary Erdoes, Asset Management Chief Executive Officer
- Michae Cavanagh, Corporate and Investment Bank Co-Chief Executive Officer
- Daniel Pinto, Corporate and Investment Bank Co-Chief Executive Officer
- Todd MacIln, Consumer and Community Banking Co-Chief Executive Officer
- Gordon Sith, Consumer and Community Banking Co-Chief Executive Officer
- Douglas Petno, Commercial Banking Chief Executive Officer

- Dr. Jacob Frenkel, JPMorgan Chase International
- Phyllis Campbell, Pacific Northwest
- Nicolas Aguzin, Latin America
- Peter Barker, California
- El Martinez, Chairman of the Southeast and Latin America
- Glenn Tilton, Midwest
- Walter Gubert, Europe, Middle East and Africa

Source: Extrapolated based on executive titles given on the corporate website.

JPM's international expansion strategy aims to increase the firm's global presence through an aggressive international expansion plan. JPM is focused on expanding its asset management, investment bank, and treasury and securities services segments in Asia, Latin America, Africa, and the Middle East. Additionally, slowly expanding into newly emerging or even frontier markets, JPM's clients in this expansion plan include multinational corporations, sovereign wealth funds, and public entities. In 2008, JPM had approximately 200 clients in Brazil, China, and India combined, but by 2012, the number of clients in these nations had expanded to 800. By 2017, JPM is expected to have more than 2,000 clients in these nations.

U.S. small businesses remain a central focus of the Chase arm of JPM. In 2011 alone, Chase provided more than $17 billion of credit to domestic small businesses, up 52 percent from 2010, indicating Chase believes the economic recovery is robust enough to tolerate any short-term downward pressures. The $17 billion of credit in 2011 makes Chase the number-1 Small Business Administration (SBA) leader nationwide for the second straight year. In addition, JPM is also the number-1 SBA lender to women- and minority-owned businesses. To help facilitate growth in the small business arm, JPM has added more than 1,200 relationship managers and business bankers since 2009 and anticipates an aggressive hiring of bankers for the foreseeable future.

With the 2011 acquisition of Sempra, JPM is currently one of the top-three firms in the world in commodity dealings. Growth from 2011 to 2012 grew by 10 percent to bring total commodity clients to more than 2,200, as well as increased commodity packaging and selling to existing clients. JPM expects commodity demand to increase with the growth of emerging markets and anticipates increased business in the various commodity asset classes the firm currently offers.

Surprising to some, JPM is actively growing its physical branches despite many predictions from outside pundits who suggest that brick-and-mortar branches are a relic of the past. JPM's own research suggests however that although 17 million JPM customers do much of their banking business online, they still value a face-to-face conversation when it comes to taking out a mortgage, applying for a credit card, or seeking general financial advice in a physical branch location. Currently 45 percent of Chase credit cards and 50 percent of retail mortgages are sold on site at branch locations.

Segments

Within its two brands, JPM operates under seven major business segments as indicated in Exhibit 2, with respective revenues given. Note that JPM's revenues have been declining in three of the seven segments.

Exhibit 3 provides a breakdown of JPM revenues and net income over the geographic regions where the bank does business. Note that North America accounts for 81 percent of revenues and 86 percent of net income. Note also the dramatic drop in North American revenues in 2011 associated with a dramatic increase in associated net income.

Investment Bank

Within JPM's investment bank segment, $8,303 million of the $26,274 million was derived from noninterest sources, with the balance of $17,971 derived from interest sources. Clients of the investment bank division include corporations, financial institutions, and government and institutional investors. Investment bank activities include advising on business strategy and structure, raising capital though debt or equity, derivative instruments, prime brokerage, and research.

Exhibit 4 provides a geographic breakdown of JPM's investment bank segment. Note the decline in revenue from North America and Asia and Pacific, but the increase in revenue from other areas globally. Total 2011 net income from this division totaled $1,678 million.

Bonds trading is an important part of JPM's Investment Bank. A *Wall Street Journal* article (11-2-12, p. C3) reported that JPM's 12.3 percent market share in the USA in bonds trading was the largest among all banks, followed by Deutsche Bank (10.5 percent), Barclays (9.9 percent), Bank of America (9.6 percent), and Goldman Sachs (8.3 percent). A part of fixed-income operations, bond-trading is risky business. That is why UBS AG recently exited the bond-trading business to focus its investment bank on less-risky businesses such as advising on mergers and stock underwriting.

EXHIBIT 2 JPM's Financial Results by Segment (in millions $)

Revenue by Product	2012	%Change	2011	2010
Consumer & Community Banking	49,945	+9	45,687	48,927
Corporate & Investment Bank	34,326	+1	33,984	33,477
Commercial Banking	6,825	+6	6,418	6,040
Asset Management	9,946	+4	9,543	8,984
Corporate/Private Equity	(1,152)	−128	4,135	7,414
Total	99,890	0	99,767	104,842

Net Income by Product	2012		2011	2010
Consumer & Community Banking	10,611	+71	6,202	4,578
Corporate & Investment Bank	8,406	+05	7,993	7,718
Commercial Banking	2,646	+12	2,367	2,084
Asset Management	1,703	+07	1,592	1,710
Corporate/Private Equity	(2,082)	−353	822	1,280
Total	21,284	+12	18,976	17,370

Return on Equity (%) by Product	2012		2011	2010
Consumer & Community Banking	25		15	11
Corporate & Investment Bank	18		17	17
Commercial Banking	28		30	26
Asset Management	24		25	26
Corporate/Private Equity	NM		NM	NM
Total				

EXHIBIT 3 JPM's Revenues and Net Income by Region Globally (in millions)

	Revenue				Net Income			
	2012	2011	2010	2009	2012	2011	2010	2009
Europe, Middle East. and Africa	$10,522	$16,212	$14,135	$16,294	$1,508	$4,844	$3,635	$5,212
Asia and Pacific	5,605	5,992	6,073	5,429	$1,048	1,380	1,614	1,286
Latin America and Caribbean	2,328	2,273	1,750	1,867	$454	340	362	463
Total International	18,455	24,477	21,958	23,590	$3,010	6,564	5,611	6,961
North America	78,576	72,757	80,736	76,844	$18,274	12,412	11,759	4,767
Total JPM	$97,031	$97,234	$102,694	$100,434	$21,284	$18,976	$17,370	$11,728

Source: Annual Report, page 300.

EXHIBIT 4 JPM's Investment Bank Revenue Breakdown
by Region (in millions)

	2011	2010	2009
Europe, Middle East, and Africa	8,418	7,380	9,164
Asia and Pacific	3,334	3,809	3,470
Latin America and Caribbean	1,079	897	1,157
North America	13,443	14,131	14,318
Net Revenue	$26,724	$26,212	$28,109
Net Income	$6,789	$6,639	$6,899

Source: 2011 *Annual Report*, page 84.

Retail Financial Services

JPM's retail financial services segment accounts for about 27 percent of 2011 net revenues with $10,405 million of the segments, $26,538 million being derived from noninterest sources, with the balance of $16,133 derived from interest sources. The retail financial services segment includes: bank branches, ATMs, mortgages, real estate, among others. JPM customers have access to more than 17,200 ATMs and 5,500 bank branches. The Chase business segment currently services more than 8 million loans in 23 states and services more than $150 billion of mortgage originations each year.

Exhibit 5 provides a breakdown of businesses within JPM's financial services segment. Note the decreases in both revenue and net income in 2011.

Card Services and Auto

JPM's credit card services and auto segment accounted for about 19 percent of 2011 net revenues with $4,892 million of the segments, $19,141 million being derived from noninterest sources with the balance of $14,249 derived from interest sources. The segment accounts for more than $132 billion in credit card loans with over 65 million open credit card accounts, making JPM one of the largest credit card issuers in the USA. JPM customers can also obtain financing through 17,200 auto dealerships and 2,000 schools and universities. Exhibit 6 provides a breakdown of businesses within JPM's credit card and auto segment. Note the reduction in revenues but increase in net income over the last three years.

Finance

JPM earned an all-time record of $19 billion in net income in 2011, up 9 percent from the previous record of $17.4 billion the prior year. The company's net income would have been considerably more, except for losses from the JPM mortgage business. Mortgage losses are expected to continue for a while longer, but the bulk of JPM bad mortgages have already been absorbed.

JPM's recent income statements are provided in Exhibit 7. Note the unusual decline in revenue associated with the increase in net income.

JPM reinstated its annual dividend of $1.00 per share in April of 2011 and increased it to $1.20 a share in April of 2012. Although JPM's goodwill has remained the same over the last

EXHIBIT 5 JPM's Retail Financial Services Revenue Breakdown by Product (in millions)

	2011	2010	2009
Lending- and deposit-related fees	$3,190	$3,061	$3,897
Asset management, administration, and commissions	1,991	1,776	1,665
Mortgage fees and related income	2,714	3,855	3,794
Credit card income	2,025	1,955	1,634
Other income	485	580	424
Net Revenue	$26,538	$28,447	$29,797
Net Income	$1,678	$1,728	$(335)

Source: 2011 *Annual Report*, page 85.

EXHIBIT 6 A Breakdown of JPM's Credit Card Business (in millions)

	2011	2010	2009
Credit card revenue	$4,127	$3,514	$3,613
Other income	765	764	93
Total revenue	$19,141	$20,472	$23,199
Net income/(loss)	$4,544	$2,872	$(1,793)

Source: 2011 *Annual Report,* page 94.

EXHIBIT 7 JPM's Income Statement (in millions)

	2012	2011	2010
Interest Income, Bank	56,063.0	61,293.0	63,782.0
Total Interest Expense	11,153.0	13,604.0	12,781.0
Non-Interest Income, Bank	52,121.0	49,545.0	51,693.0
Total Revenue	**97,031.0**	**97,234.0**	**102,694.0**
Loan Loss Provision	3,385.0	7,574.0	16,639.0
Non-Interest Expense, Bank	64,729.0	62,911.0	61,196.0
Income Before Tax	**28,917.0**	**26,749.0**	**24,859.0**
Income Tax Total	7,633.0	7,773.0	7,489.0
Income After Tax	**21,284.0**	**18,976.0**	**17,370.0**
Minority Interest	0.0	0.0	0.0
Equity In Affiliates	0.0	0.0	0.0
U.S. GAAP Adjustment	0.0	0.0	0.0
Net Income Before Extra Items	**21,284.0**	**18,976.0**	**17,370.0**
Total Extraordinary Items	0.0	0.0	0.0
Net Income	**21,284.0**	**18,976.0**	**17,370.0**

Source: Company documents.

three years, total goodwill of $48 billion indicates a history of paying more than fair market value for many acquisitions. JPM's long-term debt is declining as shown in Exhibit 8.

Competition

Banks are seemingly everywhere on every corner and online. Some analysts say bank products and services are becoming more and more like commodities, all being similar. An interesting note is that foreign banks have not yet penetrated into the U.S. marketplace. But online banks are proliferating.

JPM competes with literally hundreds of banks but a few key rivals are showcased in Exhibit 9. Note that JPM has higher revenue per employee and earnings per share (EPS) than Bank of America or Citigroup.

Bank of America

Headquartered today in Charlotte, North Carolina, and having total assets exceeding $2.5 billion, Bank of America is the second largest U.S. bank, trailing only JPM, and is the largest bank according to number of employees. Bank of America has a relationship with 99 percent of the *Fortune* 500 companies and 83 percent of the *Fortune Global* 500. The 2008 acquisition of Merrill Lynch made Bank of America the world's largest wealth management corporation and a major player in the investment banking market.

As of May 2012, Bank of America served more than 5,700 banking centers and had more than 17,000 ATMs serving customers in more than 150 countries and had branches in more than 40 countries. During 2011, Bank of America began laying off an estimated 36,000 people, contributing to intended savings of $5 billion per year by 2014. In December 2011, *Forbes* ranked Bank of America's financial health 91st out of the nation's largest 100 banks and thrift institutions. Bank of America will cut around 16,000 jobs in a quicker fashion by the end of 2012 as revenue continues to decline because of new regulations and a slow economy. This will put a plan one year ahead of time to eliminate 30,000 jobs under a cost-cutting program called Project New BAC. Bank of America generates 90 percent of its revenues in its domestic market and continues to buy businesses in the USA. The core of Bank of America's strategy is to be the number-one bank in its domestic market. It has achieved this through key acquisitions.

EXHIBIT 8 JPM's Balance Sheets (in millions)

	2012	2011	2010
Assets			
Cash & Due From Banks	53,723	59,602	27,567
Other Earning Assets, Total	1,358,307	1,271,811	1,174,042
Net Loans	711,860	696,111	660,661
Property/Plant/Equipment, Total - Net	14,519	14,041	13,355
Goodwill, Net	48,175	48,188	48,854
Intangibles, Net	9,849	10,430	17,688
Long Term Investments	0	0	0
Other Long Term Assets, Total	0	0	0
Other Assets, Total	162,708	165,609	175,438
Total Assets	**2,359,141**	**2,265,792**	**2,117,605**
Liabilities and Shareholders' Equity			
Accounts Payable	195,240	202,895	170,330
Payable/Accrued	0	0	0
Accrued Expenses	0	0	0
Total Deposits	1,193,593	1,127,806	930,369
Other Bearing Liabilities, Total	0	0	0
Total Short Term Borrowings	392,762	362,048	415,551
Policy Liabilities	0	0	0
Notes Payable/Short Term Debt	0	0	0
Current Port. of LT Debt/Capital Leases	0	0	0
Other Current Liabilities, Total	0	0	0
Total Long Term Debt	312,215	322,752	348,302
Deferred Income Tax	0	0	0
Minority Interest	0	0	0
Other Liabilities, Total	61,262	66,718	76,947
Total Liabilities	**2,155,072**	**2,082,219**	**1,941,499**
Redeemable Preferred Stock	0	0	0
Preferred Stock - Non Redeemable, Net	9,058	7,800	7,800
Common Stock	4,105	4,105	4,105
Additional Paid-In Capital	94,604	95,602	97,415
Retained Earnings (Accumulated Deficit)	104,223	88,315	73,998
Treasury Stock—Common	−12,002	−13,155	−8,160
ESOP Debt Guarantee	0	0	0
Unrealized Gain (Loss)	0	0	0
Other Equity, Total	4,081	906	948
Total Equity	**204,069**	**183,573**	**176,106**
Total Liabilities & Shareholders' Equity	**2,359,140**	**2,265,792**	**2,117,605**
Total Common Shares Outstanding	3,803.95	3,772.7	3,910.3

Source: Company documents.

Citigroup

Citigroup was formed on October 9, 1998, following the $140 billion merger of Citicorp and Travelers Group to create the world's largest financial services organization. The history of the company is comprised of many acquired firms such as the City Bank of New York (later named

EXHIBIT 9 A Synopsis of Large Banks

	JPM	Bank of America	Citigroup
Number of Employees	261K	279K	263K
Net Income ($)	17.5B	−1.31B	10.7B
Revenue ($)	90.5B	76.8B	66.3B
Revenue ($)/Employee	346K	275K	252K
EPS Ratio ($)	4.5	−0.13	3.59
Market Capitalization	129B	80.6B	74.1B

Source: Company documents.

Citibank) in 1812; Bank Handlowy in 1870; Smith Barney in 1873, Banamex in 1884; and Salomon Brothers in 1910.

Based today in New York City, Citigroup is a diversified financial services holding company broken down into two segments, Citicorp and Citi Holdings, providing global banking, advisory services, derivative services, brokerage, and much more. Citigroup today is the largest banking enterprise in the world based on geographic coverage with operations in 140 nations and more than 16,000 offices worldwide.

On Tuesday, March 13, 2012, the Federal Reserve reported Citigroup as one of the 4 financial institutions, out of 19, that have failed its stress tests. The tests make sure banks have enough capital to withstand huge losses in a financial crisis like one Citigroup faced in 2008 and early 2009 when it almost collapsed. The 2012 stress tests determine whether banks could withstand a financial crisis with unemployment at 13 percent, stock prices cut in half, and home prices decreased by 21 percent from current levels. According to Citi and the Federal Reserve stress test report, Citi failed the stress tests because of Citi's high capital return plan and its international loans rated by the Federal Reserve to be at higher risk than its domestic U.S. loans. Citi gets half their revenues from its international businesses. In comparison, Bank of America, which passed the stress test and did not ask for a capital return to investors, gets 78 percent of its revenue in the USA.

Wells Fargo & Co.

Founded in 1852 and headquartered in San Francisco, Wells Fargo is a nationwide, diversified, community-based financial services company with $1.4 trillion in assets. Wells Fargo provides banking, insurance, investments, mortgage, and consumer and commercial finance through more than 9,000 stores, 12,000 ATMs, the Internet, and has offices in more than 35 countries to support the bank's customers who conduct business in the global economy. With more than 265,000 employees, Wells Fargo serves one in three households in the USA. Wells Fargo was ranked number 26 on Fortune's 2012 rankings of the largest corporations in the USA. Wells Fargo's vision is to satisfy all our customers' financial needs and help them succeed financially.

As most large banks retreat from the trading business, Wells Fargo is expanding. The fourth-largest U.S. bank says it can earn solid returns in investment banking while taking little risk for itself. It is focusing on services that its corporate lending customers need, such as stock and bond underwriting and merger advice. For investors, it is looking at areas such as processing futures and swaps trades.

The Wells Fargo Securities unit is relatively small now, but in a few years, the unit could account for twice as much of the firm's revenue, an estimated 10 percent compared to its current 5 percent, Deutsche Bank analyst Matt O'Connor wrote in a report in May 2012. For JPM, Bank of America, and Citigroup, that percentage is closer to 20 to 25 percent. A much bigger proportion of Wells Fargo's revenue comes from traditional commercial and retail banking businesses: residential mortgages, lines of credit for corporations, and so on.

Online Banks

Online banks are growing rapidly in number and taking market share from large banks. The website http://www.mybanktracker.com/best-online-banks rates more than 30 online banks in

EXHIBIT 10 The Best Online U.S. Banks
(1= best, 18 = least best)

1. Ally	10. Discover Bank
2. Bank of Internet	11. UFB Bank
3. ING Direct	12. Simple
4. Charles Schwab Bank	13. Incredible Bank
5. Sallie Mae Bank	14. Nationwide Bank
6. USAA	15. First Internet Bank
7. TIAA Direct	16. One United Bank
8. Barclays Bank	17. Presidential Online Bank
9. State Farm Bank	18. E*TRADE

Source: Based on info at http://www.mybanktracker.com/best-online-banks.

the USA in terms of having low fees, low interest rates, excellent technology, and great customer service. Exhibit 10 reveals in rank order the top 18 Internet Banks in the USA. Note that Ally is number 1 and E*TRADE is number 18.

External Issues

Regulatory Reform

Following the 2007 to 2009 financial crisis, President Barack Obama signed the Dodd-Frank Wall Street Reform and Consumer Protection Act in 2010 that affects all aspects of the financial industry. Provisions include: prohibition of proprietary trading, restrictions on who can own hedge funds, establishing the Financial Stability Oversight Council, elimination of the Office of Thrift Supervision, and much more. The new regulations are expected to greatly increase the fees all financial institutions must pay. Provisions of Dodd-Frank aim to avoid situations in which large banks (such as AIG and Citigroup) are bailed out by the government because they are "too big to fail." Dodd-Frank did ease public perception and opinion of the financial crisis and may in fact apply to middle-size firms. However, recent research reveals that the largest institutions are so interconnected worldwide that, should a similar financial situation arise again, world governments again would be forced to save these behemoths. It is expected that there will be more than 14,000 new regulatory requirements enacted by 2015.

Mobile Payments

One of the hottest topics and business challenges facing banks today is the advent of mobile payment systems and the new competitors that enter the market associated with these payment systems. *Bank Technology News* even stated in 2012 that credit and debit cards used today are soon headed to the museum to be replaced by a linkage of mobile, Web, and point of sale options. As of 2012, there were more than five billion mobile phone users in the world, with more than 70 percent of the world's population having a mobile phone, yet only half the world's population having a bank account. Juniper Research reports that the market for global payments should exceed $600 billion by 2013. Businesses such as Intuit's GoPayment are already available for the Apple iPhones and Android platforms.

Near Field Communications (NFC) is allowing customers to pay for products using their mobile phones at retail stores. Big players such as MasterCard, American Express, Visa, eBay, and Google are also establishing mobile payment systems. Traditional banks such as JPM perhaps need to form strategic alliances to participate in this new arena because less people will be using cash, checks, and plastic cards to perform their business transactions.

Mortgage Business

As of 2012 there were 76 million homes in the USA with 52 million of these homes having a mortgage, and 4.7 million of these homes in a delinquent state. Around 2.5 million of the delinquent homes are worth less than their mortgage and around 10 million homeowners who are not delinquent are paying mortgage notes that are worth less than their home. About

25 percent of these homes are expected to go into default because homeowners either cannot afford to continue paying or are simply unwilling to pay more for a home than it is worth.

The Future

Going up and up on fees much like the U.S. Postal Service Office, are large banks on permanent decline? The *Wall Street Journal* (9-12-12, p. A1) reported that the percentage of Americans who own checking accounts dropped from 92 to 88 percent between 2010 and 2011, whereas the number of Americans who own a major credit card dropped from 74 to 67 percent, and those who own a major debit or check card dropped from 78 to 66 percent. In other words, Americans are using traditional banks less and less. In fact, the article reports that 8.2 percent of the nation's households, nearly 12 million, are managing their finances without a bank. Bank overdraft fees, according to the article, cost Americans $31.6 billion in 2011. Consumer behavior is definitely shifting from bank credit and debit cards to prepaid debit cards offered by both NetSpend and Green Dot. Pew Charitable Trusts estimates the total dollars that flow through prepaid debit cards will reach $201.9 billion in 2013, up from $28.6 billion in 2009.

A movement called "Bank Transfer Day" emerged in November 2011. In February 2012, J.D. Power & Associates reported that customers of large, regional, and mid-sized banks were defecting at a higher rate because of frustration over factors such as fees and poor customer service. According to their survey, 9.6 percent of customers said they had switched to a new banking provider within the last year, compared to 8.7 and 7.7 percent in the previous two years. The main beneficiaries of the defections are credit unions and smaller banks, which experienced an average increase of 10.3 percent in the acquisition of new customers, versus 8.1 percent a year previously. In March 2012, the National Credit Union Administration reported that credit unions added 1.3 million members in 2011, hitting a record 91.8 million. Online banks are also gaining and increasingly sustaining competitive advantage over large banks.

Cash Advance Centers Inc. is the largest payday lending company in the USA and is widely being used now in lieu of doing business with a bank. That company reports that 22 percent of its customers earn more than $75,000, so the point here is that avoiding bank fees and such is becoming popular not only with individuals of lower incomes but also with people of medium incomes. JPM needs a clear strategic plan for the future. Help JPM's top managers by preparing a recommended strategic plan for the company.

Polaris Industries, Inc., 2013

www.polaris.com, PII

Headquartered in Medina, Minnesota, Polaris (named after the North Star) designs, engineers, manufactures, and markets off-road vehicles (ORVs), snowmobiles, motorcycles, and electric on-road vehicles primarily in the USA, Canada, and Europe, with 70 percent of revenue coming from the USA. Polaris also produces On-Road Vehicles (ORV), which are predominantly Victory motorcycles. Their ORV sales grew 64 percent in 2012 to $240 million.

Polaris does business in more than 130 different nations and outside; U.S. sales were up 21 percent in 2012 and net income was up 37 percent. Completion of a 425,000-square foot manufacturing facility in Monterrey, Mexico, in 2011 serves as a platform for better Polaris penetration in Latin and South America. Polaris also produces replacement parts and other accessories such as oils, chrome accessories, electric starters, covers, cargo box accessories, and much more.

Polaris has a defense (military) segment that recently reported excellent sales of the electric Ranger and the unmanned mine roller. Sixty-nine percent of Polaris's sales came from ORVs, a 22-percent increase from the prior year. Nine percent of sales comes from snowmobiles, and 8 percent comes from on-road vehicles. Polaris is the North American leader in total power sports sales with around 20-percent market share, above rivals Harley Davidson, Honda, and Yamaha. In December 2012, Polaris acquired Teton Outfitters, LLC, a privately owned, Rigby, Idaho-based company that designs, develops and distributes KLIM Technical Riding Gear. This acquisition adds KLIM to Polaris' growing parts, garments, and accessories (PG&A) business.

For the six months that ended 6-30-13, Polaris' sales were up 12 percent overall, including Off-Road Vehicles (+7%), Snowmobiles (71%), Motorcycles (−6%), Small Vehicles (+109%), and Parts, Garments & Accessories (+30%). The company's Small Vechicles division includes its GEM and Goupil electric vehicles as well as Aixam. For Q2 of 2013, Polaris reported record second quarter net income of $80.0 million, up 15 percent from the prior year's second quarter net income of $69.8 million. Sales for the second quarter 2013 totaled a record $844.8 million, up for last year's second quarter sales of $755.4 million.

Copyright by Fred David Books LLC. (Written by Forest R. David)

History

The father of the snowmobile is considered to be Edgar Hetteen, who in 1955, with employees David Johnson, Paul Knochenmus, and Orlen Johnson, created a vehicle to ride through the snow. The primary use of the craft was to access better hunting areas that traditionally had required wearing snowshoes. An early Polaris snowmobile was called the Polaris Sno Traveler that rolled off the assembly line in Minnesota in 1956. Edgar displayed his snowmobile on a 1,200-mile trek across Alaska in 1960. However, unhappy with the performance of his Polaris vehicle, Edgar soon left the company, and started Polar Manufacturing, that later changed its name to Artic Enterprises, which ultimately went bankrupt in the 1980s. Artic emerged from bankruptcy and continues today under the Arctic Cat Brand, one of Polaris's major competitors in the snowmobile market. For the next 50 years, without Edgar, Polaris developed snowmobiles, all-terrain vehicles (ATVs), side-by-side vehicles (ORVs), and motorcycles.

Polaris began developing a smaller consumer-sized, front-engine snowmobile to compete with the SkiDoo in the early 1960s. In 1964, Polaris released the Comet, and then in 1965 the Mustang, which became a hit as a family snowmobile. In the early 1980s, Polaris created an Indy style snowmobile with a wider stance. In 1985, Polaris introduced the Trailboss, considered to be the first U.S.-made ATV. ATVs are a one-seat variation of ORVs. Today, Polaris is one of the top-selling ATV brands. In the 1990s, Polaris entered the motorcycle market and the watercraft market, producing jet skis, but exited the jet-ski market in 2004. In 2010, Polaris moved its parts plant from Wisconsin to Monterrey, Mexico, saving the company about $30 million annually in lower labor costs.

In 2011, Polaris announced an investment in Brammo, an electric vehicle company based in Ashland, Oregon. Its first production electric motorcycle, the Brammo Enertia, is assembled in Ashland and sold at dealerships. Polaris participated in the $13 million opening tranche of Brammo's Series C funding in July 2012. Polaris had been showing interest in electric propulsion, producing an electric version of its Ranger Side-by-Side and more recently buying Global Electric Motorcars (GEM) from Chrysler. As one publication put it, "This latest move likely signals the addition of clean and quiet drivetrains to ATVs and motorcycles under the global giant's brand umbrella—snowmobiles may have to wait on battery breakthroughs before they become commercially feasible."

Polaris purchased GEM from Chrysler in 2012 and also purchased France-based Goupil. Polaris recently restarted production on its Indy-named sleds (stopped in 2004 with the Indy 500) with the release of the 2013 Indy 600 and Indy 600 SP.

Internal Issues

Strategy

Polaris is a testament to the benefits of strategic planning. Led by Chief Executive Officer (CEO) Scott Wine, the company is in the mist of a 10-year strategic plan that is broken down into stated objectives, three- to five-year goals for each, annual actions for each, and last three-year results for each objective—all provided on the company website (http://phx.corporate-ir.net/phoenix.zhtml?c=108235&p=irol-progress). Polaris's overall objective is to increase sales to $5 billion and obtain a 10-percent net income margin by completion of its strategic plan in 2018. CEO Scott at the front of the company's 2011 *Annual Report* says:

> We again achieved record performance in a down market. Our success is the result of being extremely focused on our strategic plan and executing against it meticulously. Our disciplined approach has made us the best in Powersports and it's how we'll continue to deliver shareholder value well into the future.

Polaris has a history of successfully acquiring and divesting businesses to continue on a path of strategic improvement. Yet to its credit, Polaris reports minimal goodwill on its balance sheet. Some recent notable divestures include exiting the jet-ski market in 2004 after a 12-year stint. Polaris ceased production of its Breeze line of on-road vehicles in 2011 and acquired GEM and Goupil to fill this void. Currently, Polaris is producing more side-by-side ORVs because customers are favoring them over the traditional ATV style, single-driver, four-wheeler product.

Vision and Mission

Despite placing great emphasis on strategic planning, Polaris does not have a clearly stated vision or mission statement, but various statements on the company's elaborate website could be construed to represent those statements.

Organizational Structure

Polaris has a hybrid divisional-by-product-by-region organizational structure as illustrated in Exhibit 1. Note in the diagram it is somewhat unusual for the Vice-president of Sales and Marketing (a staff officer) to also be a line executive. It is also unclear who in the hierarchy has command and control over the U.S. operations analogously to the two other geographic vice-presidents. For example, who would be responsible for motorcycle sales in Texas, or for that matter, motorcycle sales in Germany? Also, notice that there is only one female in the corporate hierarchy.

Production

Polaris assembles products in Minnesota, Iowa, Wisconsin, and Mexico. To save costs and improve component part quality, many of the firm's product lines are vertically integrated. Plastic injection molding, welding, clutch assembly, and painting are all produced in house. Items such as fuel tank, tires, seats, and instruments are purchased from third-party vendors.

Polaris has an effective inventory management process called Maximum Velocity program (MVP) in which ORV orders can be placed in two-week intervals for high-volume dealers.

EXHIBIT 1 The Polaris Organizational Structure

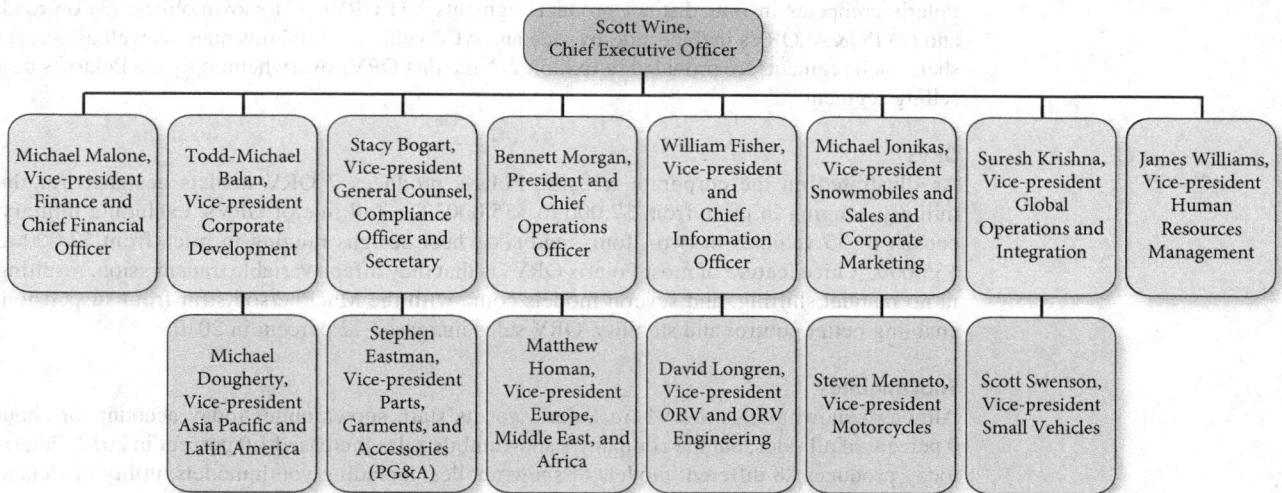

Source: Based on company documents.

Smaller dealers can use a similar process. The new process helps to keep costs down and inventories at manageable levels. Although ORV orders can be placed at any time, snowmobile orders must be placed in the spring and secured by deposit. Victory motorcycle orders are currently under MVP testing.

Sales and Marketing

Polaris has a network of about 1,650 independent dealers in North America and 15 subsidiaries and 80 distributors in over 100 countries outside of North America. The company's brands include RZR and Ranger ATVs, Indian and Victory motorcycles, and Polaris Rush snowmobiles. Snowmobiles are sold to dealers in the USA and Canada; many dealers also carry Polaris ORVs. A little more than half of all Polaris dealers in North America sell snowmobiles. ORVs are also sold through lawn and garden dealers in North America, but outside of North America, ORVs are generally handled through independent distributors. Polaris is shifting this strategy to wholly owned subsidiaries, which are now operating in Spain, China, Brazil, and India.

The Polaris Victory and Indian motorcycles are distributed through independently owned dealers outside the USA, with Melbourne and Sydney, Australia, being exceptions, in which Polaris has company owned dealers. As of 2012, Polaris had 400 dealers of Victory brand motorcycles in North America and 20 dealers of Indian motorcycles. The Polaris GEM business has around 130 dealers, and Groupil sells direct to customers in France and to dealers outside of France. The firm's military products are sold directly to the military and other government agencies.

Polaris uses group publications, billboards, and traditional television and radio for advertising. Product brochures, leaflets, posters, dealer signs, and other items are also used to help dealers market the products. Polaris spent $210 million in marketing in 2012, up from $179 million the prior year.

Research and Development (R&D)

Polaris has about 550 employees in R&D that concentrate on improving production techniques and developing new and improved products. R&D has a long tradition at Polaris because the company claims to have produced the first snowmobile with liquid cooled brakes, hydraulic breaks, three cylinder engines, and recently the MacPherson strut front suspension and Concentric Drive System in ORVs. Many of the R&D employees work in the 127,000-square foot R&D facility in Minnesota. Polaris spent about $127 million on R&D in 2012, up from $106 million the prior year.

Segments

Polaris competes in four distinct product segments: (1) ORVs, (2) snowmobiles, (3) on-road, and (4) PG&A. ORVs include side-by-side and ATV vehicles. Total revenues, as well as percent share each segment, are provided in Exhibit 2. Note that ORVs overwhelmingly are Polaris's best selling segment.

ORVs

As illustrated on the corporate website, Polaris produces 7 ORV models designed for the military, ranging in price from $7,000 to $35,000. The full line of ORVs, excluding military, consist of 35 vehicles in two-, four-, and six-wheel designs ranging in price from $7,000 to $35,000. A nice feature of most Polaris ORVs is that they offer a variable transmission, resulting in no manual shifting, and several models come with the MacPherson strut front suspension, enabling better control and stability. ORV sales increased 22 percent in 2012.

Snowmobiles

Although snowmobiles are where Polaris got its start, snowmobiles today account for about 9 percent of all sales, but the company's snowmobile sales increased 1.0 percent in 2012. Polaris today produces 28 different models of snowmobiles, including youth models, utility models to performance, and competition models used in racing. In 2012, U.S. retail prices for snowmobiles averaged $2,700 to $12,300 and are sold in Canada, Europe, and Russia. The company has a history of snowmobile innovation.

On-Road Vehicles

Polaris offers many options of its Victory brand motorcycles and many designed for cross-country trips. Acquired by Polaris in 2011, the Indian Motorcycle Company was the first motorcycle company in the USA, even predating Harley Davidson. Founded in 1901, Indian Motorcycle has earned distinction as one of the most legendary and iconic brands in the USA through unrivaled racing dominance, engineering prowess, and countless innovations and industry firsts (see www.indianmotorcycle.com). In total, Polaris makes 20 different motorcycle options available ranging in price from $12,500 to $36,000. Prices on the Polaris GEM range from $7,600 to $13,500, and the higher-end Goupil has 2012 prices ranging from $25,000 to $35,000.

PG&A

Polaris's PG&A segment is used to supply replacement parts and provide accessories for Polaris product lines. Items included in this category for ORVs include winches, bumper guards, plows, racks, mowers, tires, cargo box accessories, and many more. Snowmobile accessories include covers, traction products, electric starters, bags, and windshields. Motorcycle accessories include saddle bags, backrests, windshields, seats, and various chrome accessories. In addition to parts designed for use with specific products, the Polaris also produces apparel, including helmets, jackets, bibs, and pants.

By Region

Polaris provides a geographic breakdown of its revenues. Polaris sells products worldwide, but as revealed in Exhibit 3, 72 percent of all revenues in 2012 came from the USA and 14 percent from Canada. Polaris is trying to further expand into Western Europe and Russia, especially with its ORV and Victory motorcycle lines of products. Not revealed in Exhibit 3, Latin America and

EXHIBIT 2 Revenues by Product Category (in millions)

Year	ORV		Snowmobiles		On Road		PG&A	
2012	$2,225	69%	$283	9%	$240	8%	$408	14%
2011	1,822	69	280	11	146	5	408	15
2010	1,376	69	189	10	82	4	344	17
2009	1,021	65	179	12	53	3	313	20

Source: Based on 2012 *Form 10K*, page 30.

EXHIBIT 3 Revenues by Geographic Region (in millions)

Year	USA		Canada		Other Nations	
2012	$2,311	72%	$438	14%	460	16%
2011	1,864	70	369	14	424	16
2010	1,406	71	279	14	306	15
2009	1,074	69	239	15	252	16

Source: Based on 2012 *Form 10K*, page 31.

Asia Pacific sales grew 21 percent, respectively in 2012. However, these regions remain a negligible contribution to total revenues. With the new manufacturing plant in Mexico, Polaris hopes to improve on this weakness.

Finance

Polaris reported sales of $3.21 billion in 2012, up 21 percent from the prior year. In early 2012, Polaris announced a 14 percent increase in its quarterly cash dividend of $0.42 per a share.

Income Statements

Note in the income statements in Exhibit 4 that the company's revenue and net income have increased nicely in recent years.

EXHIBIT 4

POLARIS INDUSTRIES INC.
CONSOLIDATED STATEMENTS OF INCOME
(In thousands, except per share data)

	For the Years Ended December 31,		
	2012	2011	2010
Sales	$3,209,782	$2,656,949	$1,991,139
Cost of sales	2,284,485	1,916,366	1,460,926
Gross profit	925,297	740,583	530,213
Operating expenses:			
Selling and marketing	210,367	178,725	142,353
Research and development	127,361	105,631	84,940
General and administrative	143,064	130,395	99,055
Total operating expenses	480,792	414,751	326,348
Income from financial services	33,920	24,092	16,856
Operating income	478,425	349,924	220,721
Non-operating expense (income):			
Interest expense	5,932	3,987	2,680
Gain on securities available for sale	—	—	(825)
Equity in loss of other affiliates	179	—	—
Other (income) expense, net	(7,529)	(689)	325
Income before income taxes	479,843	346,626	218,541
Provision for income taxes	167,533	119,051	71,403
Net income	**$312,310**	**$227,575**	**$147,138**
Basic net income per share	$ 4.54	$ 3.31	$ 2.20
Diluted net income per share	$ 4.40	$ 3,20	$ 2.14
Weighted average shares outstanding:			
Basic	68,849	68,792	66,900
Diluted	71,005	71,057	68,765

Source: 2012 *Form 10K*, p. 48.

468 STRATEGIC MANAGEMENT CASES

Balance Sheets

Note in the balance sheets provided in Exhibit 5 that the company's long-term debt is relatively low and the firm is in good financial shape.

EXHIBIT 5 The Polaris Balance Sheets

POLARIS INDUSTRIES INC.
CONSOLIDATED BALANCE SHEETS
(In thousands, except per share data)

	December 31,	
	2012	2011
ASSETS		
Current Assets:		
Cash and cash equivalents	$417,015	$325,336
Trade receivables net	119,769	115,302
Inventories, net	344,996	298,042
Prepaid expenses and other	34,039	33,969
Income taxes receivable	15,730	24,723
Deferred tax assets	86,292	77,665
Total current assets	1,017,841	875,037
Property and Equipment:		
Land, buildings and improvements	133,688	123,771
Equipment and tooling	557,880	524,382
	691,568	648,153
Less accumulated depreciation	(438,199)	(434,375)
Property and equipment net	253,369	213,778
Investment in finance affiliate	56,988	42,251
Investment in other affiliates	12,817	5,000
Deferred tax assets	22,389	10,601
Goodwill and other intangible assets net	107,216	77,718
Other long-term assets	15,872	3,639
Total Assets	$1,486,492	$1,228,024
LIABILITIES AND SHAREHOLDERS' EQUITY		
Current Liabilities:		
Current portion of capital lease obligations	$2,887	$2,653
Accounts payable	169,036	146,743
Accrued expenses:		
Compensation	139,140	165,347
Warranties	47,723	44,355
Sales promotions and incentives	107,008	81,228
Dealer holdback	86,733	76,512
Other	73,529	68,856
Income taxes payable	4,973	639
Total current liabilities	631,029	586,333
Long term income taxes payable	7,063	7,837
Capital lease obligations	4,292	4,600
Long-term debt	100,000	100,000
Other long-term liabilities	53,578	29,198
Total liabilities	795,962	727,968
Shareholders' Equity:		
Preferred stock $0.01 par value, 20,000 shares authorized, no shares issued and outstanding	—	—
Common stock $0.01 par value, 160,000 shares authorized, 68,647 and 68,430 shares issued and outstanding	686	684
Additional paid-in capital	268,515	165,518
Retained earnings	409,091	321,831
Accumulated other comprehensive income, net	12,238	12,023
Total shareholders' equity	690,530	500,056
Total Liabilities and Shareholders' Equity	$1,486,492	$1,228,024

Source: 2012 Form 10K, p. 47

External Issues

The recreational vehicle industry has been one of the most consistent performers in terms of stock price over the last five years, which is pretty amazing for what some analysts say is a bunch of companies selling expensive toys. According to Morningstar, the recreational vehicle industry achieved an annualized total return of 10 percent over the past five years, which is 610 basis points higher than the S&P 500. In fact, the stocks in that sector performed in the top quartile over the last five-year, three-year, one-year, and year-to-date periods. Many analysts think that an improving economy should keep the party going for some time.

Industry Background

ORVs are designed for traversing through rough terrain such as swamps and marshlands and can often carry two to six passengers depending on the model. Their main purpose is for hunting and fishing, but they are also used on farms and ranches, in the military, and for mud riding or other rough-riding activities. ORVs were introduced in the USA in 1970 by Honda, followed later by Yamaha, Kawasaki, and Suzuki. Polaris entered the ATV market in 1985 followed by Artic Cat in 1995 and Bombardier in 1998. Both the USA and Western Europe, also a primary market for ATVs, have experienced a sales decline as customers prefer side-by-side ORVs. Polaris estimates during 2012, worldwide sales of ATVS increased 2 percent to 419,000 ATVs sold, whereas the side-by-side ORV sales increased 13 percent during the same period with around 353,000 units sold worldwide. Currently, the main competitors of Polaris in the side-by-side market are Deere & Company, Kawasaki, Yamaha, and Artic Cat.

Snowmobiles have been produced in the USA since at least the early 1950s and under the Polaris name since 1954. Originally, their designed purpose was for work in northern and snow-covered rural environments, however, like the ATV, many recreational fans have arisen providing additional markets for manufacturers. The novelty of snowmobiles peaked in the 1960s with more than 100 producers and 495,000 units produced in 1971. Today, the only makers of snowmobiles are Yamaha, BRP, Artic Cat, and Polaris. Industry-wide sales were around 131,000 units in 2012.

The on-road vehicle market consists of motorcycles and small electric vehicles. Polaris makes both the Victory and Indian motorcycles and a brand of small electric vehicles. There are generally four segments of motorcycles: (1) cruisers, (2) touring, (3) sports bikes, and (4) standard. Entering the motorcycle market in 1998 in the cruiser segment, Polaris enjoyed an overall industry doubling in sales from 1996 to 2006, but sales declined from 2007 to 2010 with the weakening economic conditions. Polaris entered the cruiser and touring market (defined as a bike with 1,400 cc and above) in 2010, and estimates this brand of bike had industry-wide sales of about 173,000 units in 2012 in North America, up 2 percent from the prior year.

Safety Regulations

Polaris products can be dangerous, especially because they are often used by youth. Both the federal and state governments continually promulgate laws to increase product safety and awareness in regard to ORVs, ATVs, snowmobiles, and motorcycles. International governments have taken similar measures. Two key commissions in the USA are the Consumer Product Safety Commission (CPSC), which has oversight on ATVs, snowmobiles, and side-by-side vehicles. The National Highway Transportation Safety Administration (NHTSA) has oversight on motorcycles and other small electric vehicles that Polaris produces. In 1988, for example, the CPSC forced Polaris and five of its competitors to recall all three- and four-wheel ATVS sold that could be used by youth younger than 16 years of age. The government is constantly imposing better suspension, breaks, and handing of vehicles. As recently as 2006, the U.S. government banned the sale of all three-wheel ATVs. Governmental oversight puts increased pressure on Polaris to closely monitor its dealers and ensure all dealers are in compliance with safety regulations.

Environmental Concerns

Recent governmental oversight has restricted the amount of lead paint that can be used on products aimed at youth 12 years of age and younger. In addition, to better protect the environment, the federal government and many state governments have restricted the use or banned all together the use of ATVs, ORVs, and snowmobiles from some national parks, federal lands, and state lands. It is unclear how these bans will impact sales.

The Environmental Protection Agency (EPA) continues to adopt and revise more stringent emission regulations for ATVs and ORVs. The laws require firms in the industry to increase its R&D expenditures to improve on emission technologies to meet not only current regulations but also future regulations. With Polaris products being sold in many different nations, it often results in all products being developed for the most stringent set of laws regarding emissions, further adding to costs.

Competition

Polaris competes in an industry that is fiercely competitive based on price, perceived quality, reliability, style, service, and warranties. In addition, dealers compete on financing, local advertising, and location of stores. Major Polaris competitors are Arctic Cat, Honda, Harley-Davidson, and Kawasaki, with John Deere also entering the side-by-side market. Note in Exhibit 6 that Honda is more than 30 times larger than Polaris, but Polaris is four times larger than Arctic Cat.

Arctic Cat

Headquartered in Plymouth, Minnesota, Arctic Cat designs, engineers, and produces snow-mobiles, side-by-sides, and ATVs under the Arctic Cat brand name. Arctic Cat's fiscal year ends March 31. With 1,300 employees, Arctic Cat also makes garments and accessories for its products. As noted previously, one of the founders of Polaris also founded rival Arctic Cat after leaving Polaris. The two companies make similar products, are structured similarly, and are located in the same region of the USA. Arctic Cat does business in the USA, Canada, and Europe through independent dealers, whereas customers in South America, the Middle East, and Asia can purchase products through third-party distributers.

For reporting purposes, Arctic Cat combines its ATVs, ORVs, and snowmobiles into one segment and lists its PGA in a separate segment. In fiscal 2013, Arctic Cat reported revenues of $250 million for snowmobiles, $227 million for its ATVs and ORVs, and $108 million for PGA. As revealed in Exhibit 6, Arctic Cat reported revenues of $671 million in fiscal 2013 and spent $37 million on marketing and $21 million on R&D.

The Arctic Cat brand is well respected in the recreational vehicles (RV) industry and controls 23 percent of the North American snowmobile market, about the same as larger rival Polaris. On the ATV side in North America, Artic Cat has just a 7.5-percent market share but recently introduced a side-by-side product line. Arctic Cat's Wildcat 4 1000 is especially popular. The company's stock's performance over the past five years is spectacular, up nearly 25 percent on an annualized basis.

Honda

Founded in 1946 and headquartered in Tokyo, Japan, Honda develops and sells motorcycles, ATVs, automobiles, and other power products such snow blowers, lawn mowers, weed eaters, generators, among many other power products. Honda is the world's largest motorcycle company and one of the world's largest automakers. Honda has recently initiated a new strategy with

EXHIBIT 6 Polaris versus Rival Firms (in millions except for debt/equity and EPS)

	Polaris	Arctic Cat	Honda
Sales	$3,028	$671	$98,090
Income	$327	$40	$3,650
Debt/Equity	0.15	0.00	0.98
EPS	4.62	3.24	1.92
Market Cap.	6,570	520	68,420
Shares Outstanding	69	13.19	1,810

EPS, earnings per share.
Source: Based on year-end 2012 company information.

its motorcycles to target the "fun segment." Honda's research reveals there is a growing demand for motorcycles in the smaller 125-cc and 700-cc sizes used for leisure, enjoyment, and everyday use. These products cost less and are cheaper to operate, having excellent fuel economy. The 125-cc size is targeted primarily at Asian and Indian customers.

In fiscal 2012, Honda reported that 17 percent of all its revenue was derived from motorcycles and ATVs, with total revenues of around 1,400 billion yen or approximately $16 billion. Like Honda's other divisions, the motorcycle and ATV division has experienced declining sales over the last five years. Sales in this division are down since 2008 in Japan, North America, and Europe with sales down around 60 percent in both the North America and European markets since 2008. Sales in Asia, South America, and the Middle East however are up 11 percent collectively since 2008. In 2012, Honda reported sales of 7,948 billion yen or around U.S. $93 billion.

The Future

In mid-2013, Polaris raised guidance for its full year 2013 earnings to a range of $5.20 to $5.30 per diluted share, up 19 percent over 2012 based on expected full year 2013 sales growth of 14 percent. Polaris acquired Indian Motorcycle Company in 2011 and has been focusing on relaunching the Indian brand. The company will soon compete directly with Harley Davidson in the 1400cc heavyweight motorcycle segment, which has a global addressable market of around 214,000 units. However, Polaris has less than one percent global market share in this segment, or just 428 units in 2012. The company is planning to increase Indian's dealer base from 20 in 2012 to nearly 140 by year-end 2013. Develop a clear strategic plan for Polaris Industries.

The Emirates Group, 2014

www.theemiratesgroup.com

Based in Dubai, United Arab Emirates (UAE), Emirates Group (Emirates) includes (a) Emirates (the airlines) and (b) Dnata, a company specializing in aviation ground-handling services and operating at 20 airports. The largest airline in the Middle East, Emirates flies to more than 130 destinations in 70 countries on six continents and offers direct flights from Dubai to Washington, DC, San Francisco, Los Angeles, and Seattle. Emirates services the world from Beijing to San Francisco and more than 100 markets in between. More than 1,200 Emirates flights depart Dubai each week, accounting for about 40 percent of all air traffic out of Dubai International Airport.

Emirates carries 40 million passengers and 2.0 million tons of cargo annually, using a fleet of more than 170 aircraft. The company has another 230 aircraft on order (worth about $84 billion) and is the world's largest operator of both the Airbus 380 and Boeing 777. Using large planes such as the Airbus 380 and Boeing 777 provides extra space and luxury for wealthy and business passengers alike. Most of the company's planes even include spacious private suites, and some planes provide a spa with showers. Emirates is well known for providing excellent service for high-end passengers in first class, but it also provides excellent service in business class and economy class. Economy-class customers receive well-thought-out meals consisting of many courses, e-mail, SMS services, telephone, and personal TV monitors with more than 1,400 channel options. Singapore Air is considered the closest competitor based on overall business model of top service at a premium price and markets served.

Emirates has more than 67,000 employees and annual revenues of more than 73.1 billion Dirham (the United Arab Emirates currency). The Dirham is pegged to the U.S. dollar so currency fluctuations are not significant. Emirates is owned by the government of Dubai operating under the Investment Corporation of Dubai name, but the company and the government of Dubai are quick to point out the airline has grown in scale not by way of protectionism but through competition. The government of Dubai treats Emirates as a wholly independent business entity on its own and attributes this to the firm's success. Dubai has an open-skies policy and more than 60 percent of all flights in Dubai are by companies other than Emirates.

In August 2013, Emirates became the first airline in the Middle East to provide Google Now cards for their passengers who book via Emirates.com. A feature of the Google Search app, Google Now is available and fully integrated for Android (devices running Android 4.1 and above) and iOS (iPhones and iPads). This new product enables Emirates' customers to see and monitor their upcoming flight, providing flight times and departure terminal. Google Now gives passengers relevant information on their destination (for example weather conditions locally, currency, local landmarks, accommodations, and attractions).

Copyright by Fred David Books LLC. (Written by Forest R. David)

History

Dubai is a city-state in the UAE, located within the emirate of the same name, one of the seven emirates that make up the UAE. Dubai has the largest population in the UAE (2,104,895) and the second-largest land territory by area (4,114 km^2) after Abu Dhabi. Dubai and Abu Dhabi, the national capital, are the only two emirates to have veto power over critical matters of national importance in the UAE legislature. The city of Dubai is located on the emirate's northern coastline and is often misperceived as a country or city-state and, in some cases, the UAE as a whole has been described as Dubai.

When the British pulled out of Dubai in the late 1950s, Sheikh Saeed bin Maktoum (the current CEO of Emirates) decreed open-seas, open-skies, and open-trade policies to develop the country. He also required that all government agencies make a profit. Dubai was aiming to eliminate its dependence on its finite oil reserves within 50 years and thus has operated under a free market society for decades. Emirates Group started in 1959 as the Dubai National Air

Transport Association (Dnata), with Dnata airport operations, Dnata cargo, and Dnata agencies as segments. After Gulf Air began cutting back service to Dubai in the 1980s, Dubai's royal family provided funding for Dnata to obtain two planes and the company became known as Emirates Group. The company's first flight was in 1985 on a leased Airbus plane. After being in operation for four years, Emeritus was serving 12 destinations, and by 1994 the airline was serving 32 destinations but still only operated 15 aircraft and was the sixth largest airline in the Middle East. During this time, 92 rival firms were serving Dubai Airport, which provided intense competition for Emirates.

The late 1990s was a time of rapid expansion for Emirates; it ordered 16 Airbus 330-200s at a cost of $2 billion, and in 1997, it ordered an additional six Boeing 777-200s. The company followed that by opening a $65-million training center with simulators for training pilots and crew. The company continued to expand, ordering an additional 22 Airbus A380s, the largest plane in the world, and six additional Boeing 777s in 2001. The 2000s saw considerable expansion in the number of planes operated and destinations served, including new flights being added every month to various places around the world. Emirates received 22 new aircraft in fiscal year 2012, the most ever obtained in a single year by the company. Emirates is perhaps the world's fastest growing and most profitable airline in the industry.

Dubai is one of the fastest-growing countries in the world because thousands of people migrate to Dubai monthly, often because there is no tax on the personal wages in Dubai. The living standard is great, the climate is great, the infrastructure is impressive, business is growing leaps and bounds, and the schools in Dubai are international and provide a great learning environment for kids of all nationalities. However, an expatriate (foreigner) may work in Dubai only if sponsored by an employer.

Internal Issues

Mission and Vision

Emirates' mission is "to become one of the top lifestyle brands in the world."

Organizational Structure

As indicated in Exhibit 1, Emirates operates from a divisional-by-product organizational design. Note that no women are among the company's top management team, which comes as no surprise given Middle Eastern culture. However, Emirates could set an example soon by promoting

EXHIBIT 1 Emirates' Organizational Structure

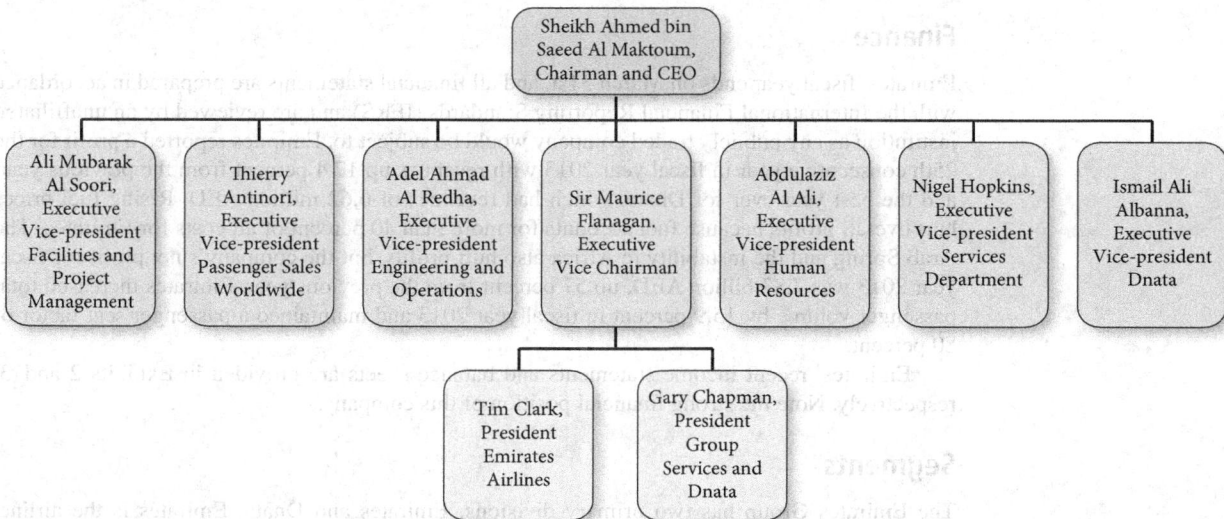

Source: Based on company documents.

one or more women to top management, to exemplify that women are as capable as men to manage business operations. The Executive Vice Chairman position perhaps is analogous to the traditional Chief Operations Officer.

Emirates Luxury

First-class passengers on Emirates flights enjoy their own private suites on Airbus 380, Airbus 350, and Boeing 777 planes. The Emirates first-class experience starts with a personal chauffeur picking up a passenger and driving him or her to the airport for a seamless check in. Customers are then able to enjoy the first-class lounge while they wait for the plane to arrive before the boarding process begins. First-class passengers have an allowance for two carry on items totaling 25 pounds combined and unlimited checked bags up to 170 pounds total weight. Once on board, the customer enjoys suites that include a personal mini-bar, vanity table, mirror, wardrobe, 23-inch TV with more than 1,400 channels including the latest movies, sliding door for extra privacy, SMS, Internet, and much more. If desired, the flight crew can covert the seat to a fully flat bed with mattress. To complement the bed, pajamas, slippers, and toiletries with Bulgari lotions are provided. First-class customers have exquisite free food and drink options, including Dom Perignon, martinis, Iranian caviar, stir-fried lobster, glazed duck breast, Arabic mezze (appetizers), and much more. First-class customers have access to the first-class lounge to mingle with other first-class passengers and enjoy hors d'oeuvres prepared by some of the world's best chefs. First-class customers can enjoy one of the two onboard shower spas as part of their experience on the Emirates Airbus 380. The spas are marketed as having walnut and marble designs with fine linens and provide complimentary massages in addition to a shower. The price in 2009 for a first-class ticket from Dubai to Melbourne, Australia was around $16,000.

Business-class travel on Emirates is possibly the best in the world. Business-class passengers enjoy many amenities, such as seats turning into a 79-inch flat bed at the push of a button, power supply for laptops, extra large tables, large screen TVs with more than 1,400 channels, SMS, Internet, mini-bar built into every seat, and privacy dividers. These amenities are provided on A380 and most Boeing 777 aircraft. Business-class passengers also enjoy delicious food and many drink options. Complimentary champagne and vintage wines are the norm, and all food is presented on Royal Doulton fine-bone china. Business-class customers also have access to the business-class lounge on the second level of all A380 aircraft where chefs fix snacks and hors d'oeuvres. Emirates' economy-class customers enjoy more than 1,400 channels on their personal TV, meals, and Internet, phone, and SMS capabilities at their seats.

Finance

Emirates' fiscal year ends on March 31st, and all financial statements are prepared in accordance with the International Financial Reporting Standards (IFRS) and are reviewed by an unaffiliated institution as any publicly traded company would be subject to. Emirates reported a profit for the 25th consecutive year in fiscal year 2013 with revenues up 17.4 percent from the previous year, and the best year ever for Dnata, which had revenues of 6.62 million AED. Rising fuel prices hurt overall profits because fuel accounts for more than 40 percent of all costs for Emirates. The Arab Spring and the instability in Africa also hurt profits, but the company's net profit for fiscal year 2013 was 7.83 billion AED, up 57 percent from the previous year. Emirates increased total passenger volume by 15.9 percent in fiscal year 2013 and maintained a passenger seat factor of 80 percent.

Emirates' recent income statements and balance sheets are provided in Exhibits 2 and 3, respectively. Note the strong financial position of this company.

Segments

The Emirates Group has two primary divisions, Emirates and Dnata. Emirates is the airline, whereas Dnata includes (a) cargo and ground handing, (b) travel services, (c) catering, and (d) freight forwarding.

EXHIBIT 2 Emirates' Income Statement (in millions of AED)

	2013 AED m	2012 AED m	2011 AED m
Revenue	71,159	61,508	52,945
Other operating income	1,954	779	1,286
Operating costs	(70,274)	(60,474)	(48,788)
Operating profit	**2,839**	**1,813**	**5,443**
Other gains and losses	—	—	(4)
Finance income	406	414	521
Finance costs	(900)	(657)	(506)
Share of results in associates and joint ventures	127	103	91
Profit before income tax	**2,472**	**1,673**	**5,545**
Income tax expense	(64)	(53)	(78)
Profit for the year	**2,408**	**1,620**	**5,467**
Profit attributable to non-controlling interests	**125**	**118**	**92**
Profit attributable to Emirates' owner	**2,283**	**1,502**	**5,375**
Profit for the year	**2,408**	**1,620**	**5,467**
Currency translation differences	9	(9)	38
Cash flow hedges	56	(259)	(282)
Actuarial losses on retirement benefit obligations	(70)	(116)	(57)
Other comprehensive income	**(5)**	**(384)**	**(301)**
Total comprehensive income for the year	**2,403**	**1,236**	**5,166**
Total comprehensive income attributable to non-controlling interests	**125**	**118**	**92**
Total comprehensive income attributable to Emirates' Owner	**2,278**	**1,118**	**5,074**

Source: Based on page 8, 2013 *Annual Report.*

EXHIBIT 3 Emirates' Balance Sheets (in millions of AED)

	2013 AED m	2012 AED m	2011 AED m
ASSETS			
Non-current assets			
Property, plant and equipment	57,039	49,198	39,848
Intangible assets	910	902	901
Investments in associates and joint ventures	485	430	386
Advance lease rentals	807	370	384
Loans and other receivables	508	917	1,704
Derivative financial instruments	92	69	—
Deferred income tax asset	15	10	—
		51,896	43,223
Current assets			
Inventories	1,564	1,469	1,290
Trade and other receivables	8,744	8,126	6,481
Derivative financial instruments	67	8	123
Short term bank deposits	18,048	8,055	3,777
Cash and cash equivalents	6,524	7,532	10,196
	34,447	25,190	21,867
Total assets	**94,803**	**77,086**	**65,090**

(continued)

EXHIBIT 3 Continued

	2013 AED m	2012 AED m	2011 AED m
EQUITY AND LIABILITIES			
Capital and reserves			
Capital	17	801	801
Retained earnings	22,729	21,256	20,370
Other reserves	(768)	(833)	(565)
Attributable to Emirates' owner	**22,762**	**21,224**	**20,606**
Non-controlling interests	**270**	**242**	**207**
Total equity	**23,032**	**21,466**	**20,813**
Non-current liabilities			
Borrowings and lease liabilities	35,752	26,843	20,502
Retirement benefit obligations	—	631	479
Deferred revenue	1,460	1,074	930
Deferred credits	294	350	401
Deferred income tax liability	—	—	2
Trade and other payables	—	—	31
Derivative financial instruments	1,016	957	642
		29,855	22,987
Current liabilities			
Trade and other payables	25,013	20,601	17,551
Income tax liabilities	24	36	22
Borrowings and lease liabilities	5,042	4,037	2,728
Deferred revenue	1,147	915	792
Deferred credits	87	136	136
Derivative financial instruments	6	40	61
	31,319	25,765	21,290
Total liabilities	**71,771**	**55,620**	**44,277**
Total equity and liabilities	**94,803**	**77,086**	**65,090**

Source: Based on page 9, 2013, *Annual Report.*

Emirates

Passenger revenue is the largest overall revenue generator as revealed in Exhibit 4. Substantial revenue also is derived from cargo, which produces 15 percent of the segment's total revenue, whereas sale of goods produces 3 percent. All other sources contribute less than 1 percent of the segment's revenues. This segment includes several maritime and mercantile holdings,

EXHIBIT 4 Emirates Revenues by Segment (in millions of AED)

REVENUE			
	2013 AED m	2011–12 AED m	2010–11 AED m
Passenger	57,477	48,950	41,415
Cargo	10,346	9,546	8,803
Excess baggage	388	332	293
Other	767		
Transport revenue	**68,978**	**58,828**	**50,511**
Sale of goods	1,196	2,017	1,774
Food	502	245	226
Other	483	418	434
Total	**71,159**	**61,508**	**52,945**

Source: Page 13, 2013, *Annual Report.*

a 49 percent ownership in a wine and spirit business in Thailand, and hotels in UAE, Australia, and Seychelles.

This segment operates more than 180 aircraft with approximately 120 on operating lease, 55 on financial lease, and 6 being fully owned by Emirates. Out of the 180 planes the company operates, 98 are Boeing's 777, one of Boeing's largest planes and the largest twin-engine plane in the world. An additional 21 aircraft are Airbus 380s, the four-engine double-decker plane that is the largest in the world. Emirates is the largest operator of Airbus 380 aircraft in the world. The company has on order 223 additional aircraft broken down to 84 Boeing 777s, 69 Airbus 380s, and 70 Airbus 350-900s. The Airbus 350s are wide-bodied, long-range planes designed to compete with Boeing's Dreamliner. Although the 350s are considered large capacity, they hold significantly less passengers than the 777 and 380 models. On average, Emirates wide-body planes are 77 months old compared to the industry average of 136 months. With 223 new planes on order, the average age of planes in the fleet should drop substantially.

More than 40 percent of all expenses are related to jet fuel. Employment expenses account for 13 percent of revenue and operating leases account for 8 percent. Maybe surprising to some, aircraft maintenance only amounted for AED 1,296 million or 2 percent of total revenues, about the same as parking and landing fees. Exhibit 4 details a revenue breakdown within the Emirates segment.

Exhibit 5 reveals the geographic breakdown of Emirates' flights. No single market accounts for more than 30 percent of revenues, creating a well-diversified company with respect to regions served. The Americas market grew at the highest rate in the most recent fiscal year, but East Asia and Australasia regions had the largest overall AED growth. Note that the Americas segment grew from last place to fourth place.

Dnata

Dnata's profits and revenues for fiscal year-end March 31, 2013 were at all time records of 6.5 billion AED and 815 million AED respectively, as revealed in Exhibit 6. Much of the revenue growth can be attributed to recent acquisitions Dnata made including Travel Republic Ltd., the largest privately-held online travel company in the United Kingdom, in 2011.

EXHIBIT 5 Geographic Breakdown of Emirates' Revenues (in millions of AED)

Year	East Asia and Australasia	Europe	West Asia and Indian Ocean	Americas	Middle East	Africa	Total
2012–2013	20,884	20,140	8,031	8,275	7,117	6,712	71,159
2011–12	18,227	17,058	7,083	6,696	6,314	6,130	61,508
2010–11	15,503	14,433	6,405	5,518	5,488	5,598	52,945

Source: Page 14, 2012–2013 *Annual Report.*

EXHIBIT 6 Dnata's Revenues by Segment (in millions of AED)

Revenue	2012–2013 AED m	2011–12 AED m	2010–11 AED m	% change
In-flight Catering	1,686	2,452	576	325.7
Airport operations	2,474	2,321	1,980	17.2
Cargo	1,077	993	882	12.6
Information Technology	755	649	546	18.9
Travel services	544	319	243	31.3
Other	—	173	100	73.0
Total	6,536	6,907	4,327	59.6

Source: Based on company documents.

EXHIBIT 7 Geographical Revenue in Percent

	2011–2012	2010–2011	2009–2010
UAE	77%	62%	45%
International	23%	38%	55%

Source: Based on page 54, 2012 *Annual Report.*

In late 2010, Dnata acquired Alpha Flight Group's in-flight catering business. This is why the segment's revenues increased so much in 2011–2012 because Travel Republic's revenues first appeared on the income statement.

In-flight catering was both the largest revenue gainer and the largest revenue percent increase by 325 percent; however, the 2010–2011 fiscal year represents only three months of providing this service in house, resulting in the large percent increase. In-flight catering through the acquisition of Alpha Flight Group provided more than 48 million meals to customers in fiscal year 2012. Note all revenue streams in the Dnata segment experienced significant increases over the two years reported. Exhibit 7 provides a breakdown of Dnata services in UAE and internationally. For the first time ever, revenues in international markets were greater than domestic revenues.

Competition

Factors impacting the airline industry include global unrest, volatility of fuel prices, mergers and acquisitions, strategic alliances, video conferencing, and entry of discount airlines such as Ryanair. More than 100 different airlines provide service to Dubai International Airport, which is projected to become the world's busiest airport by 2016. Opening for passenger travel by the end of 2013 will be the new Al Maktoum Airport in Dubai. In fiscal year 2012 alone, Emirates started long-haul flights to Seattle, Dallas–Fort Worth, Rio de Janeiro, Buenos Aries, Washington DC, Geneva, Baghdad, and St. Petersburg (Russia), among others. Emirates' largest direct competitors are Singapore Airlines, British Airways, Delta, Middle East Airlines, and flydubai. Dubai is located eight hours by air from 75 percent of the world's population.

Singapore Airlines Group
Singapore Air dates back to 1947 when the company was known as Malayan Airways Limited, operating flights to cities in and around Singapore. But in 1971 Malayan Airways split into Singapore Airlines and Malaysian Airline System, and the Singapore Airlines brand took off. Singapore Air now operates 101 planes that average six years and seven months and have 30 more planes on order. Like Emirates, Singapore Air operates the Airbus 380 (19 in operation) and the Boeing 777 (58 in operation). The Group operates 20 subsidiaries within the air travel industry, including SIA Cargo, SIA Engineering Company, SilkAir, Scoot, and Tradewinds Tours and Travel. Both SilkAir and Scoot are airlines that compliment the service of Singapore Air. Singapore Air predominantly serves Europe, Asia, and Australia, but it also flies to four cities in the United States and three in Africa.

Singapore Airline Group's fiscal year, like Emirates', ends on March 31. For fiscal year 2012, the company's profits were down $756 million to $336 million or 69 percent reduction, whereas revenues grew by $333 million to $14.8 billion, up 2 percent from the previous year. Both Singapore Air and Emirates are luxury airlines using Suites (separate from first class), first class, business class, and economy class. First-class passengers can enjoy 23-inch TVs, dining with food served on tableware designed by Givenchy, wines, and champagne. Singapore Air markets that they are the only airline to offer a stand-alone bed, not a converted seat. To complement the stand-alone bed, a sleeper suit, bedroom slippers, and linens also designed by Givenchy are provided. Soft lighting options and premium skin care products and toiletries are also provided.

Customers in first, business, and economy classes also enjoy amenities that exceed most all competing airlines. Hot, moist, hand towels are provided after meals to customers, even those in economy class. Serving all passengers since 1972 is the distinguished "Singapore Girl" that according to the company "is an enduring symbol of our impeccable service standards."

flydubai

flydubai was started by the government of Dubai in 2008 and was supported by Emirates during the firm's establishing phase, but flydubai is not part of the Emirates Group. With the backing of the Dubai government, flydubai ordered 50 Boeing 737-800s at a total price of $3.74 billion. The first planes were delivered in 2009, and flydubai was air bound for Beirut, the first market served. The company quickly grew as additional planes on order arrived. As of early 2013, the company served 52 markets, mostly in the Middle East but also a few select markets in Eastern Europe and India. In contrast to Emirates, flydubai is a discount airline provider much like a Spirit Airlines or AirTran in the USA or Ryanair or easyJet in Europe. flydubai operates 28 planes and 800 flights per week. The average age of aircraft is less than two years. The company does not currently provide financial information to the public.

Middle East Airlines

Middle East Airlines (MEA) began in 1945 in Beirut and served cities in Syria, Cyprus, Egypt, and later Saudi Arabia. The airline provides a local alternative for customers in the Middle East. In 1963, MEA merged with Air Liban and added destinations in the Middle East, West Africa, and Europe. In 2010, MEA accepted delivery of two new Airbus 320 aircrafts and resumed flights to Berlin and Brussels. In 2012, MEA joined SkyTeam and currently serves Europe, Persian Gulf, Middle East, and Africa. Notable destinations include four flights a day to Paris, London, Frankfurt, and Brussels; they also have flights to Rome, Milan, Athens, Geneva, Istanbul, and others in Europe and flights to several cities in Saudi Arabia, Amman, Iraq, Cairo, and Sharm el Sheikh. In total, MEA operates 19 aircraft with an average age of less than four years, has 10 planes on order, and serves 31 markets. The company offers Cedar Class (first class) and economy class. In 2011, MEA had revenues of $637 million with profits of $62 million.

British Airways

British Airways is a member of the Oneworld Alliance and is the largest carrier based on fleet size in the United Kingdom. The airline currently operates more than 250 aircraft with 50 more on order and serves the entire world. The airline has alliances with several airlines including Comair of South Africa and Sun Air of Scandinavia. The company had revenues of $14.8 billion in 2011. British Airways offers economy class, premium-economy class, business clas, and first class.

Delta

Headquartered in Atlanta and a member of the Sky Team Alliance, Delta is a major U.S. airline. Delta has hubs in several U.S. cities as well as in Amsterdam, Tokyo, and Paris. Operating more than 5,000 flights a day and an additional 2,500 flights through Delta Connection, Delta is one of the largest airlines in the world, and one of only a select few to provide service to all six inhabited continents. The airline provides business elite, first class, economy comfort, and economy class. Delta reported revenues of $14 billion and net income of $854 million in 2011.

Strategic Alliances

Airlines started forming strategic alliances in the 1990s to better compete with rival firms. Historically, if an airline did not serve a select market, a customer would either find an airline that did or be forced to purchase two separate tickets. Alliances largely resolve this problem because airlines can jointly benefit having a competitor (now also an alliance member) provide service for that leg of the flight. Other benefits of alliances are more efficient marketing and advertising exposure and frequent-flier programs, which attempt to hook passengers on to one particular airline for all their flying needs.

Three of the largest alliances in the world are SkyTeam, Star Alliance, and Oneworld. SkyTeam is based out of Amsterdam and was created in 2000 by founding members: Delta, Air France, Aeromexico, and Korean Air. The Sky Team Alliance consists of 19 carriers from five continents and carries more than 550 million passengers each year. Based out of New York City, Oneworld was formed in 1999 with founding members: American Airlines, British Airways, Canadian Airlines, Cathay Pacific, and Qantas. Today, 11 airlines operate within the Oneworld alliance and carry more than 335 million passengers annually. The Star Alliance was founded in 1997 by Air Canada, Lufthansa, Scandinavian Airlines, Thai Airways International, and United Airlines.

Based in Frankfurt, Germany, the Star Alliance has 28 member airlines and serves 193 different countries with annual passenger numbers more than 670 million, making Star Alliance the largest alliance in terms of passengers served.

Alliance with Quantas

Emirates is not a member of any airline alliance, whereas Quantas is a member of Oneworld. However in January 2013, Emirates and Quantas, two rival firms, formally entered into a partnership allowing Quantas Airbus 380 customers to depart from Concourse A at Dubai Airport, the world's only concourse designed for the Airbus 380. Quantas customers can enjoy the concourse, while waiting for their connecting flights to Europe. In exchange, Quantas moved their hub for European flights from Singapore to Dubai. Neither airline owns shares of the other, but they work together to better coordinate price, sales, and schedules. Quantas CEO Alan Joyce believes the partnership is a first of its kind and different from traditional alliances.

Dubai Business Culture

To be successful in business in Dubai, their culture and religion must be respected and rules must be followed. For example, a colleague should never be embarrassed or criticized in public. Women in Dubai should dress conservatively. Alcohol should never be consumed on the street, and it should be taken home only if one has a license to purchase it. Singles of the opposite sex may not live together in Dubai; gay marriages and relationships are not accepted in Dubai. If an unmarried woman becomes pregnant, then she must leave the country immediately. Other important rules to follow in Dubai include: do not cross your legs in front of someone of higher authority because it is seen as disrespectful; do not hold onto a handshake for a long time because it signifies a brotherly bond instead of a friendly gesture; do not use your left hand because it is considered dirty so use only the right hand to offer drinks, food, and so on; do not turn down a drink offer because it might insult the host; do not engage in friendly talk in pubic with any females; do not shake hands with women unless they come forward to do so; do not flirt, hug, and have other physical contact with a member of the opposite sex; do not make eye contact with women; do not ask a male Arab about any female because that is bad manners; do not point the soles of shoes at an Arab because the soles are dirty; do not refuse any gifts (if offered) but open them in private not in public; do not express a desire to communicate with any member of the opposite sex.

In Dubai, the workday starts at 8 A.M. until 1 P.M., but employees return at 7 P.M. to work more. During the Muslim Festival Ramadan, working hours in offices become shorter by two hours. In Arab cultures, clothes should be worn on all body parts including limbs. On Friday, Muslims pray and rest, so business should not be conducted on that day. During the month of Ramadan, Muslims avoid eating, smoking. and drinking during daylight.

The Future

Ironically for Emirates, the flydubai discount airline may pose the largest threat to the firm because demand for low price flights is growing rapidly globally. Flying with Emirates is high dollar, and competitors see great potential to take market share from Emirates with lower prices. It is important, therefore, for Emirates' Chairman and CEO, Sheikh Ahmed bin Saeed Al Maktoum, to have a clear strategic plan for the next three years. Design a business strategy for the Emirates Group for the next three years.

Walt Disney Company, 2013

www.disney.com, DIS

Headquartered in Burbank, California, Walt Disney Company (Disney) and its subsidiaries compete in the entertainment and media broadcasting industry worldwide. Serving customers for nearly 100 years, Disney is a diversified conglomerate, owning ABC, ESPN, theme parks, cruise lines, and more. As a member of the DOW 30 and the world's largest media conglomerate, Disney owns ABC television and cable networks such as ABC Family, Disney Channel, and ESPN (80 percent). Disney owns 8 television stations and 35 radio stations as well as Walt Disney Studios that produces films through Walt Disney Pictures, Disney Animation, and Pixar. Disney's Marvel Entertainment is a top comic book publisher and film producer. Disney owns and operates huge cruise boats, as well as 14 popular theme parks around the world.

Disney's earnings in Q3 of 2013 equaled the prior year's number, while revenue increased 4 percent, led by Disney's theme parks, resorts, and cable networks such as ESPN. For Q3 of 2013, Disney earned $1.85 billion, on revenue of $11.6 billion, up from $11.1 billion. Revenue at Disney's parks and resorts grew 7 percent to $3.7 billion. Cable networks revenue grew 8 percent to $3.9 billion, led by ESPN, A&E and U.S. Disney channels. A laggard, Disney's broadcast revenue was unchanged at nearly $1.5 billion. Overall, Disney's media networks business grew 5 percent to $5.4 billion. For Q3 of 2013, Disney's movie studio revenue fell 2 percent to $1.6 billion, due to poor results from the movies "The Lone Ranger" and "Iron Man 3."

Copyright by Fred David Books LLC. (Written by Forest R. David)

History

Walt Disney and his brother Roy arrived in California in the summer of 1923 to sell a cartoon called *Alice's Wonderland.* A distributor named M. J. Winkler contracted to distribute the *Alice Comedies* on October 16, 1923, and the Disney Brothers Cartoon Studio was founded. Over the years, the company produced many cartoons, from *Oswald the Lucky Rabbit* (1927) to *Silly Symphonies* (1932), *Snow White and the Seven Dwarfs* (1937), and *Pinocchio* and *Fantasia* (1940). The company name was changed to Walt Disney Studio in 1925. Mickey Mouse emerged in 1928 with the first cartoon in sound. In 1950, Disney completed its first live action film, *Treasure Island*, and in 1954, the company began television with the Disneyland anthology series. In 1955, Disney's most successful series, *The Mickey Mouse Club*, began, and the new Disneyland Park opened in Anaheim, California.

Disney created a series of releases from 1950s through 1970s, including *The Shaggy Dog*, *Zorro*, *Mary Poppins*, and *The Love Bug*. Walt Disney died in 1966. In 1969, Disney started its educational films and materials. Another important time of Disney's history was opening Walt Disney World in Orlando, Florida, in 1971. In 1982, the Epcot Center opened as part of Walt Disney World. The following year, Tokyo Disneyland opened.

After leaving network television in 1983, Disney introduced its cable network, The Disney Channel. In 1985, Disney's Touchstone division began the successful *Golden Girls* and Disney Sunday Movie. In 1988, Disney opened Grand Floridian Beach and Caribbean Beach Resorts at Walt Disney World along with three new gated attractions: the Disney/MGM Studios Theme Park, Pleasure Island, and Typhoon Lagoon. Filmmaking soon hit new heights as Disney led Hollywood studios in box-office gross for the first time. Some of the successful films were: *Who Framed Roger Rabbit*, *Good Morning Vietnam*, *Three Men and a Baby*, and later, *Honey, I Shrunk the Kids*, *Dick Tracy*, *Pretty Woman*, and *Sister Act*. Disney moved into new areas by starting Hollywood Pictures and acquiring the Wrather Corp. (owner of the Disneyland Hotel) and television station KHJ (Los Angeles), which was renamed KCAL. In merchandising, Disney purchased Childcraft and opened numerous highly successful and profitable Disney Stores.

By 1992, Disney's animation reached new heights with *The Little Mermaid, Beauty and the Beast,* and *Aladdin.* Also that year, Disneyland Paris opened. During the 1990s, Disney introduced Broadway shows, opened 725 Disney Stores, acquired the California Angels baseball team to add to its hockey team, opened Disney's Wide World of Sports in Walt Disney World, and acquired Capital Cities/ABC.

From 2000 to 2007, Disney created new attractions in its theme parks, produced many successful films, opened new hotels, and built Hong Kong Disneyland. Disney acquired Pixar in 2006, Marvel in 2009, and launched *Disney Dream,* a new cruise liner in 2011. Newer Disney initiatives include the April 2011 groundbreaking of Shanghai Disney Resort at a price tag of $4.4 billion and expected opening day slated for sometime in 2015. In February 2012, Disney finalized acquisition of UTV Software Communications, an Indian entertainment company. In October of 2012, Disney announced plans to acquire Lucasfilm, producers of the popular *Star Wars* movies. The acquisition is expected to cost $4.05 billion. Disney plans to release *Star Wars Episode VII* in 2015.

Internal Issues

Vision and Mission
Disney's vision is "to make people happy."

Organizational Structure
As indicated in Exhibit 1, Disney operates using a strategic business unit (SBU) organizational structure that consists of five diverse, but all family entertainment segments: (1) media networks, (2) parks and resorts, (3) studio entertainment, (4) consumer products, and (5) interactive media. The president, chief executive officer, and director of Walt Disney is Robert Iger. There is no chief operations officer (COO) in the Disney hierarchy, but Andy Bird, Chairman of Walt Disney International, functions like a COO.

Segments

Disney provides segment revenue and operating income for each of their five SBUs. Exhibit 2 displays the three most recent years of revenue and operating income per Disney SBU, along with a percentage change for each of the last two years. Note that total consolidated revenues and operating income increased in 2012 and 2011, albeit at a decreasing rate during the most recent period. Note that the consumer products and the interactive media segments are small compared to media networks and parks and resorts.

Media Networks
Media networks is the largest Disney SBU in both revenues and operating income, accounting for 45 percent of all revenues in 2012. Revenue growth in 2012 came from increased affiliate fees, higher advertising rates, increased viewership of ESPN programs and the shows *Castle, Once Upon a Time,* and *Revenge.* The positive growth was limited by lower home entertainment revenues from programs such as *Lost* and lower Disney Channel viewership. Production costs increased as college sports, as well as NFL, MLB, NBA, and Wimbledon were able to negotiate more lucrative contracts. For example, the Southeastern Conference (SEC) signed a deal with ESPN in 2008 for $2 billion for 15-year rights to broadcast football and men's and women's basketball games. However, with the 2012 additions of Texas A&M and Missouri to the SEC, the previous contract is contractually renegotiable and a new, much more expensive, contract is expected in the near future.

With media networks, Disney owns and operates the ABC Television Network that reaches 99 percent of all U.S. households. This segment also includes ABC-owned Television Stations Group, ABC Studios, Disney Channels Worldwide, ABC Family, SOAPnet, Disney ABC Domestic Television, Disney Media Distribution, Hyperion, and Radio Disney network. The ABC Television Network operates more than 220 affiliated stations across the USA. Disney channels worldwide consists of 94 kids and family entertainment channels available in 169 countries and 33 languages. ABC Family is a mixture of series and movies. SOAPnet owns character-driven

EXHIBIT 1 Disney's Organizational Chart

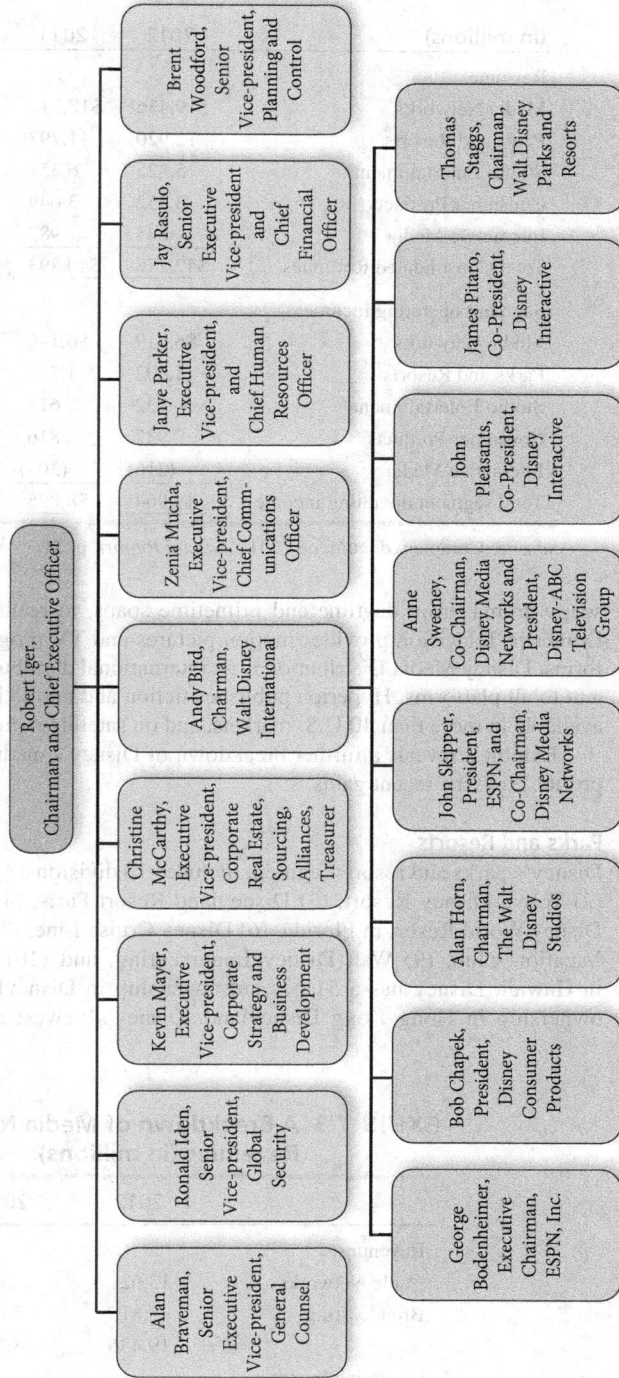

Robert Iger,
Chairman and Chief Executive Officer

- Alan Braveman, Senior Executive Vice-president, General Counsel
- Ronald Iden, Senior Vice-president, Global Security
- Kevin Mayer, Executive Vice-president, Corporate Strategy and Business Development
- Christine McCarthy, Executive Vice-president, Corporate Real Estate, Sourcing, Alliances, Treasurer
- Andy Bird, Chairman, Walt Disney International
- Zenia Mucha, Executive Vice-president, Chief Communications Officer
- Janye Parker, Executive Vice-president, and Chief Human Resources Officer
- Jay Rasulo, Senior Executive Vice-president and Chief Financial Officer
- Brent Woodford, Senior Vice-president, Planning and Control

- George Bodenheimer, Executive Chairman, ESPN, Inc.
- Bob Chapek, President, Disney Consumer Products
- Alan Horn, Chairman, The Walt Disney Studios
- John Skipper, President, ESPN, and Co-Chairman, Disney Media Networks
- Anne Sweeney, Co-Chairman, Disney Media Networks and President, Disney-ABC Television Group
- John Pleasants, Co-President, Disney Interactive
- James Pitaro, Co-President, Disney Interactive
- Thomas Staggs, Chairman, Walt Disney Parks and Resorts

Source: Based on information in company documents.

EXHIBIT 2 A Breakdown of Disney Revenues by SBU

(in millions)	2012	2011	2010	Change (%) 2012 vs. 2011	Change (%) 2011 vs. 2010
Revenues:					
Media Networks	$19,436	$18,714	$17,162	4%	9%
Parks and Resorts	12,920	11,797	10,761	10%	10%
Studio Entertainment	5,825	6,351	6,701	(8)%	(5)%
Consumer Products	3,252	3,049	2,678	7%	14%
Interactive Media	845	982	761	(14)%	29%
Total Consolidated Revenues	$42,278	$40,893	$38,063	3%	7%
Segment operating income:					
Media Networks	$6,619	$6,146	$5,132	8%	20%
Parks and Resorts	1,902	1,553	1,318	22%	18%
Studio Entertainment	722	618	693	17%	(11)%
Consumer Products	937	816	677	15%	21%
Interactive Media	(216)	(308)	(234)	30%	(32)%
Total segment operating income	$9,964	$8,825	$7,586	13%	16%

Source: Company documents. 2012 *Annual Report,* p. 31.

soapy drama, from daytime and primetime soaps, to reality shows and movies. Disney ABC Domestic Television provides motion pictures and TV programming to U.S.-based media platforms. Disney Media Distribution is an international distributor of branded and nonbranded content to all platforms. Hyperion publishes fiction and nonfiction titles for adults. Radio Disney is available in more than 40 U.S. markets, and on satellite radio, mobile apps, and the Web.

Exhibit 3 reveals a further breakdown of Disney's media networks' revenues and operating profits. Note the recent gains.

Parks and Resorts

Disney's parks and resorts segment includes 10 divisions: (1) Disneyland Resorts in California, (2) Tokyo Disney Resort, (3) Disneyland Resort Paris, (4) Hong Kong Disneyland, (5) Walt Disney World Resort in Florida, (6) Disney Cruise Line, (7) Adventures by Disney, (8) Disney Vacation Club, (9) Walt Disney Imagineering, and (10) Aluani, a Disney Resort and Spa in Hawaii. Disney has a 51 percent ownership in Disneyland Resort Paris and a 47 percent ownership in Hong Kong Disneyland. Disney's newest theme park will be in the Pudong

EXHIBIT 3 A Breakdown of Media Networks Revenues (in millions)

	2012	2011	Change (%)
Revenues:			
Cable Networks	13,621	12,877	6
Broadcasting	5,815	5,837	—
	19,436	18,714	4
Operating Income:			
Cable Networks	5,704	5,233	9
Broadcasting	915	913	—
	6,619	6,146	8

Source: 2012 *Annual Report,* p. 33.

EXHIBIT 4

	Domestic			International			Total		
	2012	2011	2010	2012	2011	2010	2012	2011	2010
Parks									
Increase in attendance	3%	1%	(1)%	6%	6%	1%	4%	2%	(1)%
Increase in Per Capital Guest Spending	7%	8%	3%	1%	2%	3%	5%	6%	3%
Hotels									
Occupancy	81%	82%	82%	85%	88%	85%	——	83%	82%
Available Room Nights (in thousands)	9,850	9,625	9,629	2,468	$2,466	2,466	12,318	12,091	12,095
Per Room Guest Spending	$257	$241	$224	$317	$294	$273	$270	$251	$234

[a]Per capita guest spending and per room guest spending include the impact of foreign currency translation. Guest spending statistics for Disneyland Paris were converted from euros into U.S. dollars at weighted average exchange rates of 1.36 and 1.35 for fiscal 2010 and 2009, respectively.
[b]Per room guest spending consists of the average daily hotel room rate as well as guest spending on food, beverages, and merchandise at the hotels. Hotel statistics include rentals of Disney Vacation Club units.
Source: Walt Disney Company, *Annual Report,* page 34 (2012).

district of Shanghai opening in 2015. Exhibit 2 revealed that Disney's parks and resorts revenue for 2012 increased 10 percent to $12.9 billion, and operating income increased 22 percent to $1.9 billion. Results for 2012 reflected increases at nearly all theme parks, except a decrease at Disneyland Paris.

The new 4,000-passenger ship, *Disney Dream*, was christened at Port Canaveral in 2011 and was designed especially for families. *Disney Dream* joins *Disney Magic* and *Disney Wonder*. Another new ship, *Disney Fantasy*, joined the Disney fleet in 2012. *Disney Dream* will sail to Disney's private island, Castaway Cay.

Revenue in this segment is generated primarily from the sale of admissions tickets to the theme parks, as well as hotel room charges per night and sales from merchandise, food, and beverages. Revenue also comes from rentals and sales from vacation club properties and sales of cruise vacations.

Exhibits 4 and 5 reveal that Disney domestic revenues from its parks and resorts division increased 11 percent in 2011, to $12.9 billion, resulting from customers spending 6 percent more, mainly from higher ticket and hotel prices. Revenue growth was 6 percent in international operations stemming from 4 percent in higher spending, a 3-percent volume increase, and a 3-percent gain on foreign currency appreciation.

Studio Entertainment
Disney produces live-action and animated motion pictures, direct-to-video programming, musical recordings, and live-stage plays. Disney motion pictures are distributed under the names: Theatrical Market, Home Entertainment Market, Television Market, Disney Music Group, and

EXHIBIT 5 Parks and Resorts: Revenue and Operating Income

(in millions)	2012	2011	2010	Change (%)
Revenues:				
Domestic	$10,339	$9,302	$8,404	11%
International	$2,581	2,495	2,357	3%
	$12,920	$11,797	$10,761	10%
Segment operating income:				
	$1,902	$1,553	$1,318	22%

Source: Walt Disney Company, *Annual Report,* page 33 (2012).

EXHIBIT 6 Studio Entertainment: Revenue and Operating Income

(in millions)	2012	2011	2010	Change (%)
Revenues:				
Theatrical Distribution	$1,470	$1,733	$2,050	(15)%
Home Entertainment	$2,221	2,435	2,666	(9)%
Television Distribution and Other	$2,134	2,183	1,985	(2)%
Total Revenues	$5,825	$6,351	$6,701	(8)%
Segment operating income:				
	$722	$618	$693	+17%

Source: Walt Disney Company, *Annual Report,* page 34 (2012).

Disney Theatrical Productions. Disney has also licensed the rights to produce and distribute features films such as *Spider-man, The Fantastic Four,* and *X-Men* to third-party studios. Disney earns a licensing fee on these films, whereas the third-party studio incurs the cost to produce and distribute the films. Currently Disney has a diverse business line in the studio entertainment SBU consisting of: Marvel, Touchstone, Pixar, Disneynature, Disney Studios Motion Pictures, and more Disney-branded services. Disney's studio entertainment revenues for 2012 decreased 8 percent to $5.8 billion and segment operating income increased 17 percent to $722 million. Exhibit 6 reveals a revenue breakdown for this segment.

Consumer Products

Disney's consumer products segment partners with licenses, manufacturers, publishers, and retailers worldwide who design, promote, and sell a wide variety of products based on new and existing Disney characters. Product offerings are: (a) character merchandise and publications licensing, (b) books and magazines, and (c) The Disney Store. Disney released in mid-2011 a new toy line that captured the fantasy, action, and adventure of *Pirates of the Caribbean: On Stranger Tides.* Disney is perhaps the largest worldwide licensor of character-based merchandise and producer and distributor of children's film-related products based on retail sales. Disney's consumer products revenues for 2012 increased 7 percent to $3.25 billion; operating income increased 15 percent to $937 million.

Interactive Media

Disney's interactive media segment creates and delivers games and media for smartphones and tablets. Interactive media revenues for 2012 decreased 14 percent to $845 million and operating income incurred a loss of $216 million. As indicated in Exhibit 8, games and subscription revenue increased 36 percent in 2011, but the segment has incurred losses for several years, as revealed in Exhibit 2.

EXHIBIT 7 Consumer Products: Revenue and operating income

(in millions)	2012	2011	2010	Change (%)
Revenues:				
Licensing and Publishing	$2,056	$1,933	$1,725	6%
Retail and Other	1,196	1,116	953	7%
Total Revenues	$3,252	$3,049	$2,678	7%
Segment operating income:				
	$937	$816	$677	15%

Source: Walt Disney Company, *Annual Report,* page 35.

EXHIBIT 8 Interactive: Revenue and Operating Income

(in millions)	2012	2011	2010	Change (%)
Revenues:				
Games Sales and Subscriptions	$613	$768	$563	(20)%
Advertising and Other	232	214	198	8%
Total Revenues	845	982	$761	(14)%
Segment operating income:				
	$(216)	$(308)	$(234)	(30)%

Finance

Income Statement

Disney's 2012 income statement is provided in Exhibit 9. Note the 17.4 percent increase in net income.

Balance Sheets

Disney's 2012 balance sheets are provided in Exhibit 10. Note that Disney has $2.45 billion of "projects in progress." Also, note the $25 billion in goodwill, fully one-third of total assets, which is not a good thing. Long-term debt is staying about the same at $10 billion, which is a lot of debt to service.

Competition

Disney competes directly with NBC Universal, Paramount Pictures, Time Warner, CBS Corp., News Corp., Carnival Corp., and Royal Caribbean and indirectly with all family entertainment oriented businesses globally. In essence, all hotels, restaurants, water parks, and attractions any-where near Disney's 14 theme parks, are rival businesses, such as Sea World, Marineland, and Silver Springs in Florida. There is a large, new (China state run) theme park scheduled to open in 2014 right beside the Disney theme park (also slated for opening in 2014) in Shanghai, China, so that will be a major competitor.

EXHIBIT 9 Disney's Recent Income Statements (in millions of dollars, except EPS)

Income Statement	2012	2011
Revenues	42,278	40,893
Costs and expenses	(33,415)	(33,112)
Restructuring	(100)	(55)
Other revenue	239	75
Net interest expense	(369)	(343)
Equity in the income	627	585
Income before taxes	9,260	8,043
Income taxes	(3,087)	(2,785)
Net income	6,173	5,258
Noncontrolling interests	(491)	(451)
Net income	$5,682	$4,807
EPS	3.13	2.52
Shares outstanding (in thousands)	1,818	1,909

EPS, earnings per share.
Source: Company documents.

EXHIBIT 10 Disney's Unaudited Balance Sheets (in millions)

	2012	2011
Assets		
Current Assets		
Cash and cash equivalents	3,387	3,185
Receivables	6,540	6,182
Inventories	1,537	1,595
Television costs	676	674
Deferred income taxes	765	1,487
Other current assets	804	634
Total current assets	13,709	13,757
Film and television costs	4,541	4,357
Investments	2,723	2,435
Parks, resorts and other property	38,582	35,515
Accumulated depreciation	(20,687)	(19,572)
	17,895	15,943
Projects in progress	2,453	2,625
Land	1,164	1,127
	21,512	19,695
Intangible assets	5,015	5,121
Goodwill	25,110	24,145
Other assets	2,288	2,614
Total Assets	**74,898**	**72,124**
Liabilities and Equity		
Current Liabilities		
Accounts payable	6,393	6,362
Current portion of borrowings	3,614	3,055
Unearned royalties	2,806	2,671
Total current liabilities	12,813	12,088
Borrowings	10,697	10,922
Deferred income taxes	2,251	2,866
Other long-term liabilities	7,179	6,795
Preferred Stock, $.01 par value, 100 million shares authorized but none issued		
Common Stock, 4.6 billion shares, 2.8 and 2.7 billion shares issues respectively	31,731	30,296
Retained earnings	42,965	38,375
Accumulated other loss	(3,266)	(2,630)
	71,430	66,041
Treasury Stock, 1.0 billion shares	(31,671)	(28,656)
Total Equity	39,759	37,385
Noncontrolling interests	2,199	2,068
Total Equity	41,958	39,453
Total Liabilities and Shareholders' Equity	**74,898**	**72,124**

Source: Company documents.

CBS Corp.

Headquartered in New York City, CBS is a large media conglomerate with operations in television, radio, online content, and publishing. CBS Broadcasting operates the number-1 rated CBS television network, along with a group of local TV stations. CBS also owns cable network Showtime and produces and distributes TV programming through CBS Television Studios and CBS Television Distribution. Also competing with Disney, other operations include CBS Radio, CBS Interactive, and book publisher Simon & Schuster. In addition, CBS Outdoor is a leading operator of billboards and outdoor advertising. Chairman Sumner Redstone controls CBS through National Amusements.

Time Warner, Inc.

Headquartered in New York City, Time Warner is the world's third-largest media conglomerate behind Walt Disney and News Corp., with operations spanning television, film, and publishing. Time Warner owns Turner Broadcasting that runs a portfolio of popular cable TV networks including CNN, TBS, and TNT. Time Warner also operates pay-TV channels HBO and Cinemax, all of which compete with Disney. Time Warner owns Warner Bros. Entertainment that includes films studios (Warner Bros. Pictures, New Line Cinema), TV production units (Warner Bros. Television Group), and comic book publisher DC Entertainment.

News Corp.

Headquartered in New York City, News Corp. is the second largest media conglomerate in the world, trailing only Walt Disney. News Corp. owns film, TV, and publishing businesses that make and distribute movies through Fox Filmed Entertainment. Owned by News Corp., FOX Broadcasting has more than 200 affiliate stations in the USA and owns and operates about 25 TV stations, as well as a portfolio of cable networks. Publishing assets of News Corp. include newspaper publishers Dow Jones (*The Wall Street Journal*) and News International (*The Times*, *The Sun*), and book publisher HarperCollins. News Corp. has stakes in British Sky Broadcasting (BSkyB) and Sky Deutschland. The company has recently split into two parts.

Carnival Corp.

Headquartered in Miami, Florida, Carnival is the world's number-1 cruise operator, owning and operating a dozen cruise lines and about 100 ships with a total passenger capacity of more than 190,000. Carnival operates in North America primarily through its Princess Cruise Line, Holland America, and Seabourn luxury cruise brand, as well as its flagship Carnival Cruise Lines unit. Brands such as AIDA, P&O Cruises, and Costa Cruises offer services to passengers in Europe, and the Cunard Line runs luxury trans-Atlantic liners. Carnival's cruise boats compete with the Disney cruise boats wherever Disney sails. Another large cruise line company, Royal Caribbean, also competes with Disney ships wherever they sail.

Paramount Pictures Corp.

Headquartered in Hollywood, California, and a subsidiary of Viacom, Paramount produces and distributes films through Paramount Pictures (*Tranformers: Dark of the Moon*) and Paramount Vantage (*Capitalism: A Love Story*). The Paramount Pictures library consists of some 3,500 films, including classic hits from the *Star Trek*, *Godfather*, and *Indiana Jones* series, and releases about a dozen new titles annually. Competing with Disney, Paramount Pictures distributes movies on video and DVD through Paramount Home Entertainment.

Lucasfilm

In October 2012, Disney acquired Lucasfilm for a whopping $4.05 billion, with Disney paying approximately half of that money in cash and issuing approximately 40 million shares at closing. Headquartered in San Francisco, California, and founded by George Lucas in 1971, Lucasfilm is a large, privately held, entertainment company that has motion-picture and television production operations. Lucasfilm's global activities include (a) Industrial Light & Magic and Skywalker Sound that serves the digital needs of the entertainment industry for visual-effects and audio post-production, (b) LucasArts, a leading developer and publisher of interactive entertainment software worldwide, (c) Lucas Licensing that manages the global merchandising activities for Lucasfilm's entertainment properties, (d) Lucasfilm Animation, (e) Lucas Online that creates Internet-based content for Lucasfilm's entertainment properties and businesses, and

(f) Lucasfilm Singapore that produces digital animated content for film and television, as well as visual effects for feature films and multi-platform games.

With the Lucasfilm acquisition, Disney obtains a substantial portfolio of cutting-edge entertainment technologies that have kept audiences enthralled for many years. Kathleen Kennedy, current co-chairman of Lucasfilm, will become President of Lucasfilm, reporting to Walt Disney Studios Chairman Alan Horn. Additionally she will serve as the brand manager for *Star Wars*, working directly with Disney's global lines of business to build, further integrate, and maximize the value of this global franchise. Kennedy will serve as executive producer on new *Star Wars* feature films, with George Lucas serving as creative consultant. *Star Wars Episode 7* is targeted for release in 2015, with more feature films expected to continue the *Star Wars* saga and grow the franchise well into the future.

The Future

Disney is busy completing its Shanghai theme park while at the same time integrating the Lucasfilm acquisition into its operations. Analysts ponder whether the Lucasfilm acquisition added more goodwill to the Disney balance sheet that already is too laden with that burden. As the world comes online, the opportunities, as well as the threats, abound for Disney. Strategic decisions have to be made in terms of what segments to bolster and what segments to focus on improving. The interactive media segment has not turned a profit in a number of years. Kevin Mayer is Disney's Executive Vice-president for Corporate Strategy and Business Development. Help Mr. Mayer by preparing a draft three-year strategic plan for Disney.

Facebook, Inc., 2015

www.facebook.com, FB

Headquartered in Menlo Park, California, Facebook is the largest social media network in the world, with over 1.3 billion current active users of its website. Facebook ended 2014 with record numbers: a total of 890 million users, 745 million daily active mobile users, and $3,851 million in revenue. Facebook's revenues from advertising totaled $3.6 billion, and $257 million in collected payments and other fees. The company spent 29 percent of its revenue dollars on research and development (R&D) in 2014, and spent a record $1,831 billion on purchasing new property and equipment.

Facebook launched its audience network in 2014, which allowed advertisers to run their Facebook ads on third-party mobile applications. Then in 2015, Facebook unveiled its own mobile advertising distributor, similar to rival Twitter's MoPub aimed at attracting more business. CEO Mark Zukerberg spent much of early 2015 personally traveling the world, to India, Latin America, Africa, Jakarta, and elsewhere, meeting with groups who petition their governments for Internet access. Given that Facebook wants to grow globally, Mr. Zukerberg describes his travels as "really cool." He wants to aggressively help phone companies build Internet connections globally. Only about half of Facebook's revenues currently come from outside the United States and Canada. Reportedly, more than 10 percent of Facebook accounts are fake.

Copyright by Fred David Books LLC. www.strategyclub.com (Written by Jason R. Willoughby, Elizabethtown Community College)

History

Facebook was founded in February 2004 by Mark Zuckerberg and his Harvard University roommates. Initially, it was to be used only by Harvard University students, but eventually Zuckerberg and the other founders gave access to the Ivy League universities and Stanford University. As Facebook grew popular, user access was given to other universities, as well as Boston area high school students. Today, Facebook has grown into a phenomenon and anyone over the age of 13 can have access to Facebook, a social media platform loved by millions.

After launching his initial (Thefacebook.com) website, three Harvard University seniors accused Zuckerberg of taking their idea to create a social network called HarvardConnection.com to create a competitive product. After the three individuals made a complaint, an investigation was initiated, and a lawsuit filed, which was settled in 2008 for 1.2 million shares ($300 million) of Facebook's IPO offering.

Facebook's initial big investment was given by the co-founder of PayPal, Peter Thiel. In 2005, the company bought the domain name facebook.com for $200,000 and dropped "the" from the original name. The investments began to grow as in 2005, as Accel invested $12.7 million and Jim Breyer added $1 million of his own money. Facebook has recently surpassed both Google and Amazon in percent market share and number of users in the social media industry.

Internal Issues

Vision and Mission

Facebook's mission statement is "to give people the power to share and make the world more open and connected." Although Facebook does not have an explicit vision statement, Zuckerberg mentions three items that reveal his desire for the company: "(1) stay connected with friends and family, (2) discover what is going on in the world, and (3) share and express what matters to the individual."

EXHIBIT 1 Facebook's Organizational Structure

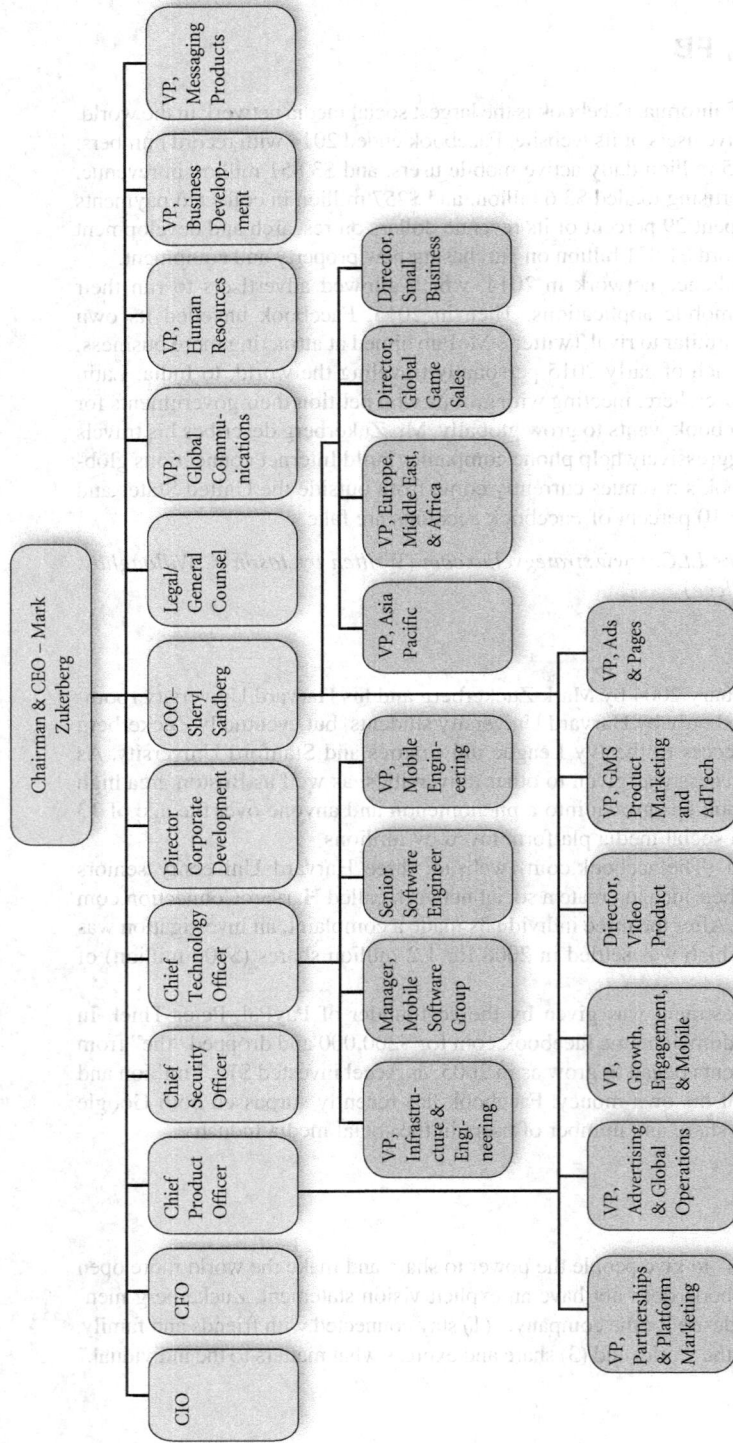

Chairman & CEO – Mark Zukerberg

- CIO
- CFO
- Chief Product Officer
- Chief Security Officer
- Chief Technology Officer
- Director Corporate Development
- COO – Sheryl Sandberg
- Legal/General Counsel
- VP, Global Communications
- VP, Human Resources
- VP, Business Development
- VP, Messaging Products

Under Chief Technology Officer:
- VP, Infrastructure & Engineering
- Manager, Mobile Software Group
- Senior Software Engineer
- VP, Mobile Engineering

Under COO – Sheryl Sandberg:
- VP, Asia Pacific
- VP, Europe, Middle East, & Africa
- Director, Global Game Sales
- Director, Small Business

Bottom row:
- VP, Partnerships & Platform Marketing
- VP, Advertising & Global Operations
- VP, Growth, Engagement, & Mobile
- Director, Video Product
- VP, GMS Product Marketing and AdTech
- VP, Ads & Pages

Source: Based on Facebook's organizational chart (http://www.theofficialboard.com/org-chart/facebook).

Code of Conduct

According to Facebook's corporate governance report, "Facebook Personnel" are expected to act lawfully, honestly, ethically, and in the best interests of the company while performing duties on behalf of Facebook. The company code of conduct applies to all Facebook personnel, including members of the board of directors (in connection with their work for Facebook), officers, and employees of Facebook, Inc. and its corporate affiliates, as well as contingent workers (e.g., agency workers, contractors, and consultants) and others working on Facebook's behalf.

Organizational Structure

Facebook has 14 subsidiaries, as follows: Facebook Benelux, Facebook Brazil, Facebook Canada, Facebook France, Facebook Germany, Facebook India, Facebook Italy, Facebook Korea, Facebook Norway, Facebook Portugal, Facebook Spain, Instagram, Oculus VR, and WhatsApp. Facebook's top executives are listed in Exhibit 1, along with an organizational chart of the company. Note the company structure is a hybrid, being divisional by region and by product. Some analysts suggest the structure is too complex, with overlapping duties, and would prefer to see something similar to a strategic business unit (SBU) structure.

Segments

As indicated in Exhibit 2, Facebook is segmented both by region, having four regions, and by revenue source, Advertising as well as Payments and Other Fees. Note that roughly one half of Facebook's revenues are generated from the United States and Canada.

Finance

Facebook's income statement is provided in Exhibit 3. Note that the firm's net income more than doubled in 2014. Facebook's balance sheet is provided in Exhibit 4. Note the company's goodwill more than doubled, partly because Facebook in 2014 acquired the messaging service WhatsApp for $19 billion.

EXHIBIT 2 Facebook's Revenue Segments (in millions of USD)

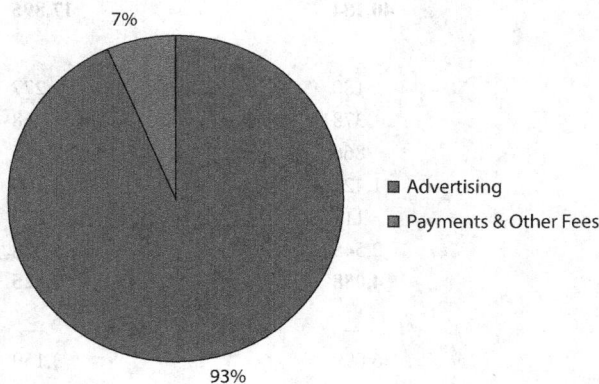

Revenue - Geography	1st Quarter 2014	2nd Quarter 2014	3rd Quarter 2014	4th Quarter 2014
USA & Canada	$1,179	$1,308	$1,514	$1,864
Europe	$698	$824	$844	$1,030
Asia-Pacific	$354	$431	$492	$554
Rest of the World	$271	$347	$353	$403

Source: Based on Facebook's 2014 *Form 10-K*.

EXHIBIT 3 Facebook's Income Statements (in millions of USD)

Report Date	December 31, 2014	December 31, 2013
Revenues	$12,466	$7,872
Operating expenses	7,472	5,068
EBIT	4,994	2,804
Interest	84	50
Other income (loss)	—	—
EBT	4,910	2,754
Tax	1,970	1,254
Income from continuing operations	2,940	1,500
Other items	(15)	(9)
Net income	**2,925**	**1,491**

Source: Based on Facebook's 2014 *Annual Report* Page 57 and Yahoo Finance.

EXHIBIT 4 Facebook's Balance Sheets (in millions of USD)

Report Date	December 31, 2014	December 31, 2013
Assets		
Cash and equivalents	$11,199	$11,449
Accounts receivable	1,678	1,109
Other current assets	793	512
Total current assets	13,670	13,070
Property, plant & equipment	3,967	2,882
Goodwill	17,981	839
Intangible assets	3,929	883
Other assets	638	221
Total assets	**40,184**	**17,895**
Liabilities		
Short-term debt	180	277
Accounts payable	378	268
Other current liabilities	866	555
Total current liabilities	1,424	1,100
Long-term debt	119	237
Other liabilities	2,545	1,088
Total liabilities	**4,088**	**2,425**
Common stock	—	—
Retained earnings	6,099	3,159
Paid in capital and other	29,997	12,311
Total equity	**36,096**	**15,470**
Total liabilities & equity	**40,184**	**17,895**

Source: Based on Facebook's 2014 *Annual Report* Page 56 and Yahoo Finance.

Marketing Strategy

Until November 2014, most Facebook users obtained free marketing and advertising of a product or service by creating posts on their "wall" to their mass audience. But a new system was installed toward the end of 2014. Individuals now wanting to gain exposure based on free advertising and marketing will no longer obtain the high-traffic distribution to their page "fans." The only way entrepreneurs and small business owners can receive high volumes of distribution of their materials is to pay Facebook for their product service exposure. The more money paid by the individual or business, the more reach their message will be distributed.

Another marketing item Facebook has initiated is product ads, which show users pictures of products and prices, once the user has visited the specific product's website, based on the users' interests and/or location. Facebook now also offers a work-oriented product similar to LinkedIn and rivals Microsoft, Google, and Salesforce.com. The new Facebook "professional" service enables users to keep their personal postings, pictures, and identity separate from the professional and work content. The new service includes online chatting with professional colleagues, which is a serious challenge to LinkedIn, the leading business-oriented social network. The new service comes with tools to share and store documents, taking aim at products and services from Microsoft, Google, and Salesforce.com. Facebook has a significant advantage in any competition, given its reported 1.35 billion users who are active monthly and 864 million who use it daily, compared to LinkedIn's claims of 332 million registered users, but only 90 million persons visited the site from July through September 2014.

Facebook's wide following is its main competitive advantage, because of what is commonly referred to as the *network effect* in business and economics. Much of the value comes from the availability of other people with similar interests that you may want to market to or interact with professionally or personally. Two disadvantages of Facebook, however, and reasons many companies have banned employees from using the service at work, is that (1) many persons lose significant productivity at work by spending too much time on Facebook and (2) Facebook has faced privacy criticisms for years. Information leaked through employees "communicating" on Facebook could potentially land in the hands of competitors, causing damage to the business. It is unclear yet whether the new Facebook "professional" service will charge users or be paid for by advertising.

For a decade, digital marketers have been constrained to an increasingly outdated technology known as the *cookie,* which are still used to measure and target digital ads. Best described as bits of code dropped into web browsers, cookies generate poor approximations of how many people view a digital ad and provides inaccurate estimates of how many times any given individual sees an ad. Cookies give unreliable measures of clicks and sales and are not used on mobile apps. However, from 2015 to 2017, Facebook-owned Atlas aims to take digital marketing beyond the cookie to (1) correct cookies' inaccuracies and (2) discover what's happening within the cookie-less world of mobile apps. Atlas strives to be able to connect offline purchases and conversions to digital ads shown across mobile apps and the Web. In essence, Facebook's Atlas is an ad server that allows ad buyers to measure, target, and optimize digital and mobile ads across digital apps (i.e., not just on Facebook).

For Facebook, Google, Yahoo!, Microsoft, and AOL, the primary revenue sources are Internet advertising. Exhibit 5 reveals the percentage of total digital display ad revenues for each company.

EXHIBIT 5 Digital Display Ad Revenues: Facebook versus Rivals

	2010	2011	2012	2013	2014
Google	12.1%	13.5%	15.4%	18.0%	21.2%
Facebook	11.5%	14.1%	14.4%	15.2%	15.5%
Yahoo!	14.0%	11.0%	9.3%	8.0%	7.0%
Microsoft	5.2%	4.9%	4.5%	4.3%	4.0%
AOL	4.7%	4.3%	3.6%	3.1%	2.7%

*These data include advertising on desktop and laptop computers, mobile phones, and tablets.

Source: Based on http://www.quora.com/Who-are-facebooks-biggest-competitors-and-why

Instagram

Facebook recently acquired Instagram, whose primary customer base is teenagers. Instagram is the Web's leading photo-sharing and video-sharing social media service and is on pace to top 100 million users in the United States by 2018. Instagram surpassed Twitter in early 2015 as the second-most used social media service in the region after its parent company, Facebook. The number of U.S. users of Instagram climbed by nearly 60 percent to 64.2 million in 2014 versus the year-earlier. Twitter ended 2014 with 48.4 million users in the United States, an increase of 12 percent. However, Instagram's user growth is expected to climb to 21 percent in 2015, 15 percent in 2016, and 10 percent in 2017, whereas Twitter's user growth is expected to decline to 9 percent in 2015, 8 percent in 2016, and 7 percent in 2017. Analysts expect that by 2018, Instagram will have 106.2 million users in the United States, up 7 percent, compared to Twitter, which is projected to have 66 million users and year-over-year growth of 6 percent. Although Instagram has customers of all ages, roughly 62 percent of all teens in the 12 to 17 age group used Instagram regularly in 2014.

Competitors

Although there are hundreds of online social media websites, the major competitors of Facebook include Instagram, Snapchat, LinkedIn, Google+, and Twitter. Snapchat is a more private medium than Facebook, which is why it's growing in popularity. Snapchat only lets you send "snaps" to the friends selected by the user. Compared to Snapchat, LinkedIn is not as nearly as popular with social media usage, but LinkedIn is gaining users and platform time from Facebook due to the professional nature of LinkedIn. Google+ and Twitter compete with Facebook for users and time spent on social media.

Snapchat

Three Stanford University students created the Snapchat photo messaging system in July 2011. In 2013, Snapchat launched an application named Snapkidz for users 13 years of age and younger, with those users only being able to save photos on their local drive; they are not able to send pictures to anyone. In October 2014, with the demand to raise more funds and users for this application, Snapchat released their first 20-second movie trailer for the film *Ouija*. This was their first paid advertising venture into the market. Currently, Snapchat caters to sending over 700 million videos and photos for current users. Snapchat is a photo messaging application whereby users can take photos, record videos, add text and drawings, and send them to a controlled list of recipients. These sent photographs and videos are known as "Snaps." Users set a time limit for how long recipients can view their Snaps (as of April 2014, the range is from 1 to 10 seconds), after which they are hidden from the recipient's device and deleted from Snapchat's servers. According to Snapchat in May 2014, the app's users were sending 700 million photos and videos per day, and Snapchat Stories content was being viewed 500 million times per day. The company has a valuation of $10 to $20 billion, depending on various sources.

LinkedIn Corporation (LNKD)

LinkedIn is a professional social networking service that has over 260 million users in 200 countries. Headquartered in Mountain View, California, LinkedIn has three major business units: talent solutions, marketing solutions, and premium subscriptions. Companies can utilize LinkedIn talent solutions for employee procurement. Individuals seeking employment can pay a premium subscription to find job openings. LinkedIn continues to acquire competing firms to help complement its current product offerings. A key recent acquisition was Digg, a social news site, in 2012. As its growth continues, LinkedIn's 2014 market penetration was highest in the United States, the United Kingdom, Canada, and Australia. India was the fastest-growing country of LinkedIn users that grew to 20 million during 2014.

Google, Inc. (GOOG)

Google+ is an identity service and a social network with up to 540 million active users. About 30 percent of Google+ customers use the application on their smartphones. Beginning at age 13,

EXHIBIT 6 Facebook vs Rival Firms

	Facebook	LinkedIn	Twitter
# Full-Time Employees	9,200	6,900	3,900
$ Net Income	$2,900 M	($15.7 M)	($578 M)
$ Revenue	$12,400 M	$2,218 M	$1,403 M
$ Revenue/Employee	$1,348,000	$321,000	$360,000
$ EPS Ratio	$1.03	$(0.37)	$(0.98)
$ Market Cap.	$251 B	$26.9 B	$24.6 B

Source: Based on Yahoo Finance 2014 data and other sources.

teens may create a Google+ account. There are services that set Google+ apart from its competitors such as circles, streams, Hangouts, Hangouts on Air, and the +1 button. One item that Google+ users and advertisers will benefit from is SEO (Search Engine Optimization), as being on Google+ will boost search results rankings.

Twitter, Inc. (TWTR)

Headquartered in San Francisco, Twitter is a social networking service that allows individuals to send tweets within their network. Tweets are 140-character messages and can be posted only by registered users. By the end of 2014, Twitter had more than 500 million users. The company has several revenue services to generate income, such as paid advertising to companies that can be compared to Google Adwords. Twitter offers a self-service advertising system for small business owners. Total revenue for 2014 was $1.4 billion compared to $664.89 million the prior year.

Exhibit 6 provides comparative data for Facebook and its direct competitors. Note both LinkedIn and Twitter reported negative net income in 2014.

External Issues

Pinning, tweeting, posting, tagging, texting, liking, and other social media lingo have become a major part of daily lives, with almost two billion people in the world being active users of social media applications. However, social media users increasingly feel commercialized when pop-up ads cover their computer screens while surfing social media platforms. Companies must figure out a way to utilize advertising that creates comfort when seen by individuals.

The age of users continues to be an external issue. Facebook currently has a policy that children age 13 or younger must have parent consent to create a page on their platform, which parallels with the Children's Online Privacy Protection Act (COPPA). Approximately 1 of 8 Americans show signs of having a social media addiction, which consists of declining social relationships, anger and depression when the Internet is not available for use, lying about usage, and experiencing high levels of happiness when using the Internet. Other characteristics of this addiction consist of waking up in the middle of the night to check Facebook, checking social media before getting out of bed, and using social media to cover up everyday life problems.

A new Facebook application enables users to comment on political debates and issues. Users connecting via the Facebook platform and the company pushing the idea of political impact caused the Egyptian government to ban Facebook in their country. Facebook created a political action committee in 2011 with the Federal Election Commission. It was named the FB PAC.

Social Media and Personal Branding

A new trend is the idea of using social media platforms to create a person brand whereby individuals are combining their social media applications to create a personal brand or image that directly relates to future employment. A common practice for human resource managers is to perform a search on potential employees. One company, Klout, has grasped the idea that society has become aware of individual brands, and has made it easier for human resource managers to review a potential employee's social media influence. Headquartered in San Francisco, Klout is a private company that measures social media analytics to rank an individual's social influence. One's Klout score can be between 1 and 100. As President Obama's score is 99, the likes of Justin Bieber and actress Zooey Deschanel have scores of 92 and 86, respectively. To put a Klout score into perspective, my (the case author) clout score is currently 53. The higher the score, the better it is for individuals looking to be hired at large corporations in the United States. Klout uses Bing, Facebook, Foursquare, Google+, Instagram, LinkedIn, Twitter, and Wikipedia data to create Klout user profiles that are assigned a unique "Klout Score."

The Future

Social media use is growing exponentially. A key question moving forward is: Where will the large amounts of data be stored? Who will control the stored data? Will government intervention play a part of using the stored data? Does Facebook have a right to store and even sell this information?

Google and Facebook are becoming closer friends. Both companies want more people online, searching around and clicking on ads. Both firms are finding new ways to make it happen—from selling smartphone data plans, to using solar-powered drone aircraft as floating cell towers, to partnering with telecom providers in the developing world to get people hooked on apps. Both companies recently gave updates on their efforts at the Mobile World Congress wireless show in Barcelona, Spain, in March 2015. At the meeting, Facebook CEO Mark Zuckerberg and Google Vice President Sundar Pichai told attendees they plan to collaborate more, but are taking very different approaches to getting the world connected. Internet.org is Facebook's fledgling effort to create new users in countries with little or low Internet use. Zuckerberg revealed at the meeting that his company has launched apps with basic free services in six countries: Zambia, Ghana, Kenya, Tanzania, Colombia, and most recently, India. The app is customized for each country and telecom operator, in order to attract new users while not hurting the telecoms' already existing base of customers. Facebook offers free versions of services users already pay for— a primary reason why Internet.org does not include the WhatsApp messaging service.

Develop a three-year strategic plan for Facebook's CEO, Mr. Mark Zukerberg.

World Wildlife Fund for Nature (WWF) 2015

www.worldwildlife.org

Headquartered in Gland, Switzerland, the World Wildlife Fund by some measures is the world's largest independent, nonprofit conservation organization working in 100 countries, supported by over 1 million members within the United States and 5 million members globally. The organization has about 6,200 full-time staff members that manage an average of 1,300 projects at any one time. Since being founded in 1961, it has invested close to $10 billion in more than 13,000 conservation projects in over 150 countries. Within the United States, the WWF operates as a nonprofit organization and is headquartered in Washington, DC. The organization generated a total of $291.49 million in operating revenue in 2014, resulting from a fundraising expense of $28.70 million. A total of $224.46 million was expended by the organization in direct support of conservation programs. The symbol of WWF is the Giant Panda (the endangered black and white bear from China).

WWF opened a new office in Myanmar in late 2014 after partnering with the national government to achieve shared goals. Myanmar, located in southeast Asia, has a very rich natural capital, including three of the world's most pristine rivers, over 250 mammal species, and more than 1,000 bird species. The country's important biodiversity includes endangered species such as tigers, elephants, and Irrawaddy dolphins. Myanmar is determined to develop a green economy that can serve as a global model of how to improve life for a country's citizens, while protecting its natural capital.

In July 2015, the U.S. Fish and Wildlife Service began investigating the circumstances surrounding the killing that month of Cecil, a lion who is thought to have been lured out of his protected habitat in Zimbabwe and killed by Walter J. Palmer, an American dentist and hunter. The killing of Cecil raised global awareness for wildlife welfare on many fronts. Well known to anyone who ever visited Hwange National Park in western Zimbabwe, Cecil was killed and beheaded—the head intended as a trophy for the hunter.

Copyright by Fred David Books LLC. www.strategyclub.com (Written by Edward Moore, Liberty University)

History

The World Wildlife Fund was formed when the Morges Manifesto document was signed in 1961 by 16 of the world's leading conservationists, stating that although the expertise to protect the environment existed, the financial support for the goal did not. As a result, the document established the WWF as an international fundraising organization. It quickly established itself on the world conservation stage and opened its first office in Morges, Switzerland, with H.R.H. Prince Bernhard as its first president. In 1961, WWF funded the British National Appeal and the United States Appeal, the first two national organizations funded under WWF. Also that inaugural year, WWF approved five projects totaling $33,000 to begin conservation work with several endangered species, including the Bald Eagle.

By 1973, WWF hired its first staff scientist as a project administrator and had projects in countries across the globe, ranging from a $38,000 grant to study tiger populations in Nepal to purchasing 37,000 acres of land in Kenya to be set aside as a feeding ground and sanctuary for nearly 30 bird species, including one million flamingoes. WWF promoted the Convention on International Trade in Endangered Species of Wild Fauna & Flora (CITES), which to date has been signed by over 170 nations, all committed to ensuring wild plants and animals from runaway trade and exploitation.

By the early 1980s, in partnership with the United Nations Environment Program and the International Union for Conservation of Nature (IUCN), WWF established a program of debt-for-nature swaps in which the WWF converts portions of national debt into funding for conservation efforts. In 1985, WWF launched Wildlands and Human Needs, a new initiative intended to highlight how economic conditions of rural people who share land with wildlife can improve without negative impact to the natural habitats the wildlife relies on. By 1989, the WWF debt-for-nature swap initiative had grown and the organization was able to negotiate a $2.1 million swap for Madagascar.

In 2004, a wildlife census in Africa showed that WWF efforts to save rhinos were paying off with the population of black rhinos reaching 3,600 and white rhinos reaching 11,000. Otherwise, these animals would likely have gone extinct. WWF soon adopted a new and challenging 10-year goal to "measurably conserve 15 to 20 of the world's most important eco-regions and in so doing, transform markets, policies, and institutions in order to reduce threats to these places and the diversity of life on Earth."

Internal Issues

Vision/Mission/Ethics

The World Wildlife Fund's mission is to conserve nature and reduce the most pressing threats to the diversity of life on Earth. The organization's vision is "to build a future in which people live in harmony with nature." WWF's mission is to conserve nature and reduce the most pressing threats to the diversity of life on Earth. In an effort to increase organizational effectiveness, WWF has recently shifted its emphasis from a narrow focus on saving specific species and landscapes to a broad focus addressing the global forces and threats that are impacting specific species and landscapes. This shift has led the organization to focus its efforts on the six key areas of forests, marine, freshwater, wildlife, food, and climate.

The code of ethics calls for the organization to remain global, independent, multicultural, and nonparty political. Importantly, it also calls for objective examination of available information and a strong focus on concrete conservation solutions. The code also highlights the strategy of partnerships and collaboration to accomplish the mission as well as a focus on cost-effective operations.

Organizational Structure

The World Wildlife Fund is structured divisionally, as illustrated in Exhibit 1. There are five divisions reporting to COO Marcia Marsh, including the newest division, simply titled Oceans.

Strategy

The World Wildlife Fund's strategy relies on a combination of fundraising, collaboration, research, conservation projects, and government influence to accomplish the following:

- Protect and restore species and their habitats.
- Strengthen local communities' ability to conserve the natural resources they depend on.
- Transform markets and policies to reduce the impact of the production and consumption of commodities.
- Ensure that the value of nature is reflected in decisions made by individuals, communities, governments, and businesses.
- Mobilize hundreds of millions of people to support conservation.

The World Wildlife Fund's strategy is to partner with organizations to positively impact seven areas: forests, oceans, freshwater, wildlife, food, climate, and species. Its work on forests, for example, focuses on the threats created by growing agriculture use as well as illegal and unsustainable logging. The WWF website places the rate of loss of forests globally at a staggering 48 football fields per minute. To help mitigate this, the WWF has set a specific goal of "conserving the world's most important forests to sustain nature's diversity, benefit our climate, and support human well-being by 2020."

The organization's work on oceans focuses on promoting healthy marine ecosystems capable of sustaining livelihoods and economies while supporting biodiversity. The WWF website says 1 billion people rely on fish as an important part of their diet and that more than 520 million livelihoods are supported by fishing and its related activities.

The WWF's 2014 Living Planet Report reported that wildlife populations of mammals, birds, reptiles, amphibians, and fish have declined by 52 percent over the last 40 years. Success stories in this area include the recovery of Africa's black rhino and black bucks in the Himalayas.

EXHIBIT 1 WWF's Organizational Structure

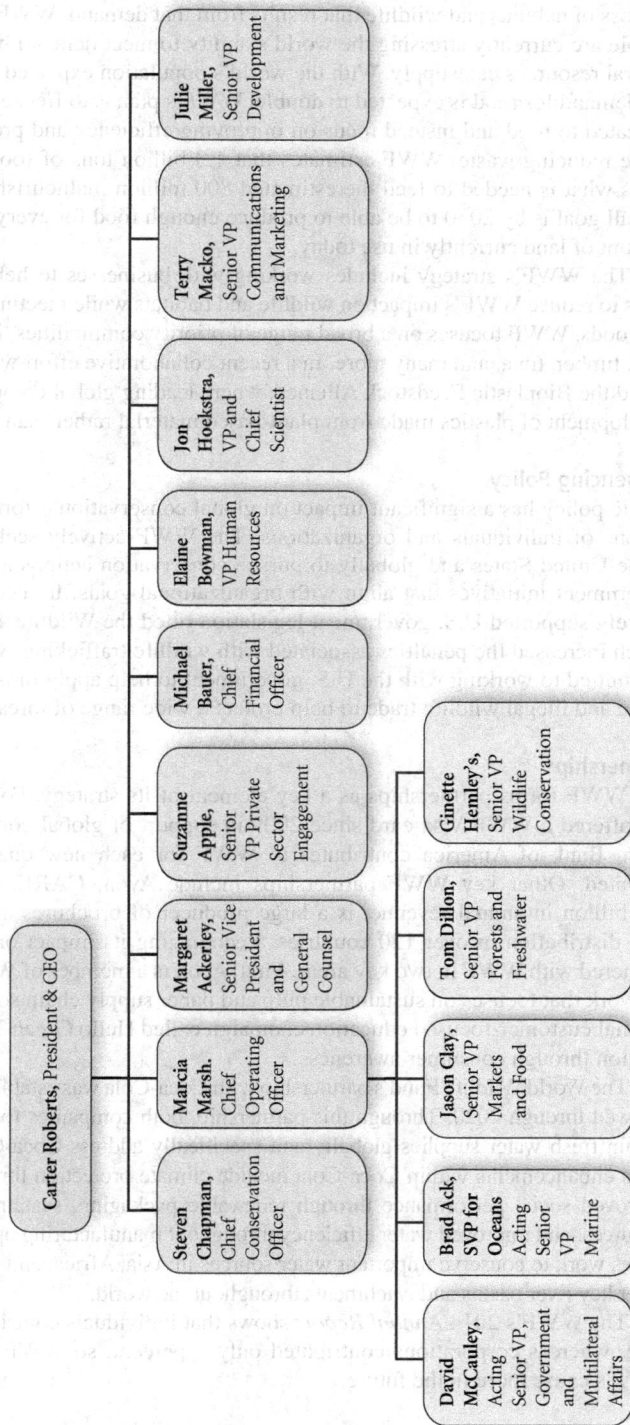

- **Carter Roberts**, President & CEO
  - **Steven Chapman**, Chief Conservation Officer
    - **David McCauley**, Acting Senior VP, Government and Multilateral Affairs
    - **Brad Ack**, SVP for Oceans Acting Senior VP Marine
    - **Jason Clay**, Senior VP Markets and Food
    - **Tom Dillon**, Senior VP Forests and Freshwater
    - **Ginette Hemley's**, Senior VP Wildlife Conservation
  - **Marcia Marsh**, Chief Operating Officer
  - **Margaret Ackerley**, Senior Vice President and General Counsel
  - **Suzanne Apple**, Senior VP Private Sector Engagement
  - **Michael Bauer**, Chief Financial Officer
  - **Elaine Bowman**, VP Human Resources
  - **Jon Hoekstra**, VP and Chief Scientist
  - **Terry Macko**, Senior VP Communications and Marketing
  - **Julie Miller**, Senior VP Development

Source: Based on information from the WWF 2014 *Annual Report* as of June 30, 2014.

Current projects include efforts to conserve snow leopards in Central Asia, and ostriches and zebras in Namibia. The goal here is to "use our best science, policy influence, market based strategies, and communications to quantify and enhance the value of wildlife."

Work in the area of food focuses on the conflict created by growing demand for food and the loss of habitats and wildlife that results from that demand. WWF studies show that 7.2 billion people are currently stressing the world's ability to meet demand by consuming 1.5 times what natural resources can supply. With the world's population expected to grow to 9 billion by 2050, the demand for food is expected to double. WWF's plan is to freeze the amount of land currently allocated to food and instead focus on improving efficiency and productivity in current systems while reducing waste. WWF estimates that 1.3 billion tons of food is wasted each year—four times what is needed to feed the estimated 800 million malnourished people in the world. The overall goal is by 2050 to be able to produce enough food for everyone, using roughly the same amount of land currently in use today.

The WWF's strategy includes working with businesses to help discover new and creative ways to reduce WWF's impact on wildlife and habitats while meeting the growing global demand for goods. WWF focuses on a broad range of priority commodities, including items such as dairy, beef, timber, tuna, and many more. In a recent collaborative effort with business, the WWF established the Bioplastic Feedstock Alliance, where leading global companies have committed to the development of plastics made from plant-based material rather than fossil fuels.

Influencing Policy

Public policy has a significant impact on global conservation efforts as it can guide and control actions of individuals and organizations. The WWF actively seeks to influence governments in the United States and globally to pursue conservation actions as well as actively supporting government initiatives that align with organizational goals. In a recent policy initiative, WWF actively supported U.S. government legislation titled the Wildlife Trafficking Enforcement Act, which increased the penalties associated with wildlife trafficking. WWF went a step further and committed to working with the U.S. government to help apply those new penalties to organized crime and illegal wildlife trade to help protect a wide range of threatened species.

Partnerships

The WWF forms partnerships as a key element of its strategy. For example, Bank of America has offered a WWF Visa card since 2009 in support of global conservation. Through this program, Bank of America contributes to WWF for each new qualifying account opened and activated. Other key WWF partnerships include Avon, CARE, and Coca-Cola. Avon, with $11 billion in annual revenue, is a large producer of brochures and consumer paper products with distribution in over 120 countries. Recognizing its impact on the environment, Avon has partnered with WWF in two key areas. First, Avon is a member of WWF's Global Forest & Trade Network that focuses on sustainable pulp and paper supply chain solutions. Second, Avon has an internal customer-focused education campaign called Hello Green Tomorrow to help curb deforestation through consumer awareness.

The World Wildlife Fund's partnership with Coca-Cola was established in 2007 and was recently renewed through 2020. Through this partnership, both companies focus on efforts to improve and sustain fresh water supplies globally and specifically address Coca-Cola's value chain. The value chain enhancements within Coca-Cola include climate protection through reduced carbon content, improved social performance through renewable packaging, sustainable sourcing of agricultural resources, and improved water efficiency throughout manufacturing operations. Externally, the companies work to conserve important water sources in Asia, Africa, and the Americas, and specifically target key river basins and catchments throughout the world.

The WWF's 2014 *Annual Report* shows that individuals contributed 32 percent of total revenue, whereas corporations contributed only 4 percent, so WWF wants businesses to rally to WWF's cause more in the future.

Finance

The World Wildlife Fund generated $291 million in revenue during 2014, up 12 percent from the previous year. The Statement of Activities shown in Exhibit 2 is similar to the income statement of a for-profit organization and reveals that $136 million of the WWF revenue was in the form of direct contributions, with another $51 million in government grants and contracts. The remaining revenue came from other sources, including WWF network revenue and non-operating income. Total operating expenses were $266 million, resulting in a surplus of nearly $26 million.

As a nonprofit, it is important for WWF to measure the efficiency with which the organization raises funds and converts those funds into programs that support its mission. Charity

EXHIBIT 2 WWF's Statement of Activities (in millions of USD)

Report Date	2014	2013
Operating Activities		
Revenues		
Contributions	$136.58	$122.18
Government Grants and Contracts	50.82	48.22
WWF Network Revenue	17.90	16.21
Other Revenue Including Royalties	5.49	6.81
In-kind Contributions	46.96	64.30
Non-operating Income Allocated to Operations	33.75	21.73
Total Revenues	**291.49**	**279.44**
Net Assets Released from Restrictions	–	–
Net Revenues	**291.49**	**279.44**
Commercial Building Operations		
Revenues	6.10	6.68
Expenses	5.85	5.52
Net Income on Commercial Building Operations	**0.25**	**1.16**
Total Revenue and Support	**291.74**	**280.60**
Operating Expenses		
Program Services		
Conservation Field and Policy Programs	159.75	144.38
Public Education	64.71	81.74
Total Program Services	**224.46**	**226.12**
Supporting Services		
Finance and Administration	12.72	12.35
Fundraising	28.71	27.66
Total Supporting Activities	**41.43**	**40.02**
Total Operating Expenses	**265.89**	**266.13**
Revenues and Support Over Operating Expenses	**25.85**	**14.46**
Non-operating Activities		
Bequests, Endowments, and Split Income Gifts	12.19	29.21
Income on Interest Rate Swaps	0.28	5.87
Income from Investments, Net	34.47	19.42
Gain/(Loss) on Foreign Currency Exchange	0.45	(0.12)
Total Non-operating Activities	**46.94**	**54.39**
Total Allocated to Operations	(33.75)	(21.73)
Change in Net Assets from Non-Operating Activities	**13.19**	**32.66**
Change in Net Assets	39.03	47.12
Net Assets at Beginning of Year	318.82	271.69
Net Assets at End of Year	**357.85**	**318.82**

Source: Based on WWF's 2014 *Annual Report.*

Navigator (www.charitynavigator.com), a nonprofit rating organization, provides guidance when evaluating this type of performance in the form of industry norms. WWF spent $224 million on programs in support of its mission in 2014, representing 77 percent of its total revenue. Data from Charity Navigator shows that 7 out of 10 nonprofit companies spend at least 75 percent on programs, placing WWF in the top tier for the conversion of revenue to programs. Total administrative and fundraising expenses for 2014 were nearly $13 million and $29 million, respectively. These two categories represent 4.8 and 10.8 percent of total expenses. The best-performing nonprofit organizations, according to Charity Navigator, keep their administrative expenses below 15 percent and fundraising expenses below 10 percent. WWF is operationally efficient in both categories when compared to industry norms.

Another metric to consider is the return on fundraising expenses. According to Charity Navigator, top-performing nonprofit companies will spend less than $0.10 to raise $1.00 in revenue. During 2014, the WWF raised a total of $291 million with a fundraising expense of $29 million, placing them in the top tier with an expense of $0.0985 for each $1.00 raised. One final metric used by Charity Navigator is the working capital ratio that measures how many years the organization could sustain its present program spending using only net assets, with the best performing organizations having a ratio of greater than 1:1. With a current program expense of $224 million and total net assets of $358 million, the WWF has a ratio of 1.59:1, placing it again in the top tier. Taken together, these financial performance metrics reveal WWF to be an efficient and effective organization in the area of fundraising and allocation to program expense while minimizing internal expenses.

The Statement of Financial Positions in Exhibit 3 is similar to the balance sheet of a for-profit organization in that it summarizes assets and liabilities, but differs in totaling net assets rather than shareholders' equity. Despite the differences, several leading financial health metrics can be calculated. For example, the current ratio for 2014 for WWF is 2.35, up from 2.28 in 2013.

Exhibit 4 reveals 10 years (only even years data are shown) of operating revenue and program spending history. Note how the distance between the two lines becomes wider toward 2014, indicating both greater profits and efficiency. Spending decreased $2 million, and net revenues increased $12 million from 2013 to 2014.

Competitors

Donors make choices about where to make contributions based on the operational efficiency of the nonprofit organizations as well as its specific causes. The Nature Conservancy, Conservation International, and the Wildlife Conservation Society are leading wildlife and habitat conservancy nonprofit organizations and as such are competitors to WWF.

The Nature Conservancy (www.nature.org)

Headquartered in Arlington, Virginia, The Nature Conservancy was founded in 1951 with the broad goal of working around the world to protect ecologically important lands and waters for both nature and people. The organization currently has more than 1 million members and since its inception it has protected more than 119 million acres of land and thousands of miles of rivers across the globe. It has a global impact with projects in all 50 states in the United States and more than 35 countries. Its work is focused on threats to conservation, including climate change, fresh water, oceans, and land. The mission statement of the organization is similar to the WWF in that it focuses on achieving conservancy through collaborative partnerships.

The organization's 2013 total revenue was $859 million with a total expense of $752 million made up of $542 million in program expenses, $122 million in administrative expenses, and $87.88 million in fundraising expenses. Using the evaluative methods from Charity Navigator, only 63 percent of revenue went to program expense, which is below the top-tier target of 75 percent. Administration made up 16 percent of total expense, with another 11.7 percent of total expense allocated to fundraising. Both of these are also short of the top-tier targets of less than 15 percent for administration and 10 percent for fundraising. In the area of fundraising efficiency, the organization spent $0.10 for each dollar raised, which was right on target.

The Nature Conservancy also operates more than 100 marine conservation projects globally. The organization's assets totaled $6.18 billion as of 2014. The Nature Conservancy is the largest

EXHIBIT 3 WWF's Statement of Financial Position (in millions of USD)

Report Date	2014	2013
Assets		
Current Assets		
Cash and Cash Equivalents	$34.66	$32.32
Short-term Investments	35.54	25.45
Accounts Receivable	19.54	23.09
Pledges Receivable	28.96	23.13
Prepaid Assets	3.45	4.04
Other Current Assets	2.06	2.99
Total Current Assets	**124.20**	**111.00**
Non-current Assets		
Long-term Investments, Net	240.28	211.99
Pledges Receivable, Net of Current, Discount, and Allowance for Uncollectable Pledges	33.28	20.41
Long-term Trust Receivables	28.67	31.29
Bond Issuance Costs, Net of Amortization	1.14	1.24
Other Non-current Assets	4.97	14.00
Land, Building, and Equipment, Net	59.01	61.00
Total Non-current Assets	**367.35**	**339.92**
Total Assets	**491.55**	**450.93**
Liabilities and Net Assets		
Current Liabilities		
Accounts Payable and Accrued Expenses	14.86	11.73
Grants Payable	28.12	27.85
Deferred Revenue	7.78	7.14
Current Portion of Long-term Debt	2.08	2.03
Total Current Liabilities	**52.83**	**48.75**
Non-current Liabilities		
Long-term Debt, Net of Current Portion	59.51	61.60
Other Long-term Liabilities	8.02	8.14
Interest Rate Sway Liability	13.34	13.62
Total Non-current Liabilities	**80.87**	**83.36**
Total Liabilities	**133.70**	**132.11**
Commitments and Contingencies		
Net Assets		
Unrestricted	171.46	153.18
Temporarily Restricted	142.93	122.79
Permanently Restricted	43.47	42.85
Total Net Assets	**357.85**	**318.82**
Total Liabilities and Net Assets	**491.55**	**450.93**

Source: Based on WWF's 2014 *Annual Report.*

environmental nonprofit by assets and by revenue in the Americas. The Nature Conservancy echoes the concerns of the WWF surrounding drinking water. Its research shows that currently half of the world's major rivers are seriously polluted and/or depleted and that within 10 years, most people on the planet will face water shortages. While the debate surrounding climate change is ongoing, a 2014 National Oceanic and Atmospheric Administration (NOAA) report has cited that 2014 was the hottest year on record since 1880, tied with 1998 and 2010.

EXHIBIT 4 10-Year Comparison of Revenue and Spending (in millions of USD)

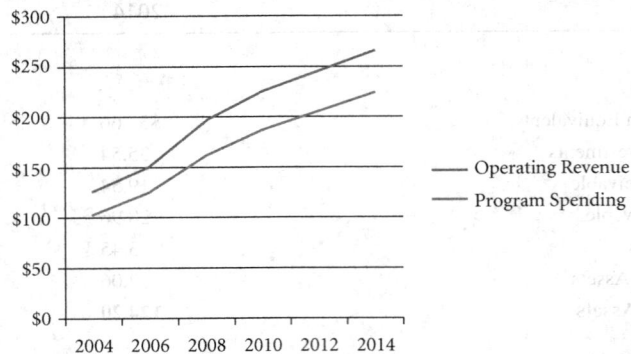

Source: Based on information on the WWF 2014 *Annual Report.*

Conservation International (www.conservation.org)

Headquartered in Arlington, Virginia, and founded in 1987, Conservation International (CI) has the broad goal of protecting nature for the benefit of everyone on our planet. The organization currently has 900 members and is working in over 30 countries. Its work is focused in three areas, including protecting our natural wealth, fostering effective governance, and promoting sustainable production. From its website, Conservation International's vision and mission statements are:

> **Vision:** We imagine a healthy, prosperous world in which societies are forever committed to caring for and valuing nature, for the long-term benefit of people and all life on Earth.

> **Mission:** Building upon a strong foundation of science, partnership and field demonstration, CI empowers societies to responsibly and sustainably care for nature, our global biodiversity, for the well-being of humanity.

The organization reported 2013 revenue of $96.82 million with a total expense of $144 million made up of $122 million in program expenses, $13 million in administrative expenses, and $8.7 million in fundraising expenses. The organization posted a deficit of $47 million during the year. The evaluative metrics from Charity Navigator reveal that 126 percent of CI's revenue went to program expense, well above the top tier target of 75 percent, but includes spending in excess of revenue. Administration made up 8.9 percent of total expense with another 6.1 percent of total expense allocated to fundraising. Both of these are well ahead of the top-tier targets of less than 15 percent for administration and 10 percent for fundraising. In the area of fundraising efficiency, the organization spent $0.09 for each dollar raised, which was also above target.

Wildlife Conservation Society (www.wcs.org)

Headquartered in New York City, the Wildlife Conservation Society (WCS) was founded in 1895 and has the broad goal of saving wildlife and wild places globally through a combination of science, conservation, education, and management of urban wildlife parks. The organizations flagship park is the Bronx Zoo. The WCS currently manages close to 500 conservation projects, manages more than 200 million acres of protected lands, and operates in more than 60 countries. The organization focuses its work on four issues facing wildlife and wild places, including climate change, resource exploitation, the connection between wildlife and human health, and sustainable development. The WCS website lists the mission statement for the organization as:

> **Mission:** WCS saves wildlife and wild places worldwide through science, conservation action, education, and inspiring people to value nature.

The Wildlife Conservation Society reported 2013 revenue of $212 million with a total expense of $1.218 billion made up of $181.07 million in program expenses, $28 million in administrative expenses, and $9.52 million in fundraising expenses. The organization posted a deficit of $6.4 million. Evaluative metrics from Charity Navigator reveal that 85.41 percent of revenue went to program expense, well above the top-tier target of 75 percent. Administration made up 12.7 percent of total expense with another 4.4 percent of total expense allocated to fundraising. Both of these are well ahead of the top-tier targets of less than 15 percent for administration and 10 percent for fundraising. The WCS was very efficient and well above target in the area of fundraising, spending only $0.045 for each dollar raised.

Future

The global condition of wildlife and wild areas has steadily declined, especially in the ocean. The WWF's 2014 *Annual Report* states that 60 percent of the world's ecosystems, including water supplies, fish stocks, and fertile soil, are in decline, and that global demand for resources already requires 1.5 times the available supply. Fully 1 in 9 people on the planet suffer from hunger, yet 90 percent of the ocean's fish stocks are overfished and global wildlife populations have declined by an average of 52 percent. WWF's global organization (www.panda.org) highlights the loss of biodiversity and cites that the current extinction rate is over 1,000 times higher than what science can attribute to natural extinction losses.

The World Health Organization (www.who.int) has also weighed in on the impact of global environmental change. Its website lists leading hazards to human health as climate change, stratospheric ozone depletion, changes in ecosystems due to loss of biodiversity, changes in hydrological systems and the supply of freshwater, land degradation, and stresses on food-producing systems.

WWF reports that unsustainable agriculture practices have nearly wiped out the forest regions of Borneo and Sumatra, while all oceans are threatened by overfishing and changing sea temperatures. At the same time, expanding territory for livestock and soy production is driving deforestation in the Amazon region.

Like all organizations, WWF must establish priorities, since no firm can do all they would like to do. Develop a 3-year strategic plan that will enable WWF to best meet the challenges of the future.

Ford Motor Company, 2015

www.ford.com, F

Headquartered in Dearborn, Michigan, Ford Motor Company is the second-largest U.S. auto-maker behind General Motors, but only the fifth-largest in the world based on vehicle sales. The company produces many different cars and trucks ranging from entry level to luxury cars. Ford's F-150 pickup truck is the most popular truck in the world for 32 years running. Ford owns stakes in several car manufacturers around the world, including Aston Martin, Jiangling, Troller, and FPV. In the past, Ford has owned portions of Jaguar, Land Rover, and Volvo. In 2011, Ford discontinued its Mercury brand that had existed since 1938. In 2015, Ford switched the body of its famous F-150 to aluminum from steel. The extra cost was $395 per truck, but fuel economy improved with the reduced weight.

Fords have been running fast lately. For Q2 of 2015, Ford reported excellent financial results, including the following:

- Global market share grew to 7.6 percent, up one-tenth percent from a year ago.
- Twelve of 16 planned global new product launches are completed; the remainder is on track.
- Introduced SYNC® 3, the all-new communications and entertainment system.
- Continued strong profit at Ford Credit; pre-tax profit of $506 million.
- Ford Smart Mobility plan moved from research to the start of implementation.
- Ford Credit launched car-sharing pilot in 6 U.S. cities and London.
- Pre-tax profit of $2.9 billion, up $269 million or 10 percent from a year ago.
- Net income of $1.9 billion, up $574 million or 44 percent from a year ago.
- After-tax earnings per share of 47 cents, up 7 cents from a year ago.
- Best company quarterly profit since 2000.
- Wholesale volume up 2 percent, driven by North America and Europe.
- Automotive revenue is about equal, with higher net pricing and volume offset by unfavorable translation effects of the strong U.S. dollar.

Copyright by Fred David Books LLC. www.strategyclub.com (Written by Forest R. David)

History

Ford traces its roots back to 1896 when Henry Ford built and marketed his first Quadricycle, a 4-wheel vehicle with a 4-horsepower engine. It was not until 1901, however, that Ford started his own car company, named the Henry Ford Company. He started Ford Motor Company in 1902 with 12 investors and $28,000 in cash. Interestingly, two of Ford's first investors in his new company were John and Horace Dodge, who later would start their own car company, called Dodge. Ford had spent nearly the entire initial investment when his first car was sold in July 1903. It did not take Ford Motor Company long, though, to start making large profits. By October 1903, Ford had turned a profit of $37,000, indicating just how popular this new equipment was going to become. The company was incorporated in 1903.

Henry Ford is world famous for his assembly line, but for the first 10 years of the company, two to three men worked on each car, and the parts were supplied by outside firms. Ford produced the famous Model T in 1908 and sold over 15 million, until production ceased in 1927. To help maintain employee morale, Ford paid workers $5 per day in 1914, double the national average. In addition, Ford reduced the workday from 9 to 8 hours. Many of Ford's workers could even afford a car they produced with the salary they earned.

In 1922, Ford acquired Lincoln Company and even began experimenting with aircraft production. In 1925, 2 years before selling the Model A automobile in 1927, Ford closed all plants for 6 months to retool and train employees on construction. By 1931, despite the great depression, Ford sold over 5 million Model A's. Ford continued to grow over the next two decades, until its IPO in 1956, which was at the time the largest IPO in history.

In 2005, Ford, along with GM, had their corporate bonds downgraded to junk status. High health-care costs, rising gas, falling market share to foreign products, a demanding United Auto Workers (UAW) union, and lack of strategic planning all contributed to the downfall. In 2007, Ford reached an agreement with the UAW on retirement benefits and other costs. The company was able to avoid a government takeover, unlike its counterpart, General Motors. Over the last several years, Ford has rebounded and continues to produce quality automobiles worldwide, as well as more and more electric and part-electric vehicles.

Internal Issues

Organizational Structure

As revealed in Exhibit 1, Ford operates using a divisional-by-geographic region organizational structure. Alan Mulally retired as CEO of Ford Motor Company on July 1, 2014, and was replaced by the then COO Mark Fields. In December 2014, the company hired a Chief Analytics Officer.

Vision/Mission

Ford does not have a published vision statement, but does have a stated mission statement, which is based on four key components and paraphrased as follows:

> *One Ford:* Align employee efforts toward a common definition of success and optimize their collective strengths worldwide.

> *One team:* Work together as one team to achieve automotive leadership, which is measured by the satisfaction of our customers, employees, and essential business partners, such as our dealers, investors, suppliers, unions/councils, and communities.

> *One plan:* Aggressively restructure to operate profitably at the current demand and changing model mix.

> *One goal:* Create an exciting and viable company delivering profitable growth for all.

Strategy

Since 2005, Ford's warranty repairs have declined 66 percent for vehicles in the first 3 months of service with average warranty costs falling 54 percent. Ford has reduced its energy use, emissions, and waste in its factories and its vehicles. The new F-150 comes with a 2.7 liter V6 EcoBoost engine, giving it the same power as a V8, with much better fuel economy. Higher engine outputs with smaller displacements are a key initiative moving forward for Ford and greatly improve fuel economy and emissions. To improve safety, many Ford products now include Blind Spot Information Systems, lane alerts, and rear parking assistance.

In 2014, Ford launched more vehicles than ever before in a single calendar year, including a new Mustang and F-150. Ford is especially proud of offering its Mustang for the first time ever in select markets in Europe and Asia, and the F-150 moving to an aluminum body will save over 700 pounds on weight with the same material strength. Currently, Ford is engaged in its largest manufacturing expansion in over 50 years by increasing capacity in six U.S. plants and by opening two new plants in Asia and one each in South America and Europe. The U.S. plants alone are expected to enjoy $6 billion of improvements. In 2013, Ford sold over 85,000 hybrid or all-electric, plug-in automobiles, up 150 percent from 2012 as the company attempts to produce, as one executive said, a Tesla for the average person. As the average age of cars increases in the United States and abroad, Ford is aggressively launching new or significantly redesigned products. In 2014, Ford introduced 23 new vehicles, up from 11 in 2013, and plans to introduce a 150 percent new product turnover by 2018.

Marketing

Ford is unveiling a slew of new high-performance models, more than 12 new go-fast models coming to market by 2020, including a super-hot new Focus model, the RS. A new high-performance "Raptor" version of its new F-150 pickup could debut, and a new Ford sports car is coming. Fast, sexy sports cars (and trucks) make for great headlines and they help develop loyal customers. Products such as the V8-powered GT version of Ford's Mustang sell well, but higher-performance models are typically niche products. That niche is growing—Ford recently reported that sales of high-performance models have risen 70 percent in the United States since

EXHIBIT 1 Ford's Organizational Structure

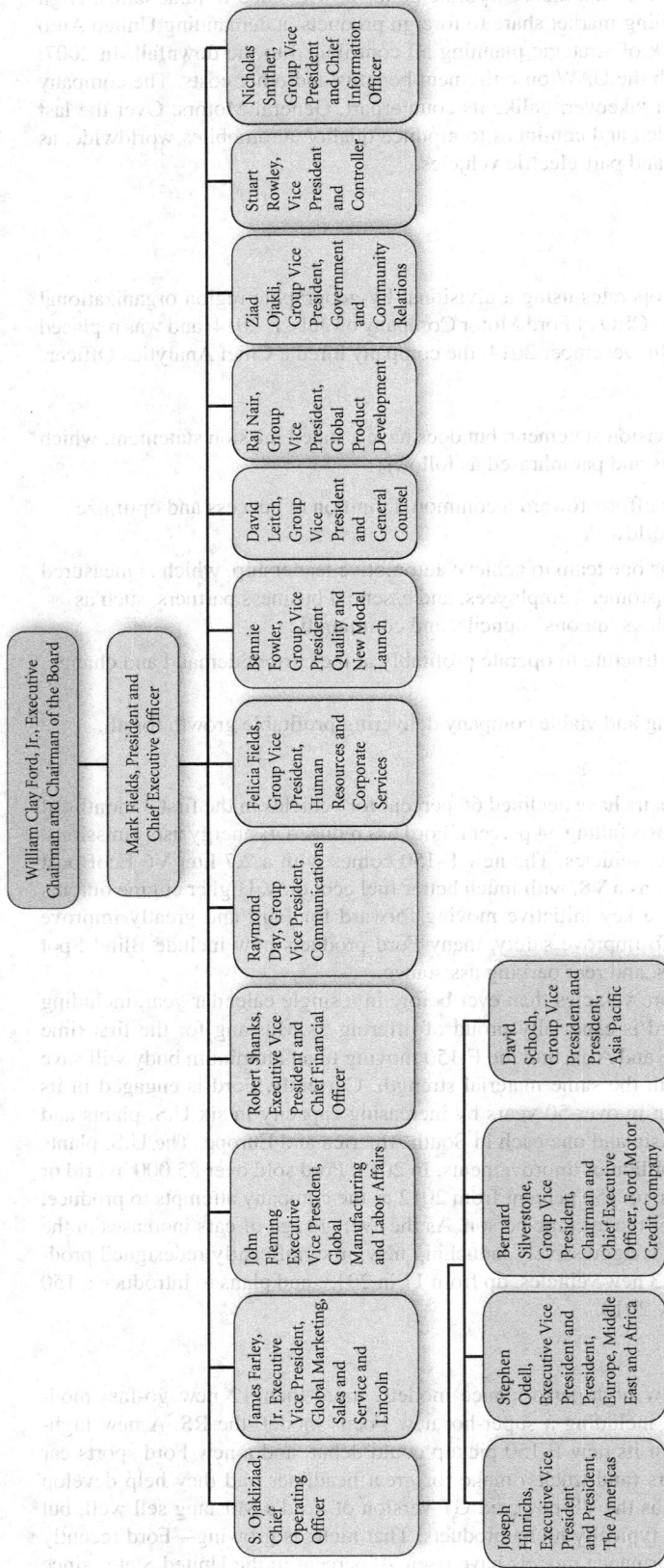

```
                    William Clay Ford, Jr., Executive
                    Chairman and Chairman of the Board

                    Mark Fields, President and
                    Chief Executive Officer
```

- S. Ojakliziad, Chief Operating Officer
- James Farley, Jr. Executive Vice President, Global Marketing, Sales and Service and Lincoln
- John Fleming Executive Vice President, Global Manufacturing and Labor Affairs
- Robert Shanks, Executive Vice President and Chief Financial Officer
- Raymond Day, Group Vice President, Communications
- Felicia Fields, Group Vice President, Human Resources and Corporate Services
- Bennie Fowler, Group Vice President Quality and New Model Launch
- David Leitch, Group Vice President and General Counsel
- Raj Nair, Group Vice President, Global Product Development
- Ziad Ojakli, Group Vice President, Government and Community Relations
- Stuart Rowley, Vice President and Controller
- Nicholas Smither, Group Vice President and Chief Information Officer

- Joseph Hinrichs, Executive Vice President and President, The Americas
- Stephen Odell, Executive Vice President and President, Europe, Middle East and Africa
- Bernard Silverstone, Group Vice President, Chairman and Chief Executive Officer, Ford Motor Credit Company
- David Schoch, Group Vice President and President, Asia Pacific

Source: Based on information in Ford's 2014 *Annual Report.*

2009, and 16 percent in Europe over the same period—but it's still small. High-performance versions of mainstream models generally make up less than 10 percent of the model's total sales. Ford reports that more than 65 percent of those who buy its "hot-hatch" Focus ST and Fiesta ST models are new to the brand, and importantly, often become loyal customers "for life."

Segments

Ford derives approximately 60 percent of its revenues from the United States, Canada, and Mexico. Virtually all the company's profits in 2014 came from these countries; the only other profitable region was Asia. Ford is in the midst of a $400 million restructuring program in Europe and anticipates Europe will become profitable sometime in 2015. South America pretax profits were slightly negative and are expected to remain so the next several years. Brazil and Argentina are the strongest markets, with Venezuela being the weakest major market.

Ford reports revenues by five regions and by process: (1) vehicle sales and (2) financial services. In 2014, Ford reported $136 billion from vehicle sales and $8.2 billion from financial services. Pretax results were just over $2.5 billion, with vehicle sales and financial services accounting for $1.8 billion. It is important to note that Ford's Pretax results were less than half the previous year for total automotive operations. See Exhibit 2.

Finance

Ford's recent income statement and balance sheet are provided in Exhibits 3 and 4, respectively. Note the decline in revenues and the dramatic decline in net income.

EXHIBIT 2 Segment Data for Ford (in millions of USD)

	2014		2013	
	Revenue	Pretax Results	Revenue	Pretax Results
North America	$82,400	$6,898	$86,500	$8,809
South America	10,800	(1,162)	8,800	(33)
Europe	29,500	(1,062)	27,300	(1,442)
Middle East & Africa	4,400	(20)	4,500	(69)
Asia Pacific	10,700	589	10,300	327
Other Automotive	NA	(755)	NA	(656)
Total Automotive minus Special Items	**135,782**	**2,548**	**139,369**	**5,368**
Financial Services	**8,295**	**1,854**	**7,548**	**1,756**

Source: Based on *2014 Quarterly and Full Year Review,* various pages.

EXHIBIT 3 Ford's Income Statement (in millions of USD)

Report Date	December 31, 2014	December 31, 2013
Revenues	$144,077	$146,917
Operating expenses	140,637	141,439
EBIT	3,440	5,478
Interest expense	797	829
Interest & other income	1,699	2,391
EBT	4,342	7,040
Tax	1,156	(135)
Noncontrolling interest	(1)	(7)
Net income	**3,187**	**7,182**

Source: Based on company documents.

EXHIBIT 4 Ford's Balance Sheet (in millions of USD)

Report Date	December 31, 2014	December 31, 2013
Assets		
Cash and equivalents	$10,757	$14,468
Marketable securities	20,393	22,100
Accounts receivable	92,819	87,309
Inventories	7,866	7,708
Total current assets	131,835	131,585
Property, plant & equipment	53,343	47,600
Long-term investments	3,357	3,679
Goodwill & intangibles	—	—
Other assets	19,992	19,315
Total assets	**208,527**	**202,179**
Liabilities		
Accounts payable	20,035	19,531
Total current liabilities	20,035	19,531
Long-term debt	119,171	114,688
Other liabilities	44,174	41,517
Total liabilities	**183,380**	**175,736**
Redeemable noncontrolling interest	342	331
Common stock	40	40
Retained earnings	24,556	23,386
Treasury stock	(848)	(505)
Pension & retirement losses and other	(20,032)	(18,231)
Paid in capital and other	21,089	21,422
Total equity	**24,805**	**26,112**
Total liabilities & equity	**208,527**	**202,179**

Source: Based on company documents.

Competitors

Competition in the automobile manufacturing business is intense among Ford, GM, Toyota, BMW, Honda, Volkswagen, Hyundai-Kia, Nissan, Mercedes, and several other firms. About 75 percent of all revenue goes to purchase raw materials, so the industry is affected substantially by prices of steel, rubber, aluminum, and other raw materials. Wages, the second-largest expense, historically have been about $70,000 per employee in the United States and account for 5 percent of total revenue expenses. Higher commodity prices and wage expenses forced GM and Chrysler into Chapter 11 bankruptcies toward the end of the economic recession. However, labor expenses were reduced after labor unions agreed to concessions.

Competition among competing models of vehicles and competing firms primarily boils down to price, fuel economy, reliability, and utility. Business customers tend to focus on utility, whether it is a construction company that needs heavy trucks or a pharmaceutical business that provides cars to its salespeople. Most consumers, however, are more focused with styling and price, but there are many exceptions and subsets of each population.

The industry is experiencing increased globalization. Firms like Ford are offering new products in existing markets and expanding into new markets. Many Japanese manufacturers are gaining market share in the United States. There are high barriers to entry, which discourages new companies from trying to enter the industry.

Exhibit 5 shows the largest automakers in the world. Other notable firms were Fiat Chrysler, BMW, Daimler, and Mazda. Although no Chinese automaker is ranked in the top 10, from 13th to

EXHIBIT 5 Top Five Automobile Manufactures based on 2014 Units Sold (10 months data, in thousands)

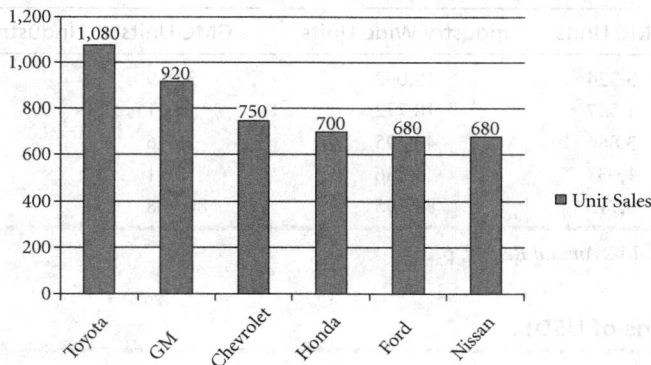

Source: Consolidated and adapted from SP Net Advantage Table.

EXHIBIT 6 Ford versus Rival Firms

	Ford	GM	Toyota
# Employees	187,000	216,000	339,000
$ Net Income	3,187 M	3,949 M	17,703 M
$ Revenue	144,007 M	155,929 M	249,472 M
$ Revenue/Employee	770,000	721,893	735,906
$ EPS Ratio	0.80	1.65	10.71
Market Cap.	63.4 B	60.8 B	213 B

Source: A variety of sources.

30th, there are 10 Chinese firms represented. Exhibit 6 provides a synopsis comparison between Ford, GM, and Toyota.

General Motors (GM) Company

Headquartered in Detroit, Michigan, GM is the largest American car manufacturing company, ranking second behind Toyota in revenues and units of vehicles sold annually. GM brands include GMC, Chevrolet, Buick, Cadillac, Opel, Wuling, Jie Fang, and Alpheon, among many others. General Motors also holds stakes in and has joint ventures with firms in Korea and China. GM is investing heavily in its electric vehicle line, which totaled 7 vehicles in 2013, and has partnered with Honda to work on hydrogen cell technologies, with a 2020 timeframe for selling vehicles.

General Motors owns OnStar, which serves 6.5 million customers across North America with an assortment of services, including alerting First Responders to your location in an accident, as well as offering driving directions. With a new application for smartphones, OnStar can reveal your tire pressure, fuel levels, and even start your car remotely.

Exhibit 7 reveals GM unit sales across world markets. Europe remains a laggard in the world vehicle market, experiencing reduced sales for both Ford and GM. South America, while enjoying an increase in industrywide sales, reported fewer unit sales of GM vehicles in 2013.

Toyota Motor Corporation

Headquartered in Aichi, Japan, with U.S. headquarters based in Torrance, California, Toyota is the largest automaker in the world in terms of revenues, and one of the largest in the U.S. market. Toyota sells vehicles in over 170 different nations and generated $214 billion in revenues over all operating segments in 2013. Popular vehicles sold in the United States include Lexus, Camry,

EXHIBIT 7 GM Segment Data (in units sold in thousands)

	2013		2012	
	GMC Units	Industry Wide Units	GMC Units	Industry Wide Units
North America	3,324	19,092	3,019	17,847
Europe	1,557	18,772	1,611	18,983
Asia/Pacific, Middle East, Africa	3,886	40,795	3,616	38,229
South America	1,037	5,936	1,051	5,849
World Wide	9,715	84,595	80,908	9,297

Source: Based on information in the 2013 GMC *Annual Report,* p. 3.

EXHIBIT 8 Toyota Segment Data (in millions of USD)

Geographic Region	2013		2012	
	Revenue	Operating Income	Revenue	Operating Income
Japan	$106,414	$4,784	$92,689	($1,718)
North America	52,161	1,842	39,441	1,547
Europe	17,290	220	16,550	148
Asia	36,399	3,121	27,674	2,131
Other	17,382	1,110	14,609	903
Intersegment elimination	(46,514)	(113)	(36,719)	(59)
Totals	183,133	10,963	154,244	2,952

Source: Based on Toyota's 2013 *Annual Report,* p. 35. (Exchange rate conversion, December 2014)

Corolla, Avalon, Rav4, 4Runner, Land Cruiser, Tacoma, Tundra, Prius, and many others, including several mini-vans.

Exhibit 8 presents the segment data for Toyota based on geographic region. It is interesting to note that revenues were up 18 percent in 2013 but operating income was up 275 percent over the same time period. In particular, operating revenues in Japan increased substantially. Toyota reported increased sales in Europe over the same time frame when both Ford and GM had losses in Europe.

Hyundai-Kia
Headquartered in Seoul, South Korea, Hyundai-Kia is the second-largest automaker in Asia and the fourth largest in the world. The firm operates the single-largest automobile manufacturing plant in the world, in Uslan, South Korea, producing over 1.5 million vehicles annually. Hyundai has become the fastest-growing automaker in the world. With extended warranties common, Hyundai has gained loyalty and significantly increased its U.S. market share. The company reported revenues in 2014 of $8.4 billion. Popular cars include the Sonata, Santa Fe, Accent, Tucson, and the Rio and Optima by Kia.

External Issues

Vehicle Variety in the USA
Exhibit 9 reveals the percent of revenue of various classes of vehicle. Cross-over utility vehicles have taken much of the demand away from SUVs, which account for only 10 percent of total U.S. market share. These vehicles look much like an SUV, but are built on car chasses and lack the towing power of an SUV. They also tend to get much better gas mileage, as automakers started applying hybrid technology to cross-overs before SUVs. Notable SUVs include the Ford Flex, Toyota Venza, and Dodge Journey. The Ford Explorer has recently been shifted to become more of a SUV style along with several other popular SUV models.

EXHIBIT 9 Breakdown on Market Share of Vehicles in the USA

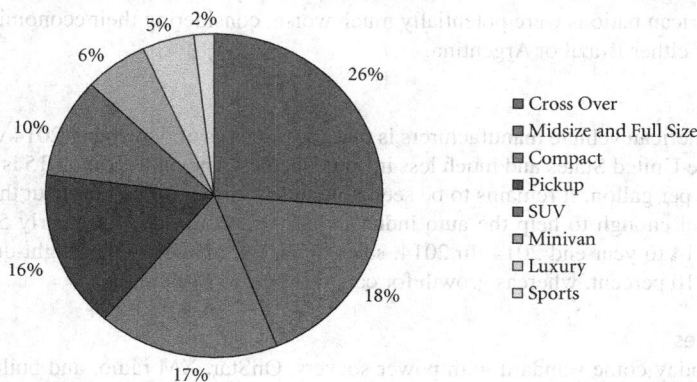

- ■ Cross Over — 26%
- ■ Midsize and Full Size — 18%
- ■ Compact — 17%
- ■ Pickup — 16%
- ■ SUV — 10%
- ■ Minivan — 6%
- □ Luxury — 5%
- □ Sports — 2%

Source: Adapted and consolidated from various IBIS reports.

The next most popular style of vehicle in the United States is compact cars. Popular products in this line include the Ford Focus, Chevrolet Cruze, and the Toyota Corolla, and can start around $17,000. Smaller cars also popular include the Ford Fiesta and the Chevrolet Sonic which can start as low as $15,000. Many of these products are four-cylinders with some having the option of six cylinders. Midsize cars are also extremely popular, taking much of the market share away from larger vehicles. The Ford Fusion, Chevy Malibu, Dodge Charger, and Toyota Camry are examples of midsize vehicles. Full-size vehicles start around $30,000 with the Ford Taurus and Chevy Impala being two of the more popular options. Pickup trucks remain popular in the United States, with the F-150 the best seller in its class. Smaller size trucks such as the GMC Canyon or Chevy Colorado are not as popular as the full-size trucks. Ford's 150 and 250, GMC's Sierra, Chevy's Silverado, Toyota's Tundra, and Dodge's Ram are all popular and dominate the U.S. truck market.

Mini-vans were once super-popular because they were considered much more sporty than a station wagon; however, mini-vans and full-size vans have experienced declining sales. This line of vehicles is most popular among taxi companies and families with kids. Luxury cars account for 5 percent of the total U.S. market share; popular brands include BMW, Lexus, Cadillac, Mercedes, and several others. Sports cars account for only 2 percent of total U.S. market share; they include cars such as the Mustang, Camaro, Dodge Charger, and Corvette.

International Vehicle Market

In 2013, China became the first country to have over 20 million vehicle deliveries in a single year, with 22 million units. As of late 2014, Chinese vehicle sales were up 8 percent over the record year in 2013. In total, China enjoyed a 28 percent share as compared to the U.S. 17.5 percent share in global vehicle sales in 2013; China expects to increase its global market share lead. China will continue to put pressure on U.S., European, and Japanese automakers as new Chinese-based auto companies are formed and grow to prominence. However, it is important to note that Ford did experience a 22 percent growth in China in 2013 (partly due to its relatively small 5 percent Chinese market share) and GM and Volkswagen each have 15 percent market share in China. Therefore, the large U.S. and European players are expected be a factor for many years to come, even in China. Demand in India has been slow, with a 3 percent decline in 2014.

Europe is starting to stabilize economically, although the euro continues to decline, losing 25 percent of its value to the dollar between 2008 and 2014, putting further pressure on U.S. car manufacturers. Ford has especially experienced difficulties in Europe recently with pretax losses in both 2013 and 2012. Ford's European sales were estimated to be up 8 percent in 2014, showing improvement in the region even though Ford is expected to once again lose money in Europe in 2014. General Motors also has lost money in Europe in recent years. France remains the real laggard in western Europe with less than 2 percent vehicle sales growth. Eastern Europe exceeded a 9 percent decline and Russia nearly a 13 percent decline over 2013.

As a whole, South America experienced nearly 14 percent decline in automobile sales, with Brazil and Argentina each accounting for around a 13 percent decline in sales. Sales in other South American nations were potentially much worse, considering their economies are not nearly the size of either Brazil or Argentina.

Fuel Prices

A positive for American vehicle manufacturers is that gas prices as of November 2014 were averaging $2.92 in the United States and much less in some locales. The outlook in 2015 is for gas to remain below $3 per gallon. It remains to be seen how much further oil can fall, but the existing drop is substantial enough to help the auto industry in 2015. Oil prices fell nearly 50 percent from summer 2014 to year-end 2014. In 2014, sales of SUVs, mini-vans, and light-duty trucks increased nearly 10 percent, whereas growth for cars was below 2 percent.

High-Tech Vehicles

Many vehicles today come standard with power sockets, OnStar, XM radio, and built in Wi-Fi hotspots. These numerous extra features are all sources of profit for automakers. GM even has plans to introduce a self-driving Cadillac model in 2017, and Google claims to be in this business. Proponents of self-driving cars indicate they are safer and will save $1.3 trillion annually in the United States, along with fuel savings and fewer accidents. In addition, over $500 billion can be saved each year in productivity gains as people can work while commuting—if the driver can take his or her mind off the road completely.

Recalls and Fines

Vehicle recalls in the United States hit 22 million in 2013, a 9-year high. Hit especially hard by the recalls were Toyota, Chrysler, and Honda, accounting for 24, 21, and 13 percent of all recalls, respectively. Ford, BMW, Toyota, and several other vehicle manufacturers are recalling products containing airbags manufactured by Takata Corporation after five deaths were linked to them. As of October 2014, a class-action suit has been filed in U.S. court against Takata and several unstated automobile manufacturers. Recalls continued their upward trend in 2014 as well, resulting in billion-dollar penalties, including a $1.2 billion penalty on Toyota in 2014. Through only half of 2014, recalls were up 70 percent over the total recall amounts in all of 2013.

Access to Vehicle Loans

As of August 2014, the total balance on auto loans in the United States was $924 billion, an all-time high, and up 11 percent from the previous year. In addition, the number of delinquent auto loans has been falling, and are expected to continue to do so through 2015. Rates are slowly going up and currently are around 4.5 percent for new cars and 8.8 percent for used cars as of 2014. The lower rates and easy access to loans has been great for automakers. The average car price in 2008 was $25,000; in 2014, the average was over $33,000. Also, a strong used-car market has helped new car sells as well.

Production in North America

As wage differences around the world shrink, there is increasing attractiveness to locate manufacturing facilities back in the United States and Mexico. Factories are closer to the market, which reduces shipping costs and there is more control over operations. In 2013, GM committed to invest $16 billion in the United States over the next 3 years and Ford planned to invest $6 billion. Kia recently spent $1.5 billion in Mexico and another $10 billion is expected to be spent in Mexico from BMW, Toyota, and Daimler AG.

Future

In early 2015, Ford started production of two new engines—the 2.0-liter and 2.3-liter EcoBoost engines—for its plant in Cleveland. The 2.0-liter engine will be available in the Ford Edge. The 2.3-liter engine will be available in the Ford Mustang, Ford Explorer, and Lincoln MKC. However, for the most recent month (February 2015) available at the time this case was written, Ford reported a 1.9 percent decline in sales in the United States to 180,383 units. Ford brand's sales fell 1.7 percent to 174,219 units in the month, and Lincoln brands dropped 7.5 percent to

6,164 units. All total for the month, sales of Ford cars and utility vehicles fell 8.1 and 2.3 percent to 56,081 and 54,420 units, respectively. However, Ford's truck sales increased 4 percent, led by a 24.6 and 18.7 surge in sales of the Transit Connect and heavy trucks, respectively. Retail sales of the F-series fell 1.2 percent in February. Even Ford's two most popular two vehicles, the Focus and the Fusion, recorded a year-over-year decline in sales. The Ford Escape reported a 9.6 decline in sales for the month. A bright spot was the Ford Explorer had a 31.8 percent surge in sales in February 2015. Ford Mustang was the company's only car that reported higher sales during the month, increasing 31.9 percent to 8,454 units in February, making it the Mustang's best February sales since 2007. Since the launch of the new Mustang model, it has been the highest-selling sports car in America. But overall in February 2015, compared to the prior year period, Ford shareholders were not pleased with all the declines. Develop a 3-year strategic plan for Ford's new CEO, Mr. Mark Fields.

Bayerische Motoren Werke (BMW) Group, 2013

www.bmwgroup.com, BMW.DE

Headquartered in Munich, Bavaria, Germany, BMW Group is a world famous German automobile-, motorcycle-, and engine-manufacturing company. In June 2012, BMW was listed in *Forbes* magazine as the number-one most reputable company in the world. Rankings were based on aspects such as "people's willingness to buy, recommend, work for, and invest in a company." The rankings were based 60 percent on public perceptions of the company and 40 on public perceptions of their products.

BMW owns and produces the Mini marque and is the parent company of Rolls-Royce Motor Cars. BMW produces motorcycles under the Motorrad and Husqvarna brands led by the K 1200 GT, R 1200 RT, and F 800 S models. BMW Group operates 29 production and assembly facilities in 14 countries and has a global dealer network in more than 140 countries. BMW's premium lineup includes sedans, coupés, convertibles, and sport wagons in the 1, 3, 5, 6, and 7 Series, as well as the M3 coupe and convertible, the X5 sport active, and the Z4 roadster. BMW has a profitable financial services segment that provides purchase financing and leasing, asset management, dealer financing, and corporate fleets. About 3,000 dealers worldwide sell BMWs.

In calendar year 2012, BMW Group sold 1.85 million cars and nearly 117,000 motorcycles worldwide, the highest annual total ever for the company and an increase of 10.6 percent over the previous record year in 2011. BMW sales in the month of January 2013 were the highest ever in a January for the company; sales grew 11.5 percent to 107,276 units and it was the first time that more than 100,000 BMW vehicles were delivered worldwide to customers in that month.

In early 2013, BMW Group and Toyota Motor Corporation extended their long-term collaboration agreement for the joint development of a fuel-cell system, joint development of architecture and components for a sports vehicle, joint research and development of lightweight technologies, and collaborative research on lithium-air batteries with a post-lithium-battery solution. BMW Group had a workforce of approximately 105,000 employees.

BMW Group reported the best-ever May 2013 sales with 166,397 BMW, MINI, and Rolls-Royce automobiles delivered to customers worldwide, up 5.8 percent from the previous May. BMW Motorrad also had a successful May 2013 with sales up 14.2 percent to 13,081 vehicles delivered. However, in August 2013, BMW customers around the world were complaining intensely about not being able to obtain spare parts for their BMW. The world's biggest maker of luxury cars, BMW has struggled from June to September 2013 to ship components on time because of a new supply-management system being introduced in its central warehouse in Germany. BMW's 40 parts-distribution centers originate at the main warehouse in Dingolfing that also directly supplies about 300 repair shops in Germany. Raimund Nestler—who lives in Ingolstadt, Germany, the home base of rival Audi AG (NSU)—has been waiting six weeks for a new part that controls engine speed. "I have always been a die-hard BMW driver and am currently driving my seventh BMW, but will consider which brand I'll buy the next time," he said by phone. "For a premium carmaker like BMW, this is particularly disappointing." BMW's stock has declined 2.5 percent in 2013 through August, valuing the company at 45.7 billion euros ($61 billion).

Copyright by Fred David Books LLC. (Written by Forest R. David)

History

BMW was established in 1917 following a restructuring of the Rapp Motorenwerke aircraft manufacturing company. At the end of World War I, BMW was forced to cease aircraft engine production by the terms of the Versailles Armistice Treaty. The company shifted to motorcycle production in 1923 and once the restrictions of the treaty started to be lifted, began producing automobiles in 1928–1929. The first car produced by BMW was the Dixi, a vehicle whose design was based on the Austin 7, from the Austin Motor Company in Birmingham, England.

BMW's circular blue and white logo, or roundel, evolved from the circular Rapp Motorenwerke logo, but as BMW grew, that emblem was combined with the blue and white colors of the flag of Bavaria. The BMW logo has also been portrayed as the movement of an aircraft propeller with the white blades cutting through a blue sky—first used in a BMW advertisement in 1929, 12 years after the roundel was created.

BMW's first significant aircraft engine was the BMW IIIa inline-six liquid-cooled engine of 1918, much preferred for its high-altitude World War I performance. With German rearmament in the 1930s, the company again began producing aircraft engines for the Luftwaffe. Especially successful World War II aircraft engines were the BMW 132 and BMW 801 air-cooled radial engine, and eventually the BMW 003 axial-flow turbojet that powered Germany's 1944- and 1945-era jets, such as the Heinkel He 162 and eventually the Messerschmitt Me 262.

After outselling Lexus in 2011 and 2012, BMW and Mercedes are vying to be the top luxury auto brand in the USA. Lexus was the top-selling luxury car brand in the USA from 1999 to 2010. Sales of the Toyota Lexus rose 32 percent to 16,211 in January 2013, led by the ES sedan, which more than doubled to 5,186 deliveries.

Internal Issues

Year 2012

In calendar year 2012, BMW sales rose 11.6 percent to 1,540,085 vehicles, the best sales level in the history of the company. Success was led by the highly successful BMW 1 Series, with a total of 226,829 vehicles sold in 2012, an increase of 28.6 percent over the previous year. The BMW X1 also did great in 2012 with a total of 147,776 vehicles sold, up 16.9 percent over the prior year. The BMW 3 Series Sedan did best with 294,039 vehicles delivered, an increase of 22.4 percent over 2011. Sales of the BMW X3 grew 27.1 percent to 149,853 units sold, whereas the BMW 5 Series reported that 337,929 vehicles were delivered to customers in 2012, up 9.0 percent from the prior year. Even sales of the BMW 6 Series grew 146.8 percent, with 23,193 vehicles being delivered to customers.

Also for 2012, global sales of the BMW MINI were a record 301,526 vehicles, up 5.8 percent. The USA remained the largest market for the MINI, with a record-breaking 66,123 cars sold in 2012, followed by the United Kingdom, with 50,367 cars sold. In the ultra-luxury-class segment, Rolls-Royce sales for the full year 2012 reached record sales result of 3,575 motor cars, the highest annual sales in the 108-year history of Rolls-Royce and the third consecutive record.

Additionally, a record total of 106,358 BMW Motorrad motorcycles were sold in 2012.

Organizational Structure

BMW operates using an autocratic, functional structure with no apparent Chief Executive Officer or Chief Operations Officer and divisional presidents. As indicated in Exhibit 1, if executives with these titles exist, they are neither listed on the corporate website nor in the *Annual Report*.

EXHIBIT 1 BMW's Organizational Structure

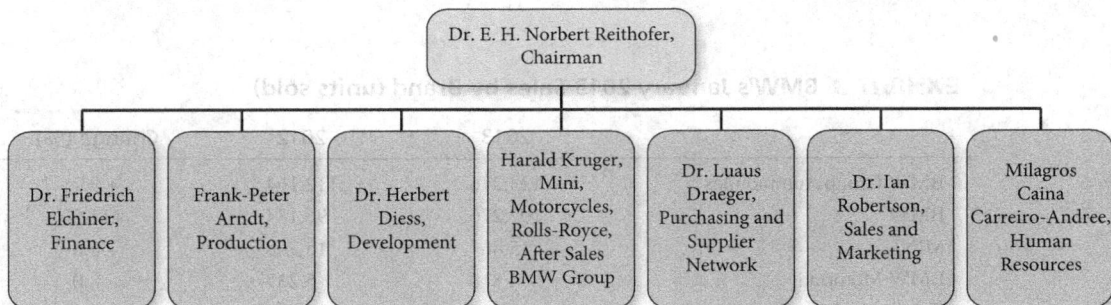

Source: Based on company documents

Segments

BMW reports their revenues by region and by brand and is doing exceptionally well in all regions and brands. For example, BMW reported its strongest January ever as sales climbed 11.5 percent to 107,276 units for January 2013, the first time ever that more than 100,000 BMW vehicles were delivered worldwide to customers in a January. There were 29,053 BMW 3 Series sold, up 27.9 percent, as well as 11,753 BMW X1 vehicles sold, up 57.8 percent. The BMW X3 continued to be popular with 10,230 vehicles delivered to customers, up 9.4 percent. Sales of the BMW 1 Series were up 8.8 percent to 14,222 units sold, and the BMW 5 Series sales grew 6.4 percent to 23,049. Sales of the BMW 6 Series grew 22.4 percent to 1,354 units. Also in January 2013, worldwide sales of the MINI reached 15,864 vehicles, up 0.6 percent, which was a new all-time high for any January ever.

As indicated in Exhibits 2 and 3, BMW's sales in January 2013 increased in all regions and all brands, except Motorrad motorcycles. Despite BMW's record January 2013, rival Audi (owned by Volkswagen AG) beat BMW in 2013 luxury-car market January sales, propelled by a 39-percent jump in Audi deliveries in China, its biggest national market. Audi sold 111,750 cars and sport utility vehicles (SUVs) worldwide in January, a 16-percent increase from a year prior, compared to BMW brand's 12-percent gain to 107,276 deliveries. Global sales at Mercedes (owned by Daimler AG) rose 9 percent in January 2013 to 94,895 vehicles, helped by demand for the A- and B-class compacts and its SUV line-up.

Exhibit 4 reveals BMW's 2012 year-end segment data by region for automobiles. Note the 2.8 percent decline in motorcycle revenues, and the decline in United Kingdom revenues.

EXHIBIT 2 BMW's January 2013 Sales by Region (units sold)

	2013	2012	Change (%)
Asia	43,114	36,422	+ 18.4
China	30,397	26,505	+ 14.7
Japan	3,250	—	+ 19.0
South Korea	2,790	—	+ 32.9
Americas	25,021	24,419	+ 2.5
United States	20,195	19,739	+ 2.3
Europe	50,594	46,831	+ 8.0
Germany	18,709	17,028	+ 9.9
Russia	2,311	1,653	+ 39.8
Africa*	37,649	32,890	+ 14.5
Oceania*	23,000	21,297	+ 8.0

*For all of 2012
Source: Based on company documents.

EXHIBIT 3 BMW's January 2013 Sales by Brand (units sold)

	2013	2012	Change (%)
BMW Group Automobiles	123,276	112,164	+ 9.9
BMW	107,276	96,184	+11.5
MINI	15,864	15,768	+ 0.6
BMW Motorrad	4,818	5,237	− 8.0
Husquarna Motorcycles	587	544	+ 7.9

Source: Based on company documents.

EXHIBIT 4 BMW's Revenues By Segment

Revenues in € million	2012	2011
Automobiles	50,165	46,681
Motorcycles	980	1,008
Other revenues	7,660	7,318
	58,805	55,007
Germany	11,974	12,494
United Kingdom	4,059	4,061
Rest of Europe	12,303	12,766
North America	12,991	10,903
Asia	14,436	12,042
Other markets	3,042	2,741
	58,805	55,007

Source: Company documents.

Finance

Exhibit 5 shows the income statement for BMW Group.

EXHIBIT 5 BMW's Income Statements

(in € million)	2012	2011
Revenues	58,805	55,007
Cost of sales	−46,252	−43,320
Gross profit	**12,553**	**11,687**
Selling expenses	−3,684	−3,381
Administrative expenses	−1,701	−1,410
Research and development expenses	−3,573	−3,045
Other operating income and expenses	703	670
Result on investments	598	181
Financial result	−99	−665
Profit from ordinary activities	**4,797**	**4,037**
Extraordinary income	—	29
Income taxes	−1,635	−2,073
Other taxes	−31	−23
Net profit	**3,131**	**1,970**
Transfer to revenue reserves	−1,491	−462
Unappropriated profit available for distribution	**1,640**	**1,508**

Source: Company documents

EXHIBIT 6 BMW's Balance Sheets

(in € million)	2012	2011
Assets		
Intangible assets	178	161
Property, plant and equipment	7,806	6,679
Investments	3,094	2,823
Tangible, intangible and investment assets	**11,078**	**9,663**

(continued)

EXHIBIT 6 Continued

(in € million)	2012	2011
Inventories	3,749	3,755
Trade receivables	858	729
Receivables from subsidiaries	6,297	5,827
Other receivables and other assets	2,061	1,479
Marketable securities	2,514	3,028
Cash and cash equivalents	4,618	2,864
Current assets	**20,097**	**17,682**
Prepayments	118	120
Surplus of pension and similar plan assets over liabilities	672	43
Total assets	**31,965**	**27,508**
Equity and liabilities		
Subscribed capital	656	655
Capital reserves	2,053	2,035
Revenue reserves	5,515	4,024
Unappropriated profit available for distribution	1,640	1,508
Equity	**9,864**	**8,222**
Registered profit-sharing certificates	32	32
Pension provisions	56	84
Other provisions	7,406	7,651
Provisions	**7,462**	**7,735**
Liabilities to banks	1,408	911
Trade payables	3,900	2,940
Liabilities to subsidiaries	8,451	6,923
Other liabilities	800	741
Liabilities	**14,559**	**11,515**
Deferred income	48	4
Total equity and liabilities	**31,965**	**27,508**

Source: Based on company documents.

Competitors

The combined sales for Toyota's Lexus, Daimler's Mercedes-Benz, BMW, Honda's Acura, GM's Cadillac, Volkswagen's Audi, and Nissan's Infiniti, which are the seven best-selling luxury brands automobiles in the world, rose 15 percent in the USA in 2012 through November. Growth in sales of luxury vehicles exceeds growth in all other automobile categories, and these brands are fiercely competitive globally.

Exhibit 7 provides a financial summary of leading luxury-car manufacturers. Note that BMW is the smallest firm in terms of number of employees, but it has the second highest earnings per share (EPS).

Volkswagen

Headquartered in Wolfsburg, Lower Saxony, Germany, Volkswagen (VW) is the largest German automobile manufacturer and the second- or third-largest automaker in the world behind GM or Toyota. The word *volkswagen* means "people's car" in German and is pronounced *folks wagen*. VW aims to double its U.S. market share from 2 percent to 4 percent by 2014 and aims to be the world's largest carmaker by 2018. VW introduced diesel-electric hybrid versions of its most popular models in 2012, including the Jetta, followed by the Golf Hybrid and the Passat. VW also owns Porsche.

Mercedes-Benz

Headquartered in Stuttgart, Baden-Wuttemberg, Germany, Mercedes-Benz is a division of the German automobile manufacturer Daimler AG. Mercedes-Benz is active in three forms of motorsport racing: Formula Three, DTM, and Formula One. The parent, Daimler AG, holds

EXHIBIT 7 A Financial Comparison of BMW with Rival Firms (in U.S. dollars)

	BMW	VW	Daimler	GM	Toyota	Nissan
Revenue ($)	76.1B	251B	153B	151B	243B	102B
Net Income ($)	5.1B	30B	7.5B	4.5B	8.3B	3.3B
Profit Margin (%)	6.65	11.9	4.9	3.0	3.4	3.2
Debt-to-Equity Ratio	1.47	1.24	1.85	0.40	1.15	1.45
EPS ($)	7.27	12.82	7.03	2.67	2.60	0.79
Number of Employees	106K	549K	275K	213K	325K	157K
Revenue per Employee ($)	717K	457K	556K	708K	747K	680K

EPS, earnings per share.
Source: Based on company information.

a 60 percent stake in Formula One team Mercedes-Benz Grand Prix, as well as a 22 percent stake in aerospace and defense consortium EADS. Daimler sells its vehicles in 40 countries, but Europe represents 40 percent of its sales.

Mercedes-Benz's U.S. sales surged 11 percent in January 2013, in its effort to overtake BMW in luxury-auto deliveries for all of 2013. Mercedes sold 22,501 vehicles in January 2013, its best January ever, and helped the C-Class sedan's 11 percent climb to 7,214 units sold. In comparison, sales for BMW increased 0.7 percent to 16,513 units, boosted by a 56 percent gain for its X5 SUV.

Toyota Motor Corporation

Headquartered in Toyota, Aichi, Japan, Toyota runs neck and neck with GM as the largest automobile company in the world. Toyota's U.S. operations are headquartered in Torrence, California. Popular Toyota models include the Camry, Corolla, Land Cruiser, and Lexus, as well as the Tundra truck. The Lexus competes directly with BMW. Lexus sales were up 23 percent in the USA in 2012 through November and are expected to gain at least 10 percent in 2013.

Volvo Car Corporation

Headquartered in Gothenburg, Sweden, Volvo, or *Volvo Personvagnar AB*, is owned by Zhejiang Geely Holding Group China, headquartered in Hangzhou, China. Geely acquired Volvo in 2010 from Ford Motor Company. Volvo manufactures and markets a wide range of vehicles, some that compete with BMW. With approximately 2,300 local dealers from around 100 national sales companies worldwide, Volvo's largest markets are the USA, Sweden, China, Germany, the United Kingdom, and Belgium. In 2011, Volvo recorded global sales of 449,255 cars, an increase of 20.3 percent compared to 2010. In 2012, Volvo signed NBA star Jeremy Lin to an endorsement agreement. Over the next two years Lin will participate in Volvo's corporate and marketing activities as a "brand ambassador" for Volvo.

Audi

Headquartered in Ingolstadt, Bavaria, Germany, Audi Aktiengesellschaft (Audi) designs, engineers, manufactures, and markets automobiles and motorcycles. Audi-branded vehicles are produced in seven production facilities worldwide. AUDI AG has been a majority owned (99.55 percent) subsidiary of VW since 1966. In September 2012, Audi began construction of its first North American manufacturing plant in Puebla, Mexico, expected to be operative in 2016 and produce the successor to the Q5.

In 2012, Audi again won the 24 Hours of Le Mans, a historic first Le Mans victory for a hybrid, which was captured by Audi's R18 e-tron quattro. Audi's other R18 hybrid took second, whereas R18 ultras took third and fifth. This sports car racing success followed Audi R18's victory at the 2011 24 Hours of Le Mans. The Audis finished in front of three Peugeot 908s by 13.8 seconds to claim victory.

Audi offers a computerized control system for its cars, called multimedia interface (MMI). This advancement came amid criticism of BMW's iDrive control, a rotating control knob and "segment" buttons—designed to control all in-car entertainment devices (radio, CD changer, iPod, TV tuner), satellite navigation, heating and ventilation, and other car controls with a screen. Some believe MMI is a considerable improvement on BMW's iDrive, although BMW has since improved their iDrive.

Business Culture in Germany

Germany survived the 2008 recession in good position thanks to their strong economy and manufacturing base. Unemployment in Germany is lower now than it was in 2008. German companies are generally run by individuals specializing in various technical areas. For example, a car company is more likely to be run by an expert mechanical engineer in Germany than an expert accountant or finance individual. This technical nature often extends down the chain of command for other key positions as well. For example, responsibility is often delegated to another technically sound individual, who then expects his or her manager to leave them alone to perform the task with little oversight. People from other cultures often view this approach as distant and cold. In addition, socializing is much more common at the peer level than up or down the hierarchy in Germany.

Meetings in Germany generally start on time with all members in attendance having well researched any aspects of the meeting that touch on their area of expertise. It is often assumed by people outside Germany that "German businesspeople have their minds made up before the meeting even starts," but this is not the case. Germans take a sense of pride in their subject matter and want to be as well prepared as possible, so they can contribute and make key points during the meeting. During a meeting, it is expected that individuals will contribute when the discussion touches on their area of expertise. This is an overriding theme in German business, where well-prepared specialists are groomed and preferred to generalists. This line of thinking also extends into teamwork in Germany. Each team member answers to the leader, but each tends to focus on his or her individual technical task, with little overlapping conversations, at least in technical nature, with other team members.

Communication in Germany tends to be direct and to the point. Supervisors tend not to sugarcoat their reviews or requirements for subordinates, instead informing them in direct words their performance reviews, expectations, and so forth. In addition, when interviewing a German worker for a job, they will tend to describe in clear terms what they are capable of doing, rather than speaking in vague terms like in other cultures. German workers tend not to oversell themselves in an interview; if they claim they are capable of a task, you can generally bet they are capable.

Dress in Germany is professional but not as clearly defined as in the United Kingdom, USA, or many Asian nations. Women often wear dress pants, rather than dresses or skirts, and men often wear sport jackets, as opposed to black or blue suits. Despite having a woman president as leader of Germany, women in Germany still lag behind women in other European nations in securing top-level management opportunities, partly because women are not majoring in the technical fields as commonly as men; senior-level jobs generally go to individuals heavily trained in key technical areas.

The Future

China overtook the USA in 2012 as BMW's biggest international market, with the company's sales in China rising 14 percent to 28,597 automobiles and motorcycles. "Looking ahead, we expect the headwinds in Europe to remain," said Ian Robertson, BMW's head of sales and marketing. "However, we are confident of healthy sales growth in other regions, especially Asia and the Americas."

BMW borrowed a new retail concept from Apple stores, which was tested in the United Kingdom, by rolling out its version on the Apple "Genius Bar" across Europe. The iPad-equipped, specially trained "BMW Genius Everywhere" staff will give customers information about vehicles and features, but they will not sell cars. The new BMW employees wear a white polo shirt that says "BMW Genius," but they are paid a salary, not a commission on sales. A pilot program for the "BMW Genius Everywhere" program began in the USA in late 2013, with a full launch by early 2014, which is when the new BMW i3 electric car is set to go on sale.

Exxon Mobil Corporation, 2013

www.exxonmobil.com, XOM

Headquartered in Irving, Texas, ExxonMobil is by some measures the largest corporation in the world. ExxonMobil produces and markets crude oil, natural gas, petroleum products, chemicals, plastics, and much more under brand names that include Exxon, Mobil, Esso, and in Canada, Imperial Oil. Exxon produces about 6.3 million barrels of oil daily by operating more than 37,000 oil wells in 21 different countries, but the firm also has huge interests in electric power generation. With more than 77,000 employees worldwide, ExxonMobil has annual revenues of about $500 billion. In 2012, Apache Corp. acquired ExxonMobil's North Sea Limited assets including the Beryl field. Exxon has ownership interests in 32 refineries in 17 countries.

In August 2013, ExxonMobil released its estimated second quarter 2013 results saying its total revenues and other income would be down 16.4 percent year-over-year to $106.5 billion; the company's Q2 2013 net income will be down 56.9 percent to $6.9 billion. Weaker refining margins and volumes associated with planned refinery turnaround and maintenance activities negatively impacted the company's Downstream earnings.

Copyright by Fred David Books LLC. (Written by Forest R. David)

History

ExxonMobil began when John D. Rockefeller's Standard Oil was established in 1870. The name Standard was used to denote high, uniform quality. The federal government forced Standard Oil to separate into 34 companies in 1911, and two of these companies eventually became Exxon and Mobil. The Mobil Oil trademark was first used in 1920 when gasoline eclipsed kerosene production because the automobile industry was growing. In 1972, Jersey Standard changed its name to Exxon Corporation. The worst company accident in Exxon's history occurred on March 24, 1989, when the tanker Exxon Valdez ran aground in Prince William Sound in Alaska.

Exxon acquired Mobil in 1998 for $73.7 billion and formed a new corporation called Exxon Mobil Corporation. The merger reunited the two largest companies of Rockefeller's Standard Oil after nearly a century of operating independently. In 2005, ExxonMobil passed General Electric as the largest company in the world based on market capitalization and reported record profits of $36 billion the same year, up 42 percent from 2004. ExxonMobil announced in 2008 plans to transition out of company-owned gas stations, but the brand names Exxon and Mobil are still be used by operators, who compensate ExxonMobil for use of its name. A complete, elaborate interactive history of ExxonMobil is provided on the corporate website.

Internal Issues

Vision and Mission

Exxon does not report a mission or vision statement, but the company has a statement of guiding principles:

> Exxon Mobil Corporation is committed to being the world's premier petroleum and petrochemical company. To that end, we must continuously achieve superior financial and operating results while simultaneously adhering to high ethical standards.

Organizational Structure

ExxonMobil appears to operate from a strategic business unit (SBU) organizational structure, with the groups being Upstream, Downstream, Chemical, and Other. Upstream is the term that refers to the search, recovery, and production of crude oil and natural gas, also commonly called *oil exploration*. Underground and underwater drilling for oil and gas is an upstream activity. Downstream operations include the refining, selling, and distribution of natural gas and products derived from crude oil such as gasoline, diesel, asphalt, plastics, antifreeze, and by-products such as sulfur. There are literally thousands of products that derive from oil that the consumer can purchase in retail stores.

As indicated in Exhibit 1, there apparently is no chief operations officer (COO) or chief accounting officer (CAO) in the Exxon hierarchy, nor an SBU head for each group. In addition, note that ExxonMobil has virtually zero women, Hispanics, or African Americans among its top corporate executives. Perhaps that is why the company's *Form 10K* lists executives' names only by first and middle initials, rather than providing first names, which would more clearly reveal the lack of diversity.

Exxon Oil Spills

Exxon has had several notable spills over its history with the worst being the Exxon Valdez, an oil tanker that spilled more than 11 million gallons of crude oil into Prince William Sound, Alaska. The spill resulted in Congress passing the Oil Pollution Act of 1990 and initially rewarded $5 billion of punitive damages, although that amount was later reduced. Exxon endured criticism to its slow response time to the spill and the use of single-hull ships. As of 2009, Exxon still employed more single-hull oil tankers than the next 10 largest oil companies combined. In 2007, there was a major Exxon oil spill in Brooklyn, New York, that spilled 17 to 30 million gallons of petroleum. In 2011, Exxon was responsible for a spill in the Yellowstone River that leaked up to 40,000 gallons of oil before the refinery was shut down. In 2012, a crude pipeline in Baton Rouge, Louisiana, burst and spilled around 80,000 gallons into the nearby rivers and creeks.

Environmental Record

Exxon's Sakhalin-I oil and gas project in eastern Russia has been claimed by scientists to threaten the western gray whale population, and they have called for a moratorium on all oil activities in the area. Scientists claimed Exxon's activities discouraged the whales in their summer and fall feeding areas and sighted a decline in whales as evidence. Similarly, Exxon's Alaskan pipeline is oftentimes criticized for possibly harming migration routes of Alaskan animals, especially caribou. Exxon also endures criticism at times regarding its impact on global warming and climate change. ExxonMobil was recently accused of paying for TV advertisements and programs that generate skepticism that global warming is principally the result of greenhouse gasses caused by burning of coal and petroleum-based fuels. *Mother Jones Magazine* says Exxon has paid more than $8 million to 40 different organizations that challenge the scientific evidence of global warming. Exxon was a member of the Global Climate Coalition, a skeptic group on the possible destructive nature of greenhouse gasses.

Segments

The oil and gas industry is commonly divided into two segments: (1) upstream and (2) downstream. Exhibit 2 reveals ExxonMobil's earnings broken down by source and geographic location. Note that the vast majority of Exxon's earnings derive from upstream processes outside the USA.

Upstream

ExxonMobil's upstream business accounted for 67 percent of all earnings after tax in 2012, down from 84 percent from 2011. Exxon continues to expand its diverse portfolio in this segment through global exploration, development, production, and marketing activities. Between now and 2016, oil and natural gas output in North America is expected to increase dramatically. About 30 percent of Exxon's production comes from North America, but by 2016 this number is expected to grow to 35 percent. Arctic technology, deepwater drilling, and oil sands recovery are expected to grow from 45 percent to 50 percent also by 2016. Melting of the Artic ice cap as a result of global warming is spurring additional drilling as well as rising disputes among Russia, Canada, and the USA regarding even ownership of new "unfrozen" areas.

In 2013, ExxonMobil and its partners began developing the Herbron oil field offshore of Newfoundland on Canada's east coast. The gravity-based structure used is expected to cost $14 billion and to recover 700 million barrels of oil or 150,000 barrels per day. Production is expected to begin toward the end of 2017. Exxon operates the Herbron facility but controls only

EXHIBIT 1 Exxon's Organizational Structure

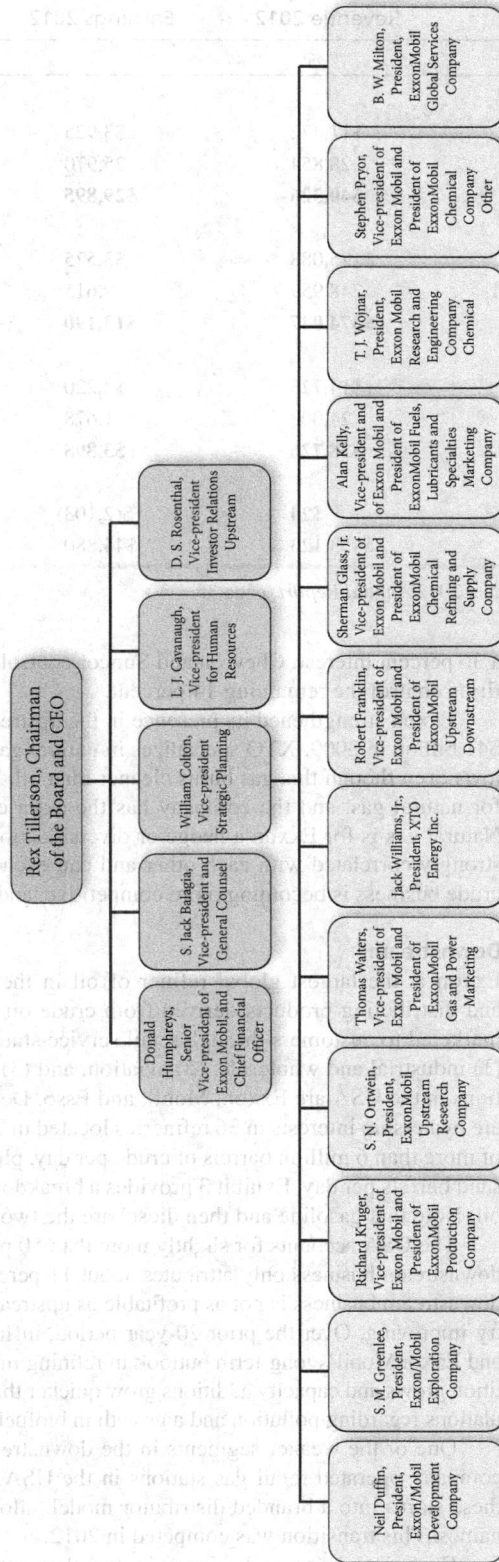

Rex Tillerson, Chairman of the Board and CEO

- Donald Humphreys, Senior Vice-president of Exxon Mobil and Chief Financial Officer
- S. Jack Balagia, Vice-president and General Counsel
- William Colton, Vice-president Strategic Planning
- L. J. Cavanaugh, Vice-president for Human Resources
- D. S. Rosenthal, Vice-president Investor Relations Upstream

Reporting units:

- Neil Duffin, President, Exxon/Mobil Development Company
- S. M. Greenlee, President, Exxon/Mobil Exploration Company
- Richard Kruger, Vice-president of Exxon Mobil and President of ExxonMobil Production Company
- S. N. Ortwein, President, ExxonMobil Upstream Research Company
- Thomas Walters, Vice-president of Exxon Mobil and President of ExxonMobil Gas and Power Marketing
- Jack Williams, Jr., President, XTO Energy Inc.
- Robert Franklin, Vice-president of Exxon Mobil and President of ExxonMobil Upstream Downstream
- Sherman Glass, Jr. Vice-president of Exxon Mobil and President of ExxonMobil Chemical Refining and Supply Company
- Alan Kelly, Vice-president and of Exxon Mobil and President of ExxonMobil Fuels, Lubricants and Specialties Marketing Company
- T. J. Wojnar, President, Exxon Mobil Research and Engineering Company Chemical
- Stephen Pryor, Vice-president of Exxon Mobil and President of ExxonMobil Chemical Company Other
- B. W. Milton, President, ExxonMobil Global Services Company

Source: Based on company information.

EXHIBIT 2 ExxonMobil's Earnings by Segment

Segment	Revenue 2012	Earnings 2012	Earnings After Tax (in millions)	
			2011	2010
Upstream				
United States	$11,472	$3,925	$5,096	$4,272
Non-United States	28,854	25,970	29,343	19,825
Total	**$40,326**	**$29,895**	**$34,439**	**$24,097**
Downstream				
United States	$125,088	$3,575	$2,268	$770
Non-United States	248,959	9,615	2,191	2,797
Total	**$374,047**	**$13,190**	**$4,459**	**$3,567**
Chemical				
United States	$14,723	$2,220	$2,215	$2,422
Non-United States	24,003	1,678	2,168	2,491
Total	**$38,726**	**$3,898**	**$4,383**	**$4,913**
Corporate and Financing				
Total	$24	$(2,103)	$(2,221)	$(2,117)
Total	**$453,123**	**$44,880**	**$41,060**	**$30,460**

Source: Based on company information at 2012 *Annual Report*, page 35.

a 36 percent interest. Chevron and Suncor control 27 and 23 percent respectively, and two other firms control the remaining 14 percent.

Exxon strengthened its presence in the upstream area with the purchase of XTO Energy for $41 billion in 2009. XTO specializes in natural gas, but natural gas prices have fallen to historic lows even though this gas burns cleaner than oil. Exxon forecasts a long-term growing demand for natural gas, and the company has the extra cash to withstand the lower prices at present. Natural gas is for Exxon a hedge or diversification away from crude because the prices are not strongly correlated with each other and can even trade opposite of each other. In addition, the crude business is becoming more competitive, and there is an increased difficulty in finding oil.

Downstream

Exxon is the largest global refiner of oil in the world with downstream operations refining and distributing products derived from crude oil to customers around the world. Products are marketed to customers through retail service stations and three business-to-business segments: (1) industrial and wholesale, (2) aviation, and (3) marine. Three of Exxon's largest service stations in the USA are Exxon, Mobil, and Esso. Delivering Exxon Mobil's downstream revenues are ownership interests in 36 refineries located in 21 countries that contain a distillation capacity of more than 6 million barrels of crude per day, plus a lubricant base stock capacity of 131 thousand barrels per day. Exhibit 3 provides a breakdown of how Exxon Mobil uses a barrel of crude oil. Note that gasoline and then diesel are the two largest uses.

The USA accounts for slightly more than 50 percent of Exxon's earnings, and Exxon's entire downstream business only attributes about 11 percent of companywide earnings. The company's downstream business is not as profitable as upstream operations even with the downstream industry improving. Over the prior 20-year period, inflation-adjusted refining margins have been flat, and ExxonMobil's long-term outlook in refining margins will likely remain weak because competition grows and capacity additions grow quicker than global demand. Increased governmental regulations regarding pollution and a growth in biofuels also hinder growth in the refining business.

One of the weaker segments in the downstream industry for ExxonMobil is its dealer and company operated retail gas stations in the USA. Starting in 2008, Exxon began transitioning these stores into a branded distributor model, allowing distributors to use the Exxon and Mobil names. This transition was competed in 2012.

Exxon's lubricants business in the downstream market continues to grow, and Exxon is the current market leader in high value synthetic lubricants in many key markets such as

EXHIBIT 3 How Exxon Uses a Barrel of Crude Oil

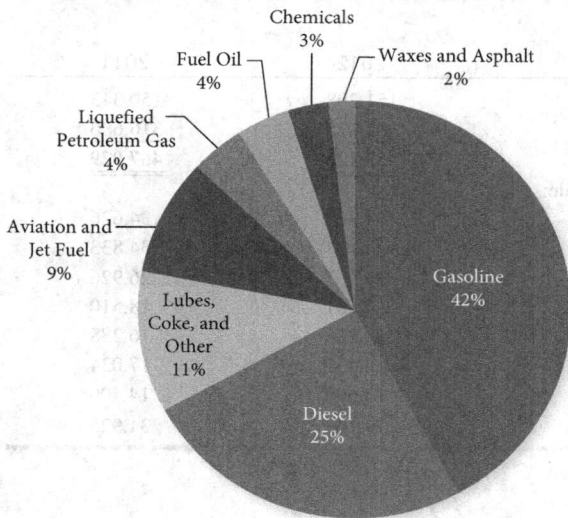

Source: Data from company website

China, India, and Russia. Despite the success in lubricants, overall the downstream business remains weak, and Exxon recently divested their downstream businesses in Argentina, Uruguay, Paraguay, Central America, Malaysia, and Switzerland. In 2012, Exxon announced restructuring of their downstream holdings in Japan.

Exxon is nearing completion of new units and improvements of existing facilities in Thailand to refine lower sulfur diesel and gasoline to meet new Thailand specifications. New plans are also in the construction phase in Singapore, Saudi Arabia, and China.

Chemical

ExxonMobil is one of the largest petrochemical companies in the world, providing materials for use in products including plastic bottles, synthetic rubber, solvents, and countless other goods. The company is the largest global manufacturer of paraxylene and benzene. Exxon is also a large producer of ethylene and propylene which, like many of the chemicals Exxon produces, are considered feedstock, meaning they are the basic ingredients used to help produce many of the products we use today such as different fuels, fibers, packaging film, automotive parts, and more. ExxonMobil's chemical business experienced modest demand growth in 2011, but its overall chemical earnings after tax declined 11 percent in 2011 from the prior year. Exxon in 2012 completed construction of its Singapore petrochemical project.

Finance

Note in the income statements provided in Exhibit 5 that the company's revenues and profits are increasing nicely.

Geographic

ExxonMobil also reports revenues by country. Note in Exhibit 4 that about 66 percent of company revenues are made outside the USA.

Note in the balance sheets provided in Exhibit 5 that Exxon has zero goodwill, which is excellent.

Competitors

ExxonMobil ranks third on the S&P Global Oil Industry Classification Standard, behind Saudi Aramco of Saudi Arabia and National Iran Oil Company (NIOC). ExxonMobil sells more than $6.4 million barrels a day, far more than the Saudi and Iran state-owned operations that dominate in reserves. However, Saudi Aramco controls liquid reserves of 24 times that of ExxonMobil and

EXHIBIT 4 ExxonMobil's Revenues by Region (in millions)

Geographic

Sales and other operating revenue	2012	2011
United States	151,298	150,343
Non-U.S.	301,825	316,686
Total	**453,123**	**467,029**
Significant non-U.S. revenue sources include:		
Canada	34,325	34,626
United Kingdom	34,134	34,833
Belgium	23,567	26,926
France	19,601	18,510
Italy	18,228	16,288
Germany	16,451	17,034
Singapore	14,606	14,400
Japan	14,162	31,925

Source: 2012 *Annual Report*, p. 122.

EXHIBIT 5 ExxonMobil's Recent Income Statements (000,000 omitted)

	2012	2011
Revenues and other income		
Sales and other operating revenue	453,123	467,029
Income from equity affiliates	15,010	15,289
Other income	14,162	4,111
Total revenues and other income	**482,295**	**486,429**
Costs and other deductions		
Crude oil and product purchases	265,149	266,534
Production and manufacturing expenses	38,521	40,268
Selling, general and administrative expenses	13,877	14,983
Depreciation and depletion	15,888	15,583
Exploration expenses, including dry holes	1,840	2,081
Interest expense	327	247
Sales-based taxes	32,409	33,503
Other taxes and duties	35,558	39,973
Total costs and other deductions	**403,569**	**413,172**
Income before income taxes	78,726	73,257
Income taxes	31,045	31,051
Net income including noncontrolling interests	47,681	42,206
Net income attributable to noncontrolling interests	2,801	1,146
Net income attributable to ExxonMobil	**44,880**	**41,060**
Earnings per common share (dollars)	**9.70**	**8.43**

Source: 2012 *Annual Report*, p. 61.

has gas reserves 3.6 times greater. Iran-based and state-owned NIOC controls 14 times the liquid reserves and 15 times the gas reserves than ExxonMobil controls.

Acquisitions and joint ventures are common in the oil industry. Notable recent acquisitions include CNOOC Canada paying $19 billion for Nexen, Energy Transfer Partners paying $8.7 billion for Sunoco, several firms purchasing EP Energy for $8 billion, and 16 other purchases with each totaling over $1.5 billion, all in 2012 alone.

ExxonMobil is the top refiner in the world and has a significant edge on both Saudi Aramco and NIOC on refining. In 2011, ExxonMobil refined 5.8 million barrels per day, Royal Dutch

Petroleum refined 4.1 million, Sinopec refined 3.9 billion, and BP refined 3.3 billion. Saudi Aramco was 10th and NIOC was 14th. The results are not surprising because the USA alone controls approximately 19 percent of the world's refineries, whereas Saudi Arabia and Iran control around 1 percent each. For comparison, China has 8 percent of the world's refineries and Russia and Japan control 6 and 4.5 percent, respectively.

Exhibit 6 provides a financial comparison of ExxonMobil with two competitors, BP and Chevron. Other large publically-traded competitors include Royal Dutch Shell, Eni SpA, Total S.A., and ConocoPhillips. Note in Exhibit 7 that Exxon generates more revenue per employee than BP or Chevron.

EXHIBIT 6 ExxonMobil's Balance Sheets (in millions)

	Dec. 31, 2012
Assets	
Current assets	
Cash and cash equivalents	9,582
Cash and cash equivalents—restricted	341
Notes and accounts receivable, less estimated doubtful amounts	34,987
Inventories	
Crude oil, products and merchandise	10,836
Materials and supplies	3,706
Other current assets	5,008
Total current assets	**64,460**
Investments, advances and long-term receivables	34,718
Property, plant and equipment, at cost, less accumulated depreciation and depletion	226,949
Other assets, including intangibles, net	7,668
Total assets	**333,795**
Liabilities	
Current liabilities	
Notes and loans payable	3,653
Accounts payable and accrued liabilities	50,728
Income taxes payable	9,758
Total current liabilities	**64,139**
Long-term debt	7,928
Postretirement benefits reserves	25,267
Deferred income tax liabilities	37,570
Long-term obligations to equity companies	3,555
Other long-term obligations	23,676
Total liabilities	**162,135**
Commitments and contingencies	
Equity	
Common stock without par value (9,000 million shares authorized, 8,019 million shares issued)	9,653
Earnings reinvested	365,727
Accumulated other comprehensive income	(12,184)
Common stock held in treasury (3,517 million shares in 2012 and 3,285 million shares in 2011)	(197,333)
ExxonMobil share of equity	165,863
Noncontrolling interests	5,797
Total equity	**171,660**
Total liabilities and equity	**333,795**

Source: 2012 *Annual Report*, p. 84.

EXHIBIT 7 Comparing ExxonMobil to BP and Chevron

	ExxonMobil	BP	Chevron
Number of employees	82,000	83,000	61,000
Revenue ($)	$488	$381	$241
Net Income ($)	$44	$17.6	$24
Net Profit Margin	9.64%	4.70%	10%
Revenue ($)/Employee	$5.9 M	$4.6 M	$3.9 M
EPS	$9.47	$5.51	$12.19
Market Capitalization	403 B	138 B	213 B
Shares Outstanding	4.56 B	3.19 B	1.96 B

EPS, earnings per share.
Source: Based on company documents.

Royal Dutch Shell

Headquartered in the Netherlands, Royal Dutch Shell plc (Shell) is a huge oil and gas producer and marketer and also has interests in chemicals and other energy-related businesses. Shell operates in three segments: (1) Upstream, (2) Downstream, and (3) Corporate. Shell has a market capitalization above $220 billion, a P/E ratio of 8, and a dividend yield of 5.3 percent. Shell's stock price has increased 18 percent since 2010. However, Shell's third quarter in 2012 cash flow from operations dropped 18 percent year-over-year. Through the first nine months of 2012, Shell's income dropped 18 percent, although the company raised its dividend by 2 percent.

Eni

Headquartered in Italy, Eni SpA is a large oil and gas company that operates under seven segments: (1) refining and marketing focuses on refining and marketing of petroleum products; (2) trading covers group services in commodity trading, shipping, and derivatives; (3) petrochemicals covers the production and sale of petrochemical products; (4) engineering and construction includes the services for the oil and gas industry; (5) exploration and production focuses on exploration, development and production of oil and natural gas; (6) gas and power covers the supply, regasification, transport, storage, distribution, and marketing of natural gas, power generation, and electricity sales; (7) other activities handles the corporate, financial, and service components. Eni sells oil and gas in 85 countries and operates numerous subsidiaries and affiliates in Nigeria, Poland, and Germany, among others.

Eni has a market value of $90 billion and trades at a P/E ratio of slightly greater than 9 with a dividend yield of about 4.5 percent. Eni's stock price recently rebounded to a 52-week high of $50 per share, after plunging to $37 during the summer of 2012. For the first nine months of 2012, Eni's operating profit was up nearly 14 percent versus the same period in 2011, and its oil and natural gas production was up 8 percent. Eni's new licenses in Liberia and its expanded presence in Asia is spurring growth.

ConocoPhillips

Headquartered in Houston, Texas, Conoco explores for, produces, transports, and markets crude oil, natural gas, natural gas liquids, liquefied natural gas, and bitumen on a worldwide basis. In May 2012, the company separated into two stand-alone, publicly traded corporations, (1) Upstream and (2) Downstream. All the firm's midstream, downstream, marketing, and chemical operations were separated into a new company named Phillips 66. As a result, ConocoPhillips continued its operations as an exploration and production company.

In April 2012, ConocoPhillips sold its Trainer Refinery to Monroe Energy LLC. As of January 1, 2012, Conoco conducted exploration activities in 19 countries and produced hydrocarbons in 13 countries, with proved reserves located in 15 countries. The company's production averaged 1.57 million billion barrels of oil equivalent (BOE) per day for the nine months ending on September 30, 2012, and proved reserves were 8.4 BOE. In August 2012, Conoco closed a transaction with LUKOIL for the sale of ConocoPhillips's indirect 30 percent interest in NaryanMarNefteGaz (NMNG).

Total S.A.

Headquartered in France, Total S.A. is a huge oil and gas company with operations in more than 130 countries, Total engages in all aspects of the petroleum industry, including (1) Upstream operations (oil and gas exploration, development and production, liquefied natural gas [LNG]) and (2) Downstream operations (refining, marketing, and the trading and shipping of crude oil and petroleum products). It also produces base chemicals (petrochemicals and fertilizers) and specialty chemicals for the industrial and consumer markets. Total has interests in coal mining and power generation and is active in solar-photovoltaic power, both in Upstream and Downstream activities. Total has subsidiaries, including Elf Aquitaine, Total Venezuela, Total E&P Nigeria SAS, and Total E&P USA, Inc., among others. For the first half of 2012, Total's sales increased 10 percent and cash flow from operations increased 6 percent year-over-year (as measured in euros). Return on equity for the first six months of the year was 17.5 percent. Total is executing on new initiatives in Thailand, the Norwegian Sea, and Italy, which should drive future production growth.

Chevron

Headquartered in San Ramon, California, and the second-largest U.S. oil company by market capitalization (behind ExxonMobil), Chevron in December 2012 reported that its upstream operations oil and natural gas production averaged 2.662 million BOE per day, 0.8 percent above the fourth quarter in 2011 level. Production for the fourth quarter in 2012 was up by about 5.8 percent from the third quarter of 2012. In the first two months of the fourth quarter, Chevron's total domestic oil production rose 39,000 barrels per day from third-quarter levels, primarily as a result of volume gains from its recently acquired Permian Basin (Texas) assets. Net international oil production was 1,986,000 barrels per day, up 107,000 barrels from the third quarter in 2012. The upsurge was driven by the completion of planned repair work in Kazakhstan and the United Kingdom.

Regarding Chevron's downstream operations, its U.S. refinery crude input fell 77,000 barrels per day, affected largely by the shutdown of its Richmond, California, refinery crude unit after a fire in August. Refinery crude-input volumes outside the USA was up slightly by 9,000 barrels per day.

In 2013, Chevron discovered two new offshore natural gas sites, Pinhoe-1 and Arnhem-1, in Western Australia's Carnarvon Basin. The discoveries, the 18th and 19th by Chevron off the Australian coast since mid-2009, adds to Chevron's leading position in this area. Drilled to a total depth of 13,396 feet (4,083 meters), the Pinhoe-1 well encountered 197 feet (60 meters) of net gas pay. The find is situated in the WA-383-P permit area, approximately 124 miles (200 kilometers) north of Exmouth Plateau area of the Carnarvon Basin. Similarly, the Arnhem-1 discovery—that lies in the WA-364-P permit area, roughly 180 miles (290 kilometers) north of Exmouth—was drilled to a total depth of 9,557 feet (2913 meters). The well came across 149 feet (45.5 meters) of net gas pay. Chevron Australia has a 50-percent operated interest in both the prospects, with the other partner being the subsidiary of Royal Dutch Shell Plc.

External Issues

The world's population is expected to grow to 8.7 billion by 2040, an increase of 28 percent from today's population and accompanied by an economic growth rate of about 3 percent per year. Energy demand is expected to increase about 35 percent by 2040. However, with increasingly energy-efficient technologies, energy consumption per unit is expected to decrease. For example, by 2040, energy for cars, trucks, ships, trains, and airplanes is likely to increase only around 45 percent. Liquid fuel is still expected to be the fuel of choice to power the world's transportation fleets by 2040.

Natural gas demand is expected to enjoy larger gains and the largest market share percent gain by 2040, although geothermal, solar, and wind may eclipse in percent gain but they are not significant players. Once thought of as unprofitable to collect, many natural gas sources found in shale and other rock formations will help supply demand for this product. Coal, despite environmental concerns, is expected to continue to be the leading choice of power generation for a number of years, but it could lose its status as the number-2 source of energy to natural gas by 2025. Nuclear power and renewables, such as wind, geothermal, and solar, are also expected to grow in their use over the next 30 years. The demand for electricity globally will increase 85 percent by 2040, while the demand for natural gas increases 65 percent.

Energy Prices

Energy prices tend to be highly volatile and are expected to continue their volatile nature in the future. Economic problems in Europe, the USA, and other areas resulted in the price of oil falling to as low as $78 dollars a barrel in May 2012, but then that price increased to more than $100 by year-end 2012. Crude demand in the USA, which accounts for 21 percent of global demand, declined around 2.6 percent in the first half of 2012. Demand in Europe, which accounts for 16 percent of the world's use of oil, has declined as well. China, the world's second largest consumer of oil, reported in mid-2012 the slowest growth for oil in more than 20 months.

For ExxonMobil, a $1 change in the price of oil produces a weighted average effect of $350 million in annual after-tax earnings on upstream production. A $0.10 change in gas would have a $200 million annual after-tax effect on upstream production. Some of the cited concerns for the current volatility in the price of oil include the USA, Europe, and China offering extra stimulus packages to spur the economy; sanctions on Iran, which has threatened to close the Strait of Hormuz where 20 percent of the world's petroleum is shipped; concerns about Iran and Israel's geopolitical relationship; and reduced production concerns in the North Sea. The Organization of the Petroleum Exporting Countries (OPEC), which accounts for nearly 80 percent of the world's oil reserves, has kept production unchanged recently, but Saudi Arabia is trying to negate the impact or the embargo on Iran by increasing its own output. Possibly reducing some oil volatility in the future is the fact that the largest non-OPEC area currently is in onshore shale in the USA and Canada along with traditional drilling in North America. Given the current price of oil, extracting oil from shale sand remains expensive and produces lower margins than traditional drilling, but this problem is fading as increased technologies emerge and oil and gas prices resume their upward trends.

Unconventional Fuel Sources

Accessing so-called unconventional resources such as shale, rock, and sands for oil was impracticable for years because of lower demand and unprofitable because of lower oil prices and the expense of extracting the product. However, with increasing demand, rising oil prices, improved technology, and competition for traditional oil fields, tapping such energy sources is a new avenue for growth among petroleum companies today. One of the largest sources of this energy is in North America, with natural gas being derived at a high rate in recent years that current prices of gas have plummeted as a result of oversupply. Many firms have engaged in mergers and acquisitions for shale, with Exxon's acquisition of XTO energy being a notable example. Currently however, with the low prices for natural gas, many companies are drilling the same shale, rock, and sands areas for liquid oil instead of natural gas.

Notable hotbeds for exploration include the Eagle Ford, Bakken, and Permian Basin. Eagle Ford is located in south Texas and is considered the hottest area in North America producing higher liquid content than traditional shale. Competition in Eagle Ford remains high with Norway's Statioil ASA, India's Reliance Industries, and China National Offshore Oil Corp. all entered with billion-dollar deals in 2011. As of 2012, there were 211 rigs operating in Eagle Ford.

Located in Montana, North Dakota, and Saskatchewan, the Bakken Shale formation is the second-most concentrated shale region in North America. The U.S. Geologic Survey estimates the region is capable of producing up to 4.3 billion barrels of oil. Companies such as Hess and Marathon are increasing their presence in the region. As of 2012, there were 160 active rigs in the Bakken formation.

The Canadian oil sands have also been economically feasible in recent years and could potentially make Canada one of the world's largest oil producers. French-based Total SA has invested $3 billion in the Athabasca oil sands in Alberta, and Devon Energy and BP have a joint venture to develop properties in the region. Sinopec and China National Offshore also have invested in the area with Sinopec investing more than $8 billion alone to acquire rights to sand deposits.

U.S. Natural Gas

Recent discoveries and advances in drilling and hydraulic fracturing are making natural gas drilling in North America increasingly assessable. If technologies developed in the United States can be applied to shale, rock, and oil sands in Europe and Asia, the results would be revolutionary. Developments in the USA include Exxon's acquisition of XTO Energy and Chevron's merger with Atlas Energy to acquire Atlas's Marcellus Shale holdings in the Appalachian Basin.

Natural gas exposes companies to less public backlash than conventional fuel options such as coal, gasoline, and diesel because it is a clean-burning low-carbon fuel.

OPEC

The largest single player in the oil market is OPEC, controlling 73 percent of the world's oil reserves. As of 2012, OPEC maintained its output level of 30 million barrels a day, helping to fix the price of oil for consumers around the world. Member nations have been quite compliant in sticking to the agreed-on output levels over the last few years, but as the price of oil has increased, compliance dropped from 83 to 80 percent. Analysts expect member nations to violate their agreements and produce more oil than agreed on, thus tempering the price appreciation of a barrel of oil. The top five OPEC nations in order of oil reserves are (1) Venezuela, (2) Saudi Arabia, (3) Iran, (4) Iraq, and (5) Kuwait. Venezuela controls approximately 25 percent of OPEC's oil, whereas Saudi Arabia controls 22 percent. All other nations control less than 13 percent each.

U.S. Refining

The USA leads the world with 125 of the world's 655 refineries, but the trend is toward fewer but larger refineries as a result of competition and the economies of scale the larger refineries offer. In 1981, considered the peak of the refining business, there were 324 refineries in the USA. This downstream product is less profitable than upstream operations, so many firms including Exxon are attempting to reduce their exposure to this market.

Argentina Reserves

In South America, everybody knows about Venezuela with Hugo Chavez and the country's Orinoco Valley. Many people also know about the numerous discoveries during the past five years in Brazil's prolific deepwater Santos Basin. However, Argentina is South America's largest natural gas producer and its oil production registers something less than 750,000 barrels per day (or about a third of Venezuela's output). ExxonMobil and Chevron of late have been excitedly pursuing shale-drilling opportunities in Argentina's Neuquen Basin. The Basin's Vaca Muerta (dead cow) shale is fast gaining worldwide attention. Including Vaca Muerta's 23 billion BOE, Argentina likely holds the world's third-largest deposits of shale gas, behind only the USA and China.

Of all the energy companies involved in Argentina, Apache is the largest with that company owning about 3.7 million acres and being active in the country's four primary producing basins: Neuquen, Austral, Cuyo, and Noroeste. But in late 2012, Chevron reached an agreement with Argentina's nationalized oil company YPF to form a $1 billion partnership to develop shale oil reserves in the Vaca Muerta. YPF is also holding talks with Norway's Statoil for the development of Argentinean properties.

The Future

ExxonMobil just acquired Plano, Texas-based Denbury Resources' Bakken Shale assets in North Dakota and Montana for $1.3 billion, along with property in Wyoming and Texas. The company now controls 50 percent of the Bakken Shale region.

A number of analysts contend that Exxon should spin-off its refining business because the refining and production business are at odds with each other; oil-refining companies look to buy oil at the lowest possible cost while production companies look to sell oil at the highest possible cost. ConocoPhillips and Marathon Oil Corp. (MRO) recently separated their refining operations into separate companies.

Exxon is trying to sell its stake in the giant southern oilfield in Iraq after clashing with the central government in Baghdad over exploration contracts it had signed with the autonomous Kurdistan region in the north. The CNPC unit of Petrochina is currently negotiating for Exxon's 60 percent in the $50 billion West Qurna-1 project. Iraq has the world's fourth-largest oil reserves and wants to at least double its production in the next few years, and ultimately challenge Russia and Saudi Arabia as the world's biggest oil nation. Exxon's departure would all but wipe out the U.S. presence in Iraq's southern oilfields. Occidental Petroleum has a small stake in the Zubair oilfield development project. Prepare a three-year strategic plan for ExxonMobil's CEO Rex Tillerson.

Embraer S.A., 2013

www.embraer.com, (Sao Paulo Stock Exchange and ticker ERJ on NYSE)

Headquartered in Sao Jose dos Campos, Brazil, Embraer specializes in developing and manufacturing civilian and military aircraft as well as providing aeronautical services. Embraer has more than 18,032 full-time workers (16,325 in Brazil) and more than $15 billion worth of aircraft on back order. One of the largest aerospace firms in the world, Embraer has carved its niche on what many airline companies are calling "right-sized" aircraft. To date, Embraer commercial jets are produced with seating options generally between 70 and 124 seats on the E-Jets and 37 to 50 passengers on the ERJ jets. By producing quality jets, sized right at affordable prices, Embraer is one of the largest exporting firms in Brazil. Both Delta and JetBlue use Embraer jets to shuttle passengers between New York, Boston, Atlanta, Washington, and similarly distanced locations. Since 1969, Embraer has delivered more than 5,000 aircraft to airlines or militaries in more than 100 countries on five continents. In mid-2013, SkyWest places an order for 200 Embraer 175 aircraft worth about $4.1 billion to begin being delivered in Q2 of 2014. SkyWest is headquartered in Utah and is the largest regional airline in the world operating such companies as United Express, USAir Express, Delta Connection, American Eagle, and ExpressJet.

On 8-27-13, RBC Capital Markets published an initiation report on Embraer S.A. (ERJ) with a stock price target of $42. Embraer had last traded in New York at $33.37, representing a 25 percent upside. There were two main reasons for RBC's Buy recommendation. First, RBC projected strong demand for regional jets and Embraer has been gaining market share from rival Bombardier, from 29 percent in 2003 to 76 percent in 2013. RBC forecasted a 17 percent year-on-year Embraer earnings growth in 2014. Second, Embraer at the time was trading at a 20 percent discount compared to rival firms, even though the company reported the second fastest earnings growth at 14.3 percent for 2012–2015 (estimated), versus its commercial aircraft rival firms at 6.1 percent and its defense peers at 1.2 percent.

Copyright by Fred David Books LLC. (Written by Forest R. David)

History

Embraer was founded in 1969 as a state-owned civilian and military aviation company known at the time as Empresa Brasileira de Aeronautica. Brazil's Aeronautics Ministry signed a contract for the purchase of 80 Bandeirante aircraft that were produced in a hanger capable of producing two planes per month with a workforce of 500 employees. After growing during the 1970s, Empresa Brasileria de Aernonautica obtained an office in Florida and formed a subsidiary named the Embraer Aircraft Company to better serve the U.S. market. In 1983, the company started Embraer Aviation International in Paris to better serve European markets and markets in the Middle East and Africa. Despite growth, macroeconomic conditions and the burden of being state-run culminated in the company struggling and facing possible bankruptcy by 1990. To avoid bankruptcy, and to cash in on revenues received from the demand for smaller aircraft in the early 1990s, the company was privatized in 1994 with a handful of financial institutions acquiring ownership in the company. The company name was also officially changed to Embraer S.A. in 1994.

After rapid growth for 15 years, Embraer opened its first plant in the USA in Melbourne, Florida, in 2011. The hanger was 7,500 square feet and designed for final assembly and included a modern paint booth. Also in 2011, Embraer's Defense and Security segment backward integrated by purchasing 64 percent of the shares of OrbiSat da Amazonia SA's radar division and created Harpia Sistemas SA to focus on unmanned aerial vehicles research. Embraer holds a 51 percent stake in Harpia with AEL Sistemas owning the remaining 49 percent.

In January 2013, Embraer and Republic Airways Holdings Inc., operator of the largest E-jets fleet in the world, revealed a contract for the sale of 47 embraer 175 jets, with options for an additional 47 aircraft, providing a potential for 94 E175s, which could reach a total value of approximately U.S. $4 billion, in 2013 economic conditions, at list price. The new aircraft will be operated by Republic Airlines, a Republic subsidiary, under the American Eagle brand in the American Airlines' regional network. The deal was approved in early 2013. The E175 is a dual-row layout, seating up to 76 passengers; the first delivery was in mid-2013.

"It is significant that our long-time, valued customer Republic Airways—a true innovator in the regional transport business—is the first customer for the enhanced E175," said Paulo Cesar Silva, President and CEO, Embraer Commercial Aviation. "The E175 is the most comfortable, technologically advanced and efficient aircraft in its class and it represents the best value for airlines because it also delivers the lowest total operating cost."

Internal Issues

Vision and Mission
Embraer in late 2012 developed a vision statement as follows: "Embraer will continue to consolidate its position as one of the primary powers in the global aeronautics and defense security industries, with market-leading positions in the segments in which it operates, and a reputation for excellence." The company's mission statement is as follows: "Embraer's business is to generate value for its shareholders by fully satisfying its customers in the global aviation market. By 'generate value,' we mean maximizing the Company's value and ensuring its perpetuity, acting with integrity and social environmental awareness."

Organizational Structure
As indicated in Exhibit 1, Embraer has two primary segments (1) Defense and Security and (2) Commercial Aviation. Instead of a Chief Operations Officer, note that the company has an Executive Vice-president of Operations.

Finance
Embraer's EPS increased 336 percent in 2012 to 0.96 as the company delivered 221 aircraft that year. Among the 221 were 106 commercial jets, 99 executive jets, 14 Super Tucanos, and 2 EMB 145 jets. Embraer's revenues increased 6 percent from 2011 to 2012, and net income increased 212 percent. American Airlines filed Chapter 11 bankruptcy protection in 2011, and they utilized ERJ 145 jets, forcing Embraer to lose up to $293 million.

Embraer's income statements and balance sheets are provided in Exhibits 2 and 3, respectively. Note in Exhibit 3 the zero goodwill, which is good.

EXHIBIT 1 Embraer's Organization Chart

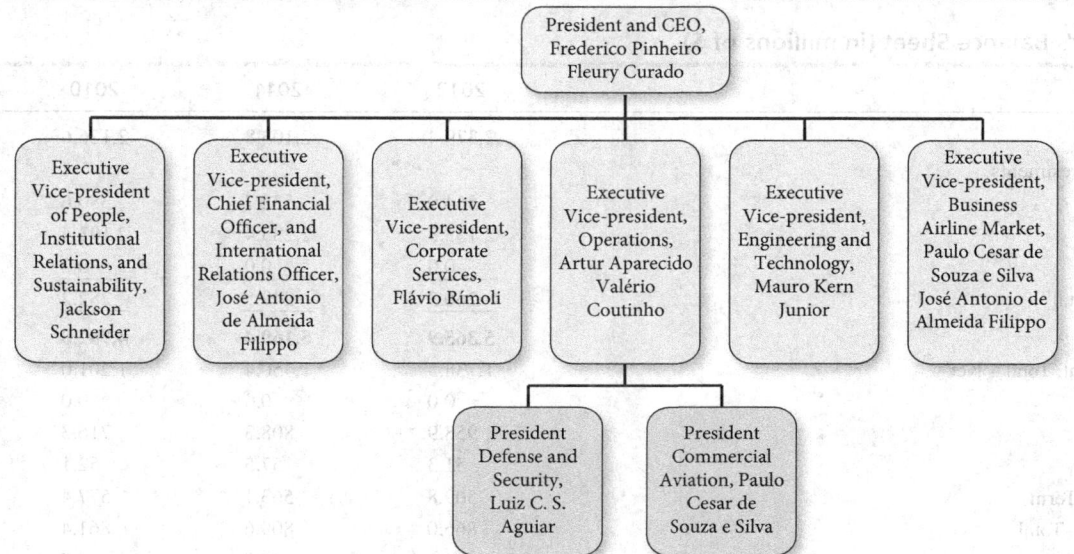

Source: Based on company documents.

EXHIBIT 2 Embraer's Income Statement (in millions of $)

	2012	2011	2010
Revenue	6,177.9	5,802.95	5,364.1
Other Revenue, Total	0.0	0.0	0.0
Total Revenue	**6,177.9**	**5,802.95**	**5,364.1**
Cost of Revenue, Total	4,683.0	4,495.86	4,338.1
Gross Profit	**1,494.9**	**1,307.1**	**1,026.0**
Selling/General/Administrative Expenses, Total	762.5	681.83	571.6
Research & Development	77.3	85.25	72.1
Depreciation/Amortization	0.0	0.0	0.0
Interest Expense (Income), Net Operating	0.0	0.0	0.0
Unusual Expense (Income)	11.4	0.0	0.0
Other Operating Expenses, Total	33.3	221.43	−9.4
Operating Income	**610.2**	**318.24**	**391.7**
Interest Income (Expense), Net Non-Operating	0.0	0.0	0.0
Gain (Loss) on Sale of Assets	0.0	0.0	0.0
Other, Net	−30.6	−143.72	−32.0
Income Before Tax	**614.1**	**247.55**	**408.1**
Income Tax - Total	265.5	127.12	62.7
Income After Tax	**348.6**	**120.42**	**345.4**
Minority Interest	−0.8	−8.82	−15.2
Equity In Affiliates	0.0	0.0	0.0
U.S. GAAP Adjustment	0.0	0.0	0.0
Net Income Before Extra. Items	**347.8**	**111.61**	**330.2**
Total Extraordinary Items	0.0	0.0	0.0
Net Income	**347.8**	**111.61**	**330.2**

Source: Based on company documents.

EXHIBIT 3 Embraer's Balance Sheet (in millions of $)

	2012	2011	2010
Assets	2,379.4	2,103.8	2,126.6
Cash and Short-Term Investments			
Total Receivables, Net	564.9	532.7	380.6
Total Inventory	2,155.3	2,283.4	2,193.4
Prepaid Expenses	0.0	0.0	0.0
Other Current Assets, Total	266.3	249.5	282.2
Total Current Assets	**5,365.9**	**5,169.4**	**4,982.8**
Property/Plant/Equipment, Total – Net	1,738.5	1,450.4	1,201.0
Goodwill, Net	0.0	0.0	0.0
Intangibles, Net	958.9	808.3	716.3
Long-Term Investments	51.3	57.5	52.1
Note Receivable - Long Term	509.8	563.1	577.4
Other Long-Term Assets, Total	866.0	809.6	861.4
Other Assets, Total	0.0	0.0	0.0
Total Assets	**9,490.4**	**8,858.3**	**8,391.0**

EXHIBIT 3 Continued

	2012	2011	2010
Liabilities and Shareholders' Equity			
Accounts Payable	758.9	829.9	750.2
Payable/Accrued	0.0	0.0	0.0
Accrued Expenses	65.4	89.2	79.5
Notes Payable/Short-Term Debt	0.0	0.0	0.0
Current Port. of LT Debt/Capital Leases	348.2	564.6	184.4
Other Current Liabilities, Total	1,619.9	1,358.0	1,374.6
Total Current Liabilities	**2,792.4**	**2,841.7**	**2,388.7**
Total Long-Term Debt	2,118.5	1,556.1	1,721.7
Deferred Income Tax	26.5	23.0	11.4
Minority Interest	92.0	110.5	103.1
Other Liabilities, Total	1,202.7	1,319.7	1,137.7
Total Liabilities	**6,232.1**	**5,851.0**	**5,362.6**
Redeemable Preferred Stock	0.0	0.0	0.0
Preferred Stock - Non Redeemable, Net	0.0	0.0	0.0
Common Stock	1,438.0	1,438.0	1,438.0
Additional Paid-In Capital	0.0	0.0	0.0
Retained Earnings (Accumulated Deficit)	1,980.3	1,737.3	1,759.8
Treasury Stock – Common	−154.2	−183.7	−183.7
ESOP Debt Guarantee	0.0	0.0	0.0
Unrealized Gain (Loss)	0.0	0.0	0.0
Other Equity, Total	−5.8	15.7	14.3
Total Equity	**3,258.3**	**3,007.3**	**3,028.4**
Total Liabilities & Shareholders' Equity	**9,490.4**	**8,858.3**	**8,391.0**
Total Common Shares Outstanding	740.47	723.67	740.47

Source: Based on company documents.

Segments

Commercial Aviation

Embraer's commercial aviation segment accounts for more than 60 percent of all company revenues. Embraer has more than 90 customers, including 30 of which are airline companies on five continents. To date, more than 900 regional jets from the ERJ 145 family are in service. ERJ planes typically offer 37 to 50 seats and are designed to carry passengers from small cities to larger airports for connecting flights. United Airlines uses the 50-seat ERJ from the USA to Mexican cities such as Torreon, Queretaro, and Veracruz. Despite rapid growth in this segment, it is Embraer's belief that this segment has reached maturity in the current markets where they operate.

To create new market share in the commercial aviation segment, Embraer is now producing a larger E-jet in four different models. The E170 and E175 models are designed for 70 to 88 passengers whereas the E190 and E195 jets are designed for 93 to 124 passengers. The company likes to promote the E-jet as a product that "taps the gap" between regional and larger aircraft. For example, a flight from Atlanta to Boston could easily be accommodated by an E-jet around noon when demand is lower because most flight demand is during the morning and afternoon hours. Advantages to the E-jet is there is no middle seat and they are large enough to stand up as a passenger walks down the aisle, just as one would be able to on a Boeing 737 or Airbus 320, unlike competitor Bombardier's planes where many people have to bend over as they make their way to their seat. A drawback with the E-jet is that it does not have the fuel capacity to fly across the USA. But forecasts indicate that demand will grow for E-jets, as indicated by Republic Airlines paying Embraer to $4 billion to provide E175 jets.

Executive Aviation

Embraer's second most profitable segment is the executive aviation, accounting for 19 percent of all revenues. Embraer entered this market in 2000 and rolled out the first plane, a Legacy 600, in 2002. Currently, Embraer provides seven different executive jet options, including the Phenom, Legacy, and Lineage models. The Phenom 100 is the smallest jet offered in the segment and carries 4 passengers up to 1,200 nautical miles. That plane retails for just under $4 million. Larger than the Phenoms are Embraer's Legacy line of jets. The Legacy 500 can carry 12 passengers up to 2,800 nautical miles and costs around $18 million. The larger Legacy 600 and 650 aircraft are capable of carrying 13 passengers over 3,000 nautical miles at altitudes of 41,000 feet. Purchase price is around $27 million.

The Lineage is a variation of the commercial Embraer 190 and is designed with an executive floor plan and additional range by adding a fuel tank. The aircraft can carry 19 passengers upward of 4,500 nautical miles with a price tag of more than $50 million. Currently less than 20 of these aircraft have been built, compared to more than 200 Legacy 600-style planes. All Embraer executive jets can be customized to include showers, bedrooms, or standard commercial jet seating layouts.

Defense and Security

Revenues from Embraer's Defense and Security segment increased 44 percent in 2012. Embraer's Defense and Security segment accounts for 15 percent of revenues. Embraer provides 48 different nations with services and products contained under the Defense and Security's umbrella, including supplying the Brazilian Air Force with more than 70 percent of its fleet. In addition to traditional manned aircraft, Embraer is also engaged in unmanned aerial vehicles and public security systems. These new endeavors were acquired through acquisitions and partnerships with existing firms.

One of Embraer's newer crafts, the Super Tucano, replaced the Tucano that was first produced in 2003 and continues to be produced today. The plane is a single-engine turbo propeller that resembles a World War II fighter plane to the untrained eye. The plane is designed for light attack and aerial reconnaissance in low-threat environments as well as serving a role in pilot training. The Embraer 99 is the military version of the ERJ 145 used in early warning and control. The plane differs mainly from the ERJ 145 in that it provides 20 percent more thrust. The firm also provides several variations of the Embraer 99, all with slightly different features and purposes. The Embraer KC-390 is a twin-engine military jet aircraft designed for troop transport. That plane's first flight is scheduled for 2014 with introduction scheduled for 2016. The company currently does not produce a fighter jet or bomber.

Agricultural

The Embraer EMB 202 Ipanema is a small single-engine plane designed for use in crop dusting. The cost is around $250,000. The agricultural segment makes up less than 2 percent of total revenues and is not separated by Embraer into its on distinct segment, just listed as "other revenues." Since 1969, more than 1,200 aircraft have been built. In 2012, 66 Ipanerna aircraft were sold in Brazil and Mercosur, up 15 percent over 2011.

The Segment Numbers

Note in Exhibit 4 the drop in Embraer aircraft deliveries in 2011 versus 2010. Exhibit 5 shows the company's percentage of revenue provided by each segment. Exhibit 6 details the geographic breakdown of Embraer's revenues. Currently North America accounts for 20 percent of total revenues, a number that is expected to increase as the company continues to provide aircraft to large U.S. carriers and additionally increases production of the executive jets such as the Phenom produced in Melbourne, Florida. The USA comprises 40 percent of the aviation world market share.

EXHIBIT 4 Embraer Aircraft Deliveries

	2012	2011	2010	2009
Commercial Aviation	106	105	100	122
Executive Aviation	99	99	144	115
Defense and Security	16	0	2	7
Total Jets	221	204	246	244

Source: Based on company documents.

EXHIBIT 5 Revenue Percent by Segment

	2012	2011	2010	2009
Commercial Aviation (%)	61	64	61	69
Executive Aviation (%)	21	19	23	17
Defense and Security (%)	17	15	15	12
Others (%)	1	2	1	2

Source: Based on company documents.

EXHIBIT 6 Geographic Revenues

	2012	2011	2010	2009
North America (%)	24	20	13	22
Europe (%)	31	25	33	33
Latin America (%)	3	11	15	7
Brazil (%)	14	17	13	11
Asia Pacific (%)	19	23	22	21
Others (%)	9	4	4	6

Source: Based on company documents.

Competitors

Embraer's three primary competitors are Bombardier, Boeing, and Airbus. But, up-and-coming aircraft manufacturing rivals such as Japan's Mitsubishi Heavy Industries, Russia's Sukhoi, and even China's COMAC are aiming to drive down prices in coming years. This industry is already highly competitive and getting more so every day.

Bombardier virtually invented the regional-jet segment when its CRJ100 entered service in 1992. Embraer broke into the space with its ERJ145 in 1996. Embraer today controls slightly more than 50 percent of the regional aircraft market, including turboprop planes, but the landscape is fluid.

Exhibit 7 shows that Embraer is only one-third of the size of Bombardier and one-tenth of the size of Boeing, which hurts Embraer in terms of economies of scale. Note in Exhibit 7 that Boeing is by far the most efficient and most profitable. However, in the 61 to 120 seat size jets, Embraer leads all rivals in producing these planes—holding a 43-percent market share.

Bombardier

Based in Montreal, Canada, Bombardier is the world's only producer of both aircraft and trains. With customers in more than 60 nations and a workforce of 70,000 employees, Bombardier is a world leader in transportation services. The company trades publicly on the Toronto Stock Exchange under ticker symbol BBD and is also listed on the Dow Jones Sustainability World and North American indexes.

About half of the total workforce at Bombardier is devoted to working in the aerospace segment. Products produced include planes for business and commercial purposes and

EXHIBIT 7 Aircraft Manufacturer Competitor Comparison

	Embraer	Bombardier	Boeing
Number of employees	18,000	61,900	171,000
Revenue	$6.2B	$18.3B	$78.9B
Net Income	$347M	$837M	$4.3B
Net Profit Margin	5.59%	4.89%	5.46%
Revenue per Employee	$344K	$295K	461K
EPS	$0.73	$0.44	5.67
Market Capitalization	5.93B	$7.02B	55.8
Shares Outstanding	185M	1.75B	754M

EPS, earnings per share.
Source: Derived from a variety of sources.

specialized amphibious aircraft. Bombardier is currently the number-one producer of business and regional aircraft in the world and the third-largest aircraft manufacturer behind Boeing and Airbus. Bombardier products in the business aircraft segment include: Learjet, Challenger, and Global aircraft. Commercial aircraft include the C-Series program, CRJ series, and Q-Series. Amphibious aircraft include the Bombardier 415 and Bombardier 415 MP.

Headquartered in Wichita, Kansas, Learjet is part of Bombardier; Learjet offers four variations of planes that range in capacity from 7 to 10 passengers and have ranges between 2,000 and 3,000 nautical miles. All Learjets have a top speed of around 540 miles per hour. The Learjet 60, a midsize Learjet, costs $13.5 million. Bombardier's Challenger series business jets come in three sizes with capacities ranging from 10 passengers to 14 passengers. The Challenger crafts have a longer range, 2,800 nautical miles to more than 4,000 nautical miles, making nonstop flights across the USA or Europe possible. Speeds are comparable with the Learjet family. The Global family of jets is available in four different models with passenger volume either 17 or 19. Top speed is around 590 miles per hour, making the Challenge series the fastest jet Bombardier manufactures. Total range varies by model ranging from 5,200 to 7,900 nautical miles making transocean travel possible.

Bombardier's commercial series of craft includes the Q-Series propeller planes and the CRJ and C-Series jets. Q-series prop planes offer seating for 60 to 90 passengers. The prop planes are designed for short haul flights but offer jetlike speed. The CRJ planes offer seating options ranging from 40 to 100 passengers depending on the model and are designed for short to midrange flights. The larger C-Series plane accommodates either 100 or 149 passengers depending on the model and are designed for midrange flights. Bombardier also offers special aircraft for surveillance and fire fighting.

Boeing
Headquartered in Chicago, Illinois, Boeing is the world's largest manufacturer of commercial jets and military aircraft combined. The company also designs and manufactures rotorcraft, missiles, satellites, launch vehicles, and much more. Boeing is the principle contractor for the International Space Station, a major provider to NASA, and serves customers in more than 150 nations.

Boeing's commercial jets range in size from the 737, with total capacity ranging from 110 to 220 seats, to the 747, with capacity of up to 550 passengers. The 737 family most closely competes with Embraer's commercial aircraft. With fuel capacity of up to 6,875 gallons, the 737 can fly 3,000 nautical miles and is rated for a maximum altitude of 41,000 feet. Prices in 2012 ranged from $71 million to $107 million for the Boeing 737. Boeing produces a wide range of business craft as well, but these planes are similarly reconfigured versions of existing passenger aircraft and not smaller business planes like Embraer and Bombardier produce.

Demand for commercial air transportation globally increased 5.3 percent in 2012, but profitability of airline companies declined from $8.8 billion (in 2011) to $6.7 billion in 2012. That profitability number is expected to increase to $8.4 billion in 2013.

Airbus

Headquartered in Toulouse, France, Airbus is a subsidiary of the European Aeronautic Defense and Space Company and produces around half of the world's commercial jet airliners. Airbus employs more than 63,000 people and has annual revenues of about $43 billion. Airbus produces a wide array of aircraft including commercial jets, business jets, freighters, and military planes. The military jets are limited to cargo and surveillance and are not designed for attacking military operations. Competing principally with Embraer is Airbus's 320 line of commercial craft and a wide array of business aircraft.

Airbus's 320 is available in four different models, with the A318 and A319 competing most closely with Embraer. The A318 is capable of carrying up to 107 passengers in two-class layouts with maximum range of 1,500 nautical miles. The A319 has a capacity between 124, which is the same capacity as one version of Embraer's E-jet, and 156 seats. The A319 has a range of 2,000 nautical miles and is the widest single-isle fuselage on the market. There are 1,352 A319s in service and another 1,526 on order. The A318 is not as popular, with 78 planes in operation and 81 on order.

Airbus also manufactures eight versions of business-class aircraft. The ACJ318 is the smallest version with total capacity of 8 passengers and an impressive range of more than 4,200 nautical miles. The largest plane offered is the ACJ380 with capacity up to 50 passengers and range more than 9,500 nautical miles. Like Boeing, Airbus business craft are virtually the same as their respective passenger craft, just reconfigured with office space, conference tables, and larger seats for business travelers.

External Issues

Growth in the Middle Class

Although many discuss the U.S. shrinking middle class, worldwide there is a rapid growth in the middle class. The middle class in Eastern Europe, China, and Latin America is expected to grow substantially over the next 20 years as a redistribution of wealth created from increasing gross domestic product (GDP) in these regions. By 2030, it is expected that emerging market cities will have more middle and high-end residents than developed cities. The size of the middle class will grow from 1.8 billion to 3.2 billion by 2022 resulting in a larger population of middle class than poor. By 2030, the number of middle-class people is expected to be 4.9 billion. Total economic benefit is expected to increase from $21 trillion to $56 trillion by 2030, all of which posits increasing demand for airlines and thus consistent demand for aircraft makers such as Embraer.

In addition, Africa is a new frontier that corporations are turning to for business. Historically, the African economy has been largely dependent on natural resources and as recently as 2010, around 67 percent of all exports were related to natural resources. Kenya, South Africa, and the Ivory Coast are three of the leading markets in Africa and overall around 33 percent of the population in Africa has grown into the middle class. The African economy is expected to outpace the world average over the next 20 years and with an increasing amount of middle-class citizens and reduction in the dependence of exports, more and more businesses and citizens will come to depend on air travel to conduct business throughout the continent. European and Middle Eastern airlines have begun to expand their routes into Africa, forcing African airline companies to respond because more than 50 percent of their planes are 10 years or older and cannot operate as efficiently as the new aircraft. In addition, most African-based aircraft offer seating configurations of 120 seats or more, although most flights contain less than 100 passengers. This limits markets served and frequency of air service. It is Embraer's expectation their smaller-sized jets will fit the bill in the new revitalizing Africa.

Business Culture in Brazil

Home to Embraer, Brazil is the largest nation in South America and fifth largest in the world in both land area and population. Brazil has a population of 146 million with more than 15 million living in the Sao Paulo and Rio de Janeiro areas. Approximately 55 percent of all Brazilians are of Portuguese descent with 38 percent a mixture of several cultures. Around 6 percent of the population is of African decent. Portuguese is the official language, and although there is no official religion, about 90 percent of the population consider themselves Roman Catholics.

Currently around 50 percent of the population of Brazil is younger than 20 years of age, and despite economic problems, Brazil has much potential to become a rich nation with its strong industrial, agricultural, and natural resource operations.

Workers in Brazil, like other areas of Latin America, hold a higher concern for rules, controls, and career security than in the USA or Europe. Brazilian society tends to be risk-adverse and reluctant to accept change, and this has contributed to a growing inequality between rich and poor in Brazil. However, the reluctance for change is complimented by a strong respect for tradition, including a strong work ethic. Employees believe in long-term rewards for a hard day's work. New ideas or ways of doing business are often met with great skepticism in Brazil.

Brazilians dress formal at work with executives wearing three-piece suits and office workers often wearing two-piece suits. Women are expected to dress conservatively and have their nails well manicured. Appointments in Brazil should be made with at least two weeks notice; last-minute appointments with either businesses or government agencies should not be attempted. Although parts of Brazil may not be the most punctual in regard to meetings starting on time, meetings in Sao Paulo and Rio De Janerio are much like those in the USA or Europe because they start on time. However, even in these two cities, casual chit chat should start the meeting and only when the host moves to the business at hand should the conversation turn to more serious matters. It is also common courtesy to purchase lunch or dinner for a host but not to provide a gift.

The Future

In a market that some analysts consider to be a duopoly, the short-hop, narrow-body jets manufactured by Embraer have outsold those from Bombardier for nearly a decade. But Bombardier is not conceding ground, especially in its traditional North American stronghold. United Airlines and smaller rival US Airways are both expected to announce airplane purchases in 2013. Bombardier received a December 2012 order worth up to $3.29 billion from Delta Air Lines. That order almost matches Embraer's deal worth up to $4 billion to supply the regional network of AMR Corp's (AAMRQ.PK) American Airlines. More orders for somebody will follow soon because U.S. carriers need new short-haul planes, to the tune of 250 to 400 planes in the next 18 months. American Eagle already has a large mixed fleet of Embraers and Bombardiers, so neither suppliers has exclusive rights.

Bombardier's market share in the regional-jet market has fallen below 30 percent, from 72 percent in 2003, but the company has a strategic plan to regain its dominance. Airlines are often hesitant to switch fleets from one supplier to another because additional training and maintenance costs can outweigh savings on the purchase. Unfortunately for Embraer, Delta, US Airways, and their regional flying partners already operate more Bombardier CRJs, whereas American and United and their partners use more Embraer jets. Embraer needs a clear strategic plan to maintain (or increase) its current market share. Perhaps Embraer needs to shift some focus to trying to supply firms such as Ryanair, Emirates, Singapore Air, and flydubai.

Apple Inc., 2015

www.apple.com, AAPL

Apple is the world's largest corporation based on a market capitalization of about $650 billion, approximately $200 billon more than Exxon, the world's second-largest company. Apple designs, manufactures, and markets the world's single-most popular smartphone, the iPhone, even though Apple has only about 15 percent of the global market share in smartphones. Apple also produces the iPad, iPod, iCloud, Mac computers, and other accessory devices. Headquartered in Cupertino, California, Apple owns iTunes, the popular app and store where customers can download music.

New for Apple with the release of the iPhone 6 and 6 Plus is Apple Pay, where customers can pay at retail stores by scanning their phone. Apple currently operates 450 Apple stores and employs 98,000. Apple's iPhone 6 and 6+ offer larger screens to better compete with Samsung. Initial sales of the iPhone 6 and 6+ broke records, with the higher margin 6+ doing best of all. Apple's new gold smartwatch released in spring 2015 sells for $4,000 to $5,000. The aluminum model is priced at $349, and the stainless steel model at $500.

On July 21, 2015, Apple announced financial results for its fiscal 2015 third quarter that ended June 27, 2015. Specifically, the company reported quarterly revenue of $49.6 billion and quarterly net profit of $10.7 billion, compared to revenue of $37.4 billion and net profit of $7.7 billion the prior year-ago quarter. International sales accounted for 64 percent of the quarter's revenue. In that third quarter Apple's year-over-year growth rate accelerated from the first half of fiscal 2015, with revenue up 33 percent and earnings per share up 45 percent. The growth was fueled by record third quarter sales of iPhone and Mac, all-time record revenue from services, and the successful launch of Apple Watch. The company's quarterly iPhone revenue was up 59 percent over last year. Apple Music was released in July 2015 and the company plans to release iOS 9, OS X El Capitan and watchOS 2 to customers in Fall 2015.

Copyright by Fred David Books LLC. www.strategyclub.com (Written by Forest R. David)

History

Founded in 1976 by Steve Jobs and Steve Wozniak, Apple began as a personal computer company providing desktop computers for businesses and the home. The first computer, the Apple 1, was hand built by Wozniak and did not come with a keyboard or an outer case to protect the computer. The products were considered a kit, and users had to supply extra parts themselves. The Apple 1 sold for the interesting price of $666.66, or around $2,800 adjusted for inflation. Apple was incorporated in 1977 after Wozniak sold his share for $800. The Apple II was first sold in 1977 and had the first major piece of business software, VisiCalc, a spreadsheet product.

Apple went public in 1980 for $22 a share and generated more money on its IPO than any firm since Ford Motor Company 25 years earlier. Following a dispute with the Board, Steve Jobs resigned from Apple in 1985 and started a new firm. With Jobs unaffiliated with Apple for the next 15 years, Apple experimented with various other products, including CD players, digital cameras, speakers, and others. Throughout the 1990s, Apple experimented with several different product lines of personal computers, with limited success. Apple's products were generally significantly more expensive than that of competitors, not compatible with much of the leading software or with the more popular Windows machines, and also were not able to multitask as well as Windows-based machines.

By 1996, Apple was struggling immensely and the firm acquired Steve Jobs' firm, NeXT. After the Board fired the existing CEO in 1997, Jobs was back, acting as interim CEO of Apple. In the same year, Jobs identified Jonathan Ive, and the two started working to rebuild Apple's products and brand name. Ive is currently the Senior VP of Design. After several Mac upgrades and new software products such as iMovie, in 2001, Apple introduced the iPod and the firm sold 100 million units in 6 years. The year 2003 brought about the iTunes store, which synced $0.99 downloads to iPods and remains an industry leader. Apple launched the iPhone in 2008 and the iPad in 2010. In 2011, Steve Jobs passed away and current CEO Tim Cook now leads Apple.

Internal Issues

Vision/Mission

Neither at its corporate website nor in its *Form 10K* does Apple provide a written vision or mission statement labeled as such. There are statements such as the following, however, that perhaps serve as Apple's vision and/or mission:

1. "We strive to provide users of Apple products the best experience possible though innovative product designs and software."

2. "Apple designs Macs, the best personal computers in the world, along with OS X, iLife, iWork and professional software. Apple leads the digital music revolution with its iPods and iTunes online store. Apple has reinvented the mobile phone with its revolutionary iPhone and App Store, and is defining the future of mobile media and computing devices with iPad."

Organizational Structure

As indicated in Exhibit 1, Apple appears to operate from a divisional-by-process design, but absent of any presidents of divisions. However, Apple does report revenues by both region and product. Some analysts suggest that titles of Apple's executives more closely mirror how the firm reports sales, and many expect to see a COO with divisional presidents reporting to that position.

Strategy

Apple was late in producing a larger screen smartphone, but did so with the launch of the iPhone 6 and 6+ in October 2014. Apple prides itself on simplicity. Apple products are generally more user friendly than those of Windows, Android, and other operating systems, but at the sacrifice of the user being able to customize or tailor the device for their specific needs. Apple's overriding strategy always has been to produce elegant, easy-to-use products, often at a premium price point. In a November 2014 interview, CEO Cook reiterated this when asked if having just 15 percent of the global smartphone market share is a concern, by responding, "Not all market share is equal, and Apple has never been about the most; we are about being the best."

Apple also has a culture of not collecting every detail about its users. For example, Apple does not read or store iMessages or FaceTime. Even if a government were to ask for these data, Apple could not provide it, for the company simply does not keep it on file. The latest version of iOS 8 is more encrypted than ever. CEO Cook compares Apple to designing to an electronic Fort Knox.

With the release of the new iPhone 6 line, Apple introduced Apple Pay, a mobile app that enables Apple customers to use their existing Master Card, Visa, or American Express card to make mobile payments at retail stores. Apple Pay's fingerprint technology is more convenient for consumers and also more secure for credit card companies such as Visa, American Express, and MasterCard. However, competitors such as Samsung currently have a similar technology on some of their phones, and all phones will likely have a similar technology moving forward. Using Apple Pay, merchants are charged the same fee as normally charged by a credit card company, which is an average of 2 percent in the United States. Transactions in the United States annually produce more credit card fees than everywhere else in the world combined, leaving open the door for Apple to possibly transition away from credit card companies in the future. Apple could offer its own in-house credit system at much lower cost to merchants, in essence becoming a financial institution.

Keeping in line with its user-friendly products strategy, Apple must approve all third-party digital content through the iTunes Store or the App Store and iBooks store. Competitors, such as Android-based phones, tend to have less control over apps offered to their customers than does Apple. Apple prides itself on well-trained and knowledgeable salespersons with excellent customer service. Apple invests heavily in R&D, over $6 billion in 2014 alone, up nearly 100 percent from 2012. In addition, Apple is expanding its retail stores around the world.

During 2014, Apple acquired several firms, including Beats Music and Beats headphones. Apple obtained a subscription streaming music service and a headphone firm in the process. Apple's acquisitions in 2014, however, increased the firm's goodwill from $1.5 to $4.6 billion.

To keep costs low, almost all Apple hardware products are manufactured in Asia and many of these are manufactured at a single location, except for a few Macs that are manufactured in

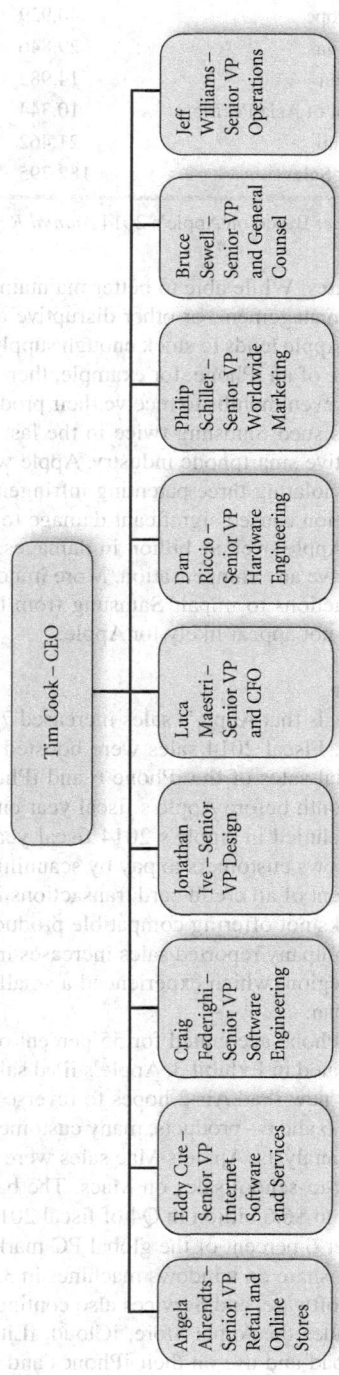

EXHIBIT 1 Apple's Organizational Structure

Tim Cook – CEO

- Angela Ahrendts – Senior VP Retail and Online Stores
- Eddy Cue – Senior VP Internet Software and Services
- Craig Federighi – Senior VP Software Engineering
- Jonathan Ive – Senior VP Design
- Luca Maestri – Senior VP and CFO
- Dan Riccio – Senior VP Hardware Engineering
- Philip Schiller – Senior VP Worldwide Marketing
- Bruce Sewell – Senior VP and General Counsel
- Jeff Williams – Senior VP Operations

Source: Based on company documents.

EXHIBIT 2 Apple Revenues by Region (in millions of USD)

Revenues	2014	2013	2012
Americas	$65,232	$62,739	$57,512
Europe	40,929	37,883	36,323
China	29,846	25,417	22,533
Japan	14,982	13,462	10,571
Rest of Asia Pacific	10,344	11,181	10,741
Retail	21,462	20,228	18,828
Net Sales	182,795	170,910	156,508

Source: Based on Apple's 2014 *Annual Report*, p. 27.

the United States. While able to better maintain quality control, this does put Apple at risk over strikes, poor management, or other disruptive activities at a single location facility. To counter this problem, Apple tends to stock enough supply to cover its demand for up to 150 days, but during a new issue of an iPhone, for example, there can be supply shortages, where customers must wait weeks or even months to receive their products.

Apple has sued Samsung twice in the last couple of years for patent infringements in the hypercompetitive smartphone industry. Apple was awarded $120 million of a $2.2 billion claim for Samsung violating three patenting infringements. However, Apple was unable to prove that Samsung's action caused significant damage to its product line. To date, Samsung has been ordered to pay Apple over $1 billion in damages, and both cases have been appealed, and Apple has yet to receive any compensation. More important for Apple than the $1 billion was the desire for the legal actions to impair Samsung from being able to sell certain products. To date, this outcome does not appear likely for Apple.

Segment Data

Exhibit 2 reveals that Apple's sales increased 7 percent in 2014, following a 9 percent increase the prior year. Fiscal 2014 sales were boosted by strong iPhone 5s and 5c sales, and also account for initial sales of the iPhone 6 and iPhone 6+, released in October 2014 in the United States, one month before Apple's fiscal year ended. However, some preorder sales of iPhone 6 and 6+ are included in Apple's 2014 fiscal year. With the iPhone 6 and 6+ also comes Apple Pay, which allows customers to pay by scanning their phones at selected retail stores. As of late 2014, 83 percent of all credit card transactions in the United States were compatible with Apple Pay, with banks not offering compatible products quickly but rather coming to agreement with Apple. The company reported sales increases in all regions in fiscal 2014, except in the Rest of Asia Pacific region, which experienced a small decline. The largest percent growth came from China and Japan.

Apple's iPhone accounted for 55 percent of total 2014 revenues, up 11 percent from fiscal 2011, as indicated in Exhibit 3. Apple's iPad sales have been steady but have not increased since 2012. Apple's new iPad Air 2 hopes to reverse this trend. However, with the larger iPhone displays with the 6 and 6+ products, many customers may opt only for having one device. In a bit of a surprise for analysts, Apple's Mac sales were up 12 percent in fiscal 2014, from stronger than expected back-to-school sales on Macs. The back-to-school sales were strong enough to boost Mac revenues to $6.6 billion in Q4 of fiscal 2014, more than iPad's revenue of $5.3 billion. Mac now owns over 6 percent of the global PC market, its largest market share since 1995. Mac has gained market share on windows machines in 33 of the last 34 quarters.

iTunes, Software, and Services also continues to grow, up 12 percent from fiscal 2013. This segment includes the Apple Store, iCloud, iLife, iWork, AppleCare, and apps that many users pay to download and use on their iPhones and iPads. Apple's iPod, once the bellwether for the firm before the release of the iPhone, has been in constant decline, with sales down 61 percent from 2012 to 2014. In summer 2014, Apple discontinued making its classic iPod 160gb device on claims they could no longer get the parts. Apple's accessories segment includes headphones, Apple TV, cases, and Apple Watch. Apple Watch will be compatible only with iPhone 5 and newer products running iOS 8.0 or newer.

EXHIBIT 3 Apple Revenues by Product (in millions of USD)

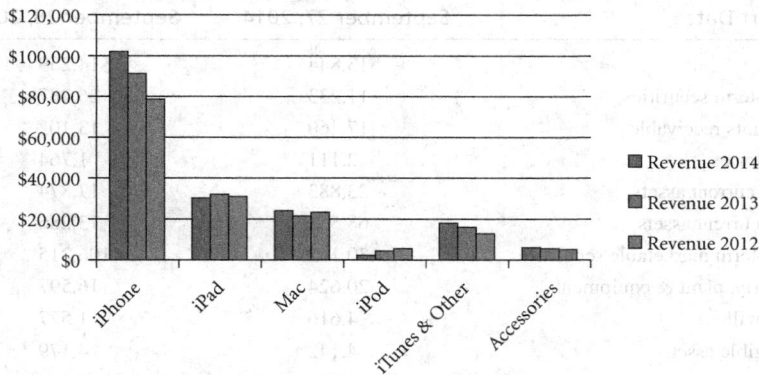

Source: Based on Apple's 2014 *Annual Report*, p. 27.

Finance

For years Apple had no long-term debt on its balance sheet. But in 2013, the firm, for the first time since 1994, used debt to finance operations, and reported $17 billion in long-term debt, and then reported $29 billion in long-term-debt in fiscal 2014, with varying maturity dates out as far as 2044. Apple is aggressively looking at financing further by debt and also for the first time with bonds backed in Euros as well. The firm reported in April 2014 that a $90 billion stock repurchase had been authorized and also raised the dividend to $0.47 per share for a 30 percent increase. Assuming $100 average stock price on the repurchases, Apple will need to purchase 900 million shares back, or around 15 percent of current shares outstanding.

Apple's current income statement and balance sheet are provided in Exhibits 4 and 5, respectively. Much of the cash on Apple's balance sheet is kept in foreign banks. In this way, Apple avoids paying U.S. corporate taxes on those earnings.

EXHIBIT 4 Income Statement (in millions of USD)

Report Date	September 27, 2014	September 28, 2013
Revenues	$182,795	$170,910
Cost of revenue	112,258	106,606
Gross profit	70,537	64,304
Operating expenses	18,034	15,305
EBIT	52,503	48,999
Interest additions	980	1,156
EBT	53,483	50,155
Tax	13,973	13,118
Net income	**39,510**	**37,037**

Source: Based on company documents.

Competitors

Apple competes in a highly competitive and rapidly changing industry that is often associated with strong customer loyalty. Apple and rival firms typically roll out new smartphones, computers, and tablets annually. Many of Apple's rivals have prices 50 to 70 percent lower on comparable products. However, in the tablet and phone market, top rival Samsung prices its top products in line with Apple prices. Competition for Apple should only increase in the future as rival firms are better able to duplicate Apple's products or even better able to persuade customers their products are just as good but significantly cheaper in price. Top competitors for Apple are Samsung and Lenovo in the smartphone, tablet, and PC markets. However, Apple faces significant competition from various other PC providers such as Dell, Sony, and Toshiba.

EXHIBIT 5 Balance Sheet (in millions of USD)

Report Date	September 27, 2014	September 28, 2013
Cash	$13,844	$14,259
Short-term securities	11,233	26,287
Accounts receivable	17,460	13,102
Inventories	2,111	1,764
Other current assets	23,883	17,874
Total current assets	68,531	73,286
Long-term marketable securities	130,162	106,215
Property, plant & equipment	20,624	16,597
Goodwill	4,616	1,577
Intangible assets	4,142	4,179
Other assets	3,764	5,146
Total assets	**231,839**	**207,000**
Accounts payable	30,196	22,367
Other current liabilities	33,252	21,291
Total current liabilities	63,448	43,658
Long-term debt	28,987	16,960
Deferred income taxes	20,259	16,489
Deferred revenue	3,031	2,625
Other liabilities	4,567	3,719
Total liabilities	**120,292**	**83,451**
Common stock	23,313	19,764
Retained earnings	87,152	104,256
Treasury stock	—	—
Paid in capital and other	1,082	(471)
Total equity	**111,547**	**123,549**
Total liabilities & equity	**231,839**	**207,000**

Source: Based on company documents.

EXHIBIT 6 2014 Percent Market Share of Key Global Players

	Apple	Android	Windows
Smart Phones	14%	81%	3%
Tablets	45%	51%	4%
Watches	0%	67%	0%

Source: Based on company documents and a variety of other sources.

Exhibit 6 provides a comparative analysis of Apple with some of its rival firms in terms of market share. Note that Apple products trail Android products substantially in market share. Apple projects to take a 35 percent market share in watches in 2015, reducing Android's share to 42 percent. In 2014, the total watch market was less than 10 million, but is expected to expand to 35 million units by year-end 2015. Exhibit 7 provides additional comparative competitive information for Apple and rival firms.

Samsung

Founded in 1938 in South Korea, Samsung specializes in semiconductors and electronic appliances. The firm did not enter the mobile communications arena until the late 1990s, but by

EXHIBIT 7 Apple versus Rival Firms

	Apple	Samsung	Lenovo
# Employees	92,000	96,900	54,000
$ Net Income	39.5 B	27.7 B	817 M
$ Revenue	182.8 B	208 B	38,707 M
$ Revenue/Employee	2 M	2 M	716,796
$ EPS Ratio	7.39	180	7.88
Market Cap.	692.7 B	—	—

Source: Based on company documents and a variety of other sources.

2010 it was producing half of its mobile phones in China. Samsung has five R&D centers in China. Samsung was 2 years behind first-mover Apple into the smartphone market with its launch in 2009 using the Bada operating system. In 2010, Samsung provided an Android-powered smartphone. In 2013, Samsung smartphones were 21 percent of the global smartphone market, making Samsung the industry leader. In addition to smartphones, Samsung also today produces tablets, televisions, Blu-rays, DVD players, cameras, refrigerators, air conditioners, washing machines, ovens, PC notebooks, printers, storage devices, and more. In addition, Samsung is engaged in providing select medical equipment such as X-rays, ultrasound, and other items.

In popular products, Samsung competes with Apple directly on the Samsung Galaxy and Note smartphones, Galaxy Tablet, TVs, watches, and laptop computers. Samsung reported revenues of over $208 billion in 2013.

Lenovo
Founded in 1984 in Beijing and headquartered in both Beijing and New York City, Lenovo acquired IBM's ThinkPad laptops and more recently IBM's lower-end servers. Lenovo did not enter the smartphone market until 2010, but its LePhone is popular in China and increasing its market share in the entry-level market space. Lenovo is also rapidly introducing the LePhone in Russia, India, Indonesia, and other neighboring Asian nations that also have developing economies. Lenovo competes with Apple primarily on PCs, since the firm has positioned itself in a lower demographic market for its smartphones.

Lenovo's 2014 revenues are expected to be in excess of $37 billion—the same as in 2013. With Lenovo's $2.9 billion acquisition of Motorola in 2014, the firm is now the world's third-largest smartphone maker, behind Samsung and Apple. Lenovo trades on the Hong Kong Stock Exchange and currently employs 54,000 people worldwide.

External Issues

In 2014, there were 234 million smartphone Internet connections in the United States. The growth rate was approximately 35 percent from 2009 to 2014, with a forecast of 313 million connections by 2019.

China
Most of the world's smartphones are manufactured in China, and the Chinese smartphone market itself increased nearly 55 percent from 2010 to 2014. Less than 1.5 million units were produced in 2003, increasing to over 500 million units in 2015. The top four smartphone manufacturers in China are Samsung, Lenovo, Apple, and HTC, accounting for over half of the total industry revenue in 2014. There is a growing fragmentation in the market as new entrants enter and now comprise 50+ percent overall market. Smartphone industry revenue will increase about 20 percent annually to around $180 billion by 2020, with over 1.5 billion units produced annually. Worldwide mobile phone shipments (all phones included) were just under 2 billion in 2014 with about 70 percent of shipped phones considered smartphones. By 2018, however, 2.2 billion mobile phones will be shipped and all but 400 million are projected to be smartphones.

Computer Manufacturing and Tablets

Computer manufacturing is a $14 billion industry in the United States alone, but sales fell over 17 percent per year between 2009 and 2014. About 62 percent of all computers manufactured in the United States are laptops, but this still leaves 38 percent of the computers manufactured being desktops. Overall projections are 5 percent declines moving forward through 2020. Tablets are projected to further make inroads into personal computers in U.S. manufacturing. However, it is important to note that at least for Apple's Q4 of 2014, Mac sales exceeded iPad sales.

Most tablets are manufactured in China, with Apple holding 27 percent of the market share, followed by Samsung and Lenovo with 12 and 8 percent, respectively, on tablets made in China. The largest players in the U.S. computer manufacturing business, which also includes servers, are HP, Dell, and IBM, with 25, 19, and 18 percent market shares, respectively. Two relative new areas that may help boost laptop sales are the new ultrabooks, extra thin laptops with no battery sacrifice, and laptops with touch glass where the user can touch the screen much like on a smartphone or tablet. Worldwide PC sales are expected to be $190 billion in 2015, tapering down to $160 billion by 2018. In 2014, PC shipments alone accounted for 56 percent of the device (PC and Tablets) shipments, but this number is expected to be reduced to 45 percent by 2018, as tablets make further inroads on PCs. (Tablets are expected to grow 9 percent a year through 2018.) Currently, Android-based phones account for just over 60 percent of smartphone operating systems, with iOS picking up much of the balance. Through 2018, the outlook is projected to remain the same.

Operating Systems

Operating systems are another large market in the United States with 2013 revenues of $45 billion expected to grow to $57 billion by 2019. Major firms by market share include Microsoft and Apple, with 62 and 20 percent of the total market. Microsoft's prominent product continues to be Windows, while Apple is the owner of iOS.

Geographic Outlook

Most smartphone markets in developed countries are expected to see growth rates subside moving forward. However, with the current culture of customers being trained to update their phones at least every 2 years, the long-term outlook for smartphone providers looks promising. The real exponential growth, though, moving forward should come from developing markets such as Brazil, India, and China. Tablet sales in the United States are projected to increase from $55 billion in 2014 to 63 billion in 2018, or a 15 percent total increase. In the Asia Pacific (not including Japan) region, tablet sales are expected to increase from $65 to $93 billion over the same time frame, or 43 percent. Sales for smartphones are expected to show similar results with respect to the major growth being in China, India, and Brazil.

During its first month in operation (July 2015), Apple Music obtained 11 million trial members, giving the App store a record-breaking month. The streaming service costs users $9.99 per month with the first 3 months free. But 2 million of those subscribers opted for the more expensive family plan costing $14.99 per month. Despite some bugs and glitches in the service, which Apple is scrambling to fix, Apple Music is a popular hit so far. If all the trial users convert to paying monthly customers, Apple will surpass most competitors. For example, 10-year-old Spotify only has 20 million paying customers, but boasts 75 million active users, Pandora has 3.3 million paid subscribers from its 79 million active user base, and Deezer has 6 million paid subscribers out of its 16 million active users. During July 2015, Apple's App store did a record-breaking $1.7 billion in transactions. Interestingly, 23 percent of the digital music market is made up of paid subscribers, who generated a collective $1.6 billion in calendar year 2014.

Future

Apple announced record financial results for 2015 fiscal first quarter that ended in December 2014. Total revenues and profits were $74.6 and $18 billion, respectively, up from $57.6 and $13.1 billion in first quarter 2014. In addition, international sales accounted for 65 percent of total revenue as the iPhone is now the most popular phone in China. International sales would have been significantly higher if not for a significant rally in the U.S. dollar against other foreign currencies over much of 2014.

Apple began shipping its Apple watch in April 2015. iPhone and Mac revenues were $51 and $7 billion, respectively, for the first quarter 2015, up 57 and 9 percent from first quarter 2014. However, iPad sales were down 22 percent over the same time frame due to people not updating their tablets as frequently, less demand than for phones, and also the new iPhone 6+ has cannibalized iPad sales.

Develop a 3-year strategic plan for CEO Tim Cook that will enable Apple to continue to compete with rivals Samsung and Lenovo. Use the template at the www.strategyclub.com website to prepare matrices and analyses. Impress Mr. Cook with your work because, according to *Financial Times,* CEO Cook was the business "Person of the Year" for 2014. In 2015, at Apple's shareholder meeting, when someone questioned the profitability of Apple's environmental initiatives, Mr. Cook responded: "We do things for other reasons than a profit motive, we do things because they are right and just. If that's a hard line for you…then you should get out of the stock."

International Business Machines (IBM) Corporation, 2015

www.ibm.com, IBM

Headquartered in Armonk, New York, IBM has over 430,000 employees worldwide that provide information technology (IT) products and services. IBM manufactures and markets computer hardware and software, and offers infrastructure, hosting, and consulting services in areas ranging from business analytics and mainframe computers to nanotechnology. IBM has more than a dozen research laboratories worldwide. For 22 consecutive years, IBM has held the record for most patents generated by a company. IBM sold its personal computer (PC) and low-end (x86) server businesses to Lenovo in 2005 and 2014 for $1.25 billion and $2.3 billion, respectively.

Disappointing Wall Street has become the trend for IBM, whose stock was the worst performer among the 30 in the Dow Jones industrial average in both 2014 and 2013—an ominous, dubious distinction for a company historically known as Big Blue. In October 2014, after 10 quarters of flat or declining sales, IBM's CEO Virginia Rometty said, "Our results this quarter are disappointing; we've got to reinvent ourselves."

In 2015, IBM paid $1.5 billion to Globalfoundries in order to divest its costly chip division. It is very unusual for any firm (in this case IBM) to pay another firm to acquire a division of your own firm. IBM is making payments to the chipmaker over three years. In the deal, privately held Globalfoundries obtained IBM's global commercial semiconductor technology business, including intellectual property and technologies related to IBM Microelectronics. Also, Globalfoundries obtained IBM's semiconductor manufacturing operations and plants in East Fishkill, New York, and in Essex Junction, Vermont, as well as access to thousands of patents and IBM's commercial microelectronics business. Globalfoundries is now IBM's exclusive server processor semiconductor technology provider for 22 nanometer (nm), 14nm, and 10nm semiconductors for the next 10 years.

In August 2015, IBM acquired Merge Healthcare, which provides medical images and clinical systems, in a $1 billion deal in order to combine that company with its Watson Health analytics unit. IBM plans to combine data and images from Merge Healthcare's medical imaging management platform with Watson's cloud-based computing platform that analyzes high volumes of data, understands complex questions posed in natural language, and proposes evidence-based answers.

A huge partner with Apple, IBM in July 2015 launched a new service that will help other corporations make the same leap from Windows to the MacBook and iPad that it has done over the last several years. The new service takes the lessons IBM just learned by installing more than 110,000 Apple devices, including iPads, MacBooks, and iPhones, across its own company, helping corporate clients make the same kind of wide-reaching tech turnover.

In June 2015, IBM acquired Compose, a database-as-a-service startup established in Birmingham, Alabama. Compose provides database services for companies so their engineers can focus on mobile and web development. Now headquartered in San Mateo, California, Compose serves about 3,600 clients and recently rebranded from MongoHQ.

Copyright by Fred David Books LLC. www.strategyclub.com (Written by Forest R. David)

History

IBM began business in the 1800s with the Tabulating Machine Company, the International Time Recording Company, and the Computing Scale Company of America, all independently operating separately as distinct corporations. In 1911, the merger of these firms was completed, creating the Computing-Tabulating-Recording Company; the name was changed to International Business Machines (IBM) in 1924. IBM has worked diligently in the last decade to shift resources and strategy away from manufacturing into service industries. For example, IBM acquired SPSS and Cognos (data analytics software) in 2009 for $1.2 billion. IBM plans to keep its high-end server business, which is less prone to commoditization by other firms' products.

In 2013, IBM acquired SoftLayer Technologies, a web hosting service, for about $2 billion. A year later, IBM initiated a partnership with Apple Inc. in enterprise mobility and also acquired the business operations of Lighthouse Security Group, LLC, a premier cloud security services provider. Financial terms were not disclosed. IBM executives accepted no bonuses in 2014 for fiscal year 2013, because the firm reported a 5 percent drop in sales and a 1 percent decline in net profit for 2013. Today, IBM is investing more than $1.2 billion, expanding its data centers and cloud-storage business and building 15 new centers, bringing the total to 40 in 2014.

The company is heavily involved in providing business consulting and business analytics services. It is investing $3 billion between 2014 and 2019 to create computer functionality to resemble how the human brain thinks. IBM says its goal is to design a neural chip that mimics the human brain, with 10 billion neurons and 100 trillion synapses, but that uses just 1 kilowatt of power.

In late 2014, IBM signed an extensive cooperative agreement with Twitter Inc. to gain access to all tweets posted now and previously to 2006, so the 10,000+ IBM consultants can help solve client problems using IBM's business analytics software. Both Twitter and IBM, as part of the agreement, are now developing data offerings for specific industries, such a banking, retail, travel, and transportation. IBM's CEO Rometty personally negotiated with Twitters' CEO Costolo to forge the partnership.

Also in late 2014, IBM introduced a new email service called IBM Verse to complement its IBM Notes software suite. With Verse, IBM hopes to address common complaints that customers have with gmail, Yahoo! email, and AOL email services, such as filter problems, spam, and weak tracking features. In early 2015, IBM announced a new product called the z13, a machine about the size of an extra-large refrigerator that reportedly is the most sophisticated computer ever built. IBM says the z13 can complete 2.5 billion transactions a day, and analysts say the product will generate $2.3 billion in revenue in 2015. Mainframe computers such as the z13 generate about 20 percent of IBM's revenues.

For the second quarter of 2015 that ended June 30, IBM's revenues fell 13 percent year-over-year to $20.8 billion, and company earnings also declined 13 percent from the year-ago period. Part of the decline was the result of IBM selling its System X server business to China's Lenovo. For Q2, IBM's sales fell 8 percent in the Americas region, but only 2 percent when backing out currency and System X effects. In IBM's Asia-Pacific segment, revenues declined 19 percent, and in the Europe/Middle East/Africa segment, revenues dropped 17 percent. In the BRIC bloc of Brazil, Russia, India, and China, IBM's revenues declined 35 percent. Even after backing out the System X and currency valuation events, IBM's organic sales to the BRIC markets fell 18 percent year-over-year.

Also in Q2, IBM's business and technology services segment revenues declined 11 percent year-over-year, while the company's software sales decreased 10 percent. The company's hardware segment revenues declined 32 percent and now comprises only 9.6 percent of Big Blue's revenues, as the company has almost totally transitioned away from hardware. On a positive note for Q2, IBM's "strategic imperatives" increased sales significantly. Specifically, the firm's cloud computing revenues rose more than 70 percent, backing out the currency and System X sale again. Similarly, business analytics revenues at IBM grew more than 20 percent, mobile services sales quadrupled, and the company's social revenues jumped 30 percent.

Values, Vision, Mission

In 2003, IBM executives and over 300,000 employees convened for the first time in 100 years to reestablish and reanalyze the company's core values and existing mission statement. Core values, according to top management at IBM, are more than ethics and legal compliance. From that 2003, 72-hour discussion, IBM decided on these three core values that all IBM employees globally are expected to live every day. Although vague, the values are:

1. Dedication to every client's success
2. Innovation that matters for our company and the world
3. Trust and personal responsibility in all relationships

At the 2003 meeting, IBM abandoned its existing more formal mission statement. As of 2015, there is still no formal mission or vision statement provided on any literature published on IBM's website. Lacking written vision and mission statements to guide strategy and direction, it is unclear whether IBM has the necessary foundation to make clear strategy decisions moving forward.

IBM is exemplary regarding workplace equality. It is no accident that IBM's CEO is a woman, Virginia Rometty. IBM provides same-sex partners of its employees with health benefits and provides an anti-discrimination clause. The Human Rights Campaign for 10 consecutive years has rated IBM 100 percent on its index of gay-friendliness. In recent years, IBM UK has ranked first in Stonewall's annual Workplace Equality Index for United Kingdom (UK) employers.

Internal Issues

Organizational Structure

Many analysts do not consider IBM's organizational structure to be exemplary. There is no chief operating officer or chief administrative office, the divisions are named in somewhat obscure ways, and the CEO is also the chairperson and president. No actual chart could be obtained, but a depiction of IBM's probable structure is given in Exhibit 1.

Strategy

Over 60 percent of IBM employees in R&D are working in fields such as "big data," cloud computing, and other key growth initiatives. This is a drastic change from 20 years ago when over 70 percent of R&D workers were focused on materials and hardware. The new IBM wants to "own the cloud," but ironically and unfortunately for IBM, the cloud will kill profit margins on mainframes, and those profit margins are still the mainstay at IBM. Michael Holland, the principal money manager of Holland & Company in New York City, says, "I am as negative on IBM as I could be. I was a long-term shareholder, and now I'm out of the stock."

IBM's 2013 *Annual Report* revealed three key "strategic imperatives" moving forward. The first of three key initiatives is to focus on the area of big data, which IBM estimates will be a $187 billion industry by year-end 2015. IBM has invested over $24 billion to date, made 30 acquisitions, and has 15,000 consultants and 400 mathematicians in this area. About two thirds of all IBM's R&D is devoted to big data. With 6,000 partners and 1,000 university partnerships, IBM is committed to evolving into a big data company.

The launch of IBM Watson Group in January 2014 promises to grow IBM revenues. Watson helps clients understand big data in a natural language, helping nontechnical people understand complex information more easily. Watson is working on recommending tailored treatments for cancer patients by scanning medical journals and patients' own DNA. Watson is a vast collection of artificial intelligence and machine-learning algorithms, sometimes called "cognitive computing." IBM has had some success with Watson-based technologies in areas such as education and health care. In 2015, IBM formed a strategic alliance with Japan's SoftBank, extending Watson's reach into that country. Until now, Watson has been operating on an English-only corpus.

IBM's second key initiative focuses on cloud computing, which IBM estimates will be a $250 billion industry by year-end 2015. Roughly 80 percent of all Fortune 500 companies today use IBM's cloud services and IBM remains a leader in this area. IBM recently acquired SoftLayer along with 14 other cloud-based firms for a total of $7 billion. Much of IBM's R&D expenses not devoted to big data are focused on the firm's cloud-computing initiative.

The third key in IBM's initiative, dubbed "systems of engagement," centers on technological social interaction products and services. IBM expects firms to double its expenses in this area by 2016. IBM's purchase of Skype and Facebook's purchase of WhatsApp are two examples of companies trying to profit off the social media revolution.

Recently, IBM announced an alliance with Apple to work in tandem to create business apps for mobile devices for IBM's corporate customers. Reeling from 8 consecutive year-over-year revenue declines, IBM is betting on Apple's popularity and simplicity to help please the IBM customer base. Roughly one third of iPad sales in 2013 were to governments or corporations. Many corporate employees use their personal Apple products at work. The new Apple IBM alliance is expected to put increasing pressure on Google and its Android platform to develop corporate partners. It remains to be seen how the difference in culture between IBM and Apple will affect the alliance. Traditionally, IBM has focused on businesses while Apple has focused on upscale personal consumers.

EXHIBIT 1 IBM's Organizational Structure

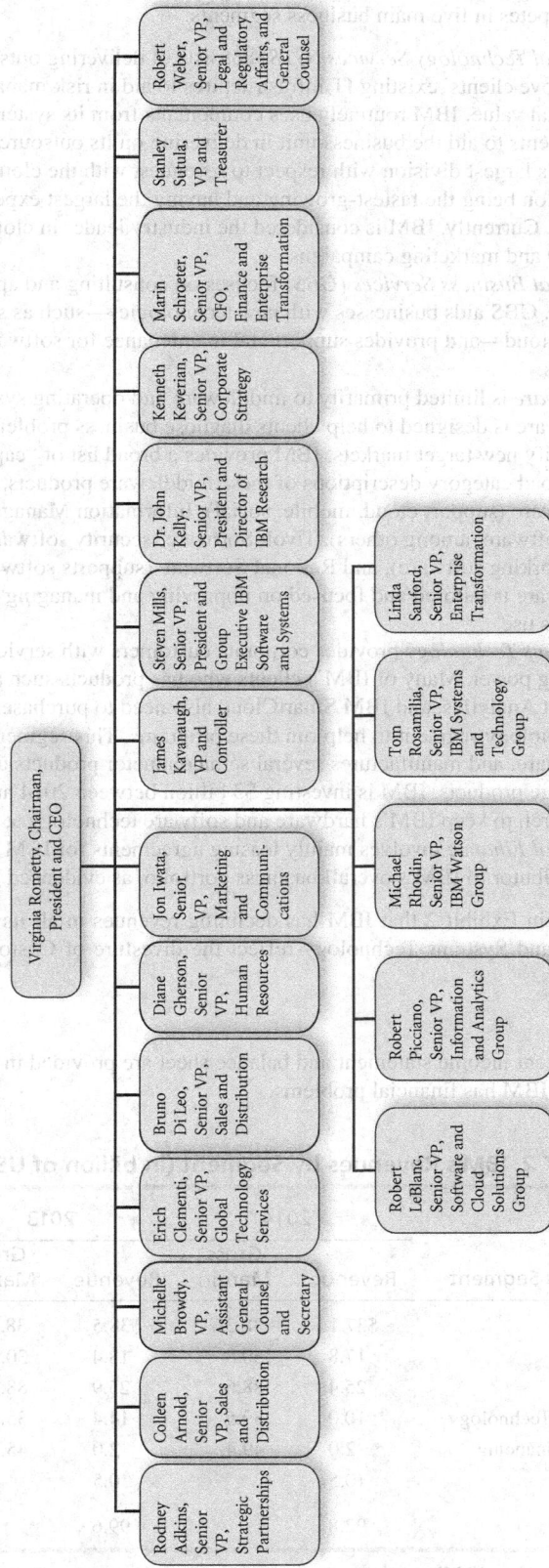

Virginia Rometty, Chairman, President and CEO

- Rodney Adkins, Senior VP, Strategic Partnerships
- Colleen Arnold, Senior VP, Sales and Distribution
- Michelle Browdy, VP, Assistant General Counsel and Secretary
- Erich Clementi, Senior VP, Global Technology Services
- Bruno Di Leo, Senior VP, Sales and Distribution
- Diane Gherson, Senior VP, Human Resources
- Jon Iwata, Senior VP, Marketing and Communications
- James Kavanaugh, VP and Controller
- Steven Mills, Senior VP, President and Group Executive IBM Software and Systems
- Dr. John Kelly, Senior VP, President and Director of IBM Research
- Kenneth Keverian, Senior VP, Corporate Strategy
- Marin Schroeter, Senior VP, CFO, Finance and Enterprise Transformation
- Stanley Sutula, VP and Treasurer
- Robert Weber, Senior VP, Legal and Regulatory Affairs, and General Counsel

Under Steven Mills:
- Robert LeBlanc, Senior VP, Software and Cloud Solutions Group
- Robert Picciano, Senior VP, Information and Analytics Group
- Michael Rhodin, Senior VP, IBM Watson Group
- Tom Rosamilia, Senior VP, IBM Systems and Technology Group
- Linda Sanford, Senior VP, Enterprise Transformation

Source: Based on IBM's Company Documents.

Segment Data

IBM competes in five main business segments:

1. *Global Technology Services (GTS)* consists of delivering outsourcing services to help improve clients' existing IT infrastructures to aid in risk management, flexibility, and financial value. IBM routinely uses components from its systems technology and software segments to aid the business unit in delivering on its outsourcing services mission. GTS is IBM's largest division with respect to revenues, with the cloud-computing portion of the division being the fastest-growing and having the largest expected demand moving forward. Currently, IBM is considered the industry leader in cloud computing through heavy R&D and marketing campaigns.
2. *Global Business Services (GBS)* focuses on consulting and application management services. GBS aids businesses with new technologies—such as smarter commerce, mobile, and cloud—and provides support and maintenance for software and other products IBM offers.
3. *Software* is limited primarily to middleware and operating system software. Middleware software is designed to help clients diagnose business problems, improve efficiency, and identify new target markets. IBM provides a broad list of "capabilities" that serve more as broad category descriptions of these middleware products. They include WebSphere Software (support cloud, mobile, social), Information Management Software (data analytics software, among others), Tivoli Software (security software), Lotus Software (social networking software), and Rational Software (supports software development). Operations software is tailored and focused on improving and managing the core processes that computers use.
4. *Systems Technology* provides corporate customers with services that require large computing power. Many of IBM's clients who use products such as IBM PureSystems, IBM Smart Analytics, and IBM SmartCloud also need to purchase services from the Systems Technology segment to help run these programs. This segment offers storage systems and software, and manufactures several semiconductor products used in IBM systems and storage products. IBM is investing $3 billion between 2014 and 2019 on semiconductor research to keep IBM's hardware and software technology at the forefront.
5. *Global Finance* involves mainly leasing agreements for IBM products; this is not a major contributor to IBM's overall business portfolio, as evidenced in Exhibit 2.

Note in Exhibit 2 that IBM has declining revenues in all its segments. The 2014 numbers for GTS and Systems Technology reflect the divesture of Customer Care BPO and System x businesses.

Finance

IBM's recent income statement and balance sheet are provided in Exhibits 3 and 4, respectively. Note that IBM has financial problems.

EXHIBIT 2 IBM's Revenues by Segment (in billion of USD)

Business Segment	2014		2013		2012	
	Revenue	Gross Margin	Revenue	Gross Margin	Revenue	Gross Margin
GTS	$37.1	38.3%	$38.5	38.1%	$40.2	36.6%
GBS	17.8	30.8	18.4	30.9	18.6	30.0
Software	25.4	88.6	25.9	88.8	25.4	88.7
Systems Technology	10.0	39.5	14.4	35.6	17.7	39.1
Global Financing	2.0	49.4	2.0	45.6	2.0	46.5
Other	(0.5)		0.5		0.6	
Totals	92.8		99.6		104.5	

Source: Based on IBM's company documents.

EXHIBIT 3 Income Statement (in millions of USD)

Report Date	December 31, 2014	December 31, 2013
Revenues	$92,793	$98,367
Cost of revenue	46,386	49,683
Gross profit	46,407	48,684
Operating expenses	25,937	28,038
EBIT	20,470	20,646
Interest expense	484	402
EBT	19,986	20,244
Tax	4,234	3,363
Income from continuing operations	15,752	16,881
Discontinued operations	(3,730)	(398)
Net income	**12,022**	**16,483**

Source: Based on IBM's company documents.

EXHIBIT 4 Balance Sheet (in millions of USD)

Report Date	December 31, 2014	December 31, 2013
Cash	$8,476	$11,066
Accounts receivable	31,831	31,836
Inventories	2,103	2,310
Deferred taxes and prepaid expenses	7,012	6,138
Total current assets	49,422	51,350
Property, plant & equipment	10,771	13,821
Long-term receivables	11,109	12,755
Goodwill	30,556	31,184
Intangible assets	3,104	3,871
Other assets	12,570	13,242
Total assets	**117,532**	**126,223**
Taxes	5,084	4,633
Short-term debt	5,731	6,862
Accounts payable	6,864	7,461
Other current liabilities	21,921	21,198
Total current liabilities	39,600	40,154
Long-term debt	35,073	32,856
Retirement obligations	18,261	16,242
Other liabilities	12,584	14,042
Total liabilities	**105,518**	**103,294**
Common stock	52,666	51,594
Retained earnings	137,793	130,042
Treasury stock	(150,715)	(137,242)
Other	(27,730)	(21,465)
Total equity	**12,014**	**22,929**
Total liabilities & equity	**117,532**	**126,223**

Source: Based on IBM's company documents.

EXHIBIT 5 IBM versus Rival Firms

	IBM	HP	Accenture
# Employees	430,000	11,900	320,000
$ Net Income	$12,000 M	707 M	$2,941 M
$ Revenue	$92.8 B	$3.7 B	$31.8 B
$ Revenue/Employee	$215,814	$310,924	$99,375
$ EPS Ratio	$11.90	$6.72	$4.66
Market Cap.	$155 B	$7.3 B	$55.4 B

Source: Based on IBM's company documents.

Competition

Exhibit 5 provides a comparison of IBM with HP and Accenture. Note that IBM is larger than both rival firms put together.

Hewlett Packard (HP)

Based in Palo Alto, California, HP provides technologies, software, PCs, workstations, tables, calculators, and many other accessories and services to individuals as well as corporations. The company has been struggling in recent years, with both revenues and profits decreasing annually from the $127 billion and $30 billion, respectively, reported back in 2011.

Hewlett Packard prides itself on three key areas: converged cloud, big data, and security and risk management. Forrester's Wave for Private Cloud recently declared HP to be the world leader in the private cloud market, earning the highest rankings for 8 of 15 categories measured. HP prides its cloud business on providing customers with an easier installation and configuration process than traditionally cloud-based products provided. HP's new cloud technology allows users to better streamline its IT operations, design workloads in a more optimal fashion, and provide an open source design. HP's new Vertica Analytics Platform is the firm's flagship big data package that enables companies to quickly analyze large volumes of data in real time. The software provides support for both C++ and R statistical language.

In the personal systems market, HP has revenues of about $30 billion annually. Personal systems consist of notebooks, desktops, and workstations. Primarily, HP competes with Lenovo, Dell, Apple, Lenovo, and Toshiba in this segment. Printing has long been a stable for HP, competing with Canon, Lexmark, Xerox, Sieko, Epson, and others. HP's printing revenues are about $22 billion annually.

The company's Enterprise Group and Enterprise Services focus on technology infrastructure, IT services, consulting, and business outsourcing. Revenues are about $50 billion in these two segments. Top competitors in this area are IBM, Cisco, Microsoft, and Accenture. Software is a growing business worldwide, and HP competes with IBM, CA Technologies, BMC Software, and others. Software is one of the few bright spots for HP, with revenues increasing to over $4 billion in 2014.

Hewlett Packard's new Apollo 8000 system is the first super-computer to be 100 percent liquid cooled and offers direct competition to IBM's high-end server market. The Apollo 8000 is priced from $500,000 to several million dollars. In addition to being liquid cooled, the new product operates 28 percent more efficiently than any other product on the market.

Accenture

Based in Dublin, Ireland, Accenture is a management consulting and technology company. Accenture employs over 320,000 people, conducts business worldwide, and reported revenues of $32 billion in 2014, up from $27 billion in 2011. Accenture had acquisitions totaling over $800 million in 2013, most notably Acquity Group, Fjord, and AvVenta. Many of the acquisitions were focused on helping Accenture's marketing consulting businesses. Accenture recently formed a joint venture formed with GE called Taleris that enables airplanes to better anticipate aircraft maintenance issues. Accenture has seen the U.S. market grow at an annualized rate of 13 percent in revenues from 2011 to 2013, but continues to focus on emerging markets, especially Brazil.

External Audit

Industry Growth Rate

Slow information technology (IT) growth continues in 2015. IDC, a global IT data provider, estimates growth from 2012 to 2017 to be around 4.6 percent annualized, as companies are reluctant to sign long-term contracts. Moving forward, the key areas of IT growth are expected in the following areas: application management, cloud computing, business consulting, network consulting and integration, and hosted application management. The areas listed are expected to grow annualized from 2012 to 2017 at 5.2, 23.5, 7.6, 6.6, and 7.4 percent, respectively. Cloud computing clearly dominates future expectations. Some analysts in fact predict over 80 percent of all IT growth between 2012 and 2017 will be cloud related.

Areas of slower growth between 2012 and 2017 are expected to come from IT outsourcing, IT consulting, and IT hardware support at projected annualized growth rates of 1.3, 4.1, and 2.9 percent, respectively. Exhibit 6 provides detailed projections from IDC on growth yields through 2017. Note that IT outsourcing is not expected to produce any real gains during the projected period. Business consulting and outsourcing are both prime areas of interest for firms moving forward the next several years; firms without a good presence in these areas will likely look to mergers and acquisitions to provide them a quick presence in these areas.

As per IT growth by geographic region, Asia has experienced the best growth rates of late, with China up 7.7 percent, Indonesia up 6.2 percent, Vietnam up 5.0 percent, and India up 3.2 percent in 2012. Europe, still recovering from its economic debt crisis, reported the smallest growth rates, with the United Kingdom up only 0.2 percent and Germany up 0.9 percent. The United States experienced IT growth of 2.8 percent in 2012.

Computers and Servers

The desktop computer, laptop computer, and server industry has declined in the United States on average 17 percent per year from 2009 to 2014, and is expected to decline another 5 percent per

EXHIBIT 6 Projected Industry Dollar and Returns for IT (in billions of USD)

Area	2014	2015	2016	2017	2014–2017 Yields (%)
Business consulting	$92	$100	$108	$117	27%
IT consulting	33	34	36	37	12
Systems integration	121	127	132	138	14
Network consulting & integration	40	43	46	49	23
Customer application development	43	45	48	50	16
Project-based Total	**329**	**349**	**369**	**391**	**19**
Business outsourcing	177	188	198	209	32
Application management	57	60	63	65	14
Hosted application management	12	12	13	15	25
IT outsourcing	126	128	129	129	2
Network & desktop outsourcing	51	53	55	57	12
Hosting infrastructure services	39	42	44	48	21
Outsourcing Total	**461**	**482**	**503**	**524**	**14**
Hardware deployment/support	67	69	71	73	9
Software deployment/support	74	76	79	82	11
IT education/training	25	26	27	28	12
Support/training Total	**165**	**171**	**177**	**183**	**11**
Total global services spending	**955**	**1,002**	**1,049**	**1,098**	**15**

Source: Based on IDC's March 2013 forecast report.

year into 2019, despite a slight increase in demand. High standardization of products makes differentiating product lines difficult, resulting in reduced prices for manufacturers. Compounding problems, new competitors are able to enter the industry fairly easily, creating downward pressure on prices. Increases in tablet and smartphone demand also erode into PC sales, but analysts expect a sizable market for PCs to remain for quite some time.

Software

The business of data analytics, data storage, and security are growing. IBM primarily competes in the data analytics and data storage arenas, both representing around 20 percent of a $170 billion industry (in sales) in the United States alone. Smartphone apps represent about 2 percent of this industry, but further growth is expected. In total, around 3 percent growth is forecasted in the software area through 2019 in this country. But this industry requires large R&D expenses to stay current, as well as an expensive labor force, protection of patents and piracy risks, and substantial marketing.

Legal and Ethical Big Data Considerations

In the last 5 years, the general public has become especially aware and suspicious of data usage. Privacy concerns have arisen and even rights to who owns the data presents a problem moving forward for corporations in the data business. The use of data, and more specifically the information that can be derived from data, has grown faster than our legal systems can keep up. Netflix, AOL, and even the Eric Snowden incident involving release of U.S. secrets have exposed issues related to the use of big data.

Your web-browsing history, emails, texts, tweets, posts, and movements around town are now tracked. To what extent do firms need permission to obtain this personal data? Can data that an individual agreed to be collected then be sold to a third party? Should the individual be compensated for data collected from her or his actions each time the data are used? What guarantees can be made to ensure privacy so certain individuals cannot be pinpointed out of a database? The volume and nature of how data can be used is growing faster than world government legal systems can adapt to. The threat of legal issues against firms using big data is increasing daily. Complicating legal issues further, will negligence attorneys use data to prosecute corporations and governments for *not* using data to predict and foresee potential problems?

Future

In early 2015, Marriott and IBM announced a deal to move 80 percent of Marriott's old-school technology to what's known as a "hybrid" cloud built by IBM. That means Marriott will use IBM's cloud to host apps that it doesn't want to host. Marriott will keep its data centers but will update them to use the latest cloud technology. Marriott's infrastructure supports over 4,000 locations worldwide. This deal was similar to the $500 million, 6-year deal IBM signed a year ago with insurance giant The Hartford.

IBM's three initiatives focus on the cloud, big data, and systems of engagement, but the future of those industries is uncertain. In fiscal 2014, IBM divested its Customer Care BPO and System x businesses. Company revenues fell 11 percent between fiscal years 2012 and 2014; the firm's stock price fell 17 percent over the same time frame while the S&P 500 increased 60 percent. Prepare a needed, 3-year strategic plan for CEO Virginia Rometty and Big Blue.

Microsoft Corporation, 2013

www.microsoft.com, MSFT

Headquartered in Redmond, Washington, Microsoft is the world's largest software company and had record revenues of $73 billion in fiscal year 2012 that ended on June 30, 2012. Microsoft develops a variety of software and hardware products and services for customers around the world, including its Windows Office, Windows 8 operating system for personal computers (PCs), Windows Phone 7 operating systems for mobile phones, Windows Server operating systems, Windows Azure, Microsoft SQL, Visual Studio, Silverlight, and the popular Xbox gaming and entertainment console. Many PC makers such as Acer, Lenovo, Dell, Hewlett-Packard, and Toshiba pre-install Microsoft software on devices. The firm also offers consulting services, cloud-based services, and training certifications as well as online products such as Bing, MSN, adCenter, and Atlas. Microsoft has strategic alliances with Nokia, NIIT, and Dominion Enterprises. The company owns Skype and recently introduced a Windows Phone and a Windows tablet computer named "Surface."

Microsoft's third quarter of fiscal 2013 results reported April 2013 were outstanding, with its Business Division's revenues up 8 percent to $6.32 billion, its Server and Tools' revenues of $5.04 billion up 11 percent, its Windows' division revenues of $5.07 billion up 23 percent, its Online Services segment revenues up 18 percent to $832 million, and its Entertainment and Devices segment revenues up 56 percent to $2.53 billion.

In August 2013, CEO Ballmer announced he would resign from Microsoft within 12 months, so the firm is scurrying to determine who will be a good replacement. The month prior, Microsoft revamped its organizational structure, dissolving its eight business lines up in favour of four new segments to focus on engineering and encourage collaboration across the company. Basically the company is now structured as a division-by-function type of structure. The divisions are expected to focus on operating systems, apps, cloud technology and devices. The move largely reversed the strategy and structure put in place by CEO Ballmer in 2005. Microsoft's stock price jumped in response the Ballmer announcing that he would resign soon.

Copyright by Fred David Books LLC. (Written by Forest R. David)

History

Founded by Bill Gates and Paul Allen in 1975, Microsoft was established to develop and sell BASIC Interpreters for the Altair 8800. The company rose to dominate the PC operating system market in the mid-1980s with their MS-DOS software, followed by the Microsoft Windows operating system, which was a graphical extension of MS-DOS. Microsoft went public in 1986, instantly creating three billionaires and 12,000 millionaires from Microsoft employees. In 1990, Microsoft introduced its software office suite, Microsoft Office that bundled MS Word and MS Excel together.

Microsoft acquired Skype Technologies for $8.6 billion in 2011 in its largest-ever acquisition. Following the release of Windows Phone 7, Microsoft underwent a gradual rebranding of its product range throughout 2011 and 2012. Its logos, products, services, and websites adopted the principles and concepts of the Metro design language. Microsoft in early 2012 introduced Windows 8, an operating system designed to power both PCs and tablet computers. Then in May 2012, Microsoft introduced its own tablet computer, the Microsoft Surface. As the company continued to diversify away from operating systems, it paid $1.2 billion to buy the social network firm Yammer and then launched its Windows Phone 8. To cope with the potential increase in demand for products and services, Microsoft is slowly but surely opening its own Microsoft Stores across the USA. Bill and Melinda Gates are today one of the richest couples on the planet, and one of the most giving couples in terms of philanthropic endeavors through the Bill and Melinda Gates Foundation.

Internal Issues

Vision and Mission

A statement at the corporate website says: "At Microsoft, our mission and values are to help people and businesses throughout the world realize their full potential."

Organizational Structure

Among the 17 executives listed in Exhibit 1, there are three women in Microsoft's management hierarchy. Note in Exhibit 1 that Microsoft uses a division-by-product organizational structure, with Steve Ballmer being chief executive officer (CEO) and Kevin Turner being chief operations officer (COO). Some analysts say that executive titles could be more effectively named. For example, President of Microsoft Corp. versus President of Microsoft Business is unclear to some observers. It is unclear from the structure where Microsoft Phone and Microsoft Tablet and Microsoft Stores reports. Such items would ideally be clear in executive titles. Perhaps a strategic business unit (SBU) structure would be more effective.

The Surface Tablet

Sales of Microsoft's Surface tablet are not good; analysts expect the company to sell between 500,000 and 600,000 Surface tablets in their second quarter of fiscal 2013, much lower than the company's original estimate of 1 to 2 million. Introducing a tablet is a good idea for three reasons: (1) Microsoft has the cash to invest heavily in research and development (R&D) for its own tablet; (2) the tablet market has been booming; and (3) the PC market is declining. But the problem perhaps is that Microsoft priced the Surface too high at $499 and up, roughly the same price as the competing Apple iPad. Microsoft likely should compete on price, not luxury, when up against Apple products. Microsoft could undercut Apple's price, and even if it *loses money* on Surface, the initial loss could be worth it if it revitalizes sales of other company products. The success of Windows 8 largely hinges on widespread adoption of the Surface tablet. The whole

EXHIBIT 1 Organizational Chart

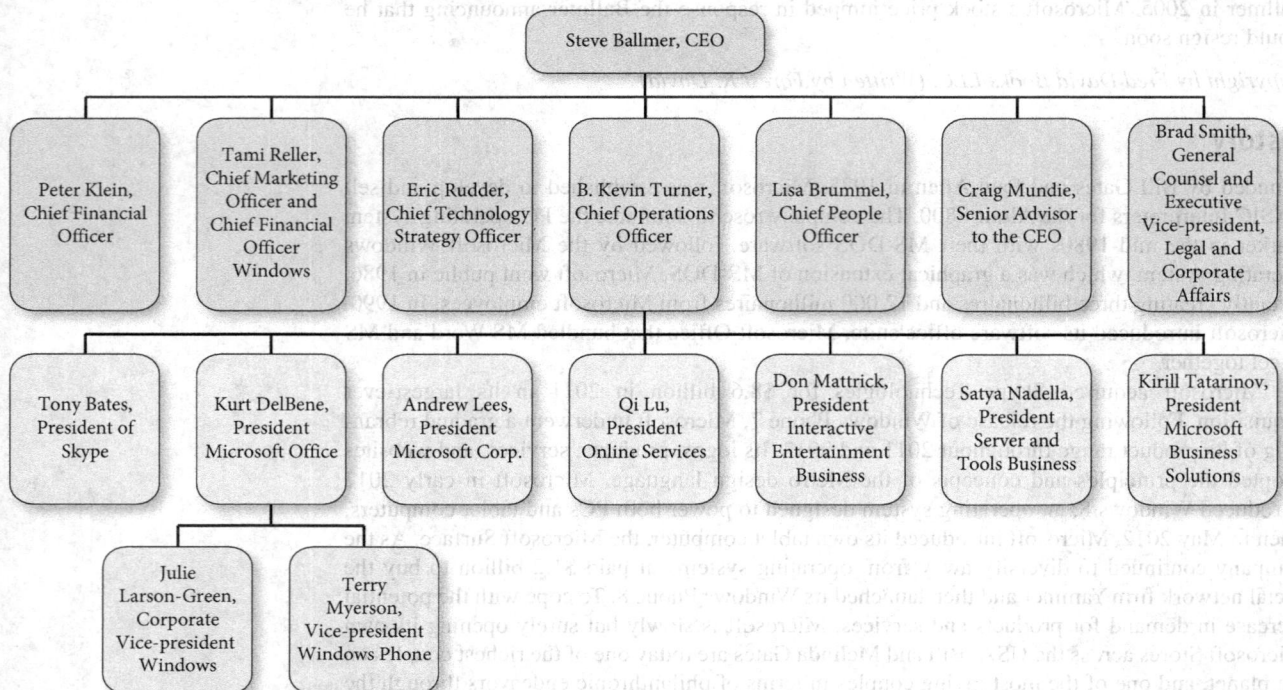

Source: Based on company documents.

point of Windows 8 was to launch Microsoft into the world of tablet computing, and with weak sales of its tablet, Microsoft's transition away from the faltering PC market may be a difficult one. Microsoft should perhaps consider McDonald's successful strategy of offering and heavily marketing inexpensive products (for example, the Dollar Menu) and by promoting low-grade items.

Segments

Microsoft has five reportable business segments as listed in Exhibit 2. Note that Microsoft Business is the largest segment in both revenues and operating income, whereas both the Windows and Windows Line (called Windows Division from here on), and Server and Tools segment, contribute greatly to the company's financial position. A sixth segment, titled Corporate Level Activity, includes all financial dealings not allocated to specific segments. The division includes costs related to marketing, product support services, legal, finance, and other business activities. Some analysts contend that the company's segments could be more effectively named to reveal their nature.

The Windows Division receives approximately 75 percent of its revenue from the Windows operating system, with the bulk of this revenue coming from equipment manufacturers such as Dell, Sony, Toshiba, and others pre-installing Windows on their machines for customers. The division in addition to providing Windows also provides related software, online services, and PC hardware products. This division could be vulnerable if worldwide PC sales continue to slump, as they did in 2012 with a 3.2-percent decline. Windows 8, launched in October 2012, provides better communication with cloud services and enables tablets and phones to run with near PC power. The whole world is becoming less dependent on traditional PCs, which historically has been Microsoft's bread and butter and is a key reason why the firm is looking to diversify.

Microsoft's Server and Tools Division is Microsoft's third most profitable division, producing name brand products such as Windows Server, Microsoft SQL, Windows Azure, Visual Studio, Enterprise Services, and others. Enterprise Services include product support and consulting services and account for 20 percent of the division's revenues. The division also offers developer tools, training, and certifications. Around 55 percent of Server and Tools revenues are derived from multiyear licensing agreements, with the remaining 25 percent coming from transactional volume licensing programs. In 2012, revenues increased by 12 percent in the division mainly attributed to growth in the SQL and Windows servers, although Enterprise

EXHIBIT 2 Microsoft's Revenues by Segment (in millions)

	2012	2011	2010
Windows Division			
Revenues	$18,373	$19,033	$19,491
Operating Income	11,460	12,211	12,895
Server and Tools			
Revenues	18,686	16,680	15,109
Operating Income	7,431	6,290	5,381
Online Services			
Revenues	2,867	2,607	2,294
Operating Income	(8,121)	(2,657)	(2,408)
Microsoft Business			
Revenues	23,991	22,514	19,256
Operating Income	15,719	14,657	11,849
Entertainment and Devices			
Revenues	9,593	8,915	6,079
Operating Income	364	1,257	517
Corporate Level Activity	(5,090)	(4,597)	(4,136)

Source: Based on 2012 *Annual Report*, p. 21–25.

Services grew 18 percent over the same period from an increase in both product support and consulting services. Overall operating income still increased 17 percent.

The company's Online Services Division designs products that aid customers in simplifying tasks and making more informed decisions online. Products include Bing and MSN, which generate sales through advertising. In fiscal year 2012, advertising revenues grew 13 percent in this segment to $2.6 billion. Online advertising revenues grew 13 percent over the fiscal year to $2.6 billion; however, operating losses totaled $8 billion resulting from $6 billion in goodwill impairment from fourth quarter of fiscal year 2012, resulting from the 2007 acquisition of aQuantive. Expectations of future sales growth and profitability are significantly lower for aQuantive than anticipated.

The company's Microsoft Business Division produced 32 percent of total companywide revenues and 72 percent of operating income in fiscal year 2012. The segment derives revenues from software and online servers that help to increase personal team and organizational productivity. Microsoft's most notable product, its Microsoft Office System, makes up more than 90 percent of this division's revenues. However, future reliance on this segment is somewhat tenuous because Google and other competitors are now offering Web-based products that work much the same as Microsoft Office products work.

The company's Entertainment and Devices Division generated 13 percent of total revenues in fiscal year 2012, led by the Xbox 360 entertainment platform. The division includes Xbox, Skype, and Windows Phone. Skype is a free popular video chat platform and for-pay phone service. Sales from Skype and Windows Phone increased 6.5 percent in fiscal year 2012, but Xbox sales declined $113 million even though Xbox LIVE revenue increased. Skype reported revenues of $860 million, net losses of $7 million, and long-term debt of $686 million in 2011, leading some analysts to say Microsoft paid too much for Skype. Overall, Microsoft has a history of using poor judgments in acquisitions, as indicated by the company's goodwill being more than $13 billion. Skype does overlap considerable with Windows Live Messenger in that both offer free chat, voice chat, and video chat. Windows Messenger though has around three times the users as Skype, but Skype offers a more refined platform for video chats. The one key difference between Microsoft's existing products and Skype is that about 8 million Skype users pay for the service through telephone connectivity, making it easy for many customers across the globe to buy phone numbers in foreign markets affordably. With the purchase price of $8.5 billion, Microsoft is in essence paying around $1,000 for each customer who is worth around $30 each, assuming most of Skype's income is from call charges, leaving much to be made up on possible advertisements or some synergy with existing Microsoft products. Compounding problems for Skype, it is estimated a large percentage of their customers come from emerging markets and do not have much money to spend. However for Microsoft, preventing Google and Facebook from obtaining Skype also played a role in the purchase.

Exhibit 3 reveals that approximately 52 percent of Microsoft's 2012 revenues are derived from the USA. Note that international revenues have increased as a percent of total revenues in each of the three years provided.

Finance

Microsoft's fiscal year ends on June 30 of each year. As indicated in the financial statements provided in Exhibits 4 and 5, Microsoft's revenues have been growing annually in recent years, a good thing. However, note in Exhibit 4 that the company's net income dropped 26.7 percent in

EXHIBIT 3 Microsoft's Revenues by Geographic Region (in millions)

	2012	2011	2010
USA	$38,846	$38,008	$36,173
Outside USA	$34,877	$31,935	$26,311
Total	$73,723	$69,943	$62,484

Source: Based on 2012 *Annual Report*, p. 80.

EXHIBIT 4 Microsoft's Income Statements (in millions)

	2012	2011	2010
Revenue	**73,723.0**	**69,943.0**	**62,484.0**
Other Revenue, Total	0.0	0.0	0.0
Total Revenue	73,723.0	69,943.0	62,484.0
Cost of Revenue, Total	17,530.0	15,577.0	12,395.0
Gross Profit	56,193.0	54,366.0	50,089.0
Selling/General/Administrative Expenses, Total	18,426.0	18,162.0	17,218.0
Research and Development	9,811.0	9,043.0	8,714.0
Depreciation and Amortization	0.0	0.0	0.0
Interest Expense (Income), Net Operating	0.0	0.0	0.0
Unusual Expense (Income)	5,895.0	-80.0	-10.0
Other Operating Expenses, Total	0.0	0.0	0.0
Operating Income	22,061.0	27,241.0	24,167.0
Interest Income (Expense),	0.0	0.0	0.0
Gain (Loss) on Sale of Assets	0.0	0.0	0.0
Other, Net	1.0	-31.0	14.0
Income Before Tax	22,267.0	28,071.0	25,013.0
Income Tax, Total	5,289.0	4,921.0	6,253.0
Income After Tax	16,978.0	23,150.0	18,760.0
Minority Interest	0.0	0.0	0.0
Equity in Affiliates	0.0	0.0	0.0
U.S. GAAP Adjustment	0.0	0.0	0.0
Net Income Before Extraordinary Items	16,978.0	23,150.0	18,760.0
Total Extraordinary Items	0.0	0.0	0.0
Net Income	**16,978.0**	**23,150.0**	**18,760.0**
Total Adjustments to Net Income	0.0	0.0	0.0
Basic Weighted Average Shares	8,396.0	8,490.0	8,813.0
Basic EPS Excluding Extraordinary Items	2.02	2.73	2.13
Basic EPS Including Extraordinary Items	2.02	2.73	2.13

EPS, earnings per share; GAAP, generally accepted accounting procedures.
Source: Based on company documents.

fiscal year 2012 and that the company's R&D expenditures have held at 13 percent of revenue for the last three years. Microsoft's sales and marketing expenditures for the last three years have dropped from 21 to 20 to 19 percent of revenues.

Note in Exhibit 5 that Microsoft's goodwill increased another $900 million to $13.4 billion in fiscal year 2012. Goodwill represents the cumulative amount the company has historically paid "above book value" for acquisitions, so such a high number is not good.

EXHIBIT 5 Microsoft's Balance Sheets (in millions)

	2012	2011	2010
Assets			
Cash and Short-Term Investments	63,040.0	52,772.0	36,788.0
Total Receivables, Net	15,780.0	14,987.0	13,014.0
Total Inventory	1,137.0	1,372.0	740.0
Prepaid Expenses	0.0	0.0	0.0
Other Current Assets, Total	5,127.0	5,787.0	5,134.0
Total Current Assets	**85,084.0**	**74,918.0**	**55,676.0**

(continued)

EXHIBIT 5 Continued

	2012	2011	2010
Property, Plant, and Equipment	8,269.0	8,162.0	7,630.0
Goodwill, Net	13,452.0	12,581.0	12,394.0
Intangibles, Net	3,170.0	744.0	1,158.0
Long-Term Investments	9,776.0	10,865.0	7,754.0
Note Receivable, Long Term	0.0	0.0	0.0
Other Long-Term Assets, Total	1,520.0	1,434.0	1,501.0
Other Assets, Total	0.0	0.0	0.0
Total Assets	**121,271.0**	**108,704.0**	**86,113.0**
Liabilities and Shareholders' Equity			
Accounts Payable	4,175.0	4,197.0	4,025.0
Payable/Accrued	0.0	0.0	0.0
Accrued Expenses	3,875.0	3,575.0	3,283.0
Notes Payable and Short-Term Debt	0.0	0.0	1,000.0
Current Portability of Long-Term Debt Capital Leases	1,231.0	0.0	0.0
Other Current Liabilities, Total	23,407.0	21,002.0	17,839.0
Total Current Liabilities	32,688.0	28,774.0	26,147.0
Total Long-Term Debt	10,713.0	11,921.0	4,939.0
Deferred Income Tax	1,893.0	1,456.0	229.0
Minority Interest	0.0	0.0	0.0
Other Liabilities, Total	9,614.0	9,470.0	8,623.0
Total Liabilities	54,908.0	51,621.0	39,938.0
Redeemable Preferred Stock	0.0	0.0	0.0
Preferred Stock, Nonredeemable, Net	0.0	0.0	0.0
Common Stock	65,797.0	63,415.0	62,856.0
Additional Paid-In Capital	0.0	0.0	0.0
Retained Earnings (Accumulated Deficit)	−856.0	−8,195.0	−17,736.0
Treasury Stock, Common	0.0	0.0	0.0
ESOP Debt Guarantee	0.0	0.0	0.0
Unrealized Gain (Loss)	1,523.0	1,658.0	1,231.0
Other Equity, Total	−101.0	205.0	−176.0
Total Equity	**66,363.0**	**57,083.0**	**46,175.0**
Total Liabilities and Shareholders' Equity	**121,271.0**	**108,704.0**	**86,113.0**

ESOP, employee stock ownership plan.
Source: Based on company documents.

Competition

Being so diversified, Microsoft has different competitors in different segments. The company's Windows Operating System faces competition from Apple and Google who have their own operating systems. Microsoft's server products face stiff competition from Hewlett-Packard, IBM, and Oracle, who all offer preinstalled operating systems on their server hardware. Microsoft's cloud-based services compete with Amazon, Google, and Salesforce.com, whereas Microsoft's SQL Azure faces intense competition from IBM, Oracle, and many other firms.

The Microsoft Office package (Word, Excel, Access, and other products) faces heavy competition from Adobe, Apple, Cisco, Google, SAP, and many other Web-based competitors offering word processing, spreadsheets, and databases. The company's Entertainment and Devices segment, producer of Xbox360, faces intense competition from heavyweights Nintendo and Sony. The average life of an entertainment console is surprisingly long at 5+ years, and game selection is one of the largest factors in deterring the success of a gaming console.

EXHIBIT 6 A Financial Comparison of Microsoft to Rival Companies

	Microsoft	Apple	Google	Oracle
Number of employees	94,000	72,800	53,546	115,000
Revenue	$72.4B	$156.5B	$47.5B	$37B
Net Income	$15.7B	$41.7B	$10.6B	$10.6B
Net Profit Margin	21.7%	26.7%	22.2%	28.7%
EPS	$1.85	$44.15	$31.91	$2.13
Market Capitalization	228B	457M	237.9B	$164B
Shares Outstanding	8.42B	940M	228M	4.7B

EPS, earnings per share.
Source: Based on company documents.

Microsoft's new Windows Phone competes with market share leader Apple with their iPhone and Google with their Android platform powering Samsung and other phones. Also, Research in Motion is revitalizing their once-popular Blackberry. Microsoft's alliance with Nokia to power Nokia phones with Windows 8 hopes to inch away at market share in the phone industry.

Exhibit 6 provides a financial comparison of Microsoft with three competitors. Note that Microsoft has the lowest earnings per share (EPS) among the firms included, partly as a result of having by far the most shares of stock outstanding.

Apple

Headquartered in Cupertino, California, Apple produces PCs, digital music players, iPhones, and other communication media to customers around the world. Some of their most popular products include the iPhone, iPad, MacBook Pro, and iPod. Apple has their own operating system for all of their products. The iPhone is the world leader in market share for all mobile phones, but Samsung is the world leader in smartphone unit volume (most phones sold) because they produce multiple options for customers, rather then a one-size-fits-all as Apple does with their current iPhone. In addition, Google's Android platform, which Samsung and other phone manufacturers use on their phones, powers more phones than Apple's operating system, which is only used to power Apple iPhones.

Apple also provides many software products with their operating system such as iLife, iWork, Final Cut Pro, Logic Studio, and of late Apple TV. Apple provides their products through online stores, retail stores such as Walmart, Best Buy, Apple Stores, and others. Apple operates about 250 Apple Stores in the USA and 140 stores internationally.

Apple's stock price fell from $700 around the launch of iPhone 5 in 2012 to $485 in early 2013. Some analysts suggest products by Samsung powered by Google's Android software are taking significant market share away from Apple. Apple launched a new phone in the middle of 2013 called the iPhone 5S, reportedly to sell at a significant discount to the iPhone 5. To be targeted at large emerging markets in which many customers have no phone and less money, the 5S phone is likely to have a polycarbonate construction instead of the glass and aluminum the iPhone 5 sports. In addition, there will be no retina display and the phone will not be compatible with newer LTE markets and will thus run on 3G. Running on 3G however, is adequate because many emerging markets will not have LTE for a number of years into the future. The iPhone 5S follows the line of thinking of the iPad Mini, providing a discounted item for customers on a limited budget. Although the 5S may hurt profit margins, producing the phone is an attempt to win market share in emerging markets before Samsung, Dell, Nokia, and other competitors win legions of fans over to their products.

Google

Headquartered in Mountain View, California, Google provides the world's most popular search engine as well as cloud computing, Google Chrome, Google Maps for GPS users, Google Earth, Google Analytics for keeping track of hits and traffic on websites, and YouTube. Many of Google's products are supported by heavy advertisements, helping to produce record revenues of $38 billion for year end 2011. Google produces Android, the world's most popular smartphone platform.

About 96 percent of all Google revenues are derived from advertising programs, with the balance coming predominantly from licensing agreements. Using technology from a firm named DoubleClick, Google can better determine user interest and effectively target advertisements, thus enabling Google to charge more for their service.

Google's Android operating system used for touch-screen smartphones and tablets currently enjoys a 75-percent market share in the smartphone marketplace. One of the key benefits of using Android products is that they are open source, meaning the software can be modified and distributed to anyone. Phone manufacturers such as Samsung or wireless carriers such as Verizon can alter the software to meet their specific needs. In addition, enthusiasts who enjoy developing applications for use in mobile devices can also alter the platform to fit their needs. The popularity and open source nature of Android has led it to becoming the top choice in the world for smartphones and tablets. The future of Android's use may eventually extend away from solely phones and tablets into television, games, and consoles and virtually any electronic device. This could potentially put further pressure on Microsoft with their Windows 8 operating system and Xbox consoles.

Oracle Corp.

Headquartered in Redwood City, California, Oracle is a producer of middleware software, application software, application server and cloud application, data integration, development tools, Java, and much more. Oracle also provides consulting services in business and information technology (IT), strategy alignment, and ongoing product enhancements. In 2012, Oracle acquired RightNow Technologies, Inc. (RightNow) and Taleo Corporation (Taleo). Oracle's stock hit a new 52-week high of $35 in January 2013.

As an example of Oracle's software products that compete with Microsoft, one of the largest Australian Supermarket chains is Coles with more than 100,000 employees and 2,000 stores throughout Australia. Coles recently installed Oracle's Exadata Database Machine and Oracle Enterprise Manager 12c running on Oracle Linux to enable critical trend reporting during retail seasonal spikes. By implementing the Oracle Exadata Database Machine, Coles's processes improved three to four times out of the box, with four to six times faster query performance so that Coles's can now meet SLAs and drive customer satisfaction. With the Oracle software, Coles can now also store 20+ TB of trending historical data, enabling new, complex analytical reports to help better predict the needs and potential issues for Coles's stores.

Nintendo

Headquartered in Kyoto, Japan, Nintendo is the world's largest video game company by revenues. Translated into English the company name is: "leave luck to heaven." Nintendo is Japan's third most valuable publically traded company and has a market value of more than $85 billion and revenues of more than $12 billion. Based in Redmond, Washington, near Microsoft's headquarters, Nintendo North America is the majority owner of the Seattle Mariners Major League Baseball team. Nintendo is a market share leader position with products such as the Nintendo 3DS and Nintendo's Wii products including the new Wii U, which features touch-screen controllers. Nintendo's European division is based in Frankfurt, Germany. Nintendo has a joint venture in China now produces and markets the iQue Player, a modified version of the Nintendo 64.

External

Smartphone Growth

Smartphone shipments have risen dramatically since 2005 from 50 million phones shipped worldwide to more than 650 million phones shipped in 2012. Shipments by 2016 are expected to be more than 1,200 million phones. Most of the growth is expected to come from emerging markets, with China leading the way. In 2012, China surpassed the USA as the world's largest smartphone market, yet there are millions of untapped customers remaining in China. India, Brazil, and other emerging markets offer millions of customers. Aside from traditional phone providers, companies such as Apple, Dell, and others are all continually offering new products and features to differentiate their handsets. Google and Microsoft are teaming up with existing phone producers to provide new and better operating systems for their respective phones.

Nokia Migrates to Windows 8

Nokia unveiled in late 2012 their latest Lumia 920 and 820 model smartphones, Nokia's first set of smartphones to run off the new Windows 8 operating system. A main advantage gained for Nokia using Windows 8 resides in the compatibility of file-sharing capabilities because both the 920 and 820 devices will sync with PCs and tablets with Windows 8. Nokia hopes the switch to Windows 8 will differentiate its products and aid in improving sales which declined 37 percent from the second quarter 2011 to the second quarter 2012.

Cloud Computing

Cloud computing, supplying computing services via the Internet without having to use hardware or platform support, continues to grow in its use and offerings. Many businesses employ the technology to save on costs because they can lease data storage and computing capacity from web-based providers. Advantages for businesses using cloud technology include reduced capital investments in equipment and software, while allowing for payments only for the capacity needed. Traditionally, firms would buy their own in-house capacity and have to forecast future needs, often resulting in purchasing more capacity than was needed. Google is the lead company using cloud technology to support many of their offerings. However, there is still some concern among businesses that cloud computing offers less security, and increased dependability on a third-party vender such as Google to continually provide the service at an appropriate network speed is questionable. Nevertheless, cloud services are expected to yield revenues of $100 billion in 2016, up from $40 billion in 2011.

The Future

Microsoft is developing technologies that increasingly enable touch screen and voice to be more readily understood by PCs, tablets, and phones. Microsoft CEO Ballmer envisions that technology will soon act on people's behalf rather than at their command, so he has directed Microsoft R&D staff to develop cloud services that enhance the experience for both businesses and individuals. Microsoft plans to better align the communication between PCs, tablets, phones, and servers by developing improved operating systems with Windows 8 delivering preliminary results in this arena.

High-definition TVs and tablets of today are expected to soon lose market share to gadgets than can read human emotions and to eye gaze technology that will allow for automatic scrolling and opening of apps. Even "skin stretch feedback" on devices will take into account people's emotions. Tom Wilson, CEO of emotions3D, for example recently remarked that such devices will "interpret moods and give consumers a more helpful and rewarding experience." Some analysts predict that the audio quality alone on smartphones will increase 16 times from 2013 to 2018. Also, as the tablet's video gaming experience increases and becomes closer to the experience on an Xbox, PlayStation or Nintendo's market share for traditional gaming consoles may decline. More useable devices for people on the go are being developed in part to reduce accidents while driving and using mobile devices.

Microsoft in early 2013 introduced its new Office 365 product, a subscription service for $99.99 or $9.99 per month pay-as-you-go option. Office 365 constantly updates itself every time you open a program. The product works great on Apple Macs and virtually all companies' computers, tablets, smartphones, and more.

Microsoft's $2 billion investment to finance part of Dell computer's buyout in early 2013 is an attempt by the firm to support the ailing PC industry—which saw shipments fall 14 percent in the first quarter of 2013 alone. Millions of consumers globally are skipping over PCs altogether and going straight to mobile devices.

Technology is changing so rapidly everyday, and new rival firms arising globally in the industry, that Microsoft needs a clear strategic plan going forward. Develop a new strategic plan for the upcoming new CEO of Microsoft.

Lenovo Group Limited, 2013

www.lenovo.com, LNVGY

Headquartered in Beijing, China, Lenovo designs, produces, and markets ThinkPad personal computers, notebook computers, tablet computers, desktop computers, mobile phones, workstations, servers, electronic storage, information technology (IT) management software, and smart televisions. Lenovo is the world's second-largest PC vendor (behind Hewlett-Packard [HP]), and markets the ThinkPad line of notebook computers and ThinkCentre line of desktops. Lenovo's U.S. headquarters is in Morrisville, North Carolina, and its registered office is in Hong Kong, China. Lenovo has operations in more than 60 countries and sells its products in around 160 countries. Lenovo ranks fourth in the global tablet market by volume. Lenovo's fiscal year ends on March 31 every year. For fiscal 2012/2013 ending March 31, 2013, Lenovo's revenues increased 14.5 percent to $33.8 billion while net income increased 33 percent to $631 million.

Lenovo sells directly to consumers and businesses through online sales, company-owned stores, chain retailers, and other distributors. Lenovo's principal facilities are in Beijing, Morrisville, and Singapore, with research centers in those locations, as well as Shanghai, Shenzhen, Xiamen, and Chengdu in China, and Yamato in Kanagawa Prefecture, Japan. Lenovo operates factories in Chengdu and Hefei, China and recently started production in Argentina.

In July 2012, Lenovo and the National Football League (NFL) announced that Lenovo had become the NFL's "Official Laptop, Desktop and Workstation Sponsor." Lenovo said that this was its largest sponsorship deal ever in the United States. Lenovo will receive advertising space in NFL venues and events and be allowed to use the NFL logo on its products and ads. Lenovo said that this sponsorship would boost its efforts to market to the key 18-to-35-year-old male demographic.

Lenovo entered the smartphone market in 2012 and quickly became a huge vendor of smartphones in the Chinese market. Entry into the smartphone market was accompanied by a change of strategy from "the one-size-fits-all LePhone strategy" to a diverse portfolio of devices. In 2012, Lenovo passed Apple to become the number 2 provider of smartphones in China with about a 15-percent market share, behind Xiaomi. In late 2013, Xiaomi was a growing smartphone rival to Lenovo, both firms being valued at $10 billion. Chinese-made smartphones are becoming serious competitors to Apple and Samsung both at home and overseas. In the second quarter of 2013, Xiaomi overtook Apple within China and became the sixth-largest smartphone maker globally with 5 percent market share compared to Apple's 18 percent. Xiaomi also derives revenue from its own digital game platform and social messaging app, MiLiao. Lenovo is contemplating making a move to acquire Xiaomi—or it could it be the other way around if Lenovo falters?

Lenovo has invested U.S. $793 million in the construction of a mobile phone manufacturing and research-and-development facility in Wuhan, China. Lenovo has expanded sales of its smartphones into Russia, Indonesia, and India, with further expansion intended. The LePhone smartphone is offered at a low price point and is customized for the Chinese market. It has benefited from strong support from Chinese mobile phone companies and content providers such as Baidu, Alibaba, and Tencent.

A 7,500-square foot flagship Lenovo store opened in Beijing in February 2013. At the same time in the USA, Lenovo introduced the ThinkPad X131e Chromebook—a rugged PC designed for K–12 education. This product simplifies software and security management for school administrators and provides students and teachers with quick access to thousands of apps, education resources, and storage.

Copyright by Fred David Books LLC. (Written by Forest R. David)

History

Liu Chuanzhi founded Lenovo in 1984 with a group of 10 engineers in Beijing. For the first 20 years of its existence, the company's English name was "Legend" but in April 2003, the company publicly announced its new name, "Lenovo," with a large media campaign involving huge outdoor billboards and primetime television advertisements. Lenovo's first successful product was the Han-card, an add-on card for PCs that allowed them to efficiently process Chinese characters. Lenovo became a publicly traded company after listing in Hong Kong in 1994, raising nearly $30 million.

Lenovo acquired IBM's PC business in 2005 amid a backlash in Congress against Chinese companies trying to purchase U.S. businesses. Lenovo's acquisition of IBM's PC division accelerated access to foreign markets while improving both its branding and technology. Lenovo paid $1.25 billion for IBM's computer business and assumed an additional U.S. $500 million of IBM's debt. This acquisition made Lenovo the third largest computer maker worldwide by volume.

In January 2011, Lenovo formed a PC joint venture with NEC, a Japanese IT company. The venture is named Lenovo NEC Holdings B.V., which is registered in the Netherlands. Lenovo owns a 51 percent stake in the joint venture, whereas NEC holds a 49 percent stake. Lenovo has a five-year option to expand its stake in the joint venture. This joint venture is intended to boost Lenovo's worldwide sales by expanding its presence in Japan, a key market for PCs. NEC spun off its PC business into the joint venture, so Lenovo is now the largest PC seller in Japan.

Lenovo recently acquired Medion, a German electronics manufacturing company, doubling its share of the German computer market to 14 percent and making it the third-largest vendor by sales after Acer and HP. The deal was the first in which a Chinese company acquired a well-known German company.

The Year 2012: Expanding Globally

Lenovo had acquired the Brazil-based electronics company CCE that sells products under the brand name Digibras for a base price of 300 million reais (U.S. $148 million) in a combination of stock and cash and an additional 400 million reais dependent on performance benchmarks. Before this acquisition, Lenovo already established a $30 million factory in Brazil, but Lenovo desired a local partner to maximize regional growth. Lenovo realizes that the 2014 World Cup that will be hosted by Brazil as well as the 2016 Summer Olympics and CCE has a reputation for quality.

Lenovo acquired the U.S.-based software company Stoneware, in its first software acquisition to date. Lenovo desires to improve and expand its cloud-computing services. For the two years before its acquisition, Stoneware partnered with Lenovo to sell its software. During this period, Stoneware's sales doubled. Stoneware was founded in 2000. Stoneware is based in Carmel, Indiana, and has 67 employees.

Lenovo has made an investment in Vertex, a technology-oriented venture capital firm in Israel. Lenovo's Chief Executive Officer (CEO), Yang Yuanging, said that this investment was just the beginning. He said, "Definitely we are interested in Israel's technology, to grow our company, to grow our business."

Lenovo recently introduced the more powerful desktop computer IdeaCentre A720, with a 27-inch touch-screen display and running Windows 8. With a TV tuner and HDMI, the A720 is also a multimedia hub of sorts. In 2013, Lenovo added a table computer to the IdeaCentre line. Lenovo sells tablet computers under the IdeaPad and ThinkPad product lines abroad and as the LePad in Mainland China. The LePad is part of an effort by Lenovo in the market for mobile Internet devices. Lenovo has established a Mobile Internet and Digital Home Business Group to compete in this space.

Lenovo is developing a new smart television product called LeTV. The PC, communications, and TV industries are currently undergoing a "smart" transformation. Lenovo recently offered a new cloud computing service that will allow users to share content between multiple devices, in addition to managing their personal information and social networking.

Internal Issues

Vision and Mission

Lenovo's vision statement reads as follows: "To create personal devices more people are inspired to own, a culture more people aspire to join and an enduring, trusted business that is well respected around the world."

Lenovo's mission statement reads as follows: "To become one of the world's great personal technology companies."

Organizational Structure

Lenovo's organizational chart is depicted in Exhibit 1. Note that there is no chief operations officer (COO), and the structure appears to be divisional by region because the only two presidents head geographic regions. There are three females among the top 13 executives. Lenovo's

EXHIBIT 1 Lenovo's Organizational Chart

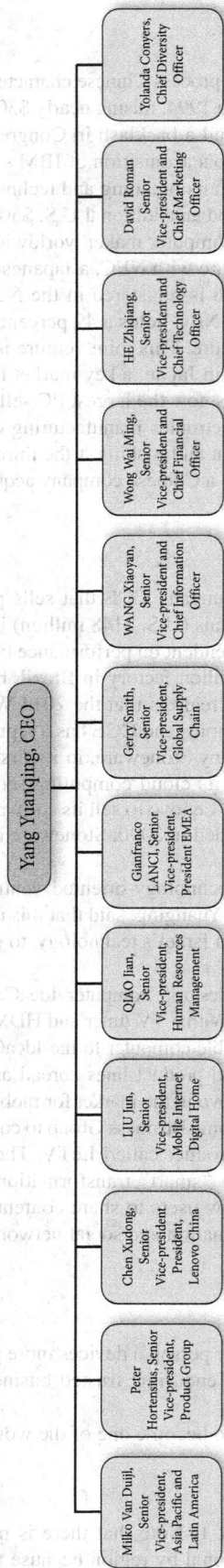

Yang Yuanqing, CEO

- Milko Van Duijl, Senior Vice-president, Asia Pacific and Latin America
- Peter Hortensius, Senior Vice-president, Product Group
- Chen Xudong, Senior Vice-president, President, Lenovo China
- LIU Jun, Senior Vice-president, Mobile Internet Digital Home
- QIAO Jian, Senior Vice-president, Human Resources Management
- Gianfranco LANCI, Senior Vice-president, President EMEA
- Gerry Smith, Senior Vice-president, Global Supply Chain
- WANG Xiaoyan, Senior Vice-president and Chief Information Officer
- Wong Wai Ming, Senior Vice-president and Chief Financial Officer
- HE Zhiqiang, Senior Vice-president and Chief Technology Officer
- David Roman, Senior Vice-president and Chief Marketing Officer
- Yolanda Conyers, Chief Diversity Officer

Note: EMEA = Europe/Middle East/Africa; APLA = Asia/Pacific/Latin America
Source: Based on company information provided at the corporate website.

new geographic based structure became effective in April 2012 with the creation of new reporting business units as follows: (1) China, (2) Asia-Pacific/Latin America (APLA), (3) Europe-Middle East-Africa (EMEA), and (4) North America. The new geographical structure, according to Lenovo, enables the firm to stay as close to its customers as possible.

Strategy

Lenovo is still primarily a PC company, but demand for PCs is falling; however, demand for smartphones is rapidly growing, so Lenovo is shifting gears. In smartphones, Lenovo is competing with Chinese rivals, such as Huawei Technologies Co Ltd. and ZTE Corp., that are already among the top-five smartphone companies globally. Although the second-biggest smartphone vendor in China, Lenovo has begun selling smartphones in Russia, Indonesia, the Philippines, and Vietnam, but the company faces stiff competition globally from Samsung Electronics Co. Ltd. and Apple Inc.

Lenovo's manufacturing operations are a departure from the usual industry practice of outsourcing to contract manufacturers. Lenovo instead focuses on vertical integration to avoid excessive reliance on suppliers and to keep down costs. Speaking on this topic, Yuanqing said, "Selling PCs is like selling fresh fruit. The speed of innovation is very fast, so you must know how to keep up with the pace, control inventory, to match supply with demand and handle very fast turnover." Lenovo benefited from its vertical integration after flooding affected hard-drive manufacturers in Thailand in 2011 because the company could continue manufacturing operations by shifting production toward products for which hard drives were still available.

Lenovo began to accentuate vertical integration after a meeting in 2009 in which Yuanqing, and the head of Lenovo's supply chain, analyzed the costs versus the benefits of in-house manufacturing and decided to make at least 50 percent of Lenovo's manufacturing in-house. Lenovo Chief Technology Officer George He said that vertical integration has an important role in product development. He stated, "If you look at the industry trends, most innovations for PCs, smartphones, tablets and smart TVs are related to innovation of key components—display, battery and storage. Differentiation of key parts is so important. So we started investing more … and working very closely with key parts suppliers."

Lenovo has partially moved production of its ThinkPad line of computers to Japan. ThinkPads are produced by NEC in Yamagata Prefecture. Akaemi Watanabe, president of Lenovo Japan, said, "As a Japanese, I am glad to see the return to domestic production and the goal is to realize full-scale production as this will improve our image and make the products more acceptable to Japanese customers." Lenovo recently started manufacturing computers in Whitsett, North Carolina.

For Lenovo's third quarter of 2012 that ending December 2012, the company reported a quarterly profit of $200.0 million, up 30 percent from a year previously. That amount exceeded its previous record of $163 million, on strong sales of smartphones and tablet computers. For the third quarter, Lenovo's revenue grew 12 percent from a year previously to $9.4 billion, but the bulk of that still came from its PC business. Lenovo shipped 9.4 million smartphones in the third quarter, all but about 400,000 of them however in China. CEO Yang says "the smartphone business outside China is 'still in the first stage' and Lenovo needs to invest to gain market share before focusing on profitability." The company's third-quarter revenues in the bigger but slower-growing PC market rose 7 percent to $7.9 billion.

Lenovo's global market share in PCs increased to 15.9 percent in the third quarter, trailing HP's 17.0 percent, but well ahead of both Dell and Acer. Lenovo's 15.9 percent was the average of their 11.1 percent market share in EMEA, 9 percent in North America, and 36.7 percent in China. Lenovo has rapidly gained market share in the PC sector and in early 2013 trails HP only by a slim margin in PC shipments. However, as PC demand growth slows, Lenovo has been diversifying into the mobile device sector to tap robust demand for smartphones and tablets, particularly at home in China, the world's biggest market for mobile phones and PCs.

About a one-tenth of Lenovo's third-quarter revenues in 2012 came from its mobile Internet and digital home (MIDH) business—mainly consisting of its smartphone sales in China, which jumped 77 percent to $998 million, although that was only 11 percent of total revenue. The company's third-quarter shipments of media tablets rose 77 percent to 800,000 units. MIDH now contributes 11 percent of Lenovo's overall revenue. At the end of the third quarter in 2012, Lenovo is number-three worldwide in Smart Connected Devices (PC's, tablets, and smartphones).

Lenovo basically has what it calls a two prong strategy: (1) Protect its commercial global PC business and its China business and (2) attack three high-growth opportunities in emerging markets with smartphones, tablets, and smart TVs. For quarter ending January 31, 2013, Lenovo's "attack" businesses delivered 50 percent of the company's revenues, a significant increase from four years ago when the company first launched the strategy and attack revenues were 32 percent. Lenovo's MIDH revenues include its smartphone, tablet, and smart TV businesses and accounted for a record 11 percent of total Lenovo revenue in the third quarter, up 77 percent year-over-year. And for the first time ever, Lenovo's smartphone business in China became profitable in third quarter.

Ethics

In fiscal 2012, Lenovo CEO Yang received a $3 million bonus as a reward for record profits, which he in-turn redistributed to about 10,000 Lenovo's employees. According to Lenovo spokesman, Jeffrey Shafer, Yang felt that it would be the right thing to "redirect [the money] to the employees as a real tangible gesture for what they done." Shafer also said that Yang, who owns about eight percent of Lenovo's stock, "felt that he was rewarded well simply as the owner of the company." The bonuses were mostly distributed among staff working in positions such as production and reception who received an average of 2,000 yuan or about U.S. $314. This was almost equivalent to a month's pay for the typical Lenovo worker in China. According to Lenovo's annual report, Yang earned $14 million, including $5.2 million in bonuses, during the fiscal year that ended in March 2012.

Finance

Lenovo's recent income statements and balance sheets are provided in Exhibits 2 and 3, respectively. Note in Exhibit 2 the 14.6 percent increase in revenues for fiscal 2012/2013, as well as the 33 percent increase in net income.

EXHIBIT 2 Lenovo's Income Statements (U.S. $ 000,000 omitted)

	FY2012/13	FY2011/12
Revenue	33,873	29,574
Cost of sates	(29,800)	(26,128)
Gross profit	**4,073**	**3,446**
Other income, net	20	1
Selling and distribution expenses	(1,888)	(1,691)
Administrative expenses	(847)	(730)
Research and development expenses	(623)	(453)
Other operating income - net	65	11
Operating profit	**800**	**584**
Finance income	44	43
Finance costs	(42)	(44)
Share of losses of associated companies	(1)	(1)
Profit before taxation	801	582
Taxation	(170)	(107)
Profit for the period	631	475
Profit attributable to:		
Equity holders of the company	635	473
Non-controlling interests	(4)	2
Dividend	248	183
Earnings per share (U.S. cents)		
Basic	**6.16**	**4.67**
Diluted	**6.07**	**4.57**

Source: Based on company documents.

EXHIBIT 3 Lenovo Balance Sheet (in millions of U.S. dollars)

	As of Mar 31, 2013	As of Mar 31, 2012
Non-current assets	4,492	4,040
Property, plant and equipment	480	392
Intangible assets	3,326	3,092
Others	686	556
Current assets	12,390	11,820
Bank deposits and cash	3,573	4,172
Trade, notes and other receivables	6,694	6,297
Inventories	1,965	1,218
Others	158	133
Current liabilities	12,091	11,809
Short-term bank loans	176	63
Trade, notes and other payables	10,576	11,251
Others	1,339	495
Net current assets	299	11
Non-current liabilities	2,111	1,603
Total equity	**2,680**	**2,448**

Source: Based on company documents.

Segments

Lenovo does an excellent job of reporting segment financial information both by geographic region and by product. Exhibit 4 reveals geographic segment information for Lenovo's 2012/2013 fiscal year that ended March 31, 2013. Note the high revenue growth in Europe/Middle East/Africa (EMEA) and the high profit margin in China. At March 31, 2013, Lenovo's worldwide personal computer (PC) market share grew from 13.0 percent to 15.3 percent, trailing only HP's 15.7 percent, and above Dell's 13.2 percent.

Competitors

A financial comparison of various Lenovo competitors is provided in Exhibit 5. Note that Apple crushes all competitors, including Lenovo, on profit margin and earnings per share (EPS). Note that HP is struggling and that Lenovo does not have that many shares outstanding versus most rival firms. Apple is the second-largest publicly traded corporation in the world by market capitalization with its $424 billion figure. Lenovo is also concerned about China's ZTE Corp., which plans to become one of the world's top-three smartphone brands. ZTE was struggling financially as 2012 ended, but the company has aggressive plans and a good product.

Apple, Inc.

Headquartered in Cupertino, California, Apple's best-known products are the Mac line of computers, the iPod, iPhone, iPad, iTunes, iLife, and iWork. Apple software includes the OS X and iOS operating systems and the Safari web browser. Apple is the world's second-largest information technology company by revenue after Samsung Electronics. Apple is also the world's third-largest mobile phone make after Samsung and Nokia. As of November 2012, Apple has 394 retail stores in 14 countries and an online Apple Store and iTunes Store. For its fiscal year that ended in September 2012, Apple posted revenue of $22.5 billion in China, nearly double the amount from the prior year. However, partly as a result of Lenovo, Apple's market share dropped to 4.2 percent of the China smartphone market in the quarter ended September 2012, from 5.8 percent the prior year. Another problem for Apple in China is that the China's largest mobile carrier, China Mobile Ltd., does not sell the iPhone, although that company had 87.9 million subscribers to high-cost, third-generation mobile services at year end 2012.

EXHIBIT 4 Lenovo's Sales and Profit by Region (in U.S. dollars)

Including MIDH and non-PC revenue & results	Revenue US$ Million		Segment Operating Profit/ (Loss) US$ Million		Segment Operating Profit Margin	
	FY13	Y/Y	FY13	FY12^	FY13	FY12^
China	14,539	17%	678	569	4.7%	4.6%
China - PC	11,751	6%	733	638	6.2%	5.8%
APLA	6,860	8%	24	0	0.3%	0.0%
EMEA	7,535	20%	147	83	2.0%	1.3%
North America	4,939	9%	168	161	3.4%	3.5%

Note: EMEA = Europe/Middle East/Africa; APLA = Asia/Pacific/Latin America.

EXHIBIT 5 A Financial Comparison of Lenovo with Rival Firms (In U.S. Dollars)

	Lenovo	Apple	Dell	HP	Toshiba	Fujitsu
Sales ($)	34 B	165 B	58 B	120 B	63 B	49 B
Income ($)	631 M	42 B	2.7B	–12.6 B	1.3 B	279 M
Profit Margin	1.86%	25.35%	4.44%	–10.5%	2.27%	0.55%
Market Capitalization ($)	11.07 B	424 B	24 B	32.5 B	18.5 B	8.5 B
Shares Outstanding	518 M	939 B	1.75 B	1.95 B	4.25 B	414 M
EPS ($)	1.10	44.10	1.47	–6.45	0.30	0.64

Note: EPS, earnings per share.
Source: Developed in February 2013 from a variety of sources.

An increasing number of companies are interested in purchasing Mac computers for all or part of their global operations. Apple focuses its business toward consumers and does not aggressively develop products and services for global enterprise customers. Organizations that have multiple-country operations oftentimes have to make separate arrangements in each region, with local partners making global deployments more complex. Apple has outstanding product design and innovation as well as financial stability, but the company lacks consistent global service and support. In September 2012, Apple unveiled the iPhone5, featuring an enlarged screen, more powerful processors, and running iOS6. The phone also includes a new mapping application (replacing Google Maps) that has attracted some criticism.

Dell, Inc.

Headquartered in Round Rock, Texas, Dell is the third-largest PC vendor in the world after HP and Lenovo. Dell employs more than 103,300 people worldwide and is a strong corporate PC supplier with good global coverage and capabilities. Dell is positioning itself beyond its PC roots however and as such is becoming less competitive on PC pricing. To diversify away from PCs—although that product, like Lenovo, is still Dell's best seller—Dell in 2012 acquired Wyse Technology and Quest Software and Gale Technologies and Credant Technologies. These acquired firms produce and market other high-technology products and services, but not PCs, smartphones, or tablets.

Fujitsu

Headquartered in Tokyo, Japan, Fujitsu is the world's third-largest IT services provider measured by revenues after IBM and HP. Fujitsu executes on a global basis and provides a good option for corporate purchasing for many organizations. Although its U.S. operations are still weak, Fujitsu has added desktops and bolstered its North American capabilities. Fujitsu is also a strong supplier of pen tablet PCs, an important segment with Windows 8. Fujitsu has a good desktop service portfolio across Europe and is strong in the Middle East, Africa, and Japan. In May 2011, Fujitsu entered the mobile phone market again and released various Windows Phone devices. Fujitsu offers a public cloud service delivered from data centers in Japan, Australia, Singapore, the United States, the United Kingdom, and Germany based on its Global Cloud Platform strategy. The platform delivers Infrastructure-as-a-Service (IaaS) virtual information and communication technology (ICT) infrastructure, such as servers and storage functionality.

Hewlett-Packard

Headquartered in Palo Alto, California, HP has a strong global PC presence and portfolio of services and products and is a viable supplier for global enterprise customers, regardless of business size. In May 2012, HP announced plans to lay off approximately 27,000 employees, after posting a profit decline of 31 percent in the second quarter of 2012. The profit decline is largely as a result of the growing popularity of smartphones, tablets, and other mobile devices that have slowed the sale of PCs. HP recently merged its printing and PC businesses under one executive, Todd Bradley. In November 2012, HP recorded a write down of around $8.8 billion related to its $11.3 billion acquisition of the U.K.-based software maker Autonomy Corp. HP accused Autonomy of deliberately inflating the value of the company before its takeover, but Autonomy flatly rejected the charge. The FBI is investigating but HP's stock has fallen to a decades' low.

Toshiba Corporation

Headquartered in Tokyo, Japan, Toshiba provides a wide range of notebook computers targeted at businesses, but its global focus has shifted increasingly toward the consumer and small-business markets. Toshiba remains strong in Canada and Australia in commercial sales, but a lack of desktop offerings makes Toshiba inappropriate if a sole PC vendor is desired for a company. Toshiba's focus has shifted toward the nonenterprise notebook market. Toshiba is no longer a major concern for Lenovo because the two firms' product lines overlap less and less every day.

Acer

Headquartered in Taiwan, China, Acer plans to build up its smartphone business, raising sales from 500,000 units in 2012 to 1.5 million in 2013, and 5 million in 2014. Acer is targeting specific operators individually instead of trying to offer models across entire markets. Acer has suffered two consecutive (2011 and 2012) annual losses, still struggling from its bad acquisitions of Gateway, Packard Bell, and eMachines. Of late however, Acer has posted strong sales of notebooks using Google's Chrome platform.

Nokia Corporation

Nokia is a communications and IT corporation headquartered in Keilaniemi, Espoo, Finland. Its principal products are mobile phones and portable IT devices. Nokia was the world's largest vendor of mobile phones from 1998 to 2012 but over the past five years, the company has suffered declining market share as a result of the growing use of smartphones from other vendors, principally the Apple iPhone and devices running on Google's Android operating system. As a result, its share price has fallen from a high of U.S. $40 in 2007 to under U.S. $3 in 2012. Since February 2011, Nokia has had a strategic partnership with Microsoft whereby Nokia smartphones will incorporate Microsoft's Windows Phone operating system (replacing Symbian). Nokia unveiled its first Windows Phone handsets, the Lumia 710 and 800 in October 2011 but sales subsequently dropped and Nokia made six consecutive loss-making quarters from second quarter 2011 to third quarter 2012.. The fourth quarter of 2012 saw Nokia return to profit after strong sales of its new Windows Phone 8 handsets, particularly the high-end Lumia 920. In October 2012, Nokia said its high-end Lumia 820 and 920 phones, which will run on Windows Phone 8 software, will soon be available across Europe and in Russia. In December 2012, Nokia introduced two new smartphones, the Lumia 620 and 920T. In January 2013, Nokia reported 6.6 million smartphone sales for the fourth quarter in 2012, consisting of 2.2 million Symbian and 4.4 million sales of Lumia devices (Windows Phone 7 and 8). In North America, only 700,000 mobile phones have been sold including smartphones.

Samsung Electronics

Based in Seoul, South Korea, Samsung makes the popular Galaxy smartphone. Samsung also makes DVD players, digital TVs, and digital still cameras; computers, color monitors, LCD panels, and printers; semiconductors such as DRAMs, static RAMs, flash memory, and display drivers; and communications devices ranging from wireless handsets and smartphones to networking gear; microwave ovens, refrigerators, air conditioners, and washing machines. Galaxy runs on Google's android mobile-operating software.

The Future

Lenovo's diverse product brands overlap more and more, which is becoming confusing to many customers. The company's current aggressive pricing may not be profitable in future years. The differentiation provided by Lenovo's ThinkVantage software tools is eroding. Alternative offerings from Microsoft and third parties are improving, and are often free, reducing the value of Lenovo's unique tools. Even for a strong firm such as Lenovo, rivals await at every turn to seize market share and customer loyalty. The global smartphone market increased by 39 percent in 2012 in terms of units shipped, according to International Data Corporation.

In the summer of 2013, Lenovo introduced another new product, a table PC that weighs 17 pounds and runs off Windows 8 and is called the Lenovo Idea Centre Horizon Table PC. The new product does everything and features a 27-inch high-definition display panel. Hundreds of fun games and educational apps come preloaded on the new product. Lenovo is engaged in discussions to acquire the maker of the BlackBerry smartphone, but a larger concern for the company perhaps is Xiaomi. Develop a clear strategic plan for Lenovo that will enable the company to continue its historical success.

Nikon Corporation, 2013

www.nikon.com, NINOY

Headquartered in Tokyo, Japan, Nikon is known worldwide for its digital and film cameras, binoculars, microscopes, and ophthalmic lenses. Nikon's major competitor is Canon, also headquartered in Tokyo. In January 2013, Nikon introduced two new cameras, the COOLPIX S9500, a multifunctional, high-power zoom model offering 22× optical zoom and equipped with wi-fi connectivity and GPS functions, and the COOLPIX S9400, a high-performance model equipped with an 18× optical zoom lens. Nikon Vision Co., Ltd. recently released the new ACULON A211 binoculars, designed for a wide range of outdoor activities, such as bird watching, nature observation, boating, and hiking. The compact digital camera market globally is shrinking and prices are falling with the proliferation of smartphones with built-in cameras. This is a major problem for Nikon going forward, as is the shrinking global market for their liquid crystal display (LCD) steppers and scanners. Nikon's fiscal year ends on March 31.

The top three digital camera producers, Canon, Nikon, and Sony, are facing potential disaster because excellent technology in smartphones today allows people to take high quality pictures without buying a high quality camera. According to International Data Corp. (IDC), in the first five months of 2013, global shipments of compact digital cameras declined 43 percent. Canon is trying to maintain its 23 percent share of the global camera market, followed by Nikon with a 21 percent and Sony with 15 percent. IDC reports that the global digital camera market peaked in 2010 and will likely endure a 30 percent drop in revenue in 2013 alone. For Nikon, digital cameras are part of its imaging products segment, a segment that generates 91.8 percent of revenues. In contrast, Canon's imaging systems segment, which includes sales of digital cameras, accounts for 39.4 percent of the company's sales.

Copyright by Fred David Books LLC. (Written by Forest R. David.)

History

The company that became Nikon was founded in 1917 as part of the huge Mitsubishi *keiretsu*, a group of businesses linked by cross-ownership. Originally the company name was Nippon Kogaku, but the name changed to Nikon in 1988. During World War II, the company grew to 19 factories and 23,000 employees, supplying binoculars, lenses, bomber sights, and submarine periscopes to the Japanese military. After the war, Nippon Kogaku reverted to producing civilian products in a single factory. In 1948, the first Nikon-branded camera, the Nikon I, was released. Nikon lenses became popular during the Korean War because U.S. photojournalist, David Duncan, popularized them. Nikon also designs and manufactures precision equipment for use in semiconductor and LCD fabrication, inspection, and measurement.

Over its long history, Nikon has developed and sold millions of photographic lenses under the Nikkor name, including projection lenses for LCD's and scanners, as well as lenses for both film and digital cameras. The Nikkor history began in 1933 with shipments of Aero-Nikkor lenses for aerial photography.

Nikon Middle East FZE started operations in Dubai, United Arab Emirates (UAE) in 2012, and in Brazil and Thailand the year before. In January 2013, to tell the story of the company, Nikon released its second movie, *The Day*, telling about the Nikon brand (http://nikonimaging.tumblr.com). That movie followed *Tears*, released by Nikon in late 2012, to personify the ultimate human emotion (tears). *The Day* reveals the fun of manipulating light with Nikon digital cameras and Nikkor lenses, using various scenes such as the morning sun, a vibrant flower, and the natural smile of a child.

Internal Issues

Vision and Mission

Nikon's vision statement is: "Our Aspirations—Meeting needs. Exceeding expectations."

Nikon's mission statement is: "Trustworthiness & Creativity."

Organizational Structure

There are no females among Nikon's top executive team. Note in Exhibit 1 that Nobuyoshi Gokyu is in essence the chief operations officer (COO) of the company, although his official title does not include that designation. Nikon operates from a strategic business unit (SBU) organizational structure by product because many subsidiaries and divisions report to the three unit executives (Ushida, Masai, and Okamoto).

Segments

Nikon operates in four business segments: (1) Precision Equipment, (2) Imaging, (3) Instruments, and (4) Other. Nikon has 86 subsidiaries and 11 associated companies that report under these four segments. Exhibit 2 reveals the various products offered with each Nikon segment. Note that digital and film cameras dominate its Imaging division, whereas microscopes dominate its Instruments division. The Imaging segment is nearly four times larger than the other segments combined, so Nikon is primary a camera company.

Note in Exhibit 3 that Nikon's sales in fiscal 2013 increased 10.0 percent to 1.01 trillion yen, but the company's precision equipment sales decreased 28 percent, Instruments decreased 3.5 percent, and Other decreased 3.7 percent. These declines were offset by the company's 29 percent in Imaging Products sales to 751 billion yen.

Strategy

As cameras in smartphones become increasingly effective, Nikon's compact camera business is a low-to-no-growth proposition, so Nikon is trying to diversify into other, more profitable areas. But this process at Nikon has perhaps been too little too late, and some analysts are concerned

EXHIBIT 1 Nikon's Organizational Chart

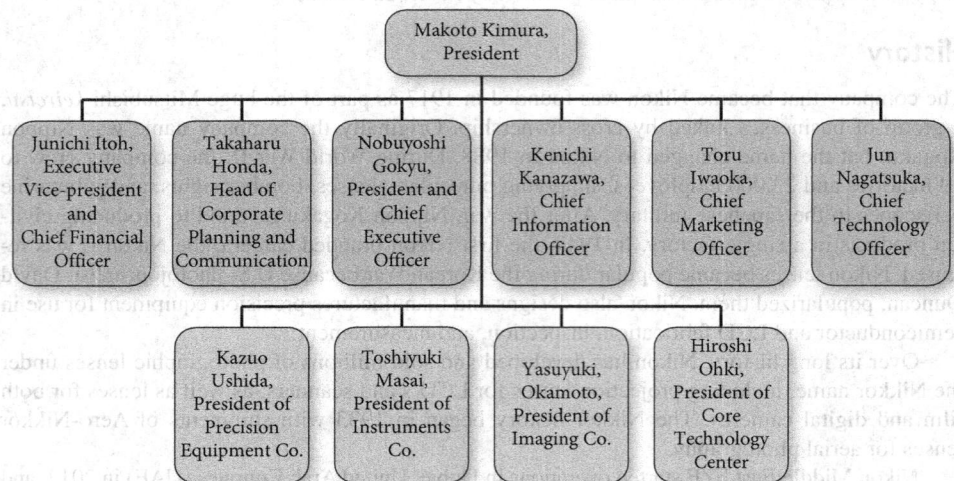

EXHIBIT 2 Nikon Products by Segment

Precision Equipment: Steppers and scanners for LCDs
Imaging: Digital and film cameras, lenses, speed lights, film scanners, software, and sport optics
Instruments: Biological, industrial, and stereoscopic microscopes, measuring instruments, semiconductor inspection equipment, and surveying instruments
Other: Ophthalmic lenses, glass, and encoders

Source: Based on company documents.

EXHIBIT 3 Nikon's Segment Sales (in millions of yen)

Fiscal Year-Ended (March 31)	2011	2012	2013
Net Sales	887,512	918,651	1,010,493
Net Sales by Industry Segment			
Precision Equipment	208,613	248,145	179,013
Imaging Products	596,375	587,127	751,240
Instruments	57,451	56,000	53,877
Other	25,071	27,379	26,363
Net Sales in Japan and Export Sales by Region[1]			
Japan	127,162	130,517	144,417
Overseas	760,350	788,134	866,075
USA	237,611	221,768	271,459
Europe	202,854	225,739	260,038
China	96,956	126,302	118,162
Other Areas	222,927	214,325	216,416
North America	—	—	—
Asia & Oceania[2]	—	—	—

[1] From the year ended March 2011, "North America" and "Asia" area has been changed to "Other Areas".
[2] From the year ended March 2008 to the year ended March 2010, "Asia" area had been changed to "Asia & Oceania" area.

Source: Based on company documents.

that Nikon may eventually go the way of Eastman Kodak. But Nikon has great name recognition, which the firm could parlay into other endeavors, such as perhaps "smartphones with wonderful cameras," but Nikon has not indicated interest in that business. Rivals Canon and Sony have diversified into numerous related products, so their camera business contributes only a small part of overall revenue. Nikon definitely needs a clear strategic plan going forward; the firm at present is stable.

Ethics

Nikon's website reveals that the company is quite giving. For example, Nikon gave money and support for the victims of Hurricane Sandy in the U.S. Northeast and similarly to victims of Typhoon Bopha in the Philippines. Many such activities are described at the corporate website. Nikon also has an effective Environmental Management System (EMS) and Policy and works hard to be a good steward of the natural environment, as elaborated on at the company website.

Finance

As indicated in Exhibit 4, Nikon's revenues increased 10.0 percent in fiscal 2013, but net income decreased 28.5 percent. The balance sheet in Exhibit 5 reveals a continued drop in the company's goodwill in 2013.

Competitors

Nikon's competitors include Canon, Casio, Eastman Kodak, Sony, Pentax, Fujifilm, Olympus, and Netherlands-based ASML Holding. Canon is Nikon's biggest and most worrisome competitor, followed by Sony. Note in Exhibit 6 that Canon is four times larger than Nikon and dramatically more profitable than any company featured in the analysis. Pentax is a brand name used by Pentax Ricoh Imaging Company for cameras and binoculars that compete with Nikon products. In late October 2011, Ricoh renamed the subsidiary Pentax Ricoh Imaging Company, Ltd.

EXHIBIT 4 Nikon's Income Statement (in millions of yen)

Fiscal Year-Ended (March 31)	2011	2012	2013
Net sales	**887,512**	**918,651**	**1,010,493**
Cost of sales	575,535	567,000	663,509
Gross profit	311,977	351,651	346,984
Selling, general and administrative expenses	257,924	271,570	295,982
Operating income	**54,052**	**80,080**	**51,001**
Non-operating income	9,860	11,917	7,849
Non-operating expenses	8,101	2,614	10,506
Other non-operating expenses	21,729	16,107	20,260
Ordinary income (loss)	**55,811**	**89,383**	**48,344**
Extraordinary gains	121	16,144	14,299
Gain on sales of property, plant and equipment	91	159	302
Gain on sales of investment securities	30	65	5,132
Extraordinary losses	9,427	19,360	788
Loss on disposals of property, plant and equipment	1,000	250	—
Loss on sales of property, plant and equipment	47	4	57
Non-recurring depreciation on noncurrent assets	—	—	—
Impairment losses	397	6,502	663
Loss on sales of investment securities	82	96	31
Losses on devaluation of investment securities	4,512	0	35
Loss on restructuring of business	—	—	—
Environmental expenses	—	—	—
Effect of application in accounting standard for asset retirement obligations	1,073	—	—
Loss on disaster	2,313	12,505	—
Income (loss) before income taxes	46,505	86,168	61,856
Current	13,096	26,627	12,081
Deferred	6,097	235	7,316
Income taxes	19,193	26,862	19,397
Income (loss) before minority interests	27,312	59,305	42,459
Net income (loss)	**27,312**	**59,305**	**42,459**

Source: Company documents.

EXHIBIT 5 Nikon's Balance Sheet (in millions of yen)

Fiscal Year-Ended (March 31)	2011	2012	2013
Assets			
Current assets			
Cash and time deposits	181,077	132,404	110,281
Notes and accounts receivable-trade	123,077	137,533	134,225
Inventories	236,407	263,033	269,411
Deferred tax assets	42,640	47,110	43,959
Other current assets	15,118	34,061	21,563
Allowance for doubtful receivables	(7,365)	(4,667)	(3,795)
Total current assets	**590,954**	**609,474**	**575,647**
Fixed assets			
Tangible fixed assets			
Buildings and structures	43,362	37,807	45,774
Machinery, equipment and vehicles	34,003	35,200	57,551
Land	14,777	14,609	15,025
Lease Assets, net	5,794	4,901	3,878
Construction in progress	7,566	23,809	15,935
Other	13,511	14,615	23,439

EXHIBIT 5 Continued

Total tangible fixed assets	**119,016**	**130,943**	**161,605**
Intangible fixed assets			
Software	26,237	27,927	27,826
Goodwil	13,235	5,157	4,443
Total intangible fixed assets	39,473	33,085	32,270
Investments and other assets			
Investment securities	56,303	55,355	66,859
Deferred tax assets	17,604	13,293	7,317
Other	6,817	18,284	21,551
Allowance for doubtful receivables	(260)	(207)	(231)
Total investments and other assets	80,465	86,727	95,496
Total fixed assets	238,954	250,755	289,371
Total assets	**829,909**	**860,230**	**865,019**
Liabilities and Net Assets			
Liabilities			
Current liabilities			
Notes and accounts payable-trade	171,735	155,338	124,676
Short-term borrowings	16,732	18,350	18,739
Commercial paper	—	—	—
Current portion of bonds	—	—	—
Lease obligations	2,422	2,163	1,703
Accrued expenses	54,545	54,751	54,505
Accrued income taxes	2,520	15,076	1,395
Advances received	63,626	54,214	50,799
Warranty reserve	7,296	7,594	8,096
Other current liabilities	23,415	34,519	39,270
Total current liabilities	**342,295**	**342,009**	**299,186**
Long-term liabilities			
Bonds	40,000	40,000	40,000
Long-term debt	24,700	22,900	22,600
Lease obligations	3,620	2,953	2,305
Liability for employees' retirement benefits	14,951	3,700	2,876
Retirement allowances for directors and corporate auditors	606	—	—
Asset retirement obligations	2,324	2,365	2,512
Other long-term liabilities	12,191	12,684	4,214
Total long-term liabilities	98,393	84,604	74,508
Total liabilities	**440,069**	**426,613**	**373,695**
Net assets			
Shareholders' equity			
Common stock	65,475	65,475	65,475
Capital surplus	80,711	80,711	80,711
Retained earnings	272,227	319,823	345,692
Treasury stock	(13,173)	(12,992)	(12,804)
Total Shareholders' equity	405,241	453,017	479,076
Valuation and translation adjustments			
Unrealized gains on available-for-sale securities	4,450	3,061	9,482
Deferred gains or losses on hedges	(696)	(1,592)	(216)
Foreign currency translation adjustments	(20,201)	(21,474)	2,187
Total Valuation and translation adjustments	(16,448)	(20,005)	11,452
Share subscription rights	427	604	795
Total net assets	389,220	433,616	491,324
Total liabilities and net assets	**829,909**	**860,230**	**865,019**

Source: Based on company documents.

EXHIBIT 6 A Financial Comparison of Nikon vs. Rival Firms (in yen)

	Nikon	Canon	Sony
Sales	1 T	3.5 T	6.8 T
Net Income	42 B	225 B	43 B
Profit Margin	4.2 %	6.5%	0.6%
Number of Employees	24 K	201 K	163 K
Debt-to-Equity Ratio	0.18	0.01	0.68
Market Capitalization	733 B	4.1 T	1.7 T
EPS	105	173	43

EPS, earnings per share.
Source: Based on information at a variety of sources on February 10, 2013.

Canon, Inc.

Headquartered within a few miles of Nikon in Tokyo, Japan, Canon makes cameras, LCD projectors, lenses, LCDs, and binoculars—competing against Nikon on all these products. But Canon has diversified and also manufactures printers, multifunction document equipment, and other computer peripherals for home and office use. Canon generates only 20 percent of its revenues in Japan. Canon manufactures digital single-lens reflex cameras, compact digital cameras, interchangeable lens, digital video cameras, ink-jet multifunction devices, single-function ink-jet printers, image scanners, television lens for broadcasting use, office network, color network and personal multifunction devices, office, color and personal copy machines, laser printers, large-sized ink-jet printers and digital production printers, exposure equipment used in semiconductor and LCDs, medical image recording equipment, ophthalmic instruments, magnetic heads, micro motors, computers, handy terminals, and document scanners.

In early 2013, Canon released three stylish, feature-packed PowerShot Digital Cameras: the PowerShot ELPH 330 HS, ELPH 115 IS, and A2500. These new models offer great photo quality and excellent video performance in compact, powerful point-and-shoot designs while providing advanced wireless connectivity for easy sharing and great performance in dimly lit situations. With about $45.6 billion in global revenue, Canon's U.S. parent company, Canon, Inc., ranked third overall in U.S. patents registered in 2011 and was one of *Fortune* Magazine's World's Most Admired Companies in 2012.

September 30, 2013 Revenue was 913 billion yen ($9.3 billion U.S. Dollars) and June 30, 2013 Revenue was 967 billion yen ($9.8 billion U.S. Dollars) for a 5.6% decline.

Sony Corporation

Headquartered within a few miles of Nikon (and Canon) in Tokyo, Japan, Sony manufactures LCD televisions, cameras, audio and video equipment, personal computers (PCs), personal navigation systems, game consoles and software, audio, videos and monitors for broadcast and commercial use, image sensors and other semiconductors, optical pickups, batteries, data recording media and systems, movie software, and animation works. Sony also has a Finance segment that provides life and nonlife insurance, banking services and credit finance services, and a new Sony Mobile segment provides that mobile phones.

Sony recently sold its U.S. headquarters for $685 million and has benefited lately from the weak Japanese currency, the yen. In fact, for each one-yen slide against the euro helps to boost Sony's annual operating profit by 6 billion yen. Nikon, too, is benefiting from the weak yen because much of its revenue comes from outside Japan. Sony recently lowered its sales forecasts for LCD television sets, Blu-ray disc players, digital cameras, camcorders, personal computers, and portable videogame machines. Smartphones have crept into all of these other consumer electronic domains, especially cameras, to the dismay of Nikon.

For the quarter ending September 2013, net loss of 19.3 billion yen ($195 million U.S. Dollars) (Note is 98.8 yen to 1.0 Dollars on November 4, 2013). Sony's new smartphone, the Xperia Z, became available in Japan in early February 2013, but Samsung's Galaxy and Apple's iPhone dominate the smartphone industry globally. Sony recently dissolved its capital-intensive LCD-panel joint ventures with rivals Samsung and Sharp.

The Future

Even though Nikon benefits from a weak yen, Nikon's Precision Equipment segment is reporting falling revenues as a result of the semiconductor-related and LCD panel-related markets shrinking. In the Imaging Products segment, the compact digital camera market continues to shrink, but the interchangeable lens digital camera market is growing. In Nikon's Instruments segment, the bioscience-related market has worsened as a result of reductions and execution deferments in government budgets in countries such as Japan and the USA, and the industrial instruments-related markets contracting resulting from restrained capital investment in the semiconductor and electronics fields. The company is suffering from the proliferation of cameras in smartphones because consumers increasingly find those cameras sufficient for their everyday needs.

Nikon needs a clear strategic plan for the future. Perhaps the firm needs to make key acquisitions to move into other areas that offer higher growth in revenues. Or perhaps the firm needs to establish cooperative agreements with Samsung, Nokia, or even Apple to offer Nikon's camera quality smartphone cameras. But that strategy could further curtail Nikon's mainstream revenue source from compact digital cameras. A thorough strategic analysis is needed to determine the best path forward for Nikon.

Netgear, Inc., 2013

www.netgear.com, NTGR

Headquartered in San Jose, California, Netgear develops and markets Ethernet switches, wireless controllers, storage devices, routers, media services, and other products associated with connecting users with the Internet. All Netgear products are produced through third-party manufacturers and marketed through thousands of retailers worldwide. Netgear prides itself on developing and marketing high performance devices that are dependable and easy to operate in homes. But this "desired competitive advantage" is difficult to maintain because consumers widely believe such products are a commodity (like gasoline). For businesses, Netgear provides networking, storage, and security devices that are cheaper and easier to use than comparable products offered by rival firms. Netgear products are sold in more than 28,000 retail locations around the world and through about 42,000 resellers. Netgear has operations in 25 nations and has 850 employees, of which 352 are in sales, marketing and technical support, 251 in research and development (R&D), 128 in finance, and 119 in operations.

Netgear's revenues for 2012 were $1.27 billion, up 7.6 percent from 2011. The company reported revenue for Q2 of 2013 of $357.7 million, up from $320.7 million the prior year when the company's new acquisition, AirCard, was not in the numbers. Q2 2013 net income was $14.0 million, down from $21.5 million the prior year. During Q2, Netgear grew its Retail Business Unit (RBU), led by its 802.11ac upgrade cycle, as well as the rollout of the Smart Home for developed markets. The integration of the AirCard business into the company's Service Provider Business Unit (SPBU) went well. On a year-over-year basis, Netgear's RBU revenue was up 3 percent. The company's strong Q2 2013 year-on-year growth for RBU in North America and Asia was offset by weakness in the European region. The company's SPBU revenue was up 58 percent sequentially, and up 20 percent over the prior year quarter. The company's Commercial Business Unit (CBU) revenue was up 25 percent sequentially, and up 10 percent over the prior year quarter.

Copyright by Fred David Books LLC. (Written by Forest R. David)

History

Netgear was incorporated in 1996 as a subsidiary of Bay Networks and was purchased by Nortel in 1998. The company became fully independent from Nortel in 2002 and remains independent today. Back in 1996, the Internet was in its infancy, especially high speed and wireless devices. As an industry pioneer, Netgear has kept tight inventory controls and used off-the-shelf hardware and software products from existing companies. Founder, chairman, and CEO Patrick Lo was quoted in 2004 as saying: "We do the system integration and let the contracted firms do the grunt work of designing circuit boards." Netgear went public in 2003. Since then, the company has grown into a $1.2 billion in sales firm. In 2011, Netgear combined its North, Central, and South U.S. salesforces to form a new Americas territory as a means to increase operational efficiencies. Today, the company operates in three distinct geographic territories: (1) Americas, (2) Europe, and (3) Middle East and Asia Pacific.

To get a flavor of what Netgear develops and markets, in late 2012, the company introduced its CG4500TM Voice/Data Gateway that received the CableLabs® DOCSIS® 3.0 certification. This unit has the capability for 24 × 4-channel bonding and is the firm's most advanced DOCSIS 3.0 Voice/Data Gateway integrating in one device. The new product allows concurrent 802.11n dual-band wireless networking that provides up to 900 Mbps (450 + 450 Mbps) aggregate speed and with simultaneous dual-band technology helps mitigate interference ensuring sustained throughput and reliable connections. With integrated MoCA, the CG4500TM Gateway enables seamless data and video distribution over the in-home coax network.

Internal Issues

Vision and Mission

Netgear's mission statement is: "To be the innovative leader in connecting the world to the Internet," recently changed from, "To be the preferred customer-driven provider of innovative networking solutions for small businesses and homes." There is a statement on the company's website that may be their vision: "Our goal is to be the leading provider of innovative networking products to the consumer, business, and service provider markets."

Location

Netgear's primary administrative, sales, marketing, and R&D facilities consist of 142,700 square feet in an office complex in San Jose, California, under a lease that expires in 2018. Netgear's international headquarters comprise 10,000 square feet of office space in Cork, Ireland, under a lease that expires in 2026. Netgear's international salespersons are based out of local sales offices or home offices in Austria, Australia, Brazil, Canada, China, Czech Republic, Denmark, France, Germany, India, Italy, Japan, Korea, Mexico, New Zealand, Poland, Russia, Singapore, Spain, Sweden, Switzerland, the Netherlands, the United Arab Emirates, and the United Kingdom. Netgear has operations personnel in Hong Kong, and R&D facilities in Atlanta, Chicago, Beijing, Guangzhou, Nanjing, Shanghai, and Taipei.

Organizational Structure

Netgear is managed in three specific business units: (1) retail, (2) commercial, and (3) service provider. The retail business unit consists of home networking, storage, and digital media products to connect users with the Internet and their content and devices. The commercial business unit consists of relatively low-cost business networking, storage, and security solutions. The service provider business unit consists of made-to-order and retail proven, whole-home networking solutions sold to service providers for sale to their customers.

Netgear recently combined their North American, Central American, and South American sales forces to form the Americas territory. Thus, the firm is today organized into the following three geographic territories: (1) Americas, (2) Europe, Middle-East, and Africa (EMEA) and (3) Asia, Pacific (APAC).

Exhibit 1 provides a diagram of Netgear's existing organizational structure. Note there is no Chief Operations Officer. Some analysts contend that the company is too dependent on Lo, with no other person being groomed as an eventual successor.

EXHIBIT 1 Organizational Chart

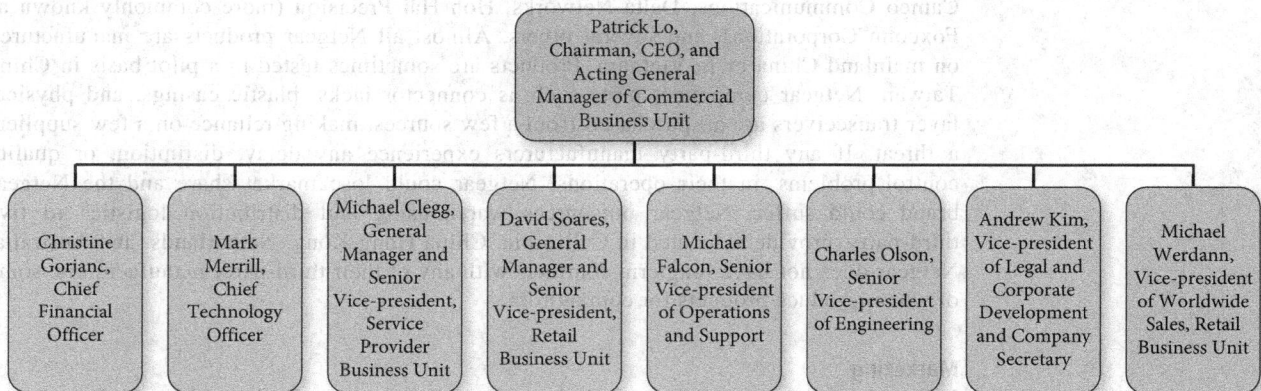

Source: Based on company documents.

Products

Netgear products that target businesses are designed with metal cases and are capable of faster speeds, up to 10 gigabits per second, and higher port counts to allow more users. Products targeting homes are designed with more pleasing aesthetics and are often offered at much lower prices than the more robust higher security business models. Netgear plans to develop a home network that will enable all devices to be connected to the Internet at all times.

Netgear's products can be grouped into three categories: (1) commercial business networking, (2) broadband access, and (3) network connectivity. Commercial business networking products include (a) Ethernet switches and wireless controllers such as routers used in WiFi applications, (b) Internet security appliances that enable Internet access with capabilities such as anti-virus and firewalls, and (c) network-attached storage, which provides file sharing with multiple PCs over a businesses own local area network.

Netgear's broadband access enables customers to move digital content over high-speed networks rather than traditional low-speed telephone lines. Products in this segment include: (a) routers, which allow the home or office networks to connect wireless to the Internet via a broadband modem, (b) gateways, which are routers integrated into a modem, (c) Internet Protocol (IP) telephony products, which enable voice communications over a network, and (d) media servers, which store multimedia content for use on PCs laptops, smartphones, and other devices.

Netgear's connectivity products enable resource sharing and include wireless access points, wireless network interface cards, Ethernet network interface cards, media adapters, and power line adapters.

R&D

High technology firms spend anywhere from 5 to 15 percent of revenue on R&D. In 2012, Netgear spent $61 million, up 25.5 percent, on R&D to develop new and improved products and respond to changing technology in a timely manner. The $61 million was 4.8 percent of Netgear's revenues, up from 4.1 percent the prior year. Netgear works closely with their technology suppliers to develop products using a methodology such as Original Design Manufacturer (ODM) or In-House Development. Under ODM, Netgear defines the product and specifications and coordinates with suppliers who develop the product. On development of a prototype, debugging and testing begins, and the product is ultimately released for production after passing final measures. The In-House Development model is similar to ODM, except entire development is coordinated by Netgear engineers.

Manufacturing

Like Apple, Inc., Netgear outsources all of their manufacturing to third parties, such as Cameo Communications, Delta Networks, Hon Hai Precision (more commonly known as Foxconn Corporation), and several others. Almost all Netgear products are manufactured on mainland China or in Vietnam. Products are sometimes tested in a pilot basis in China Taiwan. Netgear component parts such as connector jacks, plastic casings, and physical layer transceivers are all purchased from a few sources, making reliance on a few suppliers a threat. If any third-party manufacturers experience any delay, disruption, or quality control problems in their operations, Netgear could lose market share and the Netgear brand could suffer. Netgear outsources warehousing and distribution logistics to five third-party providers, located in California, China Hong Kong, Netherlands, and Australia. Netgear does not have longterm contracts with any of their third-party manufacturers, some of whom produce products for competitors.

Marketing

Netgear's global sales channel includes thousands of value added resellers (VARs), direct market resellers (DMRs), such as CDW, and 37,000 traditional retailers worldwide, such as Best Buy, Walmart, Fry's Electronics, and Staples in North America; PC World in the United Kingdom; and MediaMarket in Germany, as well as online retailers such as Amazon.

com, Dell.com, and NewEgg.com. Netgear also sells its products through broadband service providers such as BSkyB, Virgin Media UK, YouSee Denmark, Telecom Denmark, Time-Warner Cable, Comcast, TV Cabo Portugal, Telkom South Africa, J:Com of Japan, and Comhem of Sweden.

Best Buy and Ingram Micro each account for 10 percent or greater of Netgear revenues. Netgear works closely with customers on market development activities, such as co-advertising, in-store promotions and demonstrations, instant rebate programs, event sponsorship, and sales associate training. It also participates in major industry trade shows and marketing events. Netgear marketing managers work closely with the company's sales and R&D people to align product development roadmaps to meet customer technology demands.

Finance

Netgear's net income declined in 2012 to $86.5 million from the year before value of $91.4 million.

Income Statements

Netgear's recent income statements are provided in Exhibit 2. Note the steady increases in revenues but recent drop in net income.

EXHIBIT 2

NETGEAR, INC.
STATEMENTS OF OPERATIONS
(In thousands, except per share data)

	Year Ended December 31,		
	2012	2011	2010
Net revenue	$1,271,921	$1,181,018	$902,052
Cost of revenue	888,368	811,572	602,805
Gross profit	383,553	369,446	299,247
Operating expenses:			
Research and development	61,066	48,699	39,972
Sales and marketing	149,766	154,562	131,570
General and administrative	45,027	39,423	36,220
Restructuring and other charges	1,190	2,094	(88)
Litigation reserves, net	390	(201)	211
Total operating expenses	257,439	244,577	207,885
Income from operations	126,114	124,869	91,362
Interest income	498	477	426
Other income (expense), net	2,670	(1,136)	(564)
Income before income taxes	129,282	124,210	91,224
Provision for income taxes	42,743	32,842	40,315
Net income	$86,539	$91,368	$50,909
Net income per share:			
Basic	$2.27	$2.46	$1.44
Diluted	$2.23	$2.41	$1.41
Weighted average shares outstanding used to compute net income per share:			
Basic	38,057	37,121	35,385
Diluted	38,747	37,932	36,124

Source: 2012 *Form 10K*, p. 54.

Balance Sheets

Netgear's recent balance sheets are provided in Exhibit 3. Note the zero long-term debt.

Segments

Netgear reports operating income by geographic region. Before 2011, the company's operations in Central and South America were categorized under the APAC segment. Note in Exhibit 4 that Netgear's APAC segment was the largest gainer in 2012 versus the prior year, whereas EMEA reported a decline in revenues.

EXHIBIT 3 Netgear's Balance Sheet

NETGEAR, INC.
BALANCE SHEETS
(In thousands, except per share data)

	December 31, 2012	December 31, 2011
ASSETS		
Current assets:		
Cash and cash equivalents	$149,032	$208,898
Short-term investments	227,845	144,797
Accounts receivable, net	256,014	261,307
Inventories	174,903	163,724
Deferred income taxes	22,691	23,088
Prepaid expenses and other current assets	33,724	32,415
Total current assets	864,209	834,229
Property and equipment, net	19,025	15,884
Intangibles, net	27,621	20,956
Goodwill	100,880	85,944
Other non-current assets	22,834	14,357
Total assets	**$1,034,569**	**$971,370**
LIABILITIES AND STOCKHOLDERS' EQUITY		
Current liabilities:		
Accounts payable	$87,310	$117,285
Accrued employee compensation	18,338	26,896
Other accrued liabilities	126,255	120,480
Deferred revenue	27,645	40,093
Income taxes payable	1,382	4,207
Total current liabilities	**260,930**	**308,961**
Non-current income taxes payable	13,735	18,657
Other non-current liabilities	5,293	4,995
Total liabilities	**279,958**	**332,613**
Commitments and contingencies		
Stockholders' equity:		
Preferred stock: $0.001 par value; 5,000,000 shares authorized; none issued or outstanding	—	—
Common stock: $0.001 par value; 200,000,000 shares authorized; shared issued and outstanding:		
38,341,644 and 37,646,872 at December 31, 2012 and 2011, respectively	38	38
Additional paid-in capital	394,427	364,243
Cumulative other comprehensive income	4	23
Retained earnings	360,142	274,453
Total stockholders' equity	**754,611**	**638,757**
Total liabilities and stockholders' equity	**$1,034,569**	**$971,370**

Source: 2012 Form 10K, p. 53.

EXHIBIT 4 Revenues by Geographic Segment

| | Year End December (in thousands) | | | | | | | |
| | 2012 | | 2011 | | 2010 | | Percent Change | |
	$	%	$	%	$	%	2012	2011
Americas	$679,419	53.4	$587,056	49.7	$466,542	51.7	15.7	25.8
EMEA	$457,724	36%	$477,713	40.4	$340,249	37.7	(4.2)	40.4
APAC	$134,778	10.6	$116,249	9.9	$95,261	10.6	15.9	22.0
Total	$1,271,921	100%	$1,181,018	100%	$902,052	100%		

APAC, Asia Pacific; EMEA, Europe, Middle East, Africa.
Source: 2012 *Form 10K*, page 41.

Competition

Netgear operates in an extremely competitive industry, with many products being viewed by consumers as commodities, proper position on store floors being critically important, and competitive pricing being essential. Many Netgear products, such as media adapters, Ethernet, and routers, are also made by rivals Cisco Systems, Roku, Western Digital, and Apple in the USA, and by many foreign competitors such as AVM in Europe, Corega in Japan, and TP-Link in China. Netgear also develops and markets networking and streaming products, competing against rivals LG, Microsoft, Samsung, and Sony. Also competing against Netgear are many cable companies that now provide modems, and those companies may soon provide their own routers as part of their service offerings. If Netgear cannot form contracts with various cable providers, then those firms may also become competitors.

Netgear's principal competitors in the commercial business market include Allied Telesys, Barracuda, Buffalo, Data Robotics, Dell, D-Link, Fortinet, Hewlett-Packard, Huawei, Cisco Systems, the Linksys division of Cisco Systems, QNAP Systems, Seagate Technology, SonicWALL, Synology, WatchGuard, and Western Digital. Netgear's principal competitors in the home market for networking devices and television connectivity products include Apple, Belkin, D-Link, the Linksys division of Cisco Systems, Roku, and Western Digital. Netgear's principal competitors in the broadband service provider market include Actiontec, ARRIS, Comtrend, D-Link, Hitron, Huawei, Motorola, Pace, Sagem, Scientific Atlanta (a Cisco company), SMC Networks, TechniColor, Ubee, Compal Broadband, ZTE, and ZyXEL. Other current and potential competitors that Netgear considers include numerous local vendors such as Devolo, LEA, and AVM in Europe; Corega and Melco in Japan; and TP-Link in China. Even consumer electronics vendors are rivals, including LG Electronics, Microsoft, Panasonic, Samsung, Sony, Toshiba, and Vizio, who could integrate networking and streaming capabilities into their line of products, such as televisions, set top boxes, and gaming consoles.

Exhibit 5 provides a comparative summary of Netgear versus four leading competitors. Note that Netgear is a bit larger than D-Link, but much smaller than most rival firms.

EXHIBIT 5 Comparative Data for Netgear versus Rival Firms

	Netgear	Cisco Systems	D-Link	Alcatel Lucent	Western Digital
Number of Employees	791	71.8K	500	76K	103K
Net Income ($)	95.3M	7.36B	41.5M	1.4B	1.9B
Revenue ($)	1.23B	45.6B	1.15B	19.8B	13.8B
Revenue ($)/Employee	1,554K	635K	2,300K	260.5K	134K
EPS Ratio ($)	2.49	1.36	0.06	0.54	7.61
Market Capitalization	1.26B	87.64B	—	—	10.1B
Headquarters	California	California	China Taiwan	France	California

EPS, earnings per share.
Source: Based on company information.

Cisco Systems, Inc.

Nearly 40 times the size of Netgear, Cisco is headquartered in the same city as Netgear, San Jose, California. Like Netgear, Cisco structures its operations in the same three geographic segments, with its European and Middle East headquarters in the Netherlands and the Asia Pacific headquarters in Singapore. Also like Netgear, Cisco produces Internet protocol networking and other related devices to support communications and information technology. Cisco's sales by geographic region reported in its fiscal year end June 2012 were 65, 21, and 14 percent respectively for Americas, EMEA, and APAC. Also like Netgear, Cisco produces cable modems, video software, encoders, decoders, and many more products. Cisco's Linksys wireless routers compete directly with Netgear routers. As of year-end 2012, Cisco had 66,000 employees, annual revenues of $46 billion, and net income of $8 billion. Also like Netgear, Cisco relies exclusively on contract manufacturers for all their manufacturing needs.

Cisco spends about 12 percent of net sales on R&D compared to only 4 percent for Netgear. Cisco contains around $17 billion in goodwill on the balance sheet resulting in approximately 40 percent of total stockholders' equity residing from intangible assets, which is not good, versus Netgear's 17 percent.

Western Digital Corporation

Headquartered in Irvine, California, Western Digital creates and markets storage devices, home entertainment devices, and networking devices, similar to Netgear. Western Digital is known for their 2.5- and 3.5-inch form factor hard drives under the Ultrastart, XE, WD, and SiliconDrive brand names. Western Digital also produces a wide range of external hard drives in 500-gb sizes, FireWire, and Ethernet connections.

Western Digital is structured based on the same geographic regions both Netgear and Cisco. One notable exception, Western Digital, with $12.5 billion of revenue in fiscal 2012 that ended June 2012, reported that about 58 percent of their revenues come from Asian markets with 23 and 19 percent coming from the Americas and EMEA, respectively, providing the company a significantly more Asian presence than both Netgear and Cisco. The company currently spends 8 percent of revenues on R&D. The firm has $2 billion in goodwill and around 37 percent of all current assets are in inventory.

As of December 2012, Western Digital has a price-to-earnings (P/E) ratio of five, below the S&P 500 P/E ratio of 17.7, and its stock price was up 22.9 percent year-to-date. Western Digital has numerous strengths, such as robust revenue growth, reasonable debt levels, solid stock price performance, impressive record of earnings per share growth, and compelling growth in net income. Western Digital has no glaring weaknesses.

Western Digital recently acquired the hard disk drive operations of Hitachi, greatly increasing its capacity and sales volume. Like rival Seagate Technology, Western Digital has been targeting some acquisitions upstream to better control input costs. Seagate recently acquired the hard disk operations of Samsung.

D-Link Corporation

Headquartered in Taipei, China Taiwan, D-Link develops, produces, and markets networking, connectivity, and data communications hardware, offering hubs and switches, adapters, print servers, routers, and transceivers. Other D-Link products include broadband modems, virtual private network/firewall devices, data-storage systems, videoconferencing equipment, Web cameras, and business phones. D-Link sells to individuals and businesses, but the firm specializes in wi-fi and Ethernet components for the small to medium-sized office market. D-Link sells its products through distributors in more than 100 countries, but generates most of its sales in Asia.

The Future

In July 2012, Netgear acquired AVAAK, Inc., a privately-held company that develops wire-free video networking products for a total purchase consideration of $24.0 million in cash. This acquisition bolstered the company's retail business unit product offerings and expanded their presence in the smart home market. Some analysts however contend that the fate of Netgear's industry is inexorably tied to the PC and that PCs are in decline as users switch to tablets, which will not need hard disk drives. But there are external storage needs for hard-disk drives that seem to be growing and conventional storage is still cheaper than flash memory.

Every few months or so, Netgear introduces a new or improved product, including the recently introduced Netgear ProSecure® UTM25S Unified Threat Management Firewall, which provides two modular slots that fit optional interface cards, enabling IT administrators to custom tailor the firewall to their specific connectivity requirements. In addition, like other members of the ProSecure UTM family of security appliances, the UTM25S integrates with Netgear ReadyNAS® network-attached storage systems, giving businesses almost unlimited activity log and quarantine capacity for forensic, regulatory and legal requirements.

Netgear also recently introduced the CentriaTM, a powerful, all-in-one automatic backup/ media server and high-speed wi-fi router. Centria is a dual-band high-performance router with the added convenience of automatic data backup for both PCs and Macs. The backup capability of the Centria router gives a consumer peace of mind knowing that data is always backed up. If a PC or Mac goes down or is lost, a consumer can still access data from Centria using another computer. Routers are excellent for data backup because they are always on and are the central point of connection for all computers in the home. Centria can also be used as a storage repository for photos, media, and documents that may take up too much space on your computer. Centria uses an internal SATA drive or external USB drives to backup and store data.

There are companies such as Western Digital or Cisco that may be interested in acquiring Netgear. Even D-Link desires a greater market share in the United States. And Netgear itself has a history of making acquisitions. What would be some good acquisition targets for Netgear, to help solidify its competitive position and gain economies of scale. To remain attractive in this rapidly changing industry, Netgear needs a clear strategic plan going forward.

Crocs, Inc., 2013

www.crocs.com, CROX

Headquartered in Niwot, Colorado, Crocs, Inc. produces Crocs shoes, one of the most comfortable shoes ever designed. The awkward, even clumsy look of the Crocs shoe is offset by unbelievable comfort. One of the world leaders in casual footwear and apparel for men, women, and children, Crocs' shoes offer unmatched comfort derived from Croslite, a proprietary material that gives Crocs its soft, lightweight, waterproof, and odor-resistant qualities. Crocs are produced in many different styles, including boots, sandals, sneakers, flats, golf shoes, mules, and the popular original clog style, which is offered in more than 20 colors. Most of the other styles are limited to six colors or two-color combinations.

Crocs makes shoes specifically for companies in the healthcare and airline industries as well as for diabetic needs markets. Crocs has an alliance with the American Nurses Association, providing nurses with a 25 percent discount on shoes. Croc "Fuzz Collection" is designed with removable woolly liners that enable the shoe to be worn in winter or summer and the Jibbitz line, marketed primarily at children, manufactures declarative clip on items, often of Disney characters, for use in the ventilation holes of the shoes.

For the first time in its history, Crocs reported revenues of more than $1 billion at year-end 2011 and in 2012 celebrated its 10th birthday. To date, Crocs has sold more than 200 million pairs of shoes to customers in more than 90 countries through its retail stores, outlets, kiosks, and Web stores. Crocs Web stores operate under the brand names Crocs Work, Crocs Rx, Ocean Minded, and Jibbitz. As of year-end 2012, Crocs operated 121 kiosks, mostly in malls, 287 retail stores, 129 outlet stores, and 43 Web stores around the world. With more than 4,100 employees, Crocs manufactures its shoes mainly in Mexico, but it has other manufacturers in Italy, Romania, Bosnia and Herzegovina, and China.

Crocs' major rival, **Columbia Sportswear Company** (COLM), in late 2013 strengthened its presence in India by forming a distribution agreement with the New Delhi-based Chogori India Retail Ltd. As per the agreement, Chogori will serve as the sole distributor of Columbia's brands in India. Chogori owns 32 stores in 14 cities in India and is the exclusive retailer of Hi-Tec, the British footwear brand and American footwear brand, Crocs.

Copyright by Fred David Books LLC. (Written by Forest R. David)

History

Crocs was founded by friends Scott Seamans, Lyndon "Duke" Hanson, and George Boedecker Jr. in 2002 who desired to manufacture and distribute a foam clog style shoe they purchased from a company in Quebec, Canada, called Foam Creations. Foam Creations was marketing the shoe solely for use as a spa shoe, however, Boedecker, former Chief Operations Officer of International Sales at Quiznos Corp. in Canada, envisioned a brighter future for the product than limiting the marketing only to spas. Soon after securing rights to the shoe, Crocs unveiled its first official shoe under the Crocs brand named, called the *Beach*, at the 2002 Fort Lauderdale, Florida Boat Show. All 200 pairs available at the show were sold almost instantaneously. In 2004, Crocs officially purchased Foam Creations and with it rights to Croslite, the principle material that provides Crocs their comfort and medically beneficial properties. In 2006, Crocs expanded their brand by acquiring Jibbitz, from a stay-at-home mom, for $10 million, and acquired Bite Footware and Ocean Minded in 2007. In 2008, Crocs acquired two European based companies, Tidal Trade and Tagger.

In 2006, Crocs had an initial public offering (IPO), selling stock and raising funds through equity financing for the first time. Fortunately for Crocs, the 2006 IPO corresponded with the rapid advancement of sales in what *Salon* described as "somehow just caught fire" in reference to demand for the product. Crocs' stock price subsequently jumped from around $15 in 2006 to more than $75 by 2007, amounting to a 400-percent return for IPO investors in a little more than a year. However, along with increasing sales, critics of Crocs were coming equally as fast. In 2007, fashion consultant Tim Gunn was quoted in *Time Magazine* as saying "the Croc looks like a plastic hoof. How can you take that seriously?" In addition to *Time*, the *Washington Post* and *New York Times* printed critical reviews of the shoes. The ongoing negative press coincided with a weakening global economy and resulted in Crocs' stock price falling from $75 per share in late 2007 to under $0.80 per share by year-end 2008. Fortunately for Crocs, the stock and company rebounded an amazing 4,000 percent to $32 per share in 2011. Revenues also hit an all-time high of $1 billion at year-end 2011.

Along with Crocs robust rise as a powerful player in the shoe industry in 2006, the year witnessed other firms manufacturing or distributing products deemed "croc-offs" a unique play on words indicating Crocs patents were being infringed. In 2007, many of these "croc-offs" were seized in the Philippines and Denmark. However today, there are still competitors offering similar looking shoes under various brand names such as Airwalk, Poliwalks, and NothingZ. Unfortunately for Crocs, Inc., croc-offs can be purchased today at discount stores, beach stores, superstores, and similar shopping outlets.

Internal Issues

Mission Statement

According to the company website, Crocs provides two separate mission statements, one for Crocs, Inc. and one for Ocean Minded. Crocs' mission is: "To bring profound comfort, fun and innovation to the world's feet." Ocean Minded's mission is: "To become the global leader in sustainable lifestyle footwear, apparel and accessories whilst ensuring that the four pillars of the Ocean Minded brand—Quality, Authenticity, Responsibility and Community—resonate throughout our company, products, associates and actions."

Organizational Structure

Crocs' organizational structure consists of all white males, as indicated in Exhibit 1. Notice the firm operates using a division-by-region organizational design. Shares of Crocs' stock dropped 5.1 percent on 8-8-13 after Sterne Agee analysts downgraded the company to underperform, due to a perceived lack of talented top executives. The analysts also have concerns about Crocs' relationship with backjoy.com—which includes several former Crocs executives—calling it "too close for comfort."

EXHIBIT 1 Organizational Structure

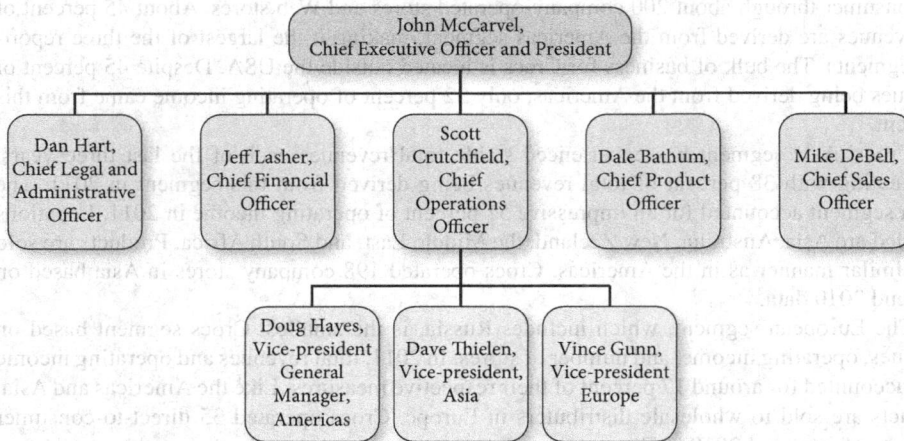

Source: Based on company documents.

Segments

In 2012, Crocs operated 43 company-owned Internet web stores, up from 42 and 37 the prior two years respectively. But the company's Internet sales dropped to 9.1 percent of total revenue in 2012 from 9.6 percent the prior year. For 2012, 57.5 percent of Crocs' revenues were derived from sales to wholesale distributors, down from 59.8 and 60.8 percent the prior two years, respectively. Distributors include Dick's Sporting Goods, Famous Footwear, Kohl's, and Nordstrom, but no single customer accounts for 10 percent or more of revenues.

By Product

Crocs footwear accounts for about 96 percent of total revenues, with accessories, primarily from Jibbitz, producing the remaining revenues. Footwear products are divided into four main categories: (1) Core-Comfort, (2) Active, (3) Casual, and (4) Style. Core-Comfort category includes the classic Crocs and all close derivatives from the original design. The Active product offerings are designed for activities such as boating, walking, and hiking. The remaining two categories of shoes are designed with style in mind, taking more of an equal role with comfort, and Crocs hopes this line of shoes will expand the pool of "wearing occasions" for customers.

Crocs also operates under three different brands: (1) Crocs, (2) Ocean Minded, and (3) Jibbitz. Although Crocs does not report revenues or operating incomes by brand, the three brands are quite distinct and even have their own mission statements. The Crocs brand is the traditional clog-looking shoe and in line with the Core-Comfort category. Crocs describes the Crocs brand shoe as being: innovative, fun, comfortable, and simple. Even going as far to state "in a world full of bells and whistles, less is more." Crocs' Ocean Minded brand, which was acquired in 2007 keeping the name Ocean Minded, includes the Active, Casual, and Style categories of shoes. The Ocean Minded brand specializes in ocean or water sports themed items. Flip flops, boat shoes, and shoes for surfing are all possible options. In addition, shoes with wooly liners, high-quality leather, hiking shoes, and more everyday shoes are also produced by Ocean Minded. Ocean Minded brand shoes have their own website at www.oceanminded.com. Finally, the Jibbitz brand produces accessories designed for use with Crocs brand shoes as well as a means to personalize purses, cell phone cases, beach bags, backpacks, and more. Jibbitz has contracts with Disney, Marvel, and Lego, among others to produce trademarked items.

By Region

Crocs' organizational structure is set up by geographic region, and so are the reporting business segments. As indicated in Exhibit 2, Crocs' revenues and operating incomes are reported under three segments: Americas, Europe, and Asia. Exhibit 2 provides a breakdown of the most recent financial information for Crocs. Note the company is doing well in all three geographic regions.

The Crocs' Americas segment includes all revenues in North and South America. Products are sold wholesale to sporting goods, department, and specialty retail stores as well as direct to the consumer through about 200 company-operated stores and Web stores. About 45 percent of all revenues are derived from the Americas segment, making it the largest of the three reporting segments. The bulk of business for Crocs is located outside the USA. Despite 45 percent of revenues being derived from the Americas, only 32 percent of operating income came from this segment.

Crocs' Asia segment has experienced stable total revenues each of the last three years, culminating with 38 percent of total revenues being derived from this segment in 2011. The Asian segment accounted for an impressive 51 percent of operating income in 2011. Locations included are Asia, Australia, New Zeeland, the Middle East, and South Africa. Products are sold in a similar manner as in the Americas. Crocs operated 198 company stores in Asia based on year-end 2010 data.

The European segment, which includes Russia, is the smallest Crocs segment based on revenues, operating income, and number of stores. In 2011, total revenues and operating income each accounted for around 17 percent of their respective measures. Like the Americas and Asia, products are sold to wholesale distributers in Europe. Crocs operated 35 direct-to-consumer stores as of year-end 2010 in European markets.

EXHIBIT 2 Crocs' Revenues by Channel

($ thousands)	Year Ended December 31,		Change
	2012	2011	%
Channel revenues:			
Wholesale:			
Americas	$ 235,988	$ 214,062	10.2%
Asia	298,350	259,104	15.1
Europe	110,947	124,995	(11.2)
Other businesses	574	191	200.5
Total Wholesale	645,859	598,352	7.9
Consumer-direct:			
Retail:			
Americas	196,711	174,840	12.5
Asia	143,062	111,650	28.1
Europe	35,052	20,167	73.8
Total Retail	374,825	306,657	22.2
Internet:			
Americas	63,153	59,175	6.7
Asia	15,999	11,012	45.3
Europe	23,465	25,707	(8.7)
Total Internet	102,617	95,894	7.0
Total revenues:	$ 1,123,301	$ 1,000,903	12.2%

Source: 2012 *Form 10K*, p. 28.

By Channel

As indicated in Exhibit 3, Crocs' revenue increased nicely in 2012 in all channels. Note in Exhibit 4 that Crocs reduced its number of kiosks in 2012 to 121 from 158 the prior year, but increased its number of retail stores and outlet stores to 287 and 129 respectively.

Finance

Crocs' stock price recently jumped 9 percent in one day after Goldman Sachs analyst Taposh Bari gave the creator of those colorful plastic shoes a "Buy" rating, saying that investors have misinterpreted the shoe brand as a fad. "We see Crocs as a lifestyle brand with global appeal that appears both proven and sustainable," he wrote in a note to investors. Crocs' stock hit a 52-week low price of $12 on November 15, 2012, but since then has increased to $18 in mid-2013. Crocs, Inc. has little debt and has more than $315 million in total cash, and a price-to-earnings to growth (PEG) ratio of only 0.90. All these factors indicate a stock that is undervalued. The company has never paid a cash dividend on shares of its stock.

As revealed in Exhibit 5, 2012 was the best year ever for Crocs with the company reporting revenues up 12.2 percent percent from 2011 to an all-time record of $1.12 billion and net income rose 17 percent to $131 million. The record growth was fueled by all three geographic operating segments and Crocs attention to focusing on selling prices, new product styles, forming new contracts with existing and new wholesale customers and a strong expansion of new Crocs stores. In addition, Crocs increased marketing efforts of Ocean Minded products to provide Crocs footwear options for all four seasons.

The balance sheets in Exhibit 6 reveal that Crocs' stockholders' equity increased 30 percent from 2011 to 2010 and an impressive 71 percent more than the two-year period ending in 2011. Crocs has acquired other firms over the years, but to their credit, the company has $0 goodwill on their balance sheet.

EXHIBIT 3 Crocs Income by Segment

($ thousands)	Year Ended December 31,		Change
	2012	2011	%
Revenues:			
Americas	$ 495,852	$ 448,077	10.7%
Asia	457,411	381,766	19.8
Europe	169,464	170,869	(0.8)
Total segment revenues	1,122,727	1,000,712	12.2
Other businesses	574	191	200.5
Total consolidated revenues	**$ 1,123,301**	**$ 1,000,903**	**12.2%**
Operating income:			
Americas	$ 85,538	$ 70,532	21.3%
Asia	140,828	123,918	13.6
Europe	21,678	37,106	(41.6)
Total segment operating income	**248,044**	**231,556**	**7.1**
Other businesses	(10,805)	(14,128)	(23.5)
Intersegment eliminations	60	66	(9.1)
Unallocated corporate and other	(91,125)	(86,415)	5.5
Total consolidated operating income	**$ 146,174**	**$ 131,079**	**11.5%**

Source: 2012 *Form 10K*, p. 33.

EXHIBIT 4 Crocs' Company-Owned Stores

	December 31, 2012	Opened	Closed	December 31, 2011
Type:				
Kiosk/Store in Store	121	39	(76)	158
Retail Stores	287	120	(13)	180
Outlet Stores	129	42	(5)	92
Total	**537**	**201**	**(94)**	**430**
Geography:				
Americas	199	44	(42)	197
Asia	241	94	(51)	198
Europe	97	63	(1)	35
Total	**537**	**201**	**(94)**	**430**

Source: 2012 *Form 10K*, p. 28.

Strategy

A competitive advantage for Crocs is the absence of any type of box packaging, saving millions on costs. Although revolutionary, Croslite remains cheaper to purchase and manufacture than other shoe materials like leather. Rival firms such as Deckers Outdoor and Timberland report cost of sales around 55 percent, whereas Crocs' cost of sales are about 42 percent.

One of the biggest changes Crocs undertook in the aftermath of the 99-percent stock depreciation was that the firm began producing their own footwear in their own facilities in Mexico, Italy, and China. Ultimately this reduced costs, provided Crocs with better quality control and enabled the company to significantly speed up production and delivery of products to customers. Crocs also expanded away from their traditional clog-style shoe into beachwear, hiking shoes, boats shoes, and other more casual and fashionable options.

EXHIBIT 5 Crocs' Income Statement

($ thousands, except share data)	For the Year Ended December 31,		
	2012	2011	2010
Consolidated Statements of Operations Data			
Revenues	**$ 1,123,301**	**$ 1,000,903**	**$ 789,695**
Cost of sales	515,324	464,493	364,631
Restructuring charges	—	—	1,300
Gross profit	607,977	536,410	423,764
Selling, general and administrative expenses	460,393	404,803	342,961
Restructuring charges	—	—	2,539
Asset impairments	1,410	528	141
Income (loss) from operations	146,174	131,079	78,123
Foreign currency transaction (gains) losses, net	2,500	(4,886)	(2,325)
Other income, net	(2,711)	(1,578)	(1,001)
Interest expense	837	853	657
Income (loss) before income taxes	145,548	136,690	80,792
Income tax (benefit) expense	14,205	23,902	13,066
Net income (loss) attributable to common stockholders	**$ 131,343**	**$ 112,788**	**$ 67,726**
Income (loss) per common share:			
Basic	$ 1.46	$ 1.27	$ 0.78
Weighted average common shares:			
Basic	89,571,105	88,317,898	85,482,055
Footwear unit sales	49,947	47,736	—
Average footwear selling price	21.55	20.04	—

Source: 2012 *Form 10K*, p. 24.

Crocs continues to expand globally. The company's unique products match well with consumer demand around the world, so there are numerous countries yet that Crocs can enter.

External Issues

The footwear industry is quite fragmented in the USA and Western Europe. Total footwear sales rose just under 5 percent in 2011 to $50.5 billion in the USA. Out of the main categories of footwear, fashion represented 48 percent, performance 27 percent, sports and leisure 13 percent, outdoor 8 percent, and work and occupational 4 percent. It is expected the leading area for growth the footwear industry in the USA and Western Europe resides in the fashion category. Markets in Asia and Eastern Europe are less developed and offer a wider range of product development and penetration strategies for firms to explore. Firms competing in the industry are increasingly expanding their product offerings. Nike, for example, is now well entrenched in the apparel business and more recently has expanded into producing golf clubs, watches, yoga mats, and other products in an attempt to grow revenues.

Shoe Composition: Health Concerns

The Swedish Society for Nature Conservation found in 2009 alarming concentrations of toxic chemicals in many popular plastic-based shoes, including flip flips, sandals, clogs, and other similar style shoes. Out of 27 shoes tested originating from the Philippines, India, Indonesia, South Africa, and other nations, 17 or 63 percent of the shoes tested contained high levels of phthalates. Although Crocs does not manufacture their shoes in any of the tested nations, many fake crocs illegally using Croc logos have historically been produced in the Philippines. The growing awareness of toxic chemicals in shoe production is of potential concern for all shoe manufacturers, including Crocs. But Crocs conceivably could turn this issue into a competitive

EXHIBIT 6 Consolidated Balance Sheets

($ thousands, except number of shares)	December 31, 2012	December 31, 2011
ASSETS		
Current assets:		
Cash and cash equivalents	$ 294,348	$ 257,587
Accounts receivable, net of allowances of $13,315 and $15,508, respectively	92,278	84,760
Inventories	164,804	129,627
Deferred tax assets, net	6,284	7,047
Income tax receivable	5,613	5,828
Other receivables	24,821	20,295
Prepaid expenses and other current assets	24,967	20,199
Total current assets	613,115	525,343
Property and equipment, net	82,241	67,684
Intangible assets, net	59,931	48,641
Deferred tax assets, net	34,112	30,375
Other assets	40,239	23,410
Total assets	**$ 829,638**	**$ 695,453**
LIABILITIES AND STOCKHOLDERS' EQUITY		
Current liabilities:		
Accounts payable	$ 63,976	$ 66,517
Accrued expenses and other current liabilities	81,371	76,506
Deferred tax liabilities, net	2,405	2,889
Income taxes payable	8,147	8,273
Current portion of long-term borrowings and capital lease obligations	2,039	1,118
Total current liabilities	157,938	155,303
Long term income tax payable	36,343	41,665
Long-term borrowings and capital lease obligations	4,596	—
Other liabilities	13,361	6,705
Total liabilities	**212,238**	**203,673**
Commitments and contingencies		
Stockholders' equity:		
Preferred shares, par value $0.001 per share, 5,000,000 shares authorized, none outstanding	—	—
Common shares, par value $0.001 per share, 250,000,000 shares authorized, 91,047,297 and 88,662,845 shares issued and outstanding, respectively, at December 31,2012 and 90,306,432 and 89,807,146 shares issued and outstanding, respectively, at December 31,2011	91	90
Treasury stock, at cost, 2,384,452 and 499,286 shares, respectively	(44,214)	(19,759)
Additional paid-in capital	307,823	293,959
Retained earnings	334,012	202,669
Accumulated other comprehensive income	19,688	14,821
Total stockholders' equity	617,400	491,780
Total liabilities and stockholders' equity	**$ 829,638**	**$ 695,453**

Source: Crocs 2012 *Form 10K*, p. F-4.

advantage by educating consumers because crocs are made of Croslite, which is a proprietary blend of materials the company does not disclose. Lack of transparency by Crocs in this regard could be a major problem for the firm. The chemicals associated with phthalates and PVC are believed to cause health complications including infertility, testicular problems, endocrine disorders, and possibly even cancer.

The Swedish Society for Nature Conservation has advised consumers to demand full disclosure of product information and to avoid products derived from PVC and phthalates. These chemicals are also currently used in many household products such as baby milk bottles, pacifiers, printer inks, nail polish, adhesives, and perfumes just to name a few. The USA and European Union have passed laws banning phthalate rich children toys. Walmart and Target are phasing out PVC in their packaging, as are various companies, including Nike. China and the Philippians still do not have laws in place regarding acceptable levels of these containments. It remains to be seen how companies such as Crocs will fare when their shoes possibly contain these pollutants, and even if they do not contain them, public perception may steer customers away, especially parents of young kids who are a primary target of Crocs.

Demographic and Economic Factors

China, Vietnam, Brazil, Nigeria, Nambia, and Chile are just a few among many countries in which Crocs shoes could be well received. Those countries have rapidly growing middle-class consumers looking for new and innovative products. As consumers worldwide become more health conscious and more interested in style and convenience, Crocs could take advantage of demographic trends. World economies are in general improving, which also bodes well for firms such as Crocs.

Competition

Crocs competes with Foot Locker, Timberland, Decker, Adidas, Columbia Sportswear (COLM), Skechers USA, Inc. (SKX), Wolverine World Wide (WWW), and Nike, as well as numerous smaller firms. Croc-off companies that produce and market imitation crocs are the company's primary competitors. It is difficult to determine names of firms producing the knock-off crocs that sell for less than $10, whereas authentic crocs sell for over $20 per pair.

Among competitors' price-to-earnings ratios in December 2012, Deckers was low at 10.2, compared to Nike at 17.4, and Wolverine World Wide and Adidas both above 15. Columbia Sportswear was nearly 17. Crocs had the lowest price earnings ratio at 8.8. Note in Exhibit 7 that Crocs' earnings per share (EPS) and revenue per employee lag far behind both Deckers and Nike. The latter ratio indicates that Crocs may have some internal efficiency problems, perhaps even too many employees. Note that Decker has less than one-half the employees of Crocs, but generates 27 percent more revenue.

Deckers Outdoor Corp.

Headquartered in Goleta, California, Deckers is publically traded on the NASDAQ and has enjoyed 35-percent increases in profits from 2009 to 2010 and 2010 to 2011. Deckers' acquisition of Sanuk in 2011 inflated company goodwill from $6 million to $120 million. Deckers

EXHIBIT 7 Crocs, Inc. versus Deckers Outdoor and Nike

	Crocs	Deckers	Nike
Price earnings ratio	8.8	10.2	17.4
Number of employees	4,157	1,900	44,000
Revenue ($)	1.1B	1.4B	43.8B
Revenue per employee	264K	736K	995K
Net income	140M	156M	2.14B
EPS	1.54	4.06	4.60
Book value	1.21B	1.34B	43.8B

EPS, earnings per share.
Source: Company documents.

designs, manufactures, and markets footwear and accessory luxury items ranging apparel to handbags. Deckers designs products for cold weather applications, hiking, amphibious footwear, and more. Deckers' popular UGG brand, accounted for 87 percent of 2011 revenues. Under the firm's Teva brand, Deckers offers what the company calls, rugged outdoor travel shoes. Other brands offered include Sanuk, TSUBO, Ahnu, and MOZO. These brands produce items ranging from high-end casual footwear to amphibious footwear products. To reduce Deckers' dependence on their UGG brand for revenue, Sanuk was purchased in 2011 for $120 million plus future payments for five years based on revenues the brand generates.

Deckers sells its products mainly through third-party retail stores, but they also own outlet stores, and in addition sell from the company website. Deckers' products are available worldwide in the United States, Europe, Canada, Australia, Asia, and Latin America. Deckers UGG brand, made with luxury sheepskin, is currently the company's most popular product. To maintain strong sales, Deckers introduces a consistent flow of new product variations in the fall and spring seasons, along with year-round styles. To expand the UGG Brand, Deckers is targeting men, expanding the brand globally, and creating additional products such as handbags to supplement the shoe sales. Pricing for the UGG brand is considered mid- to upper-priced luxury.

Teva and Sanuk are the two other principle brands offered by Deckers. The Teva brand has evolved from sports scandals to also include open- and closed-toe outdoor-themed footwear. In addition, the Teva brand has evolved to include light hiking, amphibious footwear, and travel shoes. Most recently, Deckers introduced an insulated boot under the Teva brand. Sanuk revolves almost entirely around the surf community.

Deckers' stock price hit its all-time closing high of $117.66 on October 28, 2011, but from there it has been a steep and rapid decline, down to its lowest level in three years, $28.63 on October 31, 2012. Since then, though, Deckers' stock has been increasing nicely.

Nike

Headquartered in Beaverton, Oregon, Nike specializes in the design and development of footwear, apparel, sports equipment, and accessories for men, women, and children worldwide. The company also markets their products to college and professional sports teams. Nike distributes products under the Converse, Chuck Taylor, All Star, Hurley, and One Star trademarks, among others.

The Hurley brand produces sandals and shoes designed for the surf boarding community, competes directly with Crocs Ocean Minded products. Nike's Cole Haan brand designs reflective shoes for night life and other evening outings best competing with the more stylish brands of shoes Crocs develops. Nike and Crocs both develop and market shoes for golfers.

Nike sells its products mainly through retail stores and the company website, but Nike has its own retail stores and outlet stores. To its credit and financial soundness, Nike has goodwill of only $201 million despite numerous acquisitions in Nike's history. Of late, however, Nike has been divesting brands. In late 2012, Nike sold its Cole Haan handbag and shoe brand to private equity firm Apax Partners for $570 million and also sold its Umbro football brand to Iconix Brand Group for $225 million.

Skechers USA

Headquartered in Manhattan Beach, California, Skechers' Chief Executive Officer Robert Greenberg leads this firm that designs and sells more than 3,000 styles of lifestyle and athletic footwear (oxfords, boots, sandals, sneakers, training shoes, and semi-dressy shoes) for men, women, and children. Skechers also offers fashion and street-focused footwear under the Marc Ecko, Zoo York, and Mark Nason brands. Its shoes are sold through department and specialty stores in more than 100 countries, as well as in some 330 company-owned concept and outlet stores and on its website. Sketchers footwear is manufactured primarily by Chinese contractors.

For the third quarter of 2012, Skechers sales grew 4.2 percent to $429.4 million from the prior-year quarter, reflecting excellent performance across company-owned retail businesses, domestic wholesale, and international distributors. The company's domestic wholesale sales were up 7.2 percent, reflecting a 9.1-percent increase in pairs shipped, coupled with a strong growth across kids and performance divisions. Sales grew 10.9 percent in the quarter for the company's international distributor, reflecting strong growth across Pan-Asian distributors, Middle East, Indonesia, Philippines, South Korea, China Taiwan, New Zealand, and

Australia. However, international subsidiary sales declined 14.6 percent. On a combined basis, Skechers' retail business sales grew 13.9 percent. Domestic retail sales grew 13.2 percent, and the company added 23 new domestic and 4 new outside-U.S. stores.

The Future

If Croslite is indeed free of phthalates, then (a) a huge marketing campaign by Crocs may be worthwhile in the future to educate consumers, and (b) numerous health-related specialty areas exist for Crocs to develop new products. If Croslite is not free of phthalates, Crocs, Inc. should correct this problem as quickly as possible while the exact composition of its shoes is a secret.

Crocs could in some manner follow the lead of Nike and Deckers regarding (a) diversification into accessory items, (b) expansion into other countries, and (c) development of new products. There is nothing wrong with being a fast follower, as evidenced by firms such as Samsung doing quite well following Apple's first-mover advantage strategy. The Croslite material perhaps has many undiscovered, marketable applications, so the company could devote more resources to research and development to develop innovative new products.

It may be in Crocs' best interest to take legal action against croc-off imitation shoes, especially against firms that produce nearly identical-looking shoes. Despite this and other external threats, Crocs has performed admirably in recent years, but a clear strategic plan is still needed help assure continued success. Crocs plans to open about 90 new stores in 2013 but analysts question whether this is a desired strategy. Develop a three-year strategic plan for Crocs based on sound strategic-management tools and techniques.

L'Oréal SA, 2013

www.loréal.com, LRLCF or LRLCY or OR (Paris Exchange)

Headquartered in Clichy, France, just outside Paris, L'Oréal is the world's largest beauty products company, with brands that include L'Oréal Paris and Maybelline (mass-market), Lancôme (luxury), and Redken and SoftSheen/Carson (retail and salon). L'Oréal owns Dallas-based SkinCeuticals that conducts cosmetology and dermatology research. With more than 50 percent of sales generated outside Europe, L'Oréal has focused on acquiring brands globally. L'Oréal owns UK-based natural cosmetics retailer The Body Shop International, which has about 2,550 retail stores worldwide. L'Oréal's dermatology unit, Galderma S.A., is a joint venture with Nestlé.

L'Oréal SA is structured into three branches: (1) Cosmetics, (2) The Body Shop, and (3) Dermatology. The Cosmetics branch is divided into four sectors: Consumer Products, Professional Products, Luxury Products, and Active Cosmetics. Consumer Products are marketed under L'Oréal Paris, Garnier, Maybelline, Softsheen, and Carson brands. The company's Professional Products segment includes hair care products for use by professional hairdressers, such as Kerastase, Redken, and Matrix. L'Oréal's Luxury Products are sold globally under such brands as Lancome, Diesel, Giorgio Armani, and Cacharel. The firm's Active Cosmetics division, which consists of products under Vichy and La Roche Posay brands, are for sale mainly in pharmacies.

L'Oréal has a portfolio of 27 international, diverse, and complementary brands. With sales amounting to 22.5 billion euros in 2012, L'Oréal employs 72,600 people worldwide, has 43 production plants worldwide, 146 distribution centers, more than 20,000 employees in industrial operations worldwide, and 5.8 billion units produced. The world's largest cosmetics firm by sales, L'Oréal in August 2013 offered to buy a Chinese facial mask company for about US $840m. The company, Magic Holdings International, a Hong Kong-listed cosmetics producer based in Guangzhou, is known for its facial masks, one of the fastest-growing segments in China's cosmetics market. Magic Holdings generated revenues of about €150m in 2012, up 29 percent from the previous year. L'Oréal, which makes Lancôme creams and Garnier shampoo, said it would offer $HKD6.3 (HKD = Hong Kong Dollar) per share for the Chinese company. The offer represents a 25 percent premium on the previous day's closing price. L'Oréal already has won approval from six shareholders representing 62.3 percent of Magic Holding's shares. The deal requires approval from Chinese authorities.

History

In 1907, Eugene Schueller, a young French chemist, working with La Cagoule, developed a hair dye formula called *Auréale*. Schueller formulated and manufactured his own products, which he then sold to Parisian hairdressers. In 1919, Schueller registered his company as the French Society of Inoffensive Tinctures for Hair, which became L'Oréal. The guiding principles of the company were research and innovation in the field of beauty. In 1920, L'Oréal employed three chemists. By 1950, the research teams were 100 strong; that number reached 1,000 by 1984 and is nearly 2,000 today.

L'Oréal got its start in the hair-color business, but the company soon branched out into other cleansing and beauty products. L'Oréal currently markets more than 500 brands and many thousands of individual products in all sectors of the beauty business: hair color, permanents, hair styling, body and skin care, cleansers, makeup and fragrances. The company's products are found in a wide variety of distribution channels, from hair salons and perfumeries to hyper- and supermarkets, health/beauty outlets, pharmacies, and direct mail.

L'Oréal today has five worldwide research and development centers located in: (1) Aulnay, France, (2) Chevilly, France, (3) Clark, New Jersey, (4) Kawasaki, Japan, and (5) Shanghai, China. A future facility in the USA will be in Berkeley Heights, New Jersey.

L'Oréal has recently faced discrimination lawsuits in France related to the hiring of various spokespersons and institutional racism. In the United Kingdom, L'Oréal has faced wide-spread condemnation from the Office of Communications regarding truth in their advertising and marketing campaigns concerning the product performance of one of their mascara brands.

Protest group Naturewatch states that L'Oréal continues to test new ingredients on animals. L'Oréal has the largest factory in the Jababeka Industrial Park, Cikarang, Indonesia. L'Oréal does significant business in Indonesia.

Financially, L'Oréal is strong and is excelling globally in developing, producing, and marketing cosmetics, fragrances, and personal care products. For Q1 of 2013, L'Oréal reported sales of 5.93 billion euros, up 6.5 percent overall, including 8.5 percent up in North America and 11.8 percent up in Africa and the Middle East.

Internal Issues

Vision and Mission

L'Oréal does not have a vision statement, but the company's mission statement is provided on the corporate website, as follows:

> Beauty for all—For more than a century, L'Oréal has devoted itself solely to one business: beauty. It is a business rich in meaning, as it enables all individuals to express their personalities, gain self-confidence and open up to others.
>
> Beauty is a language—L'Oréal has set itself the mission of offering all women and men worldwide the best of cosmetics innovation in terms of quality, efficacy and safety. It pursues this goal by meeting the infinite diversity of beauty needs and desires all over the world.
>
> Beauty is universal. Since its creation by a researcher, the group has been pushing back the frontiers of knowledge. Its unique Research arm enables it to continually explore new territories and invent the products of the future, while drawing inspiration from beauty rituals the world over.
>
> Beauty is a science. Providing access to products that enhance well-being, mobilizing its innovative strength to preserve the beauty of the planet and supporting local communities. These are exacting challenges, which are a source of inspiration and creativity for L'Oréal.
>
> Beauty is a commitment. By drawing on the diversity of its teams, and the richness and the complementarity of its brand portfolio, L'Oréal has made the universalisation of beauty its project for the years to come.
>
> L'Oréal, offering beauty for all.

Sustainability

Regarding sustainable development, Corporate Knights, a Global Responsible Investment Network, has selected L'Oréal for its 2012 ranking of the Global 100 Most Sustainable Corporations in the World. L'Oréal has received this distinction for the fifth consecutive year. L'Oréal has more than 84 percent of its production globally being manufactured in compliance with the ISO 9001 (quality), ISO 14001 (environment), OHSAS 18001 (safety) certifications.

In San Luis Potosi, Mexico, L'Oréal opened the largest hair color production plant in the world in 2012, the firm's second plant in Mexico. L'Oréal views Mexico as the gateway between both North and South America. The new plant is in the process of becoming LEED certified and features advanced technologies for water treatment and solar-powered equipment. L'Oréal Mexico has reduced water consumption per unit by 60 percent and carbon dioxide emissions per unit by 60 percent in recent years.

On November 12, 2012, for its 10th anniversary, Vigeo European rating agency revealed a new range of environmental-social-governance (ESG) indices measuring companies' corporate and social responsibility on a global or European level, and more specifically in France and the United Kingdom. Vigeo's France index ranks L'Oréal as "the leading company in social responsibility" among 20 companies. The France index is based on 35 criteria, consolidated in an overall score covering six areas of social responsibility: human rights, human resources, environment, business behavior, corporate governance, and community involvement. L'Oréal ranks fourth in Vigeo's Europe index (120 companies) and fifth in Vigeo's World index (120 companies).

Organizational Structure

L'Oréal's organizational chart is provided in Exhibit 1. Note there is no chief operations officer (COO), but perhaps Jean-Philippe Blanpain serves that role. Note the divisional-by-geographic-region structure in conjunction with divisional-by-product. This could prove problematic in the sense that, for example, professional products operations in the Africa, Middle East Zone could report to either Geoff Skinsley or An Verbulst-Santos.

Advertising

L'Oréal's famous advertising slogan was "Because I'm worth it." In the mid-2000s, this slogan was replaced by "Because you're worth it." In late 2009, the slogan was changed again to "Because we're worth it." The shift to "we" was made to create stronger consumer involvement in L'Oréal philosophy and lifestyle and provide more consumer satisfaction with L'Oréal products. L'Oréal owns a Hair and Body products line for kids called L'Oréal Kids, the slogan for which is "Because we're worth it too."

Segments

L'Oréal has five product groupings:

1. L'Oréal LUXE (Luxury): Lancome, Giorgio Armani, YSL Beaute, Biotherm, Kiehl's, Ralph Lauren, Shu Uemura, Cacharel, Helena Rubinstein, Diesel, Viktod&Rolf, Stella McCartney, and Maison Martin Margiela. As indicated in Exhibit 2, L'Oréal Luxe sales grew in the first quarter of 2013 by 8.1 percent, largely as a result of the acquisition of *Clarisonic*. In a market that has slowed slightly, L'Oréal Luxe is continuing to increase market share worldwide.

EXHIBIT 1 L'Oréal's Organizational Structure

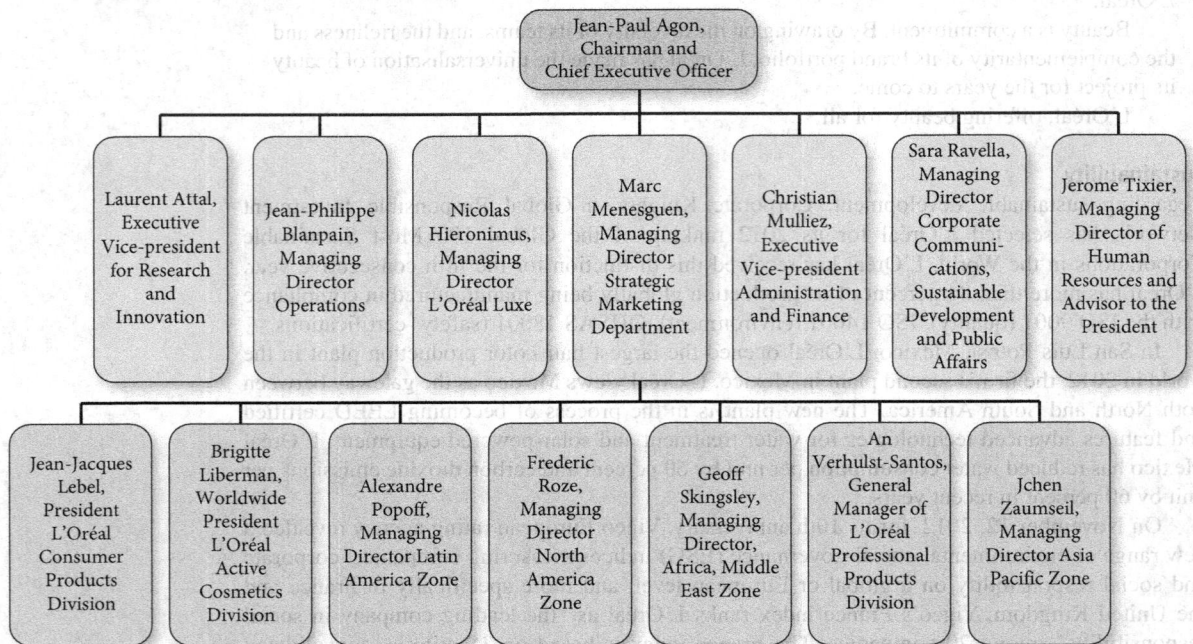

Source: Based on company documents.

EXHIBIT 2 L'Oréal's Sales by Operational Division and Geographic Zone (000,000 euros omitted)

By division	Q1 2012	Q1 2013	% Change
Professional Products	755.6	752.6	−0.4%
Consumer Products	2,769.5	2,920.8	5.5%
L'Oréal Luxe	1,315.5	1,422.0	8.1%
Active Cosmetics	468.6	497.6	6.2%
Cosmetics total	**5,309.1**	**5,593.0**	**5.3%**
BY GEOGRAPHIC ZONE			
Western Europe	1,953.9	1,990.4	1.9%
North America	1,263.4	1,371.4	8.5%
New Markets, of which:	2,091.7	2,231.1	6.7%
- Asia, Pacific	*1,124.3*	*1,188.4*	*5.7%*
- Latin America	*433.5*	*458.7*	*5.8%*
- Eastern Europe	*360.0*	*389.7*	*8.2%*
- Africa, Middle East	*173.8*	*194.3*	*11.8%*
Cosmetics total	**5,309.1**	**5,593.0**	**5.3%**
The Body Shop	180.4	181.9	0.8%
Dermatology	153.5	156.7	2.1%
Group total	**5,643.0**	**5,931.6**	**5.1%**

Source: Company documents.

2. Consumer Products: L'Oréal Paris, Garnier, Maybelline New York, Le Club Des Createurs, and Essie. In the first quarter of 2013, sales were up 5.5 percent.
3. Professional Products: L'Oréal Professionnel, INOA, Serie Expert, Serie Nature, L'Oréal Prefessionnel Homme, Tecni.art, Play ball, and Texture Expert. In quarter one of 2013, sales were down 0.4 percent.
4. Active Cosmetics: Vichy, La Roche Posay, Skinceuticals, Inmeov, Roger&Gallet, and Sanoflore. In the first quarter of 2013, sales were up 6.2 percent.
5. The Body Shop: Dermablend Coverage Cosmetics are sensitivity tested, non-comedogenic, non-acnegenic, fragrance free, water-resistant, smudge-resistant, long lasting and easy to use. For the third quarter of 2012, The Body Shop recorded like-for-like sales growth at 5.3 percent as shown in Exhibit 3. The Body Shop is growing strongly, especially in the Middle East and in South East Asia. Several important new product innovations include *BB Cream All-in-One*, a one-of-a-kind texture that transforms on application, as well as *Pore Minimiser* in its iconic *Tea Tree* range featuring Community Fair Trade organic tea tree oil from Kenya. The Body Shop continues to recruit new customers through its e-commerce channel, with 20 sites now live. The brand is rolling out its innovative Pulse boutique concept globally. In the first quarter of 2013 sales were up 0.8 percent.

Notice in Exhibit 2 that L'Oréal did especially well in the first quarter of 2013 in their L'Oréal Luxe segment and in their Africa/Middle East region.

Finance

Note in Exhibit 3 that L'Oréal's revenues and net income have increased nicely in recent years.

Note in Exhibit 4 that L'Oréal's goodwill increased almost €5 billion in 2011 which is not good, but the company has been paying off its long-term debt nicely, which is good.

Competitors

Exhibit 5 provides an overview of L'Oréal as compared to some of its leading competitors. Note that L'Oréal is by far the largest cosmetics and fragrances firm in terms of revenue, number of employees, and net income. L'Oréal also has the highest profit margin and revenue per

EXHIBIT 3 L'Oréal's Income Statement (000,000 euros omitted)

	2012	2011	2010	2009
Revenue	22,462.7	20,343.1	19,495.8	17,472.6
Other Revenue, Total	0.0	0.0	0.0	0.0
Total Revenue	**22,462.7**	**20,343.1**	**19,495.8**	**17,472.6**
Cost of Revenue, Total	6,587.7	5,851.5	5,696.5	5,161.6
Gross Profit	**15,875.0**	**14,491.6**	**13,799.3**	**12,311.0**
Selling, General, Administrative Expenses, Total	11,387.2	10,478.5	10,077.7	9,124.2
Research and Development	790.5	720.5	664.7	609.2
Depreciation and Amortization	0.0	0.0	0.0	0.0
Interest Expense (Income), Net Operating	0.0	0.0	0.0	0.0
Unusual Expense (Income)	93.7	108.1	74.0	277.6
Other Operating Expenses, Total	30.1	−11.8	79.2	0.0
Operating Income	**3,753**	**3,196.3**	**2,903.7**	**2,300.0**
Interest Income (Expense), Net Nonoperating	0.0	0.0	0.0	0.0
Gain (Loss) on Sale of Assets	0.0	0.0	0.0	0.0
Other, Net	−7.8	−5.6	−9.0	−13.1
Income Before Tax	**3,875.9**	**3,466.7**	**3,151.9**	**2,471.0**
Income Tax, Total	1,005.5	1,025.8	909.9	676.1
Income After Tax	**2,870.4**	**2,440.9**	**2,242.0**	**1,794.9**
Minority Interest	−2.7	−2.5	−2.3	−2.7
Equity In Affiliates	0.0	0.0	0.0	0.0
U.S. GAAP Adjustment	0.0	0.0	0.0	0.0
Net Income Before Extraordinary Items	**2,867.7**	**2,438.4**	**2,239.7**	**1,792.2**
Total Extraordinary Items	0.0	0.0	0.0	0.0
Net Income	**2,867.7**	**2,438.4**	**2,239.7**	**1,792.2**

GAAP, generally accepted accounting principles.
Source: Based on company documents.

employee. But every day is another day, and all of these rivals strive to overtake L'Oréal anywhere and everywhere they can.

Estée Lauder Companies, Inc.
Headquartered in New York City, Estée Lauder has annual sales of about $10 billion and net income of about $1 billion. Estée Lauder manufactures and markets skin care, makeup, fragrance, and hair care products. The company's products are sold in more than 150 countries and territories under a number of brand names, including Estee Lauder, Aramis, Clinique, Origins, M.A.C, Bobbi Brown, La Mer, and Aveda. The company is also the global licensee for fragrances or cosmetics sold under brand names, such as Tommy Hilfiger, Donna Karan, Michael Kors, Tom Ford, and Coach. The company sells its products in more than 30,000 points of sale, consisting of upscale department stores, specialty retailers, upscale perfumeries and pharmacies, and prestige salons and spas.

Avon
Headquartered in New York City, Avon Products is the world's largest direct-seller firm, and by far the largest direct seller of cosmetics and beauty-related items. Avon is the fifth-largest cosmetics and fragrance firm in the world. The company receives sales from catalogs and a website, but the vast majority of its sales come from its 6.4 million independent sales representatives in some 110 countries. Since 1892, Avon has been on the forefront of empowering women to be their own boss and be independent and become leaders in communities and business.

Avon products include cosmetics, fragrances, toiletries, jewelry, apparel, home furnishings, watches, footwear, children's products, skin care, and gift and decorative products, nutritional

EXHIBIT 4 L'Oréal's Balance Sheets (000,000 euros omitted)

	2012	2011	2010	2009
Assets				
Cash and Short-Term Investments	1,823.2	1,652.2	1,550.4	1,173.1
Total Receivables, Net	3,682.8	3,423.3	3,100.7	2,826.8
Total Inventory	2,033.8	2,052.0	1,810.1	1,476.7
Prepaid Expenses	234.3	231.3	208.9	168.1
Other Current Assets, Total	435.5	363.6	326.2	296.4
Total Current Assets	**8,209.6**	**7,722.4**	**6,996.3**	**5,941.1**
Property, Plant, and Equipment, Total (Net)	2,962.9	2,880.8	2,677.5	2,599.0
Goodwill, Net	6,478.2	6,204.6	5,729.6	5,466.0
Intangibles, Net	2,625.4	2,477.3	2,177.4	2,042.4
Long-Term Investments	8,445.3	6,901.0	5,837.5	6,672.2
Note Receivable, Long Term	86.0	0.0	0.0	0.0
Other Long-Term Assets, Total	717.8	671.5	626.2	570.8
Other Assets, Total	0.0	0.0	0.0	0.0
Total Assets	**29,525.2**	**26,857.6**	**24,044.5**	**23,291.5**
Liabilities and Shareholders' Equity				
Accounts Payable	3,318.0	3,247.7	3,153.5	2,603.1
Payable/Accrued	0.0	0.0	0.0	0.0
Accrued Expenses	0.0	1,039.0	986.8	918.2
Notes Payable and Short-Term Debt	20.8	806.0	119.0	151.5
Current Portability of Long-Term Debt and Capital Leases	180.3	284.8	648.0	238.2
Other Current Liabilities, Total	2,850.4	1,752.4	1,674.8	1,475.5
Total Current Liabilities	**6,369.5**	**7,129.9**	**6,582.1**	**5,386.5**
Total Long-Term Debt	46.9	57.5	824.3	2,741.6
Deferred Income Tax	764.4	677.7	462.0	418.0
Minority Interest	4.8	3.1	2.9	3.1
Other Liabilities, Total	1,407.9	1,355.0	1,310.3	1,147.1
Total Liabilities	**8,593.5**	**9,223.2**	**9,181.6**	**9,696.3**
Redeemable Preferred Stock	0.0	0.0	0.0	0.0
Preferred Stock, Nonredeemable, Net	0.0	0.0	0.0	0.0
Common Stock	121.8	120.6	120.2	119.8
Additional Paid-In Capital	1,679.0	1,271.4	1,148.3	996.5
Retained Earnings (Accumulated Deficit)	20,035.3	16,886.8	14,445.3	13,550.5
Treasury Stock, Common	−904.5	−644.4	−850.9	−1,071.6
ESOP Debt Guarantee	0.0	0.0	0.0	0.0
Unrealized Gain (Loss)	0.0	0.0	0.0	0.0
Other Equity, Total	0.0	0.0	0.0	0.0
Total Equity	**20,931.6**	**17,634.4**	**14,862.9**	**13,595.2**
Total Liabilities and Shareholders' Equity	**29,525.1**	**26,857.6**	**24,044.5**	**23,291.5**
Total Common Shares Outstanding	598.36	594.39	589.66	584.74
Total Preferred Shares Outstanding	0.0	0.0	0.0	0.0

ESOP, employee stock option plan.
Source: Based on company documents.

products, housewares, and entertainment and leisure products. Avon owns and sells Silpada jewelry. A few well-recognized company brand names include Avon Color, ANEW, Skin-So-Soft, Advance Techniques, Avon Naturals, and *mark*. Although a large U.S. iconic corporation, Avon is today struggling to recover from poor management strategies that led to CEO Jung resigning amid global bribery investigations. The direct-selling business model has waned in the USA, but

EXHIBIT 5   L'Oréal versus Rival Firms (in U.S. dollars)

	L'Oréal	Revlon	Avon	Estée Lauder
Number employees	72.6K	5.2K	40.6K	38.5K
Revenue ($)	27.7B	1.4B	10.7B	9.8B
Net income ($)	3.36B	40.6M	115.5M	877M
Profit Margin (%)	12.1	2.9	1.1	8.9
Revenue per employee	406K	269K	263K	255K
EPS	1.12	0.78	0.27	2.22
Market capitalization	83.3B	775.9M	6.35B	23.2B

EPS, earnings per share.
Source: Based on company documents.

it is effective in many emerging economies globally. Millions of motivated direct sellers in many countries are Avon's key competitive advantage going forward, but the company needs a clear strategic plan.

Mary Kay, Inc.

Headquartered in Addison, Texas, (outside Dallas) Mary Kay is a privately-owned cosmetic and fragrance direct-selling company. Mary Kay is the sixth-largest direct-selling company in the world, with annual sales of about $3.0 billion. Mary Kay's business model is similar to the Avon business model. Founded by Mary Kay Ash in 1963, the company is famous for the pink Cadillacs, given to high-selling representatives. Richard Rogers, Mary Kay's son, is the chairman of the board. Mary Kay products are sold in more than 35 markets worldwide, and the global Mary Kay independent sales force exceeds 2.4 million women.

In 1968, Mary Kay Ash purchased the first pink Cadillac and had it repainted to match the Mountain Laurel Blush in the Mary Kay compact. Since the Cadillac program's inception, more than 100,000 independent sales force members have qualified for the use of a Career Car or elected the cash compensation option. GM estimates that it has built 100,000 pink Cadillacs for Mary Kay. For 2012, high-sellers may select other Career Cars, including the Chevrolet Malibu, Chevrolet Equinox, Toyota Camry, and the Cadillac CTS, SRX & Escalade Hybrid, or most recently, a black Ford Mustang.

Revlon, Inc.

Headquartered in New York City, Revlon is a cosmetics leader with brands such as Almay and Revlon ColorSilk hair color, Mitchum antiperspirants and deodorants, Charlie and Jean Naté fragrances, and Ultima II and Gatineau skincare products. Revlon's beauty aids are distributed in more than 100 countries, though the USA is its largest market, generating about 55 percent of sales. Walmart is Revlon's biggest single customer, accounting for some 22 percent of sales.

Revlon manufactures, markets, and sells cosmetics, women's hair color, beauty tools, antiperspirant deodorants, fragrances, skincare, and other beauty care products. Revlon products are sold and marketed under brand names, such as Revlon, including the Revlon ColorStay, Revlon Super Lustrous, and Revlon Age Defying franchises; Almay, including the Almay Intense i-Color and Almay Smart Shade franchises; Sinful Colors in cosmetics; Revlon ColorSilk in women's hair color; Revlon in beauty tools; Mitchum in antiperspirant deodorants; Charlie and Jean Nate in fragrances, and Ultima II and Gatineau. Revlon also owns certain assets of Sinful Colors cosmetics, Wild and Crazy cosmetics, freshMinerals cosmetics, and freshcover cosmetics.

Coty, Inc.

Headquartered in New York City, Coty is one of the world's leading makers of beauty products for men and women. Led by CEO Michele Scannavini, Coty is a $4.1 billion beauty company, and the biggest seller of nail care, nail polish, and fragrances in the USA. Sarah Jessica Parker, Jennifer Lopez, Celine Dion, Gwen Stefani, Katy Perry, and Thomas Dutronc are several celebrities that promote Coty. Founder of the company, François Coty created his first perfume, La Rose Jacqueminot, in 1904.

Coty's product lineup today ranges from moderately-priced scents sold globally by mass retailers to prestige fragrances and nail polishes found in department stores. Coty's brands include Adidas, Philosophy, Rimmel, and Sally Hansen. Cody's prestige perfume labels are led by Calvin Klein. Coty's shimmery blue nail polish and Lady Gaga's perfume are high-selling products. Thomas Dutronc is the face of Coty's new Cerruti fragrance for men, which launched in 2013.

Coty's Rimmel Scandaleyes mascara, which debuted in early 2012, is another big seller. Over-the-top lashes are hot these days because false eye lashes have made a comeback and are "almost mainstream." Promotional material for Scandaleyes urges women to "ditch those falsies." Mascara makers today compete with eyelash lengthening drugs such as Latisse.

The Future

On November 14, 2012, in the Kingdom of Saudi Arabia, L'Oréal created L'Oréal KSA, a new subsidiary based on a joint venture with Al Naghi Group. L'Oréal brands have been distributed in the Kingdom of Saudi Arabia for two decades and since 2000, Al Naghi Group has been the company's sole distributor for its Consumer Products, Active Cosmetics, and Professional Products Divisions. However, L'Oréal KSA will manage a portfolio of brands including, among others, L'Oréal Professional, Kerastase, L'Oréal Paris, Garnier, Maybelline New York, and Vichy. L'Oréal KSA's will enable the company to better understand and to meet needs of woman in one of the most male-dominated countries in the world. There are other countries globally, especially in Africa and South America, that L'Oréal could engage in a similar manner. Brazil, for example, is where Avon derives most of its revenue, more even that from the USA.

There are numerous firms that could be acquired by L'Oréal to further expand and penetrate globally. Even a firm such as Avon that is struggling financially, but has a business model that is especially suited to emerging economies, may be interested in an offer from L'Oréal. Another firm could be Coty, Inc. that could fit well with the L'Oréal portfolio. And then there are cosmetic and fragrance divisions of large firms such as Procter & Gamble that could be available if L'Oréal deemed that to be attractive.

L'Oréal needs a clear strategic plan for the future. Perhaps the firm could vastly improve its selling operations online. Being the biggest and the best at year-end 2012 does not guarantee prosperity in the years to come. Develop an effective three-year strategic plan for L'Oréal.

Avon Products, Inc., 2013

www.avon.com, AVP

Headquartered in New York City, Avon is one of the world's largest direct-seller firms, and is by far the largest direct seller of cosmetics and beauty-related items. Avon is the fifth-largest cosmetics and fragrance firm in the world. The company receives sales from catalogs and a website, but the vast majority of its sales come from its 6.4 million independent sales representatives in some 110 countries. These women are all independent contractors. Avon has 39,100 employees, but only 4,800 are employed in the USA. Since 1892, Avon has been on the forefront of empowering women to be their own boss and be independent and become leaders in communities and business.

Avon products include cosmetics, fragrances, toiletries, jewelry, apparel, home furnishings, watches, footwear, children's products, skin care, and gift and decorative products, nutritional products, housewares, and entertainment and leisure products. Avon owns and sells Silpada jewelry. A few well-recognized company brand names include Avon Color, ANEW, Skin-So-Soft, Advance Techniques, and *mark*. Although a large U.S. iconic corporation, Avon is struggling today to recover from poor management strategies that led to CEO Jung resigning over global bribery investigations. The direct-selling business model has waned in the USA, but it is effective in many emerging economies globally. Avon obtains 85 percent of its revenue from outside the USA. Millions of motivated direct sellers in many countries is Avon's key competitive advantage going forward, but the company needs a clear strategic plan.

Avon reported a loss of $38.2 million in 2012 compared to a net income of $517.8 million the prior year. Avon's second-quarter 2013 net income declined 48 percent but that was above Wall Street expectations and so Avon's stock price hit a new high for the year. Avon has made an offer to settle its overseas bribery allegations for $12 million; the offer has been rejected by U.S. authorities. Avon's beauty products earned $31.9 million for Q2, down from $61.6 million a year ago. Revenue slipped 2 percent to $2.51 billion due to currency rates and North American sales. Avon's sales in North America during Q2 2013 declined 12 percent, hurt by a 13 percent drop in the number of active sales representatives. Avon's Asia-Pacific sales fell 9 percent, but the company's sales in Latin America and Europe, the Middle East and Africa rose. For the quarter, Avon's prices rose and their average order size increased.

Copyright by Fred David Books LLC. (Written by Forest R. David)

History

David McConnell started a business in 1886 that eventually came to be named Avon Products. A traveling book salesman, McConnell did not originally intend to create a beauty company, but he realized that his female customers were far more interested in the free perfume samples he offered than in his books. McConnell had also noticed that many of his female customers were isolated at home while their husbands went off to work. So, McConnell purposely recruited female sales representatives and believed they had a natural ability to network with and market to other women. At a time of limited employment options for women, the Avon earnings opportunity for women historically was a revolutionary concept for mankind. It marked the start of the company's long and rich history of empowering women around the globe.

In 1892, McConnell changed the company name when his business partner, who was living in California, suggested that he name his business the California Perfume Company, because of the great abundance of flowers in California. In 1916, the California Perfume Company was incorporated in the state of New York and filed its first trademark application for Avon on June 3, 1932. The document described the company's goods and services as perfumes, toilet waters, powder and rouge compacts, lipsticks, and other toiletry products.

Avon entered the Chinese market in 1990, but legal changes in 1998 forced Avon to sell only through physical stores called Beauty Boutiques. The company received China's first license for direct selling in 2006. Avon purchased Silpada, a direct seller of silver jewelry, in 2010 for $650 million. Brazil is the company's largest market, passing the USA in 2010. Avon closed its Atlanta distribution center in 2013 and is closing its Pasadena distribution center in 2014. Avon's revenue dropped 5 percent to $10.72 billion in 2012.

Internal Issues

Vision and Mission

Avon has stated vision and mission statements on its corporate website. Avon's vision is: "To be the company that best understands and satisfies the product, service and self-fulfillment needs of women—globally." Avon's mission statement is quite lengthy, but in summary it says: Avon's mission is focused on six core aspirations the company continually strives to achieve: (1) leader in global beauty, (2) women's choice for buying, (3) premier direct-selling company, (4) most-admired company, (5) best place to work, and (6) to have the largest foundation dedicated to women's causes.

Marketing and R&D

Avon uses both door-to-door sales people ("Avon ladies," primarily, but a growing number of men) and brochures to advertise its products. Avon training centers help women who want to become Avon representatives selling beauty products, jewelry, accessories, and clothing. The Avon training centers have a small retail section with skin care products, such as creams, serums, makeup, and washes. There are classroom areas in which the representatives learn about the products and sales techniques. Avon representative are each independent sole proprietors running their own business.

Avon spent $253.6 million on advertising in 2012, down from $311.2 million the prior year. Avon spent $75.2 million on R&D in 2012, down from $77.7 million the prior year. Avon's primary R&D facility is located in Suffern, New York.

Sustainability and Philanthropy

Avon has extensive information on its corporate website about its sustainability and philanthropy programs and operations. Avon is a huge advocate for women's rights and works tirelessly through its Foundation for Women to combat violence against women, breast cancer, and more. For example the recent 10th Annual New York Avon Walk for Breast Cancer raised more than $8.3 million. Avon is also on a mission to help prevent deforestation worldwide.

Founded in 1955, the Avon Foundation for Women is the largest corporate-affiliated philanthropic organization for women in the world. Avon has always been committed to helping women achieve their highest potential of economic opportunity and self-fulfillment by empowering them through scholarships and support for other forms of educational and occupational training and advancement. The Avon Foundation awards scholarships for Avon Sales Representatives and their families, as well as for the children of Avon associates. The Avon Foundation is currently focused on two key causes: breast cancer and domestic violence. The foundation approved $38 million in grants in 2011. In 2012, Avon launched its first global fundraising drive.

Organizational Structure

Avon's CEO is Sheri McCoy, who previously was a top executive at Johnson & Johnson. The former Avon CEO, Andrea Jung, was the longest-tenured female CEO among *Fortune* 500 companies. Jung stepped down as CEO in April 2012 and relinquished her Avon board seat at year-end 2012.

As indicated in Exhibit 1, Avon operates from a divisional-by-geographic region organizational structure. Note there is no chief operations officer (COO) so apparently all top executives report to the CEO. In fact, there has been no COO at Avon since 2006, a potential strategic mistake by CEO Jung (and McCoy).

EXHIBIT 1 Avon's Organizational Chart

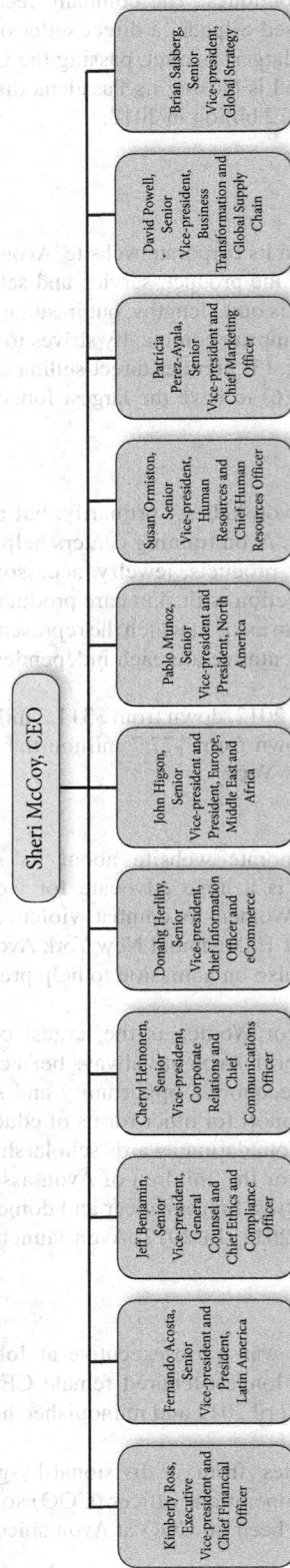

Sheri McCoy, CEO

- Kimberly Ross, Executive Vice-president and Chief Financial Officer
- Fernando Acosta, Senior Vice-president and President, Latin America
- Jeff Benjamin, Senior Vice-president, General Counsel and Chief Ethics and Compliance Officer
- Cheryl Heinonen, Senior Vice-president, Corporate Relations and Chief Communications Officer
- Donahg Herlihy, Senior Vice-president, Chief Information Officer and eCommerce
- John Higson, Senior Vice-president and President, Europe, Middle East and Africa
- Pablo Munoz, Senior Vice-president, President, North America
- Susan Ormiston, Senior Vice-president, Human Resources and Chief Human Resources Officer
- Patricia Perez-Ayala, Senior Vice-president and Chief Marketing Officer
- David Powell, Senior Vice-president, Business Transformation and Global Supply Chain
- Brian Salsberg, Senior Vice-president, Global Strategy

Source: Based on company information.

616

EXHIBIT 2 Avon's Revenue and Profits By Region

Years ended December 31	2012		2011		2010	
	Total Revenue	Operating Profit (Loss)	Total Revenue	Operating Profit (Loss)	Total Revenue	Operating Profit
Latin America	$4,993.7	$443.9	$5,161.8	$634.0	$4,640.0	$613.3
Europe, Middle East & Africa	2,914.2	312.8	3,122.8	478.9	3,047.9	474.3
North America	1,906.8	(214.9)	2,064.6	(188.0)	2,193.5	147.3
Asia Pacific	902.4	5.1	942.4	81.4	981.4	82.6
Total from operations	10,717.1	546.9	11,291.6	1,006.3	10,862.8	1,317.5
Global and other expenses	–	(232.1)	–	(151.7)	–	(244.4)
Total	**$10,717.1**	**$314.8**	**$11,291.6**	**$854.6**	**$10,862.8**	**$1,073.1**

Source: 2012 *Annual Report*, p. 33.

Segments

Comparing 2012 to 2011, Avon's geographic results are provided in Exhibit 2. Note the percent revenue decline in every geographic region, although a few particular countries with regions reported increases.

Avon's reportable segments are sometimes noted to be: (a) beauty, (b) fashion, and (c) home. Beauty consists of color cosmetics, fragrances, skin care, and personal care. Fashion consists of fashion jewelry, watches, apparel, footwear, accessories, and children's products. Home consists of gift and decorative products, housewares, entertainment and leisure products, and nutritional products. Avon's sales in its Beauty, Fashion, and Home segments decreased 5, 5, and 4 percent respectively in 2012 from the prior year. For 2012, the Beauty segment accounted for 72 percent of company sales, followed by Fashion at 18 percent and Home at 10 percent. Specifically within the Beauty segment, 2012 Fragrance, Color, Skincare, and Personal Care revenues were down 4, 6, 7, and 6 percent respectively.

Finance

Avon's cash dividends paid out dropped to $0.75 per share in 2012 from $0.92 the prior year. The company's long-term debt increased to $2.62 billion from $2.45 billion the prior year.

Avon's recent income statements and balance sheets are provided in Exhibits 3 and 4, respectively. Note that Avon's revenue and net income decreased in 2012.

Competitors

As indicated in Exhibit 3, Avon's earnings per share (EPS) and profit margin are negative. L'Oreal leads the beauty industry, but other firms also compete with Avon, especially Mary Kay, Revlon, Estee Lauder, Coty, and Procter & Gamble. A synopsis of some of these rival firms is provided.

EXHIBIT 3 Avon versus Rival Firms

	Avon	L'Oreal	Revlon
Number of Employees	39.1K	68.3K	5.2K
Revenue ($)	10.7B	27.7B	1.4B
Net income ($)	(42.5)M	3.36B	40.6M
Profit Margin (%)	—	12.1	2.9
Revenue ($)/employee	273K	406K	269K
EPS	—	1.12	0.78
Market capitalization	10.5B	83.1B	775.9M

EPS, earnings per share.

L'Oreal SA

Headquartered in France, L'Oreal is a large, global, cosmetic conglomerate with annual sales of about $30 billion and net income of about $3.5 billion. L'Oreal is structured into three segments: (1) Cosmetics, (2) The Body Shop, and (3) Dermatology. The Cosmetics unit is divided into four sectors: Consumer Products, Professional Products, Luxury Products, and Active Cosmetics. Consumer Products are marketed under L'Oreal Paris, Garnier, Maybelline New York (Maybelline NY), and Softsheen-Carson brands. Professional Products, including hair care products for use by professional hairdressers, are marketed under Kerastase, Redken, Matrix, and L'Oreal Professionnel. Luxury Products are sold under such international brands as Lancome, Diesel, Giorgio Armani, and Cacharel among others. Active Cosmetics, which consists of products under Vichy and La Roche Posay brands, are for sale mainly in pharmacies. The Body Shop segment is focused on cosmetics on the basis of natural ingredients. The Dermatology segment consists of Galderma, a joint venture between L'Oreal and Nestle.

Mary Kay, Inc.

Headquartered in Addison (outside of Dallas), Texas, Mary Kay is a privately-owned cosmetic and fragrance direct-selling company. Mary Kay is the sixth-largest direct selling company in the world, with annual sales of about $3 billion. Mary Kay's business model is similar to the Avon business model. Founded by Mary Kay Ash in 1963, the company is famous for its pink Cadillacs, given to high-selling representatives. Richard Rogers, Mary Kay's son, is the chairman of the board. Mary Kay products are sold in more than 35 markets worldwide, and the global Mary Kay independent sales force exceeds 2.4 million women.

In 1968, Mary Kay Ash purchased the first pink Cadillac and had it repainted to match the Mountain Laurel Blush in the Mary Kay compact. Since the Cadillac program's inception, more than 100,000 independent sales force members have qualified for the use of a Career Car or elected the cash compensation option. GM estimates that it has built 100,000 pink Cadillacs for Mary Kay. For 2012, high-sellers may select other Career Cars, including the Chevrolet Malibu, Chevrolet Equinox, Toyota Camry, and the Cadillac CTS, SRX, and Escalade Hybrid—or most recently, a black Ford Mustang.

Estee Lauder Companies, Inc.

Headquartered in New York City, Estee Lauder has sales of about $10 billion annually and income of about $1 billion. Estee Lauder manufactures and markets skin care, makeup, fragrance, and hair care products. The company's products are sold in more than 150 countries and territories under a number of brand names, including Estee Lauder, Aramis, Clinique, Origins, M.A.C, Bobbi Brown, La Mer, and Aveda. The company is also the global licensee for fragrances or cosmetics sold under brand names, such as Tommy Hilfiger, Donna Karan, Michael Kors, Tom Ford, and Coach. The company sells its products at more than 30,000 points of sale, consisting of upscale department stores, specialty retailers, upscale perfumeries and pharmacies, and prestige salons and spas.

Revlon, Inc.

Headquartered in New York City, Revlon is a cosmetics leader with brands such as Almay and Revlon ColorSilk hair color, Mitchum antiperspirants and deodorants, Charlie and Jean Naté fragrances, and Ultima II and Gatineau skin care products. Revlon's beauty aids are distributed in more than 100 countries, though the USA is its largest market, generating about 55 percent of sales. Walmart is Revlon's biggest single customer, accounting for some 22 percent of sales.

Revlon manufactures, markets, and sells cosmetics, women's hair color, beauty tools, antiperspirant deodorants, fragrances, skin care, and other beauty care products. Revlon products are sold and marketed under brand names, such as Revlon, including the Revlon ColorStay, Revlon Super Lustrous, and Revlon Age Defying franchises; Almay, including the Almay Intense i-Color and Almay Smart Shade franchises; Sinful Colors in cosmetics; Revlon ColorSilk in women's hair color; Revlon in beauty tools; Mitchum in antiperspirant deodorants; Charlie and Jean Nate in fragrances, and Ultima II and Gatineau. Revlon also owns certain assets of Sinful Colors cosmetics, Wild and Crazy cosmetics, freshMinerals cosmetics, and freshcover cosmetics.

Coty, Inc.

Headquartered in New York City, Coty is one of the world's leading makers of beauty products for men and women. Led by CEO Bernd Beetz, Coty is a $4.1 billion beauty company, and the biggest seller of nail care, nail polish, and fragrances in the USA. Sarah Jessica Parker, Jennifer Lopez, Celine Dion, Gwen Stefani, Katy Perry, and Thomas Dutronc are several celebrities that promote Coty. Founder of the company, François Coty created his first perfume, La Rose Jacqueminot, in 1904.

Coty's product lineup today ranges from moderately priced scents sold globally by mass retailers to prestige fragrances and nail polishes found in department stores. Coty's brands include adidas, philosophy, Rimmel, and Sally Hansen. Cody's prestige perfume labels are led by Calvin Klein. Coty's shimmery blue nail polish and Lady Gaga's perfume are high-selling products. Thomas Dutronc is the face of Coty's new Cerruti fragrance for men that was launched in the Spring 2013.

Coty's Rimmel Scandaleyes mascara, which debuted in early 2012, is another big seller. Over-the-top lashes are hot these days because false eye lashes have made a comeback and are "almost mainstream." Promotional material for Scandaleyes urges women to "ditch those falsies." Mascara makers today compete with eyelash lengthening drugs such as Latisse.

Nail care generated $735 million in sales in U.S. discount stores, pharmacy chains, and supermarkets in 2011, up 6.5 percent from 2010. Lipstick sales rise even as a nation's economy falters, partly because the economy has put the consumer in charge of her own beauty treatments without having to go to the nail bar. Sally Hansen Salon Effects nail polish strips also brings "nail art," which has been trending at beauty salons nationwide, to everyday drugstore shoppers at a mere $8 to $10. Vivienne Rudd, head of beauty and personal care for market research firm Mintel, says "the nail-art trend is largely being driven by younger shoppers; it takes a little courage to wear stripes and spots." Still, women of all ages are experimenting with the strips as they look for inexpensive fun.

Overall, nail care product sales have been booming in today's shaky economic climate. Women have been skipping the salon and playing at-home manicurist, whereas consumer products companies have been injecting innovation into the business with products like Salon Effects and the hologram, crackle, and magnetic nail finishes on the market, analysts say. The strips are available in funky prints and patterns such as leopard, florals, and tie dye.

EXHIBIT 4 Avon's Recent Income Statement (in millions)

	2012	2011	2010	2012 vs. 2011	2011 vs. 2010
Total revenue	$10,717.1	$11,291.6	$10,862.8	(5)%	4%
Cost of sales	4,169.3	4,148.6	4,041.3	–%	3%
Selling, general and administrative expenses	5,980.0	6,025.4	5,748.4	(1)%	5%
Impairment of goodwill and intangible asset	253.0	263.0	–	(4)%	*
Operating profit	314.8	854.6	1,073.1	(63)%	(20)%
Interest expense	104.3	92.9	87.1	12%	7%
Interest income	(15.1)	(16.5)	(14.0)	(8)%	18%
Other expense, net	7.0	35.6	54.6	(80)%	(35)%
Net (loss) income attributable to Avon	(42.5)	513.6	606.3	(108)%	(15)%
Diluted (loss) earnings per share attributable to Avon	$(.10)	$1.18	$1.39	(108)%	(15)%
Advertising expenses	$253.6	$311.2	$400.4	(19)%	(22)%
Gross margin	61.1%	63.3%	62.8%	(2.2)	.5

Source: 2012 Annual Report, p. 29.

The Future

Avon announced in late 2012 that it is cutting about 1,500 jobs globally and will exit the South Korea and Vietnam markets as part of a turnaround plan. The global beauty industry is growing at the rate of 6 percent, good news for Avon. The company's current ratio and debt service coverage ratios indicate that it has enough liquidity to survive in the near future, but a clear strategic plan is needed to survive.

The general feeling about Avon is negative because of the sliding profits, four-year pending legal probe related to bribery and ineffective business strategies. However, Avon has a popular global brand with a high market share in emerging markets. Although door-to-door selling may be an outdated business model in the USA, direct selling remains effective in emerging markets such as Brazil. Direct selling grew about 30 percent between 2006 and 2012 into a $150 billion global market. Many of the more than 100 countries in which Avon competes do not have good retail infrastructure, so Avon's 6.5 million person global sales force is its biggest advantage over its competitors. Avon's stock price hit a 52-week high in June 2013 of $24.30.

EXHIBIT 5 Avon's Balance Sheets

	December 31,	
(In millions, except per share data)	2012	2011
Assets		
Current Assets		
Cash, including cash equivalents of $762.9 and $623.7	$ 1,209.6	$ 1,245.1
Accounts receivable (less allowances of $161.4 and $174.5)	751.9	761.5
Inventories	1,135.4	1,161.3
Prepaid expenses and other	832.0	930.9
Total current assets	$ 3,928.9	$ 4,098.8
Property, plant and equipment, at cost		
Land	66.6	65.4
Buildings and improvements	1,165.9	1,150.4
Equipment	1,479.3	1,493.0
	2,711.8	2,708.8
Less accumulated depreciation	(1,161.6)	(1,137.3)
	1,550.2	1,571.5
Goodwill	374.9	473.1
Other intangible assets, net	120.3	279.9
Other assets	1,408.2	1,311.7
Total assets	$ 7,382.5	$ 7,735.0
Liabilities and Shareholders' Equity		
Current Liabilities		
Debt maturing within one year	$ 572.0	$ 849.3
Accounts payable	920.0	850.2
Accrued compensation	266.6	217.1
Other accrued liabilities	661.0	663.6
Sales and taxes other than income	211.4	212.4
Income taxes	73.6	98.4
Total current liabilities	2,704.6	2,891.0
Long-term debt	2,623.9	2,459.1
Employee benefit plans	637.6	603.0
Long-term income taxes	52.0	67.0
Other liabilities	131.1	129.7
Total liabilities	$ 6,149.2	$ 6,149.8

EXHIBIT 5 continued

(In millions, except per share data)	December 31, 2012	2011
Commitments and contingencies		
Shareholders' Equity		
Common stock, par value $.25 – authorized 1,500 shares; issued 746.7 and 744.9 shares	$ 188.3	$ 187.3
Additional paid-in capital	2,119.6	2,077.7
Retained earnings	4,357.8	4,726.1
Accumulated other comprehensive loss	(876.7)	(854.4)
Treasury stock, at cost (314.5 and 314.1 shares)	(4,571.9)	(4,566.3)
Total Avon shareholders' equity	1,217.1	1,570.4
Noncontrolling interests	16.2	14.8
Total shareholders' equity	**$ 1,233.3**	**$ 1,585.2**
Total liabilities and shareholders' equity	**$ 7,382.5**	**$ 7,735.0**

Source: 2012 *Annual Report*, p. F5.

Revlon, Inc., 2015

www.revlon.com, REV

Headquartered in New York City, Revlon is a large beauty and personal care products company and is a subsidiary of MacAndrews & Forbes Holding Inc. Popular Revlon products include lipsticks, skin care products, deodorant, blush, makeup, hair and nail products, and much more, marketed under such brands as Almay, SinfulColors, Pure Ice, Revlon ColorSilk, Charlie, Jean Naté, Mitchum, Gatineau, and Ultima II. Revlon sells products worldwide through its sales force, sales representatives, and independent distributors, and licenses its trademarks to select manufacturers for complementary beauty-related products and accessories. For the quarter that ended June 30, 2015, Revlon's revenues were $482 million, up from $438 million the prior quarter, and the company's net income was $26 million, up from a negative $900,000 the prior quarter. Also during Q2 of 2015, Revlon completed its acquisition of the CBBeauty Group and exited business operations in Venezuela, moving to a distributor model in that country. Revlon's sales for Q3 of 2015 were $471.5 million, about the same as the prior year Q3, but the company's Q3 2015 net income was $6.2 million, down from $14.6 million the prior year Q3. The company's stock price declined 12 percent in 2015 through November. Thus, investors are concerned about Revlon's strategic plan and performance.

Revlon hired a new CEO in 2014, Lorenzo Delpani. He needs a clear strategic plan going forward, as rivals such as Avon, L'Oreal, Mary Kay Cosmetics, and Estee Lauder compete for market share in the industry.

Copyright by Fred David Books LLC. www.strategyclub.com (Written by Meredith E. David and Forest R. David)

History

Revlon was founded in 1932 when brothers Charles and Joseph Revson, and chemist C. R. Lachman, launched a new product—a nail enamel that came in colors other than red. Somewhat bizarre, but interestingly, the name Revlon comes from replacing the *s* in *Revson* with the L from *Lachman*. One of Charles Revson's most famous quotes to describe his business was "in the factory we make cosmetics, in the drug store we sell hope." Being the only provider of different color nail polishes, Revlon had a large leg up on competition, and within 6 years the firm was a multimillion dollar organization. By the early 1940s, Revlon had expanded its product line to include many other beauty products, including lipstick, which it remains famous for today. Revlon went public in 1955 and saw its stock price increase over 200 percent in the first two months of trading. In the 1960s, Revlon restructured into six different business units based on target customer. Throughout the next 20 years, Revlon acquired many different cosmetic-related firms to expand its product offerings, but in the 1980s, it was still losing ground to major competitors Estee Lauder, Cover Girl, Procter & Gamble, and others. Thus, in 1985, Revlon was sold to Pantry Pride and left department stores to become a mass-market beauty brand. The firm hired Claudia Schiffer, Cindy Crawford, and Christy Turlington to model its products during the 1980s. In the 1990s, Revlon introduced its Color Stay line and hired model Halle Berry to promote the products. Revlon acquired Mirage Cosmetics in 2011 and Colomer Group in 2013 and hired both Emma Stone and Olivia Wilde to promote its products. Revlon divested all of its Chinese operations in 2014.

Internal Issues

Vision/Mission
Revlon has one statement as follows on the corporate website related to vision/mission: "Revlon is a global color cosmetics, hair color, beauty tools, fragrances, skincare, anti-perspirant deodorants and beauty care products company whose vision is Glamour, Excitement and Innovation through high-quality products at affordable prices."

EXHIBIT 1 Revlon's Organizational Structure

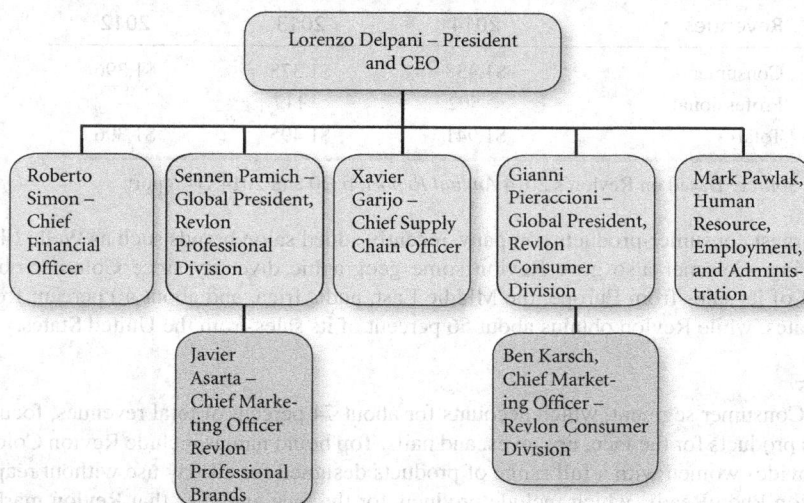

Lorenzo Delpani – President and CEO

- Roberto Simon – Chief Financial Officer
- Sennen Pamich – Global President, Revlon Professional Division
  - Javier Asarta – Chief Marketing Officer Revlon Professional Brands
- Xavier Garijo – Chief Supply Chain Officer
- Gianni Pieraccioni – Global President, Revlon Consumer Division
  - Ben Karsch, Chief Marketing Officer – Revlon Consumer Division
- Mark Pawlak, Human Resource, Employment, and Administration

Source: Based on company documents.

Organizational Structure

Like about half of the Fortune 500 companies, Revlon does not have an executive with the title COO among its top management team. As depicted in Exhibit 1, the company has two primary divisions: Professional and Consumer. The two divisions focus on selling products to (1) beauty salons (Professional Segment) and (2) individuals (Consumer Segment), respectively. The current structure was finalized in October 2013 with the acquisition of the Colomer Group for $664 million in cash. The Colomer business comprises 100 percent of Revlon's professional segment. Let's presume that the two divisional presidents report to the CAO because sometimes that is another name for the COO position.

Marketing and R&D

Revlon uses sales representatives and independent distributors primarily in marketing. In 2013, 56 percent of all Revlon sales in the United States were derived from mass merchandisers. Revlon's largest customers in this country are Walmart, CVS, Walgreens, Boot Alliance, and Target. In November 2014, Revlon launched its "Love is On" marketing campaign in all markets globally—the firm's first global marketing campaign in over 10 years. CEO Delpani suggested the new slogan because he says love is a "universally applicable theme that has no boundaries." Audio and video of related marketing ads are played to the classic song "Addicted to Love" and feature Halle Berry, Emma Stone, and Olivia Wilde.

Revlon spent $32 million on R&D in 2014 and employs 200 people in its R&D locations in New Jersey, Florida, and California. The bulk of Revlon's products are produced at its own factories in North Carolina and in South Africa. The firm produces products for its professional segment in Florida, Spain, Italy, and Mexico, as well as through various third-party contractors.

Strategy

One of CEO Delpani's first decisions after taking over in 2014 was to divest the firm's Chinese business, which accounted for only 2 percent of total sales. Delpani also cut 15 percent, or approximately 5,000, Revlon employees. The decision to exit China came on the heels of rival Avon reporting a 67 percent decline in Chinese sales in 2013, and rival L'Oreal reporting slowing sales in China, despite the market being worth an estimated $20 billion.

Revlon's acquisition of Colomer Group bolstered the company's offerings to professional salon customers. This acquisition added the Creative Nail professional and Shellac Nail polishes to Revlon's portfolio, as well as American Crew men's hair care products. Rival cosmetics companies had recently added products and services aimed at salon customers, such as Unilever in 2011 buying Alberto-Culver for about $3.7 billion, giving it the Nexxus haircare brand. P&G, the

EXHIBIT 2 Revlon's Revenues by Customer (in millions of USD)

Revenues	2014	2013	2012
Consumer	$1,438	$1,378	$1,396
Professional	502	117	–
Total	$1,941	$1,495	$1,396

Source: Based on Revlon's 2014 *Annual Report*, p. 30 and 2014 Q4 report.

world's largest consumer-products company, recently added salon brands such as Wella Illumina hair coloring. Colomer also gave Revlon some geographic diversity since Colomer obtained about half of its sales from Europe, the Middle East, and Africa, and about 40 percent from the United States, while Revlon obtains about 56 percent of its sales from the United States.

Segments

Revlon's Consumer segment, which accounts for about 74 percent of total revenues, focuses on cosmetics products for the face, lips, eyes, and nails. Top brand names include Revlon ColorStay, which provides women with a full range of products designed for all-day use without reapplication; Revlon PhotoReady, which include products for the face and eyes that Revlon markets as able to bend and reflect light to provide women flawless airbrushed appearance in any light condition; Revlon Age Defying products that are designed for women over age 35 to mask lines and wrinkles; and Revlon Super Lustrous, the flagship wax-based lipcolor, and possibly the product the company is best known for, offered in many different colors and shades of both lipstick and lip gloss. Other products include Revlon ColorBurst, Revlon Grow Luscious, and Almay. ColorBurst focuses on lip glosses in high-shine style, opposite of the matte Super Lustrous products. Revlon's Grow Luscious and Almay are designed mostly for improving the eyelashes and hypo-allergenic products, respectively. In fact, Almay has a full line of products all centered on hypo-allergenic products. Other key products included in the consumer division include hair color products under the name ColorSilk, various beauty tools for use on the nails and eye, fragrances such as Charlie and Jean Naté, deodorants under the name Mitchum, and skin care products under brands Gatineau and Ultima II. Revlon reported profits of $347 million from its Consumer division in 2013 down from $363 million the previous year.

Revlon's Professional division accounts for about 26 percent of revenues as indicated in Exhibit 2. This division is aimed at selling products directly to professional salons rather than the consumer at mass merchant and grocery stores. Notable brands include Revlonissimo NMT, Nutri Color Crème, Sensor Perm, and Revlon Professional Equave. American Crew is another product targeting men with shampoos, conditioners, gels, and other products. Revlon's CND brand offers popular nail color and treatments to professional salons in over 80 countries. Total profits for the newly acquired professional division were $5.2 million in 2013.

Revlon's revenues by region are provided in Exhibit 3. Note that the United States contributes more than half of Revlon's revenues in 2013.

Exhibit 4 reveals Revlon's revenues by geographic region in 2014. Note that U.S. sales and international sales were both up substantially over 2013 numbers. Also note that U.S. and international revenues in Exhibit 4 do not perfectly match the data in Exhibit 3; however, total revenues for 2013 *do* match, which reflects a slight reclassification of certain revenues by Revlon.

Finance

Revlon's recent income statement and balance sheet are provided in Exhibits 5 and 6, respectively. On the balance sheet, notice the negative retained earnings because the company has been incurring losses, although for 2014 there was a positive net income of $41 million.

Competitors

The beauty products business contains over 3,000 different competitors with top companies being Procter & Gamble, Unilever, L'Oreal, Estee Lauder, Mary Kay, Avon, Helen of Troy, Coty, Ultra Salons, and Revlon. The industry is comprised of many different classes of competitors

EXHIBIT 3 Revlon's Revenues by Region for Consumer Division (in millions of USD)

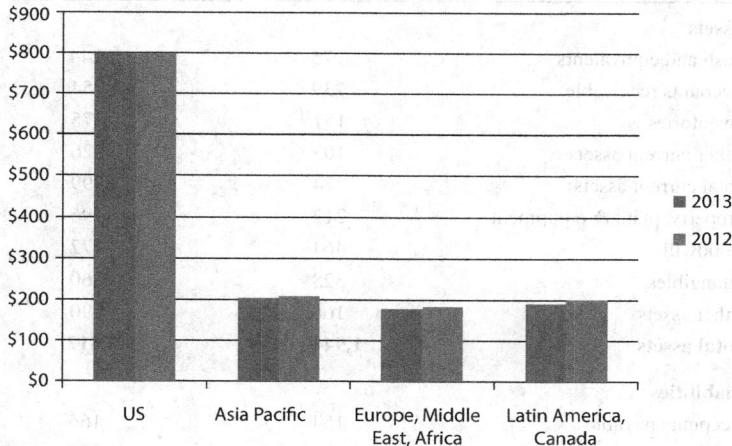

Source: Adapted from Revlon's 2013 Annual Report, p. 30.

EXHIBIT 4 Revlon's 2014 Revenues by Geographic Region (in millions of USD)

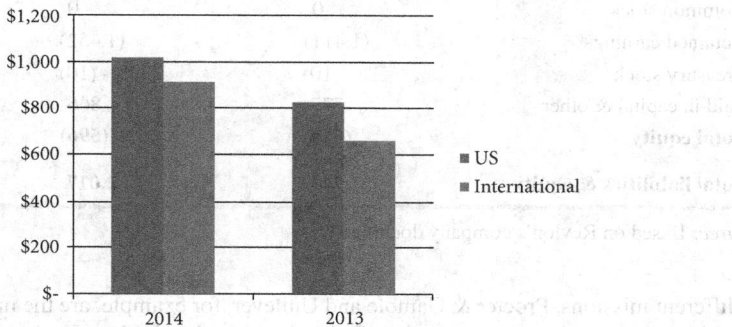

Source: Adapted from Revlon's 2014 Annual Report.

EXHIBIT 5 Revlon's Income Statement (in millions of USD)

Report Date	December 31, 2014	December 31, 2013
Revenues	$1,941	$1,494
Cost of revenue	668	544
Gross profit	1,273	950
Operating expenses	1,037	761
EBIT	236	189
Interest and other	118	118
EBT	118	71
Tax	78	46
EAT	40	25
Income from continuing operations	1	(30)
Net income	**41**	**(5)**

Source: Based on Revlon's company documents.

EXHIBIT 6 Revlon's Balance Sheet (in millions of USD)

Report Date	December 31, 2014	December 31, 2013
Assets		
Cash and equivalents	$275	$244
Accounts receivable	239	254
Inventories	157	175
Other current assets	103	126
Total current assets	774	799
Property, plant & equipment	212	196
Goodwill	464	472
Intangibles	328	360
Other assets	166	190
Total assets	**1,944**	**2,017**
Liabilities		
Accounts payable	154	166
Other current liabilities	311	387
Total current liabilities	465	553
Long-term debt	1,832	1,862
Other liabilities	291	198
Total liabilities	**2,588**	**2,613**
Common stock	0	0
Retained earnings	(1,411)	(1,452)
Treasury stock	(10)	(10)
Paid in capital & other	777	866
Total equity	**(644)**	**(596)**
Total liabilities & equity	**1,944**	**2,017**

Source: Based on Revlon's company documents.

with many different missions. Procter & Gamble and Unilever, for example, are the most diversified firms, selling many products not even classified as beauty related. Mary Kay and Avon both rely on direct (door-to-door) sales. Ultra Salons is fully vertically integrated, making its own products, selling them in its own stores, and even offering salons in its stores. A notable trend in the industry is less customer loyalty and increased commoditization. Many customers today are willing to mix and match and try various products based on attributes other than brand name. This bodes well for many firms, as customer spending has increased substantially as a result. However, R&D and marketing expenses are on the rise in the industry, as corporations try to attract buyers to their products by providing new and exciting selections. A comparative analysis of Revlon versus two rival firms is provided in Exhibit 7.

EXHIBIT 7 Revlon versus Avon and L'Oreal SA

	Revlon	Avon	L'Oreal SA
# Employees	6,900	36,700	77,452
$ Net Income	28 M	(124) M	3,480 M
$ Revenue	1.93 B	9.18 B	26.88 B
$ Revenue/Employee	279,710	250,136	347,053
$ EPS	0.10	(0.29)	1.16
$ Market Cap.	1.72 B	3.25 B	94.14 B

Source: A variety of sources, all based on company documents.

Avon Products, Inc. (AVP)

Headquartered in New York City and founded in 1886 "to help women become independent," Avon reported a net loss of $124 million in 2014. The company sells a wide array of beauty products, including cosmetics, fragrances, skin care, hair care, and others. The firm also sells jewelry, watches, apparel, houseware products, nutritional products, and more. Similar to rival Mary Kay, Avon competes in direct sales and provides products to over 65 countries. Most of Revlon's sales are generated in the United States, but over 85 percent of all sales of Avon are derived from foreign markets. Avon has been plagued with the stronger dollar in recent years. Approximately 30 percent of sales for Avon are derived from products other than cosmetics.

In late 2014, Avon and the U.S. government came to agreement on a fine totaling $135 million concerning bribes to Chinese officials in return for better business opportunities for Avon. Rumors are that Avon is currently talking with private equity firm TPG Capital about being acquired.

Avon has not been performing well. From 2011 to 2015, the company witnessed a declining revenue trend in North America, especially in the United States, mainly due to a decrease in active representatives, partly offset by large average orders. Revenue from the United States has declined considerably from about $2,293.4 million in 2009 to nearly $1,458.2 million in 2013. Avon's revenues from the United States declined another 16 percent in the third quarter of 2014.

L'Oreal SA (LRYCY)

Headquartered outside of Paris, France, and founded in 1909, L'Oreal is known worldwide for producing quality cosmetics. It is considered the world's largest cosmetics company, selling cosmetics and hair color products in drugstores and mass merchandisers worldwide. In addition to the L'Oreal brand, other top brands include Garnier, Maybelline, Lancome, and The Body Shop. L'Oreal employs 72,000 worldwide and reported revenues in excess of $26 billion in 2013. The firm receives approximately one quarter of its sales from North America, the same percent as sales derived from Europe. The weak euro and strong dollar lately has benefited L'Oreal. To better compete against rival Estee Lauder in the United States, L'Oreal acquired Los Angeles-based NYX Cosmetics in 2014. L'Oreal's U.S. headquarters is in New York City. In June 2014, L'Oreal reached agreement with the U.S. Federal Trade Commission not to make claims about its anti-aging products, unless it had credible scientific evidence supporting the claims. The settlement followed an investigation by the commission into claims being made in relation to two products, which the commission described as "false and unsubstantiated." In 2014, L'Oréal made the commitment to ensure that none of its products is linked to deforestation, and to source 100 percent renewable raw materials by 2020. L'Oreal was recently included in the Corporate Knights "Global 100" list of the 100 most sustainable companies.

Estee Lauder Companies, Inc. (EL)

Headquartered in New York City and founded in 1946, Estee Lauder is still controlled by the Lauder family. The firm does business worldwide with over 40,000 employees. As of June 30, 2014 (the end of the fiscal year), Estee Lauder Companies had sales of more than $10.9 billion. The company is known for its skin care products, makeup, fragrances, hair care products, and many other beauty related products. Top brands include Clinique, Aveda, Bumble and Bumble, Bobbi Brown, Origins, and several others. As of 2014, the firm was aggressively expanding into the men's skin care business. In general, Estee Lauder products are considered premium and of better quality than many rivals, including Revlon, Avon, and L'Oreal. Estee Lauder typically sells its products direct to consumers or through its own stores, boutiques, specialty salons, and upscale retailers. Approximately 10 percent of Estee Lauder's total revenues are derived from Macy's.

External Issues

Lipstick Industry

The lipstick industry in the United States is valued around $1.5 billion annually and is expected to grow at an annualized rate of nearly 6 percent through 2020. Key producers are Estee Lauder, Procter & Gamble, Revlon, and L'Oreal, representing 16, 10, 5, and 3 percent of the U.S. market share, respectively. The lipstick industry has 60 manufacturers. Despite lipstick being one of the most visible cosmetic products, the industry revenue of $1.5 billion pales in comparison to the over $50 billion cosmetic product industry. The lipstick industry is much more resistant to economic downturns than many other industries, even other cosmetics products. Competitors are introducing many new styles and colors of lipstick as well, creating new sales. With the relatively cheap price of lipstick for the consumer, many women have different colors and styles for various occasions, and are willing to try new colors and products, as cost is generally not prohibitive. An area of concern for lipstick and cosmetic manufacturers generally is the increased sensitivity to possibly harsh metals, chemicals, or animal byproducts used in lipstick. The new sensitivity in the composition of lipsticks has many firms increasing their R&D and advertising budget to ensure consumers are provided the products they desire. In fact, R&D and marketing budgets now comprise 25 percent of total industry revenue. Also, there is much less brand loyalty now industrywide, and many consumers are switching from brand to brand and even using multiple different lipstick or cosmetic brands simultaneously. In addition, celebrities are increasingly posting photos of themselves without makeup and adding hashtags and other messages.

Most lipstick is categorized into either sheer or matte. Sheer lipstick products contain more oil and must be applied more often to make lips look shiny. Matte lipstick is more robust and need to be applied much less frequently. Both types of lipsticks are equally popular, accounting for 85 percent of all lipstick sold. Lip stain, lip liner, and other lip products make up the remaking 15 percent of sales.

Lipstick is sold in many different mediums, with mass merchants such as cosmetic stores, grocery stores, Walmart, and drugstores accounting for nearly half of all sales. Department stores account for another 20 percent of sales and direct to the consumer accounts for 8 percent of sales. There are several companies that deal directly to the consumer, such as Mary Kay and Avon. Interestingly, despite having great global brands in the United States, only 15 percent of total revenues are obtained from outside the states. Wholesalers account for 10 percent of total sales, but are expected to increase their share moving forward as they have better bargaining power. Imports account for $200 million of the $1.5 billion U.S. lipstick industry, with a quarter of these coming from France, likely largely contributed by French-based L'Oreal.

Hair Care, Skin Care, Cosmetics

The hair care, skin care, and cosmetic industry in the United States accounts for over $55 billion in annual sales and has enjoyed a growth rate of nearly 6 percent from 2010 through 2014. Much like the lipstick market, consumers still purchased beauty products at high rates, even during the recession. Growth is projected to continue through 2020 at a rate of nearly 4 percent. Hair care and skin care products are the two largest revenue-producing contributions to the industry as a whole, with revenues each of approximately $13 billion totaling just short of 50 percent of total revenues combined. Cosmetics, perfumes, and deodorants also contribute significantly to the industry, with total market shares of 15, 10, and 8 percent, respectively. Many of the same issues facing lipstick manufacturers are also faced in the marketing and producing of cosmetic-related products. Higher marketing and R&D expenses—along with a growing concern for reduced packaging, animal safety, and product safety—negatively impacted profits. Consumers also are quick to switch from brand to brand, and are showing less brand loyalty, presenting both threats and opportunities for producers. There is also a growing influx of imported products from around the world on all price points. Generally perceived higher-quality products are imported from Europe, whereas perceived lower-quality and lower-priced products are imported from Mexico and China. Currently, about 15 percent of revenues of U.S.-based producers are derived from overseas markets. Interestingly, overseas customers, even in Asia, tend to prefer higher-quality, more expensive products, and firms that have attempted to offer lower-quality, cheaper alternative products have not fared as well.

Hair care products, the largest segment by revenues, includes hair dye, bleaches, shampoos, conditions, hair sprays, gels, mousses, and all other products related to the hair. Shaving products are also included in this segment. Hair care products have not grown as a segment as rapidly as other products (e.g., skin care). There is growing research and marketing to suggest that expensive shampoos are not worth the money, thereby hurting this product class. In addition, many women are coloring their hair at home or going longer between visits to the salon for coloring, which hurts the industry. Also, there have been relatively few new products developed to entice buyers. This is in stark contrast to other segments such as skin care, lipsticks, perfumes, and cosmetics that often introduce new products.

Skin care products continue to grow as a percent of total industry market share as more and more people are using these products, including men. In 2014, skin care products barely trailed hair care products in industrywide sales, but are expected to be the largest revenue-producing product category moving forward. Firms promote anti-aging treatments and wrinkle-reducing creams. Even creams promoted to remove back circles from under the eyes are available. Sunscreen is also in this category. Estee Lauder's CEO recently suggested that men's skin care products may outpace companywide growth at his firm moving forward.

Other products sold making up the other 50 percent of industrywide revenue include makeup, perfumes, and other products. Makeup has been a relatively slow-growing product line for firms, but with increased demand for products that are marketed as chemical free, there is room for some moderate growth. Interestingly enough, all products contain chemicals, but this is a possible area for growth moving forward. Perfumes, especially for women, have been stagnant; however, men's colognes have grown at moderated paces and are expected to continue.

No Makeup Trends

There is a growing trend promoted by many online articles, several from the *New York Times*, and from celebrities taking photos with hashtags "no makeup" that are encouraging women to be more natural in appearance. No clear data exist yet on how popular or enduring this trend may become, but it is worth noting, and possibly a factor cosmetic firms should be aware of moving forward. The growing population of women who endorse the natural look claim that "being comfortable in your own skin and low maintenance is the true beauty; to the extent you apply layers of makeup you only become more frivolous and superficial." Various theories on why the trend is developing include attractive women wanting everyone to know just how attractive they are without the use of makeup, a new fashion trend for everyone, or possibly just laziness. Whether or not the trend will be enduring, most experts agree, it is like underdressing for the job or not brushing your hair. Therefore the impact on cosmetic firms for *now* is probably limited, but it is certainly something worth monitoring.

Future

Ronald Perelman's New York City-based MacAndrews & Forbes Inc. owns about 78 percent of Revlon. Perelman is Revlon's chairman of the board. There are rumors that Perelman may want to sell Revlon. Analysts say Revlon's EBIT margins, on average, are good at 19 percent, but the company's market capitalization to EBIT ratio of just 9.6 is substantially below the 13.3 average ratio for eight of its global peers. Some analysts report that global consumer companies would be the most likely interested in buying Revlon, such as Procter & Gamble Co. and L'Oreal. Revlon would be complementary to P&G's CoverGirl business. Unilever NV and even Coty, Inc. are among others that could be interested in Revlon. For any firm to obtain the highest acquisition price for its shareholders, a clear strategic plan is needed, showing expected increases in both revenues and profits going forward. Help CEO Delpani develop an impressive strategic plan for Revlon.

Under Armour, Inc., 2013

www.ua.com, UA

Headquartered in Baltimore, Maryland, Under Armour (UA) was founded in 1996 by a former University of Maryland football player who desired a t-shirt that would whisk away perspiration rather than get soggy wet. The company has grown to be one of the most sought after brands among athletes around the world, being worn by some of the largest U.S. college football and European soccer teams. Colleges such as the Maryland Terrapins, Auburn Tigers, South Carolina Gamecocks, and many more have contracts with UA to outfit their teams. English soccer team Tottenham Hotspur, Greek team Aris F.C., and Mexican club Deportivo Toluca F.C. all are outfitted by UA. Mega stars such as Tom Brady, Cam Newton, Bryce Harper, Michael Phelps, and many more, all sponsor and market UA products.

UA designs, develops, markets, and distributes apparel, footwear, and accessories for men, women, and children worldwide. The company offers apparel in three styles: compression, fitted, and loose and designed to be worn in hot, cold, or normal weather. Footwear products include cleats for most all sports, running and basketball shoes, and even hunting boots. Accessories include gloves for football, baseball, golf, socks, and team uniforms. UA's moisture-wicking fabrications are engineered in many different designs and styles for wear in nearly every climate to provide a performance alternative to traditional products. Its products are sold worldwide and worn by athletes at all levels, from youth to professional, on playing fields around the globe. UA's European headquarters are in Amsterdam's Olympic Stadium, with additional offices in Denver, Hong Kong, Toronto, and Guangzhou, With about 1,800 employees, UA distributes its products through specialty retailers, department stores, outlet stores, and institutional athletic departments.

For the second quarter of 2013 that ended June 30, 2013, UA reported that revenues increased 23 percent to $455 million while the company's net income increased 163 percent to $18 million compared to the prior year's period. The company's apparel revenues increased 23 percent to $310 million, primarily driven by a new baselayer product and the expansion of the Storm and Charged Cotton products. The company's second quarter footwear revenues increased 21 percent to $82 million, spurred by the Highlight football cleat and the UA Spine platform. UA's Q2 2013 accessories revenues increased 30 percent to $51 million, primarily driven by headwear. For the quarter, UA's Direct-to-Consumer revenues represented 30 percent of total net revenues and grew 29 percent year-over-year. The company's Women's category is doing well with its new Studio and ArmourBra products, and the Spine running footwear is doing well.

Copyright by Fred David Books LLC. (Written by Forest R. David)

History

At age 23, Kevin Plank developed a new t-shirt in his grandmother's basement in Washington D.C. after noticing that his compression shorts always stayed dry, but t-shirts had to be changed frequently because they became sweat soaked. This observation led Plank to create a new compression t-shirt that whisked away sweat. After graduating, Plank provided this t-shirt to his former teammates who were playing in the National Football League (NFL). After positive reviews, UA had t-shirt orders totaling $100,000 in 1997. UA's first big break came when *USA Today* pictured Oakland Raiders quarterback Jeff George wearing UA apparel. In late 1997, Georgia Tech asked for 10 shirts, ultimately leading to deals with Georgia Tech, Arizona State, and North Carolina State universities.

In the 2000s, UA expanded rapidly after outfitting Warner Brothers with apparel for two films, and an advertisement placed in *ESPN Magazine* generated $750,000 in sales. In 2003, UA became the outfitter of the now defunct XFL football league and launched its first TV advertisement with the motto "Protect this House."

UA recently opened specialty stores, including a 6,000-square foot store in Illinois and has opened factory outlet stores in 34 states. In 2011, the company purchased 400,000 square feet of office space for $60.5 million. UA has new contracts with the NFL, National Basketball Association (NBA), and Major League Baseball (MLB) to produce footwear, apparel, and accessories. Many European football teams such as Trottenham Hotspur and other rugby teams are outfitted with UA products. None of UA's 5,900 employees are members of a union, and 1,900 are full-time.

Internal Issues

UA owns no fabric or process patents. Thus, UA competitors can manufacture and sell products very similar to UA products. UA's success thus hinges a lot on their brand image, trademarks, and copyrights.

Vision and Mission
Regarding UA's vision, CEO Plank recently said:

> Our investments illustrate our commitment to realizing our long-term vision of one day having our Women's business larger than Men's, Footwear larger than Apparel, and our International business larger than our U.S. business.

Organizational Structure
UA reportedly operates under four geographic segments: (1) North America, (2) Europe, the Middle East, and Africa (EMEA), (3) Asia, and (4) Latin America. However, from its organization structure revealed in Exhibit 1, it appears the company is structured divisionally by product.

Marketing
UA's marketing expenses were $205.4 million in 2012, up from $167.9 million the prior year. But these marketing expenses were 11.2 percent of revenues, down from 11.4 percent the prior year. UA's advertising expenditures in 2012 and 2011 were $205.4 million and $167.9 million respectively. UA develops and markets products primarily for use in athletics, fitness, and any outdoor activities. UA attempts to drive demand through brand equity and increasing consumer awareness of its superior product. UA's growth is largely dependent on sales from Dick's Sporting Goods, The Sports Authority, and Foot Locker, which have store-within-a-store sales

EXHIBIT 1 Under Armour's Organizational Structure

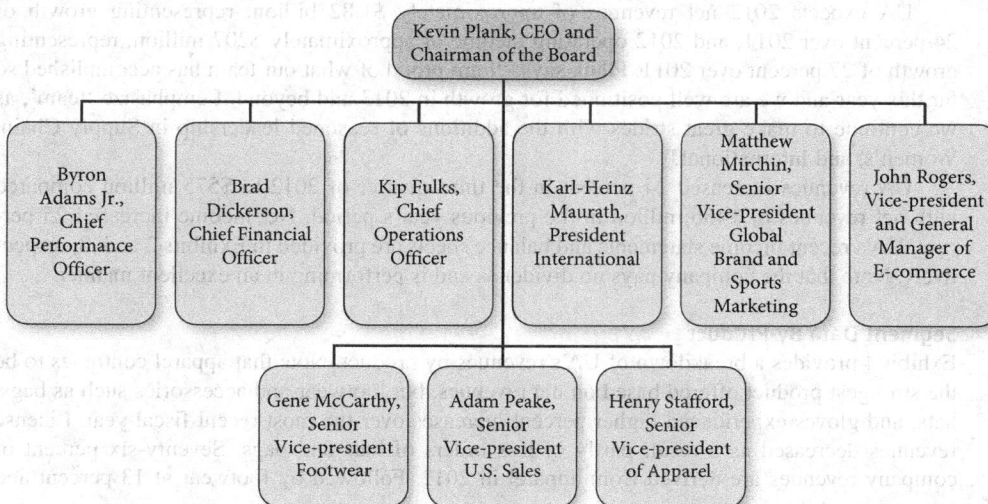

Source: Based on company documents.

channels. However, UA has been making great strides selling its products directly to consumers, with 29 percent of revenue in 2012 coming from direct sales. UA has the brand strength to attract many consumers to more profitable channels. However, 69 percent of 2012 revenue was from wholesale, and 2 percent from licenses.

A key strategy for UA is securing endorsement of its products from high-performing athletes who have significant influence in the NFL, NBA, MLB, and even high school teams. Many sports stars such as Cam Newton and Tom Brady endorse and wear UA products. It is UA's belief that this strategy is the best possible way to advertise its products because many fans become familiar with UA products seeing them worn by high-performing athletes on a year round basis. In addition to focusing on the large-market leagues, UA also focuses on brand authenticity from a more grassroots level. By hosting camps, clinics, and other activities for young athletes, it is able to gain a firsthand appreciation for UA's product quality and brand equity.

UA uses broadcast, print, and social media outlets to promote the firm's product. UA also engages in acquiring prime real estate in the 25,000 major retail stores worldwide in which their products are sold, as well as operating outlet stores in 34 different states. UA products are sold throughout the world. New UA products in 2012 included UA Studio line, the Armour Bra, cold-back technology, UA Spine footwear, and UA scent control technology.

"The biggest, baddest brand on the planet, bar none." That's how founder and CEO Plank likes to describe his vision for what UA can ultimately become. Plank and his team are excellent marketers; the company's blood-pumping ads resonate with athletes and those who aspire to become athletes. UA's bold logo and brash and edgy marketing campaigns inspire movement and physical fitness, positioning the company well within the healthier lifestyle megatrend. Plank and his team relish their underdog image versus big rival firms; they love to operate within and promote an "us-versus-them" philosophy. This competitive fire has served UA well and has encapsulated many athletes and fans.

UA has 102 factory house stores in North America, mostly located in the eastern USA. UA opened its first factory house store in Canada in 2012.

Finance

In late 2012, UA has an impressive annual growth rate of 34 percent since 2005, has a market cap of $4.32 billion, and a price-to-earnings (P/E) ratio of 49.4, above the S&P 500 P/E ratio of 17.7. UA shares were up 44.6 percent year-to-date as of December 20, 2012. Strong financially, UA has used zero of its $300 million revolving credit facility at the end of September 2012. UA's debt-to-equity ratio is low at 0.10. UA has a quick ratio of 1.84 and has improved its earnings per share by 22.7 percent in the most recent quarter compared to the same quarter a year ago. UA does not pay dividends, preferring to reinvest all earnings back into the firm.

UA expects 2012 net revenues of approximately $1.82 billion, representing growth of 24 percent over 2011, and 2012 operating income of approximately $207 million, representing growth of 27 percent over 2011. Plank says: "I am proud of what our team has accomplished so far this year and we are well positioned for growth in 2013 and beyond. I emphasize 'team', as we continue to make great strides with the additions of seasoned leadership in Supply Chain, Women's, and International."

UA revenues increased 24 percent in the third quarter of 2012 to $575 million compared with net revenues of $466 million in the previous year's period. Net income increased 25 percent. UA's recent income statements and balance sheets are provided in Exhibits 2 and 3, respectively. Note that the company pays no dividends and is performing in an excellent manner.

Segment Data By-Product
Exhibit 4 provides a breakdown of UA's revenues by product. Note that apparel continues to be the strongest product offered based on net revenues, but footwear and accessories such as bags, hats, and gloves experienced higher percent increases over the most recent fiscal year. License revenues decreased as a result partly of less orders of hats and bags. Seventy-six percent of company revenues are derived from apparel in 2012. Followed by footwear at 13 percent and accessories at 9 percent.

EXHIBIT 2

Under Armour Statements of Income
(In thousands, except per share amounts)

	Year Ended December 31,		
	2012	2011	2010
Net revenues	$1,834,921	$1,472,684	$1,063,927
Cost of goods sold	955,624	759,848	533,420
Gross profit	879,297	712,836	530,507
Selling, general and administrative expenses	670,602	550,069	418,152
Income from operations	208,695	162,767	112,355
Interest expense, net	(5,183)	(3,841)	(2,258)
Other expense, net	(73)	(2,064)	(1,178)
Income before income taxes	203,439	156,862	108,919
Provision for income taxes	74,661	59,943	40,442
Net income	$128,778	$96,919	$68,477
Net income available per common share			
Basic	$1.23	$0.94	$0.67
Diluted	$1.21	$0.92	$0.67
Weighted average common shares outstanding			
Basic	104,343	103,140	101,595
Diluted	106,380	105,052	102,563

Source: 2012 Form 10K, p. 49.

EXHIBIT 3 Under Armour Balance Sheets

Under Armour, Balance Sheets
(In thousands, except share data)

	December 31, 2012	December 31, 2011
Assets		
Current assets		
Cash and cash equivalents	$341,841	$175,384
Accounts receivable, net	175,524	134,043
Inventories	319,286	324,409
Prepaid expenses and other current assets	43,896	39,643
Deferred income taxes	23,051	16,184
Total current assets	903,598	689,663
Property and equipment, net	180,850	159,135
Intangible assets, net	4,483	5,535
Deferred income taxes	22,606	15,885
Other long-term assets	45,546	48,992
Total assets	$1,157,083	$919,210
Liabilities and Stockholders' Equity		
Current liabilities		
Accounts payable	$143,689	$100,527
Accrued expenses	85,077	69,285
Current maturities of long-term debt	9,132	6,882
Other current liabilities	14,330	6,913
Total current liabilities	252,228	183,607
Long-term debt, net of current maturities	52,757	70,842
Other long-term liabilities	35,176	28,329
Total liabilities	340,161	282,778

(continued)

EXHIBIT 3 Continued

	December 31, 2012	December 31, 2011
Commitments and contingencies		
Stockholders' equity		
Class A Common Stock, $0.0003 1/3 par value; 200,000,000 shares authorized as of December 31, 2012 and 2011; 83,461,106 shares issued and outstanding as of December 31, 2012 and 80,992,252 shares issued and outstanding as of December 31, 2011.	28	27
Class B Convertible Common Stock, $0.0003 1/3 par value; 21,300,000 shares authorized, issued and outstanding as of December 31,2012 and 22,500,000 shares authorized, issued and outstanding as of December 31, 2011.	7	7
Additional paid-in capital	321,338	268,206
Retained earnings	493,181	366,164
Accumulated other comprehensive income	2,368	2,028
Total stockholders' equity	**816,922**	**636,432**
Total liabilities and stockholders' equity	**$1,157,083**	**$919,210**

Source: 2012 *Form 10K*, p. 48

Apparel is offered in many styles and fits to cover most any environment condition. Apparel is specifically engineered to replace traditional nonperformance fabrics and replace them with the most cutting edge products available. UA currently has three gear lines that achieve the designed purpose of having a sophisticated apparel option for all weather conditions. The three products are marketed under HEATGEAR, designed for hot weather, COLDGEAR, designed for cold temperatures, and ALLSEASONGEAR, designed for between the extremes. In addition to the three temperature ratings, all products also come in three fit types: compression (tight fit), fitted (athletic fit), and loose (relaxed). All UA appeal products are designed to whisk water away from the wearer to keep them as dry and comfortable as possible in any temperature or type of activity.

UA expanded into offering footwear in 2006 and today makes footwear for virtually all sports including running and even hunting boots. Like the traditional shirts, footwear offerings are designed to cushion and manage moisture. In 2011, UA began to sell hats and bags in house; these products were previously provided by a licensee. Other accessories developed and now marketed by UA include gloves for football, baseball, golf, and running as well as mouth guards, socks, and eye wear.

Segment Data By Region
Exhibit 5 reveals UA's recent revenues and operating profits for the North American and international markets. UA reports revenues in four distinct geographic regions: (1) North America, (2) EMEA, (3) Asia, and (4) Latin America. Each geographic segment operates in the same

EXHIBIT 4 UA Segment Data by Product

	Year Ended December 31 (in Thousands),			Percent Change	
	2012	2011	2010	2012	2011
Apparel	$1,385,350	$1,122,031	$853,493	23.5%	31.5%
Footwear	238,955	181,684	127,175	31.5	42.9
Accessories	165,835	132,400	43,882	25.3	201
Total net sales	1,790,140	1,436,115	1,024,550	24.7	40.2
License revenues	44,781	36,569	39,377	22.5	(7.1)
Total revenues	1,834,921	$1,472,684	$1,063,927	24.6%	38.4%

Source: 2012 *Form 10K*, p. 29.

manner, to design, develop, market, and distribute UA products. Note that only 6 percent of UA revenues were derived from international markets so the company combines all these countries into one segment for reporting reasons. UA acknowledges that the trend in performance products is becoming increasingly global with a bright future, but 6 percent so far leaves tremendous upside for the company.

UA's North American segment includes about 18,000 retail stores; UA also owns 80 outlet stores located in 34 different states. The company's two largest customers are Dick's Sporting Goods and The Sports Authority. In addition to selling to the public, UA earns income from the sale of uniforms and practice gear to high school, college, and professional teams.

In EMEA, UA products are sold in approximately 4,000 retail outlet stores. European football teams that wear UA gear reside in many European nations including the United Kingdom, France, Germany, Greece, Italy, and Spain among others. First division rugby clubs in France, Ireland Italy, and the United Kingdom also wear UA products. Products in Europe are currently distributed out of The Netherlands.

Since 2002, UA has enjoyed a licensing agreement with Dome Corp., which produces and sells UA products in Japan, which are all tailored for Japanese consumers' specific taste. Products are sold in more than 2,500 specialty stores in Japan, as well as to several professional soccer and baseball games in Japan. Also in Asia, products are sold in both Australia and New Zealand, and in 2011, UA's first specialty store opened in Shanghai, China. Latin American customers are provided UA products through independent distributors but more commonly are served through distribution facilities in the USA. Only 6 percent of UA's 2012 revenues were generated from outside North America. The company does have two specialty stores in Shanghai, China. About 55 percent of the fabric used in UA products comes from suppliers in China, Malaysia, Mexico, and Vietnam. UA has 27 manufacturers in 14 countries.

Competition

UA has unique branding of a fabric to whisk away water from the body, but competitors such as Nike and Adidas have copied UA's designs and technology. The fabrics UA uses are not unique to them, and it does not control any patents on fabrics or processes. It is all about branding for UA. Because firms such as Nike and Adidas have much larger resources to draw on, competing long term may be difficult for UA, but so far the firm is doing well. In addition, competing for floor space at large retailers is difficult because many stores have their own store brands, in addition to private label brands, all competing for floor space.

Exhibit 6 provides some comparative information for UA and rival firms. Note that in terms of revenue UA is about the size of Columbia Sportswear, but Nike and Adidas are both more

EXHIBIT 5 UA Segment Data by Geographic Region

	Year Ended December 31 (in Thousands),				
	2012	2011	2010	Percent Change	
Net Revenues					
North America	$1,726,733	$1,383,346	$997,816	38.6%	
Other Foreign Countries	108,188	89,338	66,111	35.1%	
Total Net Revenues	1,834,921	1,472,684	1,063,927	38.4%	
Operating Profits				**2012**	**2011**
North America	$197,194	$150,559	$102,806	31.0%	46.4%
Other Foreign Countries	11,501	12,208	9,549	(5.8)	27.8
Total Operating Profit	208,695	162,767	112,355	28.2	44.9

Source: 2012 Form 10K, p. 33.

EXHIBIT 6 Comparative Information for Sports Apparel Firms

	Under Armour	Adidas	Columbia Sportswear	Nike
Number of Employees	1.9K	39.9K	4.1K	40K
Net Income ($)	98.9M	922M	94.6M	2.2B
Revenue ($)	1.54B	17.1B	1.7B	24B
Revenue ($)/Employee	855K	429K	414K	600K
EPS Ratio ($)	0.95	2.20	2.78	4.73
Market Cap.	5.2B	15.3B	1.8B	42.6B

EPS, earnings per share.
Source: Based on company documents.

than 10 times the size of UA. Note also that UA is exceptionally efficient as indicated by its high revenue per employee ratio.

Nike

Headquartered in Beaverton, Oregon, Nike is the largest apparel and footwear provider for men, women, and children worldwide. Nike outfits athletes globally in virtually every sport, including running, basketball, football, soccer, golf, and many more. In addition to apparel and footwear, Nike also produces golf clubs, athletic bags, gloves, footballs, bats, and much more. Nike owns brands such as Converse, Chuck Taylor, and All Star to name a few.

Nike reported in 2011 that 42 percent of revenues derived from U.S. operations, where the company sells its products in a wide range of mediums from retail stores, its Internet site, 156 Nike factory stores, and tens of thousands of other stores, such as Foot Locker. Nike's international sales accounted for 58 percent of revenues in 2011 and products are sold in similar ways as in the USA. Nike currently operates 308 factory stores outside the USA. Approximately 67 percent of all Nike North American revenues are derived from footwear, 28 percent from appeal, and only 5 percent from equipment. Nike's operations in international markets have a similar revenue breakdown by product, making Nike's primary revenue generator footwear, as opposed to UA being primarily an apparel producer.

Like UA, Nike outfits many professional and major U.S. college teams with their gear. Notable teams wearing Nike gear include the University of Oregon, Penn State University, and The University of Alabama. Nike has stars such as Michael Jordan, LeBron James, and Tiger Woods serving as spokespersons to help in promoting the brand. Late in 2012, Nike sold its Cole Haan handbag and shoe brand to private equity firm Apax Partners for $570 million and also sold its Umbro football brand to Iconix Brand Group for $225 million.

Adidas AG

Headquartered in Herzogenaurach, Germany, Adidas AG develops and produces a wide range of athletic appear, footwear, and accessories and operates in six business segments: wholesale, retail, TaylorMade-Adidas Golf, Rockport, Reebok-CCM Hockey, as well as other brands. Adidas sells its products through retail stores, the Internet, and through 2,401 company-owned stores worldwide. The company most closely competes with UA with its sport performance line of apparel that is modeled after UA fabrics to help keep athletes dry and comfortable for the duration of their activity.

Adidas currently has a contract with the NBA to outfit all teams with apparel, and in addition, Adidas outfits some or the largest European football clubs with apparel. Adidas employs many of soccer's biggest starts to market their products, such as Frank Lampard, Steven Gerrard, and Micheal Ballack. Tennis stars endorsing Adidas include Andy Murray, Justine Henin, Marcos Baghdatis, and many more. Andy Murray is Adidas's highest paid spokesman with a five-year contract worth $24.5 million.

Adidas had sales of more than 13 billion euros in 2011, an 11-percent increase from the previous year, with every reporting segment enjoying larger revenues than the previous fiscal year.

The retail and TaylorMade-Adidas Golf segments enjoyed the largest percent increases at 20 and 16 percent, respectively.

Columbia Sportswear Company

Headquartered in Portland, Oregon, Columbia's trademark Bugaboo parka with weatherproof shell competes with some UA products, as does Columbia's performance apparel for a variety of activities and Columbia's sportswear accessories, boots, and rugged footwear, sold under brands Columbia, Mountain Hardwear, Sorel, and Montrail. Columbia brands are used globally during outdoor activities, such as skiing, snowboarding, hiking, climbing, camping, hunting, fishing, running, and the like. Columbia operates about 50 outlet retail stores and 10 branded retail stores in the USA, as well as 10 in Europe, 2 outlet stores in Canada, and about 300 in Japan and Korea. Thousands of other stores sell Columbia products globally, including even Dick's Sporting Goods and The Sports Authority that UA counts on most.

External Issues

Economic Factors

The apparel industry has a mediocre outlook given weak economies in which consumers are faced with less discretionary income. Items expected to maintain strong sales are those that are well differentiated from competing products, where consumers value the extra features and are less price sensitive to products they deem necessary. More luxury items in both sporting activities are expected to have modest growth. In 2011, the apparel industry reported sales up 5.9 percent over 2010, however much of this gain was the result of inflation and the rising prices of commodities such as cotton, increased labor wages overseas, and increased freight fees. Nevertheless, the S&P Apparel Retail Index rose 22 percent versus a 12-percent increase for the S&P 1500 Index from March 2011 to March 2012. The S&P Footwear Index rose only 11.5 percent during this same time frame.

Apparel sales totaling $77.7 billion was imported into the USA in 2011, up nearly 9 percent from 2010. Approximately 38 percent of all apparel imported came from China. The apparel industry is extremely fragmented with many firms competing for the same customers. For example, the top 10 national brands only account for 16 percent of wholesale apparel sales in the USA with 84 percent of apparel distributed coming from smaller brands and store brand goods. Women's segment has traditionally accounted for significantly more sales at 55 percent. Men only accounted for 28 percent and children 17 percent of apparel sales in 2011.

The footwear industry grew at a slower rate than apparel in 2011. Fashion footwear accounted for 48 percent of total footwear sales, with performance footwear accounting for 27 percent, sports footwear 13 percent, outdoor footwear 8 percent, and work and safety footwear 4 percent. Fashion and sports footwear are expected to be the most significant areas of growth moving forward as people look to improve their fashion looks and the growing health-minded concerns of the public.

Technological Changes

Nike was one of the first companies to understand the importance of producing better sporting apparel and footwear for athletes, when Phillip Knight and his track coach Bill Bowerman developed a better shoe for members of the University of Oregon track team. Since the 1960s, there have been many developments and improvements in shoe and apparel design away from the traditional cotton sweat suit and basic tennis shoe. Today, apparel hugs the body and insulates the wearer from cold and keeps them cool from hot. Shoes can be synced to computers to determine performance and impact points for the runner and t-shirt fabrics can even help manage odors. These types of technological offerings keep customers purchasing new items and can create intense competition and brand loyalty.

Where to Produce

China has historically been the low-cost alternative for apparel firms when selection a nation for the production of their products. In 2011 alone, 38 percent of all apparel imports and 74 percent of all footwear imports into the USA came from China. However, with rising production costs, higher wages in China, increased transportation costs and less control over quality, Chinese imports may be waning in the eyes of large U.S. apparel corporations in favor of facilities in Mexico and the Caribbean. UA currently produces many of their items in Mexico and enjoys quicker turnaround and more quality control than some rival firms who import a large percentage of their inventory from China.

The Future

UA needs considerably more global presence to gain economies of scale versus its large rival firms. Increasing downward pressure on prices could necessitate that UA effectively expand globally. The primary strategic issue facing UA therefore is how and when and where to expand globally. Other secondary strategic issues facing UA include whether to diversify into other accessory items to reduce the firm's reliance on apparel and whether to increase its expenditures on R&D to keep pace with changing technological advancements in the apparel industry. UA is strong financially, which does enable the firm to make strategic acquisitions as needed, so the firm should identify potential acquisition candidates around the world. Effective global expansion is an important key to UA's growth and prosperity in the future. Even South America, Central America, Mexico, and Australia are all sports-minded areas in which UA products should be well received. Perhaps what UA needs most is to fulfill CEO Plank's vision: "Our long-term vision is to one day have our Women's business larger than Men's, our Footwear business larger than Apparel, and our International business larger than our USA business." Prepare a five-year strategic plan for CEO Plank to fulfill his vision for UA.

Pearson PLC, 2013

www.pearson.com, PSORF or PSON (London exchange)

Headquartered in London, United Kingdom, Pearson is the largest education company and the largest book publisher in the world. Pearson is organized into three main business groupings: (1) Pearson Education (digital learning, education publishing and services including Poptropica and eCollege; (2) Financial Times (FT) Group (business information, including the *Financial Times* newspaper); and (3) Penguin Group (consumer publishing, including the Dorling Kindersley and Penquin Classics imprints). In late 2011, Pearson acquired Global Education and Technology Group. In 2012, Pearson acquired Certiport, Inc., Author Solutions, Inc. (ASI), and EmbanetCompass.

In late 2012, Pearson agreed to merge its Penguin Books division with Bertelsmann's Random House to create the world's biggest book publisher, a newly created joint venture named Penguin Random House. Bertelsmann will own 53 percent of the joint venture and Pearson will own 47 percent. The joint venture excludes Bertelsmann's trade publishing business in Germany and Pearson retains rights to use the Penguin brand in education markets worldwide. The newly formed company is subject to customary regulatory and other approvals but is expected to complete in the second half of 2013.

In October 2013, Harish Manwani joined the board of directors of Pearson. Harish is Chief Operating Officer of the global consumer products company Unilever. Harish is a graduate from Bombay University and holds a Masters degree in management studies. Pearson chairman Glen Moreno said: "Harish brings to Pearson a deep knowledge of emerging markets, an understanding of the rapidly growing middle class in those countries, and senior experience in a successful global organization. This background is very relevant to our transformation of Pearson into the world's leading learning company." Harish replaces Dr. Susan Fuhrman on the Pearson board; Susan is President of Teachers College, Columbia University. Pearson also recently announced another appointment to its board, Linda Lorimer, Vice President of Yale University.

History

Founded by Samuel Pearson in 1844, Pearson originally was a building and engineering firm operating under the name of *S. Pearson & Son*. In 1880, control passed to grandson Weetman Pearson, an engineer later known as Lord Cowdray, who in 1890 moved the business to London and turned it into one of the world's largest construction companies. Pearson was listed on the London Stock Exchange in 1969. Pearson acquired Penguin Books in 1970 and Ladybird Books in 1972.

During the 1990s, Pearson acquired a number of TV production and broadcasting assets and sold most of its nonmedia assets, under the leadership of future U.S. Congressman Bob Turner. Pearson acquired the education division of Simon & Schuster in 1998 from Viacom and merged it with its own education unit, Addison-Wesley Longman, to form Pearson Education.

In 2000, Pearson acquired National Computer Systems and entered the educational assessment and school management systems market in the United States. That same year, Pearson acquired Dorling Kindersley, the illustrated reference publisher and integrated it within Penguin. In 2006, Pearson acquired National Evaluation Systems, Inc. (NES; Amherst, MA), a provider of customized state assessments for teacher certification in the USA. Pearson completed the acquisition of Harcourt Assessment in 2008, merging the acquired businesses into Pearson Assessment & Information. In that same year, Pearson acquired eCollege, a digital learning technology group for $477M. In 2011, Pearson created the Pearson College, a British degree provider based in London and Manchester. Also that year, Pearson acquired Connections Education.

In late 2012, Pearson acquired KEV Group, the North American leader in the management and accounting of school activity funds and online payments. KEV Group's *School Cash Suite* of products manage all aspects of every dollar that comes into secondary schools. Whether cash, check, or an online transaction, KEV's products help more than 4,000 schools reduce fraud and significantly decrease their workload. Limiting cash in a school system and increasing transparency of cash that does come in decreases the risk of bullying, reduces classroom distractions, and ensures maximum efficiency for all users.

Internal Issues

Vision and Mission

Pearson has no clearly stated vision or mission statement. However, there is a statement at the Pearson website, under the Strategy icon, that may be the firm's mission statement. It reads: "Pearson's goal is to help people make progress in their lives through learning. We aim to be the world's leading learning company, serving the citizens of a brain-based economy wherever and whenever they are learning."

Strategy

Pearson's strategy, as stated on the company website, consists of four initiatives, paraphrased as follows to focus on:

1. Long-term organic investment in content,
2. Digital products and services businesses—Add services to our content, usually enabled by technology; Pearson's digital revenues were £2bn or 33 percent of total sales.
3. International expansion—Pearson sells in more than 70 countries, but desires new particular emphasis on fast-growing markets in China, India, Africa and Latin America. In 2011, Pearson generated $1bn of revenue in developing markets for the first time, accounting for 11 percent of total sales and 22 percent of employees.
4. Efficiency—Pearson profit margins have increased to 16.1 percent and the ratio of average working capital to sales has improved from 20.1 percent to 16.9 percent.

Organizational Structure

On the Pearson website, the top management team is listed under the Board of Directors icon. Pearson's organizational chart is provided in Exhibit 1. Chief executive officer (CEO) John Fallon replaced CEO Marjorie Scardino on January 1, 2013.

Segments

Pearson is organized into four main business groupings: (1) Pearson International Education, (2) Pearson North American Education, and (3) Professional Education and FT Group. In 2012 Pearson generated total revenues of £5.059 billion, as indicated in Exhibit 2. £2.658

EXHIBIT 1 Pearson's Organizational Structure

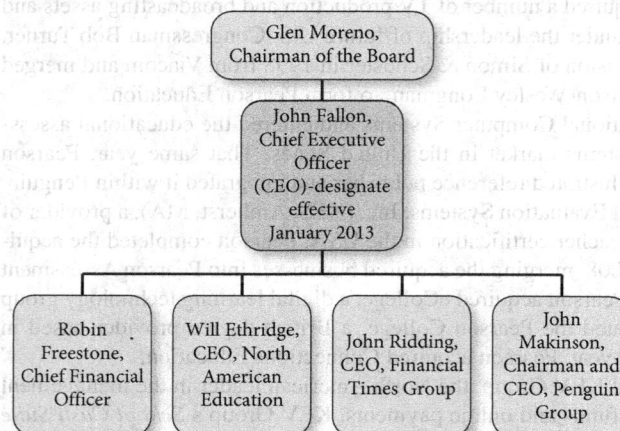

Source: Based on company documents.

EXHIBIT 2 Pearson's Segment

All figures in £ millions	2012						
	North American Education	International Education	Professional	FT Group	Corporate	Discontinued operations	Group
Continuing operations							
Sales (external)	2,658	1,568	390	443	—	—	5,059
Sales (inter-segment)	5	1	12	—	—	—	18
Adjusted operating profit	536	216	37	49	—	—	838
Intangible charges	(66)	(73)	(37)	(4)	—	—	(180)
Acquisition costs	(7)	(8)	(1)	(4)	—	—	(20)
Other net gains and losses	—	—	(123)	—	—	—	(123)
Operating profit	**463**	**135**	**(124)**	**41**	**—**	**—**	**515**

All figures in £ millions	2011						
	North American Education	International Education	Professional Education	FT Group	Corporate	Discontinued Operations	Group
Continuing operations							
Sales (external)	2,584	1,424	382	427	—	—	4,817
Sales (inter-segment)	3	—	9	—	—	—	12
Adjusted operating profit	493	196	66	76	—	—	831
Intangible charges	(57)	(60)	(11)	(8)	—	—	(136)
Acquisition costs	(2)	(9)	—	(1)	—	—	(12)
Other net gains and losses	29	(6)	—	412	—	—	435
Operating profit	**463**	**121**	**55**	**479**	**—**	**—**	**1,118**

billion were from North America, £1.568 billion from International, £390 million were from Professional, and £443 million from Financial Times (FT) Group—as indicated in Exhibit 2. Note in Exhibit 3 that Pearson had 2012 revenue declines in three regions, but sales were up in the USA slightly.

Pearson Education

Pearson Education provides textbooks and digital technologies to teachers and students across all ages. Pearson's education brands include Bug Club, Edexcel, Financial Times Publishing, Fronter, MyEnglishLab, and BBC Active. Pearson's education brands in North America include eCollege, Poptropica, FT Press, MyLabs/Mastering, SAMS Publishing, and Que Publishing. Pearson generates about 60 percent of its education sales in North America but operates in more than 70 countries. Pearson publishes across the curriculum under a range of brand names including Scott Foresman, Prentice Hall, Addison-Wesley, Allyn and Bacon, Benjamin Cummings, and Longman.

Pearson's Prentice Hall division is the market leader in higher education publishing across all discipline areas; Pearson's Addison Wesley and Benjamin Cummings are premier publishers in computing, economics, finance, mathematics, science, and statistics; Pearson's Longman brand focuses on materials in English, history, philosophy, political science, and religion; and Allyn and Bacon focuses on the social sciences, humanities, and education disciplines.

In 2013, Pearson Education reorganized into three main divisions: Pearson International Education, Pearson North American Education, and Professional Education. Pearson International is headquartered in London, with offices across Europe, Asia, and South America. Pearson North America is headquartered in Upper Saddle River, New Jersey, with major business units based

EXHIBIT 3 Pearson's Revenues By Region

	Sales	
All figures in £ millions	2012	2011
Continuing operations		
UK	705	713
Other European countries	391	394
USA	2,800	2,707
Canada	145	150
Asia Pacific	647	514
Other countries	371	339
Total continuing	**5,059**	**4,817**
Discontinued operations		
UK	160	152
Other European countries	78	77
USA	603	606
Canada	56	59
Asia Pacific	139	132
Other countries	17	19
Total discontinued	**1,053**	**1,045**
Total	**6,112**	**5,862**

in San Francisco, Boston, Columbus, Indianapolis, and Chandler (Arizona). In 2012, Pearson International Education had revenues of £1,568 million, Pearson North American Education had revenues of £2,658 million, and Professional Education had revenues of £443 million.

The North American segment had 2012 operating profits of £536 million. Student registration for MyLab grew 11 percent to almost 10 million. Student registrations in 2012 at Pearson's eCollege grew 3 percent to 8.7 million. Also in North America, Pearson's Connection Education, which operates online K-12 schools in 22 states, served more than 43,000 students, up 31 percent from 2011.

Pearson's International Education segment reported 2012 operating profits of £216 million, partly due to student enrollments in China at Wall Street English (WSE), increasing 15 percent to 61,000. WSE is Pearson's worldwide chain of English language centers for professionals with 11 new WSE centers opened in 2012. Pearson did especially well in 2012 in India with its TutorVista program and in Mexico with the launch of UTEL, a new university enabling Mexicans to enroll in online business courses. Also in the International segment, Pearson VUE test volumes grew 7 percent in 2012 to almost 8 million.

Financial Times Group
The FT Group provides business and financial news, data, comment, and analysis in print and online. FT Publishing includes: the *Financial Times* newspaper and FT.com website; a range of specialist financial magazines and online services; and Mergermarket, a financial data vendor. The FT Group also has shareholdings in Business Day and Financial Mail (BDFM) of South Africa (50 percent stake) and The Economist (50 percent stake). Pearson's FT group reported 2012 operating profits of £49 million, with digital subscriptions increasing 18 percent to almost 316,000 and with 3.5 million FT web app users. The Economist (50% owned by Pearson) reported in 2012 a 2 percent increase in worldwide printed digital circulation.

Penguin Group
Penguin Group is an international consumer publisher, which includes imprints such as Allen Lane, Avery, Berkley Books, dial, Dutton, Dorling Kindersley, Grosset & Dunlap, Hamish Hamilton, Ladybird, Plume, Puffin, Penguin, Putnam, Michael Joseph, Riverhead, rough Guides, and Viking. Penguin publishes around 4,000 titles every year and its range of titles

includes classics, reference volumes, and children's titles. In October 2012, Pearson agreed to merge Penguin Group with Bertelsmann's Random House to create the world's biggest trade book publisher—Penguin Random House. Bertelsmann will own 53 percent and Pearson will own 47 percent. Penguin reported 2012 revenue of £1,053 million and operating profits of £98 million. E-book revenue grew strongly and accounted for 17 percent of Penguin's global revenue.

Pearson now owns 47 percent of the new Penguin/Random House publishing company. In 2012, Penguin published 255 *New York Times* bestsellers.

Finance

Note in the income statements in Exhibit 4 that Pearson reported increasing revenues but declining profits in 2012. The decline in earnings resulted in a decline in 2012 retained earnings on the Pearson balance sheets, as shown in Exhibit 5.

External

Total U.S. college enrollments declined 2 percent in 2012 while the overall higher education publishing market declined 6 percent, according to the Association of American Publishers (AAP). AAP also reported a 15 percent decline in the textbook publishing market in 2012.

Competitors

The world of book publishing is changing rapidly as e-books, renting books, sharing books, avoiding books, photocopying books, scanning books, creating custom books, using e-readers

EXHIBIT 4 Pearson's Income Statements

	Year ended 31 December 2012	
All figures in £ millions	2012	2011
Sales	5,059	4,817
Cost of goods sold	(2,224)	(2,072)
Gross profit	2,835	2,745
Operating expenses	(2,216)	(2,072)
Profit on sale of associate	—	412
Loss on closure of subsidiary	(113)	—
Share of results of joint ventures and associates	9	33
Operating profit	515	1,118
Finance costs	(113)	(96)
Finance income	32	25
Profit before tax	434	1,047
Income tax	(148)	(162)
Profit for the year from continuing operations	286	885
Profit for the year from discontinued operations	43	71
Profit for the year	329	956
Attributable to:		
Equity holders of the company	326	957
Non-controlling interest	3	(1)
Earnings per share for profit from continuing and discontinued operations attributable to equity holders of the company during the year (expressed in pence per share)		
Basic	40.5p	119.6p
Diluted	40.5p	119.3p

EXHIBIT 5 Pearson's Balance Sheets

As of 31 December 2012

All figures in £ millions	2012	2011
Assets		
Non-current assets		
Property, plant and equipment	327	383
Intangible assets	6,218	6,342
Investments in joint ventures and associates	15	32
Deferred income tax assets	229	287
Financial assets–Derivative financial instruments	174	177
Retirement benefit assets	—	25
Other financial assets	31	26
Trade and other receivables	79	151
	7,073	7,423
Current assets		
Intangible assets–Pre-publication	666	650
Inventories	261	407
Trade and other receivables	1,104	1,386
Financial assets–Derivative financial instruments	4	
Financial assets–Marketable securities	6	9
Cash and cash equivalents (excluding overdrafts)	1,062	1,369
	3,103	3,821
Assets classified as held for sale	1,172	—
Total assets	**11,348**	**11,244**
Liabilities		
Non-current liabilities		
Financial liabilities–Borrowings	(2,010)	(1,964)
Financial liabilities–Derivative financial instruments	—	(2)
Deferred income tax liabilities	(601)	(620)
Retirement benefit obligations	(172)	(166)
Provisions for other liabilities and charges	(110)	(115)
Other liabilities	(282)	(325)
	(3,175)	(3,192)
Current liabilities		
Trade and other liabilities	(1,556)	(1,741)
Financial liabilities–Borrowings	(262)	(87)
Financial liabilities–Derivative financial instruments	—	(1)
Current income tax liabilities	(291)	(213)
Provisions for other liabilities and charges	(38)	(48)
	(2,147)	(2,090)
Liabilities directly associated with assets classified as held for sale	(316)	—
Total liabilities	**(5,638)**	**(5.282)**
Net assets	**5,710**	**5,962**

EXHIBIT 5 Continued

All figures in £ millions	2012	2011
Equity		
Share capital	204	204
Share premium	2,555	2,544
Treasury shares	(103)	(149)
Translation reserve	128	364
Retained earnings	2,902	2,980
Total equity attributable to equity holders of the company	**5,686**	**5,943**
Non-controlling interest	24	19
Total equity	**5,710**	**5,962**
Total Liabilities and Equity	**11,348**	**11,244**

permeate today's publishing landscape. The historical day of students carrying around encyclopedic size books is drawing to an end. Although great news for students and customers, this changing environment makes book publishing much more risky for both publishers and authors.

The situation described leads to increased competition daily on many fronts such as price, e-commerce, new entrants, ancillary offerings, acquisitions, divestitures, and weakened players. A few of Pearson's major rivals in this turbulent environment are McGraw-Hill, John Wiley, Houghton Mifflin, and Thomson Reuters, but even online book publishers such as iUniverse are attacking from new directions. Pearson is the largest and most profitable book publisher, which in a sense makes Pearson most vulnerable to competitor's duplicating and imitating their product offerings, and continually examining Pearson for potential weaknesses that can be exploited.

A financial comparison of each rival firm is provided in Exhibit 6, followed by a brief overview of each firm. Note in Exhibit 4 that Pearson's earnings per share (EPS) is lower than both McGraw-Hill and John Wiley.

McGraw-Hill Companies, Inc. (NYSE: MPH)

Headquartered in New York City, McGraw-Hill is a leading producer of textbooks, tests, and related materials, serving the elementary, secondary, and higher education markets through McGraw-Hill Education (MHE). Other businesses include S&P Ratings (indexes and credit ratings); S&P Capital IQ and S&P Indices (financial and business information); and Commodities and Commercial (Platts, J.D. Power and Associates, McGraw-Hill Construction, and Aviation Week).

EXHIBIT 6 A Comparison of Publishers

	Pearson	McGraw-Hill	John Wiley	Thomson Reuters
Sales ($)	5.09B£	6.35B	1.75B	13.45B
Net Income ($)	329M£	789M	190M	–877M
Profit Margin (%)	6.46	13.01	10.89	–6.45
Debt-to-Equity Ratio	0.41	0.67	0.64	0.43
EPS ($)	0.40£	3.03	3.14	–1.06
Market Capitalization ($)	10.6B£	14.97B	2.27B	23.83B
Number of Shares Out	817M	277M	60.15M	826M

EPS, earnings per share.
Source: Based on company documents.

McGraw-Hill announced in late 2012 that it is divesting its education division for $2.5 billion to Apollo Global Management LLC (APO). McGraw-Hill's education division had been reporting shrinking revenues over recent years, partly as a result of reduced spending on textbooks by the government (and students). Also, McGraw-Hill was facing difficulty with its plans to develop its education division into a subscription-based model through digital delivery. The new McGraw-Hill, without the education division, is being renamed McGraw-Hill Financial and will primarily focus on capital and commodities markets and include iconic brands like S&P Ratings, S&P Capital IQ, and S&P Indices. McGraw-Hill Companies expected revenues of approximately $4.4 billion from McGraw-Hill Financial in 2012, with approximately 40 percent of it coming from international avenues.

John Wiley & Sons (NYSE: JW-A)

Headquartered in Hoboken, New Jersey, John Wiley publishes scientific, technical, and medical works, including journals and reference works such as *Current Protocols* and *Kirk-Othmer Encyclopedia of Chemical Technology*. Wiley publishes more than 1,600 journal titles, produces professional and nonfiction trade books, and is a publisher of college textbooks. Wiley also publishes the *For Dummies* how-to series, the travel guide brand Frommer's, and CliffsNotes study guides, as well. Wiley has publishing, marketing, and distribution centers on four continents: North America, Europe, Asia, and Australia. For second quarter of 2012 that ended October 31, 2012, Wiley reported a slight decline in revenue compared to the same period in the previous fiscal year, and a 15-percent decrease in net income. Wiley has a market capitalization of $2.3 billion.

Houghton Mifflin Harcourt Publishing Company

Headquartered in Boston Massachusetts, Houghton Mifflin is a publisher of pre-K through grade 12 educational material, as well as textbooks and printed materials. The company provides digital content online and via CD-ROM and publishes fiction (including J. R. R. Tolkien's *The Lord of the Rings* series), as well as nonfiction titles and reference materials, and offers professional resources and educational services to teachers. Although founded back in 1832, Houghton Mifflin today is owned by private-equity concerns, including hedge fund Paulson & Co. The company filed for bankruptcy in 2012.

Thomson Reuters (NYSE: TRI)

Headquartered in New York City, Thomson Reuters is the market leader in financial data (ahead of rival information provider Bloomberg), providing electronic information and services to businesses and professionals worldwide, serving the financial services, media, legal, tax and accounting, and science markets. Nearly all Thomson Reuters' revenues come from subscription sales to its plethora of offerings.

For the third quarter of 2012, Thomson Reuters reported revenues of $3.2 billion, a 7-percent decline from the same period last year. Its net profit rose, however, by 24 percent, to $474 million. Thomson Reuters' best performing division is tax and accounting, but the firm reports flat or declining revenues in all its other divisions. Rumors circulated in 2012 that Thomson Reuters was maneuvering to buy Pearson's *Financial Times* newspaper.

The Future

The digital world is rapidly eroding Pearson's traditional book publishing business model. Luyen Chou, chief product officer for Pearson's K–12 technology group, summed it up best, when he recently said: "Pearson needs to become an 'Electronic Arts' [EA] for education. To keep up with the changing environment, we can't just digitize the static textbooks of the past; we need to excel at producing high-quality, interactive digital learning experiences and get them into the hands of students. That includes digital studios, animators, illustrators, producers, and 3-D artists. We need to build that capacity from within and we need the whole supply chain to take that from the studio to the actual users. The folks that have done that well are the Electronic Arts type companies of the world, digital studios. That's not a core competency for companies like Pearson. We have to make sure that we're complementing our data and platform with high-quality interactive learning content."

In late 2012, Blackboard Inc. and Pearson reached an agreement to expand the availability of Pearson's leading learning solution—MyLab & Mastering—with Blackboard Learn, the market-leading learning management system (LMS). Previously available in North America, the integration is now available in most markets worldwide.

The systems integration includes state-of-the-art web services that enable instructors to find and access MyLab & Mastering within their Blackboard learning system. For example, faculty can synchronize grade books, transfer information and create corresponding links in both systems, and customize courses by choosing content and rearranging items in the content area and course navigation bar. For example, Dr. Salim M. Salim, head of the Mathematics Department at Qatar University said: "The integration of MyLab & Mastering and Blackboard Learn has created not only a more enriched teaching and learning experience, but it also makes my job much more convenient. The single sign on, grade book synchronization, personalized study paths and real-time evaluations allow me and my students to easily benefit from the powerful tools both systems offer." Given the changing world of textbook publishing and publishing in general, Pearson is engaged is a competitive fight with rival McGraw-Hill for market share in the USA and indeed globally. McGraw-Hill's Connect software competes fiercely with Pearson's MyLab. Prepare a three-year strategic plan for Pearson.

Snyder's-Lance, Inc., 2013

www.snyderslance.com, LNCE

Headquartered in Charlotte, North Carolina, Snyder's-Lance (LNCE) is the second largest salty snack maker in the USA behind PepsiCo's Frito-Lay. LNCE manufactures and markets snack foods throughout the USA and Canada, including pretzels, sandwich crackers, potato chips, cookies, tortilla chips, restaurant style crackers, nuts, and other snacks. LNCE brands include Snyder's of Hanover, Lance, Krunchers!, Cape Cod, EatSmart Naturals, Jays, Tom's, Archway, O-Ke-Doke, and Stella D'oro, along with a number of private label and third party brands. LNCE revenues for 2012 declined one percent to $1.618 billion, while the firm's long-term debt doubled to over $500 million.

LNCE products are distributed widely through grocery and mass merchandisers, convenience stores, club stores, food service outlets, and other channels. LNCE has about 5,900 employees and over $1.6 billion in annual sales. No LNCE employees are covered by a collective bargaining agreement.

In fiscal 2013, LNCE completed its new 60,000 square foot R&D center in Hanover, Pennsylvania. The company reported revenue for Q2 of 2013 of $439 million, up 9.9 percent compared to prior year, and net income of $16.9 million, up from $15.0 million the prior year. The company declared a quarterly cash dividend of $0.16 per share on the company's common stock, payable on August 30, 2013 to stockholders of record at the close of business on August 21, 2013. At that time, LNCE reported that its net revenue for the full year 2013 would be up 10 to 12 percent, with 2013 capital expenditures projected to be between $78 and $83 million.

LNCE has manufacturing operations in Charlotte, as well as in Hanover, Pennsylvania; Goodyear, Arizona; Burlington, Iowa; Columbus, Georgia; Jeffersonville, Indiana; Hyannis, Massachusetts; Perry, Florida; Ashland, Ohio; Cambridge, Ontario; and Guelph, Ontario. In late 2012, LNCE opened a new distribution facility in Southaven, Mississippi and acquired Snack Factory, LLC for $343 million. That company develops and markets snacks under the Pretzel Crisps brand name.

LNCE does not have a stated vision or mission statement, but on many LNCE packages, the following phrase appears and perhaps is the firm's mission: "We make, sell, and deliver the most irresistible specialty snacks in the world."

Copyright by Fred David Books LLC. (Written by Forest R. David)

History

Snyder's of Hanover is a bit older than Lance, but both firms have a rich history dating back to the early 1900s.

Snyder's of Hanover

Business began in 1909 when Harry Warehime, founder of Hanover Canning Company (the firm's parent company until 1980), began producing OldeTyme Pretzels for the Hanover Pretzel Company. In the 1920s, Grandma Eda and Edward Snyder II began frying potato chips in a kettle at their home and selling the home cooked snack door-to-door and to fairs and farmers' markets. William Snyder in 1940 constructed a new plant in Hanover, PA. To extend the shelf life of his product for distant markets, William began to use aluminum foil bags, becoming the first chipper to implement this creative, yet practical innovation. Eleven years later, William's son, William "Billy" L. Snyder, sold the Hanover plant to Hanover Canning, headed by Alan R. Warehime. Company sales in 1961 were about $400,000.

In 1963, the Bechtel Pretzel Company, founded by Bill and Helen Bechtel in 1947, was purchased and incorporated into Snyder's Bakery. Bill developed the original recipe for the Sourdough Hard Pretzel that is still enjoyed by consumers today. In 1980, nineteen years after Snyder's was purchased, the Warehime family decided to "spin off" Snyder's of Hanover Snack Operation from Hanover Brands, enabling the companies to focus on their respective industries of snacks and vegetables. Snyder's sales in 1980 were $15.8 million. After the split, both companies began growing faster than industry averages.

Lance

Business began in 1913 when Phillip Lance, a food broker in Charlotte, obtained 500 pounds of raw peanuts for a customer. When the customer backed out of the deal, Mr. Lance kept the peanuts and began roasting them and selling them on the streets of Charlotte for a nickel a bag. Mr. Lance was later joined in business by his son-in-law, S. A. Van Every, and together they formed Lance Packing Company. Mr. Lance's wife and daughter added to the product line when they developed a peanut butter sandwich cracker. It is believed that this was the first such combination sandwich cracker offered for sale. Incorporated in 1926, Lance continued to grow as better methods of preparing peanuts and making peanut butter candy were developed. In 1935, Lance reached one million dollars in sales, and then two million in 1939 when the company's name was officially changed to Lance, Inc. By 1960, annual sales volume had grown to $26 million.

In 1979, Lance greatly expanded its product offerings with the acquisition of Midwest Biscuit Company in Burlington, Iowa. Midwest, the predecessor to Vista Bakery and Lance Private Brands, gave Lance a solid foothold in the rapidly growing private label cookie and cracker market. Lance continued to grow throughout the 1980s and 1990s and in 1999 made two acquisitions, Cape Cod Potato Chip Company and Tamming Foods. Based in Ontario, Canada, Tammong is a manufacturer of private label sugar wafers. Cape Cod is one of the nation's leaders in kettle-cooked potato chips. Sales of Cape Cod snack products grew rapidly as Lance leveraged the power of its company-owned direct-store-delivery system to increase distribution.

Since 2005, Lance experienced rapid revenue growth as the Company augmented organic growth with a series of strategic acquisitions. In 2005, Lance acquired the assets of Tom's Foods, a well-established company with a product line and distribution system very similar to Lance's. In 2008, Lance acquired Brent and Sam's Inc., a manufacturer of premium private label cookies. That same year the company acquired the Archway bakery in Ashland, Ohio. With Archway, Lance was able to add a well-known brand of cookies to its snack portfolio and increase its presence in the supermarket trade channel. In late 2009, Lance acquired the Stella D'oro brand. Stella D'oro is well-known in the Northeast and offers consumers a number of lightly sweet Italian-style cookies.

The Merger

LNCE was formed in 2010 when Lance, Inc. and Snyder's of Hanover merged. In late 2011, LNCE acquired George Greer Co., a snack food distributor, for $15.0 million in cash. Goodwill recorded as part of the purchase price allocation was $10.1 million, and identifiable intangible assets acquired as part of the acquisition were $8.4 million.

In late 2012, LNCE acquired the brand Pretzel Crisps, owned by Snack Factory, for $340 million and thus entered the fast growing deli-bakery section of grocery stores. Pretzel Crisps (http://pretzelcrisps.com/) are a thin and crunchy pretzel cracker,

Brands

LNCE contracts with other branded food manufacturers to produce their products. However, LNCE branded products represent about 59 percent of total revenue and non-branded products about 41 percent. LNCE sales are almost all within the USA, with the largest customer being Walmart, which comprises about 18 percent of revenue.

LNCE has many famous brands of its own as described below:

Snyder's of Hanover (www.snydersofhanover.com)—OldeTyme pretzels are made from wholesome ingredients, individually twisted and slow-baked to seal in the flavor.

Lance (www.lance.com)—Lance sandwich crackers are baked fresh with real peanut butter or cheese, and no preservatives, trans fat or high-fructose corn syrup.

Cape Cod (www.capecodchips.com)—Cape Cod Potato Chips are high quality, all natural, hand-stirred, kettle-cooked chips with a classic legendary, crisp, crunch.

Krunchers! (www.krunchers.net)—Krunchers is a kettle chip produced from hand picked premium potatoes, sliced to the ideal thickness, and seasoned with the finest spices.

Tom's (www.toms-snacks.com)—Tom's snacks come in unique shapes and textures, and offer exceptional freshness and quality.

Archway (www.archwaycookies.com)—Archway produces fresh-baked cookies made with high-quality ingredients.

EatSmart Naturals (www.eatsmartnaturals.com)—EatSmart Naturals are unique interesting snacks packed with wholesome ingredients made without artificial preservatives and additives.

Organizational Structure

LNCE appears to operate using a functional structure since the company's *Form 10K* lists only six top executives, as indicated in Exhibit 1. Apparently COO Carl Lee, Jr. oversees all the company's brands and operations. Most analysts contend that LNCE is too large to operate from a functional design. Thus, in the design given in Exhibit 1, note that a strategic business unit (SBU) executive is proposed for the Snyder's-Lance Brands and another for Private Brands—but certainly other alternative designs could be utilized.

Code of Ethics

Snyder's Lance has an elaborate code of ethics posted on its website. An excerpt from the code is given below:

"It is up to each of us no matter what our position or length of service with the Company to be responsible for ensuring that we operate with integrity and treat one another with professionalism and respect. Our Code of Ethics will provide clarity about what is expected from each of us." (Source: Corporate website)

Sustainability

LNCE was recently recognized as one of the top 20 companies in the USA for utilizing solar energy capacity at their facilities. LNCE ranked No. 17 with 3.5 megawatts of installed solar capacity, anchored by a 26-acre solar farm in Pennsylvania that supplies energy for its manufacturing facility in nearby.

EXHIBIT 1 The Synder's-Lance Organizational Structure

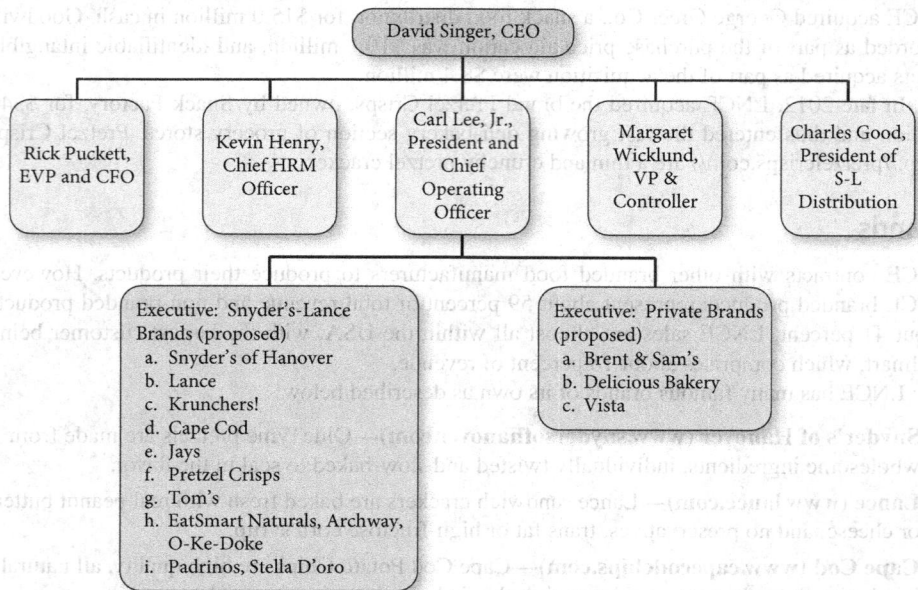

- David Singer, CEO
  - Rick Puckett, EVP and CFO
  - Kevin Henry, Chief HRM Officer
  - Carl Lee, Jr., President and Chief Operating Officer
    - Executive: Snyder's-Lance Brands (proposed)
      - a. Snyder's of Hanover
      - b. Lance
      - c. Krunchers!
      - d. Cape Cod
      - e. Jays
      - f. Pretzel Crisps
      - g. Tom's
      - h. EatSmart Naturals, Archway, O-Ke-Doke
      - i. Padrinos, Stella D'oro
    - Executive: Private Brands (proposed)
      - a. Brent & Sam's
      - b. Delicious Bakery
      - c. Vista
  - Margaret Wicklund, VP & Controller
  - Charles Good, President of S-L Distribution

LNCE's Cape Cod Potato Chips, Snyder's of Hanover Pretzels, and EatSmart Naturals recently received the following awards for being healthy.

- Cape Cod's newest variety, *Waffle Cut Sea Salt,* was selected as the potato chip winner for the 2012 *SHAPE Snack Awards* in the "Best for Parties" category. The *SHAPE Snack Awards* recognizes the best low-calorie snacks of the year and products must meet strict nutritional guidelines to be considered by editors. The awards are listed in the July 2012 issue of *SHAPE* magazine, which reaches more than 2 million readers through its print and online editions.
- Snyder's of Hanover Organic Honey Whole Wheat Pretzel Sticks were selected as a better-for-you snack option in Rodale's "*Eat This, Not That!*" list of the 21 Best Organic Snacks. Rodale is a publisher of health and wellness magazines, books, and digital properties, including *Men's Health, Women's Health, Prevention,* and *Runner's World.* The publisher reaches more than 70 million people around the world.
- Snyder's of Hanover Bacon Cheddar Pretzel Pieces and EatSmart Naturals Potato Crisps were selected by *Progressive Grocer* for the 2012 "Editors' Picks." Both snacks were recognized, out of a pool of more than 300 entries, as two of the best new consumer products introduced in 2012. They were honored as "Editors' Picks" in the August 2012 print issue of *Progressive Grocer* as well as on the *Progressive Grocer* website. The supermarket industry publication reaches more than 50,000 people each month through its print and online versions.

LNCE strives to reduce, reuse, and recycle extensively. The company recycles corrugated cardboard, shipping cartons, metal and plastic drums, office paper, stretch film, plastic jugs and buckets, meal bags, dry waste, salt, pretzel pieces, burnt chips, oil, petroleum, scrap metal, iron, potato starch, and potato peels. The company website gives the following information:

Reduce
- We use low wattage high efficiency light bulbs.
- Motion sensors have been added to areas with low traffic.
- Meters have been installed on our ovens to control gas usage.
- We've reduced the size and thickness of our cartons.
- Water meters have been installed to control usage.
- Our delivery system has been optimized to use less fuel.

Reuse
- Bulk material is delivered in reusable bags.
- Office printer paper is used for scrap paper or recycled.

Recycle
- We now use 100% renewable corn based film for our new Variety Packs.
- Our shipping cartons contain up to 50% recycled materials.
- We use 100% recycled paperboard in our Lunch Packs.
- Plastic drums and barrels are recyclable plastic.
- We repair and recycle damaged shipping pallets.
- Office and printer paper is recycled or reused.

Segment Data

LNCE owns four core brands: 1) Snyder's of Hanover Pretzels, 2) Lance Sandwich Crackers, 3) Cape Cod Potato Chips, and 4) Pretzel Crisps. The company provides of revenue breakdown of its brands versus its revenues from other brands, as indicated in Exhibit 2. Note that LNCE revenues are increasing nicely. Exhibit 3 provides a geographic breakdown of LNCE revenues. Note that almost all LNCE sales are in the USA.

Finance

LNCE has consistently paid dividends of 16 cents per quarter to its shareholders since 2000. LNCE stock offers a healthy dividend yield of 2.52 percent, compared to a snacks industry average dividend yield of only 1.55 percent.

EXHIBIT 2 LNCE Revenues by Brand Category (in millions)

	2012	2011	2010	2009
Branded Products	$ 955.5	943.2	569.5	533.6
Non-Branded Products	663.1	691.8	410.3	384.6
Total	1,618.6	1,635.0	979.8	918.2

Source: 2012 *Form 10K,* p. 28.

EXHIBIT 3 LNCE Revenues by Region (in thousands)

	2012	2011	2010	2009
USA	$ 1,564,338	1,582,967	929,633	871,964
Canada	54,296	52,069	50,182	46,199
Total	1,618,634	1,635,036	979,835	918,163

Source: 2012 *Form 10K,* p. 45.

Michael Warehime and his wife Patricia, own about 16 percent of the outstanding common stock of LNCE. Mr. and Mrs. Warehime serve as directors of LNCE, with Mr. Warehime serving as the Chairman of the Board.

LNCE's recent income statements and balance sheets are provided in Exhibits 4 and 5 respectively. Note in Exhibit 4 the company's dramatic increase in both revenues and net income in 2011. Note in Exhibit 5 the dramatic increase in number of shares outstanding in 2011.

Competitors

Major competitors of LNCE in the snack foods industry include Frito-Lay North America, a subsidiary of PepsiCo, and the U.S. Snacks Division of Kellogg. Other LNCE competitors include General Mills and Mondelez International. A summary of key competitive information is given in Exhibit 6. Note that LNCE has the least revenue per employee among the four firms featured.

Frito-Lay

Frito-Lay North America (FLNA), as PepsiCo refers to this business they own, produces Lay's potato chips, Cheetos, Quaker-brand cereals, Doritos, Tostitos, Ruffles, Fritos, SunChips, and Santitas. For the second quarter of 2012, Frito-Lay recorded revenue growth of 2.5 percent to

EXHIBIT 4 LNCE's Income Statements (in millions)

(in millions)	2012	2011	2009
Net revenue	**$ 1,618.6**	**$ 1,635.0**	**$ 979.8**
Cost of sales	1,079.7	1,065.1	601.0
Gross margin	538.9	569.9	378.8
Selling, general and administrative	440.6	495.2	359.6
Impairment charges	11.9	12.7	0.6
Gain on sale of route businesses, net	(22.3)	(9.4)	—
Other (income)/expense, net	(0.4)	1.0	6.5
Income before interest and income taxes	109.1	70.4	12.1
Interest expense, net	9.5	10.6	3.9
Income tax expense	40.1	21.1	5.6
Net income	**$ 59.5**	**$ 38.7**	**$ 2.6**

Source: 2012 *Form 10K,* p. 28.

EXHIBIT 5 LNCE's Balance Sheets

(in thousands, except share data)	2012	2011
ASSETS		
Current assets:		
Cash and cash equivalents	$ 9,276	$ 20,841
Accounts receivable, net of allowances of $2,159 and $1,884, respectively	141,862	143,238
Inventories	118,256	106,261
Income tax receivable	—	18,119
Deferred income taxes	11,625	21,042
Assets held for sale	11,038	57,822
Prepaid expenses and other current assets	28,676	20,705
Total current assets	320,733	388,028
Noncurrent assets:		
Fixed assets, net	331,385	313,043
Goodwill	540,389	367,853
Other intangible assets, net	531,735	376,062
Other noncurrent assets	22,490	21,804
Total assets	$ 1,746,732	$ 1,466,790
LIABILITIES AND STOCKHOLDERS' EQUITY		
Current liabilities:		
Current portion of long-term debt	$ 20,462	$ 4,256
Accounts payable	52,753	52,930
Accrued compensation	31,037	29,248
Accrued profit-sharing and retirement plans	354	9,249
Accrual for casualty insurance claims	4,779	6,957
Accrued selling and promotional costs	16,240	21,465
Income tax payable	1,263	—
Other payables and accrued liabilities	27,735	31,041
Total current liabilities	154,623	155,146
Noncurrent liabilities:		
Long-term debt	514,587	253,939
Deferred income taxes	176,037	196,244
Accrual for casualty insurance claims	9,759	7,724
Other noncurrent liabilities	19,551	15,146
Total liabilities	874,557	628,199
Stockholders' equity:		
Common stock, $0.83 1/3 par value. Authorized 75,000,000 shares; 68,863,974 and 67,820,798 shares outstanding, respectively	57,384	56,515
Preferred stock, $1.00 par value. Authorized 5,000,000 shares; no shares outstanding	—	—
Additional paid-in capital	746,155	730,338
Retained earnings	50,847	35,539
Accumulated other comprehensive income	15,118	13,719
Total Snyder's-Lance, Inc. stockholders' equity	869,504	836,111
Noncontrolling interests	2,671	2,480
Total stockholders' equity	872,175	838,591
Total liabilities and stockholders' equity	$ 1,746,732	$ 1,466,790

Source: 2012 *Form 10K*, p. 45–46.

EXHIBIT 6 Comparative Information for Various Snack Food Companies

	LNCE	Mondelez	General Mills	Kellogg
# of Employees	6.1K	126K	35K	31K
$ Net Income	41.6M	3.59B	1.71B	1.19B
$ Revenue	1.64B	54.3B	16.9B	13.6B
$ Revenue/Employee	270K	430K	482K	438K
$ EPS Ratio	0.61	2.01	2.56	3.31

Source: Company documents.

$5.77 billion—obviously a huge company compared to LNCE. A global company in all respects, Frito-Lay's operating profit declined 1 percent to $1.33 billion in a recent quarter. FLNA's revenue was $13.3 billion in 2011, up from $12.6 billion the prior year.

Kellogg

Kellogg, the world's largest cereal maker well known for Frosted Flakes, Pop-Tarts, and Eggo waffles, acquired Pringles chips in 2012. The deal instantly made Kellogg the world's second-biggest salty snack food maker, behind only Frito-Lay. Based in Battle Creek, Michigan, Kellogg said Pringles sales rose by 10 percent in a recent quarter. A major competitor to LNCE, Pringles has only two major manufacturing plants in the world. Those plants—in Tennessee and Belgium—are running around the clock at full capacity, and Kellogg plans to expand Pringles' production capacity. Because Pringles derives two-thirds of its revenue from overseas, Kellogg is also hoping Pringles can give it inroads into the emerging markets where the number of people with disposable income is growing. Kellogg's stable of other salty snacks include Cheez-Its and Special K crackers.

Mondelez

In October 2012, the former Kraft Foods Inc. changed its name to Mondelez International and spun-off some brands into a new company called Kraft Foods Group. Kraft Foods Group focuses on the North American foods business. Mondelez International focuses on the global snacks business, including the former Cadbury businesses, plus global brands including Dairylea and Philadelphia. Mondelez makes some of the best-known snacks brands around the globe, including cookies and crackers such as Oreo, Nabisco, Chips Ahoy!, TUC, Belvita, Club Social, and Barni. Headquartered in Deerfield Township, Illinois, near Chicago, Mondelez also produces chocolate, biscuits, gum, confectionery, coffee, and powdered beverages. Mondelez has operations in more than 80 countries. Based in Mississauga, Ontario with primary operations in Scarborough, Mondelez Canada controls the rights to Christie Brown and Company, which consists of brands like Mr. Christie and Dad's Cookies.

General Mills

Headquartered in Golden Valley, Minnesota, General Mills produces and markets many well-known brands, such as Betty Crocker, Yoplait, Colombo, Totinos, Jeno's, Pillsbury, Green Giant, Old El Paso, Haagen-Dazs, Cheerios, and Lucky Charms. The company's grain-snack brands that compete more with LNCE products include Bugles, Cascadian Farms, Chex Mix, Gardetto's, Nature Valley, and Fiber One bars. General Mills' brand portfolio includes more than 100 leading brands in the USA and more around the world.

External Issues

Industry Consolidation

Snack foods industry consolidation has resulted in intense price competition, discounting, and other techniques by competitors who generally are significantly larger and have greater resources and economies of scale than LNCE. This size disadvantage could result in LNCE losing one or more major customers, losing existing product authorizations at customer locations, losing market share and/or shelf space, and/or having to lower prices below breakeven, which could have an adverse impact on LNCE's financial results.

LNCE is exposed to risks resulting from several large customers that account for a significant portion of the firm's revenue. LNCE's top ten customers account for about 48 percent of the firm's revenue, with their largest customer, Walmart, representing about 18 percent of their 2011 revenue. The loss of one or more of these large customers could adversely affect LNCE's financial results. LNCE hopes that their large distributors (customers), such as Walmart or Kroger, do not cut deals with rival firms that could limit or even prohibit exposure of LNCE products. Exclusivity activity routinely occurs in some industries, such as PepsiCo or Coca-Cola products being exclusively available in various fast food restaurant chains.

Social/Cultural/Demographic Issues

Consumer preferences and tastes change, which requires companies to continuously monitor trends and innovate accordingly. For example, concerns of consumers regarding health and wellness and obesity affect perceptions about product attributes and ingredients. In addition, changing consumer demographics could result in reduced demand for LNCE products, such as aging of the general population; changes in social trends; changes in travel, vacation, or leisure activity patterns; weather; or negative publicity resulting from regulatory action or litigation against companies in the snack food industry. Good and bad news as well as opinions about LNCE or their rival firms products and services travels instantly on social media outlets.

Consumers are trying to eat fresher, healthier snacks, beverages, and food. The volume of packaged food consumed is declining while the volume of fresh food is increasing. Firms like PepsiCo are actively developing a variety of healthier foods and beverages that focus on such areas as nutrition, weight management, improved digestion, disease prevention, and allergy remedies. These new products generally contain fewer calories, less fat, low carbohydrates, and/or less sugar and sodium. Many new products are gluten-free and/or whole-fiber.

Future

Since Snyder's-Lance is very small compared to its major rivals, yet is performing quite well, should the company expand its manufacturing and distribution operations further penetrating Canada, and even venturing out into Mexico and Latin America and beyond? Economies of scale are critical in this business due to increasing price competition. The snack foods business is global, so to remain solely a domestic player in such an industry could be ineffective long term. In this light, the dilemma for LNCE is how, where, when, and to what extent to engage in geographic expansion. Since its largest customers, such as Walmart, are global, would it not be advantageous for the firm to negotiate deals with those firms to offer their products in other countries. Surely customers worldwide would enjoy eating the firm's snacks just as much as Americans. Prepare a three-year strategic plan for Snyder's-Lance that will grow the firm globally.

清华会计学系列英文版教材

1. 管理会计（第 6 版）Management Accounting, 6/e
   Rajiv D. Banker, Robert S. Kaplan, S. Mark Young, Anthony A. Atkinson
2. 财务会计（第 10 版）Financial Accounting and GAP Annual Report, 10/e
   Walter T. Harrison, Charles T. Horngren
3. 会计学基础（第 11 版）Essentials of Accounting, 11/e
   Robert N. Anthony, Leslie Pearlman

清华营销学系列英文版教材

1. 消费者行为学（第 10 版）Consumer Behavior, 10/e
   Leon G. Schiffman, Leslie Lazar Kanuk
2. 市场营销原理（第 15 版）Principles of Marketing, 15/e
   Philip Kotler, Gary Armstrong
3. 全球营销管理（第 8 版）Global Marketing Management, 8/e
   Warren J. Keegan
4. 营销调研精要（第 6 版）Essentials of Marketing Research, 6/e
   William G. Zikmund
5. 广告、促销与整合营销传播（第 5 版）Integrated Advertising, Promotion, and Marketing Communications, 5/e
   Kenneth E. Clow, Donald Baack

清华管理学系列英文版教材

1. 供应链管理：战略、规划与运作（第 5 版）Supply Chain Management: Strategy, Planning and Operations, 5/e
   Sunil Chopra, Peter Meindl
2. 公共关系实务（第 12 版）The Practice of Public Relations, 12/e
   Fraser P. Seitel
3. 管理学（第 12 版）Management, 12/e
   Stephen P. Robbins，Mary Coulter
4. 人力资源管理（第 11 版）Human Resource Management, 11/e
   Gary Dessler
5. 实用多元统计分析（第 6 版）Applied Multivariate Statistical Analysis, 6/e
   Richard A. Johnson, Dean W. Wichern
6. 组织行为学（第 10 版）Behavior in Organizations, 10/e
   Jerald Greenberg
7. 组织行为学（第 3 版）Essentials of Organizational Behaviour, 3/e

Laurie Mullins, Gill Christy

8. 战略管理：理论与案例（第 12 版）Strategic Management：An Integrated Approach,Theory & Cases, 12/e

Charles W. L. Hill, Melissa A. Schilling, Gareth R. Jones

清华金融学系列英文版教材

1. 金融市场与金融机构（第 3 版）Financial Markets and Institutions, 3/e

Frederic S. Mishkin, Stanley G. Eakins

2. 期权、期货和其他衍生品（第 8 版）Options, Futures, and Other Derivatives，8/e

John C. Hull

3. 投资学（第 6 版）Investments, 6/e

William F. Sharpe, Gordon J. Alexander, Jeffery V. Bailey

4. 财务管理基础（第 13 版）Fundamentals of Financial Management, 13/e

James C. Van Horne, John M. Wachowicz, Jr.

5. 货币金融学（第 2 版）Money, Banking, and the Financial System, 2/e

Glenn Hubbard, Antony Patrick O, Brien

6. 金融学基础：金融机构、投资和管理导论（第 10 版）Basic Finance: An Introduction to Financial Institutions, Investments, and Management, 10/e

Herbert B.Mayo

清华经济学系列英文版教材

1. 微观经济学（第 7 版）Microeconomics, 7/e

Robert S. Pindyck, Daniel L. Rubinfeld

2. 宏观经济学（第 6 版）Macroeconomics, 6/e

Olivier Blanchard

3. 微观经济学原理（第 5 版）Principles of Microeconomics, 5/e

Robert H. Frank, Ben S. Bernanke

4. 宏观经济学原理（第 5 版）Principles of Macroeconomics, 5/e

Robert H. Frank, Ben S. Bernanke

5. 国际经济学：理论与政策（上册　国际贸易）（第 9 版）International Economics: Theory and Policy, 9/e

Paul R. Krugman, Maurice Obstfeld

6. 国际经济学：理论与政策（下册　国际金融）（第 9 版）International Economics: Theory and Policy, 9/e

Paul R. Krugman, Maurice Obstfeld

7. 国际经济学基础 Introduction to International Economics

Dominick Salvatore

8. 国际经济学（第 8 版）International Economics, 8/e

Dominick Salvatore

9. 计量经济学导论：现代观点（第 6 版）Introductory Econometrics: A Modern Approach, 6/e

Jeffrey M. Wooldridge

清华 MBA 核心课程英文版教材

1. 亨格瑞会计学（第 10 版）Accounting, 10/e

Tracie Nobles, Brenda Mattison, Ella Mae Matsumura

2. 组织行为学（第 15 版）Organizational Behavior, 15/e

Stephen P. Robbins

3. 战略管理：概念与案例（第 16 版）Strategic Management: Concepts and Cases, 16/e

Fred R. David, Forest R.David

4. 营销管理（第 13 版）Marketing Management, 13/e

Philip Kotler

5. 管理信息系统：管理数字化公司（第 12 版）Management Information Systems: Managing The Digital Firm, 12/e

Kenneth C. Laudon, Jane P. Laudon

清华物流学系列英文版教材

1. 供应链管理原理：均衡方法（第 2 版）Principles of Supply Chain Management: A Balanced Approach,2/e

Joel D. Wisner, G. Keong Leong, Keah-Choon Tan

2. 采购与供应链管理（第 4 版）Sourcing and Supply Chain Management, 4/e

Robert Handfield, Robert Monczka, etc.

3. 采购与供应管理（第 15 版）Purchasing and Supply Management, 15/e

P. Fraser Johnson, Anna E. Flynn

教学支持说明

尊敬的老师：

　　您好！

　　为了确保您及时有效地申请培生整体教学资源，请您务必完整填写如下表格，加盖学院的公章后传真给我们，我们将会在 2~3 个工作日内为您处理。

请填写所需教辅的开课信息：

采用教材			□ 中文版　□ 英文版　□ 双语版		
作　者		出版社			
版　次		ISBN			
课程时间	始于　　年　月　日	学生人数			
	止于　　年　月　日	学生年级	□ 专科　　　　　　□ 本科 1/2 年级 □ 研究生　　　　　□ 本科 3/4 年级		

请填写您的个人信息：

学　校			
院系/专业			
姓　名		职　称	□助教　□讲师　□副教授　□教授
通信地址/邮编			
手　机		电　话	
传　真			
official E-mail（必填） （eg：XXX@ ruc. edu. cn）		E-mail （eg：XXX@ 163. com）	
是否愿意接受我们定期的新书讯息通知：	□ 是　　　　□ 否		

系/院主任：＿＿＿＿＿＿＿＿＿＿（签字）

（系/院办公室章）

＿＿＿年＿＿＿月＿＿＿日

资源介绍：

—教材、常规教辅（PPT、教师手册、题库等）资源：请访问 www. pearsonhighered. com/educator；　　　　（免费）

—MyLabs / Mastering 系列在线平台：适合老师和学生共同使用；访问需要 Access Code；　　　　（付费）

清华大学出版社

北京市海淀区清华园学研大厦 B 座 509 室

邮编：100084

电话：8610-83470332

传真：8610-83470107

E-mail：tupfuwu@ 163. com

Website：www. tup. com. cn

Pearson Education Beijing Office

培生教育出版集团北京办事处

北京市东城区北三环东路 36 号北京环球贸易中心 D 座 1208 室

邮编：100013

电话：（8610）5735 5169

传真：（8610）5825 7961